South India

written and researched by

David Abram, Devdan Sen, Nick Edwards, Mike Ford and Beth Wooldridge

with additional contributions by

Charles Young

www.roughguides.com

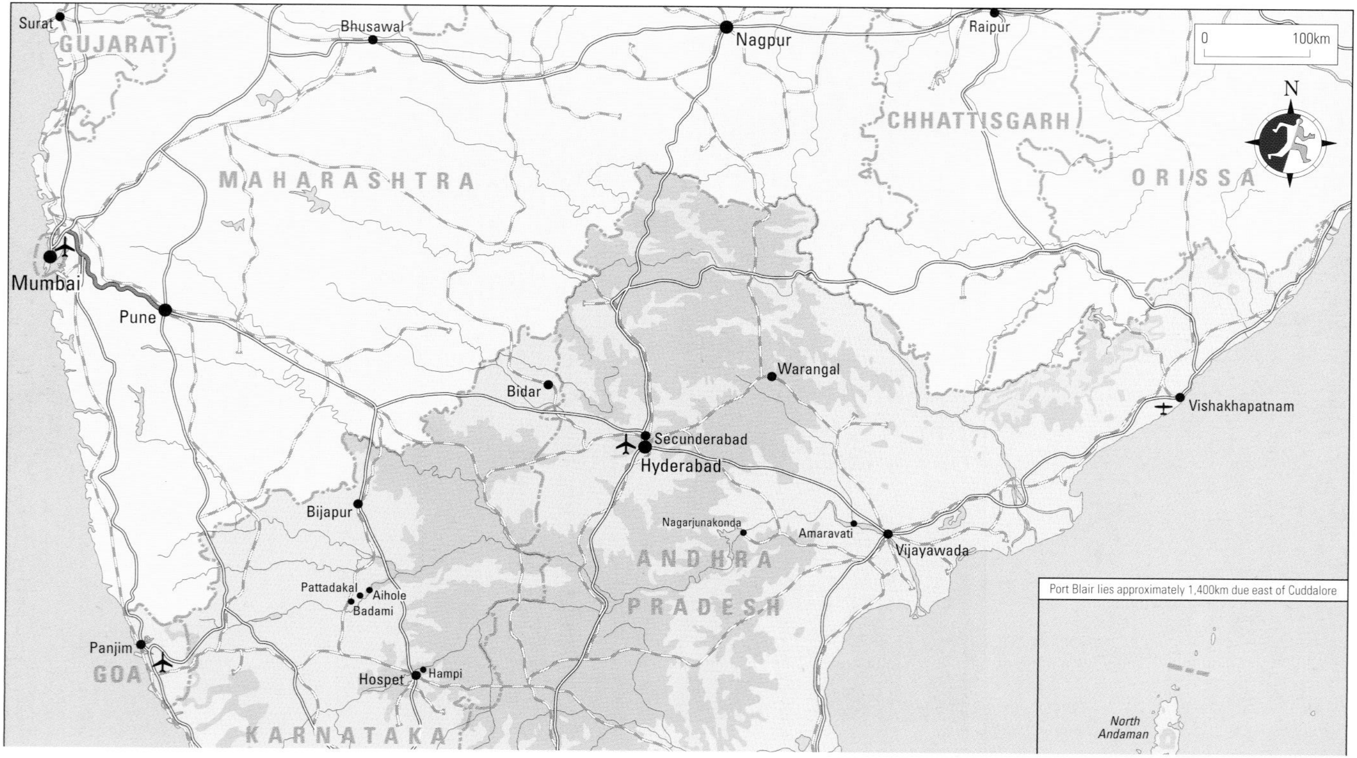

N

0 100km

GUJARAT

Surat

MAHARASHTRA

Mumbai

Pune

Bhusawal

Nagpur

CHHATTISGARH

Raipur

ORISSA

Vishakhapatnam

Warangal

Bidar

Secunderabad

Hyderabad

Nagarjunakonda

Amaravati

Vijayawada

ANDHRA PRADESH

Bijapur

Pattadakal

Aihole

Badami

Hospet

Hampi

KARNATAKA

Panjim

GOA

Port Blair lies approximately 1,400km due east of Cuddalore

North Andaman

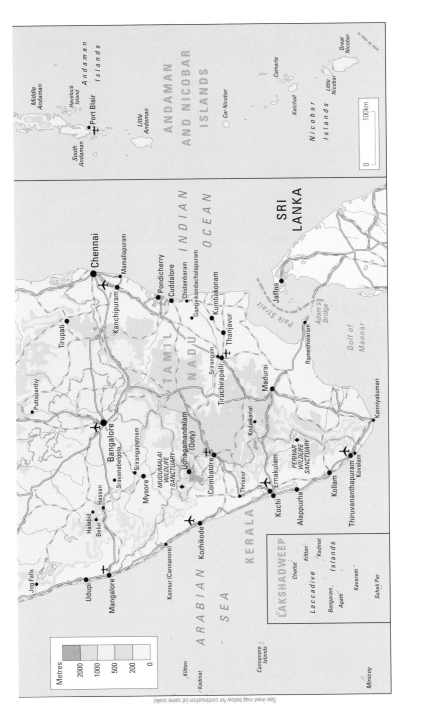

See inset map below for continuation (at same scale)

Metres
2000
1000
500
200
0

ARABIAN SEA

Jog Falls
Udupi
Mangalore
Kannur (Cannanore)
Kozhikode

KERALA

Kochi
Alappuzha
Kollam
Kovalam
Thiruvananthapuram
Ernakulam
Thrissur
Coimbatore
Udhagamandalam (Ooty)
MUDUMALAI WILDLIFE SANCTUARY
PERIYAR WILDLIFE SANCTUARY
Kodaikanal

Puttaparthy
Bangalore
Hassan
Halebid
Belur
Sravanabelgola
Mysore
Srirangapatnam

Tirupati
Kanchipuram
Chennai
Mamallapuram
Pondicherry
Cuddalore
Chidambaram
Gangaikondacholapuram
Kumbakonam
Thanjavur
Srirangam
Tiruchirapalli
Madurai
Kanniyakumari

TAMIL NADU

INDIAN OCEAN

Rameshwaram
Adam's Bridge
Palk Strait
Jaffna
Gulf of Mannar

SRI LANKA

LAKSHADWEEP
Laccadive Islands
Chetlat
Kiltan
Kadmat
Bangaram Islands
Agatti
Kavaratti
Suheli Par
Cannanore Islands
Kiltan / Kadmat
Minicoy

ANDAMAN AND NICOBAR ISLANDS

Middle Andaman
Havelock Island
A n d a m a n   I s l a n d s
South Andaman
Port Blair
Little Andaman

Car Nicobar
Camarta
Katchall
Nicobar Islands
Little Nicobar
Great Nicobar

0   100km

Introduction to

South India

Though its borders are uncertain, there's no doubt that South India, the tapering tropical half of this mighty peninsula, differs radically from the landlocked north. Stepping off a winter flight from foggy Delhi into the glasshouse humidity of Chennai or Thiruvananthapuram (Trivandrum), you enter a world far removed from the muted hues of Punjab and the great Indian river plains. In the south, the coconut groves seem a deeper green and the rice paddies positively luminescent, the faces are a darker brown and the vermilion caste marks smeared over them arrestingly red. The region's heavy rainfall means that lush paddy fields and palm groves patchwork the sun-bleached volcanic soils during all but the hottest months. But under a sun whose rays feel concentrated by a giant magnifying glass, the ubiquitous colours of South India – of silk saris, shimmering classical dance costumes, roadside political posters and frangipani flowers – radiate with a life of their own.

South India's three mightiest rivers – the Godavari, the Krishna and the Kaveri – and their countless tributaries, flow east across a low, fertile alluvial basin that has been inhabited as long as anywhere in the subcontinent. Separated from the prehistoric Indus valley civilizations of the northwest by tracts of barren hills, the earliest South Indian societies are thought to have evolved independently of their northern cousins. Periodic invasions – from the marauding Muslims whose descendants would later erect the Taj Mahal, to the evangelizing,

v

Masala movies

Emblematic of modern India at its most highly charged and lurid are the huge, hand-painted hoardings that tower over city intersections. Featuring blood-splattered macho men, curvaceous heroines in various states of distress (and undress), chubby, bulging-eyed bad guys and explosions a-plenty, they give you a pretty good taste of the kind of movies churned out by the record-beating film industries of Mumbai and Chennai. In either Hindi or Tamil, all follow formulaic hero-gets-the-girl plots, interrupted at frequent intervals by sweeping song-and-dance sequences whose ubiquitous soundtracks crackle out of cassette machines from Kashmir to Kerala. Catch the latest box-office smash at one of the big-city cinema houses, primed by our background accounts on "Bollywood" (p.132) and the Tamil film industry (p.449).

DILIP KANKARIA'S

pepper-hungry Portuguese and ineffectual French – left their marks on the territory referred to in some of India's oldest inscriptions as Dravidadesa, "Land of the Dravidians". None, however, not even the ruthlessly efficient British, ever fully subjugated the south. As a result, traditions, languages and ways of life have endured intact here for more than two thousand years – a fact that lends to any journey into the region a unique resonance.

The persistence of a distinctly Dravidian culture in part accounts for the regionalism that has increasingly dominated the political and cultural life of the South since Independence in 1947. With the exception of Goa, a former Portuguese colony, and the Andaman and Nicobar Islands, the borders of the states covered in this book – Karnataka, Kerala, Tamil Nadu and Andhra Pradesh – were drawn along linguistic lines. Each state boasts its own distinctive styles of music, dance, architecture and cuisine, not to mention religious cults and dress. Moreover, attempts by New Delhi to homogenize the country by imposing Hindi, the most widely spoken language in the North, as the medium of education and government, have consistently met with resistance, stimulating support for the regional parties whose larger-than-life leaders beam munificently from giant hoardings in every major town and city.

More pervasive even than the power of politics in South India is the influence of religion, which, despite the country's resolutely secular constitution, still permeates every aspect of life. Of the four major faiths, Hinduism is by far the most prevalent, practised by around eighty percent of the population. If the sacred peaks of the Himalayas are Hinduism's head, and the Ganges its main artery, then the temple complexes of the South are its spiritual heart and soul. Soaring high above every urban skyline, their colossal towers are emblematic of the awe with which the deities enshrined inside them have been held for centuries. Some, like the sea-washed temple at Tiruchendur in Tamil Nadu, are thought to be as old as human speech itself; others, such as the Sabarimala forest shrine in Kerala are less ancient, but attract greater numbers of pilgrims than even Mecca. For foreign visitors, however, the most extraordinary of all have to be the colossal Chola shrines of Tamil Nadu. Joining the crowds that stream through Madurai's Meenakshi-Sundareshwar temple or Shri Ramalingeshwara in Rameshwaram will take you to the very taproot of the world's last surviving classical culture, some of whose hymns, prayers and rites predate the Egyptian pyramids.

By comparison, Islam, South India's second religion, is a fledgling faith, first introduced by Arab traders along the coast in the twelfth century. Later, offshoots of the Muslim dynasties that ruled the North carved out feudal kingdoms beyond the Godavari, establishing a band of Islamic culture across the middle of the Deccan plateau. Other elements in the great South Indian melting

Teyyattam

From late October to May, archaic ritual dances known as teyyattam take place in over 400 villages and temples along the north Malabar coast. Performances often last all night, and provide a spectacular way of discovering the traditions that lie at the heart of Kerala. Each community nurtures an allegiance to a popular deity; the body and expression of the dancer, the teyyam, becomes a vessel for the deity to connect with their devotees. According to tradition, a teyyam must come from a low-caste family, but while they perform, their humble status is eliminated and social equality reigns.

The teyyam starts to learn the art when he is 9 years old and will, for the next eight years, receive training in dance, martial arts and massage. Some teyyam are required to dance deft steps whilst wearing a headdress (mudi) almost twice their size; there are also particularly rare and dangerous teyyattam where the dancer dons a headdress the height of a coconut tree. For more on tracking down teyyattam, see p.421.

INTRODUCTION | WHERE TO GO | WHEN TO GO

pot include a dozen or more denominations of Christianity, ranging from the ancient Syrian Orthodoxy believed to have been introduced by the apostle St Thomas, to the Roman Catholicism of Old Goa's Portuguese Jesuits. The region also harbours sites sacred to Jains, followers of the prophet Mahavira, a contemporary of Buddha, while in Kochi, Kerala, a vestigial population of Jews is all that remains of a once thriving mercantile community.

Since Independence, these diverse groups have coexisted more or less peacefully, rarely succumbing to the waves of communal blood-letting that have often blighted life in the northern cities. Over the past five or six years, supposedly as a reaction to the rise of Hindu extremist parties, bombs

Meals Ready

Many people come to India expecting the rich, meaty cuisine served up in British curry houses, but the reality turns out to be a lot more exciting: vegetarians, in particular, will find southern cooking a delight. Wander into almost any restaurant or canteen displaying a "Meals Ready" sign, and you'll have a tin tray with little cups, or a fresh green banana leaf, spread in front of you. In (or on) to this, legions of busy waiters will spoon a variety of rice, fresh vegetables and bean preparations, dhals, breads, yoghurt, pickles, poppadums and sauces, each flavoured with a different blend of spices, lime juice, coconut milk and sour mango. And, at the first sign that you're making any headway with this bewildering quantity of food, they'll slop another ladleful on.

Each region has its own distinctive style of set leaf or plate meal; the one thing they have in common is that they'll fill you to bursting point and cost next to nothing. For the ultimate "Meals Ready" experience, head for any branch of *Saravana Bhavan* in Chennai (see p.451), *Fry's Village Restaurant* in Kochi (see p.396), or just about anywhere that's doing a brisk trade.

and riots have erupted around the Muslim ghettos of Mumbai (Bombay) and Coimbatore (in western Tamil Nadu), but these are widely viewed as isolated flare-ups rather than a growing trend. The last decade has seen a

South India remains one of the most relaxed and congenial parts of Asia to explore

dramatic rise in caste violence, however. The age-old hierarchy introduced by the Aryans more than three thousand years ago still forms the backbone of South Indian society, crossing all religious and ethnic divides. But recent political reforms have enabled members of disadvantaged minorities to claim a fairer share of government jobs and university places, as well as political posts (the current president of India is of low-caste South Indian origin), and this has generated widespread resentment, strengthening the very divisions positive discrimination was intended to dissolve.

South India, though, remains one of the most relaxed and congenial parts of Asia to explore. It is also among the easiest. In all but the remotest districts, accommodation is plentiful, clean and inexpensive by Western standards. Freshly cooked, nutritious food is nearly always available. Getting around is usually straightforward, although the sheer size and problematic geography of the South means journeys can be long. The region's extensive rail network is a miraculous feat, moving vast numbers of people at all times of the day and night, and if a train isn't heading where you want to go, a bus probably will be. Furthermore, the widespread use of English makes communication relatively easy. South Indians are the most garrulous and inquisitive of travellers, and train rides are always enlivened by conversations that invariably begin with the refrain of "Coming from?" or "Your native place?"

The extent to which you enjoy travelling in South India will probably depend less on your luck with hotels, restaurants and transport than your reaction to the country itself. Many people expect some kind of exotic time warp, and are surprised to find a consumer culture that's as unashamedly materi-

alistic as anywhere. It is a credit to the South Indians' legendary capacity for assimilating new ideas, however, that the modern and traditional thrive side by side. Walking through downtown Bangalore, you could brush shoulders with a software programmer one moment and a saffron-clad ascetic the next, while bullock carts and stray cattle mingle with Japanese hatchbacks. There are, of course, the usual travel hassles: interminable queues, packed buses and constant encroachments on your personal space. Yet, just when your nerves feel stretched to breaking point, South India always offers something that makes the effort worthwhile: a glimpse of a wild elephant from a train window; a sumptuous vegetarian meal delicately arranged on a fresh banana leaf; or a hint of fragrant cardamom in your tea after an all-night Kathakali recital.

Where to go

South India's boundaries vary according to whom you're talking to: while some regard the Krishna River, the upper limit of India's last Hindu empire, as the real north–south divide, others place the subcontinent's main cultural fault line at the Godavari River, or further north still, at the Vindhya Hills, the barrier of arid table-topped mountains bounding the Ganges Basin. In this guide we've started with Mumbai, a hot, congested city that is the arrival point for most international flights. Mumbai gets a pretty bad press, and most people pass straight through. But those who stay find themselves witness to the reality of modern-day India, from the deprivations of the city's slum-dwellings to the glitz and glamour of Bollywood movies.

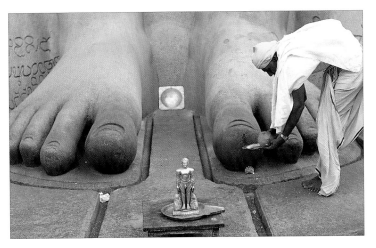

The other principal gateway is Chennai, capital of Tamil Nadu, in the deep south, which is a slightly less stressful point of entry. Although it's another major metropolis bursting at the seams, hidden under its surface are artful gems such as regular public performances of classical music and dance. With regular flights and ship departures to Port Blair, Chennai is also the major springboard for the Andaman Islands, a remote archipelago ringed by coral reefs and crystal-clear seas, 1000km east of the mainland in the Bay of Bengal.

The majority of visitors' first stop after Chennai is Mamallapuram, an ancient port littered with weatherworn sculpture sites, including the famous Shore temple. To get right off the beaten track you only have to head inland to Kanchipuram, whose innumerable Hindu shrines span the golden age of the illustrious Chola kingdom, or to Tiruvannamalai, where one of the region's massive temple complexes rises dramatically from the base of a sacred mountain, site of countless ashrams and meditation caves. Back on the coast, the former French colony of Pondicherry retains a distinctly Gallic feel, particularly in its restaurants, where you can order *coq au vin* and a bottle of Burgundy before a stroll along the promenade. The Kaveri (Cauvery) Delta, further south, harbours astonishing crops of monuments, some of the most impressive of which are around Thanjavur (Tanjore), the Cholas' former capital, dominated by the awesome Brihadishwara temple. You could profitably spend days exploring the town's watery hinterland, hunting out bronze-casting villages, crumbling ruins and other forgotten sacred sites among the web of rivers and irrigation canals. Most travellers press on south to Madurai, the region's most atmospherically charged city, where the mighty Meenakshi-Sundareshwar temple presides over a quintessentially Tamil swirl of life.

The two other most compelling destinations in Tamil Nadu are the island of Rameshwaram, whose main temple features a vast enclosure of pillared corridors, and Kannyakumari, the auspicious southernmost tip of India, where the Bay of Bengal, Indian Ocean and Arabian Sea flow together. The dark shadows visible on the horizon from here mark the start of the southern and western Ghats, which stretch for more than 1000km in a virtually unbroken chain all the way to Mumbai, forming a sheer barrier between Tamil Nadu and neighbouring Kerala. Covered in immense forests and windswept grasslands, the mountains rise to the highest peaks in peninsular India, with sides sculpted by tea terraces, coffee plantations and cardamom groves. The hill stations of Udhagamandalam (or Ooty, as it's still better known) and Kodaikanal, established by India's former colonial rulers as retreats from the searing summer heat of the plains, attract hordes of Indian visitors in the run-up to the rains, but see plenty of foreign tourist traffic during the winter, too.

Neighbouring Kerala's appeal lies less in its religious monuments, many of

which remain off-limits to non-Hindus, than its infectiously easy-going, tropical ambience. Covering a long thin coastal strip backed by a steep wall of hills, this is the wettest and most densely populated state in the South. It is also the most distinctive, with a culture that sets it squarely apart. Its surreal form of ritualized theatre (Kathakali), faintly Southeast Asian architecture and ubiquitous communist graffiti (Kerala was the first place in the world to gain a democratically elected communist government) are perhaps the most visual expressions of this difference. But spend a couple of days exploring the spicy backstreets of old Kochi (Cochin), the jungles of the Cardamom Hills around the Periyar Wildlife Sanctuary or the hidden aquatic world of the coastal backwaters, and you'll see why many travellers end up staying here a lot longer than they originally intended. If you're not pushed for time and find yourself crossing northern Kerala during the winter, set aside a few days to search for Teyyattam, a spectacular masked dance form unique to the villages around Kannur.

A short ride across the mountains takes you to Mysore in Karnataka, whose opulent maharaja's palace, colourful markets and comfortable California-like climate have made it among South India's most popular tourist destinations. Bangalore, the hectic modern capital, is not one of the highlights of the state, which are for the main part scattered over a vast area of rolling, granite-boulder-strewn uplands. Most, such as the richly carved Hoysala temples of Belur and Halebid, or the extraordinary Jain colossus at Sravanabelgola, are religious monuments. Amongst other extraordinary sights are the mausolea, mosques and Persian-style palaces of Bijapur, Karnataka, often dubbed the "Agra of the South". Almost unsurpassable, however, is the awesome scale and faded splendour of the Vijayanagar ruins at Hampi, on the Tungabhadra River. Until it was ransacked by a confederacy of Muslim sultanates in 1565, this was the magnificent capital of South India's last Hindu empire, encompassing most of the peninsula.

Only one day's journey to the west, the palm-fringed,

white-sand beaches of Goa offer a change of scenery from the rocky terrain of the Deccan. Succumbing to the hedonistic pleasures of warm seawater, constant sunshine and cheap drinks, many travellers find it hard to tear themselves away from the coast. Further east, a string of smaller former dynastic capitals punctuate the journey across the heart of the Deccan plateau to Hyderabad, capital of Andhra Pradesh, whose principal landmarks are the Charminar and Golconda fort. Andhra's other attractions, by contrast, lie much further off the beaten track. Comparatively few Western visitors ever reach them, but Puttaparthy, the ashram of India's most famous living saint, Sai Baba, and Tirupati, whose temple receives more pilgrims than anywhere else on earth, are essential stops for South Indians.

When to go

The relentless tropical sun aside, the source of South India's irrepressible fecundity lies in its high rainfall. Unlike the north of the country, which sees only a single deluge in the summer, most of peninsular India receives two annual monsoons – one sucked in from the Arabian Sea in the southwest, and the other on stormy northwesterly winds off the Bay of Bengal. The heaviest rains are reserved for the Western Ghats, a chain of mountains running parallel with the southwest coast. Cloaked for the most part in dense forest, these form a curtain that impedes the path of the first summer monsoon, which breaks in June and lasts through October. In a nutshell, you should, when planning a trip to South India, avoid the rainy seasons. The novelty of torrential downpours and the general mayhem that attend the annual deluges wears off very quickly. Road blockages, landslides and burst riverbanks can interrupt the

best-laid travel plans, not to mention the discomfort of being wet through for days on end; the widespread flooding is also none too healthy, emptying the sewers and polluting reservoirs. Broadly speaking, rule out the period between April and September, when the southwest monsoon is in full swing across the whole peninsula. From late October until April, the weather is perfect in Karnataka and Goa, but less reliable in Kerala, where, by November, the "retreating", or northwest monsoon means constant grey skies and showers. Being on the eastern side of the mountains, Tamil Nadu gets even heavier rains at this time. To enjoy the far south and the Andaman Islands at their best, come between January and March, before the heat starts to build up again. Late April and May are simply insufferable for anyone not accustomed to intense tropical heat.

Average temperatures and rainfall

	Jan	Feb	Mar	Apr	May	June	July	Aug	Sept	Oct	Nov	Dec
Bangalore (Kar)												
Av daily max (°C)	28	31	33	34	33	30	28	29	28	28	27	27
Rainfall (mm)	4	14	6	37	119	65	93	95	129	195	46	16
Chennai (TN)												
Av daily max (°C)	29	31	33	35	38	37	35	35	34	32	29	28
Rainfall (mm)	24	7	15	25	52	53	83	124	118	267	309	139
Hyderabad (AP)												
Av daily max (°C)	29	31	35	37	39	34	30	29	30	30	29	28
Rainfall (mm)	2	11	13	24	30	107	165	147	163	71	25	5
Kochi (Ker)												
Av daily max (°C)	31	31	31	31	31	29	28	28	28	29	30	30
Rainfall (mm)	9	34	50	139	364	756	572	386	235	333	184	37
Madurai (TN)												
Av daily max (°C)	30	32	35	36	37	37	36	35	35	33	31	30
Rainfall (mm)	26	16	21	81	59	31	48	117	123	179	161	143
Mumbai (M)												
Av daily max (°C)	31	32	33	33	33	32	30	29	30	32	33	32
Rainfall (mm)	0	1	0	0	20	647	945	660	309	17	7	1
Panjim (Goa)												
Av daily max (°C)	31	32	32	33	33	31	29	29	29	31	33	33
Rainfall (mm)	2	0	4	17	18	580	892	341	277	122	20	37

things not to miss

It's not possible to see everything that South India has to offer in one trip – and we don't suggest you try. What follows is a selective taste of the region's highlights: outstanding buildings, natural wonders, spectacular festivals and unforgettable journeys. They're arranged in five colour-coded categories, which you can browse through to find the very best things to see and experience. All highlights have a page reference to take you straight into the guide, where you can find out more.

01 Boating on the backwaters Page **362** • Ride a local ferryboat through Kerala's teeming Kuttanad backwater region – South India at its most luxuriant.

03 **Dussehra** Page **65** • Giant effigies of the demon Ravana are stuffed with firecrackers and burnt for the Dusshera festival (Sept–Oct). Mumbai's Shivaji Park hosts one of the biggest events.

02 **Tamil sculpture** Page **518** • The great Tamil shrines of the Kaveri Delta writhe with sensuous stone sculpture, such as this exquisite *apsara* at Srirangam's Ranganathaswamy shrine.

04 **Scuba diving** Page **610** • The remote Andaman islands lie in some of the richest, clearest seawater in the world, which provides wonderful diving opportunities.

ACTIVITIES | CONSUME | EVENTS | NATURE | SIGHTS

05 **Chariot festivals** Page **513** • Among the great spectacles of southern India are temple chariot (*rath*) festivals, such as this one at Thiruvarur in Tamil Nadu.

06 **Ayurvedic massage** Page **33** • Detox after spells in the polluted state capitals with a traditional Ayurvedic massage, at Kovalam (see p.338) or Varkala (see p.353).

07 **Jog Falls** Page **275** • India's highest waterfall, at Jog in Karnataka, peaks in the post-monsoonal period of September. Awesome views and refreshingly wet walks.

08 **Hampi** Page **289** • You'd be hard pushed to find a more exotic vision in Asia than sunrise over the Hampi's Achyutaraya temple.

10 **Feni** Page **60** • The ultimate tropical cocktail base, Goan feni, is distilled from coconut sap collected twice daily by teams of toddy tappers. Sample a drop of the hard stuff yourself.

09 **Sacred art** Page **495** • Vibrant medieval murals, such as this Garuda in Chidambaram, form part of the South's rich repertoire of sacred art.

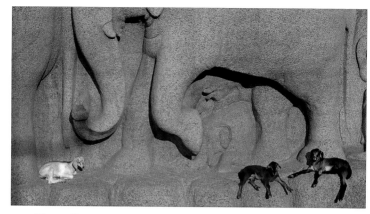

11 **Mamallapuram** Page **464** • A fishing and stone-carving village, with magnificent boulder friezes, shrines and the sea-battered Shore Temple.

13 **Mysore market** Page **238** • Jaggery, incense and garlands are made and veggies and kitsch paraphernalia are sold in Mysore's covered market.

12 **Keralan ritual theatre** Page **706** • Kerala is the place to experience Kathakali and Mohiniyattam, esoteric and otherworldly ritual theatre forms.

14 **Gokarn** Page **277** • The beautiful beaches on the edge of this temple town are popular with budget travellers fleeing the commercialism of nearby Goa.

15 Cricket Page **66** •
The nation's favourite sport is played everywhere, from street corners to the Oval Maidan in Mumbai.

16 Ashrams Page **69** • Brush up on your yoga asanas and meditation technique at one of South India's many ashrams.

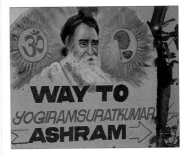

17 Kochi Page **382** • The Keralan capital's atmospheric harbourside is strung with elegant Chinese fishing nets.

18 Drum orchestras
Page **702** • Ear-splitting Keralan drum orchestras, caparisoned elephant processions, and Kathakali recitals make Kerala's intense temple festivals totally unique in India.

20 **Sravanabelgola** Page **255** • This mystical Jain colossus at Sravanabelgola forms the centrepiece of southern Karnataka's most atmospheric pilgrimage town.

19 **Madurai** Page **521** • The soaring, Disney-coloured gopuras of Madurai's Shri Meenakshi temple. To find out about temple festivals at Madurai, see p.531.

21 **Periyar Wildlife Sanctuary** Page **371** • The best bet for spotting wild Indian elephants, which graze on the shore of a reservoir high in the tropical Cardamom Hills. Safaris on foot or by boat.

22 Fishing villages Page **344** • Close to Kovalam, but beach life as few Western tourists see it: the Muslim fishing village of Vizhinjam.

24 The Nilgiri Blue Mountain Railway Page **559** • The bone-shaking ride up to Ooty on one of Asia's last steam railways is a must for Raj-philes. Worth it for the views alone.

23 Chola bronzes Page **512** • Nayak Durbar Hall Art Museum in Thanjavur holds India's finest collection of Chola bronzes. See contemporary casters at work at Swamimalai, p.505.

25 Elephanta Caves Page **123** • These ancient caves, cut from solid rock in Mumbai harbour, offer the perfect escape from the madness of the Maharashtran capital.

26 Old Goa Page **159** • Belfries and Baroque church facades loom over trees on the banks of the Mandovi, all that remains of a once-splendid colonial city.

27 Varkala Page **350** • Kerala's low-key alternative to Kovalam boasts sheer red cliffs, amazing seaviews and a legion of Ayurvedic masseurs.

28 Christmas in Kerala Page **325** • Attend Christmas Eve mass in Kerala for an insider's glimpse of one of the oldest surviving Christian traditions in Asia.

29 Golgumbaz tomb Page **308** • The mighty Golgumbaz tomb in Bijapur, merely one among a bumper crop of sublime Islamic monuments littering the Karnatakan Deccan region.

contents

using the Rough Guide

We've tried to make this Rough Guide a good read and easy to use. The book is divided into five main sections, and you should be able to find whatever you want in one of them.

colour section

The front colour section offers a quick tour of South India. The **introduction** aims to give you a feel for the place, with suggestions on where to go. We also tell you what the weather – and the food – is like. Next, our authors round up their favourite aspects of South India in the **things not to miss** section – whether it's a stunning temple, a vibrant festival or a special market. Right after this comes the Rough Guide's full **contents** list.

basics

You've decided to go and the Basics section covers all the **pre-departure** nitty-gritty to help you plan your trip. This is where to find out which airlines fly to your destination, what paperwork you'll need, what to do about money and insurance, about internet access, food, security, public transport, car rental – in fact just about every piece of **general practical information** you might need.

guide

This is the heart of the Rough Guide, divided into user-friendly chapters, each of which covers a specific region. Every chapter starts with a list of **highlights** and an **introduction** that helps you to decide where to go, depending on your time and budget.

Likewise, introductions to the various towns and smaller regions within each chapter should help you plan your itinerary. We start most town accounts with information on arrival and accommodation, followed by a tour of the sights, and finally reviews of places to eat and drink, and details of nightlife. Longer accounts also have a directory of practical listings. Each chapter concludes with **public transport** details for that region.

contexts

Read Contexts to get a deeper understanding of what makes South India tick. We include a brief history, articles about religions, art and architecture, wildlife, music and dance, a detailed further reading section that reviews dozens of **books** relating to the country, as well as a **language** section and a glossary of words and terms that are peculiar to the region.

index + small print

Apart from a **full index**, which includes maps as well as places, this section covers publishing information, credits and acknowledgements, and also has our contact details in case you want to send in updates and corrections to the book – or suggestions as to how we might improve it.

chapter map of **South India**

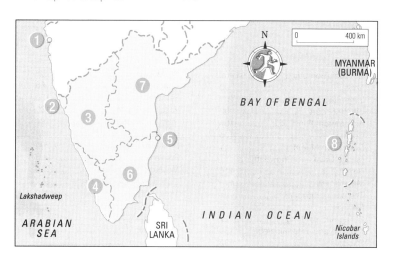

contents

colour section   i–xxiv

basics   7–87

the guide   89–630

contexts

631–733

map symbols

Maps are listed in the full index using coloured text.

REGIONAL MAPS

▬▬▬	Railway
━━━	Main road
────	Minor road
- - - -	Track or trail
────	River
── ──	Ferry
▬▬▬▬	International boundary
▬▬ ▪▪	State boundary
─ ─ ─	Chapter division boundary
〮〮〮	Mountains
▲	Peak
) (	Pass
〴〴	Rocks
🎐	Waterfall
𑃱	Viewpoint
▦	Mudflats
𑃱	Marshland
⸬	Beach
⚓	Church
◆	Place of interest
✈	International airport
✛	Domestic airport
🕯	Lighthouse

STREET MAPS

▬▬▬	Railway
━━━	Main road
━━━	Secondary road
━━━	Lane
═ ═	Track
- - - -	Path
▥▥▥▥	Steps
────	River
━━━	Wall
◉	Accommodation
■	Restaurant
▬	Building
⊞	Church
ⓘ	Tourist office
⊠	Post office
⊞	Hospital
★	Public transport stand
𑂷𑂷	Football pitch
🅿	Parking
Ⓗ	Helipad
@	Internet access
🛢	Fuel station
◄	One-way street

COMMON SYMBOLS

☪	Mosque or Muslim monument	🏛	Palace
⛰	Hindu or Jain temple	▤	Ghat
⛩	Buddhist temple	▦	Park

basics

basics

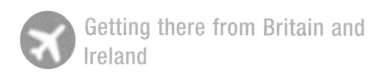

Getting there from Britain and Ireland

Most visitors to South India fly into the major international gateways of Mumbai and Chennai. Non-stop flights from London reach Mumbai in just 9 hours and Chennai in 10 hours. If cutting costs is a priority then consider an indirect flight – involving a change of plane and possibly a stopover en route; several indirect services travel via Europe or the Gulf. To satisfy the ever-increasing numbers of travellers and holiday-makers heading for Goa and Kerala, various package specialists operate seasonal charter flights. If you are covering a wider itinerary encompassing other areas of India, you may prefer to fly into Delhi – which can offer you further options and cheaper fares. However you go, though, be sure to shop around, as prices can vary wildly between agents.

Scheduled flights

British Airways and Air India fly **non-stop** daily from **London to Mumbai**. Discounted return fares range from £450 in low season (roughly Jan–June & Nov) to upwards of £600 in high season (July, Aug & Dec). BA also fly non-stop from **London to Chennai** twice weekly (Tues & Sat): flights cost from £600 low season and from £725 high season. Most days, three non-stop flights leave **London for Delhi**: Air India, British Airways and Air Canada are some of the airlines who fly the route, and prices are much the same as those to Mumbai. Air Canada, which doesn't fly to India in the summer, tends to be the cheapest of the major airlines.

Apart from some charter flights mentioned below, there are no **direct** flights to India from **regional airports**. From Manchester, your best bet is to take an **indirect** flight with Emirates to Delhi or Mumbai via Dubai. KLM and KLM UK fly out of most regional airports in the UK to Amsterdam where you can connect with their flight to Mumbai. Similarly, Air France flies to Paris from Birmingham, Bristol, Edinburgh and Glasgow for connections on to Mumbai. In general, both KLM and Air France are cheaper than BA with return tickets often discounted to as low as £420.

Of the many other indirect options, you can fly to **Chennai** with Air India (changing at Mumbai) or with Air Lanka (changing at Colombo, Sri Lanka) for £550–600. Air Lanka also flies, via Sri Lanka, to Tiruchirapalli (Trichy) and Thiruvananthapuram (Trivandrum), **Kerala**. Air India have a twice-weekly departure from London to Thiruvananthapuram, changing at Mumbai. A quicker option, however, is to take one of several departures via the Gulf, including daily flights from London on Gulf Air or Emirates. Several airlines, including Indian Airlines, Air India and a handful of Middle Eastern airlines, also fly between the Gulf and Kerala and connect with **Thiruvananthapuram**, **Kochi/Ernakulam** and **Kozhikode**. Air India also have flights, via Mumbai, to **Bangalore** in Karnataka.

Extremely cheap fares on indirect flights to **Delhi** – down to as little as £320 return out of season – can usually be found if you're prepared to fly with airlines such as Aeroflot, Tarom, Air Uzbekistan or Syrian Arab Airlines. For a full run-down of airlines and their destinations in India and South India, where applicable, see p.10.

There are no non-stop flights to India **from Ireland**, so you need to travel via another country. You can fly from **Dublin**, through to South India, with British Airways via London, KLM via Amsterdam, Air France via Paris and Swissair via Zurich. Of these, Swissair – which has one flight a week to Mumbai and charges around IR£600 at any time of the year – is the most competitive in high season. However, Royal Jordanian is the best deal with a flight out of **Shannon** – via Amman – in low season for IR£350 return (rising to IR£700 in high season). Aeroflot's daily flight from Shannon – via Moscow – is a reasonable alternative. Finally, flying KLM from **Belfast** to Delhi or Mumbai costs the same as from London.

Airlines in Britain and Ireland

As well as the agents listed below, check out the travel supplements of national papers, regional listings magazines and the *Evening Standard* in London and free giveaways like TNT. The Web is also a good source: try ⓦ www.ebookers.com, ⓦ www.travelocity .co.uk, ⓦ www.expedia.co.uk and ⓦ www .deckchair.com

Aeroflot ☏ 020/7355 2233, ⓦ www.aeroflot.com. One of the cheapest ways to get to India, but you'll have to go via Moscow and can only fly to Delhi or Calcutta.

Air Canada ☏ 0990/247226, ⓦ www.aircanada.ca. Attractive fares but they don't fly to India in the summer.

Air France ☏ 0845/084 5111, ⓦ www.airfrance.fr. One of the best of the major airlines, flying via Paris where you will need to change planes before continuing to Mumbai or Delhi.

Air India ☏ 020/8560 9996, ⓦ www.airindia.com. Daily non-stop flights from London to Delhi and Mumbai with direct connections to Chennai and indirect connections via Mumbai to Thiruvananthapuram and Bangalore.

Air Lanka ☏ 020/7930 4688, ⓦ www.airlanka.com. Competitively priced airline with connections to Chennai, Trichy and Trivandrum via Colombo – a change that may involve an overnight halt.

British Airways ☏ 0845/722 2111 or 020/7828 4895, ⓦ www.british-airways.com. Daily non-stop departures from London to Delhi and Mumbai with direct flights to Chennai (2 weekly).

Egyptair ☏ 020/7734 2395. Flights into Mumbai with a change in Cairo, where for an extra £100 or so you can get a stopover. Their prices remain unchanged throughout the year and are especially attractive in high season.

Emirates Airlines ☏ 0870/243 2222, ⓦ www.emirates.com. Flights from London and Manchester to Mumbai via the Gulf, where you can also change onto a direct flight to Kerala.

Gulf Air ☏ 020/7408 1717, ⓦ www.gulfairco.com. Flights from London and Manchester to Mumbai and Delhi via Abu Dhabi, Bahrain or Muscat in the Gulf; you can also fly to

the Gulf and change onto a direct flight to Kerala.

KLM ☏ 08705/074074, ⓦ www.klm.nl. Flights to Delhi and Mumbai, with a change at Amsterdam.

KLM UK ☏ 08705/074074, ⓦ www.klmuk.com. KLM recently bought Air UK, and the new KLM UK flies from virtually all British airports to a variety of European destinations; change in Amsterdam for KLM flights to India.

Lufthansa ☏ 0845/773 7747, ⓦ www.lufthansa.co.uk. Efficient connections through Frankfurt to Mumbai or Delhi.

Pakistan International Airlines (PIA) ☏ 020/7499 5500, ⓦ www.fly-pia.com. Change in Karachi for connections to Delhi and Mumbai.

Royal Brunei Airlines ☏ 020/7584 6660, ⓦ www.bruneiair.com. Some cheap tickets through discount agents are available, with a stop in the Gulf and connections to Delhi and Calcutta.

Royal Jordanian ☏ 020/7878 6341. Competitively priced airline with flights via Amman to Delhi and Mumbai; connections to South Indian destinations via internal airlines work well. Sometimes includes an all-inclusive overnight stop at Amman on the way back.

Swissair ☏ 020/7434 7300, ⓦ www.swissair.com. Good connections through Zurich to Mumbai and Delhi.

Syrian Arab Airlines ☏ 020/7493 2851. A cheap flight with connections through Damascus to Delhi.

Tarom Romanian Airlines ☏ 020/7224 3693, ⓦ www.tarom.digirow.net. Cheap, indirect flights through Bucharest to Delhi.

Charter flights

Various package specialists, such as Inspirations, Manos and Somak (see p.12 for a full list) operate winter (Oct–May) **charters to Goa and Kerala**, departing from London and regional airports. These deals are usually for stays of two weeks – though stays can be extended to four and in some cases six weeks. They often work out cheaper than a standard scheduled deal to Mumbai. However, your fare must include some form of accommodation (even if it isn't advertised as such), which you can occupy on arrival and then ditch when you're ready to move on. Charter tickets are generally sold through high-street travel agents, and ads in the travel pages of newspapers. Once in India, you may be offered the return leg of a charter flight for sale; this practice is particularly prevalent in Goa. Bear in mind, however, that under no circumstances is it possible to leave India on a charter flight if you entered on a sched-uled flight or overland.

Discount agents

For the best flight deals to South India you are generally advised to contact **discount agents**, who offer excess seats for airlines at rock-bottom prices; agents include STA, Usit Campus, and Trailfinders (for a full list of reliable operators, see below). Some of these specialize in **student travel** and **under-26s**, so check the restrictions on your ticket.

Smaller agents, or **bucket shops**, also known as "consolidators", generally offer unbeatable prices, but are not always reli-able. It's best to use a company that's a member of ATOL, as you'll be guaranteed a refund if the company goes bust. At the very least, ensure you get a printed receipt with your full travel itinerary when you pay for your ticket.

Discount flight agents in Britain and Ireland

Arrowguide Ltd, 29 Dering St, London W1 ☎020/7629 9516, ⓦwww.arrowguide.co.uk. A long-established and reliable consolidator specializing in cheap flights to Asia.
Bridge the World 47 Chalk Farm Rd, London NW1 ☎020/7911 0900, ⓦwww.bridgetheworld.com. Specialists in round-the-world tickets, with good deals aimed at the backpacker market.
Flightbookers, 177–178 Tottenham Court Rd, London W1P 0LX ☎020/7757 3000, ⓦwww.ebookers.com. Low fares on an extensive range of scheduled flights.
The London Flight Centre ⓦwww.topdecktravel.co.uk; 131 Earl's Court Rd, London SW5 9RH ☎020/7244 6411; 47 Notting Hill Gate, London W11 3JS ☎020/7727 4290; Shop 33, The Broadway Centre, Hammersmith tube, London W6 9YE ☎020/8748 6777. Long-established agent dealing in discount flights.
North South Travel Moulsham Mill Centre, Parkway, Chelmsford, Essex CM2 7PX ☎01245/492882, ⓦwww.northsouthtravel.co.uk. Friendly and competitive agency offering discounted fares, with profits used to support sustainable tourism and projects in the developing world.

STA Travel London call centre worldwide ☎020/7361 6144, other enquiries ☎020/7361 6150; northern call centre ☎0161/830 4713, ⓦwww.statravel.co.uk; 86 Old Brompton Rd, London SW7 3LH; 117 Euston Rd, London NW1 2SX; 38 Store St, London WC1E 7BZ; 11 Goodge St, London W1P; 38 North St, Brighton ☎01273/728282; 25 Queens Rd, Bristol BS8 1QE ☎0117/9294399; 38 Sidney St, Cambridge CB2 3HX ☎01223/366966; 75 Deansgate, Manchester M3 2BW ☎0161/834 0668; 88 Vicar Lane, Leeds LS1 7JH ☎0113/244 9212; 78 Bold Street, Liverpool L1 4HR ☎0151/707 1123; 9 St Mary's Place, Newcastle-upon-Tyne NE1 7PG ☎0191/233 2111; 36 George St, Oxford OX1 2OJ ☎01865/792 800; 27 Forrest Rd. Edinburgh ☎0131/226 7747; 184 Byres Rd, Glasgow G1 1JH ☎0141/338 6000; 30 Upper Kirkgate, Aberdeen ☎0122/465 8222; plus over 40 branches including on university campuses. Worldwide specialists in low-cost flights and tours for students and under-26s, though other customers welcome. Also over 200 offices abroad.
Trailfinders ⓦwww.trailfinders.co.uk; 1 Threadneedle St, London EC2R 8JX ☎020/7628 7628; 42–50 Earl's Court Rd, London W8 6FT ☎020/7938 3366; 194 Kensington High St, London, W8 7RG ☎020/7938 3939; 58 Deansgate, Manchester M3 2FF ☎0161/839 6969; 254–284 Sauchiehall St, Glasgow G2 3EH ☎0141/353 2224; 22–24 The Priory Queensway, Birmingham B4 6BS ☎0121/236 1234; 48 Corn St, Bristol BS1 1HQ ☎0117/929 9000. One of the best-informed and most efficient agents for independent travellers; they produce a very useful quarterly magazine worth scrutinizing for round-the-world routes (for free copy call ☎020/7938 3366); all branches open daily until 6pm, Thurs until 7pm.
Travel Cuts 295a Regent St, London W1R 7YA ☎020/7255 2082, ⓦwww.travelcuts.co.uk; 229 Great Portland St, W1N 5HD ☎020/7436 0459; 44 Queensway, London, NW2 3RS ☎020/7792 3770. Established in Canada in 1974, Travel Cuts specialize in budget, student and youth travel and round-the-world tickets, with offices in London and abroad.
Usit Campus national call centre ☎0870/240 1010, ⓦwww.usitcampus.co.uk; 52 Grosvenor Gardens, London SW1W OAG ☎020/7730 8111; 541 Bristol Rd, Selly Oak, Birmingham B29 6AU ☎0121/414 1848; 61 Ditchling Rd, Brighton BN1 4SD ☎01273/570226; 37–39 Queen's Rd, Clifton, Bristol BS8 1QE ☎0117/929 2494; 5 Emmanuel St, Cambridge CB1 1NE ☎01223/324 283); 53 Forest Rd, Edinburgh EH1 2QP ☎0131/225 6111,

telesales 668 3303; 122 George St, Glasgow G1 1RF ☏ 0141/553 1818; 166 Deansgate, Manchester M3 3FE ☏ 0161/833 2046, telesales 273 1721; 105–106 St Aldates, Oxford OX1 1DO ☏ 01865/242067. Student/youth travel specialists, with 51 branches, including in YHA shops and on university campuses all over Britain.

USIT Now 21 Aston Quay, O'Connell Bridge, Dublin 2, Ireland ☏ 01/602 1777, ⓦ www.usitnow.ie. Student and youth specialists for flights and trains, with branches in Belfast, Cork, Galway, Limerick and Waterford.

Packages and organized tours

A large number of operators offer **package holidays** to South India, covering activities such as trekking and safaris, as well as sightseeing and sunbathing. Specialist-interest tours range from steam locomotives and war history to religion and food, while general sightseeing trips take in Bangalore, Hyderabad, Chennai, Kovalam and Kochi. Some also offer wildlife trips and combined tours encompassing other regions of India. In addition, many companies will arrange **tailor-made itineraries**.

Of course, any package holiday is a lot easier than going under your own steam, particularly if you only have a short time and don't want to use it up on making your own travel bookings. On the other hand, a typical sightseeing tour can rather isolate you from the country, shutting you off in air-conditioned hotels and buses. Specialist trips such as trekking and tailor-made tours will work out rather expensive, compared with what you'd pay if you organized everything yourself, but they do cut out a lot of hassle. However, Goa beach holidays and packages to Kovalam in Kerala – particularly with charter operators – can work out cheaper than the cost of a normal flight, and usually offer tour options as extras. One-week packages to Goa including flights and accommodation, for example, are available for around £450, with further discounts off-season.

Specialist operators

Abercrombie and Kent ☏ 020/7730 9600, ⓦ www.abercrombiekent.com. Upmarket sightseeing and tailor-made holidays, trekking and wildlife trips.

Coromandel ☏ 01572/821 330. Tailor-made special-interest trips, including textile tours to village craft workshops.

Cox & Kings ☏ 020/7873 5000, ⓦ www.coxandkings.com. Tailor-made itineraries with an operator established in the days of the Raj.

Discover India ☏ 020/8429 3300. Tailor-made itineraries including pilgrimages, cricket, golf and football tours.

Essential India ☏ 01225/868544, ⓦ www.essential-india.co.uk. Courses in a wide range of subjects, from writing, painting, and pottery to Buddhism and outdoor pursuits; for individuals or groups.

Exodus ☏ 020/8675 5550, ⓦ www.exodustravels.co.uk. Experienced specialists in small-group itineraries, treks and overland tours.

Global Link ☏ 020/7409 7766. Gourmet food and wildlife tours, both budget and tailor-made.

Indian Encounters ☏ 01929/481421. Theme tours including golf, painting, textiles, plus camel safaris and tailor-made itineraries.

Inspirations ☏ 01293/822244. Specialists in Goa and Kerala packages.

Kambala ☏ 01803/732488. One of the few operators specializing in tours for the over-50s. General sightseeing and craft holidays.

Kerala Connections ☏ 01892/722440, ⓦ www.keralaconnect.co.uk. Specializing in Kerala, good for a range of accommodation and useful for suggesting itineraries.

Kuoni Travel ☏ 01306/742888, ⓦ www.kuoni.co.uk. One of the largest package and charter tour operators flying to numerous destinations in India.

Manos ☏ 020/7216 8070, ⓦ www.manos.co.uk. Specializing in Goa and Kerala packages.

Munjeeta Travel ☏ 01483/773331. Home-stay holidays lodging with Indian families.

Mysteries of India ☏ 020/8574 2727. Imaginative, tailor-made and small-group holidays, including home-stays along the backwaters and Keralan plantations.

Partnership Travel ☏ 020/8343 3446, ⓦ www.partnershiptravel.co.uk. Specialists in mid- and upmarket tailor-made itineraries in South India, particularly strong in Kerala.

Pettitts India ☏ 01892/515966, ⓦ www.pettitts.co.uk. Tailor-made holidays off the beaten track.

The Romance of India by Rail ☏ 01232/329477. Set itineraries and tailor-made tours by train.

Somak Holidays ☏ 020/8423 3000, ⓦ www.somak.co.uk. Goa beach holidays with

optional sightseeing and wildlife extensions.
Soul of India ☎01902/561485,
⊕www.soulofindia.com. Guided tours, for
individuals or groups, of sacred India, including the
Christian South.
Trans Indus Travel ☎020/8566 2729,
⊕www.transindus.co.uk. Fixed and competitively
priced tailor-made tours; specialists in wildlife,
fishing and trekking.
Western & Oriental ☎020/7313 6611,
⊕www.westernoriental.com. Well-organized,
award-winning independent tour operator with
good South India itineraries.

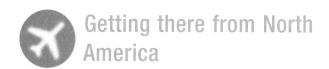

Round-the-world tickets

If you have time to spare, you could take in
India as a stopover, while flying, for example,
between Britain and Australia, or on a
round-the-world ticket, purchased from a
discount flight agent (see p.11). This makes
a lot of sense if you are planning a long trip
with several stops in Asia. A typical itinerary,
say with Quantas and British Airways
(£900–1500), open for a year, would depart
and return to London, taking in Mumbai,
Singapore, Sydney, Honolulu and LA; variations could include doing overland legs
between destinations.

Getting there from North America

India is on the other side of the planet from North America. If you live on the East
Coast it's somewhat shorter to go via Europe, and from the West Coast it's shorter via the Pacific, but either way it's a long haul, involving one or more inter-
mediate stops. You'll arrive fresher and less jet-lagged if you can manage to fit in
a few days' layover somewhere en route.

Most North American travellers arrive at
Mumbai (Bombay), one of India's busiest –
and, in general, cheapest – air gateways.
You can also get flights from North America
to Chennai, the main port of entry for the
south, to Goa on the west coast and
Thiruvananthapuram in the far south.

There are no non-stop flights to India from
North America, but Air India has direct
flights from New York and Chicago to
Mumbai, both via London; United runs a
new direct service from Washington DC to
Delhi; and Air Canada has a direct flight
from Vancouver to Delhi, again both via
London. Many more airlines offer services to
India from North America with a change of
planes either in Asia or Europe. Your choice
of airline is likely to depend on whether you
fly from the east or the west (with the
exception of the above-mentioned
Vancouver–Delhi direct flight), with a variety

of Asian airlines making the trip from the
West Coast, and several European and
Middle Eastern carriers doing the trip from
the Midwest and the East Coast (for more
details see p.14).

Air fares from North America to India are
highest from the beginning of June to late
August. They drop during the "shoulder"
seasons (Sept to early Dec and the second
half of May), but you'll get the best deals
during low season (mid-Dec to mid-May,
excluding Christmas). Direct flights are no
more expensive than those where you'll
have to change planes, but flying on weekends ordinarily adds about $100 to the
round-trip fare; price ranges quoted in the
sections below assume midweek travel.

If India is only one stop on a longer journey, you might want to consider buying a
round-the-world ticket. Some travel agents
can sell you an "off-the-shelf" RTW ticket,

touching down in about half a dozen cities; tailor-made RTW tickets usually work out more expensive. Figure on paying at least $1500 for a regular RTW ticket including India and Europe. A more extensive RTW ticket will cost up to $3000.

Airlines in North America

Aeroflot ☎ 1-888/340-6400; in Canada, ☎ 514/288-2125, ⓦ www.aeroflot.com
Air Canada ☎ 1-800/263-0882 in Canada; 1-800/776-3000 in US, ⓦ www.aircanada.ca
Air France ☎ 1-800/237-2747; in Canada, 1-800/667-2747, ⓦ www.airfrance.fr
Air India ☎ 1-800/223-2250 or 212/751-6200, www.airindia.com
Air Lanka ☎ 1-800/247-5265, ⓦ www.airlanka.com
All Nippon Airways ☎ 1-800/235-9262, ⓦ www.fly-ana.com
Asiana Airlines ☎ 1-800/227-4262, ⓦ www.flyasiana.com
British Airways ☎ 1-800/247-9297, ⓦ www.british-airways.com
Canadian Airlines in Canada, ☎ 1-800/665-1177; in US, 1-800/426-7000, ⓦ www.cdnair.ca
Cathay Pacific ☎ 1-800/233-2742, ⓦ www.cathay-usa.com
EgyptAir ☎ 1-800/334-6787 or 212/315-0900, ⓦ www.egyptair.com.eg
Emirates Air ☎ 1-800/777-3999, ⓦ www.ekgroup.com
Gulf Air ☎ 1-800/553-2824, ⓦ www.gulfairco.com
KLM/Northwest in US, ☎ 1-800/447-4747; in Canada, 1-800/361-5073, ⓦ www.klm.com
Kuwait Airways ☎ 1-800/458-9248 or 212/308-5454, ⓦ www.kuwait-airways.com
Lufthansa in US, ☎ 1-800/645-3880; in Canada, 1-800/563-5954, ⓦ www.lufthansa.com
Malaysia Airlines ☎ 1-800/552-9264, ⓦ www.malaysiaair.com
Northwest/KLM Airlines domestic, ☎ 1-800/225-2525; international, 1-800/447-4747, ⓦ www.nwa.com
Pakistan International Airlines ☎ 1-800/221-2552 or 212/370-9150, ⓦ www.piac.com
Polynesian Airlines ☎ 1-800/644-7659, ⓦ www.pacificislands.com
Qantas Airways ☎ 1-800/227-4500, ⓦ www.qantas.com
Royal Jordanian Airlines ☎ 1-800/223-0470 or 212/949-0050, ⓦ www.rja.com.jo
Sabena ☎ 1-800/955-2000, ⓦ www.sabena-usa .com

Singapore Airlines ☎ 1-800/742-3333, ⓦ www.singaporeair.com
Swissair ☎ 1-800/221-4750, ⓦ www.swissair.com
Thai Airways International in US, ☎ 1-800/426-5204; in Canada, 1-800/668-8103, ⓦ www.thaiair.com
United Airlines ☎ 1-800/538-2929, ⓦ www.united.com
Virgin Atlantic Airways ☎ 1-800/862-8621, ⓦ www.virgin-atlantic.com

Shopping for tickets

Airline tickets are sold through many channels, and there's no magic rule for predicting which will be cheapest. Whatever the airlines are offering, however, any number of specialist travel agents set out to beat it. These are the outfits you'll see advertising in the Sunday newspaper travel sections, and they come in several forms.

Consolidators buy up large blocks of tickets to sell at a discount. Besides being cheap, they don't normally impose advance purchase requirements (although at busy times you'll want to book ahead to be sure of getting a seat), but they do often charge very stiff fees for date changes; note also that airlines generally won't alter tickets after they've gone to a consolidator, so you can only make changes through the consolidator. Also, as these companies' margins are pretty tiny, they make their money by dealing in volume – don't expect them to entertain lots of questions.

Discount agents also wheel and deal in blocks of tickets offloaded by the airlines, but typically offer a range of other travel-related services such as insurance, youth and student ID cards, car rentals, tours and the like. They tend to be most worthwhile for students and under-26s. **Discount travel clubs**, offering money off air tickets, car rental and the like, are an option if you travel a lot. Most, including those we've listed opposite, charge annual membership fees.

Another way of finding cut-price flights is via the **internet**. Websites such as ⓦ www .airticketsindia.com, ⓦ www.cheaptickets.com, ⓦ www.flynow.com and, best of all, ⓦ www .travelocity.com have connections with dozens of airlines to provide competitive discounts. All you have to do is key in the dates you want to travel and their search engines will dig up the cheapest fares.

Finally, don't automatically assume that tickets bought through a travel specialist will be cheapest – once you get a quote, check with the airlines and you may turn up an even cheaper promotion. Never deal with a company that demands cash up front or refuses to accept credit cards.

Discount agents, consolidators and travel clubs

Air Brokers International ☎1-800/883-3273 or 415/397-1383, ⊛www.airbrokers.com. Round-the-world ticket specialist with good rates for itineraries that include India.

Council Travel ☎1-800/226-8624, ⊛www.counciltravel.com. Student/budget travel agency.

Discount Airfares Worldwide On-Line ⊛www.etn.nl/discount.htm. A hub of consolidator and discount agent web links, maintained by the non-profit European Travel Network.

Educational Travel Centre ☎1-800/747-5551 or 608/256-5551, ⊛www.edtrav.com. Student/youth and consolidator fares.

Hari World Travel ☎212/997-3300, ⊛www.hariworld.com. Biggest Indian consolidator, the agent for Indrail passes.

High Adventure Travel ☎1-800/350-0612 or 415/912-5600, ⊛www.airtreks.com. Round-the-world and Circle Pacific tickets. The extensive website features an interactive database called "Farebuilder" that lets you create your own RTW itinerary.

HighTime Travel ☎212/684-7700. Consolidator specializing in tickets to India.

International Travel Network/Airlines of the Web ⊛www.flyaow.com. Online air-travel information and reservations site.

Jaya Travels ☎312/606 9600, ⊛www.jayatravels.com. Chicago-based India specialist with offices nationwide.

Now Voyager, 74 Varick St, Suite 307, New York, NY 10013; ☎212/431-1616, ⊛www.nowvoyagertravel.com. Courier flight-broker and consolidator.

Rupa Travel ☎1-888/438-7872, ⊛www.rupatravel.com. New Jersey/NY India ticket consolidator.

STA Travel ☎1-800/777-0112 or 1-800/781-4040, ⊛www.sta-travel.com. Branches in most major US cities, including: 10 Downing St, New York, NY 10014 ☎212/627-3111; 7202 Melrose Ave, Los Angeles, CA 90046 ☎323/934-8722; 51 Grant Ave, San Francisco, CA 94108 ☎415/391-8407; 297 Newbury St, Boston, MA 02115

☎617/266-6014; 429 S Dearborn St, Chicago, IL 60605 ☎312/786-9050; 3701 Chesnut St, Philadelphia, PA 19104 ☎215/382-2928; 317 14th Ave SE, Minneapolis, MN 55414 ☎612/615-1800. Worldwide discount travel firm specializing in student/youth fares.

Travel CUTS ☎1-800/667-2887 Canada only, or 416/979-2406, ⊛www.travelcuts.com. Organization specializing in student fares, IDs and other travel services.

Travelers Advantage ☎1-800/548-1116, ⊛www.travelersadvantage.com. Discount travel club; annual membership of $59.95 required.

Travelocity ⊛www.travelocity.com. Online consolidator whose website has a special India section, where you'll find tour operators, accommodation options and cheap airfares.

Worldwide Discount Travel Club, 1674 Meridian Ave, Suite 206, Miami Beach, FL 33139 ☎305/534-2082. Discount travel club, with annual membership fee of $80.

From eastern and central US

Flying east, you'll stop over somewhere in Europe (most often London), the Gulf or both. Figure on at least eighteen hours' total travel time from the East Coast.

Air India and PIA discount their tickets heavily through a few specialist, understaffed New York consolidators. Marked-down tickets on European carriers – notably British Airways, Air France, KLM/Northwest and Lufthansa – are frequently sold by other discount agents. Other airlines flying between the eastern US and India include Aeroflot, Gulf Air, Kuwait Airways and Egypt Air. Or you can simply hop on any of the dozens of airlines that fly to London and pick up a flight to India from there.

Prices are most competitive out of New York, where the cheapest low-season fares to Mumbai hover around $1400 ($1750 high season). From **Washington** or **Miami**, figure on $1600/$1850; from **Chicago**, $1600/$2000; and from **Dallas/Fort Worth**, $1800/$3000. Add on roughly $100 for an onward domestic leg from Mumbai to Goa; $180 for Thiruvananthapuram; or $145 for Chennai. If you don't mind going to north India first, United's new direct service via London to Delhi is currently set at a very reasonable $1200/$2000.

From the West Coast

From the West Coast, it takes about as long to fly east or west – a minimum of 22 hours' total travel time – and if you're booking through a consolidator there may not be much difference in price either. Thai Airways, Cathay Pacific, Malaysia Airlines and Singapore Airlines are the main carriers flying over the Pacific to India, via their respective hubs. Air India doesn't do the trans-Pacific route, but can book passengers on Northwest to any of several Asian capitals and then fly them the rest of the way.

From **Los Angeles** or **San Francisco**, you're looking at a minimum of $1400 to fly to Mumbai in low season ($1700 in high season). Add-ons for domestic flights to Goa, Chennai or Thiruvananthapuram are the same as for the East Coast (see above), although you may be able to fly in at no extra cost on one of the Asian airlines, such as Air Lanka, that go direct to Chennai for the deep south.

From Canada

At the time of writing, the only **direct flight** from Canada to India was Vancouver–Delhi on Air Canada, travelling via London in under 20hr. All other routings involve a plane change and more layover time. Air Canada flies during shoulder- and high-season from all major Canadian cities to London, where passengers can join the Vancouver–Delhi flight; the rest of the year they fly through Zurich. Other airlines offering services to India, via their capitals, include British Airways, Air France, Lufthansa, KLM and Aeroflot. This list doesn't convey the full range of possibilities, however. A discount agent will probably break the journey into two, using one of dozens of carriers for the transatlantic (or trans-Pacific) leg.

Typical discounted low- and high-season fares to Mumbai are: CDN$2100/$2700 from **Montreal;** CDN$2250/$2700 from **Toronto**; and CDN$2200/$2650 from **Vancouver**. Add CDN$140 for Goa or CDN$220 for Chennai.

Packages and organized tours

Wrapping South India up into a tidy **package** makes it less daunting and more comprehensible to many first-time tourists. A tour company can also shield you from the subcontinent's many little frustrations, enabling you to cover more ground than if you were going it alone. However, tour prices are wildly out of line with the cost of living in India, and whether you take one will depend on which is tighter, your budget or your schedule. Excluding airfare, a two-week tour is likely to cost at least $2200, and a three-week trip can cost $3500 or more. Your local travel agent should be able to book any tour for you at no additional cost.

Specialist tour operators in North America

Adventure Center ☎1-800/227-8747, ⓦwww.adventurecenter.com. Trekking and cultural tours.

Cox & Kings ☎1-800/999-1758, ⓦwww.coxandkings.com. Deluxe and special-interest sightseeing.

Geographic Expeditions ☎1-800/777-8183, ⓦwww.geoex.com. Unusual tours including sea-kayaking in the Andamans.

Journeyworld International ☎1-800/635-3900. Fifteen- and twenty-day regional tours across the country, some including Sri Lanka.

Mercury Travels Limited ☎1-800/223-1474. A variety of regional and custom tours to each region of India.

Myths and Mountains ☎1-800/670-6984 or 775-832-5454, ⓦwww.mythsandmountains.com. Special-interest trips, tailor-made or group, with emphasis on culture, crafts, religion and traditional medicine.

Nature Expeditions International ☎1-800/869-0639 or 503/484-6529, ⓦwww.naturexp.com. Wildlife and cultural tours.

Rama Tours ☎1800/223-2474. A full-service operator to India, offering individual packages to Goa among its range of regional tours.

Tours of Distinction ☎1-800/888-8634. Regional and all-India tours.

Worldwide Quest Adventures ☎1-800/387-1483, ⓦwww.worldwidequest.com. Sightseeing plus trekking, cycling, and cultural tours.

Getting there from Australia and New Zealand

There are no non-stop flights to India from either Australia or New Zealand; you have to make at least one change of plane in a Southeast Asian hub city (usually Kuala Lumpur, Singapore or Bangkok). The choice of routes and airlines is bewildering, and most agents will offer you a combination of two or more carriers to get the best price.

Bear in mind when you're shopping around which city you want to fly into; your point of arrival may well affect your eventual itinerary, and there's no point in saving a few dollars on the cost of an air ticket only to lose them on an expensive or time-consuming ride across the country to get to the part of India you want to explore first.

Flying west, the main, and cheapest, India gateway city tends to be Chennai (Madras), ideal for exploration of the south, with Mumbai (Bombay) and Delhi not far behind. As a rule of thumb, the best-value tickets from Australia are on departures from the east coast. Flying from Perth to Chennai in **low/shoulder season** (Feb 1–Nov 21) costs A$1100–1300 with Singapore Airlines, Sri Lanka, Malaysian, Ansett or Air India, and from around A$1700 during **high season** (Nov 22–Jan 31). Qantas/British Airlines also offers a competitive low-season fare from the east coast to Mumbai of around A$1400, and there are daily departures connecting with these flights from most Australian cities, with less frequent departures from Cairns and Darwin (2–3 times a week). Coming from the west coast – Sydney, Melbourne or Brisbane – typically costs A$50–100 more.

Flying **from New Zealand**, the cheapest fares to India are generally with Singapore Airlines, Thai Airways, Air New Zealand and Air India (or more probably a combination of all four). Tickets range from just under NZ$2000 to around NZ$2250 if you leave from Auckland; add on approximately NZ$150 for flights from Wellington or Christchurch.

Round-the-world fares from Australia and New Zealand using the above airlines

can take in India; for example, Thai Airways, Air New Zealand, Qantas and Malaysia Airlines can route you through Delhi or Mumbai as part of a RTW deal from around A$2200/NZ$2600.

Shopping for tickets

Buying a **scheduled ticket** direct with the airline is the most expensive way to fly and most people book through an established **discount agent**, whose fares may undercut those offered by the airlines by as much as fifty percent. See p.18 for a list of recommended agents. It's also a good idea to check out the ads in the national Sunday papers or in listings magazines, and to check out online agents such as @www.travel.com.nz or @www.planit.com.au. Factors (aside from price) worth bearing in mind when you're offered a choice of routes and airlines are: the relative durations of the journeys; the number and length of stops or stopovers; and the final arrival time at your destination (a daytime arrival time is much preferable, although invariably more expensive than one in the middle of the night). You should also make a point of asking whether the quoted price includes airport tax.

Many of the companies advertising in newspapers and magazines are **bucket shops** (also known as "consolidators") who are able to offer extremely cheap deals, but who don't necessarily belong to an official bonding scheme such as ABTA or IATA, which means that if they go bust you won't get a refund. For this reason, never deal with a company that demands cash upfront or refuses to accept payment by credit card. Fully bonded operators (ie those who pay insurance to cover refunds in the event of their going under) are obliged to display the ABTA or IATA logo on their adverts. If you're unsure about your agent, give the ABTA or IATA a ring quoting the company's number (listed under the logo).

Students and **under-26-year olds** may be able to get further discounts on flight prices, especially through agents like Trailfinders or STA (although for India, there's often little difference between a youth fare and a regular discounted one). Bear in mind, too, that the lower-priced tickets will often come with restrictions (length of stay, advance booking requirements) and that penalties for changing your plans can be stiff.

Airlines and specialist agents in Australia and New Zealand

Air France in Australia ☎ 02/9244 2100; New Zealand ☎ 09/308 3352, ⓦ www.airfrance.fr
Air India Australia ☎ 02/9299 2022; New Zealand ☎ 09/303 1301, ⓦ www.airindia.com
Air New Zealand Australia ☎ 13 2476; New Zealand ☎ 0800/737000, ☎ 09/357 3000, ⓦ www.airnewzealand.com
Ansett Australia, Australia ☎ 13 1414, ☎ 02/9352 6707; New Zealand ☎ 09/336 2364, ⓦ www.ansett.com.au
Ansett New Zealand Australia ☎ 1800/022146; New Zealand ☎ 09/526 8300, ⓦ www.ansett.com.au
British Airways Australia ☎ 02/8904 8800; New Zealand ☎ 09/356 8690, ⓦ www.british-airways .com
Cathay Pacific Australia ☎ 13 1747; New Zealand ☎ 09/379 0861, ⓦ www.cathaypacific.com
KLM Australia ☎ 1300/303747; New Zealand ☎ 09/302 1452, ⓦ www.klm.com
Lufthansa Australia ☎ 1300/655727, ☎ 02/9367 3887; New Zealand ☎ 09/303 1529, ☎ 008/945 220, ⓦ www.lufthansa.com
Malaysia Airlines Australia ☎ 13 2627; New Zealand ☎ 09/373 2741 or ☎ 008/657472, ⓦ www.malaysianairlines.com
Qantas Australia ☎ 13 1313; New Zealand ☎ 09/357 8900 & ☎ 0800/808767, ⓦ www.qantas.com
Royal Jordanian Airlines Australia ☎ 02/9244 2701; New Zealand ☎ 03/365 3910, ⓦ www.rja.com.jo
Singapore Airlines Australia ☎ 13 1011 or ☎ 02/9350 0262; New Zealand ☎ 09/379 3209 or ☎ 0800/808909, ⓦ www.singaporean.com

Air Lanka/Sri Lanka Airlines Australia ☎ 02/9244 2234; New Zealand ☎ 09/308 3353, ⓦ www.airlanka.com
Swissair Australia ☎ 02/9232 1744 & 1800/221 339; New Zealand ☎ 09/358 3216, ⓦ www.swissair.com
Thai Airways Australia ☎ 1300/651960; New Zealand ☎ 09/377 3886, ⓦ www.thaiair.com

Specialist agents

Anywhere Travel ☎ 02/9663 0411, ☎ 018/401 014, ⓔ anywhere@ozemail.com.au
Asian Travel Centre ☎ 03/9245 0747, ⓦ www.planit.com.au
Australia: Adventure World ☎ 02/956 7766
Budget Travel ☎ 09/366 0061 & 0800/808040.
Flight Centres Australia: Australia ☎ 02/9235 3522, nearest branch ☎ 13 1600; New Zealand ☎ 09/358 4310, plus branches nationwide, ⓦ www.flightcentre.com.au
Northern Gateway ☎ 08/8941 1394, ⓔ oztravel@norgate.com.au
STA Travel, Australia, nearest branch ☎ 13 1776, fastfare telesales ☎ 1300/360960; New Zealand ☎ 09/309 0458, fastfare telesales ☎ 09/366 6673, ⓦ www.statravel.com.au
Student Uni Travel ☎ 02/9232 8444, ⓔ sydney@backpackers.net
Thomas Cook, Australia ☎ 02/9231 2877 or for local branch ☎ 13 1771, Thomas Cook Direct telesales ☎ 1800/801002; New Zealand ☎ 09/379 3920, ⓦ www.thomascook.com.au
Trailfinders, ☎ 02/9247 7666 or 07/3229 0887 or 07/4041 1199, ⓦ www.trailfinders.com.au
Travel.com.au ☎ 02/9249 5444 or 1800/000 447, ⓦ www.travel.com.au
Usit Beyond New Zealand ☎ 09/379 4224 or ☎ 0800/788336 plus branches in Christchurch, Dunedin, Palmerston North, Hamilton and Wellington, ⓦ www.usitbeyond.co.nz

Packages and organized tours

Doing a **package tour** of India makes the prospect of a trip less daunting, especially for first-time visitors, and can enable you to cover more ground than if you were going it alone. Of course, you'll have to be prepared to forgo independence and spontaneity, and accept that there will be only fleeting and predominantly mercenary encounters with local people.

Tours of India work best when they focus on one region of the country, or are based on an activity or a special interest. A fairly standard bestseller list is offered by many companies: Rajasthan palaces, Rajasthan camel safaris (often timed to coincide with the Pushkar Camel Fair), Agra–Varanasi–Khajuraho (frequently packaged with a few days in Nepal), wildlife parks, Goa, temples and/or beaches of the south and the Palace on Wheels railway. Quite a few companies specialize in trekking in the Himalayas, although they invariably offer many more itineraries in Nepal than in India.

Tour prices are always wildly out of line with the cost of living in India, and whether you take one will depend on which is tighter, your budget or your schedule. Excluding airfare, a two-week tour is likely to cost at least A$2200, and a three-week trip with all the bells and whistles can cost $3500 or more. To get an idea of the kind of tours and prices on offer, check out established companies such as Classic Oriental (ⓦwww.classicoriental .com.au/india.htm) or Travel.com.au (ⓦwww .travel.com.au).

Tour operators in Australia and New Zealand

Abercrombie and Kent 90 Bridport St, Albert Park, Victoria ⓣ03/9699 9766, ⓦwww.abercrombiekent.co.uk. Specialists in individual mid- to upmarket holidays, away from the main tourist trails.

Adventure World 73 Walker St, Sydney ⓣ02/9956 7766, toll-free 1800/221 931, plus branches in Melbourne, Adelaide, Brisbane and Perth; 101 Great South Rd, Remuera, Auckland ⓣ09/524 5118. Tailor-made air and accommodation packages, rail passes and regional tours. NZ agents for Peregrine.

Classic Oriental Tours, 4th Floor, 491 Kent St, Sydney ⓣ02/9266 3988, ⓦwww.classicoriental.com.au/india.htm. A wide choice of tours ranging from three-day city breaks to 22-day itineraries, with some adventure options.

India Nepal Travel Centre, 2/84 Pitt St, Sydney ⓣ02/9223 6000, ⓦwww.indianepaltravelcentre.com.au

Peregrine Adventures 258 Lonsdale St, Melbourne ⓣ03/9663 8611; offices in Brisbane, Sydney, Adelaide and Perth. Trekking specialists with a wide range of tailored group and individual tours.

San Michele Travel, 83 York St, Sydney ⓣ02/9299 1111 & 1800/222244, plus a branch in Melbourne, ⓦwww.asiatravel.com.au. Budget and upmarket air and accommodation packages, rail tours and tailor-made land tours for groups or individual travellers.

Travel.com.au, 76 Clarence st, Sydney ⓣ01/800 000 447, ⓦwww.travel.com.au. Agent for a broad range of tour operators. You can select set itineraries or tailor-make your own packages on their website.

Visas and red tape

Gone are the days when Commonwealth nationals could stroll visa-less into India and stay for as long as they pleased: nowadays everybody, except Nepalis and Bhutanis, needs a visa.

If you're going to India on business or to study, you'll need to apply for a special student or business visa, otherwise a standard tourist visa will suffice. These are valid for six months from the date of issue (not of departure from your home country or entry into India), and cost £30/US$60/ CAN$62/A$55/NZ$55. As you're asked to specify whether you need a single-entry or a multiple-entry visa, and the same rates apply to both, it makes sense to ask for the latter, just in case you decide to make a side trip to Nepal or another neighbouring country.

Much the best place to get a visa is in your country of residence, from the embassies and high commissions listed below; you should be able to download forms from the embassy and consulate websites (ⓦ http://passport.nic.in/vspassport /missions.htm). In Britain and North America, you'll need two passport photographs and an application form, obtainable in advance by post, or on the day. In Australia and New Zealand, one passport-sized photo and your flight/travel itinerary are required, together with the visa application form. As a rule, visas are issued in a matter of hours. Embassies in India's neighbouring countries, however, often drag their feet, demand letters of recommendation from your embassy (expensive if you are, for example, British), or make you wait and pay for them to send your application to Delhi. In the US, postal applications take a month as opposed to a same-day service if you do it in person – check your nearest embassy, high commission or consulate to be sure. Make sure that your visa is signed by someone at the embassy or you may be refused entry into the country.

It's also possible in many countries to pay a visa agency to process the visa on your behalf, which in the UK costs from around £25 (plus the price of the visa). In Britain, try The Visa Service, 2 Northdown St, King's Cross, London N1 (ⓣ 020/7833 2709, ⓦ www.visaservice.co.uk) or Visa Express, 31 Corsham St, London N1 (ⓣ 020/7251 4822, ⓔ visaexpress@cwcomm.net). In the US, try Express Visa Service, 2150 Wisconsin Ave, Suite 20, Washington (ⓣ 202/337-2442, ⓦ www.expressvisa.com), who charge $45 for the normal six-day service or $120 for delivery the next day.

It is no longer possible to extend a visa in India, though exceptions may be made in special circumstances. Most people whose standard six-month tourist visas are about to expire head for Colombo, capital of neighbouring Sri Lanka. However, in recent years this has been something of a hit-and-miss business, with some tourists having their requests turned down for no apparent reason. Try to find out from other travellers what the visa situation is, and always allow enough time on your current permit to re-enter India and catch a flight out of the country in case your request is refused.

If you do stay more than 180 days, before you leave the country you are supposed to get a tax clearance certificate, available at the foreigners' section of the income tax department in every major city. They are free, but you should take bank receipts to show you have changed your money legally. In practice, tax clearance certificates are rarely demanded, but you never know.

For details of other kinds of visas – foreigners of Indian origin, business travellers and even students of yoga can get five-year visas – contact your nearest Indian embassy.

Duty-free allowances for travellers arriving in India are covered on p.85.

Special permits

In addition to a visa, **special permits** are required for travel to the Andaman Islands and Lakshadweep. Arriving by plane, you'll be issued them at the airport, but tourists travelling to the Andamans by ship may have to obtain permits before leaving the port of origin (Chennai, Calcutta or Vishakapatnam; see p.453 and 596).

Indian embassies and consulates

Australia High Commission: 3–5 Moonah Place, Yarralumla, Canberra, ACT 2600 ⓣ 02/6273 3999, ⓕ 6273 1308, ⓔ hicanb@ozemail.com.au. Consulates: Level 27, 25 Bligh St, Level 27, Sydney, NSW 2000 ⓣ 02/9223 9500, ⓕ 9223 9246, ⓔ indianc@enternet.com.au; 15 Munro St, Coburg, Melbourne, Vic 3058 ⓣ 03/9384 0141, ⓕ 9384 1609. Honorary Consulates: Level 1, Terrace Hotel, 195 Adelaide Terrace, East Perth WA 6004, Australia (mailing address: PO Box 6118, East Perth, WA 6892, Australia) ⓣ 08/9221 1485, ⓕ 9221 1206, ⓔ india@vianet .net.au; Brisbane ⓣ 07/3260 2825, ⓕ 3260 2826. Bangladesh House 120, Rd 2, Dhanmondi Residential Area, Dhaka ⓣ 02/503606, ⓕ 863662; 1253–1256 Nizam Road, Mehdi Bagh, Chittagong ⓣ 031/211007, ⓕ 225178. Burma (Myanmar) Oriental Assurance Building, 545–547 Merchant St (PO Box 751), Rangoon ⓣ 01/82550. Canada High Commission: 10 Springfield Rd, Ottawa, ON K1M 1C9 ⓣ 613/744-3751, ⓕ 744-0913, ⓦ www.docuweb.ca/india. Consulates: 2 Bloor St W, #500, Toronto, ON M4W 3E2 ⓣ 416/960-0751; 325 Howe St, 2nd floor,

Vancouver, BC V6C 1Z7 ⊤604/662-8811,
ⓦwww.cgivancouver.com.
Japan 2-11, Kudan Minami 2-Chome, Chiyoda-ku,
Tokyo 102 ⊤03/3262 2391, Ⓕ3234 4866.
Malaysia 2 Jalan Taman Dlita (off Jalan Duta), PO
Box 10059, 50704 Kuala Lumpur ⊤03/253 3504,
Ⓕ253 3507.
Nepal ⓦwww.south-asia.com/Embassy-India
Lainchaur (off Lazimpath), PO Box 92, Kathmandu
⊤01/410900, Ⓕ413132. Allow a week – plus
extra fee – to fax Delhi; British nationals and some
Europeans need letters of recommendation.
Mon–Fri 9.30–11am.
New Zealand Indian High Commission: 180
Molesworth St (PO Box 4005), Wellington
⊤04/473 6390, Ⓕ499 0665.
Pakistan G-5, Diplomatic enclave, Islamabad
⊤051/814371, Ⓕ820742; India House, 3 Fatima
Jinnah Rd (PO Box 8542), Karachi ⊤021/522275,
Ⓕ568 0929.
Singapore India House, 31 Grange Rd (PO Box
9123), Singapore 0923 ⊤737 6777, Ⓕ732 6909.
Sri Lanka 36–38 Galle Rd, Colombo 3
⊤01/421605, Ⓕ446403, ⓦwww.indiahcsl.org;
31 Rajapihilla Mawatha, PO Box 47, Kandy
⊤08/24563.

Thailand ⓦwww.indiaemb.or.th46 Soi 23
(Prasarn Mitr), Sukhumvit Road, Bangkok 10110
⊤02/258 0300, Ⓕ258 4627; 113 Bumruangrat
Road, Chiang Mai 50000 ⊤053/243066,
Ⓕ247879. Visas take five working days to issue.
UK ⓦwww.hcilondon.org. High Commission: India
House, Aldwych, London WC2B 4NA ⊤020/7836
8484, Ⓕ7836 4331. Consulates: 20 Augusta St,
Jewellery Quarter, Hockley, Birmingham B18 6GL
⊤0121/212 2782; 17 Rutland Square, Edinburgh
EH1 2BB ⊤0131/229 2144. All open Mon–Fri
8.30am–noon.
USA Embassy of India (Consular Services): 2107
Massachusetts Ave NW, Washington, DC 20008.
⊤202/939-7000, Ⓕ939-7027. Consulates: 3 East
64th St, New York, NY 10021 ⊤212/774-0600,
Ⓕ861-3788, ⓦwww.indiacgny.org; 540 Arguello
Blvd, San Francisco, CA 94118 ⊤415/668-0683,
Ⓕ668-9764; 455 North Cityfront Plaza Drive, Suite
850, Chicago, Il 60611 ⊤312/595-0405 (ext 22
for visas), Ⓕ595-0416,
ⓦwww.indianconsulate.com; 201 St Charles Ave,
New Orleans, LA 70170 ⊤504/582-8106; 2051
Young St, Honolulu, HI 96826 ⊤808/947-2618.

Information, websites and maps

The Indian government maintains a number of tourist offices abroad, where you can pick up a range of pamphlets. Their main purpose is to advertise rather than inform, but they can be extremely helpful and knowledgeable.

Other sources of information include travel agents (who are in business for themselves, so their advice may not always be totally unbiased), and the Indian Railways representatives listed on p.39.

Inside India, both national and local governments run **tourist information offices**, providing general travel advice and handing out an array of printed material, from city maps to glossy leaflets covering specific destinations. The Indian government's tourist department – whose main offices are oppo-

site Churchgate train station, Mumbai – has branches in most regional capitals. These, however, operate independently of the information counters and bureaux run by the **state tourism development corporations**, usually referred to by their initials (eg KTDC in Kerala), who offer a wide range of travel facilities, including **guided tours**, **car rental** and their own **hotels** (which we identify with the relevant acronyms throughout this book).

Just to confuse things more, the Indian government's tourist office has a go-ahead corporate wing too. **ITDC** (Indian Tourism Development Corporation), is responsible for the Ashok chain of hotels and operates tour and travel services, frequently competing with its state counterparts.

Indian government tourist offices abroad

ⓦ www.tourisminindia.com

Australia Level 2, Piccadilly, 210 Pitt St, Sydney NSW ⓣ 02/9264 4855, ⓕ 9264 4860; Level 1, 17 Castle Reagh, Sydney, NSW 2000 ⓣ 02/9232 1600, ⓕ 9223 3003, ⓔ sydney@tourismindia.com.

Canada 60 Bloor St (West), #1003, Toronto, Ontario M4W 3B8 ⓣ 416/962-3787, ⓕ 962-6279, ⓔ toronto@tourismindia.com.

Netherlands Rokin 9–15, 1022 KK, Amsterdam ⓣ 020/620 8991, ⓕ 638 3059, ⓔ amsterdam@tourismindia.com.

Singapore 20 Karamat Lane, 01–01A United House, Singapore 0922 ⓣ 065/235 3800, ⓕ 235 8677, ⓔ singapore@tourismindia.com.

Thailand Singapore Airlines Bldg, 3rd floor, 62/5 Thaniya Rd (Silom), Bangkok ⓣ 02/235 2585 & 235 6670, ⓕ 236 8411.

UK 7 Cork St, London W1X 2LN ⓣ 020/7437 3677, ⓕ 7454 1048, ⓔ london@tourismindia.com.

USA 3550 Wilshire Blvd, Suite #204, Los Angeles, CA 90010 ⓣ 213/380-8855, ⓕ 380-6111, ⓔ la@tourismindia.com; Suite 1808, 1270 Ave of Americas, New York, NY 10020 ⓣ 212/751-6840, ⓕ 582-3274, ⓔ ny@tourismindia.com

South India on the internet

General

ⓦ www.123india.com
India-specific search engine providing links to a wide choice of India-related websites.
ⓦ http://travel.indiamart.com
Comprehensive site providing tourist information on tours, hotels and India's forts, monuments, museums and temples.
ⓦ www.indev.org
India Development Information Network website for information on Indian development issues: discussions, news regarding NGOs and useful links.

Tourism

Government of India, Ministry of Tourism
ⓦ www.tourisminindia.com

A very useful site providing a vast range of information, including city guides, rail and air travel timetables, details and dates of festivals. (Also, check out ⓦ www.tourismsindia.com, which links up with all the regional Indian Tourist Boards.)
ⓦ www.tourindia.com
The website – originating from the US – of the Government of India Tourist Office, which is easier to navigate than the main site.

News and media

ⓦ www.indiainfo.com
Excellent resource for links to the websites of both national and regional Indian newspapers and magazines.
ⓦ www.timesofindia.com
ⓦ www.hinduonline.com
The websites of *The Times of India* and *The Hindu* provide the most up-to-date and detailed national news coverage.

South India

ⓦ www.mumbai-central.com
ⓦ www.chennainow.com
ⓦ www.hyderabad.com
ⓦ www.mangalore.com
ⓦ www.pondicherry.com
Besides our own extensive site on India (ⓦ www.roughguides.com), these are some useful websites on South Indian cities, some with search engines, listings and news. ⓦ www.explocity.com has comprehensive city listings for Bangalore, Hyderabad and Mumbai among other places.

ⓦ www.andhraworld.com
ⓦ www.deccan.com
ⓦ www.goacom.com
ⓦ www.karnataka.com
ⓦ www.kerala.com
ⓦ www.tamilnadu.com
Useful state-wide websites with search engines and some good links.

ⓦ www.thekkady.com
ⓦ www.alappuzha.com
ⓦ www.cochin.com
Some of the best of a host of town and regional websites now available on Kerala.

Travel advice

ⓦ www.fco.gov
The British Foreign Office website is useful for checking potential or actual dangerous areas.

Ⓦhttp://travel.state.gov/travel–warnings
.html
The US State Department's travel advice for
potential hot spots.

Maps

Getting good **maps** of India, in India, can be
difficult; the government forbids the sale of
detailed maps of border areas, which include
the entire coastline. Geocentre produces an
excellent map of South India at a scale of
1:2,000,000, showing good road detail.

Another excellent map of South India is the
Nelles' India 4 (South) 1:1,500,000, which
shows colour contours, road distances, inset
city plans and even the tiniest places. Ttk, a
Chennai-based company, publishes basic
state maps, which are widely available in India,
and in some specialized travel and map shops
in the UK such as Stanfords (see below).
Regional Automobile Associations based in
Mumbai and Chennai produce books of road
maps which are useful for those planning
overland routes across India. For basic state-
by-state and city road maps try Ⓦhttp://map-
sofindia.com/maps. The Indian Railways map
at the back of the publication *Trains at a
Glance* is useful for planning railway journeys.

If you need larger-scale **city maps** than
the ones we provide in this book – which are
keyed to show recommended hotels and
restaurants – you can sometimes get them
from tourist offices. Both Ttk and the official
Indian mapping organization, the Survey of
India, Janpath Barracks A, New Delhi 110
001 (Ⓣ011/332 2288), have town plans at
scales of 1:10,000 and 1:50,000. Some of
the city and regional maps they have for sale
are grossly out of date.

Book and map outlets in the UK and Ireland

Blackwell's Map and Travel Shop, 53 Broad
St, Oxford OX1 3BQ Ⓣ01865/792792,
Ⓦwww.blackwell.bookshop.co.uk.
Daunt Books, 83 Marylebone High St, W1M 3DE
Ⓣ020/7224 2295, Ⓕ020/7224 6893; 193
Haverstock Hill, NW3 4QL Ⓣ020/7794 4006.
Heffers Map and Travel, 20 Trinity St,
Cambridge, CB2 1TJ Ⓣ01223/586586,
Ⓦwww.heffers.co.uk.
James Thin Melven's Bookshop, 29 Union St,
Inverness, IV1 1QA Ⓣ01463/233500,
Ⓦwww.jthin.co.uk.

John Smith and Sons, 26 Colquhoun Ave,
Glasgow, G52 4PJ Ⓣ0141/221 7472, Ⓕ484412,
Ⓦwww.johnsmith.co.uk.
The Map Shop, 30a Belvoir St, Leicester, LE1
6QH Ⓣ0116/247 1400.
National Map Centre, 22–24 Caxton St, SW1H
0QU Ⓣ020/7222 2466, Ⓦwww.mapsnmc.co.uk.
Newcastle Map Centre, 55 Grey St, Newcastle
upon Tyne, NE1 6EF Ⓣ0191/261 5622,
Ⓦwww.newtraveller.com.
Stanfords, 12–14 Long Acre, WC2E 9LP
Ⓣ020/7836 1321; British Airways office, 156
Regent St, W1R 5TA Ⓣ020/7434 4744; 29 Corn
St, Bristol BS1 1HT Ⓣ0117/929 9966,
Ⓦwww.stanfords.co.uk.
The Travel Bookshop, 13–15 Blenheim
Crescent, W11 2EE Ⓣ020/7229 5260,
Ⓦwww.thetravelbookshop.co.uk.
Waterstones', 91 Deansgate, Manchester, M3
2BW Ⓣ0161/837 3000, Ⓕ835 1534,
Ⓦwww.waterstonesbooks.co.uk.

Book and map outlets in the USA

ADC Map and Travel Center, 1636 I St NW,
Washington DC 20006 Ⓣ202/628 2608.
Adventurous Traveler Bookstore, PO Box
64769, Burlington, VT 05406 Ⓣ1-800/282-3963,
Ⓦwww.adventuroustraveler.com.
Book Passage, 51 Tamal Vista Blvd, Corte
Madera, CA 94925 Ⓣ415/927-0960,
Ⓦwww.bookpassage.com.
The Complete Traveller Bookstore, 199
Madison Ave, New York, NY 10016 Ⓣ212/685-
9007; 3207 Fillmore St, San Francisco, CA 92123
Ⓣ415/923-1511.
Distant Lands, 56 S Raymond Ave, Pasadena, CA
91105 Ⓣ626/449-3220, Ⓦwww.distantlands.com
Elliott Bay Book Company, 101 S Main St,
Seattle, WA 98104 Ⓣ206/624-6600,
Ⓦwww.elliottbaybook.com.
Map Link, 30 S La Petera Lane, Unit #5, Santa
Barbara, CA 93117 Ⓣ805/692-6777,
Ⓦwww.maplink.com.
Phileas Fogg's Books & Maps, #87 Stanford
Shopping Center, Palo Alto, CA 94304 Ⓣ1-
800/533-FOGG, Ⓦwww.foggs.com.
Rand McNally, Ⓦwww.randmcnally.com: 444 N
Michigan Ave, Chicago, IL 60611 Ⓣ312/321-1751;
150 E 52nd St, New York, NY 10022 Ⓣ212/758-
7488; 595 Market St, San Francisco, CA 94105
Ⓣ415/777-3131; 7988 Tysons Corner Center,
McLean, VA 22102 Ⓣ703/556-8688; Ⓣ1-800/333-
0136 ext 2111 for other locations or for mail order.
Sierra Club Bookstore, 730 Polk St, San
Francisco, CA 94110 Ⓣ415/977-5653,

ⓦ www.sierraclubbookstore.com.
Travel Books & Language Center, 4437 Wisconsin Ave NW, Washington, DC 20016 ⓣ 1-800/220-2665.
Traveler's Choice Bookstore, 22 W 52nd St, New York, NY 10019 ⓣ 212/941-1535, ⓦ tvlchoice@aol.com.

Book and map outlets in Canada

Open Air Books and Maps, 25 Toronto St, Toronto, ON M5R 2C1 ⓣ 416/363-0719.
Ulysses Travel Bookshop, 4176 St-Denis, Montréal ⓣ 514/843-9447, ⓦ www.ulysses.ca
World of Maps, 1235 Wellington St, Ottawa, ON K1Y 3A3 ⓣ 613/724-6776, ⓦ www.worldofmaps.com.
World Wide Books and Maps, 552 Seymour St, Vancouver, BC V6B 3J5 ⓣ 604/687-3320, ⓦ www.itmb.com.

Book and map outlets in Australia and New Zealand

Mapland, 372 Little Bourke St, Melbourne, VIC 3000 ⓣ 03/9670 4383.
The Map Shop, 16a Peel St, Adelaide, SA 5000 ⓣ 08/8231 2033.
Perth Map Centre, 884 Hay St, Perth, WA 6000 ⓣ 08/9322 5733.
Speciality Maps, 58 Albert St, Auckland ⓣ 09/307 2217.
Travel Bookshop, Shop 3, 175 Liverpool St, Sydney, NSW 2000 ⓣ 02/9261 8200.
Worldwide Maps and Guides, 187 George St, Brisbane, QLD 4000 ⓣ 07/3221 4330.
Mapworld, 173 Gloucester Street, Christchurch ⓣ 03/374 5399, ⓕ 03/374 5633, ⓦ www.mapworld.co.nz.

Travel insurance

In the light of the potential health risks involved in a trip to India – see opposite – travel insurance is essential. In addition to covering medical expenses and emergency flights, it also insures your money and belongings against loss or theft. A typical travel insurance policy usually provides cover for the loss of baggage, tickets and – up to a certain limit – cash or cheques, as well as cancellation or curtailment of your journey. Most of them exclude so-called dangerous sports unless an extra premium is paid: in India this can mean trekking, mountaineering, skiing, whitewater rafting and scuba-diving, though probably not jeep safaris.

Read the small print and benefits tables of prospective policies carefully; coverage can vary wildly for roughly similar premiums. Many policies can be chopped and changed to exclude coverage you don't need – for example, sickness and accident benefits can often be excluded or included at will. If you do take **medical coverage**, ascertain whether benefits will be paid as treatment proceeds or only after return home, and whether there is a 24-hour medical emergency number. When securing baggage cover, make sure that the per-article limit – typically under £500 equivalent – will cover your most valuable possession.

If you need to make a claim, you should keep **receipts** for medicines and medical treatment and, in the event you have anything stolen, you must obtain an official police report. Bank and credit cards often have certain levels of medical or other insurance included; you may automatically get travel insurance if you use a major credit card to pay for your trip. Keep photocopies of everything you send to the insurer and don't allow months to elapse before informing them. Write immediately and tell them what's happened; you can usually claim later.

Travel agents and tour operators are likely to require some sort of insurance when you

Rough Guides now offers its own travel insurance, customized for our readers by a leading UK broker and backed by a Lloyd's underwriter. It's available for anyone, of any nationality or age, travelling anywhere in the world.

There are two main Rough Guide insurance plans: Essential, for basic, no-frills cover (£23.03 worldwide) for two weeks; and Premier – with more generous and extensive benefits (£28.79 worldwide). Alternatively, you can take out annual multi-trip insurance, which covers you for any number of trips throughout the year (with a maximum of 60 days for any one trip) at £83.99 (worldwide). Unlike many policies, the Rough Guides schemes are calculated by the day, so if you're travelling for 27 days rather than a month, that's all you pay for. If you intend to be away for the whole year, the Adventurer policy will cover you for 365 days from £160 (worldwide excluding USA and Canada) and £200 (worldwide including USA and Canada). Each plan can be supplemented with a "Hazardous Activities Premium" if you plan to indulge in sports considered dangerous, such as trekking, mountaineering, skiing or scuba-diving. Rough Guides also does good deals for older travellers, and will insure you up to any age, at prices comparable to SAGA's.

For a policy quote, call the Rough Guide Insurance Line on UK freefone ☎ 0800 015 0906, US freefone ☎ 1-866/220558 or, if you're calling from outside Britain, on ☎ 44/1243 621046. Alternatively, get a quote and buy online at ⊛ www.roughguides.com/insurance

---

book a **package holiday**, though according to UK law they can't make you buy their own (other than a £1 premium for "schedule airline failure"). If you have a good all-risks home insurance policy it may cover your possessions against loss or theft even when overseas. Many private medical schemes also offer coverage plans for abroad, including baggage loss, cancellation or curtailment and cash replacement as well as sickness or accident.

Travellers from the **US** and **Canada** should carefully check their current insurance policies before taking out a new one. You may discover that you are already covered for medical and other losses while abroad. Holders of ISIC cards are entitled to be reimbursed for $3000-worth of accident cover-

age and sixty days of in-patient benefits of up to $100 a day for the period the card is valid. If you do want a specific travel insurance policy, there are numerous kinds to choose from: short-term combination policies covering everything from baggage loss to broken legs are the best bet. Coverage of prepaid airfare and accommodation expenses of up to $2500, plus $10,000 primary medical coverage will cost you $150 for up to thirty days, plus $5 per extra day.

In **Australia** and **New Zealand**, travel insurance is put together by the airlines and travel agent groups. Most adventure sports are covered, but check your policy first. A typical policy will cost AUS$150/NZ$170 for one month.

Health

A lot of visitors get ill in South India just as in the rest of the country, and some of them get very ill. However, if you are careful, you should be able to get through the region with nothing worse than a mild dose of "Delhi belly". The important thing is to keep your resistance high and to be very aware of health risks such as poor hygiene, untreated water, mosquito bites and undressed open cuts.

What you **eat** and **drink** is crucial: a poor diet lowers your resistance. Ensure you eat a balance of protein, energy, vitamins and minerals. Meat and fish are obvious sources of protein for non-vegetarians in the West, but not necessarily in India, though in southern India the fish bought along the coast should be fresh and safe. Eggs, pulses (lentils, peas and beans), rice and curd are all protein sources, as are nuts. Overcooked vegetables lose a lot of their vitamin content; eating plenty of peeled fresh fruit – provided this is fruit you have peeled yourself – helps keep up your vitamin and mineral intake. With all that sweating, too, make sure you get enough salt – put a bit extra on your food – and drink enough water. This is especially important in the consistently hot and humid south. It's also worth taking daily multivitamin and mineral tablets with you. Above all, make sure you eat enough – an unfamiliar diet may reduce the amount you eat – and **get enough sleep** and rest: it's easy to get run down if you're on the move a lot, especially in a hot climate.

It's worth knowing, if you are ill and can't get to a doctor, that almost any medicine can be bought over the counter without a prescription.

A travellers' first-aid kit

Below are items you might want to take, especially if you're planning to go trekking – all medicines are available in India itself, at a fraction of what you might pay at home:

☐ Antiseptic cream
☐ Insect repellent and cream such as Anthisan for soothing bites
☐ Plasters/band aids
☐ A course of Flagyl antibiotics
☐ Water sterilization tablets or water purifier
☐ Lint and sealed bandages
☐ Knee supports
☐ Imodium (Lomotil) for emergency diarrhoea treatment
☐ A mild oral anaesthetic such as Bonjela for soothing ulcers or mild toothache
☐ Paracetamol/aspirin (called crocin in India)
☐ Multivitamin and mineral tablets
☐ Rehydration sachets
☐ Hypodermic needles and sterilized skin wipes

Precautions

The lack of sanitation in India can be exaggerated. It's not worth getting too worked up about, though, as you'll never enjoy anything. A few **common-sense precautions**, however, are in order, bearing in mind that things such as bacteria multiply far more quickly in a tropical climate, and your body will have little immunity to Indian germs.

For details on the **water**, see the box opposite. When it comes to **food**, it's quite likely that tourist restaurants and Western dishes will bring you grief. Be particularly wary of prepared dishes that have to be reheated – they may have been on display in the heat and the flies for some time. Anything that is boiled or fried (and thus sterilized) in your presence is usually all right, though meat can sometimes be dodgy, especially in towns or cities where the electricity supply (and thus refrigerators) frequently fails. Any food that has been left out for any length of time is definitely suspect. Raw unpeeled fruit and vegetables should always be viewed with suspicion, and you should avoid salads unless you know they have been soaked in an iodine or potassium permanganate solution. Wiping down a plate before eating is sensible, and avoid straws as they are usually dusty or secondhand. As a rule of thumb, stick to cafés and restaurants that are doing a brisk trade, and where the food is thus freshly cooked, and you should be fine.

Be vigilant about **personal hygiene**. Wash your hands often, especially before eating. Keep all cuts clean – treat them with iodine or antiseptic – and cover them up to prevent infection. Be fussier than usual about sharing things like drinks and cigarettes, and never share a razor or toothbrush. It is also inadvisable to go around barefoot – and best to wear flip-flop sandals, including in the shower.

Advice on avoiding **mosquitoes** is offered under the section on malaria on p.29. If you do get bites or itches try not to scratch them: it's hard, but infection and tropical ulcers can result if you do. Tiger balm, calamine lotion, antihistamine cream and even dried soap may relieve the itching.

Finally, especially if you are going on a long trip, have a **dental check-up** before you leave home – you don't want to go down with unexpected tooth trouble in India. If you do, and it feels serious, head for Mumbai,

One of the chief concerns of many prospective visitors to India is whether the water is safe to drink. To put it simply, no, though your unfamiliarity with Indian micro-organisms is generally more of a problem rather than any great virulence in the water itself.

It is generally not a good idea to drink tap water. However, it is almost impossible to avoid untreated tap water completely: it is used to make ice, which may appear in drinks without being asked for, lassis are made with it, utensils are washed with it, and so on. Bottled water is widely available. Always check that the seal is intact, as refilling bottles is not uncommon, and crush the bottle after use to stop the trade in refills.

If you plan to go somewhere with no access to bottled drinks (which really only applies to travellers venturing well off the beaten track) find an appropriate method of treating water, whether your source is tap water or natural groundwater such as a river or stream. Boiling it for a minimum of five minutes (longer at higher altitudes) is sufficient to kill micro-organisms, but is not always practical and does not remove unpleasant tastes. Chemical sterilization is cheap and convenient, but dirty water remains dirty, and still contains organic matter or other contamination. You can sterilize water by using chlorine or iodine tablets, but these leave a nasty after-taste (which can be masked with a squeeze of lemon or lime) and are not effective in preventing such diseases as amoebic dysentery and giardia. Tincture of iodine is better, although it still doesn't do much for the taste; add five drops to one litre of water and leave it to stand for thirty minutes. If the water is cloudy, filter it before adding the iodine or add ten drops per litre. Pregnant women, babies and people with thyroid problems should avoid using iodine sterilizing tablets or iodine-based purifiers, or use an additional iodine-removal filter. The various kinds of filter only remove visible impurities and the larger pathogenic organisms (most bacteria and cysts). However fine the filter, it will not remove viruses, dissolved chemicals, pesticides, herbicides etc.

Purification, a two-stage process involving both filtration and sterilization, gives the most complete treatment. Portable water purifiers range from pocket-size units weighing 60g, up to 800g. Some of the best water purifiers on the market are made in Britain by Pre-Mac. For suppliers contact:

All Water Systems Ltd Unit 2018 Citywest Business Campus, Faggart, Co. Dublin, Ireland ☎ 01/466 0133

Nomad Travellers Store and Medical Centre 3-4 Wellington Terrace Turnpike Lane, London N8 0PX ☎ 020/8889 7014, ⓕ 8889 9529, ⓦ www.nomadtravel.co.uk

Pre-Mac (Kent) Ltd Unit 5 Morewood Close, Sevenoaks, Kent TN13 2HU England ☎ 01732/460333, ⓦ www.pre-mac.com

Travel Medicine 351 Pleasant St, Suite 312, Northampton, MA 01060, US ☎ 1-800/872 8633, ⓦ www.travmed.com

Chennai or Bangalore, and ask a foreign consulate to recommend a dentist.

Vaccinations

No **inoculations** are legally required for entry into India, but meningitis, typhoid and hepatitis A jabs are recommended, and it's worth ensuring that you are up to date with tetanus, polio and other boosters. All vaccinations can be obtained in Mumbai, Chennai and other major cities if necessary; just make sure the needle is new or provide your own.

Hepatitis A is not the worst disease you can catch in India, but the frequency with which it strikes travellers makes a strong case for immunization. Transmitted through contaminated food and water, or through saliva, it can lay a victim low for several months with exhaustion, fever and diarrhoea – and may cause liver damage. The Havrix vaccine has been shown to be extremely effective; though expensive, it lasts for up to ten years. The protection given by gamma-globulin, the traditional serum of hepatitis antibodies, wears off quickly and the injection should therefore be given as late as possible before departure: the longer your planned stay, the larger the dose.

Symptoms by which you can recognize hepatitis include a yellowing of the whites of the eyes, nausea, general flu-like malaise, orange urine (though dehydration could also cause that) and light-coloured stools. If you think you have it, avoid alcohol, try to avoid passing it on and get lots of rest. More serious is **hepatitis B**, passed on like AIDS through blood or sexual contact. There is a vaccine, but it is only recommended for those planning to work in a medical environment, or in rural areas. **Typhoid**, also spread through contaminated food or water, is endemic in India, but rare outside the monsoon. It produces a persistent high fever with malaise, headaches and abdominal pains, followed by diarrhoea. Vaccination can be by injection (two shots are required, or one for a booster), giving three years' cover, or orally – tablets, which are more expensive but easier on the arm.

Most medical authorities now recommend vaccination against **meningitis** too. Spread by airborne bacteria (through coughs and sneezes for example), it attacks the lining of the brain and can be fatal. Symptoms include fever, a severe headache, stiffness in the neck and a rash on the stomach and back. If you think you may have meningitis, seek immediate medical attention.

You should have a **tetanus** booster every ten years whether you travel or not. Tetanus (or lockjaw) is picked up through contaminated open wounds and causes severe muscular spasms; if you cut yourself on something dirty and are not covered, get a booster as soon as you can.

Assuming that you were vaccinated against **polio** in childhood, only one (oral) booster is needed during your adult life. Immunizations against mumps, measles, TB and rubella are a good idea for anyone who wasn't vaccinated as a child and hasn't had the diseases.

Rabies is a problem in India. The best advice is to give dogs and monkeys a wide berth, and not to play with animals at all, no matter how cute they might look. A bite, a scratch or even a lick from an infected animal could spread the disease; wash any such wound immediately but gently with soap or detergent, and apply alcohol or iodine if possible. Find out what you can about the animal and swap addresses with the owner (if there is one) just in case. If the animal might be infected or the wound begins to tingle and fester, act immediately to get treatment – rabies is invariably fatal once symptoms appear. There is a vaccine, recommended if you plan to work in rural areas, but it is expensive and only effective for a maximum of three months.

Medical resources for travellers

For up-to-the-minute information, make an appointment at a **travel clinic**. These clinics also sell travel accessories, including mosquito nets and first-aid kits. Information about specific diseases and conditions, drugs and herbal remedies is provided at Ⓦhttp://health.yahoo.com, as well as advice from health experts. You could also consult the *Rough Guide to Travel Health* by Dr Nick Jones.

UK

British Airways Travel Clinics Operates several clinics located in London including 156 Regent St, London W1 ☏020/7439 9584 (Mon–Fri 9.30am–5.15pm, Sat 10am–4pm; no appointment necessary). There are appointment-only branches at 101 Cheapside, London EC2 ☏020/7606 2977, and at the BA terminal in London's Victoria Station ☏020/7233 6661. Call ☏01276/685040 for your nearest clinic, or check out Ⓦwww.britishairways.com; BA operates around 28 regional clinics throughout the country. The clinics provide vaccinations, tailored advice from their online database and a complete range of travel healthcare products.

Hospital for Tropical Diseases Travel Clinic, 2nd floor, Mortimer Market Centre, off Capper Street, London WC1E 6AU (Mon–Fri 9am–5pm by appointment only; ☏020/7388 9600). A consultation costs £15 which is waived if you have your injections here. Their recorded Health Line (☏09061/337733; 50p per min) gives hints on hygiene and illness prevention as well as listing appropriate immunizations.

Malaria Helpline 24hr recorded message (☏0891/600350; 60p per minute).

MASTA (Medical Advisory Service for Travellers Abroad), London School of Hygiene and Tropical Medicine. Operates a prerecorded 24-hour Travellers' Health Line (☏ 0906/822 4100, 60p per min), giving written information tailored to your journey by return of post.

Nomad Pharmacy, surgeries 40 Bernard St, London, WC1 opposite Russell Square tube station; and 3–4 Turnpike Lane, London N8 (Mon–Fri 9.30am–6pm ☏ 020/7833 4114 to book appointment). Advice is free if you go in person, and the telephone helpline is ☏ 09068/633414 (60p a minute). They can give information tailored to your travel needs.

Trailfinders No-appointments-necessary immunization clinics at the 194 Kensington High St branch in London (Mon–Fri 9am–5pm except Thurs to 6pm, Sat 9.30am–4pm; ☏ 020/7938 3999).

North America

Canadian Society for International Health, 1 Nicholas St, Suite 1105, Ottawa, ON K1N 7B7 ☏ 613/241-5785, ⓦ www.csih.org. Distributes a free pamphlet, *Health Information for Canadian Travellers*, containing an extensive list of travel health centres in Canada.

Centers for Disease Control, 1600 Clifton Rd NE, Atlanta, GA 30333 ☏ 404/639-3311, ⓦ www.cdc.gov. Publishes outbreak warnings, suggested inoculations, precautions and other background information for travellers. The website is very useful, as well as their International Travelers Hotline: ☏ 1/888-232-3228.

International Association for Medical Assistance to Travellers (IAMAT), 417 Center St, Lewiston, NY 14092 ☏ 716/754-4883; 40 Regal Rd, Guelph, ON N1K 1B5 ☏ 519/836-0102, ⓦ www.sentex.net/~iamat. A non-profit organization supported by donations, it can provide a list of English-speaking doctors in India, climate charts and leaflets on various diseases and inoculations.

International SOS Assistance, PO Box 11568, Philadelphia, PA 19116 ☏ 1-800/523-8930, ⓦ www.intsos.com. Members receive pre-trip medical referral info, as well as overseas emergency services designed to complement travel insurance coverage.

Travel Medicine, 351 Pleasant St, Suite 312, Northampton, MA 01060 ☏ 1-800/872-8633, ⓦ www.travmed.com. Sells first-aid kits, mosquito netting, water filters and other health-related travel products.

Travelers Medical Center, 31 Washington Square West, New York, NY 10011 ☏ 212/982-1600. Consultation service on immunizations and treatment of diseases for people travelling to developing countries.

Australia and New Zealand

Auckland Hospital, Park Road, Grafton ☏ 09/797 440. General traveller health advice.

Travel-Bug Medical and Vaccination Centre, 161 Ward St, North Adelaide ☏ 08/8267 3544. Consultations, inoculations, first-aid/medical kits, post-travel examinations.

Travellers' Immunization Service, 303 Pacific Hwy, Lindfield, Sydney ☏ 02/9416 1348. Offers inoculations and general advice.

Travellers' Medical and Vaccination Centre Australia: Level 7, 428 George St, Sydney ☏ 02/9221 7133; Level 2, 393 Little Bourke St, Melbourne ☏ 03/9602 5788; Level 6, 29 Gilbert Place, Adelaide ☏ 08/8212 7522; Level 6, 247 Adelaide St, Brisbane ☏ 07/3221 9066; 5 Mill St, Perth ☏ 08/9321 1977. New Zealand: 1/170 Queen St ☏ 09/373 3531; 6 Washington Way, Christchurch ☏ 03/379 4000. General info/health line: ☏ 1902/261 560 (Australia). Inoculations/medications, area-specific advice, lists of English-speaking doctors in India, first-aid/medical kits and post-travel examinations. A full rundown of their branches, along with general travellers' health advice, appears on ⓦ www.tmvc.com.au.

Malaria

Protection against **malaria** is absolutely essential. The disease, caused by a parasite carried in the saliva of female Anopheles mosquitoes, is endemic everywhere in South India and is nowadays regarded as the big killer in the subcontinent. It has a variable incubation period of a few days to several weeks, so you can become ill long after being bitten. Programmes to eradicate the disease by spraying mosquito-infested areas and distributing free preventative tablets have proved disastrous; within a short space of time, the Anopheles mosquitoes develop immunities to the insecticides, while the malaria parasite itself constantly mutates into drug-resistant strains, rendering the old cures ineffective.

It is vital for travellers to take **preventative tablets** according to a strict routine, and to cover the period before and after your trip. The drug used is chloroquine (trade names include Nivaquin, Avloclor and Resochin), and you usually take two tablets weekly, but India has chloroquine-resistant strains, and you'll need to supplement it with daily proguanil (Paludrine) or weekly Maloprim. A new weekly drug, mefloquine (Larium), is supposed to replace all these, but is not currently recommended for journeys of more than two months because of its side-effects (see below). Australian authorities are now prescribing the antibiotic Doxycycline instead.

As the malaria parasite can incubate in your system without showing symptoms for more than a month, it is essential that you continue to take preventative tablets for at least four weeks after you return home: the most common way of catching malaria is when travellers forget to do this. **Side-effects** of anti-malaria drugs may include itching, rashes, hair loss and sight problems. In the case of Larium some people may experience disorientation, depression and sleep disturbance; if you're intending to use Larium you should begin to take it two weeks before you depart to see whether it will agree with your metabolism, though normally you only need to begin taking anti-malaria medication a week before your departure date. Chloroquine and quinine are safe during pregnancy, but Maloprim, Fansidar, mefloquine and Doxycycline should be avoided at that time.

Mefloquine should be avoided if you are going to the island resorts, as there is a worry about possible side effects for divers.

Symptoms of malaria

The first **signs of malaria** are remarkably similar to a severe flu, and may take months to appear: if you suspect anything go to a hospital or clinic immediately. The shivering, burning fever and headaches are like severe flu and come in waves, usually beginning in the early evening. Anyone who develops such symptoms should get to a doctor for a blood test as soon as possible. Malaria is not infectious, but some strains are dangerous and can occasionally be fatal when not treated promptly, in particular, the choloquine-resistant **cerebral malaria**. This virulent and lethal strain of the disease, which affects the brain and often proves fatal if left untreated, is treatable, but has to be diagnosed early. Erratic body temperature, lack of energy and aches are the first key signs, and if you get diagnosed at such an early stage, you have a much better chance of being treated without complications and the onset of more unpleasant symptoms.

Preventing mosquito bites

The best way of avoiding malaria, of course, is to **avoid mosquito bites**. Sleep under a **mosquito net** if possible – one which can hang from a single point is best (you can usually find a way to tie a string across your room to hang it from). Burn mosquito **coils**, which are easily available in South India, but tend to break in transit (there are some question marks over health risks if coils are used in a room with poor ventilation, and they should be avoided if you suffer from asthma). Increasingly common are plug-in **vapour mats**. When out after dusk, smother yourself in **mosquito repellent**: an Indian brand of repellent, Odomos, is widely available, very effective and has a pleasant lemon scent, though most travellers bring their own from home, usually one containing the noxious but effective compound DEET. DEET can cause rashes and a strength of more than thirty percent is not advised for those with sensitive skin. The new wrist and ankle bands are as effective as spray and a good alternative for sensitive skin. Although they are active from dusk till dawn, female Anopheles mosquitoes prefer to bite in the evening, so be especially careful at that time. Wear long sleeves, skirts and trousers, avoid dark colours, which attract mosquitoes, and put repellent on exposed skin. A more natural alternative for those with sensitive skin is **citronella** or Mosi-guard Natural, made in the UK from a blend of **eucalyptus oils**. In India, the New Age centre, Auroville, produces its own herbal coils, incense and spray, available in all traveller ghettos.

Dengue fever and Japanese encephalitis

Another illness spread by mosquito bites is **dengue fever**, whose symptoms are similar to those of malaria, plus aching bones. There is no vaccine available and the only treatment is complete rest, with drugs to assuage the fever. **Japanese encephalitis** (yet another mosquito-borne viral infection causing fever, muscle pains and headaches) has been on the increase in recent years in wet, rural rice-growing areas. However, there have been no reports of travellers catching the disease, and you shouldn't need the vaccine (which is expensive and has several potentially nasty side-effects) unless you plan to spend much time around paddy fields during and immediately after the monsoons.

Intestinal troubles

Diarrhoea is the most common bane of travellers. When mild and not accompanied by other major symptoms, it may just be your stomach reacting to unfamiliar food. Accompanied by cramps and vomiting, it could well be food poisoning. In either case, it will probably pass of its own accord in 24–48 hours without treatment. In the meantime, it is essential to replace the fluids and salts you're losing, so take lots of water with oral **rehydration salts** (commonly referred to as ORS, or called Electrolyte in India). If you can't get ORS, use half a teaspoon of salt and eight of sugar in a litre of water, and if you are too ill to drink, seek medical help immediately. Travel clinics and pharmacies sell double-ended moulded plastic spoons with the exact ratio of sugar to salt.

While you are suffering, it's a good idea to avoid greasy food, heavy spices, caffeine and most fruit and dairy products. Some say bananas and pawpaws are good, as are kitchri (a simple dhal and rice preparation) and rice soup and coconut water, while curd or a soup made from Marmite or Vegemite (if you happen to have some with you) are forms of protein that can be easily absorbed by your body when you have the runs. Drugs like Lomotil or Immodium simply plug you up – undermining the body's efforts to rid itself of infection – though they can be useful if you have to travel. If symptoms persist for more than a few days, a course of antibiotics may be necessary; this should be seen as a last resort, and only used following medical advice.

Sordid though it may seem, it's a good idea to look at what comes out when you go to the toilet (and it makes an endless topic of polite meal-time conversation with your fellow travellers). If your diarrhoea contains blood or mucus and if you are suffering other symptoms including rotten-egg belches and farts, the cause may be dysentery or giardia. With a fever, it could well be caused by **bacillic dysentery**, and may clear up without treatment. If you're sure you need it, a course of antibiotics such as tetracycline should sort you out, but they also destroy "gut flora" in your intestines (which help

protect you – curd can replenish them to some extent). If you start a course, be sure to finish it, even after the symptoms have gone. Similar symptoms, without fever, indicate **amoebic dysentery**, which is much more serious, and can damage your gut if untreated. The usual cure is a course of Metronidazole (Flagyl) or Fasigyn, both antibiotics which may themselves make you feel ill, and must not be taken with alcohol; avoid caffeine too. Symptoms of **giardia** are similar – including frothy stools, nausea and constant fatigue – for which the treatment again is Metronidazole. If you suspect that you have any of these, seek medical help, and only start on the Metronidazole (750mg three times daily for a week for adults) if there is blood in your diarrhoea and it is impossible to see a doctor.

Finally, bear in mind that oral drugs, such as malaria pills and the Pill, are likely to be largely ineffective if taken while suffering from diarrhoea.

Bites and creepy-crawlies

Worms may enter your body through skin (especially the soles of your feet) or food. An itchy anus is a common symptom, and you may even see them in your stools. They are easy to treat: if you suspect you have them, get some worming tablets such as Mebendazole (Vermox) from any pharmacy.

Biting insects and similar animals other than mosquitoes may also aggravate you. The obvious ones are **bed bugs** – look for signs of squashed ones around cheap hotel beds. An infested mattress can be left in the hot sun all day to get rid of them, but they often live in the frame or even in walls or floors. Other notorious culprits, particularly bothersome in parts of the Andaman Islands, are **sandflies**, whose bites can become unbearably itchy. Head and body **lice** can also be a nuisance, but medicated soap and shampoo (preferably brought with you from home) usually see them off. Avoid scratching bites, which can lead to infection, sometimes in dangerous forms such as **septicaemia** or **tropical ulcers**. Bites from ticks and lice can spread **typhus**, characterized by fever, muscle aches, headaches, and later, red eyes and a measles-like rash. If you think you have it, seek treatment (Tetracycline is usually prescribed – for adults, a single 1g dose followed by 300mg four times daily for five days).

Snakes are unlikely to bite unless accidentally disturbed, and most are harmless in any case. To see one at all, you will need to search stealthily – if you walk heavily, they usually oblige by disappearing. If you do get bitten, remember what the snake looked like (kill it if you can), try not to move the affected part and seek medical help: antivenoms are available in most hospitals. A few **spiders** have poisonous bites too. Remove **leeches**, which may attach themselves to you in jungle areas, with salt or a lit cigarette: never just pull them off.

Heat trouble

The sun and the heat can cause a few unexpected problems, especially in the tropical south. Many people get a bout of **prickly heat** rash before they've acclimatized. It's an infection of the sweat ducts caused by excessive perspiration that doesn't dry off. A cool shower, zinc oxide powder (sold in India) or talcum powder and loose cotton clothes should help. **Dehydration** is another possible problem, so make sure you're drinking enough liquid, and drink rehydration salts frequently, especially when hot and/or tired. The main danger sign is irregular urination (only once a day for instance), but dark urine could probably mean you should drink more, although it could indicate hepatitis (see above).

The **sun** can burn, or even cause sunstroke, and a high-factor sunblock is vital on exposed skin, especially when you first arrive, and on areas newly exposed by haircuts or changes of clothes. A light hat is also a very good idea, especially if you're doing a lot of walking around.

Finally, be aware that overheating can cause **heatstroke**, which is potentially fatal. Signs are: a very high body temperature without a feeling of fever, accompanied by headaches and disorientation. Lowering body temperature (a tepid shower for example) and resting in an air-conditioned room is the first step in treatment.

HIV and AIDS

The rapidly increasing presence of **AIDS** has only recently been acknowledged by the Indian government as a national problem.

The reluctance to address the issue is partly due to the disease's association with sex, a traditionally closed subject in India. As yet only NGOs and foreign agencies such as the WHO have embarked on awareness and prevention campaigns. As elsewhere in the world, high-risk groups include prostitutes and intravenous drug users. It is extremely unwise to contemplate casual sex without a condom – carry some with you (preferably brought from home as Indian ones may be less reliable; also, be aware that heat affects the durability of condoms), and insist upon using them.

Should you need an injection or a transfusion in India, make sure that new, sterile equipment is used; any blood you receive should be from voluntary rather than commercial donor banks. Try to bring needles from home in your first-aid kit. If you have a shave from a barber, make sure he uses a clean blade, and don't submit to processes such as ear-piercing, acupuncture or tattooing unless you can be sure that the equipment is sterile.

Getting medical help

Pharmacies can usually advise on minor medical problems, and most doctors in India speak English. Also, many hotels have a doctor on call. Basic medicaments are made to Indian Pharmacopoea (IP) standards, and most medicines are available without prescription – although always check the sell-by date. Hospitals vary in standard. Private clinics and mission hospitals are often better than state-run ones, but may not have the same facilities. Hospitals in the big cities are generally pretty good; university or medical-school hospitals are best of all. Private hospitals may require patients (even emergency cases) to buy necessities such as medicines, plaster casts and vaccines and to pay for X-rays, before procedures can be carried out, though costs are a fraction of private health care in the West (be sure to keep all original documents and receipts to claim money back on insurance if need be). However, government hospitals provide all surgical and aftercare services free of charge, and in most other state medical institutions, charges are usually so low that for minor treatment the expense may well be lower than the initial "excess" on your insurance. You will need a companion to stay, or

Ayurved, a Sanskrit word meaning the "knowledge for prolonging life", is a five-thousand-year-old holistic medical system, is widely practised in India and especially popular in the South, where Kerala is a particular stronghold. Ayurvedic doctors and clinics in large towns deal with foreigners as well as their usual patients, and some pharmacies specialize in Ayurvedic preparations, including toiletries such as soaps, shampoos and toothpaste.

Ayurved assumes the fundamental sameness of self and nature and as such it is a sister science to yoga, stemming from the same period of Vedic philosophy. It accords great importance to the harmony of mind, body and spirit and acknowledges the psychosomatic causes behind many diseases. Unlike the allopathic medicines of the West, which depend on finding out what's ailing you and then killing it, Ayurved looks at the whole patient: disease is regarded as a symptom of imbalance, so it's the imbalance that's treated, not the disease.

Ayurvedic theory holds that the body is controlled by three *doshas* (forces), themselves made up of the basic elements of space, fire, water, earth and air, which reflect the forces within the self. The three *doshas* are: *pitta*, the force of the sun, which is hot and rules the digestive processes and metabolism; *kapha*, likened to the moon, the creator of tides and rhythms, which has a cooling effect, and governs the body's organs and bone structure; and *vata*, wind, which relates to movement, circulation and the nervous system. People are classified according to which *dosha* or combination of them is predominant. The healthy body is one that has the three forces in the correct balance for its type. To diagnose an imbalance, the Ayurvedic doctor not only goes into the physical complaint but also into family background, daily habits and emotional traits.

Imbalances are typically treated with herbal remedies designed to alter whichever of the three forces is out of whack. This commonly involves the application of oils or ingestion of specially prepared medicines. Made according to traditional formulae, using indigenous plants, Ayurvedic medicines are cheaper than branded or imported ones. Traditional, strictly vegetarian diets are also advised for long-term benefits. In addition, the doctor may prescribe various forms of yogic cleansing to rid the body of waste substances. To the uninitiated, these techniques will sound rather off-putting – for instance, swallowing a long strip of cloth, a short section at a time, and then pulling it back up again to remove mucus from the stomach.

Many places advertising Ayurvedic treatments in the more touristy spots are just glorified massage parlours using a few herbal oils and traditional techniques; however, even these can provide welcome relaxation. Those who seek out more bona fide clinics for lengthier purification regimes, or for the treatment of individual ailments, are often full of praise for the efficacy of these ancient methods.

you'll have to come to an arrangement with one of the hospital cleaners, to help you out in hospital – relatives are expected to wash, feed and generally take care of the patient.

Addresses of foreign consulates (who will advise in an emergency), and of clinics and hospitals can be found in the Listings sections for major towns in this book.

Costs, money and banks

India is still one of the least expensive countries for travellers in the world – and generally the South is even cheaper than the North so a little foreign currency goes a long way. That means you can be confident of getting consistently good value for money, whether you're setting out to keep your budget to a minimum or to enjoy the opportunities that spending a bit more will make possible.

While we attempt below to suggest the kind of sums you can expect to pay for varying degrees of comfort, it is vital not to make a rigid assumption at the outset of a long trip that whatever money you bring to India will last for a certain number of weeks or months. On any one day it may be possible to spend very little, but cumulatively you won't be doing yourself any favours if you don't make sure you keep yourself well rested and properly fed. As a foreigner in India, you will find yourself penalized by double-tier entry prices to museums and historic sites (see box) as well as in upmarket hotels and airfares, both of which are levied at a higher rate and in dollars

What you spend depends on you: where you go, where you stay, how you get around, what you eat and what you buy. On a budget of as little as £5/US$7.50 per day, you'll manage if you stick to the cheapest of everything and don't move about too much; double that, and you can permit yourself a few splurge meals, the occasional mid-range hotel and some souvenirs. If you're happy spending £20–25/US$30–37 per day, however, you can really pamper yourself; to spend much more than that, you'd have to be doing a lot of travelling, consistently staying in the best hotel in town and eating in the top restaurant.

Accommodation costs from £1.50/US$2 per night upwards (see p.46), while a vegetarian meal in an ordinary restaurant is unlikely to cost even that much. Rice and dhal can be had for well under 30p/45¢, but you wouldn't want to live on that alone. Transport in town costs pennies (even by taxi), while a twelve-hour train journey might cost £3/$4 in second class, £12/$17 in first.

Where you are makes a difference: Mumbai is notoriously pricey, especially for accommodation, while tourist enclaves like the Goa beaches will not be cheap for things like food, and there will be more souvenirs to tempt you. Out in the sticks, on the other hand, and particularly away from your fellow tourists, you will find things incredibly cheap, though your choices will obviously be more limited.

Some independent travellers tend to indulge in wild and highly competitive penny-pinching, which Indian people find rather pathetic – they know how much an air ticket to Chennai or Mumbai costs, and they have a fair idea of what you can earn at home. Bargain where appropriate, but don't begrudge a few rupees to someone who's worked hard for them: consider what their services would cost at home, and how much more valuable the money is to them

Entrance fees

In 2000, the Archeological Survey of India announced a double-tiered entry system, with foreign visitors (including non-resident Indians) required to pay $5–10 or its rupee equivalent to enter major archeological sites. This means that foreigners can find themselves paying many times the entrance fee levied to domestic visitors. Due to considerable outcry from tour agencies and tourists, the Indian government is currently reviewing this policy, and discount pass schemes may emerge; ask at a Government of India tourist office for the latest.

Foreign visitors may be charged in either dollars or rupees; where, as is the case at some sites, foreigners are charged in dollars at that day's exchange rate, we give the dollar rate current at the time of going to press, so bear in mind that this may fluctuate. Prices for Indian visitors are given in square brackets throughout the Guide.

than it is to you. Even if you get a bad deal on every rickshaw journey you make, it will only add at most one percent to a £1000/$1500 trip. Remember too, that every pound or dollar you spend in India goes that much further, and luxuries you can't afford at home become possible here: sometimes it's worth spending more simply because you get more for it. At the same time, don't pay well over the odds for something if you know what the going rate is. Thoughtless extravagance can, particularly in remote areas that see a disproportionate number of tourists, contribute to inflation, putting even basic goods and services beyond the reach of local people.

Currency

India's unit of currency is the **rupee**, usually abbreviated "Rs" and divided into a hundred paise. Much of the money is paper, with notes of 1, 2, 5, 10, 20, 50, 100 and 500 rupees, though denominations smaller than Rs10 are gradually becoming less common. Coins start at 5 paise (for temple offerings), then range up to 10, 20, 25 and 50 paise, and 1, 2 and 5 rupees.

Banknotes, especially lower denominations, can get into a terrible state, but don't accept torn **banknotes**; no one else will be prepared to take them, so you will be left saddled with the things, though you can change them at the Reserve Bank of India and large branches of other big banks. Don't pass them on to beggars; they can't use them either, so it amounts to an insult. However, notes full of holes (from the obligatory bank staples), tatty edges or covered in plastic pass without comment.

Large denominations can also be a problem, as change is often in short supply, particularly in small towns. Many Indian people cannot afford to keep much lying around, and you shouldn't necessarily expect shopkeepers or rickshaw-wallahs to have it (and they may – as may you – try to hold onto it if they do). Paying for your groceries with a Rs100 note may well entail waiting for the grocer's errand boy to go off on a quest around town trying to change it. Keeping a wad of Rs1 notes handy isn't a bad idea (you can get bundles of a hundred stapled together in banks).

At the time of writing, the **exchange rate** was approximately Rs68 to £1, or Rs47 to US$1.

Travellers' cheques, credit cards and ATMs

Carry a mixture of cash and travellers' cheques to cover all eventualities, with a few small denominations for the end of your trip and for the odd foreign-currency purchase. US dollars are the easiest **currency** to convert, with pounds sterling coming a close second. Major hard currencies can be changed easily in tourist areas and big cities, less so elsewhere. If you enter the country with over US$10,000 or the equivalent, you are supposed to fill in a currency declaration form.

Travellers' cheques aren't as liquid as cash, but obviously more secure (and you get a slightly better exchange rate for them at banks). Not all banks, however, accept them, and those that do can be quirky about exactly which ones they *will* change. Well-known brands such as Thomas Cook and American Express are your best bet, but in some places even American Express is only accepted in US dollars and not as pounds sterling.

Hold on to **exchange receipts** ("encashment certificates"); they will be required if you want to change back any excess rupees when you leave the country, and to buy air tickets and reserve train berths with rupees. The State Bank of India now charges for tax clearance forms (see p.20 to find out if you'll need one.)

A **credit card** is a handy backup, as an increasing number of hotels, restaurants, large shops and tourist emporia as well as airlines now take plastic, with American Express, Access/Mastercard, Visa and Diners Club being the most commonly accepted brands. If you have a selection of cards, take them all; you'll get much the same exchange rate as you would in a bank, and bills can take a surprisingly long time to be charged to your account at home. The Bank of Baroda and Standard Chartered Grindlays issue rupees against a Visa card at all their branches. Even train tickets can now be paid for by credit card at major stations. Don't expect to be able to use plastic outside of the big cities or major tourist centres though.

Several banks now have **ATM machines** but only in the cities, and not all ATMs will accept foreign cards even if they sport Visa and Mastercard signs; you are best advised to enquire first before sticking your card into the slot. Mumbai branches of the Hong Kong Bank (HSBC) and Bank of America have 24hr ATMs that take Visa and Mastercard, while some of Standard Chartered Grindlays banks also have foreigner-friendly ATM machines.

It is illegal to carry rupees into or out of India, and you won't get them at a particularly good rate in the West anyhow (though you might in Thailand, Malaysia or Singapore).

Travellers' cheques and credit card contacts

Both Amex and Thomas Cook have branches in other cities throughout South India; see the relevant account in the guide and pick up a full list when you purchase your cheques.

American Express

Ⓦwww.americanexpress.com
Lost and stolen cards ⓣ011/614 5920 or 687 5050 (open 24hr)
Bangalore Janardhan Tower, 2 Residency Rd ⓣ080/227 1485
Chennai G-17, Spencer Plaza, 768–769 Anna Salai ⓣ044/852 3628 & 852 3573
Mumbai Regal Cinema Building, Chatrapati Shivaji Maharaj Road, Colaba ⓣ022/204 8291-5

Thomas Cook

Ⓦhttp://64.27.75.224/index.html
Lost and stolen cards ⓣ0044-1733/294451
Bangalore 70 Mahatma Gandhi Rd ⓣ080/558 8038 & 55 Mahatma Gandhi Rd ⓣ080/559 4168
Chennai Ceebros Centre, 45 Montieth Rd, Egmore ⓣ044/855 3276 & 855 4913
Mumbai Dr Dadabhai Naoroji Road, Fort ⓣ022/204 8556-7
Thiruvananthapuram Tourindia, MG Road ⓣ0471/330437

Banks

Changing money in regular **banks**, especially government-run banks such as the State Bank of India (SBI), can be a time-consuming business, involving form-filling and queuing at different counters, so change substantial amounts at any one time. Banks in main cities are likely to be most efficient, though not all change foreign currency, and some won't take **travellers' cheques** or

currencies other than dollars or sterling (banks usually charge a percentage of the transaction while ANZ Grindlays charge Rs200). You'll have no such problems with **private companies** such as Thomas Cook and American Express who have offices in most state capitals.

In the major cities and the main tourist centres, there are usually several **licensed currency exchange bureaus** where the rates are not usually as good as at a bank but where there's generally a lot less hassle. In small towns, the SBI is your best bet but you may want to ask around for an alternative. Note that if you arrive at a minor airport you may not be able to change anything except to cash US dollars or sterling.

Outside normal **banking hours** (Mon–Fri 10am–2pm, Sat 10am–noon), large hotels may change money, probably at a lower rate, and exchange bureaus have longer opening hours. Banks at Mumbai and Chennai **airports** stay open 24 hours but none of these is very conveniently located. Otherwise, there's always the black market if you're desperate.

Wiring money to India is a lot easier than it used to be. Indian banks with branches abroad, such as the State Bank of India and the Bank of Baroda, can wire money by telex from those branches to large ones in India in two working days. Western Union (information on ⓣ1-800/325-6000 in the US or ⓣ0800/833833 in the UK) can transfer cash or banker's drafts paid into their overseas branches to any one of 43 offices in India within fifteen minutes, for a typically hefty fee of around 7.5 percent of the total amount; similar services are offered by American Express, Thomas Cook, and foreign banks with branches in India such as Standard Chartered (and Standard Chartered Grindlays) and HSBC.

The black market

A **black market** still exists today, but only in the major tourist areas of the biggest cities, with little if any premium over the bank rate, though it is a lot faster. Small denominations are not popular, with the best rates given for notes of £50, US$100 or DM1000; you will, of course, have to haggle.

Always do this kind of business with shopkeepers rather than shady "hello my friend" types on the street, and proceed with caution.

Never hand over your pile until you have counted and checked the rupees and have them in your hand; make sure they really are the denominations they should be. Unusually high rates suggest a con, as does any attempt to rush you, or sudden claims that the police are coming. Remember what you are doing is illegal; you can be arrested and you may be set up.

Baksheesh

As a presumed-rich sahib or memsahib, you will, like wealthy Indians, be expected to be liberal with the **baksheesh**, which takes three main forms.

The most common is **tipping**: a small reward for a small service, which can encompass anyone from a waiter or porter to someone who lifts your bags onto the roof of a bus or keeps an eye on your vehicle for you. Large amounts are not expected – five to ten rupees should satisfy all the aforementioned. Taxi drivers and staff at cheaper hotels and restaurants do not necessarily expect tips, but always appreciate them, of course, and they can keep people

sweet for the next time you call. Some may take liberties in demanding *baksheesh*, but it's often better just to acquiesce rather than spoil your mood and cause offence over trifling sums.

More expensive than plain tipping is paying people to **bend the rules**, many of which seem to have been invented for precisely that purpose. Examples might include letting you into a historical site after hours, finding you a seat or a sleeper on a train that is "full" or speeding up some bureaucratic process. This should not be confused with bribery, a more serious business with its own risks and etiquette, which is best not entered into.

The last kind of *baksheesh* is **alms-giving**. In a country without a welfare system, this is an important social custom. People with disabilities and mutilations are the traditional recipients, and it seems right to join local people in giving out small change to them. Kids demanding money, pens or the like are a different case, pressing their demands only on tourists. In return for a service it is fair enough, but to yield to any request encourages them to go and pester others.

Getting around

Inter-city transport in South India may not be the fastest or the most comfortable in the world, but it's cheap, goes more or less everywhere and generally gives you the option of train or bus, sometimes plane, and occasionally even boat. Transport around town comes in even more permutations, ranging from cycle rickshaws just about everywhere to double-decker buses in Mumbai.

Whether you're on road or rail, public transport or your own vehicle, India offers the chance to try out some classics: narrow-gauge railways, steam locomotives, the Ambassador car and the Enfield Bullet motorbike, they're all here. Some people come to India for these alone.

By train

Travelling by train is one of the great experiences of South India. It's a system which

looks like chaos, but it works, and works well. Trains are often late of course, sometimes by hours rather than minutes, but they do run, and with amazing efficiency too: when the train you've been waiting for rolls into the station, the reservation you made halfway across the country several weeks ago will be on a list pasted to the side of your carriage, and when it's time to eat, the packed meal you ordered down the line will be ready at the next station, put on the train and delivered to your seat.

At the end of each chapter in this book, you'll find a Travel Details section summarizing major transport connections in the relevant state. In addition, boxes at the end of each major city detail Moving On from that city.

It's worth bearing in mind, with journeys frequently lasting twelve hours or more, that an overnight train can save you a day's travelling and a night's hotel bill, assuming you sleep well on trains. While sleeper carriages can be more crowded during the day, between 9pm and 6am anyone with a bunk reservation is entitled to exclusive use of their bunk. When travelling overnight, however, always padlock your bag to your bunk – metal attachments or chains are usually provided under the lower bunk.

Routes and classes

The rail network covers almost the whole of South India; only a few places (such as most of Goa and some parts of the Ghats) are inaccessible by train. **Inter-city** trains, called "**express**" or "**mail**", vary a lot in the time taken to cover the same route. Slow by Western standards, they're still much faster than local "**passenger**" trains, which you need only use to get right off the beaten track. There is also an increasing number of special "**super-fast**" a/c trains, usually named *Rajdhani* or *Shatabdi Express*, which cover routes between major cities in as little as half the normal time. Note that express and mail trains cost a fair amount more than ordinary passenger trains, so if travelling unreserved you must buy the right ticket to avoid being fined.

Most lines are either metre-gauge or broad-gauge (1.676m, or 4ft 6in), the latter being faster; many metre-gauge lines are now being converted to broad-gauge. The only narrow-gauge line (often referred to as "the toy train"), in the South, runs to Ootacamund (Ooty), and you will only find **steam locomotives** in routinely scheduled service on the steep sections of this narrow-gauge mountain railway. All other trains are now hauled by diesel engines.

Classes of train travel

Indian Railways (ⓦwww.indianrailway.com or ⓦwww.southernrailways.org) distinguishes between no fewer than seven **classes** of travel, though you'll seldom have more than the following four to choose from on mainline services: second-class unreserved, second-class sleeper, first and a/c first (or a/c two- or three-tier sleeper class). In general, most travellers (not just those on low budgets) choose to travel second class, and prefer not to be in a/c compartments; an open window keeps you cool enough, and brings you into contact with the world outside, while air-conditioning by definition involves being sealed away behind glass, which is often virtually opaque. Doing without a sleeper on an overnight journey is, however, a false economy. Bed rolls (sheet, blanket and pillow) are available in first class and a/c second for that extra bit of comfort – book these with your ticket, or before you board the train.

Second-class unreserved is painfully crowded and noisy with no chance of a berth overnight, but incredibly cheap, for example, just Rs77 (that's just over £1 or under $2) for a thousand-kilometre journey on a slow passenger train (Rs174 on an express or mail train). However, the crush and hard wooden seats, if you are lucky or nifty enough to get one, make it viable only for short hops or for the extremely hardy. Far more civilized, and only around fifty percent more expensive, is **second-class sleeper** (Rs270 for 1000km), which must be booked in advance even for daytime journeys. If you have an unreserved ticket and travel in a sleeper carriage, even if it is not full, you will be charged a Rs60 fine as well as the difference in fare. Sleeper class can be pretty crowded during the day but never lacks activity, be it peanut-, chai- or coffee-sellers, travelling musicians, beggars or sweepers passing through each carriage. Overnight trips in second-class sleeper compartments are reasonably comfy (provided the berths are foam and not wooden), and there's the option of more privacy for women in ladies' compartments on most long-haul journeys.

First class (Rs914 for 1000km), in comfortable compartments of two to four berths, is used mainly by English-speaking business travellers. It costs about three and a half times as much as second-class sleeper and insulates you to a certain extent from the chaotic hustle and bustle – which you may or may not consider to be an advantage.

Air-conditioned travel falls into four categories but only one or two will be available on any particular service. The best value is **a/c chair car** (Rs522 for 1000km), with comfortable reclining seats at only double the price of second-class sleeper. The famous "superfast" *Rajdhani* and *Shatabdi* expresses, which cost around double that of a normal express, mostly consist of such compartments, and you will also find the odd carriage tacked onto some normal expresses. **Air-conditioned three-tier** sleepers (Rs783 for 1000km) cost slightly less than normal first class, but are not all that common, while **a/c two-tier** sleepers (Rs1253 for 1000km) are more abundant and cost half as much again as first class. Top of the tree and costing around two and a half times as much as first class is **a/c first class** (Rs2506 for 1000km), which offers little more than extra space on top of the obvious cool air.

Here are the ticket prices for some specific journeys in different classes: Chennai to Bangalore (361km) would cost Rs530 in a/c chair car on the *Shatabdi Express*, while on a normal express it would be Rs266 for a/c chair car or Rs135 for a second class sleeper; Trivandrum to Mangalore (635km) would cost only Rs62 if you slogged it in unreserved second class on a passenger train, while on an express the ticket would be Rs138 in unreserved, Rs693 in first class or Rs941 in an a/c two-tier sleeper.

Timetables and tickets

Indian Railways publish an annual **timetable** of all mail and express trains – in effect, all the trains you are likely to use. Called *Trains at a Glance*, it is available for Rs25 from information counters and newsstands at all main stations, and from Indian Railways agents abroad. *Southern Railways at a Glance* gives details of all local and interstate trains in South India, and national timetables. *Thomas Cook*'s *International Timetable* Vol II (the blue one) has a limited selection of timetables, while the elusive monthly *Indian Bradshaw* covers every scheduled train in the country. In theory, this is available at major termini, but it is often difficult to get hold of; complete regional timetables are widely available, however. Southern Railways' timetable is ample for the region, with details of passenger trains a summary of routes in the rest of the country.

All rail **fares** are calculated according to the exact distance travelled. *Trains at a Glance*

prints a chart of fares by kilometres, and also gives the distance in kilometres of stations along each route in the timetables, making it possible to calculate what the basic fare will be for any given journey. However, endless pouring over the columns reveals little more than that fares are very cheap indeed.

Each individual train has its own name and number, which is prominently displayed in station booking halls. When buying a ticket, it makes sense to pay the tiny, extra fee to reserve a seat or sleeper (the fee is already included in the price of a first-class sleeper). To do so, you fill in a form specifying the train you intend to catch, its number, your date of travel and the stations you are travelling to and from, plus, amusingly to most travellers, your age and sex.

Most stations (listed in *Trains at a Glance*) have computerized booking counters, and you will be told immediately whether or not seats are available.

Indian railways sales agents abroad

Australia Adventure World, 73 Walker St (PO Box 480), North Sydney, NSW 2059 ☎ 02/9956 7766, ⓦ www.adventureworld.com.au

Bangladesh Omaitrans International, 70/1 Inner Circular Rd, Kakrail, Dhaka ☎ 02/834401

Canada Hari World Travel Inc, 1 Financial Place, Adelaide St East, Toronto M5C 2V8 ☎ 416/366-2000

Malaysia City East West Travels, Sdn Bhd No 135-A, Jalan Bunus, 50100 Kuala Lumpur ☎ 03/293 0569

South Africa 13 M K Bobby Naidoo Travel Agency, PO Box 2878, Durban, SA 44001 ☎ 021/309 3628

Thailand SS Travels Service, 10/12–13, SS Building, Convent Rd, Bangkok 10500 ☎ 02/236 7188

UK SD Enterprises Ltd, 103 Wembley Park Drive, Wembley, Middx HA9 8HG ☎ 020/8903 3411, ⓦ www.indiarail.co.uk

USA Hari World Travels Inc, 25 W 45th St # 1003 New York, NY 10036 (☎ 212/957-3000); with additional locations in Atlanta (☎ 404/233-5005), and Chicago (☎ 773/381-5555)

Reserving tickets

Reservation offices in the main stations are often in a separate building and generally open Mon–Sat 8am–8pm and Sun 8am–2pm. In larger cities, the major stations have special **tourist sections**, to cut the queues for foreigners and Indian citizens resident abroad buying tickets, with helpful English-speaking staff; however, if you don't pay in pounds sterling or US dollars (travellers' cheques or cash), you must produce an encashment certificate to back up your rupees. Elsewhere, buying a ticket can often involve a long wait, though women may get round this at ticket counters which have "ladies' queues". Some stations also operate a numbered system of queuing, allowing you to repair to the chai stall or check the timetable until your number is called. Alternatively, many travel agents will secure tickets for a reasonable Rs25–50 fee. Failure to buy a ticket at the point of departure will result in paying a stiff penalty when the ticket inspector finds you.

It's important to plan your train journeys in advance, as demand often makes it impossible to buy a long-distance ticket on the same day that you want to travel. Travellers following tight itineraries tend to buy their departure tickets from particular towns the moment they arrive, to avoid having to trek out to the station again. At most large stations, it's possible to reserve tickets for journeys starting elsewhere in the country. You can even book tickets for specific journeys (if you buy an Indrail pass) before you leave home, with Indian Railways representatives abroad (see box on p.39). They accept bookings of up to six months in advance, with a minimum of one month for first class, and three months for second.

If you have to **cancel your ticket**, the fare is refunded up to a day before departure, minus a fee for the reservation (Rs10 in second class, Rs20 in sleeper, Rs30 a/c chair car or first, and Rs50 in a/c first). Cancelling between a day and four hours before scheduled departure, gets you 75 percent back; you can still claim a fifty percent refund if you present your ticket up to twelve hours after the train actually leaves on a journey of over 500km, six hours on 200–500km trips or three hours on a short journey.

If there are **no places available** on the train you want, you have a number of choices. First, some seats and berths are set aside as a "**tourist quota**" – ask at the tourist counter if you can get in on this, or try the stationmaster. This quota is usually only available at major or originating stations.

Indrail passes

Indrail passes – sold to foreigners and Indians resident abroad – cover all fares and reservation fees for periods ranging from half a day to ninety days. Even if you travel a lot, this works out considerably more expensive than buying your tickets individually (especially in second class), but it will save you queuing for tickets, and allow you to make and cancel reservations with impunity (and without charge). It will also generally smooth your way in, for example, finding a seat or berth on a "full" train: pass-holders, for example, get priority for tourist quota places. Indrail passes are available, for pounds sterling or US dollars, at main station tourist counters in India, and outside the country at Indian Railways agents (see box on p.39). If you're travelling from Britain, Mr Dandapani of SD Enterprises Ltd (see p.39) is an excellent contact, providing information on all aspects of travel on Indian railways.

RATES IN US$

	a/c First Class		First Class or a/c Sleeper or a/c Chair Car		Second Class	
	Adult	**Child**	**Adult**	**Child**	**Adult**	**Child**
1 day*	95	48	43	22	19	10
4 days*	220	110	110	55	50	25
7 days	270	135	135	68	80	40
15 days	370	185	185	95	90	45
21 days	396	198	198	99	100	50
30 days	495	248	248	126	125	65
60 days	800	400	400	200	185	95
90 days	1060	530	530	265	235	120

*For sale outside India only; half-day & two-day passes are also available. Note that these prices are liable to rise a further ten percent.

Failing that, other special quotas, such as one for VIPs, may remain unused – however, if you get a booking on the **VIP quota** and a pukka VIP turns up, you lose the reservation. Alternatively, a "reservation against cancellation" (**RAC**) ticket will give you priority if sleepers do become available – the ticket clerk should be able to tell you your chances. With an RAC ticket you are allowed onto the train and can sit until the conductor can find you a berth. The worst sort of ticket to have is a **wait-listed** one which will allow you on to the train but not in a reserved compartment; in this case go and see the ticket inspector as soon as possible to persuade him to find you a place if one is free: something usually is, but you'll be stuck in unreserved if it isn't. Wait-listed ticket holders are not allowed on to Shatabdi and Rajdhani trains. In practice, if your number on the waiting list is not far into double figures, you have a good chance of getting a place. Alternatively, and especially if you get on where the train starts its journey, *baksheesh* may persuade a porter to "reserve" you an unreserved seat, or, better still, a luggage rack where you can stretch out for the night. You *could* even fight your way on and grab one yourself, although we don't rate your chances. As for attempting to **travel unreserved**, for journeys of any length, it's too uncomfortable to be worth seriously considering.

Ladies' compartments exist on all overnight trains for women travelling on their own or with other women; they are usually small and can be full of noisy kids, but can give untold relief to women travellers who otherwise have to endure incessant staring in the open section of the carriage. On the other hand, particularly if you like (or are with) children, they can be a good place to meet Indian women. Some stations also have ladies-only waiting rooms.

Cloakrooms

Most stations in India have "cloakrooms" (sometimes called "parcel offices"), for passengers to leave their baggage. These can be extremely handy if you want to go sightseeing in a town and move on the same day. In theory, you need a current train ticket or Indrail pass to deposit luggage, but they don't always ask; they may however refuse to take your bag if you can't lock it. Losing your reclaim ticket causes problems; the clerk will be assumed to have stolen the bag if he can't produce it, so there'll be untold running around to obtain clearance before you can get your bag without it. Make sure, when checking baggage in, that the cloakroom will be open when you need to pick it up. The standard charge is currently Rs7 for the first 24 hours, Rs8 per 24hr after that.

By air

Though obviously more expensive than going by train or bus, **flying** can save a lot of time: Mumbai–Chennai, for example, can take around thirty hours' hard travelling by train, yet a mere 1hr 45min by plane. Delays and cancellations can whittle away the time advantage, especially over small distances, but if you're short of time and plan to cover a lot of ground, you should definitely consider flying.

India has just one national internal air carrier, **Indian Airlines** (IA, ⊛ www.nic.in /indian-airlines), which serves 147 routes country-wide and also flies to Southeast Asia. In addition, Air India runs shuttles between the four main cities (from the international, not the domestic, terminals), which provides useful links to Mumbai and Chennai for those entering India via Delhi or Calcutta. Jet Airways (⊛ www.jetairways.com) is the only private operator with an extensive and constantly expanding network throughout the country and standards compare favourably with IA. Sahara (⊛ www.airsahara.net) also has some schedules for southern cities. Prices are similar whichever company you use and, unfortunately, as a foreigner you have to pay substantially higher prices than Indians and in hard currency too. Short flights can be cheap, sometimes less than £50/$75, but longer ones are no less than equivalent distances anywhere else and often more expensive than the competitive deals you find in Europe or the USA. IA has a number of special deals that are worth knowing about: in addition to 25 percent discount for under-30s and students, and 50 percent for over-65s, they offer two multi-flight discounts; Jet Airways also has similar deals (see box on p.42).

One problem with flying is that you may have to spend a massive amount of time queuing at the airline office to get a reservation; it's often quicker to book through a

These fares only work on a circular route and don't allow back-tracking.

Indian Airlines

Discover India Fare Unlimited travel on all internal flights: 15 days $500; 21 days $750 (no single route twice)

India Wonderfare Seven days' travel in one given region; $300

Jet Airways

Visit India Fare Unlimited travel on their routes: 15 days $550; 21 days $800; 7 days regional fare (eg south India) $330

hotel or travel agent, which is the norm for booking on private carriers. If you haven't got a confirmed seat, be sure to get to the airport early and keep checking your position in the queue; even if you have got a confirmed seat, be sure to always reconfirm 72 hours before your flight.

Airlines have offices or representatives in all the places they fly to; all are listed in this book in the relevant city sections. IA tickets must be paid for in hard currency or with a credit card. Children under 12 pay half fare, and under-2s (one per adult) pay ten percent. There are no cancellation charges if you pay in foreign currency, but tickets are not replaceable if lost. **Timetables** for all internal flights (with fares) are published in *Divan* and *Excel* magazines, and shown on teletext in the UK, while all operators stock their own timetables.

By bus

Although trains are the definitive form of transport in South India, and generally more comfortable than **buses**, there are places where trains don't go, where they are awkward and inconvenient, or where buses are simply faster (as in most places without broad-gauge track). Alternatively, you might just fancy a change or the train you want might be booked up. In that case, the bus is for you; and you'll be pleased to know that they go almost everywhere, more frequently than trains (though mostly in daylight hours), and there are state-government-operated services everywhere, and plenty of private firms besides.

Buses vary somewhat in price and standards. Government-run ramshackle affairs,

packed to the gunnels with people, livestock and luggage, cover both short and very long distances. In more widely travelled areas there usually tend to be additional private buses offering more leg-room and generally travelling faster – not necessarily a plus point when you consider the dilapidated state of the vehicles.

Some clue as to comfort can be gained from the description given to the bus. "Ordinary" buses usually have minimally padded fixed upright seats arranged with a double and triple on either side of the aisle. "**Deluxe**", or "**luxury**", and even "**super-deluxe**", are fairly interchangeable terms and when applied to government buses may hardly differ from "ordinary". Usually they refer to private services, though, and should then guarantee a softer, sometimes reclining, individual seat. You can check this out when booking, and it's also worth asking if your bus has a video or music system, as their deafening noise ruins any chances of sleep. The South generally has fewer smart private buses, and those available are aimed primarily at foreigners. However, smaller private bus companies may be only semi-legal and have little backup in case of breakdown or accident. You should also bear in mind that even luxury coaches can have broken seats, recliners that don't recline and windows that don't close, so be prepared, and always try to avoid the back seats – they accentuate bumpy roads, launching you into the air several times a minute. Try and sit in the middle of the bus for safety.

Luggage travels in the hatch on private buses, sometimes at a small extra charge, but you can usually squeeze it into an unobtrusive corner inside state-run vehicles, although you may sometimes be requested to have it travel on the roof (you may be able to travel up there yourself if the bus is too crowded, though it's dangerous and illegal); check that it's well secured (ideally, lock it there yourself or watch it being tied on) and not liable to get squashed. *Baksheesh* is in order for whoever puts it up there for you.

Buying a bus ticket is usually less of an ordeal than buying a train ticket, although at large city bus stations there may be twenty or so counters, each assigned to a different route. When you buy your ticket you'll be given the registration number of the bus and, sometimes, a seat number. As at railway stations, there is usually a separate, quicker, ladies' queue, although the sign to indicate it may not be in English. You can always get on ordinary state buses without a ticket, and at bus stands outside major cities you can usually only pay on board, so you have to be sharp to secure a seat. Prior booking is usually available and preferable for express and private services and it is a good idea to check with the agent exactly where the bus will depart from. You can usually pay on board private buses too, though that reduces your chances of a seat.

By boat

Apart from flat-bottomed river ferries, which are common along the Konkan coast (particularly in Goa), the boat services you're most likely to use in South India are those plying the backwaters of **Kerala**, where the majority of settlements are still most easily reached by water. Foreign visitors generally stick to the route connecting the area's two main towns, Alappuzha and Kollam, along which the local tourist office operates popular sightseeing boats, but it can be fun to catch run-of-the-mill village ferries to smaller, less developed areas.

The other region of South India still heavily reliant on ferries is the **Andaman Islands**, around 1000km east of Chennai in the Bay of Bengal. A new road runs the length of this remote archipelago, crossing larger estuaries by means of small river ferries, but to reach any of the offshore islands you'll have to wait around in the capital, Port Blair, for one of the sporadic government ferry services. If you can't afford the air fare (or can't get a ticket on the over-subscribed flight), boats – from Chennai or Vishakapatnam (and Calcutta) – are the only other way to reach the Andamans. The crossing is frequently uncomfortable and lasts three or four days (see p.610).

A decade or so ago, you could catch a rusty old steamer from Mumbai to **Goa**, but the Indian Navy requisitioned the boat for the invasion of Sri Lanka in 1989, and since then the service has been suspended.

For more detailed information on the routes outlined above, see the relevant chapters of the guide. At the time of writing, these were the only ferry services in operation in South India. Sri Lanka can for the moment only be reached by air, while the scheduled ship cruise to the Lakshadweep Islands from Kochi (Kerala) is very expensive.

By car or motorbike

It is much more usual for tourists in South India to be driven than it is for them to drive; car rental firms operate on the basis of supplying **chauffeur-driven vehicles**, and taxis are available at cheap daily rates. Arranged through tourist offices, local car rental firms, or branches of Hertz, Budget or Europcar, a chauffeur-driven car will run to about £20/US$30 per day. On longer trips, the driver sleeps in the car. The big international chains are the best bet for self-drive car rental; in India they charge around thirty percent less than chauffeur-driven, with a Rs1000 deposit against damage, though if you pay in your home country it can cost a whole lot more. In one or two places, motorbikes or mopeds may be rented out for local use, but for biking around the country, it is a much better idea to buy (see below).

Driving in India is not for beginners. If you do drive yourself, expect the unexpected, and expect other drivers to take whatever liberties they can get away with. Traffic circulates on the left, but don't expect road regulations to be obeyed. Traffic in the cities is heavy and undisciplined; vehicles cut in and out without warning, and pedestrians, cyclists and cows wander nonchalantly down the middle of the road as if you don't exist. In the country the roads are narrow, in terrible repair and hogged by overloaded Tata trucks that move aside for nobody, while something slow-moving like a bullock cart or a herd of goats can easily take up the whole road. To overtake, sound your horn – the driver in front will signal if it is safe to do so; if not, he will wave his hand, palm downwards, up and down. A huge number of potholes don't make for a smooth ride either. Furthermore, during the monsoon, roads can become flooded and dangerous; rivers burst their banks and bridges get washed away. Ask local people before you set off, and proceed with caution, sticking to main highways if possible.

You should have an **international driving licence** to drive in India, but this is often overlooked if you have your licence from home (but beware of police in Goa, who are quick to hand out fines). Insurance is compulsory, but not expensive. Car seat-belts and motorcycle crash-helmets are not compulsory but very strongly recommended; helmets are best brought from home. Accident rates are high, and you should be on your guard at all times. It is very dangerous to drive at night – not everyone uses lights, and bullock carts don't have any. If you have an **accident**, it might be an idea to leave the scene quickly and go straight to the police to report it; mobs can assemble fast, especially if pedestrians or cows are involved.

Fuel is reasonably cheap, but the state of the roads will take its toll, and mechanics are not always very reliable, so a knowledge of **vehicle maintenance** is a help, as is a check-over every so often to see what all those bone-shaking journeys are doing to your conveyance. Luckily, if you get a flat tyre, puncture-wallahs can be found almost everywhere.

To import a car or motorbike into India, you'll have to show a *carnet de passage*, a document intended to ensure that you won't sell the vehicle illegally. These are available from foreign motoring organizations such as the AA. It's also worth bringing a few basic spares, as spare parts for foreign makes can be hard to find in India, although low-quality imitations are widely available. All in all, the route is arduous, and bringing a vehicle to India something of a commitment.

The classic Indian automobile is the Hindustan Ambassador (basically a Morris Oxford), nowadays largely superseded by more modern vehicles such as the Japanese-style Maruti Suzuki. Renting a car, you'll probably have a choice of these two or others. If you're interested in buying one, the Ambassador is not famed for its mod cons or low mpg, but has a certain style and historical interest, and later models make little sense as prices are higher and quality lower than in the West.

By motorbike

Buying a motorbike is a much more reasonable proposition, and again, if it's an old British classic you're after, the Enfield Bullet (350 model), sold cheapest in Pondicherry on the coast of Tamil Nadu, leads the field. If low price and practicality are your priorities, however, a smaller model, perhaps even a moped or a scooter, might better fit the bill. Many Japanese bikes are now made in India, as are Vespas and Lambrettas, and motorbikes of various sorts can easily be bought new or secondhand. Garages and repair shops are a good place to start; Bales Road in Chennai is particularly renowned. Obviously, you will have to haggle for the price, but you can expect to pay half to two-thirds the original price for a bike in reasonable condition. Given the right bargaining skills, you can sell it again later for a similar price – perhaps to another foreign traveller, by advertising it in hotels and restaurants. A certain amount of bureaucracy is involved in transferring vehicle ownership, but a garage should be able to put you on to a broker ("auto consultant") who, for a modest commission (around Rs300), will help you find a seller or a buyer, and do the necessary paperwork. A motorbike can be taken in the luggage car of a train for the same price as a second-class passenger fare. You could, of course, bring your own bike all the way **overland** from Europe but remember it is that much further again to the south of India and you will need to consider spares. Helmets are best brought from home, even if you are planning to get a bike once in India.

Some **knowledge of mechanics** is necessary to ensure that you are not being sold a pup so if you are not too savvy yourself, make sure you take someone with you to give the engine, forks, brakes and suspension the once-over. Bear in mind that experienced overlanders often claim that making sure the seat is comfy is the crucial element to an enjoyable trip. Beside the appalling road conditions encountered (see above) and the ensuing fatigue, **renting a bike**, unless you are well versed in maintenance, can be a bit of a nightmare, with breakdowns often in the most inconvenient places. If you do break down in the middle of nowhere, you may need to flag down an empty truck to transport the bike to the nearest town for repairs. Motorbike rental is available in some tourist towns and useful for local use, but the quality of the bikes is never assured.

If you are unsure of negotiating your own bike or travelling around on your own you may consider joining a **motorbike tour**. Try contacting:

Blazing Trails UK ☎01293/533338, ⊛www.jewelholidays.com

Classic Bike Adventure "Casa Tres Amigos", Assagao 403 507, Spain, ☎0832/244467, ☏262076, ⊛www.classic-bike-india.com

By bicycle

Ever since Dervla Murphy's *Full Tilt*, a steady but increasing trickle of travellers has either done the overland trip **by bicycle**, or else bought a bike in India and ridden it around the country. In many ways it is the ideal form of transport, offering total independence without loss of contact with local people. You can camp out, though there are cheap lodgings in almost every village – take the bike into your room with you – and, if you get tired of pedalling, you can put it on top of a bus as luggage, or transport it by train (it goes in the luggage van: get a form and pay a small fee at the station luggage office).

Bringing a bike from abroad requires no *carnet* or special paperwork, but spare parts and accessories may be of different sizes and standards in India, and you may have to improvise. Bring basic spares and tools and a pump. Panniers are the obvious thing for carrying your gear, but fiendishly inconvenient when not attached to your bike, and you might consider sacrificing ideal load-bearing and streamlining technology for a backpack you can lash down on the rear carrier.

Buying a bike in India presents no great difficulty; most towns have cycle shops and even cycle markets. The advantages of a local bike are that spare parts are easy to get, locally produced tools and parts will fit and your vehicle will not draw a crowd every time you park it. Disadvantages are that Indian bikes tend to be heavier and less state-of-the-art than ones from abroad – bikes with gears, let alone mountain bikes, are virtually unheard of. Selling should be quite easy: you won't get a tremendously good deal at a cycle market, but you may well be able to sell privately, or even to a rental shop.

Bicycles can be **rented** in most towns, usually for local use only: this is a good way to find out if your legs and bum can survive the Indian bike before buying one. Rs10–30 per day or Rs2–3 per hour is the going rate, occasionally more in tourist centres, and you may have to leave a deposit, or even your passport as security.

IBT, 4887 Columbia Drive S, Seattle WA 98108-1919 (☎206/767-0848, ⊛www.ibike

.org) publishes information and offers advice on bicycle travel around the world.

City transport

Transport around town takes various forms, with **buses** the most obvious. These are usually single-decker, though double-deckers (some articulated) exist in Mumbai and elsewhere. City buses can get unbelievably crowded, so beware of pickpockets, razor-armed pocket-slitters and "Eve-teasers" (see p.80); the same applies to **suburban trains** in Mumbai (Chennai is about the only other place where you might want to use trains for local city transport).

You can also take **taxis**, usually rather battered Ambassadors (painted black and yellow in Mumbai). With any luck, the driver will agree to use the meter; in theory you're within your rights to call the police if he doesn't, but the usual compromise is to agree a fare for the journey before you get in. Naturally, it helps to have an idea in advance what the fare should be, though any figures quoted in this or any other book should be treated as being the broadest of guidelines only. From places such as main stations, you may be able to find other passengers to share a taxi to the town centre; many stations, and certainly most airports, operate pre-paid taxi schemes with set fares that you pay before departure; more expensive pre-paid limousines are also available.

The **auto-rickshaw**, that most Indian of vehicles, is the front half of a motor-scooter with a couple of seats mounted on the back. Cheaper than taxis, better at nipping in and out of traffic, and usually metered (again, in most places they probably won't use them and you should agree a fare before setting off), auto-rickshaws are a little unstable and their drivers often rather reckless, but that's all part of the fun. In major tourist centres rickshaws can, however, hassle you endlessly on the street, often shoving themselves right in your path to prevent you ignoring them, and once they've got you on board, they may take you to several shops before reaching your destination. Moreover, agreeing a price before the journey will not necessarily stop your rickshaw-wallah reopening discussion when the trip is under way, or at its end. In general it is better to hail a rickshaw than to take one that's been following you, and to avoid those that hang around outside posh hotels.

One or two cities also have larger versions of auto-rickshaws known as **tempos**, with six or eight seats behind, which usually ply fixed routes at flat fares. Here and there, you'll also come across horse-drawn carriages, or **tongas**. Tugged by underfed and often lame horses, these are the least popular with tourists.

If you want to see a variety of places around town, consider hiring a taxi, rickshaw or auto-rickshaw for the day. Find a driver who speaks English reasonably well, and agree a price beforehand. You will probably find it a lot cheaper than you imagine: the driver will invariably act as a guide and source of local knowledge, and tipping is usually in order.

Accommodation

There are far more Indians travelling around South India at any one time – whether for holidays, on pilgrimages or for business – than there are foreign tourists, and a vast infrastructure of hotels and guesthouses caters for their needs. On the whole, accommodation for foreign tourists, like so many other things in South India, provides extremely good value for money, though in the major cities, especially, prices are soaring for luxury establishments that provide Western-style comforts and service.

Throughout this book we recommend places to stay in cities, towns and villages that range from lavish lakeside palaces to the most basic dormitory accommodation.

Inexpensive hotels

While accommodation prices in India are generally on the up, there's still an abundance of **cheap hotels**, catering for backpacking tourists and less well-off Indians. Most charge Rs100–200 for a double room, and some outside the big cities have rates below Rs100 (£1.50/$2.20). The cheapest option is usually in a dormitory of a hostel or hotel, where you'll be charged anything from Rs30 to Rs100. With prices as low as Rs20 per person, ashrams and *dharamshalas* are even better value.

Budget accommodation varies from filthy fleapits to homely guesthouses and, naturally, tends to be cheaper the further you get off the beaten track; it's at its most expensive in Mumbai, where prices are at least double those for equivalent accommodation in most other cities.

Cold showers or "bucket baths" are the order of the day – not really a problem in most of South India for most of the year. It's always wise, though, to check out the state of the bathrooms and toilets before taking a room. Bed bugs and mosquitoes are other things to check for – splotches of blood around the bed and on the walls where people have squashed them are tell-tale signs.

If a taxi driver or rickshaw-wallah tells you that the place you ask for is full, closed or has moved, it's more than likely that it's because he wants to take you to a hotel that pays him commission – added, in most cases, to your bill. Hotel touts, more prevalent in the North than in the South, operate in some major tourist spots, working for commission from the hotels they take you to. This can become annoying, but sometimes paying the little extra can be well worth it, especially if you arrive alone in a new place at night. One way to avoid the hassle is to stay put – some of the airports have retiring rooms and so do most of the larger railway stations.

All accommodation prices in this book are coded using the symbols below. The prices given are for a double room; in the case of dorms, we give the actual price in rupees. Most mid-range and all expensive and luxury hotels charge a luxury tax of around ten to fifteen percent, and a local tax of around five percent. All taxes are included in the prices we quote.

India doesn't have a tourist season as such, and most accommodation keeps the same prices throughout the year. Certain resorts, however, and some spots on established tourist trails do experience some variation and will be more expensive, or less negotiable, when demand is at its peak. For the hill stations, this will be in the summer (April–July); for Goa and other beach resorts in the South, it'll be the winter (Dec–Jan), especially around Christmas and New Year. We indicate such fluctuations where appropriate.

① up to Rs100	**④** Rs300–400	**⑦** Rs900–1500
② Rs100–200	**⑤** Rs400–600	**⑧** Rs1500–2500
③ Rs200–300	**⑥** Rs600–900	**⑨** Rs2500 and upwards

Mid-range hotels

Even if you value your **creature comforts**, you don't need to pay through the nose for them. A large clean room, freshly made bed, your own spotless (often sit-down) toilet and hot and cold running water can still cost under Rs300 (£4/$6). Extras that can bump up the price include local taxes, TV, mosquito nets, a balcony and, above all, **air-conditioning** (rarely found for much under Rs600). Abbreviated in this book and in India itself as **a/c**, air-conditioning is not necessarily the advantage you might expect – in some hotels you can find yourself paying double for a system that is so dust-choked, wheezy and noisy as to preclude any possibility of sleep – but providing it entitles a hotel to consider itself mid-range. Some also offer a halfway-house option known as "**air-cooled**" found in drier climes as coolers do not work in areas of extreme humidity such as along the coasts of South India and the Bay of Bengal. Additionally, many medium-priced hotels have attached restaurants, and even room service.

New hotels tend to be lined inside, on floors and walls, with marble (or some imitation), which can make them feel totally characterless. They are, however, much cleaner than older hotels, where dirt and grime clings to cracks and crevices, and damp quickly devours paint. Some mid-range hotels feel compelled to furnish their rooms with wall-to-wall carpeting which often smells due to the humidity and damp caused by heavy rains.

Most state governments run their own "**tourist bungalows**" – similar to mid-range hotels – either directly, or through their Tourist Development Corporation. These usually offer pricier a/c rooms as well as cheaper dorms, and are often good value, though the standard varies a lot from state to state and even within states. Some, such as Karnataka's, for example, tend to be rather run-down, whereas Kerala's range even includes four-star luxury.

If you're on a medium budget, it's not a bad idea to consider staying at the state-run hotel in any town; we've consistently indicated such places throughout this guide by including the state acronym in the name – eg KTDC (Kerala Tourist Development Corporation) *Surya*. Bookings for state-run hotels can be made in advance by telephone, through state tourist offices or with most of the state Tourist Development Corporation offices or hotels.

Upmarket hotels

Most luxury hotels in India fall into one of two categories: old-fashioned institutions brimming with class, and modern jet-set chain hotels, on the whole confined to large cities and tourist resorts. Most luxury hotels belong to a chain, although there are now several independent hotels, especially around Goa and Kerala, that offer superb facilities. The faded grandeur of the **Raj** lingers on in the venerable edifices of British imperial hangouts, more prevalent in the North than in South India where you are more likely to come across it in the timeless atmosphere of clubs, most of which are in hill stations.

Modern deluxe establishments – slicker, brighter, faster and far more businesslike – tend to belong to chains, which can be Indian as often as they are international. The *Taj* in Mumbai for example, the country's grandest hostelry, has a number of offshoots, including hotels in Chennai, Kochi, Bangalore, Hyderabad and several "Garden Retreats", including Kumarakom and Varkala. Other chains include Oberoi, Hilton International, Meridien, Hyatt and Sheraton, the Welcomgroup and the Government of India Tourist Development Corporation's Ashok chain. You'll find such hotels in most state capitals and some resorts favoured by rich Indian and foreign tourists. It's becoming more common for these to quote tariffs in US dollars, starting at $110, and sometimes bringing the price for a double room up to an astonishing $500. In palaces and heritage hotels, however, you'll still get excellent value for money, with rates only just beginning to approach those of their counterparts back home.

Heritage hotels combine traditional-style, and in some cases, antique architecture with modern amenities, to offer an interesting and much more attractive alternative than the large deluxe hotels. They are located along the popular western coastal strip, especially in Kerala. Although some – especially those along the sea – tend to shun air-conditioning and come with "open to the sky" showers, standards are generally very high. In fact, most feature Ayurvedic massage and rejuvenation programmes. A handful of old mansions in Kochi have been converted very successfully into hotels, and the Kochi-based Casino Group runs several heritage hotels in Kerala and one in Lakshadweep. You can expect to pay around $100 for a double room low season (roughly Jan–Jun & Nov), and up to $250 for the most luxurious rooms in high season (July, Aug & Dec).

Other places

Many train stations have "**retiring rooms**" for passengers to sleep in, but you have to put up with station noises. These rooms can be particularly handy if you're catching an early morning train, but tend to get booked up well in advance. They vary in price, but generally charge roughly the same as a budget hotel, and have large, clean, if somewhat institutional rooms; dormitories, where you can bank on being woken at the crack of dawn by a morning chorus of throat-clearing, are often available. Occasionally you may come across a main station with an a/c room, in which case you will have found a real bargain.

In one or two places, you can **rent rooms in people's homes**. Munjeeta Travel in Woking (see box on p.12) organizes "Homestay Tours" across India – an excellent way to get to know an Indian family and see how they live. You can also contact the free international hosting organization Servas (ⓦwww.servas.org) to sign up as a member with your local branch – you then get given a list of hosts in the country you plan to visit, whom you contact directly; India currently has over six hundred such hosts.

Camping is possible too, although in most of the country it's hard to see why you'd want to be cooped up in a tent overnight, when you could be sleeping on a cool *charpoi* (a sort of basic bed) on a roof terrace for a handful of rupees – let alone why you'd choose to carry a tent around India in the first place, except possibly on treks. It's not usual simply to pitch a tent in the countryside, though many hotels allow camping in their grounds. The YMCA runs a few sites, as do state governments and the Scouts and Guides.

YMCAs and **YWCAs**, confined to big cities, are plusher and pricier, comparable to a mid-range hotel. They are usually good value, but are often full, and some are exclusively single-sex. Official and non-official **youth hostels**, some run by state governments, are spread haphazardly across the country. They give HI cardholders a discount, but rarely exclude non-members, nor do they usually impose daytime closing. Prices match the cheapest hotels; where there is a youth hostel, it usually has a dormitory and may well be the best budget accommodation available – which goes especially for the **Salvation Army** ones.

Finally, some temples offer accommodation for pilgrims and visitors, and may put up tourists. A donation is often expected, and certainly appreciated. Pilgrimage sites, especially those far from other accommodation, also have **dharamshalas** where visitors can stay – very cheap and very simple, almost always with basic, communal washing facilities. Some of the Jain as well as Hindu sites in South India are very well organized, with booking offices in town that offer quite reasonable budget accommodation for as little as Rs20.

Accommodation practicalities

Check-out time at the pricier hotels is noon. Always confirm this when you arrive: many expect you out by 8am. The majority of lower to mid-range places operate a 24-hour system, under which you are simply obliged to leave by the same time as you arrived. Some places let you use their facilities after the official check-out time, sometimes for a small charge, while a few won't even let you leave your baggage after then unless you pay for another night.

Unfortunately, not all hotels offer **single rooms**, so it can often work out more expensive travelling alone; in hotels that don't, you may be able to negotiate a slight discount. However, it's not unusual to find rooms with three or four beds – great value for families and small groups.

In cheap hotels and hostels, you needn't expect any **additions to your basic bill**, but as you go up the scale (above $200–300), you'll find taxes and service charges creeping in, sometimes adding as much as a third on top of the original tariff. Service is generally ten percent, but taxes are a matter for state governments and, as such, vary from state to state.

Like most other things in India, the price of a room may well be open to **negotiation**. If you think the price is too high, or if all the hotels in town are empty, try haggling. You may get nowhere – but nothing ventured, nothing gained.

Eating and drinking

Indian food has a richly deserved reputation throughout the world for being aromatic and delicious. The broad spectrum of cultures in South India is reflected in the cuisine of the various regions, and a culinary tour will prove that food in the South is some of the finest there is in the subcontinent. As well as offering wonderful fresh fish, South India can be particularly special if you're a vegetarian. Indians are used to people having special dietary requirements: yours will be respected, and no one will think you strange for having them. Indeed, some of the very best food India – and especially the South – has to offer is vegetarian, and even the most confirmed meat-eaters will find themselves tucking into delicious lentils and veg curries with relish.

For the first-time visitor, South India, with its bewildering range of regional cuisine (see below), can challenge all preconceptions of Indian food. What Westerners call a **curry** covers a variety of dishes, each made with a different *masala* or mix of spices. The word curry probably originates from the *karhi* leaf, a type of laurel, found in much of Indian cooking especially in the South. Curry powder does not exist in India, the nearest equivalent being the northern *garam masala* ("hot mix"), a combination of dried, ground black pepper and other spices, added to a dish at the last stage of cooking to spice it up. Commonly used **spices**, most grown along the lush spice belt of the Western Ghats particularly in Kerala, include pepper, cardamom, cloves, cinnamon, chilli, turmeric, garlic, ginger, coriander – both leaf and seed – cumin and saffron. Some are used whole, so beware of chewing on them.

It's the Indian penchant for **chilli** that alarms many Western visitors, though if you have a fondness for the hotter curries served in Indian restaurants in Britain, you may find those in India mild on the whole. The majority of newcomers develop a tolerance for it, but if you don't, stick to mild dishes and eat rice and plenty of *dahi* (curd) to counter the effects. Fresh lime squeezed onto hot curries also tends to reduce the fire. Curd rice, a typical southern dish, is calming and good for an upset stomach, as is tender coconut water (*yellaniru* in Kanada). Beer is one of the best things for washing chilli out of your mouth; the essential oils that cause the burning sensation dissolve in alcohol, but not in water. A softer option – a *lassi* (sweet or salty curd drink) – to accompany your meal can also help cool things down.

Most religious Hindus, and a large majority of people in the far South, do not consume the flesh of animals, while some orthodox Brahmins will not eat food cooked by anyone outside their household (or onions or garlic, as they inflame the baser instincts). Jains are even stricter and will go as far as shunning tomatoes, which remind them of blood. Veganism as such is not common, however, so if you're vegan keep your eyes open for dairy products which are prevalent in all forms of cooking, from sweets to *ghee* (the unclarified butter often used in more elaborate cuisine).

Many eating places state whether they are vegetarian or non-vegetarian – "**veg**" and "**non-veg**" – and we have adopted these terms throughout our eating reviews. Sometimes, especially in the South, you will come across restaurants advertising both "veg" and "non-veg", indicating they have two separate kitchens and, often, two distinct parts to the restaurant so as not to contaminate and offend their vegetarian clientele. You'll also see "**pure veg**" advertised, which means that no eggs or alcohol are served. As a rule, meat-eaters should exercise caution in India: even when meat is available, especially in the larger towns, its quality is not assured and you won't get much in a dish anyway – especially in railway canteens where it's mainly there for flavouring. Note, what is called "mutton" is in fact goat. Hindus, of course, do not eat beef, and Muslims shun pork, so you'll only find those in a few Christian enclaves such as the beach areas of Goa, in the few Tibetan communities and amongst the Kodavas of the Kodagu (Coorg) hill country of Karnataka, who love pork. In Kerala, due to a liberal mix of religions and cultures, attitudes to food can be more relaxed, and both beef and pork appear on the same menu. Fish, especially along the coast, is popular and is consumed by most, except strict vegetarians.

Set "**meals**" – rather more plain food usually served on a banana leaf instead of a plate – are served all over South India, the equivalent of a North Indian thali. After the meal, the banana leaf is either assigned to compost or as fodder for cows. In some circles, tradition is so entrenched that the banana leaf is preferred even in an urban environment. "Meals" restaurants are usually found clustered around major bus stations and busy bazaars; they serve endless quantities of rice and vegetables and are normally excellent value. Not all "meals" restaurants are vegetarian. Some serve chicken and fish, and a good way of approaching a "meal" is to order a vegetarian meal, with fish or chicken on the side. Most "meals" restaurants often come with a plain canteen and a more upmarket section, some with air-conditioning. You may even encounter "meals" restaurants that come with vegetarian and non-vegetarian sections. Occasionally found along main highways, though more prevalent in north India, *dhabas* are a Punjabi tradition and cater mainly to truck drivers serving basic but delicious wholesome food including dhal (lentil soup pronounced "da'al") and *roti* (oven-baked unleavened bread).

In the South – perhaps even more so than elsewhere – **eating with your fingers** is *de rigueur* (you want to feel the food as well as taste it), and cutlery may not always be available. Wherever you eat, however, remember to use only your right hand (see p.73), and wash your hands before you start. Use the tips of your fingers to avoid getting food on the palm of your hand.

Restaurants vary in price and quality, and offer a wide variety of dishes. If you're in a group, order a variety of dishes and sample each one. Deluxe restaurants, such as those in five-star hotels, are expensive by Indian standards, but they offer the chance to sample top-quality classic Indian cuisine: rich, subtle and mouthwatering, at a fraction of the price you'd pay at home – assuming you could find Indian food that good. Try one out at least once but avoid the wine, which is invariably overpriced.

An alternative type of eating-place – catering specifically for foreign travellers with unadventurous tastebuds, or simply a hankering for home – is the **tourist restaurant**, found in beach resorts, hill stations and travellers' meccas. Here you can get Western food galore: pancakes and fritters, omelettes and toast, chips, fried prawns, cereal, and fruit salad. They tend to be a bit pricey, can miss the mark by a long way and are not, of course, authentically Indian.

Finally, should you be lucky enough to be invited into someone's home, you will get to taste the most authentic Indian food of all. Most Indian women are expert cooks, trained from childhood by mothers, grandmothers and aunties, and aided by daughters and nieces. They can quite easily spend a whole day cooking – grinding and mixing the spices themselves – and using only the freshest ingredients.

For advice on water in India, see p.27.

South Indian food

Occasionally, a sweeping generalization is made, that the cuisine of North India is rich and spicy, while that of the South is plain. Considering the incredible **regional variety**, ranging from the rich northern-style Mughlai cooking, developed within the opulent courts of Muslim Hyderabad, to more simple vegetarian dishes in Tamil Nadu, this generalization is quite simply not true. The street food of Mumbai is renowned; Goan cuisine reflects strong Portuguese influences; and Karnataka draws heavily from the plain cooking of its southern neighbours as well as from the rich, aromatic cooking of Hyderabad. Kerala's cuisine is remarkably varied. Tamil Nadu, the most vegetarian and perhaps the most austere, however, offers pockets of variety in regions such as Chettinad – with its memorable version of fried chicken – and the small, diminishing Franco-Indian population of Pondicherry – whose unique cuisine, now rare outside the family home, threatens to disappear altogether.

Most quintessential of all South Indian food are *iddlis* (steamed rice cakes), *vadas* (deep-fried lentil cakes) and *dosas* (rice pancakes), which come either with filling (*masala*) or plain (*sada*) – dished up with *sambar* (lentil soup) and coconut chutney. They are served as breakfast, snacks and frequently as part of "meals" dishes, throughout South India.

Those with a penchant for North Indian food and **tandoori** (clay oven) preparations will find dishes such as chicken *tikka* (boneless cubes of *tandoori* chicken, marinated with yoghurt, spices and herbs) and other favourites feature on the menus of more upmarket restaurants and five-star hotels.

Goan cuisine

The hot and sour curry **vindaloo**, found on menus in Indian restaurants worldwide, is possibly the most famous of all Goan dishes. *Vindaloo* originates from the Portuguese *vinho d'alho*, literally "garlic wine", and consists of meat or fish seasoned with vinegar, but is traditionally made with pork. Goan food is particularly distinctive in that it uses palm vinegar, a Portuguese introduction, in many of its preparations. In fact, the **Portuguese influence** spread far beyond the borders of their once colonial enclave, when they introduced vegetables and spices from the New World. These included green and red peppers – chillies – which eventually replaced black pepper as the source of heat in Indian cooking.

Pork specialities from Goa, include: *chouriço* (red sausages), *leitao* (suckling pig) and *balchao* (pork in a rich brown sauce). Essentially a *vindaloo*, *sarpotel* (pork with liver and heart, vinegar, chillies, spices and tamarind) combines the best of both Portuguese and Indian influences, as does *assado* (a spicy, pan-cooked beef preparation, usually served with salad and potatoes). Although meats like pork and beef feature heavily in Goan cuisine, being a coastal region, its seafood is exceptional. Much like the food of Kerala, Goan cooking relies heavily on coconuts especially ground coconut, an ingredient that appears in assorted dishes, from fish curries to cakes. Best prepared with *pomfret*, a flat fish found in coastal waters throughout India, the classic Goan fish curry is cooked with spices mixed with coconut and tamarind, and is usually served with plain, boiled rice. Another fish curry, *caldeen*, marinades the fish in vinegar before cooking it in a spicy sauce made with coconut and chillies. Goa's wonderfully fresh seafood includes shellfish such as clams, lobster and prawn cooked in a variety of ways. Specialities are pies, hot curries and soups such as *sopa de camarão*, a prawn soup cooked with puréed potatoes, egg yolk and milk, and *apa de camarão*, a spicy prawn pie with a rice and semolina crust. Goa is also celebrated for its cakes and desserts such as *bebinca*, a custard made with *gram* (chickpea) flour, eggs and coconut milk.

Hyderabadi haute cuisine

Some connoisseurs may argue, and not without a certain justification, that haute cuisine originating from Hyderabad, Andhra Pradesh, represents the **pinnacle** of all **Indian Muslim cooking**. Although the grandeur of a once luxurious court has faded, traditions still linger on and if you find yourself in the city, a culinary tour will leave indelible impressions. Many Hyderabadi dishes will already be familiar to visitors. Preparations such as *korma* (an aromatic but mild and creamy curry), *pilaf* (aromatic fried rice also known as *pilau*) and *biryani* (aromatic baked rice) feature prominently in India and are recognized worldwide.

During the height of the Nizam's rule (nineteenth/early twentieth century) Hyderabad attracted Muslims from all over India and abroad, who left their influence on food preparation in the region. Spice mixtures present in some preparations are derived from Persian recipes and, with the city's proximity to the spice belts of the Malabar Coast, are combined with indigenous ingredients to give a unique, rich and aromatic cuisine. With the help of tamarind and local spices, Persian dried lamb with beans is recreated as the delicious *dalcha*, and the fiery *til ki chutney*, inspired by the Middle Eastern *tahini*, is made of sesame seeds. Common ingredients used in Hyderabadi cuisine include: cassia buds, *karhi* leafs, chillies, cinnamon, cardamom, tamarind, peanuts, coconut milk and curds (*dahi*). Mixing these spices is a high art, best illustrated by *potli ka masala*, an unusual mixture consisting of *khas* (vetivert) and dried rose petals, ground and sprinkled onto prepared food, and sometimes present on meat dishes such as *nahari* (a slow cooked stew of lamb with tongue and trotters). Other meat dishes include *lukmi*, which is a type of deep-fried ravioli, and *chippe ka gosht*, where lamb, marinated in yoghurt and coconut, is cooked slowly in an earthenware pot to give it its distinctive earthy flavour. As with Muslim cooking everywhere,

Hyderabadi cuisine is heavily meat-orientated with a large variety of kebabs and meat preparations. However, there are delicious vegetarian dishes such as *bagheri baingan*, also known as *Hyderabadi baingan* (small aubergines cooked with peanut paste), as well as several rice preparations including *khichari* (rice cooked with lentils and *ghee*), which is traditionally served at breakfast.

Food from Karnataka

Sandwiched between the meat-loving Muslim enclaves of Hyderabad and the central Deccan and the lush, rice-eating coastal regions to the south, Karnataka enjoys the **best of both worlds** in terms of food. In restaurants in Bangalore, you can eat the most sumptuous chicken *biryanis* inspired by Andhra Pradesh cuisine and served on banana leafs, while your neighbour on the next table tucks into a vegetarian "meal" complete with unlimited quantities of vegetables, *sambar* (lentil soup), rice and *rasam* (pepper water). By far the most famous of all of Karnataka's cooking comes from the town of Udupi, to the north of Mangalore, where the Udupi Brahmins have gained a legendary reputation as excellent restaurateurs and hotel-keepers and for their vegetarian cuisine developed, in part, as offerings made to their famous Krishna temple. They have become synonymous with quality, and, throughout the South, restaurants and hotels boast they are "Udupi-run". Udupi food is presented as a classic "meal" on a banana leaf but complemented with excellent rice preparations and a variety of delicious vegetable curries, liberally sprinkled with *ghee* (clarified butter) and accompanied by pickle. Udupi "meals" restaurants are well worth seeking out, not just because of their legendary food, but also for their excellent value. Their restaurants are also good for the ubiquitous *iddlis*, *vadas* and *dosas* and, it is said, the *masala dosa*, wrapped around a filling of potatoes and vegetables, was invented by an Udupi Brahmin. While Bangalore offers the most choice, a visit to Mysore is an opportunity to sample a good selection of Karnatakan cuisine, offering a handful of good Andhra and Udupi restaurants. The city's best-known dish is its Mysore *pak*, a sweet made from a rich, crumbly mixture of maize flour and *ghee*. Regional variety within Karnataka includes

the meat-dominated specialities of the Kodavas (see p.260) and the North Indian-style food of the central Deccan in the north of the state, where spicy curries are accompanied by *joleata roti*, a *chapati* (unleavened flat bread) made from a locally grown maize.

Keralan cooking

Colourful communities living in close proximity to each other have given Kerala a legacy of a rich and varied cuisine, complemented by the great spice belts along the Western Ghats and the rich source of **fish** to be had along the Malabar Coast and the Kuttanad backwaters. Kerala has always been a key centre for the **spice trade**, and attracted traders throughout history from all over the world. These different cultures, including Arabs, Phoenicians, Egyptians, Greeks, Romans and Chinese, were all instrumental in the development of Keralan cuisine. Syrian Christians and an ancient Iraqi Jewish community, along with indigenous Keralan Christians, Hindus and Muslims have, more recently, helped create a tolerant and liberal atmosphere that is reflected in the food – Kerala is, in fact, the only state in India where the slaughter of beef is tolerated. A veritable hothouse enclosed by a lush mountain range and the highest tea estates in the world, Kerala offers a huge variety of vegetables, from beans to bitter gourds, and fruit, including mangoes, bananas and jackfruit, which lie at the heart of the diverse cuisine of this region. One dish that is universally Keralan is *appam* – rice pancakes mixed with coconut, and cooked in a wok, known as *cheena chatti* (Chinese pot), to give it a soft centre and crisp edges which can make it look like a large fried egg. Variously known as *kallappam* or *wellayappam*, *appam* is traditionally served with an "*eshtew*" (a stew) of chicken and potatoes in a creamy white mild sauce, flavoured with spices such as pepper and cloves and complemented with coconut milk. While the *eshtew* may or may not have been inspired by European imports, the Malabar pudding – made of sago and topped with liquid jaggery and coconut milk instead of sugar and cream – has far more obvious European roots. The most famous of all Keralan dishes, however, is its wonderful fish curry or *molee*, cooked in a delicious cream of tomatoes, ground coconut and coconut milk. The coastal waters proffer a huge variety of seafood including marlin and shark. The day's catch is proudly displayed on the stands of the many seaside tourist restaurants of Kovalam and Varkala. Some of the best fish comes from the backwaters, where the black *karimeen*, a flat sole-like fish that hugs the muddy bottoms, is justifiably prized. Also known as fish tamarind, *kodampoli* (*Garcinia indica*) provides the distinctive flavour in the fiery fish curry *meen vevichathu*, which is cooked in an earthenware pot.

Muslim fishermen of the Mopla community favour shellfish, as well as beef, while the Christian fishing communities around Kovalam specialize in catching pomfret, mackerel, squid, prawns and other seafood, which they then sell on the beach to the highest bidder.

Rice features heavily in various forms in the Keralan diet. The *pilaf* (aka *pulau*) is especially popular among Muslims, and is served with seafood, especially prawns along the coast; occasionally tapioca, known locally as *kappa*, appears as an alternative staple to accompany coastal fish curries or is served as deep-fried chips.

Snacks and street food

Feeling peckish should never be a problem, with all sorts of **snack meals** and **finger food** to choose from. Served in restaurants and cafés throughout the South, *vadas*, *iddlis* and *dosas*, are the most popular snacks. *Appams*, offered along the seafront at Kochi, are served by vendors from portable stands, and are a favoured regional snack.

Street finger food includes *bhel puris* (a Mumbai speciality of small vegetables – stuffed *puris* with tamarind sauce), *pani puris* (the same *puris* dunked in peppery and spicy water – only for the seasoned), *bhajis* (deep-fried cakes of vegetables in chickpea flour), *samosas* (meat or vegetables in a pastry triangle, fried) and *pakoras* (vegetables or potato dipped in chickpea flour batter and deep-fried). Kebabs are common in the north and around Hyderabad, most frequently *shish kebab* (minced lamb grilled on a skewer) but also *shami kebab* (small minced lamb cutlets). With all street snacks, though, remember that food left lying around attracts germs – make sure it's freshly cooked. Be especially careful with snacks

You may be relieved to know that the red stuff people spit out all over the streets – predominantly in the North and major cities in the South – isn't blood, but juice produced by chewing paan – a digestive, commonly taken after meals, and also a mild stimulant.

A paan consists of chopped or shredded nut (always referred to as *betel* nut, though in fact it comes from the areca palm), wrapped in a leaf (which *does* come from the betel tree). It is prepared with ingredients such as *katha* (a red paste), *chuna* (slaked white lime), *mitha masala* (a mix of sweet spices, which can be ingested) and *zarda* (chewing tobacco, not to be swallowed on any account, especially if made with *chuna*). The triangular package thus formed is wedged inside your cheek and chewed slowly, and in the case of *chuna* and *zarda paans*, spitting out the juice as you go. Paan is an acquired taste; novices should start off, and preferably stick with, the sweet and harmless *mitha* variety, which is perfectly all right to ingest.

Paan and paan masala (a mix of betel nut, fennel seeds, sweets and flavourings) are sold by paan-wallahs, often from tiny stalls squeezed between shops. Paan-wallahs develop big reputations and some of the more extravagant concoctions come with silver and, in some rare cases, even gold foil; these are often produced at weddings.

---

involving water such as *pani puris* and cooking oil that is often recycled. Generally, it's a good idea to acclimatize to Indian conditions before you start eating street snacks.

You won't find anything called "Bombay mix" in India, but there's no shortage of dry spicy snack mixes, often referred to as *channa chur*. Jackfruit chips are sometimes sold as a savoury snack, though they are rather bland, and cashew nuts are a real bargain. Peanuts, also known as "monkey nuts", usually come roasted and unshelled. Look out for *gram* vendors who sell dry roasted chickpeas – known as *gram*. Another sweeter street snack seen throughout the south in bright yellow piles is banana chips fried in coconut oil.

Non-Indian food

Chinese food has become widespread in towns all over the country, where it is generally cooked by Indian chefs and not what you'd call authentic. However, India does have a small Chinese population, and in Mumbai, Bangalore and Chennai, you can expect to come across very good Chinese cuisine. Chinese communities tend to adapt their cooking to their environment and, in India, Chinese food comes with a hint of spice.

Outside of upmarket hotels, **Western food** is often dire, and expensive compared with

Indian food, although the international chains serve the same standard fare as elsewhere in the world at much cheaper prices. Branches of *Pizza Hut*, *Domino's*, *KFC* and *McDonald's* can be found in Mumbai, Chennai and Bangalore in ever-increasing numbers. *Wimpy's*, home-grown chains such as *Kwality's* and independently owned fast-food cafés like *Pizza Corner* can be found in most cities and large towns. Tourist centres, however, such as Goa, Pondicherry and Kovalam offer a reasonable choice of Western food, from patisseries serving cakes and croissants to restaurants offering lasagne on candle-lit terraces. Small cheese factories are beginning to emerge, providing an alternative to the dreary processed cheese produced by Amul; cheeses and breads made at Auroville are sold throughout the South. Cities such as Bangalore and Mumbai also offer a choice of **Tex-Mex**, **Thai**, **Japanese**, **Italian** and **French** cuisine, but these are often only available in the restaurants of luxury hotels.

Breakfast

Westerners seem to get especially homesick around breakfast time; but getting your fry-ups and hash browns is likely to be a problem. Each region has its own **traditional** way of greeting the day and in the South *iddli*, *vada*, *dosa* and *uppma* (semolina and nuts)

is the most common equivalent, while members of the *India Coffee House* chain can be depended upon for some decent coffee and toast.

In those towns which have established a reputation as hangouts for "travellers", budget hotels and restaurants serve up the usual hippy fare – banana pancakes, muesli, etc – as well as omelettes, toast, porridge (not always oatmeal), cornflakes and even bacon and eggs.

Sweets

Most Indians have rather a sweet tooth and Indian **sweets**, usually made of milk, can be very sweet indeed. Although the emphasis on milk products is stronger in the North

A glossary of dishes and cooking terms

Owing to the very distinct languages of South India, an effective glossary of food terms is almost impossible, but the following list represents a highlight of food and the terms you are likely to come across as a visitor.

apa de camarão	spicy prawn pie with a rice and semolina crust (Goa)	*dahi rice*	a pleasant and light preparation – sometimes lightly spiced – of boiled rice with yoghurt (*dahi*)
appam	wok-cooked rice pancake speckled with holes, soft in the middle; a speciality of the Malabar coast of Kerala (Kerala)	*dhal*	lentils, pronounced "da'al" and found in one form or another throughout India; in the South often replaced by *sambar* (universal)
assado	a spicy pan-cooked beef preparation (Goa)	*dhansak*	meat and lentil curry, a Parsi speciality; medium-hot (Mumbai)
bagheri baingan	small aubergine cooked with peanut paste and spices (Hyderabad)	*dosa*	rice pancake – should be crispy; when served with a filling it is called a *masala dosa* and when plain, a *sada dosa* (Andhra Pradesh, Karnataka, Tamil Nadu, universal)
bebinca	custard made with *gram* (chickpea) flour, eggs and coconut juice (Goa)		
biryani	rice baked with saffron or turmeric, whole spices and meat (sometimes vegetables), and often hard-boiled egg (North India and Hyderabad)	*eshtew*	a stew, usually made with chicken, cooked with potatoes in a creamy white sauce of coconut milk (Kerala)
Bombay duck	dried bummelo fish (Mumbai)	*ghee*	clarified butter sometimes used for festive cooking, and often sprinkled onto food before eating (universal)
caldeen	fish marinated in vinegar and cooked in a spicy sauce of coconut and chillies (Goa)		
chapati	unleavened bread made of wholewheat flour and baked on a round griddle-dish called a *tawa* (universal)	*iddli*	steamed rice cake, usually served with *sambar*; *malligi* (jasmine) *iddlis* around Mysore are exceptionally fluffy and so named because of their lightness – the scent of jasmine is said to waft on the breeze (Andhra Pradesh, Karnataka, Kerala, Tamil Nadu, universal)
chop	minced meat or vegetable surrounded by breaded mashed potato (universal)		
cutlet	cutlet – often minced meat or vegetable fried in the form of a flat cake (universal)	*jaggery*	unrefined sugar made from palm sap (universal)
		jeera rice	rice cooked with cumin seeds (*jeera*) (universal)

than in the South, sweets, including regional specialities, are popular throughout the country, with sweet shops thriving in all cities and large towns.

Of the more solid type, *barfi*, a kind of fudge made from boiled-down and condensed milk, varies from moist and delicious to dry and powdery. It comes in various flavours, from plain, creamy white to livid green *pista* (pista-chio), and is often sold covered with silver leaf (which you eat). Smoother-textured, round *penda* and thin diamonds of *kaju katri*, plus moist *sandesh* and the harder *paira*, are among many other sweets made from boiled-down milk. Numerous types of gelatinous *halwa*, are especially popular in Hyderabad, all of which are totally different in taste and texture to the Middle Eastern variety. Of the

karhi leaf	a type of laurel from which the leaf and the seeds are widely used as a spice throughout South India (universal)	*pulau*	also known as *pilaf* or *pullao*, rice, gently spiced and pre-fried (universal)
keema	minced meat (Hyderabad)	*puri*	crispy, puffed-up, deep-fried wholewheat bread (universal)
khichari	rice cooked with lentils in various ways, from plain, to aromatic and spicy (Hyderabad, universal)	*rasam*	spicy, pepper water often drunk to accompany "meals" in the South
kofta	balls of minced vegetables or meat in a curried sauce (Hyderabad)	*roti*	loosely used term; often just another name for *chapati*, though it should be thicker, chewier and baked in a *tandoor* (universal)
korma	meat braised in yoghurt sauce, mild (Hyderabad)		
kulcha	fried flat bread to accompany curries (Hyderabad)	*sambar*	soupy lentil and vegetable curry with asafoetida and tamarind; used as an accompaniment to *dosas*, *iddlis* and *vadas* (universal)
molee	curry with coconut, usually fish, originally Malay (hence the name), now a speciality of Kerala; hot (Kerala)		
		sarpotel	pork dish with liver and heart, cooked in plenty of vinegar and spices (Goa)
mulligatawny	curried vegetable soup, a classic Anglo-Indian dish rumoured to have come from "Mulligan Aunty" but probably South Indian; medium-strength (universal)	*uppma*	popular breakfast cereal made from semolina, spices and nuts, and served with *sambar* (Kerala, Tamil Nadu)
naan	white, leavened bread kneaded with yoghurt and baked in a *tandoor* (universal)	*uttapam*	thick rice pancake often cooked with onions (Karnataka, Tamil Nadu, Kerala, universal)
papad or *poppadum*	crisp, thin chickpea flour cracker (universal)	*vada*	also known as *vadai*, a doughnut-shaped deep-fried lentil cake, which usually has a hole in its centre
paratha	wholewheat bread made with butter, rolled thin and griddle-fried; a little bit like a chewy pancake, sometimes stuffed with meat or vegetables (universal)		
		vindaloo	Goan meat – seasoned with vinegar – (sometimes fish) curry, originally pork; very hot (but not as hot as the kamikaze UK version) (Goan, universal)
pomfret	a flatfish popular in Bombay and Calcutta (universal)		

regional varieties, Mysore *pak*, made from a rich crumbly mixture of maize flour and *ghee*, is one South Indian sweet that is exported to the rest of India.

Getting softer and stickier, those circular orange tubes, dripping syrup in sweet-shop windows, called *jalebis*, and made of deep-fried treacle, are as sickly as they look. *Gulab jamuns* (deep-fried cream cheese sponge balls soaked in syrup) are just as unhealthy. Common in both the North and the South, *ladu* consists of balls made from semolina flour with raisins and sugar and sometimes made of other grains and flour.

Chocolate is improving rapidly in India, and Cadbury's and Amul bars are available everywhere. None of the indigenous brands of imitation Swiss and Belgian chocolates appearing on the cosmopolitan markets are worth eating.

Among the large **ice-cream** vendors, Kwality (now owned and branded as Wall's), Vadilal's, Gaylord and Dollops stand out. Uniformed men push carts of ice cream around and the bigger companies have many, usually quite obvious, imitators. Some have no scruples – stay away from water ices unless you have a seasoned constitution. Now common throughout southern towns and cities, ice-cream parlours selling elaborate concoctions including sundaes have really taken off. When travelling, especially around coastal Karnataka and parts of Kerala, look out for a local variation known as *gad-bad* (literally "mix-up") where layers of ice cream come interspersed with chopped nuts and dried and glacéd fruit. Be sure to try *kulfi*, a pistachio of mango- and cardamom-flavoured frozen sweet which is India's answer to ice cream but is more popular in the north than in South India. *Bhang kulfi*, not available everywhere but popular during the festival of Holi, is laced with cannabis, so has an interesting kick to it, but should be approached with caution.

Fruit

What fruit is available varies with region and season, but there's always a fine choice. Ideally, you should **peel all fruit,** including apples, or soak it in a strong iodine or potassium permanganate solution for thirty minutes. Roadside vendors sell fruit which they often cut up and serve sprinkled with salt and even *masala*. Don't buy anything that looks as if it's been hanging around for a while.

Mangoes are usually on offer, but not all are sweet enough to eat fresh – some are used for pickles or curries. Indians are picky about their mangoes, which they feel and smell before buying; if you don't know the art of choosing the fruit, you could be sold the leftovers. Among the varieties appearing at different times in the season – from spring to summer – look out for Alphonso, which is grown in the vicinity of Mumbai, and, Langra, which is grown all over South India. Oranges and tangerines are generally easy to come by, as are sweet melons and thirst-quenching watermelons, although the South is famous for its numerous kinds of bananas on sale all year round. Some bananas, such as the *nendrakai* variety of Kerala, come raw and are meant for cooking. Try the delicious red bananas of Kovalam, or the *nanjangod* variety grown in the vicinity of Mysore, which are considered by many Mysore city-dwellers as the best and most extravagant at around Rs5 per fruit! Certainly, while travelling on the buses through the Western Ghats, bananas provide a good fallback, especially for upset stomachs, complemented by tender-coconut water.

Tropical fruits such as coconuts, papayas (pawpaws) and pineapples are common, while things such as lychees and pomegranates are very seasonal. Among less familiar fruit, the *chiku*, which looks like a kiwi and tastes a bit like a pear, is worth a mention, as is the watermelon-sized jackfruit (*chakkai* in Malayalam), a favourite with Keralans, whose spiny green exterior encloses sweet, slightly rubbery yellow segments, each containing a seed. The custard apple, a knobbly green case housing a scented white pulp with large black seeds, is another interesting seasonal fruit.

Drinks

With some of the world's prime coffee-growing areas, unlike the rest of the country **coffee** is certainly as common as tea in South India, more so in some spots. South Indian coffee is traditionally prepared with sugar, topped with large quantities of milk to produce a distinctive taste. A whole ritual is attached to the drinking of milky Keralan coffee, poured in flamboyant sweeping motions between tall glasses to cool it down. One of the best places to get a decent cup of South Indian coffee is in the India Coffee House co-operative chain, found in every southern town. Good vacuum-packed filter coffee from Coorg (Kodagu) in Karnataka is now available but is yet to have an impact in cafés and restaurants.

The rest of India sometimes seems to run on **tea** (**chai**) – grown in Darjeeling, Assam in the North and in the Nilgiri Hills in South India – and sold by chai-wallahs on just about every street corner. Ginger and/or cardamoms are often added. If you're quick off the mark, you can get them to hold the sugar. English tea it isn't, but many travellers find it an irresistible brew and the rest get used to it: "Just don't think of chai as tea," advise some waverers. Sometimes, especially in tourist spots and upmarket hotels, you might get a pot of European-style "tray" tea, generally consisting of a tea bag in lukewarm water – you'd do better to stick to the pukka Indian variety, unless you are in a traditional tea-growing area. In some of the highest estates in the world, on the borders of Kerala and Tamil Nadu, the tea gardens of the Nilgiris produce fine, strong tea with a long tradition and a justifiable reputation.

With **bottled water** so widely available, you may have no need of **soft drinks**. These have long been surprisingly controversial in India. Coca-Cola and Pepsi returned to India in the early Nineties after being banned from the country for seventeen years. That policy was originally instigated, in part, to prevent the expatriation of profits by foreign companies; since their return, militant Hindu groups such as the RSS have threatened to make them the focus of a new boycott campaign against multinational consumer goods. The absence of Coca-Cola and Pepsi spawned a host of Indian colas such as Campa Cola (innocuous), Thums Up (not unpalatable), Gold Spot (fizzy orange) and Limca (rumoured to have dubious connections to Italian companies and to contain additives banned there). All contain a lot of sugar but little else: adverts for Indian soft drinks have been known to boast "Absolutely no natural ingredients!" None will quench your thirst for long.

More recommendable are straight water (treated, boiled or bottled; see also p.27), and cartons of Frooti Jumpin, Réal and similar brands of fruit juice drinks, which come in mango, guava, apple and lemon varieties. If the carton looks at all mangled, it is best not to touch it as it may have been recycled. Tender-coconut water from **green coconuts**, common around coastal areas especially in the South, are cheaper than any of these, and sold on the street by vendors who will hack off the top of the coconut for you with a machete and give you a straw to suck up the coconut water (you then scoop out the flesh and eat it).

India's greatest cold drink, **lassi** – originally from the north but now available throughout India – is made with beaten curd and drunk either salted, sweetened with sugar or mixed with fruit. It varies widely from smooth and delicious to insipid and watery, and is sold at virtually every café, restaurant and canteen in the country. Freshly made milk shakes are also common at establishments with blenders. They'll also sell you what they call a fruit juice, which is usually fruit, water and sugar (or salt) liquidized and strained; also, street vendors selling fresh fruit juice in less than hygienic conditions are apt to add salt and garam masala. In central and northern cities, especially in Hyderabad, *sharbat*, flavoured drinks made with sugar, fruit and, often, rose essence, are inspired by Middle Eastern roots and remain popular especially among Muslim communities.

With all such drinks, however appetizing they may seem, exercise great **caution** in deciding where to drink them, unless you're confident your body has acclimatized; find out where the water is likely to have come from and hold the ice.

Alcohol

Prohibition, once widespread in India, is now only partially enforced in a few states, including Tamil Nadu which retains some semblance of prohibition in the form of "dry" days, high taxes, restrictive licences and health warnings on labels ("Liquor – ruins country, family and life," runs Tamil Nadu's). Kerala's licensing laws have also resulted in restrictive licences and prohibitive fees to all except the government agencies, such as the Kerala Tourist Development Corporation, who have a virtual monopoly on the beer parlours throughout the state.

Except for the new pub scene in cosmopolitan cities such as Bangalore, most Indians drink to get drunk as quickly as possible and this trend has had a terrible toll on family life, especially among the working classes and peasantry. Because of this, politicians searching for votes have from time to time played the prohibition card. In states like Tamil Nadu, which persist with draconian drinking policies, the illicit trade in liquor flourishes, and every now and then papers report cases of mass contamination from illicit stills that have led tragically to an extraordinary number of deaths.

Beer is widely available, if rather expensive by local standards. Price varies from state to state, but you can usually expect to pay around Rs40–80 for a 650ml bottle. Kingfisher and Black Label are the leading brands, but there are plenty of others. All lagers, which tend to contain chemical additives including glycerine, are usually pretty palatable if you can get them cold. In certain places, notably unlicensed restaurants in Tamil Nadu, beer comes in the form of "special tea" – a teapot of beer, which you pour into and drink from a teacup to disguise what it really is. A cheaper, and often delicious,

alternative to beer in Kerala and one or two other places is *toddy* (palm wine).

Spirits usually take the form of "Indian Made Foreign Liquor" (IMFL), although the recently legitimized foreign liquor industry is expanding rapidly. Some Scotch, such as Seagram's Hundred Pipers, is now being bottled in India and sold at a premium; Smirnoff vodka is also available and other known brands are soon to follow. Some of the brands of Indian whisky are not too bad and are affordable in comparison; gin and brandy can be pretty rough, while Indian rum is sweet and distinctive. In Goa, *feni* is a spirit distilled from coconut or cashew fruit. Steer well clear of illegally distilled arak, however, which often contains methanol (wood alcohol) and other poisons. A look through the press, especially at festival times, will soon reveal numerous cases of blindness and death as a result of drinking bad hooch (or "spurious liquor" as it's called). Licensed country liquor, sold in several states under such names as *bangla*, is an acquired taste.

Telephones, mail and internet access

There is no need to be out of touch with the rest of the world while you're in India. The mail service is pretty reliable if a little slow; international phone calls are surprisingly easy; and internet/email services are nowadays widely available.

Telephones

Privately run **phone services** with international direct dialling facilities are widespread. Advertising themselves with the acronyms STD/ISD (standard trunk dialling/international subscriber dialling), they are extremely quick and easy to use; some stay open 24 hours per day. Both national and international calls are dialled direct. To call abroad, dial the international access code (00), the code for the country you want – 44 for the UK, for example – the appropriate area code (leaving out any initial zeros), and the number you

want; then you speak, pay your bill, which is calculated in seconds, and leave. Prices vary between private places and are slightly cheaper at official telecommunications offices; many have fax machines too. Calling from hotels is usually more expensive. "Call back" (or "back call", as it is often known) is possible at most phone booths and hotels, although check before you call and be aware that this facility rarely comes without a charge of between Rs3 and 10 per minute at booths, but is invariably free at hotels.

Direct dialling rates are very expensive during the day – Monday to Saturday 8am

International codes

	From India:	To India:
UK	☏00 44	☏00 91
Irish Republic	☏00 353	☏00 91
US and Canada	☏00 1	☏011 91
Australia	☏00 61	☏0011 91
New Zealand	☏00 64	☏00 91

to 7pm – but this falls to half rate on Sundays, national holidays, and daily from 7am to 8am and 7pm to 8.30pm, when the charge is reduced further.

Home country direct services are now available from any phone to the UK, the US, Canada, Ireland, Australia, New Zealand and a growing number of other countries. These allow you to make a collect or telephone credit card call to that country via an operator there. If you can't find a phone with home country direct buttons, you can use any phone toll-free, by dialling 000, your country code and 17 (except Canada which is 000-127).

To **call India** from abroad, dial the international access code 00, followed by 91 for India, the local code minus the initial zero, then the number you want.

When you land and switch on your **mobile phone**, your network will search for a local partner, you confirm that you want to use them, then you can use the phone as usual. It's worth investigating costs before deciding to take your mobile to India, but bear in mind that it may be useful in an emergency. **Prepaid cards** for pay-as-you-go phones are handy and available in most of the major cities and towns; prices start from Rs1000 and as low as Rs500 for a top-up card.

Mail services

Mail can take anything from three days to four weeks to get to or from India, depending largely on where exactly you are; ten days is about the norm. Stamps are not expensive, and aerogrammes and postcards cost the same to anywhere in the world. Ideally, you should have mail franked in front of you. Most post offices are open Mon–Fri 10am–5pm and Sat 10am–noon, but big city GPOs where the Poste Restante is usually located keep longer hours (Mon–Fri 9.30am–6pm, Sat 9.30am–1pm). You can also buy stamps at big hotels.

Poste restante (general delivery) services throughout the country are pretty reliable, though exactly how long individual offices hang onto letters is more or less at their own discretion; for periods of longer than a month, it makes sense to mark mail with your expected date of arrival. Letters are filed alphabetically; in larger offices, you sort through them yourself. To avoid misfiling, your name should be printed clearly, with the surname in large capitals and underlined, but it is still a good idea to check under your first name too, just in case. Have letters addressed to you c/o Poste Restante, GPO (if it's the main post office you want), and the name of the town and state. Sometimes too, as in Chennai, local tourist offices might be more convenient than the GPO. Don't forget to take ID with you to claim your mail. American Express offices also keep mail for holders of their charge card or travellers' cheques.

Having parcels sent out to you in India is not such a good idea – chances are they'll go astray. If you do have a parcel sent, have it registered.

Sending a parcel out of India can be quite a performance. First you have to get it cleared by customs at the post office (they often don't bother, but check), then you take it to a tailor and agree a price to have it wrapped in cheap cotton cloth (which you may have to go and buy yourself), stitched up and sealed with wax. In big city GPOs, people offering this service will be at hand. Next, take it to the post office, fill in and attach the relevant customs forms (it's best to tick the box marked "gift" and give its value as less than Rs1000 or "no commercial value", to avoid bureaucratic entanglements), buy your stamps, see them franked, and dispatch it. Parcels should not be more than a metre long, nor weigh more than 20kg. Surface mail is incredibly cheap, and takes an average of three months to arrive – however, it may take half, or four times that. It's a good way to dump excess baggage and souvenirs, but don't send anything fragile this way.

As in Britain, North America and Australasia, books and magazines can be sent more cheaply, unsealed or wrapped around the middle, as **printed papers** ("book post"). Alternatively, there are numerous courier services, although it is safest to stick to known international companies such as DHL or Fedex, which have offices in all the state capitals. Packages sent by air are expensive. Couriers are not as reliable as they should be, and there have been complaints of packages going astray. Remember that all packages from India are likely to be suspect at home, and searched or X-rayed: don't send anything dodgy.

Internet and email

In all the large cities there are **internet** and **email** facilities accessible to the general public, usually at cybercafés, though many hotels and STD booths offer this service as well. The charges for internet use range from Rs10 to Rs80 per hour for reading mail and browsing, extra for printing (especially if you do not have access to a registered account); most centres offer membership deals which can cut costs. The shops that advertise email alongside unrelated business concerns

are cheaper, but you have to send and receive mail through their own private account, which means your messages are open to public scrutiny.

If you're planning to be away from home for a while, you may want to set up a **free email** account before leaving. This takes five or ten minutes, costs nothing and allows you to receive electronic mail wherever you are in the world. All you have to pay is the cybercafé's charges after you've finished using their machine. Microsoft own the phenomenally popular Hotmail service (Ⓦ www.hotmail.com), but due the volume of traffic through this server, smaller web-based email providers such as Yahoo (Ⓦ www.yahoo.com) tend to be quicker and less prone to interruptions. The fastest free email service in India is Ⓦ www.rediff.com, a generic free email service. To sign up, access the internet and key in one of site addresses listed above. For more advice on using the internet, see *Rough Guide to the Internet*.

Media

With over one billion people and a literacy rate of around fifty percent, India produces a staggering 4700 daily papers in over 300 languages and another 39,000 journals and weeklies. There are a large number of English-language daily newspapers, both national and regional. The most prominent of the nationals are the Hindu, the Statesman, the Times of India, the Independent, the Economic Times and the Indian Express (usually the most critical of the government). All are pretty dry and sober, and concentrate on Indian news, though their flowery prose can be entertaining (see Contexts p.718). Asian Age, published simultaneously in India, London and New York, is a conservative tabloid that sports a motley collection of the world's more colourful stories. All the major Indian newspapers have websites (see p.22), with the Times of India, The Hindu and the Hindustan Times providing the most up-to-date and detailed news services.

India's press is the freest in Asia, and attacks on the government are often quite outspoken. However, as in the West, most papers can be seen as part of the political establishment and are unlikely to print anything that might upset the "national consensus".

In recent years, a number of *Time/Newsweek*-style **news magazines** have hit the market with a strong emphasis on politics. The best of these are *India Today*, published independently, and *Frontline*, published by *The Hindu*. Others include *Outlook*, which presents the most readable broadly themed analysis, *Sunday* and *The Week*. As they give more of an overview of stories and issues than the daily papers, you will probably get a better idea from them of what is going on in Indian politics, and most tend to have a higher proportion of international news too. *Business India* is more financially orientated, and *the India Magazine* more cultural. Film fanzines and gossip mags are very popular (*Screen* and *Filmfare* are the best, though you'd have to be reasonably *au fait* with Indian movies to follow a lot of it), but magazines and periodicals in English cover all sorts of popular and minority interests, so it's worth having a look through what's available. One publication of special interest is *Amar Chitra Katha*'s series of Hindu legends, Indian history and folk tales in comic form for children.

Foreign publications such as the *International Herald Tribune*, *Time*, *Newsweek*, *The Economist* and the international edition of the British *Guardian* are all available in the main cities and in the most upmarket hotels, but they are rather costly. For a read through the British press, try the British Council in Mumbai, Chennai, Bangalore, Hyderabad or Thiruvananthapuram, the USIS being the American equivalent. Expat-orientated bookstalls stock slightly out-of-date and expensive copies of magazines like *Vogue* and *NME* for homesick Westerners.

BBC World Service radio can be picked up on short wave, although reception quality is highly variable. The wavelength also changes at different times of day. In the morning, try 5965Khz (49m/5.95–6.20Mhz) or 9605Khz (31m/9.40–9.90Mhz); in the afternoon, 9740Khz (31m/9.40–9.90Mhz) or 11750 (25m/11.70Mhz). A full list of the World Service's many frequencies appears on the BBC website (🌐 www.bbc.co.uk /worldservice).

The government-run **TV** company, Doordarshan, which broadcasts a sober diet of edifying programmes, has tried to compete with the onslaught of mass access to cable and **satellite TV** but is losing ground fast. The main broadcaster in English is Rupert Murdoch's **Star TV** network, which incorporates the BBC World Service, and Zee TV (with Z News), which presents a progressive blend of Hindi-orientated chat, film, news and music programmes. Star Sports and ESPN churn out a mind-boggling amount of cricket with occasional forays into other sports – ESPN broadcasts Premier and Champions League football, for example. Others include CNN, the Discovery Channel, National Geographic, MTV, the immensely popular Channel V hosted by scantily clad Mumbai models and DJs, and an increasing number of reasonable film channels like Star Movies, HBO and AXN. Most hotels from the top end of the budget range upwards have cable TV these days but it is rather hit and miss how many channels you will get in any particular location.

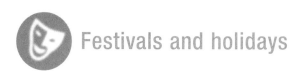

Festivals and holidays

Virtually every temple in every town or village across the country has its own festival. While mostly religious in nature, merrymaking rather than solemnity are generally the order of the day, and onlookers are usually welcome. Indeed, if you are lucky enough to coincide with a local festival, it may well prove to be the highlight of your trip. Music and dance, originally nurtured within the temple environment, are often key features of temple festivals and, in winter, multi-day music festivals known as "conferences", spring up in most major southern cities where you can hear the cream of Carnatic classical music. The biggest and most splendid of festivals, such as Madurai's three annual festivals and

India has only four national public holidays: January 26 (Republic Day); August 15 (Independence Day); October 2 (Gandhi's birthday); and December 25 (Christmas Day). Each state, however, has its own calendar of public holidays; most businesses close on the major holidays of their own religion, marked with an asterisk below.

The Hindu calendar months are given in brackets below as most of the festivals listed are Hindu.

Key: B=Buddhist; C=Christian; H=Hindu; J=Jain; M=Muslim; N=non-religious; P=Parsi; S=Sikh.

Jan–Feb (Magha)

H Pongal (1 Magha): Tamil harvest festival celebrated with decorated cows, processions and *rangolis* (chalk designs on the doorsteps of houses). *Pongal* is a sweet porridge made from newly harvested rice and eaten by all, including the cows. The festival is also known as Makar Sankranti and is celebrated in Karnataka, Andhra Pradesh and the east of India.

H Vasant Panchami (5 Magha): One-day spring festival in honour of Saraswati, the goddess of learning, celebrated with kite-flying, yellow saris and the blessing of schoolchildren's books and pens by the goddess.

C Feast of Mar Thoma: A colourful procession of decorated carts leads to this ancient site where St Thomas first landed.

N Republic Day (Jan 26)*:

N Goa Carnival: Goa's own Mardi Gras features float processions and *feni*-induced mayhem in the state capital, Panjim.

H Floating Festival (16 Magha) at Madurai (Tamil Nadu).

N Elephanta Music and Dance Festival (Mumbai).

H Elephant Festival at Thiruvananthapuram's Shiva temple which boasts a spectacular elephant procession.

Feb–March (Phalguna)

B Losar (1 Phalguna): Tibetan New Year celebrations among Tibetan communities throughout India including Karnataka.

H Shivratri (10 Phalguna): Anniversary of Shiva's *tandav* (creation) dance, and his wedding anniversary. Popular family festival but also a *sadhu* festival of pilgrimage and fasting, especially at important Shiva temples.

H Holi (15 Phalguna)*: Water festival held during Dol Purnima (full moon) to celebrate the beginning of spring, most popular in North India but heartily celebrated in Mumbai and parts of northern Karnataka, where you can expect to be bombarded with water, paint, coloured powder and other mixtures.

C Carnival (Mardi Gras): The last day before Lent, forty days before Easter, is celebrated in Goa, as in the rest of the Catholic world.

H Puram, Guruvayur: Although the temple here is off-limits to non-Hindus, the elephant procession with over forty elephants and the elephant race are well worth the visit.

March–April (Chaitra)

H Ramanavami (9 Chaitra)*: Birthday of Rama, the hero of the *Ramayana*, celebrated with readings of the epic and discourses on Rama's life and teachings.

C Easter (movable feast)*: Celebration of the resurrection of Christ. Good Friday is a particularly celebrated day.

P Pateti: Parsi new year, also known as No Ruz, celebrating the creation of fire. Feasting, services and present-giving.

P Khorvad Sal (a week after Pateti): Birthday of Zarathustra (aka Zoroaster).

H Chittirai, Madurai (Tamil Nadu): Elephant-led procession.

H Arat Festival, Thiruvananthapuram: Held again during Oct/Nov, this festival celebrates the deities of the rajas of Travancore who are led to the sea in a procession of elephants.

April–May (Vaisakha)

HS Baisakhi (1 Vaisakha): To the Hindus, it's the solar new year, celebrated with music and dancing; to the Sikhs, it's the anniversary of the foundation of the *Khalsa* (Sikh brotherhood).

J Mahavir Jayanti (13 Vaisakha)*: Birthday of Mahavira, the founder of Jainism. The main Jain festival of the year.

H Puram Festival, Thrissur (Kerala): frenzied drumming and elephant parades.

B Buddha Jayanti (16 Vaisakha)*: Buddha's birthday. He achieved enlightenment and *nirvana* on the same date.

July–Aug (Shravana)

H **Naag Panchami (3 Shravana)**: Snake festival in honour of the *naga* snake deities. Mainly celebrated in Rajasthan and Maharashtra.

H **Raksha Bandhan/Narial Purnima (16 Shravana)**: Festival to honour the sea god Varuna. Brothers and sisters exchange gifts, the sister tying a thread known as a *rakhi* to her brother's wrist. Brahmins, after a day's fasting, change the sacred thread they wear.

N **Independence Day (15 Aug)***: India's biggest secular celebration, on the anniversary of its Independence from Britain.

Aug–Sept (Bhadraparda)

H **Ganesh Chaturthi (4 Bhadraparda)**: Festival dedicated to Ganesh, especially celebrated in Maharashtra. In Mumbai, huge processions carry images of the god to immerse in the sea.

H **Onam**: Keralan harvest festival, celebrated with snake-boat races. The Nehru Trophy snake-boat race at Alappuzha (held on the second Saturday of August), is the most spectacular, with long boats each crewed by 150 rowers.

H **Janmashtami (23 Bhadraparda)***: Krishna's birthday, an occasion for feasting and celebration, especially in Vaishnava centres like Udupi and in Mumbai.

H **Avani Mula festival, Madurai (Tamil Nadu)**: Celebration of the coronation of Shiva.

Sept–Oct (Ashvina)

H **Dussehra (1–10 Ashvina)***: Ten-day festival (usually two days' public holiday) associated with vanquishing demons, in particular Rama's victory over Ravana in the *Ramayana*, and Durga's over the buffalo-headed Mahishasura. Dussehra celebrations include performances of the *Ram Lila* (life of Rama). Best seen in the South in Mysore (Karnataka).

N **Mahatma Gandhi's Birthday (2 Oct)***: Rather solemn commemoration of Independent India's founding father.

Oct–Nov (Kartika)

H **Diwali (Deepavali) (15 Kartika)***: Festival of lights, especially popular in the North but celebrated everywhere, to mark Rama and Sita's homecoming in the *Ramayana*. Festivities include the lighting of oil lamps and firecrackers and the giving and receiving of sweets.

J **Jain New Year (15 Kartika)**: Coincides with Diwali, so Jains celebrate alongside Hindus.

S **Nanak Jayanti (16 Kartika)***: Guru Nanak's birthday marked by prayer readings and processions around Sikh *grudwaras*.

Nov–Dec (Margashirsha, or Agrahayana)

N **Hampi Festival (Karnataka)**: Government-sponsored music and dance festival.

Dec–Jan (Pausa)

CN **Christmas (Dec 25)***: The Christian festival the whole world celebrates, popular in Christian areas of Goa and Kerala, and in big cities.

N **Carnatak Music Festivals, Chennai**: For around a month every year, the city hosts around thirteen large music programmes called conferences, each lasting several days.

N **Mamallapuram Dance festival**: Colourful dance and music festival runs for several days on a stage in front of the famous bas relief.

N **Kerala Kalamandalam Festival, Cheruthuruthy**: The annual festival of music and dance is a showcase for this leading arts institution, featuring the best of Kerala and attracting musicians and dancers from all over the country.

Movable

H **Kumbh Mela**: Major three-yearly festival held at one of four holy cities: Nasik, Ujjain, Haridwar or Prayag. The Maha Kumbh Mela or "Great" Kumbh Mela, the largest religious fair in India, is held every twelve years in Allahabad; the next festival is due to take place in 2013.

M **Ramadan (first day: Nov 28, 2001; Nov 17, 2002)**: The start of a month during which Muslims may not eat, drink or smoke from sunrise to sunset, and should abstain from sex. Towards the end of the month it takes its toll, so be gentle with Muslims you meet at this time.

M **Id-ul-Fitr (Dec 28, 2001; Dec 17, 2002)***: Feast to celebrate the end of Ramadan, after the lunar month is complete.

M **Id ul-Zuha**: Pilgrimage festival to commemorate Abraham's preparedness to sacrifice his son Ismail. Celebrated with slaughtering and consumption of sheep.

M **Muharram**: Festival to commemorate the martyrdom of the (Shi'ite) Imam, the Prophet's grandson and popular saint, Hussain.

Mysore's celebrated Dussehra festival around September or October, are major attractions. In Karnataka and Tamil Nadu, the focus of a temple festival is usually a *rath* (chariot) in which the deities are borne aloft in procession through the streets. However, in Kerala, instead of a *rath*, the deity is carried on a pageant of elephants. A few festivals feature elephant races while others, especially along the coast of Kerala, host spectacular boat races and regattas. These are only a few of the festivals which occur, and as we cannot list every festival in every village across South India here, look at the box features in individual chapters for local festivals.

There is a list of the main national and regional celebrations on p.64–65. It requires a little explanation. Hindu, Sikh, Buddhist and Jain festivals follow the Indian **lunar calendar** and their dates therefore vary from year to year against the plain old Gregorian calendar. Determining them more than a year in advance is a highly complicated business best left to astrologers. Each lunar cycle is divided into two *paksa* (halves): "bright" (waxing) and "dark" (waning), each consisting of fifteen *tithis* ("days" – but a *tithi* might begin at any time of the solar day). The *paksa* start respectively with the new moon (*ama* or *bahula* – the first day of the

month) and the full moon (*purnima*). Lunar festivals, then, are observed on a given day in the "light" or "dark" side of the month. The lunar calendar adds a leap month every two or three years to keep it in line with the seasons. Muslim festivals follow the **Islamic calendar**, whose year is shorter and which thus loses about eleven days per annum against the Gregorian. Christianity – following the Gregorian calendar – is especially strong in Goa and Kerala where the feasts of saints are celebrated and carols are sung in churches packed to the brim during Christmas.

Sports and outdoor pursuits

India is not perhaps a place that most people associate with sports – they won only one bronze medal at the Sydney Olympics in 2000, oddly enough in women's wrestling. However, cricket, hockey and football (soccer, that is) all have their place.

Cricket is by far the most popular of these, and a fine example of how something quintessentially British (well, English) has become something quintessentially Indian. Travellers to India will find it hard to get away from cricket – it is everywhere and enjoys extensive coverage on television. Cricketing heroes such as the maestro batsman Sachin Tendulkar are held in the highest esteem and live under the constant scrutiny of the media and public. The reputations of some top players, such as ex-captain Muhammed Azharrudin, have taken a bashing through

well-reported match-fixing scandals but the popularity of the game remains undiminished. Expectations are high and disappointments acute; India versus Pakistan matches are especially emotive. In 1999, the right-wing Hindu group Shiv Sena threatened to disrupt Pakistan's tour of India and even dug up the pitch in Delhi, but to no avail. Despite the occasional riot, the tour was a resounding success and one of the most exciting and eagerly fought cricketing contests ever held between the two sides. Test matches are rare but inter-state cricket is easy to catch – the most prestigious competition is the Ranji Trophy. Besides spectator cricket, you'll see games being played on open spaces all around the country. Occasionally, you may even come across a match blocking a road, and will have to be patient as the players grudgingly let your vehicle continue.

Horseracing can be a good day out, especially if you enjoy a flutter. There are several racecourses around the south, mostly in larger cities such as Mumbai, Hyderabad, Mysore and Bangalore; look in local newspapers, such as *Bangalore Today*, and any local listings magazine to find out when race meetings are being held. Other (mainly) spectator sports include **polo**, originally from upper Kashmir, but taken up by the British to become one of the symbols of the Raj. Princes of Rajasthan were considered in the Thirties, Forties and Fifties to be the best polo players in the world but since the Sixties, when the Privy Purses were cut, they have been unable to maintain their stables, and the tradition of polo has declined. Today, it is mainly the army which plays polo so you may catch a game near a major southern cantonment.

After years in the doldrums, Indian **hockey**, which used regularly to furnish India with Olympic medals, is making a strong comeback. The haul of medals dried up in the Sixties when international hockey introduced astro-turf which was, and still is, a rare surface in India. However, hockey is still very popular, especially in schools and colleges and, interestingly, amongst the tribal girls of Orissa who supply the Indian national team with a regular influx of players. Indian **athletics** are improving all the time and, today, India boasts world-class women sprinters who bagged several medals at the 1998 Asian Games.

Volleyball is very popular throughout India. Standards aren't particularly high, and joining a game should be quite easy. **Football** (soccer) is similarly liked, with a keenly contested national championship. The best teams are based in Calcutta but Goa and Kerala are two of the areas with most interest in the world's favourite sport after that.

Tennis in India has always been a sport for the middle-classes and is increasing in popularity as that class expands. The country boasts a player or two of world-class standing, such as the duo of Bhupati and Paes who briefly achieved a world number-one ranking in the mens' doubles in 1999. Motorsport, especially car-racing, is popular in the south and there is a popular race track on the outskirts of Chennai. **Golf** is extremely popular and relatively inexpensive in India, again amongst the middle classes.

Amongst the contact sports unique to India **kushti**, a form of Indian wrestling, has a small but dedicated following and is a favourite of devotees of the monkey god, Hanuman. However, the most dramatic and ferocious of all is the popular Keralan martial art of **kalarippayat** (see p.332) which utilizes both hand-to-hand combat and the use of weapons. **Kabadi**, where two teams of seven try to "tag" each other in an enclosed court, to continuous cries of "kabadik-abadikabadi" is another traditional Indian pastime. Although still an amateur sport, kabadi is taken very seriously with state and national championships, and now features in the Asian Games but it is not as popular in South India as it is further north.

As far as outdoor pursuits that foreigners might want to engage in are concerned, the two available in South India are trekking and scuba diving/snorkelling. Although there are far more **trekking** possibilities in the mountainous north, low level treks are available in the Western Ghats and Nilgiri Hills, which most people should have no trouble with. It is not necessary to have any specialized gear for such low altitudes but it is a good idea to have the following equipment: clothes to wear in layers, sturdy shoes or boots, a waterproof jacket, backpack, compass and map, pocket knife, sleeping bag, sunblock, toiletries and toilet paper, torch, water bottle, basic medical kit and some emergency provisions. It is usually best to take a guide if you are planning to get off the beaten track. Suggestions on specific routes are given in the relative chapters.

Scuba diving and snorkelling, on the other hand, are pastimes which you really have to be in South India to enjoy. Served by well-equipped and reputable diving centres, the Andaman islands, and Lakshadweep offer world-class diving on a par with just about anything in Asia. Don't come here expecting rock-bottom prices though. Compared with Thailand, India's dive schools are pricey, typically charging around Rs15,000 ($350) for a four-day PADI-approved open-water course.

For independent travellers, the most

promising destination for both scuba diving and snorkelling is the **Andaman islands** in the Bay of Bengal, around 1000km east of the mainland. Part of a chain of submerged mountains that stretch north from Sumatra to the coast of Burma (Myanmar), this isolated archipelago is ringed by gigantic coral reefs whose crystal-clear waters are teeming with tropical fish and other marine life. Given the prohibitively high cost of diving courses, most visitors stick to snorkelling, but if you already have your PADI permit, it's well worth renting equipment from one of the three dive schools in the islands (see p.610). If you want to do an open-water course, book ahead as places can be in short supply during the peak season, between December and February.

The other group of Indian islands surrounded by clear seas and abundant marine life is **Lakshadweep**, a classic coconut-palm-covered atoll, some 400km west of Kerala in the Arabian Sea. The shallow lagoons, extensive coral reefs and excep-

tionally good visibility make this a perfect option for both first-timers and more experienced divers. The catch is that permit restrictions mean foreigners are only allowed to visit one island, Bangaram, where accommodation is confined to a single, phenomenally expensive five-star resort. There's no way around this problem as you have to have pre-booked a room in the hotel in order to procure the necessary permit.

For anyone on a limited budget, a better option is **Goa**. Visibility is not so great along this stretch of coast, but you can escape the worst of the silt by heading further out to sea by boat, where a handful of islands and two wrecks shelter prolific fishlife. Most of the dive sites are shallow (between 10 and 20m), and thus ideal for beginners.

As with other countries, qualified divers should take their current certification card and/or log book; if you haven't used it for one year or more, you may have to take a short test costing around Rs300 ($7).

Yoga, meditation and ashrams

Of all India's exports, the ancient techniques of yoga and meditation, refined over more than two thousand years of tradition and still widely practised as part of everyday religious life in the subcontinent, have arguably been the most influential. The source of many Western stereotypes about the "mystic east", they have also ensured a steady supply of spiritual questers over the centuries – particularly since Allen Ginsberg's drug-fuelled visions in Varanasi and the Beatles' much-publicized sojourn with Maharishi Yogi in Rishikesh.

The West's long-standing obsession with Indian gurus and godmen doubtless says more about the shortcomings of occidental culture than the essence of the subcontinent, but modern India remains – despite the rampant materialism that has taken hold in the late twentieth century – a land of

countless living saints, wandering *sadhus* and yogis with mysterious powers. This is particularly true of the South, which, even more than the famous religious sites of the Ganges plains, has always attracted foreigners seeking spiritual nourishment. While you may not be tempted to don saffron and disappear into the forest for a decade, a short spell in an ashram learning yoga and meditation can, if nothing else, be an ideal antidote to the chaos and pollution of the southern cities, or the overt hedonism of beach life.

Yoga is taught virtually everywhere in the South, and in addition, there are several internationally known yoga centres where you can train to become a teacher. **Meditation** is similarly practised all over the region and specific courses are available in temples, meditation centres and monasteries. South India also has innumerable **ashrams** — communities where people work, live and study together, drawn by a common (usually spiritual) goal. The most established of these is the Shri Aurobindo Ashram in Pondicherry, but there are dozens of others dotted around the southern states, from the headquarters of India's most famous living holy man, Sai Baba, in Andhra Pradesh, to the home of the celebrated "Hugging Guru", Amritananda Mayi, in the backwaters of Kerala.

Details of yoga and meditation courses and ashrams are provided throughout the Guide section of the book. Most centres offer courses that you can enrol on at short notice; however, many of the more popular ones listed below need to be booked well in advance.

Yoga

The word "yoga" literally means "to unite" and the aim of the discipline is to help the practitioner unite his or her individual consciousness with the Divine. This is achieved by raising awareness of one's self through spiritual, mental and physical discipline. *Hatha* yoga is based on physical postures called **asanas**, and although the most popular form in the West, it is traditionally just the first step leading on to more subtle stages of meditation which commence when the energies of the body have been awakened and sensitized by stretching and relaxing. Other forms of yoga include *raja* yoga, which includes moral discipline; and *bhakti* yoga, the yoga of devotion, which entails a commitment to one's guru or teacher. Traditional centres for yoga in the South include Mysore, in Karnataka (see p.70) and Tiruvanammalai in Tamil Nadu (see p.70), but numerous institutions throughout the region

have good teachers and advanced practitioners. In many of the travellers' haunts, such as Goa and Kovalam, posters in cafés advertise local teachers.

Meditation

Meditation is often practised after a session of yoga, when the energy of the body has been awakened, and is an essential part of Hindu and Buddhist practices. It is considered the most powerful tool for understanding the true nature of mind and self, an essential step on the path to enlightenment. **Vipassana** meditation is a technique originally taught by the Buddha, whereby practitioners learn to become more aware of physical sensations and mental processes. Courses last for a minimum of ten days and are austere, involving 4am kick-offs, around ten hours of meditation a day, no solid food after noon, segregation of the sexes and no talking for the duration (except with the leaders of the course). Courses are free for all first-time students to allow everyone an opportunity to learn and benefit from the technique. Vipassana is taught in more than 25 centres throughout India including ones in Bangalore, Chennai and Hyderabad.

Courses and ashrams

Ashrams range in size from several thousand people to just a handful, and their rules, regulations and restrictions vary enormously. While some offer on-site accommodation, charge Western prices and have set programmes, others will require you to stay in the nearest town or village, operate through donations and only offer guidance and teaching as and when requested. The following well-known establishments routinely welcome foreign visitors:

Astanga Yoga Nilayam, 876 1st Cross, Lakshmipuram, Mysore, Karnataka 570004. Run by Pattabhi Jois, courses last at least a month and need to be booked in advance. The great yoga master Sri Tirumalai Krisnamacharya taught here until his death in 1989. Dynamic yoga affiliated with martial arts.

Mata Amritananda Mayi Math, between Kollam and Alappuzha, Kerala (see p.354). Dubbed the "Hugging Guru" because she ritually embraces all who come to see her, Amritananda Mayi is a self-proclaimed reincarnation of Lord Krishna, and the focal point of a rapidly growing cult with a huge following in the US. Her ashram, in the depths of the

Keralan backwaters, has a large contingent of Westerners, and a sizeable transient population who come here by boat en route between Kollam and Alappuzha for the daily *darshan* (literally "viewing") sessions, when the guru goes into hugging mode.

Prasanthi Nilayam, Puttaparthy, Andhra Pradesh ⊕ 08555/87583 (see p.599). The ashram of Sai Baba, one of India's most revered and popular gurus, with a worldwide following of millions. Puttaparthy is four to five hours by bus from Bangalore. Visitors sometimes comment on the strict security staffing and rigid rules and regulations. Cheap accommodation is available at the ashram in dormitories or "flats" for four people. You cannot book in advance though, phone to check availability; see p.600 for more details. Sai Baba also has a smaller ashram in Bangalore and one in Kodaikanal.

Saccidananda Ashram, Thanneepalli, Kullithalai near Tiruchirapelli, Tamil Nadu ⊕ 04323/3060 (see p.518). Also known as Shanivanam (meaning "Peace Forest" in Sanskrit), this unusual ashram is situated on the banks of the sacred Cauvery River in the heart of Tamil Nadu. It was founded by Father Bede Griffiths, a visionary Benedictine monk, to develop a sympathetic fusion of Christianity and Hinduism. Visitors can join in the services and rituals or just relax here. Accommodation is in simple huts dotted around the grounds and meals are communal. Very busy during the major Christian festivals.

Sankaramandam Math, Kanchipuram, Tamil Nadu (see p.520). The sacred city of Kanchipuram is the seat of a line of holy men, or Archaryas, dating back more than two thousand years. Their monastery, or *math*, houses the *samadhi* of the highly revered Sri Chandrasekharendra Sarasvati Swami, the 68th Archarya, who died in January 1994 at the age of a 101. His successor gives *darshan* to the public during the morning. All are welcome.

Shri Aurobindo Ashram, Pondicherry, Tamil Nadu (see p.491). The anti-imperial revolutionary, Aurobindo Ghose, fled the British and his native Bengal in 1910 to settle in the French colony of Pondicherry, where he ditched politics to propagate his tortuous amalgamation of Hinduism and occultism. In this, he was aided by his half-Egyptian, half-Turkish chief organizer, Mirra Alfassa, known to her devotees as "The Mother". Their massive marble sarcophagi form the focal point of the ashram today, patronized by a predominantly Bengali following. Accommodation available in Western-style guest houses; see also Auroville p.492.

Shri Ramana Maharishi Ashram, Tiruvannamalai, Tamil Nadu (see p.486). Ramana Rishi, one of twentieth-century India's most famous saints, spent the best part of two decades meditating in a cave on the lower slopes of Arunachala, a sacred "red" mountain overlooking a vast Chola temple complex. Later, he founded an ashram nearby, where his *samadhi* now attracts devotees from all over the world. In addition, around half a dozen other ashrams have sprung up in the town, offering a range of courses.

Sivananda Yoga Vedanta Dhanwanthari Ashram, PO Neyyar Dam, Thiruvanthapuram Dist, Kerala, 695 576 ⊕ 0471/290493, ⓔ YogaIndia@sivananda.org (see p.349). This yoga-based ashram, deep in the Keralan hills, was set up by a swami known as "The Flying Guru" (because he used to throw flowers and peace leaflets into war zones from a small airplane). In addition to excellent introductory courses in yoga and meditation for beginners, it offers more advanced training for teachers. The regime is also very strict.

Vipassana. The Vipassana movement has three regional centres in South India: Dhamma Khetta, Nagarjun Sagar Rd, Kusum Nagar Vanasthali Puram, Hyderabad 500 070, Andhra Pradesh ⊕ 040/402 0290, ⓔ bprabhat@hd1.vsnl.net.in; Dhamma Setu, c/o Sri Roopchand Agarwal, Gotewalla R.G. Brothers, 148 Mint St, Chennai 600 079, Tamil Nadu ⊕ 044/587399; Bangalore Vipassana Centre, Dhamma Sumana, c/o Mrs Jaya Sangoi, 13/1 Vijaya II Main, 5th Block; Kumara Park (W), Bangalore, Karnataka 560 020 ⊕ 080/336 0896, ⓕ 221 5776, ⓔ maitri@cyberspaceindia.com.

Crime and personal safety

In spite of the crushing poverty and the yawning gulf between rich and poor, India is on the whole a very safe country in which to travel. As a tourist, however, you are an obvious target for the tiny number of thieves (who may include some of your fellow travellers), and stand to face serious problems if you do lose your passport, money and ticket home. Common sense, therefore, suggests a few precautions.

If you can tolerate the encumbrance, carry valuables in a money belt or in a pouch around your neck at all times. In the latter case, the cord should be hidden under your clothing and not be easy to cut through (a metal guitar string is good). Beware of **crowded locations**, such as packed buses or trains, in which it is easy for pickpockets to operate – slashing pockets or bags with razor blades is not unheard of in certain locations – and don't leave valuables unattended on the beach when you go for a swim. Backpacks in dormitory accommodation are also obvious targets.

Budget travellers would do well to carry a **padlock**, as these are usually used to secure the doors of cheap hotel rooms and it's reassuring to know you have the only key; strong combination locks are ideal. You can also lock your bag to seats or racks in trains, for which a length of chain also comes in useful. Don't put valuables in your luggage for bus or plane journeys: keep them with you at all times. If your baggage is on the roof of a bus, make sure it is well secured. On trains and buses, the prime time for theft is just before you leave, so keep a particular eye on your gear then, beware of deliberate diversions and don't put your belongings next to open windows. Remember that routes popular with tourists tend to be popular with thieves too.

However, don't get paranoid. Crime levels in India are a long way below those of Western countries, and violent crime against tourists is extremely rare. Virtually none of the people who approach you on the street intend any harm: most want to sell you something (though this is not always made apparent immediately), some want to practise their English, others (if you're a woman) to chat you up, while more than a few just want your address in their book or a snap taken with you. Anyone offering wonderful-sounding money-making schemes, however, is almost certain to be a con artist.

Be wary of **credit card fraud**; a credit card can be used to make duplicate forms to which your account is then billed for fictitious transactions, so don't let shops or restaurants take your card away to process – insist they do it in front of you. Even **monkeys** rate a mention here: it is not unknown for them to steal things from hotel rooms with open windows or even to snatch bags from unsuspecting shoulders. It's not a bad idea to keep US$100 or so separately from the rest of your money, along with your travellers' cheque receipts, insurance policy number and phone number for claims and a photocopy of the pages in your passport containing personal data and your Indian visa. This will cover you in case you do lose all your valuables.

If the worst happens and you get robbed, the first thing to do is report the theft as soon as possible to the local **police**. They are very unlikely to recover your belongings, but you need a report from them in order to claim on your travel insurance. Dress smartly and expect an uphill battle; city cops in particular tend to be jaded from too many insurance and travellers' cheque scams.

Losing your passport is a real hassle, but does not necessarily mean the end of your trip. First, report the loss immediately to the police, who will issue you with the all-important "complaint form" you need to travel around and check into hotels, as well as claim back any expenses incurred in replacing your passport from your insurer. A complaint form, however, will not allow you to change money or travellers' cheques. If you've run out of cash, your best bet is to

Ⓑ

BASICS | Crime and personal safety

Future is black if sugar is brown
– *Indian anti-drugs poster.*

India is a centre for the production of cannabis and to a lesser extent opium, and derivatives of these drugs are widely available. The use of cannabis is frowned upon by respectable Indians – if you see anyone in a movie smoking a *chillum*, you can be sure it's the baddie. *Sadhus*, on the other hand, are allowed to smoke *ganja* (marijuana) legally as part of their religious devotion to Shiva, who is said to have originally discovered its narcotic properties. If you indulge as a foreigner, it is best to be discreet, even if you see others behaving more openly.

Bhang (a preparation made from marijuana leaves, which, it is claimed, sometimes contains added hallucinogenic ingredients such as datura) is legal and widely available in bhang shops: it is used to make sweets and drinks such as the notoriously potent *bhang lassis* which have waylaid many an unwary traveller. Use of other illegal drugs such as LSD, ecstasy and cocaine is largely confined to tourists in party locations such as Goa.

All of these drugs except *bhang* are strictly controlled under Indian law, with a minimum sentence of ten years for possession. Anyone arrested with less than three grams of cannabis, which they are able to prove is for their own use, is liable to a six-month maximum, but cases can take years to come to trial (two is normal and eight not unheard of). Police raids and searches are particularly common in the beach areas of Goa, and around Idukki and Kumily in Kerala. "Paying a fine now" may be possible with one or two officers upon arrest – though it will probably mean all the money you have – but once you are booked in at the station, your chances are slim. A minority of the population languishing in Indian jails are foreigners on drugs charges.

ask your hotel manager to help you out (staff will have seen your passport when you checked in, and the number will be in the register). The next thing to do is telephone your nearest embassy or consulate in India (see p.136). Normally, passports have to be applied for and collected in person, but if you are stranded, it is usually possible to arrange to receive the necessary forms in the post. However, you still have to go to the embassy or consulate to pick it up. "Emergency passports" are the cheapest form of replacement, but are normally only valid for the few days of your return flight. If you're not sure when you're leaving India, you'll have to obtain a more costly "full passport"; these can only be issued by embassies and larger consulates in Mumbai, and not those in Chennai or Panjim.

Cultural hints and etiquette

Cultural differences extend to all sorts of little things. While allowances will usually be made for foreigners, visitors unacquainted with Indian customs may need a little preparation to avoid causing offence or making fools of themselves. The list of dos and don'ts here is hardly exhaustive: when in doubt, watch what the Indian people around you are doing.

Eating and the right-hand rule

The biggest minefield of potential faux pas has to do with **eating**. This is usually done with the fingers, and requires practice to get absolutely right. Rule one is: **eat with your right hand only**. In India, as right across Asia, the left hand is for wiping your bottom, cleaning your feet and other unsavoury functions (you also put on and take off your shoes with your left hand), while the right hand is for eating, shaking hands, and so on.

Quite how rigid individuals are about this tends to vary, with brahmins (who at the top of the hierarchical ladder are one of only two "right-handed castes") and southerners likely to be the strictest. While you can hold a cup or utensil in your left hand, and you can usually get away with using it to help tear your *chapati*, you should not eat, pass food or wipe your mouth with your left hand. Best is to keep it out of sight below the table.

This rule extends beyond food. In general, do not pass anything to anyone with your left hand or point at anyone with it either, and Indians definitely won't be impressed if you put it in your mouth. In general, you should accept things given to you with your right hand – though using both hands is a sign of respect.

The other rule to beware of when eating or drinking is that your lips should not touch other people's food – *jhuta* or sullied food is strictly taboo. Don't, for example, take a bite out of a *chapati* and pass it on. When drinking out of a cup or bottle to be shared with others, don't let it touch your lips, but rather pour it directly into your mouth. This custom also protects you from things like hepatitis. It is customary to wash your hands before and after eating.

Temples and religion

Religion is taken very seriously in South India; it's important always to show due respect to religious buildings, shrines, images and people at prayer. When entering a temple or mosque, remove your shoes and leave them at the door (socks are acceptable and protect your feet from burning-hot, stony ground). Some temples – Jain ones in particular – do not allow you to enter wearing or carrying leather articles and forbid entry to menstruating women. Dress conservatively (see below), and try not to be obtrusive; cover your head with a cap or cloth when entering a *dargah* (Sufi shrine) or Sikh *gurudwara*. At a mosque, you'll not normally be allowed in at prayer time and women are sometimes not let in at all. In a Hindu temple, you are often not allowed into the inner sanctum. At a Buddhist stupa or monument, you should always walk round clockwise (with the stupa on your right). Hindus are very superstitious about taking **photographs** of images of deities and inside temples; if in doubt, resist. Do not take photos of funerals or cremations.

Dress

Indian people are very conservative about **dress**. Women are expected to dress modestly, with legs and shoulders covered. Trousers are acceptable, but shorts and short skirts are offensive to many. Men should not walk around bare-chested and should avoid wearing shorts (a sign of low caste), except around the obvious beach resorts. These rules go double in temples and mosques.

Never mind sky-clad Jains or *naga sadhus*, **nudity** is not acceptable in India. The mild-mannered people of Goa may not say anything about nude bathing (though it is in theory prohibited), but you can be sure they don't like it.

In general, Indians find it hard to understand why rich Western sahibs should wander round in ragged clothes or imitate the lowest ranks of Indian society, who would love to have something more decent to wear. Staying well groomed and dressing "respectably" vastly improves the impression you make on local people, and reduces sexual harassment too.

Other possible gaffes

Kissing and **embracing** are regarded in India as part of sex: do not do them in public. It is not even a good idea for couples to hold hands, though Indian men can sometimes be seen holding hands as a sign of "brotherliness". Be aware of your feet. When entering a private home, you should normally remove your shoes (follow your host's example); when sitting, avoid pointing the soles of your feet at anyone. Accidental contact with someone's foot is always followed by an apology.

Indian English can be very formal and even ceremonious. Indian people may well call you "sir" or "madam", even "good lady" or "kind sir". At the same time, you should be aware that your English may seem rude to them. In particular, **swearing** is taken rather seriously in India, and casual use of the F-word is likely to shock.

Meeting people

Westerners have an ambiguous status in Indian eyes. In one way, you represent the rich sahib, whose culture dominates the world, so the old colonial mentality has not completely disappeared: in that sense, some Indians may see you as "better" than them. On the other hand, as a non-Hindu, you are an outcaste, your presence in theory polluting to an orthodox or high-caste Hindu, while to members of all religions, your morals and your standards of spiritual and physical cleanliness are suspect: in that sense Indians may see themselves as "better" than you. Even if you are of Indian origin, you may be considered to suffer from Western

corruption, and people may test you out on that score.

As a traveller, you will constantly come across people who want to strike up a conversation. English not being their first language, they may not be familiar with the conventional ways of doing this, and thus their opening line may seem abrupt if at the same time very formal. "Excuse me gentleman, what is your mother country?" is a typical one. It is also the first in a series of questions that Indian men seem sometimes to have learnt from a single book in order to ask Western tourists. Some of the questions may baffle at first – "What is your qualification?" "Are you in service?" – some may be queries about the ways of the West or the purpose of your trip, but mostly they will be about your family and your job.

You may find it bewildering or even intrusive that complete strangers should want to know that sort of thing, but these subjects are considered polite conversation between strangers in India and help people place one another in terms of social position. Your family, job, even income, are not considered "personal" subjects in India, and it is completely normal to ask people about them. Asking the same questions back will not be taken amiss – far from it. Being curious does not have the "nosy" stigma in India that it has in the West.

Things that Indian people are likely to find strange about you are: lack of religion (you could adopt one), travelling alone, leaving your family to come to India, being an unmarried couple (letting people think you are married can make life easier) and travelling second class or staying in cheap hotels when, as a tourist, you are relatively rich. You will probably end up having to explain the same things many times to many different people; on the other hand, you can ask questions too, so you could take it as an opportunity to ask things you want to know about India. English-speaking Indians, and members of the large and growing middle class in particular, are usually extremely well informed and well educated and often far more *au fait* with world affairs than Westerners, so you may even be drawn into conversations that are way out of your depth.

Shopping

So many beautiful and exotic souvenirs are on sale in South India, at such low prices, that it's sometimes hard to know what to buy first. On top of that, all sorts of things (such as made-to-measure clothes) that would be vastly expensive at home are much more reasonably priced. Even if you lose weight during your trip, your baggage might well put on quite a bit – unless of course you post some of it home.

Where to shop

Quite a few items sold in tourist areas are made elsewhere and, needless to say, it's more fun (and cheaper) to pick them up at source. Best local buys are noted in the relevant sections of the guide, along with a few specialities that can't be found outside their regions. South India is awash with street and beach **hawkers**, often very young kids. Although they can be annoying and should be dealt with firmly if you are not interested, do not write them off completely as they sometimes have decent souvenirs at lower than shop prices and are open to hard bargaining.

Virtually all the state governments in India run handicraft "**emporia**". There is also an exceptionally well-stocked Central Cottage Industries Emporium in Mumbai. Goods in these places are generally of a high quality, even if their fixed prices are a little expensive, and they are worth a visit to get an idea of what crafts are available and how much they should cost.

Other famous places to shop in South India include the weekly flea market in **Anjuna**, Goa, where goods from all over the country are sold alongside the latest fluoro rave gear and techno tapes, and **Kovalam**, in southern Kerala, where vendors import handicrafts from northern states such as Rajasthan and Gujarat. For sheer variety, however, **Mumbai** is hard to beat. With its tourist-orientated streetside boutiques, swish CD and fashion shops, antique markets and huge *khadi* store, this is the perfect place to stock up on souvenirs before you leave.

Bargaining

Whatever you buy (except food, household items and cigarettes), you will almost always be expected to **haggle** over the price. Bargaining is very much a matter of personal style, but should always be light-hearted, never acrimonious. There are no hard and fast rules – it's really a question of how much something is worth to you. It's a good plan, however, to have an idea of how much you want, or ought, to pay. "Green" tourists are easily spotted, so try and look as if you know what you are up to, even on your first day, or leave it till later.

Don't worry too much about initial prices. Some guidebooks suggest paying a third of the opening price, but it's a flexible guideline depending on the shop, the goods and the shopkeeper's impression of you. You may not be able to get the seller much below the first quote; on the other hand, you may end up paying as little as a tenth of it. If you bid too low, you may be hustled out of the shop for offering an "insulting" price, but this is all part of the game, and you'll no doubt be welcomed as an old friend if you return next day.

Don't start haggling for something if you know you don't want it, and never let any figure pass your lips that you are not prepared to pay. It's like bidding at an auction. Having mentioned a price, you are obliged to pay it. If the seller asks you how much you would pay for something, and you don't want it, say so.

Metalware and jewellery

South Indian artisans have been casting **bronze statues** of Hindu deities for over two thousand years – notably in the Kaveri (Cauvery) Delta of Tamil Nadu, where the Chola dynasty took the form to heights never since surpassed. Traditionally, bronzes were commissioned by wealthy temples, but today the casters are kept busy by demand from rich NRIs (Non-Resident Indians) and tourists who can afford to pay the huge sums for these striking metal icons. The images are produced by the "lost-wax" process, used since medieval times, in which a model is first carved out of beeswax, then surrounded in clay, and finally fired. The wax melts to leave a terracotta mould. Top quality images will have finely detailed fingers and eyes, and the metal should not have pits or spots. Still the best place to watch bronze casters in action is the village of **Swamimalai**, near Kumbakonam in Tamil Nadu (see p.505), where showrooms display awesome dancing Shivas and other Chola-style bronzes. Some Chola bronzes are priceless, such as those in the temples of Tamil Nadu, but affordable miniatures are available direct from the artisans. For more on Chola bronzes, see p.680.

Brass and copperware can be exquisitely worked, with trays, plates, ashtrays, cups and bowls among the products available. **Bidri** work (see box on page p.314), named after Bidar (Karnataka), where it originated, is a method of inlaying a gunmetal alloy with fine designs in brass or silver, then blackening the gunmetal with sal ammoniac, to leave the inlay work shining. *Bidri* jewellery boxes, dishes, bracelets and hookah pipes, among other things, are widely sold, particularly in Karnataka and Andhra Pradesh. **Stainless steel** is less decorative and more workaday: *thali* sets, tiffin and spice tins are among the possible buys, available throughout the region.

Among precious metals, silver is generally a better buy than **gold**. The latter is usually 22 carat and very yellow, but relatively expensive due to taxes (smuggling from the Gulf to evade taxes is rife), added to this is its investment value – women traditionally keep their wealth in this form, and a bride's jewellery is an important part of her dowry. **Silver** varies in quality, but is usually reasonably priced, with silver jewellery generally heavier and rather more folksy than gold. Gold and silver are usually sold by weight, the workmanship costing very little. While silversmiths are ubiquitous in South India, goldsmiths are thinner on the ground, with the largest single concentration around the Kaplishvara temple in the Mylapore district of Chennai (see p.444) and in Kozikhode in northern Kerala. This is also a prime place to sight the gaudy but distinctively Tamil **dance jewellery** worn by Bharatiya Natyam performers. Made from gold-coated silver, studded with artificial rubies, the most striking items are the headpiece, or *thalasaman*, the *adigay*, a long chain worn around the neck with a large floral or peacock-shaped pendant known as a *padakkam*, and the heavy ornamental belt, or *odyanan*.

Gemstones can be something of a mine-field; scams abound, and you would be most unwise even to consider buying gems for resale or as an investment without a basic knowledge of the trade. That said, some precious and semi-precious stones can be a good buy in India, particularly those which are indigenous, such as garnets, black stars and moonstones.

Woodwork and stone carving

Ornate carvings of gods and goddesses are a speciality of Mysore, where members of the *gudigar* caste work with fragrant **sandal-wood**, their preferred medium for a thousand years or more. At one time, deities could *only* be figured from this rare wood, but dwindling forests have forced the price up, and these days fake sandalwood – cheaper soft wood that's been rubbed with essential oil – is almost as common as the real thing. In Kerala, deep red **rosewood**, inlaid with lighter coloured woods to create geometric patterns, is used for carving elephants and heavy furniture, samples of which are to be found at most state-run emporia. For more authentic Kathakali masks and old wooden jewellery **boxes**, however, the bric-a-brac and antiques market in the former Jewish quarter of Kochi (Fort Cochin) is the best place to look. Embossed with brass, these traditionally contained a woman's dowry goods. Metal trunks have largely superseded them, but Keralan cabinet-makers still turn out reproductions for the tourist market.

The fishing village of **Mamallapuram** (see p.464), just south of Chennai, is renowned as India's **stone-carving** capital. Countless workshops line its sandy lanes, and the sound of chisels chipping granite is a constant refrain from dawn until well into the night. Pieces range from larger-than-life-size icons for temples to pocket-size gods sold to the many tourists who pour through every day. Whatever their size, though, the figures are always precisely carved according to measurements meticulously set out in ancient canonical texts, which explains why little innovation has taken place over the centuries. The only recent developments in Mamallapuram's stone carving has been in the design of *chillums*, and small pendants, bought wholesale for the summer festival hippy market back in Europe.

Textiles and clothing

Textiles are so much a part of Indian culture that Gandhi wanted a spinning wheel put on the flag. The kind of cloth he had in mind was the plain white homespun material worn by Nehru, whose hat, jacket and *dhoti* remain a mark of support for the Congress Party to this day. Homespun, handloom-woven, hand-printed cloth is called **khadi**, and is sold in government shops called Khadi Gramodyog all over India. Methods of dying and printing this and other cloth vary from the tie-dying (*bhandani*) of Rajasthan to block printing and screen printing of calico (from Calicut – now Kozhikode, Kerala) cotton and silk.

Saris are normally made of cotton for everyday use, although **silk** is used for special occasions (worn more frequently throughout the South). Western women are notoriously inept at wearing this most elegant of garments – it takes years of practice to carry one off properly – but silk is usually a good buy in India, provided you make sure it is the real thing (the old test was to see whether it was possible to pull the whole garment straight through a wedding ring; however, some synthetics apparently go through too, so burn a thread and sniff it to be sure). The best silk in India comes from **Kanchipuram** (see p.475), in northern Tamil Nadu, whose hallmarks are contrasting borders (known as Ganga–Jamuna borders after India's two most sacred rivers) and ornate designs featuring *gopurams* (temple gate towers). Kanchi's weavers are also famous for **brocade** – top-quality silk hand-woven with expensive gold or silver thread.

In Andhra Pradesh, cloth is more likely to be patterned using the **ikat** technique, where yarn is resist- or tie-dyed before being woven. The geometric images of flowers, animals and birds that result have attractive blurred, or "flame", edges that conjure up Southeast Asia, to where *ikat* was exported in the medieval era.

Less expensive cloth to look out for, especially while you're in Goa, includes that touted by the **Lamanis** – the semi-nomadic low-caste minority from northern Karnataka who traditionally lived by transporting salt across the Deccan Plateau. These days, the women and girls make most of the family money through the sale of textiles carefully tailored for the tourist trade. Their rainbow cloth, woven with geometric designs and inlaid with cowrie shells or fragments of mirror and mica, is fashioned into shoulder bags, caps and money belts. If you haggle hard and can put up with all the shouting and tugging that inevitably accompanies each purchase, you can usually pick up it up at bargain prices.

From Tamil Nadu, an authentic souvenir to take home is the kind of **Madras-check lunghis** worn by most of the men (at least in the countryside); Keralans tend to prefer jazzier varieties, with day-glo colours rendered on slinky polyester. Particularly beautiful and high quality lunghis of creamy cotton or **calico** are to be found in **Kozhikode**, Kerala (see p.414). Indeed the town's former name of Calicut came about because of its trade in the material. For women, **salwar kamise**, the elegant pyjama suits worn by Muslims, unmarried girls and middle-class students, make ideal travel outfits, although in the sticky heat of the far south you may find them too heavy. Long loose shirts – preferably made of khadi, and known as *kurta* or *panjabi* – are more practical. Tourist shops sell versions in various fabrics and colours. Block-printed bedsheets, as well as being useful, make good wall-hangings. You will find every region has its own fabrics, its own methods of colouring them and making them up – the choice is endless.

On top of this, with **tailoring** so cheap in India, you can choose the fabric you want, take it to a tailor, and have it made into whatever you fancy. For formal Western-style clothes, you'll want to see quite a posh tailor in a big city, but tailors in almost every village in the country can run you up a shirt or a pair of pyjama-type trousers in next to no time. Many tailors will also copy a garment you already have.

Carpets and rugs

South India is generally less renowned for its carpets than the North, but the former

Muslim kingdoms of the Deccan, notably around Eluru and Warangal in Andhra Pradesh, have retained weaving traditions dating from the seventeenth century, when Moghul artisans drifted south in the wake of their conquering armies. They brought with them techniques and designs from medieval Persia, and these still feature prominently in today's flat-weave durries. The colours tend to be pale pastels, with floral motifs overlaid on cameo backgrounds. In accordance with an old Persian tradition, each design is named after a patron of the weaving industry. The carpets themselves are hard to come by – they are only produced in small numbers by a few families – but you can usually track some down in the Muslim bazaars of Hyderabad, the Andhran capital.

A little visited spot which has a lively hand-loom and weaving industry is **Tusara**, near Kozhikode (Calicut) in Kerala (see p.417). There you can not only watch the artisans at work but actually design your own rug or wall-hanging and learn how to make it. For everyday domestic use, **rag rugs**, made from recycled clothing, are good buys. Available just about everywhere, they cost little enough in Europe and North America, but in India are fantastically cheap; many visitors buy large ones and post them home by surface mail.

Of course, you do not have to go all the way north to buy a **Kashmiri** rug or carpet. Many Kashmiris have set up shop in the main tourist centres of the South and you can find high quality goods there, though not all the dealers are known for their scruples and it is best to learn something about what you are trying to buy before you lay out a lot of cash. A pukka Kashmiri carpet should have a label on the back stating that it is made in Kashmir, what it is made of (wool, silk, or "silk touch", the latter being wool combined with a little cotton and silk to give it a sheen), its size, density of knots per square inch (the more the better) and the name of the design. To tell if it really is silk, scrape the carpet with a knife and burn the fluff – real silk shrivels to nothing and has a distinctive smell. Even producing the knife should cause the seller of a bogus silk carpet to demur.

Paintings and antiques

The former Chola capital of Thanjavur (Tanjore), in the Kaveri (Cauvery) Delta area of Tamil Nadu, is famous throughout the South for its school of religious painting, which emerged in the nineteenth century under patronage from the local maharaja. "Painting" is actually something of a misnomer, as the images are partly raised in low plaster relief, and inlaid with precious stones, glass pieces, pearls, mica and ivory. The Tanjore school's preferred subject is Balakrishna (Krishna as a crawling baby stealing butter balls), and depictions of Vishnu's other incarnations. You'll come across these all over the region, but only in **Thanjavur** itself (see p.505) are you likely to see the artists in action. Prices range from around Rs2000 to Rs200,000 depending on the size, the quality of the painting and the value of the inlays and gold leaf.

The villages of Machilipatnam and Kalahasti, southeast of Vijayawada in Andhra Pradesh, are the source of a rare kind of devotional painting known as **Kalamkari**. Stylized images of deities and mythological scenes are outlined in black on lengths of thick cotton and coloured with beautiful natural dyes. Ochre, russet, blue-green, soot black and red are the predominant colours of the ornate hangings, which were traditionally produced for temples.

At the opposite end of the market, **leaf skeleton paintings** from southern Kerala are widely available in handicraft and souvenir shops, though they too vary somewhat in quality.

When it comes to **antiques**, if they really are genuine – and, frankly, that is unlikely – you'll need a licence to export them, which is virtually impossible to get. The age and status of antiques can be verified by the **Archaeological Survey of India**, Sion Fort, Sion, Mumbai 400022 ☎022/407 1102; Fort St George, Chennai 600009 ☎044/560396; 5th floor, F Wing, Kendriya Sadan, 17th Main Rd, Keramangala, Bangalore 560034 ☎080/553 7348. These offices also issue export clearance certificates.

Toys and puppets

Wooden **toys** crop up in various craft villages around Andhra Pradesh, among them Kondapalli, near Vijayawada, and Ettikopakka in the Vishakaptnam district, where brightly coloured figures, thought to have originally been made for temple rituals, are produced on lathes. Sticks of lac dye are used to decorate them; the heat generated by friction as the crayons are pressed against the revolving wood causes the pigment to melt. When this dries it forms a hard, bright shell. A similar technique has been refined in the village of Chennapatna, between Mysore and Bangalore in Karnataka, where artisans fashion toy replicas of buses, trains, planes and everyday household objects for children to play with.

Shadow puppets, *tolu bommalaatam* in Tamil, are another traditional South Indian means to amuse and instruct kids. Made of translucent leather, dyed and decorated with geometric perforations, they are manipulated with bamboo sticks by teams of puppeteers seated behind a back-lit cloth screen – a technique that was exported by medieval Tamil traders and which has subsequently taken root in parts of Indonesia, including Bali. Music and percussion accompanies performances of mythological epics such as the *Ramayana* and *Mahabharata*. Squeezed out by cinema, puppetry is sadly a dying art in South India these days, but you can still see performances at the Dakshina Chitra folk museum near Chennai (see p.474), while souvenir-sized shadow puppets are sold at most government emporia in Tamil Nadu.

Odds and sods

Of course, not everything typically Indian is old or traditional. **CDs** and **audio cassettes** of Hindustani classical, Carnatic, *Bhangra*, *filmi* and Western music are available in most major towns and cities for a fraction of what you'd pay back home. By far the best-stocked stores are in Mumbai, Bangalore and Chennai.

Books are also excellent buys in India, whether by Indian writers (see Contexts p.710) or writers from the rest of the English-speaking world. Once again, they are usually much cheaper than at home, if not so well printed or bound. Hardback volumes of Indian sacred literature are particularly good value.

Bamboo flutes are incredibly cheap, while other **musical instruments** such as *tabla*, *sitar* and *sarod* are sold in music shops in the larger cities. The quality is crucial; there's no point going home with a *sitar* that is virtually untunable, even if it does look nice. Students of music purchase their instruments from master craftsmen or established shops. A good place to start looking is Chennai, where you can pick up quality Carnatic percussion instruments such as *mridangam*, the double-headed drum that gives South Indian music its distinctive rhythms, *vinas*, the southern cousin of the sitar, and *nadasvaram*, a kind of over-sized oboe used in temple rituals. For more on Carnatic music, see Contexts p.694.

Other possible souvenirs include kitchen implements like tiffin boxes, wind-up clockwork tin toys, film posters, tea (especially Orange Pekoe from the plantations of the Nilgiri mountains), essential oils (such as eucalyptus, citronella or sandalwood) from Coonor in Tamil Nadu (see p.557), spices and peacock feather fans (though these are considered unlucky).

Things not to bring home include ivory and anything made from a rare or protected species, including snakeskin and turtle products. As for drugs – don't even think about it.

Women travellers

South India is not a place that provides huge obstacles to women travellers, petty annoyances being more the order of the day. In the days of the Raj, upper-class eccentrics started a tradition of lone women travellers, taken up enthusiastically by the flower children of the hippy era. Women today still do it, and most come through the challenge perfectly unscathed. However, few women get through their trip without any hassle, and it's good to prepare yourself to be a little thick-skinned.

South Indian streets are almost without exception male-dominated – something that may take a bit of getting used to, particularly when you find yourself subjected to incessant **staring**, whistling and name-calling. This can usually be stopped by ignoring the gaze and quickly moving on, or by firmly telling the offender to stop looking at you. Most of your fellow travellers on trains and buses will be men who may start up most unwelcome conversations about sex, divorce and the freedom of relationships in the West. These cannot often be avoided, but demonstrating too much enthusiasm to discuss such topics can lure men into thinking that you are easy about sex, and the situation could become threatening. At its worst in larger cities, all this can become very tiring. You can get round it to a certain extent by joining women in public places, and you'll notice an immense difference if you join up with a male travelling companion. In this case, however, expect Indian men to approach him (assumed, of course, to be your husband – an assumption it is sometimes advantageous to go along with – you could even consider wearing a wedding ring) and talk to him about you quite happily as if you were not there. Beware, however, if you are (or look) Indian with a non-Indian male companion: this may well cause you grief and harassment, as you will be seen to have brought shame on your family by adopting the loose morals of the West.

In addition to staring and suggestive comments and looks, **sexual harassment**, or "Eve teasing" as it is bizarrely known, is likely to be a nuisance, but not generally a threat. Expect to get groped in crowds, and to have men "accidentally" squeeze past you at any opportunity. It tends to be worse in cities than in small towns and villages, but anywhere being followed can be a real problem.

In time you'll learn to gauge a situation – sometimes wandering around on your own may attract so much unwanted attention that you may prefer to stay in one place until you've recharged your batteries or your male fan club has moved on. It's always best to dress modestly whenever in public – a *salwar kamise* is perfect, or baggy clothing – and refrain from smoking and drinking in public, which only reinforces suspicions that Western women are "loose" and "easy".

Returning an unwanted touch with a punch or slap is perfectly in order (Indian women often become aggressive when offended), and does serve to vent a little frustration. It should also attract attention and urge someone to help you, or at least deal with the offending man – a man transgressing social norms is always out of line, and any passer-by will want to let him know it. If you feel someone getting too close in a crowd or on a bus, brandishing your left shoe in his face can be very effective.

To go and watch a Bollywood movie at the cinema is a fun and essential part of your trip to India, but unfortunately such an occasion is rarely without hassle. The crowd is predominantly male and mostly young at that. If you do go and see a film, go with a group of people and/or sit in the balcony area – it's a bit more expensive but the crowd is much more sedate up there.

Violent sexual assaults on tourists are extremely rare, but unfortunately the number of reported cases of rape is rising. Though no assault can be predicted, you can take **precautions**: at night avoid quiet, dimly lit streets and alleys; if you find a trustworthy rickshaw/taxi driver in the day keep him for the night journey; and try to get someone to accompany you to your hotel whenever possible. While Indian women are still quite timid about reporting rape – it is considered as much a disgrace to the victim as to the perpetrator – Western victims should always report it to the police, and before leaving the area try to let other tourists, or locals, know, in the hope that pressure from the community may uncover the offender and see him brought to justice. At present there's nowhere for tourists who've suffered sexual violence to go for sanctuary; most victims seek support from other travellers, or go home.

The **practicalities** of travel take on a new dimension for lone women travellers. Often you can turn your gender to your advantage. For example, on buses the driver and conductor will often take you under their wing, watch out for you and buy you chai at each stop, and there will be countless other instances of kindness wherever you travel. You'll also be more welcome in some private houses than a group of Western males, and may find yourself learning the finer points of Indian cooking round the family's clay stove. Women frequently get preference at bus and train stations where they can join a separate "ladies' queue", and use ladies' waiting rooms. On overnight trains you can aim for the enclosed ladies' compartments, which are peaceful havens – unless filled with noisy children – or share a berth section with a family so as to draw you into the security of the group, making you less exposed to lusty gazing. In hotels watch out for "peep-holes" in your door (and in the common bathrooms), be sure to cover your window when changing and when sleeping, and avoid the sleazy permit-room hotels of the southern cities.

Lastly, bring your own supply of tampons, not widely available outside Indian cities.

Women's organizations in South India

Forum against the Oppression of Women 29 Bhatia Bhawan, Babrekan Rd, Gokale Rd (North), Dadar, Mumbai 400028 (☎ 022/422 2436). Support centre which also organizes workshops.
Streelekha (International Feminist Bookshop and Information Centre), 15/55, 1st floor, Cambridge, Jeevan Kendra Layout, Bangalore 560 008, Karnataka. Stocks books, journals, posters and provides space for women to meet.
Women's Centre 104B Sunrise Apartments, Nehru Rd, Valoka, Santa Cruz East, Mumbai 400055 (☎ 022/614 0403). A drop-in centre for women to meet, hold workshops and gain access to literature on women's issues.

 Gay travellers

Homosexuality is not generally open or accepted in India, and "carnal intercourse against the order of nature" (anal intercourse) is a ten-year offence under article 377 of the penal code. Laws against "obscene behaviour" are used to arrest gay men for cruising or liaising anywhere that could be considered a public place. The same law could in theory be used against lesbians.

The homosexual scene in India was brought into the spotlight in 1998 with the nationwide screening of the highly controversial film *Fire* by Deepa Mehta, about two sisters-in-law living together under the same roof who become lesbian lovers. Flying in the face of the traditional emphasis on heterosexual family life, the film created a storm. Right-wing extremists attacked cinemas that showed it, and in the wake of the attacks, many gays and lesbians came out for the first time to hold candlelit protest vigils in Delhi, Mumbai, Calcutta, Chennai and Bangalore.

For lesbians, **making contacts** will be rather difficult; even the Indian Women's Movement does not readily promote lesbianism as an issue that needs confronting. The only public faces of a hidden scene are the organizations listed below and a few of the nationwide women's organizations (see p.81).

Meeting places for gay men are marginally easier to find, with established gay bars cropping up in the more Westernized cities such as Mumbai and Bangalore. Contact the organizations listed given below, and they will tell you about gay events and parties.

Contacts in South India

Write in advance for information – most addresses are PO boxes:

Bombay Dost 105A Veena-Beena Shopping Centre, Bandra Station Rd, Bandra (West), Mumbai 400050. Publishes a newsletter and has contacts nationwide.

Khush Club, PO Box 573551, Mumbai 400058. Organizes gay social events regularly in Mumbai.

Gay Info Centre c/o Owais, PO Box 1662, Secunderabad HPO 500003, Andhra Pradesh. Provides literature, contacts and resources on homosexuality in India.

Good As You 201 Samaraksha, 2nd Floor Royal Corner, 1+2 Lalbang Rd, Bangalore, Karnataka. Gay support group.

Men India Movement PO Box 885, Kochi 682005, Kerala. Gay men's support group.

Saathi PO Box 571, Putlibowli PO, Hyderabad, Andhra Pradesh. Gay support group.

Sneha Sangama PO Box 3250, Bangalore 560032, Karnataka. Gay men's support group.

Stree Sangam PO Box 16613, Matunga, Mumbai 400019. A support group for lesbian and bisexual women.

Disabled travellers

Disability is common in India; many conditions that would be treatable in the West, such as cataracts, are permanent disabilities here because people can't afford the treatment. Disabled people are unlikely to get jobs, and the choice is usually between staying at home being looked after by your family and going out on the street to beg for alms.

For the **disabled traveller**, this has its advantages: disability and disfigurement, for example, do not get the same embarrassed reaction from Indian people that they do from some able-bodied Westerners. On the other hand, you'll be lucky to see a state-of-the-art wheelchair or a loo for the disabled (major airports usually have both, though the loo may not be in a usable state), and the streets are full of all sorts of obstacles that would be hard for a blind or wheelchair-bound tourist to negotiate independently. Kerbs are often high, pavements uneven

and littered, and ramps non-existent. There are potholes all over the place and open sewers. Some of the more expensive hotels have ramps for the movement of luggage and equipment, but if that makes them accessible to wheelchairs, it is by accident rather than design.

If you walk with difficulty, you will find street **obstacles** and steep stairs hard going. Another factor that can be a problem is the constant barrage of people proffering things at you (hard to wave aside if you are for instance on sticks or crutches), and all that queuing, not to mention heat, will take it out of you if you have a condition that makes you tire quickly. A light, folding camp-stool is one thing that could be invaluable if you have limited walking or standing power.

Then again, Indian people are likely to be very helpful if, for example, you need their help getting on and off buses or up stairs. Taxis and rickshaws are easily affordable and very adaptable; if you rent one for a day, the driver is certain to help you on and off, and perhaps even around the sites you visit. If you employ a guide, they may also be prepared to help you with steps and obstacles.

If complete independence is out of the question, going with an able-bodied companion might be on the cards. Contact one of the specialist organizations listed below for further advice on planning your trip. Otherwise, some package tour operators try to cater for travellers with disabilities – Bales and Somak among them – but you should always contact any operator and discuss your exact needs with them before making a booking. You should also make sure you are covered by any insurance policy you take out.

Organizations for the disabled

Britain and Ireland

Can Be Done 7–11 Kensington High St, London W8 5NP ☎020/8907 2400. Specialist tour operators for the disabled.
Carefree Holidays 64 Florence Rd, Northampton NN1 4NA ☎01604/634301. Specialist tour operators for the disabled.
Holiday Care Service 2nd Floor, Imperial Buildings, Victoria Rd, Horley, Surrey RH6 7PZ ☎01293/774535. Provides information and lists of tour operator and should be able to help you get in touch with someone.
National Rehabilitation Board 25 Clyde Rd, Ballsbridge, Dublin 4 ☎01/668 4181.

Tripscope, Alexandra House, Albany Road, Brentford, Middlesex TW8 0NE ☎08457/585641, ☎020/8580 7022, ✉tripscope@cableinet.co.uk, ⊕www.justmobility.co.uk/tripscope. This registered charity provides a national telephone information service offering free advice on UK and international transport for those with a mobility problem.

US and Canada

Jewish Rehabilitation Hospital, 3205 Place Alton Goldbloom, Chomedy Laval, Quebec, H7V 1RT (☎450/688-9550 ext 226). Their medical library provides guidebooks and travel information on India and various other countries for travellers with disabilities.
Society for the Advancement of Travel for the Handicapped (SATH), 347 Fifth Ave, Suite 610, New York NY10016 (☎212/447 7284, ⊕www.sittravel.com).
Travel Information Service, Moss Rehab Hospital, 1200 West Tabor Rd, Philadelphia, PA 19141 (☎215/456-9600).
Twin Peaks Press, Box 129, Vancouver, WA 98666 (360/694-2462 or 1-800/637-2256). Publisher of *Directory of Travel Agencies for the Disabled*, *Travel for the Disabled*, *Directory of Accessible Van Rentals*, and *Wheelchair Vagabond*, which is loaded with personal tips.

Australia and New Zealand

ACROD, PO Box 60, Curtin, ACT 2605 (☎02/6682 4333).
Barrier Free Travel, 36 Wheatley St, North Bellingen, NSW 2454 (☎02/6655 1733).
Disabled Persons Assembly, 173 Victoria St, Wellington (☎04/801 9100).

India

India Rehabilitation Co-ordination – India, A–2 Rasadhara Co-operation Housing Society, 385 SVP Rd, Mumbai 400004.

Travelling with children

Travelling with kids can be both challenging and rewarding. Indians are very tolerant of children so you can take children almost anywhere without restriction, and they always help break the ice with strangers.

The main problem with children, especially small children, is their extra vulnerability. Even more than their parents, they need protecting from the sun, unsafe drinking water, heat and unfamiliar food. All that chilli in particular may be a problem, even with older kids, if they're not used to it. Remember too, that diarrhoea, perhaps just a nuisance to you, could be dangerous for a child: rehydration salts (see p.31) are vital if your child goes down with it. Make sure too, if possible, that your child is aware of the dangers of rabies; keep children away from animals, and consider a rabies jab. Advice on malaria is given on p.29.

For babies, nappies (diapers) and places to change them can be a problem. For a short visit, you could bring disposable ones with you; for longer journeys, consider going over to washables. A changing mat is another necessity. And if your baby is on powdered milk, it might be an idea to bring some of that; you can certainly get it in India, but it may not taste the same. Dried baby food too could be worth taking – mix it with hot (boiled) water that any café or chai-wallah should be able to supply you with.

For touring, hiking or walking, child-carrier backpacks are ideal; they start at around £35 and can weigh less than 2kg. If the child is small enough, a fold-up buggy is also well worth packing – especially if they will sleep in it (while you have a meal or a drink...). If you want to cut down on long journeys by flying, remember that children under two travel for ten percent of the adult fare, and under-12s for half price.

Voluntary organizations

While in India, you may consider doing some voluntary charitable work. Several charities welcome volunteers who make a medium-term commitment, say over two months.

If you do want to spend your time working for a **NGO (Non-Government (voluntary) Organization)**, you should make arrangements before you arrive by contacting the body in question. If you are working within the time limit of an ordinary tourist visa and are not working anywhere sensitive that may require a special permit, you shouldn't need to apply for a special visa. Missionaries, however, do require a special visa (consult the Indian consulate).

Voluntary work resources and charities

The following organizations provide useful resources:

Charities Aid Foundation (CAF), Kings Hill, West Malling, Kent ME19 4TA, UK ℡01732/520000, ⓦwww.cafonline.org/cafindia/i_search.cfm. CAF provides useful information and contacts for numerous NGOs and aid agencies working in India; their online database is very useful.

Indev, The British Council, 17 Kasturba Gandhi Marg, New Delhi 110 001 ☎011/371 1401, ⊛www.indev.org. Indev, an initiative of the British Council, provides useful resources through discussions and a mammoth databank, accessed through their website, with over 1000 Indian NGOs.

Peace Corps of America ☎1-800/424-8580, ⊛www.peacecorps.gov. The US-government sponsored aid and voluntary organization, with projects all over the world.

SOS Children's Villages of India, A-7 Nizamuddin (West), New Delhi 110013 ☎0111/464 7835 & 464 9734, ⊛www.soscvindia.org. SOS has 32 villages and numerous allied projects in different parts of India,

including in Karnataka, giving shelter to distressed children by providing a healthy environment and education including vocational training. Volunteers are welcomed at some of their centres – contact them first.

Voluntary Service Overseas (VSO), 317 Putney Bridge Road, London SW15 2PN, UK ☎020/8780 2266 & 87807200, ⊛www.vso.org.uk. A British government-funded organization that places volunteers on various projects around the world and in India.

Voluntary Service Overseas (VSO) ⊛www.vsocan.com. Canada 806-151 Slater Street Ottawa ON K1P 5H3, Canada (☎1-888-876-2911). Canadian-based organization affiliated to the British VSO.

Directory

AIRPORT DEPARTURE TAX There is a standard departure tax of either Rs750 – for most international flights – or Rs210, for domestic flights and flights to Pakistan, Bangladesh, Nepal, Sri Lanka, Myanmar (Burma), the Maldives and Afghanistan. Recently the tax has started to be included in the ticket price of all flights, wherever purchased, but there is no harm in double-checking that it has been covered when you reconfirm your flight. This tax also applies to international sea departures.

CIGARETTES Indian cigarettes, such as Wills, Gold Flake, Four Square and Charms, are okay once you get used to them, and hardly break the bank (Rs10–30 per pack), but if you find them too rough, stock up on imported brands such as Marlboro and Benson and Hedges, or some rolling tobacco, available in the bigger towns and cities. One of the great smells of India is the *bidi*, the cheapest smoke, made of a single low-grade tobacco leaf. If you smoke roll-ups, stock up on good papers as Indian Capstan cigarette papers are thick and don't stick very well and Rizlas, where available, are pretty costly.

DUTY-FREE ALLOWANCE Anyone over 17 can bring in one US quart (0.95 litre – but nobody's going to quibble about the other 5ml) of spirits, or a bottle of wine and 250ml spirits; plus 200 cigarettes, or 50 cigars, or 250g tobacco. You may

be required to register anything valuable on a Tourist Baggage Re-export Form to make sure you can take it home with you, and to fill in a currency declaration form if carrying more than US$10,000 or the equivalent. There is a market for duty-free spirits in big cities: small retailers are the best people to approach.

ELECTRICITY Generally 220V 50Hz AC, though direct current supplies also exist, so check before plugging in. Most sockets are triple round-pin (accepting European-size double round-pin plugs). British, Irish and Australasian plugs will need an adaptor, preferably universal; American and Canadian appliances will need a transformer too, unless multi-voltage. Power cuts and voltage variations are very common; voltage stabilizers should be used to run sensitive appliances such as laptops.

INITIALS AND ACRONYMS Widely used in Indian English. Thus, the former Prime Minister, Vishwana Pratap Singh, was always "VP", and many middle-class Indian men bear similar monikers. Likewise, Andhra Pradesh (not Arunchal Pradesh) is AP and MG Road anywhere you go means Mahatma Gandhi Road. State and national or state organizations such as ITDC, KSTDC and so on are always known by their acronyms.

LAUNDRY In India, no one goes to the laundry: if they don't do their own, they send it out to a

85

dhobi-wallah. Wherever you are staying, there will either be an in-house *dhobi*-wallah, or one very close by to call on. The *dhobi*-wallah will take your dirty washing to a *dhobi ghat*, a public clothes-washing area (the bank of a river for example), where it is shown some old-fashioned discipline: separated, soaped and given a damn good thrashing to beat the dirt out of it. Then it's hung out to dry in the sun and, once dried, taken to the ironing sheds where every garment is endowed with razor-sharp creases and then matched to its rightful owner by hidden cryptic markings. Your clothes will come back from the *dhobi*-wallah absolutely spotless, though this kind of violent treatment does take it out of them: buttons get lost and eventually the cloth starts to fray. For more on *dhobi wallahs*, see the box on p.121. If you'd rather not entrust your Saville Row made-to-measure to their tender mercies, there are dry-cleaners in large towns.

NUMBERS A hundred thousand is a *lakh* (written 1,00,000); ten million is a *crore* (1,00,00,000). Millions, billions and the like are not in common use.

OPENING HOURS Standard shop opening hours in India are Mon–Sat 9.30am–6pm. Most big stores, at any rate, keep those hours, while smaller shops vary from town to town, religion to religion and one to another, but usually keep longer hours. Government tourist offices are open in principle Mon–Fri 9.30am–5pm, Sat 9.30am–1pm, though these may vary slightly; state tourist offices are likely to be open Mon–Fri 10am–5pm, but sometimes operate much longer hours.

PASSSENGER TAX
Tax of Rs200 is levied on passengers arriving in India; check in advance whether this is included in the price of your ticket. The tax is payable in rupees.

PHOTOGRAPHY Beware of pointing your camera at anything that might be considered "strategic", including airports, anything military and even bridges, train stations and main roads. Remember too that some people prefer not to be photographed, so it is wise to ask before you take a snapshot of them. More likely, you'll get people, especially kids volunteering to pose. Camera film, sold at average Western prices, is widely available in India (but check the date on the box, and note that false boxes containing outdated film are often sold – Konica have started painting holograms on their boxes to prevent this). It's fairly easy to get films developed, though they don't always come out as well as they might at home. If you're after slide film, slow film or fast film, buy it in the big cities, and don't expect to find specialist brands

Things to take

Most things are easy to find in India and cheaper than at home, but here is a list of useful items worth bringing with you:

❑ Padlock and chain (to lock rooms in budget hotels, and attach your bag to train fittings)
❑ Universal electric plug adapter and a universal sink plug (few sinks or bathtubs have them)
❑ Mosquito net
❑ Sheet sleeping bag (made by sewing up a sheet – so you don't have to worry about the state of the ones in your hotel room)
❑ Pillowcase
❑ Washing line
❑ Quick-dry towel
❑ Hat
❑ Small flashlight
❑ Earplugs (for street noise in hotel rooms and music on buses)
❑ High-factor sunblock
❑ Pocket alarm clock
❑ Inflatable neck-rest or pillow, to help you sleep on long journeys
❑ Multipurpose penknife
❑ Needle and some thread (but dental floss is better than cotton for holding baggage together)
❑ Plastic, or nylon, bags (to sort your baggage, make it easier to pack and unpack, and keep out damp and dust)
❑ Small umbrella (local ones tend not to retract)
❑ Tampons
❑ Condoms
❑ First-aid kit
❑ Multivitamin and mineral tablets

such as Velvia. Also, remember to guard your equipment from dust. Konica studios through South India have hi-tech equipment and process film in one hour (Rs200–250).

TIME India is all in one time zone: GMT+5hr 30min. This makes it 5hr 30min ahead of London, 10hr 30min ahead of New York, 13hr 30min ahead of LA, 4hr 30min behind Sydney and 6hr 30min behind NZ; however, summer time in those places will vary the difference by an hour.

TOILETS A visit to the loo is not one of India's more pleasant experiences: toilets are often filthy and stink. They are also major potential breeding grounds for disease. In addition, there is the squatting position to get used to, as the traditional Asian toilet has a hole in the ground, with two small platforms either side for feet instead of a seat. Paper, if used, often goes in a bucket next to the loo rather than down it. Indians use a jug of water and their left hand instead of paper, a method you may also come to prefer, but if you do use paper, keep some handy – it isn't usually supplied, and it might be an idea to stock up before going too far off the beaten track as it is not available everywhere.

guide

guide

Mumbai

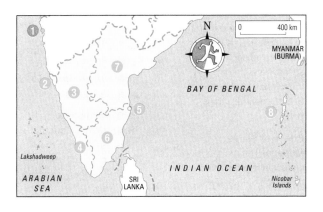

CHAPTER 1 # Highlights

* **Victoria Terminus** A fantastically eccentric pile, perhaps the greatest railway station ever built by the British. See p.101

* **The Gateway of India** The departure-point for the last British troops leaving India, now a favourite spot for an evening stroll. See p.108

* **Regional cuisines** There's nowhere better to sample India's many and diverse cooking styles: Parsi berry pulao to Bombay bhel puri. See our eating listings p.127

* **Prince of Wales Museum** The main enticement is the fine collection of Indian art, including erotic Gita Govinda paintings. See p.111

* **Maidans (parks)** Where Mumbai's citizens escape the hustle and bustle to play cricket, eat lunch and hang out. See p.114

* **Elephanta Island** A magnificent rock-cut Shiva temple on an island in Mumbai harbour. See p.123

* **Nightlife** The best pubs and clubs in India and great international cuisine. See p.130–133

* **Bollywood blockbusters** Check out the latest Hindi mega movie in one of the city centre's gigantic air-con cinemas. See p.132

Mumbai

Young, brash and oozing with the cocksure self-confidence of a maverick money-maker, **MUMBAI** (formerly **Bombay**) revels in its reputation as India's most dynamic and Westernized city. Behind the hype, however, intractable problems threaten the Maharashtran capital, foremost among them being a chronic shortage of space. Crammed onto a narrow spit of land that curls from the swamp-ridden coast into the Arabian Sea, Mumbai has, in less than five hundred years since its "discovery" by the Portuguese, metamorphosed from an aboriginal fishing settlement into a sprawling megalopolis of over sixteen million people. Whether you are being swept along broad boulevards by endless streams of commuters, or jostled by coolies and hand-cart pullers in the teeming bazaars, Mumbai always feels like it is about to burst at the seams.

The roots of the population problem lie, paradoxically, in the city's enduring ability to create wealth. Mumbai alone generates 38 percent of India's GNP, its port handles half the country's foreign trade, and its movie industry is the biggest in the world. Symbols of prosperity are everywhere, from the phalanx of office blocks clustered on Nariman Point, Maharashtra's Manhattan, to the yuppie couples nipping around town in their shiny new Maruti hatchbacks. The flip side to the success story, of course, is the city's much chronicled poverty. Each day, hundreds of economic refugees pour into Mumbai from the Maharashtran hinterland. Some find jobs and secure accommodation; many more (around a third of the total population) end up living on the already overcrowded streets, or amid the appalling squalor of Asia's largest slums, reduced to rag-picking and begging from cars at traffic lights.

However, while it would definitely be misleading to downplay its difficulties, Mumbai is far from the ordeal some travellers make it out to be. Once you've overcome the major hurdle of finding somewhere to stay, you may begin to enjoy its frenzied pace and crowded, cosmopolitan feel. Conventional **sights** are thin on the ground. After a visit to the most famous colonial monument, the **Gateway of India**, and a look at the antiquities in the **Prince of Wales Museum**, the most rewarding way to spend time is simply to wander the city's atmospheric streets. **Downtown**, beneath rows of exuberant **Victorian-Gothic** buildings, the pavements are full of noisy vendors and office-wallahs hurrying through clouds of wood-smoke from *gram*-sellers' braziers. In the eye of the storm, encircled by the roaring traffic of beaten-up red double-decker buses, lie other vestiges of the Raj, the **maidans**. Depending on the time of day, these central parks are peppered with cricketers in white flannels, or the bare bums of squatting pavement-dwellers relieving themselves on the parched brown grass. North of the city centre, the broad thoroughfares splinter into a

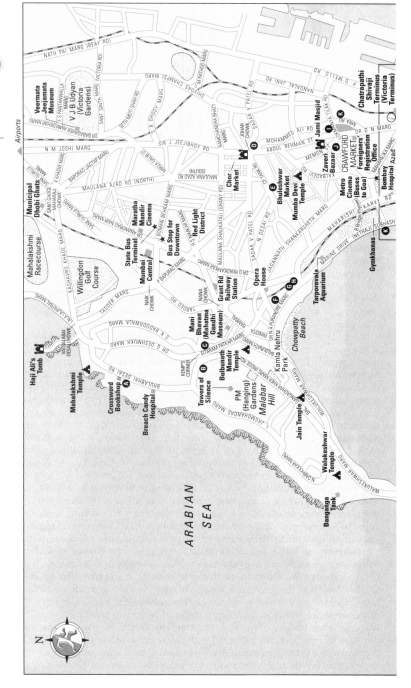

Airports

NATH PAI MARG (REAY RD)

Veermata
Jeejamata
Museum

V J B Udyan
(Victoria
Gardens)

Chatrapathi
Shivaji
Terminus

Chatrapathi
Shivaji
Terminus
(Victoria
Terminus)

K Jami Masjid

D

Zaveri
Bazaar **I**

J Foreigners'
Registration
Office

CRAWFORD
MARKET

Metro
Cinema
(Buses
to Goa)

Bombay
Hospital Azad

Mahalakshmi
Racecourse

Municipal
Dhobi Ghats

Willingdon
Golf
Course

Maratha
Mandir
Cinema

State Bus
Terminal

Bus Stop for
Downtown

Mumbai
Central

Red Light
District

E

Bhuleshwar
Market

Mumba Devi
Temple

Chor
Market

Opera
House

Grant Rd
Railway
Station

G **H**

F

Tarporevala
Aquarium

Gymkhanas

*Chowpatty
Beach*

Haji Ali's
Tomb **M**

Mahalakshmi
Temple

Crossword
Bookshop **A**

Breach Candy
Hospital

Towers of
Silence

Bulbunath
Mandir
Temple

B

PM
(Hanging)
Gardens

*Malabar
Hill*

Kamla Nehru
Park

Mani
Bhavan
(Mahatma
Gandhi
Museum) **C**

Jain Temple

Walukeshwar
Temple

Bananga
Tank

*ARABIAN
SEA*

N

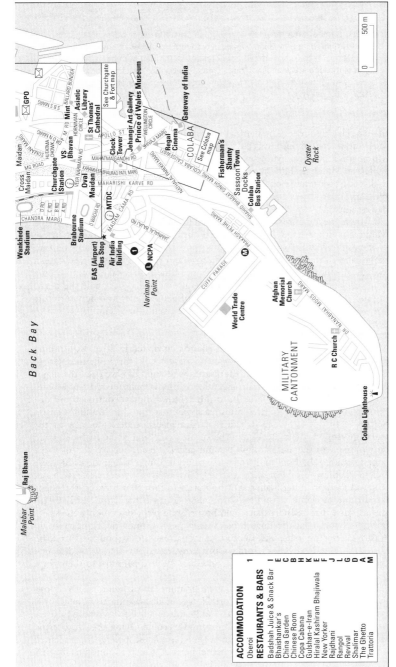

▲ *Launch to Elephanta Island*

MUMBAI

Back Bay

Malabar Point ● **Raj Bhavan**

Wankhede Stadium

Cross Maidan
MG ROAD

Churchgate Station

Brabourne Stadium

EAS (Airport) Bus Stop ✈

Air India Building

❶ NCPA

Nariman Point

Oval Maidan

Clock Tower

MTDC

Oyster Rock

World Trade Centre

CUFFE PARADE

Afghan Memorial Church

R C Church ⛪

MILITARY CANTONMENT

Colaba Lighthouse ▲

✉ GPO

Mint
Asiatic Library
St Thomas' Cathedral

See Churchgate & Fort map

Jehangir Art Gallery
Prince of Wales Museum

Gateway of India

COLABA

See Colaba map

Regal Cinema

Fisherman's Shanty

Colaba Bus Station

Sassoon Docks

VS Bhavan

HORNIMAN CIRCLE

WELLINGTON CIRCLE

APOLLO ST

MAHATMA GANDHI RD

MAHARISHI KARVE RD

M

0   500 m

ACCOMMODATION	
Oberoi	1

RESTAURANTS & BARS

Badshah Juice & Snack Bar	I
Bhaishankar's	E
China Garden	C
Chinese Room	B
Copa Cabana	H
Gulshan-e-Iran	K
Hiralal Kashiram Bhajiwala	F
New Yorker	J
Rajdhani	L
Rangol	G
Revival	D
Shalimar	A
The Ghetto	
Trattoria	M

95

In 1996 Bombay was renamed Mumbai, as part of a wider policy instigated by the ultra-right-wing Shiv Sena Municipality to replace names of any places, roads and features in the city that had connotations of the Raj. Mumbai is the Marathi name of the local deity, the mouthless "Maha-amba-aiee" (Mumba for short), who is believed to have started her life as an obscure aboriginal earth goddess. See p.122.

maze of chaotic streets. The **central bazaar** districts afford glimpses of sprawling Muslim neighbourhoods, as well as exotic **shopping** possibilities, while Mumbai is at its most exuberant along **Chowpatty Beach**, which laps against exclusive **Malabar Hill**. When you've had enough mayhem, the beautiful rock-cut Shiva temple on **Elephanta Island** – a short trip by launch across the harbour from the promenade, **Apollo Bunder** – offers a welcome half-day escape.

If you're heading for south India, you'll probably have to pass through Mumbai at some stage. Its international airport, **Sahar**, is the busiest in the country; the **airline offices** downtown are handy for confirming onward flights, and all the region's principal air, road and rail networks originate here. Whether or not you choose to stay for more time than it takes to jump on a train or plane to somewhere else depends on how well you handle the burning sun, humid atmosphere and perma-fog of petrol fumes, and how seriously you want to get to grips with the India of the twenty-first century.

Some history

Mumbai originally consisted of seven **islands**, inhabited by small Koli fishing communities. At different times, various dynasties held this insignificant outlying district; the city of Puri on **Elephanta** is thought to have been the major settlement in the region, until King Bimba, or Bhima, built the town of Mahim on one island, at the end of the thirteenth century. Hindus controlled the area until it was captured in the fourteenth century by the Muslim Gujarat Sultanate. In 1534, Sultan Bahadur of Ahmedabad ceded the city to the **Portuguese**, who felt the land to be of little importance, and concentrated development in the areas around Mahim and Bassein. They handed over the largest island to the English in 1661, as part of the dowry when the Portuguese Infanta Catherine of Braganza married Charles II; four years later Charles received the remaining islands and the port, and the town took on the anglicized name of Bombay from the Portuguese "Buan Bahia" or Good Bay. This was the first part of India that could properly be termed a colony; elsewhere on the subcontinent the English had merely been granted the right to set up "factories", or trading posts. Because of its natural safe harbour and strategic position for trade, the **East India Company**, based at Surat, wanted to buy the land; in 1668 a deal was struck, and Charles leased Mumbai to them for a pittance.

The English set about an ambitious programme of fortifying their outpost, living in the area known today as Fort. However, life was not easy. There was a fast turnover of governors, and malaria and cholera culled many of the first settlers. A chaplain of the East India Company, Reverend Ovington, wrote at the end of the seventeenth century: "One of the pleasantest spots in India seemed no more than a parish graveyard, a charnel house...Which common fatality has created a Proverb among the English there, that two monsoons are the age of a man". **Gerald Aungier**, the fourth governor (1672–77), set out to plan "the city which by God's assistance is intended to be built", and by the start of the eighteenth century the town was the capital of the East India Company. He is credited with encouraging the mix that still contributes to the city's success, welcoming Hindu traders from Gujarat, Goans (escaping Jesuit persecution), Muslim weavers and, most visibly, the business-minded Zoroastrian **Parsis**.

Much of the British settlement in the old Fort area was destroyed by a devastating fire in 1803, and the European population remained comparatively low well into the 1800s. The arrival of the **Great Indian Peninsular Railway** in the 1850s improved communications, encouraging yet more immigration from elsewhere in India. In 1852 the first of many land-reclamation projects (still ongoing) fused the seven islands; just a year later the rail link between Bombay and the cotton-growing areas of the Deccan plateau opened. This crucial railway, coupled with the cotton crisis in America following the Civil War, gave impetus to the great Bombay cotton boom and established the city as a major industrial and commercial centre. With the opening of the Suez Canal in 1859, and the construction of enormous docks, Bombay's access to European markets improved further. **Sir Bartle Frere**, governor from 1862 to 1867, oversaw the construction of the city's distinctive colonial-Gothic buildings; the most extravagant of all, **Victoria Terminus** railway station – now officially Chatrapathi Shivaji Terminus or CST – is a fitting testimony to this extraordinary age of expansion.

The Dons

Criminals have always been a part of the Mumbai's life, but the 1980s saw an intensification of organized crime in the city. Previously, gangsters had confined their activities to small-scale racketeering in poor neighbourhoods. After the post-1970s real estate boom however, many petty "landsharks" became powerful godfather figures, or dons, with drug- and gold-smuggling businesses as well as involvement in extortion and prostitution. Moreover, corrupt politicians who employed the gangs' muscle-power to rig elections had become highly placed political puppets with debts to pay – a phenomenon dubbed criminalization. The dividing line between the underworld and politics grew increasingly blurred during the Nineties – in 1992, no fewer than forty candidates in the municipal elections had criminal records.

The gangs have also become integral in the dirty war between India and Pakistan, with Karachi-based Dawood Ibrahim heavily implicated with the Pakistani security services – he is thought to be behind the bombings of 1993 (see p.99) – and Bombay's leading don Chhota Rajan with the Indian forces. In fact, many see the bungling of Rajan's recent extradition from Thailand, and his subsequent escape from a guarded hospital room – he drugged his Thai police guards and climbed out of the window using his bed sheets – as payment for services rendered.

The late Eighties saw the entrance of the dons into Bollywood, when the rise of video and TV made regular film financiers nervous of investing in the industry. Mob money poured in and it's an open secret that the film industry is one of the favoured forms of money-laundering with the dons – rival films mysteriously put back their release dates in order to give mob-backed movies a clear run at the box office. In 2000, however, the authorities began to take action, and Bollywood mogul Bharat Shah (who usually has around ten billion rupees invested in films at any one time) was arrested recently for financial links to the Dawood Ibrahim gang.

However, Mumbai is still the playground for mafia gangs – each with their own personalities and legends. If you read any newspapers while you're in the city you won't escape this phenomenon; the media revels in the shocking and bloodthirsty exploits of the gangsters, and the unfolding sagas run like a Bollywood blockbuster.

Not all Mumbai's grandest architecture is owed to the Raj– wealthy Jains and Parsis have also left their mark throughout the downtown area. As the most prosperous city in the nation, Bombay was at the forefront of the Independence struggle; Mahatma Gandhi used a house here, now a museum, to co-ordinate the struggle through three decades. Fittingly, the first British colony took pleasure in waving the final goodbye to the Raj, when the last contingent of British troops passed through the Gateway of India in February 1948. Since Independence, Mumbai has prospered as India's commercial and cultural capital and this period has seen the population grow tenfold to more than sixteen million.

However, as early as 1982, Mumbai's infrastructure was starting to buckle under the tensions of over-population. A bitter and protracted **textile strike** had impoverished tens of thousands of industrial workers, unemployment and crime were spiralling and the influx of immigrants into the city showed no signs of abating. Among the few beneficiaries of mounting discontent was the extreme right-wing Maharashtran party, the **Shiv Sena**. Founded in 1966 by Bal "the Saheb" Thackery, a self-confessed admirer of Hitler, the Sena's uncompromising stand on immigration and employment found favour with the disenchanted mass of lower-middle-class, mainly Marathi-speaking Hindus in the poorer suburbs. The party's venom, at first focused on the city's sizeable south Indian community, soon shifted to its fifteen-percent Muslim minority. Communal antagonism flared briefly in 1984, when ninety people died in riots, and again in 1985 when the Shiv Sena routed the Congress party in municipal elections. Between December 1992 and late January 1993, two waves of **rioting** in Mumbai affected not only the Muslim ghettos and poor industrial suburbs, but, for the first time, much of downtown too. According to

The festivals of Mumbai

Mumbai has its own versions of all the major Hindu and Muslim festivals, plus a host of smaller neighbourhood celebrations imported by its immigrant communities. Exact dates vary from year to year; check in advance at the government tourist office.

Makar Sankranti (Jan). A celebration of prosperity, when sweets, flowers and fruit are exchanged by all, and kites are flown in the parks as a sign of happiness.

Elephanta Music and Dance Festival (Feb). MTDC-organized cultural event including floodlit performances by classical artists with the Shiva cave temple as a backdrop.

Gudi Padva (March/April). The Maharashtran New Year.

Gokhulashtami (July/Aug). Riotous commemoration of Krishna's birthday; terracotta pots filled with curd, milk-sweets and cash are strung from tenement balconies and grabbed by human pyramids of young boys.

Nowroz (July/Aug). The Parsi New Year is celebrated with special ceremonies in the Fire Temples, and feasting at home.

Ganesh Chathurthi (Aug/Sept). Huge effigies of Ganesh, the elephant-headed god of prosperity and wisdom, are immersed in the sea at Chowpatty Beach in a ritual originally promoted by freedom-fighters to circumvent British anti-assembly legislation. Recently it has seemed in danger of being hijacked by Hindu extremists such as the Shiv Sena, tingeing it more with chauvinism than celebration.

Nariel Purnima (Sept). Koli fishermen launch brightly decorated boats to mark the end of the monsoon.

Dussehra (Oct). Rama's victory over the evil king of Lanka, Ravana, is marked in Mumbai by re-enactments of scenes from the *Ramayana* on Chowpatty Beach.

(conservative) official statistics, 784 people died, and around 5000 were injured – seventy percent of them Muslim.

Just as Mumbai was regaining its composure, disaster struck again. On March 12, 1993, ten massive **bomb blasts** ripped through the heart of the city, killing 317 people. No one claimed responsibility, but the involvement of "foreign hands" (ie Pakistan) was suspected. The city recovered from the explosions with astonishing speed, with hoardings erected beside the motorways ("Bombay Bounces Back!", "It's My Bombay", "Bombay, I Love You") attempting to restore the pride and ebullience with which India's most confident city had formerly gone about its business.

Arrival and information

Unless you arrive in Mumbai by train at **Chatrapathi Shivaji Terminus** (formerly Victoria Terminus), be prepared for a long slog into the centre. The international and domestic **airports** are north of the city, way off the map, and ninety minutes or more by road from the main hotel areas, while from **Mumbai Central** train or **bus station**, you face a laborious trip across town. Finding a place to stay can be even more of a hassle; phone around before you set off into the traffic.

By air

For many visitors, **Sahar** (30km), Mumbai's busy **international airport**, provides their first experience of India. The complex is divided into two "modules", one for Air India flights and the other for foreign airlines. Once through customs and the lengthy immigration formalities, you'll find a 24hr State Bank of India exchange facility, rather unhelpful government (ITDC) and state (MTDC) tourist information counters, car rental kiosks, cafés and a pre-paid taxi stand in the chaotic arrivals concourse. There's also – very usefully – an **Indian Railways booking office** which you should make use of if you know your next destination; it'll save you a long wait at the reservation offices downtown. If you're on one of the few flights to land in the afternoon or early evening – by which time most hotels tend to be full – it's worth paying on the spot for a room at the **accommodation booking desk** in the arrivals hall. All of the domestic airlines also have offices outside the main entrance, and there's a handy 24hr **left luggage** "cloakroom" in the car park nearby (Rs20–50 per day, depending on the size of your bag; maximum duration 90 days).

From the domestic terminal it is less than a fifteen-minute walk (across the main road) or Rs15 auto-rickshaw ride to Vile Parle station from where **suburban trains** run every few minutes (5am–midnight; 35–40min; Rs5) to Churchgate. The international terminal lies about 3km from the next station out of town on the same line, Andheri, and linked to it by buses #308, 338 and 409 or a Rs25 rickshaw ride. This is a fast and cheap way into town, and convenient unless you are really loaded down with luggage.

Many of the more upmarket hotels, particularly those near the airport, send out **courtesy coaches** to pick up their guests. **Taxis** are comfortable and not too extravagant. To avoid haggling over the fare or being duped by the private taxi companies outside the airport, pay in advance at the taxi desk in the arrivals hall. The price on the receipt, which you hand to the driver on arrival at your destination, is slightly more than the normal meter rate (around Rs260 to Colaba or Nariman Point, or Rs93 to Juhu), but at least you can be sure you'll be taken by the most direct route. Taxi-wallahs invariably try to persuade you to stay at a different hotel from the one you ask for. Don't agree to this; their commission will be added on to the price of your room.

Internal flights land at Mumbai's more user-friendly **domestic airport**, **Santa Cruz** (26km to the north), which is divided into separate modern terminals: the cream-coloured one (Module 1A) for Indian Airlines, and the blue-and-white (Module 1B) for private carriers. If you're transferring directly from here to an international flight at Sahar, 4km northeast, take the free "fly-bus" that shuttles every fifteen minutes between the two. The Indian government and MTDC both have 24hr information counters in the arrivals hall, and there's a foreign exchange counter and accommodation desk tucked away near the first-floor exit. Use the yellow-and-black metered taxis that queue outside the exit. The touts that claim to be running a pre-paid taxi system overcharge hugely – a journey to Colaba should cost around Rs250, no more.

Don't be tempted to use the **auto-rickshaws** that buzz around outside the airports; they're not allowed downtown and will leave you at the mercy of unscrupulous taxi drivers on the edge of Mahim Creek, the southernmost limit of their permitted area.

By train

Trains to Mumbai from most central, southern and eastern regions arrive at **Victoria Terminus** (officially renamed Chatrapathi Shivaji Terminus or CST), the main railway station at the end of the Central Railway line. From here it's a ten- or fifteen-minute ride to Colaba; either pick up a taxi at the busy rank outside the south exit, opposite the new reservation hall, or make your way to the main road and catch one of the innumerable buses.

Mumbai Central, the terminus for Western Railway trains from northern India, is further out from the centre; take a taxi from the main forecourt, or cross the hectic road junction next to the station and catch a BEST bus from the top of Dr DN Marg (Lamington Road); #66 and #71 run to VT (CST) and #70 to Colaba Causeway. It costs around the same to take a suburban train from Mumbai Central's local platform, across the footbridge. Four stops on is Churchgate station, the end of the line, a short taxi ride from Colaba (Rs20–30).

Some trains from south India arrive at more obscure stations. If you find yourself at **Dadar**, way up in the industrial suburbs, and can't afford a taxi (Rs120), cross the Tilak Marg road bridge onto the Western Railway and catch a suburban train into town, or take BEST bus #1 or #70 to Colaba, #66 to Central. **Kurla** station, where a few Bangalore trains pull in, is even further out, just south of Santa Cruz airport; taking a suburban train for Churchgate is the only reasonable alternative to a taxi (Rs220). From either, it's worth asking at the station when you arrive if there is another long-distance train going to Churchgate or Victoria Terminus shortly after – it's a far preferable to trying to cram into either a suburban train or bus.

By bus

Nearly all inter-state **buses** arrive at **Mumbai Central** bus stand, a stone's throw from the railway station of the same name. Again, you have a choice between municipal black-and-yellow taxis, the BEST buses (#66, #70 & #71), which run straight into town from the stop on Dr DN Marg (Lamington Road), two minutes' walk west from the bus station, or a suburban train from Mumbai Central's local platform over the footbridge.

Inspired by St Pancras station in London, F.W. Stevens designed Victoria Terminus, the most barmy of Mumbai's buildings, as a paean to "progress". Built in 1887 as the largest British edifice in India, it's an extraordinary amalgam of domes, spires, Corinthian columns and minarets that was succinctly defined by the journalist James Cameron as "Victorian-Gothic-Saracenic-Italianate-Oriental-St Pancras-Baroque". In keeping with the current re-Indianization of the city's roads and buildings, this icon of British imperial architecture has been renamed Chatrapathi Shivaji Terminus, in honour of a Maratha warlord who dedicated his life to fighting the Muslim Moghuls and professing Hindu cultural identity. However, this is a bit of a mouthful and the locals mostly still mostly use VT (pronounced "vitee") when referring to it, though it's always CST officially.

Few of the two million or so passengers who fill almost a thousand trains every day notice the mass of decorative detail. A "British" lion and Indian tiger stand guard at the entrance, and the exterior is festooned with sculptures executed at the Bombay Art School by the Indian students of John Lockwood Kipling, Rudyard's father. Among them are grotesque mythical beasts, monkeys and plants and medallions of important personages. To minimize the sun's impact, stained glass was employed, decorated with locomotives and elephant images. Above it all, "Progress" stands atop the massive central dome.

An endless frenzy of activity goes on inside: scuttling passengers; hundreds of porters in red with impossibly oversize headloads; TTEs (Travelling Ticket Examiners) in black jackets and white trousers clasping clipboards detailing reservations; spitting checkers busy handing out fines to those caught in the act; chaiwallahs with trays of tea; trundling magazine stands; crowds of bored soldiers smoking *beedis*, and the inexorable progress across the station of sweepers bent double. Amid it all, whole families spread out on the floor, eating, sleeping or just waiting and waiting.

Most **Maharashtra State Road Transport Corporation** (MSRTC) buses terminate at Mumbai Central though those from Pune, Nasik (and surrounding areas) end up at the **ASIAD** bus stand, a glorified parking lot near the railway station in **Dadar**.

Buses from Goa drop off at various points between central and downtown Mumbai. Most of the private companies currently work from the roadside in front of the Metro Cinema, at the north end of MG Road, while Kadamba (the Goan state transport corporation) buses stop nearby on the opposite (east) side of Azad Maidan, where they have a small ticket kiosk. Both places are an inexpensive taxi ride from the main hotel district.

Information

The best source of **information** in Mumbai is the excellent **Government of India tourist office** (Mon–Fri 8.30am–6pm, Sat 8.30am–2pm; ☎022/203 3144) at 123 M Karve Rd, opposite Churchgate station's east exit. The staff here are exceptionally helpful and hand out a wide range of leaflets, maps and brochures both on Mumbai and the rest of the country. There are also 24hr tourist **information counters** at Sahar International (☎022/832 5331) and Santa Cruz (☎022/615 9320) airports.

Maharashtra State Tourism Development Corporation Ltd (**MTDC**) main office, on Madam Cama Road (Mon–Sat 8.30am–7pm; ☎022/202 6731), opposite the LIC Building in Nariman Point, sells tickets for city sightseeing tours and can reserve rooms in MTDC resorts. They too have information counters at Sahar International and Santa Cruz airports, as well as at VT and Dadar railway stations and near the Gateway of India.

If you need detailed **listings**, ask at any tourist office for a free copy of the slick *Mumbai This Fortnight* which is user-friendly and has a wealth of useful information, despite being a commercial venture. If you want to spend any time in the city, invest in a copy of the *Pocket Mumbai Guide* (Rs20), which, although badly produced, contains more detailed information on bus and local train services as well as a useful rail map.

For **what's on** you're better off checking out the "The List" section of *Mid-Day* (Mumbai's main local rag), the "Metro" page in the *Indian Express*, or the "Bombay Times" section of the *Times of India*. All are available from street vendors around Colaba and the downtown area and cost Rs2–3.

For a detailed **map** of Mumbai, look for Karmarkar Enterprise's *Most Exhaustive A–Z* street plan (Rs60). It's fiendishly hard to find in bookstores (Crossword, on Bhulabai Desai Road, usually have one or two in stock), but the pavement guidebook- and magazine-wallahs along VN Road, between Churchgate and Flora Fountain, may have copies. Otherwise, the Discover India Series has produced a good, up-to-date map and listings book called the *Road Guide to Mumbai* (Rs60), that is widely available.

City transport

Only a masochist would travel on Mumbai's hopelessly overtaxed public **transport** for fun. For much of the day, traffic on the main roads crawls along at little more than walking speed, or grinds to a halt in endless jams at road junctions. On the plus side, it might take forever to ride across town on a dusty red double-decker **bus**, but it will never set you back more than a few rupees. Local **trains** get there faster, but are a real endurance test even outside rush hours. **Rickshaws** do not run downtown. A less stressful way of seeing the historical and cultural highlights of the city is on a **walking tour** (Sun); contact the Bombay Heritage Walks Society (☎022/834 4622).

Buses

BEST (Bombay Electric Supply and Transport; 24hr information line ☎022/414 3611) operates a **bus** network of labyrinthine complexity, extending to the furthest-flung corners of the city. Unfortunately, neither route booklets, maps nor "Point to Point" guides (which you can consult at the tourist office or at newsstands) make things any clearer. Finding out which bus you need is difficult enough. Recognizing it in the street can be even more prob

Tours

Of MTDC's sightseeing tours around Mumbai, the "City" tour (Tues–Sun 2–6pm; Rs75) is the most popular, managing to cram Colaba, Marine Drive, the Hanging Gardens, Kamla Nehru Park and Mani Bhavan into half a day; the "Suburban" tour (Tues–Sun 9.15am–6.15pm; Rs120) takes in Kanheri caves, Krishnagiri Upavan National Park, a lion safari and Juhu in a full day. MTDC also run an hour-long evening tour of the illuminated sights on an open-top bus, departing daily at 7pm and 8.30pm (Rs70 upper-deck, Rs20 lower-deck). Tickets should be booked in advance from the MTDC office (see p.101) at Nariman Point (the main departure area).

lematic, as the numbers are written in Maharathi (although in English on the sides). Aim, wherever possible, for the "Limited" services, which stop less frequently, and avoid rush hours at all costs. Tickets should be bought from the conductor on the bus.

Useful bus routes

#1/3/6(Ltd)/11(Ltd)/103/124 Colaba bus station to Mahatma Phule (Crawford) Market, via VT (Nagar Chowk)

#43 Colaba bus station to GPO

#70 Colaba to Dadar Station (W), via Mumbai Central

#106/107 Colaba to Kamala Nehru Park, via Chowpatty Beach

#124 Colaba to Vatsalabai Desai Chowk, via Mumbai Central

#132 Colaba to Breach Candy, via Vatsalabai Desai Chowk

#81 Churchgate to Santa Cruz, via Vatsalabai Desai Chowk (for Haji Ali's tomb and Mahalakshmi temple)

#66 VT to Mumbai Central

#91(Ltd) Mumbai Central to Kurla station

Trains

Mumbai would be paralyzed without its local **trains**, which carry millions of commuters each day between downtown and the sprawling suburbs in the north. One line begins at VT, running up the east side of the city as far as Thane. The other leaves Churchgate, hugging the curve of Back Bay as far as Chowpatty Beach, where it veers north towards Mumbai Central, Dadar, Santa Cruz and Vasai, beyond the city limits. Services depart every few minutes from 5am until midnight, stopping at dozens of small stations. Carriages remain packed solid virtually the whole time, with passengers dangling precariously out of open doors to escape the crush, so start to make your way to the exit at least three stops before your destination. The apocalyptic peak hours are worst of all. Women are marginally better off in the "ladies carriages"; look for the crowd of saris and *salwar kamises* grouped at the end of the platform.

Taxis

With rickshaws banished to the suburbs, Mumbai's ubiquitous black-and-yellow **taxis** are the quickest and most convenient way to nip around the city centre. In theory, all should have meters and a current rate card (to convert the amount shown on the meter to the correct fare); in practice, particularly at night or early in the morning, many drivers refuse to use them. If this happens, either flag down another or haggle out a fare. As a rule of thumb, expect to be charged Rs5 per kilometre after the minimum fare of around Rs13, together with a small sum for heavy luggage (Rs5 per article). The latest addition to Mumbai's hectic roads is the **cool cab**, a blue taxi that boasts air-conditioning, and charges higher rates for the privilege.

Boats

Ferry-boats regularly chug out of Mumbai harbour, connecting the city with the far shore and some of the larger islands in between. The most popular with visitors is the **Elephanta Island** launch (see p.123) which departs from the Gateway of India. Boats to **Mandve** (9 daily; 6.30am–6.15pm; 90min; Rs40), for Alibag, the transport hub for the rarely used **coastal route south**, leave from the Gateway of India.

Car rental

Cars with drivers can be rented per eight-hour day (Rs800–1000 for a non-a/c Ambassador, upwards of Rs1200 for more luxurious a/c cars), or per kilometre, from ITDC. They have an (occasionally) staffed counter at the Government of India tourist office and on the eleventh floor of the Nirmal Building at Nariman Point. Otherwise, go through any good travel agent (see p.137). Ramniranjan Kedia Tours and Travels (℡022/437 1112) are recommended if you want to book a vehicle on arrival at Sahar international airport.

Self-drive is also now available in Mumbai, though the service seems to be intended more for middle-class Indians out to impress their friends ("They'll never know it's rented!") than tourists. You will be a lot safer if you leave the driving to someone more at home with the city's racetrack rules of the road. If you are willing to risk it, Autoriders International Ltd (in association with Hertz) at 139 Auto World, Tardeo Road (℡022/496 1714, ℻492 1172), or Avis (℡022/285 7327, ⓦ www.avis.co.in) in the *Oberoi* are recommended.

Accommodation

Even though Mumbai offers all kinds of **accommodation**, finding a room at the right price when you arrive can be a real problem. Budget travellers, in particular, can expect a hard time: standards at the bottom of the range are grim and room rates exorbitant. A windowless cell with wood-partition walls and no running water costs Rs300 and above, while a comfortable room in the centre of town, with an attached toilet and shower, and a window, will set you back the best part of Rs1000. The best of the relatively inexpensive places tend to fill up by noon, which can often mean a long trudge in the heat with only an overpriced fleapit at the end of it, so you should really phone ahead as soon as (or preferably well before) you arrive. Prices in upmarket places are further inflated by the state-imposed "**luxury tax**" (between four and thirty percent depending on how expensive the room is), and "**service charges**" levied by the hotel itself; such charges are included in the price symbols shown below.

Colaba, down in the far, southern end of the city, has dozens of possibilities in each price range and is where the majority of foreign visitors head first. A short way across the city centre, **Marine Drive**'s accommodation is generally a little more expensive, but more salubrious, with Back Bay and the promenade right on the doorstep. If you're arriving by train and plan to make a quick getaway, a room closer to **VT** station is worth considering. Alternatively, **Juhu**, way to the north near the airports, boasts a string of flashy four- and five-stars, with a handful of less expensive places behind the beach. For those who just want to crawl off the plane and straight into bed, plenty of options can be found in the suburbs around **Sahar** and **Santa Cruz** airports, a short taxi ride from the main terminal buildings.

Finally, if you would like to **stay with an Indian family**, ask at the government tourist office in Churchgate, or at their information counters in Sahar

Accommodation price codes

All accommodation prices in this book have been categorized using the price codes below. Prices given are for a double room, and all taxes are included. For more details, see p.46.

① up to Rs100	④ Rs300–400	⑦ Rs900–1500
② Rs100–200	⑤ Rs400–600	⑧ Rs1500–2500
③ Rs200–300	⑥ Rs600–900	⑨ Rs2500 and upwards

and Santa Cruz (see p.101) about the popular "paying guest" scheme. Bed and breakfast-style accommodation in family homes, vetted by the tourist office, is available throughout the city at rates ranging from Rs500–1200.

Colaba

A short ride from the city's main commercial districts, railway stations and tourist office, **Colaba** makes a handy base. It also offers more in the way of food and entertainment than neighbouring districts, especially along its busy main thoroughfare, "**Colaba Causeway**" (Shahid Bhagat Singh – SBS – Marg). The streets immediately south and west of the Gateway of India are chock-full of accommodation, ranging from grungy guesthouses to India's most famous five-star hotel, the *Taj Mahal Intercontinental*. Avoid at all costs the nameless lodges lurking on the top storeys of wooden-fronted houses along **Arthur Bunder Road** – the haunts of not-so-oil-rich Gulf Arabs and touts who depend on commission from these rock-bottom hostels to finance their heroin habits. If, like many, you find all this sleaze a turn-off, Colaba's quieter, leafier backstreets harbour plenty of respectable mid-range hotels.

The hotels below are marked on the **map** of Colaba on p.109.

Aga Bheg's & Hotel Kishan, ground & 2nd Floor, Shirin Manzil, Walton Road ℡ 022/284 2227 or 283 8386. *Aga Bheg's* has lurid pink walls and little wooden blue beds, though it's clean, cool, and with a thankfully quiet and relaxed atmosphere. *Hotel Kishan*'s more tasteful a/c rooms are incredibly good value. ⑤ –⑥

Ascot, 38 Garden Rd ℡ 022/284 0020, ℻ 204 6449, ℮ ascothotel@vsnl.com. One of Mumbai's oldest hotels. Comfortable, spacious rooms, with cable TV and room service. ⑧

Diplomat, 24–26 PK Boman Behram Marg ℡ 022/202 1661, ℻ 283 0000, ℮ diplomat@bom3.vsnl.net.in. Hemmed in by the *Taj* across the road and in need of a face-lift, but the rooms are pleasant. ⑧ –⑨

Fariyas, 35 Arthur Rd ℡ 022/204 2911, ℻ 283 4492, ⓦ www.fariyas.com. Next on the scale down from the *Taj*. Relaxing roof garden, luxurious decor with themed suites, pool, health club, business centre, central a/c and all the trimmings. The *Tavern* pub is very popular with trendy Bombayites. Rates in dollars only. ⑨

Goodwin, Jasmine Building, Garden Road ℡ 022/287 2050, ℻ 287 1592, ℮ services@vsnl.com. Top class three-star with restaurant, bar and 24hr room service. The *Garden* (℡ 022/283 1330, ℻ 204 4290), next door, is similar but slightly inferior. Both ⑥

Gulf, 4/36 Kamal Mansion, Arthur Bunder Road ℡ 022/285 6672, ℻ 283 2694, ℮ gulfhotel @hotmail.com. Seedy neighbourhood, but respectable and elegantly decorated, with clean, modern rooms. ⑧

Harbour View, 3rd and 4th Floors, 25 PJ Ramchandani Marg ℡ 022/282 1089, ℻ 284 3020, ℮ parkview@bom3.vsnl.net.in. Decent hotel tucked away above the Strand cinema, boasting comfortable, modern standard rooms and slightly more expensive (and larger) sea-facing ones. All rooms a/c. ⑧ –⑨

Lawrence, 3rd Floor, 33 Rope Walk Lane, off K Dubash Marg, opposite Jehangir Art Gallery ℡ 022/284 3618. Mumbai's best-value cheap hotel if you don't mind the great hike up the stairs. Six immaculate double rooms (one single) with fans, and not-so-clean shared shower-toilet. Breakfast included in the price. Best to book in advance. ④ –⑤

Prosser's, 2–4 Henry Rd ℡ 022/283 4937. Noisy, with mostly wood-partitioned rooms that are clean and air-cooled. ④ –⑥

Regency, 18 Lansdowne House, Mahakari Bhusan Marg, behind the Regal cinema ℡ 022/202 0292, ℻ 287 3375. Well-appointed rooms (though bathrooms need redoing) and cheaper attic garrets with character. ⑦

Regent, 8 Best Rd ℡ 022/287 1854, ℻ 202 0363, ℮ hotelregent@vsnl.com. Luxurious, international-standard hotel on small scale, with all mod cons but smallish rooms. ⑨

Salvation Army, Red Shield House, 30 Mereweather Rd, near the *Taj* ℡ 022/284 1824. Rock-bottom bunk beds in cramped, stuffy dorms (lockers available), large good-value doubles (some a/c), and a sociable travellers' scene. Cheap canteen food. Priority given to women, but your stay is limited to one week or less. ① –⑤

Sea Shore, 4th Floor, 1-49 Kamal Mansion, Arthur Bunder Road ℡ 022/287 4237. Among the best budget deals in Colaba. The sea-facing rooms with windows are much better than the airless cells on the other side. Friendly management and free, safe baggage store. Common baths only, though some rooms have a/c. If it's full you can always try the wooden partitioned rooms at the seedy *India* (☎022/283 3769; ④–⑤) or the grubby but bearable ones at the *Sea Lord* (☎022/284 5392; ④–⑤) in the same building. ⑤–⑦

Shelley's, 30 PJ Ramchandani Marg ☎022/284 0229, ☞284 0385, ⓦwww.shellyshotel.com. Charmingly old-fashioned hotel in the colonial mould despite renovations to the rooms. Pukka dining hall and pricier rooms with sea views. ⑦–⑧

Taj Mahal Intercontinental, PJ Ramchandani Marg ☎022/202 3366, ☞287 2711, ⓦwww.tajhotels.com. The stately home among India's top hotels, and the haunt of Mumbai's *beau monde*. Opulent suites in an old wing or a modern skyscraper, plus shopping arcades, outdoor pool, swish bars and restaurants. Starts at $290. ⑨

Whalleys', Jaiji Mansion, 41 Mereweather Rd ☎022/282 1802. Well-established, popular hotel in a rambling colonial building, with 27 rooms (of varying sizes), shared or attached shower-toilets, pleasant verandah and some a/c. Reasonable value with breakfast included. ⑦

YWCA, 18 Madam Cama Rd ☎022/202 5053, ☞202 0445, ⓔywcaic@bom8.vsnl.net.in. Relaxing, secure and quiet hostel with spotless dorms, doubles or family rooms. Rate includes membership, breakfast and filling buffet dinner. Dorm beds also available (Rs650). One month's advance booking (by money order) advisable. ⑦

Marine Drive and Nariman Point

At the western edge of the downtown area, Netaji Subhash Chandra Marg, or **Marine Drive**, sweeps from the skyscrapers of Nariman Point in the south to Chowpatty Beach in the north. Along the way, four- and five-star hotels take advantage of the panoramic views over Back Bay and the easy access to the city's commercial heart, while a couple of inexpensive guesthouses are worth trying if Colaba's cheap lodges don't appeal. Compared with Colaba, Marine Drive, and the arterial **VN Road** that connects it with Churchgate, are more open and relaxed. Families and office cronies plod along the promenade in the evening, approached more often by *gram*- and balloon-wallahs than junkies and money-changers.

The hotels below are marked on the **map** on p.109, apart from the *Oberoi*, which is marked on p.95.

Ambassador, VN Road ☎022/204 1131, ☞204 0004, ⓔambassador@vsnl.com. Luxurious four-star with excellent views from upper front-side rooms and a revolving Thai/Chinese rooftop restaurant. Dollars only. ⑨

Bentley, 3rd Floor, Krishna Mahal, Marine Drive ☎022/281 1787. Run-down hotel on the corner of D Road. No lift, no a/c, no attached bathrooms and no frills (except windows), but clean rooms, some of which have sea-facing balconies – at a price. 24hr checkout, and breakfast included. ⑤

Chateau Windsor, 5th Floor, 86 VN Rd ☎022/204 4455, ☞202 6459, ⓔinfo@chateauwindsor.com. Spotless single, double or group rooms (some on the small side), shared or attached bathrooms and optional a/c. It's very popular, so reservations are recommended. ⑦–⑧

Marine Plaza, 29 Marine Drive ☎022/285 1212, ☞282 8585, ⓦwww.sarovarparkplaza.com. Glitzy pad on the seafront, with every luxury mod con, glass-bottomed swimming pool, health club, Chinese restaurant, pub and 24hr coffee-shop. ⑨

Norman's, 127 Marine Drive ☎022/281 4234, ☞281 3362. Small, moderately priced ground-floor guesthouse, with neat, clean rooms, some attached shower-toilets and a/c. ⑦–⑧

Oberoi, Nariman Point ☎022/232 5757, ☞204 3282, ⓦwww.oberoihotels.com. The *Taj*'s main competitor – India's most expensive hotel – is glitteringly opulent, with a pool, a Polynesian restaurant and your own personal butler. Rates start at $320. ⑨

Around Victoria (Chatrapathi Shivaji) Terminus

Arriving in Mumbai at **VT** after a long train journey, you may not feel like embarking on a room-hunt around Colaba. Unfortunately, the area around the station and the nearby GPO, though fairly central, has little to recommend it. The majority of places worth trying are mid-range hotels grouped around the crossroads of P D'Mello (Frere) Road, St George's Road and Shahid Bhagat Singh (SBS) Marg, immediately southeast of the post office (5min on foot from the station). VT itself also has **retiring rooms** (Rs150), although these are booked up by noon.

The hotels below are marked on the **map** on p.112.

City Palace, 121 City Terrace ☏ 022/261 5515, ℱ 267 6897. Large and popular hotel bang opposite the station. "Ordinary" rooms are tiny and windowless, but have a/c, are perfectly clean and proudly sport "electronic push button telephone instruments". ❼

Grand, 17 Sprott Rd, Ballard Estate ☏ 022/269 8211, ℱ 262 6581, ☒ www.grandhotelbombay.com. Solid and very comfortable with a faintly 1930s feel. Central a/c, restaurant and 24hr foreign exchange. ❽

Lord's, 301 Adi Mazban Path, Mangalore Street ☏ 022/261 8310. Above *City Kitchen* restaurant, this is a drab, but reasonably clean and cheap for the area. Mostly shared bathrooms. –❸ –❹

Manama, opposite George Hospital, 221/225 P D'Mello Rd ☏ 022/261 3412, ℱ 261 3860. Very friendly, clean, popular budget option with run-of-the-mill rooms, some a/c. Currently being renovated. Book ahead. ❻

Prince, 34 Walchand Hirachand Rd, near Red Gate ☏ 022/261 2809, ℱ 265 8049. The best all-round economy deal in this area: modest, neat and respectable. Avoid the airless partition-rooms upstairs. ❻

Railway, 249 P D'Mello Rd ☏ 022/261 6705, ℱ 265 8049. Spacious, clean and friendly, and the pick of the mid-range bunch around VT, though correspondingly pricey. ❼ –❽

Ship, 3rd Floor, 219 P D'Mello Rd ☏ 022/261 7613. The cheapest option near VT, with cavernous, crowded dorms (including one for women) and tiny partitioned rooms which are incredibly claustrophobic unless you get one with a window – though they do come with TV. Dorm beds (Rs130) come with in-built locker underneath. ❸

Juhu Beach

Since the early 1970s, a crop of exclusive **resort hotels** has been creeping steadily down the road that runs behind **Juhu Beach**, twenty minutes' drive from Santa Cruz airport. Most offer the predictable hermetically sealed five-star package, with bars, restaurants and a pool to lounge beside. It's hard to believe that anyone would come to India expressly for this sort of thing, but if money's no object and you want to keep well away from all the hustle, bustle and poverty, you'll be spoiled for choice. **Vile Parle** (pronounced *Vee*lay *Par*lay) is the nearest suburban railway station to Juhu. Both the hotels below lay on courtesy buses from the airports.

Centaur Juhu Beach, Juhu Tara Road ☏ 022/611 3040, ℱ 611 6343, ☒ www.centaurhotel.com. Gigantic five-star with a palatial foyer, sea views, pool and various speciality restaurants. ❾

Holiday Inn, Balraj Sahani Marg ☏ 022/670 4444, ℱ 620 4452, ☒ www.holidayinnbombay.com. Overlooking the beach, this revamped five-star boasts two pools, terrace garden, shops, bars and formula furnishings. Dollars only. ❾

Around the airports

Hotels near Sahar and Santa Cruz **airports** cater predominantly for transit passengers and flight crews, at premium rates. If you arrive in Mumbai at an inconvenient hour when most of the hotels in the city proper are closed or full, you may want to arrange less expensive accommodation in the nearby suburbs of **Santa Cruz**, **Vile Parle** or **Andheri**. Bookings can be made through the accommodation desk in the arrivals concourse at Sahar, or by phone. Nearly all the hotels below have courtesy buses to and from the terminal building.

Airport Palace, Vakola Bridge, Bull's Royce Colony Road ☏ 022/614 0057. Small, airless non-a/c rooms, but all with fresh bed linen and lockable doors. ❺

Air View, 12th Nehru Road, Santa Cruz East ☏ 022/612 0060. Quiet hotel near rail and bus stations. Clean rooms with either fan or a/c. ❺ –❻

Ashwin, near Marol Fire Station, Andheri Kurla Road, Andheri East ☏ 022/836 7267, ℱ 836 7258. One of several medium-sized, international-standard hotels right outside Sahar. Rooms are comfortably deluxe and there's a good multi-cuisine restaurant. ⑥

Centaur, Western Express Highway, Santa Cruz ☏022/615 6660, ⓕ611 6535, ⓔcentaur .airport@vsnl.com. Circular building directly outside the domestic airport, with five stars, three restaurants, two bars and one pool. ⑨

Kamat's Plaza, 70-C Nehru Rd, Vile Parle ☏022/612 3390, ⓕ612 5974. Plush four-star with a swimming pool. ⑧–⑨

Kumaria Presidency, Andheri Kurla ☏022/835 2601, ⓕ837 3850, Facing the international airport. One of a string of three-stars bookable through the accommodation desk in the airport arrivals hall. ⑥

Leela, Sahar ☏022/691 1234, ⓕ691 1455, ⓦwww.theleela.com. Ultra-luxurious, the best in the area in fact, with an art gallery, four restaurants, a nightclub and amazing sports facilities. Dollars only. ⑨

Samrat, 3rd Road, Khar, Santa Cruz East, near Khar railway station ☏022/648 5441, ⓕ649 3501. Another comfortable transit hotel in a quiet suburban backstreet. No courtesy bus. ⑥–⑧

Shangri-La, Nanda Parker Road, Ville Parle East ☏022/612 8983. Cheerful budget hotel near the domestic airport with lots of clean and basic a/c and non-a/c rooms, some refurbished. Good Chinese restaurant tacked alongside. ④–⑤

The City

Between the airports to the north and the southern tip of Mumbai lies a thirty-kilometre, seething mass of streets, suburbs and relentless traffic. Even during the relatively cool winter months, exploring it can be hard work, requiring plenty of pit stops at cold-drink stalls along the way. The best place to start is down at the far south end of the peninsula in **Colaba**, home to most of the hotels, restaurants and best-known sights, including the **Gateway of India**. Fifteen minutes' walk north takes you past the **Prince of Wales Museum** to the **Fort** area, home of all the banks and big stores, plus the cream of Mumbai's ostentatious Raj-era buildings. The extravagant Victoria Terminus (Chatrapathi Shivaji Terminus) overlooks its northern limits, close to the impressive onion-dome of the **GPO**. The hub of the suburban train network, **Churchgate station**, stands 4km west, across the big maidans that scythe through the centre of town. Churchgate, and the **tourist office**, is a stone's throw from the sweeping curve of Back Bay. With **Nariman Point**'s skyscrapers at one end, lively **Chowpatty Beach** and the affluent apartment blocks of **Malabar Hill** at the other, the Bay is Mumbai at its snazziest. But the area immediately north and east is ramshackle and densely populated. The **central bazaars** extend from **Crawford Market**, beyond VT station, right up to **J Boman (JB) Behram Marg**, opposite the other mainline railway station, **Mumbai Central**.

Colaba

At the end of the seventeenth century, **Colaba** was little more than the last in a straggling line of rocky islands extending to the lighthouse that stood on Mumbai's southernmost point. Today, the original outlines of the promontory (whose name derives from the Koli who first lived here) have been submerged under a mass of dilapidated colonial tenements, hotels, bars, restaurants and handicraft shops. If you never venture beyond the district, you'll get a very distorted picture of Mumbai. In spite of being the main tourist enclave and a trendy hang-out for the city's rich young things, Colaba has retained the distinctly sleazy feel of the bustling port it used to be, with dodgy money-changers, dealers and pimps hissing at passers-by from doorways.

The Gateway of India

Mumbai's most famous landmark, the **Gateway of India**, was built in 1924 by George Wittet, responsible for many of the city's grandest constructions.

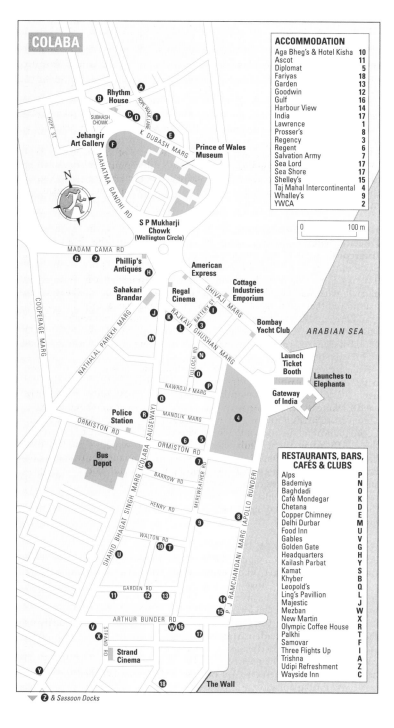

COLABA

Rhythm House

SUBHASH CHOWK

Jehangir Art Gallery

Prince of Wales Museum

HOPE ST

ROPE WALK LANE

K DUBASH MARG

MAHATMA GANDHI RD

N

S P Mukharji Chowk
(Wellington Circle)

MADAM CAMA RD

Phillip's Antiques

American Express

Cottage Industries Emporium

Sahakari Brandar

Regal Cinema

SHIVAJI MARG

Bombay Yacht Club

ARABIAN SEA

COOPERAGE MARG

NATHALAL PAREKH MARG

RAJKAVI GHUSHAN MARG

BATTERY ST

TULLOCH RD

NAWROJI F MARG

Launch Ticket Booth

Launches to Elephanta

Gateway of India

Police Station

MANDLIK MARG

ORMISTON RD

ORMISTON RD

Bus Depot

BARROW RD

SHAHID BHAGAT SINGH MARG (COLABA CAUSEWAY)

MEREWEATHER RD

P J RAMCHANDANI MARG (APOLLO BUNDER)

HENRY RD

WALTON RD

GARDEN RD

ARTHUR BUNDER RD

STRAND RD

Strand Cinema

The Wall

2 & Sassoon Docks

ACCOMMODATION

Aga Bheg's & Hotel Kisha	10
Ascot	11
Diplomat	5
Fariyas	18
Garden	13
Goodwin	12
Gulf	16
Harbour View	14
India	17
Lawrence	1
Prosser's	8
Regency	3
Regent	6
Salvation Army	7
Sea Lord	17
Sea Shore	17
Shelley's	15
Taj Mahal Intercontinental	4
Whalley's	9
YWCA	2

0	100 m

RESTAURANTS, BARS, CAFÉS & CLUBS

Alps	P
Bademiya	N
Baghdadi	O
Café Mondegar	K
Chetana	D
Copper Chimney	E
Delhi Durbar	M
Food Inn	U
Gables	V
Golden Gate	G
Headquarters	H
Kailash Parbat	Y
Kamat	S
Khyber	B
Leopold's	Q
Ling's Pavillion	L
Majestic	J
Mezban	W
New Martin	X
Olympic Coffee House	R
Palkhi	T
Samovar	F
Three Flights Up	I
Trishna	A
Udipi Refreshment	Z
Wayside Inn	C

Commemorating the visit of King George V and Queen Mary in 1911, India's own honey-coloured Arc de Triomphe was originally envisaged as a ceremonial disembarkation point for passengers alighting from the P&O steamers. Ironically, today it is more often remembered as the place the British chose to stage their final departure from the country – on February 28, 1948, the last detachment of troops remaining on Indian soil set sail from here. Nowadays, the only boats bobbing about at the bottom of its stone staircase are the launches that ferry tourists across the harbour to Elephanta Island (see p.123).

The spruced-up square surrounding the Gateway is a popular place for a stroll during the evenings. At one end, an equestrian statue of **Shivaji**, the Maratha military adventurer who dogged the last years of the Moghul emperor Aurangzeb in the second half of the seventeenth century, looks sternly on. Shivaji has been appropriated as a nationalist symbol (the prototypical "Son of the Soil") by the extreme right-wing Shiv Sena, which explains the garland of marigolds often draped around the statue's neck as a sign of respect.

Behind the Gateway

Directly behind the Gateway, the older hotel in the **Taj Mahal Intercontinental Hotel** complex (see p.106) stands as a monument to local pride in the face of colonial oppression. Its patron, the Parsi industrialist J.N. Tata, is said to have built the old Taj as an act of revenge after he was refused entry to what was then the best hotel in town, the "whites only" Watson's. The ban proved their undoing. Watson's disappeared long ago, but the Taj, with its grand grey and white stone facade and red-domed roof, still presides imperiously over the seafront, the preserve of visiting diplomats, sheikhs and Mumbai's jet-set. Lesser mortals are allowed in to sample the opulent tea shops and restaurants.

From the Taj, you can head down the promenade, PJ Ramchandani Marg, better known as **Apollo Bunder** (nothing to do with the Greek sun god; the name is a colonial corruption of the Koli words for a local fish, *palav*, and quay, *bunda*), taking in the sea breezes and views over the busy harbour. Alternatively, Shivaji Marg heads northwest towards **Wellington Circle** (SPM Chowk), the hectic roundabout in front of the Regal cinema. The latter route takes you past the old **Bombay Yacht Club**, another idiosyncratic vestige of the Raj. Very little seems to have changed here since its smoky common rooms were a bolt hole for the city's *burra-sahibs*. Dusty sporting trophies and models of clippers and dhows stand in glass cases lining its corridors, polished from time to time by bearers in cotton tunics. If you want to look around, seek permission from the club secretary; accommodation is available only to members and their guests.

Southwards along Colaba Causeway

To walk from Wellington Circle to the south of the peninsula, you have first to run the gauntlet of street-vendors and hustlers who crowd the claustrophobic pavements of **Colaba Causeway** (this stretch of Shahid Bhagat Singh Marg). It's hard to believe that such a chaotic city thoroughfare, with its hole-in-the-wall cafés, clothes stores and incense stalls, was reclaimed from the sea.

On the corner of the Colaba Causeway and Arthur Bunder Road you'll find the **Shree Bhid Mahadeo Mandir**, a Shiva temple built in 1923 round a sacred tree. It's a tiny place plastered with many different gods, with a small but colourful Shiva shrine by the tree; one of the Brahmins speaks English and will happily answer any questions. You can also make a puja here and they won't hassle you for big donations – Rs10 is sufficient.

Turning left down **Arthur Bunder Road**, you'll pass many Muslim perfumeries, hotels and restaurants. At the end of the road is the *Voodoo Lounge*, which in previous incarnations (it's now a gay bar) played host to a number of Sixties bands including the Stones, Led Zeppelin and Pink Floyd. Taking a right past here you'll come out by a small sea-wall which is named **The Wall** in honour of Pink Floyd. It's a nice place at sunset, when locals and transients can be found chilling out, making it a good place to meet people. From here, a short walk south will bring you into the **fisherman's shanty town**; you can wander through this communally mixed area that demonstrates a religious tolerance that does credit to the city – it's not dangerous but remember it's a residential area so have your namastes (greetings) ready.

From here head east back onto Colaba Causeway and a five-minute walk will bring you to the wholesale seafood market at **Sassoon Docks**, a kilometre or so south of central Colaba, which provides an unexpected splash of rustic colour amid the drab urban surroundings. Koli fisherwomen, their cotton saris hitched dhoti-style, squat beside baskets of glistening pomfret, prawns and tuna, while coolies haul plastic crates of crushed ice over rickety gangplanks to the boats moored at the quay. The stench, as overpowering as the noise, comes mostly from bundles of dried fish that are sold in bulk. "**Bombay duck**", the salty local snack, has found its way to many a far shore, but you'll be hard pushed to find any in Colaba's own restaurants. **Photography** is strictly forbidden, as the market is close to a sensitive military area.

From the docks, hop on any bus heading south down Colaba Causeway (#3, #11, #47, #103, #123, or #125) to the **Afghan Memorial Church of St John the Baptist**, built (1847–54) as a memorial to the British victims of the First Afghan War. Hemmed in by the cantonment area, the pale yellow church, with its tall steeple and tower, would look more at home beside the playing fields of Eton than the sultry waters of the Arabian Sea. If the door is unlocked, take a peep at the marble plaques and stained glass windows inside.

Downtown Mumbai

Aldous Huxley famously described Mumbai as "one of the most appalling cities of either hemisphere", with its "lavatory bricks and Gothic spires". The critic Robert Byron, although a wholehearted fan of New Delhi, was equally unenthusiastic, feeling moved to refer to **downtown Mumbai** in 1931 as "that architectural Sodom", claiming that "the nineteenth century devised nothing lower than the municipal buildings of British India. Their ugliness is positive, daemonic." Today, however, the massive erections of Empire and Indian free enterprise appear not so much ugly, as intriguing.

Prince of Wales Museum (Chatrapati Shivaji Museum) and Jehangir Art Gallery

Set back from Mahatma Gandhi (MG) Road in an attractive garden is the unmissable **Prince of Wales Museum of Western India** (Tues–Sun 10.15am–6pm; Rs150, camera Rs15). This distinctive Raj-era building, crowned by a massive white Moghul-style dome, houses a superb collection of paintings and sculpture that you'll need several hours, or a couple of visits, to get the most out of. Its foundation stone was laid in 1905 by the future King George V, then Prince of Wales; the architect, George Wittet, went on to design the Gateway of India. The museum is undoubtedly the finest example of his work; the epitome of the hybrid **Indo-Saracenic** style, it is said to be an

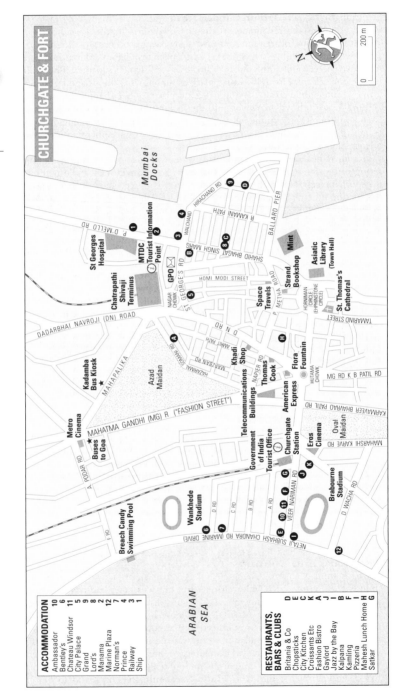

CHURCHGATE & FORT

ACCOMMODATION

Ambassador	10
Bentley's	6
Chateau Windsor	11
City Palace	5
Grand	9
Lord's	8
Manama	2
Marine Plaza	12
Norman's	7
Prince	4
Railway	3
Ship	1

RESTAURANTS, BARS & CLUBS

Britania & Co	D
Chopsticks	E
City Kitchen	C
Croissants Etc	K
Fashion Bistro	A
Gaylord	J
Jazz by the Bay	B
Kalpana	F
Kamling	I
Pizzeria	H
Mahesh Lunch Home	G
Satkar	

ARABIAN SEA

Mumbai Docks

"educated" interpretation of fifteenth- and sixteenth-century Gujarati architecture, mixing Islamic touches with typically English municipal brickwork.

The **central hall**, overlooked by a carved wooden balcony, provides a snapshot of the collection with a few choice Moghul paintings, jade work, weapons and miniature clay and terracotta figures from the Mauryan (third century BC) and Kushana (first to second century AD) periods. From Bengal (first century BC) are horrible-looking *yakshis* (godlings or sprites) devouring lizards. Sculpture galleries on either side of the hall open onto the front garden; the one to the right houses the museum's **natural history** section, which contains a large and well-kept – if somewhat unfashionable – collection of stuffed birds, fish and animals.

The main **sculpture room** on the **ground floor** displays some excellent fourth- and fifth-century heads and figures from the Buddhist state of Gandhara, a former colony of Alexander the Great (hence the Greek-style statues). Important Hindu sculptures include a seventh-century Chalukyan bas-relief from Aihole depicting Brahma seated on a lotus, and a sensuously carved torso of Mahisasuramaraini, the goddess Durga with tripod raised ready to skewer the demon buffalo. On the way up to the **first floor** a display on the astonishingly urban **Indus Valley Civilization** (3500–1500 BC) has models

Dabawallahs

Mumbai's size and inconvenient shape create all kind of hassles for its working population – not least having to stew for over four hours each day in slow municipal transport. One thing the daily tidal wave of commuters do not have to worry about, however, is finding an inexpensive and wholesome home-cooked lunch. In a city with a wallah for everything, it will find them. The members of the Mumbai Tiffin Box Suppliers Association, known colloquially, and with no little affection, as "dabawallahs", see to that. Every day, around 4000 *dabawallahs* deliver freshly cooked food from 125,000 suburban kitchens to offices in the downtown area. Each lunch is prepared early in the morning by a devoted wife or mother while her husband or son is enduring the crush on the train. She arranges the rice, dhal, *subzi*, curd and *parathas* into cylindrical aluminium trays, stacks them on top of one another and clips them together with a neat little handle. This tiffin box, not unlike a slim paint tin, is the lynchpin of the whole operation. When the runner calls to collect it in the morning, he uses a special colour code on the lid to tell him where the lunch has to go. At the end of his round, he carries all the boxes to the nearest railway station and hands them over to other *dabawallahs* for the trip into town. Between leaving the wife and reaching its final destination, the tiffin box will pass through at least half a dozen different pairs of hands, carried on heads, shoulder-poles, bicycle handlebars and in the brightly decorated handcarts that plough with such insouciance through the midday traffic. Tins are rarely, if ever, lost, and always find their way home again (before the husband returns from work) to be washed up for the next day's lunch.

To catch *dabawallahs* in action, head for VT or Churchgate stations around late morning time, when the tiffin boxes arrive in the city centre. The event is accompanied by a chorus of "lafka! lafka!" – "hurry! hurry!" – as the *dabawallahs*, recognizable in their white Nehru caps and baggy khaki shorts, rush to make their lunch-hour deadlines. Most collect about one rupee for each tin they handle, netting around Rs1000 per month in total. *Daba* lunches still work out a good deal cheaper than meals taken in the city restaurants, saving precious paise for the middle-income workers who use the system, and providing a livelihood for the legions of poorer immigrants from the Pune area who operate it.

of typical settlements, mysterious seal moulds in an as-yet-undeciphered script, and jewellery. The main attraction, though, has to be the superb collection of **Indian painting**, including illustrated manuscripts and erotic Gita Govinda paintings in the pre-Moghul Sultanate style. **Moghul schools** are well represented, too, with fine portraits and folios from the reign of Akbar (1556–1605), and sublime drawings of animals and birds from the Jehangir (1605–28) school. The well-known portrait of the emperor Shah Jahan (1628–57) and his forefathers is also on display.

Jade, porcelain and ivory can be seen on the **second floor**, along with a collection of **European art** that includes a minor Titian and a Constable. Among the weapon collection are the swords of emperors Shah Jahan and Aurangzeb, a shield of Akbar ornamented with the zodiac, and various daggers, maces and guns. The poorly lit **Indian textiles room** showcases brocaded saris, turbans, and antique Kashmiri shawls, intricately patterned with flowers, birds, animals and abstract designs.

Technically in the same compound as the Prince of Wales Museum, though approached from further up MG Road, the **Jehangir Art Gallery** (daily 11am–7pm; free) is Mumbai's best-known venue for contemporary art, with five small galleries specializing in twentieth-century arts and crafts from around the world. You never know what you're going to find – most exhibitions last only a week and exhibits are often for sale.

Around Oval Maidan

Karmaveer Bhaurao Patil Marg's southern edge holds a statue of Dr B.R. Ambedkar (1891–1956) who, though born into an outcast Hindu community, converted to Buddhism. A great number of "untouchables" followed suit; many are now part of a militant movement calling themselves dalits, "the oppressed", eschewing Gandhi's reconstructed name of Harijans, "god's people". Some of Mumbai's most important Victorian buildings line the eastern side of the vast green **Oval Maidan**, behind the statue, where impromptu cricket matches are held almost every day (foreign enthusiasts are welcome to take part, but should beware the maidan's demon bowlers and less-than-even pitches). Partially obscured by police huts, the dull yellow **Old Secretariat** now serves as the City Civil and Sessions Court. Indian civil servant G.W. Forrest described it in 1903 as "a massive pile whose main features have been brought from Venice, but all the beauty has vanished in transhipment". Inside, you can only imagine the originally highly polished interior, which no longer shines, but buzzes with activity. Lawyers in black gowns, striped trousers and white tabs bustle up and down the staircases, whose corners are emblazoned with expectorated paan juice, and offices with perforated swing-doors give glimpses of text-book images of Indian bureaucracy – peons at desks piled high with dusty be-ribboned document bundles.

Across A S D'Mello Road from the Old Secretariat, two major buildings belonging to **Mumbai University** (established 1857) were designed in England by Sir Gilbert Scott, who had already given the world the Gothic extravaganza of London's St Pancras railway station. Access through the main gates is monitored by caretakers who only allow you in if you say you're using the library. Funded by the Parsi philanthropist Cowasjee "Readymoney" Jehangir, the **Convocation Hall** greatly resembles a church. Above its entrance, a huge circular stained-glass window features a wheel with spokes of Greek pilasters that separate signs of the zodiac. The library (daily 10am–10pm) is beneath the 79.2-metre-high **Rajabhai clock tower** which is said to be modelled on Giotto's campanile in Florence. Until 1931, it chimed tunes such as *Rule Britannia* and *Home Sweet Home*. It's worth applying for a visitor's ticket to the library (Rs5 a day, Rs10 for three days) just to see the interior. The magnificent vaulted wooden ceiling of the reading room, high Gothic windows and stained glass still evoke a reverential approach to learning.

Hutatma Chowk (Flora Fountain)

A busy five-point intersection in the heart of the Fort area, the roundabout formerly known as **Flora Fountain** has been renamed **Hutatma Chowk** ("Martyr's Square") to commemorate the freedom fighters who died to establish the state of Maharashtra in the Indian Union. The chowk centres on a statue of the Roman goddess **Flora**, erected in 1869 to commemorate Sir Bartle Frere. It's hard to see quite why they bothered – the Raj architecture expert, Philip Davies, was not being unkind when he said "The fountain was designed by a committee, and it shows."

Facing Hutatma Chowk is a **statue of Dadabhai Naoroji** (1812–1917) showing the first Indian member of the British parliament (1892–95). You may want to tarry here a while to consult Machindra Govind Pawar, who for years has sat next to the statue daily (except Sunday) between 8am and 8pm. Signs explain his business, offering cures for "rheumatism, hair falling, piles, fistula and sex weakness". Sri Pawar, who hails from Pune, says he is a practitioner of *Ayurved*, and operates on a basis that sounds like commercial suicide: he accepts no payment until his patients are cured.

Horniman Circle and the Town Hall

Horniman Circle, formerly Elphinstone Circle, is named after a pro-Independence newspaper editor. It was conceived in 1860 as a centrepiece of a newly planned Bombay by the then Municipal Commissioner, Charles Forjett, on the site of Bombay "Green". Forjett, a Eurasian, had something of a peculiar reputation; he was fond of disguising himself in "native" dress and prowling about certain districts of the city to listen out for seditious talk. In 1857, at the time of the First War of Independence (as it is now known by Indians; the British call it the Indian Mutiny), Forjett fired two suspected revolutionaries from a cannon on the Esplanade (roughly the site of the modern maidans).

It is often said that the design of Horniman Circle was based on Tunbridge Wells or Leamington Spa in England, with elegant Neoclassical buildings centring on a garden with a fountain. East of the square, the impressive Doric **Town Hall** on SBS Marg houses the vast collection of the **Asiatic Library** (see p.137).

St Thomas' Cathedral

The small, simple **St Thomas' Cathedral** (daily 6.30am–6pm), on Tamarind Street, is reckoned to be the oldest English building in Mumbai, blending Classical and Gothic styles. Governor Aungier self-righteously envisaged it with "the main design of inviting the natives to repair thereunto, and observe the gravity and purity of our own devotions". After his death, the project was abandoned; the walls stood 5m high for forty-odd years until enthusiasm was rekindled by Richard Cobbe, a chaplain to the East India Company, in the second decade of the eighteenth century. He believed the church's unfinished walls represented "a mark of derision for the natives for whose conversion they were partly raised [and] a reproach and a scandal to the English in Bombay". It was finally opened on Christmas Day 1718, complete with the essential "cannon-ball-proof roof". In those days, the seating was divided into useful sections for those who should know their place, including one for "Inferior Women".

St Thomas' whitewashed and polished brass-and-wood interior looks much the same as when the staff of the East India Company worshipped here in the eighteenth century. Lining the walls are memorial tablets to English parishioners, many of whom died young, either from disease or in battle.

Marine Drive and Chowpatty Beach

Netaji Subhash Chandra Marg, better known as **Marine Drive**, is Mumbai's seaside prom, an eight-lane highway with a wide pavement built in the 1920s on reclaimed land. Sweeping in an arc from the skyscrapers at Nariman Point in the south, Marine Drive ends at the foot of Malabar Hill and the old Chowpatty Beach. The whole stretch is a favourite place for a stroll; the promenade next to the sea has uninterrupted views virtually the whole way along, while the apartment blocks on the land side – most of which are ugly, unpainted concrete and called something-or-other Mahal – are some of the most desirable and expensive addresses in the city.

It's a great place for people-watching. Early in the morning yuppies in shorts speed-walk or jog before breakfast while street kids, mothers and babies and limbless beggars take up position at the traffic lights at major junctions to petition drivers and passengers for a rupee. Those one rung further up the social ladder have something to sell: twisted fun balloons or a newspaper. Some kids perfunctorily wipe a rag over the bodywork and do their best to wrest a few coins from momentarily captive people, ninety percent of whom stare resolutely ahead.

Evening sees servants walking their bosses' Pekinese or poodles, and children playing under the supervision of their *ayahs* (nannies). Sometime after 6pm the place magically transforms; the British called it the "Queen's Necklace". The massive red sun disappears into the sea, street lights snap on, five-star hotels glow and neon lights blink. Innumerable couples materialize to take romantic strolls down to the beach, stopping on the way to buy from a peanut vendor or to pay off a *hijra* or eunuch, threatening to lift up his sari and reveal all.

Just beyond the huge flyover, B Bridge, are a series of cricket pitches known as **gymkhanas**, where there's a good chance of catching a match any day of the week. A number are exclusive to particular religious communities. The first doubles as a swanky outdoor wedding venue for Parsi marriages; others include the Catholic, Islamic and Hindu pitches, the last of which has a classic colonial-style pavilion.

Chowpatty Beach

Chowpatty Beach is a Mumbai institution, which really comes to life at night and on Saturday. People do not come here to swim (the sea is foul) but to wander, sit on the beach, let the kids ride a pony or a rusty Ferris wheel, have a massage, get ears cleaned or hair cut, listen to musicians, buy drugs, have a go on a rifle range, consult an astrologer, watch dreadlocked ascetics perform public austerities, get conned, and picnic on *bhel puri* and cups of kulfi. Gupta Bhelwallas's *bhel puri* stall satisfied the discerning Mumbai palate with a secret concoction of the sunset snack for over a century; unfortunately, at the time of writing all the *bhel puri* wallahs had been evicted from the beach in an attempt to clean the place up, but since they are a well-loved part of the scene it's hoped they will be relocated nearby soon. There are also plenty of good ice-cream

bars and restaurants across Marine Drive, opposite the beach (see p.130), where you'll find Wagh's Fine Art Studio, whose curious collection of plaster figures in the window includes a much larger than life Gandhi plus Alsatian dog.

Once a year in September the **Ganesh Chathurthi** festival (see p.98) draws gigantic crowds to participate in the immersion of idols, both huge and small, of the elephant-headed god Ganesh.

Just west of Chowpatty Beach is the **Breach Candy swimming pool**, where membership is strictly restricted to the upper echelons of society. However, tourists are allowed to join for the day (Rs200), and use both the British-style indoor pool and the India-shaped outdoor pool. The complex overlooks the beach, with relaxing sun loungers and a good restaurant.

Mani Bhavan Mahatma Gandhi Museum

Mani Bhavan, 19 Laburnum Rd (daily 9.30am–6pm), was Gandhi's Bombay base between 1917 and 1934. Set in a leafy upper-middle-class road, the house is now a permanent memorial to the Mahatma with an extensive research library. Within the lovingly maintained polished wood interior, the walls are covered with photos of historic events and artefacts from the man's extraordinary life – the most disarming of which is a friendly letter to Hitler suggesting world peace. Gandhi's predictably simple sitting-cum-bedroom is preserved behind glass. Laburnum Road is a few streets along from the Bharatiya Vidya Bhavan music venue on KM Munshi Marg – if coming by taxi ask for the nearby Gamdevi Police Station.

Malabar Hill

Malabar Hill, the long, steep-sided promontory enfolding Chowpatty Beach at the north end of Back Bay, is Mumbai's ritziest neighbourhood. Since the eighteenth century, its lush forests, fresh sea breezes and panoramic views have made the hill an attractive location for the grand mansions and bungalows of the city's merchants and governors. These days however, high-rise, high-rent apartment blocks have squeezed out all but a handful of the old colonial buildings to make way for Mumbai's "new money" set – the in-crowd of politicians, millionaires, film stars and gangsters who flit across the glossy pages and gossip

The towers of silence

High on the top of Malabar Hill, screened from prying eyes by an imposing wall and a dense curtain of vegetation, stand the seven Parsi Towers of Silence, or *dokhmas*. If you know only one thing about the Parsis, it is probably that they dispose of their dead by leaving the corpses on top of tall cylindrical enclosures for their bones to be picked clean by vultures. This ancient mortuary ritual, thought to predate the 2500-year-old faith, was advocated by the prophet Zoroaster as a means of avoiding pollution of the four sacred elements (air, water, earth and, the holiest of all, fire). Recently, Parsis have been debating whether to switch to electric cremation as a sound, and more sanitary, alternative – supposedly because scraps of human flesh discarded by the over-fed vultures have been appearing on balconies, rooftops and gardens near the Towers. Whatever they decide, no one will thank you for trying to peep at the *dokhmas* themselves, which are off-limits to all living people other than the pall-bearers who put the corpses in place. Not to be put off, *Time-Life* once published a colour photograph of a funeral taken from the buildings overlooking the site. Enraged Parsis retorted by asking how the photographer would feel if he saw pictures of *his* mother's body being pecked to bits by birds?

columns of India's popular magazines. Somehow, though, a few jaded remnants of the city's past have managed to weather the changes.

Before heading up the hill from the busy roundabout at the far end of Chowpatty Beach, make a short diversion through the narrow backlanes to **Balbunath Mandir**, one of Mumbai's most important Hindu temples. You'll have no trouble finding the entrance: just look for the melee of stray cattle and flower-sellers that forms here around puja times. The building itself, a clumsy modern agglomeration of towers, turquoise arches and staircases, makes a much less interesting spectacle than the stream of *pujaris* (priests) and pilgrims on the greasy stone steps leading to it.

The municipal parks and the Jain temple

From the Balbunath temple, the most pleasant and direct route up to Malabar Hill's main thoroughfare, **Ridge Road**, now renamed **Bal Gangadhar** (or BG) **Kher Marg**, is via the tangle of crumbling concrete paths through the woods below it. The trail emerges near a pair of dull but popular public parks. The larger, known as the "**Hanging Gardens**" (renamed "Pherozeshah Mehta Gardens") is full of loving couples smooching ostentatiously around its gravel paths and manicured flowerbeds. By contrast, the smaller **Kamala Nehru Children's Park** (across the road) is unlikely to appeal to anyone over the age of seven. The views of Back Bay are, in any case, better admired from the congenial terrace bars of the *Naaz Café* nearby.

A kilometre or so straight down the ridge from the parks stands Malabar Hill's **Jain temple**. Mumbai's Jains originally came from Gujarat in the late seventeenth century to escape persecution by the Hindu Marathas. Since then, their legendarily sharp business sense has helped make these ultra-strict vegetarians one of the city's most prosperous minorities. According to an ancient dictum, Jains should, every day after bathing, walk barefoot to their local temple in a length of stitchless cloth to pray, a gesture of humility and renunciation that contrasts with the lavish decoration of the temples themselves. This temple, though on the small side, is no exception. Mirrors and colourful paintings cover the walls surrounding the approach to the central chamber, where the polished marble image of **Adinath**, the first of the 24 Jain teacher-prophets, or *tirthankaras*, is enshrined. In front of the image, devotees make rice patterns as offerings. The temple also runs a stall selling freshly baked pure-veg biscuits, sweets and cakes. It's to the left of the main entrance, near the racks where shoes and leather articles have to be deposited.

Walukeshwar Mandir and Banganga Tank

Beyond the Jain temple, Malabar Hill tapers off to a narrow spit that shelves steeply down to Back Bay on one side, and the rocky sea shore on the other. **Walukeshwar Mandir**, among the few of Mumbai's ancient Hindu sites not buried under layers of conurbation, can be reached via a lane left off the main road. According to the Ramayana, Rama paused here during his journey south to rescue Sita from the clutches of the evil Ravana, and fashioned a lingam out of sand to worship Shiva. Over time, the Walukeshwar, or "Sand-Lord" shrine, became one of the western Indian coast's most important religious centres, venerated even by the marauding Malabar pirates who menaced the islands. Today's temple, erected in 1715 after the original had been destroyed by the Portuguese, is unremarkable and best bypassed in favour of the more impressive **Banganga tank** below it. Hemmed in by a towering wall of apartment blocks, the spring that feeds the tank is believed to have been created by an arrow fired from Rama's own fabled bow. Today, it's a minor pilgrimage site, busy only on "white" (full-) or "black" (no-) moon days of the month. At other times, Banganga's stone *ghats*, numerous subsidiary shrines, and scum-covered greenish waters see little more than a trickle of bathers, drawn mostly from the slum encampments which have sprung up on the broken land lining the shore. A path picks its way past these shacks, and the washing lines of the dhobis who live in them, to the **cremation ghats** nearby.

North of Malabar Hill

Two of Mumbai's most popular religious sites, one Hindu, the other Muslim, can be reached by following Bhulabhai Desai Road **north from Malabar Hill** as far as Prabhu Chowk, through the exclusive suburb of **Breach Candy** (bus #132 from Colaba). Alternatively, make for Mumbai Central and head due northwest to **Vatsalabai Desai Chowk** (also bus #132).

Mahalakshmi Mandir is joined to Bhulabhai Desai Road by an alley lined with stalls selling puja offerings and devotional pictures. Mumbai's favourite *devi*, **Lakshmi**, goddess of beauty and prosperity – the city's most sought-after attributes – is here propitiated with coconuts, sweets, lengths of shimmering silk and giant lotus blooms. At weekends, queues for *darshan* extend right the way across the courtyard and down the main steps beyond. Gifts pile so high that the temple *pujaris* run a money-spinning sideline reselling them. Their little shop, to the left of the entrance, is a good place to buy cut-price saris and brocades infused with lucky Lakshmi-energy. While you're here, find out what your future holds by joining the huddle of devotees pressing rupees onto the rear wall of the shrine room. If your coin sticks, you'll be rich.

A temple has stood on this rocky outcrop for well over a thousand years. Not until the eighteenth century however, when the hitherto swampy western edge of the city was drained, was the present building erected. Legend has it that the goddess herself told a contractor working on the project that unless her icon – which she said would soon reappear from the sea where it had been cast by Muslim invaders – was reinstated in a temple on the site, the breach-wall would not hold back the waves. Sure enough, the next day a Lakshmi deity was fished out of the silt by workmen, to be installed on this small headland, where it has remained to the present day.

Another site shrouded in myth is the mausoleum of the Muslim saint, Afghan mystic **Haji Ali Bukhari**, occupying a small islet in the bay just north of the Mahalakshmi temple. Islamic lore has two legends regarding its founding, though both agree he was sailing to India after performing *Haj* at Mecca; the first says that the coffin was washed ashore on these rocks after it had, on strict instructions from the saint, been cast into the sea off the coast of what is now Pakistan. The other is that the saint, when he realized he wouldn't reach India before his death, asked his disciples – the Fazla brothers – to build his tomb where he died. The construction took the brothers one year and was completed in 1865. The tomb is said to be very effective in answering prayers and the locals say that believers of all faiths make supplications here – it's even claimed British generals gave thanks to the saint after winning battles. It's connected to the mainland by a narrow concrete **causeway**, only passable at low tide. When not immersed in water, its entire length is lined with beggars who change one-rupee pieces into ten-paise coins for pilgrims. The prime sites, closer to the snack bars that flank the main entrance, near the small mosque, and the gateway to the **tomb** itself, are allocated in a strict pecking order. If you want to make a donation, spare a thought for the unfortunates in the middle. After all the commotion, the tomb itself comes as something of a disappointment. Its

On the face of it, the idea of going out of your way to ogle Mumbai's dirty washing sounds like a very perverse pastime. If you're passing, however, the municipal dhobi ghats, near Mahalakshmi suburban railway station, are well worth hopping off the train to see. This huge open-air laundry is the centre of one of those miraculous Indian institutions which, like the *dabawallah's* operation (see p.113), is usually regarded by Westerners with disbelief. Each morning, washing from all over Mumbai is brought here to be thrown into soapy piles and thumped by the resident *dhobiwallahs* in the countless concrete tanks, barrels and shanty shacks inside the compound. The next day, after being aired, pressed, folded in newspaper and bound with cotton thread, the bundles are returned to whence they came. The secret behind this smooth operation is a symbol marked on each item of clothing; each *dhobiwallah* has their own code – invisible to the untrained eye but understood by all in the washing business – that ensures the safe passage of laundry. The bird's-eye view over the V-shaped rows of *dhobi ghats* from Mahalakshmi Road bridge is one of Mumbai's most bizarre photo opportunities.

white Moghul domes and minarets look a lot less exotic close up than when viewed from the shore, silhouetted against the sun as it drops into the Arabian Sea.

A couple of kilometres further up the coast, the densely packed districts of central Mumbai are broken by a huge, empty expanse of dusty brown grass. The optimistically named **Mahalakshmi racecourse**, founded in 1879, is the home of the Mumbai Turf Club and a bastion of the city's Anglophile elite. Regular meetings take place here on weekends between November and March. If you fancy a hack yourself, the Amateur Riding Club also rents out horses during the week (except Wednesdays).

The central bazaars

Lining the anarchic jumble of streets north of Lokmanya Tilak (formerly Carnac) Road, Mumbai's teeming **central bazaars** are India at its most intense. You could wander around here for months without seeing the same shop-front twice. In practice, most visitors find a couple of hours mingling with the crowds in the heat and din quite enough. Nevertheless, the market districts form a fascinating counterpoint to the wide and Westernized streets of downtown, even if you're not buying.

In keeping with traditional divisions of guild, caste and religion, most streets specialize in one or two types of merchandise – a pain if you want to see a smattering of all the goods on offer in a relatively short time. If you lose your bearings, the best way out is to ask someone to wave you in the direction of **Abdul Rehman Street**, the busy road through the heart of the district, from where you can hail a cab.

Crawford Market

Crawford (aka Mahatma Phule) **Market**, ten minutes' walk north of VT station, is an old British-style covered market dealing in just about every kind of fresh food and domestic animal imaginable. Thanks to its pompous Norman-Gothic tower and prominent position at the corner of Lokmanya Tilak Road and Dr DN Marg, the Crawford Market is also a useful landmark and a good place to begin a foray into the bazaars.

Before venturing inside, check out the **friezes** wrapped around its exterior – a Victorian vision of sturdy-limbed peasants toiling in the fields designed by

Rudyard Kipling's father, Lockwood, as principal of the Bombay School of Art in 1865. The **main hall** is still divided into different sections: pyramids of polished fruit and vegetables down one aisle, sacks of nuts or oil-tins full of herbs and spices down another. Sitting cross-legged on a raised platform in front of each stall is its eagle-eyed owner, wearing starched *khadi* pyjamas and a Nehru cap, with a fresh red *tilak* smeared on his forehead.

Around the back of the market, in the atmospheric **wholesale wing**, the pace of life is more hectic. Here, noisy crowds of coolies mill about with large reed-baskets held high in the air (if they are looking for work) or on their heads (if they've found some).

One place animal lovers should definitely steer clear of is Crawford Market's **pet** and **poultry** section, on the east side of the building. You never quite know what creatures will turn up here, cringing in rank-smelling, undersized cages. The **tobacco** market, by contrast, is altogether more fragrant. Look out for the Muslim hookah merchants selling picturesque smoking paraphernalia.

North of Crawford Market

The streets immediately **north of Crawford Market** and west of **Mohammed Ali Road**, the main drag through Mumbai's Muslim ghettos, form one vast bazaar area. Ranged along both sides of narrow **Mangaldas Lane**, the cloth bazaar, are small shops draped with lengths of bright silk and cotton. Low doorways on the left open on to a colourful **covered market** area, packed with tiny stalls where you'll be badgered to sit and take tea while merchants tempt you with dozens of different saris and scarves.

Eastwards along Mangaldas Lane from Carnac Road, the pale green-washed domes, arches and minarets of the **Jami Masjid**, or "Friday Mosque" (c.1800), mark the start of the Muslim neighbourhoods. **Memon Street**, cutting north from the mosque, is the site of the **Zaveri Bazaar**, the jewellery market.

By the time the gleaming golden spire that crowns the **Mumba-Devi temple**'s cream and turquoise tower appears at the end of the street, you're deep in a maze of twisting lanes hemmed in by tall, wooden-balconied buildings. The temple is one of the most important centres of Devi-worship in India. Reached via a tiny courtyard where *pujaris* regale devotees with religious songs, its shrine houses a particularly revered, and unusual, deity. Her present resting place was built early in the nineteenth century, when she was relocated from her former home to make way for VT Station. Mumba Devi's other claim to fame is that her name is the original root of the word "Bombay", as well as the newer, and more politically correct, Maharashtran version, "**Mumbai**".

Chor Bazaar, Mutton Road and the red-light district

Jump in a taxi at the Mumba-Devi temple for the two-kilometre trip north to the other concentration of markets around **Johar Chowk**, just north of SP Patel Road. The most famous of these, **Chor** (literally "thieves") **Bazaar** (where vendors peevishly insist the name is a corruption of the Urdu *shor*, meaning "noisy"), is the city's largest **antiques** cum flea market. Friday, the Muslim holy day, is the best day to be here. From 9am onwards, the neighbourhood is cluttered with hawkers and hand-carts piled high with bric-a-brac and assorted junk being eagerly rummaged by men in skullcaps. At other times, the antique shops down on **Mutton Road** are the main attraction. Once, you could hope to unearth real gems in these dark, fusty stores, but your chances of finding a genuine bargain nowadays are minimal. Most of the stuff is pricey Victoriana – old gramophones, chamber pots, chipped china – salvaged from the homes of Parsi families on the decline. The place is also awash with **fakes**, mainly small bronze votive statues, which make good souvenirs if you can knock the price down.

Press on north through Chor Bazaar and you'll eventually come out onto **Grant Road** (Maulana Shaukatali Road). Further north and west, in the warren of lanes below JB Behram Marg, lies the city's infamous **red-light district**. **Kamathipura**'s rows of luridly lit, barred shop fronts, from where an estimated 25,000 prostitutes ply their trade, are one of Mumbai's more degrading and unpleasant spectacles. Many of these so-called "**cage girls**" are young teenagers from poor tribal areas, and from across the border in Nepal, who have been sold by desperate parents into **bonded slavery** until they can earn the money to pay off family debts. The area is definitely no place to wander around on foot.

Elephanta

An hour's boat ride from Colaba, the tranquil, forested island of **ELEPHANTA** is one of the most atmospheric places in Mumbai. Populated only by a small fishing community, it makes a wonderful contrast to the seething claustrophobia of the city, even when crowded with day-trippers at weekends. Originally known as **Gharapuri**, the "city of Ghara priests", the island was renamed in the sixteenth century by the Portuguese in honour of the carved elephant they found at the port (see p.124). Its chief attraction is its unique **cave temple**, whose massive **Trimurti** (three-faced) **Shiva sculpture** is as fine an example of Hindu architecture as you'll find anywhere.

"**Deluxe**" **boats** set off from the Gateway of India (Oct–May hourly 9am–2.30pm; Rs85 return including government guide); book through the kiosks near the Gateway of India. Ask for your guide at the caves ticket office on arrival – they take about thirty minutes. **Ordinary ferries** (Rs65 return), also from the Gateway of India, don't include guides, and are usually packed. The journey takes about an hour on either boat.

Cool drinks and souvenir stalls line the way up the hill, and at the top, the MTDC *Chalukya* restaurant offers food and beer, and a terrace with good views out to sea, but you cannot stay overnight on the island.

The Cave

Elephanta's impressive excavated eighth-century **cave** (9.30am–4pm; $5 [Rs5]), covering an area of approximately 5000 square metres, is reached by climbing more than one hundred steps to the top of the hill. Inside, the massive columns, carved from solid rock, give the deceptive impression of being structural. To the right, as you enter, note the panel of **Nataraj**, Shiva as the cosmic dancer. Though spoiled by the Portuguese who, it is said, used it for target practice, the panel remains magnificent; Shiva's face is rapt, and in one of his left hands he removes the veil of ignorance. Opposite is a badly damaged panel of Lakulisha, Shiva with a club (*lakula*).

Each of the four entrances to the simple square main **shrine** – unusually, it has one on each side – is flanked by a pair of huge fanged *dvarpala* guardians (only those to the back have survived undamaged), while inside a large *lingam* is surrounded by coins and smouldering joss left by devotees. Facing the northern wall of the shrine, another panel shows Shiva impaling the demon **Andhaka**, who wandered around as though blind, symbolizing his spiritual blindness. Shiva killed him as he attempted to steal a divine tree from heaven. The panel behind the shrine on the back wall portrays the marriage of **Shiva**

and Parvati. Moving east, the next panel shows Ganghadaran, Shiva receiving the descending river Ganga, his lover, to live in his hair, while Parvati, his wife, looks on. A powerful six-metre bust of **Trimurti**, the three-faced Shiva, who embodies the powers of creator, preserver and destroyer, stands nearby, and to the west a sculpture shows Shiva as **Ardhanarishvara**, half male and half female. Near the second entrance on the east, another panel shows Shiva and Parvati on **Mount Kailasha** with Ravana about to lift the mountain. His curved spine shows the strain.

Uptown and the outskirts

Greater Mumbai has crept inexorably northwards to engulf villages and swampland in a pall of chimneys, motorways and slums. These grim industrial areas hold few attractions, but possibilities for full- or half-day excursions include the quirky **Victoria and Albert museum** and botanical gardens in Byculla, and the **beach** at **Juhu**. All lie within reach of a suburban railway station, although you will, in most cases, have to take a rickshaw or taxi for the last few kilometres. Beyond them to the north lie the Buddhist caves chiselled out of the hillside at **Kanheri**, and the crumbling Portuguese fort at **Bassein**.

Byculla and the Veermata Jeejamata (Victoria and Albert) museum

As the bedrock of Mumbai's once-gigantic weaving industry, **Byculla**, immediately north of the central bazaar, epitomizes the grim legacy of nineteenth-century industrialization: idle chimney stacks, overcrowding and pavements strewn with ragged, sleeping bodies. The cotton-mills and sweat-shops are still here, churning out cheap clothes for the massive domestic market, but few can claim the turnovers they enjoyed a hundred years ago. Today, eclipsed by their old Gujarati rivals in Surat and Ahmedabad, all but the larger nationalized mills teeter on the brink of bankruptcy.

Visitors are welcome to look around the few of Byculla's cotton-mills still in business, but a more common reason to come up here is to see the **Veermata Jeejamata (Victoria and Albert) museum** (daily except Wed 10.30am–4.30pm; Rs2) on Dr Babasaheb Ambedkar Marg. Inspired by its namesake in London, this grand Victorian-Gothic building was built in 1871 to house artefacts relating to Mumbai's history and development. Engravings, photographs and old maps are displayed in a small gallery on the first floor, along with sundry *objets d'art*. Downstairs in the main hall, the exhibits are more eclectic. Among the Victorian china and modest assortment of south Indian bronzes are cases filled with papier-mâché parakeets, pick-axe heads and plastic models of vegetables. More instructive is the scale model of a Parsi Tower of Silence (see box on p.118), with a gruesome description of the mortuary rituals performed on the real ones on Malabar Hill.

The museum's oldest and most famous exhibit, however, is the **stone elephant** in the small garden to the rear of the building. Now somewhat forlorn and neglected in the shadows, this was the very beast that inspired the Portuguese to name the island in the harbour "Elephanta" (see p.123). The crumbling figure was brought here for safe-keeping in 1863 from its original, and more fittingly prominent, site alongside the landing stage that leads up to the cave temple.

A wrought-iron gateway beyond the elephant opens onto one of Mumbai's most popular venues for an old-fashioned family day out. The peaceful and green **botanical gardens** (daily except Wed 8am–6pm) hold a huge collection of South Asian flora, plus Mumbai's only **zoo** (Rs4), where, after a trip around the predictably small and smelly cages, kids can enjoy an elephant or camel ride.

Both museum and botanical gardens can be reached either by BEST **bus** (#3 or #11(Ltd) from Colaba, or #19 from Flora Fountain and Crawford Market); or by suburban train to Byculla station, on the opposite (western) side of the motorway.

Juhu Beach

With its palm trees, glamorous seaside apartment blocks and designer clothes stores, **Juhu**, 30km north of downtown, is Mumbai's answer to Sunset Boulevard. Unless you're staying in one of the many five-star hotels lining its five-kilometre strip of white sand, however, this affluent suburb holds little appeal. Sunbathing and swimming are out of the question, thanks to an oily slick of raw sewage that seeps into the Arabian Sea from the slum bastis surrounding Mahim Creek to the south. A more salubrious way to enjoy Juhu is to walk along the strand after office hours, when young families turn out in droves to enjoy the sunsets and sea breezes, attracting a bevy of *bhel puri*-wallahs, side shows, mangy camels and carts, and lads hawking cheap Taiwanese toys. The rows of brightly painted stalls along the beach whip up delicious varieties of *falooda*, a fruit, ice cream and *vermicelli* milkshake unique to Mumbai.

Further north up Juhu Road, the headquarters of the International Society for Krishna Consciousness (ISKCON) deals with matters more spiritual. Its richly appointed **Krishna temple** (daily 4am–1pm & 4–9pm) draws local Hindus in their Sunday-best shirtings and saris, and well-heeled Westerners wearing kaftans, *kurtas* and *dhotis*. Rich visitors get to stay in what must surely rank as the world's most glamorous *dharamshala* – a modern, multistorey hotel complex with its own vegetarian restaurant, conference hall and theatre.

Kanheri Caves

The chief reason to make the day's excursion to the suburb of Borivli, 42km out at the northern limits of Mumbai's sprawl, is to visit the Buddhist **Kanheri Caves** (daily 9am–5.30pm; US$5 [Rs5]), ranged over the hills in virtually unspoilt forest. It's an interminable journey by road, so catch one of the many **trains** (50min) on the suburban line from Churchgate (marked "BO" on the departure boards; "limited stop" trains are 15min faster) to Borivli East. When you arrive, take the Borivli East exit, where a **bus** (for Kaneri Cave via SG Parles; Rs10), **auto–rickshaw** (about Rs60) or **taxi** (about Rs90) will take you the last 15km. Bring water and food as the stalls here only sell warm soft drinks.

Kanheri may not be as spectacular as other cave sites, but some of its sculpture is superb – though to enjoy the blissful peace and quiet that attracted its original occupants you should avoid the weekend and the crowds of daytrippers. Most of the caves, which date from the second to the ninth centuries AD, were used simply by monks for accommodation and meditation (*viharas*) during the four months of the monsoon, when an itinerant life was impractical – the season when the forest is at its most beautiful. They are connected by steep winding paths and steps; engage one of the friendly local guides at the entrance to find your way about, but don't expect any sort of lecture as their English is limited. Due to a recent spate of muggings in some of the remoter caves, it is not advisable to venture off the beaten track alone.

In **Cave 1**, an incomplete *chaitya* hall (a hall with a stupa at one end, an aisle and row of columns at either side), you can see where the rock was left cut, but unfinished. Two stupas stand in **Cave 2**; one was vandalized by a certain N. Christian, whose carefully incised Times-Roman graffiti bears the date 1810. A panel shows seated Buddhas, portrayed as a teachers. Behind, and to the side, is the *bodhisattva* of compassion, Padmapani, while to the right the *viharas* feature rock-cut beds.

Huge Buddhas, with serenely joyful expressions and unfeasibly large shoulders, stand on either side of the porch to the spectacular **Cave 3**. Between them, you'll see the panels of "donor couples", thought to have been foreigners that patronized the community. Inside, leading to a stupa at the back, octagonal columns in two rows, some decorated with animal motifs, line the magnificent Hinayana *chaitya* hall.

The sixth-century **Cave 11** is a large assembly hall, where two long "tables" of rock were used for the study of manuscripts. Seated at the back, in the centre, is a figure of the Buddha as teacher, an image repeated in the entrance, to the left, with a wonderful flight of accompanying celestials. Just before the entrance to a small cell in **Cave 34**, flanked by two standing Buddhas, an unfinished ceiling painting shows the Buddha touching the earth. There must be at least a hundred more Buddha images on panels in **Cave 67**, a large hall. On the left side, and outside in the entrance, these figures are supported by *nagas* (snakes representing *kundalini*, yogic power).

Bassein Fort

Trundling over the rickety iron bridge that joins the northern fringes of Mumbai to the Maharashtran mainland, you could easily fail to notice the ruined fort at **Bassein** (or Vasai), 61km north of the city centre. Yet these mouldy stone walls, obscured by a carpet of palms and lush tropical foliage at the mouth of the milky-blue River Ulhas, once encompassed India's most powerful and prosperous colonial settlement. It was ceded to the Portuguese by Sultan Bahadur of Gujarat in 1534, in return for help in the Gujarati struggle against the Moghuls, and quickly became the hub of the region's maritime trade, "The Court of the North", from which the Portuguese territories at Goa, Daman and Diu were administered. In 1739, however, the **Marathas** laid siege to the city for three months, eventually wiping out the garrison, and a final death blow was dealt in 1780 by the cannons of the **British**. Bassein's crumbling remnants were left to be carried off for raw building material or reclaimed by the coastal jungle, and only a handful of weed-infested buildings still stand today.

If you don't mind spending hours in a crowded suburban **train** (around 1hr 15min from Churchgate), Bassein makes an atmospheric day-trip from the city. Only a few express trains stop at the nearest mainline station, Vasai Road, from where the onward trip (11km) involves jumping in and out of **shared autorickshaws** – Rs5 for each leg. These stop halfway at a busy market crossroads, where you catch another ride for the last stretch from a stand 100m up a road left from the crossroads. Ask for the "*kila*", the Marathi word for "fort". Stock up on food and drink at Vasai Road; there's nowhere very sanitary to eat in Bassein.

The **fort** is entered through a large gateway in its slanting stone battlements. Once inside, the road runs past a modern monument to the Maratha leader, Shivaji, before heading towards the woods and the old Portuguese town. The ruins are a melancholy sight: *peepal* and tall palm trees poke through the chancels of churches and convents, while water buffalo plod listlessly past piles of rubble, and monkeys leap and crash through the canopy overhead.

By contrast, the small **fishing village**, under the archway from the rickshaw stand, is thriving. The spiritual legacy of the Portuguese has endured here longer than their architectural one, as shown by the painted Madonna shrines tucked into wall-niches and crucifixes gleaming on the singlets of the fishermen lounging in the local bar. On the **beach**, a short way down the narrow sandy footpath through the main cluster of huts, large wooden frames are hung with pungent-smelling strips of dried pomfret, while nearby, fishing boats bob around in the silt-laden estuary water.

Eating

In keeping with its cosmopolitan credentials, Mumbai (and Colaba above all) is crammed with interesting **eating places**, whether you fancy splashing out on a buffet lunch-with-a-view from a flashy five-star revolving restaurant, or simply tucking into piping-hot roti kebab by gaslight in the street.

Colaba

Colaba (see map on p.109) has even more places to eat than it does hotels. In the space of just 1km, you can sample an amazing array of **regional cuisines**: pure-veg "Hindu hotels" serving delicious Gujarati and south Indian food stand cheek by jowl with Muslim cafés whose menus will delight die-hard carnivores. Nearby, within a stone's throw of the *Taj* and its expensive gourmet restaurants, are Mumbai's oldest and best-loved Chinese joints. Other than during the monsoons (when choppy seas keep the fishing fleet in the polluted waters of the harbour), these offer fresh, safe **seafood** dishes of tiger prawns, crab or delicate white pomfret. Still in Colaba, traditional Iranian restaurants serve minced lamb and mutton specialities, while revamped café-bars dish up draught beer and reasonable Western food for tourists and local yuppies. Non-vegetarians will enjoy succulent meats, smothered in the split-lentil stew known as dhansak, in Parsi restaurants, while Goan and Mangalorean "lunch-homes" crop up everywhere too – good for a pork vindaloo or a fiery fish curry.

The majority of Colaba's cafés, bars and restaurants – among them the popular travellers' haunts, *Leopold's* and the *Café Mondegar* – are up at the north end of the Causeway. Those below are divided into **price categories** based on the cost of a main dish: inexpensive (below Rs75), moderate (Rs75–200) and expensive (above Rs200).

Street food

Mumbai is renowned for distinctive street foods – and especially bhelpuri, a quintessentially Mumbai masala mixture of puffed-rice, deep-fried *vermicelli*, potato, crunchy *puri* pieces, chilli paste, tamarind water, chopped onions and coriander. More hygienic, but no less ubiquitous, is pao bhaji, a round slab of flat bread stuffed with meat or vegetables simmered in a vat of hot oil, and kanji vada, savoury doughnuts soaked in fermented mustard and chilli sauce. And if all that doesn't appeal, a pit stop at one of the city's hundreds of juice bars probably will. There's no better way to beat the sticky heat than with a glass of cool milk shaken with fresh pineapple, mango, banana, *chikoo* (small brown fruit that tastes like a pear) or custard apple. Just make sure they hold on the ice – made, of course, with untreated water.

Restaurants, bars and cafés are listed below by district. The most expensive restaurants, particularly in the top hotels, will levy "service charges" that can add thirty percent to the price of your meal. Phone numbers have been given where we recommend you reserve a table for dinner.

Inexpensive

Bademiya, behind the *Taj* on Tulloch Road. Legendary Colaba kebab-wallah serving delicious flame-grilled chicken, mutton and fish steaks, in hot tandoori *rotis*, from benches on the sidewalk.

Kamat, Colaba Causeway. Friendly little eatery serving the best South Indian breakfasts in the area.

Majestic, near Regal cinema, Colaba Causeway. Large, traditional South Indian joint patronized by off-duty taxi-wallahs, junior office staff and backpackers.

Mezban, Apollo Bunder Road, off Colaba Causeway. Cheap but delicious Arabic, Punjabi and Mughlai food in light, airy surroundings. Excellent non-veg items and the pizzas aren't bad either.

New Martin, near the Strand cinema, Strand Road. Unpromising formica booths, but famed for delicious Goan dishes such as prawn *pulao*, sausages, pork vindaloo and spicy fish curry. Also does take-aways.

Olympic Coffee House, 1 Colaba Causeway. *Fin-de-siècle* Iranian café with marble tabletops, wooden wall panels and a mezzanine floor for "ladies". Decor more alluring than the menu of greasy meat dishes, but nonetheless, a good place for a coffee break, though not – strangely – coffee.

Udipi Refreshment, Colaba Causeway. One of many inexpensive south Indian and Gujerati thali joints that line the Causeway south of KP's. One will set you back only Rs20–25.

Moderate

Alps, Nawroji Fardunji Road. Trendy, ersatz American restaurant serving lamb-burgers, fries, sizzling steaks and copious "mixed-grills" to Western chart-music. Cheap beer by the pitcher, too.

Baghdadi, Tulloch Road. Male-dominated place famous for its meat: mostly mutton and chicken steeped in spicy garlic sauce. Chauffeurs pick up takeaways here for their bosses in the *Taj*.

Food Inn, 61 Colaba Causeway. Not much of a looker from the outside, but serves excellent Punjabi dishes – especially non-veg. Frequented mainly by locals who think *KP's* has lost its touch.

Kailash Parbat ("KP's"), 1 Pasta Lane, near the Strand cinema. Uninspiring on the outside, but the *alu parathas* for breakfast, pure veg nibbles, hot snacks and sweets (across the road) are worth the walk. A Colaba institution – try their famous *makai-ka* (corn) *rotis*.

Leopold's, Colaba Causeway. Colaba's most famous – and over-priced – café-bar is determinedly Western, with a clientele to match. Three hundred items on the menu from scrambled eggs to "chilly chicken", washed down with cold beer (Rs110). There's also a bar upstairs.

Expensive

Ling's Pavilion, 19/21 Lansdowne Road, behind the Regal cinema ☏ 022/285 0023. Swanky Chinese restaurant: soft lighting, marble floors and gourmet Cantonese cuisine.

Palkhi, Walton Road ☏ 022/284 0079. Over-the-top, quasi-medieval decor and traditional Mughlai cooking for the health-conscious (lighter on oil and spices). Lots of veg options too.

Tanjore, *Taj Mahal* ☏ 022/202 3366. Opulent interior, rich Mughlai cuisine and classical Indian music and dance in the evening. Expense-account prices.

Downtown

In the following list, *Britania & Co*, *City Kitchen* and *Mahesh Lunch Home* feature on the **Churchgate and Fort map** (see p.112); the others appear on the **Colaba map** (p.109).

Britania & Co, opposite the GPO, Sprott Road, Ballard Estate. Definitive Iranian-Parsi food and decor. Try their special "*berry pulao*" or Bombay duck dishes. A real find, and cheap too.

Chetana, 34 K Dubash Marg ☏ 022/284 4968. Painstakingly prepared Rajasthani/Gujarati food, including set thalis (Rs150) at lunch time and numerous à la carte dishes – absolutely the last word in fine veg cuisine. Expensive, but not extravagant. Reserve for dinner.

City Kitchen, 301 SBS Marg. Highly rated hole-in-the-wall Goan restaurant. Serves all the usual dishes – mostly fish and meat simmered in coconut milk and fiery spices. Inexpensive.

Copper Chimney, 18 K Dubash Marg ☏ 022/204 1661. Renowned eatery with wonderful ceramic murals and stylish versions of standard north Indian dishes; the tandoori kebabs are recommended. Reservations essential at weekends. Superb but expensive.

Kalpana, 254 Shahid Bhagatsingh Road, 3min east from VT. Great place to get your bearings if you've just flopped off a train at VT. Inexpensive Punjabi dishes and great thali (veg and non-veg) served in a light, airy dining hall with comfortable seating.

Khyber (sign not in English), opposite Jehangir Art Gallery, Kala Ghoda ☏ 022/267 3227. Ultra-fashionable, with opulent Arabian Nights interior and uncompromisingly rich Mughlai-Punjabi cuisine. The chicken *makhanwallah* is legendary. Reservations essential.

Mahesh Lunch Home, 8-B Cawasji Patel St, Fort. Inexpensive Keralan restaurant serving authentic veg "meals" and delicious non-veg options – chicken fried in ginger or fish masala on groaning platefuls of rice.

Café Samovar, Jehangir Art Gallery, MG Road. Very pleasant, peaceful semi-open-air café, with varying menu of food and drink: *roti kebabs*, prawn curry, fresh salads and dhansak, chilled guava juice and beer.

Trishna, 7 Ropewalk Lane, Kala Ghonda ☎ 022/267 2176. Visiting dignitaries and local celebs from the President of Greece and Imran Khan to Bollywood stars have eaten here (as photos attest). Wonderful fish dishes in every sauce going, and prices to match the clientele. Very small, so book in advance.

Wayside Inn, opposite Jehangir Art Gallery, K Dubash Marg. Upmarket Parsi café, with red-chequered table cloths and solid English cooking. Nice place for a coffee after visiting the museum.

Churchgate and Nariman Point

The restaurants listed below are marked on either the **Churchgate and Fort map** on p.112 or the **Mumbai map** on p.94.

Chopsticks, 90a VN Rd ☎ 022/204 9284. Wide choice of pricey meat, seafood and veg in fiery Szechuan and milder Cantonese style. Try the excellent *dim sum* or dishes with such inscrutable names as "ant climbing up the tree". Buffet lunch Rs200.

Croissants Etc, Industrial Insurance Building, opposite Churchgate station. Filled croissants, pricey pastries and other Western food, including delicious cakes.

Gaylord, VN Road ☎ 022/282 1259). Parisian-style terrace café in the heart of Mumbai. Tandoori, sizzlers and some Western food. Wholewheat bread, baguettes and sticky buns in the patisserie.

Kamling, VN Road ☎ 022/204 2618. Favourite for the title of oldest, best and most authentic Chinese in town. Southeast Asian flight crews and well-heeled locals tuck into delicious Cantonese dishes – try the mouthwatering "chimney soup" or the (expensive) seafood specialities.

The Outrigger, *Oberoi Hotel*, Nariman Point ☎ 022/202 4343. Polynesian specialities (Chinese with more fruit thrown in), tribal masks and a full-size canoe. Expensive.

The Pearl of the Orient, *Ambassador Hotel*, VN Road ☎ 022/291131. Revolving Oriental restaurant in glam four-star hotel with panoramic views. Reserve for dinner – expensive.

The Pizzeria, Corner of Veer Nariman and Marine Drive. Delicious freshly baked pizzas served on newly renovated terrace overlooking Back Bay, or to take away. Plenty of choice, and moderate to expensive prices.

Purohit's, VN Road ☎ 022/204 6241. Justly popular traditional restaurant serving a good range of mid-price Gujarati thalis, Punjabi main dishes and South Indian *chaat*.

Rangoli, inside NCPA Centre, Nariman Point ☎ 022/202 3366. Excellent-value Continental-Oriental buffet lunches (Rs350) are its forte, but the à la carte menu is gourmet-standard though fairly pricy. Be warned that the waiters may put on a "show" in the evening.

Satkar, opposite Churchgate station's western exit. Busy pure-veg terrace restaurant: great for south Indian "fast food" and crowd-watching.

Trattoria, *Hotel President*, 90 Cuffe Parade ☎ 022/215 0808. Surprisingly authentic Italian cuisine. Pizza and pasta with fresh herbs, real Parmesan, bitter chocolate ice cream, and a big buffet lunch on Sundays (noon–3pm; Rs400).

Crawford Market and the central bazaars

Badshah Juice and Snack Bar, opposite Crawford Market, Lokmanya Tilak Road. Mumbai's most famous *falooda* joint also serves delicious *kulfi*, ice creams and dozens of freshly squeezed fruit juices. The ideal place to round off a trip to the market.

Bhaishankar's, near Bhuleshwar Market, CP Tank Circle. One of Mumbai's oldest and most respected sweet shops. Try their Bengali *barfi*, cashew *kalin-*

gar or masala milk (made with pistachio, almonds, saffron and nutmeg).

Gulshan-e-Iran, Palton Road ☎ 022/265183. Popular Muslim breakfast venue on the main road that does inexpensive biryanis, kebabs, chutneys and fresh bread. Open all day.

Hiralal Kashiram Bhajiwala, Kumbhar Tukda, Bhuleshwar Market. Cheap restaurant serving great *farsan* savouries, including *ponk vadas* (millet and garlic balls), *batata vadas* (made with sweet potatoes) and *kand bhajis* (deep-fried purple-yam), all with a tasty, fiery chutney.

Rajdhani, Mangaldas Road (in the silk bazaar opposite Crawford market). Outstanding, eat-till-you-burst Gujarati thalis dished up by barefoot waiters to discerning aficionados. A

little more expensive than usual, but well worth it.

Shalimar, Bhindi Bazaar Junction. Outstanding Mughlai, tandoori and (not as good) Chinese food in a cool Art Deco marbelled interior. Great food and reasonable prices make it very popular with Muslim Mumbayakas.

Chowpatty Beach and Kemp's Corner

Chowpatty Beach is a popular venue for a picnic, crowded with vendors selling kulfi in clay cups and bhel puri, kanji vada and pao bhaji. **Kemp's Corner**, crouched under the hectic G Deshmukh flyover, fifteen minutes' walk north, boasts a clutch of very good places to eat – handy for visitors to Malabar Hill. The restaurants listed below feature on the **map** on p.117.

China Garden, Om Chambers, 123 August Kranti Marg ☎022/363 0841. Malabar Hill's glitterati don their finest for this place, which has expensive, authentic Chinese, Korean, Thai and Japanese food.

Chinese Room, Kwality House, Kemp's Corner ☎022/380 6771. A less expensive alternative to *China Garden*, specializing in quality Sezchuan, Hunan and Cantonese cooking, with great seafood.

Gupta Bhelwalla, around Chowpatty Beach. *The most legendary stall in India, where colourful variations of hot/cold, sweet/sour bhel puri* are whipped up in front of you with flair. Utterly delicious. May take some tracking down due to the clearing of food stands on Chowpatty Beach.

New Yorker, Fulchand Niwas, 25 Chowpatty Seaface. Western food – baked potatoes, pizzas,

burgers, and some Tex-Mex options – dished up in a bustling a/c café. Moderate.

Paramount, Marine Drive, near the Aquarium. Small Iranian café, which while it has a certain charm, with marble-top tables, wood-panelled and mirrored walls, applies strict rules: signs request that you "Do not spit", "Do not comb your hair", "Do not stretch legs on other pieces of furniture" and, most advisedly, "Do not sit unnecessarily a long time". Inexpensive.

Revival, above *London Pub*, Chowpatty Seaface, near the footbridge. Expensive but good-value 1930s retro restaurant serving imaginative and tasty Italian (with authentic ingredients) and Indian veg food.

Nightlife and entertainment

Mumbai never sleeps. No matter what time of night you venture out, there are bound to be others going about some business or other. The city has always led the **nightlife** scene in India and there are bars and clubs to suit every taste: jazz dens compete with salsa, tabla–dance fusions and funk. Mumbai's alternative but decidedly yuppie crowd meet at the *Ghetto Bar* before heading down to the gay, glitzy or groovy clubs around Colaba and Juhu.

Of course, Mumbai is also a cultural centre, attracting the finest **Indian classical music** and **dance** artists from all over the country; ⓦ www.dreammerchants .org/theatreguide/tg.htm has good listings and includes bus routes and stations. There are frequent concerts and recitals at venues such as: Bharatiya Vidya Bhavan, KM Munshi Marg (☎022/363 0224), the headquarters of the international cultural (Hindu) organization; Cowasjee Jehangir (CJ) Hall opposite the Prince of Wales Museum (☎022/282 2457); Birla Matushri, 19 Marine Lines (☎022/203 6707); Tejpal Auditorium, 7 AK Nayak Marg (☎022/207 2061); Shanmukhananda Hall, 6 J Yagnik Marg (☎022/403 1357); and the National Centre for the Performing Arts, Narimon Point (NCPA; ☎022/288 3838) auditorium. NCPA also offers modern Gujarati, Hindi, Marathi and English-language **plays** as well as Western **chamber music**, while a smattering of platinum-selling Western rock artists appear at Mumbai stadium.

On the principle that laughter is the best medicine, Mumbai doctor Madan Kataria has created a new kind of therapy: hasya (laughter) yoga. There are now over 300 Laughter Clubs in India and many more worldwide; around 50,000 people joined the Laughter Day celebrations in Mumbai in January 2001.

Fifteen-minute sessions start with adherents doing yogic breathing whilst chanting "Ho ho ha ha," which develops into spontaneous "hearty", "silent" and "swinging" laughter. Sessions mostly take place between 6am and 7am, a time that, according to the good doctor, "keeps you in good spirits throughout the day, energizes your body and charges you with happiness". There are many clubs in Mumbai itself: to find out about them, check ⊛ www.indiabuzz.com/laughter/yogi.htm.

Bars and cabarets

Mumbai has an unusually easy-going attitude to **alcohol**; popping into a bar for a beer is very much accepted (for men at least) even at lunch time. Chowpatty Beach and Colaba Causeway, where you'll find *Leopold's* and the *Café Mondegar*, form the focus of the travellers' social scene, but if you want to sample the pulse of the city's nightlife venture up to Bandra and Juhu.

There is also a seamier side to the city's nightlife, concentrated around (illegal) late-night **cabarets** in the Grant Road area. In these dens of iniquity, women dance before men-only crowds in clothes that might in the West be considered Victorian in their propriety but would be unheard of anywhere else in India.

Café Mondegar, Colaba Causeway. Draught beer by the glass or pitcher, imported beer and deliciously fruity cocktails in a small café-bar. The atmosphere is very relaxed, the music tends towards rock classics and the clientele is a mix of Westerners and students; murals by a famous Goan cartoonist give the place a nice ambience.

Gables, Arthur Bunder Road, Colaba. Small and dark bar serving very cheap beer (from Rs45) and liquors to a tranquil male Indian clientele.

The Ghetto, 30 Bhulabhai Desai Road, near Breach Candy, Mahalakshmi (bus #132 from downtown). The alternative Mumbai scene where young, arty theatre types gather to play their music with attitude and write profound thoughts on the walls – the uniformed waiters do, unfortu-nately, ruin the effect. Cheap beer by the pitcher.

Jazz by the Bay, next to *The Pizzeria*, 143 Marine Drive. The official Channel V TV hangout is a convenient place to crawl to after stuffing yourself with pizza. There's nightly live music, with both Indian and foreign artists performing, except on Sundays and Mondays when it's karaoke. Rs150 entrance; free Tues.

Leopold Pub, 1st Floor, *Leopold's*, Colaba Causeway. Swanky, self-consciously Western-style bar-nightclub, with bouncers, serving expensive beers to Mumbai's smart set. No single men admitted.

The Tavern, *Fariyas Hotel*, Colaba. Another "English-style" pub, complete with wooden beams, loud music and imported beer.

Nightclubs

The **nightclub** scene in Mumbai is the best in India and the late-Nineties saw the rise of a funkier, groovier scene as the moneyed jet-set began to hear the latest house, trance, fusion and funk that was hitting the decks in Goa and the West. Though this scene was scuppered by new licensing laws that require everything (including discos) to be shut by 1am, it looks likely that extending opening hours will be a way for the Maharashtra to refill empty state coffers. One of the best options at present is to find one of the private student **Goa trance parties** that take place at weekends in and around Mumbai – try frequenting student bars and ask the DJ.

Most discos and clubs charge per couple on the door, and in theory have a "couples-only" policy. In practice, if you're in a mixed group or don't appear

For anyone brought up on TV, it's hard to imagine the power that movies continue to wield in India. Every village has a cinema within walking distance and, with a potential audience in the hundreds of millions, the Indian film industry is the largest in the world, producing around 900 full-length features each year. Regional cinema, catering for different language groups (in particular the Tamil cinema of Chennai), though popular locally, has little national impact. Only Hindi film – which accounts for one-fifth of all the films made in India – has crossed regional boundaries to great effect, most particularly in the north. The home of the Hindi blockbuster, the "all-India film", is Mumbai, famously known as Bollywood.

To overcome differences of language and religion, the Bollywood movie follows rigid conventions and genres; as in myth, its characters have predetermined actions and destinies. Knowing a plot need not detract from the drama, and indeed, it is not uncommon for Indian audiences to watch films numerous times. Unlike the Hollywood formula, which tends to classify each film under one genre, the Hindi film follows what is known as a "masala format", and includes during its luxurious three hours a little bit of everything, especially romance, violence and comedy. Frequently the stories feature dispossessed male heroes fighting evil against all odds with a love interest thrown in. The sexual element is repressed, with numerous wet sari scenes and dance routines featuring the tensest pelvic thrusts. Other typical themes include male bonding and betrayal, family melodrama, separation and reunion and religious piety. Dream sequences are almost obligatory, too, along with a festival or celebration scene – typically Holi, when people shower each other with paint – a comic character passing through, and a depraved, alcoholic and mostly Western "cabaret", filled with strutting villains and lewd dancing.

The exploits of Mumbai's film stars – on and off screen – and their lavish lifestyles in the city's clubs and millionaires' ghetto of Malabar Hill, are the subject of endless titillating gossip. Fanzines such as Stardust, Star and Style, Film World and Cine Blitz are snaffled up by millions, while the industry looks to the more sober Screen. Following the careers of the stars requires dedication; each may work on up to ten movies at once.

One way in which Bollywood has moved closer to Hollywood in recent years has been the rise in budgets to tens of millions of dollars, with foreign settings and an increase in on-screen sauciness. But, with pirate videos and a thirty percent drop in audiences, a number of big-budget movies are failing to make money, and many now lose up to Rs100 million. Coupled with the recent mafia scandals involving financing (see p.97), Bollywood is in big trouble, and an overhaul of the industry is desperately needed.

Visitors to Mumbai should have ample opportunity to sample the delights of a movie. To make an educated choice, buy *Bombay* magazine, which contains extensive listings and reviews. Otherwise, look for the biggest, brightest hoarding, and join the queue. Seats in a comfortable air-conditioned cinema cost around Rs20, or less if you sit in the stalls (not advisable for women). Of the two hundred or so cinemas, only eight regularly screen English-language films. The most central and convenient are the Regal in Colaba, the Eros opposite Churchgate station, the Sterling, the New Excelsior and the New Empire, which are all a short walk west of CST station.

---

sleazy you won't have any problems. At the five-star hotels, entry can be restricted to hotel guests and members.

Copa Cabana, Marine Drive. Dark, smoky atmosphere, Latino music and lots of tequila. Free shooters for the ladies on Weds till 10pm and Thurs is 2 for 1 on Indian liquors.

Fashion Bistro, 16 Marzban Rd, next to Sterling Cinema. Mannequins display designer creations in one room, with a bar and tiny dance floor in another. Deafeningly loud Western chart-music with a

Seventies and Eighties night on Fri. Rs200–300 cover charge per couple.

Headquarters, 166 MG Rd, opposite Regal Cinema, Colaba. Great little student club with good DJs, hip decor and a storming Goa-trance night on Fri. It is, however, fairly pricy with a Rs200–400 cover charge – though couples get in free Tues, Thurs & Sun. Tues–Sun 8pm–1.30am.

The 1900s, *Taj Mahal*. Pounding disco, free to guests but otherwise for members only. If you can get in, you'll see the cream of Mumbai society at their air-kissing best.

Razzberry Rhinoceros, *Juhu Hotel*, Juhu Beach. Much UV lighting and a good-size dance floor

playing trance (Fri), drum'n'bass (alternate Wed) and the latest Western sounds (Sat & alternate Weds). Also has live rock bands on Thursdays as well as occasional blues, jazz or reggae bands on Sun. Cover charge Rs100–400 per couple and closes at 1.30am – though the coffee shop over-looking the beach stays open till 5 or 6am.

Three Flights Up, Apollo Bunder, Colaba. Used to have the longest bar in Asia and, despite moving to new (smaller) premises, is the biggest club in Mumbai. The music is Western disco, there's a no-smoking policy on the dance floor and fantastic a/c.

Shopping

Mumbai is a great place to shop, whether for last-minute souvenirs, or essentials for the long journeys ahead. Locally produced **textiles** and export-surplus clothing are among the best buys, as are **handicrafts** from far-flung corners of the country. With the exception of the swish arcades in the five-star hotels, prices compare surprisingly well with other Indian cities. In the larger shops, rates are fixed and **credit cards** are often accepted; elsewhere, particularly deal-ing with street-vendors, it pays to haggle. Uptown, the **central bazaars** – see p.121 – are better for spectating than serious shopping, although the **antiques** and Friday flea market in the Chor, or "thieves" bazaar, can sometimes yield the odd bargain. The **Zaveri** (goldsmiths') **bazaar** opposite Crawford Market is the place to head for new gold and silver jewellery. The city features a number of swish modern **shopping centres**, including India's largest, Crossroads, at 28 Pandit MM Rd near the Haj Ali mosque. In Colaba, there's also Sahakari Brandar which sells a range of good-value handicrafts and household goods. An attached supermarket stocks a cornucopia of dry and tinned goods.

Opening hours in the city centre are Monday to Saturday, 10am to 7pm. The Muslim bazaars, quiet on Friday, are otherwise open until around 9pm.

Antiques

The **Chor Bazaar** area, and Mutton Street in particular, is the centre of Mumbai's **antique trade**. For a full account, see p.122. Another good, if much more expensive, place to sift through the fakes for a real gem or two is **Phillip's** famous antique shop, on the corner of Madam Cama Road, opposite the Regal cinema in Colaba. This fascinating, old-fashioned store has changed little since it opened in 1860. Innumerable glass lamps and chandeliers hang from the ceil-ing, while antique display cases are stuffed with miniature brass, bronze and wood Hindu sculpture, silver jewellery, old prints and aquatints. Most of the stuff on sale dates from the twilight of the Raj – a result of the Indian gov-ernment's ban on the export by foreigners of items more than a century old.

In the **Jehangir Art Gallery** basement, a branch of the antiques chain Natesan's Antiqarts offers a tempting selection of antique (and reproduction) sculpture, furniture, paintings and bronzes.

Clothes and textiles

Mumbai produces the bulk of India's **clothes**, mostly the lightweight, light-coloured "shirtings and suitings" favoured by droves of uniformly attired office-wallahs. For cheaper Western clothing, you can't beat the long row of stalls on the pavement of MG Road, opposite the Mumbai Gymkhana. "**Fashion Street**" specializes in reject and export-surplus goods ditched by big manufacturers, selling off T-shirts, jeans, leggings, summer dresses, and trendy sweatshirts. Better-quality cotton clothes (often stylish designer-label rip-offs) are available in shops along **Colaba Causeway**, such as Cotton World, down Mandlik Marg.

If you're looking for **traditional Indian clothes**, head for the Khadi Village Industries Emporium at 286 Dr DN Marg, near the Thomas Cook office. As Whiteaway & Laidlaw, this rambling Victorian department store used to kit all the newly arrived *burra-sahibs* out with pith helmets, khaki shorts and quinine tablets. These days, its old wooden counters, shirt and sock drawers stock dozens of different hand-spun cottons and silks, sold by the metre or made up as vests, *kurtas* or block-printed *salwar kamises*. Other items include the ubiquitous white Nehru caps, *dhotis*, Madras-check *lunghis* and fine brocaded silk saris. Actually buying the stuff requires a number of separate manoeuvres: you select an item, get a chit, go to the cash desk, have the additions checked, pay for the goods, get a receipt, and go to the collection point, where your goods will be beautifully wrapped in paper bags just bursting to fall apart.

Another good place to pick up quality Indian clothes is the cloth bazaar on Mangaldas Lane, opposite Crawford Market, where touts lead you through a maze of stalls to backstreet shops crammed with inexpensive silk scarves, embroidered Kashmiri shawls and Gujarati tie-dye wall-hangings.

Handicrafts

Regionally produced **handicrafts** are marketed in assorted state-run emporia at the World Trade Centre, down on Cuffe Parade, and along Sir PM Road, Fort. The quality is consistently high – as are the prices, if you miss out on the periodic holiday discounts. The same goes for the **Central Cottage Industries Emporium**, 34 Shivaji Marg, near the Gateway of India in Colaba, whose size and central location make it the single best all-round place to hunt for souvenirs. Downstairs you'll find inlaid furniture, wood and metal work, miniature paintings and jewellery, while upstairs specializes in toys, clothing and textiles – Gujarati appliqué bedspreads, hand-painted pillowcases and Rajasthani mirror-work, plus silk ties and Noel Coward dressing gowns. **Mereweather Road**, directly behind the *Taj*, is awash with Kashmiri handicraft stores stocking over-priced papier-mâché pots and bowls, silver jewellery, woollen shawls and rugs. Avoid them if you find it hard to shrug off aggressive sales pitches.

Perfume is essentially a Muslim preserve in Mumbai. Down at the south end of Colaba Causeway, around Arthur Bunder Road, shops with mirrored walls and shelves are stacked with cut-glass carafes full of syrupy, fragrant essential oils. **Incense** is hawked in sticks, cones and slabs of sticky *dhoop* on the sidewalk nearby (check that the boxes haven't already been opened and their contents sold off piecemeal). For bulk buying, the hand-rolled, cottage-made bundles of incense sold in the Khadi Village Industries Emporium on Dr DN Marg (see above) are a better deal; it also has a handicraft department where, in addition to furniture, paintings and ornaments, you can pick up glass bangles, block-printed and calico bedspreads, and wooden votive statues produced in Maharashtran craft villages.

Books

Mumbai's excellent English-language **bookshops** and bookstalls are well stocked with everything to do with India, and a good selection of general classics, pulp fiction and travel writing. Indian editions of popular titles cost a fraction of what they do abroad and include lots of interesting works by lesser-known local authors. If you don't mind picking through dozens of trigonometry textbooks, back issues of National Geographic and salacious 1960s paperbacks, the **street stalls** between Flora Fountain and Churchgate station can also be good places to hunt for secondhand books.

Chetana, 34 Dubash Rd (Rampart Row). Exclusively religion and philosophy.
Crossword, Mahalakshmi Chambers, 22 Bhulabhai Desai Rd, Breach Candy ☎ 022/492 2458. Mumbai's largest and most reputed retailer, a bus ride (#132) from the downtown area.
Nalanda, ground floor, *Taj Mahal*. An exhaustive range of coffee-table tomes and paperback literature.
Pustak Bharati, Bharatiya Vidhya Bhavan, KM Munshi Marg. Excellent small bookshop specializing in Hindu philosophy and literature, plus details of Bhavan's cultural programmes.
Shankar Book-Stand, outside the *Café Mondegar*, Colaba Causeway. Piles of easy-reads, guidebooks, classic fiction, and most of the old favourites on India.
Strand, next door to the Canara Bank, off PM Road, Fort. The best bookshop in the city centre, with the full gamut of Penguins and Indian literature.

Music

The most famous of Mumbai's many good **music shops** are near the Moti cinema along SV Patel Road, in the central bazaar district. Haribhai Vishwanath, Ram Singh and RS Mayeka are all government-approved retailers of traditional Indian instruments, including sitars, sarods, tablas and flutes.

For **cassettes and CDs** try Rhythm House, Subhash Chowk, next to the Jehangir Art Gallery. This is a veritable Aladdin's cave of classical, devotional and popular music from all over India, with a reasonable selection of Western rock, pop and jazz.

Listings

Airlines, domestic Alliance Air ☎ 022/611 4426; Air India ☎ 022/287 6565, ⓦ www.airindia.com; Indian Airlines, Air India Building, Nariman Point (Mon–Sat 8.30am–7.30pm, Sun 10am–1pm & 1.45–5.30pm; ☎ 022/202 3031); counter at the airport ☎ 022/615 6850; Jet Airways, Amarchand Mansion, Madam Cama Road ☎ 022/285 5788; Sahara Airlines Unit 7, Ground Floor, Tulsiani Chambers, Nariman Point ☎ 022/283 5671.
Airlines, international Aeroflot, Ground Floor, Tulsiani Chambers, Free Press Journal Road, Nariman Point ☎ 022/287 1942; Air France, Maker Chambers VI, 1st Floor, Nariman Point ☎ 022/202 5021; Air India, Air India Building, Nariman Point ☎ 022/202 4142; Air Lanka, 12-D, Raheja Centre, Nariman Point ☎ 022/282 3288; Alitalia, Industrial Insurance Building, VN Road, Churchgate ☎ 022/204 5026; British Airways, 202-B Vulcan Insurance Building, VN Road, Churchgate ☎ 022/282 0888; Cathay Pacific, Bajaj Bhavan, 3rd Floor, 226, Nariman Point ☎ 022/202 9561; Delta, *Taj Mahal*, Colaba ☎ 022/288 5652; Emirates, 228 Mittal Chambers, Nariman Point ☎ 022/287 1645; Gulf Air, Maker Chamber V, Nariman Point ☎ 022/202 1626; KLM, Khaitan Bhavan, 198 J Tata Rd, Churchgate ☎ 022/283 3338; Kuwait Airways, 86 VN Rd, Churchgate ☎ 022/204 5331; Japan Airlines, Raheja Centre, Nariman Point ☎ 022/287 4937; Lufthansa, 1st Floor, Express Towers, Nariman Point ☎ 022/202 7178; Pakistan International Airlines, Mittal Tower, B Wing, 4th Floor, Nariman Point ☎ 022/202 1373; Qantas Airways, 42 Sakhar Bhavan, Nariman Point ☎ 022/202 0343; Royal Nepal Airlines, 222, Maker Chamber V, Nariman Point ☎ 022/283 6197; SAS and Thai Airways, 15 World Trade Centre, Cuffe Parade, Colaba ☎ 022/215 5301; Saudia, Ground Floor, Express Towers, Nariman Point ☎ 022/202 0199; Scandinavian Airlines, Ground Floor, Podar House, 10 Marine Drive, Churchgate ☎ 022/202 7083; South African Airways, Podar House, 10 Marine Drive, Churchgate ☎ 022/282 3454; Swissair, Maker Chamber VI, 220 Nariman Point ☎ 022/287 2210; Syrian Arab Airlines, 7 Brabourne

135

Stadium, VN Road, Churchgate ☎ 022/282 6043; TWA and Australian Airlines, Amarchand Mansion, M Carve Road ☎ 022/282 3080.

Airport enquiries Sahar International Airport ☎ 022/836 6700. Santa Cruz Domestic Airport: Terminal 1A for Indian Airlines ☎ 022/615 6633; 1B for all other airlines ☎ 022/615 6600.

Ambulance ☎ 022/266 2913 or ☎ 101 for general emergencies or ☎ 105 for heart cases.

Banks and currency exchange The logical place to change money when you arrive in Mumbai is at the State Bank of India's 24hr counter in Sahar airport. Rates here are standard but you'll have to pay for an encashment certificate – essential if you intend to buy tourist quota train tickets or an Indrail pass at the special counters in Churchgate or VT stations. All the major state banks downtown change foreign currency (Mon–Fri 10.30am–2.30pm, Sat 10.30am–12.30pm); some also handle credit cards and cash advances. Several 24hr ATMs handle international transactions, usually Visa, Delta and Mastercard – it's best to check with your bank which you can use beforehand. It's also worth noting that there's often a limit on how much you can take out: it can be as low as Rs4000. ATM machines can be found at: Air India Building, Nariman Point and 293 DN Rd, Fort (Citibank); and 52/60 MG Rd, near Hutama Chowk, Fort and Asha Mahal, Kemp's Corner Flyover, Breach Candy (HSBC). The fast and efficient American Express office (daily 9.30am–6pm; ☎ 022/204 8291, on Shivaji Marg, around the corner from the Regal cinema in Colaba, offers all the regular services (including poste restante) to travellers' cheque- and card-holders and is open to anyone wishing to change cash. Thomas Cook's big Dr DN Marg branch (Mon–Sat 9.30am–6pm; ☎ 022/204 8556), between the Khadi shop and Hutatma Chowk, can also arrange money transfers from overseas.

Consulates and high commissions Although the many consulates and High Commissions in Mumbai can be useful for replacing lost travel documents or obtaining visas, most of India's neighbouring states, including Bangladesh, Bhutan, Burma, Nepal and Pakistan, only have embassies in New Delhi and/or Calcutta (see relevant city account). All of the following are open Monday to Friday: Australia, 16th Floor, Maker Tower "E", Cuffe Parade (9am–5pm; ☎ 022/218 1071); Canada, 41–42 Maker Chambers VI, Nariman Point (9am–5.30pm; ☎ 022/287 6027); China, 1st floor, 11 M.L. Dahanukar Marg (10am–4.30pm; ☎ 022/282 2662); Denmark, L & T House, Narottam Moraji Marg, Ballard Estate (10am–12.45pm; ☎ 022/261 4462); Germany,

10th Floor, Hoechst House, Nariman Point (9–11am; ☎ 022/283 2422); Republic of Ireland, Royal Bombay Yacht Club Chambers, Apollo Bunder (10am–noon; ☎ 022/202 4607); Netherlands, "International" Building, New Marine Lines, Cross Road, 1 Churchgate (9am–5pm; ☎ 022/201 6750); Norway, Navroji Mansion, 31 Nathelal Parekh Marg (10am–1pm; ☎ 022/284 2042); Philippines, 61 Sakhar Bhavan, Nariman Point (10am–1pm; ☎ 022/202 4792); Singapore, 9th Floor, 94 Sakhar Bhavan, Nariman Point (9am–noon; ☎ 022/204 3205); South Africa, Gandhi Mansion, 20 Altamount Rd (9am–noon; ☎ 022/389 3725); Spain, Ador House, 3rd floor, 6 K Dubash Marg, Kala Ghoda (10.30am–1pm; ☎ 022/287 4797); Sri Lanka, Sri Lanka House, 34 Homi Modi St, Fort (9.30am–11.30am; ☎ 022/204 5861); Sweden, 85 Sayani Rd, Subash Gupta Bhawan, Prabhadevi (9.30am–12.30pm; ☎ 022/288 4563); Switzerland, Maker Chamber IV, 10th floor, Nariman Point (8am–11am; ☎ 022/204 3003); Thailand, Malabar View, 4th floor, Dr Purandure Marg, Chowpatty Sea Face (9am–noon; ☎ 022/363 1404); United Kingdom, 2nd Floor, Maker Chamber IV, Nariman Point (8am–11.30am; ☎ 022/283 0517); USA, Lincoln House, 78 Bhulabhai Desai Rd (7am–11am; ☎ 022/363 3611).

Hindi lessons Kalina University, in north Mumbai, and a number of private academies run short courses. Ask at the tourist office in Churchgate (☎ 022/203 3144) for more details.

Hospitals The best hospital in the centre is the private Mumbai Hospital (☎ 022/206 7676), New Marine Lines, just north of the government tourist office on M Karve Road. Breach Candy Hospital (☎ 022/363 3651) on Bhulabhai Desai Road, near the swimming pool, is also recommended by foreign embassies.

Internet access A couple of cramped 24hr places (Rs40 per hour) can be found in Colaba, just round the corner from Leopold's on Nawroji F Marg, though it's worth paying the Rs5 extra at Access Infotech, located down a small alley further down Colaba Causeway on the left, which is faster and more comfortable. Near VT, several places can be found on Sahid Bhagat Singh Marg where Nikhil Communication Centre at no. 268 costs Rs40 per hour and is open till 1am. On-line is another good name and they have two cafés: 82 Veer Nariman Rd, Churchgate and 39 Sea Face, Chowpatty (both Rs50/hr).

Left luggage If your hotel won't let you store bags with them, try the cloakrooms at Sahar and Santa Cruz airports (see p.99), or the one in VT station (Rs7–10 a day). Anything left here, even rucksacks, must be securely fastened with a pad-lock and can be left for a maximum of one month. Libraries Asiatic Society, SBS Marg, Horniman Circle, Ballard Estate (Mon–Sat 10.30am–7pm); British Council (for British newspapers), A Wing, 1st Floor, Mittal Tower, Nariman Point (Tues–Sat 10am–6pm); Alliance Francaisede Mombai, Theosophy Hall, 40 New Marine Lines; Max Mueller Bhavan, Prince of Wales Annexe, off MG Road (Mon–Fri 9.30am–6pm). The KR Cama Oriental Institute, 136 Mumbai Samachar Marg (Mon–Fri 10am–5pm, Sat 10am–1pm), specializing in Zoroastrian and Iranian studies has a public collection of 22,000 volumes in European and Asian languages. Mumbai Natural History Society, Hornbill House (Mon–Fri 10am–5pm, Sat 10am–1pm, closed 1st & 3rd Sat of the month), has an international reputation for the study of wildlife in India. Visitors may become temporary members which allows them access to the library, natural history collection, occasional talks and the opportunity to join organized walks and field trips. Pharmacies Real Chemist, 50/51 Kaka Arcade (☎ 022/200 2497) and Royal Chemists, M Karve Road (☎ 022/534 0531), both close to Mumbai Hospital, are open 24hr. Kemps in the *Taj Mahal* also opens late.

Photographic studios and equipment The Javeri Colour Lab, opposite the Regal cinema in Colaba, stocks colour-print and slide film, as do most of the big hotels. A small boutique behind the florists in the Shakhari Bunder covered market does instant Polaroid passport photographs.

Police The main police station in Colaba (☎ 022/285 6817) is on the west side of Colaba Causeway, near the crossroads with Ormiston Road.

Postal services The GPO (Mon–Sat 9am–8pm, Sun 9am–4pm) is around the corner from VT Station, off Nagar Chowk. Its poste restante counter (Mon–Sat 9am–6pm, Sun 9am–3pm) is among the most reliable in India, although they trash the letters after four weeks. The much less efficient parcel office (10am–4.30pm) is behind the main building on the first floor. Packing-wallahs hang around on the pavement outside. DHL (☎ 022/850 5050) have eleven offices in Mumbai, the most

convenient being the 24hr one under the *Sea Green Hotel* at the bottom of Marine Drive.

State tourist offices: Goa, Mumbai Central Railway Station ☎ 022/308 6288; Gujarat, Dhanraj Mahal, Chhatrapati Shivaji Maharaj Marg, Apollo Bunder ☎ 022/202 4925; Himachal Pradesh, 36 World Trade Centre, Cuffe Parade ☎ 022/218 1123; Jammu & Kashmir, 25 World Trade Centre ☎ 022/218 9040; Kerala Tourism Information Counter, "Kairali", Nirmal Building, Nariman Point ☎ 022/202 6817; Madhya Pradesh, 74 World Trade Centre ☎ 022/218 7603; Rajasthan, 230 Dr DN Marg, Fort ☎ 022/204 4162; Tamil Nadu, G2(A), Royal Grace, Lokmanya Tilak Colony Marg No. 2, Dadar (East) ☎ 022/411 0118; and Uttar Pradesh, 38 World Trade Centre ☎ 022/218 5458.

Swimming pools The snooty sports club at Breach Candy, north of Malabar Hill, is a popular place to beat the heat. A day's membership costs around Rs200.

Telephones and faxes STD booths abound in Mumbai. For rock-bottom phone and fax rates however, head for Videsh Sanchar Bhavan (open 24hr), the swanky government telecom building on MG Marg, where you can make reverse charge calls to destinations such as the UK, US and Australia. Receiving incoming calls costs a nominal Rs10. Numbers in the city change constantly, so if you can't get through after several attempts, try directory enquiries on ☎ 197.

Travel agents The following travel agents are recommended for booking domestic and international flights, and long-distance private buses where specified: Ambassador Travels, 14, Embassy Centre, Nariman Point ☎ 022/283 1046; Cox and Kings India Ltd, 271/272, Dr DN Marg ☎ 022/204 3065; ⊛ www.coxkings.com; Magnum International Tours & Travels, Frainy Villa, 10 Henry Rd, Colaba ☎ 022/285 2343, ⊜ magnum.intnal @axcess.net.in; Peerless Hotels & Travels Ltd, Ground Floor, Churchgate Chambers, 5 New Marine Lines ☎ 022/265 1500; Sita World Travels Pvt Ltd, 8 Atlanta Building, Nariman Point ☎ 022/284 0666, ⊜ boml.sita@sma.springtrpg .ems.vsnl.in; Thomas Cook (see p.136)

Moving on from Mumbai

Most visitors feel like getting out of Mumbai as soon as they can. Fortunately, Mumbai is equipped with "super-fast" services to arrange or confirm **onward travel**. All the major international and domestic **airlines** have offices in the city, the railway networks operate special tourist counters in the main reservation halls, and dozens of **travel agents** and road transport companies are eager to help you on your way by **bus**.

Travel within India

Mumbai is the nexus of several major internal flight routes, train networks and highways, and is the main transport hub for traffic heading towards south India. The most travelled trails lead north up the Gujarati coast to **Rajasthan** and **Delhi**; northwest into the **Deccan** via Aurangabad and the caves at Ellora and Ajanta; and south, through Pune and the hills of the Western Ghats towards **Goa** and the Malabar coast. Public transport is cheap and frequent, but book in advance and be prepared for delays.

By plane

Indian Airlines and other **domestic carriers** fly out of Santa Cruz to destinations all over India. Computerization has made booking less of a lottery than it used to be, but availability on popular routes (especially Mumbai–Goa–Mumbai) should never be taken for granted. Check with the airlines as soon as you arrive; **tickets** can be bought directly from their offices (see p.135), or through any reputable travel agent, although you'll have to pay the mandatory Rs600 **airport tax** when you get to Santa Cruz.

In theory, it is also possible to book domestic air tickets abroad when you buy your original long-haul flight. However, as individual airlines tend to have separate agreements with domestic Indian carriers, you may not be offered the same choice (or rates) as you will through agents in Mumbai. Note, too, that Indian Airlines is the only company offering 25 percent discounts (on all flights) to customers under the age of thirty.

By train

Two main networks converge on Mumbai: the **Western Railway** runs to north and west India; the **Central Railway** connects Mumbai to central, eastern and southern regions.

Nearly all services to Gujarat, Rajasthan, Delhi and the far north leave from **Mumbai Central** station, in the mid-town area. Second-class tickets can be booked here through the normal channels, but the quickest place for foreign nationals to make reservations is at the efficient tourist counter (no. 28) on the first floor of the Western Railway's booking hall, next door to the India government tourist office in Churchgate (Mon–Fri 9.30am–4.30pm, Sat 9.30am–2.30pm; ☎ 022/203 8016, extension 4577 for foreigners). This counter also has access to special "**tourist quotas**", which are released the day before departure if the train leaves during the day, or the morning of the departure if the train leaves after 5pm. If the quota is "closed" or already used up, and you can't access the "**VIP quota**" (always worth a try), you will have to join the regular queue.

Mumbai's other "Tourist Ticketing Facility" is in the snazzy air-conditioned Central Railway booking office to the rear of VT (Mon–Sat 9am–1pm & 1.30–4pm; counter no. 22 or 21 on Sun), the departure point for most trains heading east and south. Indrail passes can also be bought here, and there's an MTDC tourist information kiosk in the main concourse if you need help filling in your reservation slips.

Just to complicate matters, some Central Railway trains to **south India**, including the fast Dadar–Madras Chennai Express #6063 to Madras, do not depart from VT at all, but from **Dadar station**, way north of Mumbai

Central. Seats and berths for these trains are reserved at VT. Finally, if you're booking tickets to Calcutta, make sure your train doesn't leave from **Kurla station**, which is even more inconvenient, up near the airports. Getting to either of these stations on public transport can be a major struggle, though many long-distance trains from VT or Churchgate stop there and aren't as crowded.

By bus

The main departure point for long-distance **buses** leaving Mumbai is the frenetic **Central bus stand** on JB Behram Marg, opposite Mumbai Central railway station. States with bus company counters here (daily 8am–8pm; ☎022/307 6622), include Maharashtra, Karnataka, Madhya Pradesh, Goa and Gujarat. Few of their services compare favourably with train travel on the same routes. Reliable timetable information can be difficult to obtain, reservations are not available on standard buses, and most long-haul journeys are gruelling overnighters. Among the exceptions are the **deluxe buses** run by MSRTC to Pune, Nasik and Kolhapur; the small extra cost buys you more leg-room, fewer stops and the option of advance booking. The only problem is, most leave from the **ASIAD** bus stand in Dadar, thirty minutes or so by road or rail north of Mumbai Central.

Other possibilities for road travel include the "super-fast" **luxury coaches** touted around Colaba. Most are run by private companies, guaranteeing breakneck speeds and possible long waits for the bus to fill up. ITDC also operate similarly priced services to the same destinations, which you can book direct

Recommended trains from Mumbai

The services listed below are the most direct and/or the fastest. This list is by no means exhaustive and there are numerous slower trains that are often more convenient for smaller destinations – see p.141.

Destination	Name	No.	From	Frequency	Departs	Total time
Agra	Punjab Mail	#2137–38	CST	Daily	7.10pm	21hr 30min
Aurangabad	Devgiri Express	#1003	CST	Daily	6.10pm	7hr 25min
Bangalore	Udyan Express	#6529	CST	Daily	7.55am	24hr 40min
Bhopal	Flrozpur Punjab Mail	#2137	CST	Daily	7.10pm	14hr 10min
Calcutta	Gitanjali Express	#2859	CST	Daily	6am	32hr 55min
	Mumbai–Howrah Express	#8001	CST	Daily	8.15pm	36hr
Chennai	Mumbai–Chennai Express	#6011	CST	Daily	2pm	26hr 45min
Cochin*	Kanniyakumari Express	#1081	CST	Daily	3.35pm	38hr 10min
Goa	Mumbai–Madgaon Express	#KR011	CST	Daily	10.30pm	12hr
Hyderabad	Hussainsagar Express	#7001	CST	Daily	9.55pm	15hr 15min
Jaipur	Bandra–Jaipur Express	#9707	Bandra	Daily	9.25pm	23hr
Jodhpur	Bandra–Bikaneer Express	#4708	Bandra	Daily	3.10pm	19hr 25min
New Delhi	Rajhani Express	#2951	MC	Daily	4.55pm	17hr
	Paschim Express	#2925	MC	Daily	11.35am	23hr 20min
	Golden Temple Mail	#2903	MC	Daily	9.30pm	23hr 30min
Pune	Shatabdi Express	#2027	CST	Daily	6.40pm	3hr 25min
Trivandrum	Kanniyakumari Express	#1081	CST	Daily	3.35pm	44hr 45min
Udaipur	Saurashtra Express**	#9215	MC	Daily	7.45am	24hr 40min
Varanasi	Mahanagiri Express	#1093	CST	Daily	11.55pm	28hr

*details also applicable for Ernakulam Town
**change at Ahmedabad to the Delhi Sarai Rohila Express #9944

Since the inauguration of the controversial Konkan Railway, the best-value way to travel the 500km from Mumbai to Goa has been by train. However, tickets for the twelve-hour ride down the coast tend be in short supply, and virtually impossible to obtain at short notice, so it's best to try and book with an Indian Railways agent back home before setting off. Otherwise, you'll probably find yourself having to shell out for a flight. This can be done in your home country when you buy your long-haul ticket or on arrival in India, although bear in mind that seats frequently sell out weeks ahead, particularly around peak season. Considering how hellish the bus ride can be, and how hard getting hold of train tickets is, it's well worth paying the extra to travel by plane, ideally before you leave home, which could save you days waiting around in Mumbai.

By plane

At present, four airlines – Air India, Indian Airlines, Jet Airways and Sahara – operate daily services to Goa. If you can afford it, this is the most painless way to go, but demand for seats is fierce (particularly around Christmas/New Year) and you may well have to wait several days. If you didn't pre-book when you purchased your international ticket, check availability with the airlines as soon as you arrive; tickets can be bought directly from their offices (see Listings), or through any reputable travel agent in Mumbai, although bear in mind that an agent may charge you the dollar fare at a poorer rate of exchange than that offered by the airline company.

All Goa flights leave from Chatrapathi Shivaji Domestic Airport, 30km north of the city centre. One-way fares for the forty-minute flight start at $53 with Indian Airlines, and rise to $83 with Sahara, or $93 ($72 for under 30s) with swisher Jet. In addition, Air India operates an Airbus service to Mumbai on Mondays and Thursdays for $85. Few people seem to know about this flight, so you can nearly always get a seat on it.

By train

The new Konkan Railway line runs daily express trains from Mumbai to Goa. However, these services are not always available as they are invariably booked for at

---

From their main offices downtown or through the more conveniently situated Government of India tourist office, 123 M Karve Rd, Churchgate. Two night buses leave Nariman Point every evening for the twelve-hour trip to **Aurangabad**, and there are morning departures to **Nasik** and **Mahabaleshwar**, which take six and seven hours respectively.

Leaving India

In spite of its prominence on trans-Asian flight routes, Mumbai is no longer the bargain basement for **international air tickets** it used to be. Discounted fares are very hard to come by – a legacy of Rajiv Gandhi's economic reforms of the 1980s. If you do need to book a ticket, stick to one of the tried and tested agents listed on p.137.

All the major airlines operating out of Mumbai have offices downtown where you can buy scheduled tickets or confirm your flight; see p.135 for a list of addresses. The majority are grouped around Veer Nariman Road, opposite the *Ambassador Hotel*, or else on Nariman Point, a short taxi ride west of Colaba.

least a month in advance. If you don't have a reservation, it may be possible to get a place on your planned day of travel by joining the waiting list. But by the far the best option, if you know your travel dates in advance, is to book a ticket with an Indian Railways agent in your home country several months ahead; for more, see Basics on p.37.

Don't be tempted to travel "unreserved" class on any Konkan service as the journey as far as Ratnagiri (roughly mid-way) is overwhelmingly crushed. The most convenient of the Konkan services is the overnight Mumbai–Madgaon Express #KR0111 (10.40pm; 12hr) which departs from VT (CST). The other, only slightly faster train is the Madavi Express #KR0103, leaving CST at 5.15am.

Fares in second class cost around Rs250 (£4/$6), or Rs750 (£13/$19) for a three-tier berth in first class.

By bus

The Mumbai–Goa bus journey ranks among the very worst in India. Don't believe travel agents who assure you it takes thirteen hours. Depending on the type of bus you get, appalling road surfaces along the sinuous coastal route, make eighteen to twenty hours a more realistic estimate.

Bus tickets start at around Rs290 for a push-back seat on a beaten-up Kadamba (Goan government) or MSRTC coach. Tickets for these services are in great demand in season, so book in advance at Mumbai Central or Kadamba's kiosks on the north side of Azad Maidan, near St Xavier's College (just up from CST station; ☏022/262 1043). More and more private overnight buses (around 25 daily) also run to Goa, costing around Rs375–400 for a noisy front-engined Tata bus, Rs400–450 for an a/c bus with pneumatic suspension and on-board toilet, and Rs600–675 for a service with coffin-like sleeper compartments which quickly become unbearably stuffy. Tickets should be booked at least a day in advance through a reputable travel agent (see p.137), though it's sometimes worth turning up at the car park opposite the Metro cinema, Azad Maidan, where most buses leave from, on the off-chance of a last-minute cancellation. Make sure, in any case, that you are given both your seat and the bus registration numbers, and that you confirm the exact time and place of departure with the travel agent, as these frequently vary between companies.

Travel details

Trains

Direct services to: Agra (4 daily; 23hr 15min–27hr); Ahmedabad (4 daily; 7hr 10min–12hr); Aurangabad (2 daily; 7hr 20min); Bangalore (3 daily; 24hr 30min); Bhopal (4 daily; 14hr); Calcutta (4 daily; 33–40hr); Chennai (3 daily; 24–29hr); Coimbatore (1 daily; 10hr); Delhi (11 daily; 17–33hr); Hyderabad (2 daily; 15–17hr); Indore (1 daily; 14hr 35min); Jaipur (2 daily; 18–23hr); Jodhpur (1 daily; 22hr; change at Ahmedabad); Kolhapur (3 daily; 11–12hr); Nagpur (4 daily; 14–15hr); Nasik (15 daily; 4hr); Pune (25 daily; 3hr 15min–5hr); Thiruvananthapuram (2 daily; 42hr); Udaipur (1 daily; 25hr; change at Ahmedabad); Ujjain (1 daily; 12hr 25 min); Varanasi (2 daily; 29–36hr).

Buses

Only state bus services are listed here; for details of private buses, see above.
Mumbai Central to: Aurangabad (2 daily; 10hr); Bangalore (3 daily; 24hr); Bijapur (3 daily; 12hr); Goa (2 daily; 18–19hr); Indore (2 daily; 16hr); Ujjain (1 daily; 17hr).
ASIAD Dadar to: Kolhapur (4 daily; 10hr); Nasik (17 daily; 5hr); Pune (half-hourly; 4hr).

Flights

For a list of airline addresses and travel agents, see p.135. In the listings below, AI represents Alliance Air, IA is Indian Airlines, JA Jet Airways, and SA Sahara Airlines.

Santa Cruz airport to: Ahmedabad (AI, IA, JA 6–7 daily; 1hr); Aurangabad (IA, JA 2 daily; 1hr 30min); Bangalore (AI, IA, JA 11 daily; 1hr 30min); Bhopal (SA, AL 2 daily; 1hr 25min); Calcutta (AI, IA, JA, SA 5–6 daily; 2hr 25min); Calicut (AI, IA, JA 2–5 daily; 1hr); Chennai (AI, JA 8–9 daily; 1hr 45min); Cochin (AI, IA, JA 4 daily; 1hr 50min); Coimbatore (IA, JA 2 daily; 1hr 50min); Delhi (AI, IA, JA, SA, 22–26 daily; 1hr 45min–2hr); Goa (AI, IA, JA, SA 3–4 daily; 1hr 55min); Hyderabad (AI, IA, JA 6–8 daily; 1hr 15min); Indore (JA, SA 3–4 daily; 1hr 10min); Jaipur (AL, JA, SA 7–8 daily; 1hr 35min); Johdpur (AL 4 weekly; 2hr 20min); Madurai (IA 1 daily; 1hr 55min); Mangalore (AL, JA 4 daily; 1hr 15min); Nagpur (AL, IA 2 daily; 1hr 55min); Pune (JA 2–3 daily; 35min); Thiruvananthapuram (AI, IA, JA 3–5 daily; 2hr); Udaipur (AA, IA, JA 2–3 daily; 1hr 45min); Varanasi (IA, SA 1–2 daily; 3hr 5min).

2

Goa

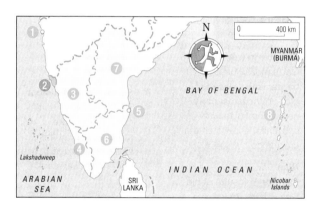

CHAPTER 2

Highlights

✳ **Old Goa** Belfries and Baroque church facades loom over the trees on the banks of the Mandovi, all that remains of a once splendid colonial city. See p.159

✳ **Beach shacks** Tuck into a fresh kingfish, tandoori pomfret or lobster, washed down with *feni* or an ice-cool Kingfisher beer. See p.199

✳ **Flea market, Anjuna** Goa's most vibrant bazaar is the place to pick up the latest party gear, shop for touristy souvenirs, and watch the crowds go by. See p.180

✳ **Nine Bar, Ozran Vagator** Epicentre of hip Goa, where Trance music accompanies the sunsets over Vagator beach. See p.183

✳ **Arambol** An alternative resort with exquisite beaches and a ramshackle fishing village. See p.189

✳ **Perreira-Braganza House, Chandor** The region's most impressive colonial-era mansion, crammed with period furniture and fittings. See p.197

✳ **Sunset stroll, Palolem** Tropical sunsets don't come much more romantic than at this idyllic palm-fringed cove in the hilly deep south. See p.205

Goa

I f one word could be said to encapsulate the essence of **GOA**, it would have to be the Portuguese *sossegarde*, meaning "carefree". The pace of life in this former colonial enclave, midway down India's southwest coast, has picked up over the past twenty years but, in spite of the increasing chaos of its capital, beach resorts and market towns, Goa has retained the laid-back feel that has traditionally set it apart from the rest of the country. Its 1.4 million inhabitants are unequivocal about the roots of their distinctiveness; while most of the subcontinent was colonized by the stiff-upper-lipped British, Goa's European overlords were the **Portuguese**, a people far more inclined to enjoy the good things in life than their Anglo-Saxon counterparts.

Goa was Portugal's first toe-hold in Asia, and served as the linchpin for a vast trade network for over 450 years. However, when the Lusitanian empire began to flounder in the seventeenth century, so too did the fortunes of its capital. Cut off from the rest of India by a wall of mountains and hundreds of miles of unnavigable alluvial plain, it remained resolutely aloof from the wider subcontinent. While India was tearing itself to pieces in the run-up to Independence in 1947, the only machetes being wielded here were cutting coconuts. Not until 1961, after an exasperated Indian Prime Minister, Jawaharlal Nehru, gave up trying to negotiate with the Portuguese dictator Salazar and sent in the army, was Goa finally absorbed into India.

Those who visited in the late 1960s and 1970s, when the overland travellers' trail wriggled its way south from Bombay, found a way of life little changed in centuries: Portuguese was still very much the lingua franca of the well educated elite, and the coastal settlements were mere fishing and coconut cultivation villages. Relieved to have found somewhere inexpensive and culturally undemanding to recover from the travails of Indian travel, the travellers got stoned, watched the mesmeric sunsets over the Arabian Sea and partied madly on full-moon nights, giving rise to a holiday culture that soon made Goa synonymous with hedonistic **hippies**.

Since then, the state has largely shaken off its reputation as a drop-out zone, but hundreds of thousands of visitors still flock here each winter, the vast majority to relax on Goa's beautiful **beaches**. Around two dozen stretches of soft white sand indent the region's coast, from spectacular 25-kilometre sweeps to secluded palm-backed coves. The level of development varies wildly; while some are lined by ritzy Western-style resorts, the most sophisticated structures on others are palm-leaf shacks and old wooden outriggers that are heaved into the sea each afternoon.

Wherever you travel in Goa, vestiges of former Portuguese domination are ubiquitous, creating an ambience that is at once exotic and strangely familiar.

This is particularly true of Goan food which, blending the Latin love of meat and fish with India's predilection for spices, is quite unlike any other regional cuisine in Asia. Equally unique is the prevalence of **alcohol**. Beer is cheap, and six thousand or more bars around the state are licensed to serve it, along with the more traditional tipple, *feni*, a rocket-fuel spirit distilled from cashew fruit or coconut sap.

Travelling around the Christian heartland of central Goa, with its white-washed churches and wayside shrines, it's all too easy to forget that **Hinduism** remains the religion of more than two-thirds of the state's population. Unlike

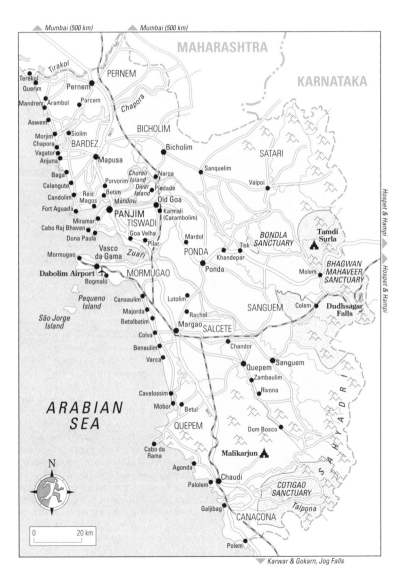

Accommodation price codes

All accommodation prices in this book have been categorized using the price codes below. The prices given are for a double room, and all taxes are included. For more details, see p.46.

① up to Rs100	④ Rs300–400	⑦ Rs900–1500
② Rs100–200	⑤ Rs400–600	⑧ Rs1500–2500
③ Rs200–300	⑥ Rs600–900	⑨ Rs2500 and upwards

in many parts of the country, however, religious intolerance is rare here, and traditional practices mingle easily with more recently implanted ones. Faced by the threat of merger with neighbouring states, Goans have always put regional cohesion before communal differences at the ballot box. A potent stimulus for regional identity was the campaign through the 1980s to have **Konkani**, the language spoken by the vast majority of Goans, recognized as an official state language, which it eventually was in 1992. Since then, the **immigration** issue has come to dominate the political agenda. Considerably more prosperous than neighbouring states, Goa has been deluged over the past couple of decades with economic refugees, stirring up fears that the region's cultural distinctiveness will disappear. Among the main employers of migrant labour in recent years has been the **Konkan Railway**, completed in 1997 to form a super-fast land link with Mumbai – another conduit of economic prosperity that has brought lasting changes.

Which beach you opt for when you arrive largely depends on what sort of holiday you have in mind. Heavily developed resorts such as **Calangute** and **Baga**, in the north, and **Colva** (and to a lesser extent **Benaulim**), in the south, offer more "walk-in" accommodation, shopping and tourist facilities than elsewhere. Even if you don't fancy crowded bars and purpose-built hotels, it can be worth heading for these centres first, as finding places to stay in less commercialized corners is often difficult. **Anjuna**, **Vagator**, and **Chapora**, where accommodation is generally more basic and harder to come by, are the beaches to aim for if you've come to Goa to party. However, the bulk of budget travellers taking time out from tours of India end up in **Palolem**, in the far south, or **Arambol**, beyond the increasingly long reach of the charter buses. Although fast becoming resorts in their own right, these two fishing villages have largely preserved the laid-back atmosphere most people come to Goa for.

Foremost among the attractions away from the coast are the ruins of the Portuguese capital at **Old Goa**, 10km from Panjim – a sprawl of Catholic cathedrals, convents and churches that draws crowds of Christian pilgrims from all over India. Another popular day excursion is to Anjuna's Wednesday **flea market**, a sociable place to shop for souvenirs and dance wear. Further inland, the thickly wooded countryside around **Ponda** harbours numerous temples, where you can check out Goa's peculiar brand of Hindu architecture. The district of Salcete, and its main market town, **Margao**, is also littered with Portuguese mansions, churches and seminaries. Finally, wildlife enthusiasts may be tempted into the interior to visit the nature reserve at **Cotigao** in the far south. The best **time to come** to Goa is during the dry, relatively cool winter months between late October and late March. At other times, either the sun is too hot for comfort, or the monsoon rains make life miserable. During peak season, from mid-December to the end of January, the weather is perfect, with temperatures rarely nudging above 32°C. Finding a room or a house to rent at

2

GOA

Some of Goa's festivals are on fixed dates each year; ask at a tourist office for dates of the others. The biggest celebrations take place at Panjim and Margao.

Festa dos Reis (Jan 6). Epiphany celebrations include a procession of young boys decked out as the Three Kings to the Franciscan chapel of Reis Magos, near Panjim on the north bank of the Mandovi, 3km east of Fort Aguada. Other processions are held at Cansaulim and Chandor.

Carnival (Feb/March). Three days of *feni*-induced mayhem, centering on Panjim, to mark the run-up to Lent.

Shigmo (Feb/March). The Goan version of Holi is celebrated with big parades and crowds; drum and dance groups compete and huge floats, which threaten to bring down telegraph wires, trundle through the streets.

All Saints (March). On the fifth Monday in Lent, 26 effigies of saints, martyrs, popes, kings, queens and cardinals are paraded around the village of Velha Goa, near Panjim. A fair also takes place.

Igitun Chalne (May). *Dhoti*-clad devotees of the goddess Lairya enter trances and walk over hot coals at the village of Sirigao, Bichloim.

Sanjuan (June 24). The festival of St John is celebrated all over Goa, but is especially important in the coastal villages of Arambol and Terekol. Youngsters torch straw dummies (representing St John's baptism, and thus the death of sin), while revellers in striped pants dive into wells after drinking bottles of *feni*.

Janmashtami (Aug). Ritual bathing in the River Mandovi, off Diwadi Island, to celebrate the birth of Krishna.

Dussehra (Sept/Oct). Nine days of festivities in which more effigies are burned on bonfires, and children perform episodes from the life of Rama.

Diwali (Oct/Nov). The five-day Hindu "festival of lights" features processions all over the region, often accompanied by fireworks, and the exchange of sweets by neighbours, regardless of their faith.

Christmas (Dec 24–25). Celebrated everywhere in Goa. Late-night mass is usually followed by music, dancing and fireworks.

that time, however – particularly over Christmas and New Year when tariffs double, or triple – can be a real hassle.

Some history

The sheer inaccessibility of Goa by land has always kept it out of the mainstream of Indian history; on the other hand, its control of the seas and the lucrative spice trade made it a much coveted prize for rival colonial powers. Until a century before the arrival of the Portuguese adventurer **Vasco da Gama**, who landed near Kozhikode in Kerala in 1498, Goa had belonged for over a thousand years to the kingdom of **Kadamba**. In the interim it had been successfully conquered by the Karnatakan Vijayanagars, the Muslim Bahmanis, and Yusuf Adil Shah of Bijapur, but the capture of the fort at Panjim by **Afonso de Albuquerque** in 1510 signalled the start of a Portuguese occupation that was to last 450 years.

As Goa expanded, its splendid capital (now Old Goa) came to hold a larger population than Paris or London. Though Ismail Adil Shah laid siege for ten months in 1570, and the Marathas under Shivaji and later chiefs came nailbitingly close to seizing the region, the greatest threat was from other European maritime nations. While the Dutch made several unsuccessful attacks, the British at first preferred the avenue of diplomacy. Their **East India**

Company signed the **Convention of Goa** in 1642, granting them the right to trade with the colony, and use its harbours.

Meanwhile, conversions to **Christianity**, started by the Franciscans, gathered pace when St Francis Xavier founded the **Jesuit** mission in 1542. With the advent of the **Inquisition** soon afterwards, laws were introduced censoring literature and banning any faith other than Catholicism – even the long-established Syrian Christian community were branded heretics. Hindu temples were destroyed, and converted Hindus adopted Portuguese names, such as da Silva, Correa and de Sousa, which remain common in the region. The transnational influence of the Jesuits eventually alarmed the Portuguese government; the Jesuits were expelled in 1749, which made it possible for Indian Goans to take up the priesthood. However, standards of education suffered, and Goa entered a period of decline. The Portuguese were not prepared to help, but neither would they allow native Goans equal rights. An abortive attempt to establish a Goan Republic was quelled with the execution of fifteen Goan conspirators.

A spin-off of the British conflict with Tipu Sultan of Mysore (a French ally) at the end of the eighteenth century, was the **British occupation** of Goa, which lasted sixteen years from 1797. The occupation was solely military; the Goan authorities never gave up their administration. Despite a certain liberalization,

Police, trouble and nudism

While the vast majority of visitors to Goa never encounter any trouble, tourism-related crime is definitely more prevalent than in other parts of the country. Theft is the most common problem – usually of articles left unattended on the beach. Don't assume your valuables are safe in a padlocked house or hotel room, either. Break-ins, particularly on party nights, are on the increase. The most secure solution is to rent a deposit box in a bank, which costs around Rs100, or to opt for one of the few guesthouses with lockers.

The other eventuality to avoid, at all costs, is getting on the wrong side of the law. Drugs are the most common cause of serious trouble. Many travellers imagine that, because of Goa's free-and-easy reputation, drug use is legal: it isn't. Possession of even a small amount of cannabis is a criminal offence, punishable by large fines or prison sentences of up to ten years. Arrests, however, rarely result in court appearances. The Goan police tend to ensure that offenders are given the opportunity of leaving the country first, having relieved them of nearly all their spare cash and valuables. That said, Fort Aguada prison had, at the last count, half a dozen foreigners serving long sentences for drugs offences.

Though violent crime is rare, women should think twice before wandering down deserted beaches and dark tracks on their own. Sexual harassment usually takes the form of unsubtle ogling, but there have also been several incidents of rape in recent years. Wherever you're staying, therefore, take the same common-sense precautions as you would at home: keep to the main roads when travelling on foot or by bicycle, avoid dirt tracks and unfrequented beaches (particularly on party nights) unless you're in a group, and when you're in your house after dark, ensure that all windows and doors are locked.

Finally, remember that nudism is prohibited. In case tourists miss the "NO NUDISM" signs posted at the entrances to most beaches, police regularly patrol the busier resorts to ensure that decorum is maintained. If you are tempted to drop your togs, check that there are no families within eyeshot. No one is likely to object openly, but when you consider that wet Y-fronts and saris are about as risqué as beachwear gets for most Indians, you'll understand why men in G-strings and topless women cause such a stir.

White Maruti van taxis serve as the main means of travelling between resorts. You'll find them lined up outside most charter hotels, where a board invariably displays "fixed rates" to destinations in and around the region. These fares only apply to peak season, however, and at other times you should be able to negotiate a hefty reduction.

By ferry

If auto-rickshaws are the quintessentially Indian mode of transport, flat-bottomed ferries are their Goan equivalent. Crammed with cars, buses, commuters on scooters, fisherwomen and clumps of bewildered tourists, these rusting blue-painted hulks provide an essential service, crossing the coastal backwaters where bridges have not yet been built. They're also incredibly cheap, and run from the crack of dawn until late in the evening.

The most frequented river crossings in Goa are Panjim to Betim, across the Mandovi (every 15min); Old Goa to Divar Island (every 15min); Siolim to Chopdem, across the Chapora River for Arambol and Pernem (every 15min); Querim to Terekol, over the Terekol River (every 30min); and Cavelossim, in the far south of Salcete, to Assolna (every 20–30min).

By train

Following years of controversy, the Konkan Railway was completed in 1997, running down the coast from Mumbai to link with the southern rail network at Mangalore. This now serves as Goa's principal long-distance transport artery, but is rarely convenient for shorter journeys within the state. The relative infrequency of services and distance of the line from most of the resorts means you're invariably better off catching the bus.

By bus

The Goan transport corporation, Kadamba, runs long-distance services throughout the state from their main stands at Panjim, Mapusa and Margao. Private buses, serving everywhere else including the coastal resorts, are cheap, frequent, and more relaxed than many in India, although you should still brace yourself for a crush on market days and when travelling to major towns and tourist centres. Details on how to get around by bus are listed in the relevant accounts, and on p.213.

By motorcycle taxi

Goa's unique pillion-passenger motorcycle taxis, known locally as "pilots", are ideal for nipping between beaches or into town from the resorts. Bona fide opera-

such as the restoration of Hindus' right to worship and the final banishment of the dreaded Inquisition in 1820, the nineteenth century saw widespread civil unrest. During British occupation many Goans moved to Bombay, and elsewhere in British India, to find work.

The success of the post-Independence Goan struggle for freedom owed as much to the efforts of the Indian government, who cut off diplomatic ties with Portugal, as to the work of freedom fighters such as **Menezes Braganza** and **Dr Cunha**. After a "liberation march" in 1955 resulted in a number of deaths, the state was blockaded. Trade with Bombay ceased, and the railway was cut off, so Goa set out to forge international links, particularly with Pakistan and Sri Lanka. That led to the building of Dabolim airport, and a determination to improve local agricultural output. In 1961, prime minister Jawaharlal Nehru

tors ride black bikes (usually Rajdoots) with yellow mudguards and white number plates. Fares, which should be settled in advance, are comparable with auto-rickshaw rates: roughly Rs5 per kilometre.

By rented motorcycle

Renting a motorcycle in Goa gives a lot of freedom but can be perilous. Every season, an average of one person a day dies on the roads; many are tourists on two-wheelers. Make sure, therefore, that the lights and brakes are in good shape, and be especially vigilant at night: many Goan roads are appallingly pot-holed and unlit, and stray cows and bullock carts can appear from nowhere.

Officially, you need an international driver's licence to rent, and ride, anything more powerful than a 25cc moped. Owners and rental companies rarely enforce this, but some local police use the rule to extract exorbitant baksheesh from tourists. If you don't have a licence with you, the only way around the problem is to avoid big towns such as Panjim, Margao and Mapusa (or Anjuna on market day), and only to carry small sums of money when driving. If you are arrested for not having the right papers, it's no big deal, though police officers may try to convince you otherwise; keep cool, and be prepared to negotiate. Some unlicensed operators attempt to rent out machines to unwary visitors; always make sure you get some evidence of rental and insurance.

Rates vary according to the season, the vehicle, and how long you rent it for; most owners also insist on a deposit and/or passport as security. The range is pretty standard, with the cheapest choice, a 50cc moped, costing Rs100 per day. These are fine for buzzing to the beach and back, but to travel further try the stalwart Enfield Bullet 350cc, popular mainly for its pose value (upwards of Rs250 per day); the smaller but more reliable Honda Kinetic 100cc, which has automatic gears and is a good first-time choice (Rs150–200/day); or the best all-rounder, the Yamaha RD 100cc: light, fast enough, reliable, economical and with manual gears (Rs150–225/day). The notoriously unreliable Indian makes, Rajdoot and Bajaj, are best avoided.

Tours

On paper, GTDC's guided tours from Panjim, Margao, Calangute and Colva seem like a good way of getting around Goa's highlights in a short time. However, they're far too rushed for most foreign tourists, appealing essentially to Indian families wishing to combine a peek at the resorts with a whistle-stop puja tour of the temples around Ponda. Most also include a string of places inland that you wouldn't otherwise consider visiting. Leaflets giving full itineraries are available at any GTDC office, where you can also buy tickets: full-day tours cost Rs95.

finally ran out of patience with his opposite number in Lisbon, the right-wing dictator Salazar, and sent in the armed forces. Mounted in defiance of a United Nations resolution, "**Operation Vijay**" met only token resistance, and the Indian army overran Goa in two days. Thereafter, Goa (along with Portugal's other two enclaves, Daman and Diu) became part of India as a self-governing **Union Territory**, with minimum interference from Delhi.

Since Independence, Goa has continued to prosper, bolstered by iron-ore exports and a booming tourist industry, but is struggling to hold its own against a tidal wave of **immigration** from other Indian states. Its inhabitants voted overwhelmingly to resist a merger with neighbouring Maharashtra in the 1980s, and successfully lobbied for Konkani to be granted official-language status in 1987, when Goa was finally declared a fully fledged state of the Indian Union.

Since then, however, its political life has been dogged by chronic **instability**. In the 1990s, no fewer than twelve chief ministers held power over a succession of shaky, opportunistic coalitions, which saw standards of government plummet to depths hitherto unseen in the region. Elections were invariably followed by periods of deal cutting, in which old scores were settled and revenge exacted for past defections and betrayals. As a result, policy-making has been rendered near impossible, while **corruption** has eroded the fabric of government.

Among the main beneficiaries of the ongoing chaos have been the extreme right-wing Hindu fundamentalists, the **BJP** (Bharatiya Janata Party). In the past, their pro-merger stance made them unpopular with the Goan electorate – even Hindus – despite the party's dominance in the national arena. But at the time of writing – in the wake of the political coup of November 1999 when a Congress splinter group came to power under the leadership of Francisco Sardinha, and was then ousted by another ad hoc group – the BJP occupied one quarter of the seats in the Goan assembly.

Panjim and central Goa

Take any mid-sized Portuguese town, add a sprinkling of banana trees and auto-rickshaws, drench annually with torrential tropical rain, and leave to simmer in fierce humid sunshine for at least one hundred and fifty years, and you'll end up with something like **PANJIM** (also known by its Maarathi name, **Panaji** – "land that does not flood"). The Goan capital has a completely different feel from any other Indian city. Stacked around the sides of a lush terraced hillside at the mouth of the River Mandovi, its skyline of red-tiled roofs, whitewashed churches, and mildewing concrete apartment blocks has more in common with Lisbon than Lucknow. This lingering European influence is most evident in the small squares and cobbled lanes of the town's old Latin quarter, **Fontainhas**. Here, Portuguese is still very much the lingua franca, the shopfronts sport names like José Pinto and de Souza, and the women wear knee-length dresses that would turn heads anywhere else in the country.

For centuries, Panjim was little more than a minor landing stage and customs house, protected by a hilltop fort, and surrounded by stagnant swampland. It only became capital in 1843, after the port at Old Goa had silted up, and its rulers and impoverished inhabitants had fled the plague. Although the last Portuguese viceroy managed to drain many of the nearby marshes, and erect imposing public buildings on the new site, the town never emulated the grandeur of its predecessor upriver – a result, in part, of the Portuguese nobles' predilection for erecting their mansions in the countryside rather than the city. Panjim expanded rapidly in the 1960s and 1970s, without reaching the unmanageable proportions of other Indian state capitals. After Mumbai, or even Bangalore, its uncongested streets seem easy-going and pleasantly parochial. Sights are thin on the ground, but the palm-lined squares and atmospheric Latin quarter, with its picturesque Neoclassical houses and Catholic churches, make a pleasant backdrop for aimless wandering.

Some travellers see no more of Panjim than its noisy bus terminal – which is a pity. Although you can completely bypass the town when you arrive in Goa, either by jumping off the train or coach at Margao (for the south), or Mapusa (for the northern resorts), or by heading straight off on a local bus, it's definitely worth spending time here – if only a couple of hours en route to the ruined former capital at Old Goa.

PANJIM

RESTAURANTS

A Pastelaria	I
Delhi Durbar	A
Goenchin	J
Horseshoe	G
Megson's	E
Rosoyo	D
Satkar	F
Venite	C
Vihar	B
Tony's	H

ACCOMMODATION

Afonso	8
GTDC Tourist Hostel	2
Nova Goa	6
Orav's	5
Panjim Inn	9
Park Lane Lodge	7
Park Plaza	1
Republica	3
The White House	4

GOA | Panjim and central Goa

Railway Station (11 km), Old Goa & Ponda

Mapusa

Betim

Mandovi River

Private Bus Stand

Santa Monica (boat cruises)

PATO

Babasaheb Ambedkar Park

Kadamba Bus Stand

Laundry

GTDC Tourist Home

Water Tower

State Archeological Museum

PATO BRIDGE

Ourem Creek

Footbridge

HPO

SÃO TOMÉ

Secretariat

Abbé de Faria Statue

AVDA DOM JOAO CASTRO

DR RS RD

Mhamay Kamat Mansion

Panjim Church

Indian Government Tourist Office

High Court

Chapel of St Sebastian

FONTAINHAS

Azulejos Shop

Historical Archives

Pond

Church Square (Municipal Gardens)

Jama Masjid

Mahalakshmi Temple

Vaca de Boca Spring

Bishop's Palace

State Bank

Thomas Cook

Menezes Braganza Institute

Police HQ

British Consular Assistant

Rickshaws

Peroze Framroze Forex

Air India

Jet Airways

Ashok Samrat Cinema

HDFC Bank & ATM

Indian Airlines

Goa Medical College & Hospital

High School

Caculo Island

Campal Gardens

Kala Academy

Airport (29 km), Vasco Da Gama & Margao

0   200 m

153

The area **around Panjim** attracts far fewer visitors than the coastal resorts, yet its paddy fields and wooded valleys harbour several attractions worth a day or two's break from the beach. **Old Goa** is just a bus ride away, as are the unique temples around **Ponda**, an hour or so southeast, to where Hindus smuggled their deities during the Inquisition. Further inland still, the forested lower slopes of the Western Ghats, cut through by the main Panjim–Bangalore highway, shelter the impressive **Dudhsagar falls**, which you can only reach by four-wheel-drive jeep.

Arrival, information and local transport

European charter planes and domestic flights arrive at Goa's **Dabolim airport**, 29km south of Panjim on the outskirts of Vasco da Gama, Goa's second city. Pre-paid taxis into town (45min; Rs475), booked at the counter in the forecourt, can be shared by up to four people.

Long-distance and local **buses** pull into Panjim at the town's busy **Kadamba bus terminal**, 1km east of the centre in the district of Pato. Ten minutes' walk from here, across Ourem Creek to Fontainhas, brings you to several budget hotels. If you plan to stay in the more modern west end of town, flag down a motorcycle taxi or jump into an auto-rickshaw at the rank outside the station concourse.

GTDC's **information** counter, inside the concourse at the main Kadamba bus stand (daily 9.30am–1pm & 2–5pm; ☎0832/225620) is useful for checking train and bus timings, but little else. The more efficient **India Government Tourist Office** is across town on Church Square (Mon–Fri 9.30am–6pm, Sat 9.30am–1pm; ☎0832/223412).

The most convenient way of **getting around** Panjim is by **auto-rickshaw**; flag one down at the roadside or head for one of the ranks around the city. The only city **buses** likely to be of use to visitors run to Dona Paula from the main bus stand via several stops along the esplanade (including the Secretariat), and Miramar beachfront. If you feel up to taking on Panjim's anarchic traffic, **bicycles** can be rented (Mon–Sat only; Rs3/hr) from a stall up the lane opposite the Head Post Office.

River cruises

GTDC runs two return trips from Santa Monica jetty, directly beneath the Mandovi Road bridge (daily: 6pm & 7.15pm; Rs90). Aim for the earlier one, as it usually catches the last of the sunset. Snacks and drinks are available, and the price includes a display of Konkani and Portuguese dance accompanied by folk singers in traditional Goan costume, and sometimes a live Hindi cover band. Two-hour "Full Moon" cruises also leave daily at 8.30pm, regardless of the lunar phase. Operating in direct competition to GTDC are Emerald Waters' cruises from the quay outside the *Mandovi Hotel*. In addition to evening departures (daily: 5.45pm, 7pm, 8.15pm & 9.30pm; Rs90), also with live folk music and dance, and a bar, they offer longer sightseeing trips during the day.

   Bookings for the GTDC cruises can be made through their agents, Goa Sea Travels, opposite the *Tourist Hostel*. Emerald Waters' ticket counter is opposite the *Hotel Mandovi*.

Accommodation

The majority of Goa's Indian visitors prefer to stay in Panjim rather than the coastal resorts, which explains the huge number **hotels** and **lodges** crammed into the town centre. Finding a place to stay is only a problem during the festival of St Francis (Nov 24–Dec 3), Dusshera (Sept/Oct) and during peak season (mid-Dec to mid-Jan), when tariffs double. At other times, hotels try to fill rooms by offering substantial discounts. The most atmospheric options are in Fontainhas, down by Ourem Creek, and in the back streets behind the esplanade. Standards are generally good, and even the cheapest rooms should have a window, a fan, running water and clean sheets. Most other hotels are bland places in the modern, west end of town.

Note that **checkout times** here vary wildly. Find out what yours is as soon as you arrive, or your hard-earned lie-in could end up costing you an extra day's rent.

Alfonso, St Sebastian Chapel Square, Fontainhas ☏ 0832/222359. Recently refurbished colonial-era house in a picturesque backstreet. Spotlessly clean, cool en-suite rooms, friendly owners and rooftop terrace with views. Single occupancy rates available. ⑤–⑥

GTDC Tourist Hostel, Avda Dom Joao Castro ☏ 0832/223396 or 227103. Spacious rooms in a bustling government-run hotel next to the main road and river. Shops, a hair salon and tourist information in the lobby. Some a/c. ⑤–⑥

Nova Goa, Dr Atmaram Borkar Road ☏ 0832/226231, ℱ 224958, ℮ novagoa@goa1.dot.net.in. Panjim's brightest, newest top-class hotel in the heart of the shopping area and with the usual comforts, plus bath tubs and a pool. Popular mainly with visiting Portuguese and corporate clients. ⑧–⑨

Orav's, 31 Janeiro Rd, Fontainhas ☏ 0832/46128. Modern building in the old quarter, with good-sized, comfortable rooms and small balconies on the front side overlooking the rooftops. ④

Panjim Inn, E-212, 31 Janeiro Rd, Fontainhas ☏ 0832/226523, ℱ 228136, ⓦ www.panjiminn.com. Grand colonial-era town house, now managed as an upmarket but homely hotel, with period furniture, sepia family photos, balconies and a common veranda, where meals and drinks are served to guests. An even more beautiful Hindu house across the road, *Panjim Pousada*, renovated by the same owner, offers the chance to sample what Panjim must have felt like

a century ago, with a leafy inner courtyard and huge breadfruit tree overhanging the rear veranda. Easily the best place in its class. ⑥–⑦

Park Lane Lodge, near Chapel of St Sebastian ☏ 0832/220238 or 227154, ℮ pklaldg@goatelecom .com. Spotless and characterful but cramped family guesthouse in old colonial-style house. Pepper and coffee plants add atmosphere to a narrow communal terrace, and there's a TV lounge upstairs; also safe deposit facilities, internet access, laundry service and good off-season discounts. ④

Park Plaza, Azad Maidan ☏ 0832/422601–5, ℱ 225635. A newish hotel on a quiet square near the river. Close to the commercial centre, with all the usual amenities, including a restaurant, and courteous staff. Good full- and half-board packages for single travellers. ⑦

Republica, Jose Falcao Road, near GTDC *Tourist Hostel* ☏ 0832/224630. Rock-bottom budget travellers' lodge with grubby rooms, attached shower-toilets and river views from a large wooden veranda. A last resort option only. ②–③

The White House, PO Box 329, behind GTDC *Tourist Hostel* ☏ 0832/255239 or 223928. Renamed to coincide with Clinton's 2000 India visit, this quirky 1920s lodge, close to the riverfront and run by a garrulous landlord, caters mainly for salesmen and the odd budget traveller. Its rooms are roughish and musty during the rainy season, but reasonably good value. ②–④

The Town

Until a decade or so ago, most visitors' first glimpse of **Panjim** was from the decks of the old Bombay steamer as it chugged into dock at the now-defunct ferry ramp. These days, however, despite the recent inauguration of the Konkan Railway, the town is most usually approached by road – from the north via the huge ferro-concrete bridge that spans the Mandovi estuary, or from the south on the recently revamped NH-7, which links the capital with the airport and railhead at Vasco da Gama. Either way, you'll have to pass through the suburb of **Pato**, home of the main Kadamba bus terminal, before crossing Ourem

Creek to arrive in Panjim proper. West of **Fontainhas**, the picturesque Portuguese quarter, the commercial centre's grid of long straight streets fans out west from Panjim's principal landmark, **Church Square**. Further north, the main thoroughfare, **Avenida Dom Joao Castro**, sweeps past the Head Post Office and **Secretariat** building, before bending west along the waterfront.

Church Square

The leafy rectangular park opposite the India Government tourist office, known as **Church Square** or the **Municipal Garden**, forms the heart of Panjim. Presiding over its east side is the town's most distinctive and photogenic landmark, the toothpaste-white Baroque facade of the **Church of Our Lady of the Immaculate Conception**. Flanked by rows of slender palm trees, at the head of a crisscrossing laterite walkway, the church was built in 1541 for the benefit of sailors arriving here from Lisbon. The weary mariners would stagger up from the quay to give thanks for their safe passage before proceeding to the capital at Old Goa – the original home of the enormous bell that hangs from its central gable.

The Secretariat

The road that runs north from the church brings you out at the riverside near Panjim's oldest surviving building. With its sloping tiled roofs, carved-stone coats of arms and wooden verandas, the stalwart **Secretariat** looks typically colonial. Yet it was originally the summer palace of Goa's sixteenth-century Muslim ruler, the Adil Shah. Later, the Portuguese converted it into a temporary rest house for the territory's governors (who used to overnight here en route to and from Europe) and then a residence for the viceroy. Today, it accommodates the Goan State Legislature, which explains the presence of so many shiny chauffeur-driven Ambassador cars outside, and the armed guards at the door.

A hundred metres east, a peculiar statue of a man holding his hands over the body of an entranced reclining woman shows **Abbé Faria** (1755–1819), a Goan priest who emigrated to France to become one of the world's first professional hypnotists.

An even more impressive edifice than the Mhamay Kamat mansion is the **Menezes Braganza Institute**, now the town's Central Library, which stands behind the esplanade, 1km west of the Secretariat past the Abbé de Faria statue. Among the colonial leftovers in this grand Neoclassical building, which was erected as part of the civic makeover initiated by the Marquis of Pombal and Dom Manuel de Portugal e Castro in the early nineteenth century, are the panels of blue-and-yellow-painted ceramic tiles, known as **azulejos**, lining the lobby of the west (Malacca Road) entrance. These larger-than-life illustrations depict scenes from Luis Vaz Camões' epic poem, *Os Luisiades*. The tone of the tableaux is intentionally patriotic (valiant Portuguese explorers being tossed on stormy seas and a nobleman standing defiantly before a dark-faced Raja of Calicut), but the tale was, in fact, intended as an invective against the Portuguese discoveries, which Camões rightly believed was milking his mother country dry and leaving its crown easy prey for the old enemy, Spain.

Fontainhas and Sao Tomé

Panjim's oldest and most interesting district, **Fontainhas**, lies immediately west of Pato, overlooking the banks of the oily green Ourem Creek. From the footbridge between the bus stand and town centre, a dozen or so blocks of

Neoclassical houses rise in a tangle of terracotta rooftops up the sides of **Altinho Hill**. At siesta time, Vespas stand idle on deserted street corners, while women in Western clothes exchange pleasantries with their neighbours from open windows and leafy verandas. Many buildings have retained their traditional coat of ochre, pale yellow, green or blue – a legacy of the Portuguese insistence that every Goan building (except churches, which had to be white) should be colourwashed after the monsoons.

At the southern end of the neighbourhood, the pristine whitewashed **Chapel of St Sebastian** is one of many Goan churches to remain faithful to the old colonial decree. It stands at the end of a small square where Fontainhas' Portuguese-speaking locals hold a lively annual street *festa* to celebrate their patron saint's day in mid-November. The eerily lifelike crucifix inside the chapel, brought here in 1812, formerly hung in the Palace of the Inquisition in Old Goa. Unusually, Christ's eyes are open – allegedly to inspire fear in those being interrogated by the Inquisitors.

Sao Tomé ward is the other old quarter, lying north of Fontainhas on the far side of Emilio Gracia Road. This is the area to head for if you fancy a bar crawl: the narrow streets are dotted with dozens of hole-in-the-wall taverns, serving cheap, stiff measures of *feni* under strip lights and the watchful gaze of colourful Madonnas. You'll feel less conspicuous in the neighbourhood's best known hostelry, the *Hotel Venite* (see p.158).

The State Archeological Museum

The most noteworthy feature of Panjim's **State Archeological Museum** (Mon–Fri 9.30am–1.15pm & 2–5.30pm) is its imposing size, which stands in glaringly inverse proportion to the collections inside. In their bid to erect a structure befitting a state capital, Goa's status-obsessed bureaucrats ignored the fact that there was precious little to put in it. The only rarities to be found amid the lame array of temple sculpture, hero stones, and dowdy colonial-era artefacts are a couple of beautiful Jain bronzes rescued by Customs and Excise officials from smugglers and, on the ground floor, the infamous Italian-style table used by Goa's Grand Inquisitors, complete with its original, ornately carved tall-backed chairs. On your way out, look out too for the photos of the prehistoric rock carvings at Kajur and Usgalimal, lining the walls of the main entrance hall. Their discovery in a remote corner of the state in 1993 effectively redrew the Konkan coast's archeological map by proving that more than 12,000 years ago – well before the arrival of settled agriculturalists from the north – the region supported a population of hunter-gatherers.

Eating and drinking

Catering for the droves of tourists who come here from other Indian states, as well as more price-conscious locals, Panjim is packed with good **places to eat**, from hole-in-the-wall fish-curry-rice joints to swish air-conditioned restaurants serving top-notch Mughlai cuisine. In a week you could feasibly attempt a gastronomic tour of the subcontinent without straying more then five minutes from the Municipal Gardens. Vegetarians are best catered for at the numerous *udipi* canteens dotted around town, most of which open around 7am for blow-out **breakfasts** – great if you have just staggered into town after a night on the bus. Beer, *feni* and other spirits are available in all but the purest "pure veg" places, especially in the hole-in-the-wall taverns around Sao Tomé.

A Pasteleria, Dr Dada Vaidya Road. Panjim's best bakery does dozens of Western-style cakes, biscuits and sticky buns, including brownies and fruit loaves. Its savoury selection of tasty egg puffs, and succulent, spicy chicken or prawn patties is good, too. Takeaway only.

Delhi Durbar, behind the *Hotel Mandovi*. A provincial branch of the famous Mumbai restaurant, and the best place in Panjim – if not all Goa – to sample traditional Mughlai cuisine of mainly meat steeped in rich, spicy sauces (try their superb *rogan ghosh* or melt-in-the-mouth chicken tikka). Most main dishes are pricey at around Rs120, but this place is well worth a splurge.

Goenchin, off Dr Dada Vaidhya Road. Glacial a/c and dim lighting, but the best and most authentic Chinese food in Goa. Count on Rs300 per head.

Horseshoe, Rua de Ourem, Fontainhas. The town's only Portuguese–Goan restaurant, serving a limited, but very reasonably priced, menu of old standards such as *caldo verde* soup and grilled sardines. The food is so-so, but the decor and atmosphere make this a worthwhile option. Most mains around Rs50.

Megson's, next to *Moti Mahal*, 18 June Rd. The state's top deli, with a great selection of traditional Goan foods: spicy sausages, prepared meats, tangy cheese from the Nilgiris, olive oil, and the best *bebinca* you can buy (ask for *Linda* brand).

Rosoyo, 18 June Rd. Run by *Megson's*, this busy little fast-food joint is *the* place to sample tasty, hygienic Mumbai-style street food: crunchy *bhel puri* or delicious *pau bhaji*. They also serve wonderful Gujarati snacks such as *thepla* – chappatis griddle-cooked with curry leaves and cumin, and served with South Indian *chatni* – plus a range of shakes and ice creams. You'll be hard pushed to spend Rs50 here.

Satkar, 18 June Rd. Newest and much the most congenial of Panjim's numerous South Indian snack joints. They do a huge range of dishes, including Chinese and North Indian, but most people go for their fantastic masala dosas and piping hot, crunchy samosas, which get the vote as the best in town.

Tony's, Emilio Gracia Road/31 Janeiro Rd, Fontainhas. A blue-painted street-stall run by retired footballer and his wife, who serve up the freshest, tastiest and most authentic Goan food in town. Dishes include sublime fish cutlets, chicken *xacuti*, chilli beef, *sorpatel* and – on Saturdays only – perfect *sanna*, made with real palm *toddi*. Around Rs30 per person for a filling meal; no veg options. Takeaway only.

Venite, 31 Janeiro Rd. Deservedly popular hotel restaurant, serving great fresh seafood, including affordable lobster and crab, along with Western dishes, desserts, *feni* and cold beers. Wooden floors, balcony seats, candles and an eclectic cassette collection add to the ambience. Good breakfasts, too. Closed Sun.

Vihar, 31 Janeiro Rd, around the corner from *Venite*. Arguably the best *udipi* in Panjim, and more conveniently situated than *Satkar*. Try their super tasty *rawa* masala dosas.

Listings

Airlines Air India, *Hotel Fidalgo*, 18 June Rd ℡ 0832/224081; Air France, Air Seychelles, American Airlines, Bimab Bangladesh, Gulf Air, Kenyan Airways, Royal Jordanian, Sri Lankan Airlines, all c/o Jetair, Rizvi Chambers, 1st Floor, H Salgado Road ℡ 0832/222438, 226154 or 223172; British Airways, Shiv Tower, EDC Plaza, Patto ℡ & ℗ 0832/420335 or 420320; Indian Airlines, Dempo Building, Dr D Bandodkar Road ℡ 0832/223831; Jet Airlines, Sesa Ghor, ECD Plaza, next to GTDC *Pato Tourist Home*, Patto ℡ 0832/431472; KLM (also PIA), 2nd floor, Mahalaxmi Chambers ℗ 0832/426678, 224802 or 222633, ℗ 224802; Sahara Airlines, *Hotel Fidalgo*, Room 133, 18 June Rd ℡ 0832/230634; Swissair & Sabena, Ground Floor, Sesa Ghor, EDC Plaza, Plot #20, Patto ℡ 0832/422255, ℗ 432233.

Banks and ATMs The most efficient places in Panjim to change money are: Thomas Cook, near the Indian Airlines office, at 8 Alcon Chambers, Devanand Bandodkar Road (Mon–Sat 9am–6pm, Oct–March also Sun 10am–5pm; ℡ 0832/221312, ℗ 221313); and the Pheroze Framroze Exchange Bureau on Dr P Shirgaonkar Road (Mon–Sat 9.30am–7pm & Sun 9.30am–1pm). Unlike most private companies, the latter's rates are competitive and they don't charge commission on either currency or travellers' cheques. The HDFC Bank on 18 June Rd has a handy 24hr ATM, where you can make withdrawals using Visa or Mastercard. Changing money in the regular, government-run banks tends to take a lot longer, but the rates are invariably best: State Bank of India is opposite the *Hotel Mandovi*, Avda Dom Joao Castro; the Bank of Baroda (where you can draw money on Visa cards), is on Azad Maidan; and the Corporation Bank is on Church Square, around the corner from the Government Tourist Office.

Books The bookshops in the *Hotel Fidalgo* and the *Hotel Mandovi* stock a range of English-language fiction in paperback, and special-interest titles and coffee-table tomes on Goa.

British Consular Assistant The British High Commission of Mumbai has a Consular Assistant in Panjim (see p.136): Shilpa Sarah Caldeira's office is on the third floor of 302 Manguirish Building (opposite Gulf Supermarket), 18 June Rd ℡0832/228571, ℻232828, ℮bcagoa@goa1.dot.net.in.

Hospital Panjim's largest hospital, the Goa Medical College (aka the GMC), in the west of town at the far end of Avda Dom Joao Castro, is grim and overstretched; if you're able to travel, head for the more modern and better equipped Salgaonkar Hospital. Ambulances (℡0832/46300 or 44566) are likely to get you there a lot less quickly than a standard taxi.

Music and dance Regular recitals of classical Indian music and dance are held at Panjim's school for the performing arts, the Kala Academy in Campal, at the far west end of town on Devanand Bandodkar Road. For details of forthcoming events, consult the boards in front of the auditorium or the listings page of local newspapers.

Pharmacies Panjim's best pharmacy is Hindu Pharma (℡0832/43176), next to the *Hotel Aroma* on Church Square, which stocks Ayurvedic, homeopathic and allopathic medicines.

Police Police Headquarters is on Malaca Road, central Panjim.

Post Panjim's reliable poste restante counter (Mon–Sat 9.30am–1pm & 2–5.30pm) is in the Head Post Office, 200m west of Pato Bridge. To get your stamps franked, walk around the back of the building and ask at the office behind the second door on the right. For parcel stitching, ask at Deepak Stores on the corner of the next block north.

Travel agents AERO Mundial, Ground Floor, *Hotel Mandovi*, Dr D Bandodkar Road ℡0832/223773; Menezes Air Travel, Rua de Ourem ℡ & ℻ 0832/222214. For air and Damania catamaran tickets, try MGM International, Mama Camotim Building (near Secretariat); or Tradewings Ltd, Mascarenhas Buildings (near Jolly Shoes), Dr Atmaram Borkar Road ℡0832/22243.

Old Goa

At one time a byword for splendour, with a population of several hundred thousand, Goa's erstwhile capital, **OLD GOA**, was virtually abandoned following malaria and cholera epidemics that plagued the city from the seventeenth century onwards. Today you need considerable imagination to picture the once-great capital as it used to be. The maze of twisting streets, piazzas and ochre-washed villas has gone, and all that remains is a score of extraordinarily grandiose churches and convents. Granted World Heritage Status by UNESCO, Old Goa today attracts bus-loads of foreign tourists from the coast, and Christian pilgrims from around India, in roughly equal numbers. While the former come to admire the gigantic facades and gilt altars of the beautifully preserved churches, the main attraction for the latter is the tomb of **St Francis Xavier** (see p.164), the renowned sixteenth-century missionary, whose remains are enshrined in the **Basilica of Bom Jesus**.

If you are staying on the coast and contemplating a day-trip inland, this is the most obvious and accessible option. Just thirty minutes by road from the state capital, Old Goa is served by buses every fifteen minutes from Panjim's Kadamba bus stand; alternatively, hop into an auto-rickshaw, or rent a taxi. GTDC also slot the site's highlights into several of their guided coach **tours**; further details and tickets are available at any GTDC hotel or tourist office.

Arch of the Viceroys and the Church of St Cajetan

On arriving at the river landing stage to the north, seventeenth-century visitors passed through the **Arch of the Viceroys** (1597), constructed to commemorate Vasco da Gama's arrival in India and built from the same porous red laterite as virtually all Old Goa's buildings. Above it a Bible-toting figure rests his foot on the cringing figure of a "native", while its granite facade, facing the

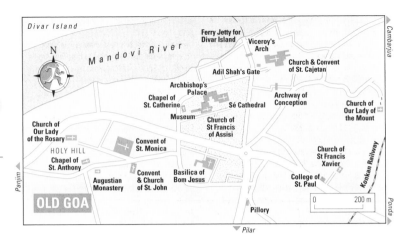

river, holds a statue of da Gama himself. It is hard to imagine today that these overgrown fields and simple streets with a few cool drinks stands were once the focus of a lively market, with silk and gem merchants, horse dealers and carpet weavers. The one surviving monument, known as **Adil Shah's Gate**, predates the Portuguese and possibly even the Muslim period. Hindu in style, it consists simply of a lintel supported by two columns in black basalt, to which are attached the remains of perforated screens. You can find it by turning left at the crossroads immediately above the Arch of the Viceroys.

A short way up the lane from the Gate, the distinctive domed **Church of St Cajetan** (1651) was modelled on St Peter's in Rome by monks from the Theatine order, who believed in Divine Providence; they never sought charity, but simply expected it. While it does boast a Corinthian exterior, you can also spot certain non-European elements in the decoration, such as the cashew-nut designs in the carving of the pulpit. Hidden beneath the church is a crypt where the embalmed bodies of Portuguese governors were once kept in lead coffins before they were shipped back to Lisbon. Forgotten for over thirty years, the last batch (of three) was only removed in 1992 on the eve of the state visit to Goa of Portuguese president Mario Soares.

The Sé (St Catherine's Cathedral)

The Portuguese Viceroy Redondo (1561–64) commissioned the **Sé**, or **St Catherine's Cathedral**, southwest of St Cajetan's, to be "a grandiose church worthy of the wealth, power and fame of the Portuguese who dominated the seas from the Atlantic to the Pacific". Today it stands larger than any church in Portugal, although it was beset by problems, not least a lack of funds and Portugal's temporary loss of independence to Spain. It took eighty years to build and was not consecrated until 1640.

On the Tuscan-style exterior, the one surviving tower houses the **Golden Bell**, cast in Cuncolim (south Goa) in the seventeenth century. During the Inquisition, its tolling announced the start of the gruesome *auto da fés* that were held in the square outside, when suspected heretics were subjected to public torture and burned at the stake. Reconstruction of parts of the roof, which once had overhanging eaves, has damaged some paintings inside. The scale and detail of the Corinthian-style interior is overwhelming; huge pillars divide the central nave from the side aisles, and no fewer than fifteen altars are arranged around the walls, dedicated among others to Our Ladies of Hope, Anguish and Three Needs. An altar to St Anne treasures the relics of the **Blessed Martyrs of Cuncolim**, whose failed mission to convert the Moghul emperor Akbar culminated in their murder by Muslims, while a chapel behind a highly detailed screen holds the **Miraculous Cross**, which stood in a Goan village until a vision of Christ appeared on it. Said to heal the sick, it is kept in a box; a small opening on the side allows devotees to touch it. The staggeringly ornate gilded main **altar** comprises nine carved frames and a splendid crucifix. Panels depict episodes from the life of St Catherine of Alexandria (died 307 AD), including an interchange of ideas with the pagan Roman emperor Maxim, who wished to marry her, and her subsequent flogging and martyrdom.

The Archbishop's Palace

Adjoining the Sé Cathedral, with which it is an exact contemporary, the **Archbishop's Palace** is unique as the last surviving civil building of colonial Goa's golden era. Though in a lamentable state of disrepair, its steeply inclined roofs and white facade still perfectly embody of the solidity and imposing strength of the so-called "chã" style of architecture, derived from military constructions of the day, of which the most extreme example was the Viceroy's Fortress Palace (Palacio da Fortaleza), which has since vanished without trace. Presenting their most austere aspect to the river, these two fortified palaces formerly dominated the skyline of the waterfront, appropriately enough for a city perennially under threat of attack.

Nineteenth-century photos show that the city-facing side of the building was originally enfolded by a low wall, which surrounded a garden. This has long been dismantled, but the two grand **entrance porches** remain intact. The one on the right (as you look at the building) is original, complete with red decorative frescoes lining the side walls, among the last remaining paintings of their kind left in Goa. During the Portuguese heyday, guards in blue livery would have stood on its steps, as they did in the Viceroys's palace and most *hidalgo* houses.

The palace is officially closed to visitors so if you want to have a nose around, you'll have to bully or bribe the ASI caretaker into letting you.

The Church of St Francis of Assisi and Archeological Museum

Southwest of the Cathedral is the ruined **Palace of the Inquisition**, in operation up until 1774, while to the west stands the **Convent of St Francis of Assisi**, built by Franciscan monks in 1517 and restored in the mid-eighteenth century. Today, the core of its **Archeological Museum** (daily except Fri 10am–5pm; Rs5) is a gallery of portraits of Portuguese viceroys, painted by local artists under Italian supervision. Other exhibits include coins, domestic Christian wooden sculpture, and downstairs in the cloister, pre-Portuguese Hindu sculpture. Next door, the **Church of St Francis** (1521) features fine decorative frescoes and paintings on wood showing the life of St Francis of Assisi.

Basilica of Bom Jesus

Close to the convent of St Francis, the 1605 church of **Bom Jesus**, "Good" or "Menino Jesus" (Mon–Sat 9am–6.30pm, Sun 10am–6.30pm), is known principally for the **tomb of St Francis Xavier**. In 1946, it became the first church in India to be elevated to the status of Minor Basilica. On the west, the

Written histories of Goa are rife with accounts of atrocities committed by the Portuguese. None, however, compare with those perpetrated in the name of Christianity by the dreaded Santo Officio, or "Holy Office". Better known as the Inquisition (from the Latin verb *inquiro*, "to inquire into"), the dreaded tribunal became the most brutal, systematic and macabre instrument of cultural bigotry ever devised by a European colonial power. As one eighteenth-century historian put it, "(the) Holy Office combined all that the ferocity of savages and the ingenuity of civilized man had till then invented."

The original targets of the Inquisition were not, as is often assumed, Hindus, but *Christianos nuevos* ("new Christians") – mainly Iberian Jews and Muslims who had been forcibly converted during the religious persecution of the medieval era, but who had since lapsed into their former faiths. Jews, in particular, had fled in large numbers to the new colonies of Africa, South America and Asia, where they had become the dominant mercantile community. It was to complain of their lax religious ways that Francis Xavier wrote to the King Joao III of Portugal in 1546, encouraging him to dispatch the Holy Inquisition to Goa, which he duly did four years later, in 1560.

By this time, the religious intolerance that had been making life difficult for the *Christianos nuevos* in Europe had also infected attitudes to local Hinduism in the *Estado da India*. Temple worship had been banned, shrines destroyed and brahmin priests banished. With the arrival of the two Grand Inquisitors and their spies from Lisbon, however, the range of "crimes" for which one could imprisoned broadened considerably. Substances and plants connected with Hindu ritual – turmeric powder (*haldi*), basil (*tulsi*) leaves, incense or marigolds – were banned, as was cooking rice "without salt", wearing a *dhoti* or *choli* (sari top), selling arms or horses to Muslims, sodomy ("the unnameable sin") and refusing to eat pork. Other offences that could land their perpetrators a long stretch of hideous incarceration – or worse – included astrology, alchemy or polygamy.

Goa being the most notoriously licentious and decadent European enclave in Asia, it wasn't long before the Inquisition's jails began to fill. Deep in the bowels of the Holy Office HQ (known to terrified locals as simply "*Orlem Ghor*", "Big House"), suspects would be tortured into confessing their heresy. Among the devices used for such purposes were, according to one record, "stretching racks, thumbscrews, leg crushers, holy water, burning sulphur, candles, quicklime and spiked wheels over which the victims were drawn with weights on their feet".

The only surviving first-hand account of the Goan Inquisition is attributed to a French physician named Charles Dellon, who found himself at the mercy of the Santo Officio in 1673, aged 24. His alleged crime was blasphemy; he'd supposedly mocked certain Christian rituals and criticized the Inquisition itself (although the fact he'd seduced the Governor of Daman's mistress can't have helped him any). Dellon languished in solitary confinement, without light or sanitation, for a total of three years while his case was debated. In the end, his life was spared, but not before he'd twice attempted suicide (by trying to slash his wrists with a sharpened coin) and endured one of the infamous autos da fé – literally "trials of faith" – staged every few years by the Inquisition.

three-storey Renaissance facade encompasses Corinthian, Doric, Ionic and Composite styles.

The interior is entered beneath the choir, supported by columns. On the northern wall, in the centre of the nave, is a cenotaph in gilded bronze to **Dom Jeronimo Mascaranhas**, the Captain of Cochin and benefactor of the church. The main altar, extravagantly decorated in gold, depicts the infant Jesus

His blow-by-blow account of this ordeal, in which he and 150 others were paraded in front of the city before being told whether or not they would be burned to death, remains a spine-chilling read, not least for its depiction of the grotesque theatricality with which the whole event was enacted. On the morning of the trial, a petrified Dellon, crippled by a "universal and violent trembling", was handed long black-and-white-striped robes to wear. Over these was tied a thigh-length yellow tabard, called a *sambenito*, emblazoned with the cross of St Andrew. Heretics accused of the most heinous crimes ("sorcery", or "*crimen magicae*") were required to don similar grey robes, known as *samarras*, bearing images of their heads engulfed in flames and tormented by trident-wielding devils. To complete the ensemble, tall mitres (*carocha*) daubed with ghoulish images and slogans were placed on the prisoners' heads.

From the dungeons, the accused were marched barefoot to the Great Hall of the Holy Office, where each was allotted a "Godfather" – a kind of warder drawn from the aristocracy. Among the pews, coffin-like boxes and dummies were held aloft by Inquisition agents; these were the remains and effigies of heretics who had died in captivity, or else been condemned posthumously. With the great bell of the Sé cathedral tolling in the background, the procession would then be led by Dominican friars carrying banners and a huge crucifix across Terreiro de Gales square to the Church of Saint Francis of Assisi, watched by huge crowds of onlookers. Inside the church, the terrified assembly knelt in front of the Viceroy and Grand Inquisitor, while the Augustinian prelate delivered a sermon. When he'd finished, the judgements were read aloud. Dellon was sentenced to five years of galley slavery in Lisbon, while two of his fellow prisoners were to be burned at the stake beside the Mandovi.

Before embarking on his voyage back to Europe, the Frenchman had to swear on oath that he would never speak of what had happened to him at the hands of the Santo Officio in Goa. Ten years later, however, he reneged on this promise. One of the most harrowing accounts of captivity ever written, his *Relation de l'Inquisition de Goa* (see "Books" p.710), first published in Paris in 1687, was an immediate bestseller. Translations into English, German and Dutch appeared the following year, to glowing reviews by key Enlightenment figures such as Voltaire (who lifted material from it for *Candide*), Thackery and Montesqieu. As a result, *Relation* contributed in no small part to the eventual suppression of the regime it described with such amazing exactitude.

Until 1774 – the point up to which detailed records survive –16,176 people (an average of 75 per year) were arrested by the Goan Inquisition. The majority of these were Hindus, although of those condemned to death, 71 percent were *Christianos nuevos* of Jewish descent. Its activities were curtailed towards the end of the eighteenth century, but the Inquisition was not fully repealed until 1814, as part of a treaty between the Portuguese and British.

Few remnants of this gruesome chapter in Goa's history survive. The Palace of the Inquisition was pulled down during the shift of the capital upriver, and most of its written records incinerated in 1814. You can, however, sit at the old table used by the Inquisitors for their grim deliberations, while the crucifix that formerly hung above it – rendered with open eyes to instil fear into the heart of the accused – can still be seen in a small chapel in Fontainhas, Panjim (see p.157).

under the protection of St Ignatius Loyola; to each side are subsidiary altars to Our Lady of Hope and St Michael. In the southern transept, lavishly decorated with twisted gilded columns and floriate carvings, stands the **Chapel and Tomb of St Francis Xavier**. Constructed of marble and jasper in 1696, it was the gift of the Medici, Cosimo III, the Grand Duke of Tuscany; the middle tier contains panels detailing the saint's life. An ornate domed reliquary in silver contains his remains; on his feast day, December 3, the saint's finger is displayed to devotees.

Holy Hill

A number of other important religious buildings, some in ruins, stand opposite Bom Jesus on **Holy Hill**. The **convent of St Monica**, constructed in 1627, destroyed by fire in 1636 and rebuilt the following year, was the only Goan convent at the time and the largest in Asia. It housed around a hundred nuns, the Daughters of St Monica, and also offered accommodation to women whose husbands were called away to other parts of the empire. The **church** adjoins the convent on the south. As they had to remain away from the public gaze, the nuns attended mass in the choir loft and looked down upon the congregation.

Inside, a **Miraculous Cross** rises above the figure of St Monica at the altar. In 1636, it was reported that the figure of Christ had opened his eyes,

---

St Francis Xavier

Francis Xavier, the "Apostle of the Indies", was born in 1506 in the old kingdom of Navarre, now part of Spain. After taking a masters' degree in philosophy and theology at the University of Paris, where he studied for the priesthood until 1535, he was ordained two years later in Venice. He was then recruited by (Saint) Ignatius Loyola (1491–1556) along with five other priests into the new "Society of Jesus", which later became known as the Jesuits.

When the Portuguese king, Dom Joao III (1521–57), received reports of corruption and dissolute behaviour among the Portuguese in Goa, he asked Ignatius Loyola to despatch a priest who could influence the moral climate for the better. In 1541 Xavier was sent to work in the diocese of Goa, constituted seven years earlier, and comprising all regions east of the Cape of Good Hope. Arriving after a year-long journey, he embarked on a busy programme throughout southern India. Despite frequent obstruction from Portuguese officials, he founded numerous churches, and is credited with converting 30,000 people and performing such miracles as raising the dead and curing the sick with a touch of his beads. Subsequently he took his mission further afield to Sri Lanka, Malacca (Malaysia), China and Japan where he was less successful.

When Xavier left Goa for the last time, it was with the ambition of evangelizing in China; however, he contracted dysentery aboard ship and died on the island of San Chuan (Sancian), off the Chinese coast, where he was buried. On hearing of his death, a group of Christians from Malacca exhumed his body – which, although the grave had been filled with lime, they found to be in a perfect state of preservation. Reburied in Malacca, it was later removed and taken to Old Goa, where it has remained ever since, enshrined in the Basilica of Bom Jesus.

However, Saint Francis' incorruptible corpse has never rested entirely in peace. Chunks of it have been removed over the years by relic hunters and curious clerics: in 1614, the right arm was dispatched to the Pope in Rome (where it allegedly wrote its name on paper), a hand was sent to Japan, and parts of the intestines to southeast Asia. One Portuguese woman, Dona Isabel de Caron, even bit off the little toe of the cadaver in 1534; apparently, so much blood spurted into her mouth, it left a trail to her house and she was discovered.

Every ten years, the saint's body is carried in a three-hour ceremony from the Basilica of Bom Jesus to the Sé Cathedral, where visitors file past, touch and photograph it. During the 1995 "exposition", which was rumoured to be the last one, an estimated two million pilgrims flocked for *darshan* or ritual viewing of the corpse, these days a shrivelled and somewhat unsavoury spectacle.

motioned as if to speak, and blood had flowed from the wounds made by his crown of thorns. The last Daughter of St Monica died in 1885, and since 1964 the convent has been occupied by the Mater Dei Institute for nuns.

Nearby, the **Convent of St John of God**, built in 1685 by the Order of Hospitallers of St John of God to tend to the sick, was rebuilt in 1953. At the top of the hill, the **Chapel of Our Lady of the Rosary**, built in 1526 in the Manueline style (after the Portuguese king Manuel I, 1495–1521), features Ionic plasterwork with a double-storey portico, cylindrical turrets and a tower that commands fine views across the river from the terrace where Albuquerque surveyed the decisive battle of 1510. Its cruxiform interior is unremarkable, except for the marble tomb of **Catarina a Piró**, believed to be the first European woman to set foot in the colony. A commoner, she eloped here to escape the scandal surrounding her romance with Portuguese nobleman Garcia de Sá, who later rose to be governor of Goa. Under pressure from no less than Francis Xavier, Garcia eventually married her, but only *in articulo mortis* as she lay on her deathbed. Her finely carved tomb, set in the wall beside the high altar, incorporates a band of intricate Gujarati-style ornamentation, probably imported from the Portuguese trading post of Diu.

Ponda and around

Characterless, chaotic **PONDA**, 28km southeast of Panjim and 17km northeast of Margao, is Ponda *taluka*'s administrative headquarters and main market town, but not somewhere you're likely to want to stay. Straddling the busy Panjim–Bangalore highway (NH-4), the town's ugly concrete centre is permanently choked with traffic, and guaranteed to make you wonder why you ever left the coast. Of the few visitors who stop here, most do so en route to the nearby **Hindu temples** or **wildlife reserves** farther east, or to take a look at Goa's best-preserved sixteenth-century Muslim monument, the **Safa Masjid**, 2km west on the Panjim road. Built in 1560 by the Bijapuri ruler Ibrahim Adil Shah, this small mosque, with its whitewashed walls and pointed terracotta tile roof, is renowned less for its architecture than for being one of only two Islamic shrines in Goa to survive the excesses of the Portuguese Inquisition.

Practicalities

Ponda is served by regular **buses** from Panjim (via Old Goa) and Margao, and lies on the main route east to Karnataka. The Kadamba bus stand is on the main square, next to the auto-rickshaw rank.

There are plenty of **places to stay** if you get stuck here. Best of the budget lodges is the *Padmavi* (no phone; ●) at the top of the square. For more comfort, try the *President* (☎0832/312287; ●–●), a short rickshaw ride up the Belgaum road, which has large, clean en-suite rooms, some with air-conditioning. More upmarket is the three-star *Atash* (☎0832/313224, ●313239; ●), 4km northwest on the NH-4 at **Farmagudi**, whose comfortable a/c rooms have satellite TV, and there's also a restaurant and car parking facilities. However, the best mid-range deal within striking distance of Ponda has to be GTDC's *Tourist Resort* (☎0832/312932; ●–●), also at Farmagudi (look for the signpost on the roundabout below the Shivaji memorial), whose en-suite chalets, stacked up the side of a steep hill overlooking the highway, are spacious, clean and reasonably priced. There's also a small terrace restaurant serving a standard menu of spicy mixed cuisine.

Temples around Ponda

Scattered among the lush valleys and forests **around Ponda** are a dozen or so **Hindu temples** founded during the seventeenth and eighteenth centuries, when this hilly region was a Christian-free haven for Hindus fleeing persecution by the Portuguese. Although the temples themselves are fairly modern by Indian standards, their deities are ancient and held in high esteem by both local people and thousands of pilgrims from Maharashtra and Karnataka.

The temples are concentrated in two main clusters: the first to the north of Ponda, on the NH-4, and the second deep in the countryside, around 5km west of the town. Most people only manage the **Shri Manguesh** and **Shri Mahalsa**, between the villages of **Mardol** and **Priol**. Among the most interesting temples in the state, they lie just a stone's throw from the main highway and are passed by regular **buses** between Panjim and Margao via Ponda. The others are farther off the beaten track, although they are not hard to find on motorbikes: locals will wave you in the right direction if you get lost.

Mardol and Priol

Although the **Sri Manguesh** temple originally stood in a secret location in Cortalim, and was moved to its present site between **MARDOL** and **PRIOL** during the sixteenth century, the structure visitors see today dates from the 1700s. A gateway at the roadside leads to a paved path and courtyard that gives on to a water tank, overlooked by the white temple building, raised on a plinth. Also in the courtyard is a seven-storey *deepmal*, a tower for oil lamps. Inside, the floor is paved with marble, and bands of decorative tiles emblazon the white walls. Flanked by large *dvarpala* guardians, embossed silver doorways with floriate designs lead to the sanctum, which houses a *shivalingam*.

Two kilometres south, the **Mahalsa Marayani** temple was also transferred from its original site, in this case Salcete *taluka* further south, in the seventeenth century. Here, the *deepmal* is exceptionally tall, with 21 tiers rising from a figure of Kurma, the tortoise incarnation of Vishnu. Original features include a marble-floored wooden *mandapa* (assembly hall) with carved pillars, ceiling panels of parakeets and, in the eaves, sculptures of the incarnations of Vishnu.

Dudhsagar waterfalls

Measuring a mighty 600m from head to foot, the famous **waterfalls** at **DUDHSAGAR**, on the Goa–Karnataka border, are some of the highest in India, and a spectacular enough sight to entice a steady stream of visitors from the coast into the rugged Western Ghats. After pouring across the Deccan plateau, the headwaters of the Mandovi River form a foaming torrent that fans into three streams, then cascades down a near-vertical cliff face into a deep green pool. The Konkani name for the falls, which literally translated means "sea of milk", derives from clouds of foam kicked up at the bottom when the water levels are at their highest. Overlooking a steep, crescent-shaped head of a valley carpeted with pristine tropical forest, Dudhsagar is set amid breathtaking **scenery** that is only accessible on foot or by jeep; the old Vasco–Castle Rock railway actually passes over the falls on an old stone viaduct, but services along it are infrequent.

Practicalities

The best time to visit Dudhsagar is immediately after the monsoons, from October until mid-December, although the falls flow well into April. Unfortunately, the train line, which climbs above the tree canopy via a series of spectacular cuttings and stone bridges, only sees two services per week in each direction (Tues & Sat; depart Margao 7.21am), neither of them returning the same day. As a result, the only practicable way to get there and back is by four-wheel-drive **Jeep** from **Colem** (reachable by train from Vasco, Margao and Chandor, or by taxi from the north coast resorts for around Rs1000). The cost of the onward thirty- to forty-minute trip from Colem to the falls, which takes you across rough forest tracks and two or three river fords, is around Rs250–350 per person; the drive ends with an enjoyable fifteen-minute hike, for which you'll need a sturdy pair of shoes. Finding a Jeep-wallah is easy; just turn up in Colem and look for the "Controller of Jeeps" near the station. However, if you're travelling alone or in a couple, you may have to wait around until the vehicle fills up, or else fork out Rs2000 or so to cover the cost of hiring the whole Jeep yourself. Note that it can be difficult to arrange transport of any kind from Molem crossroads, where regular taxis are in short supply.

North Goa

Beyond the mouth of the Mandovi estuary, the Goan coast sweeps **north** in a near-continuous string of beaches, broken only by the odd saltwater creek, rocky headland, and three tidal rivers – two of which, the Chapora and Arondem, have to be crossed by ferry. The most developed resorts, **Calangute** and **Baga**, occupy the middle and northern part of the seven-kilometre strip of pearl-white sand that stretches from the Aguada peninsula in the south to a sheer laterite promontory in the north. Formerly, the infamous colonies of Goa hippies gathered in these two villages during their annual winter migration; now both heave during high season with British charter tourists, bus loads of trippers from out of state and itinerant vendors hawking fruit and trinkets on the beach. The "scene", meanwhile, has shifted northwards, to the beaches around **Anjuna**, **Vagator** and **Chapora**, where the Christmas–New Year parties take place.

Most of the tourist traffic **arriving in north Goa** from Mumbai is siphoned off towards the coast through **Mapusa**, the area's main market town. For short hops between towns and resorts, **motorcycle taxis** are the quickest and most convenient way to get around, but **buses** also run to all the villages along the coast, via the **ferry crossings** at Siolim, 7km north of Anjuna, and Querim (for Terekol).

Mapusa

The ramshackle market town of **MAPUSA** (pronounced *Map*sa) is the district headquarters of Bardez *taluka*. If you arrive by road from Mumbai and plan to stay in one of the north Goan resorts, you can jump off the bus here and pick up a local service straight to the coast, rather than continue on to Panjim, 13km south.

A dusty collection of dilapidated modern buildings scattered around the west-facing slope of a low hill, Mapusa is of little more than passing interest in itself, although on Fridays it hosts a lively **market** (hence the town's name, which derives from the Konkani words for "measure", *map*, and "fill up", *sa*). Calangute and Anjuna may be better-stocked with souvenirs, but this bazaar is more authentic. Visitors who have flown straight to Goa, and have yet to experience the rest of India, wander in on Friday mornings to enjoy the pungent aromas of fish, incense, spices and exotic fruit stacked in colourful heaps on the sidewalks. Local specialities include strings of spicy Goan sausages (*chouriço*), bottles of *todi* (fermented palm sap) and large green plantains. You'll also encounter sundry freak shows, from run-of-the-mill snake charmers and kids dressed up as *sadhus* to wide-eyed flagellants, blood oozing out of slashes on their backs.

Practicalities

Other than to shop, you may want to visit Mapusa to arrange **onward transport**. All buses between Goa and Maharashtra pass through, so you don't need to travel to Panjim to book a ticket to Mumbai, Pune, Bangalore or Mangalore. Reservations for private buses can be made at the numerous agents' stalls at the bottom of the square, next to where the buses pull in; the **Kadamba terminal** – the departure point for long-distance state buses and local services to Calangute, Baga, Anjuna, Vagator, Chapora, and Arambol – is five minutes' walk down the main road, on the southwest edge of town. You can also get to the coast from Mapusa on one of the **motorcycle taxis** that wait at the bottom of the square. Rides to Calangute and Anjuna take twenty minutes, and cost Rs40. **Taxis** charge considerably more, but you can split the fare with up to five people.

As soon as you step off the bus, you'll be pestered by touts trying to get you to rent a **motorbike**. They'll tell you that rates here are lower than on the coast – they're not. Another reason to wait a while is that Mapusa is effectively a "no-go zone" for rented motorbikes, especially on Friday, when the police set up road-blocks on the outskirts of town to collar tourists without international licences (see p.151).

Accommodation and eating

Nearly all long-distance buses pull in to Mapusa in the morning, leaving plenty of time to find **accommodation** in the coastal resorts nearby. If you have to spend the night here, though, there are plenty of places within easy walking distance of the Kadamba bus stand. The best budget deal is GTDC's *Tourist Hotel* (℡ 0832/262794 or 262694; ❺), on the roundabout below the square, which has spacious and clean rooms, a Goa **tourist information** counter, and a small Damania Shipping office. The *Vilena*, across town near the Municipality Building on Mapsa Road (℡ 0832/263115; ❷–❺), also offers good-value economy rooms (with or without attached bathrooms), in addition to more comfortable a/c ones, and has a dimly lit bar and small rooftop restaurant. On the north side of the main square, the *Hotel Satyaheera* (℡ 0832/262849 or 262949; ❺), is the town's top hotel, with mostly a/c rooms.

Mapusa's most relaxing **restaurant** is the *Ruchira*, on the top floor of the *Hotel Satyaheera*, which serves a standard Indian menu with Goan and Chinese alternatives, and cold beer. The *Hotel Vrindavan*, on the east side of the main square, dishes up Mapusa's best inexpensive South Indian snacks, along with an impressive range of ice creams and shakes. Cheaper but less salubrious Goan thali joints can be found in the streets east of the main square.

Candolim and Fort Aguada

Compared with Calangute, 3km north along the beach, **CANDOLIM** (from the Konkani *kandoli*, meaning "dikes", in reference to the system of sluices that the area's first farmers used to reclaim land from nearby marshes)

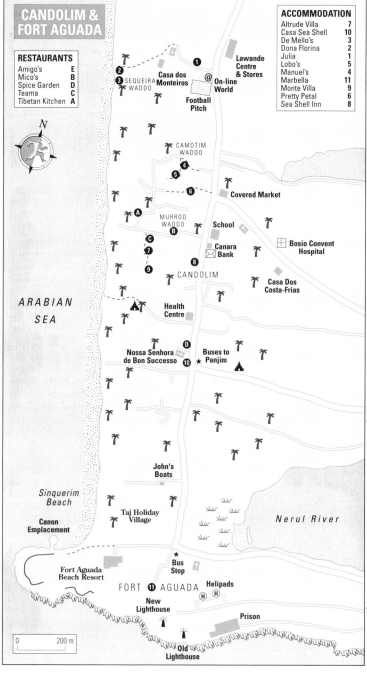

Calangute (2 km)

CANDOLIM & FORT AGUADA

RESTAURANTS
Amigo's	E
Mico's	B
Spice Garden	D
Teama	C
Tibetan Kitchen	A

ACCOMMODATION
Altrude Villa	7
Casa Sea Shell	10
De Mello's	3
Dona Florina	2
Julia	1
Lobo's	5
Manuel's	4
Marbella	11
Monte Villa	9
Pretty Petal	6
Sea Shell Inn	8

N

SEQUEIRA WADDO

Casa dos Monteiros

Lawande Centre & Stores

@ On-line World

Football Pitch

CAMOTIM WADDO

Covered Market

MURROD WADDO

School

Canara Bank

Bosio Convent Hospital

CANDOLIM

Casa Dos Costa-Frias

ARABIAN SEA

Health Centre

Nossa Senhora de Bon Successo

Buses to Panjim

John's Boats

Sinquerim Beach

Taj Holiday Village

Nerul River

Canon Emplacement

Bus Stop

Fort Aguada Beach Resort

FORT ① AGUADA

Helipads

New Lighthouse

Prison

Old Lighthouse

0   200 m

Panjim (13 km)

Panjim (13 km), Nerul & Coco Beach

Fort Aguada

is a surprisingly sedate resort, attracting mainly middle-aged package tourists from the UK and Scandinavia. Over the past five years or so, however, its ribbon development of hotels and restaurants has sprouted a string of multi-storeyed holiday complexes, and during peak season the few vestiges of authentically Goan culture that remain here are drowned in a deluge of Kashmiri handicraft stalls, luridly lit terrace cafés and shops crammed with postcards and beachwear. Long gone are the days when this was a tranquil bolt hole for burgundy-clad *sanyasins* from the Rajneesh ashram at Pune. Now the beach where they used to hold yoga positions is lined with sun beds, parasols and shack cafés, and the surf sees more jet-skis and paragliders than fishing boats. On the plus side, Candolim has lots of pleasant places to stay, many of them tucked away down quiet sandy lanes and better value than comparable guesthouses in nearby Calangute, making this a good first stop if you've just arrived in Goa and are planning to head further north after finding your feet.

Immediately south, a long peninsula extends into the sea, bringing the seven-kilometre white sandy beach to an abrupt end. **FORT AGUADA**, which crowns the rocky flattened top of the headland, is the best-preserved Portuguese bastion in Goa. Built in 1612 to protect the northern shores of the Mandovi estuary from Dutch and Maratha raiders, it is home to several natural springs, the first source of drinking water available to ships arriving in Goa after the long sea voyage from Lisbon. On the north side of the fort, a rampart of red-brown laterite juts into the bay to form a jetty between two small sandy coves. This picturesque spot, known as **Sinquerim Beach**, was among the first places in Goa to be singled out for upmarket tourism. Taj Group's *Fort Aguada* resorts, among the most expensive hotels in India, lord over the beach from the lower slopes of the steep-sided peninsula.

The ruins of the **fort** can be reached by road; head through the *Taj Holiday Village*, and turn right when you see the sign. Nowadays, much of the site serves as a prison, and is therefore closed to visitors. It's worth a visit, though, if only for the superb views from the top of the hill where a four-storey Portuguese **lighthouse**, erected in 1864 and the oldest of its kind in Asia, looks down over the vast expanse of sea, sand and palm trees of Calangute beach on one side, and across the mouth of the Mandovi to Cabo Raj Bhavan, and the tip of the Mormugao peninsula, on the other.

Practicalities

Buses to and from Panjim stop every ten minutes or so at the stand opposite the *Casa Sea Shell*, in the middle of Candolim. A few head south here to the *Fort Aguada Beach Resort* terminus, from where services depart every thirty minutes for the capital via Nerul village; the rest all go direct to Panjim via Nerul bridge, immediately east of the junction, or else hasten north along the main drag to Calangute. **Taxis** can be located outside any of the major resort hotels listed below, or flagged down on the road. During the season, there is often a shortage of **motorcycles for rent** here, and you may find yourself having to search for a bike in Calangute (see p.174).

Accommodation

Candolim is charter-holiday land, so **accommodation** tends to be expensive for most of the season. That said, if bookings are down you can find some great bargains here. The best place to start looking is at the end of the lane that leads to the sea opposite the Canara Bank, at the north side of the village.

Altrude Villa, Murrod Waddo ☎ 0832/277703. Large, airy rooms with attached tiled bathrooms and private verandas. The larger ones on the first floor have sea views. ⑤ –⑦

Casa Sea Shell, Fort Aguada Road, near *Bom Sucesso* ☎ 0832/277879. A new block, identical to *Sea Shell Inn*, but with its own pool, picturesquely situated beside a small chapel. The rooms are large, with spacious tiled bathrooms, and the staff and management welcoming and courteous. Arguably the best choice in this class. ⑥

De Mello's, Monteiro's Road ☎ 0832/277395. Gaudy pink-and-orange place in the dunes that takes the overspill from the (pricier) *Dona Florina* next door. Smallish rooms with not very private balconies, but only a stone's throw from the beach and very quiet. ⑤

Dona Florina, Monteiro's Road ☎ 0832/275051 or 277398, ⊕ 276878. Large, ten-year-old guest house in superb location, overlooking the beach in the most secluded corner of the village. Sanyasins from the Rashneesh ashram from Pune have long been its mainstay, hence the higher than usual rates – worth paying if you want idyllic sea views. No vehicle access. ⑥ –⑦

Julia, Escrivao Waddo ☎ 0832/277219. At the north end of the village. Comfortable en-suite rooms, tiled floors, balconies, a relaxing, sociable garden, and easy access to the beach. ④

Lobo's, Camotim Waddo ☎ 0832/279165. In a peaceful corner of the village, this is a notch up from *Manuel's*, opposite, with larger rooms, a long common veranda on the ground floor and very friendly owners. ④

Manuel's, Camotim Waddo ☎ 0832/277729. Small family guesthouse that's been around for years and is welcoming, clean and cheap, although somewhat boxed in by other buildings. All rooms have fans and attached shower-toilets. ③ –④

Marbella, Sinquerim ☎ 0832/275551, ⊕ 276509. Individually styled suites and spacious rooms (from Rs1000) in a beautiful house built to resemble a traditional Goan mansion. The decor, fittings and furniture are gorgeous, especially in the top-floor "Penthouse" (Rs2000), and the whole place is screened by greenery. Unashamedly romantic and well worth splashing out on. ⑦

Monte Villa, Murrod Waddo ☎ 0832/276344, ⓔ montvila@goatelecom.com. Seven lovely en-suite rooms, 2min from the beach, recently revamped by friendly Gulf returnees. Scrupulously clean and with some sea views. Ask for "M5", which has a breezy corner balcony. Internet access available. ④ –⑤

Pretty Petal, Camotim Waddo ☎ 0832/276184. Not as twee as it sounds: very large, modern rooms, all with fridges and balconies, and relaxing, marble-floored communal areas overlooking lawns. Their top-floor apartment (#113), with windows on four sides and a huge balcony, is the best choice, though more expensive.

Sea Shell Inn, Fort Aguada Road, opposite the Canara Bank ☎ 0832/276131. Homely, immaculately clean rooms in a roadside hotel featuring safe deposit lockers, laundry facility and a popular terrace restaurant. The tariff includes use of a nearby pool – a very good deal. ⑤

Eating and drinking

Candolim's numerous beach **cafés** are a cut above your average seafood shacks, with pot plants, state-of-the-art sound systems and prices to match. Basically, the farther from the *Taj* complex you venture, the more realistic the prices become.

Amigo's, 3km east of Candolim at Nerul bridge. Well off the beaten track and rarely patronized by tourists, this rough-and-ready riverside shack, tucked away under the bridge, is famous locally for its superb fresh seafood, served straight off the boats on no-nonsense stone tables. Fish curry and rice is their stock in trade, but they also do stuffed pomfret, calamari chilli-fry, red snapper and, best of all, Jurassic-sized crabs in butter-garlic sauce. Count on Rs150 for the works, with drinks.

Casa Sea Shell, in *Casa Sea Shell* hotel. This is the place to head for top-notch tandoori and North Indian dishes, although they also offer a good choice of Chinese and European food. Excellent service and moderate prices.

Mico's, Murrod Waddo. Succulent barbecued meats and seafood are the speciality of this stylish but unpretentious new restaurant, set around a beautifully renovated Portuguese-era house just off the main road. They also serve a range of tasty, healthy starters (including great satay chicken, hummus and tsatsiki), tender steak in whisky sauce and a great Thai-style curry made with fresh coconut, lemongrass and ginger. Main courses from Rs90 (for Indian veg),to Rs500 (for a grilled fresh lobster).

Sea Shell, at the *Sea Shell Inn*, Fort Aguada Road. A congenial terrace restaurant that cooks seafood and sizzling meat meals to order – also good for vegetarians and anyone fed up with spicy Indian food. Try one of their delicious cocktails.

Spice Garden, opposite Canara Bank. The food here is not up to much, but the live music is well worth dropping in for. A local guitarist does singa-long numbers (and beautiful Konkani wedding songs if cajoled), interspersed with Tom Jones covers from the owner, complete with dramatic gestures and heavy vibrato: a must.

Teama, Murrod Waddo, opposite *Altrude Villa*. One of the best places in the area to sample authentic Goan food. Try their prawn curry and rice house

speciality, or milder fish *caldin*. Most of the main meals cost around Rs120–175, and they have a good breakfast menu. Occasional live music during the season.

Tibetan Kitchen, Murrod Waddo. A swish offshoot of the established Calangute restaurant, serving filling and tasty (but non-spicy) Tibetan and Chinese specialities, and a good range of Western dishes, in comfortable surroundings behind the dunes. Most main dishes under Rs100.

Calangute

A mere 45-minute bus ride up the coast from the capital, **CALANGUTE** is Goa's busiest and most commercialized resort, and the flagship of the state government's bid for a bigger slice of India's package-tourist pie. In the 1970s and early 1980s, this once-peaceful fishing village epitomized Goa's reputation as a haven for hedonistic hippies. Indian visitors flocked by the bus-load from Bombay and Bangalore to giggle at the tribes of dreadlocked Westerners lying naked on the vast white sandy beach, stoned out of their brains on local *feni* and cheap *charas*. Calangute's flower-power period, however, has long passed. Hoteliers today joke about the days when they used to rent out makeshift shacks on the beach to backpackers. Now many of them manage tailor-made tourist settlements, complete with air-conditioned rooms, swimming pools and lush lawns, for groups of suitcase-carrying fortnighters.

The charter boom, combined with a huge increase in the number of Indian visitors, for whom this is Goa's premier resort, has placed an impossible burden on Calangute's rudimentary infrastructure. Each year, as another crop of construction sites blossoms into resort complexes, what little charm the village has retained gets steadily more submerged under ferro-concrete and heaps of garbage. The pollution problems are compounded by an absence of adequate provision for waste disposal and sewage treatment, and ever-increasing water-consumption levels. One worrying sign that Calangute has already started to stew in its own juices has been a dramatic rise in **malaria** cases: virex, and the more serious falciparum strain, are now both endemic here, and rife during the early part of the season.

The town and beach

The road from the **town** to the beach is lined with Kashmiri-run handicraft boutiques and Tibetan stalls selling Himalayan curios and jewellery. The quality of the goods – mainly Rajasthani, Gujarati and Karnatakan textiles – is generally high, as are the prices. Haggle hard and don't be afraid to walk away from a heavy sales pitch – the same stuff crops up every Wednesday at Anjuna's flea market. The **beach** itself is nothing special, with steeply shelving sand, but is more than large enough to accommodate the huge numbers of high-season visitors. Most of the action centres on the beachfront below GTDC's unsightly *Tourist Resort*, where crowds of Indian women in saris and straw hats stand around watching their sons and husbands frolic in the surf. Nearby, stray cows nose through the rubbish left by the previous bus party, while an endless stream of ice-cream and fruit sellers, *lunghi*-wallahs, ear cleaners and masseurs, work their way through the ranks of trippers.

To escape the melee of the main beachfront area, head fifteen minutes or so south, towards the rows of old wooden boats moored below the dunes at Maddo

N

BAGA

Drop Anchor
Bar ⑤

Lina Travel

ENEM Financial
Services

Tito's Nightclub

ARABIAN
SEA

Wendell Rodrick's Shop

ACCOMMODATION

Alidia (Alirio & Lidia)	6
Angelina	10
Camizala	21
Casa Leyla	20
Cavala	5
CoCo Banana	19
Coelho's	24
Divine	2
Dona Emeldina's	8
Gabriel's	25
Golden Eye	23
Hacienda	13
Joanita	14
Lina	1
Melissa	3
Nani's & Rani's	4
Nilaya Hermitage	15
NV's	22
Pousada Tauma	18
Ronil Royale	11
Sunset Cottages	12
Varma's Beach Resort	17
Villa Fatima	7
Villa Goesa	16
Zinho's	9

CALANGUTE

Bus Stop
Taxis
Shyam
Bookstore
Wall St
Bus Finances
Stop
Casa dos
Proença
Vanessa
Cinema
Motorcycle
Taxis
Bank of
Baroda
Buses to Panjim
Market

RESTAURANTS & CAFÉS

After Eight	I
Aubergine	D
Fiesta	C
Infanteria Pastelaria	F
J&A's Little Italy	A
Le Restaurant	E
Lila Café	B
Milky Way	H
Plantain Leaf	E
Souza Lobo	G

St Anthony's
Chapel

0   100 m

Kerkar Art
Gallery
㉔ ㉕

CALANGUTE & BAGA

Waddo (literally "toughies' quarter", referring to the fishermen, who used to be very tough indeed before the relatively recent advent of the outboard motor).

At the other end of the village's social hierarchy, one of Calangute's wealthiest families in the early eighteenth century built an extraordinary mansion, the **Casa dos Proença**, which still stands just north of the market area, beyond the Bank of Baroda. Its most distinctive feature is a wonderful tower-shaped veranda whose sides are covered in screens made from oyster shells (*carepas*). The gallery is surmounted by a grand pitched roof, designed to funnel the air entering the room through the windows and other openings (now glazed) – an ingenious natural air-conditioning system that was in time adopted all over the Portuguese empire.

Practicalities

Buses from Mapusa and Panjim pull in at the small bus stand-cum-market square in the centre of Calangute. Some continue to Baga, stopping at the crossroads behind the beach en route. Get off here if you can (as the main road veers sharply to the right); it's closer to most of the hotels. **Motorcycle taxis** hang around opposite the temple in the market area, and around the little sandy square behind GTDC's *Tourist Resort*, next to the steps that drop down to the beachfront. Ask around here if you want to rent a **motorcycle**. Rates are standard; the nearest **petrol station** (or "pump") is five minutes' walk from the beach, back towards the market on the right-hand side of the main road. **Bicycles** are also widely available for around Rs50 per day.

There's a State Bank of India on the main street, but the best place to **change money** and travellers' cheques is Wall Street Finances (Mon–Sat 8.30am–7pm, Sun 10am–2pm), opposite the petrol pump and in the shopping complex on the beachfront. If they are closed, try the fast and friendly ENEM Finances in Baga, who open late (daily 8am–9pm), but offer poorer rates. For Visa encashments, go to the Bank of Baroda, just north of the temple and market area; a commission fee of Rs100, plus one percent of the amount changed, is levied on all Visa withdrawals.

Accommodation

Calangute is chock-full of **places to stay**. Demand only outstrips supply in the Christmas–New Year high season, and at Diwali (Sept–Oct), when the town is inundated with Indian tourists; at other times, haggle a little over the tariff, especially if the place looks empty.

Even the cheapest rooms tend to have a veranda or a balcony, and an attached bathroom; nowhere is far from the shore, but sea views are more of a rarity. The top hotels are nearly all gleaming white, exclusive villa complexes with pools, and direct beach access. High-season rates in such places can be staggeringly steep, as they cater almost solely for package tourists.

Camizala, 5-33B Maddo Waddo ☎ 0832/279530 or 276263. Lovely, breezy little place with only four rooms, common verandas and sea views. About as close to the beach as you can get, and the ward is very quiet (see *Casa Leyla* review below). Cheap considering the location. ③

Casa Leyla, Maddo Waddo ☎ & ℻ 0832/276478. A great place if you're a family looking for somewhere with plenty of space for a let of at least one week. The rooms are huge and well furnished, with fridges, kid-friendly beds and chairs, and basic self-catering facilities, while the house itself, whose upper storey sits up in the palm canopy, is set deep in the secluded fishing ward, behind the quietest stretch of the beach. ④ –⑤

CoCo Banana, 1195 Umta Waddo ☎ & ℻ 0832/276478, down the lane past *Meena Lobo's* restaurant. Very comfortable, spacious chalets, all with bathrooms, mosquito nets, extra-long mattresses and verandas, around a central garden. Run by a very sorted Swiss-Goan couple who have been here for years. ⑤ –⑥

Coelho's, just south of *Golden Eye*, near the ice factory, Gaura Waddo ℡0832/277646. Twelve very spacious rooms in a large new house, on the peaceful (sea-facing) side of the village, 2min from the beach. Individual balconies, and a wonderful roof terrace with sea views. ④–⑤

Gabriel's, next door to *Coelho's*, Gauro Waddo ℡0832/279486, ℉ 277484. A congenial, quiet guesthouse midway between Calangute and Candolim, run by a gorgeous family who go out of their way to help their guests, many of whom return year after year. Shady garden, pleasant views from rear side across the *toddi* dunes, top little restaurant and very close to the beach. ④

Golden Eye, A-1/189 Gaura Waddo ℡0832/277308, ℉ 276187. Large rooms, balconies, sea views and a terrace restaurant, all smack on the beach. One of the first purpose-built hotels in Calangute. ⑥

NV's, south Calangute ℡0832/279749 or 281334, ℮nv-goa@hotmail.com. Homely, traditional Goan guesthouse right on the beach, run by a fisher family and holding its own despite proximity of a large package resort. Eleven rooms, four with breezy common balcony. A good budget option. ③–⑤

Pousada Tauma, Porba Waddo ℡ 0832/279061, ℉ 279064, ⓦwww.pousada-tauma.com. New luxury resort complex, comprising double-storey laterite villas ranged around a pool, in the middle of Calangute, but screened from the din by lots of vegetation. Understated decor, and a very exclusive atmosphere, preserved by five-star prices. Their big draw is a first-rate Keralan Ayurvedic health centre (open to non-residents). ⑨

Varma's Beach Resort, 2min east of GTDC *Tourist Resort* ℡0832/276077, ℉ 276022. Attractive a/c rooms, with balconies overlooking a leafy garden. Close to the centre of the village, but secluded. ⑧

Villa Goesa, Cobra Waddo ℡0832/277535, ℉276182, ℮alobo@goatelecom.com. A stone's throw from the beach and very swish, set around a lush garden of young palms and lawns. Occasional live music and a cocktail bar. All rooms have balconies. ⑦

White House, 185/B Gaura Waddo, near *Goan Heritage* ℡0832/277938, ℉ 276308. Immaculate, large rooms in modern block close to the beach, with balconies, bathrooms and some views. If full, try the equally comfortable *Dona Cristalina* along the lane (℡0832/297012). ⑤ –⑥

Eating and drinking

Calangute's **bars** and **restaurants** are mainly grouped around the entrance to the beach and along the Baga road. As with most Goan resorts, the accent is firmly on **seafood**, though many places tack on a few token veg dishes. Western breakfasts (pancakes, porridge, muesli, eggs) also feature prominently.

After Eight, Gauro Waddo, midway between Calangute and Candolim, down a lane leading west off the main road, between the Lifeline Pharmacy and a small chapel. Superb gourmet restaurant run by two ex-Taj (Mumbai) whizz kids, in a quiet garden. Steaks are their most popular dish, and chef Chakraborthy has a sublime touch with seafood, served with original, delicate sauces. Most main courses around Rs250.

Gabriel's, in *Gabriel's* guesthouse, Guara Waddo. Authentic Goan cooking (pork *sorpotel*, chicken *xacuti*, stuffed squid and prawn masala), and very popular Italian dishes (with home-made pasta) served on a cosy roof terrace well away from the main road. A tiny bit pricier than average (most mains around Rs80) but worth it, and they do real espresso coffee.

Infantaria Pastelaria, next to St John's Chapel, Baga Road. Roadside terrace café that gets packed out at breakfast time for its piping hot croissants, freshly baked apple pie and real coffee. During the season they do full-on breakfast buffets too, with cereals and fresh fruit (Rs80 including

drinks). Indian-Continental dinner menu served upstairs in the evening. Takeaways from the street-facing counter.

NV's, south Calangute. A ten-minute trek down the beach, but well worth it for no-nonsense platefuls of grilled fish, calamari and crab, all fresh from the family boat and at rock-bottom prices.

Plantain Leaf, near Vanessa Cinema, market area. The best *udipi* restaurant outside Panjim, serving the usual range of delicious dosas and other spicy snacks in a clean, cool marble-lined canteen, with relentless background *filmi* music. Try their tasty *idly-fry* – South India's answer to chips – or the filling thalis (Rs35).

Souza Lobo, on the beachfront. One of Goa's oldest restaurants and deservedly famous for its superb seafood, served on crisp gingham tablecloths by legions of fast-moving waiters in matching Madras-checked shirts. Blow-out fish sizzlers and mouthwatering tiger prawns or lobsters are the house specialities, but they do a mean stuffed avocado for veggies. Get there early, and avoid weekends. Most main dishes Rs100–150.

Calangute's **nightlife** is surprisingly tame for a resort of its size. All but a handful of the bars wind up by 10pm, leaving punters to prolong the short evenings back at their hotels, find a shack that's open late, or else head up to Baga (see below). The other places that consistently work into the wee hours are a couple of dull hippy hangouts in the woods to the south of the beach road: *Pete's Bar*, a perennial favourite next door to the *Angela P. Fernandes Guest House*, is generally the most "lively", offering cheap drinks, backgammon sets and relentless Bob Marley. Further afield, *Bob's Inn*, between Calangute and Candolim, is another famous old bar, renowned above all for its extrovert owner, who claims with some justification to have been Goa's first hippy.

Finally, don't miss the chance to sample some pukka Indian culture while you are in Calangute. The **Kerkar Art Gallery**, in Gaurwaddo, at the south end of town (℡ 0832/276017), hosts evenings of **classical music and dance** (Tues 6.45pm; Rs250 on door or in advance), held in the back garden on a sumptuously decorated stage, complete with incense and evocative candlelight. The recitals, performed by students and teachers from Panjim's Kala Academy, are kept comfortably short for the benefit of Western visitors, and are preceded by a short introductory talk.

Baga

BAGA, 10km west of Mapusa, is basically an extension of Calangute; not even the locals agree where one ends and the other begins. Lying in the lee of a rocky, wooded headland, the only difference between this far northern end of the beach and its more congested centre is that the scenery here is marginally more varied and picturesque. A small river flows into the sea at the top of the village, below a broad spur of soft white sand, from where a dirt track strikes across an expanse of paddy fields towards Anjuna.

Until the early 1990s, few buildings stood at this far northern end of the beach other than a handful of old red-tiled fishers' houses nestling in the dunes. Since the package boom, however, Baga has developed more rapidly than anywhere else in the state and today looks less like a Goan fishing village than a small-scale resort on one the Spanish Costas, with a predominantly young, charter-tourist clientele to match. But if you can steer clear of the lager louts and bar brawls, Baga boasts distinct advantages over its neighbours: a crop of excellent restaurants and a nightlife that's consistently more full-on than anywhere else in the state, if not all India.

Accommodation

Accommodation is harder to arrange on spec in Baga than in Calangute, as most of the hotels have been carved up by the charter companies; even rooms in smaller guesthouses tend to be booked up well before the season gets under way. If you're keen to stay, you may have to hole up farther down the beach for a night while you hunt around for a vacancy. The rough-and-ready places dotted around the fishing village usually have space; look for signs on the main square. Cheap houses and rooms for rent are also available on the quieter north side of the river, although these are like gold dust in peak season. If you come then, beware of "compulsory gala dinner supplements" or some similarly named ruse to slap stiff surcharges (typically Rs750 per head) on to your room tariff.

Alidia (Alirio & Lidia), Baga Road, Saunta Waddo ℡ 0832/276835 or ℡ &℗ 279014, ℮ alidia @goaworld.com. Attractive modern chalet rooms with good-sized verandas looking on to the dunes. Double or twin beds. Quiet, friendly and the best deal in this bracket. ④–⑥

Angelina, near *Tito's*, Saunta Waddo
☏ 0832/279145. Spacious, well-maintained rooms
with large tiled bathrooms and big balconies, off
the road but still in the thick of things. A/c available. ③ —⑥

Cavala, on the main road ☏ 0832/277587 or
276090, ℉ 277340, ⊚ www.cavala.com. Modern
hotel in tastefully traditional mould; simple rooms,
and separate balconies, but a little close to the
road for comfort. ⑥ —⑦

Divine, near *Nani's & Rani's*, north of the river
☏ 0832/279546. Run by fervent Christians (the
signboard features a burning cross and bleeding
heart), the rooms are on the small side, but clean;
some have attached shower-toilets. ③

Dona Emeldina's, Sauto Waddo ☏ 0832/276880.
Pleasantly old-fashioned cottages with verandas
opening on to lawns, run by a garrulous
Portuguese-speaking lady. A bargain in low and
mid-season (Rs550–650), but pricey over
Christmas, due to its proximity to the party enclave
– a dubious distinction. If she's fully booked, check
out her other place, the cheaper but less appealing
Baga Queen nearby. ⑦

Hacienda, Baga Road ☏ 0832/277348. Nothing
special but good value, with big, airy rooms, balconies, running hot water and a neat little garden.
⑤ —⑥

Joanita, Baga Road ☏ 0832/277166. Clean, airy
rooms with attached baths and some double beds,
around a quiet garden. A good choice if you want
to be in the village centre but off the road. ③ —④

Lina, north of the river ☏ 0832/281142. Baga's
most secluded guest house, deep in a peaceful
palm grove on the edge of dense woodland. Quiet,
with only four simple en-suite rooms, and cheap
for the area. ③

Melissa, 620 Anjuna Rd ☏ 0832/279583. Eight
recently built rooms in a clean, quiet block on the
north side of the river, all with attached shower-
toilets. Good off-season discounts, too. ③

Nani's and Rani's, north of the river
☏ 0832/276313 or 277014. A handful of red-tiled,
whitewashed budget cottages in a secluded garden behind a huge colonial-era house. Fans, some
attached bathrooms, well-water, outdoor showers
and internet facility. ② —④

Nilaya Hermitage, Arpora Bhati
☏ 0832/276793–4 or 275187–8, ℉ 276792,
ⓔ nilaya@goa1.dot.net.in. Set on the crest of a
hilltop 6km inland from the beach, with matchless
views over the coastal plain, this place ranks
among India's most exclusive hotels, patronized by
a very rich international jet set. On site are a
steam room, gym, clay tennis court, and a restaurant that's open to lesser mortals who can't afford
to stay here. Rooms from around $245 for two,
including meals and airport transfers. ⑨

Ronil Royale, Baga Road ☏ 0832/276101,
℉ 276068. Baga's most upmarket hotel, a ten-
minute walk from the beach, has Portuguese-style
apartments overlooking two small pools, with a
swish restaurant. ⑨

Sunset Cottages, Sauta Waddo ☏ 0832/276802,
℉ 275001. The best mid-budget choice in this
generally overpriced area below *Tito's*. In season
it's rammed with beery Brits, but the smallish
rooms are well kept and the management friendly.
⑤ —⑥

Villa Fatima, Baga Road ☏ 0832/277418. Thirty-
two attached rooms in a large, three-storey backpackers' hotel centred on a sociable garden terrace. Their rates are reasonable, varying with room
size. All attached bathrooms. ④ —⑥

Zinho's, 7/3 Saunta Waddo ☏ 0832/277383.
Tucked away off the main road, close to *Tito's*. Half
a dozen modest size, clean rooms above a family
home. Near to the beach and good value. ④

Eating

Baga has the best range of **restaurants** in Goa, from standard beach shacks to
swish pizzerias and terrace cafés serving real expresso coffee. Because of the stiff
competition, prices are generally reasonable and the quality of cooking high.
Even if they wouldn't be seen dead here during the day, many old Goa hands
come to Baga to eat in the evenings. For a splurge, splash out on a candle-lit
dinner at *J&A's Little Italy*, or a romantic Italian meal at *Fiesta*.

Aubergine, 3km inland at Arpora. Sophisticated,
intimate garden restaurant created by Goan
designer Wendell Rodricks. The Norman chef,
Patrick Le Clerc, aims to provide simple, wholesome dishes that blend Indian ingredients with
French flair – try the wonderful the *papillotte de
poisson farci beurre nantais* (fish fillet with prawn
stuffing steamed in banana leaf with white wine
and butter). And his chocolate mousse is unmissable. Mains Rs135–225; real Cuban cigars
Rs90–440.

Fiesta, Tito's Lane. Baga's most extravagantly
decorated restaurant enjoys a perfect spot at the
top of a long dune with sea views. The menu's

Mediterranean, with a generous measure of Portuguese. Most mains around Rs180; wine Rs70 per glass, or by the bottle (Rs550).

J&A's Little Italy, Baga Creek. Mouthwatering, authentic Italian food (down to the imported Parmesan and olive oil) served in the riverside garden of an old fisherman's cottage. Cooked in a wood-fired oven, their pizzas are delicious (try the amazing "smoked beef" house speciality), and dishes of the day include fresh lasagne. Count on Rs250–300 per head for the works; extra for wine (Rs60 per glass).

Le Restaurant, Baga Road. Hot contender for the title of best restaurant in Goa, as much for its classic French cooking as the reasonable prices and fun atmosphere, whipped up by the three Gallic partners against a backdrop of classy red curtains and Christmas lights. Steaks are the chef's forte, but they offer plenty of seafood and veg alternatives. Main courses around Rs150.

Lila Café, Baga Creek. Laid-back bakery-cum-snack-bar, run by a German couple who've been here for years. Their healthy home-made breads and cakes are great, and there's an adventurous lunch menu featuring spinach à la crème, aubergine pate and smoked water buffalo ham, rounded off with real espresso coffee. Open 8am–8pm.

Milky Way, midway between Calangute and Baga. Baga's best breakfast venue (occupying the same garden as *Le Restaurant*), serving mountainous bowls of fresh fruit and home-made curd, as well as pancakes, muesli and omelettes.

Nani's and Rani's, at *Nani's and Rani's* guesthouse on the north side of the river. Friendly family-run restaurant serving unremarkable but inexpensive, tasty food on a sociable veranda overlooking the river. Popular with budget travellers.

Nightlife

Nightlife revolves around *Tito's*, on a sandy hillock above the beach. Women are allowed in for free; "unaccompanied" men have to pay Rs100–250, depending on the crowd. Be warned, however, that in recent years this has become something of a pick-up joint, frequented by groups of so-called "rowdies" from Delhi and Mumbai, with the lager fuelled antics you'd find in a rough British nightclub. A marginally more sedate option, run by the same owners is *Mambo's*, further down the hill, where karaoke is the big attraction. At the far end of Baga beach, *Drop Anchor* is deservedly the most popular place for a quiet drink. Also owned by the *Tito's* family, it serves up cocktails in addition to the usual range of beers and spirits, and has a terrace with easy chairs on the sand.

Anjuna

With its fluorescent-painted palm trees and infamous full-moon parties, **ANJUNA**, 8km west of Mapusa, is Goa at its most "alternative". Fractal patterns and day-glo lycra may have superseded cotton kaftans, but most people's reasons for coming are the same as they were in the 1970s: drugs, dancing and lying on the beach slurping tropical fruit. Depending on your point of view, you'll find the headlong hedonism a total turn-off or heaven-on-sea. Either way, the scene looks here to stay, despite government attempts to stamp it out, so you might as well get a taste of it while you're in the area, if only from the wings, with a day-trip to the famous **flea market**.

One of the main sources of Anjuna's enduring popularity as a hippy hangout is its superb **beach**. Fringed by groves of swaying coconut palms, the curve of soft white sand is safer for bathing than most of the nearby resorts, especially at the more peaceful southern end, where a rocky headland keeps the sea calm and the undertow to a minimum. North of the market ground, the beach broadens, running in an uninterrupted kilometre-long stretch of steeply shelving sand to a low red cliff. The village bus park lies on top of this high ground, near a crop of small cafés, bars and Kashmiri handicraft stalls. Every lunch time, tour parties from Panjim pull in here for a beer, before heading home again, leaving the ragged army of sun-weary Westerners to enjoy the sunset.

ANJUNA 🌴

Police Post

Traveland

❶

❷ Bus Stop ★

❸ Bank of Baroda

Speedy Travel ◇ Motorcycle Repairs

❺ ❼ ❻ Sports Field

Orchard Stores

❽ ❹

RESTAURANTS

Axirwaad	A
Lafranza's	C
Orgasmic	B
Rose Garden Motel	D
Sea Breeze	E

❿ ❾ St Anthony's Chapel

Sacred Heart High School

Orgasmic Centre Oxford Stores ⓑ

Guru Bar ⑪ ⑫

ACCOMMODATION

Anjuna Beach Resort	1
Casa da Capitao	9
Coutinho's Nest	6
Don João Resort	3
Hill View	2
Laguna Anjuna	8
Manali	7
Martha's	13
Palacete Rodrigues	4
Palmasol Guest House	10
Sailor's Inn	11
Sea Wave Inn	5
White Negro	12

⑬ C

N

Sports Ground

D

E Fleamarket Ground

Bruno's Laundry

Shore Bar

Sunset Point

0   200 m

Ⓐ Mapusa | Calangute, Assago & Animal Sanctuary | Baga

2

GOA | North Goa

The season in Anjuna starts in early November, when most of the long-staying regulars show up, and peters out in late March, when they drift off again. During the Christmas and New Year rush, the village is inundated with a mixed crowd of round-the-world backpackers, refugees from the British club scene and revellers from all over India, lured by the promise of the big beach parties. A large contingent of these are young Israelis fresh out of the army and full of devil-may-care attitudes to drugs and other people's sleep. Outside peak season, however, Anjuna has a surprisingly simple, unhurried atmosphere – due, in no small part, to the shortage of places to stay. Most visitors who come here on market day or for the raves travel in from other resorts.

Whenever you come, keep a close eye on your valuables. **Theft**, particular-ly from the beach, is a big problem. Party nights are the worst; if you stay out late, keep your money and papers on you, or lock them somewhere secure. Thieves have even been known to break into local houses by lifting tiles off the roof.

Practicalities

Buses from Mapusa and Panjim drop passengers at various points along the tarmac road across the top of the village, which turns right towards Chapora at the main Starco's crossroads. If you're looking for a room, get off here as it's close to most of the guesthouses. The crossroads has a couple of small **stores**, a **motorcycle taxi** rank, and functions as a de facto village square and **bus stand**.

The *Manali Guesthouse* and Oxford Stores **change money** (at poor rates). The Bank of Baroda on the Mapusa road will make encashments against Visa

179

Anjuna's Wednesday flea market is the hub of Goa's alternative scene, and *the* place to indulge in a spot of souvenir shopping. A decade or so ago, the weekly event was the exclusive preserve of backpackers and the area's semi-permanent population, who gathered here to smoke chillums, and to buy and sell clothes and jewellery they probably wouldn't have the nerve to wear anywhere else: something like a small pop festival without the stage. These days, however, everything is more organized and mainstream. Pitches are rented out by the metre, drugs are banned and the approach roads to the village are choked solid all day with a/c buses and Ambassador cars ferrying in tourists from resorts farther down the coast.

The range of goods on sale has broadened, too, thanks to the high profile of migrant hawkers and stall-holders from other parts of India. Each region or culture tends to stick to its own corner. At one end, Westerners congregate around racks of New Age and dance gear, batik and designer beachwear. Nearby, hawk-eyed Kashmiris sit cross-legged beside trays of silver jewellery and papier-mâché boxes, while Tibetans, wearing jeans and T-shirts, preside over orderly rows of prayer wheels, turquoise bracelets and sundry Himalayan curios. Most distinctive of all are the Lamani women from Karnataka, decked from head to toe in traditional tribal garb, and selling elaborately woven multicoloured cloth, which they fashion into everything from jackets to money belts, and which makes even the Westerners' party gear look positively funereal. Elsewhere, you'll come across dazzling Rajasthani mirrorwork and block-printed bedspreads, Keralan woodcarvings and a scattering of Gujarati appliqué.

What you end up paying for this exotic merchandise largely depends on your ability to haggle. Lately, prices have inflated as tourists not used to dealing in rupees will part with almost anything. Be persistent, though, and cautious, and you can usually pick things up for a reasonable rate. Even if you're not spending, the flea market is a great place to sit and watch the world go by. Mingling with the sun-tanned masses are bands of strolling musicians, itinerant beggars, performing monkeys and snake-charmers, as well as the inevitable hippy jugglers, clad in regulation waistcoats and billowing pyjama trousers.

cards, but doesn't do foreign exchange, nor is it a good place to leave valuables, as thieves have previously climbed through an open window and stolen a number of "safe custody" envelopes. The **post office**, on the Mapusa road, 1km inland, has an efficient poste restante counter. *Manali Guest House* also offers **internet access** (Rs60/hr), but Colours, next to Speedy Travel, has a much faster connection and a/c for the same price.

Accommodation

Most of Anjuna's very limited **accommodation** consists of small unfurnished houses, although finding one is a problem at the best of times – in peak season it's virtually impossible. By then, all but a handful have been let to long-staying regulars who book by post several months in advance. If you arrive hoping to sort something out on the spot, you'll probably have to make do with a room in a guesthouse at first, although most owners are reluctant to rent out rooms for only one or two days at a time. Basically, unless you mean to stay for at least a couple of months, you're better off looking for a room in Calangute, Baga or nearby Vagator or Chapora.

Anjuna Beach Resort, De Mello Waddo ⓣ0832/274499, ⓔ fabjoe@goa1.dot.net.in. Fifteen spacious, comfortable rooms with bal-

conies, fridges, attached bathrooms and solar hot water in a new concrete building. Those on the upper floor are best. Good value. ⓞ

Casa da Capitao, near St Anthony's Chapel ⊤0832/273832. Three basic but spruce, purple-painted rooms amid lots of greenery, and with large sitouts. ❹

Coutinho's Nest, Soronto Waddo ⊤0832/274386. Small, very respectable family guesthouse on the main road. Their immaculately clean rooms are among the village's best budget deals. Shared shower-toilets only. ❸

Don João Resort, Soronto Waddo ⊤0832/274325, Ⓕ273447, Ⓦwww.goacom.com/hotels/donjoao.html. An unsightly multistorey hotel, slap in the middle of the village, and aimed squarely at the charter market, with a poolside restaurant, fridges in the rooms and inflated rates: precisely the kind of place Anjuna could do without. ❻

Hill View, De Mello Waddo ⊤0832/273235. One of the newer and more pleasant budget places, run by a landlady who puts Israeli guests into a separate "unbreakable" block. Quiet location, and good value. ❸

Hilton, on the main road near the bus park ⊤0832/274432 or 273477. Five double rooms in a characterless outbuilding, 500m behind the beach. Some attached shower-toilets. ❹

Laguna Anjuna, De Mello Waddo ⊤0832/274305. Recently opened "alternative designer" resort, in a similar mould to the famous *Nilaya* at Arpora (see p.177), but somewhat less expensive ($120 in peak season). It comprises 25 colourfully decorated laterite "cottages", grouped behind a convoluted pool, with a restaurant, pool room and bar.

Manali, south of *Starco's* ⊤0832/274421, Ⓔmanali@goatelecom.com. Anjuna's best all-round budget guesthouse has simple rooms

opening on to a yard, fans, safe deposit, money-changing, library, internet connection, a sociable terrace-restaurant and shared bathrooms. Very good value, so book in advance. ❷

Martha's, 907 Montero Waddo ⊤0832/273365. Eight immaculate en-suite rooms, including two pleasant houses, run by a warm and friendly family. Basic amenities include kitchen space, fans and running water. ❺

Palacete Rodrigues, near *Oxford Stores* ⊤0832/273358, Ⓕ274310. Two-hundred-year-old residence converted into an upmarket guesthouse. Carved wood furniture, and a relaxed, traditional Goan feel. Single occupancy available. ❻

Palmasol Guest House, Praia de St Anthony, behind middle of beach ⊤0832/273258, Ⓕ222261. Huge, comfortable rooms in an immaculately kept old house very near the beach. The larger ones have running water, verandas, cooking space and a relaxing garden; cheaper alternatives in the back yard. ❹–❻

Sailor's Inn, southwest of St Anthony's Chapel ⊤0832/273439. Four plain, clean rooms, very close to the sea shore, and with spacious sitouts, in a quiet spot, although you pay for proximity to the beach. ❺–❻

Sea Wave Inn, De Mello Waddo ⊤0832/274455. Smart, spacious, high-ceilinged rooms in a new block. Tiled bathrooms and balconies. Not the best location, but good value at this price. ❻

White Negro, 719 Praia de St Anthony, south of the village ⊤0832/273326, Ⓔmjanets@goa1.dot.net.in. A row of fourteen spotless back-to-back chalets catching the sea breeze, all with attached bathrooms and 24hr running water. Also a lively restaurant and friendly management. Good value. ❼

Water shortages

Because of the extra inhabitants it attracts over the winter, Anjuna has become particularly prone to water shortages. These tend not to affect many visitors, as the drought only begins to bite towards the end of March when the majority have already left. For the villagers, however, the problem causes genuine hardship. Use well water very sparingly and avoid water toilets if possible – traditional dry ("pig") ones are far more ecologically friendly.

Eating and drinking

Anjuna is awash with good **places to eat and drink**. The beach shacks tend to be overpriced by comparison with those elsewhere in the state (especially on flea market days, when they hike their prices) but many will feel the location is worth paying for. Responding to the tastes of its many "alternative" visitors, the village also boasts a crop of quality wholefood café serving healthy veg dishes and juices. The most sophisticated restaurant in the area, however, has to be the *Axinwaad*, 4km inland at Assagao.

Hedonism has figured prominently in European images of Goa from the mid-sixteenth century, when mariners and merchants returned to Lisbon with tales of unbridled debauchery among the colonists. The French traveller François Pyrard was first to chronicle this as moral decline, in a journal peppered with accounts of wild parties and sleaze scandals.

Following the rigours of the Inquisition, a semblance of morality was restored, which prevailed through the Portuguese era. But traditional Catholic life in Goa's coastal villages sustained a rude shock in the 1960s with the first influx of hippies to Calangute and Baga beaches. Much to the amazement of the locals, the preferred pastime of these would-be *sadhus* was to cavort naked on the sands together on full-moon nights, amid a haze of *chillum* smoke and loud rock music blaring from makeshift PAs. The villagers took little notice of these bizarre gatherings at first, but with each season the scene became better established, and by the late 1970s the Christmas and New Year parties, in particular, had become huge events, attracting thousands of foreign travellers.

In the late 1980s, the local party scene received a dramatic face lift with the coming of acid house and techno. Ecstasy became the preferred dance drug as the club-reggae scene gave way to rave culture, with ever greater numbers of young clubbers pouring in for the season on charter flights. Goa soon spawned its own distinctive brand of psychedelic music, known as Goa Trance. Distinguished by its multilayered synth lines and sub-bass rhythms, the hypnotic style combines the darkness of hard techno with an ambient sentiment. Cultivated by artists such as Juno Reactor and Hallucinogen, the new sound was given wider exposure when big-name DJs Danny Rampling and Paul Oakenfold started mixing Goa Trance in clubs and on national radio back in the UK, generating a huge following among music lovers who previously knew nothing of the place which had inspired it.

In spite of the growing interest in Goa Trance, the plug was pulled on the state's party scene in 1994–95. For years, drug busts and bribes provided the notoriously corrupt local cops with a lucrative source of baksheesh. But after a couple of drug-related deaths, a series of sensational articles in the local press and a decision by Goa Tourism to promote upmarket over backpacker tourism, the police began to demand impossibly large bribes – sums that the organizers could not hope to recoup. Although the big New Year and Christmas events continued unabated, smaller parties, hitherto held in off-track venues such as "Disco Valley" behind Middle Vagator beach, started to peter out, much to the dismay of local people, many of whom had become financially dependent on the raves and the punters they pulled in to the villages.

Against this backdrop, news of the Y2K amplified-music ban between 10pm and 7am seemed to sound the death knell for Goa's party scene. At the time, locals and expats alike still believed the ruling would have little impact – that the police would simply use it as a pretext to exort still larger bribes from bar owners and party organizers. But they were wrong. Since winter 1999–2000, the nights on Goa's coast have, with a few notable exceptions, been silent. Only a handful of cafés and clubs can muster large enough payoffs to stay open through the small hours, and most of these are mainstream venues in Baga.

So if you've come to Goa expecting an Indian equivalent of Ko Pha Ngan or Ibiza-on-the-Arabian Sea, you'll be sorely disappointed. Only over Christmas and New Year, when tourist numbers ensure organizers can recoup the massive outlay on bribes, do parties take place, and these are a far cry from the free-and-easy events that once filled the beaches on full-moon nights.

Axirwaad, #483 Rua de Boa Vista, Bouta Waddo, Assagao. Located 4km east along the main Mapusa road, this atmospheric restaurant occupies an lofty old Portuguese-era *palacio*, decked out and lit with blue colours and textiles to create an underwater ambience. The menu (mains around Rs150) blends East and West, and all points in between. On Thursdays, it metamorphoses into a "Lounge Groove Space", serving tapas and Arab mezes, with guest DJs.

Lafranza's, south end of village on the road to the market ground. The budget travellers' choice: big portions of tasty fresh fish and fries, with plenty of veg options.

Martha's Breakfast Home, at *Martha's* guesthouse, 907 Montero Waddo. Secluded, ultrafriendly breakfast garden serving fresh Indian coffee, crepes and delicious waffles.

Orgasmic, near Oxford Stores. Gaudily decorated with coloured pea lights and flouro paints, this is where the Anjuna's wealthy, healthy alternative clique like to dine on gourmet vegetarian food. If you're hankering for safe, adventurous salads, you'll be spoilt for choice (Rs100 for a big bowl). They also do great tofu dishes and even sushi.

Rose Garden Motel, on the beach south of the *Shore Bar*. Not to be confused with the *Rose Garden Restaurant* in the village. The exhaustive menu here features superb, reasonably priced seafood sizzlers and tasty Indian veg dishes.

Sea Breeze, market ground. Does a roaring trade in cold beer and snacks on Wednesdays. At other times the vast tandoori fish selection is tasty and good value, especially for groups; order in advance.

Sun 'n' Sand, market ground. Renowned for its whopping fresh-fruit salads served with crumbled coconut and curd. Great for inexpensive, healthy breakfasts.

Nightlife

Thanks to a recent ban on amplified music after 10pm, Anjuna no longer deserves the reputation it gained through the 1980s as a legendary rave venue, but big **parties** do still take place here from time to time, especially around the Christmas–New Year full-moon period. Smaller events may also happen whenever the organizers can muster the increasingly large pay-offs demanded by local police.

At other times, **nightlife** centres on the *Nine Bar*, above Vagator beach, where big Trance sounds attract a fair-sized crowd for sunset. On Wednesdays after the flea market, the *Shore Bar*, in the middle of Anjuna beach, offers more of the same on a larger scale, with hundreds of foreigners making the most of the police-free zone on the bar's steps. The music gains pace as the evening wears on, winding up around 10pm, when there's an exodus over to the *Primrose Café* in Vagator, which stays open until after midnight. *Axirwaad* in Assagao is the place to be on Thursday nights, when the restaurant becomes a cool lounge club, with cutting-edge fusion from visiting DJs.

Vagator

Barely a couple of kilometres of clifftops and parched grassland separate Anjuna from the southern fringes of its nearest neighbour, **VAGATOR**. A desultory collection of ramshackle farmhouses and picturesque old Portuguese bungalows scattered around a network of leafy lanes, the village is entered via a branch off the Mapusa road, which passes a few small guesthouses and restaurants before running down to the sea. Dominated by the red ramparts of Chapora fort, Vagator's broad white sandy beach – **Big Vagator beach** – is undeniably beautiful, spoiled only by the daily deluge of whisky-swilling tour parties that spill across it at lunch times.

Far better, then, to head to the next cove south. Backed by a steep wall of crumbling palm-fringed laterite, **Ozran** (or "Little") **Vagator beach** is more secluded and much less accessible than either of its neighbours. To get there, walk ten minutes from Big Vagator, or drive to the end of the lane off the main Chapora–Anjuna road, from where a footpath drops sharply down to a wide

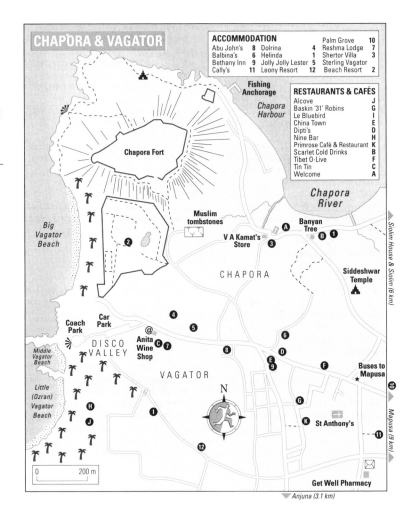

CHAPORA & VAGATOR

ACCOMMODATION

Abu John's	8	Dolrina	4
Balbina's	6	Helinda	1
Bethany Inn	9	Jolly Jolly Lester	5
Cally's	11	Leony Resort	12

Palm Grove	10
Reshma Lodge	7
Shertor Villa	3
Sterling Vagator Beach Resort	2

RESTAURANTS & CAFÉS

Alcove	J
Baskin '31' Robins	G
Le Bluebird	I
China Town	E
Dipti's	D
Nine Bar	H
Primrose Café & Restaurant	K
Scarlet Cold Drinks	B
Tibet O-Live	F
Tin Tin	C
Welcome	A

Fishing Anchorage

Chapora Harbour

Chapora Fort

Chapora River

Big Vagator Beach

Muslim tombstones

V A Kamat's Store

Banyan Tree

CHAPORA

Siddeshwar Temple

Coach Park

Car Park

@ Anita Wine Shop

DISCO VALLEY

VAGATOR

Middle Vagator Beach

Little (Ozran) Vagator Beach

N

Buses to Mapusa

St Anthony's

Get Well Pharmacy

0   200 m

Siolim House & Siolim (6 km)

Mapusa (9 km)

Anjuna (3.1 km)

stretch of level white sand (look for the mopeds and bikes parked at the top of the cliff). At this southern end of the beach (dubbed "Tel Aviv Beach"), a row of makeshift **cafés** provides shade and sustenance (and relentless Trance music) for a predominantly Israeli crowd. In spite of the Goan nudism laws, topless bathing is the norm; not that the locals, nor the odd groups of inebriated men who file past around mid-afternoon, seem in the least perturbed.

Like Anjuna, Vagator is a relaxed, comparatively undeveloped resort that appeals, in the main, to budget travellers with time on their hands. Accommodation is limited, however, and visitors frequently find themselves travelling to and from Baga every day until a vacancy turns up in one of the guesthouses.

Practicalities

Buses from Panjim and Mapusa, 9km east, pull in every fifteen minutes or so at the crossroads on the far northeastern edge of Vagator, near where the main road peels away towards Chapora. From here, it's a one-kilometre walk over the hill and down the other side to the beach, where you'll find most of the village's accommodation, restaurants and cafés. The *Primrose Café*, on the south side of the village, has a **foreign exchange** licence (for cash and travellers' cheques) but their rates are well above those on offer at the banks in Mapusa and Calangute. If you need medical attention, contact Dr Jawarhalal Henriques at Zorin, near the petrol pump in Chapora (ⓣ 0832/274308).

Accommodation

Accommodation in Vagator revolves around a few family-run budget guesthouses, a pricey resort hotel and dozens of small private properties rented out for long periods. The usual charge for a house is between Rs2000 and Rs4500 per month; ask around the cafés and back lanes south of the main road. **Water** is in very short supply here, and you'll be doing the villagers a favour if you use it frugally at all times (see p.181).

Abu John's, halfway between the crossroads and the beach (no phone). Self-contained chalets in a quiet garden, all with bathrooms and running water. A comfortable mid-range option. ⑤

Balbina's, Menndonca Waddo (no phone). Cosy little place below the main road, with views of the fort across the valley and a terrace café for guests. Quiet, and the rooms (all attached) are well maintained. ③

Bethany Inn, next to the Chapora crossroads ⓣ 0832/273973, ⓕ 273731, ⓔ bethany @goatelecom.com. Seven immaculately clean rooms with fridges, balconies and attached bathrooms. Tastefully furnished, and efficiently managed by two young brothers, originally from Pune. Internet access available. ⑤ –⑥

Cally's, near St Anthony's Church, behind Bella Bakery ⓣ 0832/273704. A new block owned by the same family as *Dolrina*, twenty minutes back from the beach, with clean tiled bathrooms and views from relaxing verandas across the fields. Good value. ② –③

Dolrina, north of the road near the beach ⓣ 0832/273382. Nestled under a lush canopy of trees, Vagator's largest and most popular budget guesthouse is run by a friendly Goan couple and features attached or shared bathrooms, a sociable common veranda, individual safe deposits and roof space. Single occupancy rates, and breakfasts available. ⑤

Jolly Jolly Lester, halfway between the crossroads and Big Vagator beach ⓣ 0832/273620. Eleven pleasant doubles with tiled bathrooms, plus a small restaurant, set in a lovingly kept garden and surrounded by woodland. Single occupancy possible. ⑤

Leoney Resort, on the road to Disco Valley ⓣ 0832/273634, ⓕ 273595, ⓔ romi@goatelecom .com. Smart chalets and pricier (but more spacious) octagonal "cottages" on sleepy side of village, ranged around a pool. Restaurant, laundry, lockers and foreign-exchange facilities. A comfortable option. No advance bookings Dec–Jan. ⑦

Reshma Lodge (Mrs Bandobkhar's), next to the Anita Wine Shop ⓣ 0832/273568. Inexpensive rooms in a newish building with running water, owned and managed by a friendly local lady. ④

Sterling Vagator Beach Resort, behind Big Vagator beach ⓣ 0832/274377. Upmarket resort hotel pitched at wealthy Indians, but extremely shabby for the price. A/c "cottages" (with TVs, fridges and attached bathrooms) grouped around a large pool at the top of the hill, or behind the beach at sea level; two multi-cuisine restaurants, safe deposit and money changing. ⑨

Eating, drinking and nightlife

Vagator boasts an eclectic batch of **restaurants**, with wildly varying menus and prices, and an equally dramatic turnover of chefs. Western tourists tend to stick to the pricier ones lining the road through the village, while Indian visitors frequent the more impersonal, cheaper places down on the beach itself. The bar to head for a sundowner is *Nine Bar* (formerly *Ram Das Swami's*), on the clifftop above Ozran beach, where alternative Goa struts its stuff, accompanied by a wall of techno. When it closes (at 9pm), everyone makes their way over to the *Primrose Café*, which offers much the same atmosphere, without the views.

Alcove, next to *Ram Das Swami's*, above Ozran beach. This unsightly clifftop complex enjoys the best location for miles, with spellbinding sea views through the palms. The food is also a cut above the competition, and the service slick. Try their fish dish of the day, washed down with a cocktail.

Baskin "31" Robins, near *Primrose Café*. Thirty-one flavours of melt-in-the-mouth American ice cream. The nut crunch is to die for.

Le Bluebird, on the road out to *Nine Bar*. Tucked away in the most appealing corner of the village is Vagator's famous French-run restaurant, which serves classier-than-average continental food at traveller-friendly prices. Seafood is their strong point, but they offer a better range of veg dishes than you'd find in a real French restaurant, as well as crepes, Bordeaux claret and champagne (around Rs2000 per bottle).

China Town, next to *Bethany Inn*. For the past few seasons, this small roadside restaurant, tucked away just south of the main drag, has been the village's most popular budget place to eat, serving particularly tasty seafood dishes in addition to a large Chinese selection, as well as all the usual Goa-style travellers' grub.

Dipti's, on the Mapusa road. Extraordinary magic mushroom plastic art meets Ajanta-mural-decor is the hallmark of this cosy bar, which serves a full Indian–Goan–Chinese–Continental menu. It's also a friendly place for a quiet cocktail.

Jolly Jolly Lester, halfway between the village crossroads and Big Vagator beach. Not to be confused with *Julie Jolly's*, near the *Primrose Café*.

This one's smaller, offering a better selection of inexpensive seasonal seafood, salads and tasty Western-style veg dishes.

Nine Bar, above Ozran beach. Boasting a crystal trance sound system, this clifftop café enjoys a prime location, with fine sea views from its terrace through the palm canopy, where Nepali waiters serve up cold beer and the usual range of budget travellers' grub to a generally spaced out clientele. They've recently enlarged the place to accommodate a dance floor and chill-out area.

Primrose Café and Restaurant, on the southern edge of the village. Goa's posiest café-bar livens up around 8pm and serves tasty German whole-food snacks, light meals and cakes, as well as drinks.

Tibet O-Live, east side of the village, on the main road. Run by a team of friendly young lads from Darjeeling, this place shuttles between Manali in the summer and Goa in the winter, and has earned a strong reputation in both for its ultra-tasty, inexpensive pizzas. They also serve mouth-watering fried *momos* (the spinach and cheese ones are best).

Tin Tin, west side of the village, near the clifftop car park. The kind of theme bar that makes you wonder why you ever left home: large and lavishly decorated, and crammed with a mainly young package tourist clientele, hence the higher than average prices, which the expat British co-owner justifies with a popular "big portions" policy. The menu is exhaustive, but best bets are the dishes of the day chalked on boards.

Chapora

Crouched in the shadow of a Portuguese fort on the opposite, northern side of the headland from Vagator, **CHAPORA**, 10km from Mapusa, is a lot busier than most north-coast villages. Dependent on fishing and boat-building, it has, to a great extent, retained a life of its own independent of tourism. The workaday indifference to the annual invasion of Westerners is most evident on the main street, lined with as many regular stores as travellers' cafés and restaurants. It's unlikely that Chapora will ever develop into a major resort either; tucked away under a dense canopy of trees on the muddy southern shore of a river estuary, it lacks both the space and the white sand that have pulled crowds to Calangute and Colva.

If you have your own transport, however, Chapora is a good base from which to explore the region: Vagator is on the doorstep, Anjuna is a short ride to the south, and the ferry crossing at Siolim – gateway to the remote north of the state – is barely fifteen minutes away by road. The village is also well connected by bus to Mapusa, and there are plenty of sociable bars and cafés to hang out in. The only drawback is that accommodation tends, again, to be thin on the ground. Apart from the guesthouses along the main road, most of the places to stay are long-stay houses in the woods.

Chapora's chief landmark is its venerable old **fort**, most easily reached from the Vagator side of the hill. At low tide, you can also walk around the bottom of the headland, via the anchorage and the secluded coves beyond it to Big Vagator, then head up the hill from there. The red-laterite bastion, crowning the rocky bluff, was built by the Portuguese in 1617 on the site of an earlier Muslim structure (thus the village's name – from *Shahpura*, "town of the Shah"). Deserted in the nineteenth century, it lies in ruins today, although the **views** up and down the coast from the weed-infested ramparts are still superb.

Practicalities

Direct **buses** arrive at Chapora three times daily from Panjim, and every fifteen minutes from Mapusa, with departures until 7pm. **Motorcycle taxis** hang around the old banyan tree at the far end of the main street, near where the buses pull in. Air, train, bus and catamaran **tickets** may be booked or reconfirmed at Soniya Tours and Travels, next to the bus stand.

Siolim Zagor

While much of India has had to learn to live with the spectre of religious violence, Goa's Christians and Hindus, despite the sabre-rattling of their respective right-wing politicians, manage to coexist peacefully and in a spirit of mutual respect unsurpassed on the subcontinent. Emblematic of this communal harmony, and indeed of the richness of Goa's melting pot culture in general, is the extraordinary Zagor festival, held in Siolim, just east of Chapora, on the first Sunday after Christmas.

Although ostensibly a Christian celebration, coinciding with the feast day of Nossa Senhora de Guia, the night-long event blends together elements from both religions. It centres on a small Hindu shrine, housed under *peepal* tree down a lane near the ferry ramp. This sacred spot is associated with an important local deity called Zagoryo, believed to be the guardian of the village dams (*bunds*) which hold the river off the rice paddy. During the festival, each household makes offerings to Zagor to give thanks and ensure the village is protected from flooding over the coming year: Christians give candles, Hindus give oil and both offer cakes of pressed rice called *pohe*.

The festivities, however, start with a sombre candle-lit procession through Siolim, in which an effigy of Zagor is carried around the various *waddos* of the village, stopping at wayside crosses and shrines along the way to receive offerings. Everyone then gathers at a *mand*, or sacred arena, in a Catholic house for a dance drama. The actors in this ancient ritual, assuming hereditarily assigned roles, are always drawn from two old Siolim families: the Shirodkars (Hindus) and D'Souzas (Catholics); it enacts stories from the legend of the Zagor deities. At dawn, when the play is complete and the priests have recited mantras and Christian scriptures to invoke the god's protection, Zagor is carried amid much pomp back to his shrine, where offerings of roasted maize, *feni* and fermented rice pikelets (called *sanna*) are placed before his small domed shrine.

Traditionally, local satirists used to take over at this point, performing zupatteos: songs poking fun at politicians, priests and anyone else who deserved to be taken down a peg or two. These days, however, the culmination of Zagor tends to be Konkani *tiatr* play, followed by a set of crowd-pleasing Konkani classics from local rock star, Remo Fernandes, who was born and still lives in Siolim.

Aside from being a model of religious tolerance, Zagor is a great spectacle and enormous fun. Surprisingly few tourists participate, but foreigners are welcomed enthusiastically, both to the religious dance drama and resolutely secular, *feni*-fuelled party that succeeds it.

If you want to check into a cheap guesthouse while you sort out more permanent **accommodation**, try the basic *Shertor Villa* (℡0832/424335; ②–③), off the west side of the main street. Nearly all its rooms, ranged around a sheltered back yard, come with fans and running water. If this place is full, try the *Helinda* (℡0832/274345; ②–③), at the opposite end of the village, which has rock-bottom options and a couple of more comfortable rooms with attached shower-toilets, as well as a good restaurant. The only luxury place hereabouts is the *Siolim House* (℡0832/272138 or 272942, ℻272323, ⓦwww.siolimhouse.com; ⑨), 5km inland from Chapora along the south bank of the river, in Siolim village. Housed in a recently restored *palacio*, the hotel captures the period feel of the Portuguese era, with elegant, simply furnished rooms ranged around a central pillared courtyard. It also has a twelve-metre pool in the garden, and an unobtrusive restaurant serving fine Goan food.

Finding cheap **meals** in Chapora itself is easy: just take your pick from the crop of inexpensive little cafés and restaurants on the main street. The popular *Welcome*, halfway down, offers a reasonable selection of cheap and filling seafood, Western and veg dishes, plus relentless reggae and techno music, and backgammon sets. If you're suffering from chilli-burn afterwards, *Scarlet Cold Drinks* and the *Sai Ganesh Café*, both a short way east of the main street, knock up deliciously cool fresh fruit milkshakes.

Pernem and the far north

Bounded by the Chapora and Arondem rivers, **Pernem** is Goa's northernmost district and one of its least explored regions. Apart from the fishing village of **Arambol**, which during the winter plays host to a large contingent of hippy travellers seeking a rougher, less pretentious alternative to Anjuna and Vagator, the beautiful Pernem coastline of long sandy beaches, lagoons and coconut plantations is punctuated with few settlements equipped to cope with visitors. However, the wonderfully picturesque journey north to **Terekol fort**, on the Maharashtran border, can easily be covered in a day-trip, while the long empty beaches at **Aswem** or **Mandrem** are perfect spots to pull off the road for a swim.

Before the Portuguese took over Pernem in 1778, the Chapora River marked the border between old Christian Goa (the *Velhas Conquistas*) and wider Hindu India. The 250 years of colonial rule that preceded the acquisition of the *Novas Conquistas*, of which Pernem was a part, ensured this divide was as much cultural as political, and even today the transition between the two is clearly discernible. Once across the river, most villages are grouped around brightly painted, colonnaded temples, the calendars in the provision stores sport images of Ganesh or Lakshmi rather than Our Lady, and the women tend to wear saris instead of dresses.

Travelling north from Siolim, the entrepôt to Pernem proper is the ferry landing stage at **Chopdem**. Head straight on for 200m or so until you arrive at a T-junction. A right turn here will take you along the quick route to Arambol.

Aswem and Mandrem

At the northern limits of Morjim beach, where the village's wooden fishing fleet is beached, stands a clump of eroded black rocks and a solitary white crucifix, around which locals harvest mussels at low tide each evening. Beyond it, the coast empties completely save for a handful of shacks and the odd palm-leaf hut encampment, nestling in the shade of small *toddi* plantations and tangles of prickly cactus. When the Siolim–Chapora bridge is built, this stretch of coast, known as **ASWEM**, is bound to be more quick-ly transformed than any other in Pernem, but for the time being, migratory sea birds still well outnumber tourists. That said, visitors unused to such "pris-tine" Indian beaches may find the lumps of rotting fish and human excre-ment left by the villagers a disincentive, not to mention the used syringes routinely dumped by the drug users who hole up here, out of range of the Panjim narcotics police.

If you're after peace and solitude during the day, it's also best to avoid the col-lection of shack restaurants and handicraft hawkers who congregate beneath the laterite bluff at the far northern end of Aswem beach, to which groups of tourists are brought by boat or minibus on package excursions from other resorts. When the trippers have gone home, however, this can be a pleasantly peaceful spot. Basic **accommodation** is available at the grandly named *Hotel Arabian Sea* (☎ 0832/296424, ⓕ 297375; ⓪–④), comprising a single block of three simple rooms with shared shower-toilets, and a few ramshackle bamboo "treehouses".

The next village up the coast, **MANDREM**, is also showing signs of low-key development, most of it in a small but lively riverside enclave behind the dunes known as **Junasa Waddo**. Top of the range here is the functional *Mandrem Beach Resort* (☎ 0832/297115; ⓪–④), to date the northernmost out-post of charter tourism in Goa. Its en-suite rooms are spacious and light, although somewhat incongruously modern for the area. A more stylish alter-native, with colourfully decorated rooms, relaxing cane furniture and large verandas, is the *River Cat Villa* (☎ 0832/297346, mobile ☎ 98230/92107, ⓕ 297375, ⓔ rinoopeter7@yahoo.com; ⓪–④). Its rates are a notch lower than the *Beach Resort*'s, but several of the rooms have shared bathrooms. Back towards the village, *Dunes* (☎ 0832/297219, ⓕ 297375, ⓔ dunes13@rediffmail .com; ⓪) is the best budget option: a camp of comfortable leaf huts and tepees, kitted out with proper beds, fans, mattresses and electric lights. The toilets and showers are immaculate, and the beach is only a stone's throw away.

All three of these places offer **food**, but the most congenial restaurant in Junasa Waddo is the *Oasis*, near the *River Cat Villa*, where you can eat top tan-doori seafood on a lovely terrace overlooking the river. For *pao-bhaji* breakfasts, you'll have to head back into Mandrem village, 3km along the main road to Arambol, where there's a great little *udipi* restaurant serving all the usual Goan snacks and thali rice-plate meals at lunch time. This busy little bazaar also has the area's best stocked provisions **stores**, and a cheap **laundry** (above the jew-eller's shop in the small courtyard just off the main street; Rs5 per item of clothing).

Arambol (Harmal)

The largest coastal village in Pernem district, and the only one really geared up for tourism, is **ARAMBOL** (or Harmal), 32km northwest of Mapusa. If you're happy with basic amenities but want to stay somewhere lively, this might be your best bet. The village's two beaches are beautiful and still relatively unex-ploited – thanks to the locals, who a few years back managed to block pro-posals put forward by a local landowner to site a sprawling five-star resort here. Parties do occasionally happen, drawing revellers across the river from Anjuna and Vagator, but these are rare intrusions into an otherwise tranquil, out-of-the-way corner of the state.

The one unpleasant aspect of Arambol is **crime**. The rate of thefts has gone through the roof here over the past few seasons. Dozens of travellers lose their passports and money each season, mostly from rented houses, so make sure your valuables are secure when you go out, especially after dark.

When a strong and steady on-shore breeze blows through the night in early November at Morjim – the long, empty beach west of the ferry ramp at Chopdem – the locals call it a turtle wind because such weather normally heralds the arrival of Goa's rarest migrant visitors: the Olive Ridley marine turtles (Lepidochelys olivacea).

For as long as anyone can remember, the spoon-shaped spit of soft white sand at Temb, the far southern end of the beach, has been the nesting ground of these beautiful sea reptiles. Each winter, a succession of females emerges from the surf during the night and, using their distinctive flippers, crawls to the edge of the dunes to lay their annual clutch of 105–115 eggs. Just over two months later, the fresh hatchlings clamber out and crawl blinking over their siblings to begin the perilous trek back to the water, guided into the sea by reflected moonlight. Little more is known about how these enigmatic creatures spend the rest of their long lives (turtles frequently live for over a century), but it is thought that the females return to the beaches where they were born to lay their own eggs. Some have been known to travel as far as 4500km to do this.

Once a thriving species, with huge populations spread across the Pacific, Atlantic and Indian oceans, the Olive Ridley is nowadays endangered. Aside from a wealth of traditional predators (such as crows, ospreys, gulls and buzzards, who pick off the hatchlings during their dash for the sea), the newborns and their parents are vulnerable to a host of man-made threats. In Morjim, as in most of Asia, the eggs are traditionally considered a delicacy and local villagers collect them to sell in Mapusa market. Many (perhaps as many as 35,000 worldwide) are killed accidentally by fisherman, caught up in fine shrimp nets or attracted by squid bait used to catch tuna. Floating litter, which the hapless turtles mistake for jellyfish, has also taken its toll over the past two decades, as have tar balls from oil spills, which coat the animals' digestive tracks and hamper the absorption of food. The growth of tourism poses an additional danger: electric lights behind

Modern Arambol is scattered around an area of high ground west of the main coast road, where most of the buses pull in. From here, a bumpy lane runs downhill, past a large school and the village church, to the more traditional end of the village, clustered under a canopy of widely spaced palm trees. The main **beach** lies 200m farther along the lane. Strewn with dozens of old wooden fishing boats and a line of tourist café-bars, the gently curving bay is good for bathing, but much less picturesque than its neighbour around the corner.

To reach "**Paradise beach**", follow the track over the headland to the north. Beyond a rather insalubrious smelling, rocky-bottomed cove, the trail emerges to a broad strip of soft white sand hemmed in on both sides by steep cliffs. Behind it, a small freshwater lake extends along the bottom of the valley into a thick jungle. Hang around the banks of this murky green pond for long enough, and you'll probably see a fluorescent-yellow human figure or two appear from the bushes at its far end. Fed by boiling hot springs, the lake is lined with sulphurous mud, which, when smeared over the body, dries to form a surreal, butter-coloured shell. The resident hippies swear it's good for you and spend much of the day tiptoeing naked around the shallows like refugees from some obscure tribal initiation ceremony – much to the amusement of Arambol's Indian visitors.

Practicalities

Buses to and from Panjim (via Mapusa) pull into Arambol every half-hour until noon, and every 90min thereafter, at the small bus stop on the main road.

the beaches throw the hatchlings off course as they scuttle towards to sea, and sand compressed by sunbathers' trampling feet damages nests, preventing the babies from digging their way out at the crucial time. On average, only two out of a typical clutch of more than one hundred survive into adulthood to reproduce. In Goa, the resulting decline has been dramatic. Of the 150 nesting females that used to return each year to Morjim, for example, only thirteen showed up in 1999.

However, under the auspices of the Forest Department, a new scheme has been launched to revive turtle populations. Locals are employed to watch out for the females' arrival in November, and guard the nests after the eggs have been laid until they hatch. You'll see them camped under palm-leaf shades on the beach, with the nests fenced in and marked by Forest Department signs. One of the main reasons the fishing families at Temb have so enthusiastically espoused the initiative is that its success promises to bring about the creation of an official nature sanctuary at Morjim, blocking forever plans to build unwanted tourist resorts on their beach. So far, the government-led conservation attempt seems to have been successful. In 1999, 778 hatchlings were monitored at Morjim and Goa's other turtle nesting site, Galjibag, in the far south.

Watching the nesting turtles is an unforgettable experience, although one requiring a certain amount of dedication, or luck. No one knows for sure when an Olive Ridley female will turn up, but with a strong turtle wind blowing at the right time, the chances are good. Much more predictable are the appearances of the hatchlings, who emerge exactly 54 days after their mothers laid the eggs. If you ask one of the wardens looking after the nests, they can tell you when this will be.

For more on international attempts to save marine turtles, including the massive synchronized *arribida* (arrival) of around 200,000 at the Bhita Kanika Sanctuary, Orissa, on the east coast of India, visit the website of the World Wildlife Fund (ⓦ www.wwf.org), which tells you how you can join environmental groups such as the Marine Conservation Society.

A faster private **minibus** service from Panjim arrives daily opposite the chai stalls at the beach end of the village. **Boats** leave here every Wednesday morning for the ninety-minute trip to the flea market at Anjuna. Tickets should be booked in advance from the *Welcome Restaurant* by the beach (Tues–Sun 8–9am & 8–9pm; Rs150), which also rents out motorcycles and scooters. The **post office**, next to the church, has a poste restante box; there are also several places offering **internet access** in the village, the cheapest and newest of them just past the junction on the main road. Reliable **money changers** include: Delight, on the east side of the main road, and Tara Travel, directly opposite, where you can also reconfirm and book air and catamaran tickets.

Apart from a couple of purpose-built chalets on the edge of the village, most of Arambol's **accommodation** consists of simple houses in the woods behind the beach. Some of the more expensive places have fully equipped kitchens and showers, but the vast majority are standard-issue bare huts, with "pig" toilets and a well in the back garden. Long-stay visitors either bring their own bedding and cooking stuff, or kit themselves out at Mapusa market. Good places to start room-hunting when you've just arrived are the *Villa Oceanic* (ⓣ0832/292296; ❷–❸), in the middle of the village, and the nearby *Ave Maria* (ⓣ0832/29764; ❸), the closest Arambol has to bona fide guesthouses.

The choice of **places to eat** has broadened impressively over the past few years. Pick of the bunch is the excellent *Double Dutch Bakery Café*, tucked away among the *toddi* trees in a clearing just below the main street (look for the yellow sign board). Run by an expat Dutch couple, it serves a tempting selection of delicious, healthy breakfasts, and home-made snacks, cakes and pastries during the day. They've also recently started offering evening meals of a standard not yet matched in the village, including great Indonesian dishes and a sumptuous Mughlai chicken. Arambol's other outstanding restaurant is the *Relax Inn*, north of the main entrance to the beach, through a gap in the bushes. Frequented by the village's resident German paragliding fraternity, it dishes up generous portions of fresh Goan-style seafood, with fries and copious salads. You generally have to wait longer than usual to be served, because they prepare each dish to order, sauces included. For inexpensive Indian rice-based meals, best bets are the no-nonsense chai stalls at the bottom of the village. *Sheila's* and *Siddi's* tasty thalis both come with *puris*, and they have a good travellers' breakfast menu of pancakes, eggs and curd. *Dominic's*, also at the bottom of the village (near where the road makes a sharp ninety-degree bend), is renowned for its fruit juices and milkshakes, while *Sai Deep*, a little further up the road, does generous fruit salads with yoghurt.

Terekol

North of Arambol, the sinuous coast road climbs to the top of a rocky, undulating plateau, then winds down through a swathe of thick woodland to join the River Arondem, which it then follows for 4km through a landscape of vivid paddy fields, coconut plantations and temple towers protruding from scruffy red-brick villages. The tiny enclave of **TEREKOL**, the northernmost tip of Goa, is reached via a clapped-out car ferry (every 30min; 5min) from the hamlet of Querim, 42km from Panjim.

After the long and scenic drive, the old **fort** that dominates the estuary from the north is a bit of an anticlimax. Hyped as one of the state's most atmospheric historic monuments, it turns out to be little more than a down-at-heel country house recently converted into a low-key luxury hotel. If your visit coincides with the arrival of a guided tour, you may get a chance to look around the gloomy interior of the **Chapel of St Anthony**, in the fort's claustrophobic cobbled square; at other times it's kept locked.

Practicalities

The few visitors that venture up to Terekol tend to do so by motorbike, heading back at the end of the day to the relative comfort of Calangute or Baga. If you run out of fuel, the nearest service station is at Arambol. One of GTDC's daily **tours** from Panjim (see p.151) comes up here, as does one daily Kadamba **bus** from the capital; alternatively, the 7am bus from Siolim, on the Chapora River, pulls in at the Querim ferry an hour later.

Accommodation is limited to the posh *Hotel Tirakhol Fort Heritage* (⊤ 0832/782240, Ⓕ 782326; ❼), whose rooms are pleasant and comfortable, but way overpriced at Rs800 for the no-frills (windowless) options, and around Rs2000 (plus taxes) for a luxury suite with sea views. The **restaurant** downstairs, kept busy in the daytime by bus parties, offers seafood, Indian and Chinese dishes, as well as beer.

South Goa

Beyond the unattractive port city of **Vasco da Gama**, and its nearby airport, the southern reaches of the state harbour some of the region's finest **beaches**, with attractive Portuguese-style villages nestled in a hilly interior. Many visitors base themselves initially at **Benaulim**, 6km west of Goa's second city, **Margao**. The most traveller-friendly resort in the area, Benaulim stands slap in the middle of a spectacular 25-kilometre stretch of pure white sand, backed by a broad band of coconut plantations. Although increasingly carved up by Mumbai time-share companies, low-cost accommodation here is plentiful and of a consistently high standard. Nearby **Colva**, by contrast, has degenerated over the past five or six years into an insalubrious charter resort, frequented by huge numbers of day-trippers. More polluted and far less relaxing than its neighbours, it's not somewhere you'd choose to hole up for a beach holiday.

With the gradual spread of package tourism down the coast, **Palolem**, a couple of hours' south of Margao down the main highway, has emerged as most budget travellers' first choice, despite its relative inaccessibility. Set against a backdrop of forest-cloaked hills, its beach is spectacular and development relatively low-key.

Vasco da Gama

VASCO DA GAMA (commonly referred to as "Vasco"), 29km by road southwest of Panjim, sits on the narrow western tip of the Mormugao peninsula, overlooking the mouth of the Zuari River. Acquired by the Portuguese in 1543, this strategically important site was formerly among the busiest ports on India's west coast. It remains a key shipping centre, with container vessels and iron-ore barges clogging the choppy river mouth, but holds nothing of interest for visitors, particularly since the completion of the Konkan Railway, when Goa's main railhead shifted from here to Margao. The only conceivable reason you might want to come to Vasco is to catch a bus to **Dabolim airport**, 4km southeast.

Dabolim airport

Dabolim, Goa's airport, lies on top of a rocky plateau, 4km southeast of Vasco da Gama. A large new civilian terminal was recently constructed at this naval aerodrome to accommodate Goa's rapidly increasing air traffic, but long delays are still common – so if you're catching a flight from here, aim to check in well in advance.

Facilities in the terminal buildings include State Bank of India foreign exchange desks (open for flights), post office counters, and counters for domestic airlines. There's also a handy pre-paid taxi counter outside the main exit. Fixed fares to virtually everywhere in the state are displayed behind the desk; pay here and give the slip to the driver when you arrive.

Facilities in Dabolim's first floor departures hall include another pint-size State Bank of India (Mon, Tues, Thurs & Fri 10.30am–1.30pm, Sat 10.30am–noon), a sub-post-office and branches of several domestic airlines: Indian Airlines (daily 7.15am–2pm; ☏0832/512788), Gujarat Airways (daily 9.30am–5pm; ☏0832/516060), Sahara Airlines (daily 9.30am–5pm; ☏0832/510043) and Jet (daily 9.30am–5pm; ☏0832/511005). There's a very ordinary and overpriced cafeteria, too, but it doesn't open in time for early morning domestic departures, so if you're looking for a filling breakfast, head across the road from the front of the terminal building to the staff canteen, where you can grab piping hot *bhaji pao* and *batata wada* for a few rupees. Finally, don't forget that if you're leaving Goa by international charter you have to pay Rs300 airport tax at the State Bank counter before you check in.

Practicalities

Vasco is laid out in a grid, bordered by Mormugao Bay to the north, and by the railway line on its southern side. Apart from the cluster of oil storage tanks, the town's most prominent landmark is the **railway station** at the south end of the main Dr Rajendra Prasad Avenue. **Arriving by bus** from Panjim or Margao, you'll be dropped off in the inconveniently situated interstate Kadamba terminus, 3km east of the town centre. Local **minibuses** ferry passengers from here to the more central market bus stand, at the top of the square, where buses from Dabolim airport also pull in. **Auto-rickshaws** and Ambassador and motorcycle **taxis** hang around on the corner of Swatantra Path and Dr Rajendra Prasad Avenue, near the station and the small **cycle rental** stall. If you need to **change money**, head for the State Bank of India (Mon–Fri 10am–2pm, Sat 10am–noon) at the north end of F L Gomes Road. GTDC's **tourist information** counter is in the lobby of their *Tourist Hostel* (daily 9.30am–5pm).

Thanks to its business city status, Vasco boasts a better-than-average batch of **hotels**. Most are plush mid-range places, although there are several no-frills lodges near the railway station. Best of the budget bunch is the neat and clean *Annapurna*, on Dattatreya Deshpande Road (℡0832/513375 or 513715; ⑤). If it's full try the GTDC *Tourist Hostel*, off Swatantra Path near the station (℡0832/510829 or 513119; ⑤–⑥). Moving upscale, the *Citadel*, Pe Jose Vaz Road (℡0832/513190 or 512222, ℻513036; ⑥), currently offers the best value for money among Vasco's many modern mid-range places. At the other end of town opposite Hindustan Petroleum, the *Maharaja* (℡0832/513075–8, ℻512559; ⑥–⑦) has similar tariffs and spotless rooms, but dismal views over the refinery. Finally, for fully air-conditioned comfort, complete with plush bars, restaurants and a gym, check in to Vasco's top hotel, the *La Paz*, on Swatantra Path (℡0832/512121, ℻513302; ⓦwww.hotellapazgardens.com; ⑨).

All of the hotels listed above have **restaurants**, but for traditional Indian snacks and thalis, the *Annapurna*'s ground-floor vegetarian cafeteria is hard to beat. At the other end of the centre, next door to *Hotel La Paz*, the excellent *Welcome Restaurant,* a more modern snack bar, serves a huge selection of dosas, as well as the usual range of bhajis and a full Punjabi menu; most main dishes cost between Rs30 and Rs50.

Margao (Madgaon) and around

MARGAO, the capital of prosperous Salcete *taluka*, is regarded as Goa's second city, even though it's marginally smaller than Vasco da Gama, 30km northwest. Surrounded by fertile farmland, the town has always been an important agricultural market, and was once a major religious centre, with dozens of wealthy temples and *dharamshalas* – however, most of these were destroyed when the Portuguese absorbed the area into their Novas Conquistas ("New Conquests") during the seventeenth century. Today, Catholic churches still outnumber Hindu shrines, but Margao has retained a distinctly cosmopolitan feel, largely due to a huge influx of migrant labour from neighbouring Karnataka and Maharashtra. The resultant overcrowding has become a real problem in the town centre, whose 1950s municipal buildings and modern concrete blocks stew under a haze of traffic pollution.

If you're arriving in Goa on the Konkan Railway from Mumbai or South India, you'll almost certainly have to pause in Margao to pick up onwards transport by road. The other reason to come here is to shop at the town's excellent **market**. Stretching from the south edge of the main square to with-

Head Post Office

RESTAURANTS & CAFÉS

Banjara	B
Bombay Café	F
Gaylin	A
Kamat	C
Longuinho's	D
Shri Damodar	E

Poste
Restante

Bus
Stand

Khadi
Shop

Bank of Baroda

★ Buses for Colva
& Benaulim

Municipal
Building

Music
Shop

Bazaar

Fish
Market

State
Bank
of India

Bob-
cards

ACCOMMODATION

GTDC Tourist Hostel	6
Mabai	2
Nanutel	1
Rukrish	5
Saaj	4
Woodlands	3

MARGAO

0   100 m

GOA | South Goa

Vasco da Gama ▲ & Mumbai (500 km)

Colva & Benaulim ◀

New Railway Station (3 km) ▶

Karwar ▼   ▼ Quepem

in a stone's throw of the old railway station, the bazaar centres on a labyrinthine covered area that's a rich source of authentic souvenirs, and a good place to browse. While you're here, take a short rickshaw ride north to the stately **Church of the Holy Spirit**, in the heart of a dishevelled but picturesque colonial enclave. Presiding over the dusty Largo de Igreja square, the church, built by the Portuguese in 1675, is one of the finest examples of late-Baroque architecture in Goa, boasting a pristine white facade and an interior dripping with gilt, crystal and stucco.

For a taste of Goa's wonderful vernacular colonial architecture, you'll have to head inland where a scattering of picturesque farming villages **around Margao** harbour a crop of decaying old Portuguese *palacios*, as well as handful of idiosyncratically Goan Hindu temples.

Practicalities

Margao's new **railway station**, the only stop in Goa for most long-distance express services on the Konkan Railway, lies 3km south of the centre. The reservation office (Mon–Sat 8am–4.30pm, Sun 8am–2pm) is divided between the ground and first floor; bookings for the superfast Rajdhani Express to Delhi are made at the hatch to the left of the main entrance. Tickets for trains to Mumbai are in short supply, so make your reservation as far in advance as possible, get here early in the day to avoid agonizing long queues, and bring a book. Several of the principal trains that stop in Margao do so at unsociable times of night, but there's a 24hr information counter (℡0832/712790), and round-the-clock pre-paid auto-rickshaw stand outside the exit.

Local private buses to Colva and Benaulim leave from in front of the *Kamat Hotel*, on the east side of Margao's main square. Arriving on long-distance government services you can get off either here or (at a more leisurely pace) at the main **Kadamba bus stand**, 3km further north, on the outskirts of town. The latter is the departure point for interstate services to Mangalore, via Chaudi and Gokarn, and for services to Panjim and north Goa. Paulo Travel's deluxe coach to and from Hampi works from a lot next to the *Nanutel Hotel*, 1km or so south of the Kadamba bus stand on Padre Miranda Road.

GTDC's **information office** (Mon–Fri 9.30am–5.30pm; ℡0832/222513), which sells tourist maps and keeps useful lists of train and bus times, is inside the lobby of the *Tourist Hostel*, on the southwest corner of the main square. **Exchange** facilities are available at the State Bank of India (Mon–Fri 10am–2pm, Sat 10am–noon), off the west side of the square; the Bobcard office in the market sub-branch of the Bank of Baroda, on Luis Gomes Road, does Visa encashments. The **GPO** is at the top of the municipal gardens, although its **poste restante** is in a different building, 200m west on the Rua Diogo da Costa.

Accommodation

With Colva and Benaulim a mere twenty-minute bus ride away, it's hard to think of a reason why anyone should choose to **stay** in Margao. If you do get stuck here, however, one of the following hotels are worth a try, although most tend to be full by early evening.

GTDC Tourist Hostel, behind the Municipal Building ℡0832/721966. Standard good-value government block, with en-suite rooms (some a/c) and a restaurant. A safe budget option. ❺

Mabai, 108 Praca Jorge Barreto ℡0832/721658. The *Woodlands*' only real competitor is frayed around the edges, but clean and central. Some a/c. ❹

Nanutel, Padre Miranda Road ℡0832/733176, ℻733175. The town's top hotel, pitched at visiting businesspeople, with 55 centrally a/c rooms, pool, bookshop, travel desk and a quality restaurant. ❻–❼

Rukrish, opposite the Municipal Building ℡0832/721709. Best of the rock-bottom lodges in the town centre, with passably clean rooms – some overlooking the main road and market. ❶–❷

Saaj, Miguel Loyola Furtado Road ℡0832/711757. A newcomer that's marginally brighter and cheaper than its main competitor, the nearby *Woodlands*. ❸–❺

Woodlands, Miguel Loyola Furtado Road ℡0832/721121. Margao's most popular mid-range hotel, around the corner from the *Tourist Hostel*. Its bargain "non-deluxe" rooms are often booked up. Reservations recommended. Some a/c. ❸–❺

Eating and drinking

After a browse around the bazaar, most visitors make a beeline for *Longuinho's*, the long-established hang-out of Margao's English-speaking middle classes. If you are on a budget, try one of the South Indian-style pure-veg cafés along Francisco Luis Gomes Road. A couple of these, notably the *Bombay Café*, open early for breakfast.

Banjara, De Souza Chambers ℡0832/722088. This swish basement restaurant is the classiest North Indian joint outside Panjim, specializing in rich Mughlai and tandoori dishes. Tasteful wood and oil-painting decor, unobtrusive *ghazaal* background music, imported liquors and slick service. Most main courses around Rs100.

Bombay Café, Francisco Luis Gomes Road. Popular with office workers and shoppers for its cheap veg snacks, served on tin trays by young lads in grubby cotton uniforms.

Gaylin, behind Grace Church. Smart, air-conditioned Chinese restaurant serving a good selection of Cantonese and Szechuan dishes (mostly steeped in hot red Goan chilli paste). Count on around Rs150–200 for three courses; extra for drinks.

Kamat, Praça Jorge Barreto, next to the Colva/Benaulim bus stop. The town's busiest *udipi*

canteen, serving the usual South Indian selection, as well as hot and cold drinks. Their masala dosas are the best for miles.

Longuinho's, opposite the *Tourist Hostel*, Rua Luis Miranda. Relaxing, old-fashioned café serving a reasonable selection of moderately priced meat, fish and veg mains, freshly baked savoury snacks, cakes and drinks. The food isn't up to much these days, and the old Goan atmosphere has been marred by the arrival of satellite TV, but it's a pleasant enough place to catch your breath over a beer.

Shri Damodar, opposite Gandhi Market, Francisco Luis Gomes Road. One of several inexpensive cafés and ice-cream parlours ranged around the temple square. This one is the cleanest, and has an air-cooled "family" (read "women's") room upstairs.

Lutolim

Dotted around the leafy lanes of **LUTOLIM**, 10km northeast of Margao, are several of Goa's most beautiful **colonial mansions**, dating from the heyday of the Portuguese empire when this was the country seat of the territory's top brass. Lying just off the main road, the village is served by eight daily **buses** from Margao, which drop passengers off on the square in front of a lopsided-looking church. The cream of Lutolim's houses lie within walking distance of here, nestled in the woods, or along the road leading south. However, you shouldn't turn up at any of them unannounced; visits have to be **arranged in advance** through the Margao tourist office.

Pick of the crop in Lutolim is **Miranda house**, a stone's throw from the square. Fronted by a plain classical facade, the mansion was built in the 1700s, though renovated later following raids by a clan of rebel Rajput bandits. Today, it is occupied by a famous Goan cartoonist and his family, direct descendants of the wealthy areca planters who originally owned the surrounding estate. **Roque Caetan Miranda house**, two minutes' walk south of the square, and **Salvador Costa house**, tucked away on the western edge of the village, are other mansions worth hunting out; the latter is occupied by an elderly lady who only welcomes visitors by appointment.

Lutolim's other attraction is the quirky model village-cum-heritage centre, a short way east of the square, called **Ancestral Goa** (daily 9am–6pm; Rs20). Set up to show visitors a cross-section of local village life as it was a hundred years ago, it's a well-meaning but ultimately dull exhibition of miniature houses and dressed dummies.

Chandor

Thirteen kilometres east of Margao across the fertile rice fields of Salcete lies sleepy **CHANDOR** village, a scattering of tumbledown villas and farmhouses ranged along shady tree-lined lanes. The main reason to venture out here is the splendid **Perreira–Braganza/Menezes–Braganza house** (daily except holidays; recommended donation Rs50), regarded as the grandest of Goa's colonial mansions. Dominating the dusty village square, the house, built in the 1500s by the wealthy Braganza family for their two sons, has a huge double-storey facade, with 28 windows flanking its entrance. Braganza de Perreira, the great-grandfather of the present owner, was the last knight of the king of Portugal; more recently, Menezes Braganza (1879–1938), a famous journalist and freedom fighter, was one of the few Goan aristocrats to actively oppose Portuguese rule. Forced to flee Chandor in 1950, the family returned in 1962 to find their house, amazingly, untouched. The airy tiled interiors of both wings contain a veritable feast of **antiques**. Furniture enthusiasts, and lovers of rare Chinese porcelain, in particular, will find plenty to drool over, while anyone interested in religious relics should request a glimpse of St Francis Xavier's diamond-encrusted toenail, recently retrieved from a local bank vault and enshrined in the east wing's tiny chapel. The house's most famous feature, however, is its ostentatiously grand ballroom, or **Great Salon**, where a pair of matching high-backed chairs, presented to the Perreira-Braganzas by King Dom Luís of Portugal, occupy pride of place.

Visitors generally travel to Chandor by taxi, but you can also get there by bus from Margao (8 daily; 45min). It's generally fine to turn up without an appointment, but to ensure someone from the family is in to receive you, phone ahead (☎0832/784227 or 9822/160009).

Colva

A hot-season retreat for Margao's moneyed middle classes since long before Independence, **COLVA** is the oldest and largest – but least appealing – of south Goa's resorts. Its leafy outlying *vaddos*, or wards, are pleasant enough, dotted with colonial-style villas and ramshackle fishing huts, but the beachfront is dismal: a lacklustre collection of concrete hotels, souvenir stalls and fly-blown snack bars strewn around a bleak central roundabout. The atmosphere is not improved by heaps of rubbish dumped in a rank-smelling ditch that runs behind the beach, nor by the stench of drying fish wafting from the nearby village.

Practicalities

Buses leave Margao (from outside the *Kamat Hotel* on Praça Jorge Barreto) every thirty minutes for Colva, dropping passengers at the main beachfront, and at various points along the main road. Auto-rickshaws charge Rs100 from the railway station.

To rent a **motorcycle**, ask around the taxi rank, or in front of *Vincy's Hotel*, where 100cc Yamahas are on offer at the usual rates. **Petrol** is sold by the Bisleri bottle from a little house behind the Menino Jesus College, just east of *William's Resort*. This is the only petrol stop in Colva, but the stuff sold may well be adulterated.

Meeting Point Travel (⊤0832/723338, ⑤732004), between *William's Resort* and the crossroads, exchanges **travellers' cheques** and **cash** at a little under bank rates, and Sanatan Travels, 200m east of the church does encashments on Visa and Mastercard. Both also book and reconfirm domestic and international flights, and arrange deluxe bus, catamaran and train tickets to other parts of India.

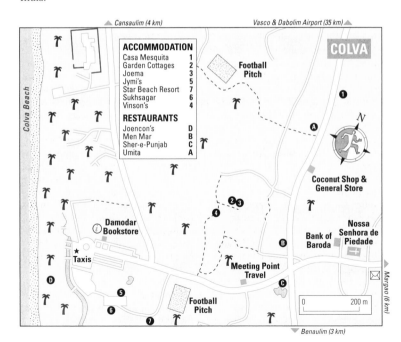

The **post office**, opposite the church in the village, has a small but reliable poste restante box. Damodar Book Store, on the beachfront, stocks a good selection of reasonably priced secondhand paperbacks in English. They also do part-exchange, and have the best range of postcards in Colva.

Accommodation

Mirroring the village's rapid rise as a package tour resort, Colva's plentiful **accommodation** ranges from bare cockroach-infested cells to swish campuses of chalets and swimming pools, with a fair selection of good-value guesthouses in between. Most of the budget rooms lie amid the more peaceful palm groves and paddy fields north of here: the quarter known as Ward 4, which is accessible via the path that winds north from *Johnny Cool's* restaurant, or from the other side via a lane leading west off the main Colva–Vasco road.

Casa Mesquita, 194 Vasco Rd, Ward 3 ☎0832/788173. Large rooms, with rickety four-poster beds (if you're lucky) but no fans or attached shower-toilets, in fading old colonial-style house. Mosaic-floored verandas add to the old world atmosphere. Western water-toilet, and some cheap dorm beds available on request. A touch grubby, but cheap and full of period feel. ❶–❷

Garden Cottages, Ward 4 (no phone). Immaculately maintained, attractive budget guesthouse in Colva's most tranquil quarter. Spacious twin-bedded en-suite rooms with fans, and a garden. ❷–❸

Joema, Ward 4 (no phone). Established in 1973, which probably makes this the oldest guesthouse in Colva. They've since added four small and simple but scrupulously clean attached rooms around the back. Easy, friendly Goan family atmosphere, with kids and pigs charging around, and a relaxing café-restaurant from mid-November. ❷–❸

Jymi's, opposite *Sukhsagar* ☎0832/788016. Large, long-established budget travellers' hotel,

with passable en-suite rooms. A good place to hole up until you find somewhere nicer, as it usually has vacancies. ❹

Star Beach Resort, near Football Ground ☎0832/788166 or 780092, ℮resortgoa@yahoo.com. Spacious rooms in new complex, with a large (crystal clear) pool, in-house generator, Ayurvedic health centre and inexpensive a/c. Not such a great deal at the beginning of the season, but they only increase their rates by Rs100 over Christmas. ❼

Sukhsagar, opposite the *Penthouse* restaurant ☎0832/721888, ℻731666. Nothing special from the outside, but its en-suite rooms are clean, light and airy, and the best deal in this price range. There's also a pleasant palm-shaded garden to relax in. Some a/c. ❻

Vinson's, Ward 4 (no phone). The newest of this ward's good-value cheapos. Quiet and secluded. ❷–❸

Eating and drinking

When the season is in full swing, Colva's beachfront sprouts a row of large seafood **restaurants** on stilts, some of them very ritzy indeed, with tablecloths, candles and smooth music. The prices in these places are top-whack, but the portions are correspondingly vast, and standards generally high. Budget travellers are equally well catered for, with a sprinkling of **shack-cafés** at the less frequented ends of the beach, and along the Vasco road.

Joencon's, second restaurant south from the beachfront. The classiest of Colva's beach restaurants. Agonizingly slow service and pricey, but the food is superb: try their flamboyant fish sizzlers, mouthwatering tandoori sharkfish or Chinese and Indian veg specialities.

Men Mar, Vasco Road. Their lassis, prepared with fresh fruit and home-made curd, are delicious. Open for breakfast.

Sher-e-Punjab, near the main crossroads, between the beachfront and church. Off-shoot of

the popular Panjim Punjabi joint, serving an exhaustive menu of inexpensive, deliciously spicy Indian food. Butter chicken is their signature dish, but there are plenty of tasty vegetarian options, including rich dhal *makhani*; and their naan bread is possibly the best in the village.

Umita, Vasco Road. Down-to-earth Goan and Indian veg cooking served up by a friendly Hindu family. Try their blow-out "special" thalis or whopping fresh fruit and curd breakfasts. Opens early.

Nightlife

Catering for an uncomfortable mixture of boozy Indian men from out of state and young European charter tourists, Colva's **nightlife** is less than enticing these days, despite the presence at the south end of the beach of Goa's few surviving "discos". *Splash* boasts a big MTV satellite screen and music to match, with a late bar and dance floor that livens up around 10pm. Less sophisticated than *Mambo's* and *Tito's* in Baga, however, it can be unpleasant for women. In theory, single men ("stags") aren't allowed on the dance floor, but this doesn't stop them trying their luck. If you'd prefer to get plastered somewhere cheaper and less pretentious, try *Johnny Cool's*, midway between the beach and Colva crossroads. *Men Mar*, on the Vasco Road, also serves beers, snacks and lassis until around 10.30pm.

Cobra warning

You'll rarely see a villager in Colva or Benaulim crossing a rice field at night. This is because paddy is prime territory for snakes, especially cobras. If you do intend to cut across the fields after dark, take along a strong flashlight, make plenty of noise and hit the ground ahead of you with a stick to warn any lurking serpents of your approach.

Benaulim

According to Hindu mythology, Goa was created when the sage Shri Parasurama, Vishnu's sixth incarnation, fired an arrow into the sea from the top

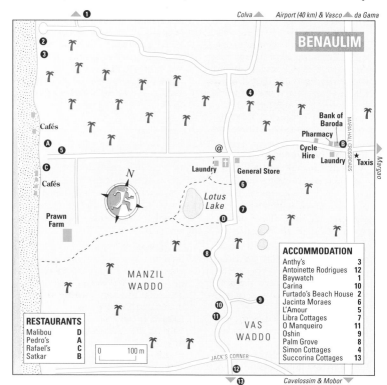

Goa may not suffer from the same Hindu–Muslim tensions that dominate political life in the north, but both its Hindu majority and Christian minority remain riven by caste conflict, as a recent dispute in a village near Benaulim called Cuncolim has underlined.

The dispute, between landowning Christian Gaunkars (brahmins) and their lower caste Shudra (formerly known as "Untouchable") neighbours in Cuncolim village (Salcete district), hinges on ritual rights and privileges in the local church. For centuries, religious life in Christian Cuncolim – famous as the home of the five Jesuit priests martyred in their attempt to convert the Moghul emperor Akbar – has been dominated by members of the 3000-strong Guankar community. Originally converts from the Hindu Kshatriya ('warrior') caste, the local landowners have traditionally claimed exclusive rights to be buried in the church cemetery, sing in the choir, lead the saints' day processions and don sacred red-and-white robes, known as *opa murca*, for important religious occasions. They have also, most critically, monopolized membership of the local confraternity – the Confraria do Santissimo Sacramento and Nossa Senhora de Saude – which organizes church festivals.

While traditionally upholding the dominance of the Gaunkars, the Portuguese colonial administration and, after Independence, the Catholic Church, had to be seen to promote greater equality and assert the rights of the lower castes. However, their efforts consistently met with stern rebuffs, provoking a more confrontational approach from the local Shudras.

A few years back, the low-caste villagers in Cuncolim held a funeral in the church cemetery, the first burial of a non-Gaunkar there since the Church of Our Lady of Health was built in 1604. The following night, however, the body was exhumed, wrapped in cloth and dumped outside the church, on the road to the Shudra quarter. Firmly engrained pollution customs would have prevented them from carrying out the crime themselves, but no one in Cuncolim doubted that local Gaunkars were behind the outrage.

What really fired the powder keg of Cuncolim's caste conflict, however, was the decision, by the new young, jeans-wearing village priest, Father Socorso Mendes, to admit two Shudra men into the Confraria. Immediately, a deputation of furious Gaunkars stormed the priest's house, threatening to "cut him into pieces and send them to (his) mother" if the two weren't thrown out. When the priest refused, an angry mob formed a cordon around the church to demonstrate.

The stand-off was diffused by the intervention of senior clergymen, but the village has grown more divided since. The Gaunkars have even gone so far as to lobby their Hindu counterparts in the village, arguing that if the lower orders are allowed to gain equal rights in the church, it is only a matter of time before the same happens in the nearby temple. The subsequent declaration of solidarity by the Hindu Gaunkars, in turn, provoked a boycott of all their businesses in the village by members of the lower castes (both Christian and Hindu). Soon, the football and hockey teams and youth clubs all collapsed, as opposing castes refused to have anything to do with each other.

Cuncolim's problems are by no means exceptional. Throughout Goa, churches have become the arena in which growing tensions and changing political relations between castes are expressed. Recent decades have seen increased prosperity among Shudras and other lower castes, many of whom have raised their standard of living through reserved government jobs and wage employment abroad. This new-found affluence, and exposure to more democratic ways of life via the media and in other countries, has inevitably put the political disparities of traditional village life under pressure. The challenge for the Catholic Church in Goa now is how quickly it can adapt institutions originally devised to accommodate ancient Hindu beliefs to meet the expectations of its more equality-conscious congregations.

GOA | South Goa

of the Western Ghats and ordered the waters to recede. The spot where the shaft fell to earth, known in Sanskrit as Banali ("place where the arrow landed") and later corrupted by the Portuguese to **BENAULIM**, lies in the dead centre of Colva Beach, 7km west of Margao. Fifteen years ago, this atmospheric fishing- and rice-farming village, scattered around the coconut groves and paddy fields between the main Colva–Mobor road and the dunes, had barely made it onto the backpackers' map. Since the completion of the nearby Konkan railway, however, huge numbers of big-spending middle-class Indians have started to holiday here, in the rash of gigantic luxury resorts and time-share apartment blocks that now fill the rice fields. As a result, the village's famously *sossegarde* feel, which previously made it the number-one choice for independent travellers, is only discernible amid the scruffier fishers' quarters and along some of the back lanes leading to Colva.

Nevertheless, if you time your visit well (avoiding Diwali and the Christmas peak season), Benaulim is still hard to beat as a place to unwind. The seafood is superb, accommodation and motorbikes cheaper than anywhere else in the state, and the beach breathtaking, particularly around sunset time, when its brilliant white sand and churning surf reflect the changing colours to magical effect. Shelving away almost to Cabo da Rama on the horizon, the beach is also lined with Goa's largest, and most colourfully decorated, fleet of wooden outriggers, and these provide welcome shade during the heat of the day. Hawkers, itinerant masseurs and fruit-wallahs appear at annoying short intervals, but you usually escape them by renting a bike and pedalling south on the hard tidal sand beyond the *Taj Exotica*, where tourism has made less of an impact.

Practicalities

Buses from Margao, Colva, Varca, Cavelossim and Mobor roll through Benaulim every half-hour, dropping passengers at the Maria Hall crossroads. Ranged around this busy junction are two well-stocked **general stores**, a couple of **café–bars**, a **bank**, **pharmacy** and the taxi and auto-rickshaw rank, from where you can pick up **transport** to the beach 2km west.

Signs offering **bicycles** and **motorbikes** for rent are dotted along the lane leading to the sea: rates are standard, descending in proportion to the length of time you keep the vehicle. Worth bearing in mind if you're planning to continue further south is that motorbikes are much cheaper to rent (and generally in better condition) here than Palolem, where there's a relative shortage of vehicles. **Petrol** is sold by the litre from a table at the roadside, two minutes' walk south down the road leading to *Royal Palm Beach Resort*, but tends to be laced with solvent and smokes badly. Local boys will try to get you to pay them to fill your bike up in Margao, but invariably pocket half of the money in the process, so if you've a valid licence do it yourself (Margao's main petrol pump is on the west side of the Praça Jorge Barreto – see map on p.195).

If you need to **change money**, the most convenient places are GK Tourist Centre, at the crossroads in the village centre, and the *L'Amour Beach Resort*, which in principle offers the same rates as Thomas Cook. With a Visa card, you can also make encashments at the Bank of Baroda (Mon–Fri 9.30am–2.30pm, Sat 9.30am–12.30pm), on Maria Hall crossroads. Otherwise, the nearest foreign exchange facilities are at Margoa and Colva. Finally, international and domestic **flights** can be booked, altered or reconfirmed at Sarken Tour Operators, and at *L'Amour*, which also does deluxe bus and train ticketing for cities elsewhere in India.

For **internet access**, the best outfit is GK Tourism, who offer four terminals, a faster-than-average connection and blissfully cool air-conditioning (Rs60/hr).

Accommodation

Aside from the unsightly time-share complexes and five-stars that now all but encircle the village, most of Benaulim's **accommodation** consists of small budget guesthouses, scattered around the leafy lanes 1km or so back from the beach. The majority are featureless annexes of spartan tiled rooms (dubbed locally as "cottages"), with fans and, usually, attached shower-toilets; the only significant difference between them is their location. The best way to find a vacancy is to hunt around on foot or by bicycle, although if you wait at the Maria Hall crossroads or the beachfront with luggage, someone is bound to ask if you need a room. During peak season, the village's few mid-range hotels (namely *L'Amour*, *Failaka*, *Palm Grove* and *Carina*) tend to be fully booked, so reserve in advance if you want to stay in one of these.

Anthy's, Sernabatim ☎ 0832/733824. Technically in Colva, but one of the few places hereabouts actually located in the dunes. Well-maintained rooms, with tiny bathrooms, breezy verandas and the beach on your doorstep. ❸–❺

Antoinette Rodrigues, near Jack's Corner, 1695 Vas Waddo ☎0832/731735. Large new block backing on to the soccer pitch just before the fishers' quarter, named after and run by its friendly owner. The rooms are pleasant, with separate balconies and green views; best is the pricier corner one, which is larger, has a lockable steel cupboard and a fridge – well worth the extra Rs50. ❹

Baywatch, Sernabatim ☎ 0832/730075. An unfortunate name, but very pleasant little complex in the dunes between Benaulim and Colva, with immaculate rooms opening on to a deep common veranda. Among the best places in its category if prices and standards are maintained. ❸–❺

Carina, Tamdi-Mati, Vas Waddo ☎ 0832/734166, ☏ 711400, ✉ carinabeachresort@yahoo.com. This good-value upmarket hotel lies in a tranquil location on the south side of Benaulim and offers a pool, bar-restaurant, foreign exchange facilities and room service. Some a/c. ❻–❼

Furtado's Beach House, Sernabatim ☎0832 /705265 or 770043. Not to be confused with *Furtado's* in the village proper. This one is slap on the beach, with en-suite rooms and road access. Very popular, mainly with refugees from Colva's charter hotels. The best fallback if nearby *Anthy's* is full. ❸

Jacinta Moraes, 1608/A Vas Waddo ☎ 0832/770187. Half a dozen largish clean rooms, and two new family apartments behind the main block, all with fans, attached shower-toilets, sound plumbing and Western toilets. Friendly and central, though some will consider it too close to the *Royal Palms* resort for comfort. ❷

L'Amour, on the beachfront ☎ 0832/733720. Benaulim's longest established hotel is a comfortable thirty-room cottage complex, with terrace restaurant, travel agent, money-changing and some a/c. No single occupancy. ❻–❼

Libra Cottages, Vas Waddo ☎ 0832/731740. In much the same mould as *Jacinta Moraes*, only a bit brighter, with a couple more rooms, including two economy options around the back. Very good value. ❸

O Manqueiro, Vas Waddo ☎ 0832/734164. Dependable budget guesthouse in the secluded south of the village, run by a family with a predilection for plastic fruit. Their best rooms (Rs400 per double) are in the recently constructed "Millennium" block, which have small balconies, but new beds and mattresses – as opposed to rooms above the family house next door (Rs200), which are very basic indeed (rickety beds, old mattresses, common toilets and wood partition walls). ❷–❹

Oshin, Mazil Waddo ☎ 0832/770069. Large, triple-storey complex set well back from the road, with views from balconies over the tree tops from top floor rooms. Spacious and clean, with en-suite bathrooms. A notch above most places in this area, and good value. ❹

Palm Grove, Tamdi-Mati, 149 Vas Waddo ☎ 0832/722533, ✉ palmgrovecottages@yahoo.com. Secluded hotel surrounded by beautiful gardens, with a luxurious new block around the back, some a/c, a pleasant terrace restaurant and friendly management. A bike-ride back from the beachfront, but by far the most pleasant place in its class. ❹–❼

Simon Cottages, Sernabatim Ambeaxir ☎ 0832/734283. Currently among the best budget deals in Benaulim: large rooms, all with shower-toilets and sit-outs, opening on to a sandy courtyard in a secluded spot at the unspoilt north side of the village. You can book through Silver Stores at Maria Hall crossroads during shop hours. ❷–❸

Succorina Cottages, House #1711/A, Vas Waddo ☎ 0832/712072. Immaculate rooms in a new house, 1km south of the crossroads in the fishing village, with glimpses of the sea across the fields. You'll need at least a bicycle to stay here, but it's a perfect place to get away from the tourist scene. ❷–❸

Benaulim's proximity to Margao market, along with the presence of a large Christian fishing community, means its **restaurants** serve some of the most succulent, competitively priced seafood in Goa. The best shacks flank the beachfront area, where *Johncy's* catches most of the passing custom. However, you'll find better food at lower prices in the smaller joints further along the beach, which seem to change owners and chefs annually; the only way the find out which ones offer the best value for money is to wander past and see who has the most customers.

L'Amour, at hotel of same name on the beachfront. Just about the slickest restaurant in Benaulim, serving an exhaustive multi-cuisine dinner menu (mains Rs80–125), as well as drinks. With background noise limited to chinking china and hushed voices, it's also a relaxing place for breakfast: fresh fruit, muesli, yoghurt and pancakes.

Malibou, on the lane leading south through Vas Waddo, near *Palm Grove*. Cosy little corner café-restaurant that's a popular late-night drinking spot. Attentive service, fresh seafood and they have a tandoor to bake pomfret, kebabs and spicy chicken.

Palm Grove, at hotel of same name, Tamdi-Mati, Vas Waddo. Mostly Goan seafood, with some Indian and continental options, dished up alfresco in cosy garden café-restaurant that's lit with fairy lights.

Pedro's, on the beachfront. Long waits, but the food – mostly fish steaks served with delicious home-made sauces – is freshly cooked, tasty and inexpensive (Rs50 for a generous cut of kingfish).

Rafael's, on the beachfront. Rough-and-ready beach café serving all the usual stuff, plus fried rice, salads and deliciously stodgy oven-hot coconut pudding. Worth patronizing if only because it's the oldest café in the village, and hasn't changed a jot since it opened.

Satkar, Maria Hall crossroads. No-frills locals' *udipi* canteen on the crossroads that's the only place in the village where you can order regular Indian snacks – samosas, masala dosas, pakoras and spicy chickpea stew (*channa*) – at regular Indian prices. And the *bhaji pao* breakfast here is a must.

Cavelossim and Mobor

Sleepy **CAVELOSSIM**, straddling the coast road 11km south of Colva, is the last major settlement in southwest Salcete: its only claim to fame. A short way beyond the village's picturesque church square, a narrow lane veers left (east) across an open expanse of paddy fields to the Cavelossim–Assolna **ferry crossing** (last departures: 8.30pm from Cavelossim, 8.45pm from Assolna), near the mouth of the Sal River. Make the crossing at low tide, and you'll probably see scores men wading up to their necks in the water, collecting clams, mussels and oysters from the river silt. The discovery that the bed of the Sal between here and nearby Betul was phenomenally rich in **shellfish** was only made a couple of years back. Present stocks are expected to last for another three or four years, although the boom may be brought to a premature end if the Directorate of Fisheries (whose job is ostensibly to promote the welfare of local fishermen) press ahead with plans to dredge the river. If you're heading south to Canacona, turn left off the ferry – *not* right as indicated on local maps – and continue as far as Assolna bazaar, clustered around a junction on the main road. A right turn at this crossroads puts you on track for Palolem and Canacona.

Carry straight on at the junction just past the square in Cavelossim, however, and you'll eventually arrive at **MOBOR**, where Colva beach fades into a rounded sandy spur at the mouth of the Assolna River. This would be an exquisite spot if it weren't the site of south Goa's largest, and most obtrusive, package tourist enclave. Crammed together on to a narrow spit of dunes between the surf and estuary, the controversial *Leela Palace*, *Holiday Inn* and *Dona Sylvia* resort hotels combine to create a holiday camp ambience that has as little to do with Goa as their architecture. Moreover, most have at some time been served writs by the region's green lobby for infringing environmental laws. Unless you've hundreds of dollars to waste on the hugely inflated tariffs they charge walk-in customers, look for accommodation elsewhere.

The far south: Canacona

Ceded to the Portuguese by the Rajah of Sund in the Treaty of 1791, Goa's **far south – Canacona district** – was among the last parts of the territory to be absorbed into the Novas Conquistas, and has retained a distinctly Hindu feel. The area also boasts some of the state's most outstanding scenery. Set against a backdrop of the jungle-covered Sahyadri hills (an extension of the Western Ghat range), a string of pearl-white coves and sweeping beaches scoop its indented coastline, enfolded by laterite headlands and colossal piles of black boulders.

With the exception of the village of **Palolem**, whose near-perfect beach attracts a steady flow of day-trippers and longer-staying travellers during high season, the coastal settlements hereabouts remain rooted in a traditional fishing and *todi*-tapping economy. However, the red gash of the **Konkan Railway** threatens to bring its days as a tranquil rural backwater to an end. For the last year or two, it has been possible to reach Canacona by direct "super-fast" express trains from Mumbai, Panjim and Mangalore: the developers' bulldozers and concrete mixers are sure to follow.

The region's main transport artery is the NH-17, which crawls across the Sahyadri and Karmali Ghats towards Karnataka via the district headquarters, **Chaudi**. Bus services between here and Margao are frequent; off the highway, however, bullock carts and bicycles far outnumber motor vehicles. The only way to do the area justice, therefore, is by motorcycle, although you'll have to rent one further north (Benaulim's your best bet for this) and drive it down here as few are available in situ.

Palolem

PALOLEM, 35km south of Margao, pops up more often in glossy holiday brochures than any other beach in Goa, not because the village is a major pack-age tour destination, but because its crescent-shaped bay, lined with a swaying curtain of coconut palms, is irresistibly photogenic. Hemmed in by a pair of wooded headlands, it forms a perfect curve of white sand, arcing north from a pile of gargantuan boulders to the spur of **Sahyadri Ghat**, which tapers into the sea, draped in thick forest and studded with large black rocks. Beyond it, a narrow causeway runs through the shallows to a islet whose only permanent inhabitants are a colony of by black-faced langur monkeys.

Until relatively recently, this idyllic spot was south Goa's best-kept secret. Over the past five or six years, however, Palolem has become a fully fledged resort, with shack-restaurants and palm-leaf huts lining the entire beach. Around 1500 visitors stay here in peak season at any one time, most of them independent travellers seeking an escape from the more commercial tourist scene further north. Their ranks are swollen by droves of day-trippers, both domestic and foreign, who trav-el down in minibus taxis or pleasure boats, and disappear again around sunset.

That this overwhelming seasonal influx has not entirely spoilt the village is a tribute to the enlightened attitude of the local community, which has consis-tently resisted plans to develop Palolem. The local municipality strictly forbids any concrete construction in the palm groves behind the beach – hence all the leaf huts, tents and bamboo platforms. Because of this relative independence of the charter trade, Palolem's season is considerably longer than normal. While Benaulim and Colva's shack owners are busily building their shelters in early November, Palolem's have usually been up and running for weeks. Even so,

Chaudi (4 km)

PALOLEM

Cycle Rental
PUNDALIK GAITONDI ROAD
School
Ma-Rita's Shack
Dylan's Bar

RESTAURANTS
Classic   C
Cool Breeze B
Hira   A
Sun 'n' Moon D

A R A B I A N   S E A

COLOM

Rajbag (2 km) & Chaudi (5 km)

Patnem (500 m) & Rajbag

Colom Beach

ACCOMMODATION

Bhakti Kutir	12	La Alegro	9
Ciaran's Camp	8	Maria's	4
Coco Huts	10	Norgoa	2
Cozy Nook	11	Palolem Beach Resort	7
Cupid Castle	5	Sea Gull	3
D'Mello	1	Unic Resort	6

0   200 m

outside December and January, it remains peaceful here, with the pace of life set more by the traditional rhythms of *toddi* tapping than the arrival and departure of tourists.

Long before foreign sun worshippers started to show up here, Palolem's *raison d'être* was its home distilleries, and **coconut feni** remains the main cottage industry. Once each week, the telltale roar of stills emanates from little shacks at the less frequented corners of the village. Head down to the beach the next morning, and you'll see the fruits of this work being loaded onto boats for "export" to Karnataka. The locals keep plenty of the best stuff for themselves, though, both for consumption at home and in the little bars dotted around the groves behind the beach.

Arrival and information

Frequent **buses** run between Margao and Karwar (in Karnataka) via Chaudi (every 30min; 2hr), where you can pick up an **auto-rickshaw** (Rs50) or **taxi** (Rs80) 2km west to Palolem. Alternatively, get off at the Char Rostay ("Four-Way") crossroads, 1.5km before Chaudi, and walk the remaining kilometre or so to the village. Regular buses also go all the way to Palolem from Margao; these stop at the end of the lane leading from the main street to the beachfront.

The last bus from Palolem to Chaudi/Margao leaves at around 4.30pm; check with the locals for the precise times, as these change seasonally. **Bicycles** may be rented from a stall halfway along the main street

Water shortages in Palolem

The vast increase in visitor numbers in Palolem has been blamed for the severe water shortages that have afflicted Canacona district over the past three years. The municipality seems unwilling or unable to do anything about the problem, so the onus falls on tourists to use as little water as possible during their stay. One of the most effective ways you can do this is to avoid water toilets, which dump a colossal quantity of untreated sewage into often poorly manufactured septic tanks below the ground. Traditional pig loos, still common in the village, are a far cleaner, greener option.

for the princely sum of Rs5 per hour (with discounts for longer periods). The village has several **public telephones**: avoid the one in the *Beach Resort*, which charges more than double the going rate for international calls, and head for the much cheaper ISD/STD booths 100m down the lane (next to the bus stop). This is also where you'll find the best **internet cafés** in the village. Several agents in Palolem are licensed to **change money**; Sarken Tours inside the *Nature Restaurant* and LKP Forex in the *Beach Resort* offer the best rates.

Accommodation

Local resistance to large-scale development explains why – with the exception of the *Beach Resort*'s tent camp, *Bhakti Kutir* in nearby Colom (see below) and a handful of small budget guesthouses – most of the village's **accommodation** consists of simple palm leaf huts. Costing anywhere between Rs100 and Rs350 per night, they vary in size and standards of comfort, but tend to have shared showers and toilets. The other option is to look for a room in a family home. Most, although not all, of these also have limited shared washing facilities and pig toilets. The easiest way to find a place is to walk around the palm groves behind the beach with a rucksack; sooner or later someone will approach you. Rates vary from Rs100 to Rs200 per night, depending on the size of the room, and the time of year.

The cheapest places, however, are to be found in Colom, around the headland south of Palolem village, where Hindu fishing families rent the odd room out to tourists. Further south still, behind Patnem beach, the shack owners erect rudimentary leaf-huts slap on the beach.

Bhakti Kutir, on the headland above Colom fishing village ℡ 0832/643460 or 643472, ℻ 643469, ℮ bhaktikutir@yahoo.com. Homely, eco-friendly thatched village huts equipped with Western amenities (including completely biodegradable chemical toilets), in a secure, leafy compound five minutes' walk from the south end of Palolem beach. Beautifully situated and sensitively designed to blend with the landscape by German-Goan owners. ❹–❻

Ciaran's Camp, middle of the beach ℡ 0832/643477 or 644074, ℮ johnciaran@hotmail.com. One of Palolem's longest established hut camps: twenty structures, sharing five toilets, equipped with fans, mozzie nets, mirrors and tables. Free library, laundry, bar, restaurant and safe lockers. ❸

Coco Huts, south end of Palolem beach ℡ 0832/643104. Thai-style bamboo and palm-thatch huts on stilts, lashed to *toddi* trees around a sandy clearing, slap on the beach. The "rooms" have fans, electric lights and safe lockers, but toilets are shared, and the leaf walls offer little privacy. ❹–❻

Cozy Nook, north end of the beach, near the island ℡ 0832/643550. After *Bhakti Kutir*, this is the most attractively designed set up in the village, comprising 25 bamboo huts (sharing 7 toilets, but with good mattresses, mozzie nets, safe lockers and fans) opening on to the lagoon on one side and the beach on the other – an unbeatable spot, which explains the higher than average tariffs. ❸–❹

Cupid Castle, on the road to the beachfront ℡ 0832/643326. An original name, but these recently built rooms are characterless, and a little too close to the beachfront for comfort. Nonetheless, they're clean, spacious, and have attached bathrooms. ❹

D'Mello, Pundalik Gaitondi Road ℡ 0832/643057. A mix of attached and non-attached rooms on three storeys, some in a concrete annexe set back from the main road. ❹

La Alegro, north side of the beach ℡0832/643498. En-suite rooms slap on the beach. Very basic and not all that well maintained, but the location's great. The same owner also has five more (cheaper) identikit rooms around the back. ❸

Maria's, south of the village, near the *Classic* restaurant ℡ 0832/643732 or 643856, ℮ selvin16@yahoo.com. Five simple rooms opening onto an orchard of banana, fruit and spice trees. All attached shower-toilets, and very friendly management. Nice little bar-restaurant, ISD phone and internet access on site. A good deal. ❷

Norgoa, Gaitondi Road (no phone). Half a dozen basic rooms of varying size, with shared shower-toilets, on the main road through the village. They also have six budget-priced bamboo "huts" in the front garden. ❶–❸

Palolem Beach Resort, on the beachfront ℡ 0832/643054, ℻ 643054, ℮ yogesh@goa1.dot.net.in. Twin-bedded canvas tents, each with their own locker, lights and fans, grouped under a shady *toddi* grove in a walled compound. In addition, there's a handful of small en-suite rooms. The big drawback here is noise from the busy terrace restaurant. ❸–❺

Sea Gull, next door to *Cupid Castle* ℡ 0832/643978. Dark but serviceable rooms with

attached shower-toilets behind a bar near the beachfront area. ❸

Unic Resort, Tembi Waddo ℡ 0832/643059. A relative newcomer that, strictly speaking, is in Colom, a 10min walk inland from the beach; you can also get here via the backroad to Chaudi (see map, p.206). The rooms are plain but clean, with fans and en-suite bathrooms, and there's a secluded German-run restaurant on an adjacent terrace. ❹

Eating and drinking

With the beach now backed by brightly lit shack cafés, finding somewhere to **eat** in Palolem is not a problem. Finding quality cooking, however, can be a hit and miss business, mainly because most of the fresh fish has to bought in from Margao and Karwar (the locals only catch mackerel in their hand-nets). Currently the most popular places among travellers, and a cut above the competition, are *Sun 'n' Moon*, just behind the beach, and *Cool Breeze*, on the beach road; after hours, die-hard drinkers head through the palm trees to bars, which stay open until the last customer has staggered home. Travellers on tight budgets should note the row of tiny **bhaji stalls** outside the *Beach Resort*, and also the *Hira Restaurant* in the village proper, where you can order tasty and filling breakfasts of *pao bhaji*, fluffy bread rolls, omelettes and chai for next to nothing.

Beach Resort, Palolem beach front. The one place definitely to avoid: indifferent, overpriced food and grating background music.

Bhakti Kutir, between Palolem beach and Colom fishing village. Laid-back terrace café-cum-restaurant with sturdy wooden tables and a German-bakery style menu. Cooked dishes here are pricey (mains around Rs100), but delicious (their omelettes are made with imported cheese), and the ingredients are usually local and organically produced.

Classic (aka "German Bakery"), south of the centre. Former German-Bakery-owned establishment that's lost its franchise and gone downhill as a result. Service standards have dropped over the past few seasons and several lapses in hygiene have been reported (they seem to hold on to some of their pastries too long).

Cool Breeze, beach road. Co-run by a British couple, this is currently the classiest restaurant in the village. Their tandoori chicken and seafood, in particular, have set new standards for Palolem, and the prices are reasonable. Come early, or you could face a long wait for a table.

Cozy Nook, far north end of the beach. Wholesome Goan-style cooking served on a small terrace that occupies a prime position opposite the island. Their filling set four-course dinners

(7–9pm; Rs110) are deservedly popular, offering imaginative and carefully prepared dishes such as pan-fried fish, aubergine with shrimps and fresh beans. They also do a tasty veg equivalent (Rs90), as well as a full seafood, north-Indian curry and snack menu.

Hira, Pundalik Gaitondi Road. Tiny locals' café at the south end of the village, serving "cheap and best" *bhaji*–bread breakfasts, good South Indian-style filter coffee and freshly fried samosas, with a complimentary *Navhind Times* passed around if you're lucky.

Maria's, south side of the village, near *Classic* restaurant. Authentic Goan food, such as chicken vindaloo, fried calamari and spicy vegetable side dishes, prepared entirely with local produce and served alfresco on a terrace. Maria's garrulous husband, Joseph, serves a mean *feni*, too, flavoured with cumin, ginger or lemongrass.

Sun 'n' Moon, Palolem beach. This small restaurant, tucked away in the palm grove behind the beach, gets packed out in the evenings, thanks to the consistently good, inexpensive food, and the attentive service of the owner, Sanjay, and his mum. Mountainous seafood sizzlers are the house speciality, but they also do tasty tandoori meat, fish and vegetarian dishes. There's even an internet booth these days.

Chaudi

CHAUDI (aka Chauri, or Canacona), 33km south of Margao, is Canacona district's charmless headquarters. Packed around a noisy junction on the main

Wherever possible, try and book plane tickets directly through the airline as private agents charge the dollar fare at poor rates of exchange; addresses of airline offices in Panjim are listed on p.158. Seats on all Konkan Railway services can be booked at the KRC reservation office on the first floor of Panjim's Kadamba bus stand (Mon–Sat 8am–8pm, Sun 8am–2pm), or at KRC's main reservation hall in Margao station (Mon–Sat 8am–4.30pm, Sun 8am–2pm; ☏0834/712780). Make your bookings as far in advance as possible, and try to get to the offices soon after opening time – the queues can be horrendous. Seats on the Konkan Railway from Goa to Mumbai are in notoriously short supply as the lion's share of the quotas goes to longer-distance travellers from Kerala, with the result that peak periods tend be reserved up to two months in advance. Book Kadamba bus tickets at their offices in Panjim and Mapusa bus stands (daily 9–11am & 2–5pm); private companies sell theirs through the many travel agents immediately outside the bus stand in Panjim, and at the bottom of the square in Mapusa. Information on all departures and fares is available from Goa Tourism's counter inside Panjim's bus stand.

For a full rundown of destinations reachable from Goa by bus, train and plane, see Travel Details at the end of this chapter.

To Mumbai

If you're heading north to Mumbai, the quickest and easiest way is by plane. Between three and six planes leave Goa's Dabolim airport daily. One-way fares for the forty-minute flight range from $53 with Indian Airlines, or $83 with Sahara, to $93 ($72 for under 30s) with swisher Jet. In addition, Air India operate an Airbus service to Mumbai on Mondays and Thursdays. Few people seem to know about this flight, so you can nearly always get a seat on it; the one drawback is that you have to check in three hours before departure as Air India is an international carrier. Wherever possible, try to book tickets directly through the airline (for addresses see Listings on p.158). Private agents charge you the dollar fare at poor rates of exchange, although when you take into account the cost of the taxi and hassle involved in travelling to the airline office, the net saving of booking direct may seem irrelevant.

Since the inauguration of the Konkan Railway in 1996, journey times to Mumbai from Goa have been slashed from twenty-four to twelve hours. Two services run daily, the most convenient of them being the Konkan–Kanya Express (#0112), which departs from Margao at 6.15pm, arriving at CST (still commonly known as "Victoria Terminus", or "VT") at 6.35am the following day. The other fast train from Margao to Mumbai CST is the Madgaon–Mumbai Express (#0104).

The cheapest, though most nightmarish, way to get to Mumbai is by night bus, which takes fourteen to eighteen hours, covering 500km of rough road at often terrifying speeds. Fares vary according to levels of comfort, and luxury buses arrive two or three hours sooner. Book Kadamba bus tickets at their offices in the Panjim and Mapusa bus stands (daily 9–11am & 2–5pm); private companies sell theirs through the many travel agents immediately outside the bus stand in Panjim, and at the bottom of the square in Mapusa. The most popular private service to Mumbai, and the most expensive, is the 24-seater run by a company called Paulo Travels. A cramped berth on this bus (which bizarrely you may have to share) costs Rs600, and it is worth pointing out that women travellers have complained of harassment during the journey. For tickets, contact Paulo Holiday Makers, near the Kadamba bus stand, Panjim (☏0832/223736) or at *Hotel Nanutel*, opposite *Club Harmonia*, Margao (☏0834/721516). Information on all departures and fares is available from Goa Tourism's counter inside Panjim's bus stand (see Arrival, information and local transport, p.154).

To Hampi

Two or three clapped-out government buses leave Panjim's Kadamba stand (platform 9) each morning for Hospet, the last one at 10.30am. Brace yourself for a long, hard slog; all being well, it should take nine or ten hours, but delays and breakdowns are frustratingly frequent. Tickets for Kadamba and KSRTC (Karnatakan State Road Transport Corporation) services should be booked at least one day in advance at the hatches in the bus stand.

From Margao, you can also travel to Hampi on a swish new night bus, complete with pneumatic suspension and berths. The service, operated by a firm called Paulo Travels, leaves from a lot next to the *Nanutel Hotel* on Margao's Rua da Padre Miranda, at 6pm, arriving in Hampi early the next morning. Tickets cost around Rs375 and can be bought from most reputable travel agents around the state. Although the coach is comfortable enough, the coffin-like berths can get very hot and stuffy, making sleep very difficult; moreover, there have been compaints from women of harassment during the night on this service.

A much less stressful option than the bus is the twice-weekly train service, which leaves from Vasco (at 6.50am) and Margao (7.21am) stations on Tuesdays and Saturdays, arriving in Hospet just over eight and a half hours later at 4pm. Tickets can be bought on the day at either point of departure. This is a wonderful rail journey, taking you one of the wildest stretches of the Western Ghats, including the Dudhsagar Falls area (see p.166). Travelling in the other direction, trains leave Hospet at 10.45am on Mondays and Fridays, and arrive in Margao at 6.45pm.

To Gokarna, Mangalore and southern Karnataka

From Goa, the fastest and most convenient way to travel down the coast to Gokarn is via the Konkan Railway. At 2.10pm, train #KR001 leaves Margao, passing through Chaudi at 3pm en route to Gokarn Road, the town's railhead, where it arrives at around 4.20pm. The station lies 9km east of Gokarn itself, but buses and rickshaws are on hand to shuttle passengers the rest of the way. As this is classed as a passenger service, you don't have to buy tickets in advance; just turn up at the station 30–45min before the departure time and pay at the regular ticket counter. As ever, it is a good idea to check timings in advance, through any tourist office or travel agent.

Buses take as much as two-and-a-half hours longer to cover the same route. A direct service leaves Margao's interstate stand in the north of town daily at 1pm. You can also get there by catching any of the services that run between Goa and Mangalore, and jumping off either at Ankola, or at the Gokarn junction on the main highway, from where frequent private minibuses and tempos run into town.

The Konkan highway is straightforward by motorcycle, with a better-than-average road surface, and frequent fuel stops along the way. Travelling on a rented bike also gives you the option of heading down sandy side lanes to explore some of the gorgeous beaches glimpsed from the road. Aside from the obvious dangers involved in mtorcycling on Indian highways, the main drawback is crossing the border, which can involve a baksheesh transaction.

To Delhi

The Konkan Railway has also improved train services to Delhi, which can now be reached on the superfast Rajdhani Express #2431 in a little under 26 hours (Tues & Thurs only). A slower daily service, the Mangala Lakshadweep Express #2617, takes nearly 38 hours to cover the same distance. Alternatively, you can fly to the capital with Indian Airlines or Jet in 2hr 45min from around $245 one-way.

Panjim–Mangalore highway, it is primarily a transport hub, of interest to visitors only because of its proximity to Palolem, 2km west. Buses to and from Panjim, Margao, and Karwar in Karnataka *taluka* trundle in and out of a scruffy square on the main street, from where taxis and auto-rickshaws ferry passengers to the villages scattered across the surrounding fields. The area's only **pharmacy** stands just off the crossroads, handy if you're staying in Palolem.

If you spend much time in Palolem, you're sure to nip into Chaudi to shop for provisions, or simply soak up its gritty Indian atmosphere, which comes as a bit of a shock after the dreamy beaches nearby. The small covered **market** is an essential source of fresh fruit and vegetables; several stalls sell stoves, cooking equipment and other hardware, while the excellent **Udipi Hotel**, a short way south of the main crossroads, is one of the few places for miles where you can eat pukka South Indian food: try their filling Rs15 thalis, or spicy fried pakora and samosas – all freshly prepared, and piping hot if you come around 5pm. They also do delicious lassis, sweetened with traditional syrups.

Agonda

AGONDA, 10km north of Chaudi, can only be reached along the sinuous coast road connecting Cabo da Rama with NH-14 at Chaudi. No signposts mark the turning and few of the tourists that whizz past en route to Palolem pull off here, but the beach, fringed along its entire length by *todi* trees, is superb. Its remote location is not the only reason this three-kilometre spread of white sand has been bypassed by the bulldozers. Villagers here are opposed to any kind of tourist development. In 1982, when a group of absentee landlords sold off a chunk of the beach to a Delhi-based hotel chain, the locals refused to vacate the plot, insisting the proposed five-star hotel and golf course would ruin their traditional livelihoods. Faced with threats of violent resistance, and protracted legal battles, the developers eventually backed down, and the unfinished concrete hulk they left behind is today the only unsightly structure for miles.

This acrimonious episode may in part explain the relative scarcity in Agonda of facilities for visitors. At present, there are only two **places to stay**, both situated at the far (south) end of the beach. The better of the pair is the *Dunhill Beach Resort* (℡0832/647328; ❷–❸), which has twelve simple en-suite rooms with small verandas opening onto a sandy enclosure. It's a clean and peaceful place, and the family who run it serve spicy Goan-fried mackerel, calamari, rice and curry to order on their small terrace. If they're full, *Caferns* (℡0832/647235; ❷) down the road is a good fall-back.

Cotigao Wildlife Sanctuary

The **Cotigao Wildlife Sanctuary**, 10km southeast of Chaudi, was established in 1969 to protect a remote and vulnerable area of forest lining the Goa–Karnataka border. Encompassing 86 square kilometres of mixed deciduous woodland, the reserve is certain to inspire tree lovers, but less likely to yield many wildlife sightings: its tigers and leopards were hunted out long ago, while the gazelles, sloth bears, porcupines, panthers and hyenas that allegedly lurk in the woods rarely appear. You do, however, stand a good chance of spotting at least two species of monkey, a couple of wild boar and the odd gaur (the primeval-looking Indian bison). Best visited between October and March, Cotigao is a peaceful and scenic park that makes a pleasant day-trip from Palolem, 12km northwest. Any of the buses running south on the NH-14 to Karwar via Chaudi will drop you within 2km of the gates. However, to explore the inner reaches of the sanctuary, you really need your own transport. The wardens at the reserve's small **Interpretative Centre** will show you how to get to a 25m-high treetop watchtower, overlooking a **waterhole** that attracts a handful of animals around dawn and dusk. Written permission for an overnight **stay**, either in the watchtower or the Forest Department's small *Rest House* (❶), must be obtained from the Deputy Conservator of Forests, 3rd Floor, Junta House, Panjim (☎0832/45926), as far in advance of your visit as possible. If you get stuck, however, the wardens can arrange a tent, blankets and basic food.

Travel details

Trains

Margao to: Chaudi (3 daily; 50min); Colem (2 weekly; 55min); Delhi (1–2 daily; 26–35hr); Ernakulam/Kochi (2 daily; 12–15hr 40min); Gokarn (1 daily; 2hr 10min); Hospet (2 weekly; 8hr 40min); Hubli (2 weekly; 5hr 30min); Mangalore/Kanakadi (5 daily; 4–6hr); Mumbai (2 daily; 12hr); Thiruvanantapuram (2 daily; 16hr 15min); Udupi (4 daily; 3hr 40min); Vasco da Gama (2 weekly; 30min).

Buses

Panjim to: Arambol (12 daily; 1hr 45min); Aurangabad (1 daily; 16hr); Baga (every 30min; 45min); Bijapur (7 daily; 10hr); Calangute (every 30min; 40min); Candolim (every 30min; 30min); Chaudi (hourly; 2hr 15min); Gokarna (2 daily; 5hr 30min); Hampi (2 daily; 9–10hr); Hospet (3 daily; 9hr); Hubli (hourly; 6hr); Hyderabad (1 daily; 18hr); Kolhapur (hourly; 8hr); Mahabaleshwar (1 daily; 12hr); Mangalore (4 daily; 10hr); Mapusa (every 15min; 25min); Margao (every 15min; 55min); Mumbai (6 daily; 14–18hr); Mysore (2 daily; 17hr); Old Goa (every 15min; 20min); Ponda (hourly; 50min); Pune (7 daily; 12hr); Vasco da Gama (every 15min; 45min–1hr).

Mapusa to: Anjuna (hourly; 30min); Arambol (12 daily; 1hr 45min); Baga (hourly; 30min); Calangute (hourly; 45min); Chapora (every 30min; 30–40min); Mumbai (6 daily; 13–17hr); Panjim (every 15min; 25min); Vagator (every 30min; 25–35min).

Margao to: Agonda (4 daily; 2hr); Benaulim (every 30min; 15min); Cavelossim (8 daily; 30min); Chandor (hourly; 45min); Chaudi (every 30min; 1hr 40min); Colva (every 15min; 20–30min); Gokarna (1 daily; 4hr 30min); Hampi (1 nightly; 10hr); Karwar (every 30min; 2hr); Lutolim (8 daily; 30min); Mangalore (5 daily; 7hr); Mapusa (10 daily; 2hr 30min); Mobor (8 daily; 35min); Mumbai (2 daily; 16–18hr); Panjim (every 30min; 50min); Pune (1 daily; 12hr).

Vasco da Gama to: Bangalore (1 daily; 16hr); Colva (2 daily; 30min); Mangalore (2 daily; 11hr); Margao (every 15min; 40min); Panjim, via Sao Jacinto (every 15min; 45min–1hr); Pilar (every 15min; 30min).

Benaulim to: Cavelossim (hourly; 20min); Colva (every 30min; 20min); Margao (every 30min; 15min); Mobor (hourly; 25min).

Chaudi to: Gokarna (1 daily; 3hr); Karwar (every 30min; 1hr); Margao (every 30min; 1hr 40min); Palolem (2 daily; 15min); Panjim (hourly; 2hr 15min).

Flights

Dabolim airport (Vasco da Gama) to: Bangalore (2 daily; 1hr 30min–2hr 25min); Chennai (Madras) (2 weekly; 3hr); Cochin (2 weekly; 1hr); Delhi (4 weekly; 2hr 25min); Hyderabad (4 weekly; 2hr 55min); Mumbai (3–6 daily; 40min).

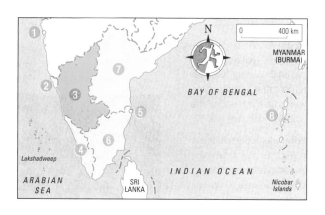

Karnataka

CHAPTER 3 # Highlights

∗ **Mysore** The sandal-
wood city has bundles of
old-fashioned charm and
lots to see, including the
opulent Maharaja's
Palace. See p.234

∗ **Halebid & Belur** Two
wonderfully ornate
Hoysala temples, set in
the slow-paced
Karnataka countryside.
See p.251 & p.253

∗ **Udupi** A coastal town
which, as well as boast-
ing an important Krishna
temple that attracts thousands, is the home of the
masala dosa. See p.273

∗ **Jog Falls** India's highest
waterfalls offer fresh air,
superb views and the
chance to take a dip
after the downhill hike.
See p.275

∗ **Gokarn** A quiet Hindu
holy town, blessed with
a series of exquisite
crescent beaches, ideal
for serious unwinding.
See p.277

∗ **Hampi** The remains of
the Vijayanagar kingdom,
scattered among fertile
plantations bisected by
the Tungabadra and
punctuated by weird
rock formations.
See p.289

∗ **Bijapur** Known as the
"Agra of the South" for
its splendid Islamic
architecture, most
famously the vast dome
of the Golgumbaz.
See p.305

3

Karnataka

Created in 1956 from the princely state of Mysore, **KARNATAKA** – the name is a derivation of the name of the local language, Kannada, spoken by virtually all of its 46 million inhabitants – marks a transition zone between northern India and the Dravidian deep south. Along its border with Maharashtra and Andhra Pradesh, a string of medieval walled towns, studded with domed mausoleums and minarets, recall the era when this part of the Deccan was a Muslim stronghold, while the coastal and hill districts that dovetail with Kerala are quintessential Hindu South India, profuse with tropical vegetation and soaring temple *gopuras*. Between the two are scattered some of the peninsula's most extraordinary historic sites, notably the ruined Vijayanagar city at Hampi, whose lost temples and derelict palaces stand amid an arid, boulder-strewn landscape of surreal beauty.

Karnataka is one of the wettest regions in India, its **climate** dominated by the seasonal monsoon, which sweeps in from the southwest in June, dumping an average of 4m of rain on the coast before it peters out in late September. Running in an unbroken line along the state's palm-fringed coast, the **Western Ghats**, draped in dense deciduous forests, impede the path of the rain clouds east. As a result, the landscape of the interior – comprising the southern apex of the triangular Deccan trap, known here as the **Mysore Plateau** – is considerably drier, with dark volcanic soils in the north, and poor quartzite-granite country to the south. Two of India's most sacred rivers, the Tungabhadra and Krishna, flow across this sun-baked terrain, draining east to the Bay of Bengal.

Broadly speaking, Karnataka's principal attractions are concentrated at opposite ends of the state, with a handful of lesser-visited places dotted along the coast between Goa and Kerala. Road and rail routes dictate that most itineraries take in the brash state capital, **Bangalore**, a go-ahead, modern city that epitomizes the aspirations of the country's new middle classes, with glittering malls, fast-food outlets and a nightlife unrivalled outside Mumbai. The state's other major city, **Mysore**, appeals more for its old-fashioned ambience, nineteenth-century palaces and vibrant produce and incense markets. It also lies within easy reach of several important historical monuments. At the nearby fortified island of **Srirangapatnam** – site of the bloody battle of 1799 that finally put Mysore state into British hands, with the defeat of the Muslim military genius **Tipu Sultan** – parts of the fort, a mausoleum and Tipu's summer palace survive.

A cluster of other unmissable sights lies further northwest, dotted around the dull railroad town of **Hassan**. Around nine centuries ago, the Hoysala kings sited their grand dynastic capitals here, at the now middle-of-nowhere villages of **Belur** and **Halebid**, where several superbly crafted temples survive intact.

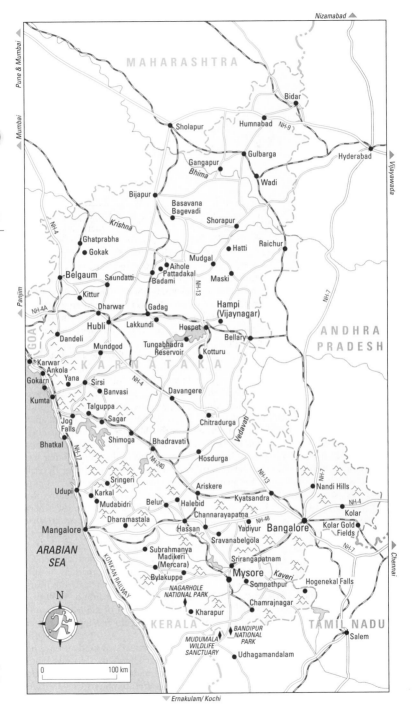

More impressive still, and one of India's most extraordinary sacred sites, is the eighteen-metre Jain colossus at **Sravanabelgola**, which stares serenely over idyllic Deccani countryside.

West of Mysore, the Ghats rise in a wall of thick jungle cut by deep ravines and isolated valleys. You can either traverse the range by rail, via Hassan, or explore some of its scenic backwaters by road. Among these, the rarely visited coffee- and spice-growing region of **Kodagu (Coorg)** has to be the most entrancing, with its unique culture and lush vistas of misty wooded hills and valleys. Most Coorgi agricultural produce is shipped out of **Mangalore**, the nearest large town, of little interest except as a transport hub whose importance can only increase now the new Konkan Railway is more or less operating a full service. Situated midway between Goa and Kerala, it's also a convenient – if uninspiring – place to pause on the journey along Karnataka's beautiful **Karavali coast**. Interrupted by countless mangrove-lined estuaries, the state's 320-kilometre-long red laterite coast has always been difficult to navigate by land, and traffic along the recently revamped highway remains relatively light. Although there are plenty of superb beaches, facilities are, with rare exceptions, nonexistent, and locals often react with astonishment at the sight of a foreigner. Again, that may well change with the impact of the Konkan Railway – with as yet unguessable consequences for the fishing hamlets, long-forgotten fortresses and pristine hill and cliff scenery along the way. For now, few Western tourists visit the famous Krishna temple at **Udupi**, an important Vaishnavite pilgrimage centre, and fewer still venture into the mountains to see India's highest waterfall at **Jog Falls**, set amid some of the region's most spectacular scenery. However, atmospheric **Gokarn**, further north up the coast, is an increasingly popular beach hideaway for budget travellers. Harbouring one of India's most famous *shivalinga*, this seventeenth-century Hindu pilgrimage town enjoys a stunning location, with a high headland dividing it from a string of exquisite beaches.

Winding inland from the mountainous Goan border, NH-4A and the rail line comprise sparsely populated **northern Karnataka**'s main transport artery, linking a succession of grim industrial centres. This region's undisputed highlight is the ghost city of Vijayanagar, better known as **Hampi**, scattered around boulder hills on the south banks of the Tungabhadra River. The ruins of this once splendid capital occupy a magical site, while the village squatting the ancient bazaar is a great spot to hole up for a spell. The jumping-off place for Hampi is **Hospet**, from where buses leave for the bumpy journey north across the rolling Deccani plains to **Badami**, **Aihole** and **Pattadakal**. Now lost in countryside, these tiny villages were once capitals of the **Chalukya** dynasty (sixth–eighth centuries). The whole area is littered with ancient rock-cut caves and finely carved stone temples.

Further north still, in one of Karnataka's remotest and poorest districts, craggy hilltop citadels and crumbling wayside tombs herald the formerly troubled buffer zone between the Muslim-dominated northern Deccan and the Dravidian Hindu south. The bustling, walled market town of **Bijapur**, capital of the Bahmanis, the Muslim dynasty that oversaw the eventual downfall of Vijayanagar, harbours South India's finest collection of Islamic architecture, including the world's second largest free-standing dome, the Golgumbaz. The first Bahmani capital, **Gulbarga**, site of a famous Muslim shrine and theological college, has retained little of its former splendour, but more isolated **Bidar**, to which the Bahmanis moved from Gulbarga in the sixteenth century, definitely deserves a detour en route to or from Hyderabad, four hours to the east by bus. Perched on a rocky escarpment, its crumbling red ramparts harbour

All accommodation prices in this book have been categorized using the price codes below. Prices given are for a double room, and all taxes are included. For more details, see p.46.

① up to Rs100   ④ Rs300–400   ⑦ Rs900–1500
② Rs100–200   ⑤ Rs400–600   ⑧ Rs1500–2500
③ Rs200–300   ⑥ Rs600–900   ⑨ Rs2500 and upwards

Persian-style mosaic-fronted mosques, mausoleums and a sprawling fort complex evocative of Samarkhand and the great silk route.

Some history

Like much of southern India, Karnataka has been ruled by successive Buddhist, Hindu and Muslim dynasties. The influence of Jainism has also been marked; India's very first emperor, **Chandragupta Maurya**, is believed to have converted to Jainism in the fourth century BC, renounced his throne, and fasted to death at Sravanabelgola, now one of the most visited Jain pilgrimage centres in the country.

During the first millennium AD, this whole region was dominated by power struggles between the various kingdoms, such as Vakatakas and the Guptas, who controlled the western Deccan and at times extended their authority as far as the Coromandel coast in Tamil Nadu. From the sixth to the eighth centuries, briefly interrupted by thirteen years of Pallava rule, the **Chalukya** kingdom included Maharashtra, the Konkan coast on the west, and the whole of Karnataka. The **Cholas** were powerful in the east of the region from about 870 until the thirteenth century, when the Deccan kingdoms were overwhelmed by General Malik Kafur, a convert to Islam.

By the medieval era, Muslim incursions from the north had forced the hitherto warring and fractured Hindu states of the south into close alliance, with the mighty **Vijayanagars** emerging as overlords. Founded by the brothers Harihara and Bukka, their lavish capital, Vijayanagar, ruled an empire stretching from the Bay of Bengal to the Arabian Sea, and south to Cape Comorin. The Muslims' superior military strength, however, triumphed in 1565 at the Battle of Talikota, when the **Bahmanis** laid siege to Vijayanagar, reducing it to rubble and plundering its opulent palaces and temples.

Thereafter, a succession of Muslim sultans held sway over the north, while in the south of the state the independent **Wadiyar Rajas** of Mysore, whose territory was comparatively small, successfully fought off the Marathas. In 1761, the brilliant Muslim campaigner Haider Ali, with French support, seized the throne. Haider Ali and his son, Tipu Sultan, turned Mysore into a major force in the south, before Tipu was killed by the British at the **battle of Srirangapatnam** in 1799.

Following Tipu's defeat, the British restored the Wadiyar family to the throne, which they kept until riots in 1830 led the British to appoint a commission to rule in their place. Fifty years later, the throne was once more returned to the Wadiyars, who remained governors until Karnataka was created by the merging of the states of Mysore and the Madras Presidencies in 1956. In the years since its creation, the state has been spared the excesses of communal and political unrest, although the scene can be volatile. Long a Congress stronghold, the party of the Gandhi dynasty was routed in the Nineties, first by a reunited Janata Dal and more recently by the fundamentalist BJP alliance, who have held the local balance of power since 1998, though there are signs of the national resurgence of Congress here too.

Bangalore and around

Once across the Western Ghats the cloying air of Kerala and the Konkan coast gradually gives way to the crisp skies and dry heat of the dusty **Mysore Plateau**. The setting for E.M. Forster's acclaimed Raj novel, *A Passage to India*, this southern tip of the Deccan – a vast, open expanse of gently undulating plains dotted with wheat fields and dramatic granite boulders – formed the heartland of the region's once powerful princely state. Today it remains the political hub of the region, largely due to the economic importance of **BANGALORE**, Karnataka's capital, which, with a population racing towards eight million is one of the fastest-growing cities in Asia. A major scientific research centre at the cutting edge of India's technological revolution, Bangalore has a trendy high-speed self-image quite unlike anywhere else in South India.

In the 1800s, Bangalore's gentle climate, broad streets, and green public parks made it the "Garden City". Until well after Independence, senior citizens, film stars and VIPs flocked to buy or build dream homes amid this urban idyll, which offered such unique amenities as theatres, cinemas and a lack of restrictions on alcohol. However, during the last decade or so, Bangalore has undergone a massive transformation. The wide avenues, now dominated by tower blocks, are teeming with traffic, and water and electricity shortages have become the norm. Even the climate has been affected, and pollution is a real problem.

Many foreigners turn up in Bangalore without really knowing why they've come. Some pass through on their way to see Satya Sai Baba at his ashram in **Puttaparthy** in Andhra Pradesh, or at his temporary residence at the **Whitefield** ashram on the outskirts of the city. What little there is to see is no match for the attractions elsewhere in the state, and the city's very real advantages for Indians are two-a-penny in the West. That said, Bangalore is a transport hub, especially well served by plane and bus, and there is some novelty in a Westernized Indian city that not only offers good shopping, eating and hotels, but is the only place on the subcontinent to boast anything resembling a pub culture. For dusty and weary travellers, Bangalore can offer a few days in a relaxed cosmopolitan city that, though it may not be quite like home, may provide a few reminders of it.

Some history

Bangalore began life as the minor "village of the half-baked *gram*" and to this day *gram* (chickpeas) remain an important local product. In 1537, Magadi **Kempe Gowda**, a devout Hindu and feudatory chief of the Vijayanagar empire, built a mud fort and erected four watchtowers outside the village, predicting that it would, one day, extend that far; the city now, of course, stretches way beyond. During the first half of the seventeenth century, Bangalore fell to the Muslim Sultanate of Bijapur; changing hands several times, it returned to Hindu rule under the Mysore Wadiyar Rajas of Srirangapatnam. In 1758, Chikka Krishnaraja Wadiyar II was deposed by the military genius Haider Ali, who set up arsenals to produce muskets, rockets and other weapons for his formidable anti-British campaigns. Both he and his son, **Tipu Sultan**, greatly extended and fortified Bangalore, but Tipu was overthrown by the British in

⓷

▲ *& Whitefield Ashram* ⓬ ▲ *Chennai & Airport (13 km)*

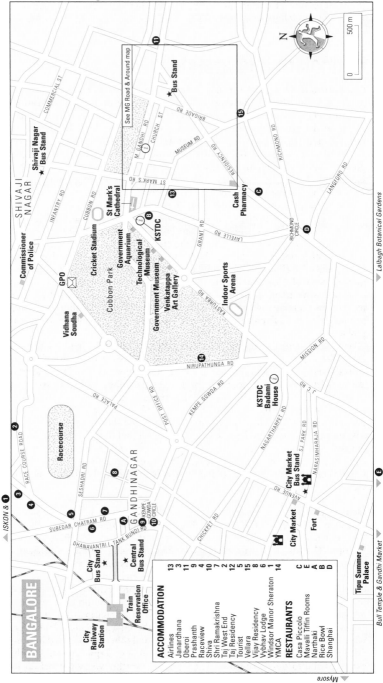

BANGALORE

N

0 ⟷ 500 m

⓫

★ **Bus Stand**

See MG Road & Around map

⓯

Cash Pharmacy

St Mark's Cathedral

⓭

Commissioner of Police

SHIVAJI NAGAR

★ Shivaji Nagar Bus Stand

GPO ✉

Cricket Stadium

Government Aquarium

Cubbon Park

Technological Museum

KSTDC **B**

Government Museum

Venkatappa Art Gallery

A

Indoor Sports Arena

C

D

Vidhana Soudha

Racecourse

GANDHINAGAR

⓮

KSTDC Badami House

★ City Market Bus Stand

City Market

Fort

Tipu Summer Palace

City Bus Stand ★

★ Central Bus Stand

Train Reservation Office

City Railway Station

E

▼ *Bull Temple & Gandhi Market*   ▼ *Lalbagh Botanical Gardens*

◀ *Mysore*

ACCOMMODATION
Airlines	13
Janardhana	3
Oberoi	11
Prashanth	9
Raceview	4
Shiva	10
Shri Ramakrishna	7
Taj West End	2
Taj Residency	12
Tourist	5
Vellara	15
Vijay Residency	8
Vybhav Lodge	6
Windsor Manor Sheraton	1
YMCA	14

RESTAURANTS
Casa Piccolo	C
Mavalli Tiffin Rooms	E
Narthaki	A
Rice Bowl	B
Shanghai	D

It comes as a surprise to many visitors to learn that India is the second-largest exporter of computer software after the US. Generating sales of around $720 million per year, the apex of this hi-tech boom was the Electronic City Industrial Park on the outskirts of Bangalore, dubbed Silicon Valley by the Indian press. Today, due to the meteoric rise of Hyderabad, in neighbouring Andhra Pradesh, as the new computer capital of India, and due to Bangalore's own growth pangs, the city is losing some of its attraction to new investors.

Bangalore's meteoric industrial rise began in the early 1980s. Fleeing the crippling costs of Mumbai and Delhi, a group of hi-tech Indian companies relocated here, lured by the comparatively cool climate and an untapped pool of highly skilled, English-speaking labour (a consequence of the Indian government's decision to concentrate its telecommunications and defence research here in the 1960s). Within a decade, Bangalore had become a major player in the software market, and a magnet for multinationals such as Motorola and Texas Instruments (who have their own satellite link with head office in Dallas).

For a while, Bangalore revelled in a spending frenzy that saw the centre of the city sprout gleaming skyscrapers, swish stores and shopping malls. Soon, however, the price of prosperity became apparent. At the height of the boom, millions of immigrants poured in, eager for a slice of the action; it is estimated that in less than five years the population more than doubled to 7.5 million. However, too little municipal money was invested in infrastructure, and today Bangalore is buckling under the weight of numbers with rocketing levels of traffic pollution. Although power cuts, which became routine again in the late Nineties, have been cut back once more by increasing the output of the city's power grid, the new-found problems have had an adverse effect on business and industry. Some multinationals are now moving out as quickly as they moved in, forcing the city's big-spending expats and computer whizz kids to leave with them. Old Bangaloreans, meanwhile, wonder what became of their beloved "Garden City".

1799. The British set up a cantonment, which made the city an important military station, and passed the administration over to the Maharaja of Mysore in 1881. After Independence, the erstwhile Maharaja became Governor of Mysore state. Bangalore was designated capital of Mysore in 1956, and retained that status when Karnataka state was created in 1973.

Arrival, information and getting around

Recently expanded and revamped to accommodate increased traffic and planned international flights, **Bangalore airport**, 13km north of the city centre, serves cities in South India and beyond; for details of departures, see p.317. The **KSTDC desk** in the arrivals hall (daily 7.30am–1.30pm & 2–7.30pm; ⊕080/526 8012) stocks leaflets on Karnataka and can book hotel rooms. Branches of the State Bank of Mysore (daily 8am–7pm) and Vijaya Bank (daily 8.30am–12.30pm) **change money**, and there's an STD telephone booth. You can get **into the city** by taxi (Rs150; book at the pre-paid desk), by one of the auto-rickshaws (Rs50) that gather outside or by bus – numerous local services run along the main road only several hundred metres from the terminal.

Bangalore City railway station is west of the centre, near Kempe Gowda Circle, and across the road from the main bus stands (for the north of the city, get off at Bangalore Cantonment railway station). As you come into the entrance hall from the platforms, the far left-hand corner holds an **ITDC booth** (daily 7am–5.30pm; ⊕080/220 4277), where you can rent cars and book tours; they will book you a hotel for a fee of ten percent of the day's room rate. The **KSTDC tourist information office** (daily 10am–8pm; ☎ 080/287 0068), to the right, also books tours and can provide useful advice. You'll find a rank of metered taxis outside or, alternatively, pre-paid auto-rickshaws charge Rs25–40 to travel to MG Road, depending on the time of day.

Innumerable **long-distance buses** arrive at the big, busy **Central (KSRTC) bus stand**, opposite the railway station. A bridge divides it from **City bus stand**, used by local services and by long-distance private operators.

Information

For information on Bangalore, Karnataka and neighbouring states, go to the excellent **Government of India tourist office** (Mon–Fri 9.30am–6pm, Sat 9am–1pm; ☎ 080/558 5417, ✉ goitoblr@satyam.net.in), in the KSFC Building, 48 Church St (parallel to MG Road between Brigade and St Mark's roads). You can pick up a free city map here and the staff are very useful in helping you put together tour itineraries.

Apart from the desks at the City railway station and airport (see above), **Karnataka State Tourist Development Corporation** has two city offices: one at Badami House, NR Square ☎ 080/227 5883, where you can book the tours outlined below, and the head office on the second floor of 10/4 Mitra Towers, Kasturba Road, Queen's Circle (daily except Sun and 2nd Sat of the month; ☎ 080/221 2901). For up-to-the-minute information about **what's on**, plus restaurants and shops, check the trendy and ubiquitous free listings paper *Bangalore This Fortnight* and their monthly magazine *Bangalore* that features articles and reviews. The monthly *Bangalore Trail Blazer* is another good source of information, with a directory and a short listings and review section.

If you want to visit any of Karnataka's **national parks**, try the Wildlife Office, Forest Department, Aranya Bhavan, Malleswaram (☎ 080/334 1993), or better still approach Jungle Lodges & Resorts (see box opposite), who promote ecotourism and offer various wildlife packages.

Getting around

The easiest way of getting around Bangalore is by metered **auto-rickshaw**; fares start at Rs9 for the first kilometre and Rs4 per kilometre thereafter. Most meters do work and drivers are usually willing to use them, although you will occasionally be asked for a flat fare, especially during rush hours.

Bangalore's extensive **bus** system, run by the Bangalore Metropolitan Transport Corporation, radiates from the City (Kempe Gowda) bus stand (☎ 080/222 2542), near the railway station. Most buses from platform 17 travel past MG Road. Along with regular buses, BMTC also operates a deluxe express service, Pushpak, on a number of set routes (#P109 terminates at Whitefield ashram) as well as a handful of night buses. Other important city bus stands include the KR Market bus stand (☎ 080/670 2177) to the south of the railway station and Shivajinagar (☎ 080/286 5332) to the north of Cubbon Park – the #P2 Jayanagar service from here is handy for the Lalbagh Botanical Gardens.

You can book **chauffeur-driven cars and taxis** through several agencies, including the Cab Service, Sabari Complex, 24 Residency Rd (☎ 080/558 6121) and the 24hr Dial-a-Car service (☎ 080/526 1737, ✉ dialacar@hotmail .com). Typical rates for car rental are around Rs150 per hour, Rs400 for four hours (which includes 40km) and Rs550 for eight hours (80km); the extra mileage charge is around Rs5 per kilometre. Most taxi companies start calculating their time and distances from when the car leaves their depot. If you

KSTDC operates a string of guided tours from Bangalore. Though rushed, these can be handy if you're short of time. The twice-daily City Tour (7.30am–1.30pm or 2–7.30pm; Rs75) calls at the museum, Vidhana Soudha, Ulsoor Lake, Lalbagh Gardens, Bull Temple and Tipu Sultan's palace, and winds up with a long stop at the Government handicrafts emporium. There are other local tours featuring more obscure temples, mainly aimed at devotees, or alternative sights such as the ISKCON temple, planetarium and musical fountain. Outstation tours include a long day-trip to Srirangapatnam and Mysore (daily 7.15am–11pm; Rs230 or a/c Rs300), and a weekend tour to Hampi (Fri 8pm–Sun 10pm; Rs775). Their day-trip to Belur, Halebid and Sravanabelgola is not recommended unless you're happy to spend more than eight hours on the bus. Other tours on offer include a three-day trip to Jog Falls, five days to Goa, Gokarna and Jog Falls and similar length ventures to various Tamil Nadu temple towns.

Jungle Lodges & Resorts, Shrungar Shopping Centre, MG Road (⊤080/559 7021, ⨍558 6163, ⓔjungle@giasbg01.vsnl.net.in), under the banner of "Eco Tourism", offers package holidays to several wildlife destinations throughout the state. These include well-situated luxury camps at the Biligiri Rangaswamy Wildlife Sanctuary (see box on p.244), the Dandeli Wildlife Sanctuary (see p.283), the Cauvery Fishing Camp at Bheemeshwari, and the Kabini River Lodge near Nagarhole National Park (see p.248). In addition they run the Devbagh Beach Resort at Karwar. Their charges are all-inclusive and also cover excursions into the forests and local sightseeing, but transport to and from the sanctuaries is extra. However, while their charges to Indians in rupees are good value, foreigners have to pay much higher rates in US dollars; typical prices are Rs1000 per night for Indians and $60 per night for foreigners.

need a taxi for a one-way journey, be prepared to pay for the return fare as well. A new metered taxi system is planned for the future which will make renting a cab simpler. See Listings, p.232, for details of self-drive car rental.

A word of warning: most taxi companies start calculating their time and distance fare from when the car leaves their depot until it returns there, so you are best advised to find out how far you are from the depot before ordering the cab. If you need a taxi for a one-way journey be prepared to pay for the return fare as well.

For **long-distance car rental** and **tailor-made itineraries**, try Gullivers Tours & Travels, South Black 201–202 Manipal Centre, 47 Dickenson Rd (⊤080/558 8001), Clipper Holidays, 406 Regency Enclave, 4 Magrath Rd (⊤080/559 9032), any KSTDC office or the ITDC booth at the railway station.

Accommodation

Arrive in Bangalore towards the end of the day, and you'll be lucky to find a room at all, let alone one at the right price, so book at least a couple of days ahead or at least phone around as soon as you arrive. **Budget accommodation** is concentrated around the railway station (which itself has good-value, but often full, retiring rooms; Rs100–400) and Central bus stand. Standards in this area can be very low; the better options are on the east side, dotted around Dhanavanthri (Tank Bund) Road and the parallel Subedar Chatram Road. **Mid-range** and **expensive hotels** are more scattered; some are around the Racecourse, a short rickshaw trip northeast of the station; of the many near MG Road, the *Victoria* is definitely the most characterful.

Around the City railway station and Central bus stand

Prashanth, 21 E Tank Bund Rd ☏ 080/287 4041. Among the better lodges opposite the Central bus stand; all rooms have windows and shower-toilets. The *Mayura* nearby is the best fall-back. ④–⑤

Shiva, 14 Dhanavantri Rd ☏ 080/228 1778. The poshest option in the immediate vicinity of the bus stand. Balconies cost extra. ⑥–⑦

Shri Ramakrishna, Subedar Chatram Road ☏ 080/226 3041. Modern mega-lodge with 250 simple (en-suite) rooms in a colossal concrete block, set round a courtyard, with a good South Indian restaurant. ③

Tourist, Ananda Rao Circle ☏ 080/226 2381. Only a little further to walk from the station, one of Bangalore's best all-round budget lodges, with small rooms, long verandas, and friendly family management. No reservations and it does fill up quickly. ②

Vijay Residency, 18 3rd Cross, Main Road ☏ 080/220 3024. A chain hotel and the most plush and comfortable – if a bit ostentatious. Within striking reach of the railway station, with foreign exchange and restaurant. ⑦–⑧

Vybhav Lodge, 60 Subedar Chatram Rd ☏ 080/287 3997. Good, clean, budget lodge offering small attached rooms with TV, dotted around a little courtyard. Very good value. ③

Around the Racecourse and Cubbon Park

Janardhana, Kumara Krupa Road ☏ 080/225 4444, ⒻS 225 8708. Neat, clean and spacious rooms with balconies and baths. Well away from the chaos and good value at this price (despite hefty service charges). ⑤

Raceview, 25 Race Course Rd ☏ 080/220 3401. Run-of-the-mill mid-range hotel whose upper front rooms overlook the racecourse. Safe deposit, foreign exchange and some a/c. ⑤–⑥

Taj West End, Race Course Road ☏ 080/225 5055, ⒻS 220 0010, ⒺS westend.bangalore @tajhotels.com. Dating back to 1887 with fabulous gardens and long colonnaded walkways. The most characterful rooms are in the old wing, where deep verandas overlook acres of grounds. ⑨

Windsor Manor Sheraton, 25 Sankey Rd ☏ 080/226 9898, ⒻS 226 4941. Ersatz palace run by Welcomgroup as a luxurious five-star, mainly for businesspeople. Facilities include voice mail, modems, gym, Jacuzzi and pool. ⑨

YMCA, Nirupathanga Road, Cubbon Park, midway between the bus stand and MG Road ☏ 080/221 1848. Large, clean rooms and cheaper dorm beds for men. Rock-bottom rates, but often full. ②–④

Around MG Road

Airlines, 4 Madras Bank Rd ☏ 080/227 3783. Respectable hotel in its own grounds, with lively terrace restaurant. Not particularly good value but usually has availability. There's an odd "amenities" charge system whereby the basic price is roughly doubled. Some a/c. ⑤–⑦

Ajantha, 22-A MG Rd ☏ 080/558 4321, ⒻS 558 4780. Good value, with larger than average en-suite rooms. Located down a quiet lane but close to shops. Often booked up days in advance. ④–⑤.

Berry's, 46 Church St ☏ 080/558 7211, ⒻS 558 693). Not the best deal, with large but rather tatty rooms. The views are great though and there are nearly always vacancies. ⑥

Bombay Ananda Bhavan, 68 Vittal Mallya ☏ 080/221 4583, ⒻS 227 7705, ⒺS anandabhavan @satyam.net.in. Family-run, Raj-era mansion in a lovely garden, with large characterful rooms (shutters and stucco ceilings). Book well in advance. ⑧–⑨

Brindavan, 40 MG Rd ☏ 080/558 4000. Old-style mid-range hotel with some a/c rooms and an excellent South Indian "meals" restaurant. A little dowdy, but still reasonable value for money, especially for singles. ④–⑦

Goutam, 17 Museum Rd ☏ 080/558 8764. Large, faceless concrete block south of MG Road. The biggest of the "economy" hotels in this area, so more likely than most to have vacancies, the only reason to consider it. Overpriced and poor service. ⑤

Oberoi, 37–9 MG Rd ☏ 080/558 5858, ⒻS 558 5960, ⒺS unitresvn@oberoiblr.com. Ultra-luxurious five-star, with a clutch of swish restaurants, beautiful landscaped garden and a pool. ⑨

Taj Residency, 41/3 MG Rd ☏ 080/558 4444, ⒻS 558 4748, ⒺS residency.bangalore@tajhotels.com. Not quite in the same league as the *Oberoi*, but a fully fledged five-star, with all the trimmings. ⑨

Vellara, 283 Brigade Rd, opposite Brigade Towers ☏ 080/556 9116. Good-value rooms from no-frills "standard", to light and airy "deluxe" on the top floor (with sweeping city views). ④–⑤

Victoria, 47–8 Residency Rd ☏ 080/558 4077, ⒻS 558 4945. Set in its own leafy compound in the centre of town, with heaps of old-world style and a popular garden restaurant cum bar, serving English brekky. Single rooms are good value, the doubles adequate, while a "deluxe" buys you a veranda. Book well ahead. ⑦

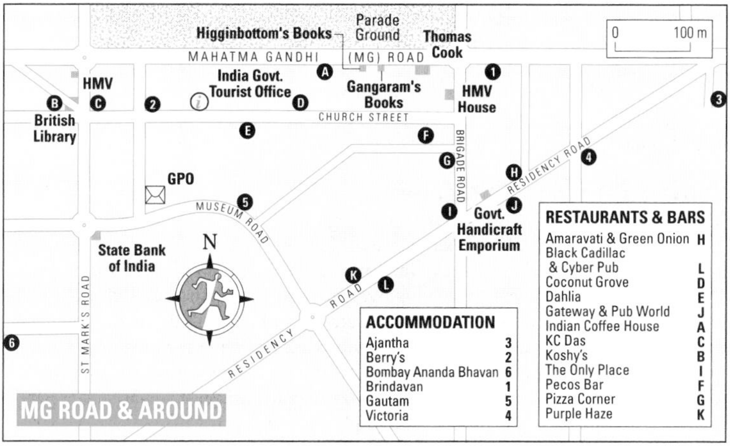
MG ROAD & AROUND
Parade Ground
Higginbottom's Books
Thomas Cook
MAHATMA GANDHI (MG) ROAD
HMV
India Govt. Tourist Office
Gangaram's Books
HMV House
British Library
CHURCH STREET
BRIGADE ROAD
RESIDENCY ROAD
GPO
MUSEUM ROAD
Govt. Handicraft Emporium
State Bank of India
N
ST MARK'S ROAD
0 100 m
ACCOMMODATION
Ajantha 3
Berry's 2
Bombay Ananda Bhavan 6
Brindavan 1
Gautam 5
Victoria 4
RESTAURANTS & BARS
Amaravati & Green Onion H
Black Cadillac & Cyber Pub L
Coconut Grove D
Dahlia E
Gateway & Pub World J
Indian Coffee House A
KC Das C
Koshy's B
The Only Place I
Pecos Bar F
Pizza Corner G
Purple Haze K

The City

The **centre** of modern Bangalore lies about 5km east of Kempe Gowda Circle, and the principal train and bus stations, at the area around **MG Road**. On MG Road you'll find most of the mid-range accommodation, restaurants, shops, tourist information and banks. Leafy **Cubbon Park**, with its less-than-exciting museums, lies on its western edge, while the oldest, most "Indian" part of the city extends south from the City railway station, a warren of winding streets at their most dynamic in the hubbub of the **City** and **Gandhi markets**. Bangalore's tourist attractions are spread out; monuments such as **Tipu's Summer Palace** and the **Bull Temple** are some way south of the centre. Most, if not all, can be seen on a half-day tour but if you plan to explore on foot be warned that Bangalore has some of the worst pavements in India.

Cubbon Park and museums

A welcome green space in the heart of the city, shaded by massive clumps of bamboo, **Cubbon Park** is entered from the western end of MG Road, presided over by a statue of Queen Victoria. On Kasturba Road, which runs along its southern edge, the poorly labelled and maintained **Government Museum** (Tues–Sun 10am–5pm; Rs4) features prehistoric artefacts, Vijayanagar, Hoysala and Chalukya sculpture, musical instruments, Thanjavur paintings and Deccani and Rajasthani miniatures. It includes the adjacent **Venkatappa Art Gallery**, which exhibits twentieth-century landscapes, portraits, abstract art, wood sculpture and occasional temporary art shows. Next door, the **Technological and Industrial Museum** (daily 10am–6pm; Rs10) is geared towards kids and further towards the junction with MG Road, the octagonal **Government Aquarium** (Tues–Sun except 2nd Tues of month 10am–5.30pm; Rs2) contains a few murky tanks downstairs and some more visible tropical fish upstairs.

Vidhana Soudha

Built in 1956, Bangalore's vast State Secretariat, **Vidhana Soudha**, northwest of Cubbon Park, is the largest civic structure of its kind in the country. K. Hanumanthaiah, chief minister at the time, wanted a "people's palace" that, following the transfer of power from the royal Wadiyar dynasty to a legislature, would "reflect the power and dignity of the people". In theory its design is entirely Indian, combining local models from Bangalore, Mysore and Somnathpur with features from Rajasthan and the rest of India. Its overall effect, however, is not unlike bombastic colonial architecture built in the so-called Indo-Saracenic style – incorporating onion-domes and Oriental features.

Lalbagh Botanical Gardens

Inspired by the splendid gardens of the Moghuls and the French botanical gardens at Pondicherry in Tamil Nadu, Sultan Haider Ali set to work in 1760 laying out the **Lalbagh Botanical Gardens** (daily 8am–8pm; Rs2 before 6pm), 4km south of the centre. Originally covering forty acres, just beyond his fort – where one of Kempe Gowda's original watchtowers can still be seen – the gardens were expanded under Ali's son Tipu, who introduced numerous exotic species of plants and today the gardens house an extensive horticultural seedling centre. The British brought in gardeners from Kew in 1856 and – naturally – built a military bandstand and a glasshouse, based on London's Crystal Palace, which hosts wonderful flower shows. Now spreading over 240 acres, the gardens are pleasant to visit during the day, but tend to attract unsavoury characters after 6pm. Great sunsets and views of the city to the north are to be had from the central hill, topped by a small shrine.

Tipu's Summer Palace

A two-storey structure built in 1791, mostly of wood, **Tipu's Summer Palace** (daily 9am–5pm; $5 [Rs5]), southwest of the City Market and 3km from MG Road, is similar to the Daria Daulat Palace at Srirangapatnam (see p.243), but in a far worse state, with most of its painted decoration destroyed. Next door, the **Venkataramanaswamy temple**, dating from the early eighteenth century, was built by the Wadiyar rajas. The *gopura* entrance-way was erected in 1978.

Bull Temple

About 6km south of the City bus stand (buses #34 and #37), in the Basavanagudi area, Kempe Gowda's sixteenth-century **Bull Temple** (open to non-Hindus; daily 7.30am–1.30pm & 2.30–8.30pm) houses a massive monolithic Nandi bull, its grey granite made black by the application of charcoal and oil. The temple is approached along a path lined with mendicants and snake charmers; inside, for a few rupees, the priest will offer you a string of fragrant jasmine flowers. For more information on Kempe Gowda, the city's founder, see p.221.

ISKCON temple

A hybrid of ultra-modern glass and vernacular South Indian temple architecture, the gleaming new temple of the ISKCON (International Society of Krishna Consciousness), the **Sri Radha Krishna Mandir**, Hare Krishna Hill, Chord Road (daily 7am–1pm & 4pm–8.30pm), 8km from the centre, is a fantastic and lavish showpiece crowned by a gold-plated dome. Barriers, designed with huge crowds in mind, guide visitors on a one-way journey through the huge well-organized complex to the inner sanctum, where images of the god Krishna and his consort Radha are displayed. Collection points throughout and inescapable merchandizing are evidence of ISKON's highly successful commercialization. Regular **buses** to the temple depart from both the City and Shivajinagar bus stands.

Eating

With unmissable sights thin on the ground, but tempting cafés and restaurants on every corner, you could easily spend most of your time in Bangalore **eating**. Nowhere else in South India will you find such gastronomic variety. Around **MG Road**, pizzerias (including *Pizza Hut*), ritzy ice-cream parlours and gourmet French restaurants stand cheek by jowl with regional cuisine from Andhra Pradesh and Kerala, Mumbai *chaat* cafés and snack bars where, in true Bangalorean style, humble thalis from as little as Rs25 masquerade as "executive mini-lunches".

Amaravati, Residency Road Cross, MG Road. Excellent Andhra cooking with "meals" served on banana leafs and specialities including biryanis and fried fish. Hectic at lunch time but well worth any wait.

Casa Piccolo, Devata Plaza, 131 Residency Rd. A dozen different tasty pizzas and big portions of *wienerschnitzel*, steaks, fried chicken, Mexican food and ice cream but no alcohol. Outside tables and flower baskets give the place a European ambience. Patronized by the well-heeled, sunglass-wearing studenty set and travellers.

Coconut Grove, Church Street ☎ 080/558 8596. Mouthwatering and moderately priced gourmet Keralan coastal cuisine: vegetarian, fish and meat preparations served in traditional copper thalis on a leafy terrace. Try their tender coconut juice cocktail, thala chickory bom. Recommended.

Dahlia, Brigade Gardens, Church Street. Japanese café tucked in a modern business complex, serving authentic dishes from further east at reasonable prices.

Gateway, 66 Residency Rd ☎ 080/558 4545. The *Northern Gate* serves a fairly undistinguished selection of Mughlai and other North Indian dishes, while the *Karavalli* specializes in west-coast dishes from Goa to Kerala, including seafood and veg. A very attractive room in traditional southern style with a wooden ceiling – plus tables outside under an old tamarind tree. Reservations essential. Expensive.

Green Onion, Next door to the *Amaravati*, this small modern triangular-shaped establishment offers a tasty range of kebabs, curries, Chinese and sweets at fair prices in a café-style atmosphere.

Indian Coffee House, MG Road. The usual cheap South Indian snacks, egg dishes and good filter coffee, served by waiters in turbans and cummerbunds. Best for breakfast.

KC Das, 38 Church St (corner of St Mark's Road). Part of the legendary chain of Bengali sweet shops serving traditional steam-cooked sweets, many soaked in syrup and rose water. Try their definitive *rasgullas*. Eat in or take away.

Koshy's, St Mark's Road, next to British Library. Spacious old-style café with cane blinds, pewter teapots and cotton-clad waiters. Bangalore's most congenial meeting place. Serves full meals, snacks and alcohol.

Mavalli Tiffin Rooms, Lalbagh Road. Indian fast-food restaurant, serving superb-value set menus (4–8.30pm), and good snacks (including the best masala dosas in Bangalore) during the day. Also pure fruit juices and lassis sweetened with honey.

Narthaki, just off Subedar Chatram Road. The best restaurant in the station/bus stand area. Filling Andhra meals are served on the first floor. On the second there is a restaurant bar with a full menu of Indian and Chinese dishes. The chicken chilli is a belter.

The Only Place, Mota Royal Arcade, Brigade Road. Highly rated Western food, including a near-legendary lasagne, pizzas and great apple pie, at reasonable prices.

Pizza Corner, Brigade Road. The most central location of this bright new chain. Quality pizza with great "lunch munch" specials and unlimited coke refills. Some of the profits go to charity.

Rice Bowl, 40/2 Lavelle Rd. Plush air-conditioned Chinese restaurant, one of the best in town; try their chop suey and, for dessert, lychees with ice cream.

Shanghai, G3–4 Shiva Shankar Plaza, 19 Lalbagh Rd, Richmond Circle. Among the city's top Chinese restaurants. Excellent beancurd veg soup and Hunan peppered fish, deep-fried with ginger, garlic and spring onions in a black pepper sauce.

Nightlife

The big boom may be over, but Bangalore's bright young things still have money to spend, and **nightlife** in the city is thriving. A night on the town generally kicks off with a bar crawl along **Brigade Road**, **Residency Road** or **Church Street**, where there are scores of swish **pubs**, complete with MTV, lasers and thumping sound systems. If you persevere, you can get away from the noise and find a spot to have a quiet drink. Drinking alcohol does not have the seedy connotations here as it does elsewhere in India; you'll even see young Indian women enjoying a beer with their mates. There is, however, a ban on alcohol sales between 2.30 and 5.30pm, imposed in 1993 by ex-Chief Minister Veerappa Moily because of the number of schoolkids skipping school to booze. Pubs close at 11pm but, once in, you generally get served till later. For quiet, elegant drinking head for the bars of five-star **hotels** such as the *Jockey Club* at the *Taj Residency* or its competition, the *Polo Club* at the *Oberoi*, and for a taste of colonial grandeur, the *Colonnade* at the *Taj West End*.

See the listings magazines to catch Bangalore's small but steady stream of **live music** and **theatre**, some of which is homegrown; there are also a handful of **discos**, which usually follow a couples-only policy.

Bangalore is also a major centre for **cinema**, with a booming industry and dozens of theatres showing the latest releases from India and abroad. Check the listings page of the *Deccan Herald*, the *Evening Herald*, the free listings monthly, *Trail Blazer*, and *Bangalore Fortnightly*, to find out what's on. Western movies are often dubbed into Hindi, although their titles may be written in English; check the small print in the newspaper. Cinema fans should head for **Kempe Gowda Circle**, which is crammed with posters, hoardings and larger-than-life-size cardboard cutouts of the latest stars, strewn with spangly garlands. To arrange a visit to a local movie studio phone Chamundeshwari Studio (℡080/226 8642) or Shree Kanteera Studio (℡080/337 1008).

Pubs and clubs

B-52, Cha Che Towers, 50 Residency Rd. Thumping high-rise pub with karaoke, disco and pool tables. Booze with a view.

Black Cadillac, 50 Residency Rd. Long-term favourite theme pub with some tables outside that also attract families.

The Club, Mysore Road ℡080/337 1008. The talk of the town, 14km from the centre, and popular with a wealthy young crowd. Features regular discos and the occasional live gig with a few big names passing through. You'll need to take a taxi.

Cyber Pub, above *Black Cadillac*, Residency Road. If you think you can cope with extremely loud music in a hi-tech bar while surfing the web, head up here for a unique experience.

Down Town, next to Galaxy Cinema, Residency Road. Large pub that also serves food and wine, and has a couple of pool tables at the back.

Guzzlers Inn, 48 Rest House Rd, off Brigade Road. Popular and established pub offering MTV, Star Sport, snooker, pool and draught beer.

JJ's, MSIL Building, Airport Road Cross ℡080/526 1929. A café which offers a varied evening programme including discos, folk dance and live jazz on Sunday nights led by the musician-owner.

Nasa, 1/4 Church St. Karaoke and sci-fi decor with lasers in a mock space shuttle. The usual combination of big-screen MTV and in-your-face music.

Oasis, Church Street. Low light and an unobtrusive sound-system: the chill-out option.

Pecos, Rest House Road, off Brigade Road. Small and relaxed pub on two floors with 1960s and 1970s music; popular with a mixed arty set.

A Pinch of Jazz, The Central Park, 47 Dickenson Rd ℡080/558 4242. Upmarket jazz café serving Cajun cuisine and live soft-jazz covers.

Pub World, opposite Galaxy Cinema, Residency Road. A well-presented newish place popular with trendy young professionals. Actually four pubs from different regions under one roof. The usual high-volume music.

Purple Haze, opposite *Black Cadillac*, Residency Road. Still one of the trendiest of the downtown pubs with a smart but jumping upstairs bar sporting Jimi Hendrix-themed graphics. More chance of decent rock here than most places.

Shopping

Bangalore has many fine shops, particularly if you're after **silk**. A wide range of silk is available at Karnataka Silk Industries Corporation and Vijayalakshmi Silk

Kendra, both on Gupte Market, Kempe Gowda Road, and at Deepam Silk Emporium on MG Road. **Handicrafts** such as soapstone sculpture, brass, carved sandalwood and rosewood are also good value; emporia include: Central Cottage Industries Emporium, 144 MG Rd; the expensive Cottage Industries Exposition Ltd, 3 Cunningham Rd; Gulshan Crafts, 12 Safina Plaza, Infantry Road, and the Karnataka's own state emporium, Cauvery, at the MG Road and Brigade Road crossing. For **silver**, try looking on and around Commercial Street (north of MG Road) and at KR Market on Residency Road, as well as at Jewels de Paragon between MG Road and Kasturba Road. The long-established Natesan's Antiqarts, 64 MG Rd, sells antiques and beautifully made reproduction sculpture, furniture and paintings at international art house prices. If you want to take a look at expensive Indian haute couture try Ffolio at Embassy Chamber, Vittal Mallya Road, which features several well-known Indian designers.

Bangalore is also a great place for **bookshops**. The first floor of Gangarams, 72 MG Rd, offers a wide selection on India (coffee-table art books and academic) plus the latest paperback fiction, and a great selection of Indian greetings cards. Another good option is Higginbotham's, 68 MG Rd, and you can browse in air-conditioned comfort at LB Publishers, 91 MG Rd. Around the corner from the ITDC office, Premier, 46/1 Church St, crams a huge number of books into a tiny space. The shop belonging to established publishers Motilal Banarsidas at 16 St Mark's Rd, close to the junction with MG Road, offers a superb selection of heavyweight Indology and philosophy titles. Sankars at 15/2 Madras Bank Rd is an airy new shop with a good range of titles of fiction, art, education and religion. The best **music** shops in the city centre, selling Indian and Western tapes, are HMV, on Brigade Road or St Mark's Road, where you can pick up an excellent four-cassette pack introducing South Indian or Carnatic music, and Rhythms, at 14 St Mark's Rd, beneath the *Nahar Heritage* hotel.

Listings

Airlines domestic Indian Airlines, Cauvery Bhavan, Kempe Gowda Road ☏ 080/221 1914, airport ☏ 526 6233; Jet Airways, 1-4 M Block, Unity Building, JC Road ☏ 080/227 6620, airport ☏ 526 6898; Sahara Airlines, 35 Church St ☏ 080/558 4457, airport ☏ 526 2531.

Airlines international Air Canada, Sunrise Chambers, 22 Ulsoor Rd ☏ 080/558 5394; Air France, Sunrise Chambers, 22 Ulsoor Rd ☏ 080/558 9397; Air India, Unity Building, JC Road ☏ 080/227 7747; Alitalia, 44 Safina Plaza, Infantry Road ☏ 080/559 1936; American Airlines, Sunrise Chambers, 22 Ulsoor Rd ☏ 080/559 4240; British Airways, 7 St Mark's Rd ☏ 080/227 1205; Delta/Sabena/Swiss Air/Singapore Airlines, Park View, 17 Curve Rd, Tasker Town ☏ 080/286 7868; Gulf Air, Sunrise Chambers, 22 Ulsoor Rd ☏ 080/558 4702; KLM, *Taj West End*, Race Course Road ☏ 080/226 8703; Lufthansa, 44/2 Dickenson Rd ☏ 080/558 8791; Malaysian Airlines, Richmond Circle ☏ 080/221 3030; Pakistan International Airlines, 108 Commerce House, 911 Cunningham Rd ☏ 080/226 0667; Qantas, Westminster, Cunningham Road ☏ 080/226 4719; Royal Brunei, Stic Travels, Imperial Court, Cunningham Road ☏ 080/226 7613; Thai Airlines, G-5 Imperial Court, Cunningham Road ☏ 080/225 6194; United Airlines, Richmond Towers, 12 Richmond Rd ☏ 080/224 4625.

Banks and exchange A reliable place to change money is Thomas Cook, 55 MG Rd, on the corner of Brigade Road, though if it's busy Weizmann Forex Ltd, 56 Residency Rd, near the other end of Brigade Road, is just as efficient and quieter (both Mon–Sat 9.30am–6pm); the slower State Bank of India is at 87 MG Rd (Mon–Fri 10.30am–2.30pm & Sat 10.30am–12.30pm). ANZ Grindlays at Raheja Towers on MG Road (same hours) changes money and advances cash on credit cards, or try the fast and efficient Wall Street Finanaces, 3 House of Lords, 13–14 St Mark's Rd (Mon–Sat 9.30am–6pm; ☏080/227 1812). Also for Visa and Mastercard advances – but not travellers' cheques – go to Bank of

Baroda, 70 MG Rd (Mon–Fri 10.30am–2.30pm & Sat 10.30am–12.30pm).

Car rental You can find self-drive car rental at Europcar, Sheriff House, 85 Richmond Rd (☎ 080/221 9502, ☎ 299 0453); Avis, *The Oberoi*, 37–39 MG Rd (☎ 080/558 3503, ☎ crs@avisdel.com); and Hertz, 167 Richmond Rd, near Trinity Circle (☎ 080/559 9408) with charges from Rs900 per day. For long-distance car rental and tailor-made itineraries, try Gullivers Tours & Travels, South Black 201–202 Manipal Centre, 47 Dickenson Rd (☎ 080/558 8001); Clipper Holidays, 406 Regency Enclave, 4 Magrath Rd (☎ 080/559 9032); any KSTDC office, and the ITDC booth at the railway station.

Hospitals Victoria, near City Market ☎ 080/670 1150; Sindhi Charitable, 3rd Main St, S R Nagar ☎ 080/223 7318.

Internet access At the last count Bangalore had a staggering 700 email/internet bureaus – most charge Rs20–30/hr and offer half-hour and some even shorter slots. The Cyber Café, 13–15 Brigade Rd (☎ 080/550 0949) is the most obvious and the most popular; you need to get a ticket at the door to book your slot on the machines and there is coffee, but they don't encourage more than one person per computer. Other alternatives include Cyber Inn, Residency Road and Brigade Road Cross (☎ 080/559 9962), Cyber Craft, 33 Rest House Rd (☎ 080/558 8341) and Cyber Den, first floor, S112A Manipal Centre, Dickenson Road (☎ 080/558 6671). Take2Net, Brigade Gardens, Church Street has Rs10/hr rates before 11am and after 9pm.

Libraries The British Council (English-language) library, 39 St Mark's Rd (Tues–Sat

Moving on from Bangalore

Bangalore is South India's principal transport hub. Fast and efficient computerized booking facilities make moving on relatively hassle-free, although availability of seats should never be taken for granted; book as far in advance as possible. For an overview of travel services to and from Bangalore, see Travel Details on p.316.

Bangalore's recently upgraded airport is the busiest in South India, with international and domestic departures and plans for more. The most frequent flights are to Mumbai, operated by Air India, Jet Airways, Indian Airlines and Sahara Indian, and there are also seven daily flights to Delhi. Jet Airways and Indian Airlines operate several flights a day to Chennai and at least one daily flight each to Calcutta, Goa, Cochin, Hyderabad and Pune. There is also one daily flight to each of Mangalore (Jet) and Trivandrum (IA). Finally, Indian Airlines has several weekly international flights to destinations in Southeast Asia and the Gulf States, while Air India operates a route to New York via London on most days.

Most of the wide range of long-haul buses from the Central stand can be booked in advance at the computerized counters near bay #13 (7.30am–7.30pm). Aside from KSRTC, state bus corporations represented include Andhra Pradesh, Kerala, Maharashtra, Tamil Nadu and the Kadamba Transport Corporation, a Government of Goa undertaking. Timings and ticket availability for the forthcoming week are posted on a large board left of the main entrance. For general enquiries, call ☎ 080/287 3377. Several private bus companies run luxury coaches to destinations such as Mysore, Bijapur, Ooty, Chennai, Kochi/Ernakulam, Trichur, Kollam and Trivandrum. Agencies opposite the bus stand sell tickets for private coach companies such as Sharma (c/o MM Travels, ☎ 080/209 4099), National (☎ 080/225 7202) and Shama, which advertise overnight deluxe buses to Goa (Rs250) as well as sleeper coaches (Rs400) and services to Mumbai for Rs350–450. The most reliable of the private bus companies is Vijayananda Travels at Sri Saraswathi Lodge, 3rd Main 2nd Cross, Gandhinagar (☎ 080/228 7222) with several other branches in Bangalore, who operate their distinctive yellow-and-black luxury coaches to destinations such as Mangalore and Hospet for Hampi.

While Southern Railways converts to broad gauge, some rail routes in Karnataka continue to suffer disruption, especially along the route from Hassan to Mangalore. Check the situation when you arrive. Bangalore City station's reservations office

10.30am–6.30pm; ☎ 080/221 3485), has newspapers and magazines that visitors are welcome to peruse in a/c comfort, as does the Alliance Française (French), 16 GMT Rd ☎ 080/225 8762, and Max Mueller Bhavan (German), 3 Lavelle Rd ☎ 080/227 5435.

Pharmacies Open all night: Al-Siddique Pharma Centre, opposite Jama Masjid near City Market; Janata Bazaar, in the Victoria Hospital, near City Market; Sindhi Charitable Hospital, 3rd Main S R Nagar. During the day, head for Santoshi Pharma, 46 Mission Rd.

Photographic equipment Adlabs, Mission Road, Subbaiah Circle, stocks transparency film. GG Welling, 113 MG Rd and GK Vale, 89 MG Rd sell transparency and Polaroid film.

Police ☎ 100.

Post office on the corner of Raj Bhavan Road and

Cubbon Street, at the northern tip of Cubbon Park, about ten minutes' walk from MG Road (Mon–Sat 10am–7pm, Sun 10.30am–1.30pm).

Swimming pools Five-star hotel pools open to non-residents include the *Taj Residency* (Rs500 includes sauna, Jacuzzi and health club) and *Taj West End* (Rs500).

Travel agents For flight booking and reconfirmation and other travel necessities, try Gullivers Tours & Travels, South Black 201–202 Manipal Centre, 47 Dickenson Rd (☎ 080/558 8001); Merry Go Round Tours, 41 Museum Rd, opposite *Berry's Hotel* (☎ & ☎ 080/558 6946); Marco Polo Tours, Janardhan Towers, 2 Residency Rd (☎ 080/227 4484, ☎ 223 6671) or Sita Travels, 1 St Mark's Rd (☎ 080/558 8892).

Visa extensions Commissioner of Police, Infantry Road, ☎ 080/225 6242 (Mon–Sat 10am–5.30pm).

(Mon–Sat 8am–2pm & 2.15–8pm, Sun 8am–2pm; phone reservations ☎ 132) is in a separate building, east of the main station (to the left as you approach). Counter #14 is for foreigners. If you have an Indrail Pass, go to the Chief Reservations Supervisor's Office on the first floor (turn left at the top of the stairs), where "reservations are guaranteed". If your reservation is "waitlisted", or you are required to confirm the booking, you may have to go on the day of departure to the Commercial Officer's office, in the Divisional Office – yet another building, this time to the west, accessible from the main road. There are two 24hr telephone information lines: one handles timetable enquiries (☎ 131), the other reels off a recorded list of arrivals and departures (☎ 133).

Recommended trains from Bangalore

The following trains are recommended as the fastest and/or most convenient from Bangalore:

Destination	Name	No.	Departs	Total time
Delhi	Rajdhani Express*	#2429	4 weekly 6.35pm	34hr 30min
	Karnataka Express	#2627	daily 6.25pm	41hr 40min
Chennai	Shatabdi Express*	#2008	daily except Tues 4.25pm	5hr
	Lalbagh Express	#2608	daily 6.30am	5hr 25min
Hospet (for Hampi)	Hampi Express	#6592	daily 10pm	9hr 50min
Hyderabad	Rajdhani Express*	#2429	4 weekly 6.35pm	11hr 55min
(Secunderabad)	Secunderabad Express	#7086	daily 5.05pm	13hr 25min
Kochi (Ernakulam)	Kanniyakumari Express	#6526	daily 9pm	12hr 50min
Mumbai	Udyan Express	#6530	daily 8.30pm	23hr 55min
Mysore	Shatabdi Express*	#2007	daily except Tues 11am	2hr
	Chennai–Mysore Express	#6222	daily 7.10am	2hr 50min
	Tipu Express	#6206	daily 2.15pm	2hr 30min
	Chamundi Express	#6216	daily 6.15pm	2hr 55min
Trivandrum	Kanniyakumari Express	#6526	daily 9pm	16hr 10min

*= a/c only

Around Bangalore

Bangalore is surrounded by some very pleasant countryside, which includes good walking country in the Nandi Hills to the north, and the Bannerghatta National Park to the south. Many visitors to Bangalore, however, are on their way to or from Mysore. The **Janapada Loka Folk Arts Museum**, between the two, gives a fascinating insight into Karnataka culture, while anyone wishing to see or study classical dance in a rural environment should check out the **Nrityagram Dance Village**.

Janapada Loka Folk Arts Museum

The **Janapada Loka Folk Arts Museum** (daily 9am–6pm; free), 53km southwest of Bangalore on the Mysore road, includes an amazing array of Karnatakan agricultural, hunting and fishing implements, weapons, ingenious household gadgets, masks, dolls and shadow puppets, carved wooden *bhuta* (spirit-worship) sculptures and larger-than-life temple procession figures, manuscripts, musical instruments and *Yakshagana* theatre costumes. In addition, an incredible 1600 hours of **audio and video recordings** of musicians, dancers and rituals from the state are available for viewing on request.

To get to the museum, take one of the many slow Mysore buses (not the non-stop ones) from Bangalore. After the town of Ramanagar, alight at the 53-kilometre stone by the side of the road. A small **restaurant** serves simple food, and dorm **accommodation** (①) is available, though you can just jump back onto a bus to Mysore. For more details contact the Karnataka Janapada Trust, 7 Subramanyaswami Temple Rd, 5th Cross, 4th Block, Kumara Park West, Bangalore.

Nrityagram Dance Village

NRITYAGRAM DANCE VILLAGE is a delightful, purpose-built model village, 30km west of Bangalore. It was designed by the award-winning Goan architect Gerard de Cunha, and founded by the late Protima Gauri – who died in an avalanche during a pilgrimage to Kailash in Tibet in 1998. Protima Gauri, who had left Nrityagram sometime before her death, had enjoyed a colourful career in media and film, and eventually came to be well respected as an exponent of Odissi dance. The school continues without her and attracts pupils from all over the world. It hosts regular performances, as well as lectures on Indian mythology and art, and also offers courses in different forms of Indian dance. **Guided tours** of the complex cost Rs250 (Tues–Sun 10am–5pm). **Accommodation** for longer stays (②) promises "oxygen, home-grown vegetables and fruits, no TV, telephones, newspapers or noise". Contact their Bangalore office for further details (☎080/558 5440, ⒲www.allindia.com/nrityaga).

Mysore

A centre of sandalwood-carving, silk and incense production, 159km southwest of Bangalore, **MYSORE**, the erstwhile capital of the Wadiyar Rajas, is one of South India's most-visited places. Considering the clichés that have been heaped upon the town, however, first impressions can be disappointing. Like anywhere else, you are not so much greeted by the scent of jasmine blossom or gentle wafts of sandalwood when you stumble off the bus or train, as by the

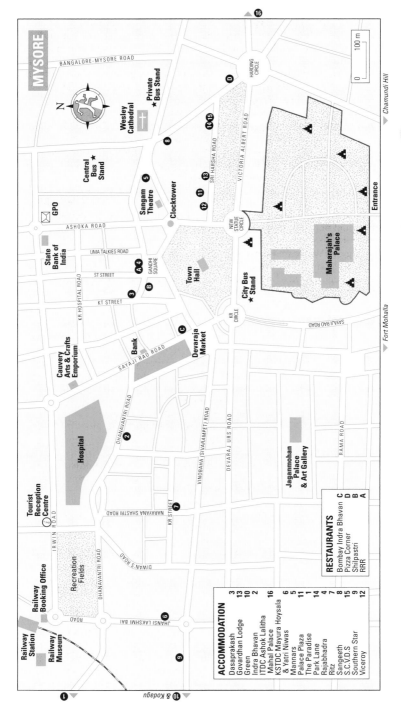

MYSORE

Bangalore-Mysore Road

N

Wesley
Cathedral

★ Private
Bus Stand

Central ★
Bus Stand

GPO

State
Bank of
India

Sangam
Theatre

Ashoka Road

Clocktower

Uma Talkies Road

ST Street

Gandhi
Square

A·4

B

3

KT Street

KR Hospital Road

Cauvery
Arts & Crafts
Emporium

Bank

C

Devaraja
Market

Sayaji Rao Road

Dhanavantri Road

Hospital

2

Tourist
Reception
Centre

Irwin
Road

Railway
Booking Office

Railway
Station

Railway
Museum

Recreation
Fields

Dhanavantri Road

Diwan's Road

Narayana Shastri Road

7

KR Street

Vinobaha (Sivarampet) Road

Devaraj Urs Road

Jaganmohan
Palace
& Art Gallery

Rama Road

Jhansi Lakshmi Bai
Road

6

9

▼ 10 & Kodagu

▼ Fort Mohalla

▼ Chamundi Hill

Harding
Circle

D

Victoria Albert Road

14 15

Sri Harsha Road

13

11

12

8

New
Statue
Circle

Town
Hall

City Bus ★
Stand

KR
Circle

Maharajah's
Palace

Entrance

Sayaji Rao Road

▲ 16

0   100 m

3

KARNATAKA | Mysore

ACCOMMODATION

Dasaprakash	3
Govardhan Lodge	13
Green	10
Indra Bhavan	2
ITDC Ashok Lalitha	
Mahal Palace	16
KSTDC Mayura Hoysala	
& Yatri Niwas	6
Mannars	5
Palace Plaza	11
The Paradise	1
Park Lane	14
Rajabhadra	4
Ritz	7
Sangeeth	8
S.C.V.D.S	15
Southern Star	9
Viceroy	12

RESTAURANTS

Bombay Indra Bhavan	C
Pizza Corner	D
Shilpastri	B
RRR	A

235

usual cacophony of careering auto-rickshaws and noisy buses, bullock carts and tongas. Nevertheless, Mysore is a charming, old-fashioned and undaunting town, dominated by the spectacular **Maharaja's Palace**, around which the boulevards of the city radiate. Nearby, the city centre with the colourful and frenetic **Devaraja Market** provides an inviting stroll. On the outskirts of Mysore, **Srirangapatnam** still harbours architectural gems from the days of the great Indian hero, Tipu Sultan, and the magnificent Hoysala temple of **Somnathpur** lies little more than an hour's drive away.

In the tenth century Mysore was known as "Mahishur" – "the town where the demon buffalo was slain" (by the goddess Durga). Presiding over a district of many villages, the city was ruled from about 1400 until Independence by the Hindu **Wadiyars**, and its fortunes were inextricably linked with those of Srirangapatnam, which became the Wadiyar headquarters from 1616 (see p.242). Their rule was only broken from 1761, when the Muslim Haider Ali and his son Tipu Sultan took over. Two years later, the new rulers demolished the labyrinthine old city to replace it with the elegant grid of sweeping, leafy streets and public gardens that survive today. However, following Tipu Sultan's defeat in 1799 by the British colonel Arthur Wellesley (later the Duke of Wellington), Wadiyar power was restored. As the capital of Mysore state, the city thereafter dominated a major part of southern India. In 1956, when Bangalore became capital of newly formed Karnataka, its maharaja was appointed governor.

Arrival and information

Mysore's nearest airport is at Bangalore: five or six daily trains from the state capital arrive at the **railway station**, 1500m northwest of the centre, with connections to and from Chennai. Mysore has three **bus** stands: major long-distance KSRTC services pull in to **Central**, near the heart of the city, where there's a friendly KSTDC booking counter for their tours, also good for information regarding bus times. The **Private** stand, just a dusty patch of road, lies a little way south, opposite the *Ritz Hotel*, and is used by buses to and from Somnathpur. Local buses, including services for Chamundi Hill and Srirangaptnam, stop at the **City** stand, next to the northwestern corner of the Maharaja's Palace.

Five minutes' walk southeast of the railway station, on a corner of Irwin Road in the Old Exhibition Building, the helpful **tourist reception centre** (daily 10am–5.30pm; ☏0821/422096) will make an effort to answer queries and can arrange transport, though there's not much you can take away with you. The **KSTDC office** (daily 7.30am–8.30pm; ☏0821/423652), at the hotel *Mayura Hoysala*, 2 Jhansi Laxmi Bai Rd, is of little use except to book one of their **tours**. The whistle-stop city tour (7.30am–8.30pm; Rs115) makes for a long day, covering Jaganmohan Palace Art Gallery, the Maharaja's Palace, St Philomena's Cathedral, the Zoo, Chamundi Hill, Somnathpur, Srirangapatnam and Brindavan Gardens. It only leaves with a minimum of ten passengers, so you may not know for sure whether it will run when you buy your ticket. Their long-distance tour to Belur, Halebid and Sravanabelgola (7.30am–9pm; Rs210) is not recommended as it is too long for a single day and you spend far too much time on the bus; it's a similar story with their Ooty tour (7.30am–9pm; Rs215). However, their **car rental** rates, at Rs4 per kilometre (for a minimum of 250km per day), are quite reasonable if you want to put together your own itinerary. The Tourist Corporation India at Gandhi Square (☏0821/443023) acts as KSTDC agent and arranges tours and car rental.

The main **post office** (poste restante) is on the corner of Ashoka and Irwin roads (Mon–Sat 10am–7pm, Sun 10.30am–1.30pm). If you need to **change money**, there's a State Bank of Mysore on the corner of Sayaji Rao and Sardar Patel Road, and the Indian Overseas Bank, Gandhi Square, opposite *Dasaprakash Hotel*. Seagull Travels, Ramanashri Hotel Complex, near Woodland Cinema, Harding Circle are also licensed moneychangers but give poor rates and no exchange certificates. Mysore is gradually catching on to cyber progress and among several reliable places are Coca-Cola Cyber Space (daily 6.30am–midnight; ☎0821/515574), next to the private bus stand, and the cheaper 24hr Internet Online (☎0821/421536) on Chandragupta Road near *Mannars Hotel*.

Accommodation

The city has plenty of **hotels** to suit all budgets. Finding a room is only a problem during Dussehra (see box on p.240), when popular places are booked up weeks in advance. Cheap lodges are concentrated on and around **Dhanavantri Road**, a little way south of the tourist reception centre on Irwin Road, and close to **Gandhi Square** further east. Most, however, are pokey and not particularly clean. Mid-range to expensive hotels are more spread out, but a good place to start is **Jhansi Lakshmi Bai Road**, which runs south from the railway station. If you're looking for a palace, then head straight for ITDC's opulent *Ashok Lalitha Mahal*.

Dasaprakash, Gandhi Square ☎0821/442444, ⓕ443456. Slightly faded large hotel complex round a spacious courtyard; busy, clean and efficient, though lacking character. Some a/c rooms, cheap singles and a veg restaurant. ❸–❻

Govardhan, opposite the Opera cinema, Sri Harsha Road ☎0821/434118, ⓕ420998. Basic budget rooms close to Ghandi Square. Frayed around the edges, but clean enough. ❷–❸

Green, Chittaranjan Palace, 2270 Vinoba Rd, Jayalakshmipuram ☎0821/512536, ⓕ516139. On the western outskirts, a former royal palace refurbished as an elegant, eco-conscious two-star, in large gardens, awarded the prize for best garden in Mysore in 1998. Spacious rooms, lounges, verandas, a croquet lawn and well-stocked library. All profits to charities and environmental projects. Their auto-rickshaw will pick you up with prior arrangement and they can also be contacted through the Charities Advisory Trust in London ☎020/7431 3739. ❻–❽

Indra Bhavan, Dhanavantri Road ☎0821/423933, ⓕ422290, ⓔhotel_Indra_bhavan @rediffmail.com. Dilapidated and characterful old lodge popular with Tibetans, with en suite singles and doubles. Their "ordinary" rooms are a little grubby, but the good-value "deluxe" have clean tiled floors and open onto a wide common veranda. ❷–❹

ITDC Ashok Lalitha Mahal Palace, T Narasipur Road ☎0821/571265, ⓕ571770. On a slope overlooking the city in the distance, and visible

for miles around, this white, Neoclassical palace was built in 1931 to accommodate the maharaja's foreign guests. Now it's a Raj-style fantasy, popular with tour groups and film crews. Tariffs are astronomical by Indian standards, ranging from $70 to $740 per night for the "Viceroy Suite". The tea lounge, restaurant and pool (Rs130) are open to non-residents. Free snooker table in bar. ❾

KSTDC Mayura Hoysala, 2 Jhansi Laxmi Bai Rd ☎0821/425349. Reasonably priced rooms and suites in a colonial-era mansion with a terrace restaurant and beer garden. Good value but the food is uninspiring and there is no room service. ❹–❻

KSTDC Yatri Niwas, 2 Jhansi Laxmi Bai Rd ☎0821/423492. The government-run *Mayura Hoysala*'s economy wing: simple rooms around a central garden, with a beer garden and lounge restaurant next door, and dorm beds for Rs70. ❶–❸

Mannars, Chandragupta Road ☎0821/448060. Budget hotel near the bus stand and Gandhi Square. No frills, though deluxe rooms have TV. Deservedly popular with backpackers. ❷–❸

Palace Plaza, Sri Harsha Road ☎0821/430034, ⓕ421070. A modern multistorey block close to all amenities where the cheaper rooms are poky but reasonable value. There are also a few a/c deluxes with extraordinary round beds and mirrored ceilings – no doubt meant for honeymooners. The restaurant is good. ❹–❻

The Paradise, 104 Vivekananda Rd, Yadavgiri ☏ 0821/410366, ℻ 514400, ✉ paradise@blr.vsnl .net.in. *Dasaprakash*'s upmarket hotel; new and modern with luxurious rooms and all facilities including an excellent South Indian vegetarian restaurant. ❺–❻

Park Lane, Sri Harsha Road ☏ 0821/434340. Eight pleasant clean rooms backing onto a popular beer-garden/restaurant. One of the best deals at this price, but can get noisy and has some dodgy plumbing. Avoid room 8 (it's next to the generator). ❷

Rajabhadra, Gandhi Square ☏ 0821/443023. Best value of several look-a-like lodges on the square. The front rooms are great if you don't mind being in the thick of things. Some singles. ❷

Ritz, Bangalore–Nilgiri Road ☏ 0821/422668. Wonderful colonial-era hotel, a stone's throw from the Private bus stand. At the top of this category, but worth the extra. Only four rooms, so book ahead. ❹

S.C.V.D.S., Sri Harsha Road ☏ 0821/421379, ℻ 426297. Spanking new lodge with cable TV in most rooms and some a/c. Very friendly and offers a Rs50 discount to foreigners. ❸–❻

Sangeeth, 1966 Narayana Shastry Rd, near the Udipi Krishna temple ☏ 0821/424693. One of Mysore's best all-round budget deals: bland and a bit boxed-in, but central, friendly and very good value. ❷–❸

Southern Star, Vinobha Road ☏ 0821/426426, ℻ 421689, ✉ southernstar@vsnl.com. Modern and comfortable monolithic hotel, affiliated to *Quality Inn*, with all facilities including two restaurants, a bar and a swimming pool. ❾

Viceroy, Sri Harsha Road ☏ 0821/428001, ℻ 433391. Snazzy new business-oriented hotel, with most mod cons and views over the park to the palace from front rooms. Mostly a/c. Quality restaurant on the ground floor. ❻–❼

The City

In addition to its official tourist attractions, Mysore is a great city simply to stroll around. The characterful, if dilapidated, pre-Independence buildings lining market areas such as **Ashoka Road** and **Sayaji Rao Road** lend an air of faded grandeur to the busy centre, teeming with vibrant street life. The best place to get a sense of what's on offer is the Government Cauvery Arts and Crafts Emporium, Sayaji Rao Road (closed Thurs), which stocks a wide range of local crafts that can be shipped overseas. Elsewhere, souvenir stores spill over with the famous **sandalwood**. The city's famous **Devaraja Market**, on Sayaji Rao Road, is one of South India's most atmospheric produce markets: a giant complex of covered stalls bursting with bananas (the delicious *nanjangod* variety), luscious mangoes, blocks of sticky jaggery and conical heaps of lurid *kunkum* powder.

Silk weaving in Mysore

As an important centre of silk production, Mysore has several silk factories, the most prestigious of which is the Karnataka Silk Industries Corporation's Silk Weaving Factory (Mon–Sat 10am–4pm) on HD Kote Road, 4km from the centre. Visitors are welcome and the showroom offers silk – mostly saris – at fixed but competitive prices. You will need a chit from the office to enter the complex; there are no conducted tours. The large factory founded in the 1920s by the Maharaja of Mysore, runs in shifts signalled by wailing sirens, and consists of huge workshops filled with automated machines. You can see the silk being loomed, some batches with pure gold thread, before it goes into the dyeing process. The machine tenders are happy to explain the operation to you but with the machines working flat out, you'll be lucky if you can hear a word over the deafening din. They also have a showroom at *KSTDC Yatri Niwas* hotel.

Mysore centre is dominated by the walled **Maharaja's Palace** (daily 10.30am–5.30pm; Rs10), a fairy-tale spectacle, topped with a shining brass-plated dome surmounting a single tower; it's especially magnificent on Sunday nights and during festivals, when it is illuminated by no fewer than five thousand light bulbs. Designed in the hybrid Indo-Saracenic style by Henry Irwin, the British consultant architect of Madras state, it was completed in 1912 for the twenty-fourth Wadiyar Raja, on the site of the old wooden palace that had been destroyed by fire in 1897. Twelve temples surround the palace, some of them of much earlier origin. Although there are six gates in the perimeter wall, entry is on the south side only. Shoes and cameras must be left at the cloakroom inside.

An extraordinary amalgam of styles from India and around the world crowds the lavish **interior**. Entry is through the Gombe Thotti or **Dolls' Pavilion**, once a showcase for the figures featured in the city's lively Dussehra celebrations and now a gallery of European and Indian sculpture and ceremonial objects. Halfway along the pavilion, the brass **Elephant Gate** forms the main entrance to the centre of the palace, through which the maharaja would drive to his car park. Decorated with floriate designs, it bears the Mysore royal symbol of a double-headed eagle, now the state emblem. To the north, past the gate, are dolls dating from the turn of the century, a wooden *mandapa* glinting with mirrorwork, and at the end, a ceremonial wooden elephant *howdah* (frame to carry passengers). Elaborately decorated with 84kg of 24-carat gold, it appears to be inlaid with red and green gems – in fact the twinkling lights are battery-powered signals to let the *mahout* know when the maharaja wished to stop or go.

Walls leading into the octagonal **Kalyana Mandapa**, the royal wedding hall, are lined with a meticulously detailed frieze of oil paintings illustrating the great Mysore Dussehra festival of 1930, executed over fifteen years by four Indian artists. The hall itself is magnificent, a cavernous space featuring cast-iron pillars from Glasgow, Bohemian chandeliers and multicoloured Belgian stained glass arranged in peacock designs in the domed ceiling. A mosaic of English floor tiles repeats the peacock motif. Beyond here lie small rooms cluttered with grandiose furniture, including a pair of silver chairs and others of Belgian cut-crystal made for the maharaja and Lord Mountbatten, the last Viceroy of India. One of the rooms has a fine ceiling of Burma teak carved by local craftsmen.

Climbing a staircase with Italian marble balustrades, past an unnervingly realistic life-size plaster-of-Paris figure of Krishnaraja Wadiyar IV, lounging comfortably with his bejewelled feet on a stool, you come into the **Public Durbar Hall**, an Orientalist fantasy often compared to a setting from *A Thousand and One Nights*. A vision of brightly painted and gilded colonnades, open on one side, the massive hall affords views out across the parade ground and gardens to Chamundi Hill. The maharaja gave audience from here, seated on a throne made from 280kg of solid Karnatakan gold. These days, the hall is only used during the Dussehra festival, when it hosts classical concerts. Paintings by the celebrated artists Shilpi Siddalingaswamy and Raja Rama Varma, from the Travancore (Kerala) royal family, adorn the walls. The whole is crowned by white marble, inlaid with delicate floral scrolls of jasper, amber and lapis lazuli in the Moghul style. Somewhat out of sync with the opulence, a series of ceiling panels of Vishnu, painted on fire-proof asbestos, date from the 1930s. The

Following the tradition set by the Vijayanagar kings, the ten-day festival of Dussehra (Sept/Oct), to commemorate the goddess Durga's slaying of the demon buffalo, Mahishasura, is celebrated in grand style at Mysore. Scores of cultural events occur, including concerts of South Indian classical (Carnatic) music and dance performances, in the great Durbar Hall of the Maharaja's Palace. On Vijayadasmi, the tenth and last day of the festival, a magnificent procession of mounted guardsmen on horseback and caprisoned elephants – one carrying the palace deity, Chaamundeshwari, on a gold *howdah* – marches 5km from the palace to Banni Mantap. There's also a floating festival in the temple tank at the foot of Chamundi Hill and a procession of chariots around the temple at the top. A torchlight parade takes place in the evening, followed by a massive firework display and much jubilation in the streets.

smaller **Private Durbar Hall** features especially beautiful stained glass and gold-leaf painting. Before leaving you pass two embossed silver doors – all that remains of the old palace.

Nearby, behind the main palace building but within the same compound, a line of tacky souvenir shops leads to a small **museum** (same hours; Rs15) run by the royal family which shows paintings from the Thanjavur and Mysore schools, some inlaid with precious stones and gold leaf. After a lengthy judicial tussle, in 1998 the courts decided in favour of formally placing the main palace in the hands of the Karnataka state government but the royal family, who still hold a claim, are set to appeal.

Jaganmohan Palace: Jayachamarajendra Art Gallery

Built in 1861, the **Jaganmohan Palace** (daily 8am–5pm; Rs5; no cameras), 300m west of the Maharaja's Palace, was used as a royal residence until it was turned into a picture gallery and museum in 1915 by Maharaja Krishnaraja Wadiyar IV. Most of the "contemporary" art on show dates from the 1930s, when a revival of Indian painting was spearheaded by E.B. Havell and the Tagore brothers Abandrinath and Ganganendranath in Bengal.

On the ground floor, a series of faded black-and-white photos of ceremonial occasions shares space with elaborate imported clocks. Nineteenth- and twentieth-century paintings dominate the first floor; among them is the work of the pioneering oil painter Raja Ravi Varma who, although not everyone's cup of tea, has been credited with introducing modern techniques to Indian art. Inspired by European masters, Varma gained a reputation in portraiture and also depicted epic Indian themes from the classics, such as the demon king Ravana absconding with Rama's wife Sita. Games on the upper floor include circular *ganjeeb* playing cards illustrated with portraits of royalty or deities and board games delicately inlaid with ivory. There's also a cluster of musical instruments, among them a brass *jaltarang* set and glass xylophone, and harmonicas and clarinet played by Krishnaraja Wadiyar IV himself. Another gallery, centring on a large wooden Ganesh seated on a tortoise, is lined with paintings, including Krishnaraja Wadiyar sporting with the "inmates" of his *zenana* (women's quarter of the palace) during Holi.

Chamundi Hill

Chamundi Hill, 3km southeast of the city, is topped with a temple to the chosen deity of the Mysore Rajas: the goddess Chamundi, or Durga, who slew the demon buffalo Mahishasura. It's a pleasant, easy bus trip (#201 from the City bus stand) to the top: sit on the left side for the best views; the walk down, past a huge Nandi – Shiva's bull – takes about thirty minutes. Pilgrims, of course, make the trip in reverse order. The walk isn't very demanding, but by the end of it, after more than a thousand steps, your legs are likely to be a bit wobbly. Take plenty of drinking water, especially if you're walking in the middle of the day.

Don't be surprised if, at the top of the hill, which is dominated by the temple's forty-metre *gopura*, you're struck by a feeling of *déjà vu*: at the **Godly Museum** at the summit, one of the displays states, "5000 years ago at this time you had visited this place in the same way you are visiting now. Because world drama repeats itself identically every 5000 years." Another exhibit goes to the heart of our "problematic world: filthy films, lack of true education, blind faith, irreligiousness, bad habits and selfishness". Suitably edified, proceed along a path from the bus stand, past trinket and tea stalls, to the temple square. Immediately to the right, at the end of this path, are four bollards painted with a red stripe; return here after visiting the temples, when you want to take the path back down the hill.

Non-Hindus can visit the twelfth-century **temple** (daily 8am–noon & 5–8pm; leave shoes opposite the entrance), staffed by friendly priests who will plaster your forehead in vermilion paste. The Chamundi figure inside is solid gold; outside, in the courtyard, stands a fearsome if gaily coloured statue of the demon Mahishasura. On leaving, if you continue by the path instead of retracing your steps, you can return to the square via two other temples and various buildings storing ceremonial paraphernalia and animal figures used during Dussehra. You'll also come across loads of scampering monkeys and the odd dreadlocked *sadhu*, who will willingly pose for your holiday snaps – for a consideration. The magnificent five-metre **Nandi**, carved from a single piece of black granite in 1659, is an object of worship himself, adorned with bells and garlands and tended by his own priest. Minor shrines, dedicated to Chamundi and the monkey god Hanuman among others, line the side of the path and, at the bottom, a little shrine to Ganesh lies near a chai-shop. From here it's usually possible to pick up an auto-rickshaw or bus, back into the city, but at weekends the latter are often full. If you walk on towards the city, passing a temple on the left, with a big water tank (the site of the floating festival during Dussehra), you come after ten minutes to the main road between the *Lalitha Mahal Palace* and the city; there's a bus stop, and often auto-rickshaws, at the junction.

Eating

Mysore has scores of **places to eat**, from numerous South Indian "meals" joints dotted around the market to the opulent *Lalita Mahal*, where you can work up an appetite for a gourmet meal with a few lengths of the pool. To sample the celebrated Mysore *pak*, a sweet, rich, crumbly mixture made of ghee and maize flour, queue at *Guru Sweet Mart*, a small stall at KR Circle, Savaji Rao Road, which is considered the best sweet shop in the city. Another speciality from this part of the world is *malligi iddli*, a delicate light fluffy *iddli* usually served in the mornings and at lunch at several of the downtown "meals" restaurants.

Akshaya, *Hotel Dasaprakash*, Gandhi Square. Very good South Indian veg "meals" joint, serving various thalis (try the "special"), ice creams and cold drinks. Low on atmosphere, but the food is delicious and cheap.

Bombay Indra Bhavan, Savaji Rao Road. Comfortable and popular veg restaurant that serves both south and North Indian cuisine and sweets. Their other branch on Dhanavantri Road (see Accommodation) is equally if not more popular and also has an a/c section.

Gopika, *Govardhan Lodge*, Sri Harsh Road. Inexpensive "meals" restaurant on the ground floor of a busy hotel; opens early for Indian breakfasts of *iddlis*, *wada*, pakora and big glasses of hot-milk coffee.

Lalitha Mahal, T Naraispur Road. Sample the charms of this palatial five-star with an expensive hot drink in the atmospheric tea lounge, or an à la carte lunch in the grand dining hall, accompanied by live sitar music. The old-style bar also boasts a full-size billiards table.

Park Lane, Sri Harsha Road. Congenial courtyard restaurant-cum-beer garden (see Accommodation), with moderately priced veg and non-veg food (meat sizzlers are a speciality), pot plants and live Indian classical music every evening. Popular with travellers, but they actively discourage Indians and foreigners from sitting together.

Pizza Corner, Bangalore-Nilgiri Road, near Harding Circle. New branch of the Bangalore chain serving high-quality pizza amid typically Western decor.

Ritz, Bangalore–Nilgiri Road. Central and secluded hotel restaurant, and a nice escape from the city streets for a drink, or veg and non-veg meals. The best tables are in courtyard at the back. Opens at 8.30am for "omelette-bread-butter-jam" break-fasts.

RRR, Gandhi Square. A plain "meals" restaurant in front with a small but plush a/c room at the back which gets packed at lunch times and at week-ends. Well worth the wait for its excellent set menus on banana leaves, chicken biryani and fried fish.

Shilpastri, Gandhi Square. Quality North Indian-style food, with particularly tasty tandoori (great chicken tikka). Plenty of good veg options, too, including lots of dhals and curd rice. Serves alcohol.

Around Mysore

Mysore is a jumping-off point for some of Karnataka's most popular destina-tions. At **Srirangapatnam**, the fort, palace and mausoleum date from the era of Tipu Sultan, the "Tiger of Mysore", a perennial thorn in the side of the British. To the southeast, the superb **Hoysala temple** of **Somnathpur** is an architectural masterpiece, while the little-visited hilltop Jain shrine at **Gomatagiri** is a veritable oasis of tranquillity northwest of the city.

If you're heading south towards Ooty, **Bandipur National Park**'s forests and hill scenery offer another escape from the city, although your chances of spot-ting any rare animals are actually quite slim. The same is true of **Nagarhole National Park**, three hours southwest of Mysore in the Coorg region.

Srirangapatnam

The tiny island of **Srirangapatnam**, in the Kaveri (Cauvery) River, 14km north of Mysore, measures only 5km by 1km. Long a site of Hindu pilgrim-age, it is named for its tenth-century Sriranganathaswamy Vishnu temple, which in 1133 served as a refuge for the philosopher Ramanuja, a staunch Vaishnavite, from the Shaivite Cholas in Tamil Nadu. The Vijayanagars built a fort here in 1454, and in 1616 it became the capital of the Mysore Wadiyar Rajas. However, Srirangapatnam is more famously associated with **Haider Ali**, who deposed the Wadiyars in 1761, and even more so with his son, **Tipu Sultan**. During Tipu's seventeen-year reign – which ended with his death in 1799, when the future Duke of Wellington took the fort at the bloody battle of Seringapatnam – he posed a greater threat than any other Indian ruler to British plans to dominate India.

Tipu Sultan and his father were responsible for transforming the small state of Mysore into a major Muslim power. Born in 1750, of a Hindu mother, Tipu Sultan inherited Haider Ali's considerable military skills. However, unlike his illiterate father, he was an educated, cultured man who introduced radical agri-cultural reforms. His burning life-long desire to rid India of the hated British invaders naturally brought him an ally in the French. He obsessively embraced

If you're contemplating a long haul, the best way to travel is by train, usually with a change at Bangalore. Six or seven express services leave Mysore each day for the Karnatakan capital, taking between 2hr and 3hr 30min to cover the 139km. The fastest of these, the a/c Shatabdi Express (#2008, daily except Tues 2.20pm) continues on to Chennai (7hr 5min); most of the others terminate in Bangalore, where you can pick up long-distance connections to a wide range of Indian cities (see p.316), though the daily Mysore–Thanjavur Express #6232 swings round south to Thanjavur (3.30pm; 14hr 50min) and every Friday the Swamajayanti Express goes all the way to Hazrat Nizamuddin in Delhi (4.20pm; 53hr). Reservations can be made at Mysore's computerized booking hall inside the station (Mon–Sat 8am–2pm & 2.15–8pm, Sun 8am–2pm). There's no tourist counter; take a good book. Due to continuing work upgrading the line, trains to Hassan are subject to disruption but theoretically there are four passenger trains a day (3–4hr), though it's better to take the bus unless you verify that they are running properly.

Reservations are not required for Bangalore (except on the Shatabdi Express), so you shouldn't ever have to do the trip by bus, which takes longer and is a lot more terrifying. If you do have to take a bus, KSRTC services leave at least every 30min from Central Bus stand, but there are few private coaches on that route. Most destinations within a day's ride of Mysore can only be reached by road. Long-distance services operate out of the Central bus stand, where you can book computerized tickets up to three days in advance. English timetables are posted on the wall inside the entrance hall, and there's a helpful enquiries counter in the corner of the compound. Regular buses leave here for Hassan, jumping-off place for the Hoysala temples at Belur and Halebid, and for Channarayapatna/Sravanabelgola (every 30min; 2–3hr). Heading south to Ooty (5hr), there's a choice of eight buses, all of which stop at Bandipur National Park. Direct services to Hospet, the nearest town to Hampi (the overnight bus leaves at 7pm and takes 10hr), and several cities in Kerala, including Kannur, Kozhikode and Kochi, also operate from Mysore and there is the option of deluxe private buses on these routes too. The only way to travel direct to Goa is on the 4pm overnight bus that arrives at Panjim at 9am. Most travellers, however, break this long trip into stages, heading first to Mangalore (12–15 daily; 7hr), and working their way north from there, usually via Gokarn – which you can also reach by direct bus (1 daily; 14hr) – or Jog Falls. Mangalore-bound buses and coaches tend to pass through Madikeri, capital of Kodagu (Coorg), which is also served by hourly buses most of which travel through the Tibetan enclave of Bylakuppe. For details of services to Somnathpur and Srirangapatnam, see the relevant accounts below.

Mysore doesn't have an airport (the nearest one is at Bangalore), but you can confirm and book Indian Airlines flights at their office in the KSTDC *Mayura Hoysala* (Mon–Sat 10am–1.30pm & 2.15–5pm; ☎0821/421846).

③

KARNATAKA | Around Mysore

---

his popular name of the **Tiger of Mysore**, surrounding himself with symbols and images of tigers; much of his memorabilia is decorated with the animal or its stripes, and, like the Romans, he is said to have kept tigers for the punishment of criminals.

Tipu Sultan's Srirangapatnam was largely destroyed by the British, but parts of the fort area in the northwest survive, including gates, ramparts, arsenals, the grim dungeons (where chained British prisoners were allegedly forced to stand neck-deep in water) and the domed and minareted Jami Masjid mosque.

The former summer palace, the **Daria Daulat Bagh** (Sat–Thurs 10am–5pm; $5 [Rs5]), literally meaning "wealth of the sea", is situated 1km east of the fort and was used to entertain Tipu Sultan's guests. At first sight, this low, wooden colonnaded building set in an attractive formal garden fails to impress because most of it is obscured by sunscreens. However, the superbly preserved interior, displaying ornamental arches, tiger-striped columns and floral decoration on every inch of the teak walls and ceiling, is remarkable. A much-repainted mural on the west wall relishes every detail of Haider Ali's victory over the British at Pollilore in 1780. Upstairs, a small collection of Tipu Sultan memorabilia, European paintings, Persian manuscripts on handmade paper and a model of Srirangapatnam are on show.

An avenue of cypress trees leads from an intricately carved gateway to the **Gumbaz mausoleum**, 3km east of the palace. Built by Tipu Sultan in 1784 to commemorate Haider Ali, and to serve as his own resting place, the lower half of the grey granite edifice is crowned by a dome of whitewashed brick and plaster. Ivory-inlaid rosewood doors lead to the tombs of Haider Ali and Tipu Sultan, each covered by a pall (tiger stripes for Tipu), and an Urdu tablet records

Wildlife sanctuaries around Mysore

Mysore lies within striking distance of three major wildlife sanctuaries – Bandipur, Nagarhole, and Mudumalai, across the border in Tamil Nadu – all of which are part of the vast Nilgiri Biosphere Reserve. In recent years, however, all three have been affected by the presence of the bandit Veerapan (see p.570) and large parts of these forest tracts are often closed to visitors. If you are thinking of going there, check with the tourist office to see which parts are open. In early 2001 a curfew during the hours of darkness even extended to the Mysore–Ooty road while an army operation to flush him out was in progress. You will require a good deal of forward planning if you want to get the most out of the sanctuaries. A few upmarket private "resorts" on the edge of the parks and one or two tourist complexes allow visitors to experience some of the delights in an area renowned for its elephants. Forest Department accommodation at Bandipur (see p.246) and Nagarhole (see p.248) must be booked as far in advance as possible through the Chief Warden, Aranya Bhavan, Ashokapuram (⊕ 0821/480901), 6km south of the centre of Mysore, on bus #61 from the City stand. To arrange accommodation at Mudumalai, you'll have to phone ahead (see p.569). Note that the Forest Department's rest houses can only be booked in Ooty.

Two lesser wildlife sanctuaries are within striking distance of Mysore. The closer, some 2km southwest of Srirangapatnam is the Ranganathittu Bird Sanctuary (daily 9am–6pm; Rs100). It's a must for ornithologists, especially during October and November, when the lake, fed by the Kaveri River, attracts huge flocks of migrating birds. At other times it's a tranquil spot to escape the city, where you can enjoy boat rides through the backwaters to look for crocodiles, otters and dozens of species of resident waders, wildfowl and forest birds. The easiest way to get there is by rickshaw from Srirangapatnam. The Biligiri Rangaswamy Wildlife Sanctuary, 90km to the east of Mysore, lies in an unspoiled corner of the state inhabited by the Soliga tribe. Covering an area of 525 square kilometres, the deciduous forests spread over the picturesque Biligiri Rangaswamy Hills harbour a myriad forms of wildlife, including elephant, panther, tiger, wild dog, sloth bear and several species of deer. Despite the thick cover, the sanctuary is a bird-watcher's dream with over 270 species, including the majestic crested hawk eagle. Accessible by bus via Nanjangod and Chamarajnagar, the sanctuary is being promoted by Jungle Lodges & Resorts, Bangalore (⊕ 080/558 6163), a government-sponsored organization which aims to promote wildlife in the state through comfortable, upmarket camps and resorts. For an all-inclusive stay including elephant ride and forest walks, their luxurious camp at the sanctuary charges Indian visitors Rs1000 per person per night and foreigners US$60.

Tipu Sultan's martyrdom. The interior walls are also painted in striking tiger colours.

At the heart of the fortress, the great temple of **Sriranganathaswamy** still stands proud and virtually untouched by the turbulent history that has flowed around it, and remains, for many devotees, the prime draw. Developed by succeeding dynasties, the temple consists of three distinctive sanctuaries and is entered via an impressive five-storey gateway and a hall that was built by Haider Ali. The innermost sanctum, the oldest part of the temple, is open to all and contains an image of the reclining Vishnu.

Practicalities

Frequent **buses** from Mysore City bus stand (including #316), and all the Mysore–Bangalore **trains**, pull in near the temple and fort. Srirangapatnam is a small island, but places of interest are quite spread out; tongas, auto-rickshaws and bicycles are available on the main road near the bus stand. The KSTDC **hotel**-cum-restaurant, *Mayura River View* (☏0821/52114; ❹–❺), occupies a pleasant spot beside the Kaveri, 3km from the bus stand, and another good option is the smart and elegant *Fort View Resorts* (☏08236/52777; ❻–❼), set in its own grounds not far from the fort entrance.

Gomatagiri

Few of Mysore's residents have ever been out to the hill of **Gomatagiri**, 18km to the northwest of the city near the small town of Bettadoor where, on a rocky granite outcrop, a monolithic five-metre-high statue of **Gomateshvara** stands atop a 25-metre mound gazing serenely over the surrounding countryside. Also known as Bahubali, the son of the first Jain *tirthankara*, Gomateshvara is shown here, as he is in sites all over southern Karnataka, naked and in a state of deep meditation with his arms limp by his sides. An idyllic spot among eucalyptus groves, Gomatagiri sees no tourists and the only other building here besides the temple on top of the hill is the Jain guesthouse where the welcoming caretaker-cum-priest lives; he will gladly open the temple for you.

Small shrines litter the base of the outcrop and house the footprints of the 24 Jain *tirthankaras*. Steps hewn out of rock lead up to the temple and the eleventh-century statue with distant views out towards the Brindavan Gardens and the Krishnaraja Sagar dam on the Kaveri River. The only time the peace of the place is at all disturbed is during the **Mastakabhisheka ceremony** around September every year, when the statue is anointed with a nectar of milk.

Practicalities

If you are tempted to stay here, **accommodation** is limited to the very basic rooms of the guesthouse (❶), none of which have beds, so bring a mat. With ample notice, the caretaker priest will provide simple vegetarian food. Bus #264 from Mysore's City bus stand runs past Gomatagiri five times a day with the first bus at 6.30am and the last at 6.30pm. The journey takes one hour and the bus continues to a village a short distance past Gomatagiri; after a short break the bus returns the way it came to Mysore.

Somnathpur

Built in 1268 AD, the exquisite **Keshava Vishnu temple** (daily 9am–5pm; $5 [Rs5]), in the sleepy hamlet of **SOMNATHPUR**, was the last important temple to be constructed by the Hoysalas; it is also the most complete and, in many respects, the finest example of this singular style (see p.677). Somnathpur itself, just ninety minutes from Mysore by road, is little more than a few neat tracks and some attractive simple houses with pillared verandas.

Like other Hoysala temples, the Keshava is built on a star-shaped plan, but, as a triple shrine, it represents a mature development from the earlier constructions. ASI staff can show you around and also grant you permission to clamber on the enclosure walls, to get a marvellous bird's-eye view of the modestly proportioned structure. It's best to do this as early as possible, as the stone gets very hot to walk on in bare feet.

The temple is in the style of a *trikutachala* or "three-peaked hill", with a tower on each shrine – a configuration also seen in certain Chalukya temples, and three temples on Hemakuta Hill at Vijayanagar (Hampi; see p.296). Each shrine, sharing a common hallway, is dedicated to a different form of Vishnu. In order of "seniority" they are Keshava in the central shrine, Venugopala to the right and Jagannath to the left. The Keshava shrine features a very unusual *chandrasila* or "moonstone" step at its entrance and, diverging from the usual semicircular Hoysala style, has two pointed projections.

The Keshava's high plinth (*jagati*) provides an upper ambulatory, which on its outer edge reproduces the almost crenellated shape of the structure and allows visitors to approach the upper registers of the profusely decorated walls. Among the many superb images here are an unusually high proportion of Shaivite figures for a Vishnu temple. As at Halebid, a lively frieze details countless episodes from the *Ramayana*, *Bhagavata Purana* and *Mahabharata*. Intended to accompany circumambulation, the panels are "read" (there is no text) in a clockwise direction. Unusually, the temple is autographed; all its sculpture was the work of one man, named Malitamba.

Outside the temple stands a *dvajastambha* column, which may originally have been surmounted by a figure of Vishnu's bird-vehicle Garuda. The wide ground-level ambulatory that circles the whole building is edged with numerous, now empty, shrines.

Practicalities

There are no direct **buses** from Mysore to Somnathpur. Buses from the Private stand run every fifteen minutes to T Narasipur (1hr), served by half-hourly buses to Somnathpur (20min). Everyone will know where you want to go, and someone will show you which scrum to join. Alternatively, join one of KSTDC's guided tours (see p.236).

You can stay at the government-owned but privately run *Tourist Rest House* (no phone; ➊), but the ultra basic rooms are grubby and cannot be booked in advance. Also the only **food** available is biscuits or maybe a samosa at one of the chai stalls or fruit from a street-seller; you'll have to go back to the cheap "meals" hotels at T Narasipur for anything more substantial.

Bandipur National Park

Situated among the broken foothills of the Western Ghat mountains, **Bandipur National Park** (6am–6pm; Rs150 [Rs10]; Rs10 extra for camera, Rs100 for video) 80km south of Mysore, covers 880 square kilometres of dry deciduous forest, south of the Kabini River. The reserve was created in the 1930s from the local maharaja's hunting lands, and expanded in 1941 to adjoin the Nagarhole National Park to the north, and Madumalai and Wynad sanctuaries to the south in Tamil Nadu. These now collectively comprise the huge **Nilgiri Biosphere Reserve**, one of India's most extensive areas of protected forest.

Access to Bandipur National Park is **severely restricted** at present, due to activities of the bandit, Veerapan – an alleged kidnapper and smuggler – although parts, such as Gopalswamy Betta, remain open to visitors with their own vehicles. Visitors should check, however, with forest authorities before travelling around the park. In any case, Bandipur, in spite of its good accommodation and well-maintained metalled Jeep tracks, is a disappointment as a tourist destination. Glimpses of anything rarer than a langur or spotted deer are infrequent outside the core area, which is off-limits to casual visitors, and the noisy diesel bus laid on by the Forest Department to transport tourists around the accessible areas of the park scares off what little fauna remain. If you're hoping to spot a tiger, forget it.

On the plus side, Bandipur is one of the few reserves in India where you stand a good chance of sighting wild **elephants**, particularly in the wet season (June–Sept), when water and forage are plentiful and the animals evenly scattered. Later in the monsoon, huge herds congregate on the banks of the Kabini River, in the far north of the park, where you can see the remnants of an old stockade used by one particularly zealous nineteenth-century British hunter as an elephant trap. Bandipur also boasts some fine scenery: at **Gopalswamy Betta**, 9km from the park headquarters, a high ridge looks north over the Mysore Plateau and its adjoining hills, while to the south, the **Rolling Rocks** afford sweeping views of the craggy, 260-metre-deep **Mysore Ditch**.

Practicalities

The **best time to visit** is during the rainy season (June–Sept); unlike neighbouring parks, Bandipur's roads do not get washed out by the annual deluge, and elephants are more numerous at this time. By November to December, however, most of the larger animals have migrated across the state border into Mudumalai, where water is more plentiful in the dry season. Try to avoid weekends, as the park attracts bus loads of noisy day-trippers.

Getting to Bandipur by bus is easy; all the regular KSRTC services to Ooty from Mysore's Central bus stand (12 daily; 2hr 30min) pass through the reserve (the last one back to Mysore leaves at 5pm), stopping outside the Forest Department's reception centre (daily 9am–4.30pm). If you miss the last bus from Mysore you can change at Gundulapet, 18km away, from where you can also take a taxi to the main reception centre (Rs200).

KSTDC's *Mayura Prakruthi* at Melkamanahally (⊕08229/7301; ④–⑤), 4km before Bandipur, has pleasant cottages with large, comfortable rooms and a restaurant. If the park is officially open, you can confirm accommodation bookings within the sanctuary at the Forest Department's reception centre. The rooms on offer are basic, but good value, ranging from the "VIP" *Gajendra Cottages* (⑨), which have en-suite bathrooms and verandas, to beds in large, institutional dorms. The *chowkidars* will knock up simple meals by arrangement. Upmarket options include *Tusker Trails*, a **resort** run by members of the royal family of Mysore, at Mangala village, 3km from Bandipur (bookable through their office at Hospital Cottage, Bangalore Palace, Bangalore; ⊕080/353 0748, ⊕334 2862; ⑨), which has cottages, a swimming pool and a tennis court and organizes trips into the forest. *Bush Betta*, off the main Mysore highway (booked through Gainnet, Raheja Plaza, Richmond Road, Bangalore; ⊕080/551 2631; ⑨), offers comfortable cottages and guided tours. Beds in the park are very limited, and it is essential to book accommodation in advance through the **Forest Department** office in Bangalore (Aranya Bhavan, 18th Cross, Malleswaram; ⊕080/334 1993), or at Mysore (Project Tiger, Aranya Bhavan, Ashokapuram; ⊕0821/480901).

Unless you have your own vehicle, the only **transport** around the park is the hopeless Forest Department bus, which makes two tours daily (7.30am & 4.30pm; 1hr). You may see a deer or two, but nothing more, on the half-hour **elephant ride** around the reception compound. Visitors travelling to Gopalswamy Betta should note that car rental is not available at Bandipur, but at Gundulapet, from where they will try and charge a lot more than the official Rs500. You must exit the park before nightfall.

Nagarhole National Park

Bandipur's northern neighbour, **Nagarhole** (Snake River) **National Park**, extends 640 square kilometres north from the Kabini River, which was dammed in 1974 to form a picturesque artificial lake. During the dry season (Feb–June), this perennial water source attracts large numbers of animals, making it a potentially prime spot for sighting wildlife. The forest here is of the moist, deciduous type – thick jungle with a thirty-metre-high canopy – and more impressive than Bandipur's drier scrub.

However, disaster struck Nagarhole in 1992, when friction between local pastoralist "tribals" and the park wardens over grazing rights and poaching erupted into a spate of arson attacks. Thousands of acres of forest were burned to the ground. The trees have grown back in places, but it will be decades before animal numbers completely recover. An added threat to the fragile jungle tracts of the region is a notorious gang of female wood-smugglers from Kerala, which has developed a fearsome and almost mythical Amazon-like reputation. Meanwhile, Nagarhole is only worth visiting at the height of the dry season, when its muddy river banks and grassy swamps, or *hadlus*, offer better chances of sighting gaur (Indian bison), elephant, *dhole* (wild dog), deer, boar and even the odd tiger or leopard, than any of the neighbouring sanctuaries.

Practicalities

Nagarhole is open year-round, but avoid the monsoons, when floods wash out most of its dirt tracks and a proliferation of leeches makes hiking impossible. To get there from Mysore, catch one of the two daily **buses** from the Central stand to **Hunsur** (3hr), which is 10km from the park's north gate, where you can pick up transport to the Forest Department's two rest houses (❷–❺). The **rest houses** have to be booked well in advance through the Forest Department offices in Mysore or Bangalore (see p.247). Turn up on spec, and you'll be told accommodation is "not available". It is also important to arrive at the park gates well before dusk, as the road through the reserve to the lodges closes at 6pm, and is prone to "elephant blocks".

The Nagarhole **visitor centre** is open 24hr and charges Rs150 [Rs10] for entrance for the park, plus Rs10 for a camera and Rs100 for a video. They do not organize elephant rides, but schedule four bus tours – two in the morning starting at 6am, and two in the afternoon – for a minimum of two people.

Other **accommodation** around Nagarhole includes the highly acclaimed and luxurious *Kabini River Lodge* (book through Jungle Lodges & Resorts in Bangalore; ☎080/559 7021; ⓞ), approached via the village of Karapura, 3km from the park's south entrance. Set in its own leafy compound on the lakeside, this former maharaja's hunting lodge offers expensive all-inclusive deals that include transport around the park with expert guides. It's impossible to reach by public transport, so you'll need to rent a taxi – in rural South India, this signifies a car with no meter – to get there and you will also have to book well in advance. Another upmarket option but not quite in the same league, the *Jungle Inn* at Veerana Hosahalli (℡08222/52781; 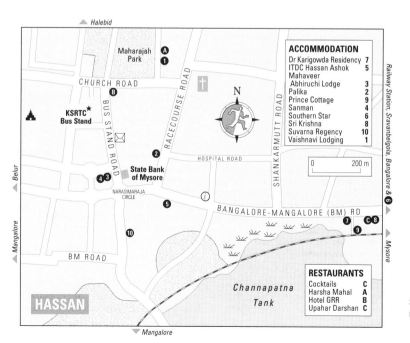; booked through their Bangalore office on ℡080/224 3172), is close to the park entrance and arranges wildlife safaris, with a very hefty surcharge for foreign visitors. Some tour groups prefer the luxury of *Orange County* (see p.265), near the town of Siddapura in Kodagu 75km to the north, despite the long drive.

Hassan and around

Although there is not a lot to recommend it in its own right, the grubby town of **Hassan**, set amid an ocean of rural plains, is the obvious centre for visits to the stunning Hoysala temples of **Belur** and **Halebid**, as well as the famous Jain centre of **Sravanabelagola**.

Hassan

Unprepossessing **HASSAN**, 118km northwest of Mysore, is visited in disproportionately large numbers because of its proximity to the Hoysala temples at **Belur** and **Halebid**, both northwest of the town, and the Jain pilgrimage site of **Sravanabelgola** to the southeast. Some travellers end up staying a couple of nights, killing time in neon-lit thali joints and dowdy hotel rooms, but with a little forward planning you shouldn't have to linger here for longer than it takes to get on a bus somewhere else. Set deep in the serene Karnatakan countryside, Belur, Halebid and Sravanabelgola are much more congenial places to stay.

Practicalities

Hassan's **KSRTC bus stand** is in the centre of town, at the northern end of Bus Stand Road which runs south past the post office to **Narsimharaja Circle**. Here you'll find the State Bank of Mysore, where you can change money, but not Thomas Cook travellers' cheques, and also most of the town's accommodation. Local auto-rickshaws operate without meters and charge a minimum of Rs10. Winding its way east–west via the Narsimharaja Circle, is the Bangalore–Mangalore Road (BM Road) along which you will find the **tourist office** (1km) at Wartah Bhavan (Mon–Sat 10am–5.30pm; ☎08172/68862), good for information on bus and railway timings and the usual cluster of booklets, but not much else. The **railway station**, served by four slow passenger trains a day to Mysore, is a further 2km down the road. Note that, at the time of going to press, the line from here across the Ghats to Mangalore on the coast had been temporarily suspended due to engineering work involved with upgrading the line. See the box opposite for details of how to get to Sravanabelgola, Belur and Halebid.

Accommodation

Considering the number of tourists who pass through, Hassan is oddly lacking in good accommodation. Most of the budget options are of a pitiful standard: the few exceptions are within walking distance of the bus stand, around **Narsimharaja Circle**. Wherever you stay, call ahead, as most hotels tend to be full by early evening.

DR Karigowda Residency, BM Road, 1km from railway station ☎08172/64506, ℱ63222. An immaculate mid-range place: friendly, comfortable and amazing value. Single occupancy possible; no a/c. ❸

ITDC Hassan Ashok, BM Road, near Narsimharaja Circle, on the left as you approach from the railway station ☎08172/68731, ℱ68324. An overpriced hotel for tour groups and VIPs featuring an uninspiring but comfortable veg and non-veg restaurant, craft shops and bar. ❽–❾

Mahaveer Abhiruchi Lodge, BM Road, near Narsimharaja Circle ☎08172/68885. Cleanish rooms with TVs and mosquito nets) and good but dilapidated veg restaurant, the *Abhiruchi*. ❷–❸

Palika, Race Course Road ☎08172/67145. Large and somewhat characterless block with sizeable rooms; the cheaper ones are good value. ❹

Prince Cottage, BM Road, behind Bhanu Theatre ☎08172/65385. Small, neat guesthouse tucked away off the main road. Good value and handy for the railway station. ❷

Sanman, Municipal Office Road ☎08172/68024. Above a busy restaurant, decent rooms with squeaky clean white-tiled floors, frames for mozzie nets, attached bathrooms, and small balconies looking on to main bazaar. ❷

Southern Star, BM Road, 500m from railway station ☎08172/51816, ℱ68916, ℮ sshassan@vsnl.com. New hotel with all mod cons belonging to the *Quality Inn* chain, but better value than most. The smartest place in town. ❼–❽

Sri Krishna, BM Road ☎08172/63240, ℱ60195. A large new hotel with some a/c rooms. The spacious non-a/c rooms are a great deal and the restaurant downstairs produces excellent South Indian cooking. ❻–❼

Suvarna Regency, PB 97, BM Road ☎08172/64006, ℱ63822. A ritzy place with lots of lights, shiny marble lobby, comfortable rooms and a rooftop barbecue. Good value and a better choice than the *Ashok*. Some a/c. ❺–❻

Vaishnavi Lodging, Harsha Mahal Road ☎08172/63885. Hassan's best budget lodge, with big clean rooms and a veg restaurant. Reservations essential. Turn left out of the bus stand, right onto Church Road and it's on the corner of the first left turn. ❷

Eating

Most of the **hotels** listed above have commendable restaurants, or you can take your pick from the string of cheap snack bars and thali joints outside the bus stand.

Cocktails, BM Road near Krishna. A new multi-storey development with a terraced restaurant and bar offering a run of the mill but varied menu.

Golden Gate, *Suvarna Regency*, PB 97, BM Road. Plush restaurant and bar with a garden extension, and the best Hassan has to offer; the varied menu is not cheap.

Harsha Mahal, below *Harsha Mahal Lodge*, Harsha Mahal Road. No-nonsense veg canteen

that serves freshly cooked *iddli* and dosa breakfasts from 7.30am.

Hotel GRR, opposite the bus stand. Traditional, tasty and filling "mini-meals" served on plantain leaves, with a wide choice of non-veg dishes and some ice creams.

Upahar Darshan, BM Road. A cheap South Indian restaurant serving good "meals" and fresh dosas and *iddlis*.

Moving on from Hassan

Hassan is well connected to most points in southwest Karnataka, with frequent buses to Mysore from the KSRTC bus stand. Hassan lies midway on the main bus route between Mangalore (180km) and Bangalore (187km), serviced by several ordinary and occasional luxury buses, and more comfortable private buses of which Vijayananda Travels, *Suvarna Regency*, PB 97, BM Road (☎08172/65807), which runs the private VRL service, is by far the best.

Apart from taking a tour, the only way to see Sravanabelgola (53km), Belur (37km) and Halebid (30km) in one day is by car, which some visitors share; most of the hotels can fix this up (around Rs1000 per day or Rs4 per kilometre for a minimum of 250km). Travelling by bus, you'll need at least two days. Belur and Halebid can be comfortably covered in one day; it's best to take the first (8am) of the hourly buses to Halebid (1hr) and move on to Belur (30min; 16km), from where services back to Hassan during the evening are more frequent (6.30am–6.15pm; 1hr 10min). Sravanabelgola, however, is in the opposite direction, and not served by direct buses; you have to head to Channarayapatna aka "CR Patna" (from 6.30am; 1hr) on the main Bangalore highway and pick up one of the regular buses (30min) or any number of minibuses from there. If you want to get to Sravanabelgola in time to visit the site and move on the same day (to Mysore or Bangalore), aim to catch one of the private luxury buses to Bangalore that leave from the road just below the *Vaishnavi Lodge* before dawn (5.30–6am); they all stop briefly in Channarayapatna. Bear in mind, too, that there are places to stay in both Belur and Halebid; arrive in Hassan early enough, and you can travel on to the temple towns before nightfall, although you should phone ahead to check rooms are available.

Halebid

Now little more than a scruffy hamlet of brick houses and chai stalls, **HALEBID**, 32km northwest of Hassan, was once the capital of the powerful Hoysala dynasty, who held sway over south Karnataka from the eleventh until the early fourteenth centuries. Once known as **Dora Samudra**, the city's name was changed to *Hale-bidu*, or "Dead City", in 1311 when Delhi Sultanate forces under the command of Ala-ud-Din-Khalji swept through and reduced it to rubble. Despite the sacking, several large Hoysala temples survive, two of which, the Hoysaleshvara and Kedareshvara, are covered in exquisite carvings. A small **archeological museum** (daily except Fri 10am–5pm) next to the Hoysaleshvara temple houses a collection of Hoysala art and other finds from the area.

The Hoysaleshvara temple

The **Hoysaleshvara** temple (daily 9am–5pm; $5 [Rs5]) was started in 1141, and after some forty years of work was left unfinished, which possibly accounts for the absence of the type of towers that feature at Somnathpur. It is no longer known which deities were originally worshipped, though the double shrine is thought to have been devoted at one time to Shiva and his consort. In any event, both shrines contain *shivalingam* and are adjoined by two linked, partly enclosed *mandapa* hallways in which stand Nandi bulls.

Like other Hoysala temples, it is raised on a high plinth (*jagati*) which follows the star-shaped plan and provides an upper ambulatory; the *mandapas* are approached by flights of steps flanked by small, free-standing, towered shrines. Inside, the lower portions of the black polished stone pillars were lathe-turned, though the upper levels appear to have been hand-carved to reproduce the effect of turning.

Hoysaleshvara also features many Vaishnavite images. The **sculptures**, which have a fluid quality lacking in the earlier work at Belur, include Brahma aboard his goose-vehicle Hamsa, Krishna holding up Mount Govardhana, Krishna playing the flute and Vishnu (Trivikrama) bestriding the world in three steps. One of the most remarkable images is of the demon king **Ravana** shaking Shiva's mountain abode, Mount Kailasa: the mount is populated by numerous animals and figures, and Shiva is seated atop with Parvati. Secular themes, among them dancers and musicians, occupy the same register as the gods, and you'll come across the odd erotic tableau featuring voluptuous, heavily bejewelled maidens. A narrative frieze, on the sixth register from the bottom, follows the length of the Nandi *mandapas* and illustrates scenes from the *Bhagavata* and Vishnu *Puranas*, *Mahabharata* and *Ramayana*.

The Jain bastis and the Kedareshvara temple

About 600m south of the Hoysaleshvara, a group of Jain *bastis* (temples) stands virtually unadorned; the only sculptural decoration consists of ceiling friezes inside the *mandapas* and elephants at the entrance steps, where there's an impressive donatory plaque. The thirteenth-century temple of **Adi Parshwanatha**, marked by a large entrance *mandapa*, is dedicated to the twenty-third *tirthankara*, while the newer **Vijayanatha** built in the sixteenth-century, easily recognized by its predominant *manasasthamba* pillar in front, is dedicated to the *tirthankara* Shantinatha. The *chowkidar* at the Parshwanatha temple will demonstrate various tricks made possible by the carved pillars' highly polished surfaces; some are so finely turned they sound metallic when struck.

To the east, there's a smaller Shiva temple, **Kedareshvara** (1217–21), also built on a stellate plan. Unfortunately, due to instability, it's not possible to go inside. Many fine images decorate the exterior, including an unusual stone Krishna dancing on the serpent demon Kaliya – more commonly seen in bronze and painting.

Practicalities

Frequent **buses** run between Halebid (the last at 6.15pm) and Hassan, and to Belur (the last at 8.45pm). The private minibuses that work from the crossroads outside the Hoysaleshvara temple take a lot longer and only leave when crammed to bursting.

The monuments lie within easy walking distance of each other, but if you fancy exploring the surrounding countryside, rent a **bicycle** from the stalls by the bus stand (Rs3 per hour). The road running south past the temples leads through some beautiful scenery, with possible side-hikes to hilltop shrines, while the road to Belur (16km) makes for another pleasant bicycle ride.

Accommodation in the village is limited to KSTDC *Mayura Shantala* (☎ 08177/73224; ❷), which is opposite the main temple and set in a small

The Hoysala dynasty ruled southwestern Karnataka between the eleventh and thirteenth centuries. From the twelfth century, after the accession of King Vishnu Vardhana, they built a series of distinctive temples centred primarily at three sites: Belur and Halebid, close to modern Hassan, and Somnathpur, near Mysore.

At first sight, and from a distance, Hoysala temples appear to be modest structures, compact and even squat. On closer inspection, however, their profusion of fabulously detailed and sensuous sculpture, covering every inch of the exterior, is astonishing. Detractors are prone to class Hoysala art as decadent and overly fussy, but anyone with an eye for craftsmanship is likely to marvel at these jewels of Karnatakan art.

The intricacy of the carvings was made possible by the material used in construction: a soft steatite soapstone that on oxidization hardens to a glassy, highly polished surface. The level of detail, similar to that seen in sandalwood and ivory work, became increasingly freer and more fluid as the style developed, and reached its highest point at Somnathpur. Beautiful bracket figures, often delicate portrayals of voluptuous female subjects, were placed under the eaves, fixed by pegs top and bottom. A later addition (except possibly in the Somnathpur temple), these serve no structural function.

Another technique more usually associated with wood is the unusual treatment of the massive stone pillars: lathe-turned, they resemble those of the wooden temples of Kerala. They were probably turned on a horizontal plane, pinned at each end, and rotated with the use of a rope. It may be no coincidence that, to this day, wood turning is still a local speciality. Only the central shaft of each pillar seems to have been turned; in the base and capitals, a less precise, presumably handworked imitation of turning is evident.

The architectural style of the Hoysala temples is commonly referred to as vesara, or "hybrid" (literally "mule"), rather than belonging to either the northern, *nagari*, or southern Dravidian styles. However, they show great affinity with *nagari* temples of western India, and represent another fruit of contact, like music, painting and literature, facilitated by the trade routes between the north and the south. All Hoysala temples share a star-shaped plan, built on high plinths (*jagati*) that follow the shape of the sanctuaries and *mandapas* to provide a raised surrounding platform. Such northern features may have been introduced by the designer and artists of the earliest temple at Belur, who were imported by Vishnu Vardhana from further north in Andhra Pradesh. Also characteristic of the Hoysala style is the use of *ashlar* masonry, without mortar. Some pieces of stones are joined by pegs of iron or bronze, or mortice and tenon joints. Ceilings inside the *mandapas* are made up of corbelled domes, looking similar to those of the Jain temples of Rajasthan and Gujarat; in the Hoysala style they are only visible from inside.

garden by the road. It offers two comfortable doubles with verandas, plus a four-bedded room, all of which should be booked in advance. Plans are afoot to construct a larger complex further south; ask at any KSTDC tourist office. After 6pm, when the chai stalls at the crossroads are closed, the only place to **eat** is at the KSTDC *Mayura Shantala* where the food, including thalis, is uninspiring but the garden is pleasant.

Belur

BELUR, 37km northwest of Hassan, on the banks of the Yagachi, was the Hoysala capital – prior to Halebid – during the eleventh and twelfth centuries. Still in use, the **Chennakeshava temple** (7.30am–8.30pm; $5 [Rs5]) is a fine and early example of the singular Hoysala style (see Contexts p.677). The temple was built by King Vishnuvardhana in 1117 to celebrate his conversion from Jainism, victory over Chola forces at Talakad and independence from the Chalukyas. Today, its grey-stone *gopura* (gateway tower) soars above a small, bustling market town – a popular pilgrimage site from October to December, when bus-loads of Ayappan devotees stream through en route to Sabarimala (see p.378). The **car festival** held around March or April takes place over twelve days and has a pastoral feel, attracting farmers from the surrounding countryside, who conduct a bullock-cart procession through the streets to the temple. If you have time to linger, Belur, with marginally better facilities than those found at Halebid, is a far better place to base yourself in order to explore the Hoysala region.

Built on a star-shaped plan, Chennakeshava stands in a huge walled courtyard, surrounded by smaller shrines and columned *mandapa* hallways. Lacking any form of superstructure, and terminating at the first floor, it has the appearance of having a flat roof. If it ever had a tower, it would have disappeared by the Vijayanagar (sixteenth-century) period; above the cornice, a plain parapet, presumably added at the same time as the east entrance *gopura*, shows a typically Vijayanagar Islamic influence. Both the sanctuary and *mandapa* are raised on the usual plinth (*jagati*). Double flights of steps, flanked by minor towered shrines, afford entry to the *mandapa* on three sides; this hallway was originally open, but in the 1200s pierced stone screens carved with geometric designs and scenes from the *Puranas* were inserted between the lathe-turned pillars. The main shrine opens four times a day for worship (8.30–10am, 11am–1pm, 2.30–5pm & 6.30–8.30pm) and it's worth considering using one of the guides who offer their services at the gates (Rs30) to explain the intricacies of the carvings.

The quantity of **sculptural decoration**, if less mature than in later Hoysala temples, is staggering. Carvings on the plinth and lower walls, in successive and continuous bands, start at the bottom with depictions of elephants, followed by garlands and arches with lion heads. As you progress, the carvings illustrate stylized vegetation with dancing figures; birds and animals; pearl garlands; projecting niches containing male and female figures and seated *yakshas*, or spirits; miniature pillars alternating with female figures dressing or dancing; miniature temple towers interspersed with dancers; and above them lion heads. Above the screens, a series of 42 figures, added later, shows celestial nymphs hunting, playing music, dancing and beautifying themselves.

Columns inside, each unique, feature extraordinarily detailed carving, with more than a hundred deities on the central **Narasimha pillar**. The inner sanctum contains a black image of Chennakeshava, a form of Krishna who holds a conch (*shankha*, in the upper right hand), discus (*chakra*, upper left), lotus (*padma*, lower right) and mace (*gada*, lower left). He is flanked by consorts Shri Devi and Bhudevi. Within the same enclosure, the **Kappe Channigaraya temple** has some finely carved niche images and a depiction of Narasimha (Vishnu as man-lion) killing the demon Hiranyakashipu. Further west, fine sculptures in the smaller **Viranarayana** shrine include a scene from the *Mahabharata* of Bhima killing the demon Bhaga.

Practicalities

Buses from Hassan and Halebid pull into the small bus stand in the middle of town, ten-minutes' walk along the main street from the temple, whereas some through buses don't bother to pull into the bus stand but stop on the highway next to it. There are auto-rickshaws available, but a good way to explore the area, including Halebid, is to rent a **bicycle** (Rs3 per hour) from one of the stalls by the bus stand. The **tourist office** (Mon–Sat 10am–5pm) is located within the KSTDC *Mayuri Velapuri* compound near the temple. They have all the local bus times, and sometimes the tourist officer is available as a guide – his knowledge of the temples is quite remarkable.

The KSTDC *Mayuri Velapuri* (℡08177/22209; ❷) is the best **place to stay**, with immaculately clean and airy rooms in its new building, or dingy ones in the older wing. The two dorms are rarely occupied (Rs35 per bed), other than between March and May, when the hotel tends to be block-booked by pilgrims. Down the road, the *Annapurna* (℡08177/22039; ❷) has adequate if dull rooms above an uninspiring restaurant; the *Swagath Tourist Home* (℡08177/22159; ❶), further up the road towards the temple, is extremely basic, boxed in and does not have hot water, but is fine as a fall-back. Of the hotels around the bus stand, the *Vishnu Lodge* (℡08177/22263; ❷–❸) above a restaurant and sweet shop, is the best bet, with spacious rooms (some with TV) but tiny attached bathrooms where hot water is only available in the mornings.

The most salubrious **place to eat** is at KSTDC *Mayuri Velapuri*'s newly built restaurant, but the menu is limited. There are several other options, many located beneath hotels strung along the main road, in addition to the veg *dhabas* by the temple, and the *Indian Coffee House* on the main road by the temple gates. If you have a weakness for Indian sweets, head for *Poonam's* below the *Vishnu Lodge*.

Sravanabelgola

The sacred Jain site of **SRAVANABELGOLA**, 49km southwest of Hassan and 93km north of Mysore, consists of two hills and a large tank. On one of the hills, Indragiri (also known as Vindhyagiri), stands an extraordinary eighteen-metre-high monolithic statue of a naked male figure, **Gomateshvara**. Said to be the largest free-standing sculpture in India, this tenth-century colossus, visible for miles around, as well as the nearby *bastis* (Jain temples), make Sravanabelgola a key pilgrimage centre, though surprisingly few Western travellers find their way out here. Spend a night or two in the village, however, and you can climb Indragiri Hill before dawn to enjoy the serene spectacle of the sun rising over the sugar-cane fields and outcrops of lumpy granite that litter the surrounding plains – an unforgettable sight.

Sravanabelgola is linked in tradition with the Mauryan emperor Chandragupta, who is said to have starved himself to death on the second hill in around 300 BC, in accordance with a Jain practice. The hill was renamed Chandragiri, marking the arrival of Jainism in southern India. At the same time, a controversy regarding the doctrines of Mahavira, the last of the 24 Jain **tirthankaras** (literally "crossing-makers", who assist the aspirant to cross the "ocean of rebirth"), split Jainism into two separate branches. *Svetambara*, "white-clad" Jains, are more common in North India, while *digambara*, "sky-clad", are usually associated with the South. Truly ascetic *digambara* devotees go naked, though few do so away from sacred sites.

All the *tirthankaras* are represented as naked figures, differentiated only by their individual attributes: animals, inanimate objects (such as a conch shell), or symbols (such as the *swastika*). Each of the 24 is also attached to a particular *yaksha* (male) or *yakshi* (female) spirit; such spirits are also evident in Mahayana Buddhism, suggesting a strand of belief with extremely ancient origins. *Tirthankara*s are represented either sitting cross-legged in meditation – resembling images of the Buddha, save for their nakedness – or *kayotsarga*, "body

Gomateshvara, or Bahubali, who was the son of the legendary King Rishabdev of Ayodhya (better known as Adinath, the first *tirthankara*), had a row with his elder brother, Bharat, over their inheritance. After a fierce fight, he lifted his brother above his head, and was about to throw him to the ground when he was gripped by remorse. Gently setting Bharat down, Gomateshvara resolved to reject the world of greed, jealousy and violence by meditating until he achieved *moksha*, release from attachment and rebirth. This he succeeded in doing, even before his father.

As a *kevalin*, Gomateshvara had achieved kevalajnana, or "sole knowledge", acquired through solitude, austerity and meditation. While engaged in this non-activity, he stood "body upright" in a forest. So motionless was he that ants built their nest at his feet, snakes coiled happily around his ankles, and creepers began to grow up his legs.

Every twelve years, at an auspicious astrological conjunction of certain planets, the Gomateshvara statue is ritually anointed in the Mahamastakabhisheka ceremony – the next one is scheduled for some time between September and December of 2005 (the precise date has yet to be announced). The process lasts for several days, culminating on the final morning when 1008 *kalashas* (pots) of "liberation water", each with a coconut and mango leaves tied together by coloured thread, are arranged before the statue in a sacred diagram (mandala), on ground strewn with fresh paddy. A few priests climb scaffolding, erected around Gomateshvara, to bathe him in milk and ghee. After this first bath, prayers are offered. Then, to the accompaniment of temple musicians and the chanting of sacred texts, a thousand priests climb the scaffold to bathe the image in auspicious unguents including the water of holy rivers, sandal paste, cane juice, saffron and milk, along with flowers and jewels. The ten-hour 1993 ceremony reached a climax when a helicopter dropped 20kg of gold leaf and 200 litres of milk on the colossus, along with showers of marigolds, gem stones and multi-hued powders. The residue formed a cascade of rainbow colours down the statue's head and body, admired by *lakhs* of devotees, Jain *sadhus* and *sadhvis* (female *sadhus*) and the massed cameras of the world. A satellite township, Yatrinagar, provides accommodation for 35,000 during the festival, and eighteen surrounding villages shelter pilgrims in temporary *dharamshalas*.

upright", where the figure stands impassive; here Gomateshvara stands in the latter, more usual, posture.

The monuments at Sravanabelgola probably date from no earlier than the tenth century, when a General Chamundaraya is said to have visited Chandragiri in search of a Mauryan statue of Gomateshvara. Failing to find it, he decided to have one made. From the top of Chandragiri he fired an arrow across to Indragiri Hill; where the arrow landed he had a new Gomateshvara sculpted from a single rock.

Indragiri Hill

Gomateshvara is approached from the tank between the two hills by 620 steps, cut into the granite of **Indragiri Hill**, which pass numerous rock inscriptions on the way up to a walled enclosure. Shoes must be deposited at the stall to the left of the steps, and you can leave bags at the site office nearby. Anyone unable to climb the steps can be carried up by a chair known as a *dholi*. Take plenty of water, especially on a hot day, as there is none available on the hill. Entered through a small wagon-vaulted *gopura*, the **temple** is of the type known as *betta*, which, instead of the usual *garbhagriha* sanctuary, consists of an open courtyard enclosing the massive sculpture. Figures and shrines of all the *yaksha* and *yakshi* spirits stand inside the crenellated wall, but the towering figure of Gomateshvara dominates. With his elongated arms and exaggeratedly wide shoulders, his proportions are decidedly non-naturalistic. The sensuously smooth surface of the white granite "trap" rock is finely carved, particularly the hands, hair and serene face. As in legend (see box), ant-hills and snakes sit at his feet and creepers appear to grow on his limbs.

Bhandari Basti and monastery (math)

The road east from the foot of the steps at Chandragiri leads to two interesting Jain buildings in town. To the right, the **Bhandari Basti** (1159), housing a shrine with images of the 24 *tirthankaras,* was built by Hullamaya, treasurer of the Hoysala Raja Narasimha. A high wall encloses the temple, forming a plain ambulatory which contains a well. Two *mandapa* hallways, where naked *digambara* Jains may sometimes be seen discoursing with devotees clad in white, lead to the shrine at the back. Pillars in the outer *mandapa* feature carvings of female musicians, while mythical beasts adorn the entrance to the inner, *navaranga,* hallway.

At the end of the street, the *math* (monastery) was the residence of Sravanabelgola's senior *acharya,* or guru. Thirty male and female monks, who also "go wandering in every direction", are attached to the *math;* normally a member of staff will be happy to show visitors around. Among the rare palm-leaf manuscripts in the library, some more than a millennium old, are works on mathematics and geography, and the *Mahapurana,* hagiographies of the *tirthankaras.* Next door, a covered walled courtyard contains a number of shrines; the entrance is elaborately decorated with embossed brass designs of *yali* mythical beasts, elephants, a two-headed eagle and an image of Parshvanath, the 23rd *tirthankara,* here shown as Padmavati. Inside, the courtyard is edged by a high platform on three sides, on which a chair is placed for the *acharya.* A collection of tenth-century bronze *tirthankara* images is housed here, and vibrant murals detail the various lives of Parshvanath. The hills where the *tirthankaras* stood to gain *moksha* are represented in a model, somewhat resembling a jelly mould, with tacked-on footprints.

Chandragiri Hill

Leaving your shoes with the keeper at the bottom, take the rock-cut steps to the top of the smaller **Chandragiri Hill**. Miraculously, the sound of radios and rickshaws down below soon disappears. Fine views stretch south to Indragiri and, from the north on the far side, across to a river, paddy and sugar-cane fields, palms and the village of **Jinanathapura**, where there's another ornate Hoysala temple, the Shantishvara *basti.*

Rather than a single large shrine, as at Indragiri, Chandragiri holds a group of *bastis* in late Chalukya Dravida style, within a walled enclosure. Caretakers, who don't speak fluent English, will take you around and open up the closed shrines. Save for pilasters and elaborate parapets, all the temples have plain exteriors. Named after its patron, the tenth-century **Chamundaraya** is the largest of the group, dedicated to Parshvanath. Inside the **Chandragupta** (twelfth century), superb carved panels in a small shrine tell the story of Chandragupta and his teacher Bhadrabahu. Traces of painted geometric designs survive and the pillars feature detailed carving. Elsewhere in the enclosure stands a 24-metre-high *manastambha,* or "pillar of fame", decorated with images of spirits, *yakshis* and a *yaksha.* No fewer than 576 inscriptions dating from the sixth to the nineteenth centuries are dotted around the site, on pillars and the rock itself.

Sravanabelgola, along with Belur and Halebid, features on **tours** from Bangalore and Mysore (see p.225 and p.236). However, if you want to look around at a civilized pace, it's best to come independently (see p.251). The **tourist office** (Mon–Sat 10am–5.30pm), at the bottom of the steps, has little to offer and the management committee office next door only serves to collect donations and hand out tickets for the *dholis*.

If you want **accommodation**, there are plenty of **dharamshalas**, managed by the temple authorities, offering simple, scrupulously clean rooms, many with their own bathrooms and sit-outs, ranged around gardens and courtyards, and most costing less than Rs125 per night. The 24hr accommodation office (T08176/57258) is located inside the *SP Guest House*, next to the bus stand (look for the clock tower); they will allocate you a room here. *Yatri Niwas* (⑥), which is close by and also booked through the accommodation office, is about as expensive as it gets, but is only marginally better than the best of the guest houses. *Hotel Raghu*, opposite the main tank, houses the best of the many small local **restaurants**.

Crisscrossed by winding back roads, the idyllic (and mostly flat) countryside around Sravanabelgola is perfect cycling terrain. **Bicycles** are available for hire (Rs3 per hour) at Saleem Cycle Mart, on Masjid Road, opposite the northeast corner of the tank or stalls on the main road. If you're returning to Hassan, you'll have to head to **Channarayapatna**, aka "CR Patna", by bus or in one of the shared vans that regularly ply the route and depart only when bursting; change at CR Patna for a bus to Hassan.

Kodagu (Coorg)

The hill region of **Kodagu**, formerly known as **Coorg**, lies 100km west of Mysore in the Western Ghats, its eastern fringes merging with the Mysore Plateau. Comprising rugged mountain terrain interspersed with cardamom jungle, coffee plantations and swathes of lush rice paddy, it's one of South India's most beautiful areas. Little has changed since Dervla Murphy spent a few months here with her daughter in the 1970s (the subject of her classic travelogue, *On A Shoestring To Coorg*), and was entranced by the landscape and people, whose customs, language and appearance set them apart from their neighbours.

Today tourism is still very low-key, and the few travellers who pass through rarely venture beyond **Madikeri** (Mercara), Kodagu's homely capital. However, if you plan to cross the Ghats between Mysore and the coast, the route through Kodagu is definitely worth considering. Most of the area around Kodagu is swathed in lush coffee plantations. Some coffee-plantation owners open their doors to visitors; to find out more contact the Codagu Planters Association, Mysore Road, Madikeri (T08272/29873). A good time to visit is during the festival season in early December or during the **Blossom Showers** around March and April when the coffee plants bloom with white flowers, although for some the strong scent can be overpowering.

Kodagu is relatively undeveloped, and "sights" are few, but the countryside is idyllic and the climate refreshingly cool, even in summer. With the help of local operators, there is now a growing trickle of visitors who come to Kodagu to **trek** through the unspoilt forest tracts and ridges that fringe the district (see box on p.263). On the eastern borders of Kodagu on the Mysore Plateau, large

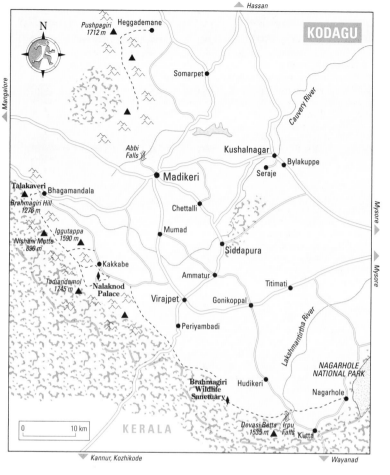

Tibetan settlements around Kushalnagar have transformed a once barren countryside into fertile farmland dotted with busy monasteries, some of which house thousands of monks.

Some history

Oblique references to Kodagu crop up in ancient Tamil and Sanskrit scriptures, but the first concrete evidence of the kingdom dates from the eighth century, when it prospered from the salt trade passing between the coast and the cities on the Deccan Plateau. Under the Hindu **Haleri Rajas**, the state repulsed invasions by its more powerful neighbours, including Haider Ali and his son Tipu Sultan, the infamous Tiger of Mysore. A combination of hilly terrain, absence of roads (a deliberate policy on the part of defence-conscious Kodagu kings) and the tenacity of its highly trained army, ensured that Kodagu was the only Indian kingdom never to be conquered.

Peace and prosperity prevailed through the 1700s, when the state was ruled by a line of eccentric rajas, among them the paranoid Dodda Vira (1780–1809),

Theories abound as to the origins of the Kodavas, or Coorgis, who today comprise less than one-sixth of the hill region's population. Fair-skinned and with their own language and customs, they are thought to have migrated to southern India from Kurdistan, Kashmir and Rajasthan, though no one knows exactly why or when. One popular belief holds that this staunchly martial people, who since Independence have produced some of India's leading military brains, are descended from Roman mercenaries who fled here following the collapse of the Pandyan dynasty in the eighth century; some even claim connections with Alexander the Great's invading army. Another theory is that the Kodavas were originally from Arabia, having been pushed out by the early Muslims and made to flee into exile.

Whatever their origins, the Kodavas have managed to retain a distinct identity apart from the freed plantation slaves, Moplah Muslim traders and other immigrants who have settled here. More akin to Tamil than Kannada, their language is Dravidian, yet their religious practices, based on ancestor veneration and worship of nature spirits, differ markedly from those of mainstream Hinduism. Land tenure in Kodagu is also quite distinctive, with taxation based on type of land and, unlike in some other traditional societies, women have a right to inheritance and ownership; they are also allowed to remarry. Kodava martial traditions are grounded in the family where, according to custom, one son was raised to work the land while another joined the army. Even today, they are allowed to carry weapons without licence.

Spiritual and social life for traditional Kodavas revolves around the Ain Mane, or ancestral homestead. Built on raised platforms to overlook the family land, these large, detached houses, with their beautiful carved wood doors and beaten-earth floors, generally have four wings and courtyards to accommodate various branches of the extended family, as well as shrine rooms, or Karona Kalas, dedicated to the clan's most important forebears. Key religious rituals and rites of passage are always conducted in the *Ain Mane*, rather than the local temple. However, you could easily travel through Kodagu without ever seeing one, as they are invariably away from roads, shrouded in thick forest.

You're more likely to come across traditional Kodava costume, which is donned for all auspicious occasions, such as marriages, funerals, harvest celebrations and clan get-togethers. The men wear dapper knee-length coats called *kupyas*, bound at the waist with a scarlet and gold cummerbund, and daggers (*peechekathis*) with ivory handles. Most distinctive of all, though, is the unique flat-bottomed turban; sadly, the art of tying these is dying, and most men wear ready-made versions (which you can buy in Madikeri bazaar). Kodava women's garb of long, richly coloured silk saris, pleated at the back and with a *pallav* draped over their shoulders, is even more stunning, enlivened by heaps of heavy gold and silver jewellery, and precious stones. Women also wear headscarves, in the fields as well as for important events, tying the corners behind the head, Kashmiri style.

The Kodava diet is heavily carnivorous, their favourite meat being pork: an important dish at festive occasions where it is often served as a dryish dish known as *pandi curry*, but sometimes substituted by *nooputtakoli curry* made with chicken, and usually accompanied with a rice preparation, *tumbuttu pandi*. Their traditional breakfast, consisting of a type of chapati known as *aki oti* served with honey and *pajji*, a chutney, is far lighter.

Like all traditional Indian cultures, this one is on the decline, not least because young Kodavas, predominantly from well-off land-owning families, tend to be highly educated and move away from home to find work, weakening the kinship ties that have for centuries played such a central role in the life of the region. However, in recent years there has been a rekindling of Kodava pride with calls for a state separate from Karnataka.

who reputedly murdered most of his relatives, friends, ministers and palace guards. The monarchy was more accountable during the reign of his successor, Chickavirarajah Rajendra, known as **Vira Raja**, but eventually lapsed into decadence and corruption. Emulating his father's brutal example, Vira Raja imprisoned or assassinated his rivals and indulged his passion for women and spending. The king's ministers eventually appealed to the British Resident in Mysore for help to depose the despot. Plagued by threats from Vira Raja, the colonial administration was eager for an excuse to intervene; they got it in 1834, when the unruly raja killed his cousin's infant son. Accusing him of maladministration, the British massed troops on the border and forced a short siege, at the end of which Vira Raja (and what remained of his family) fled into exile.

Thereafter, Kodagu became a princely state with nominal independence, which it retained until the creation of Karnataka in 1956. During the Raj, **coffee** was introduced and, despite plummeting prices on the international market, this continues to be the linchpin of the local economy, along with pepper and cardamom. Although Kodagu is Karnataka's wealthiest region, providing the highest revenue, it does not reap the rewards, and this, coupled with the distinct identity and fiercely independent nature of the Kodavas, has resulted in the Kodagu freedom movement, known as **Kodagu Rajya Mukti Morcha**, seeking its own statehood. Methods used by the KRMM include cultural programmes and occasional strikes, known as *bandhs*, designed to close down all commercial activity in protest; they rarely use violence but a new order is emerging within the movement which has left some of the older members disgruntled.

Madikeri (Mercara) and around

Nestling beside a curved stretch of craggy hills, **MADIKERI** (**Mercara**), capital of Kodagu, undulates around 1300m up in the Western Ghats, roughly midway between Mysore and the coastal city of Mangalore. Few foreigners travel up here, but it's a pleasant enough town, with red-tiled buildings and undulating roads that converge on a bustling bazaar.

The **Omkareshwara Shiva** temple, built in 1820, features an unusual combination of red-tiled roofs, Keralan Hindu architecture, Gothic elements and Islamic-influenced domes. The fort and palace, worked over by Tipu Sultan in 1781 and rebuilt in the nineteenth century, now serve as offices and a prison. Also worth checking out are the huge square **tombs of the Rajas** which, with their Islamic-style gilded domes and minarets, dominate the town's skyline. **St Mark's church** holds a small **museum** of British memorabilia, Jain, Hindu and village deity figures and weapons (Tues–Sun 9.30am–1.30pm & 2.30am–5.30pm). At the western edge of town, **Rajas' Seat**, next to KSTDC *Hotel Mayura Valley View*, is a belvedere, said to be the Kodagu kings' favoured place to watch the sunset.

Madikeri is the centre of the lucrative coffee trade, and although autorickshaws will take you there and back for around Rs150, a walk to **Abbi Falls** (8km) is a good introduction to coffee-growing country. The pleasant road, devoid of buses, winds through the hill country past plantations and makes for a good day's outing. At the littered car park at the end of the road, a gate leads through a private coffee plantation sprinkled with cardamom sprays and pepper vines, to the bottom of the large stepped falls that are most impressive during and straight after the monsoons.

Practicalities

You can only reach Madikeri by road, but it's a scenic three-hour **bus** ride via **Kushalnagar** from **Mysore**, 120km southeast (unless you mistakenly get on

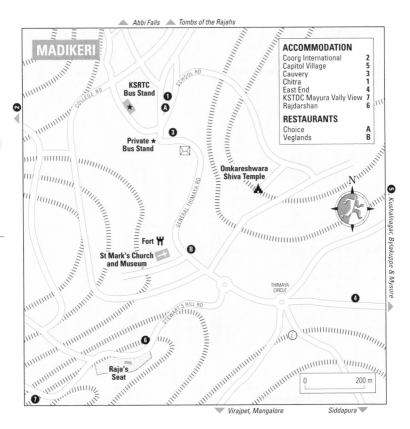

MADIKERI

ACCOMMODATION

Coorg International	2
Capitol Village	5
Cauvery	3
Chitra	1
East End	4
KSTDC Mayura Vally View	7
Rajdarshan	6

RESTAURANTS

Choice	A
Veglands	B

KSRTC Bus Stand

Private Bus Stand

Omkareshwara Shiva Temple

Fort

St Mark's Church and Museum

THIMAYA CIRCLE

Raja's Seat

0   200 m

COLLEGE RD

SCHOOL RD

GENERAL THIMAYA RD

STEWART'S HILL RD

KARNATAKA

Kodagu

Kushalnagar, Bylakuppe & Mysore

▼ Virajpet, Mangalore   Siddapura ▼

one of the few buses that goes via Siddapura, which take more than an hour longer). Regular services, including de luxe buses, also connect Madikeri with **Mangalore**, 135km northwest across the Ghats. The KSTRC state **bus stand** is at the bottom of town, below the main bazaar; private buses from villages around the region pull into a parking lot at the end of the main street.

The small local **tourist office** (Mon–Sat 10.30am–5.30pm; ☏ 08272/28580) stands five minutes' walk along the Mysore road below Thimaya Circle, next to the *PWD Travellers'* Bungalow; staff can suggest itineraries, but it is otherwise quite limited. If you're thinking of **trekking** in Kodagu contact Ganesh Aiyanna at the *Hotel Cauvery* (☏ 08272/25492) who is very helpful and organizes itineraries and trips for around Rs500 per day. Coorg Travels at *Vinayaka Lodge* (☏ 08272/25817) is also flexible and friendly and will help put together a tour. For information on Kodagu's **forests** and forest bungalows contact the Conservator of Forests (see box opposite). Netraiders.com (☏ 08272/21131) near Chowk in the heart of the bazaar offers internet access for Rs40 per hour.

Accommodation and eating

Accommodation in Madikeri can be hard to come by, particularly in the budget range, most of which is concentrated around the bazaar and bus stand. The upmarket and some of the budget hotels generally have **restaurants**. The moderately expensive restaurant at *Rajdarshan* is one of the best; surprisingly,

The finest of Kodagu's treks lie to the south of the region along the Keralan border, where an ancient path snakes through forests and across mountain ridges linking Nagarhole to Talakaveri in the southwest. The trek, which takes around a week, starts at the entrance to Nagarhole National Park and continues, with tempting diversions, to Talakaveri. Passing by the Shri Ramneshwarna Temple with a side-trip through forest to the Irpu Falls, the trail runs to Nalaknod Palace, an old hunting lodge now used as a camp and for bee-keeping. It continues to the hill temple of Nishani Motte before arriving at Brahmagiri Hill and Talakaveri (see p.265). From Kakkabe, the small town near the Nalaknod Palace, there are two alternative routes to Talakaveri – one takes a more gentle, lower route while the other tackles challenging high ground over Kodagu's highest peak, Tadiandamol (1745m), and the peak of Iggutappa (1590m), where there are a couple of old temples. You are best advised to take a guide to help avoid elephants, and for route-finding through sometimes difficult terrain.

Kakkabe, 50km to the south of Madikeri, is a good base for climbing both Tadiandamol and Iggutappa, with excellent accommodation and food at the *Palace Estate* (☏08272/38346; ❸), where Mr A.P. Pooramma will assist in planning treks and negotiating guides (around Rs150/day). One direct bus leaves Madikeri at 7am for Kakkabe. Other possible treks in Kodagu include a climb to the hill of Devasi Betta close to Irpu Falls, through the Brahmagiri Wildlife Sanctuary, for which you will need permission from the sanctuary office. Elsewhere, connecting trails from Talakaveri can be taken to the top of Kodagu's second highest peak, Pushpagiri (1712m), to the north of the region. Pushpagiri can also be climbed via the village of Heggademane to the north of Madikeri, and is accessible by bus.

Walking routes are best explored with the help of the handful of specialist agencies, some working out of Madikeri, such as Ganesh Aiyanna at the *Hotel Cauvery* (☏08272/25492), who is very informative and helpful, or Coorg Travels at *Vinayaka Lodge* (☏08272/25817). If you want to try to arrange your own itinerary, approach the Conservator of Forests, Deputy Commissioner's Office, at the fort (☏08272/25708), for permission to enter the forests and to stay at their forest bungalows, and for a mandatory guide (Rs150–300/day). Even if you intend to do it yourself, it is well worth talking to Ganesh Aiyanna and to the helpful Kodagu Wildlife Society, PO Box 111, Chain Gate Road (☏08272/23505), 2km east of the centre. Although not local, experienced Clipper Holidays, with offices in Bangalore (☏080/559 9032) and Cochin (☏0484/364443), have been organizing forest treks in Kodagu for years, while Madhushudan Shukla at Woody Adventures in Bangalore (☏080/225 9159) specializes in a variety of outdoor sports, including trekking in Kodagu.

The best season to trek in the area is between October and March; April and May are not as hot as some other parts of Karnataka, but avoid the monsoons between June and September, when the trails can get muddy and the leaches rampant.

they do not serve coffee although they do have a good bar. The *Choice Hotel* on School Road is a restaurant only, serving breakfast items and a decent range of veg and non-veg dishes. There are a couple of "meals" joints on the main road and in the centre of town, and *Veglands* is a good and highly popular vegetarian restaurant.

Capitol Village ☏08272/25975. Six kilometres from the centre and booked through the *Hotel Cauvery* in Madikeri, this is the best place to stay in the area, but you'll need your own transport. The "village" consists of a cottage complex

surrounded by a splendid variety of horticulture on the edge of a coffee plantation. It's quiet and secluded and excellent value. ❻

Cauvery, School Road ☏08272/25492, ☏25735. Below the Private bus stand, this large and friendly place is almost hidden behind their *Capitol* restaurant. ⑥

Chitra, School Road ☎ 08272/25372, ⓕ 25191. Best value in town. Neat, well-kept rooms, the slightly pricier ones with cable TV. Excellent non-veg restaurant cum bar downstairs. ③ –④

Coorg International, Convent Road ☎ 08272/28071, ⓕ 28073. Ten minutes by rickshaw from the centre, this is one of the few upmarket options. It's a large but slightly characterless hotel with comfortable Western-style rooms, a multi-cuisine restaurant, exchange facilities, and shops. ⑦

East End, General Thimaya Road (aka Mysore Road) ☎ 08272/29996. A large, plain, tiled-roof colonial bungalow turned into a hotel with a hint of character, but more renowned for its popular bar and restaurant. ③

KSTDC Hotel Mayura Valley View ☎ 08272/28387. Well away from the main road, past Rajas' Seat, and with excellent views. The rooms are huge and the restaurant serves beer. Hail a rickshaw to get there, as it's a stiff twenty-minute uphill walk from the bus stand. ⑤

Rajdarshan ☎ 08272/29142. A modern and salubrious place with a landscaped garden, restaurant and bar, just down the hill on the left from the *Hotel Mayura Valley View*. ⑥ –⑦

Tibetan settlements and coffee plantations

Madikeri provides an excellent base from which to explore the delights of Kodagu, including the **Tibetan settlements** that straddle the district border to the east. Cooperatives line the Madikeri–Mysore highway and maroon-clad monks ride tractors to work the fields around the town of **Kushalnagar**, 22km from Madikeri, and the Tibetan villages, known as "camps", scattered around **Bylakuppe**, 6km across the district border. Although the term "camp" suggests a sense of transition, the Tibetans who first settled here as refugees in the 1960s represent one of the largest settlements outside their homeland and have adapted remarkably well to a starkly different environment. There are now around five thousand monks out of a total Tibetan population in the area exceeding 15,000.

Today, several key monasteries punctuate the landscape: chief amongst these is the great *gompa* of **Sera Je**, 5km to the south of the main highway, a huge complex which acts as a university for the monks. At the centre of Sera is a large main hall built on three floors, designed to accommodate the vast congregation of monks who gather here for instruction and ceremony. Despite the colossal image of the Buddha Shakyamuni at the head of the hall, there is nothing especially attractive about the monastery, which has a functional air to it; however, the village has a buzz and the monks are welcoming.

The only transport to and from the main highway is by **auto–rickshaws** that regularly ply the route; the turn–off to Sera Je is midway between Bylakuppe and Kushalnagar. Another important monastery in the vicinity of Bylakuppe is **Tashi Lhunpo**, which is 1km off the main road past the police station. Tashi Lhunpo is much smaller than Sera Je, and is renowned as the seat of the Panchen Lama – Tibet's second most revered spiritual leader after the Dalai Lama. Two other monasteries near the main road are also well worth a visit: **Nyingmapa** has peaceful grounds around a huge colourful prayer hall housing three enormous gilt Buddhas and two startling dragon columns, while the newer **Namdroling** sports a dazzling golden temple. If you're arriving by bus from Mysore, ask to be let down at Bylakuppe, recognizable by the Tibetan farm cooperatives. If you're coming from the west, however, you'll reach Kushalnagar first, where there are more auto–rickshaws available at the bus stand. If you want an auto–rickshaw all to yourself, it'll cost Rs30 to Sera or you can share one at Rs10 per head.

Sera Je's new and welcoming *Guest House* (②), which serves to raise funds and has pleasant clean rooms and a café, is one of the few places to stay and eat around **BYLAKUPPE**. The best place for food is the *Tibet Restaurant*, popular with young monks, which is due to move in late 2001 from Kushalnagar to halfway along the Sera Je road. Namgyal, the proprietor, and his brother are welcoming and a fount of local information, plus they serve great *thukpas*, *momos*, *shabhaleys*, *mothuk* and fried rice.

There's more **accommodation** at **KUSHALNAGAR**; the most comfortable of the hotels is the *Kannika International* (Ⓣ 08276/74728, Ⓕ 73318; ❺–❻), set back from the main road near the bus stand, with its own garden, restaurant and bar with tables on the porch, and airy rooms with TV. Cheaper options on the main road around the bus stand include the basic *Radhakrishna Lodge* (Ⓣ 08276/74822; ❶) with adequate budget rooms, and the *Ganesh* (Ⓣ 08276/74528; ❷). For a bit more quiet follow the lane along the side of the bus stand past the communications tower to the *Mahalaxmi Lodge* (Ⓣ 08276/74622; ❷). Kushalnagar is also well connected **by bus** to Mangalore (via Madikeri), Bangalore, Mysore and Hassan as well as to several destinations in Tamil Nadu. Bus times are posted in English and deluxe and express buses stop here as well.

The sleepy coffee town of **SIDDAPURA** on the banks of the Kaveri (Cauvery) River, lies 32km to the south of Madikeri in the heart of coffee country, and provides the delights of staying on a plantation – at a price. Across the river, the **Dubare Reserve Forest** makes for good short exploratory treks with the chance of seeing wildlife and the occasional elephant; contact the Conservator of Forests, Deputy Commissioner's Office, The Fort, Madikeri (Ⓣ 08272/25708) for more information and take a guide. Alternatively, the resort of *Orange County* at Karadigodu, 3km from Siddapura (Ⓣ 08274/58481, code 914 from Madikeri; ❾) arranges forest walks for guests. Approached by a small road that winds through lush plantations where tall trees provide essential cover for the coffee plants, *Orange County* lies at the edge of a wealthy estate and is the most luxurious place to stay in the whole of Kodagu. Booked through their Bangalore office (Ⓣ 080/558 2380), *Orange County* offers mock-Tudor cottages set within a manicured estate where activities include treks and horse-riding and there's a pleasant pool (for residents only) and a good restaurant serving some Kodava dishes as part of a varied menu. Popular with affluent Indians, and tour groups, *Orange Country* can provide a base from which to visit Nagarhole National Park 75km to the south (see p.248), and should be booked in advance.

Bhagamandala and Talakaveri

A good bus excursion from Madikeri takes you to the quiet village of **BHAGAMANDALA** (35km west), and from there to the sacred site of **TALAKAVERI**, which is said to be the source of the holy Kaveri (Cauvery) River. The hill scenery is superb, and you can opt to walk part of the way on blissfully quiet country roads.

Wear something warm, and take the 6.30am bus from Madikeri's private stand to Bhagamandala. You should arrive around 8am, with just enough time to grab a good breakfast of *parathas* and local honey at the *Laxmi Vilas* tea shop, next to the bus stop from which the bus to Talakaveri leaves at 8.30am. At Bhagamandala, the holy spot where the Kaveri merges with two streams, Kanike and Sujyothi, the **Bhagandeshwara temple** is a fine example of Keralan-style architecture, with tiled roofs and courtyards.

At Talakaveri, the bus stops on the slopes of Brahmagiri Hill by the entrance to the sacred tank and **temple**. During **Kaveri Shankrama** in October, thousands of pilgrims come here to witness a spring – thought to be the goddess Kaveri, known as Lopamudra, the local patron deity – suddenly spurting into a small well. To bathe in the tank at this time is considered especially sin-absolving. The belief is that if the spring dries up, all the rivers of southern India will dry up too. Whenever you come, you're likely to find wild-haired *sadhus* and bathing pilgrims, and the surrounding walls swathed in drying *dhotis* and saris. Two small shrines stand at the head of the tank, one containing an image of Ganesh and the other a metal *lingam* with a *naga* snake canopy. Steep granite steps to the right lead up to the peak of **Brahmagiri Hill**, which affords superb 360° views over Kodagu.

Mangalore

Many visitors only come to **MANGALORE** on their way somewhere else. As well as being fairly close to Madikeri and the Kodagu (Coorg) hill region, it's

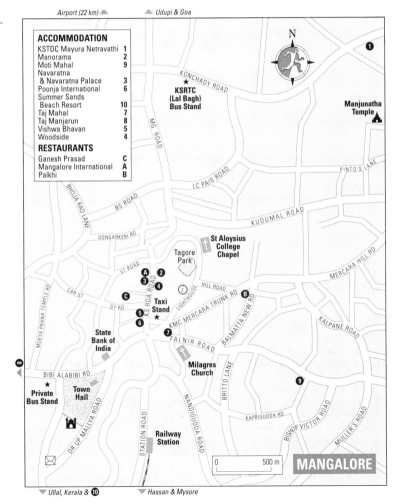

also a stopping-off point between Goa and Kerala, and is the nearest coastal town to the Hoysala and Jain monuments near Hassan, 172km east.

Mangalore was one of the most famous ports of South India, renowned overseas as early as the sixth century as a major source of pepper; the fourteenth-century Muslim writer Ibn Battuta noted its trade in pepper and ginger and the presence of merchants from Persia and the Yemen. In the mid-1400s, the Persian ambassador Abdu'r-Razzaq saw Mangalore as the "frontier town" of the Vijayanagar empire, which was why the Portuguese captured it in 1529. In Haider Ali's time, during the eighteenth century, the city became a shipbuilding centre. Nowadays, the modern port, 10km north of the city proper, is principally known for the processing and export of coffee and cocoa (much of which comes from Kodagu), and cashew nuts from Kerala and Karnataka, as well as granite. It is also a centre for the production of *beedi* cigarettes. Mangalore's heady ethnic mix lived more or less in harmony until 1998, when communal riots saw sections of the large Christian community in the city attacked by right-wing Hindu fundamentalists.

Arrival and information

Mangalore's busy KSRTC **bus stand** (known locally as the "Lal Bagh" bus stand) is 2km north of the town centre, Hampankatta, at the bottom of Kadri Hill. Private buses arrive at the much more central stand near the Town Hall. **Bajpe airport**, 22km north of the city (bus #22 or 47A, Indian Airlines city bus or taxis for Rs250), is served by both Indian Airlines and Jet Airways from Mumbai and Bangalore. The **railway station**, on the south side of the city centre, sees daily services from cities all over India, including Delhi, Agra, Hyderabad, Bangalore, Chennai, and Thiruvananthapuram.

Hampankatta, close to the facilities of Light House Hill Road, acts as the traffic hub of the city, from where you can catch **city buses** or **auto-rickshaws**, although their drivers prefer not to use their meters. The **tourist office** (Mon–Sat 10am–1.30pm & 2.30–5.30pm; ☎0824/442926) on the ground floor of the *Hotel Indraprastha* on Light House Hill Road is helpful for general information and some bus times, but carries no information on trains: for this you need to go to the railway station.

You can **change money** at Trade Wings, Light House Hill Road (Mon–Sat 9.30am–5.30pm; ☎0824/426817) who encash travellers' cheques, and at TT Forex (same hours; ☎0824/421717), 1st Floor, Utility Royal Towers, KS Rao Road. The State Bank of India (Mon–Fri 10.30am–2.30pm & Sat 10.30am–12.30pm), near the Town Hall on Hamilton Circle is somewhat slower.

Mangalore's **GPO** (Mon–Sat 10am–7pm, Sun 10.30am–1.30pm) is a short walk from the centre, at Shetty Circle. For **email** try the friendly and popular Kohinoor Computer Zone, Plaza Towers, Light House Hill Road (Mon–Sat 8am–2am; ☎0824/429340) down the road from the tourist office, or Cyber Zoom, 1st Floor, Utility Royal Towers, KS Rao Road (Mon–Sat 9.30am–6.30pm; ☎0824/449213).

Accommodation

Mangalore's **accommodation** standards are forever improving; it even has a modern five-star hotel. The main area for hotels, **KS Rao Road**, runs south from the bus stand and has an ample choice to suit most pockets. You can also stay out of town by the beach in **Ullal**.

KSTDC Mayura Netravathi, 1500m east of the bus stand, Kadir Hill ☎0824/211192. Rambling, old government hotel, the best of the budget bunch, with large, good-value en-suite rooms (most with twin beds and mozzie nets), although some are a little on the grubby side and it's a trek from the centre. None of the rickshaw-wallahs knows where it is, so ask for the "Circuit House", next door. ❷

Manorama, KS Rao Road ☎0824/440306. A 65-room concrete block with spartan, large and very clean rooms (some a/c). Good value: the best of the central options. ❸–❻

Moti Mahal, Falnir Road ☎0824/441411. Large hotel (some a/c) with 24hr room service and coffee shop, bar, pool, shops, exchange and travel desk. *Mangala* non-veg and *Madhuvan* veg restaurants serve Indian, Chinese and Western food. ❻–❼

Navaratna Palace, KS Rao Road ☎0824/441104. Shares a reception with its adjacent sister *Navaratna* but has better rooms (some a/c) for little extra cost. Also two good a/c restaurants: *Heera Panna* and *Palimar* (pure veg). ❹–❼

Poonja International, KS Rao Road ☎0824/440171, ☎441081. Smart mostly a/c highrise with all facilities and stunning views from the upper floors. Buffet South Indian breakfast included. ❻–❽

Summer Sands Beach Resort, Chota Mangalore, Ullal, 10km south of the city ☎0824/467690, ☎467693. Spacious rooms and cottages (some a/c) near the beach, originally built as a campus for expats, with a pool and a bar-restaurant serving local specialities, Indian and Chinese food. Foreign exchange for guests. Recommended. Take bus #44A from town. ❻–❽

Taj Mahal, Hampankatta ☎0824/421751. Large dowdy economy hotel overlooking a busy crossing but handy for the railway station; the restaurant, including a plain canteen and an a/c section, is renowned for its wholesome thalis. ❸–❺

Taj Manjarun, Old Port Road, 2km from railway station ☎0824/420420, ☎420585. Modern business hotel; some rooms with sea view and all a/c. Travel desk, exchange, pool, bar and 24hr coffee shop. The pricey restaurant, *Galley*, serves Indian and Western food; *Embers* is a poolside barbecue. ❼–❽

Vishwa Bhavan, KS Rao Road ☎0824/440822. Cheap, plain rooms, some with attached baths, around a courtyard close to all amenities. Best of the real cheapies. ❶

Woodside, KS Rao Road ☎0824/440296. Old-fashioned hotel offering a range of rooms (their economy doubles are the best deal), but "no accommodation for servants". Some a/c. ❸–❻

Kambla

If you're anywhere between Mangalore and Bhatkal from October to April and come across a crowd gathering around a water-logged paddy field, pull over and spend a day at the races – Karnatakan style. Few Westerners ever experience it, but the unique and spectacular rural sport of kambla, or bull racing, played in the southernmost district of coastal Karnataka (known as Dakshina Kannada), is well worth seeking out.

Two contestants, usually local rice-farmers, take part in each race, riding on a wooden plough-board attached to a pair of prize bullocks. The object is to reach the opposite end of the field first, but points are also awarded for style, and riders gain extra marks – and roars of approval from the crowd – if the muddy spray kicked up from the plough-board splashes the special white banners, or *thoranam*, strung across the course at a height of 6 to 8m.

Generally, race days are organized by wealthy landowners on fields specially set aside for the purpose. Villagers flock in from all over the region, as much for the fair, or *shendi*, as the races themselves: men huddle in groups to watch cock fights (*korikatta*), women haggle with bangle sellers and kids roam around sucking sticky *kathambdi goolay*, the local bon-bons. It is considered highly prestigious to be able to throw such a party, especially if your bulls win any events or, better still, come away as champions. Known as *yeru* in Kannada, racing bulls are thoroughbreds who rarely, if ever, are put to work. Pampered by their doting owners, they are massaged, oiled and blessed by priests before big events, during which large sums of money are often won and lost.

The city and beaches

Mangalore's strong Christian influence can be traced back to the arrival further south of St Thomas (see p.667). Some 1400 years later, in 1526, the Portuguese founded one of the earliest churches on the coast close to the old port; the present **Most Holy Rosary church**, however, with a dome based on St Peter's in Rome, dates only from 1910. Fine restored fresco, tempera and oil murals, the work of an Italian artist, Antonio Moscheni, adorn the Romanesque-style **St Aloysius College chapel**, built in 1885, on Lighthouse Hill Road, near the centre.

At the foot of Kadri Hill, 3km north and served by numerous city buses, Mangalore's tenth-century **Manjunatha temple** is an important centre of the Shaivite and Tantric **Natha-Pantha cult**. Thought to be an outgrowth of Vajrayana Buddhism, the cult is a divergent species of Hinduism, similar to certain cults in Nepal. Enshrined in the sanctuary, a number of superb **bronzes** include a 1.5-metre-high seated Lokeshvara (Matsyendranatha), made in 958 AD and considered the finest southern bronze outside Tamil Nadu. To see it close up you'll have to visit at *darshan* times (6am–1pm & 4–8pm), although the bronzes can be glimpsed through the wooden slats on the side of the sanctuary. If possible, time your visit to coincide with **mahapooja** at 8am, noon or 8pm, when the priests give a fire blessing to the accompaniment of raucous music. Manjunatha's square and towered sanctuary, containing an unusual *lingam*, is surrounded by two tiled and gabled colonnades with louvred windows, showing strong affinity with the temple complexes further south in Kerala. Nine water tanks adjoin the temple. Opposite the east entrance, steps lead via a laterite path to a curious group of minor shrines. Beyond this complex stands the **Shri Yogishwar Math**, a hermitage of Tantric *sadhus* set round two courtyards, one of which contains shrines to Kala Bhairava (a form of Dakshinamurti, the southern aspect of Shiva and deity of death), Durga and god of fire, Agni. Nearby, cut into the side of the hill, a tiny unadorned cave is credited with being one of the "night halts" for the Pandava brothers from the *Mahabharata*.

If you're looking to escape the city for a few hours, head out to the village of **ULLAL**, 10km south, whose long sandy **beach**, backed by wispy fir trees, stretches for miles in both directions. It's a deservedly popular place for a stroll, particularly in the evening when families and courting couples come out to watch the sunset, but a strong undertow makes swimming difficult, and at times unsafe. You're better off using the pool at the excellent *Summer Sands Beach Resort* (see opposite), immediately behind the beach (Rs60 for non-residents). A further 2km past the *Summer Sands*, a banyan-lined road leads to the Shiva temple of **Someshwar**, built in Keralan style, overlooking a rocky promontory, and another popular beach which is subject to gangs of gawking youths. Towards the centre of Ullal and around 700m from the main bus stand, is the *dargah* (burial shrine) of **Seyyid Mohammad Shareeful Madani**, a sixteenth-century saint who is said to have come from Medina in Arabia and floated across the sea on a handkerchief. The extraordinary nineteenth-century building with garish onion-domes houses the saint's tomb, which is one of the most important sufi shrines in southern India. Visitors are advised to follow custom and cover their heads and limbs and wash their feet before entering. Local **buses** (#44A) run to Ullal from the junction at the south end of KS Rao Road. As you cross the Netravathi River en route, look out for the brick chimney-stacks clustered on the banks at the mouth of the estuary. Using quality clay shipped downriver from the hills, these factories manufacture the famous terracotta red **Mangalorean roof tiles**, which you see all over southern India.

Eating

The best **places to eat** are in the bigger hotels. If you're on a tight budget, try one of the inexpensive café-restaurants opposite the bus stand, or the excellent canteen inside the bus stand itself, which serves great dosas and other South

Moving on from Mangalore

Mangalore is a major crossroads for tourist traffic heading along the Konkan coast between Goa and Kerala, and between Mysore and the coast. The city is also well connected by air to Mumbai, Bangalore and Chennai. Jet Airways flies to Mumbai (1–2 daily) and to Bangalore (daily), while Indian Airlines flies to Mumbai (daily) and Chennai via Bangalore (3 weekly). The Indian Airlines office is at Airlines House, Hathill Road, Lalbagh (☎ 0824/454669) and the Jet Airways office at DS Ram Bhavan Complex, Kodiabail (☎ 0824/441181).

With the inauguration of the single-track coastal Konkan Railway, services have opened up to Goa and Mumbai. One passenger train #KR2 departs Mangalore at 7.10am, travelling north along the coast and takes 6hr 20min to travel to Madgaon (Goa) via Udupi and Gokarn. The *Matsyagandha Express* (#2620), which departs at 2.50pm, is the fastest service to Goa (4hr 50min), but does not stop at Gokarn. Until the through service is introduced you have to change at Madgaon for Mumbai. The service south is more established and, if you're travelling to Kerala, the train is far quicker and more relaxing than the bus. Two services leave Mangalore station every day for Trivandrum, via Kozhikode, Ernakulam/Cochin, Kottayam and Kollam. Leaving at the red-eyed time of 3.15am, the *Parsuram Express* (#6350) is the faster of the two but the *Malabar Express* (#6330), which leaves at 4.30pm, is convenient as an overnight train to Trivandrum, arriving there at 9.35am. A better choice of train connections for the coastal run south can be had from Kasargode, an easy bus ride across the Kerala border. For those travelling to Chennai, the overnight Mangalore–Chennai mail (#6602) departs at 11.15am and follows the Kerala coast till Shoranur where it turns east to Palakaad before journeying on to Erode and arriving at Chennai at 6.20am. The *West Coast Express* (#6628) departs from Mangalore at 8.10pm. and follows the same route but also stops at Coimbatore.

The traditional way to travel on to Goa was always by bus, though that is now being usurped by the Konkan Railway. Six buses leave the KSRTC Lal Bagh stand daily, taking around 10hr 30min to reach Panjim. You can jump off at Chaudi (for Palolem) en route, and some buses also go via Margao (for Colva beach), but it's best to check, as most travel direct to the Goan capital. Tickets should be booked in advance (preferably the day before) at KSRTC's well-organized computer booking hall (daily 7am–8pm), or from the Kadamba office on the main concourse. The Goa buses are also good for Gokarn; hop off at Kumta on the main highway, and catch an onward service from there. The only direct bus to Gokarn leaves Mangalore at 1.30pm. There are plenty of buses to Udupi and several south along the coast to Kasargode and Kannur in Kerala. Many private services also plough up and down the coast to these destinations and some head inland to Jog Falls, as well as Bangalore and other major towns.

For Mysore, Bangalore, Hassan and Madikeri, it's best to take the bus as the train service inland to Hassan is slow and still disrupted due to work on the line. The best private bus service to Bangalore is on the distinctive yellow luxury coaches of VRL; two buses leave at night (10pm, 8hr; Rs220) and tickets are available through Vijayananda Travels, PVS Centenary Building, Kodiyalbail, Kudmulranga Rao Road (☎ 0824/493536). Agents along Falnir Road include Kohinoor Travels (☎ 0824/426400) and Ideal Travels (☎ 0824/424899) who also run luxury buses to Bangalore and a bus to Ernakulam (9pm, 9hr; Rs270). Bangalore-bound luxury buses travel through Madikeri and there are hourly KSRTC buses to Mysore.

Indian snacks. Also recommended for delicious, freshly cooked and inexpensive "meals" is the *Ganesh Prasad*, down the lane alongside the uninspiring *Vasanth Mahal*. The rooftop *Palkhi* on Mercara Trunk Road is an airy family restaurant with a wide menu. For something a little more sophisticated, head for the a/c *Xanadu*, at the *Woodside Hotel*, also on KS Rao Road, which offers classy non-veg cuisine and alcohol. It's too dingy for lunch, but fine for dinner, when its kitsch fish tanks and resident duck are illuminated. One of the best of the hotel restaurants, however, is the *Moghul Darbar* at the *Mangalore International* also on KS Rao Road, which has both a plush a/c and a comfortable and non-a/c section. Although they do not serve alcohol, they offer an excellent mixed menu – if you order a vegetarian thali and add fish to it you have a feast.

Around Mangalore: Jain bastis and temple towns

The **Jain bastis** (temples) of southwest Karnataka – **Mudabidri**, **Karkala** and **Dharamastala** – some of which date back to the ninth century, continue to form part of a pilgrimage circuit attracting Jains from all over India. Although the most famous of all the Jain *bastis* is at Sravanabelgola on the outskirts of Hassan (see p.255), the greatest concentration of these shrines lies to the east and northeast of Mangalore and can be taken in on day-trips.

Of the important Hindu pilgrimage centres near Mangalore, the great *matha* (a centre of pilgrimage and learning), at **Sringeri** to the east, continues to play a pivotal role in ongoing developments in Hindu theology.

Mudabidri

The most extensive of the *bastis* can be found in the small quiet town of **MUDABIDRI**, 35km to the north of Mangalore. According to legend, a Jain ascetic settled here in the eighth century when he saw significance in the sight of a tiger playing with a cow. Most of the eighteen *bastis* and several *mathas* (monasteries) at Mudabidri were built between the fifteenth and sixteenth centuries. The most impressive, close to the town centre, is the **Chandranatha Basti**, completed in 1430 AD and known as Tribhuvana Tilaka Chudamani Basti, or more commonly as the "thousand-pillar hall". Approached by an imposing entrance gate and fronted by a tall, multistorey stone lamp, the main temple consists of two large interconnected columned halls. The surrounding veranda has stone columns supporting a sloping stone roof that is, in turn, crowned by a roof coated with copper tiles supported by carved wooden angle brackets.

Karkala

An eighteen-kilometre bus ride north of Mudabidri, the small town of **KARKALA** is famous for the thirteen-metre high statue of **Gomateshvara**, standing placid and naked atop a rocky granite outcrop on the outskirts, 1km away from the town centre. Steps hewn out of rock lead up to the dramatic freestanding image, which was built in 1432 by Veerapandyadeva, a local ruler, and inspired by the monolith at Sravanabelagola (see p.255). At the bottom of the hill lies the **Chaturmukha Basti**, built in 1586 and so called because of its identical four (*chatur*) faces (*mukha*) or directions. The main object of the symmetry is the columned hall where four doors punctuate the porch, each with a view of three deities within the inner sanctum. By circumambulating the sanctuary, the devotee is thus able to take in twelve *tirthankaras* in all.

Dharamastala

A popular Hindu pilgrimage town set against a pleasant backdrop of paddy fields, wooded hills and plantations, **DHARAMASTALA**, 75km east of Mangalore, has another monolithic stone image of **Gomateshvara**, completed in 1973 by the artist Ranjal Gopal Shenoy. Although impressive, the fourteen-metre-high statue, which borrows heavily from its predecessors and took five years to create, lacks the refinement of those at Karkala and Sravanabelgola. It stands on a hill, above the frenetically busy **Manjunatha temple** (daily 6.30am–1pm & 7–8pm), where both Hindus and Jains worship. An important Shaivite shrine, managed by Vaishnava priests, the temple was founded in 1780 by the influential Hegdes, a family of Jains who still run the temple and were responsible for the statue of Gomateshvara. According to custom, pilgrims to Dharamastala bathe in the **Netravati River**, 3km away.

Sringeri

On the banks of the Tunga River, the scenic village of **SRINGERI**, on the edge of coffee plantations 100km northeast of Mangalore, is notable for its ancient *matha*, established in the ninth century by the great Hindu reformer and theologian Shankara. Shankara is supposed to have spent twelve years of his life in Sringeri. The village itself has been at the centre of religious and social events, formerly exerting a strong influence over the Vijayanagar empire based at Hampi. During the festival of Navaratri, held each September/October, which commemorates the goddess Sharada's triumph over evil, the village swells with the influx of pilgrims.

The modern **Sharada temple** at Sringeri, devoted to a form of the goddess Saraswati, receives a steady stream of pilgrims. Steps lead down to the Tunga River, where devotees congregate to feed the sacred fish. More interesting architecturally is the sixteenth-century **Vidyashankara temple**, a short distance to the south of the Sharada temple, on a picturesque location above the river. Built on a high plinth decorated with friezes of animals, figures and gods, the temple enshrines a *lingam* that is considered to be the *samadhi* (memorial) to Shankara. The twelve pillars of the *mandapa* support a set of heavy ceiling-slabs and feature lavish details including riders on mythical beasts, depicting each of the twelve signs of the zodiac. The walls of the temple are richly adorned with carvings depicting the gods, while the niches hold various aspects of Shiva and the incarnations of Vishnu, including Krishna playing the flute.

Practicalities

Regular buses from the KSRTC bus stand in Mangalore ply the route to Dharamastala, Mudabidri and Karkala, which can also be approached directly from Udupi 35km to the southeast. Several buses continue on to Sringeri, but if you miss these you can change at Karkala. The road between Karkala and Sringeri is particularly beautiful, as it passes through a lush forest-belt on its way up the Western Ghats. Mudabidri and Karkala can be taken in as long day-trips from Mangalore. At both places **accommodation** is limited to the form of basic government-run *Tourist Cottages* (❷), which you can book in the tourist office in Mangalore. Both Dharamastala and Sringeri have **room reservation offices** located near the temple entrances, which will assign you temple-run rooms (❶). These are usually excellent value and can range from very basic rooms with shared bathrooms to comfortable doubles with attached baths. Private accommodation (❷–❸), is available near the bus stands, where the choice of restaurants is limited to basic "meals".

North of Mangalore: coastal and western Karnataka

Whether you travel the **Karnatakan (Karavali) coast** on the newly operational Konkan Railway or along the busy NH-14, southern India's smoothest highway, the route between Goa and Mangalore ranks among the most scenic anywhere in the country. Crossing countless palm- and mangrove-fringed estuaries, the recently upgraded road, dubbed by the local tourist board as "The Sapphire Route", scales several spurs of the Western Ghats, which here creep to within a stone's throw of the sea, with spellbinding views over long, empty beaches and deep blue bays. Highlights are the pilgrim town of **Udupi**, site of a famous Krishna temple, and **Gokarn**, a bustling village that provides access to exquisite unexploited beaches. A couple of bumpy back roads wind inland through the mountains to **Jog Falls**, India's highest waterfall, most often approached from the east. Infrequent buses crawl from the coast through rugged jungle scenery to this spectacular spot, but you'll enjoy the trip more by motorbike; it is possible to rent one in Goa and ride down the coast from there, stopping off at secluded beaches, falls and viewpoints en route.

Just across the Ghats from the coast are several places worth visiting: the temple towns of **Sirsi**, with its unique Kavi art, and ancient **Banvasi** are quiet escapes from the main tourist trail, while the **Dandeli Wildlife Sanctuary** is renowned for its population of black panthers. Workaday **Hubli**, the area's main transport hub, offers varied side-trips to those on a longer itinerary.

Udupi

UDUPI (also spelt Udipi), 58km north of Mangalore, is one of South India's holiest Vaishnavite centres. The Hindu saint **Madhva** (1238–1317) was born here, and the **Krishna temple** and *mathas* (monasteries) he founded are visited by *lakhs* of pilgrims each year. The largest numbers congregate during the late winter, when the town hosts a series of spectacular **car festivals** and gigantic, bulbous-domed chariots are hauled through the streets around the temple. Even if your visit doesn't coincide with a festival, Udupi is a good place to break the journey along the Karavali coast. Thronging with *pujaris* and pilgrims, its small sacred enclave is wonderfully atmospheric, and you can take a boat from the nearby fishing village at **Malpé beach** to **St Mary's Island**, the deserted outcrop of hexagonal basalt where Vasco da Gama erected a crucifix prior to his first landfall in India.

Incidentally, Udupi also lays proud claim to being the birthplace of the nationally popular **masala dosa**; these crispy stuffed pancakes, made from fermented rice flour, were first prepared and made famous by the Udupi brahmin hotels.

The Krishna temple and maths

Udupi's **Krishna temple** lies five minutes' walk east of the main street, surrounded by the eight **maths** founded by Madhva in the thirteenth century. Legend has it that the idol enshrined within was discovered by the saint himself, after he prevented a shipwreck. The grateful captain of the vessel concerned offered Madhva his precious cargo as a reward, but the holy man asked instead for a block of ballast, which he broke open to expose a perfectly formed image of Krishna. Believed to contain the essence (*sannidhya*) of the god, this deity draws a steady stream of pilgrims and is the focus of almost constant ritual activity. It is cared for by *acharyas*, or pontiffs, from one or other of the *maths*. The only people allowed to touch the idol, they perform pujas (5.30am–8.45pm) that are open to non-Hindus; men are only allowed in the main shrine bare-chested. As the *acharya* approaches the shrine, the crowd divides to let him through, while brahmin boys fan the deity with cloths, accompanied by a cacophony of clanging bells and clouds of incense smoke.

A stone tank adjacent to the temple, known as the **Madhva Sarovara**, is the focus of a huge festival every two years (usually Jan 17–18), when a new head priest is appointed. Preparations for the **Paryaya Mahotsava** begin thirteen months in advance, and culminate with the grand entry of the new *acharya* into the town, at the head of a huge procession. Outside in the street, a window in the wall affords a view of the deity; according to legend, this is the spot where a Harijan, or "untouchable", devotee, denied entry due to his caste, was worshipping Krishna from outside when the deity turned to face him. A statue of the devotee stands opposite. Nearby, there's a magnificent gold-painted wooden temple chariot (*rath*), carved in the distinctive Karnatakan style, its onion-shaped tower decked with thousands of scraps of paper, cloth and tinsel.

At the **Regional Resources Centre for the Performing Arts**, in the MGM College, staff can tell you about local festivals and events that are well off the tourist trail; the collection includes film, video and audio archives. The pamphlet *Udupi: an Introduction*, on sale in the stalls around the sacred enclave, is another rich source of background detail on the temple and its complex rituals.

Malpé, Thottam and St Mary's Island

Udupi's weekend picnic spot, **Malpé beach**, 5km north of the centre, is disappointing, marred by a forgotten concrete structure that was planned to be a government-run hotel. After wandering around the smelly fish market at the harbour you could haggle to arrange a boat (around Rs800) to take you out to **St Mary's Island**, an extraordinary rock face of hexagonal basalt. Vasco da Gama is said to have placed a cross here in the 1400s, prior to his historic landing at Kozhikode in Kerala. From a distance, the sandy beach at **Thottam**, 1km north of Malpé and visible from the island, looks tempting; in reality it's an open sewer.

Practicalities

Udupi's three **bus stands** are dotted around the main street in the centre of town: the "City" stand handles private services to nearby villages, including Malpé, while the adjacent "Service" stand is for long-distance private buses including numerous services to Mangalore. From the KSRTC stand, long-distance government buses run to Mangalore, Bangalore, Gokarn, Jog Falls and Goa, and other towns along the coastal highway. Udupi's **railway station** is at Indrali on Manipal Road, 3km from the centre; there are four or five trains in each direction daily. Money can be **exchanged** at the KM Dutt branch of Canara Bank on the main road just south of the bus stands, and **email** facilities are available at nearby Netpoint, one of several such outlets.

Udupi has a good choice of **places to stay and eat**. The *Hotel Sharada International* (T 08252/22910; ③–⑤), 1km out of town on the highway, has a range of rooms from singles to carpeted a/c, as well as veg and non-veg restaurants and a bar. *Kediyoor*, near the Service bus stand (T 08252/22381, F 22380; ④–⑥) is much the same, but with three restaurants – the a/c *Janata* serves excellent thalis – while the *Janardhana*, close to the KSRTC stand

(⊤08252/23880, Ⓕ23887; ❸–❻), is a little simpler, with clean rooms, some of them a/c. The *Classic* restaurant in the building next door offers great seafood (chowder and so on), meat and veg dishes in a classy upstairs lounge and their *Wild Rain* bar is a lively place for a drink. A couple of minutes' walk east of the main road, the *Hotel Swadesh Heritage*, Maruthi Vethika (⊤08252/29605, Ⓕ20205, ⒺUswadesh-vip@zetainfotech.com; ❹–❼) is Udupi's most luxurious hotel (at least until the nearby *Sriram International* opens), with complimentary breakfasts, reasonable a/c rooms and two restaurants and a bar. Their vegetarian thalis are excellent. If you're looking for somewhere cheaper, try the basic but friendly and clean *Vyavahar Lodge*, on Kankads Road (⊤08252/22568; ❷), between the bus stand and temple, or, better still, try and get one of the great-value front rooms overlooking the tank and temple at the new *Sri Vidyasamudra Chatra* (⊤08252/20820; ❶).

Jog Falls

Hidden in a remote, thickly forested corner of the Western Ghats, **Jog Falls**, 240km northeast of Mangalore, are the highest **waterfalls** in India. These days, they are rarely as spectacular as they were before the construction of a large dam upriver, which impedes the flow of the Sharavati River over the sheer red-brown sandstone cliffs. However, the surrounding scenery is spectacular at any time, with dense scrub and jungle carpeting sparsely populated, mountainous terrain. The views of the falls from the scruffy collection of chai stalls on the opposite side of the gorge is also impressive, unless, that is, you come here during the monsoons, when mist and rain clouds envelop the cascades. Another reason not to come here during the wet season is that the extra water and abundance of leeches at this time make the excellent **hike** to the valley floor dangerous. So if you can, head up here between November and January, and bring stout footwear. The trail starts just below the bus park and winds steeply down to the water. Confident hikers also venture further downriver, clambering over boulders to other pools and hidden viewpoints, but you should keep a close eye on the water level and take along a local **guide** to point out the safest path.

Practicalities

Getting to and from Jog Falls by public transport is not easy at present, but should be soon with the completion of the NH-240 across the Ghats, which will cut the journey time from **Kumta** to three hours. Currently there are two **buses** daily to Udupi and on to Mangalore (7.30am & 8.15pm; 7hr), one to Karwar (11.30am; 6hr), one to Gokarn (5.30pm; 5hr) and hourly services to Shimoga, from where you can change onto buses for Hospet and Hampi. Better connections can be had at nearby Sagar (30km southeast) with buses to Shimoga, Udupi, Mysore, Hassan and Bangalore. Of the two direct buses to Bangalore from Jog Falls, the "semi-deluxe" departs at 7.30pm (9hr) and the ordinary at 8.30am. The **tourist office** at *Tunga Tourist Home* (Mon–Sat 10am–5.30pm) is good for bus times and advice in case you need to rent a **car** or a Jeep, both available at Jog Falls. With a car or motorbike, you can approach the falls from the coast along one of several scenic routes through the Ghats. The easiest and best maintained of these heads inland from Bhatkal to Jog Falls, but for a truly unforgettable experience, risk the tortuous, bumpy back route from **Kumta**, which takes you through some breathtaking landscape. There are very few villages and no fuel stops along the way, so stock up beforehand, and make sure your vehicle is in good shape.

Accommodation is limited. If you can get in, the *PWD Inspection Bungalow* (①), on the north side of the gorge, has great views from its spacious, comfortable rooms, but is invariably full and has to be booked in advance from the assistant engineer's office in Siddapur. Across the falls on the main side of the settlement, the large concrete complex of the KSTDC *Mayura Gerusoppa* (☎08186/44732; ②–③), located past the non-functioning public swimming pool, has vast rooms with fading plaster and bathrooms with rickety plumbing, but the staff are friendly and there's an adequate restaurant and good views. Their annexe, the KSTDC *Tunga Tourist Home* at the bus stand is more basic (②) and doesn't have the garden or view. On the opposite side of the road, the Karnataka Power Corporation also let their four comfy a/c rooms (☎08186/44742; ⑤) when available. The youth hostel (Rs50), ten minutes' walk down the Shimoga road, has basic facilities but recent renovations have made it more appealing. Most travellers make do with a raffia mat on the floor of one of the houses behind the chai stalls.

The KSTDC canteen next to the *Tunga Tourist Home* at the bus stand serves reasonable South Indian vegetarian **food** including *iddlis* and dosas. The KSTDC *Mayura Gerusoppa* has a more comfortable restaurant with a varied menu but still manages to remain uninspiring, while the chai stalls around the square serve basic thalis and (eggy) snacks.

Gokarn

Set behind a broad white-sand beach, with the forest-covered foothills of the Western Ghats forming a blue-green backdrop, **GOKARN** (also spelled Gokarna), seven hours by bus north of Mangalore, is among India's most scenically situated sacred sites. Yet this compact little coastal town – a Shaivite centre for more than two millennia – remained largely "undiscovered" by Western tourists until a little under a decade ago, when it began to attract dreadlocked and didgeridoo-toting travellers fleeing the commercialization of Goa. Now, it's firmly on the tourist map, although the Hindu pilgrims pouring through still far outnumber the foreigners that flock here in winter.

Even if you're not tempted to while away weeks on isolated beaches, Gokarn is well worth a short detour from the coastal highway. Like Udupi, it is an old-established pilgrimage place, with a markedly traditional feel: shaven-headed brahmins sit cross-legged on their verandas murmuring Sanskrit verses, while Hindu pilgrims file through a bazaar crammed with religious paraphernalia to the sea for a holy dip.

Arrival and information

The new KSRTC **bus stand**, 300m from the main road and within easy walking distance of Gokarn's limited accommodation, means that buses no longer have to negotiate the narrow streets of the bazaar. Gokarn's **railway station**, currently served by just one daily passenger train in each direction, is at Madanageri, from where buses and tempos are available to take you the 9km into town.

You can **change money** at the *Om Hotel* near the new bus stand but the best rates to be had are at the Pai STD booth on the road into town near the bus stand, one several licensed dealers. The tiny Om bureau almost opposite is the best of the various **internet** joints but none have very reliable connections. **Bicycles** are available for rent from a stall next to the *Pai Restaurant*, for Rs3 per hour or Rs30 for a full day. However, due to the roughness of the tracks you will find it near impossible to cycle to beaches other than the town beach, or along the long route to Om beach.

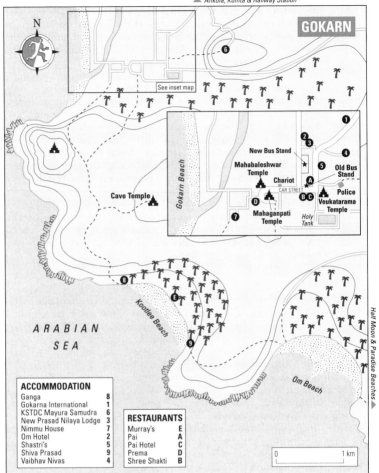

Ankola, Kumta & Railway Station

GOKARN

KARNATAKA | North of Mangalore

See inset map

New Bus Stand

Mahabaleshwar
Temple

Gokarn Beach

Chariot

CAR STREET

Cave Temple

Old Bus
Stand

Police

Veukatarama
Temple

Mahaganpati
Temple

Holy
Tank

ARABIAN
SEA

Kootlee Beach

Om Beach

Half Moon & Paradise Beaches

ACCOMMODATION

Ganga	8
Gokarna International	1
KSTDC Mayura Samudra	6
New Prasad Nilaya Lodge	3
Nimmu House	7
Om Hotel	2
Shastri's	5
Shiva Prasad	9
Vaibhav Nivas	4

RESTAURANTS

Murray's	E
Pai	A
Pai Hotel	C
Prema	D
Shree Shakti	B

0   1 km

Accommodation

Gokarn has a couple of bona fide **hotels** and a small but reasonable choice of
guesthouses. As a last resort, you can nearly always find a bed in one of the
pilgrims' hostels, or **dharamshalas**, dotted around town. With dorms, bare,
cell-like rooms and basic washing facilities, these are intended mainly for
Hindus, but Western tourists are welcome if there are vacancies: try the *Prasad
Nilaya*, just down the lane from *Om Hotel*. After staying in the village for a couple of days, however, many visitors strike out for the **beaches**, where there is
very limited accommodation (see relevant account). Some people end up
sleeping rough on the beaches, but the nights can be chilly and robberies are
common. Leave your luggage and valuables behind in Gokarn (most guesthouses will store your stuff for a fee), and if you plan to spend any time on the
beaches, consider investing in a cheap mattress from the bazaar – you can
always sell it when you leave.

Gokarna International, on main road into town ☎08386/56622. Gokarna's newest and smartest hotel is friendly and offers unbeatable value. Good range of rooms from cheap singles to deluxe a/c; some have bathtubs, TV and balconies overlooking the palms. Also two good restaurants, one with a bar. ②–⑥

KSTDC Mayura Samudra, high on a bald hill above Gokarn (look for the sign on the left as you arrive) ☎08386/56236. Only three large rooms with crumbling plaster and bathrooms with rickety plumbing, each with a sitout and garden overlooking the coast and out to sea. The staff are friendly and helpful and serve meals to order. A good option if you have transport or are willing to tackle the short but steep hike up from the bazaar past the police barracks. ②

New Prasad Nilaya Lodge, near the new bus stand ☎08386/57135. A relatively new place with clean, bright and spacious rooms with attached baths and food to order. Very reasonable. ②–③

Nimmu House, a minute's walk from the temples towards Gokarn beach (☎08386/56730). Gokarn's best budget guesthouse, run by the friendly and helpful lady whose name it bears, with clean rooms (some attached). The new block has very reasonable doubles, there is a reliable left-luggage facility and a peaceful yard to sit in. ①–②

Om Hotel, near the new bus stand ☎08386/56445. Conventional economy hotel pitched at middle-class Indian pilgrims, with plain, good-sized en-suite rooms, some a/c, and a dingy bar-cum-restaurant. ②–⑤

Shastri Guest House, 100m from the new bus stand ☎08386/56220. The best of the uniformly drab and run-down guesthouses lining the main street, this is a quiet place offering some rooms with attached bath, and rock-bottom single-occupancy rates. ②

Vaibhav Nivas, off the main road, five minutes from the bazaar ☎08386/56714. Friendly, cheap and justifiably popular place despite the tiny rooms, most with shared baths. The new extension includes some rooms with attached baths. You can eat here, too, and leave luggage if you're heading off to the beaches (Rs5 per locker including a shower on return). ①–②

The Town

Gokarn **town**, a hotchpotch of wood-fronted houses and red terracotta roofs, is clustered around a long L-shaped bazaar, its broad main road – known as **Car Street** – running west to the town beach, a sacred site in its own right. Hindu mythology identifies it as the place where Rudra (another name for Shiva) was reborn through the ear of a cow from the underworld after a period of penance. Gokarn is also the home of one of India's most powerful *shivalingam* – the **pranalingam**, which came to rest here after being carried off by Ravana, the evil king of Lanka, from Shiva's home on Mount Kailash in the Himalayas. Sent by the gods to reclaim the sacred object, Ganesh, with the help of Vishnu, tricked Ravana into letting him look after the *lingam* while he prayed, knowing that if it touched the ground it would take root and never be moved. When Ravana returned from his meditation, he tried to pick the *lingam* up, but couldn't, because the gods had filled it with "the weight of three worlds".

The *pranalingam* resides in Gokarn to this day, enshrined in the medieval **Shri Mahabaleshwar temple**, at the far west end of the bazaar. It is regarded as so auspicious that a mere glimpse of it will absolve a hundred sins, even murder of a brahmin. Local Hindu lore also asserts that you can maximize the *lingam*'s purifying power by shaving your head, fasting and taking a holy dip in the sea before *darshan*, or ritual viewing of the deity. For this reason, pilgrims traditionally begin their tour of Gokarn with a walk to the beach. They are aided and instructed by their personal *pujari* – one of the bare-chested priests you see around town, wearing sacred caste threads and with single tufts of hair sprouting from their shaven heads – whose job it is to guide the pilgrims. Next, they visit the **Shri Mahaganpati temple**, a stone's throw east of Shri Mahabaleshwar, to propitiate the elephant-headed god Ganesh. Sadly, owing to some ugly incidents involving insensitive behaviour by a minority of foreigners, tourists are now banned from the temples, though you can still get a good view of proceedings in the smaller Shri Mahaganpati from the entrance. En route, check out the splendid **rath**, or chariot, that stands at the end of the bazaar next to the Mahaganpati temple. During important festivals, notably Shiva's "birthday", **Shivratri** (Feb), deities are installed inside this colossal carved-wood cart and hauled by hand along the main street, accompanied by drum bands and watched by huge crowds.

The beaches

Notwithstanding Gokarn's numerous temples, shrines and tanks, most Western tourists come here for the beautiful **beaches** situated south of the more crowded town beach, beyond the lumpy laterite headland that overlooks the town. The hike to them takes in some superb coastal scenery, but be sure to carry plenty of water and wear a hat.

To pick up the trail, head along the narrow alley opposite the south entrance to the Mahaganpati temple, and follow the path uphill through the woods. After twenty minutes, you drop down from a sun-baked rocky plateau to **Kootlee beach** – a wonderful kilometre-long sweep of pure white sand sheltered by a pair of steep-sided promontories. Despite appearances, locals consider the water here to be dangerous. The palm-leaf chai stalls and seasonal cafés that spring up here during the winter give some respite from the heat of the midday sun, and some of them offer very basic accommodation in huts. Two places have more solid, lockable brick or mud huts but are likely to be booked out by long-term visitors: the *Ganga*, to the right as you first approach the beach (℡08386/57195; ●), and *Shiva Prasad* at the far end (℡08386/57150; ●). *Murray's Tea Shop* (aka the "Spanish tea shop" after his wife), set behind a line of neatly planted palms midway down the beach, serves good pasta, sandwiches, sweets and creamy lassis in a relaxed atmosphere. A couple of the other cafés now offer seafood and other more substantial meals.

It takes around twenty minutes to hike from Kootlee to the next beach, scaling the headland to the south and following the steep gravel path as it zigzags down the other side to the sea. The views along the way are stunning, especially when you first glimpse exquisite **Om beach**, so-named because its distinctive twin crescent-shaped bays resemble the auspicious Om symbol. During the Nineties this was the all but exclusive preserve of a hard-core hippy fringe, many of whom spend months here wallowing in a *charas*-induced torpor. However, the overall increased popularity of the area means it is now frequented by a more diverse crowd and the arrival of a dirt road from Gokarn (7km), combined with the recent acquisition of the land by developers, may slowly transform it into more of a resort. As it is, hammocks and basic huts still populate the palm groves and about a dozen chai houses provide ample food and drink.

If the concrete mixers do descend, it's unlikely they'll ever reach Gokarn's two most remote beaches, which lie another forty- to sixty-minute walk over the hill. Tantalizingly inaccessible, **Half-Moon** and **Paradise** beaches, reached via difficult dirt paths across a sheer hillside, are, despite the presence of one or two chai houses on each and the occasional shack, mainly for intrepid sun lovers happy to pack in their own supplies. If you're looking for near-total isolation, this is your best bet.

Eating

Gokarn town offers a good choice of **places to eat**, with a crop of busy "meals" joints along Car Street and the main road. Most popular, with locals and tourists, is the brightly lit *Pai Restaurant*, which dishes up fresh and tasty veg thalis, masala dosas, crisp *wadas*, teas and coffees until late. The other commendable "meals" canteen, around the corner on Car Street, is also called the *Pai Hotel*; it's much smaller, but their snacks are excellent, and the milk coffee delicious. *Shree Shakti Cold Drinks*, also on Car Street, serves mouthwatering fresh cheese, hygienically made to an American recipe and served with rolls, garlic and tomato; the friendly owner also makes his own peanut butter, and serves filling toasties and lassis. Round this off with an ice cream, either here, or at any number of places along the road. Every café does its own version of *gad-bads*, several layers of different ice creams mixed with chopped nuts and chewy dried fruit. One of the best is served at the tiny *Prema Restaurant* opposite the Mahabaleshwar temple's main gates, which has a traveller-friendly menu. The new *Gokarna International* hotel has two fine eateries: the non-veg *Downtown* offers a range of tasty meat dishes and a full bar, while the smaller *Purohit* serves South Indian veg staples. The restaurant bar at the *Om* does good fish and is more pleasant if you can find a seat in the small courtyard rather than the dingy interior.

Moving on from Gokarn

Gokarn is well connected by direct daily bus to Goa (5hr), and several towns in Karnataka, including Bangalore (13hr), Hospet/Hampi (10hr) and Mysore (14hr), via Mangalore (7hr) and Udupi (6hr). Although there are only three direct buses north along the coast to Karwar (2hr) close to the border with Goa, you can change at Ankola on the main highway for more services. For more buses to Hospet and Hampi and the best connections to Jog Falls, change at Kumta; tempos regularly ply the route between Gokarn and Kumta (32km) as well as Ankola. The KSRTC counter in the new bus stand is helpful for current bus timings.

You'll get the best train connections to Goa, Mangalore, Udupi and Kerala by going first to either Kumta or Ankola, though in the near future Gokarna Road station is due to have more services than the current one in each direction; for now only the #KR2 passenger train to Madgaon at 11.30am and #KR1 to Mangalore at 3.56pm make a stop here.

Sirsi and around

The large, bustling administrative centre of **SIRSI**, 83km east of Gokarn, sees few visitors, but provides a good stop on long journeys to and from the coast and has onward connections to the Tibetan settlements of Mundgod and Hubli in the north, Jog Falls to the south, and Hospet to the east (for those travelling on to Hampi). The town's main point of interest is the striking **Marikamba temple**, but the chief reason for stopping here is to visit the fascinating temple complex at nearby **BANVASI**.

The Town

Marikamba temple, 500m from the bus stand in Sirsi, sees a steady stream of devotees coming to propitiate Durga, the ferocious multi-armed goddess who, as usual, is depicted slaying a demon and astride a tiger. Although the most frenetic period of visitor activity is in the evenings, the temple is best seen during the day so as to appreciate the remarkable murals, which are some of the finest surviving examples of **Kavi art**. A rare form of wall-art once prevalent throughout the coastal Konkan region of west Karnataka but now practically extinct, Kavi art utilizes an unusual technique where the top layer of plaster, dyed with a blood-red pigment, is etched away to create detail revealed by the lower white layer of plaster.

An imposing nineteenth-century facade, finished in red, leads into a grand courtyard with the temple at its centre; the cloisters are lavishly decorated with gods and goddesses. Parts of the inner sanctum, which houses an image of Durga, date back to the sixteenth century, but numerous additions hide any traces of the original structure. Marikamba's *rath* (chariot) festival is held here once every other year in February, and is one of the grandest in Karnataka; the next *rath* festival here will be held in 2003. During the festival the deity is placed on the *rath* and processed through the town.

Banvasi

The ancient town of **BANVASI**, 22km to the southeast of Sirsi, dates back to the third century BC when it was a centre of Buddhist learning. However, little remains from that period and the brick stupas that once graced the banks of the Varada River have all but disappeared. From the fourth century onwards, under the Kadambas, a dynasty that ruled the region for around two hundred years, Banvasi became the capital of Kannada, the forerunner of modern Karnataka, and is still held in high esteem as the home of the Kannada script.

The **Madhukeshvara temple**, at the far end of Banvasi's winding Car Street, 1.5km from the bus stand, is still in use today. It dates back to the Kadamba period, although most of the major additions are attributed to the late Chalukya period of the twelfth century. The inner sanctum of the main temple – dedicated to Shiva as the lord (*ishvara*) of the bees (*madhuka*), who is represented here with a honey-coloured *lingam* – is said to date back to the fourth century and the adjoining pillared stone hall to the sixth century. To the right of the inner sanctum stands a marble image of Datatreya, a three-headed combination representing the Hindu trinity of Brahma the creator, Vishnu the preserver and Shiva the destroyer. A most imposing Nandi, Shiva's bull and vehicle, sits outside in ever-faithful attendance facing the *lingam*.

The entrance hall (*mukhamandapa*) has numerous pillars, all unique in style except for the four highly polished reflective granite pillars that surround the stone dance circle, now no longer in use. Leading to the middle chamber, a stone throne with lavishly carved pillars, built in 1628, is still used for placing idols during special occasions such as Vasant Utsava, the summer festival held around April every year. Immediately to the right of the main temple, the temple dedicated to Parvati was built in the late twelfth century. The extensive courtyard has an interesting collection of stone images, including gods known as the Ashtadigpalakas (the guardians of the eight directions), each with his own animal vehicle. The Ashtadigpalakas, who predate modern Hinduism and represent the sacrificial Vedic period, include: Indra (east) on his elephant; Agni (southeast) on his ram; Yama, the god of death (south), on his buffalo; Niraruti (southwest), whose vehicle is a man; Varuna (west) on a crocodile; Yayu (northwest) on a deer; Kubera (north) on a horse, and Ishana, one of the prototypes of Shiva (northeast), on his bull. Each of the gods is shown with his consort. At one side of the courtyard, stands a small temple dedicated to Shiva's son, the elephant god Ganapati (aka Ganesh).

A small **museum** by the main gates holds a collection of sculpture from around Banvasi, including a striking fifteenth-century image of the Jain Gomateshvara and Buddhist plaques from the second century. Outside the main temple stands the majestic temple *rath* (chariot) built in 1608 and used to transport the gods during Vasant Utsava. A path opposite the temple entrance leads down between some shacks to the river and is a favourite picnic spot for visiting pilgrims.

Practicalities

Several **buses** travel between Sirsi and Banvasi but none after 6pm. Buses from Sirsi's KSRTC bus stand connect the town to numerous destinations including Gokarn via Kumta, Hospet, Jog Falls, Karwar, Mundgod and Hubli. Private companies operate deluxe buses from near the bus stand to destinations such as Hubli and Bangalore.

The best mode of transport around town is by **auto-rickshaw**; **taxis** are available near the bus stand, and if you book through a hotel, you may find them cheaper. Although there is no accommodation in Banvasi, hotels in Sirsi are good value. Ignore the dives around the bus stand and head 2km out to College Road, where you'll find a handful of good options, including the *Madhuvana* (℡08384/37496, ℱ35863; ❷–❹), a large, clean and well-run hotel with excellent-value suites and a very good vegetarian restaurant. The *Samrat*, next door (℡08384/36278; ❶–❷), has simple, slightly faded rooms, including some for groups up to five. By far the best of Sirsi's hotels, the *Panchavati* on Yellapur Road (℡08384/36755, ℱ38301; ❷–❺), is 4km from the centre but well worth the ride. Set in large, pleasant grounds on the edge of town, it offers good facilities, including a restaurant and some a/c rooms. Of the dingy bars serving non-veg food in the vicinity of College Road, the *Parijata*, just round the corner towards the bus stand in Hospet Road, is the most salubrious.

Dandeli Wildlife Sanctuary

Lying between Hubli 75km to the east and Panjim 145km to the west, the scruffy town of **DANDELI** on the banks of the Kali River in Uttar Kanada (Northern Karnataka), provides access to the **Dandeli Wildlife Sanctuary** (best Dec–April, closed June–Sept 6–8am & 4–6pm; Rs150 [Rs10]), an extensive, unspoiled forest on the edge of the Deccan Plateau. Despite its close proximity to Goa and its situation at a major crossroads on the route to Hampi via Hubli, the sanctuary sees few visitors except for occasional Jeep-loads from nearby Maharashtra, and it remains a low-key and undeveloped wildlife destination.

Spread across 834 square kilometres, the large mixed-deciduous forest, famed for its teak, spills over the lip of the Deccan Plateau where it gives way to the hills, ravines and deep river valleys of the Western Ghats. At the heart of the forest, 22km from the entrance gate, the 100-metre-high **Cyntheri Rock** rises out of the **Kanari River**. The river provides an excellent vantage point for observing the animals. The sanctuary is famous for its black panthers, but sightings are rare, especially with the deep cover; you stand a better chance of seeing sambar deer, spotted deer, flying squirrels, wild boar and Indian bison – distinguished by distinctive white bands across parts of their body. Dandeli also shelters elephants, sloth bears and a small handful of tigers, while the rivers, including the **Kali River**, which sweeps past the town of Dandeli, is home to mugger crocodiles. **Sunset Point**, 6km from the gate, and remote **Sykes Point** provide sweeping views of the jungle-covered ridges of the Western Ghats.

The main Hubli–Karwar highway, which passes by Dandeli, is one of the most beautiful in Karnataka as it descends through the verdant **Anasi National Forest**, which forms part of the same forest-belt as that of the Dandeli Wildlife Sanctuary. Travelling through the area you may notice the striking features of the **Siddis**, a group of African descent who live in the region and maintain their own customs and language; they were brought over in the nineteenth century by a local raja, to act as bodyguards.

Practicalities

Dandeli's KSRTC bus stand, in the centre of town, is well connected, with frequent buses to Hubli and to Karwar on the coast; in addition the two KSRTC buses a day travelling between Goa and Hubli stop here.

The forest checkpost, at the gate of the wildlife sanctuary, is around 18km from the town of Dandeli; you will need to arrange your own vehicle, either privately or through the Forest Department in Dandeli, before getting here (Jeeps cost from Rs150/hr). To stay at any of the Forest Department's rest houses in the sanctuary, you also need to contact office, which is located on the main Karwar road, near the Kali River (☎08284/31585, ☏30300).

Cheap, simple **accommodation** is available around the bus stand, but for a little more comfort try the popular but often full *Government Guest House* (☎08284/31299; ❸), which has attractive clean rooms. The Forest Department run the *Nature Camp* (❶), located at the forest gates next to the interpretation centre. Permanent tented accommodation is offered here at a rate of Rs100 for a four- to five-person tent; however, the camp does seem to be geared towards accommodating groups of schoolchildren. Across the Kali River from Dandeli lies the *Kali River Camp* (☎08284/30266; ❼), with ten spacious rooms in the main concrete building and nine luxurious tents with attached baths along the river – bring plenty of mosquito repellent. The food at the *Kali River Camp*, served in an open thatched restaurant, is excellent, and as are their Jeep safaris. One of the newest ventures to open is the *Bison River Resort* (☎08383/46539; ❾) on the other side of the sanctuary at Bangur Nagar, which offers its luxury cabins at half-price during the off-season – fine for a pampered break but, of course, you can't go and see any animals. Jungle Lodges & Resorts in Bangalore (☎080/559 7021, ☏558 6163) offer a package that includes accommodation, Jeep safari and a coracle ride along the Kali River.

Hubli and around

Karnataka's second most industrialized city, **HUBLI**, 418km northwest of Bangalore, has little to offer tourists except for its transport connections for those travelling between Mumbai, Goa, the coast of Uttar Kanada (Northern Karnataka), Hampi and other points in the interior. But you can use it as a base from which to explore the various sites in the area.

These include the large Tibetan monastery of **Drepung** on the outskirts of the town of Mundgod, 48km south of Hubli. Improbably located in the rolling countryside of central Karnataka, where summer temperatures can soar well above 40°C – a stark contrast with the cold climate of Tibet – the busy and rarely visited complex at Drepung is home to several hundred monks. Representing the ancient scholastic monastery that once flourished outside Lhasa, along

with Sera Je at Bylakuppe (see p.264), Drepung is one of the most important Tibetan monasteries in India and plays a vital role in continuing religious traditions. The environs of Drepung, as around Bylakuppe, have been settled by Tibetan refugees, who have industriously farmed the once barren land since the 1960s. Although few travellers come this way, visitors are welcome.

Immediately to the west of Hubli, the leafy university town of **DHARWAR** is far less polluted than the city and, although it attracts few foreigners, is nationally renowned for its Hindustani classical music connections, as it is home to several famous musicians and vocalists. In musical terms, this region marks the watershed between the Carnatic classical music system of South India, and the Hindustani system of North India (see Contexts p.694). The main concert season is in winter, and performances are held at various venues around Dharwar and Hubli; check local papers for listings.

Travelling east towards Hospet and Hampi, the cotton town of **GADAG**, 53km east of Hubli, is an important stop on the train line (for connections to Badami and Bijapur) as well as the highway. During the cotton season, between February and June, the town is a hive of activity, but at other times returns to its quiet ways. Few travellers stop here but for those with the time and inclination, Gadag and its environs make a good diversion from the well travelled route to and from Hampi, with a handful of rarely visited Chalukya temples dating back to the eleventh century. The best of the Gadag monuments are the **Trikuteshwara** and **Saraswati** temples, which share a compound in the southern part of the town. The inner sanctum of the Trikuteshwara temple houses a triple *lingam*; adjoining Saraswati shares the same hall and boasts a porch with impressive carvings. You may find parts of the complex locked, in which case you will need to look for the priest, who will unlock it for you.

Gadag's other temples are in a terrible state of repair, and travelling to the village of **LAKKUNDI**, a further 11km east along the Hospet highway, is more rewarding. Less threatened by urban growth, Lakkundi's Chalukya temples, from the same period as those in Gadag, include a **Jain** *basti*, dominating the north of the village, with an impressive tower and sanctuary walls. A short distance away, the **Kashi Vishwanatha temple**, dedicated to Shiva as lord of

Recommended trains from Hubli

The services listed below are the most direct and/or the fastest. This list is by no means exhaustive and there are numerous slower trains, that are often more convenient for smaller destinations – see p.316.

Destination	Train	Number	Frequency	Departs	Total Time
Bangalore	Hubli–Bangalore Inter City Express	#2726	Daily	6.20am	7hr 30min
Hospet	Hubli–Bangalore Hampi Express	#6591	Daily	5pm	3hr
Mumbai	Bangalore–Mumbai Chalukya Express/ Mysore–Mumbai Sharavathi Express	#1018/1036	Mon, Tues, Fri, Sat	2.50pm	17hr 5min*

* Stops in Pune

Kashi (Varanasi), consists of two temples facing each other sharing the same plinth. Unfortunately, the connecting porch has collapsed, but the animal and flower friezes along the plinth are impressive and so are the carvings along the doorways and pillars. Close to the bus stand, a square stepped bathing tank with a columned bridge halfway through was designed to provide privacy for women bathers.

Practicalities

Hubli's **railway station**, close to the town centre and within walking distance of several of the hotels, is well connected to Bangalore, Mumbai, Pune and Hospet (see box on p.285). Services on the newly converted line to Goa were just about to be restored at the time of writing. Hubli's spanking new KSRTC **bus stand**, over 2km south of town, has regular services linking the city with Goa, coastal Karnataka, Badami, Hospet, Mumbai and Bangalore. It can be reached by numerous buses from the chaotic city bus stand, about 1km west of the railway station, and others from outside the station itself. There are more buses than trains for Hospet, numerous buses to Dharwar and several to Dandeli and Karwar. Many buses connect Lakkundi to Gadag as well as to Hospet. Most long-distance services are overnight and private operators can be found across the main road from the bus stand. Janata Travel (☏0836/354968) operates buses for Mumbai and Pune. Perhaps the most reputable of the private outfits, Vijayananda Travels (☏0836/350630), distinguishable by their yellow-and-black signs, operate luxury buses to Mumbai, Pune, Gulbharga, Bijapur, Sirsi and Bangalore. For Drepung, there are several buses from the KSRTC bus stand to Mundgod or you should head for the *Modern Lodge* opposite the railway station, where the Tibetan community congregates, and two or three shared Jeeps depart every morning. The best method of getting around the city is by **auto-rickshaw**; these have meters, but at the railway station and bus stands they are controlled by *dalals* (middlemen) who fix high prices.

Accommodation around the railway station includes the huge *Hotel Ajanta* on JC Nagar (☏0836/362216; ❷–❸), which has small plain rooms and rickety plumbing and, opposite the bus stand, the large and well-organized *Shree Renuka Lodge* (☏0836/251384, ⒡253615; ❷–❹), offering a range of reasonable budget rooms. Between the railway station and the bus stand, Lamington Road has a few more options, including the pleasant *Kailash* (☏0836/352935, ⒡352732; ❺), an efficient business hotel, which has good deals on a/c rooms and a plain restaurant. *Vipra*, opposite, is a good deal cheaper with a range of simple rooms (☏0836/362336, ⒡368412; ❷–❸). For a lot more comfort *Naveen* at Unkal (☏0836/372283; ❼–❾), 6km west of the centre, despite its lavish use of concrete, is quite attractive, with cottages, a pleasant lakeside setting and a swimming pool; transport can be provided from the railway station or bus stand by prior arrangement.

Most hotels have their own **restaurants**, for example the *Shree Renuka*, which has two sections, one serving South Indian vegetarian food and the other Chinese and North Indian cuisine. The best of the independent restaurants is the vegetarian *Kamat Hotel*, by the traffic island at the head of Lamington Road towards the bus stand. The downstairs restaurant serves excellent South Indian food, while the plush restaurant upstairs, *Kosher*, serves vegetarian North Indian and Chinese dishes; there is another branch opposite the railway station. Netzone (☏0836/365322) on JC Nagar, almost opposite the *Ajanta*, has internet facilities for Rs40 per hour.

Hospet

Charmless **HOSPET**, ten hours by bus east of Goa, is of little interest except as a transport hub: in particular, it is the jumping-off place for the extraordinary ruined city of Hampi (Vijayanagar), 13km northeast. If you arrive late, or want somewhere fairly comfortable to sleep, it makes sense to stay here and catch a bus or taxi out to the ruins the following morning. Otherwise, hole up in Hampi, where the setting more than compensates for the basic facilities.

Practicalities

Hospet's **railway station**, 1500m north of the centre, is served by the overnight *Hampi Express* #6592 from Bangalore and services from Hyderabad, via Guntakal Junction. The line continues west to Hubli for connections to the coast and Goa. For connections to Badami and Bijapur, travel to Gadag and change onto the slow single track running north. Auto-rickshaws are plentiful or you can get into town by cycle rickshaw (Rs10) or by foot if unencumbered.

The **long-distance bus stand** is in the centre, just off MG (Station) Road, which runs south from the railway station. The most frequent services are from Bangalore and Hubli, and there are daily arrivals from Mysore, Badami, Bijapur, Hassan, Gokarn (via Kumta), Mangalore and Goa. For a summary of services see Travel Details on p.316. **Bookings** for long-distance routes can be made at

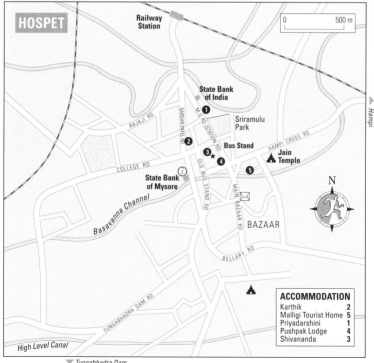

the ticket office on the bus stand concourse (daily 8am–noon & 3–6pm), where there's also a **left luggage** facility.

The **tourist office** at the Rotary Circle (Mon–Sat: June–March 10am–5.30pm; April & May 8am–1.30pm; ☎08394/28537) offers limited information and sells tickets for the KSTDC conducted tours (see below). You can **exchange** travellers' cheques and cash at the State Bank of Mysore (Mon–Fri 10.30am–2.30pm & Sat 10.30am–12.30pm), next to the tourist office, and cash only at the State Bank of India (same hours) on Station Road. Full exchange facilities are available at the *Hotel Malligi*, while Neha Travels (☎08394/25838) at the Elimanchate Complex, next to the *Hotel Priyadarshini* on MG Road, also changes any currency, travellers' cheques and advances money on credit cards. They also have branches in Hampi and book airline and train tickets, cars, and run private **luxury buses to Goa**. Their sleeper coach departs at 7pm and takes fourteen hours (Rs400). Luxury buses are also available for Bangalore (10hr; Rs200) departing between 10pm and 11pm at night. You can also buy tickets for these buses at Malleshwara Travels (☎08394/25696) opposite the bus stand.

Accommodation and eating

Accommodation in Hospet, concentrated around MG Road, ranges from budget to mid-price. By far the most popular place to stay is the incredibly versatile *Malligi Tourist Home*, with something to suit most budgets, but the *Priyadarshini* is also good value and nearer the bus and railway stations.

There's little to do in Hospet, so you'll probably pass a fair amount of time **eating and drinking**. Many of the hotels have good dining rooms, but in the evening, the upscale though affordable *Waves*, a terrace restaurant opposite owned by the *Malligi*, is the most congenial place to hang out, serving tandoori and chilled beer from 7pm to 11pm (bring lots of mosquito repellent). *Shanbhog*, an excellent little Udupi restaurant next to the bus station, is a perfect pit stop before heading to Hampi, and opens early for breakfast.

Karthik, Pampa Villa, off MG Road ☎08394/24938, ☎20028. A new, characterless block featuring unremarkable rooms but with a surprise around the back in the form of an extraordinary nineteenth-century stone villa housing two huge suites. ❸–❼

Malligi Tourist Home, 6/143 Jambunatha Rd, 2min walk east of MG Road (look for the signs) and the bus stand ☎08394/28101, ☎27038. Friendly, well-managed hotel with cheaper, clean, comfortable rooms (some a/c) in the old block and two new wings across the immaculate lawn, with luxurious air-conditioned rooms. There is also a great new swimming pool (Rs25 per hour for non-residents) in their Waves complex beneath the restaurant/bar. They sell the otherwise hard-to-find journal *Homage to Hampi*, and offer foreign exchange. The al fresco *Madhu Paradise* restau-

rant/bar in the old block serves great veg food and they have an efficient travel service. ❷–❽

Priyadarshini, MG Road, up the road from the bus stand, towards the railway station ☎08394/28838. Rooms from rock-bottom singles to doubles with TV and a/c (some balconies). Large and bland, but spotless and very good value. They have two good restaurants: the veg *Naivedyam* and, in the garden, non-veg *Manasa*, which has a bar. Their travel service handles bus and train tickets. ❷–❻

Pushpak Lodge, near bus stand, MG Road ☎08394/21380. This is the best rock-bottom lodge, with basic but clean attached rooms. ❷

Shivananda, beside bus stand, ☎08394/20700. Well-maintained hotel with spotless rooms, all attached with cable TV and some a/c. Very good value. ❸–❻

Getting to Hampi

KSTDC's daily guided **tour** only stops at three of the sites in Hampi and spends an inordinate amount of time at the far less interesting Tungabhadra Dam. Even so, it can be worth it if you're short of time. It leaves from the tourist office at Rotary Circle (Taluk Office Circle), east of the bus station (9.30am–5.30pm; Rs80 including lunch).

Frequent **buses to Hampi** run from the bus stand between 6.30am and 7.30pm; the journey takes thirty minutes. If you arrive late, either stay in Hospet, or take a taxi (Rs100–150) or one of the rickshaws (Rs60–80) that gather outside the railway station. It is also possible to catch a bus to **Kamalpura**, at the south side of the site, and explore the ruins from there, catching a bus back to Hospet from Hampi Bazaar at the end of the day. **Bicycles** are available for rent at several stalls along the main street, but the trip to, around, and back from the site is a long one in the heat. Auto-rickshaws, best arranged through hotels such as the *Malligi* or *Priyadarshini*, will also take you to Hampi and back and charge up to Rs200. For the adventurous, Bullet **motorbikes** are available on rent (or sale) from Bharat Motors (℡08394/24704) near *Rama Talkies*. Finally, some hotels in Hospet can also organize for you to hook up with **trained guides** in Hampi; ask at the *Malligi* or *Priyadarshini*.

Hampi (Vijayanagar)

The city of Bidjanagar [Vijayanagar] is such that the pupil of the eye has never seen a place like it, and the ear of intelligence has never been informed that there existed anything to equal it in the world... The bazaars are extremely long and broad... Roses are sold everywhere. These people could not live without roses, and they look upon them as quite as necessary as food... Each class of men belonging to each profession has shops contiguous the one to the other; the jewellers sell publicly in the bazaars pearls, rubies, emeralds and diamonds. In this agreeable locality, as well as in the king's palace, one sees numerous running streams and canals formed of chiselled stone, polished and smooth... This empire contains so great a population that it would be impossible to give an idea of it without entering into extensive details.

Abdu'r-Razzaq, the Persian ambassador who visited Vijayanagar in 1443

The ruined city of **Vijayanagar** (the City of Victory) – also known as **HAMPI**, the name of a local village – spills from the south bank of the Tungabhadra River, littered among a surreal landscape of golden-brown granite boulders and leafy banana fields. According to Hindu mythology, the settlement began its days as Kishkinda, the monkey kingdom of the Ramayana, ruled by the monkey kings Vali and Sugriva and their ambassador, Hanuman; the weird rocks – some balanced in perilous arches, others heaped in colossal, hill-sized piles – are said to have been flung down by their armies in a show of strength.

Between the fourteenth and sixteenth centuries, this was the most powerful Hindu capital in the Deccan. Travellers such as the Portuguese chronicler Domingo Paez, who stayed for two years after 1520, were astonished by its size and wealth, telling tales of markets full of silk and precious gems, beautiful, bejewelled courtesans, ornate palaces and joyous festivities. However, in the second half of the sixteenth century, the dazzling city was devastated by a six-month Muslim siege. Only stone, brick and stucco structures survived the ensuing sack – monolithic deities, crumbling houses and abandoned temples dominated by towering *gopuras* – as well as the sophisticated irrigation system that channelled water to huge tanks and temples.

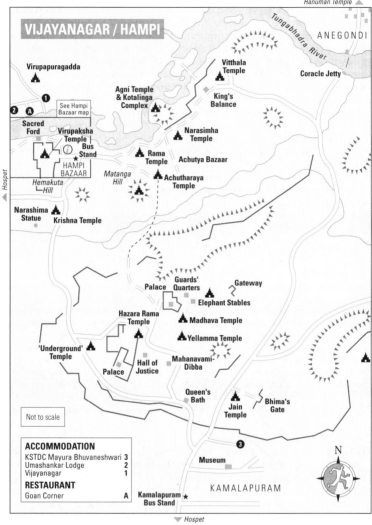

VIJAYANAGAR / HAMPI

Hanuman Temple

Tungabhadra River

ANEGONDI

Virupapuragadda

Vitthala Temple

Coracle Jetty

Agni Temple & Kotalinga Complex

King's Balance

❶
❷ Ⓐ

See Hampi Bazaar map

Sacred Ford

Virupaksha Temple

Narasimha Temple

Bus Stand

HAMPI BAZAAR

Rama Temple

Achutya Bazaar

Matanga Hill

Achutharaya Temple

Hemakuta Hill

Narashima Statue

Krishna Temple

Hospet

Guards' Quarters

Gateway

Palace

Elephant Stables

Hazara Rama Temple

Madhava Temple

Yellamma Temple

'Underground' Temple

Mahanavami-Dibba

Palace

Hall of Justice

Queen's Bath

Bhima's Gate

Jain Temple

Not to scale

ACCOMMODATION

KSTDC Mayura Bhuvaneshwari	3
Umashankar Lodge	2
Vijayanagar	1

RESTAURANT

Goan Corner	A

❸

Museum

Kamalapuram Bus Stand

KAMALAPURAM

N

Hospet

Thanks to the Muslim onslaught, most of Hampi's monuments are in disappointingly poor shape, seemingly a lot older than their four or five hundred years. Yet the serene riverine setting and air of magic that lingers over the site, sacred for centuries before a city was ever founded here, make it one of India's most extraordinary locations. Even so, mainstream tourism has thus far made little impact: along with streams of Hindu pilgrims and tatty-haired *sadhus* who hole up in the more isolated rock crevices and shrines, most visitors are budget travellers straight from Goa. Many find it difficult to leave, and spend weeks chilling out in cafés, wandering to whitewashed hilltop temples and gazing at the spectacular sunsets.

The **best time to come** to Hampi, weather-wise, is from October to March, when daytime temperatures are low enough to allow long forays on foot through the ruins. From Christmas through early January, however, the site is swamped by an exodus of travellers from Goa that has been increasing dramatically over the past few years; there have even been Anjuna-style full-moon parties, complete with techno sound-systems and bus-loads of ravers, mostly from Israel. The influx also attracts its share of dodgy characters, and crime has become a problem in the village at this time; so if you want to enjoy Hampi at its best, come outside peak season.

Some history

This was an area of minor political importance under the Chalukyas; the rise of the **Vijayanagar empire** seems to have been a direct response, in the first half of the fourteenth century, to the expansionist aims of Muslims from the north, most notably Malik Kafur and Muhammad-bin-Tughluq. Two Hindu brothers from Andhra Pradesh, Harihara and Bukka, who had been employed as treasury officers in Kampila, 19km east of Hampi, were captured by the Tughluqs and taken to Delhi, where they supposedly converted to Islam. Assuming them to be suitably tamed, the Delhi Sultan despatched them to quell civil disorder in Kampila, which they duly did, only to abandon both Islam and allegiance to Delhi shortly afterwards, preferring to establish their own independent Hindu kingdom. Within a few years they controlled vast tracts of land from coast to coast. In 1343 their new capital, Vijayanagar, was founded on the southern banks of the Tungabhadra River, a location long considered sacred by Hindus. The city's most glorious period was under the reign of **Krishna Deva Raya** (1509–29), when it enjoyed a near monopoly on the lucrative trade in Arabian horses and Indian spices passing through the coastal ports.

Thanks to its natural features and massive fortifications, Vijayanagar was virtually impregnable. In 1565, however, following his interference in the affairs

Police, thieves and mosquitoes

Hampi is generally a safe site to wander around, but a spate of armed attacks on tourists over the past few years means that you ought to think twice before venturing on your own, especially after dark, to a number of known trouble spots. Foremost among these is Matanga Hill, to the right of Hampi Bazaar as you face away from the Virupaksha temple, dubbed by local guides as "sunrise point" because it looks east. Muggers have been jumping Westerners on their way to the temple before dawn here, escaping with their cameras and money into the rocks. Although there have been fewer such incidents in the last couple of years, it's still advisable to go in a group, and to leave valuables behind. Incredibly, photographs of known rogues are posted by the police at lodges and one must wonder, as the thieves are familiar to them, why they are allowed to be at large in the first place. As some precaution, the police request foreigners to register with them at the Hampi Police Outpost (℡08394/41240) at the Virupaksha temple.

The other hassle to watch out for in Hampi is the police themselves, who are not averse to squeezing the odd backhander from tourists. You'll see *chillums* smoked in the cafés, but possession of hashish (*charas*) is a serious offence in Karnataka, liable to result in a huge bribe, or worse. There have also been reports of local cops arresting and extracting *baksheesh* from Western men who walk around shirtless. Another reason to stay fully dressed in Hampi, particularly in the evenings, is that it is a prime malaria zone. Sleep under a mosquito net if you have one, and smother yourself in insect repellent well before sunset.

of local Muslim Sultanates, the regent Rama Raya was drawn into a battle with a confederacy of Muslim forces, 100km away to the north, which left the city open to attack. At first, fortune appeared to be on the side of the Hindu forces, but there were as many as 10,000 Muslims in their number, and loyalties may well have been divided. When two Vijayanagar Muslim generals suddenly deserted, the army fell into disarray. Defeat came swiftly; although members of his family fled with untold hoards of gold and jewels, Rama Raya was captured and suffered a grisly death at the hands of the Sultan of Ahmadnagar. Vijayanagar then fell victim to a series of destructive raids, and its days of splendour were brought to an abrupt end.

Practicalities

Buses from Hospet terminate close to where the road joins the main street in Hampi Bazaar, halfway along its dusty length. A little further towards the Virupaksha temple, the **tourist office** (Mon–Sat 10am–5.30pm; ℡08394/41339) can put you in touch with a **guide** – ask for Shankar – but not much else. Shankar runs a convenience store just behind the office. Most visitors coming from Hospet organize a guide from there (see p.289).

Rented **bicycles**, available from stalls near the lodges, cost Rs5 per hour or Rs50 for a 24hr period. Bikes are really only of use if you're planning to explore Anegondi across the river – accessible by **coracle** for Rs5 – you can also rent bicycles at Kamalapuram for Rs50 per day. You can rent a motorbike for Rs300 per day, not including fuel, from Neha Travels who have three outlets in Hampi; the main office is at D131/11 Main St (daily 9am–9pm; ℡08394/41590). They can also **change money** (including travellers' cheques) but at lowish rates, advance cash on credit cards and they book airline and **train tickets** as well as run **luxury buses** to Bangalore and luxury sleeper coaches to Goa; although these drop people off right in Hampi Bazaar, you have to pick them up from Hospet thanks to the powerful taxi and rickshaw mafia.

Run by Shri Swamy Sadashiva Yogi, the Shivananda Yoga Ashram overlooking the river, past the site of the new footbridge and coracle crossing, offers courses in **yoga and meditation** as well as homeopathic treatment, magnetotherapy and **Ayurvedic treatment**, in particular for snakebites.

Accommodation

If you're happy to make do with basic amenities, Hampi is a far more enjoyable place to stay than Hospet, with around fifty congenial **guesthouses** and plenty of cafés to hang out in after a long day in the heat. As you wander through the lanes, you may find yourself solicited by local residents offering rooms in their own homes. Staying in the village also means you can be up and out early enough to catch the sunrise over the ruins – a mesmerizing spectacle. Some travellers shun Hampi Bazaar for the burgeoning community of lodges at **Virupapuradadda** across the river or at the more comfortable *Kiskinda Resorts* at Hanomana Halli, 2km from Anegondi, which has been the scene of several raves. Outside of **high season**, which lasts for six weeks starting around Christmas, you may well get a substantial discount on the room rates quoted below.

Gopi Guest House, a short walk down the lanes behind *Shanti* ℡08394/41695. There's a pleasant rooftop café here, and all ten rooms have attached baths. ②

KSTDC Mayura Bhuvaneshwari, Kamalapuram, 2.5km from Hampi Bazaar ℡08394/41574. The only remotely upscale place to stay within reach of the ruins. The modern block with clean en-suite rooms and competitively priced a/c rooms is agreeable enough. There's a pleasant garden, a good restaurant and a bar serving cold beers, but it feels detached from Hampi Bazaar and the village lacks charm. ④–⑤

Laxmi, just behind the main drag ☎08394/41728. A friendly guesthouse boasting clean rooms with shared baths. ❶

Rahul Guest House, south of Main Street, near the bus stand ☎08394/41648. Now has some new attached rooms in addition to the small and spartan old ones, which share rudimentary washing and toilet facilities, along with a pleasant shaded café. ❶–❸

Shambu, around the corner from the *Gopi Guest House* (no phone). Comparable to the *Gopi*, but slightly cheaper. ❷–❸

Shanti Guest House, just north of the Virupaksha temple ☎08394/41568. Follow the lane around the side of the temple enclosure, and the lodge is 30m further on the right. Run by the affable Shivaram, this is still the most popular place to stay, comprising a dozen or so twin-bedded cells ranged on two storeys around a leafy inner courtyard. It's basic (showers and toilets are shared), but spotless, and all rooms have fans and windows. Roof space is also available if the lodge is fully booked. ❷

Shri Rama Guest House, next to the Virupaksha temple ☎08394/41219. Rock-bottom attached rooms mainly for Hindu pilgrims, but foreigners are also welcome. ❶

Umashankar Lodge, Virupapuragadda (no phone). One of the better places to stay across the river. Small but clean attached rooms set round a lush lawn. ❷

Vicky's, at the end of the lane furthest northeast from the temple ☎08394/41694. Small clean rooms, some attached. Friendly and especially popular for its rooftop restaurant. ❶–❷

Vijayanagar, above coracle jetty, Virupapuragadda ☎08394/77640. Very cheap and rather poky cells with mattresses on the floor and shared bathrooms. Laid-back restaurant. ❶

The site

Although spread over 26 square kilometres, the ruins of Vijayanagar are mostly concentrated in two distinct groups: the first lies in and around **Hampi Bazaar** and the nearby riverside area, encompassing the city's most sacred enclave of temples and *ghats*; the second centres on the **royal enclosure** – 3km south of the river, just northwest of **Kamalapuram** village – which holds the remains of palaces, pavilions, elephant stables, guard houses and temples. Between the two stretches a long boulder-choked hill and swathe of banana plantations, fed by ancient irrigation canals.

Frequent buses run from Hospet to Hampi Bazaar and Kamalapuram, and you can start your tour from either; most visitors prefer to set out on foot or bicycle from the former. After a look around the soaring **Virupaksha temple**, work your way east along the main street and river bank to the beautiful **Vitthala temple**, and then back via the **Achyutaraya** complex at the foot of Matanga Hill. From here, a dirt path leads south to the royal enclosure, but it's easier to return to the bazaar and pick up the tarred road, calling in at **Hemakuta Hill**, a group of pre-Vijayanagar temples, en route.

On KSTDC's whistle-stop **guided tour** (see p.288) it's possible to see most of the highlights in a day. If you can, however, set aside at least two or three days to explore the site and its environs, crossing the river by **coracle** to **Anegondi** village, with a couple of side-hikes to hilltop viewing points: the west side of Hemakuta Hill, overlooking Hampi Bazaar, is best for sunsets, while **Matanga Hill**, though plagued by thieves in recent years, offers what has to be one of the world's most exotic sunrise vistas.

Hampi Bazaar, the Virupaksha temple and riverside path

Lining Hampi's long straight main street, **Hampi Bazaar**, which runs east from the eastern entrance of the Virupaksha temple, you can still make out the remains of Vijayanagar's ruined, columned bazaar, partly inhabited by today's lively market. Landless labourers live in many of the crumbling 500-year-old buildings.

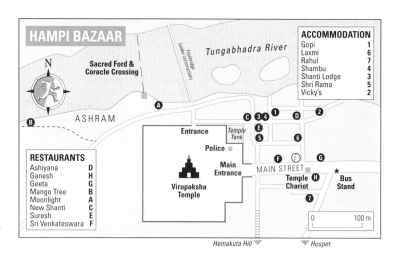

Dedicated to a local form of Shiva known as Virupaksha or Pampapati, the functioning **Virupaksha temple** (daily 8am–12.30pm & 3–6.30pm; Rs2) dominates the village, drawing a steady flow of pilgrims from all over southern India. Also known as **Sri Virupaksha Swami**, the temple is free for all who come for *arati* (worship; daily 6.30–8am & 6.30–8pm) when the temple has the most atmosphere. The complex consists of two courts, each entered through a towered *gopura*. The larger gateway, on the east, is approximately 56m high, each storey with pilastered walls and sculptures flanking an open window. It is topped by a single wagon-vault and *kalasha*, pot-shaped finial. In the southwest corner a water channel runs along a large columned *mandapa*.

A colonnade surrounds the inner court, usually filled with pilgrims dozing and singing religious songs; in the middle the principal temple is approached through a *mandapa* hallway whose carved columns feature rearing animals. Rare Vijayanagar-era paintings on the *mandapa* ceiling include aspects of Shiva, a procession with the sage Vidyaranya, the ten incarnations of Vishnu and scenes from the *Mahabharata*; the style of the figures is reminiscent of local shadow puppets. Faced by a brass image of Nandi, a *shivalingam* is housed in the small sanctuary, its entrance decorated with painted *makaras*, semi-aquatic mythical animals whose bodies end with foliage instead of a tail. Blue water spouts from their mouths, while above them flicker yellow flames. Just outside the main temple's wall, immediately to the north, is a small earlier temple, thought to have been the "ancestor" of the Virupaksha.

The sacred **ford** in the river is reached from the Virupaksha's north *gopura*; you can also get there by following the lane around the temple past *Shanti Lodge*. A *mandapa* overlooks the steps that originally led to the river, now some distance away. Although threatened by a new footbridge, **coracles** ply from this part of the bank, just as they did five centuries ago, ferrying villagers to the fields and tourists to the popular *Uma-Shankar Café* on the other side. The path through the village also winds to an impressive ruined bridge, and on to the hilltop Hanuman shrine – an enjoyable circular walk described on p.296.

To reach the Vitthala temple, walk east from the Virupaksha, the length of Hampi Bazaar. At the end, a path on the left, staffed at regular intervals by conch-blowing *sadhus* and an assortment of other ragged mendicants, follows

Vijayanagar's main festivals include, at the Virupaksha temple, a Car Festival with street processions each February, and in December the marriage ceremony of the deities, which is accompanied by drummers and dances. The Hampi Festival, organized by the tourist department, takes place in early November usually between the 3rd and the 5th and involves classical music and dance from both Carnatic and Hindustani (North Indian) traditions performed on temple stages and at Anegondi. The festival, which is beginning to attract several well-known musicians and dancers, has been growing in size and prestige, and hotels in the area can get booked well in advance. Unfortunately, the traditional music festival, Purandaradas Aradhana (Jan/Feb), which is usually held at the Vitthala temple, to celebrate the birth anniversary of the poet-composer Purandaradasa, has been temporarily suspended.

the river past a café and numerous shrines, including a Rama temple – home to hordes of fearless monkeys. Beyond at least four Vishnu shrines, the paved and colonnaded **Achutya Bazaar** leads due south to the **Tiruvengalanatha temple**, whose beautiful stone carvings – among them some of Hampi's famed erotica – are being restored by the ASI. Back on the main path again, make a short detour across the rocks leading to the river to see the little-visited waterside **Agni temple**; next to it, the Kotalinga complex consists of 108 (an auspicious number) tiny *linga*, carved on a flat rock. As you approach the Vitthala temple, to the south is an archway known as the **King's Balance**, where the rajas were weighed against gold, silver and jewels to be distributed to the city's priests.

Vitthala temple

Although the area of the **Vitthala temple** (daily 6am–6pm; $10 [Rs10]; ticket is also valid for the Lotus Mahal on the same day) does not show the same evidence of early cult worship as Virupaksha, the ruined bridge to the west probably dates from before Vijayanagar times. The bathing *ghat* may be from the Chalukya or Ganga period, but as the temple has fallen into disuse it seems that the river crossing (*tirtha*) here has not had the same sacred significance as the Virupaksha site. Now designated a World Heritage Monument by UNESCO, the Vitthala temple was built for Vishnu, who according to legend was too embarrassed by its ostentation to live there. The tower of the principal Vishnu shrine is made of brick – unusual for South India – capped with a hemispherical roof; in front is an enclosed *mandapa* with carved columns, the ceiling of which has partly collapsed. Two doorways lead to a dark passageway surrounding the sanctuary.

The open *mandapa* features slender monolithic granite **musical pillars** which were constructed so as to sound the notes of the scale when struck. Today, due to vandalism and erosion from being repeatedly beaten, heavy security makes sure that no one is allowed to play them. Guides, however, will happily demonstrate the musical resonance of other pillars on an adjacent structure. Outer columns sport characteristic Vijayanagar rearing horses, while friezes of lions, elephants and horses on the moulded basement display sculptural trickery – you can transform one beast into another simply by masking one portion of the image.

In front of the temple, to the east, a stone representation of a wooden processional **rath**, or chariot, houses an image of Garuda, Vishnu's bird-vehicle. Now cemented, at one time the chariot's wheels revolved. The three *gopura*

entrances, made of granite at the base with brick and stucco multistorey towers, are now badly damaged.

Anegondi and beyond

With more time, and a sense of adventure, you can head across the Tungabhadra
to **ANEGONDI**, a fortress town predating Vijayanagar and the city's fourteenth-century headquarters. The most pleasant way to go is to take a **putti**, a
circular rush-basket coracle, from the ford 1500m east of the Vitthala temple;
the *puttis*, which are today reinforced with plastic sheets, also carry bicycles.

Forgotten temples and fortifications litter Anegondi village and its quiet surroundings. The ruined **Huchchappa-matha temple**, near the river gateway,
is worth a look for its black stone lathe-turned pillars and fine panels of
dancers. **Aramani**, a ruined palace in the centre, stands opposite the home of
the descendants of the royal family; also in the centre, the **Ranganatha temple** is still active.

A huge wooden temple chariot stands in the village square. To complete the
five-kilometre loop back to Hampi from here (best attempted by bicycle), head
left (west) along the road, winding through sugar-cane fields towards the sacred
Pampla Sarovar, signposted down a dirt lane to the left. The small temple
above this square bathing tank, tended by a *swami* who will proudly show you
photos of his pilgrimage to Mount Kailash, is dedicated to the goddess
Lakshmi and holds a cave containing a footprint of Vishnu. If you are staying
around Anegondi, this quiet and atmospheric spot is best visited early in the
evening during *arati* (worship).

Another worthwhile detour from the road is the hike up to the tiny whitewashed **Hanuman temple**, perched on a rocky hilltop north of the river, from
where you gain superb views over Hampi especially at sunrise or sunset. The
steep climb up to it takes around half an hour. Keep following the road west
for another 3km and you'll eventually arrive at an impressive old **stone bridge**
dating from Vijayanagar times. The track from the opposite bank crosses a large
island in the Tungabhadra, emerging after twenty minutes at the sacred ford and
coracle jetty below the Virupaksha temple. This rewarding round walk can, of
course, be completed in reverse, beginning at the sacred ford. With a bike, it
takes around three hours, including the side-trips outlined above; allow most
of the day if you attempt it on foot, and take plenty of water.

Hemakuta Hill and around

Directly above Hampi Bazaar, **Hemakuta Hill** is dotted with pre-Vijayanagar
temples that probably date from between the ninth and eleventh centuries (late
Chalukya or Ganga). Three are of the *trikutachala* (three-peaked hills) type, with
three shrines facing into a common centre. Aside from the architecture, the
main reason to clamber up here is to admire the **views** of the ruins and surrounding countryside. Looking across miles of boulder-covered terrain and
banana plantations, the sheer western edge of the hill is Hampi's prime sunset
spot, attracting a crowd of blissed-out tourists most evenings, along with a couple of entrepreneurial chai-wallahs.

A couple of interesting monuments lie on the road leading south towards the
main, southern group of ruins. The first of these, a walled **Krishna temple
complex** to the west of the road, dates from 1513. Although dilapidated in
parts, it features some fine carving and shrines. On the opposite side of the
road, a fifty-metre-wide processional path leading east through what's now a
ploughed field, with stray remnants of colonnades straggling on each side, is all
that remains of an old market place.

Hampi's most-photographed monument stands just south of the Krishna temple in its own enclosure. Depicting Vishnu in his incarnation (*avatar*) as the Man-Lion, the monolithic **Narashima** statue, with its bulging eyes and crossed legs strapped into meditation pose, is one of Vijayanagar's greatest treasures.

The southern and royal monuments

The most impressive remains of Viyayanagar, the city's **royal monuments**, lie some 3km south of Hampi Bazaar, spread over a large expanse of open ground. Before tackling the ruins proper, it's a good idea to get your bearings with a visit to the small **Archeological Museum** (daily except Fri 10am–5pm; free) at Kamalapuram, which can be reached by bus from Hospet or Hampi. Turn right out of the Kamalapuram bus stand, take the first turning on the right and the museum is on the left – two minutes' walk. Among the sculpture, weapons, palm-leaf manuscripts and painting from Vijayanagar and Anegondi, the highlight is a superb scale-model of the city, giving an excellent bird's-eye view of the entire site.

To walk into the city from the museum, go back to the main road and take the nearby turning marked "Hampi 4km". After 200m or so you reach the partly ruined massive **inner city wall**, made from granite slabs, which runs 32km around the city, in places as high as 10m. The outer wall was almost twice as long. At one time, there were said to have been seven city walls; coupled with areas of impenetrable forest and the river to the north, they made the city virtually impregnable.

Just beyond the wall, the **citadel area** was once enclosed by another wall and gates of which only traces remain. To the east, the small *ganigitti* (oil-woman's) fourteenth-century **Jain temple** features a simple stepped pyramidal tower of undecorated horizontal slabs. Beyond it is **Bhima's Gate**, once one of the principal entrances to the city, named after the Titan-like Pandava prince and hero of the *Mahabharata*. Like many of the gates, it is "bent", a form of defence that meant anyone trying to get in had to make two 90° turns. Bas-reliefs depict episodes such as Bhima avenging the attempted rape of his wife, Draupadi, by killing the general Kichaka. Draupadi vowed she would not dress her hair until Kichaka was dead; one panel shows her tying up her locks, the vow fulfilled.

Back on the path, to the west, the plain facade of the fifteen-metre-square **Queen's Bath** belies its glorious interior, open to the sky and surrounded by corridors with 24 different domes. Eight projecting balconies overlook where once was water; traces of Islamic-influenced stucco decoration survive. Women from the royal household would bathe here and umbrellas were placed in shafts in the tank floor to protect them from the sun. The water supply channel can be seen outside.

Continuing northwest brings you to **Mahanavami-Dibba**, or "House of Victory", built to commemorate a successful campaign in Orissa. A twelve-metre pyramidal structure with a square base, it is said to have been where the king gave and received honours and gifts. From here he watched the magnificent parades, music and dance performances, martial art displays, elephant fights and animal sacrifices that made celebration of the ten-day Dussehra festival famed throughout the land (the tradition of spectacular Dussehra festivals is continued at Mysore; see p.240). Carved reliefs of dancers, elephant fights, animals and figures decorate the sides of the platform. Two huge monolithic doors on the ground nearby may have once been part of a building atop the platform, of which no signs remain. To the west, another platform – the largest at Vijayanagar – is thought to be the basement of the **King's Audience Hall**.

Stone bases of a hundred pillars remain, in an arrangement that has caused speculation as to how the building could have been used; there are no passageways or open areas.

The two-storey **Lotus Mahal** (daily 6am–6pm; $10 [Rs10]; ticket is also valid for the Vitthala temple on the same day), a little further north and part of the **zenana enclosure** (women's quarters), was designed for the pleasure of Krishna Deva Raya's queen: a place where she could relax, particularly in summer. Displaying a strong Indo-Islamic influence, the pavilion is open on the ground floor, whereas the upper level (no longer accessible by stairs) contains windows and balcony seats. A moat surrounding the building is thought to have provided water-cooled air via tubes.

Beyond the Lotus Mahal, the **elephant stables**, a series of high-ceilinged, domed chambers, entered through arches, are the most substantial surviving secular buildings at Vijayanagar – a reflection of the high status accorded to elephants, both ceremonially and in battle. An upper level, with a pillared hall, is capped with a tower at the centre; it may have been used by the musicians who accompanied the royal elephant processions. Tender coconuts are usually for sale under the shade of a nearby tree. East of here, recent archeological excavations have revealed what are thought to have been the foundations of a series of Vijayanagar administration offices, which until 1990 had remained buried under earth deposited by the wind.

Walking west of the Lotus Mahal, you pass two temples before reaching the road to Hemakuta Hill. The rectangular enclosure wall of the small **Hazara Rama** (One Thousand Ramas) temple, thought to have been the private palace temple, features a series of medallion figures and bands of detailed friezes showing scenes from the *Ramayana*. The inner of two *mandapas* contains four finely carved polished black columns. Many of the ruins here are said to have been part of the Hazara Rama Bazaar, which ran northeast from the temple. Much of the so-called **Underground Temple**, or Prasanna Virupaksha, lies below ground level and spends part of the year filled with rainwater. Turning north (right) onto the road that runs west of the Underground Temple will take you back to Hampi Bazaar, via Hemakuta Hill.

Eating

During the season, Hampi spawns a rash of travellers' cafés and temporary tiffin joints, as well as a number of laid-back shack bars tucked away in more secluded corners. Among the many **restaurants** in the bazaar, *Welcome* near the bus stand and *Sri Vendateswara* on the main street, are firm favourites with Western tourists, serving a predictable selection of pancakes, porridge, omelettes and veg food. Other popular restaurants include the *Geeta* and *Ganesh*, also on the main street, and the *New Shanti Restaurant*, opposite *Shanti Lodge* (but not owned by the same people), is another typical travellers' joint, renowned for its fresh pasta and soft cheese. Steer clear of the latter if there have been lots of power cuts. The friendly *Suresh*, behind the *Shri Rama Tourist Home*, serves delicious *shak-shuka* on banana leaves and is a good place for breakfast.

You can also get filling thalis and a range of freshly cooked snacks in the *Rahul Guest House*; other lodges with restaurants include *Vicky's* and *Gopi*. The *Moonlight*, a thatched café overlooking the river and the coracle jetty, offers the usual travellers' menu, and has a pleasant location a short walk past the Shanti. However, the prize for Hampi's best all-round café has to go to the *Mango Tree*, hidden away in the banana plantations beyond the coracle jetty and the

Shivananda Yoga Ashram. The food is fairly run-of-the-mill, but the relaxing riverside location is hard to beat. Across the river in Virupapuragadda, the most popular place, especially with Israelis, is *Goan Corner* – perched on the ridge to the left of the coracle jetty, it churns out pasta, bland curries and Israeli favourites.

You can get authentic Western-style bread and **cakes** through *Shanti Lodge*; place your order by early evening, and the cakes and pies are delivered the following day. Officially, as a sacred site, Hampi is supposed to be alcohol-free, but the rooftop *Durga* restaurant near the temple serves beer on certain days.

Monuments of the Chalukyas

Now quiet villages, **BADAMI**, **AIHOLE** and **PATTADAKAL** in northwest Karnataka were once the capital cities of the **Chalukyas**, who ruled much of the Deccan between the fourth and eighth centuries. The astonishing profusion of **temples** in the area beggars belief, and it is hard to imagine the kind of society that can have made use of them all. Most visitors use Badami, which can offer a few basic lodges, as a base; Aihole boasts a single rest house, and no rooms are available at Pattadakal. The **best time to visit** is between October and early March; in April and May, most of this part of northwest Karnataka becomes much too hot and government offices only open between 8am and 1pm.

Badami and Aihole's cave temples, stylistically related to those at Ellora, are some of the most important of their type. Among the many free-standing temples are some of the earliest in India and, uniquely, it is possible to see both northern (*nagari*) and southern (Dravida) architectural styles side by side. Clearly much experimentation went on, as several other temples (commonly referred to, in art historical terms, as "undifferentiated") fit into neither system. None is now thought to date from before the late sixth century, but at one time scholars got very excited when they believed the famous Lad Khan temple at Aihole, for example, to be even older.

Although some evidence of **Buddhist** activity around Badami and Aihole exists, the earliest cave and structural temples are assigned to the period of the Chalukya rise to power in the mid-sixth century, and are mostly **Hindu**, with a few Jain examples. The first important Chalukyan king was Pulakeshin I (535–66), but it was Pulakeshin II (610–42) who captured the Pallava capital of Kanchipuram in Tamil Nadu and extended the empire to include Maharashtra to the north, the Konkan coast on the west and the whole of Karnataka. Although the Pallavas subsequently briefly took most of his territory, including the capital Badami, at the end of his reign, Pulakeshin's son Vikramaditya I (655–81) later recovered it, and the Chalukyas continued to reign until the mid-eighth century. Some suggest that the incursion of the Pallavas accounts for the southern elements seen in the structural temples.

Badami and around

Surrounded by a yawning expanse of flat, farmed land, **BADAMI**, capital of the Chalukyas from 543 AD to 757 AD, extends east into a gorge between two red sandstone hills, topped by two ancient fort complexes. The south is riddled with cave temples, and to the north stand early structural temples. Beyond Badami, to the east, is an artificial lake, **Agastya**, said to date from the fifth century. The (small) selection of places to stay and restaurants makes

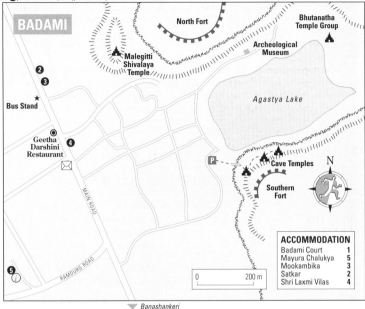

Banashankeri

Badami an ideal base from which to explore the Chalukyan remains at Mahakuta, Aihole and Pattadakal as well as the temple village of Banashankari on the outskirts of town. The whole Badami area is also home to numerous troupes of monkeys, especially around the monuments, and you are likely to find the cheeky characters all over you if you produce any comestibles – not a wise move.

Practicalities

Badami **bus stand** – in the centre of the village on Main (Station) Road – sees daily services to Gadag (2hr), Hospet (5hr), Hubli (3hr), Bijapur (4hr) and Kolhapur, and frequent buses to Aihole and Pattadakal. The **railway station** is 5km north, along a road lined with *neem* trees; tongas (Rs30 or Rs5 per head shared) as well as buses and auto-rickshaws are usually available for the journey into town. A slow meter-gauge line connects Badami to Bijapur to the north, and to Gadag in the south, from where you can change for trains or buses to Hospet and Hampi.

The new and friendly **tourist office** (Mon–Sat: June–March 10am–5.30pm; April–May 8am–1pm; ℡08357/20414) on Ramdurg Road next to KSTDC *Hotel Mayura Chalukya*, can put you in touch with a **guide**. If you need to **change money**, *Hotel Mookambika* opposite the bus stand will change US dollars and sterling, but no travellers' cheques; the other place to try is the *Hotel Badami Court*. Ambika Tours & Travels at *Hotel Mookambika* runs **tours** taking in Badami, Mahakuta, Aihole and Pattadakal in Ambassador taxis for a reasonable Rs600. One of the best ways of exploring the closer sites, including Mahakuta and the temple village of Banashankari, is to rent a **bicycle** (Rs3/hr) from stalls in front of the bus stand, but cycling to Aihole and Pattadakal will prove challenging.

Accommodation and eating

Of Badami's handful of **places to stay and eat**, by far the most comfortable is the *Hotel Badami Court* (℡08357/20230; **❼**–**❽**), 2km west of town towards the railway station. Ranged around a garden on two storeys, its 27 en-suite rooms are plain but spacious; they serve meals and expensive beer. Their swimming pool is open to non-residents for Rs80 per hour. Far cheaper, the KSTDC *Hotel Mayura Chalukya* (℡08357/65046; **❷**), at the south side of town on Ramdurg Road, has ten basic rooms with decrepit plumbing and peeling plaster, but a new wing is nearing completion and, despite fearless scavenging monkeys, the gardens are pleasant and there's a restaurant. Opposite the bus stand, the *Mookambika Deluxe* (℡08357/65067; **❹**–**❼**) is the best option in the centre of town, but is rather overpriced from its simple doubles on the ground floor to comfortable new a/c rooms upstairs. Their plain upstairs **restaurant** and livelier *Kanchan* bar and restaurant next door share the same kitchen and provide a wide menu of excellent veg and non-veg Indian and Chinese food. Other options include the grungy budget lodges opposite the bus stand, among them the *Satkar* (℡08357/20417; **❷**) and the *Shri Laxmi Vilas* (℡08357/20077; **❷**), which has a reasonable restaurant.

For food and especially breakfast, try the *Geetha Darshini*, 100m south of the bus stand; it's a South Indian fast-food restaurant without seating, but there are counters to stand at. The *iddlis*, *vadas* and dosas are out of this world.

Southern Fort cave temples

Badami's earliest monuments, in the Southern Fort area, are a group of sixth-century **caves** (daily sunrise–sunset; $5 [Rs5]) cut into the hill's red sandstone, each connected by steps leading up the hillside. About 15m up the face of the rock, **Cave 1**, a Shiva temple, is probably the earliest. Entrance is through a triple opening into a long porch raised on a plinth decorated with images of Shiva's dwarf attendants, the *ganas*. Outside, to the left of the porch, a *dvarpala* door guardian stands beneath a Nandi bull. On the right is a striking 1.5-metre-high image of a sixteen-armed dancing Shiva. He carries a stick-zither-type *vina*, which may or may not be a *yal*, a now-extinct musical instrument, on which the earliest Indian classical music theory is thought to have been developed. In the antechamber, a panel on the left shows Harihara (Shiva and Vishnu combined), accompanied by consorts Lakshmi and Parvati and the gods' vehicles Nandi and Garuda. On the right Ardhanarishvara (Shiva combined with Parvati; half-male, half-female) is accompanied by Nandi and the skeleton Bringi. Ceiling panels include a coiled Naga snake deity, flying couples and Shiva and Parvati. Inside, a columned hall, divided into aisles, leads to a small, square sanctuary at the back, containing a *lingam*.

A little higher, the similar **Cave 2**, a Vishnu shrine, is approached across a courtyard with two *dvarpala* door guardians at the end. The porch contains a panel to the left of Varaha, the boar incarnation of Vishnu, and, to the right, of Trivikrama, Vishnu as a dwarf brahmin who inflates in size to cross the earth in three steps. On the ceiling nearby, Vishnu is shown riding his bird Garuda. A central square of the ceiling features a lotus encircled by sixteen fish; other decoration includes swastika designs and flying couples. Traces of painting show how colourful the caves originally were.

Steps and slopes lead on upwards, past a natural cave containing a smashed image of the Buddhist Bodhisattva, Padmapani (He who Holds the Lotus), and steps on the right in a cleft in the rock lead up to the fort. **Cave 3** (578 AD) stands beneath a thirty-metre-high perpendicular bluff. The largest of the group, with a facade measuring 21m from north to south, it is also considered the finest, for the quality of its sculptural decoration. Eleven steps lead up to the plinth decorated with dwarf *ganas*. Treatment of the pillars is extremely elaborate, featuring male and female figures, lotus motifs and medallions portraying amorous couples.

To the east of the others, a Jain temple, **Cave 4**, overlooks Agastya Lake and the town. It's a much simpler shrine, dating from the sixth century. Figures, both seated and standing, of the 24 *tirthankaras*, mostly without their identifying emblems, line the walls. Here, the rock is striped.

After seeing the caves you can climb up to the fort and walk east where, hidden in the rocks, a carved panel shows Vishnu reclining on the serpent Adisesha, attended by a profusion of gods and sages. Continuing, you can skirt the gorge and descend on the east to the Bhutanatha temples at the lakeside. Before you get to them, there's another rock carving of a reclining Vishnu and his ten incarnations.

North Fort

North of **Agastya Lake**, a number of structural temples can be reached by steps, and the small **Archeological Museum** (daily except Fri 10am–5pm; Rs2) nearby contains sculpture from the region. Although now dilapidated, the **Upper Shivalaya temple** is one of the earliest Chalukyan buildings. Scenes from the life of Krishna decorate the base and various images of him can be seen between pilasters on the walls. Only the sanctuary and tower of the **Lower Shivalaya** survive. Perched on a rock, the **Malegitti Shivalaya** (late seventh century) is the finest southern-style early Chalukyan temple. Its shrine is adjoined by a pillared hallway with small windows hewn out of stone and a single image on each side: Vishnu on the north and Shiva on the south.

Banashankari

A pleasant excursion by foot, bicycle or rickshaw is to the temple village of **Banashankari**, 5km to the northwest of Badami; it is believed to date back to the sixth century, although much of it was built during the Maratha period of the eighteenth century. Banashankari is worth a visit more for the peaceful atmosphere than for its architectural interest. Dedicated to Shiva's consort Parvati, the shrine, with large bathing tank, is the most important living temple of the region. It attracts a steady stream of devotees throughout the year, especially during the *rath* (chariot) festival (held either in January or February), when the deity is led through the streets in a procession. At this time the quiet atmosphere of the village gives way to the fun and excitement of a large and hectic country fair, complete with circus acts, stalls selling everything from toys to food and a colourful cattle fair down the road towards Badami.

Mahakuta

Another crop of seventh-century Chalukyan temples lies 15km out of Badami on the route to Pattadakal at **Mahakuta**. Four buses a day and the occasional shared tempo run to the site, but the two- to three-hour **walk**, via an ancient, paved pilgrim trail, is well worth while, although it can get very hot; take plenty of water and an umbrella to keep off the sun. The path starts a short way beyond the Archeological Museum, just before you reach the first temple complex and tank. Peeling left up the hill, it winds past a series of crumbling shrines, gateways and old watercourses and peters out into the flat plateau. The turning down to Mahakuta is easy to miss: look for a stone marker-post that reads "RP", which leads you to a steep, roughly paved stairway. At the bottom, the main temple complex is ranged around a crystal-clear spring-fed tank, popular with bathers (it is open to all) and an enjoyable dip at the end of a hot walk. On a rise above the tank next to a shady courtyard dominated by a huge banyan tree, stands the whitewashed **Mahakutesvara temple** with its silver-crowned lingam. Around the base of the temple are wrapped some fine stone friezes – those on the southwest corner, depicting Shiva and Parvati with Ravana, the demon king of Lanka, are particularly accomplished. More carvings adorn the entrance and ceilings of the **Mallikarjuna temple** on the opposite side of the tank, while in the clearing outside the nearby **Sangameshwar temple** stands a gigantic stone-wheeled chariot used during the annual festival in May.

A living Shiva temple, attracting local devotees, pilgrims and a sprinkling of *sadhus*, Mahakuta may be in the minor league of Chalukyan architecture, but has, with its brooding banyan trees, a timeless atmosphere. There are a couple of teashops but no official guesthouse; if you want to stay, you may be able to negotiate one of the very basic rooms outside the temple gates.

Aihole

No fewer than 125 temples, dating from the Chalukyan and the later Rashtrakuta periods (sixth–twelfth centuries), are found in the tiny village of **AIHOLE** (Aivalli), near the banks of the Malaprabha River. Lying in clusters within the village, in surrounding fields and on rocky outcrops, many of the temples are remarkably well preserved, despite being used as dwellings and cattle-sheds. Reflecting both its geographical position and spirit of architectural experimentation, Aihole boasts northern (*nagari*) and southern (Dravida) temples, as well as variants that failed to survive subsequent stylistic developments.

Two of the temples are **rock-cut caves** dating from the sixth century. The Hindu **Ravanaphadigudi**, northeast of the centre, a Shiva shrine with a triple entrance, contains fine sculptures of Mahishasuramardini, a ten-armed Nateshan (the precursor of Shiva Nataraja) dancing with Parvati, Ganesh and the Sapta Matrikas (Seven Mothers). A central lotus design, surrounded by mythical beasts, figures and foliate decoration, adorns the ceiling. Near the entrance is Gangadhara (Shiva with the Ganga River in his hair) accompanied by Parvati and the skeleton Bringi. A two-storey cave, plain save for decoration at the entrances and a panel image of Buddha in its upper veranda, can be found partway up the hill to the southeast, overlooking the village. At the top of that hill, the Jain **Meguti** temple, which may never have been completed, bears an inscription on an outer wall dating it to 634 AD. The porch, *mandapa* hallway and upper storey above the sanctuary, which contains a seated Jain image, are later additions. You can climb up to the first floor for fine views of Aihole and surrounding country.

The late seventh to early eighth century **Durga temple** (daily 6am–6pm; $5 [Rs5]), one of the most unusual, elaborate and large in Aihole, stands close to others on open ground in the Archeological Survey compound, near the centre of the village. It derives its name not from the goddess Durga but from the Kannada *durgadagudi*, meaning "temple near the fort". Its apsidal-ended sanctuary shows influence from earlier Buddhist *chaitya* halls; another example of this curved feature, rare in Hindu monuments, can be seen in one of the *rathas* at Mamallapuram in Tamil Nadu (see p.468). Here the "northern"-style tower is probably a later addition, and is incongruously square-backed. The temple is raised on a plinth featuring bands of carved decoration. A series of pillars – many featuring amorous couples – forms an open ambulatory that continues from the porch around the whole building. Other sculptural highlights include the decoration on the entrance to the *mandapa* hallway and niche images on the outer walls of the now-empty semicircular sanctum. Remains of a small and early *gopura* gateway stand to the south. Nearby, a small **Archeological Museum** (daily except Fri 10am–5pm) displays early Chalukyan sculpture and sells the booklet *Glorious Aihole*, which includes a site map and accounts of the monuments.

Further south, beyond several other temples, the **Ladh Khan** (the name of a Muslim who made it his home) is perhaps the best known of all at Aihole. Now thought to have been constructed at some point between the end of the sixth century and the eighth, it was dated at one time to the mid-fifth century and was seen as one of the country's temple prototypes. The basic plan is square, with a large adjoining rectangular pillared porch. Inside, twelve pillars support a raised clerestory and enclose a further four pillars; at the centre stands a Nandi bull. A small sanctuary containing a *shivalingam* is next to the back wall. Both *lingam* and Nandi may have been later additions, with the original inner sanctum located at the centre.

Practicalities

Six daily **buses** run to Aihole from Badami (1hr 30) via Pattadakal (45min) from 5.30am to 9pm; the last bus returns around 6pm. The only place to **stay and eat** (apart from a few chai-shops) in Aihole is the small, clean and spartan KSTDC *Tourist Rest House* (☎ 08351/34541; ❶) about five minutes' walk up the main road north out of the village, next to the ASI offices. They have a "VIP" room, two doubles with bath plus two doubles and four singles without. Simple, tasty food is available by arrangement – and by candlelight during frequent power cuts. The *Kiran Bar* on the same road, but in the village, serves beer and spirits and has a restaurant.

Pattadakal

The village of **PATTADAKAL**, on a bend in the Malaprabha River 22km from Badami, served as the site of Chalukyan coronations between the seventh and eighth centuries; in fact it may only have been used for such ceremonials. Like Badami and Aihole, Pattadakal boasts fine Chalukyan architecture, with particularly large mature examples; as at Aihole, both northern and southern styles can be seen. Pattadakal's main group of monuments (daily 6am–6pm; $10 [Rs10]) stands in a well-maintained compound, next to the village, and has recently attained the status of a World Heritage Site.

Earliest among the temples, the **Sangameshvara**, also known as **Shri Vijayeshvara** (a reference to its builder, Vijayaditya Satyashraya; 696–733), shows typical southern features, such as the parapet lined with barrel-vaulted miniature roof forms and walls divided into niches flanked by pilasters. To the south, both the **Mallikarjuna** and the enormous **Virupaksha**, side by side, are in the southern style, built by two sisters who were successively the queens of Vikramaditya II (733–46). The temples were inspired by the Pallava Kailashanatha temple at Kanchipuram in Tamil Nadu, complete with enclosure wall with shrines and small *gopura* entrance way. Along with the Kanchi temple, the Virupaksha was probably one of the largest and most elaborate in India at the time. Interior pillars are carved with scenes from the *Ramayana* and *Mahabharata*, while in the Mallikarjuna the stories are from the life of Krishna.

Both temples have open Nandi *mandapa* hallways and sanctuaries housing black polished stone *lingam*.

The largest northern-style temple, the **Papanatha**, further south, was probably built after the Virupaksha in the eighth century. It features two long pillared *mandapa* hallways adjoining a small sanctuary with a narrow internal ambulatory. Outside walls feature reliefs (some of which, unusually, bear the sculptors' autographs) from the *Ramayana*, including, on the south wall, Hanuman's monkey army.

About 1km south of the village, a fine **Rashtrakuta** (ninth–tenth century) **Jain temple** is fronted by a porch and two *mandapa* hallways with twin carved elephants at the entrance. Inexplicably, the sanctuary contains a *lingam*. In the first *mandapa*, on the right, a stone staircase leads up to the roof, where there's a second, empty sanctuary. The porch is lined with bench seats interspersed with eight pillars; the doorway is elaborately decorated with mythical beasts.

Pattadakal is connected by regular state **buses** and hourly private buses to Badami (45min) and Aihole (22km; 45min). Aside from a few tea-shops and cold drinks and coconut stalls, there are no facilities. For three days at the end of January, Pattadakal hosts an annual **dance festival** featuring dancers from all over the country.

Bijapur and the north

Boasting some of the Deccan's finest Muslim monuments, **BIJAPUR** is often billed as "The Agra of the South". The comparison is partly justified: for more than three hundred years, this was the capital of a succession of powerful rulers, whose domed mausoleums, mosques, colossal civic buildings and fortifications recall a lost golden age of unrivalled prosperity and artistic refinement. Yet there the similarities between the two cities end. A provincial market town of just 220,000 inhabitants, modern Bijapur is a world away from the urban frenzy of Agra. With the exception of the mighty **Golgumbaz**, which attracts bus loads of day-trippers, its historic sites see only a slow trickle of tourists, while the ramshackle town centre is surprisingly laid-back, dotted with peaceful green spaces and colonnaded mosque courtyards. The best **time to come** here is between November and early March; in summer Bijapur gets unbearably hot and in April and May offices shut at 1pm. On February 6 and 7 Bijapur hosts an annual **music festival** which attracts several well-known musicians from both the Carnatic (South Indian) and the Hindustani (North Indian) classical music traditions.

Some history

Bijapur began life in the tenth century as **Vijayapura**, the Chalukyas' "City of Victory". Taken by the Vijayanagars, it passed into Muslim hands for the first time in the thirteenth century with the arrival of the Sultans of Delhi. The Bahmanis administered the area for a time, but it was only after the local rulers, the **Adil Shahis**, won independence from Bidar by expelling the Bahmani garrison and declaring this their capital that Bijapur's rise to prominence began.

Burying their differences for a brief period in the late sixteenth century, the five Muslim dynasties that issued from the breakdown of Bahmani rule – based at Galconda, Ahmednagar, Bidar and Gulbarga – formed a military alliance to defeat the Vijayanagars. The spoils of this campaign, which saw

BIJAPUR

N

Gulbarga ▲

Sholapur ▲

Sholapur ▲

RESTAURANTS

Mysore	B
Niyaz	C
Shrinidhi	A
Surabhi	D

0   500 m

Railway Station

Paderah Gate

Gadag ▶

Golgumbaz

⑨

④ ⑧

⑤ ⑩

Bahmani Gate

Stadium

Jama Masjid

Astar Mahal

Bara Kaman

Gagan Mahal

Mithari Mahal

Hospet ▶

Fateh Gate

Sat Manzil

CITADEL

② ⓒ ⑦

GPO

⑥

Cycle Rental

★

KSRTC Bus Stand

GANDHI CHOWK

Ⓐ Ⓑ

Bank

Sharpur Gate

Upli Buruj

Badami, Belgaum & Hubli ▶

Malik-e-Maidan

Atke Gate

AZAD ROAD

Ibrahim Rauza

①

ACCOMMODATION

Godavari	1
KSTDC Mayura Adil Shahi	7
KSTDC Mayura	3
Adil Shahi Annexe	4
Madhuvan	5
Megharaj	6
Rajdhani	2
Sagar Deluxe	8
Samrat	9
Sanman	9

the total destruction of Vijayanagar (Hampi), funded a two-hundred-year building boom in Bijapur during which the city acquired its most impressive monuments. However, old enmities between rival Muslim sultanates on the Deccan soon resurfaced, and the Adil Shahis' royal coffers were gradually squandered on fruitless and protracted wars. By the time the British arrived on the scene in the eighteenth century, the Adil Shahis were a spent force, locked into a decline from which they and their capital never recovered.

Arrival, information and city transport

State and interstate **buses** from as far afield as Mumbai and Aurangabad (see Travel Details on p.316), pull into the KSRTC bus stand on the southwest edge of the town centre; ask at the enquiries desk for exact timings, as the timetables are all in Kannada. Most of the Bangalore buses travel through Hospet including two overnight super-deluxe coaches. Other services run to Hyderabad, along with several to Gulbharga and Bidar and to Badami to the south. Most visitors head off to their hotel in (unmetered) auto-rickshaws, though there are also horse-drawn tongas for about the same price. Just a stone's throw away from the Golgumbaz, outside the old city walls, the **railway station**, 3km northeast of the bus stand, is a more inspiring point of arrival. However, only five passenger trains per day pass through in either direction: south to Badami and Gadag, where you can change for Hospet, Bangalore or the west coast, and north to Sholapur, for Mumbai and most points north. The only reliable source of information on train departures is the station itself, although most hotels keep a timetable in reception.

Besides the usual literature, the **tourist office** (Mon–Sat 10am–5.30pm; ℡08352/50359) behind the *Hotel Adil Shahi Annexe* on Station Road can help with arranging itineraries and guides. If you need to **change money** (or travellers' cheques), the most reliable service is at Girikand Tours and Travels (℡08352/20510) on the first floor at Nishant Plaza, Rama Mandir Road; you can also use the Canara Bank, a short walk north up the road from the vegetable market, but service is painfully slow and you will need to take photocopies of the relevant pages of your passport. **Internet** services are available at Cyber Park, opposite the post office.

Bijapur is flat, compact, relatively uncongested, and generally easy to negotiate by **bicycle**; rickety Heros are available for rent from several stalls outside the bus stand for around Rs2 per hour. **Auto-rickshaws** don't have meters and charge a minimum of Rs10; although most of Bijapur is covered by a fare of Rs30, they are a much more expensive way of getting around the monuments, when they charge around Rs200 for a four-hour tour. **Taxis**, available from near the bus stand, charge Rs5 per kilometre.

Accommodation and eating

Accommodation standards are pretty low in Bijapur, although finding a room is rarely a problem. Most budget tourists head for the KSTDC *Mayura Adil Shahi*, which, despite its shabbiness, has a certain charm; it's also cheap and central. **Eating** is largely confined to the hotels, with the odd independent establishment. At Gandhi Chowkh, the *Shrinidhi Hotel* and the *Mysore Hotel* both serve good South Indian vegetarian food, while the basement *Niyaz* opposite the *Sagar Deluxe* hotel serves meat. The *Hotel Megharaj* and *Surabhi*, both on Station Road, dish up good cheap vegetarian "meals".

Godavari, Athani Road ⓣ08352/53105, ⓕ56225. This monolithic modern but fading hotel is something of a landmark, and its prices have been pegged back to reflect its very average status. ❷–❺

KSTDC Mayura Adil Shahi, Anand Mahal Road ⓣ08352/50934. Stone-floored rooms ranged around a leafy courtyard-garden could be a lot nicer; all have slightly grubby attached bathrooms and tatty mozzie nets but clean sheets and towels. Hot and cold drinks are served on the verandas by helpful staff. The food at the restaurant – a standard mix of veg- and non-veg Indian, with some Chinese and Continental dishes – is ordinary, but they do serve chilled beer and it's pleasant to eat in the garden. ❷

KSTDC Mayura Adil Shahi Annexe, Station Road ⓣ08352/50401. Almost as dowdy as the main wing, but with larger, cleaner rooms, all a/c with TV and individual sit-outs. No restaurant. ❺

Madhuvan, Station Road ⓣ08352/55571. The cleanest and best-appointed place in town, with a variety of rooms, from ordinary doubles to more comfortable a/c "deluxe" options, but expensive for what it is. The restaurant, however, serves good-value thalis at lunch time. Can change money for residents. ❻–❼

Megharaj, Station Road ⓣ08352/51458. Run by the affable ex-wrestler Sundara, who unfortunately doesn't speak a word of English, the hotel has good-value doubles upstairs and even some a/c rooms. The vegetarian restaurant in the basement is cheap and good. ❷–❺

Rajdhani, opposite Laxmi Talkies, near Old Head Post Office, Station Road ⓣ08352/53468. Most bearable of the rock-bottom lodges in the centre, with clean rooms and a 24hr checkout. Sandwiched between two cinemas. ❷

Sagar Deluxe, next to *Bara Kaman*, Busreshwar Chowk ⓣ08352/59234. Centrally located hotel with unremarkable but cheap doubles and some deluxe and a/c rooms. ❷–❻

Samrat, Station Road ⓣ08352/51620. Newish lodge at the east end of town. Institutional, and not all that neat, but a fall-back if the *Mayura Adil Shahi* is full. However, you can do better and the restaurant is best avoided. ❷–❸

Sanman, opposite the Golgumbaz, Station Road ⓣ08352/51866. Best value among the budget places, and well placed for the railway station. Good-sized rooms with mozzie nets and clean attached shower-toilets. The Udupi canteen is a stop for the bus parties, so their South Indian snacks are all freshly cooked; try the popular puri korma or delicious sadar masala dosas. ❷

The town and monuments

Unlike most medieval Muslim strongholds, Bijapur lacked natural rock defences and had to be strengthened by the Adil Shahis with huge **fortified walls**. Extending some 10km around the town, these ramparts, studded with cannon emplacements (*burjes*) and watchtowers, are breached in five points by *darwazas*, or strong gateways, and several smaller postern gates (*didis*). In the middle of the town, a further hoop of crenellated battlements encircled Bijapur's **citadel**, site of the sultans' apartments and durbar hall, of which only fragments remain. The Adil Shahis' **tombs** are scattered around the outskirts, while most of the important **mosques** lie southeast of the citadel.

It's possible to see Bijapur's highlights in a day, although most people stay for three or four nights, taking in the monuments at a more leisurely pace. Our account covers the sights from east to west, beginning with the **Golgumbaz** – which you should aim to visit at around 6am, before the bus parties descend – and ending with the exquisite **Ibrahim Rauza**, an atmospheric spot to enjoy the sunset.

The Golgumbaz

The vast **Golgumbaz** mausoleum (daily 6am–6pm; $5 [Rs5]), Bijapur's most famous building, soars above the town's east walls, visible for miles in every direction. Built towards the end of the Adil Shahis' reign, the Golgumbaz is a fitting monument to a dynasty on its last legs – pompous, decadent and ill-proportioned, but conceived on an irresistibly awesome scale.

The cubic tomb, enclosing a 170-square-metre hall, is crowned with a single hemispherical **dome**, the largest in the world after St Peter's in Rome (which is only 5m wider). Spiral staircases wind up the four seven-storey octagonal towers that buttress the building to the famous **Whispering Gallery**, a three-metre-wide passage encircling the interior base of the dome from where, looking carefully down, you can get a real feel of the sheer size of the building. Get here just after opening time and you can experiment with the extraordinary acoustics; by 7am, though, the cacophony generated by bus-loads of whooping and clapping tourists means you can't hear yourself think, let alone make out whispering 38m away. A good antidote to the din is the superb **views** from the mausoleum's ramparts, which overlook the town and its monuments to the dark-soiled Deccan countryside beyond, scattered with minor tombs and ruins.

Set on a plinth in the centre of the hall below are the gravestones of the ruler who built the Golgumbaz, **Muhammed Adil Shahi**, along with those of his wife, daughter, grandson and favourite courtesan, Rambha. At one corner of the grounds stands the simple gleaming white shrine to a sufi saint of the Adil Shahi period, **Hashim Pir** which, around February, attracts *qawwals* (singers of devotional *qawwali* music) to the annual *urs*, lasting three days.

The Jama Masjid

A little under 1km southwest of the Golgumbaz, the **Jama Masjid** (Friday Mosque) presides over the quarter that formed the centre of the city during Bijapur's nineteenth-century nadir under the Nizam of Hyderabad. It was commissioned by Ali Adil Shahi, the ruler credited with constructing the city walls and complex water-supply system, as a monument to his victory over the Vijayanagars at the Battle of Talikota in 1565, and is widely regarded as one of the finest mosques in India. As it is a living mosque, you should cover your head and limbs when entering.

Approached via a square *hauz* (ablutions tank), the main **prayer-hall** is sur-mounted by an elegantly proportioned central dome, with 33 smaller shallow domes ranged around it. Simplicity and restraint are the essence of the colon-naded hall below, divided by gently curving arches and rows of thick plaster-covered pillars. Aside from the odd geometric design and trace of yellow, blue and green tile-work, the only ornamentation is found in the mihrab, or Mecca-facing prayer niche, which is smothered in gold leaf and elaborate calligraphy. The marble floor of the hall features a grid of 2500 rectangles, known as *musal-lahs* (after the *musallah* prayer mats brought to mosques by worshippers). These were added by the Moghul emperor Aurangzeb, allegedly as recompense for making off with the velvet carpets, long golden chain and other valuables that originally filled the prayer-hall.

The Mithari and Astar Mahals

Continuing west from the Jama Masjid, the first monument of note is a small, ornately carved gatehouse on the south side of the road. Although of modest size, the delicate three-storey structure, known as the **Mithari Mahal**, is one of Bijapur's most beautiful buildings, with ornate projecting windows and minarets crowning its corners. Once again, Ali Adil Shahi erected it, along with the mosque behind, using gifts presented to him during a state visit to Vijayanagar. The Hindu rajas' generosity, however, did not pay off. Only a cou-ple of years later, the Adil Shahi and his four Muslim allies sacked their city, plundering its wealth and murdering most of its inhabitants.

The lane running north from opposite the Mithari Mahal brings you to the dilapidated **Asar Mahal**, a large open-fronted hall propped up by four green-painted pillars and fronted by a large stagnant step-well. Built in 1646 by

Muhammed Adil Shahi as a Hall of Justice, it was later chosen to house hairs from the Prophet's beard, thereby earning the title **Asar-i-Sharif** (Place of Illustrious Relics). In theory, women are not permitted inside to view the upper storey, where fifteen niches are decorated with mediocre, Persian-style pot-and-foliage murals, but, for a little *baksheesh*, one of the girls who hang around the site will unlock the doors for you.

The citadel

Bijapur's **citadel** stands in the middle of town, hemmed in on all but its north side by battlements. Most of the buildings inside have collapsed, or have been converted into government offices, but enough remains to give a sense of how imposing this royal enclave must once have been.

The best-preserved monuments lie along, or near, the citadel's main north–south artery, Anand Mahal Road, reached by skirting the southeast wall from the Asar Mahal, or from the north side via the road running past KSTDC's *Mayura Adil Shahi Hotel*. The latter route brings you first to the **Gagan Mahal**. Originally Ali Adil Shahi's "Heavenly Palace", this now-ruined hulk later served as a durbar hall for the sultans, who would sit in state on the platform at the open-fronted north side, watched by crowds gathered in the grounds opposite. West off Anand Mahal Road, the five-storey **Sat Manzil** was the pleasure palace of the courtesan Rambha, entombed with Muhammed Adil Shahi and his family in the Golgumbaz. In front stands an ornately carved water pavilion, the **Jal Mandir**, now left high and dry in an empty tank.

Bara Kaman

Just north of the citadel on the far side of the main road, a quiet lane leads to one of Bijapur's less-visited sights, the peaceful **Bara Kaman**. Another mausoleum, for Ali Rauza, its construction was commenced in 1658 but the building remained uncompleted after his death in 1673. However, many chunky stone columns, some still linked by arches, remain to this day. They surround a central courtyard with a single tomb in the middle, set upon a huge square plinth that rises high above tranquil landscaped gardens.

Malik-i-Maidan and Upli Buruj

Guarding the principal western entrance to the city is one of several bastions (*burje*) that punctuate Bijapur's battlements. This one, the Burj-i-Sherza (Lion Gate) sports a colossal cannon, known as the **Malik-i-Maidan**, literally "Lord of the Plains". It was brought here as war booty in the sixteenth century, and needed four hundred bullocks, ten elephants and an entire battalion to haul it up the steps to the emplacement. Inscriptions record that the cannon, whose muzzle features a relief of a monster swallowing an elephant, was cast in Ahmednagar in 1551.

A couple more discarded cannons lie atop the watchtower visible a short walk northwest. Steps wind around the outside of the oval-shaped **Upli Burj** (Upper Bastion), to a gun emplacement that affords unimpeded views over the city and plains.

The Ibrahim Rauza

Set in its own walled compound less than 1km west of the ramparts, the **Ibrahim Rauza** represents the highpoint of Bijapuri architecture (daily 6am–6pm; Rs2, Fri free). Whereas the Golgumbaz impresses primarily by its scale, the appeal of this tomb complex lies in its grace and simplicity. Beyond the reach of most bus parties, it's also a haven of peace, with cool colonnaded verandas and flocks of iridescent parakeets careering between the mildewed domes, minarets and gleaming golden finials.

Opinions differ over whether the tomb was commissioned by Ibrahim Adil Shah (1580–1626), or his favourite wife, Taj Sultana, but the former was the first to be interred here, in a gloomy chamber whose only light enters via a series of exquisite pierced-stone (*jali*) windows. Made up of elaborate Koranic inscriptions, these are the finest examples of their kind in India. More amazing stonework decorates the exterior of the mausoleum and the equally beautiful **mosque** opposite, the cornice of whose facade features a stone chain carved from a single block. The two buildings, bristling with minarets and domed cupolas, face each other from opposite sides of a rectangular raised plinth, divided by a small reservoir and fountains. Viewed from on top of the walls that encloses the complex, you can see why its architect, Malik Sandal, added a self-congratulatory inscription in his native Persian over the tomb's south doorway, describing his masterpiece as "… A beauty of which Paradise stood amazed".

Moving on from Bijapur

Moving on from Bijapur is getting easier with efficient private companies such as VRL, recognizable by their distinctive yellow-and-black luxury coaches, travelling to Bangalore (3 buses from 7pm) and operating other overnight services to Mangalore via Udupi and Mumbai. VRL can be booked through Vijayanand Travel, Terrace floor, Shastri Market, Gandhi Circle (⊛08352/51000) or their other branch just south of the bus stand. KSRTC also runs deluxe buses to Bangalore, Hubli, Mumbai and Hyderabad (via Sholapur). The five trains to Gadag depart between 4.15am and 6.25pm, while those to Sholapur leave between 3.30am and 9.05pm.

Gulbarga

GULBARGA, 165km northeast of Bijapur, was the founding capital of the Bahmani dynasty and the region's principal city before the court moved to Bidar in 1424. Later captured by the Adil Shahis and Moghuls, it has remained a staunchly Muslim town, and bulbous onion-domes and mosque minarets still soar prominently above its ramshackle concrete-box skyline. The town is also famous as the birthplace of the *chisti*, or saint, Hazrat Bandah Nawaz Gesu Daraz (1320–1422), whose tomb, situated next to one of India's foremost Islamic theological colleges, is a major shrine.

In spite of Gulbarga's religious and historical significance, its **monuments** pale in comparison with those at Bijapur, and even Bidar. Unless you're particularly interested in medieval Muslim architecture, few are worth breaking a journey to see. The one exception is the tomb complex on the northeast edge of town, known as the **Dargah**. Approached via a broad bazaar, this marble-lined enclosure, plastered in mildew-streaked limewash, centres on the tomb of Hazrat Gesu Daraz, affectionately known to his devotees as **Bandah Nawaz**, or "the long-haired one who brings comfort to others". The saint was spiritual mentor to the Bahmani rulers, and it was they who erected his beautiful double-storey mausoleum, now visited by hundreds of thousands of Muslim pilgrims each year. Women are not allowed inside, and must peek at the tomb – surrounded by a mother-of-pearl inlaid wooden screen and draped with green silk – through the pierced-stone windows. Men, however, can enter to leave offerings and admire the elaborate mirror-mosaic ceiling. The same gender bar applies to the neighbouring tomb, whose interior has retained its exquisite Persian paintings. The Dargah's other important building, open to both sexes, is the **madrasa**, or theological college, founded by Bandah Nawaz and enlarged during the two centuries after his death. The syllabus here is dominated by the Koran, but the saint's own works on sufi mysticism and ethics are also still studied.

After mingling with the crowds at the Dargah, escape across town to Gulbarga's deserted **fort**. Encircled by sixteen-metre-thick crenellated walls, fifteen watchtowers and an evil-smelling stagnant moat, the great citadel now lies in ruins behind the town's artificial lake. Its only surviving building is the beautiful fourteenth-century **Jama Masjid**, whose elegant domes and arched gateways preside over a scrubby wasteland. Thought to have been modelled by a Moorish architect on the great Spanish mosque of Cordoba, it is unique in India for having an entirely domed prayer hall.

Practicalities

Daily KSRTC **buses** from Bijapur, Bidar and Hospet pull in to the state bus stand on the southwest edge of town. Private minibuses work from the road-side opposite, their conductors shouting for passengers across the main con-course. Don't be tempted to take one of these to Bidar; they only run as far as the fly-blown highway junction of Humnabad, 40km short, where you'll be stranded for hours. Gulbarga's main-line **railway station**, with services to and from Mumbai, Pune, Hyderabad, Bangalore and Chennai, lies 1.5km east of the bus stand, along **Mill Road**. **Station Road**, the town's other main artery, runs due north of here past three hotels and the lake to the busy **Chowk** crossroads, at the heart of the bazaar.

Gulbarga's main sights are well spread out, so you'll need to get around by **auto-rickshaw**; fix fares in advance. For medical help, head for the town **hospital**, east of the centre next door to the *Hotel Santoosh*, which has a well-stocked pharmacy. There is nowhere in Gulbarga to change money.

Accommodation and eating

Gulbarga is well provided with good-value **accommodation**, and even trav-ellers on tight budgets should be able to afford a clean room with a small bal-cony. The one place to avoid is the grim and neglected KSTDC *Mayura Bahmani*, set in the public gardens, more of a drinking den than a hotel, and plagued by mosquitoes.

All the hotels listed below have **restaurants**, mostly pure-veg places with a no-alcohol rule. *Kamat*, the chain restaurant, has several branches in Gulbarga including a pleasant one at Station Chowk, specializing in vegetarian "meals" as well as *iddlis* and dosas; try *joleata roti*, a local bread cooked either hard and crisp or soft like a chapati. The restaurant-only *Punjab Hotel*, at Station Chowk, has a varied Indian and Chinese veg menu, while carnivores can indulge at *Shree Nagarjuna*, just south of Mill Road at the first junction from Station Chowk, which also has a bar.

Adithya, 2-244 Main Rd, opposite Public Gardens ⓣ 08472/24040, ⓕ 26617. Unbeatable-value economy doubles, or posher a/c options, in a new building. Their impeccably clean pure-veg Udupi restaurant, *Pooja*, on the ground floor, does great thalis and snacks. ❸ –❻

Pariwar, Station Road, ten minutes' walk from the station ⓣ 08472/21522, ⓕ 22039. One of the town's smarter hotels, but not great value unless you get an economy room: they fill up by noon, so book ahead. The *Kamakshi Restaurant* (6am–10pm) serves quality vegetarian South Indian food, but no beer. Some a/c. ❹ –❻

Raj Rajeshwari, Vasant Nagar, Mill Road ⓣ 08472/25881. Just 5min from the bus stand, friendlier and better value than the *Pariwar*. Well-maintained modern building with large en-suite rooms with balconies, plus a reasonable veg restaurant (strictly no alcohol). ❸ –❻

Santosh, Bilgundi Gardens, University Road

08472/22661. Upscale, efficient chain hotel peacefully located on the eastern outskirts, with big, comfortable rooms (some a/c), sit-outs, veg- and non-veg restaurants and a bar. Recommended. ③ –⑥

Savita Lodge, Mill Road ☎ 08472/21560. Best of the basic bunch right by the bus stand. Small but wholesome attached rooms. ②

Southern Star, near the Fort, Super Market ☎ 08472/24093. New and comfortable with two restaurants and a bar and some a/c rooms; the rooms at the back look onto the ramparts of the fort but across the stagnant and putrid moat. ② –⑤

Bidar

In 1424, following the break-up of the Bahmani dynasty into five rival factions, Ahmad Shah I shifted his court from Gulbarga to a less constricted site at **BIDAR**, spurred, it is said, by grief at the death of his beloved spiritual mentor, Bandah Nawaz Gesu Daraz (see p.311). Revamping the town with a new fort, splendid palaces, mosques and ornamental gardens, the Bahmanis ruled from here until 1487, when the Barid Shahis took control. They were succeeded by the Adil Shahis from Bijapur, and later the Moghuls under Aurangzeb, who annexed the region in 1656, before the Nizam of Hyderabad finally acquired the territory in the early eighteenth century.

Lost in the far northwest of Karnataka, Bidar, 284km northwest of Bijapur, is nowadays a provincial backwater, better known for its fighter-pilot training base than the monuments gently decaying in, and within sight of, its medieval walls. Yet the town, half of whose 140,000 population are still Muslim, has a gritty charm, with narrow red-dirt streets ending at arched gates, with vistas across the plains. Littered with tile-fronted tombs, rambling fortifications and old mosques, it merits a visit if you're travelling between Hyderabad (150km east) and Bijapur, although expect little in the way of Western comforts, and more than the usual amount of curious approaches from locals. Lone women travellers, especially, may find the attention more hassle than it's worth.

Practicalities

Bidar lies on a branch line of the main Mumbai–Secunderabad–Chennai rail route, and can only be reached by slow passenger **train**. The few visitors that come here invariably arrive **by bus**, at the KSRTC bus stand on the far northwestern edge of town, which has hourly direct services to Hyderabad (3hr 30min) and Gulbarga (3hr), and several a day to Bijapur (7hr) and Bangalore (12hr). There is no tourist office or exchange facility but there are signs of Bidar's entry into the twenty-first century (and proximity to Hyderabad) in the shape of several **internet** outlets such as Swamy's Cyber Cafe, 100m southeast of the bus stand on Udgir Road.

Bidar's sights are too spread out to be comfortably explored on foot. However, auto-rickshaws tend to be thin on the ground away from the main streets, and are reluctant to wait while you look around the monuments, so it's a good idea to rent a **bicycle** for the day from Rouf's only 50m east of the bus stand next to the excellent *Karnatak Juice Centre*.

Most **places to stay** are an auto-rickshaw ride away in the centre, so it makes sense to opt for the new *Hotel Mayura* (☎ 08482/28142; ② –⑥) opposite the bus stand, which is one of the two best in Bidar and has large rooms with optional air-conditioning. The other decent hotel is its older sister the *Ashoka* (☎ 08482/26249; ② –⑥), 150m from the bus stand past Dr Ambedkar Chowk, which is comfortable with good-value deluxe rooms, some with a/c. The KSTDC *Mayura Barid Shahi* (☎ 08482/26571; ②) on Udgir Road, less than

1km from the bus stand, remains very shabby despite some renovation, and none of the handful of grim central lodges is worth considering.

Finding somewhere good to **eat** is not a problem in Bidar, again thanks to the restaurants at the *Mayura* and *Ashoka*, which both offer a varied selection of North Indian veg and meat dishes (try the *Mayura's* pepper chicken) and serve cold beer. The open-air garden restaurant of the *Mayura Barid Shahi* is a lot nicer than its interior and serves mostly North Indian food (try the veg *malai kofta*, or chicken tikka) with a handful of Chinese options plus chilled beer and ice cream. Also recommended, and much cheaper, is the popular *Udupi Krishna* restaurant, five minutes east of the *Mayuri Barid Shahi*, overlooking the *chowk*, which serves up unlimited pure-veg thalis for lunch; they have a "family room" for women, too, and open early (around 7.30am) for piping hot South Indian breakfasts.

The old town

The heart of Bidar is its medieval **old town**, encircled by crenellated ramparts and eight imposing gateways (*darwazas*). This predominantly Muslim quarter holds many Bahmani-era mosques, *havelis* and *khanqahs* – "monasteries" set up by the local rulers for Muslim cleric-mystics and their disciples – but its real highlight is the impressive ruins of **Mahmud Gawan's Madrasa**, or theological college, whose single minaret soars high above the city centre. Gawan, a scholar and Persian exile, was the *wazir*, or prime minister, of the Bahmani state under Muhammed Bahmani III (1463–82). A talented linguist, mathematician and inspired military strategist, he oversaw the dynasty's expansion into Karnataka and Goa, bequeathing this college as a thank-you gift to his adoptive kingdom in 1472. The distinctively Persian-style building, originally surmounted by large bulbous domes, once housed a world-famous library. However, this burnt down after being struck by lightning in 1696, while several of the walls and domes were blown away when gunpowder stored here by Aurangzeb's occupying army caught fire and exploded. Today, the *madrasa* is little more than a shell, although its elegant arched facade has retained large patches of the vibrant Persian glazed tile-work that once covered most of the exterior surfaces. This includes a beautiful band of Koranic calligraphy, and striking multicoloured zigzags wrapped around the base of the one remaining *minar*, or minaret.

Bidri

Bidar is celebrated as the home of a unique damascene metalwork technique known as Bidri, developed by the Persian silversmiths that came to the area with the Bahmani court in the fifteenth century. These highly skilled artisans engraved and inlaid their traditional Iranian designs onto a metal alloy composed of lead, copper, zinc and tin, which they blackened and polished. The resulting effect – swirling silver floral motifs framed by geometric patterns and set against black backgrounds – has since become the hallmark of Muslim metalwork in India.

Bidri *objets d'art* are displayed in museums and galleries all over the country. But if you want to see pukka bidri-wallahs at work, take a walk down Bidar's Siddiq Talim Road, which cuts across the south side of the old town, where skull-capped artisans tap and burnish vases, goblets, plates, spice boxes, betel-nut tins and ornamental *hookah* pipes, as well as less traditional objects – coasters, ashtrays and bangles – that crop up (at vastly inflated prices) in silver emporiums as far away as Delhi and Calcutta.

KARNATAKA | Bijapur and the north

The fort

Presiding over the dark-soiled plains from atop a sheer-faced red laterite escarpment, Bidar's **fort**, at the far north end of the street running past the *madrasa*, was founded by the Hindu Chalukyas and strengthened by the Bahmanis in the early fifteenth century. Despite repeated sieges, it remains largely intact, encircled by 10km of ramparts that drop away in the north and west to three-hundred-metre cliffs. The main southern entrance is protected by equally imposing man-made defences: gigantic fortified gates and a triple moat formerly crossed by a series of drawbridges. Once inside, the first building of note (on the left after the third and final gateway) is the exquisite **Rangin Mahal**. Mahmud Shah built this modest "Coloured Palace" after an unsuccessful uprising of Abyssinian slaves in 1487 forced him to relocate to a safer site inside the citadel. The palace's relatively modest proportions reflect the Bahmanis' declining fortunes, but its interior comprises some of the finest surviving Islamic art in the Deccan, with superb wood-carving above the door arches and Persian-style mother-of-pearl inlay on polished black granite surfaces. If the doors to the palace are locked, ask for the keys at the nearby ASI **museum** (daily 8am–1pm & 2–5pm; free), which houses a missable collection of Hindu temple sculpture, weapons and Stone Age artefacts.

Opposite the museum, an expanse of gravel is all that remains of the royal gardens. This is overlooked by the austere **Solah Khamb** mosque (1327), Bidar's oldest Muslim monument, whose most outstanding feature is the intricate pierced-stone *jali* calligraphy around its central dome. From here, continue west through the ruins of the former royal enclosure – a rambling complex of half-collapsed palaces, baths, *zenanas* (women's quarters) and assembly halls – to the fort's west walls. You can complete the round of the **ramparts** in ninety minutes, taking time out to enjoy the views over the red cliffs and across the plains.

Ashtur: the Bahmani tombs

As you look from the fort's east walls, a cluster of eight bulbous white domes floats alluringly above the trees in the distance. Dating from the fifteenth century, the mausoleums at **Ashtur**, 3km east of Bidar (leave the old town via Dulhan Darwaza gate), are the final resting places of the Bahmani Sultans and their families, including the son of the ruler who first decamped from Gulbarga, Alauddin Shah I. His remains by far the most impressive **tomb**, with patches of coloured glazed tiles on its arched facade and a large dome whose interior surfaces writhe with sumptuous Persian paintings. Reflecting sunlight onto the ceiling with a small pocket mirror, the *chowkidar* picks out the highlights, among them a diamond, barely visible among the bat droppings.

The tomb of Allaudin's father, the ninth and most illustrious Bahmani Sultan, Ahmad Shah I, stands beside that of his son, decorated with Persian inscriptions. Beyond this are two more minor mausoleums, followed by the partially collapsed tomb of Humayun the Cruel (1458–61), cracked open by a bolt of lightning. Continuing along the line, you can chart the gradual decline of the Bahmanis as the mausoleums diminish in size, ending with a sad handful erected in the early sixteenth century, when the sultans were no more than puppet rulers of the Barid Shahis.

Crowning a low hillock halfway between Ashtur and Bidar, on the north side of the road, the **Chaukhandi of Hazrat Khalil Ullah** is a beautiful octagonal-shaped tomb built by Allaudin Shah for his chief spiritual adviser. Most of the tiles have dropped off the facade, but the surviving stonework and calligraphy above the arched doorway, along with the views from the tomb's plinth, deserve a quick detour from the road.

The Badri Shahi tombs

The **tombs of the Badri Shahi** rulers, who succeeded the Bahmanis at the start of the sixteenth century, stand on the western edge of town, on the Udgir road, 200m beyond and visible from the bus stand. Although not as impressive as those of their predecessors, the mausoleums, mounted on raised plinths, occupy an attractive site. Randomly spaced rather than set in a chronological row, they are surrounded by lawns maintained by the ASI. The most interesting is the tomb of **Ali Barid** (1542–79), whose Mecca-facing wall was left open to the elements. A short distance southwest lies a mass grave platform for his 67 concubines, who were sent as tribute gifts by vassals of the Deccani overlord from all across the kingdom. The compound is only officially open for afternoon promenading (daily 4.30–7.30pm; Rs2) but the gateman may let you in earlier if he's around.

Travel details

When this book went to press, the changeover from metre- to broad-gauge track was still disrupting some train services in Karnataka and in particular those to Hassan; check the current situation with Indian Railways.

Trains

Bangalore to: Ahmedabad (3 weekly; 34hr 30min–38hr 45min); Calcutta (2 weekly; 38hr 15min); Chennai (5–7 daily; 5hr–7hr 35min); Delhi (1–2 daily; 34hr 30min–49hr 50min); Gulbarga (2–3 daily; 11hr 35min–12hr 15min); Hospet (1 daily; 9hr 50min); Hubli (2–4 daily; 8hr 30min–13hr); Hyderabad (Secunderabad) (1–3 daily; 11hr 55min–15hr 50min); Kochi (Ernakulam) (1–2 daily; 12hr 50min–13hr 5min); Mumbai (2–3 daily; 23hr 55min–25hr 55min); Mysore (6–7 daily; 2–3hr); Pune (2–4 daily; 19hr 25min–21hr 20min); Trivandrum (1–2 daily; 18hr 5min–18hr 10min).

Bijapur to: Badami (5 daily; 4hr); Gadag (5 daily; 6hr); Sholapur (5 daily; 3hr 30min).

Hassan to: Mangalore (1 daily, but subject to disruptions in service; 8hr); Mysore (3 daily; 3–4hr).

Hospet to: Bangalore (1 daily; 8hr 15min); Gadag (3 daily; 1hr 15min–1hr 30min); Hubli (3 daily; 2hr 30min–3hr).

Hubli to: Bangalore (2–4 daily; 7hr 45min–13hr 25min); Hospet (3 daily; 2hr 30min–3hr); Mumbai (4 weekly; 17hr 5min); Pune (5 weekly; 12hr 15min–13hr 30min).

Karwar to: Ernakulam (2–3 daily; 13hr 55min–15hr 10min); Goa (6 daily; 1hr–1hr 40min); Mangalore (5 daily; 3hr 50min– 5hr); Trivandrum (1–2 daily; 19hr 40min–20hr 5min).

Mangalore to: Chennai (2 daily; 19hr 5min–19hr 25min); Goa (5 daily; 4hr 50min–6hr 30min); Gokarn (1 daily; 4hr 20min); Kochi (Ernakulam) (2 daily; 10hr 35min–11hr 15min); Kollam (2 daily; 14hr 5min–15hr 5min); Kozhikode (2 daily; 5hr

35min–6hr 10min); Trivandrum (2 daily; 15hr 40min–17hr 5min).

Mysore to: Bangalore (6–7 daily; 1hr 55min–3hr 30min); Hassan (3 daily; 3–4hr).

Buses

Bangalore to: Bidar (2 daily; 16hr); Bijapur (5 daily; 13hr); Chennai (14 daily; 8hr); Coimbatore (2 daily; 9hr); Goa (5 daily; 14hr); Gokarn (2 daily; 13hr) Gulbarga (6 daily; 15hr); Hassan (every 30min; 4hr); Hospet (3 daily; 8hr); Hubli (3 daily; 9hr); Hyderabad (5 daily; 16hr); Jog Falls (1 nightly; 8hr); Karwar (3 daily; 14hr); Kochi (Ernakulam) (6 daily; 12hr); Kodaikanal (1 nightly; 13hr); Kozhikode (Calicut) (6 daily; 9hr); Madikeri (9 daily; 6hr); Madurai (2 daily; 12hr); Mangalore (19 daily; 8hr); Mumbai (2 daily; 24hr); Mysore (every 15min; 3hr); Ooty (6 daily; 7hr); Pondicherry (2 daily; 9hr).

Bijapur to: Aurangabad (4 daily; 12hr); Badami (4 daily; 4hr); Bangalore (5 daily; 13hr); Bidar (4 daily; 8hr); Gulbarga (hourly; 4hr); Hospet (15 daily; 5hr); Hubli (hourly; 6hr); Hyderabad (5 daily; 10hr); Mumbai (10 daily; 12hr); Pune (10 daily; 8hr); Sholapur (every 30min; 2hr 30min).

Hassan to: Channarayapatna (hourly; 1hr); Halebid (hourly; 1hr); Hospet (1 daily; 10hr); Mangalore (hourly; 4hr); Mysore (every 30min; 3hr).

Hospet to: Badami (2 daily; 5hr); Bangalore (3 daily; 8hr); Bidar (2 daily; 10hr); Gokarn (3 daily; 10hr); Hampi (every 30min; 30min); Hyderabad (6 daily; 12hr); Mangalore (1 daily; 12hr); Mysore (2 daily; 10hr); Panjim (3 daily; 10hr); Vasco da Gama (3 daily; 10–11hr).

Hubli to: Bangalore (3 daily; 9hr); Dandeli (12 daily; 2hr 30min); Goa (18 daily 5–6hr); Gokarn (3 daily; 5hr); Hospet (hourly; 4hr); Mumbai (10 daily; 12–15hr); Sirsi (every 30min; 3hr).

Mangalore to: Bangalore (19 daily; 8hr); Bijapur (1 daily; 16hr); Chaudi (6 daily; 8hr); Gokarn (3 daily; 7hr); Kannur (6 daily; 4hr); Karwar (9 daily; 8hr); Kasargode (hourly; 1hr); Kochi (Ernakulam) (1 daily; 9hr); Madikeri (hourly; 4hr); Mysore (hourly; 7hr); Panjim (6 daily; 10–11hr); Udupi (every 10 min; 1hr).

Mysore to: Bangalore (every 15min; 3hr); Channarayapatna (every 30min; 2hr); Jog Falls (via Shimoga) (every 90min; 7hr); Kannur (5 daily; 7hr); Kochi (5 daily; 12hr); Kozhikode (5 daily; 5hr); Madikeri (hourly; 3hr); Mangalore (hourly; 7hr); Ooty (8 daily; 5hr); Srirangapatnam (every 15 min; 20min).

Flights

Bangalore to: Calcutta (2 daily; 2hr 25min–3hr 30min); Chennai (6–8 daily; 45min–1hr 5min); Delhi (7 daily; 2hr 30min); Goa (2 daily; 55min–1hr 30min); Hyderabad (2–3 daily; 1hr); Kochi (Ernakulam) (2–3 daily; 50–55min); Mangalore (1–2 daily; 40min–1hr 5min); Mumbai (11–12 daily; 1hr 30min); Pune (2 daily; 1hr 20min); Trivandrum (1 daily; 2hr 5min).

Mangalore to: Bangalore (1–2 daily; 40min–1hr 5min); Chennai (3 weekly; 1hr 55min); Mumbai (2–3 daily; 1hr 15min).

Kerala

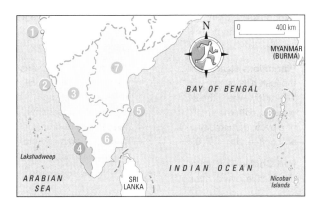

CHAPTER 4

Highlights

* **Varkala** Sit on the cliffs and watch dolphins swim, or eat South Indian snacks near the busy temple tank. See p.350

* **The backwaters** Explore the waterways of the densely populated coastal strip by boat; local ferries chug through some of the most diverse corners. See pp.362–363

* **Plantations** Head into the lush hills of Thekaddy, where the air is heady with the smell of cloves, cardamom and coffee. See p.378

* **Fort Cochin** This atmospheric little island, strung with Chinese fishing nets, draws on Jewish, Portuguese, British and Keralan culture. See p.392

* **Kathakali performance** An essential part of the Kerala experience, this noisy and colourful ritualized drama is stunning; arrive early to watch the characters come alive as intricate make-up is applied. See p.395

* **Thrissur** April/May sees the spectacular festival of Puram, involving caparisoned elephants, huge bands of drummers, fireworks and dramatic costumes. See p.402

Kerala

Asliver of dense greenery sandwiched between the Arabian Sea and the forested Western Ghat mountains, the state of **KERALA**, around 550km long and 120km wide at its broadest point, is blessed with unique geographical and cultural features. Its overpowering tropical greenness, with 41 rivers and countless waterways fed by two annual monsoons, intoxicates every new visitor. Equally, Kerala's arcane rituals and spectacular festivals stimulate even the most jaded traveller, continuing centuries of tradition that have never strayed far from the realms of magic. It is not surprising that the state tourism department have coined the phrase "God's own Country" to advertise Kerala; this state does have an alluring hint of paradise about it.

Kerala's cities and towns are all within easy reach of each other, small scale and relatively relaxed. The most popular tourist destination is undoubtedly the great port of **Kochi** (formerly Cochin), where Kerala's extensive history of peaceable foreign contact is evident in the atmospheric old quarters of Mattancherry and Fort Cochin – hubs of a still-thriving tea and spice trade. The capital, **Thiruvananthapuram** (aka Trivandrum), almost as far south as you can go, and a gateway to the nearby palm-fringed beaches of **Kovalam**, provides varied opportunities to sample Kerala's rich cultural and artistic life.

More so than anywhere else in India, the greatest joy of exploring Kerala is actually in the travelling itself, especially by **boat**. Ferries, cruisers, wooden longboats and even houseboats ply the **backwaters**, slowly meandering through the spellbinding **Kuttanad** region near historic **Kollam** (Quilon) and **Alappuzha** (Alleppey), on the southern tip of the huge **Vembanad Lake** that stretches northwards to **Kochi**. As you drift between swathes of palm trees and past tiny villages in the drowsy heat, you cannot fail to be lulled by the extraordinarily unhurried pace of life.

It's easy to escape the humid heat of the lowlands by taking off to the **hills**. Roads wind through a landscape dotted with churches and temples past spice, tea, coffee and rubber plantations, as well as natural forest, en route to wildlife reserves such as **Peppara** and **Periyar**, roamed by herds of mud-caked elephants. To the north, there is the former British hill station of **Munnar**, surrounded by endlessly rolling fields of tea, and the beautiful forested district of **Wayanad**, which features a large tribal population.

Kerala is short on the historic monuments prevalent elsewhere in India, mainly because teak has always been the building material of choice. Moreover, the ancient temples that remain today are still in use, and are more often than not closed to non-Hindus. Nonetheless, distinctive buildings throughout the state eschew grandiosity in favour of elegant understatement. Following an

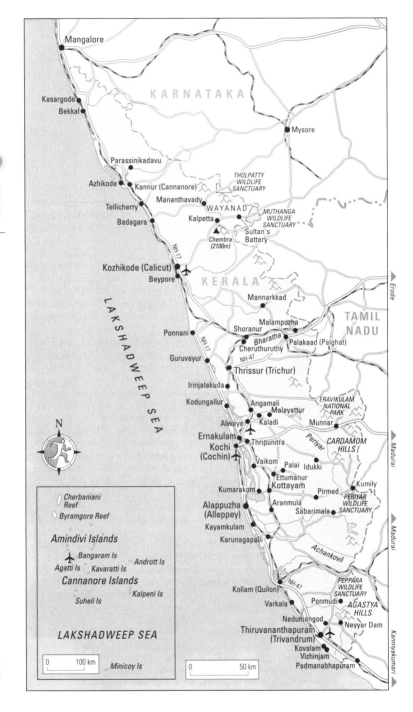

Mangalore

KARNATAKA

Kasargode
Bekkal

Mysore

Parassinikadavu

Azhikode   Kannur (Cannanore)

Mananthavady

Tellicherry   WAYANAD

Badagara   Kalpetta

*Chembra
(2100m)*   Sultan's
Battery

*THOLPATTY
WILDLIFE
SANCTUARY*

*MUTHANGA
WILDLIFE
SANCTUARY*

Kozhikode (Calicut)

Beypore   KERALA

Mannarkkad

TAMIL
NADU

Ponnani   Shoranur   Malampuzha

Bharatha   Palakaad (Palghat)

Cheruthuruthy

NH-47

Guruvayur

Thrissur (Trichur)

Irinjalakuda

Kodungallur   Angamali   Malayattur

Alwaye   Kaladi

Ernakulam

Kochi
(Cochin)   Thripunitra

Vaikom   Palai   Idukki

Munnar

*ERAVIKULAM
NATIONAL
PARK*

Periyar

*CARDAMOM
HILLS*

Ettumanur
Kumarakom   Kottayam   Pirmed

Kumily

Alappuzha
(Alleppey)   Aranmula

Sabarimala   *PERIYAR
WILDLIFE
SANCTUARY*

Kayamkulam

Karunagapalli

Achankovil

*PEPPARA
WILDLIFE
SANCTUARY*

Kollam (Quilon)   NH-47

Varkala   Ponmudi   *AGASTYA
HILLS*

Nedumangod   Neyyar Dam

Thiruvananthapuram
(Trivandrum)

Kovalam
Vizhinjam
Padmanabhapuram

LAKSHADWEEP SEA

N

*Cherbaniani
Reef*

Byramgore Reef

Amindivi Islands

Bangaram Is   *Andrott Is*

Agatti Is   *Kavaratti Is*

Cannanore Islands

Kalpeni Is

Suheli Is

LAKSHADWEEP SEA

0   100 km   *Minicoy Is*

0   50 km

NH-17

Erode

Madurai

Madurai

Kanniyakumari

unwritten law, few buildings, whether palaces, houses or temples, are higher than the surrounding trees; from high ground in urban areas this creates the illusion you're surrounded by forest. Typical features of both domestic and temple architecture include long, sloping tiled and gabled roofs that minimize the excesses of both rain and sunshine, and pillared verandas. The definitive example of such architecture is the **Padmanabhapuram palace**, just south of the border in neighbouring Tamil Nadu, easily reached from Thiruvananthapuram.

Phenomenal amounts of money are lavished upon many, varied and often all-night **entertainments** associated with Kerala's temples. Fireworks fill the sky, while processions of gold-bedecked elephants are accompanied by some of the loudest (and deftest) drum orchestras in the world. The famous **Puram** festival in Thrissur is the most astonishing, but smaller events take place throughout the state – often outdoors – with all welcome to attend.

Theatre and **dance** styles abound in Kerala; not only the region's own female classical dance form, **Mohiniattam** (dance of the enchantress), but also the martial-art-influenced **Kathakali** dance drama, which has for four centuries brought gods and demons from the *Mahabharata* and *Ramayana* to Keralan villages (see p.706). Its 2000-year-old predecessor, the Sanskrit drama **Kutiyattam**, is still performed by a handful of artists, while localized rituals known as **teyyatam**, in which dancers wearing tall masks become "possessed" by temple deities, continue to be a potent ingredient of village life in northern Kerala. Few visitors ever witness these extraordinary all-night performances first hand, but between November and May you could spend weeks hopping between colourful village festivals in northern Kerala, experiencing a way of life that has altered little in centuries.

Travelling around Kerala is relatively easy as the state is so compact: it amounts to just over one percent of the total landmass of India. There are efficient rail services from the main coastal towns to the rest of the country, but local passenger trains are not necessarily the most efficient method of travelling within the state itself. Depending on their budget, most visitors take to the local ferries, hire a car or jump on buses to get around. Although a bus journey doesn't have the charm of a Kuttanad boat ride, you will remember it all the same – Kerala's bus drivers are notoriously competitive and pass each other in the most improbable of places at sickening speeds, especially along the newly revamped coastal highway.

The **best time** to visit Kerala is between December and April and during August and September, when the skies are clear and humidity at its least debilitating. From May, the humidity becomes uncomfortable in the pre-monsoon build up, and the rains usually hit the coast in early June. This is considered the auspicious time to begin a course in Ayurvedic treatment if you want to really experience the benefits, but a beach holiday is out as the sand disappears under high tides and crashing waves. The second annual monsoon that sweeps through Tamil Nadu from October until December leaves Kerala overcast, a definite problem if working on a golden tan is your main priority.

Accommodation price codes

All accommodation prices in this book have been categorized using the price codes below. Prices given are for a double room, and all taxes are included. For more details, see p.46.

❶ up to Rs100	❹ Rs300–400	❼ Rs900–1500
❷ Rs100–200	❺ Rs400–600	❽ Rs1500–2500
❸ Rs200–300	❻ Rs600–900	❾ Rs2500 and upwards

The god **Parasurama**, or "Rama with the battleaxe", the sixth incarnation of Vishnu, is credited with creating Kerala. Born a brahmin, he set out to re-establish the supremacy of the priestly class, whose position had been usurped by arrogant *kshatryas*, the martial aristocracy. Brahmins were forbidden to engage in warfare, but despite this he embarked upon a campaign of carnage, which only ended when Varuna, the all-seeing god of the sea, gave him the chance to create a new land from the ocean, for brahmins to live in peace. Its limits were defined by the distance Parashurama could throw his axe; the waves duly receded up to the point where it fell. Fossil evidence suggests that the sea once extended to the Southern Ghats, so the legend reflects a geological truth.

Ancient Kerala is mentioned as the land of the Cheras in a third-century BC Ashokan edict, and also in the *Ramayana* (the monkey king Sugriva sent emissaries here in search of Sita), and the *Mahabharata* (a Chera king sent soldiers to the Kurukshetra war). The Tamil *Silappadikaram* (The Jewelled Anklet) was composed here and provides a valuable picture of life around the time of Christ. Early foreign accounts, such as those by Pliny and Ptolemy, testify to thriving trade between the ancient port of Muziris (now known as Kodungallur) and the Roman empire.

Little is known about the early history of the Cheras; their dominion covered a large area, but their capital Vanji has not been identified. Other contemporary rulers included the Nannanas in the north and the Ay chieftains in the south, who battled with the Pandyas from Tamil Nadu, in the eighth century. At the start of the ninth century, the Chera king Kulashekhara Alvar – a poet-saint of the Vaishnavite *bhakti* movement known as the *alvars* – established his own dynasty. His son and successor, Rajashekharavarman, is thought to have been a saint of the parallel Shaivite movement, the *nayannars*. The great Keralan philosopher Shankaracharya, whose *advaitya* (non-dualist) philosophy influenced the whole of Hindu India, also lived at this time.

Eventually, the prosperity acquired by the Cheras through trade with China and the Arab world proved too much of a temptation for the neighbouring **Chola** empire; at the end of the tenth century, they embarked upon a hundred years of sporadic warfare with the Cheras. Around 1100, the Cheras lost their capital at Mahodayapuram in the north, and shifted south to establish a new capital at Kollam (Quilon).

When the **Portuguese** ambassador and general Vasco da Gama and his fleet first arrived in India in 1498, people were as much astounded by their recklessness in sailing so close to Calicut during monsoon, as by their physical and sartorial strangeness. Crowds filled the streets of Calicut to see them, and a Moroccan found a way to communicate with them. Eager to meet the king – whom they believed to be a Christian – the Portuguese were escorted in torrential rain to his palace. However, Vasco da Gama soon established that the gifts he had brought from the king of Portugal had not made the good impression he had hoped for. The *zamorin* (raja) wanted silver and gold, not a few silk clothes and a sack of sugar.

Vasco da Gama, after such diplomatic initiatives as the kidnapping, mutilation and murder of assorted locals, came to an agreement of sorts with the *zamorin*, after which he pressed on to demand exclusive rights to the spice trade. He was determined to squeeze out the Keralan Muslim (Mappila) traders who for centuries had been a respected section of the community – acting as middlemen between local producers and traders in the Middle East. Exploiting an existing enmity between the royal families of Cochin and Calicut, Vasco da Gama turned to Cochin, which became the site of India's first Portuguese

Catching one of the numerous festivals – Utsavam – held throughout the year, will make a visit to Kerala all the more rewarding. Kerala's festivals are too numerous to list here, but local tourist offices usually provide current information, and the state tourist department publishes a useful little booklet, *Fairs and Festivals of Kerala*, every year.

Perhaps one of the greatest spectacles of the festivals are the elephant processions, which feature particularly strongly in temple festivals known as Puram – the celebration of local deities, usually a goddess. One of the highlights of the elephant parades is the Kudamattom ritual, when the colourful parasols atop the elephants are changed in synchronized motion. The Puram festivals originate from the tradition of carrying the local deity in a procession, accompanied by drums and fanfare, to receive offerings at the end of the harvest period. The most remarkable of all the *Puram* festivals are held in the town of Thrissur (April/May), when deities from the surrounding countryside are brought together in celebration. *Puram* festivals are not exclusive to Thrissur: they are held in several towns and villages throughout central Kerala including Cherai on the northern outskirts of Kochi/Ernakulam, and in and around Palakaad. The annual eight-day elephant procession at Ernakulam's Shiva temple (Jan/Feb) is not to be missed, nor is the Arat festival held in Thiruvananthapuram, when the deity is led to sea escorted by elephants (March/April & Oct/Nov). At Guruvayur (Feb/March), an elephant race is held, and, although the temple itself is off-limits to non-Hindus, the public part of the festival showcases over forty elephants. Onam, the annual harvest festival found throughout Kerala (Aug/Sept), also features elephant processions and water carnivals – one of the best of these is at Aranmula, near the town of Kottayam, which holds a snakeboat race consisting of long boats each with two lines of rowers. The most famous and spectacular of all the snakeboat races, the Nehru Trophy Boat Race, is held at Alappuzha (Aug) and, unlike the light-hearted festival spirit of Aranmula, is taken very seriously.

Many Keralan festivals feature classical music and dance, and provide an excellent opportunity to catch a Kathakali performance in a genuine setting (see p.706 for further detail on Kathakali dance). On the outskirts of Ernakulam, the Shri Purnatrayisa temple in the small town of Thripunitra runs an all-night Kathakali show during its annual festival (Oct/Nov). The royal family of Travancore are great patrons of the arts and hold a yearly Carnatic music festival at the Puttan Malika palace in Thiruvananthapuram. Probably the best place to experience one of the numerous performing art forms of Kerala and other regions of South India, however, is at Cheruthuruthy near Thrissur, where an annual performing arts festival is held every year towards the end of December.

Christmas, when the climate is pleasant, is also a good time to travel in Kerala. Fort Cochin has several churches, including the historic church of St Francis, which hosts an extremely popular carol service where the congregation spills onto the street. Another notable Christian festival is held yearly in early January at Mar Thoma Pontifical Shrine near Kodungallur; here devotees process to the ancient site with colourfully decorated carts laden with gifts.

---

fortress in 1503. The city's strategic position enabled the Portuguese to break the Middle Eastern monopoly of trade with western India. Unlike previous visitors, they introduced new agricultural products such as cashew and tobacco, and for the first time turned coconut into a cash crop, having recognized the value of its by-products: coir rope and matting.

The rivalry between Cochin and Calicut also allowed other colonial powers to move in; both the Dutch, who forcibly expelled the Portuguese from their forts, and the British, in the shape of the East India Company, firmly established themselves early in the seventeenth century. During the 1700s, first Raja Marthanda Varma, then Tipu Sultan of Mysore, carved out independent territories, but the defeat of Tipu Sultan by the British in 1792 left them in control right up until Independence.

Kerala today can claim some of the most startling **radical** credentials in India. In 1957 it was the first state in the world to elect a communist government democratically and, despite having one of the lowest per capita incomes in the country, it currently has the most equitable land distribution, due to uncompromising reforms made during the 1960s and 1970s. In 1996, the Left Democratic Front, led by the Communist Party of India (Marxist), retook the state from the Congress-led United Democratic Front, which had been in power for five years. Poverty is not absent, but it appears far less acute than in other parts of India. Kerala is also justly proud of its reputation for health care and education, with a literacy rate that stands, officially at least, at one hundred percent. Industrial development is negligible, however, with potential investors from outside tending to fight shy of dealing with such a politicized workforce. Many Keralans find themselves obliged to leave home to seek work, especially in the Gulf. The resultant influx of petro-dollars seems only to have the negative effect of increasing inflation.

Thiruvananthapuram (Trivandrum)

Kerala's capital, the coastal city of **THIRUVANANTHAPURAM** (formerly, and still more commonly known as **TRIVANDRUM**), is set on seven low hills, 87km from the southern tip of India. Despite its administrative importance – demonstrated by wide roads, multistorey office blocks and gleaming white colonial buildings – it's a decidedly easy-going city, with an attractive mixture of narrow backstreets, traditional red-tiled gabled houses and acres of palm trees and parks breaking up the bustle of its modern concrete centre.

Although it has few significant monuments, as a window on Keralan culture Thiruvananthapuram is an ideal first stop in the state. The oldest and most interesting part of town is the **Fort** area, which encompasses the **Shri Padmanabhaswamy temple** and **Puttan Malika palace** to the south. Important showcases for painting, crafts and sculpture, the **Shri Chitra Art Gallery** and **Napier Museum** stand together in a park to the north. In addition, schools specializing in the martial art Kalarippayat, and the dance/theatre forms of Kathakali and Kutiyattam, demonstrate the Keralan obsession with physical training and ability.

Many travellers, however, choose to pass straight through Thiruvananthapuram, lured by the promise of Kovalam's palm-fringed beaches. A mere twenty-minute bus ride south, this popular resort is close enough to use as a base to see the city, although the recent upsurge in package tourism means it's far from the low-key, inexpensive travellers' hangout it used to be.

Arrival, information and tours

The international airport (connected to most major Indian cities, as well as to Sri Lanka, the Maldives and the Middle East), with tourist information and foreign exchange facilities, is 6km southwest of town and serviced by an airport bus and bus #14 to and from the **City bus stand**. Auto-rickshaws will run you into the centre for around Rs40, and there is also a handy pre-paid taxi service.

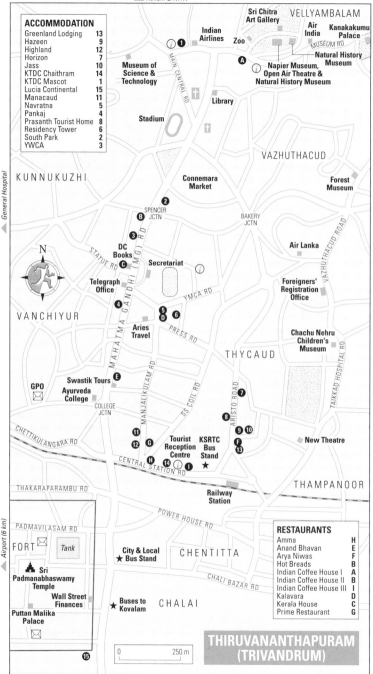

Kollam & NH17

ACCOMMODATION
Greenland Lodging	13
Hazeen	9
Highland	12
Horizon	7
Jass	10
KTDC Chaithram	14
KTDC Mascot	1
Lucia Continental	15
Manacaud	11
Navratna	5
Pankaj	4
Prasanth Tourist Home	8
Residency Tower	6
South Park	2
YWCA	3

Sri Chitra Art Gallery

VELLYAMBALAM

Indian Airlines

Air India

Kanakakumu Palace

Zoo

MUSEUM RD

Natural History Museum

Napier Museum, Open Air Theatre & Natural History Museum

Museum of Science & Technology

Library

Stadium

General Hospital

KUNNUKUZHI

VAZHUTHACUD

Connemara Market

Forest Museum

SPENCER JCTN

BAKERY JCTN

DC Books

STATUE RD

MAHATMA GANDHI (MG) RD

Secretariat

Air Lanka

Telegraph Office

YMCA RD

Foreigners' Registration Office

VANCHIYUR

Aries Travel

PRESS RD

THYCAUD

Chachu Nehru Children's Museum

GPO

Swastik Tours

Ayurveda College

MANJALIKULAM RD

SS COIL RD

ARISTO ROAD

TAIKKAD HOSPITAL RD

VAZHUTHACUD ROAD

COLLEGE JCTN

CHETTIKULANGARA RD

Tourist Reception Centre

KSRTC Bus Stand

New Theatre

CENTRAL STATION RD

THAKARAPARAMBU RD

Railway Station

THAMPANOOR

Airport (6 km)

PADMAVILASAM RD

POWER HOUSE RD

FORT

Tank

City & Local Bus Stand

CHENTITTA

CHALI BAZAR RD

Sri Padmanabhaswamy Temple

Wall Street Finances

Buses to Kovalam

CHALAI

RESTAURANTS
Amma	H
Anand Bhavan	E
Arya Niwas	F
Hot Breads	B
Indian Coffee House I	A
Indian Coffee House II	B
Indian Coffee House III	I
Kalavara	D
Kerala House	C
Prime Restaurant	G

Puttan Malika Palace

0   250 m

THIRUVANANTHAPURAM (TRIVANDRUM)

327

Kovalam

If you are heading straight out to Kovalam from the airport, you may find that a pre-paid taxi is almost as cheap as an auto-rickshaw. **Auto-rickshaws** (whose drivers don't always use their meters; they should start at Rs6) run to Kovalam for Rs60–100; normal **taxis** charge around Rs150. **Local buses** (to Kovalam for example) depart from **City bus stand**, East Fort, fifteen minutes' walk south from the KSRTC bus and railway stations.

In the city the long-distance KSRTC **Thampanoor bus stand** (T 0471/323886) and **railway station** (T 0471/329246 & 132) face each other across Station Road in the southeast – a short walk east of Overbridge Junction, where the long north–south **MG Road** bisects the city.

Information and tours

All the **tourist offices** at the **airport** are open during flight times. The Government of India's counter (T 0471/501498) offers general information regarding Kerala and the adjacent states, while the Kerala state tourism department (KTDC) has two counters, one at the domestic terminal (T 0471/501085) and the other at the international terminal (T 0471/502298), offering Kerala-specific information on, for example, backwater cruises. The Government of Kerala also has an office in the main block at the **Thampanoor bus stand** (Mon–Sat 10am–5pm; T 0471/327224) which is good for general information and maps and sells tickets for backwater cruises between Kollam and Alappuzha. They have another counter at the **railway station** (T 0471/334470).

The **Kerala Tourist Development Corporation (**KTDC) is designed primarily to sell its own products and facilities and to promote cultural events (W and W www.ktdc.com). The KTDC's main visitor centre, opposite the Government Museum at Park View (T 0471/321132), can book accommodation in their good-value **hotel** chain, and they sell tickets for various **guided tours**. Most of these, including the city tour (daily 8am–7pm; Rs95), are far too rushed, but if you're pushed for time try the **Cape Comorin** tour (daily 7.30am–9pm; Rs230), which takes in Padmanabhapuram Palace (Tues–Sun), Kovalam, Suchindram temple, and Kanniyakumari. They also offer their own **backwater cruises** (see p.362) with flexible itineraries; for further information contact their head office at Mascot Square (T 0471/318976, F 314406, E ktdc@vsnl.com). Several smaller independent companies are starting backwater cruises within striking distance of Thiruvananthapuram, for those without the time to explore the much more rewarding Kuttanad region; try Island Queen at Pazhikkara, Pachalloor (T 0471/481559).

The city of the snake anantha

Thiruvananthapuram was the capital of the kingdom of Travancore from 1750 until 1956, when the state of Kerala was created. Its name (formally readopted to replace "Trivandrum"), derives from *thiru-anantha-puram*, or "the holy city of Anantha", the coiled snake on which the god Vishnu reclines in the midst of the cosmic ocean.

Vishnu is given a special name for this non-activity – *Padma-nabha* (lotus-navel) – and is invariably depicted lying on the sacred snake with a lotus growing from his navel. The god Brahma sits inside the lotus, which represents the beginning of a new world era. Padmanabha is the principal deity of the royal family of Travancore and of Thiruvananthapuram's Shri Padmanabhaswamy temple.

Accommodation

Thiruvananthapuram's mid-range and expensive **hotels** are, in general, cheaper than in most state capitals, but are not concentrated in any one district. Budget hotels are grouped mainly in the streets around **Central Station Road** and all operate a 24hr checkout system. Good areas to start looking are **Manjalikulam Road**, five minutes' walk west from the railway station, or the lanes off **Aristo Junction**; note that the best of the budget places tend to be full by late afternoon. If you prefer to base yourself at the beach, head for **Kovalam** (see p.336).

Greenland Lodging, Aristo Road, Thampanoor ☏ 0471/328114. Large and efficient budget lodge and the best there is within a stone's throw of both the bus stand and the railway station; non-a/c and spotless rooms with attached bathrooms. Book ahead or arrive before noon. ❷

Hazeen, off Aristo Road ☏ 0471/325181. A decent budget hotel within easy reach of the railway station which features the usual green-walled rooms, but the bed linen is fresh and the tiled bathrooms immaculate. ❷

Highland, Manjalikulam Road ☏ 0471/333200. Dependable mid-range option, well managed and a short walk from the stations with a range of clean non-a/c and a/c rooms. In a multistorey block, it's the easiest place in the area to find. ❹–❻

Horizon, Aristo Road, 10min north of the railway station ☏ 0471/326888, ☏ 324444. Plush and efficient business hotel offering smart non-a/c rooms and a/c suites. Two restaurants – one on the leafy rooftop – and a bar. The tariff includes breakfast. ❼–❽

Jass, Thycaud, Aristo Junction ☏ 0471/324881, ☏ 324443. Reasonable two-star in a quiet central location near the bus and railway stations. A range of decent non-a/c and a/c rooms, all with cable TV and Western toilets. ❺–❻

KTDC Chaithram, Station Road ☏ 0471/330977. Large tower-block hotel opposite the railway station and adjacent to Thampanoor bus stand, with spacious rooms (some a/c), a/c veg restaurant, bank, travel agent, car rental, beauty parlour, cybercafé, bookshop and bar. Good value at this price. ❺–❼

KTDC Mascot, near Indian Airlines at Mascot Junction ☏ 0471/318990. Atmospheric period building with long corridors and huge non-a/c and a/c rooms; there's a swimming pool, bar and restaurant, and it's conveniently located near all the museums. ❼–❽

Lucia Continental, East Fort ☏ 0471/463443, ☏ 463347. A swish complex near the temple, with 104 deluxe a/c rooms plus "fantasy suites". Boasts a restaurant, coffee shop, disco, swimming pool and travel agent. ❽–❾

Manacaud, Manjalikulam Road ☏ 0471/330360. Nothing special, but the best maintained of several hotels on this lane. Attached bathrooms but, with small windows and no a/c, the rooms are quite airless. Quieter, but not such good value as identical lodges on Aristo Road. ❸

Navaratna, southeast of Secretariat, YMCA Road ☏ 0471/331784. Run-of-the-mill place located in the centre of town, offering pleasant enough a/c and non-a/c rooms. The restaurant is reasonably priced, if dull, and serves everything from beef and pork to duck. ❸–❻

Pankaj, opposite Secretariat, MG Road ☏ 0471/464645. Stylish and well-maintained three-star hotel. Some rooms have beautiful views over trees, as does the good Keralan restaurant. Tariff includes breakfast; foreigners pay in dollars. ❾

Prasanth Tourist Home, Aristo Road, opposite Horizon Hotel ☏ 0471/327180. One of a crop of rock-bottom and very basic family-run guesthouses near the station. The non-a/c rooms have attached bathrooms and are ranged around a courtyard. Satil and Salvha, next door, are similar. ❷

Residency Tower, Press Road ☏ 0471/331661, ☏ 331311. A centrally located, mid-range business hotel with reasonable a/c rooms, several restaurants and a bar. ❼–❽

South Park, MG Road ☏ 0471/333333, ☏ 331861. Comfortable, business-orientated Welcomgroup four-star with centrally a/c rooms, efficient travel agency, multicuisine restaurant and 24hr coffee shop. Popular with tour groups and flight crews so book in advance. Foreigners pay in dollars. ❾

YWCA, Spencer Junction ☏ 0471/477308. Spotless en-suite doubles on the top floor of an office block. Friendly, safe and central with neat non-a/c rooms, but the puritanical order and quiet is slightly overwhelming and the place is locked at 10.30pm sharp. For women and married couples only; single rates are available. ❸

The City

The historical and spiritual heart of Thiruvananthapuram is in the **Fort area**, at the southern end of **MG Road**, which encloses the **Shri Padmanabhaswamy Vishnu temple**. Following MG Road north leads you through the main shopping district, which is busy all day, and especially choked when one of the frequent, generally orderly, political demonstrations converges on the grand colonial **Secretariat** building halfway along. The whole centre

Festivals of Thiruvananthapuram

Each year the Nishangandi Dance and Music festival (22–27 February) is held at Kanakakannu Palace, originally built as a cultural venue for the maharajahs of Thiruvananthapuram. The large amphitheatre in the formal gardens is a very pleasant place to take in an evening of classical dances and music by artists invited from all over India (ask at a KTDC Tourist Office for details).

The Arattu festival, centred around the Shri Padmanabhaswamy temple, takes place biannually, in Meenam (March/April) and Thulam (Oct/Nov). Ten days of festivities inside the temple (open to Hindus only) culminate in a procession through the streets of the city, taking the deity, Padmanabhaswamy, to the sea for ritual immersion. Five caparisoned elephants, armed guards and a group playing the *nagasvaram* (double-reed wind instrument) and *tavil* drum, are led by the Maharaja of Travancore in his symbolic role as *kshatrya*, the servant of the god. Instead of the richly apparelled figure that might be expected, the Maharaja (no longer officially recognized) wears a simple white *dhoti*, with his chest bare, save for the sacred thread. Rather than riding, he walks the whole way bearing a sword. To the accompaniment of a 21-gun salute and music, the procession sets off from the east gate of the temple at around 5pm, moving at a brisk pace to reach Shankhumukham Beach at sunset, about an hour later. The route is lined with devotees, many of whom honour both the god and the Maharaja. After the seashore ceremonies, the cavalcade returns to the temple at about 9pm, to be greeted by another gun salute. An extremely loud firework display rounds off the day.

For ten days in March, Muslims celebrate Chandanakkutam Maholsavam at the Beemapalli mosque, 5km southwest of the city on the coastal road towards the airport. The Hindu-influenced festival commemorates the anniversary of the death of Beema Beevi, a woman revered for her piety. On the first, most important, day, pilgrims converge on the mosque carrying earthenware pots decorated with flowers and containing money offerings. Activities such as the sword form of *daharamuttu* take place inside the mosque, while outside there is dance and music. In the early hours of the morning, a flag is brought out from Beema Beevi's tomb and taken on a procession, accompanied by a *panchavadyam* drum and horn orchestra and caparisoned elephants, practices normally associated with Hindu festivals. Once more, the rest of the night is lit up with fireworks.

The great Keralan festival of Onam (late August/September), takes place throughout the state over ten days during the time of year when the weather is at its most pleasant. Onam is when Keralans remember the reign of King Mahabali, a legendary figure who, it is believed, achieved an ideal balance of harmony, wealth and justice during his tenure. Unfortunately, the gods became upset and envious at Mahabali's success and so Vishnu came to pack him off to another world. However, once a year the king was allowed to return to his people for ten days, and Onam is a joyful celebration of the royal visit. Families display their wealth and feasts and snakeboat races (see p.359) are held and, in Thiruvananthapuram, there is a week-long cultural festival of dance and music culminating in a colourful street carnival (ask at a KTDC office for details).

can be explored easily on foot, though you might be glad of a rickshaw ride (Rs15–20) back to the bus stands from the museums and parks, which are close to the top end of the road.

Fort area

The solid but unremarkable fort gateway leads from near the Kovalam bus stand at East Fort to the **Shri Padmanabhaswamy temple**, which is still controlled by the Travancore royal family. Unusually for Kerala it is built in the Dravidian style of Tamil Nadu, with a tall *gopura* gateway, surrounded by high fortress-like walls. It is closed to non-Hindus, and little can be seen from outside, apart from the seven-storey *gopura*.

Most of the temple buildings date from the eighteenth century, as do the additions made by Raja Marthanda Varma to the much older shrine within. According to legend, the temple was founded after Vishnu – disguised as a beautiful child – merged into a huge tree in the forest, which immediately crashed to the ground. There it transformed into an image of the reclining Vishnu, a full 13km long. Divakara, a sage who witnessed this, was frustrated by his limited human vision, and prayed to Vishnu to assume a form that he could view in its entirety. Vishnu complied, and the temple appeared. The area in front of the temple, where devotees bathe in a huge tank, is thronged with stalls selling religious souvenirs such as shell necklaces, puja offerings, jasmine and marigolds, as well as the ubiquitous plaster-cast models of Kathakali masks. As you approach the temple, the red-brick CVN Kalari Sangam, a **Kalarippayat martial arts** gymnasium, is on the left. Here you can watch the students practising Kalarippayat fighting exercises (Mon–Sat 6.30–8am). Visitors may join courses held in the gym, although prior experience of martial arts and/or dance is a prerequisite; three-month courses are also available for Rs500, not including accommodation – see the head teacher for details. You can also come here for a traditional **Ayurvedic massage**, and to consult the gym's expert Ayurvedic doctors (Mon–Sat 10am–1pm & 5–7.30pm, Sun 10am–1pm).

A path along the north side of the tank leads past the northern, western and southern entrances to the temple, which are guarded by bare-chested doormen armed with sticks – apparently to keep dogs away. It's an atmospheric walk, particularly in the early morning and at dusk, when devotees make their way to and from prayer (a closed iron gate bars the northern side, but everybody climbs through the gap). These little streets, in the old days of Kerala's extraordinary caste system, would have been a "no go" area – possibly on pain of death – to some members of the community.

Behind the temple on West Fort, set back from the road across open ground, the Margi School of **Kathakali** dance drama and **Kutiyattam** theatre (see p.708) is housed in Fort High School. With prior notice you can watch classes, and this is the place to ask about authentic Kathakali performances.

Puttan Malika palace

The **Puttan Malika palace** (daily 8.30am–12.30pm & 3.30–5.30pm; Rs20, Rs25 extra for camera), immediately southeast of the temple, became the seat of the Travancore rajas after they left Padmanabhapuram at the end of the nineteenth century. To generate funds for much-needed restoration, the Travancore royal family has opened the palace to the public for the first time in more than two hundred years. Although much of it remains off-limits, you can wander around some of the most impressive wings, which have been converted into a **museum**. Cool chambers, with highly polished plaster floors and lined with delicately carved wooden screens, house a crop of dusty Travancore heirlooms. Among the predictable array of portraits, royal regalia and weapons are some genuine treasures, such as a solid crystal throne given by the Dutch, and some fine murals. The real highlight, however, is the typically understated, elegant Keralan architecture. Beneath sloping red-tiled roofs, hundreds of wooden pillars, carved into the forms of rampant horses, prop up the eaves, with airy verandas projecting onto the surrounding lawns.

The royal family has always been a keen patron of the arts, and the tradition is upheld with an open-air **Carnatic music festival**, held in the grounds during the festival of Navaratri (Oct/Nov). Performers sit on the palace's raised porch, flanked by the main facade, with the spectators seated on the lawn. For details, ask at the KTDC tourist office.

MG Road: markets and shopping

An assortment of **craft shops** along **MG Road**, north of Station Road, sell sandalwood, brass and Keralan bell-metal oil lamps (see box on p.410). The Gandhian **Khadi Gramodyog**, between Pazhavangadi and Overbridge junctions, stocks handloom cloth (dig around for the best stuff), plus radios and cassette machines manufactured by the Women's Federation. **Natesan's Antique Arts**, further up, is part of a chain that specializes in paintings, temple woodcarvings and so forth. Prices are high, but they usually have some beautiful pieces, among them some superb reproduction Thanjavur paintings and traditional inlaid chests for Kathakali costumes.

At first glance most of the **bookstores** in the area seem largely intended for exam entrants but some, such as the a/c **Continental Books** on MG Road, stock a good choice of titles in English – mostly relating to India – and a fair selection of fiction too. Smaller, but with a wide array of English-language fiction and assorted subjects, such as philosophy, history and music, **DC Books**, on Statue Road, on the first floor of a building above Statue Junction, is well worth a browse. Other bookshops along MG Road include the chain store **Higginbothams** and **Paico Books**.

Almost at the top of MG Road, on the right-hand side, the excellent little **Connemara Market** is the place to pick up odds and ends, such as dried and fresh fish, fruit, vegetables, coconut scrapers, crude wooden toys, coir, woven winnowing baskets and Christmas decorations. The workshops of several **tailors** are within the market.

Public Gardens, Zoo and museums

A minute's walk east from the north end of MG Road, you come to the entrance of Thiruvananthapuram's **Public Gardens** (Tues & Thurs–Sun 10am–5pm, Wed 1–5pm; cover ticket for all museums except the zoo Rs5, available only at the Natural History Museum). As well as serving as a welcome refuge from the noise of the city – its lawns are usually filled with courting couples, students and picnicking families – the city's best museums are here in the park. The **Zoo** (Tues–Sun 10am–5pm; Rs4, Rs5 extra for camera) is in a nice enough location, but the depressing state of the animals, and the propensity of some visitors to get their kicks by taunting them, make it eminently missable.

Give the dusty and uninformative **Natural History Museum** a miss, and head straight for the extraordinary **Government (Napier) Museum** of arts and crafts, completed in 1880 and an early experiment in what became known as the "Indo-Saracenic" style. The building features tiled double-storey gabled roofs, garish red, black and salmon-patterned brickwork, tall slender towers and, above the main entrance, a series of pilasters forming Islamic arches. The spectacular interior boasts stained-glass windows, a wooden ceiling and loud turquoise, pink, red and yellow stripes on the walls. The architect, Robert Fellowes Chisolm (1840–1915), set out to incorporate Keralan elements into colonial architecture; the museum was named after his employer, Lord Napier, the governor of the Madras Presidency. Highlights include fifteenth-century Keralan wood-carvings from Kulathupuzha and Thiruvattar, gold necklaces and belts, minutely detailed ivory work, a carved temple chariot (*rath*), wooden models of Guruvayur temple and an oval temple theatre (*kuttambalam*), plus twelfth-century Chola and fourteenth-century Vijayanagar bronzes.

The attractive **Shri Chitra Art Gallery**, with its curved veranda and tiled roof, houses some splendid paintings from the Rajput, Moghul and Tanjore schools, as well as from China, Tibet and Japan. The oil paintings by Raja Ravi Varma (1848–1906), who is widely credited with having introduced the medium of oil painting to India, have been criticized for their sentimentality and Western influence, but his treatment of Hindu mythological themes is both dramatic and beautiful. Also on display are the paintings of the Russian artist-philosopher and mystic Nicholas Roerich, who arrived in India at the turn of the century. His paintings draw heavily on the deep, strong colours of his Russian background, amalgamating them with the mythical landscape of the Himalayas, where he died in 1947.

Away from the centre

The **Chachu Nehru Children's Museum** (Tues–Sun 10am–5pm; free) in Thycaud in the east of the city serves as a rather dusty testament to the

Kalarippayat

Started in the thirteenth-century, Kalarippayat is the ferocious martial art of Kerala that uses hand-to-hand combat and weapons. It is now widely believed to have been developed by the bodyguards of medieval warlords and chieftains. There are many other theories surrounding the origins, however, including one that the martial art was introduced by the warrior sage Parasuram, who reclaimed the land of Kerala from the ocean by throwing his *mazhu* (battle axe) into the ocean. Others believe that Lord Shiva himself was the founder of Kalarippayat, and that Parasuram and Agasthya, another illustrious sage linked to the form, were Shiva's disciples. Yet another theory amongst the practitioners of Kalarippayat is that Bodhi Dharma, the Buddhist monk from South India, took the form to China and the Far East, when he made his epic journey to spread the faith.

In the eighteenth century Kalarippayat was banned by the British, but it has since made a strong comeback. Kalarippayat has two distinct schools – the southern system and the northern system. The southern system places particular emphasis on footwork and the use of hands in combat, involving a complicated range of moves, blows and locks. The northern system is more complex and uses four basic stages of training for battle. The first stage, Meythari, is a series of twelve levels of body exercise. The second stage, Kothari, uses wooden replica weapons. The third stage, Ankathari, involves training with real medieval weapons such as the *udaval* (sword), *paricha* (shield), *kadaras* (dagger), *kuntham* (spear), *gadha* (mace) and *urumi* (a long flexible sword). The final stage, Verum Kaythari, involves barehanded combat against an armed enemy and is for advanced practitioners only. Kalarippayat demonstrations are never dull, and injuries, although rare, do happen. Traditionally practised by the martial Nair caste, Kalarippayat is popular today with Hindus, Muslims and Christians alike. For details of a place to learn Kalaripppayat, see p.331.

enthusiasm of some anonymous donor back in the 1960s. One room contains ritual masks, probably from Bengal, Rajasthan and Orissa, but the rest of the place is taken up with stamps, health-education displays and over two thousand dolls featuring figures in Indian costume, American presidents, Disney characters and British Beefeaters.

Also on the eastern side of town, visitors can, by arrangement, watch classes in the martial art of **Kalarippayat** (see box on p.333), at the PS Balachandran Nair Kalari martial arts gymnasium, Kalariyil, TC 15/854, Cotton Hill, Vazhuthakad (daily 6–8am & 6–7.30pm). Built in 1992, along traditional lines, the *kalari* fighting pit is overlooked from a height of 4m from a viewing gallery. Students (some as young as 8) train both in unarmed combat and in the use of weapons. Traditionally, the art of battle with long razorblade-like *urumi* is only taught to the teacher's successor. The school arranges short courses in Kalarippayat, and can also provide guides for forest trekking.

Eating

Thiruvananthapuram offers menus for all tastes and budgets, although smart restaurants specializing in Keralan cuisine are thin on the ground. Most of the mid to top-range hotels include a few local dishes in their pretty uniform multicuisine menus, and the *Pankaj* and *Horizon* both have pleasant rooftop restaurants. If you want to experience full-flavoured Keralan "meals" or need a cheap dosa-type snack, just head for one of the dozens of crowded, formica-tabled meals houses at lunch time.

Amma, Central Station Road. Blissful a/c and conveniently near the stations, offering the usual South Indian snacks menu and no fewer than seven different types of *uttappam* (rice pancake).

Anand Bhawan, opposite Secretariat, MG Road. Cheap, simple restaurant near the *Pankaj*, offering hot, fresh regional veg "meals".

Arya Nivaas, Aristo Junction, Thumpanoor. Spotless vegetarian restaurant in a new hotel where you can get "meals" for less than Rs30 and an assortment of dishes such as biriyani.

Hot Breads, Anna's Arcade, Spencer Junction, MG Road. Yummy fresh and hot savoury and sweet breads, pastries and snacks, including pizzas, cheese rolls and croissants.

Indian Coffee House (I), LMS Junction. Opposite the entrance to the Public Gardens, this is a clean and busy place in which to down a refreshing cold coffee after visiting the museums; excellent omelettes, South Indian snacks and meals available all day.

Indian Coffee House (II), Spencer Junction, MG Road. Small, colonial-style building, set back from the road and a sociable place to meet local students. Serves good-value snacks, freshly cooked meals and real filter coffee.

Indian Coffee House (III), Central Station Road. Next to the bus station and unbeatable for break-

fast or a quick snack. Turbaned waiters serve dosas, *wadas*, omelettes and hot drinks in a bizarre spiral building designed by an eccentric British architect. Obligatory cultural and gastronomic pit-stop.

Kalavara, Press Road. Situated on the same stretch as several bookshops, *Kalavara* is an upstairs restaurant above a fast-food counter, which features a mixed menu and local cuisine, including pork and beef dishes. You can expect to pay around Rs70 for a main dish.

Kerala House, next to DC Books, Statue Road. Full of atmosphere, popular and highly recommended by locals as the place to get Kerala cuisine "as mamma makes it". Lunch is the usual great value "meals" and dinner is a la carte – the fish curry and steamed *kappa* (tapioca) is particularly good. Moderately priced.

KTDC Chaithram, Station Road. Two hotel restaurants: one pure veg and the other Mughlai-style. The former, a tastefully decorated air-cooled place, is the best of the two, offering good-value Keralan specialities and a standard range of rice-based North Indian dishes. Moderately priced and recommended.

Prime Restaurant, Prime Square, near the train station. A comfortable restaurant with tasty North and South Indian dishes on the menu and generous portions. Inexpensive.

Sandha, *Pankaj Hotel*, opposite Secretariat, MG
Road. A fifth-floor restaurant with a multicuisine

menu and good-value lunch buffet; there is also a
ground-floor restaurant open for breakfast.

Listings

Airlines Indian Airlines has offices at Air Centre,
Mascot Junction (⊤0471/316870), and the airport
(⊤0471/451537) while Jet Airways is at Akshaya
Towers, 1st Floor, Sasthamangalam Junction
(⊤0471/321018). Air India is at Museum Road,
Vellayambalam Circle (⊤0471/310310 or
501205), and the airport (⊤0471/501426), while
Air Lanka is based at Spencer Building, Palayam,
MG Road (⊤0471/322309) and has an office at
the airport (⊤0471/501147). Gulf Air, which operates regular flights to various Gulf states is across
town in Vellayambalam (⊤0471/328003 or
501205); Air Maldives is also on Spencer Road
(⊤0471/463531) with an office at the airport
(⊤0471/501344). Other Middle East airlines
include Saudi Arabian Airlines at Baker Junction
(⊤0471/321321) and Oman Airways at
Sasthamangalam (⊤0471/328137). British
Airways is at Vellayambalam (⊤0471/326604) and
KLM at Spencer Junction (⊤0471/463531).
Ayurvedic health centres Ayurvedic treatment in
one form or another is to be found throughout
Kerala. For more information on pukka places and
treatment, contact the Ayurvedic Medical College
Hospital, MG Road ⊤0471/460823. For
Kayachikistsa or traditional Ayurvedic massage and
foot therapy contact Agastheswara, Ayurvedic Health
Centre, Jiji Nivas, Killi, Kattakkada ⊤0471/291270.
Banks and exchange Several banks and agencies change money, including the State Bank of
India, near the Secretariat on MG Road (Mon–Fri
10am–2pm, Sat 10am–noon), which accepts only
travellers cheques and currency. The State Bank of
Travancore (Mon–Fri 10am–2pm, Sat
10am–12pm) at Statue Junction and at the
domestic airport recognizes travellers cheques,
currency, Visa and Mastercard. Wall Street
Finances (Mon–Sat 10am–6pm; ⊤0471/450659),
is located behind the *Lucia Continental Hotel* in
East Fort and the Central Reserve Bank in the
lobby of the KTDC *Chaithram Hotel*. American
Express cashes travellers' cheques and advances
money on credit cards through the Great Indian
Tour Company, Mullassery Tavern, Vanross
Junction (⊤0471/331516), east off MG Road.
Thomas Cook has a counter at the airport and an
office at Tourindia, MG Road (⊤0471/330437).
Car rental Inter-Car, Ayswarya Buildings, Press

Road ⊤0471/330964; Nataraj Travels,
Thampanoor (⊤0471/323034); The Great Indian
Tour Company, Mullassery Towers, Vanross
Junction (⊤0471/331516; Travel India, opposite
the Secretariat, MG Road ⊤0471/478208.
Dance and drama For Kathakali and Kutiyattam
check with the Margi School (see p.331), or the
tourist office on Station Road (see p.328), which
organizes free dance performances at the open-air
Nishagandhi Auditorium (Sept–March Sat 6.45pm).
Hospitals General Hospital, near Holy Angels
Convent, Vanchiyur ⊤0471/44387); Ramakrishna
Mission Hospital, Sastamangalam ⊤0471/322123.
Internet access is widely available in
Thiruvanathapuram, but on the pricey side (as is
internet access throughout southern Kerala) at
Rs60–80 per hour. The most efficient place is
Hotel Chaithram (see p.329; Rs60/hr). Alternatively,
try Megabyte on MG Road and Tandem
Communications at Statue Junction.
Pharmacies Central Medical Stores, amongst oth-
ers, at Statue Junction, MG Road.
Post office The GPO, with poste restante (daily
8am–6pm), is in the Vanchiyur district, a short dis-
tance west of MG Road. The Telegraph Office,
opposite the Secretariat on MG Road, is open
around the clock.
Travel agents Aries Travels (specialists for tours
to the Maldives), Ayswarya Building, Press Road
(⊤0471/330964); Swastik Tours and Travel,
Puthenchantai, MG Road ⊤0471/331691,
ⓕ331270; Great Indian Tour Company, Mullassery
Towers, Vanross Junction ⊤0471/331516;
Airtravel Enterprises (good for air tickets), New
Corporation Building, MG Road, Palayam
⊤0471/323900; Tourindia (pioneering cruise and
tour operators), MG Road ⊤0471/330437; Travel
India, opposite the Secretariat, MG Road
⊤0471/478208.
Yoga The Sivananda Yoga Ashram at 37/1929
Airport Rd, Palkulangara, West Fort
(⊤0471/450942) holds daily classes at various
levels, which you can arrange on spec. Better still,
head for Neyyar Dam, 28km east of town, where
their world-famous Dhanwanthari ashram offers
excellent two-week introductory courses amid
idyllic mountain surroundings (see box on p.349
for more).

Thiruvananthapuram is the main transport hub for traffic along the coast and cross-country. Towns within a couple of hours of the capital – such as Varkala and Kollam – are most quickly and conveniently reached by bus. Although for longer hauls you're better off travelling by train as both the private and state (KSRTC) buses tend to hurtle along the recently upgraded coastal highway at terrifying speeds; they're also more crowded.

For an overview of travel services to and from Thiruvananthapuram, see Kerala Travel Details, on p.424.

By air

Thiruvananthapuram's airport sees daily Jet Airways and Indian Airlines flights to Chennai, Cochin and Bangalore. Indian Airlines also flies daily to Mumbai and twice daily to Delhi. Air India also flies to Mumbai seven days a week to connect with international flights. Indian Airlines flies five times a week to Malé in the Maldives and Air Maldives flies the same route daily with additional flights on Fridays and Sundays. Indian Airlines (2 weekly) and Air Lanka (6 weekly) both fly to Colombo in Sri Lanka. See p.335 for a list of airline offices.

By bus

From the long-distance KSRTC Thampanoor bus stand (☎ 0471/323886), frequent services run north through Kerala to Kollam and Ernakulam/Kochi via Alappuzha (3hr 15min). Three buses a day go up to Kumily for the Periyar Wildlife Reserve and there is one bus hourly to Kanniyakumari. Most state buses heading off eastwards or southwards are operated by the Tamil Nadu State Road Transport Corporation (TNSRTC); there are daily services to Madurai and Chennai. Tickets for all the services listed above may be booked in advance at the reservations hatch on the main bus stand concourse; note that TNSRTC has its own counter.

By train

Kerala's capital is well connected by train to other towns and cities in the country, although getting seats at short notice on long-haul journeys can be a problem.

South of Thiruvananthapuram

Despite the fact that virtually the entire 550-kilometre length of the **Keralan coast** is lined with sandy beaches, rocky promontories and coconut palms, **Kovalam** is one of the only places where swimming in the sea is not considered eccentric by locals, and which offers accommodation to suit all budgets. To experience the slow rhythms of daily life away from the exploits of the Kovalam beach scene, you can take an easy wander through the shady toddy groves to villages such as **Pachalloor** and **Vizhinjam**. A finely preserved example of Keralan architecture is also within easy reach of Thiruvananthapuram; 63km to the south is the magnificent palace of **Padmanabhapuram**, former capital of the kingdom of Travancore.

Kovalam

The coastal village of **KOVALAM** may lie just 10km south from Thiruvananthapuram, but as Kerala's most developed **beach resort** it's becoming ever more distanced from the rest of the state. Each year greater numbers

Reservations should be made as far in advance as possible from the efficient computerized booking office at the station (Mon–Sat 8am–2pm & 2.15–8pm, Sun 8am–2pm). Sleepers are sold throughout Kerala on a first-come, first-served basis, not on local stations' quotas.

The following trains are recommended as the fastest and/or most convenient from Thiruvananthapuram.

Recommended trains from Thiruvananthapuram

Destination	Name	Number	Frequency	Departs	Total time
Bangalore	Kanniyakumari–Bangalore Express	#6525	daily	9.10am	19hr 25min
Calcutta	Trivandrum–Howrah Express*	#6323	Wed & Sat	12.45pm	48hr
	Trivandrum–Guwahati Express*	#5627	Sun	12.45pm	47hr
Chennai	Trivandrum–Chennai Mail*	#6320	daily	1.30pm	17hr 45min
	Trivandrum–Guwahati Express*	#5627	Sun	12.45pm	18hr 55min
Delhi	Rajdhani Express**	#2431	Fri & Sat	7.30pm	44hr 30min
	Kerala Express	#2625	daily	11am	52hr 30min
Ernakulam/Kochi	Kerala Express	#2625	daily	11am	4hr 30min
Kanniyakumari	Kanniyakumari Express	#1081	daily	7.15am	2hr 15min
Kollam	Kanniyakumari Express**	#1082	daily	7.30am	1hr 30min
Kozhikode	Trivandrum–Cannanore Express	#6347	nightly	9pm	9hr 50min
Mangalore	Trivandrum–Mangalore-Parasuram Express***	#6349	daily	6am	16hr 30min
	Malabar Express***	#6329	daily	5.40pm	17hr 25min
Mumbai	Trivandrum–Mumbai Express	#6332	Sat	4.20am	40hr
	Kanniyakumari Express*	#1082	daily	7.30am	45hr 35min

* via Kollam, Kottayam, Ernakulam, Palakaad and Chennai
** a/c only
*** via Varkala, Kollam, Kottayam, Ernakulam, Thrissur, Kozhikode, Kannur, Kasargode

of Western visitors – budget travellers and jet-setters alike – arrive in search of sun, sea and palm-fringed beaches. For many travellers it has become, with Goa and Mamallapuram, the third essential stop on a triangular tour of tropical South Indian "paradises" – or indeed another leg of the trail along the coasts of South Asia.

Europeans have been visiting Kovalam since the 1930s, but not until hippies started to colonize the place some thirty years later were any hotels built. As the resort's popularity began to grow, more and more paddy fields were filled and the first luxury holiday complexes sprang up. These soon caught the eye of European charter companies scouting for "undiscovered" beach hideaways to supplement their Goa brochures, and by the mid-1990s plane loads of package tourists were flown here direct from the UK. This influx has had a dramatic impact on Kovalam. Prices have rocketed, rubbish lies in unsightly piles at the roadsides, and in high season the beach – recently enlarged to make way for even more hip cafés, Kashmiri souvenir stalls and overpriced fish restaurants – is packed nose-to-tail. Add to this a backdrop of rapidly deteriorating concrete hotels, and you can see why Kovalam's detractors call it "the Costa del Kerala".

The ancient system of Ayurvedic herbal medicine, dating back to the sixth century BC, has been making a healthy resurgence over the last few decades (see p.33), and nowhere more so than in Kerala. Institutes such as the Ayurvedic Medical College on MG Road in Thiruvananthapuram have been making tremendous steps with their research, which has resulted in Keralan Ayurveda being well regarded in medical circles.

The most common form of Ayurveda in Kerala is massage, which uses oils and herbs in a course of treatment, either for rejuvenation or as remedies. Ayurveda, which aims to eliminate the toxic imbalances that cause the body to become susceptible to ill-health, concentrates on the well-being of the individual as a whole and not just the affected part. The best time for treatment is during the monsoon from June till November, when the atmosphere remains cool and free of dust. Rejuvenation therapy, or *Rasayan Chikitsa*, advocates face and head massage using medicated oils and creams, body massage using hands and feet, and medicated baths. *Kayakalpa Chikitsa*, whose primary objective is to control the ageing process, concentrates on diet. *Sweda Karma*, used in the treatment of certain rheumatic illnesses, uses medicated steam baths to improve tone and reduce fat. Other therapeutic treatments include *Dhara*, for mental disorders and *Pizhichil* for the treatment of rheumatic diseases and nervous disorders, both of which which involve courses of between seven and twenty-one days. Among numerous remedies available in Keralan Ayurveda, *Snehapanam* prescribes medicated ghee and is aimed at curing osteoarthritis and leukemia.

Ayurvedic massage is advertised everywhere in Kovalam, and you'll constantly be approached by men professing to be well-qualified Ayurvedic practitioners – they even show you impressive certificates. These centres offer cheap massages, usually costing Rs150–500. However, most of the so-called "Ayurvedic centres" along Lighthouse Beach are seasonal, as are the "doctors" and "masseurs". There have been an increasing number of complaints about sexual harassment during sessions and serious skin reactions to dodgy Ayurvedic oils.

If you are interested in benefiting from an Ayurvedic massage here, the only centres in Kovalam that currently hold official state approval are those at the *Ashok Hotel* and the KTDC *Samudra*, which both charge from Rs600 a session. Alternatively, contact the Ayurveda College in Thiruvanathapuram (℡0471/460823) for a recommended practitioner in Kovalam.

Throughout Kerala, you'll find that almost all upmarket hotels have an Ayurvedic massage centre, and many offer designer all-inclusive "Ayurvedic rejuvenation programmes", which range from five days to a month and include a special diet and a consultancy with an Ayurvedic doctor. The doctors at such establishments are likely to be pukka (ask to see their qualifications) as the reputation of the hotel is at stake. Otherwise, in Thiruvananthapuram (see "Listings" on p.335) and Cochin (p.398) there are well-established Ayurvedic hospitals where they'll point you in the direction of a reliable local practitioner.

Arrival, information and getting around

Heading along the upgraded approach road from the capital (now littered with publicity hoardings), the frequent #9 **bus** from Thiruvananthapuram (East Fort; 20min) loops through Kovalam and stops at the gates of the *Ashok* complex, at the northern end of the middle bay. Anyone carrying heavy bags who wants to stay by the sea (and not at the *Ashok*), should alight earlier, either at the road to the lighthouse, or the road leading down to the *Sea Rock* hotel. It's also possible to take an **auto-rickshaw** or **taxi** all the way from Thiruvananthapuram; auto-rickshaws cost between Rs60 and Rs100 but will try to get away with a lot more, while taxis charge around Rs150.

The friendly **tourist facilitation centre** (daily 10am–5pm, closed Sun in low season; ℡0471/480085), just inside the gate to the *Ashok Hotel*, is a new place with plenty of leaflets to give out and up-to-date information about cultural events. They also run a small **reading room** next door (same hours) that stocks British and American newspapers, as well as novels.

There are now several places to **change money** at Kovalam but private exchange rates tend to vary, so it's best to do some research first. Of the **banks**,

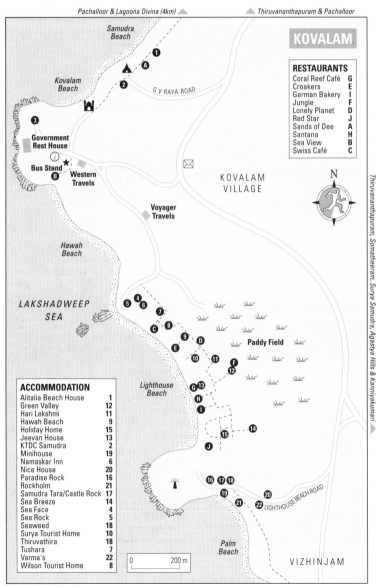

Pachalloor & Lagoona Divina (4km) ▲   ▲ Thiruvananthapuram & Pachalloor

KOVALAM

Samudra Beach

Kovalam Beach

G V RAYA ROAD

Government Rest House

Bus Stand

Western Travels

Voyager Travels

KOVALAM VILLAGE

N

Hawah Beach

LAKSHADWEEP SEA

Paddy Field

Lighthouse Beach

ACCOMMODATION

Alitalia Beach House	1
Green Valley	12
Hari Lekshmi	11
Hawah Beach	9
Holiday Home	15
Jeevan House	13
KTDC Samudra	2
Minihouse	19
Namaskar Inn	6
Nice House	20
Paradise Rock	16
Rockholm	21
Samudra Tara/Castle Rock	17
Sea Breeze	14
Sea Face	4
Sea Rock	5
Seaweed	18
Surya Tourist Home	10
Thiruvathira	18
Tushara	7
Varma's	22
Wilson Tourist Home	8

RESTAURANTS

Coral Reef Café	G
Croakers	E
German Bakery	I
Jungle	F
Lonely Planet	D
Red Star	J
Sands of Dee	A
Santana	H
Sea View	B
Swiss Café	C

LIGHTHOUSE BEACH ROAD

Palm Beach

VIZHINJAM

0   200 m

Thiruvananthapuram, Somatheeram, Surya Samudra, Agastya Hills & Kanniyakumari ▶

the Central Bank of India (Mon–Fri 10am–2pm, Sat 10am–noon) is at the *Ashok* and there is a branch of the Andhra Bank at the KTDC *Samudra* complex near the main gates (same hours). Among other places, you can also change money at *Wilson Tourist Home* any time (the most competitive rates), at Great Indian Travel Services, Lighthouse beach (℡0471/481110), and at Western Travels at the bus stand (℡0471/481334).

Opposite the bus stand, Western Travels (daily 8am–8pm; ℡0471/481334) and Great Indian Travel Services (8am-8pm; ℡ 0471/481110) are reliable agents for flight confirmations and ticketing, and can arrange **car rental**. Among other agencies, Voyager Travels, behind Howrah Beach, specializes in **motorbike rental** – an Enfield Bullet will cost around Rs550 per day, and a scooter Rs350. **Surfboards** can be rented on Lighthouse Beach for Rs50 per hour. Alternatively, for around Rs300 you can also take a ride on a traditional **kettumaran** (*kettu* meaning tied; *maran* logs), which gave the catamaran its name. Widely used by the the fishermen of Kovalam, the rudimentary boat consists of five logs tied together, and feels fairly fragile in a choppy sea.

Dozens of places offer **internet** services with charges of around Rs60 per hour, but the most efficient place with super fast connections is at *Croakers Restaurant*, Lighthouse Beach. Kovalam doesn't have a major **bookshop**, but the German Bakery has a reasonable selection of books for rent, swap or sale and there is a noticeboard to find out what's on in the area.

Accommodation

Kovalam is crammed with **accommodation**, ranging from standard budget rooms with just a double bed and bathroom to five-star hilltop chalets. Only decent rock-bottom rooms are hard to find, as all but a handful of the many budget travellers' guesthouses that formerly crowded the beachfront have been recently upgraded to suit the standards of the large number of package tourists that flock here over Christmas and the New Year. This also means that hotels are block-booked weeks in advance; it pays to phone and reserve a room before you arrive, which also saves you from the menace of the touts that hang around the bus stand. If you follow a tout, remember that their "commission" is tacked onto your room tariff. The main concentration of mid-range rooms is around the lively Lighthouse Beach area, while the quieter Samudra Beach has a couple of upmarket hotels and few simple ones to offer. The best of the resorts such as *Lagoona Davina* (see p.344) and *Surya Samudra* (see p.342) are a little further away and require transport.

Prices are extortionate compared with the rest of Kerala, soaring in peak season (Dec to mid-Jan), when you'll be lucky to find a basic room for less than Rs250. At other times, some gentle haggling should bring the rate down, especially if you stay for over a week. Rates quoted below are for the high season.

Alitalia Beach House, Samudra Beach ℡0471/480042. Basic double rooms (some a/c) with attached bathrooms in one of the few budget places on Samudra Beach, where the advantage is being away from the razzmatazz of the main strip further south. ❸–❺

Ashok, on the headland by Samudra Beach ℡0471/480101, ℻ 481522. Four complexes of chalets and "cottages" in Charles Correa's award-winning hilltop block. Bars, restaurants, pools, yoga centre and tennis courts make this Kovalam's swankiest option, but it's plagued by VIP security personnel and tour groups. ❾

Green Valley, Lighthouse Beach ℡0471/480636. Set amid the paddy fields, this is one of the best budget places in Kovalam, with pleasant en-suite a/c rooms ranged around leafy and secluded courtyards and an inexpensive restaurant on site. However, the proximity to the paddy fields means there is a bit of a mozzie problem. ❸

Hari Lekshmi, behind Lighthouse Beach ℡0471/481341. Run by a very pleasant English lady, this little guesthouse offers four spotless white rooms with attached bathrooms, and there's a relaxing communal veranda and a kitchen. Fantastic value and highly recommended. ❷

Hawah Beach, behind *Croaker's Restaurant*, Lighthouse Beach ☎0471/480431. Rather a prison block feel to the corridor with small, basic rooms with attached bathrooms but no views. The inexpensive room rates and the proximity to the beach are the main incentives to stay here. ❷

Holiday Home, behind Lighthouse Beach ☎0471/480497. In a quiet little garden, two rows of well-appointed cottage-like rooms, built in traditional Keralan style with spacious individual wooden verandas. No sea views, but great value nonetheless. ❸

Jeevan House, behind *Coral Reef Café*, Lighthouse Beach ☎0471/484481, ℻662. Right on the beach, this place offers large plain rooms and cottages (some a/c), each equipped with a fridge; more expensive rooms have good views of the sea. The drawback is that it's very popular with tour groups and directly behind a noisy restaurant. ❻–❼

KTDC Samudra, Samudra Beach ☎0471/480089, ℻480242. Posh government-run three-star, set away from other hotels overlooking its own cove. Deluxe a/c rooms, manicured gardens, a lovely swimming pool and bar, a good Ayurvedic massage centre, restaurant and friendly but slow service. ❾

Mini House, Lighthouse Beach Road ☎0471/485198. Two large non-a/c rooms with balconies, in a great location right over the rocks and breaking sea, but don't underestimate the relentless noise. A third room without the view is much cheaper. ❻–❼

Namaskar Inn, Hawah Beach ☎0471/481903. Tucked in by *Sea Face* hotel, this place has two prize rooms, each occupying an entire floor and filled with sunlight, tastefully decorated with a huge carved bed, wooden floorboards and two walls of windows looking out to sea. The other rooms are standard en-suite doubles with no sea views. ❺–❼

Nice House, Lighthouse Beach Road, opposite *Varma's* ☎0471/480684. This family-run place has absolutely no views, but it is thankfully free of tour groups, and the communal verandas are pleasant. The attached rooms are non-a/c, spotless and slightly overpriced, especially the more expensive ones at the front. ❸–❺

Paradise Rock, Lighthouse Beach Road ☎0471/480658. Variously priced, large en-suite rooms which overlook the main beach; for Rs200 extra you get a sea-facing balcony but no a/c. Clean and welcoming. ❸–❹

Rockholm, Lighthouse Beach Road ☎0471/480636. A range of well-appointed rooms along the clifftop, some of which have fantastic views. Popular with tour groups. ❼

Samudra Tara/Castle Rock, Lighthouse Beach Road ☎0471/481608. Three-storey concrete block set above the beach, with comfortable rooms and private balconies. ❹–❼

Sea Breeze, in the coconut grove behind Lighthouse Beach ☎0471/480 0240. Gaudily painted pink and blue block, with huge sunny communal balconies overlooking a tropical garden. The non-a/c rooms are clean and simple with attached bathrooms. Quiet, secluded and recommended. ❼

Sea Face, Lighthouse Beach ☎0471/481835. An ugly modern block with three-star pretensions and comfortable rooms; its saving grace is the good swimming pool. ❽–❾

Sea Rock, Hawah Beach ☎0471/480422. One of Kovalam's oldest established hotels – a block of rooms slap on the seafront, with standard double rooms (a sea view costs extra) and a popular restaurant. ❽

Sea Weed, Lighthouse Beach Road ☎0471/480391. Neat, clean and breezy hotel that claims to "get away from all the madness". Some of the rooms ranged around the leafy courtyard have a/c and, as usual, those with views cost extra. There is a pleasant rooftop restaurant. ❻–❼

Surya Tourist Home, Lighthouse Beach ☎0471/481012. One of a clutch of identikit, no-frills places tucked behind the main beach, with small but clean rooms and no sea views. Avoid the restaurants in the hotels along this row; they attract very few customers and so the ingredients may not be fresh. ❸

Thiruvathira, Lighthouse Beach Road ☎0471/480787. Attached rooms, private verandas and limited sea views and a/c in the more expensive rooms. The comfortable non-a/c rooms at the back are cheaper and offer good value, unlike the expensive ones. ❸–❽

Tushara, behind Lighthouse Beach ☎0471/481694, ℻481693. A respectable hotel where all the well-appointed rooms have private balconies, but face onto a courtyard and offer no views. The tariff includes continental breakfast. ❻

Varma's, Lighthouse Beach Road ☎0471/480478. The most attractive of the upper-range options, this place is modern but furnished in traditional Keralan style with tasteful rooms featuring carved wood, tiles and sea-facing balconies (some a/c). The management is very friendly and helpful. ❼–❽

Wilson Tourist Home Lighthouse Beach
⊤0471/480051. Popular place worth the extra for
spacious en-suite rooms (some a/c), balconies
(some with swinging chairs), garden, friendly staff
and its proximity to the beach. They do foreign
exchange. ④–⑦

Accommodation south of Kovalam

Two of the most luxurious of Kovalam's resorts lie around 8km to the south, by road. The German-run *Surya Samudra* at Pulinkudi (⊤0471/480413, ⑨481124; ⑩) consisting of beautifully presented antique Keralan wood cottages (all non-a/c), which spread discretely along a rocky hillside and look down onto two small beaches. There is an Ayurvedic centre and an extraordinary swimming pool cut into the rock. Nearby, *Somatheeram* at Chowera (⊤0471/481601, ⑨462935; ⑨), was formerly an Ayurvedic hospital and now offers high-quality massage and Ayurvedic treatment in four-star surroundings; comfortable cottages and apartments in exquisite Keralan houses spill down its landscaped hillside to a private beach. If it's full, try its sister concern around the corner, *Manatheeram* (⊤0471/481610, ⑨481611; ⑨), which is marginally cheaper and shares the same Ayurvedic facilities. Next to *Surya Samudra*, the *Bethsaida Hermitage* (⊤0471/481554; ⑧–⑨) prides itself as an eco-friendly beach resort, built in 1996 without sacrificing a single tree. Set in a superb location, the resort is made up of pleasant but small cottages built in traditional style, its own beach and a great restaurant which serves both South and North Indian dishes. *Bethsaida Hermitage* also offers Ayurvedic treatment and yoga. The resort belongs to a Christian charitable trust and a percentage of the profits goes to several projects, including an orphanage.

For a bit of quiet, head south to Poovar at the mouth of the River Neyyar, 20km south of Kovalam (taxis charge Rs200). Here, the *Treasure Island* resort (⊤0471/212063, ⑨210019; ⑧–⑨), pre-booked through *Wilson Tourist Home* in Kovalam (⊤0471/480051), occupies a very secluded spot on a palm-studded island. The cottages are pleasantly simple but stylish, set in a coconut plantation; there is a swimming pool and you can explore this beautiful stretch of the coastline by boat or on foot.

Kovalam's beaches

Kovalam consists of a succession of small crescent beaches; the southernmost, known for obvious reasons as **Lighthouse Beach**, is where most visitors spend their time. Roughly ten minutes' amble through the sand from end to end, it's bordered with cheek-to-cheek low-rise concrete guesthouses and restaurants. The red-and-white **lighthouse** (daily 2–4pm), on the promontory at the southern end of the beach, gives superb views across to Vizhinjam mosque (see p.345). On Lighthouse Beach you can hire surfboards and also take a ride out on a wooden outrigger (see p.340).

Hawah, the middle beach, overlooked from a rocky headland by the five-star *Ashok* resort, functions each morning as a base for local fishermen, who drag a massive net through the shallows to scoop up thrashing multi-hued minnows, coiling endless piles of coir rope as they work. North of the *Ashok*, in full view of its distinctive sloping terraces, the final, northernmost beach, **Samudra**, is the least affected of all by the changing times, dotted only with a few rudimentary wooden fishing vessels.

Whether the local residents like it or not, seeing Westerners in skimpy bathing suits has become relatively normal, although hardly acceptable. If you are walking in the coconut groves behind the beaches or between Howrah Beach and Samudra Beach, where you will pass a mosque, it is only polite to

KERALA | South of Thiruvananthapuram

Due to unpredictable rip currents and a strong undertow, especially during the monsoons, swimming from Kovalam's beaches is not always safe. The recent introduction of lifeguards (noticeable by their blue shirts), has reduced the annual death toll, but at least a couple of tourists drown here each year, and many more get into difficulties. Follow the warnings of the safety flags at all times, and keep a close eye on children. There is a first-aid post midway along Lighthouse Beach.

dress in a respectful manner. The cultural gulf is further accentuated at the weekends, when coach loads of day-trippers from Thiruvananthapuram hit the beach to splash about in modesty-preserving sarees and trousers.

If you want to escape the beach scene, head into the deliciously shady and cool **coconut groves** behind the hotel strip on Lighthouse Beach. A little concrete path up the hill behind Hawrah Beach takes you deep into another world, far removed from the Western-style hedonism down on the beach. Here ladies gossip in shrill Malayalam while they wash clothes and children in the village tank, palm leaves are woven and left to dry in the sun, fishing nets are mended to the whirring of the tailor's sewing machine and children play raucous games of cricket with a coconut shell and stick.

Eating, drinking and nightlife

Lighthouse Beach is lined with identikit cafés and restaurants like *Garzia*, *Coaker's* and *Coral Reef*. Most specialize in **seafood**: you pick from the fresh fish, lobster, tiger prawns, crab and mussels on display, which are then weighed, grilled over a charcoal fire or cooked in a tandoor (traditional clay oven), and served with salad and chips. Meals are pricey by Indian standards – typically around Rs150 per head for fish, and double that for lobster or prawns – and the service is often painfully slow, but the ambience of the beachfront terraces is convivial. Beer, spirits and local *feni* (distilled palm wine) are served, albeit very discreetly due to tight liquor restrictions, to a background of soft reggae or Pink Floyd. The rave scene that you see in Goa and Gokarn has so far failed to take off in Kovalam, although most restaurants organize their own beach parties at Christmas and New Year. For upmarket service and more comfort try the restaurants at one of the more expensive hotels, such as the excellent terrace restaurant at the *Rockholm* and the popular rooftop one at the *Hotel Sea Weed*; for even more upmarket options, try the *Ashok* or the *Surya Samudra* (see box opposite). For **breakfast** you can chose from any number of typical budget-traveller cafés with the usual brown-bread menus, or search out a traditional breakfast of *iddli* and *sambar* at one of the cheap local cafés along the main road and near the bus stand.

Nightlife in Kovalam is pretty laid-back, and revolves around the beach where Westerners lounge about drinking and playing backgammon until the wee hours. A couple of restaurants also offer **video nights**, screening pirate copies of the latest American hits. You may be offered *charas*, but bear in mind cannabis is illegal in Kerala, as everywhere else in India, and that the local police regularly arrest foreigners for possession.

German Bakery, Lighthouse Beach. Breezy rooftop terrace at the south end of the beach, serving tasty (mostly healthy) Western food and lots of tempting cakes (try the waffles with chocolate sauce) and great fruit lassis. Breakfasts include a "full English" and "French" (croissants with espresso and a cigarette).

Jungle, behind Lighthouse Beach, next to *Hari Lekshmi*. Set back in a toddy secluded grove (bring mozzie repellent) and owned by an Italian, offering genuine Lavazza coffee, cappuccinos and imported pasta with delicious home-made sauces.

Lonely Planet, behind Lighthouse Beach, near *Green Valley*. Congenial, generally inexpensive, veg restaurant tucked away in the paddy fields by a little pond (bring mozzie repellent in the evening). The place to come if you're pining for Indian food and one of the few where you can get *iddlis* for breakfast.

Red Star, Lighthouse Beach, near the lighthouse. A shack right on the beach, popular with those in search of dishes and seafood with local flavour and more than a tiny pinch of spice. The cook whips up inexpensive South Indian snacks, lassis and good Keralan "meals" at lunch time for Rs30, as well as fiery fish curries.

Sands of Dee, Samudra Beach. Run-of-the-mill place, but the best of the few seafood restaurants on less developed Samudra Beach; there's a beach party and a bonfire every Sunday evening.

Santana, Lighthouse Beach. The best of the seafood joints on this beach, with a great barbecue, tandoori fish and chicken, and good music. Stays open later than most.

Sea View, Hawah Beach. Congenial atmosphere and a good place for a snack lunch, or for seafood in the evenings; the day's catch may include lobster and huge king prawns.

Swiss Café, Lighthouse Beach. Hip and very chic, with an excellent sound system and rustic ambience; the place is packed at sunset during "happy hour". Offers European food to rich European customers (Rs350–700 for a main meal), with an elaborate menu of healthy, fresh dishes, lots of fish and *rosti* is served with everything. Goan fish curry is available for the mildly adventurous.

Pozhikkara beach and Pachalloor village

Heading north along Samudra for around 4km, you'll pass through fishing hamlets before eventually arriving at a point where the sea merges with the backwaters to form a saltwater lagoon. Although only thirty minutes' walk from the *Ashok*, the sliver of white sand dividing the two, known as **Pozhikkara beach**, is a world away from the headlong holiday culture of Kovalam. Here the sands are used primarily for landing fish and fixing nets, while the thick palm canopy shelters a mixed community of Hindu fishermen and Christian coir-makers. The tranquil village of **PACHALLOOR**, behind the lagoon, is a good alternative base to Thiruvananthapuram or Kovalam.

There are two **guesthouses** here, including the original and idyllic – and now upmarket – *Lagoona Davina* (℡0471/380049; ⊙, full board available). Six individually decorated en-suite rooms open onto the water and two cheaper cottages ($65 per cottage) lie behind. Lazing in a hammock under the palm trees, you can watch the villagers paddling past in their long dug-outs and sand-wallahs diving to fill up buckets with silt. The guesthouse organizes its own **backwater trips** (Rs350 per head for 2hr); accompanied by a knowledgeable guide, you're punted around the neighbouring villages, with stops to see coir being made and to identify an amazing wealth of tropical fruit trees, spices and birds. The **food** served at *Lagoona Davina* is exceptional – a fusion of authentic Keralan village dishes and European *nouvelle cuisine*. You can also have an Ayurvedic massage or take yoga lessons with the resident doctor, and there is a boutique with exquisite outfits made by Davina herself. If you book in advance, you'll be met at the airport, or take a taxi 6km along the highway towards Kovalam, and bear right along the "bypass" where the road forks, just after the Thiruvallam bridge. After another 1km or so, a sign on the right-hand side of the road points through the trees to the guesthouse. The other guesthouse at Pachalloor, the *Beach and Lake Resort* (℡0471/381055; ⊙–⊙), lies across the water from *Lagoona Davina* on the beach side, and has five rooms but no restaurant and little atmosphere.

Vizhinjam (Vilinjam)

The unassuming village of **VIZHINJAM** (pronounced Virinyam), on the opposite (south) side of the headland from Lighthouse Beach, was once the capital of the Ay kings, the earliest dynasty in south Kerala. During the ninth century the Pandyans intermittently took control, and it was also the scene of major Chola-Chera battles in the eleventh century. A number of small simple shrines survive from those times, and can be made the focus of a pleasant afternoon's stroll along quiet paths through the coconut groves. They're best approached from the village centre, beyond a fishing community, rather than via the coast road. However, if you do walk along the coast road from Kovalam to the north side of Vizhinjam, you can't fail to be struck by the contrast, from the conspicuous consumption of a tourist resort to a poor fishing village.

A huge modern pink **mosque** on the promontory overlooks the tightly packed thatched huts on the bay below. For centuries, the Muslim fishermen here were kept at arm's length by the Hindu orthodox, perpetually forced into debt by the combination of low prices for their produce and exorbitant interest charged by moneylenders on loans for boats and nets (as much as ten percent per day). Cooperatives have recently started to arrange interest-free loans and sell fish on behalf of individuals, but the mutual antipathy between the two communities persists. A flare-up occurred as recently as the early 1990s, when a series of violent riots resulted in the deaths of numerous local people. Today, Hindus and Muslims are divided by a three-hundred-metre stretch of no-man's-land, patrolled by police, which only tourists can cross without risking a severe beating. Needless to say, you're not likely to be popular if you use Vizhinjam as a photo opportunity.

On the far side of the fishing bay in the village centre, 50m down a road opposite the police station, a small unfinished eighth-century rock shrine features a carved figure of Shiva with a weapon. The **Tali Shiva** temple, reached by a narrow path from behind the government primary school, may mark the original centre of Vizhinjam. This simple shrine is accompanied by a group of *naga* snake statues, a reminder of Kerala's continuing cult of snake worship that survives from pre-Brahminical times.

The sacred grove known as **Kovil Kadu** (temple forest) lies near the sea, ten minutes' walk from the main road in the village, along Hidyatnagara Road. Here a small enclosure contains a square Shiva shrine and a rectangular shrine dedicated to the goddess **Bhagavati**. Thought to date from the ninth century, these are probably the earliest structural temples in Kerala, although the Bhagavati shrine has been renovated.

Padmanabhapuram

Although now officially in Tamil Nadu, **PADMANABHAPURAM**, 63km southeast of Thiruvananthapuram, was the capital of Travancore between 1550 and 1750, and therefore has a far more intimate connection with the history of Kerala and is administered by the government of Kerala. For anyone with even a minor interest in Keralan architecture, the small palace here is an irresistible attraction. However, **avoid weekends**, when the complex gets overrun with bus parties. Occasionally parts of the palace are closed to visitors for restoration.

Set in neat, gravelled grounds in a quiet location away from the main road, the predominantly wooden **Padmanabhapuram Palace** (Tues–Sun 9am–4.30pm; Rs6, Rs10 extra for camera) epitomizes Keralan architecture. If you are walking from the bus station, cross the main road outside the station, turn left and follow a road on the right for a pleasant ten- to fifteen-minute walk through the paddy fields to a village that backs onto the substantial walls of the palace compound. For taxis and private cars, there is a small car park right outside the main entrance.

Against a backdrop of steep-sided hills, the exterior of the palace displays a perfect combination of clean lines and gentle angles, with the sloping tiled roofs of its various interconnecting buildings broken by triangular projecting gables that enclose delicately carved screens. The palace is excellently maintained by the Archaeological Survey of India. All visitors have to be shown around by the informative **guides**, who do not charge a fee but expect a tip. At busy times they will rush you through the palace, especially if there are only a few of you, so as to catch up with the next group.

In the **entrance hall** (a veranda), a brass oil lamp hangs from an ornate teak, rosewood and mahogany ceiling and is carved with ninety different lotus flowers. Beautifully ornamented, the revolving lamp inexplicably keeps the position in which it is left, seeming to defy gravity. The raja rested from the summer heat on the cool, polished-granite bed in the corner. On the wall is a collection of *onamvillu* (ceremonial bows) decorated with images of Padmanabha – the god Vishnu reclining (see box on opposite) – which local chieftains would present to him during the Onam festival.

Directly above the entrance hall, on the first floor, is the **mantrasala** (council chamber), gently illuminated by the light filtering through panes of coloured mica. Herbs soaking in water were put into the boxed bench seats along the front wall, as a natural air-cooling system. The highly polished black floor was made from a now-lost technique using burnt coconut, sticky sugarcane extract, egg whites, lime and sand.

The oldest part of the complex is the **Ekandamandapam**, or "the lonely place". Built in 1550, it was used for rituals for the goddess Durga which typically employed elaborate floor paintings known as *kalam ezhuttu* (see p.388). A loose ring attached to a column is a tour de force of the carpenter: both ring and column are carved from a single piece of jackwood. Nearby is a *nalekettu*, a four-sided courtyard found in many Keralan houses, open to the sky and surrounded by a pillared walkway. A trapdoor once served as the entrance to a secret passageway leading to another palace, since destroyed.

The Pandya-style stone-columned **dance hall** stands directly in front of a shrine to the goddess of learning, Saraswati. The women of the royal household had to watch performances through screens on the side, and the staff, through holes in the wall from the gallery above. Typical of old country houses, steep, wooden ladder-like steps, ending in trapdoors, connect the floors. Belgian mirrors and Tanjore miniatures of Krishna adorn the chamber forming part of the **women's quarters**, where a swing hangs on plaited iron ropes. A four-poster bed, made from sixteen kinds of medicinal wood, dominates the **raja's bedroom**. Its elaborate carvings depict a mass of vegetation, human figures, birds and, as the central motif, the snake symbol of medicine, associated with the Greek physician deity Asclepius.

The **murals** for which the palace is famous – alive with detail, colour, graceful form and religious fervour – adorn the walls of the **meditation room** directly above the bedroom, which was used by the raja and the heirs apparent. Unfortunately, this is now closed – allegedly because the stairs are shaky, but in fact to preserve the murals, which have been severely damaged by generations of hands trailing along the walls.

Further points of interest in the palace include a **dining hall** intended for the free feeding of up to two thousand brahmins, and a 38-kilo stone which, it is said, every new recruit to the raja's army had to raise above his head 101 times.

In front of a depiction of the god in the meditation, or prayer room, at Padmanabhapuram Palace lies a sword. In 1750, Raja Marthanda Varma symbolically presented this weapon to Padmanabha – the god Vishnu – who reclines on the sacred serpent Anantha in the midst of the cosmic ocean, thereby dedicating the kingdom of Travancore to Vishnu. From that day, the raja took the title of Padmanabhadasa ("servant of Padmanabha"), and ruled as a servant of the god.

Thus Travancore belonged to Vishnu, and the raja was merely its custodian – a spiritual, and presumably legal, loophole that is said to have proved invaluable in restricting the power of the British in Travancore. Travancore, therefore, remained under direct control of the raja, with the British presence restricted to that of a resident only.

Practicalities

Frequent buses run to Padmanabhapuram from Thiruvananthapuram's Thampanoor station; hop on any service heading south towards Nagercoil or Kanniyakumari and get down at Thakkaly (sometimes written Thuckalai). If you're determined to see Padmanabhapuram, Kanniyakumari and Suchindram in one day, leave the city early to arrive when the palace opens at 9am. Note that two express buses leave Thakkaly for the capital during the afternoon, at 2.30pm and 3.30pm. Another way to see Padmanabhapuram is on KTDC's Kanniyakumari tour which starts at Thiruvananthapuram (Tues–Sun 7.30am–9pm; Rs230) but you can pick it up at the main bus stop in Kovalam where it stops en route.

The area around the bus station, being on the NH-47, is noisy and dirty. It's better to get **refreshment** from the chai-cum-food and "cool drinks" shops inside the outer walls of the palace, or look for the barrows selling delicious fried *kappa* (tapioca) chips. Just outside the inner gate you can usually find tender **coconuts**.

North of Thiruvananthapuram

When it gets too hot at sea level, **Ponmudi** and the **Peppara Wildlife Sanctuary**, just northeast of Thiruvananthapuram, make a refreshing overnight break: in a couple of hours you can find yourself deep in hill country, climbing up through the rubber and cardamom plantations to emerge in cooler air and endless slopes of lime-green tea bushes. Alternatively, the richly forested **Agastya Hills** are 25km northeast of Thiruvananthapuram and make a pleasant day-trip, forming a beautiful backdrop to the **Neyyar Dam**, on the banks of which is the excellent **Sivananda Yoga centre**. Just before you turn off to the Agastya Hills, it is well worth visiting the fascinating **Koikkal Kottaram** at Nedumangod. This palace is the epitome of traditional Keralan architectural elegance, and is now open to the public as a museum of local archeology, history and culture.

If you want to stick to the coastline, you could do no better than to head up to the quiet and relaxed village of **Varkala**, where pilgrims rub shoulders with foreign visitors eager to sunbathe and strike a yogic pose. A little further north, the busy town of **Kollam** is one of the main departure points for boat trips through the unforettable Keralan **backwaters**.

Koikkal Kottaram

The beautiful palace of **Koikkal Kottaram** (Tues–Sun 10am–5pm; Rs3, Rs10 extra for camera), 20km northeast of Thiruvananthapuram and just short of the turning to Neyyar Dam and Agastya Hills (see below), sits on the outskirts of the lively market town of Nedumangod, 1km north of the KSTRC bus station. This little known palace is cared for by the Archeological Survey of India, who provide knowledgeable guides to take you around the collections and exhibits; the guides are free but a tip is appreciated.

The palace was originally constructed for Umyamma Rani, a local queen who reigned from 1677 until 1684. It retains all the distinctive features of traditional **Keralan architecture**: a bowed tiled roof, intricately carved teak features outside and in, cool stone floors and dark rooms, a private central courtyard for the ladies and a wonderfully effective natural air-conditioning system using sloping wooden slats. There is also a secret passage leading out from the courtyard that the queen could use as an escape when her enemies laid siege to the palace, a common war tactic in seventeenth-century Kerala. In the beautiful manicured gardens around the palace, a maze of trees is currently being cultivated.

The ground-floor rooms contain a vast coin collection that is imaginatively displayed to chart the development of international trade along the Malabar coastline. The coins were mostly discovered during recent archeological excavations in the area and include Roman Pinari coins, tiny punch-marked coins with the royal seals of local rajas, and more modern British examples from the Victorian period. Other rooms around the courtyard contain Keralan household and farming implements dating from the eighteenth and nineteenth centuries, as well as three ornamental palanquins for the royal ladies to be carted about in.

Upstairs, the make-up and costumes for Kathakali, Ottan Thullal and teyyatam (see p.709) dance performances are displayed on ferocious-looking models, and there is an exquisite *Kettuvialaku* (platform) for the goddess Durga, carried around town during local spring festivities. Also displayed are the musical instruments and implements used in the colourful and archaic rituals that frequently take place in Keralan temples, such as the iron weaponry employed to represent aspects of deities and the elaborate jewellery worn by officiating priests.

Agastya Hills

Within easy distance of Kovalam, 25km to the northeast and feasible on a daytrip, the jagged, forested **AGASTYA HILLS** form a verdant backdrop to the **Neyyar Dam** (signs warn you not to take photographs of the dam itself for national security reasons). In an idyllic position on the banks of the dam, the **Sivananda Yoga Vedanta Dhanwanthari Ashram** (see box opposite) is one of the country's leading **yoga** ashrams.

Nearby are **ornamental gardens**, boasting outsize, garishly painted plaster images of gods and heroes. A tiny, two-acre **safari park** on a corner of the dam, approached by boats from near the Forest Department, is home to seven lions, whose roars during feeding time at sunset echo through the hills. You are strongly advised not to swim in the dam as it is infested with crocodiles.

Across the dam the forest beckons. The only way to enter the Agastya Hills reserve, however, is through the Forest Department, who will, on request, organize a **boat** and an obligatory **guide**. The guide service is free but you

Located amid the serene hills and tropical forests, around the Neyyar Dam, the Sivananda Yoga Vedanta Dhanwanthari is one of India's leading yoga ashrams. It was founded by Swami Shivananda as a centre for meditation, yoga and traditional Keralan martial arts and medicine. Dubbed the "Flying Guru" because he used to pilot light aircraft over war-stricken areas of the world scattering flowers and leaflets calling for peace, Sivananda was a renowned exponent of Advaitya Vedanta, the philosophy of non-duality, as espoused by the Upanishads and promoted later by Shankara in the eleventh century.

Aside from training teachers in advanced *raja* and *hatha* yoga, the ashram offers excellent introductory courses for beginners. These comprise four hours of intensive tuition per day (starting at 5.30am), with background lectures that provide helpful theory. During the course, you have to stay at the ashram and comply with a regime that some Western students find disconcertingly strict (smoking, alcohol, drugs, sex and even "rock music" are prohibited, the diet is pure veg, and you have to get up at the crack of dawn). However, if you are keen to acquire the basic techniques and knowledge of yoga, this is a good place to start. For more details, contact either the ashram itself (☎0471/290493) or its branch in Thiruvananthapuram, 37/1929 Airport Rd, West Fort (☎0471/450942). You can also consult its publication, *Sivananda Yoga Life*, published by the Sivananda Yoga Vedanta centre, 51 Felsham Rd, London SW15 1AZ (☎020/8780 0160, ✉Siva@dial.pipex.com).

should have prior permission to **trek** in the park from the Forest Department offices at Vazhuthacud in Thiruvananthapuram. On occasions, the local range officer does give permission, especially if you arrange it through the manager at the tourist bungalow, KTDC *Agastya House* (see below). Longer treks into the forest can be arranged through the department or through the *Agastya Garden Hill Resort* (see below) but, so far, there has been little demand.

Practicalities

Buses from the KSRTC Thampanoor bus stand in Thiruvananthapuram depart every half-hour for the Neyyar Dam. If you are coming from Kovalam, take a bus to Balaramapuram or Neyyattinkara on NH-47, then change for Aruvikara and the Neyyar Dam. The only decent **accommodation** at Neyyar Dam, is the KTDC *Agastya House* (☎0471/272160; ❹), which has huge rooms and verandas (with views), and a decent restaurant serving South Indian meals and snacks. During the weekend, avoid the rooms upstairs as the popular beer bar below gets noisy. For a bit more comfort, head for **Kalipara**, the large, black, rocky hill with a small temple on top. The *Agastya Garden Hill Resort* (☎0471/273151; ❻) has comfortable (albeit rather expensive) mock–rustic cottages with incredible views. On the downside, it is situated next to a rocky cliff-face and gets very hot in summer. The resort has introduced treks in the Agastya Hills reserve forest, and boat tours, but with a dearth of competition, these are vastly overpriced.

Ponmudi and Peppara Wildlife Sanctuary

In the tea-growing region of the **Cardamom** (or Ponmudi) **Hills**, about 60km northeast of Thiruvananthapuram and 77km from Kovalam, at an altitude of 1066m, lies the hill station of **PONMUDI**, comprising a range of cottages, rooms and a restaurant on the top of a hill that commands breathtaking views out across the range as far as the sea.

The main reason why anyone comes up here is that it serves as the only practical base for visits to the 53 square kilometres of forest set aside as the **Peppara Wildlife Sanctuary**, which protects elephants, *sambar*, lion-tailed macaques, leopards and other assorted wildlife. Although Peppara is theoretically open all year, the main season is from January until May; check before you go with the District Forest Officer, Thiruvananthapuram Forest Division, Thiruvananthapuram (☏0471/320674).

The beautiful drive up, via the small towns of Nedumangad and Vithura, runs along very narrow roads past areca nut, clove, rubber and cashew plantations, with first the Kavakulam and then the Kallar River close at hand. The bridge at **Kallar Junction** marks the start of the real climb. Twenty-two hairpin bends (numbered at the roadside) lead slowly up, starting in the foothills, heading up past great lumps of black rock and thick clumps of bamboo (*iramula*), then through the Kallar teak forest. Finally you wind through the tea plantations; the temperature is noticeably cooler and, once out of the forest, the views across the hills and the plains below become truly spectacular – on a clear day you can see the sea. There really is very little to do up here, but the high ridges and tea estates make good rambling country.

Practicalities

Four daily **buses** run from Thiruvananthapuram to Ponmudi, via Vithura; the first is at 5.30am and the last at 10.15am. There are many more buses back from Ponmudi to Thiruvananthapuram, starting at 6am until the last leaves at 6.30pm. The nearest **tourist office** is currently in Thiruvananthapuram, where information on Ponmudi is readily available. A snazzy new tourist office should be open in Ponmudi by 2002.

The *Government Guest House* (☏0472/890230; ❸–❹) has twenty-four **rooms** and seven cottages, all with attached bathrooms and hot water. Simple and inexpensive but delicious meals have to be ordered a couple of hours in advance; otherwise the cold drinks and snack shop is open daily until 4pm, or you can walk down the road to the teashop on the bend (400m from the hotel). The main building, which originally belonged to the raja of Travancore, has lost any charm it may once have possessed, and the huge plate-glass windows of its canteen-like restaurant rattle disconcertingly in the wind, but views across the hills and misty valleys from the terrace make up for all that. Weekends get relatively lively, thanks to the beer parlour (open daily 10am to 6pm).

Varkala

Long known to Keralans as a place of pilgrimage, **VARKALA**, 54km northwest of Thiruvananthapuram and 20km southeast of Kollam, is drawing more and more foreign visitors, who see the beautiful beach and cliffs, just beyond the village, as a quiet, unspoiled alternative to Kovalam. Centred on a clifftop row of budget guesthouses and palm-thatch cafés, the tourist scene has so far been relatively low-key, despite the arrival of the *Taj Group*'s luxury resort and the occasional package tour group. The best time to get here is between October and early March; during the monsoons the beach is virtually unusable.

Arrival and information

Varkala's railway station, 2km east of the village, is served by daily **trains** from Thiruvananthapuram, Kollam (hourly; 45min) and most other Keralan towns

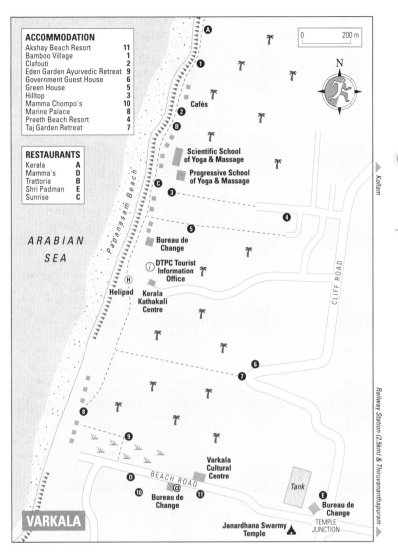

ACCOMMODATION

Akshay Beach Resort	11
Bamboo Village	1
Clafouti	2
Eden Garden Ayurvedic Retreat	9
Government Guest House	6
Green House	5
Hilltop	3
Mamma Chompo's	10
Marine Palace	8
Preeth Beach Resort	4
Taj Garden Retreat	7

RESTAURANTS

Kerala	A
Mamma's	D
Trattoria	B
Shri Padman	E
Sunrise	C

ARABIAN SEA

Papanasam Beach

Cafés

Scientific School of Yoga & Massage

Progressive School of Yoga & Massage

Bureau de Change

DTPC Tourist Information Office

Helipad

Kerala Kathakali Centre

Varkala Cultural Centre

BEACH ROAD

Bureau de Change

Tank

Bureau de Change

Janardhana Swarmy Temple

TEMPLE JUNCTION

VARKALA

Kollam

Railway Station (2.5km) & Thiruvananthapuram

on the main coastal line. From here, an auto-rickshaw to the beach costs Rs20–30. Regular **buses** run from Thiruvananthapuram's Thampanoor stand, and from Kollam (1hr–2hr 30min). A few go all the way to the beach, but most stop briefly in the village centre, a five-minute auto-rickshaw ride away from the main accommodation. If you can't get a direct bus to Varkala, take any "superfast" or "limited stop" bus along the main highway NH-47, and change at Kallamballam from where you can hop onto a local bus to Varkala, or resort to an auto-rickshaw (Rs70) or a taxi (Rs100).

The new government-run **DTPC tourist information centre** (daily 8am–6pm) next to the helipad on the clifftop, is very welcoming and informative and you avoid all the problems of agency middlemen, who are very prevalent in Varkala. Here you can arrange rail, road and air travel, organize backwater cruises, buy tickets for Katakali performances, and book a ride on an elephant. They will also pre-book taxis at the official government rate, which is especially useful if you need to leave at night or early in the morning.

You can hire **two-wheelers** everywhere in Varkala; the going rate for a scooter is Rs200, Rs300 for a motorbike and Rs300–450 for an Enfield. **Elephant rides** are the big tourist attraction in Varkala; private travel agencies will offer you expensive day-long elephant rides in a nearby forest. However, when you get there you will find that you are only allowed a trundle for an hour. The official government rate is Rs250 per hour per person, and a taxi to the forest is Rs50 return.

There are several places to **change money** in Varkala including the friendly and versatile bureau de change outlets on the corner of Temple Junction (aka Holy Cross) in the centre of town, on Beach Road, and on the southern end of the clifftop, next to the tourist information office. There are **internet** centres all around Varkala, all charging Rs50–60/hr, with a Rs15 minimum charge.

Accommodation

Varkala has a fair choice of **places to stay**, from basic rooms with shared (or outside) shower-toilets to establishments offering a bit more comfort. If you're on a tight budget, head first for the clifftop area (rickshaws can make it up there), where there are several family-run guesthouses and lodges in the coconut trees behind the row of cafes. On the way, it's worth stopping to see if the wonderful *Government Guest House* has vacancies. Otherwise, choose from a scattering of places along Beach Road. Accommodation is tight in **peak season** (late Nov–Jan), when you should call ahead.

Akshay Beach Resort, Beach Road (☎0472/602668). Clean guesthouse with en-suite rooms (some with a/c), massage and helpful management. A dull location, but handy for the beach. ❸–❻

Bamboo Village, North Clifftop (no phone). Four lovely, airy bamboo huts on stilts with little balconies and dinky attached bathrooms. They are very popular and have a congenial social scene of their own, as well as being great value. There is no phone so you have to turn up on spec and hope one is free. ❷–❸

Clafouti, North Clifftop (☎0472/601414). Spotless tiled rooms ranged around a courtyard, each with private balconies; the more expensive ones have sea views. There is a cheaper row of cottages facing the *Trattoria* restaurant. ❹–❻

Eden Garden Ayurvedic Retreat, off Beach Road (☎0472/603910). Marooned in the paddy fields behind the beach, with slightly run-down en-suite rooms ranged around a fishpond with relaxing sit-outs (beware of mosquitoes). Offers Ayurvedic treatment including massage and food; there is also a German Bakery on site. ❸–❹

Government Guest House, a 5min walk north of the temple, behind the *Taj* hotel (☎0472/602227). Former maharajah's holiday palace, converted into a characterful guesthouse, with eight enormous non-a/c rooms and meals available on request. Superb value, but a bit run-down. For more comfort try the new *Tourist Bungalow* behind, which is part of the same complex; their large plain non-a/c rooms are excellent value. ❷

Green House, clifftop area (☎0472/604659). Secluded and only 2min from the cliff edge, situated behind a small temple in an unhurried and friendly hamlet. The rooms are basic and the cheaper ones share a common bathroom, Popular with the backpacker crew, and there are plenty of similarly priced fallbacks nearby (try *White House* or *Red House*). ❷

Hilltop, north end of the clifftop area (☎0472/601237). A great spot, with pleasant, breezy rooms, attached shower-toilets and relaxing terrace restaurant. The cheaper rooms are at the back, while the upstairs rooms, which are quite a bit more expensive, have sea views. ❺–❻

Mamma Chompos, Beach Road (☎0472/603995). Run by an Italian couple on a converted farm compound with reasonable rooms and communal bathrooms. Further up the hill a new block of simple rooms with attached bathrooms nestles amongst the palm trees. There's a great Italian restaurant on site. ❹

Marine Palace, behind Papanasam Beach (⏱0472/603204). En-suite rooms in a rather dilapidated pale green building near the sea. Pricier front rooms have sea views and balconies; the thatched annexe is cheaper and the restaurant is congenial. ④–⑥
Preeth Beach Resort, clifftop area, off Cliff Road (⏱0472/600942). Large, well-maintained complex shaded by a palm grove, with a range of well-appointed rooms (some a/c), each with a private balcony. There is a good restaurant in the leafy courtyard. ⑤–⑧
Taj Garden Retreat, near the *Government Guest House*, off Cliff Road (⏱0472/603000, ⎗602296). Very comfortable and centrally a/c rooms, a good restaurant and bar, a fitness and Ayurveda centre and a pleasant swimming pool, but it's all a bit ostentatious for a laid-back place like Varkala. The tariff includes breakfast and dinner buffets. ⑨

The village

Known in Malayalam as Papa Nashini (sin destroyer), Varkala's beautiful white-sand **Papanasam Beach** has long been associated with ancestor worship. Devotees come to the beach after praying at the **Janardhana Swamy temple** (said to be over 2000 years old), to bring the ashes of departed relatives for their "final rest". Non-Hindus are not permitted to enter the inner sanctum but are welcome in the grounds. A small government hospital at the north end of the temple, opened by Indira Gandhi in 1983, was set up to benefit from being built on the same site as three **natural springs**, and to take advantage of the sea air, which is said to boost the health of asthma sufferers.

Backed by sheer red laterite cliffs and drenched by rolling waves off the Arabian Sea, the coastline is imposingly scenic and the beach relatively peaceful, despite the usual presence of hawkers. The religious significance of the beach means attitudes to (especially female) public nudity are markedly less liberal than other coastal resorts in India; bikinis don't necessarily cause offence, but you'll attract a lot less attention if you wear a full-length cotton sarong while bathing. **Dolphins** are often seen swimming quite close to the coast, and, if you're lucky, you may be able to swim with them by arranging a ride with a fishing boat – ask at the DTPC tourist office. Sea otters are occasionally seen playing on the cliffs by the sea.

Few of Varkala's Hindu pilgrims wander up to the **clifftop area**. It is reached by several steep and treacherous footpaths, or the more gradual paths up from behind the Marine Palace restaurant, and by the metalled road from the village that was built to service a helipad in advance of Mrs Gandhi's visit. However, those who do invariably seem less enthralled by the splendid sea views than by the sight of *sari*- and *kurta*-clad Westerners meditating and pulling **yoga** poses under the palm trees. This faintly cheesy New Age scene centres on two schools based here on the clifftop. The small Scientific School of Yoga & Massage, offers **Ayurvedic massage** (Rs300 per session), **meditation courses**, "lifetime" courses in **yoga** (Rs750 for an unlimited number of lessons) and fortnight-long courses in massage ($100). The school runs a small shop, Prakruthi Stores, which stocks local honey, essential oils, herbs and handmade soaps, as well as books on yoga, meditation and massage. Progress Yoga Centre also offers massage sessions (Rs250–400), and short courses in **reiki**, **reflexology**, yoga and Ayurvedic massage.

Sivagiri Hill, at the eastern edge of the village, harbours a more traditional **ashram** that attracts pilgrim devotees of Shri Narayana Guru, a saint who died here in 1922. Born into the low *ezhava* caste, he fought orthodoxy with a philosophy of social reform ("one caste, one religion, one God for man") that included the consecration of temples, with an open-door policy to all castes and had a profound effect on the "upliftment" of the untouchables.

Aimed unashamedly at the tourist market, the **Varkala Cultural Centre** (⏱0472/603612) near the tank, a few metres down Beach Road from Temple

Junction, holds **Kathakali** (as well as Bharatanatyam) dance performances most evenings in season (6.30pm–8pm). Alternatively, the DTPC has just started their own nightly show at the Kerala Kathakali Centre, just behind the helipad on the clifftop; tickets are available on the day from the DTPC Tourist Information Office. The Rs125 admission fee includes sitting in on the fascinating process of applying Kathakali make-up (daily 5pm–6.30pm). Although in a real performance the make-up process is much more elaborate and usually takes much longer, the session that precedes a performance here provides an insight into the art. For those who would like to learn more, the centres also offer short courses on make-up.

Eating

Seafood lovers will do well in Varkala's increasingly sophisticated clifftop café-restaurants, some of which have upper storeys raised on stilts for better sea views. Prices are quite high and the service can be very slow, but the superb location more than compensates, especially in the evenings when the sea twinkles with the lights of countless fishing boats. Most of the restaurants offer identical menus with fresh fish, including shark and marlin, on display. It is increasingly hard to find a menu outside the village proper that includes Indian cuisine, as more restaurants cater to homesick European tastebuds – pizza is rapidly taking over as the local dish.

Due to Kerala's antiquated licensing laws which involve huge amounts of tax, **beer** is discreetly available but at a price (Rs75–90), as none of the cafés are supposed to sell it and periodically get raided, resulting in official or unofficial fines. One alternative is to retire to the comforts of the *Taj Garden Retreat*'s bar and superb restaurant, but you will have to pay through the nose.

Clafouti, north clifftop. Little tables under rustling palm trees, and a wonderful French bakery counter stacked full of real croissants, pain aux raisins, baguettes, and sweet pies. In the evening there is a set three-course menu (about Rs150) which is changed daily, and a range of moderately priced French and seafood dishes.

Kerala, north clifftop. As the name suggests, this place serves up *iddli-dosa* breakfasts, unlimited "meals" at lunch (Rs30) and thalis, *barottas* and dosas in the evening. Although nowhere as spicy as the real thing, this place is about as authentic as you'll hope get in the clifftop area.

Mammas, Beach Road. You are greeted with the vigorous kneading of fresh dough and the wonderful smell of pizzas cooking in the traditional wood fired oven; the place is relaxed and popular, and the menu delicious.

Shri Padman, next to temple, Varkala village. The large rear terrace of this unpromising, grubby-looking "meals" joint is one of the main travellers' hang-out in Varkala. The (Indian veg) food is cheap and delicious (try the coconut-rich *navrattan*, deep-fried cheese, garlic chapatis or filling biriyanis), and the location atmospheric, especially at breakfast time, when villagers come to the tank to bathe.

Sunrise, north clifftop. This is the place to get great value set breakfasts – Israeli, French or South Indian. In the evening, try their speciality *ho mok*, a Keralan dish of fish, coconut and spices steamed in a banana leaf and served with rice.

Trattoria, north clifftop. If you can ignore the tropical climate, you might well be in Italy, as large groups of friends and families enjoy long lunches around tables covered with red-and-white checked tablecloths and generous bowls of pasta. The menu has fish, calamari, mussels and prawn dishes amongst the pizza and pasta – only the wine is missing.

Kollam (Quilon) and around

One of the oldest ports on the Malabar Coast, **KOLLAM** (pronounced Koillam, and previously known as Quilon), 74km northwest of Thiruvananthapuram and 85km southeast of Alappuzha, was formerly at the centre of the international spice trade. The sixteenth-century Portuguese writer Duarte Barbossa described it as a "very great city with a right good

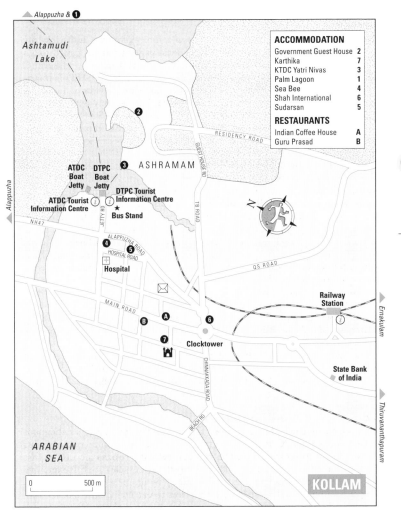

haven", which was visited by "Moors, Heathen and Christians in great numbers", and stated that "a great store" of pepper was to be found there. In fact, the port flourished from the very earliest times, trading amicably with the Phoenicians, Arabs, Persians, Greeks, Romans and Chinese.

Nowadays, Kollam is chiefly of interest as one of the entry or exit points to the backwaters of Kerala (see box on p.362), and most travellers simply stay overnight en route to or from Alappuzha. The **town** itself, sandwiched between the sea and the Ashtamudi (eight inlets) lake, is less exciting than its history might suggest. It's a typically sprawling Keralan market community, with a few characterful old tiled wooden houses and winding backstreets, kept busy with the commercial interests of coir, cashew nuts (a good local buy), pottery, aluminium and fishery industries. The missable ruins of **Tangasseri** fort (3km from the centre) are the last vestiges of colonial occupation.

Arrival and information

The **railway station** is on the east of town, a three-kilometre auto-rickshaw ride (Rs15–20) from the jetty. Numerous local passenger trains pass through daily on their way to and from Ernakulam, Thiruvananthapuram and beyond. On platform 4, the tiny District Tourism Promotion Council (DTPC) **information counter** (Mon–Sat 9am–12.30pm & 1.30–5pm) will book hotels for travellers; you have to pay one night in advance, but the only extra charge is for the phone calls. They also have a tourist office (Mon–Sat 9am–5.30pm; ℡0474/742558) at the **boat jetty** (for boat details, see box on p.362) but they will only provide details regarding their own tourist ferry service. In contrast, the local Allepuzha Tourism Development Council (ADTC) office on the opposite side of the road is very friendly and dispenses unbiased information about both tourist and local ferry services; they also have a good number of **kettu vallum** boats available for personalized backwater cruises (see p.362). Both outfits operate a **daily cruise** from Kollam to Alappuzha, which departs at 10.30am, takes eight hours (Rs150) and stops for lunch and tea. While the cruise is popular, many visitors feel that you get a far better impression of backwater life by hopping between villages on the very cheap **local ferries**. Tickets for both the DTPC and ATDC ferries can be brought on the morning of the trip in the respective tourist office; tickets for the local ferries are purchased at the booth on the jetty. Note that the ATDC ferry leaves from a pier 100m to the west of the main jetty.

The DTPC also organizes **guided tours** (daily 9am–1pm; Rs300) by boat and by foot through the complex of waterways and footpaths of nearby **Monroe Island** on Ashtamundi Lake, providing a fascinating glimpse of Keralan village life.

The jetty and KSRTC **bus stand** are close together on the edge of Ashtamudi Lake. Bookable express **buses** are available south to Thiruvananthapuram (1hr 30min) and north to Kochi (3hr) via Alappuzha (1hr 15min).

Accommodation and eating

The most congenial **places to stay** are outside the town, across Ashtamundi Lake from the DTPC main boat jetty (easy to get to by auto-rickshaw, but more difficult to return from). The **railway retiring rooms** are on the first floor of the railway station (Rs100) and boast spacious, clean and inexpensive non-a/c double rooms, but they tend to fill up by noon.

Apart from the hotel restaurants, other places to **eat** include the *Indian Coffee House* on Main Road, and *Guru Prasad*, a little further along the same road, which serves great South Indian veg "meals". The best of the hotel restaurants can be found in the *Sudarsan*, which has a good-value "meals" restaurant along with its more upmarket a/c restaurant. However, the congenial lakeside restaurant at the KTDC *Yatri Niwas* is where most travellers end up whiling away a long evening, eating tasty barbecue fish.

Government Guest House, 3km northeast of town, by Ashtamudi Lake (℡0474/743620). Characterful Euro-Keralan building, once the British Residency, with curved tiled roof and gracious verandas, in a vast compound. Ye olde British furniture in cavernous spaces, but there are just five rooms. Simple meals are served by arrangement, although most people head over to the *Yatri Niwas* to eat. You can reserve backwater cruise tickets here. Book in advance – some travellers come to Kollam purely to stay here. ❷–❹

Karthika, off Main Road, near the mosque (℡0474/751821). A large and popular budget hotel with clean, plain rooms (some a/c), ranged around a courtyard in which the centrepiece is, rather unexpectedly, three huge nude figures. Very handy for the railway station and the jetty. Cable TV costs Rs20 to hire for a night. ❸

KTDC Yatri Nivas, across from the jetty (☎0474/745538). Modern, clean rooms (two a/c) with attached bathrooms and nice balconies, in a great location overlooking the lake; the best fall-back if the *Government Guest House* is full. The restaurant is very popular with travellers, serving good South Indian nosh, and there is a beer par-lour. ❸–❹

Palm Lagoon, Vellimon West (☎0474/523974). In a beautiful location on Ashtamudi Lake but a good 15km from town, with pleasant thatched cottages and breakfast or full board. Good Ayurvedic treat-ment facilities available, and the opportunity to explore the backwaters. Book directly or through DTPC for directions and a discount. ❻

Sea Bee, Jetty Road (☎0474/744696). Big busi-ness hotel, near the bus station and jetty. Decent rooms (some a/c), a dingy restaurant, bar and for-eign exchange. ❸–❼

Shah International, TB Road (☎0474/742362). A modern hotel block with a shabby reception and dodgy-looking piping running along the corridor ceilings but, surprisingly, the large rooms (some a/c and cable TV) are spotless and bright with attached bathrooms. ❸–❼

Sudarsan, Parameswar Nagar (☎0474/744322). Central and popular, but definitely not as palatial as the posh foyer would lead you to believe. Wide range of rooms, some with a/c and cable TV. A busy, dark a/c restaurant with a white plaster *Last Supper* at one end and a TV at the other, offering a large Indian and Chinese menu, and a bar. ❺–❽

Kayamkulam and Karunagapalli

KAYAMKULAM, served by (non-express) buses between Kollam and Alappuzha, was once the centre of its own small kingdom, which after a battle in 1746 came under the control of Travancore's king Marthanda Varma. In the eighteenth century the area was famous for its **spices**, particularly pepper and cinnamon. The Abbé Reynal claimed that the Dutch exported some two mil-lion pounds of pepper each year, one-fifth of it from Kayamkulam. At this time, the kingdom was known also for the skill of its army of 15,000 Nayars (Kerala's martial caste).

Set in a tranquil garden, the dilapidated eighteenth-century **Krishnapuram palace** (Tues–Sat 10am–4.30pm; Rs2) is imbued with Keralan grace and con-structed largely of wood, with gabled roofs and rooms opening out onto shady internal courtyards. It's now a museum, but unlike the palace at Padmanabhapuram (see p.345), with which it shares some similarities, the whole place is in great need of restoration and the exhibits are poorly labelled and neglected. The best way to learn about the palace and its collections is to hire one of the unofficial guides hanging around the palace entrance. They are knowledgeable but, despite their claim to "accept no money", they will expect a tip.

A display case contains puja-ceremony utensils and oil lamps, some of which are arranged in an arc known as a *prabhu*, placed behind a temple deity to pro-vide a halo of light. Fine miniature *panchaloha* ("five-metal" bronze alloy, with gold as one ingredient) figures include the water god Varuna, several Vishnus and a minuscule worshipping devotee. Small stone columns carved with ser-pent deities were recovered from local houses.

The prize exhibit is a huge **mural** of the classical Keralan school, in muted ochre-reds and blue-greens, measuring over fourteen square metres, which depicts **Gajendra Moksha** – the salvation of Gajendra, king of the elephants. In the tenth-century Sanskrit *Bhagavata Purana*, the story is told of a Pandyan king, Indrayumna, a devotee of Vishnu cursed by the sage Agastya to be born again as an elephant. One day, while sporting with his wives at the edge of a lake, his leg was seized by a crocodile whose grip was so tight that Gajendra was held captive for years. Finally, in desperation the elephant called upon his chosen deity Vishnu, who immediately appeared, riding his celestial bird–man vehicle, Garuda, and destroyed the crocodile.

The centre of the painting is dominated by a dynamic portrayal of Garuda about to land, with huge spread wings and a facial expression denoting *raudra* (fury), in stark contrast with the compassionate features of the multi-armed Vishnu. Smaller figures of Gajendra, in mid-trumpet, and his assailant are shown to the right. As with all paintings in the Keralan style, every inch is packed with detail. Bearded sages, animals, mythical beasts and forest plants surround the main figures. The outer edges are decorated with floriate borders which, at the bottom, form a separate triptych-like panel showing Balakrishna, the child Krishna, attended by adoring females.

At a quiet spot just outside the small town of **KARUNAGAPALLI**, 23km north of Kollam towards Alappuzha, it is possible to watch the construction and repair of traditional **kettu vallam**, or "tied boats". These long cargo boats, a familiar sight on the backwaters, are built entirely without nails. Each jack-wood plank is **sewn** to the next with coir rope, and then the whole is coated with a caustic black resin made from boiled cashew kernels. With careful maintenance they last for generations.

Karunagapalli is best visited as a day-trip from Kollam; regular **buses** pass through on the way to Alappuzha. One daily **train**, the #6525 Kanniyakimari–Bangalore Express, leaves Kollam at 11.55am, arriving at Karunagapalli at 12.30pm, but you will have to get a bus back. On reaching the bus stand or railway station, take an auto-rickshaw 1km north along the national highway, then turn left into a lane for 4km to the riverside village of **Alumkattaru**, and the boatyard of the *vallam asharis*, the boat carpenters. The boat-builders are friendly and willing to let visitors watch them work. In the shade of palm trees at the edge of the water, some weave palm leaves, others twist coir strands into rope and craftsmen repair the boats. Soaking in the shallows nearby are palm leaves, used for thatch, and coconut husks for coir rope. If you wanted to buy a *vallam*, it would set you back around two *lakh* (Rs200,000).

Alappuzha

Under its former appellation of Alleppey, **ALAPPUZHA**, roughly midway between Kollam (85km south) and Kochi (64km north), is another romantic and historic name from Kerala's past. It was one of the best-known and wealthy ports along the Malabar Coast, to the extent that successful British traders who had settled here during the Raj did not want to leave at Independence. A sizeable community of British expatriates remained resident here until the 1950s, enticed by thriving trading opportunities; their luck ran out in 1957, however, when the newly elected communist government clamped down on private businesses, and they were forced to return to Britain. With such a long trading history, tourist literature is fond of referring to Alappuzha as the "Venice of the East", but while it may be full of interconnecting **canals**, there the resemblance ends. Alappuzha is a bustling, messy town of ramshackle wood and corrugated-iron-roof houses, chiefly significant in the coir industry, which accounts for much of the traffic on its oily, green-brown waterways.

Despite its insalubrious canals, Alappuzha is prominent on the tourist trail as one of the major centres for **backwater boat trips**, served by ferries to and from Kollam and Kottayam in particular. Most visitors stay just one night, catching a boat or bus out early the next morning. No special sights demand attention here, but the bazaar along the main street, **Mullakal Road**, is worth

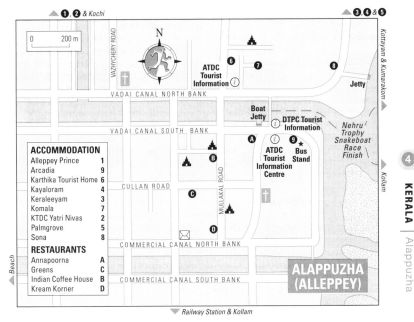

Map labels (from image):

ACCOMMODATION
Alleppey Prince 1
Arcadia 9
Karthika Tourist Home 6
Kayaloram 4
Keraleeyam 3
Komala 7
KTDC Yatri Nivas 2
Palmgrove 5
Sona 8

RESTAURANTS
Annapoorna A
Greens C
Indian Coffee House B
Kream Korner D

ALAPPUZHA (ALLEPPEY)

a browse, with a better-than-average crop of lurid Keralan *lunghis*. However, if you do have an afternoon to spare, just 5–10 minutes walk northeast of the centre the congestion of Alappuzha eases and you can wander along the **lakeside** under a shady canopy of palm trees, enjoying the extraordinarily slow pace Keralan village life.

Alappuzha really comes alive on the second Saturday of August, in the depths of the rainy season, when it serves as the venue for one of Kerala's major spectacles – the **Nehru Trophy snakeboat race**. This event, first held in 1952, is based on the traditional Keralan enthusiasm for racing magnificently decorated *chundun vallam* (longboats), with raised rears designed to resemble the hood of a cobra. Each boat carries 25 singers and 100–130 oarsmen power the craft along, all rowing to the rhythmic *Vanchipattu* (song of the boatman). There are a number of prize categories, including one for the women's race; sixteen boats compete for each prize. The atmosphere is tremendous as Alappuzha is packed with thousands of cheering spectators all dressed in their Sunday best, out to enjoy the colourful pre-race pageant in the morning as much as the races themselves. Women are not advised to go to these events on their own.

Similar races can be seen at Aranmula (p.369), and at Champakualm, 16km by ferry from Alappuzha. The ATDC information office (see below) will be able to tell you the dates of these other events, which change every year.

Arrival and information

The KSRTC **bus stand** on the east of the town, has good local and long-distance connections; the **boat jetty** is just one minute's walk west from the bus stand. The **railway station**, 3km south west of the jetty, sees few major services.

Alappuzha has several rival **tourist departments**. The main ATDC tourist information office (daily 8am–8pm; ☎0477/243462, ⓦ www.atdcalleppey.com)

KERALA | Alappuzha

359

is opposite the main jetty, next to Canara Bank, and they have a smaller office on the other side of the canal, just off Komala Road. The DTPC office (daily 7.30am–9pm; ☏0477/251796) at the DTPC jetty handles **hotel bookings** for all KTDC and private hotels throughout Kerala and in other parts of South India for the charge of the telephone call and on receipt of one night's room rate. ATDC and DTPC both sell tickets for their **ferries**, **backwater cruises** and **charter boats** (maximum 20 people) – good for group excursions into less visited backwaters. The Government of Kerala's tourist office, at the DTPC jetty (Mon–Sat 10am–5pm; ☏0477/260722) is useful for travel information. Other ferry and charter organizations include Kerala Backwaters at Choondapally Buildings, near the Nehru Trophy finishing point (☏0477/241693), Tour Kerala, Muttal Building, Nehru Trophy Ward (☏0477/242955), and Alappuzha Tour & Co, Punchiri Building, Jetty Road (☏0477/242040).

Money–changing facilities are available at the Bank of India on Mullakal Road, and the Indian Bank on Mullakal Road, which recognizes Visa and Mastercard, as well as currency and travellers cheques. The State Bank of India is on Beach Road, and Canara Bank next to the Zion Food Shop, near the jetty; it accepts travellers' cheques and Visa, but not currency. **Internet** is not widely available in Alappuzha, however Seiki Internet café opposite the *Komala Hotel* charges Rs40/hr and offers by far the fastest service, while the Zion Food Shop opposite the main jetty charges Rs60/hr.

Accommodation

If you need to stay near the town centre, Alappuzha's choice of **lodgings** is uninspiring but there are some great places to stay if you are willing to travel into the outskirts and pay a bit more. For a traditional atmosphere, try *Sona* or *Keraleeyam,* the latter specializing in Ayurvedic treatment. The *Alleppey Prince*, which has a pool, is an old favourite and within striking distance of town, while the luxurious *Kayaloram* on the southern edge of the lake ranks amongst Kerala's finest settings.

Alleppey Prince, AS Road (aka Ernakulam Road or NH-47), 2km north of the jetty ☏0477/243752. The poshest option close to the town centre: all rooms are a/c. Private backwater trips, and classical music or Kathakali staged by the pool. Book ahead. ➐–➑

Arcadia, by the KSRTC bus station ☏0477/241354. Soulless place with corridors of clean rooms (some a/c) close to the jetty; the restaurant serves excellent fish. Overpriced but popular as it's so convenient for the ferry. ➍–➎

Karthika Tourist Home, Kathiyani Road, across the canal, opposite the jetty ☏0477/251354. Plain rooms, some with attached bathrooms and wicker chairs. Room 31 has large bay windows. Try this place if the *Komala* is full. ➋

Kayaloram, Punnamada Kayal ☏0477/232040, ☏252918. An incredible location in a grove of palms with views onto the lake; the twelve cool wood cottages are built in Keralan style with open-to-the-sky baths, and ranged around a great pool. Ayurvedic treatment courses and daily sunset

cruises are available. Book through their city office at Punchiri Buildings, Jetty Road (☏0477/262931) and you will be taken there by boat from the Nehru Trophy jetty. ➒

Keraleeyam, Nehru Trophy Road, Thathampally ☏0477/231468, ☏251068. Traditional Keralan house with oodles of character that has been an Ayurvedic centre for sixty years. Elegant rooms are arranged around a communal living area, and there is a delightful cottage. There is a resident Ayurvedic doctor, and rejuvenation courses are individually tailored, including a special diet. Right on Punnamada Kayal, the Nehru Trophy channel, and you can get here by boat from the jetty. ➐

Komala, Zilla Court Ward, north of the jetty canal, 5min by rickshaw from the bus stand ☏0477/243631. Large and well-managed hotel, easily the best budget and mid-range place. A good range of clean rooms (some with a/c) and the nicest South Indian restaurant in town. ➋–➎

KTDC Yatri Nivas, AS Road, near *Alleppey Prince* ☏0477/244460. A modern complex with large,

One of the most memorable experiences available to travellers in India – even those on the lowest of budgets – is the opportunity to take a boat journey on the backwaters of Kerala. The area known as Kuttanad stretches for 75km from Kollam in the south to Kochi in the north, sandwiched between the sea and the hills. This bewildering labyrinth of shimmering waterways, composed of lakes, canals, rivers and rivulets, is lined with dense tropical greenery and preserves rural Keralan lifestyles that are completely hidden from the road.

Views constantly change, from narrow canals and dense vegetation to open vistas and dazzling green paddy fields. Homes, farms, churches, mosques and temples can be glimpsed among the trees, and every so often you might catch the blue flash of a kingfisher or the green of a parakeet. Pallas fishing eagles cruise above the water looking for prey, and cormorants perch on logs to dry their wings. If you're lucky enough to be in a boat without a motor, at times the peace will be broken only by the squawking of crows and the occasional film song from a distant radio. Day-to-day life is lived on and beside the water. Some families live on tiny pockets of land, with just enough room for a simple house, yard and boat. They bathe and wash their clothes – sometimes their buffaloes too, muddy from ploughing the fields – at the water's edge. Traditional Keralan longboats, *kettu vallam*, glide along, powered both by gondolier-like boatmen with poles and by sail. Often they look on the point of sinking, with water lapping perilously close to the edge, and laden with heavy-weight cargo. Fishermen work from tiny dugout canoes, long rowing boats or operate massive Chinese nets on the shore.

Coconut trees at improbable angles form shady canopies, and occasionally you pass under simple curved bridges. Here and there basic drawbridges can be raised on ropes, but major bridges are few and far between. Most people rely on boatmen to ferry them across the water to connect with roads and bus services, resulting in a constant crisscrossing of the waters from dawn until dusk (a way of life beautifully represented in the visually stunning film *Piravi*, by Keralan director Shaji). Poles sticking out of the water indicate dangerous shallows.

Threats to the ecosystem

The African moss that often carpets the surface of the narrower waterways, incidentally, may look attractive, but is a menace to small craft traffic and starves underwater life of light. It is also a symptom of the many serious ecological problems currently affecting the region, whose population density ranges from between two and four times that of other coastal areas in southwest India. This has put growing pressure on land, and hence a greater reliance on fertilizers, which eventually work their way into the water causing the buildup of moss. Illegal land reclamation, however, poses the single greatest threat to this fragile ecosystem. In a little over a century, the total area of water in Kuttanad has been reduced by two-thirds, while mangrove swamps and fish stocks have been decimated by pollution and the spread of towns and villages around the edges of the backwater region.

Routes and practicalities

There are numerous backwater routes to choose from, on vessels ranging from local ferries, through chauffeur-driven speedboats offered by the KTDC, to customized *kettu vallam* cruises. The most popular excursion is the full-day journey between Kollam and Alappuzha. You can cover part or all of the route in a day, returning to your original point of departure by bus during the evening, or more comfortably, stay the night at either end. All sorts of private hustlers offer their services, but the easiest to organize is by taking a trip on the tourist boats run by the Alleppey Tourism Development Co-op (ATDC) and the District Tourism Promotion Council (DTPC). The double-decker boats leave from both Kollam and

KERALA | Alappuzha

Alappuzha daily, departing at 10.30am (10am check in); tickets cost Rs150 and can be bought in advance or on the day only at the ATDC/DTPC counters on either of the jetties (beware of unauthorised vendors selling fake tickets). Both companies make three stops during the 8hr journey, including one for lunch, and another at the renowned Mata Amritanandamayi Mission at Amritapuri. Foreigners are welcome to stay at the ashram, which is the home of the renowned female guru, Shri Amritanandamayi Devi, known as the "hugging Mama" because she gives each of her visitors and devotees a big, power-imparting hug during the daily *darshan* sessions.

Although it is by far the most popular backwater trip, many tourists find the Alappuzha–Kollam route too long and at times uncomfortable, with crowded decks and intense sun. There's also something faintly embarrassing about being cooped up with a crowd of fellow tourists madly photographing any signs of life on the water or canal banks, while gangs of kids scamper alongside the boat screaming "one pen! . . . one pen . . . !" You can sidestep the tourist scene completely, however, by catching local ferries. These are a lot slower, and the crush can be worse, but you are far less conspicuous than on the ATDC/DTPC boat and you gain a more intimate experience of life on the backwaters. The trip from Alappuzha to Kottayam (11 daily; Rs6) is particularly recommended; the first ferry leaves at 7.30am and the last at 9.30pm. Arrive early so you can get a place on the bow, which affords uninterrupted views. There are also numerous daily ferries that ply routes between local villages, allowing you to hop on and off as you like. The scenery on these routes is more varied than between Kollam and Alappuzha, beginning with open lagoons and winding up on narrow canals through densely populated coconut groves and islands, and the ticket costs one-tenth of the price of the ATDC/DPTC tour. Whichever boat you opt for, take a sun hat and plenty of water, and check the departure times in advance, as these can vary from year to year.

Groups of up to ten people can charter a *kettu vallam* moored at Karunagapalli for a day's cruise on the backwaters. The boat has comfortable cane chairs and a raised central platform where passengers can laze on cushions; there is a toilet on board and cool drinks are available. Sections of the curved roof of wood and plaited palms open out to provide shade and allow uninterrupted views. Whether powered by local gondoliers or by sail, the trip is as quiet and restful (at least for the passenger) as you could possibly want. At around Rs3000 for the day, including lunch, the luxury is well worth it. For longer trips, you take a *kettu vallam* that has been converted into a houseboat with one or two bedrooms, bathroom (with shower) and a kitchen. A cook will also be provided. To book either, call Tourindia, MG Road, Thiruvananthapuram (☎0471/331057).

Almost every mid- to top-range hotel situated near the backwaters has its own private *kettu vallum* boat available for residents to hire. Alternatively, DTPC (☎0477/251796) and ATDC (☎0477/243462, ✉) operate fleets (ATDC has fifteen rice boats available, DTPC only has three) from Alleppey, and there are dozens of private *kettu vallam* operators in both Alleppey and Kollam who will arrange a trip if you turn up on spec. However, overnight *kettu vallam* cruises are not cheap, at Rs3000–5000 for two people for a 2–3 day cruise, depending on the length and number of meals you will have. Competition is stiff, and private agencies charge very similar prices, although you may be able to barter to bring the price down slightly, especially in the low season.

As a word of warning, as simple as the life in the backwaters appears to be, take care of your belongings at all times; there have been recent reports of theft, especially during the night when the crew sleep on dry land and the large windows are open. If possible, lock your valuables away (or put them under the bed in your bag) and keep belongings away from the windows.

immaculate rooms; the more expensive ones have a/c and cable TV. There's a decent South Indian restaurant and a beer parlour next door at their *Aaram Motel.* ❸–❻

Palmgrove, Punnamada ☎ 0477/235004 & 233474. On Punnamada Kayal, 2.5km from the jetty. Quaint and very simple bamboo huts and attached open-to-the-sky baths, which are dotted

around a manicured palm grove. The restaurant is in an open hut, serving South Indian food only. This place isn't nearly in the same league as some other "resorts" along the backwaters, but then it is a lot more affordable. You can get here by bus or by boat. ❻

Sona, lakeside, Thathampally ☎ 0477/235211. Beautiful old Keralan home which once belonged

Moving on from Alappuzha

As Alappuzha is not on the main railway network, but rather on a branch line, the choice of trains servicing the town is limited. There are, however, train connections to Thiruvananthapuram and Kollam in the south, and to Kochi/Ernakulam, Thrissur, Palakaad and other points in the north. Bus connections are adequate, especially to Kochi/Ernakulam where there is a greater choice of trains to northern destinations and Tamil Nadu. Although buses travel to Kollam, the best way of getting there is by boat. Regular ferry services connect to Kottayam from where you can get buses to Periyar, or several destinations along the coastal highway.

By bus

The shambolic KSRTC bus stand, on the east of town and a minute's walk from the boat jetty, is served by half-hourly buses to Kollam (2hr), Thiruvananthapuram (3hr 30min), and Kochi/Ernakulam (1hr 30min). Less frequent buses run to Kottayam (4hr), Thrissur (8hr) and Palakaad (11hr).

By boat

Tourist boats travel regularly to Kollam with the ATDC and DTPC boats operating a similar schedule (Mon–Sat; Rs150 per person), departing at 10.30am and arriving at Kollam at 6.30pm. Much cheaper local ferries travel to Kottayam, the first starting at 5am and the last at 5.30pm.

By train

As the backwaters prevent trains from continuing south beyond Alappuzha, only a few major daily services and a handful of passenger trains depart from the railway station, 3km southwest of the jetty. For points further north along the coast including Mangalore, take an early train and change at Ernakulam, as the Alleppey–Cannanore Express #6307, which continues to Kozhikode and Kannur, arrives at those destinations far too late at night. Most trains south to Thiruvananthapuram leave at inconvenient hours except for the Ernakulam–Trivandrum Express #6341 (departs daily at 7.25am).

The following trains are recommended as the fastest and/or most convenient from Alappuzha.

Recommended trains from Alappuzha

Destination	Name	Number	Frequency	Departs	Total time
Kochi/Ernakulam	*Bokaro–Tata Express	#8690	daily	6am	1hr 3min
	*Alleppey–Chennai Express	#6042	daily	3pm	1hr
	*Trivandrum–Mumbai CST Express	#6332	Fri	7.35am	1hr 15min
Chennai	*Alleppey–Chennai Express	#6042	daily	3pm	15hr 30min
Thiruvan–anthapuram	Ernakulam–Trivandrum Express	#6341	daily	7.20am	3hr 20min

* these trains continue to Thrissur and Palakaad

to a Swiss woman, with a beautiful garden and four rooms with mosquito nets and plenty of family atmosphere and home cooking. The warm and hospitable owners love to share their knowledge of local history on the town and backwaters. Recommended. ⑤

Eating

One of the most popular places to eat in Alappuzha is *Komala Hotel*'s *Arun* **restaurant**, but there are plenty of other decent, and cheaper, places including the *Zion Food Shop* snack bar at the DTPC jetty. For a splurge, catch a rickshaw out to the *Alleppey Prince*, whose a/c *Vembanad* restaurant offers the town's classiest menu, and beer by the pool. The *KTDC Aaram Motel* around the corner is a lot cheaper and also serves beer.

Annapoorna, opposite the DTPC jetty. A very good cheap vegetarian "meals" restaurant; the "meals" at lunch time include a number of coconutty Keralan veg curries.

Arun, *Komala Hotel*, Zilla Court Ward. Tasty Chinese noodles and North Indian veg (including delicious *dhal makhini*, *malai kofta* and *subzis*), but avoid the Continental food. If it's busy, settle in for a wait.

Greens, Cullan Road, off Mullakal Road. Alappuzha's popular new veg restaurant is cheap and clean with a little garden out front. It's fresh South Indian snacks and inexpensive unlimited lunchtime "meals" all the way – the excellent

coconut *uttappam* and a fresh lime soda will set you back just Rs17.

Indian Coffee House, Mullakal Road. Part of the all-India chain of co-operatives with a predictable menu of decent filter coffee, omelettes, dosas and *idlis*, but with the addition of meat dishes.

Kream Korner, Mullakal Road. Non-veg restaurant-cum-ice-cream parlour. Mostly chicken and mutton, with a selection of snacks, milkshakes and ice creams.

Thoppi, *Karthika Hotel*. Very modest but clean and friendly place with an ambitious, inexpensive Indian and Chinese menu. They open early for standard "omelette-bread-butter-jam" breakfasts.

Kottayam and around

The busy commercial centre of **KOTTAYAM**, 76km southeast of Kochi and 37km northeast of Alappuzha, is strategically located between the backwaters and the stunning Lake Vembanad to the west and the spice, tea and rubber plantations, forests and mountains of the Western Ghats to the east. Most visitors come here on the way to somewhere else – foreigners take short backwater trips to Alappuzha or set off to the **Periyar Wildlife Sanctuary**, while Ayappa devotees pass through en route to the forest temple at Sabarimala (see box on p.373).

Kottayam's long history of **Syrian Christian** settlement is reflected by the presence of two thirteenth-century churches on a hill 5km northwest of the centre, which you can get to by rickshaw. Two eighth-century Nestorian stone crosses with Pahlavi and Syriac inscriptions, on either side of the elaborately decorated altar of the **Valliapalli** (big) church, are probably the earliest solid evidence of Christianity in India. The visitors' book in the church contains entries from as far back as the 1890s, including one by the Ethiopian emperor, Haile Selassie, and a British viceroy. The interior of the nearby **Cheriapalli** (small) church is covered with lively paintings, thought to have been executed by a Portuguese artist. If the doors are locked, ask for the key at the church office (9am–1pm & 2–5pm).

Arrival and information

Kottayam's KSRTC **bus stand**, 500m south of the centre on TB Road (not to be confused with the private bus stand for local buses on KK Road aka Shastri

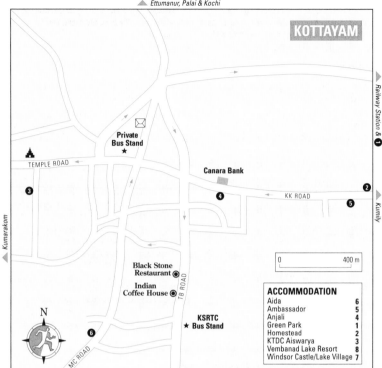

Ettumanur, Palai & Kochi

KOTTAYAM

Private
Bus Stand
★

TEMPLE ROAD

Canara Bank

KK ROAD

Black Stone
Restaurant ◉

Indian
Coffee House ◉

TB ROAD

KSRTC
★ Bus Stand

N

MC ROAD

Kumarakom

Railway Station &

Kumily

0   400 m

ACCOMMODATION

Aida	6
Ambassador	5
Anjali	4
Green Park	1
Homestead	2
KTDC Aiswarya	3
Vembanad Lake Resort	8
Windsor Castle/Lake Village	7

Boat Jetty, ❼, ❽, Thiruvananthapuram & Alappuzha

Road), is an important stop en route to and from major towns in South India. Four of the frequent buses to Kumily/Periyar (3–4hr) each day go on to Madurai in Tamil Nadu (7hr), and there are regular services to Thiruvananthapuram, Kollam and Ernakulam. The **railway station** (2km north of the centre) sees a constant flow of traffic between Thiruvananthapuram and other points north. **Ferries** from Alappuzha and elsewhere dock at the weed-clogged jetty, 3km south of town. For details of backwater trips from Kottayam, see p.363. For travelling around Kottayam itself there are plenty of **auto-rickshaws** around all the stations.

Surprisingly, there is no official source of tourist information in Kottayam. The Canara Bank (Mon–Fri 10am–2pm, Sat 10am–12pm), on KK Road opposite the Anjali Hotel, is the only place to **change money** and travellers' cheques, and cash advances are issued on Visa and Mastercard.

Accommodation and eating

Kottayam has a good choice of mid-range **hotels** but if you're in search of utter luxury, head out to one of the five-star resorts that nestle on the banks of the nearby Vembanad lake (see below) in Kumarakom. You will be hard pushed to find a decent budget hotel here, apart from the *Ambassador*, and the pleasant little *Moolappura Guest House* is the only budget place in Kumarakom.

There are basic "meals" **restaurants** in the centre of Kottayam, such as the *Black Stone*, close to the bus station on TB Road, and a fairly dingy *Indian Coffee*

House on TB Road, but the best is the vegetarian *Thali* restaurant at *Homestead Hotel*. For an evening out, the lovely lakeside *Vembanad Lake Resort*, where you eat on a *kettu vallam* rice boat, definitely wins; for elegant dining and a Keralan menu try the *Lake Village*.

Aida, Aida Junction, MC Road ℡ 0481/568391. A large friendly hotel with a good range of rooms including some a/c and reasonably priced singles; facilities include two restaurants, a bar, Star TV, money changing, and tours arranged on request. ⑤

Ambassador, KK Road ℡ 0481/563293. A well-run economy hotel with clean rooms; the ones with a/c are very good value. ②–③

Anjali, KK Road, 2km from railway station, close to the square, downtown ℡ 0481/563669. Dark but comfortable Casino Group business hotel in the centre of town, with international and Chinese restaurants and bar. All a/c. ⑦–⑧

Green Park, Kurian Uthup Road, Nagampadam, near station and private bus stand ℡ 0481/563331. Modern and efficient business hotel, with decent non-a/c and a/c rooms, a bar and two restaurants. Good value. ⑤–⑥

Homestead Hotel, opposite *Manorama*, KK Road, 1km from the station ℡ 0481/560467. Well-appointed central hotel with a range of options from clean budget to comfortable a/c rooms. Their

vegetarian restaurant does excellent "meals". ④–⑥

Vembanad Lake Resort, Kodimatha, 5min walk from ferry and 2km from town and bus station ℡ 0481/564866, ℻ 561633. Western-style motel, with large, simply furnished modern chalets (five a/c) in pleasant gardens beside an inlet of Lake Vembanad. The restaurant has good Indian, Western and Chinese dishes, including seafood. Eat outside in a lakeside garden or on a moored *kettu vallam* long boat – gorgeous at night. ⑥

Windsor Castle/ Lake Village, Kodimatha ℡ 0481/303622, ℻ 303624. Ignore the white tower block of characterless luxury rooms in the "castle" part of the hotel, and head behind it to the second part of the hotel, the "Lake Village". This is set alongside a lagoon with comfortable a/c Keralan-style chalets and a very pleasant open-air restaurant that specializes in Keralan cuisine. There are two swimming pools, a theatre for dance performances, an Ayurvedic centre and dugout boat rides through large gardens. ⑧–⑨

Around Kottayam

Some of Kerala's most attractive scenery lies within easy access of Kottayam. Probably the ideal destination for a day-trip – it also has some wonderful accommodation – is the **Kumarakom** bird sanctuary, in the backwaters to the west. **Aranmula**, to the south, is one of the last villages still making *kannady* metal mirrors, and has a Krishna temple that organizes a ritual "non-competitive" boat race. The Mahadeva temple at **Ettumanur**, a short way north of Kottayam, is known to devotees as the home of a dangerous and wrathful Shiva and to art lovers as a sublime example of temple architecture, adorned with wood-carvings and murals. A short way northeast of Ettumanur is the little town of Palai, where the beautiful Church of St Thomas boasts exquisite eighteenth-century frescoes.

Kumarakom

KUMARAKOM, 16km west of Kottayam, is technically an island on Vembanad Lake. Although right in the thick of a tangle of lush tropical waterways, it can be reached quite easily by bus from Kottayam (every 10min). The peak time to visit the **Bird Sanctuary** (daily dawn–dusk; free), which is no longer negotiable by boat since the channels have been choked by African moss, is between November and March when it serves as a winter home for many migratory birds, some from as far away as Siberia. Species include the darter or snake bird, little cormorant, night heron, golden-backed woodpecker, crow pheasant, white-breasted water hen and tree pie. Enthusiasts should visit the sanctuary at dawn, which is the quietest and best time for viewing, with early rays of sunlight falling through the lush tropical canopy. Although

Arundhati Roy's remarkable novel, The God of Small Things, published in 1997, is set in a riverside village on the outskirts of Kottayam. It earned her the Booker Prize as well as the ire of certain sections of the local populace who reacted strongly to her description of small-town Kerala. The intricate, haunting and intensely personal tale gives a glimpse of social tensions in Keralan life, and has an astutely observed interplay of character and environment. Roy was brought up in the same village as Ayemenem, the protagonist, and some of her family are still living there. Although the house in Ayemenem in the book is fictional, one of the most obvious landmarks in the book is the so-called "History house", sitting squat on the shore of Vembanad lake in Kumarakom. This was where the central characters, the twins, watch the local police beat up their friend Velutha, an untouchable servant. The "History house", built by British colonial settlers, was where Arundhati Roy played as a child and it now forms the central body of the *Taj Garden Retreat Hotel* (see below).

An architect by training, Roy comes from a proactive family; in the 1990s her mother, Mary Roy, fought and won a landmark legal battle to secure the right for Christian women in Kerala to divorce their husbands. Arundhati Roy is a dedicated supporter of low-caste Keralan poets and writers who write in the state vernacular, Malayalam. In 1998, she became an important spokesperson for the anti-nuclear campaign that followed the "blast" – India's nuclear tests – and for which she wrote a passionate pamphlet on the issue, "For the Greater Common Good". She has also taken up the cause of the 33 million or so people who have been displaced by India's hydroelectric dam projects in the Narmada Valley in Central India.

the island is quite small, a guide is useful; you can arrange one through the KTDC *Water Scapes* or another of the luxury hotels.

Next to the sanctuary, set in waterside gardens, a refurbished colonial bungalow that once belonged to a family of Christian missionaries and rubber planters forms the nucleus of a luxury **hotel**, *The Taj Garden Retreat* (℡0481/524377; ⑥). There are a couple of dozen "cottages" and a *kettu vallam* longboat grouped around a landscaped garden, and direct water access to the lake. However, it's not nearly as impressive as the very friendly and understated *Coconut Lagoon Hotel* (℡0481/524491, ℗524495; ⑥), 1km northwest and reached by launch (you can telephone for the boat from a kiosk at the canal side). Superbly crafted from fragments of ruined Keralan palaces, with beautiful woodcarvings and brass work, the building alone merits a visit. It was designed in traditional Keralan style, and its air of low-key elegance is set off perfectly by the location on the edge of Vembanad Lake. Even if you can't afford to stay here, you could try the wonderful Keralan specialities at the **restaurant**. A new rival, the *Kumarakom Lake Resort*, 3km from the village and just before the *Taj* (℡0481/524900, ℗524987; ⑨). This ostentatious place takes the concept of a "heritage" resort to the extreme with two beautiful 300-year-old palaces recovered and reconstructed on site, and ultra-luxurious cottages made up from bits of old Keralan houses, each with an outdoor bathroom hidden in a lush tropical garden behind. The Ayurveda centre here has two doctors, four massage rooms; the swimming pool boasts a Jacuzzi, its water lapping the edge of the lake. Nearby, the brand new KTDC *Water Scapes* is right on the lake (℡0481/525861, ℗525862; ⑥), and consists of comfortable a/c cottages built on stilts. Unfortunately, very few of the cottages have a decent view over the lake and there are too many ugly metal walkways and buildings on the lakefront; it is, however, slightly cheaper than its competitors and convenient for the bird sanctuary. Alternatively, you can drift across the lake on one of their luxury *kettu vallams* moored here (book through *Water Scapes*; ③).

If you're on a budget, take advantage of the excellent *Moolappura Guest House*, just 200m before the bus stand at the *Taj* (☎0481/525980; ⑤), which has just two simple rooms with attached bathrooms in the family house. The family is very warm and welcoming; they offer rides on their dugout boats, personal tours in the bird sanctuary, and can even boast a professional chef among their number, who whips up delicious Keralan and continental dishes.

Besides the hotels, the only other place to eat is KTDC's uninspiring café at the *Tourist Complex* near where the bus from Kottayam pulls in, close to the *Taj* hotel gates.

Aranmula

The village of **ARANMULA** is another appealing day-trip – so long as you start early – from Kottayam, 30km south of the town and 10km beyond Chengannur. The temple dedicated to Parthasarthy, which was the divine name under which Krishna acted as Arjuna's charioteer during the bloody Kurekshetra war recorded in the *Mahabharata*, and the guise in which he expounded the *Bhagavad Gita*. About 1800 years old, the temple is a major site on the Vishnivite pilgrimage trail in Kerala, and as Vishnu is represented here in the form of Annadanaprabhu (One Who Gives Food), it is said the no pilgrim will go hungry worshipping at the temple. Each year, towards the end of the Onam festival (Aug/Sept), a **Snakeboat Regatta** is celebrated as part of the temple rituals, and crowds line the banks of the Pampa River to cheer on the thrusting longboats (similar to those seen at Alappuzha; see p.359).

Aranmula is also known for manufacturing extraordinary *kannady* **metal mirrors** (Aranmula kannadi), produced using the "lost wax" technique with an alloy of copper, silver, brass, lead and bronze (see p.680). Once a perquisite of royal households, these ornamental mirrors are now exceedingly rare; only two master craftsmen, Subramanian Achary and Arjun Achary and their families, still make them. The most modest models cost in the region of Rs500, while custom-made mirrors can cost as much as Rs50,000.

The **Vijana Kala Vedi Cultural Centre** in Aranmula, offers ways of "experiencing traditional India through the study of art and village life". Introductory courses are offered in Kathakali, Mohiniattam and Bharatanatyam dance, wood-carving, mural painting, cooking, Kalarippayat, Ayurvedic medicine and several Indian languages. Courses cost upwards of US$200 per week and are booked by writing to: The Director, Vijana Kala Vedi Cultural Centre, Tarayil Mukku Junction, Aranmula, Kerala 689533.

Ettumanur

The magnificent Mahadeva temple at **ETTUMANUR**, 12km north of Kottayam on the road to Ernakulam, features a circular shrine, fine wood-carving and one of the earliest (sixteenth-century) and most celebrated of Keralan **murals**. The deity is Shiva in one of his most terrible aspects, described as *vaddikasula vada*, "one who takes his dues with interest" and is "difficult to please". His predominant mood is *raudra* (fury). Although the shrine is open to Hindus only, foreigners are allowed to see the painting, which may be photographed only after obtaining a camera ticket from the hatch to the left of the main, *gopura* entranceway. The four-metre mural depicts Nataraja – Shiva – executing a cosmic *tandava* dance, trampling evil underfoot in the form of a demon. Swathed in cobras, he stands on one leg in a wheel of gold, with his matted

The history of Kerala's Christians – who today represent 21 percent of the population – is said to date back to the first century AD, some three centuries before Christianity received official recognition in Europe. These days there are five main branches, among a bewildering assortment of churches. They are Nestorians (confined mainly to Thrissur and Ernakulam), Roman Catholics (found throughout Kerala), Syrian Orthodox Church (previously known as the Jacobite Syrians), Marthoma Syrians (a splinter group of the Syrian Orthodox) and the Anglican Church of South India.

A legend, widely believed in Kerala but the object of academic scepticism, states that St Thomas the Apostle – "Doubting Thomas" – landed on the Malabar Coast in 52AD, where he converted several brahmins and others, and founded seven churches. Muziris, his first port of call, has been identified as Kodungallur (see p.408); the traditional accounts of Jews who later arrived there in 68AD state that they encountered a community of Christians known as Nazranis, or "followers of the Nazarene" (Jesus). The Nazranis found little opposition from the largely Hindu population, and were able to amalgamate some age-old indigenous Hindu religious practices into their newfound religion.

In the fourth century, their number was augmented by an influx of Syrian Christians belonging to seven tribes from Baghdad, Nineveh and Jerusalem, who were under the leadership of the merchant Knayi Thoma (Thomas of Cana). Assisted by the development of commerce, the Syrian Christians were to play a vital role in the spread of Christianity in Kerala. As they went around building churches, the Syrians introduced architectural conventions from the Middle East, and so incorporated the nave and chancel with a gabled facade, which resulted in a distinctive style of Keralan Christian church. They also absorbed some architectural styles from the Nazranis by retaining the *dhwajastamba* (flag mast), the *kottupura* (gate house) and the *kurisuthara* (altar with a mounted cross).

A significant faction of the Syrian Christian community, the Nestorians (after Nestorius, the patriarch of Constantinople) were the dominant Christian group in Kerala after the sixth century and at one stage had centres in various parts of India. However, the assertive spread of Portuguese Catholicism centuries later reduced the Nestorians to a small community, which survives today in Thrissur (see p.402).

Christians gradually came to the forefront as traders, and eventually gained special privileges from the local rulers. The early communities followed a liturgy in the Syriac language (a dialect of Aramaic). Latin was introduced by missionaries who visited Kollam in the Middle Ages, and once the Portuguese turned up, in 1498, a large community of Latin Christians developed, particularly on the coast, and came under the jurisdiction of the pope. In the middle of the seventeenth century, with the ascendancy of the Dutch, part of the Church broke away from Rome, and local bishops were appointed through the offices of the Jacobite patriarch in Antioch.

During the nineteenth century, the Anglican Church amalgamated with certain "free" Churches, to form the Church of South India. At the same time, elements in the Syrian Church advocated the replacement of Syriac with the local language of Malayalam. The resultant schism led to the creation of the new Marthoma Syrian Church.

Today, numerous roadside shrines known as *kurisupalli*, or "chapels of the cross", and large and popular churches bear testimony to the continuing strength of the Christian communities throughout the state. Christmas is an important festival in Kerala; during the weeks leading up to December 25, innumerable star-shaped lamps are put up outside shops and houses, illuminating the night and identifying followers of the faith.

locks fanning out amid a mass of flowers and snakes. Outside the wheel, a crowd of celestials are in attitudes of devotion. Musical accompaniment is courtesy of Krishna on flute, three-headed Brahma on cymbals, and playing the copper *mizhavu*, the holiest and most ancient type of Keralan drum, is Shiva's special rhythm expert Nandikesvara.

Ettumanur's ten-day **annual festival** (Feb/March) reflects the wealth of the temple, with elaborate celebrations including music. On the most important days, the eighth and tenth priests bring out figures of elephants, fashioned from 460kg of gold, presented in the eighteenth century by Marthanda Varma, Raja of Travancore.

Palai

The small town of **Palai**, 30km northeast of Kottayam, is home to the Church of St Thomas, a stunning Portuguese-style building that features a well-preserved wall of beautiful **frescoes**. Well off the tourist trail, Palai is better visited as a day-trip as it has no accommodation and only a few South Indian "meals" restaurants. Buses from Kottayam and Kochi pull in and leave Palai frequently from the KSRTC bus stand next to the bell tower in the centre of town. From here the church is a two-kilometre walk or auto-rickshaw ride east along the main road and over a small bridge; turn right onto a lane which winds up to St Thomas's.

A chapel – modelled along the lines of a Hindu temple – was built to service the spiritual needs of the five Christian families resident in the Parish of St Thomas in 1003. In the sixteenth century the chapel was destroyed and a new building was erected, but burned down a century later during protracted conflict with local Muslim settlers. The present building, built in the eighteenth century, has a soaring and startlingly white ornamental facade, and a squat spire and nave.

Inside the church is a bizarre spiralling pulpit, carved from a single piece of teak that was mysteriously found already cut and floating down a river nearby; the ceilings are richly painted with gold leaf. An elaborate altar dates from 1853, filled with plastic flowers and three rather kitsch models of St Thomas, the Virgin Mary and Jesus, complete with flashing lights. However, to see the *piece de resistance*, hidden behind the altar, you will have to ask the resident caretaker for a candle. Extraordinarily well preserved in the darkness is a wall of exquisite eighteenth-century frescoes painted with plant pigments, depicting the life of St Thomas and Jesus as the Lamb of God.

The larger and modern church alongside was built in 1981; the local congregation has swelled to 1000 members in a parish of 7000 Marthoma Christians. A finger-bone relic of St Thomas is kept here and brought out for public viewing once a year on the Feast of the Magi (mid October).

Periyar Wildlife Sanctuary

One of the largest and most visited wildlife reserves in India, the **Periyar Wildlife Sanctuary** occupies 777 square kilometres of the Cardamom Hills region of the Western Ghats. Located close to the Kerala–Tamil Nadu border, the park makes a convenient place to break the long journey across the Ghats between Madurai and the coast. It's also a good base for day-trips into the Cardamom Hills, with a couple of tea factories, spice plantations, view points and forest waterfalls, and even the trailhead for the Sabarimala pilgrimage (see box opposite), within striking distance. The **best time to visit** is from December until April, when the dry weather draws animals from the forest to drink at the lakeside.

The majority of the many visitors come to the park in the hope of seeing **tigers** and **leopards** – and are disappointed, as the few that remain very wisely keep their distance, and there's only a slight chance of a glimpse even at the height of the dry season (April/May). However, there are plenty of other animals and Periyar is a good place to see **elephants**; if you're lucky, you may come across a herd swimming across a channel. Other animals include wild pig, *sambar*, Malabar flying squirrel, gaur, stripe-necked mongoose, numerous species of birds and wild boar, which are plentiful and easily visible on the shores of the lake.

The pothole-filled road that winds through the undulating hills **to Periyar** from Ernakulam and Kottayam makes for a very long slow drive, but it gives wonderful views across the Ghats. The route

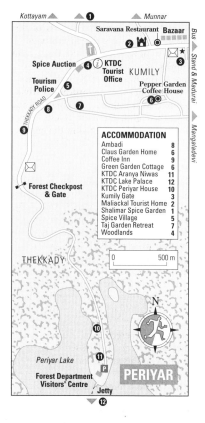

is dotted with grand churches among the trees, and numerous jazzy roadside shrines to St Francis, St George or the Virgin Mary – a charming Keralan blend of ancient and modern. Once you've climbed through the rubber-tree forests into Idukki District, the mountains get truly spectacular, and the wide-floored valleys are carpeted with lush tea and cardamom plantations.

Practicalities

Travellers heading for the **Periyar Wildlife Sanctuary** have first to make their way to the tea and spice market village of **Kumily**, 4km short of the **Thekkady** park entrance, on the northwest of the reserve. Kumily is served by state and private **buses** from Kottayam (every 30min; 4hr), Ernakulam (10 daily; 6hr), and Madurai in Tamil Nadu (frequent service; 5hr 30min); most of these terminate at the scruffy bus stand east of Kumily bazaar.

From the bus stand, **minibuses** (Rs4) shuttle visitors to the park gate, although some continue through to the KTDC *Aranya Nivas*, at Thekaddy inside the sanctuary. **Auto-rickshaws** will also run you from the bus stand to the *Aranya Nivas* for Rs25 plus Rs5 park entry, but if you are arriving late remember the gates close at 6pm, after which you'll have to show proof of your accommodation booking before they will let you in. If you are staying at the

During December and January, Kerala is jam-packed with crowds of men in black or blue *dhotis*; you will see them milling about train stations, driving in overcrowded and gaily decorated Jeeps and cooking a quick dhal-rice for twenty on the side of the road by their tour bus. They are all pilgrims on their way to the Shri Ayappa forest temple (also known as HarIharaputra or Shasta) at Sabarimala, in the Western Ghat mountains, around 200km from both Thiruvananthapuram and Kochi. The Ayappa devotees can seem disconcertingly ebullient, chanting "*Swamiyee Sharanam Ayappan*" (give us protection, god Ayappa) in a call and response style reminiscent of Western sports fans.

Although he is primarily a Keralan deity, Ayappa's appeal has spread phenomenally in the last thirty years across South India, to the extent that this is said to be the second largest pilgrimage in the world, with as many as a million devotees each year. A curious story relates to the birth of Ayappa. One day, when the two male gods, Shiva and Vishnu, were together in a pine forest, Shiva asked to see Vishnu's famed female form Mohini, the divine enchantress. Vishnu refused, having a fair idea of what this could lead to. However, Shiva was undeterred, and used all his powers of persuasion to induce Vishnu to transform. As a result of the inevitable passionate embrace, Vishnu became pregnant, and the baby Ayappa emerged from his thigh.

Pilgrims, however, are required to remain celibate. They must also abstain from intoxicants and keep to a strict vegetarian diet for a period of 41 days prior to setting out on the four-day walk through the forest from the village of Erumeli (61km, as the crow flies, northwest), to the shrine at Sabarimala. Rather less devoted devotees take the bus to the village of Pampa, and join the five-kilometre queue. When they arrive at the modern temple complex – a surreal spread of concrete sheds and walkways in the middle of the jungle – pilgrims who have performed the necessary penances may ascend the famous eighteen gold steps to the inner shrine. There they worship the deity, throwing donations down a chute that opens onto a subterranean conveyor belt, where the money is counted and bagged for the bank. In recent years, the mass appeal of the Ayappa cult has brought in big bucks for the temple, which now numbers among India's richest, despite being open for only a few months each year. Funds also pour in from the shrine's innumerable spin-off businesses, such as the sale of coconut oil and milk (left by every pilgrim) to a soap manufacturer.

The pilgrimage reaches a climax during the festival of Makara Sankranti when crowds of over 1.5 million congregate at Sabarimala. On January 14, 1999, 51 devotees were buried alive when part of a hill crumbled under the crush of a stampede. The devotees had gathered at dusk to catch a glimpse of the final sunset of *Makara Jyoti* (celestial light) on the distant hill of Ponnambalamedu.

Although males of any age and even of any religion can take part in the pilgrimage, females between the ages of 9 and 50 are barred. This rule, still vigorously enforced by the draconian temple oligarchy, was contested in 1995 by a bizarre court case. Following complaints to local government that facilities and hygiene at Sabarimala were sub-standard, the Local Collector, a 42-year-old woman, insisted she be allowed to inspect the site. The temple authorities duly refused, citing the centuries-old ban on women of menstrual age, but the High Court, which earlier upheld the gender bar, was obliged to overrule the priests' decision. The Collector's triumphant arrival at Sabarimala soon after made headline news, but she was still not allowed to enter the shrine proper.

For advice on how to visit Sabarimala, via a back route beginning at Kumily near the Periyar Sanctuary, see p.378.

KTDC *Lake Palace*, the last boat is officially at 4pm but they will arrange a later boat during daylight hours.

KTDC runs hectic and uncomfortable **weekend tours** to Periyar from Kochi, calling at Kadamattom and Idukki Dam en route (Sat 7.30am–Sun 8pm), and an even more rushed tour from Thiruvananthapuram. Unless you enjoy being cooped up in video buses, give them a miss. Numerous tour operators in Thiruvananthapuram, Kovalam and Kochi also offer tailor-made packages.

Kumily

As beds inside the sanctuary (see box opposite) are in such short supply, most visitors end up staying in or near **KUMILY**, 2km north of the park gates, a growing town where tourism appears to be gradually replacing the spice trade as the main source of income. However, the spice industry remains alive and well and several agencies offer tours to plantations as a lucrative sideline. Almost every shop on Thakkady Road sells freshly collected spices; just to walk along the street and breathe in the air filled with the scent of cloves, nutmeg, cinnamon and cardamom is a heady experience. In the middle of the melee of the bazaar stands the main **cardamom auction** area, where you can watch local tribal women sifting and sorting the fragrant green pods in heart-shaped baskets.

Tea factory, **spice plantation** and **viewpoint tours** are the big tourist attraction around Kumily; aside from every hotel offering a tour of a farm and "nice viewing place", you will also be besieged by tourist agencies all offering the same package at very competitive rates. Unfortunately, some places such as Abraham's Plantation have become heavily commercialized and expensive as a result of tourism; the best way to organize a tour is to ask at your hotel – most of the staff will have an uncle or brother who has a good plantation. The going rate for a three-hour tour, including a guide and Jeep hire and a decent halt at a viewpoint looking over the Tamil Nadu plains is Rs300–350.

Idduki district's DTPC has a low-key **tourist office** (Mon–Sat 10am–5pm; ⊤0486/322620) on the first floor of the Panchayat Building, Thekkady Junction. Besides offering information on the district itself, they organize conducted tours, including a Spice Valley tour (6.30am–9.30pm; Rs200) that takes in the tea fields at Munnar and several spice plantations. The other source of information is the **tourism police**, with an office at the bus stand and a main office at Ambady Junction. Although their prime purpose is to maintain law and order, they also offer information. However, as a word of caution, it has recently been reported that they only provide details about the hotels, tea factories, homestays and plantations that pay them commission.

Both the State Bank of Travancore (⊤0486/322041), near the bus stand, and the Central Bank of India, KK Road (⊤0486/322053), **change money**. For **internet** facilities try Rissas Communications/Media at Thekkady Junction (Rs45/hr). Although hilly, this is good cycling territory; **bicycle rental** is available from stalls in the market for around Rs30 per day. DC Books in Thekkady has a good selection of titles in English, covering fiction, wildlife, religion, culture and art.

Accommodation

Kumily has **accommodation** to suit all pockets and new hotels and "resorts" emerge each season. Thankfully, most of the accommodation lies well outside the noisy bazaar area, dotted along the Thekkady Road leading to the park. Homestays such as *Green Garden* are a popular option – ask around the bazaar for a good homestay and you'll soon be pointed in the right direction; most

The star attraction of Periyar has to be the prospect of staying in the Forest Department watchtowers, reached by boat from Thekkady and the best way to get a hands-on experience of the jungle. For the *Lake Palace*, *Periyar House* and the *Aranya Nivas* you should book in advance at the KTDC offices in Thiruvananthapuram or Ernakulam – essential if you plan to come on a weekend, a public holiday, or during peak season (Dec–March), when rooms are often in short supply.

Forest Department Rest House, Edappalayam. Very basic accommodation in the woods on the far side of the lake (you have to catch the 4pm boat and then hike, so a guide is recommended). Bring your own food and bedding. Reserve in advance at the Forest Department's visitor centre in Thekkady; you'll be lucky to get in on a weekend or in December. An unforgettable experience. ●

Forest Department Watchtowers, Edappalayam and Manakkavala. Even more primitive than the *Rest House*, but the best way of sighting game: the towers overlook waterholes in the buffer zone. Book through the visitor centre, and take along food, candles, matches, a torch, a sleeping bag and warm clothes. Again, you have to catch the 4pm boat and trek from the jetty, so a guide is useful. Don't consider this if it's been raining, when leeches plague the trail. ●

KTDC Aranya Nivas, just above the boat jetty, Thekkady ☎0486/322023, ℻322282. Plusher than *Periyar House*, a colonial manor with some huge rooms, a pleasant garden, a great swimming pool, an excellent multicuisine restaurant, and a cosy bar. Upper-deck tickets for two boat trips are included in the tariff. ●

KTDC Lake Palace, across the lake (booked through *Aranya Nivas*). The sanctuary's most luxurious hotel with six suites in a converted maharajah's game lodge surrounded by forest, with wonderful views. Charming old-fashioned rooms, great dining and a lovely lawn. This has to be one of the few places in India where you stand a chance of spotting tiger and wild elephant while sipping tea on your own veranda. Full board only. ●

KTDC Periyar House, midway between the park gates and the boat jetty, Thekkady ☎0486/322026, ℻322526. Comfortable hotel close to the lake, with a restaurant, bar and balcony overlooking the monkey-filled woods leading down to the waterside. Not as nice a location as its neighbour *Aranya Nivas*, but a lot cheaper. Ask for a lake-facing room. ●–●

charge about Rs300 and offer excellent plantation tours and home-cooked food.

Ambadi, next to turn-off for Mangaladevi temple, Thekkady Road ☎0486/322193. Pleasant hotel which has seen better times. Decent rooms sporting coir mats and wood carvings, and the non-a/c "cottages" are good value. The restaurant serves good chicken. ●–●

Claus Garden Home, 5min walk south of the main bus stand (no phone) behind the *Taj*. Difficult to find, but worth the effort. Simple rooms, kitchen and communal bathrooms in a cosy house with sociable verandas and mandala murals, and surrounded by pepper plantations. Self-catering only. ●

Coffee Inn, Thekkady Road (no phone). Surly staff but good budget accommodation: a handful of simple rooms (one en suite) around a covered terrace and garden. Their "Wild Huts" annexe has six rooms (and two raffia tree houses) with shared shower and toilet, and a spacious enclosed garden with a pond. ●–●

Green Garden Cottage, next door to Claus Garden Home ☎0486/322935. One of the best organized of the homestay options with four large, spotless cottages in the family compound, each with attached bathrooms. Pleasant, quiet and great value. ●

Kumily Gate, behind the bus stand ☎0486/322279. Greenish modern block with large, clean rooms and a restaurant and popular

KERALA | Periyar Wildlife Sanctuary

noisy bar on site. Expensive for what it is, but good for late arrivals and it appears to be quite acceptable to haggle here. **②**

Maliackal Tourist Home, KK Road ℡0486/322589. Good clean rooms, handy for the bus stand. The most expensive rooms have cable TV and balconies (but no views). **③–④**

Shalimar Spice Garden, Murikaddy ℡& ℡0486/322132. Approached by a suspension bridge, in a secluded spot on the edge of a cardamom and pepper estate, 5km from Kumily (Rs50 by Jeep). Beautiful and tranquil place run by an Italian, with lovely cottages built using traditional Keralan teak structures; there's a pool and good restaurant **⑤**

Spice Village, Thekkady Road ℡0486/322315, ℡322317. Thatched huts and traditional Keralan wood cottages spread through a spice garden with a fine restaurant and a pool. You can join master classes in Keralan cookery, and there are lots of activities on offer. Popular with tour groups, so book ahead. **⑨**

Taj Garden Retreat, Ambalambika Road ℡0486/322273. Luxurious, pseudo-rustic cottages and a main building built to emulate a jungle lodge with great views. There's an elegant restaurant and a pool. **⑨**

Woodlands, Thakkady Road ℡0486/322077. One of the cheapest places to stay in Kumily, and very rudimentary, although clean enough for a short stay, and with friendly management. Campfires can be arranged, a campsite is available, and there's a kitchen for self-catering. **②**

Eating

Nearly every hotel establishment has its own café-restaurant, ranging from the *Taj Garden Retreat's* smart à la carte, to the more traveller-oriented *Coffee Inn*.

Coffee Inn café, Thakkady Road. Well-established place serving delicious home-made backpacker nosh. With a pleasant wooden terrace and garden, it's a popular place for a lingering breakfast after the early morning boat ride in the sanctuary.

Hotel Saravana, Kumily Bazaar. One of several eternally busy and cheap no-frills "meals" joints along the main bazaar. Their thalis, served on plantain leaves, are tasty, cheap and always freshly cooked, and they serve up deliciously crisp dosas.

Pepper Garden Coffee House, in the plantation en route to *Claus Garden Home*. Wonderful coffees, teas (both grown in the garden), lassis and excellent breakfasts, including steamed *puttu* with mung beans and bananas; thalis, Chinese, South Indian and pasta for lunch and dinner. In the evening there is a bonfire, live tabla and flute, and it's open until midnight. Inexpensive.

Spice Village, Thekkady Road. A plush restaurant that caters primarily for the tour groups and rich Indian visitors who stay here; the accent is on multicuisine but the chef's speciality is Keralan cuisine. During peak season the dinner buffet will cost about Rs350 with a beer.

The Sanctuary

THE SANCTUARY ($2/Rs50 [Rs10]; ticket valid for one day only; if you are staying inside the park you must go to the Forest Centre by the jetty each day to buy a new pass) lies at cool altitudes of 900m to 1800m with temperatures between 15°C and 30°C. The sanctuary centres on a vast artificial **lake**, created by the British in 1895 to supply water to the drier parts of neighbouring Tamil Nadu, around Madurai. The royal family of Travancore, anxious to preserve their favourite hunting grounds from the encroachment of tea plantations, declared it a forest reserve, and built the Edapalayam Lake Palace to accommodate their guests in 1899. It expanded as a wildlife reserve in 1933, and once again when it became part of **Project Tiger** in 1979 (see Contexts, p.686).

Seventy percent of the protected area, which is divided into core, buffer and tourist zones, is covered with evergreen and semi-evergreen forest. The **tourist zone** – logically enough, the part accessible to casual visitors – surrounds the lake, and consists mostly of semi-evergreen and deciduous woodland interspersed with grassland, both on hilltops and in the valleys. Although excursions on the lake are the standard way to experience the park, you can get much more out of a visit by walking with a local guide in a small group, or staying in basic accommodation in the forest and well away from the noisy crowds. **Treks** (3hr; Rs350 per group, maximum 5 people), are arranged either through the visitor centre (start 7am) or you can hire private guides, who operate on a more flexible time basis. They'll approach you in Kumily or near the park gates at Thekkady. Your guide point out anything of interest, and reassure you that the fresh elephant dung on the path is nothing to worry about. The Forest Department also offers overnight trips and more elaborate week-long programmes in the forest. Avoid the period immediately after the monsoons, when **leeches** make hiking virtually impossible.

Tickets for the **boat trips** (daily 7am, 9.30am, 11.30am, 2pm & 4pm; 2hr; Rs40 for lower deck, Rs80 for upper deck) on the lake are sold through the Forest Department at their hatch just above the main **visitor centre** in Thekkady, above the jetty. If you're on a tight budget, ask at the visitor centre if there are any spaces on the Forestry Commission patrol boat (Rs15), but you'll have to go on the lower deck and they may not give you much time to check out any animals you spot. Although it is unusual to see many animals from the boats – engine noise and the presence of a hundred other people make sure of that – you might spot a family group of elephants, wild boar and sambar deer by the water's edge. The upper deck is best for game viewing, although the seats are invariably block-booked by the upscale hotels. Turn up half an hour early, however, and you may be allocated any no-show places. To maximize your chances of seeing anything, take the 7am boat (wear something warm). At this hour, the mist rises over the lake and hills as you chug past dead trees – now bird perches – never cleared when the valley was flooded to make the dam. Note that after heavy rain, chances of good sightings are very slim as the animals only come to the lake when water sources inside the forest have dried up.

Elephant rides into the park cost Rs30 per head (30min); book at the Forest Department office at the jetty.

The birds of Periyar

Although animals are not often visible due to the dense forest cover, birds are plentiful in Periyar with over 260 species known to be in the sanctuary. The most notable amongst these are the darters, which are also known as snakebirds due to the snake-like appearance of their necks while swimming. They belong to the cormorant family, and can be seen perching on top of dead tree trunks protruding from the water, sometimes allowing boats to get quite close. Other common aquatic birds include the cormorant, grey heron, squat and tailless little grebe – also known as dabchick. Of the several types of kingfisher, the lesser pied kingfisher has distinctive white flashes around its neck, and the blue-eared and storkbilled kingfishers are both a more common blue. The osprey or fish hawk is often seen, cruising above the water. Occasionally, you may be fortunate enough to see a grey-headed fishing eagle, recognizable by its white body, which contrasts with its deep brown back and wings. Other common birds of prey in Periyar include the brahminy kite, which is a handsome gold bird with a regal, white neck and crest. Amongst many of Periyar's other birds, are the Nilgiri wood pigeon, bluewinged parakeet, white-bellied tree pie, laughing thrushes and flycatchers, the white-necked stork and the white cattle egret. You will be very lucky, however, if you catch site of the great Indian hornbill, a majestic multicoloured bird with a large yellow beak.

The Cardamom Hills

Nestled amid soaring, mist-covered mountains and dense jungle, Periyar and Kumily are convenient springboards from which to explore Kerala's beautiful **Cardamom Hills**. Guides will approach you at Thekkady with offers of trips by Jeep-taxi; if you can get a group together, these work out to be pretty good value. Among the more popular destinations is the **Mangaladevi temple**, 14km east of Kumily. The rough road to this tumbledown ancient ruin deep in the forest is sometimes closed due to flood damage but, when open, the round trip takes about five hours. With a guide you can also reach remote waterfalls and mountain viewpoints, offering panoramic vistas of the Tamil Nadu plains. Rates vary according to the season, but expect to pay around Rs500 for the Jeep-taxi, and an additional Rs150 for the guide. An easy day-trip by bus (or as part of a local plantation tour) from Kumily is to the grand viewpoint of **Chellarcovil**, right on the edge of the mountains, with the endless green plains of Tamil Nadu falling away below. To get here, take a bus or Jeep to the village of Anakkara, 15km north of Kumily, and jump on a rickshaw for the last 4km through the paddy fields to Chellarkovil; hang onto your driver if you don't want to walk back to the bus

Of places that can be visited under your own steam, the fascinating **High Range Tea Factory** (⊤04868/77038 or 77043) at Puttady (pronounced "Poo-*tee*-dee"), 19km north of Kumily, is a rewarding diversion on the road to Munnar. Regular buses leave from Kumily bus stand; get off at the Puttady crossroads, and pick up a rickshaw from there to the factory. Driven by whirring canvas belts, old-fashioned English-made machines chop, sift and ferment the leaves, which are then dried in wood-fired furnaces and packed into sacks for delivery to the tea auction rooms in Kochi. The affable owner, Mr P.M. James, or one of his clerks, will show you around; you don't have to arrange a visit, but it's a good idea to phone ahead to check they are open.

The other possible day-trip from Kumily, though one that should not be undertaken lightly (or, because of Hindu lore, by pre-menopausal women), is to the Sri Ayappan forest shrine at **Sabarimala** (see box on p.373). This remote and sacred site can be reached in a long day-trip, but you should leave with a pack of provisions, as much water as you can carry and plenty of warm clothes in case you get stranded. Jeep-taxis wait outside Kumily bus stand to transport pilgrims to the less frequented of Sabarimala's two main access points – a windswept mountaintop 13km above the temple (2hr; Rs50 per person if the Jeep is carrying ten passengers). Peeling off the main Kumily–Kottayam road at **Vandiperiyar**, the route takes you through tea estates to the start of an appallingly rutted forest track. After a long and spectacular climb, this emerges at a grass-covered plateau where the Jeeps stop. You proceed on foot, following a well-worn path through superb, old-growth jungle – complete with hanging creepers and monkeys crashing through the high canopy – to the temple complex at the foot of the valley. Allow at least two hours for the descent, and an hour or two more for the climb back up to the road head, for which you'll need plenty of drinking water. The alternative route from Kumily to Sabarimala involves a Jeep ride on a forest road to **Uppupara** (42km), with a final walk of 6km through undulating country. Given the very real risks involved with missing the last Jeep back to Kumily (the mountaintop is prime elephant and tiger country), it's advisable to get a group together and rent a 4WD for the day (Rs560 or Rs4 per kilometre, plus waiting time).

Munnar and around

MUNNAR, 130km east of Kochi and 110km north of the Periyar Wildlife Sanctuary, is the centre of Kerala's principal tea-growing region. Although billed in tourist bumf as a "hill station", these days it is becoming less of a Raj-style resort than a scruffy, workaday settlement of corrugated-iron-roofed cottages,

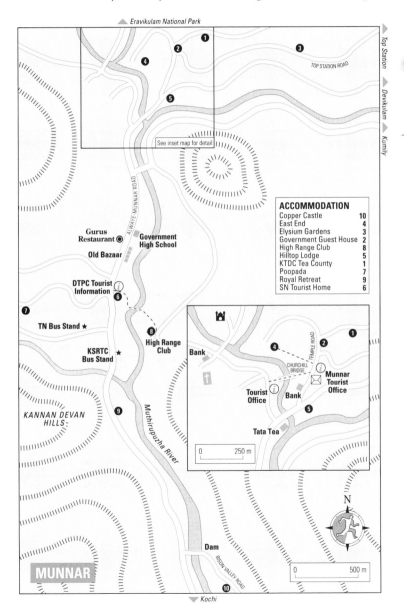

Eravikulam National Park

Top Station

Devikulam

Kumily

TOP STATION ROAD

See inset map for detail

ALWAYE-MUNNAR ROAD

Gurus Restaurant
Government High School

Old Bazaar

DTPC Tourist Information

TN Bus Stand ★

KSRTC Bus Stand ★

High Range Club

KANNAN DEVAN HILLS

Muthirapuzha River

ACCOMMODATION

Copper Castle	10
East End	4
Elysium Gardens	3
Government Guest House	2
High Range Club	8
Hilltop Lodge	5
KTDC Tea County	1
Poopada	7
Royal Retreat	9
SN Tourist Home	6

TEMPLE ROAD

Bank

CHURCHILL BRIDGE

Munnar Tourist Office

Tourist Office

Bank

Tata Tea

0   250 m

N

Dam

BISON VALLEY ROAD

0   500 m

MUNNAR

Kochi

hotels and factories couched in a valley, surrounded by great expanses of rolling green **tea plantations**. Nonetheless, the town still has something of a colonial look about it, with the odd verandaed British bungalow clinging to a side of the valley, and the famous **High Range Club** perched on the southeast edge of town; it has lovely flowerbeds and golf course (open to non-residents). Beyond the club sprawl some of Munnar's vast plantations, most of which are owned by the industrial giant Tata. At their regional headquarters in the centre of town, you can arrange visits to **tea factories** in the area (℡0486/530561).

In spite of more recent developments, it's easy to see why the pioneering Scottish planters who first developed this hidden valley in the 1900s felt so at home. At an altitude of around 1600m, the town enjoys a refreshing climate, with crisp winter mornings and relentlessly heavy rain during the monsoons. Hemmed in by soaring mountains – including peninsular India's highest peak, **Anamudi** (2695m) – it also boasts a spectacular setting. When the river mist clears, the surrounding summits form a wild backdrop to the carefully manicured plantations carpeting the valley floor and sides.

Munnar's greenery and cool air mainly draws well-heeled honeymooners from Mumbai and Bangalore. However, more and more foreigners are stopping here for a few days, enticed by the spell-binding bus ride from Periyar, which takes you across the high ridges and lush tropical forests of the Cardamon Hills, or for the equally spectacular climb across the Ghats from Madurai. Munnar is particularly popular with young travellers who head up here for the excellent **off-road cycling**; there are no official routes, just miles and miles of hills to climb up and speed down. The **hiking** scene is also growing as the countryside around Munnar offers walks for all levels of fitness, from gentle rambles through the tea fields to mountain climbing, including the scenic hamlet of **Top Station** and **Eravikulam National Park**.

Arrival and information

Munnar can be reached by **bus** from Kochi, Kottayam, Kumily and Madurai (see "Travel Details", p.424). The service to Madurai is either direct, or involves changing at Tehni. State-run and private services pull into the stand in the bazaar at the northern end of town, near the tourist information service. For hotels south of the centre you should ask to be dropped off at Old Munnar, at the friendly but ineffectual **DTPC tourist information** (Mon–Sat 10am–5pm; ℡0486/530679); here you can get a map of the town and immediate hills. If you need information on transport, accommodation or day-trips, seek out helpful Joseph Iype, who runs the efficient **tourist information service** (℡0486/530349) in the main bazaar. Immortalized in Dervla Murphy's *On a Shoestring to Coorg*, this self-appointed tourist officer has become something of a legend. In addition to handing out useful **maps** and newspaper articles, he'll arrange **auto-rickshaws** and **taxis** for excursions, and will bombard you with background information on the area. A short walk across Churchill Bridge, over the filthy Muthirapuzha River, the Munnar tourist information centre (℡0486/531051) is a government-sponsored private body, whose primary concern appears to be the promotion of its own guided tour (daily 9am–1pm & 2pm–6pm; Rs250 full day, Rs150 for half-day). Designed mainly for Indian tourists, the tour takes in a spice plantation, boating, a dairy farm, view points and Top Station in the morning, and Rajmalai Wildlife Sanctuary, waterfalls, an amusement park in the afternoon and sunset at a viewpoint.

You can **change money** at the State Bank of Travancore on Temple Road, or the State Bank of India. As adventure tourism takes off here, more and more places offer **cycle hire**; you can rent gearless bicycles in the market for about

Rs4 per hour. If you want proper mountain bikes, ask at the DTPC office (Rs10 per hour or Rs50 per day) or at *KTDC Tea County* (see below) – their top-notch bikes are officially for residents only, but its worth enquiring if there are any spare that you can hire for the day.

Accommodation and eating

Munnar has plenty of **accommodation**, although budget options are limited and are unfortunately too close to the bus station for a peaceful sleep. Upmarket visitors generally **eat** in their hotels; both *Royal Retreat* and *KTDC Tea County* have highly recommended restaurants with eclectic menus and attentive service, while *Gurus*, in the old bazaar opposite the government high school, is a characterful old-style coffee shop serving South Indian snacks. For tasty, filling and cheap meals, however, you can't beat the *Poopada*, whose small, no-frills restaurant is open to non-residents. *Saravana* in the main market serves good vegetarian "meals" while *East End*'s plush mid-priced restaurant is the best in the town centre, with a very varied menu.

Copper Castle, Bison Valley Road, Kannan Devan hills ☎0486/530633, ☎530438. Comfortable and modern hotel wedged into the side of a hill high above the valley; the deluxe rooms and restaurant both boast excellent views. Unless you have your own car, this place is inconveniently far from town. ⑥–⑧

East End, Temple Road, across the river from the bus stand ☎0486/530451, ☎530227. Immaculate upmarket hotel close to the centre of town, with Raj-style "cottages" in a big garden, and a recommended mid-priced multicuisine restaurant with a good varied menu. ⑤–⑦

Elysium Gardens, Top Station Road ☎0486/530510. In a quiet and pleasant spot with cottages and good, newly renovated rooms, all with cable TV and hot water. Decent South Indian restaurant dominated by a massive sign warning that "the Lord promotes, not man". ⑤–⑦

Government Guest House, Mattupatty Road, near the main bazaar, on the far side of the river ☎0486/530385. Characterful old British bungalow with well-refurbished and comfortable rooms; meals are provided by arrangement. The tariff appears to fluctuate daily, so you may well be able to negotiate a good discount. ⑦

High Range Club, Kannan Devan hills ☎0486/530253, ☎530333. A celebrated club for a hundred years, now offering cosy rooms in the large Raj-era club house hung with hunting trophies. The place to stay to enjoy tea or gin, and you can play billiards, golf, tennis, squash, or just read a good book in the beautiful gardens. Full board only, so indulge yourself. ⑧

Hilltop Lodge, on corner of Temple Road and Thekkady Road ☎0486/530616. Popular with the mountain-biking crew, but with a constant racket of traffic outside. This place offers the best budget deal with small clean rooms, all with attached bathrooms (blankets and hot water cost a bit extra). ②

KTDC Tea County, Top Station Road ☎0468/530460, ☎530970. The grandest address in Munnar, with a range of luxurious chalet style rooms and suites ranged along a hilltop, affording views across the valley. There's a good Indian restaurant, a bar, and a range of sporting and adventure activities, including paragliding and rock climbing. ⑦–⑧

Poopada, Kannan Devan hills, on the Manukulam Road ☎0486/530223. The front looks a tad dilapidated but the good-sized en-suite rooms are in fine condition. This place has about the best cheap eating in town, along with fine valley views and secluded location. Booking recommended on weekends. ⑥–⑦

Royal Retreat, Kannan Devan hills ☎0486/530240. Pleasant sunny yellow complex at the south end of town; spacious and comfortable rooms, some with brick fireplaces and cane furniture. ⑦–⑧

Shree Narayana ("SN") Tourist Home, Kannan Devan hills, on the main road near the tourist office ☎0486/530212. A popular and cheerful lodge set in forested grounds by a river, with slightly shabby rooms, attached bathrooms and hot water. Unfortunately, a recent price hike means this place isn't such good value anymore. ⑤–⑥

Eravikulam National Park

Encompassing 100 square kilometres of moist evergreen forest and grassy hilltops in the Western Ghats, the **Eravikulam National Park** (daily 7am–6pm; Rs50

[Rs10]; cars/taxis Rs10, auto-rickshaws Rs5) lies 13km northeast of Munnar (auto-rickshaws charge Rs150 return). It is the last stronghold of one of the world's rarest mountain goats, the **Nilgiri tahr**. Innate friendliness made the tahr pathetically easy prey during the hunting frenzy of the colonial era: during a break in his campaign against Tipu Sultan in the late 1790s, the future Duke of Wellington reported that his soldiers were able to shoot the unsuspecting goats as they wandered through his camp. By Independence, the tahr was virtually extinct; today, however, numbers are healthy, and the animals have regained their tameness, largely thanks to the efforts of the American biologist, Clifford Rice, who studied them here in the early 1980s. Unable to get close enough to properly observe the creatures, Rice followed the advice of locals and attracted them using salt, and soon entire herds were congregating around his camp. The tahrs' salt addiction also explains why so many hang around the park gates at **Vaguvarai**, where visitors – despite advice from rangers – slip them salty snacks.

The park gates mark the start of an excellent **hike** up the most accessible of the Anamudi massif's three peaks, for which you'll need sturdy footwear, plenty of water, a fair amount of stamina and a head for heights. Due to past environmental erosion, you now need to purchase a permit before setting off, available from the Wildlife DFO in Munnar (℡0486/530487). To start the trek, follow the road as it winds through the sanctuary, cutting across the switchbacks until you reach the pass forming the Kerala–Tamil Nadu border (auto-rickshaws and Jeep-taxis will drive you this far; you have to pay the vehicle fee to enter the park). Leave the road here and head up the ridge to your right; the path, which becomes very steep, peters out well before you reach the summit, and many hikers find the gradient too hair-raising to continue. But the panoramic views from the top are well worth the effort, and you may be rewarded with a glimpse of tahr grazing the high slopes.

Another popular excursion is the 34-kilometre uphill climb by bus through the subcontinent's highest tea estates to **Top Station**, a tiny hamlet on the Kerala–Tamil Nadu border with superb views across the plains. It's renowned for the very rare **Neelakurunji plant** (*Strobilanthes*), which grows in profusion on the mountainsides but only flowers once every twelve years, when crowds descend to admire the cascades of violet blossom spilling down the slopes. Top Station is accessible by **bus** from Munnar (8 daily starting at 5.30am; 1hr), and taxi-Jeeps will do the round trip for Rs600.

Trekking to Kodaikanal

A superb trek, one which is probably best done with a guide, takes around three days and follows the forested hill country from Munnar to the hill station of Kodaikanal, 85km to the southeast in Tamil Nadu. Joseph Iype of the Tourist Information Service in Munnar (see p.380) will be happy to assist with organization, and several agencies such as Clipper Holidays in Kochi (℡0484/364443) as well as Trio Travels, also in Kochi (℡0484/369571), will also organize the trek on request.

Kochi and Ernakulam and around

The venerable city of **KOCHI** (long known as Cochin) is Kerala's prime tourist destination, spread across islands and promontories in a stunning location between the Arabian Sea and the backwaters. Its main sections – modern **Ernakulam**, in the east, and the old districts of **Mattancherry** and **Fort Cochin** on a peninsula

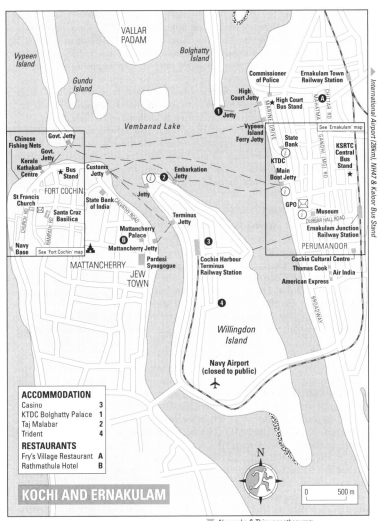

4

VALLAR
PADAM

*Vypeen
Island*

*Bolghatty
Island*

*Gundu
Island*

Commissioner
of Police

Ernakulam Town
Railway Station

High
Court Jetty

★ High Court
Bus Stand

MARINE DRIVE

CHITTAR RD

MAHATMA

❶ Jetty

Vembanad Lake

Vypeen
Island
Ferry Jetty

State
Bank

KSRTC
Central
Bus
Stand ★

GANDHI (MG) RD

See 'Ernakulam' map

Chinese
Fishing Nets

Govt. Jetty

KTDC

Govt.
Jetty

Kerala
Kathakali
Centre

★ Bus
Stand

Customs
Jetty

Embarkation
Jetty

❷

ⓘ

Main
Boat Jetty

ⓘ

FORT COCHIN

Jetty

GPO ✉

St Francis
Church

State Bank
of India

CALVATHY ROAD

ⓘ

Museum

✉

Santa Cruz
Basilica

CHURCH RD

RAMPATH RD

Terminus
Jetty

DURBAR HALL ROAD

Ernakulam Junction
Railway Station

Mattancherry
Palace

❸

Navy
Base

See 'Fort Cochin' map

Ⓑ

PERUMANOOR

Mattancherry Jetty

⚓

MATTANCHERRY

Pardesi
Synagogue

Cochin Harbour
Terminus
Railway Station

Cochin Cultural Centre

Thomas Cook

Air India

JEW
TOWN

American Express

BROADWAY

❹

*Willingdon
Island*

Navy Airport
(closed to public)
✈

ACCOMMODATION

Casino	3
KTDC Bolghatty Palace	1
Taj Malabar	2
Trident	4

RESTAURANTS

Fry's Village Restaurant	A
Rathmathula Hotel	B

N

KOCHI AND ERNAKULAM

0   500 m

International Airport (28km), NH47 & Kaloor Bus Stand

▼ *Alappuzha & Thiruvananthapuram*

in the west – are linked by a complex system of ferries, and distinctly less romantic bridges. Although most visitors end up staying in Ernakulam, Fort Cochin and Mattancherry are the focus of interest, where the city's extraordinary history of foreign influence and settlement is reflected in a jumble of architectural styles. During a wander through their narrow lanes, you'll stumble upon spice markets, Chinese fishing nets, a synagogue, a Portuguese palace, India's first European church and fort, quaint Dutch homes and a village green that could have been transported from England's home counties. The city is also one of the few places in Kerala where, at any time of year, you can be assured of seeing **Kathakali dance**, either in one of several special tourist theatres or at a more authentic performance by a temple-based company (see box on p.395).

383

Kochi sprang into being in 1341, when a flood created a natural safe port that swiftly replaced Muziris (Kodungallur, 50km north), as the chief harbour on the Malabar Coast. The royal family transferred here from Muziris in 1405, after which the city grew rapidly, attracting Christian, Arab and Jewish settlers from the Middle East. The name probably derives from *kocchazhi*, meaning the new, or small, harbour.

The history of European involvement in Kochi from the early 1500s onwards is dominated by the aggression of, successively, the Portuguese, Dutch and British, competing to control the port and its lucrative spice trade. From 1800, the state of Cochin was part of the British Madras Presidency; from 1812 until Independence in 1947, its administration was made the responsibility of a series of *diwans*, or financial ministers. In the 1920s, the British expanded the port to make it suitable for modern ocean-going ships; extensive dredging created Willingdon Island, between Ernakulam and Fort Cochin.

Arrival, information and local transport

Kochi's brand new **international airport** is at Nedumbassery, near Alwaye (aka Alua), 26km to the north of Ernakulam. Kochi is served by daily flights from **Mumbai**, **Bangalore**, **Thiruvananthapuram** and **Delhi**, and six each week from **Chennai**. There are two weekly flights from **Goa**, **Hyderabad**, **Kozhikode** and **Coimbatore**, as well as the **Lakshadweep Islands** and the Gulf States of **Doha**, **Dubai**, **Kuwait**, **Sharjah** and **Muscat**. Of the three **railway stations – Ernakulam Junction** (⏱131) is closest to the centre and is the most important; Ernakulam Town lies 4km to the north. No trains run to Fort Cochin or Mattancherry. The Cochin Harbour Terminus, on Willingdon Island, is useful only for people staying in one of the luxury hotels on the island.

The KSRTC **Central bus station** (⏱0484/372033), beside the rail line a short way east of MG Road and north of Ernakulam Junction, is the principal and most convenient station for long-distance buses. There are two bus stands for private buses, which are not officially permitted to use the state highways; these buses, which have been responsible for numerous accidents, stop more frequently and compete with each other, overtake very dangerously, and tend to be more crowded than KSRTC buses. The **Kaloor stand** (rural destinations to the south and east) is across the bridge from Ernakulam Town railway station on the Alwaye Road, and the **High Court stand** (buses to Kumily, for Periyar Wildlife Reserve, and north to Thrissur, Guruvayur and Kodungallur) lies opposite the High Court ferry jetty.

Although **auto-rickshaws** are plentiful and reliable in Ernakulam, and to a slightly lesser extent across the water in Mattancherry and Fort Cochin, everyone uses Kochi's excellent and very cheap **ferry system**. **Bicycles** for exploring Mattancherry and the rest of old Kochi can be rented from a small shop on Bazaar Road between *Hotel Seagull* and Fort Cochin or from *Adams Old Inn* (Rs5 per hour).

Tours and backwater trips

KTDC's half-day **Kochi boat cruise** (daily 9am–12.30pm & 2–5.30pm; Rs50) is a good way to orientate yourself with the city. However, it doesn't stop for long in either Mattancherry or Fort Cochin, so give it a miss if you are pushed for time. Departing from the High Court Jetty on Shanmugham Road, Ernakulam, it calls at Willingdon Island, the synagogue, Mattancherry Dutch Palace, St Francis Church, the Chinese fishing nets and Bolghatty Island. Book at the KTDC Reception Centre on Shanmugham Road (⏱0484/353234).

Half the fun of visiting Kochi is about getting on the inexpensive local ferries. Apart from providing the incomparable benefits of a cooling sea breeze and the chance to approach the city sights from a novel perspective, you also avoid the headache of finding a rickshaw, taxi or bus and sitting in endless traffic jams

The main map (see p.383) shows Ernakulam's four jetties. Theoretically, all the routes below should work in reverse. However, play safe, and don't rely on getting the last boat. A pamphlet giving the exact ferry timings is available from the ticket hatches by the jetties, and from the helpful tourist desk at the Main Boat Jetty in Ernakulam.

Ernakulam to Mattancherry
From Ernakulam (Main Jetty), via Fort Cochin (Customs Jetty), for Chinese fishing nets, St Francis Church, Dutch Cemetery; Willingdon Island (Terminus Jetty); and Mattancherry Jetty for Jewish Synagogue and Dutch Palace. Journey time 20min. First boat at 6am, last at 9.10pm.

Ernakulam to Vypeen
From Ernakulam (Main Jetty). This frequent service has two routes, some ferries go via Willingdon Island (Embarkation Jetty; 25min), and most go straight to Vypeen (Govt Jetty; 15min).
First boat 7am, then every 30min until 9.30pm.

Fort Cochin to Vypeen
From Fort Cochin (Govt Jetty) to Vypeen (Govt Jetty). Journey time 15min.
First boat 6.30am, every 10min until 9pm.

Willingdon Island to Fort Cochin
From the Tourist Office Jetty (Willingdon Island) to Customs Jetty (Fort Cochin). Journey time 15min.
First boat 6.30am, then every 30min until 6.15pm.

Ernakulam to Bolghatty Island
From Ernakulam (High Court Jetty). Journey time 10min.
First boat 6.30am, last 9pm; speedboat taxis may also be available at the jetty (Rs20; free if you are staying at Bolgatty Palace hotel).

Ernakulam to Varapuzha
Local ferry service that provides a chance to see the backwaters (see box on p.362) if you can't travel further south than Kochi or afford the organized cruises. Six boats daily, starting at 7.40am until 6.45pm; 2hr each way. There's little to see at Varapuzha, apart from paddy fields and coconuts, so it makes sense to take the 2.30pm boat and stay on it, returning to Ernakulam just after dusk at 6.30pm.

The KTDC tourist office and a couple of private companies also operate popular **backwater trips** (see box on p.362) out of Kochi. Taking in a handful of coir-making villages north of the city, these are a leisurely and enjoyable way to experience rural Kerala from small hand-punted canoes. KTDC's daily tours cost Rs315, including the car or bus trip to the departure point, 30km north, and a knowledgeable guide. Better value is a similar trip run by the tourist desk at the Main Boat Jetty (daily depart 9am, return 1.30pm, or depart 2pm, return 6.30pm; Rs275; ⊕0484/371761) or their **sunset cruise** (daily 5.30pm–7pm; Rs400) on a houseboat. Reservations for any of the tours must be made at least a day in advance. Both KTDC and the tourist desk also offer *kettu vallam* **houseboat cruises** along the backwaters of Cochin district, charging Rs3500–4500 per couple for a 24hr trip, including all meals.

Information

If you are based on Willingdon island, head for the helpful Government of India **tourist office** (Mon–Fri 9am–5.30pm, Sat 9am–noon; ☎0484/668352), between the *Taj Malabar Hotel* and Tourist Office Jetty. They offer information on Kerala and beyond, and can provide reliable guides; they also have a desk at the airport. KTDC's **reception centre**, on Shanmugham Road, Ernakulam (☎0484/353234) reserves accommodation in their hotel chain and organizes sightseeing and backwater tours (see above). Another KTDC counter can be found at the airport, and there is a DTPC desk at the Old Collectorate, Park Avenue, Ernakulam (☎0484/371488). The tiny independent **tourist desk** (daily 8am–7pm; ☎0484/371761) at the entrance to the Main Boat Jetty in Ernakulam is extremely helpful and friendly, and the best place to check ferry and bus timings; you can pick up free city and state maps. A mine of information on ritual theatre and temple festival dates around the state, the award-winning tourist desk office also publishes a useful South India information guide and offers daily boat tours and houseboats at very competitive rates, and they run a fantastic guesthouse near Cannanore (see p.421; book in Kochi).

Useful **publications** include the *Jaico Timetable* (Rs7) and the bimonthly *Cochin Shopper's Digest* (free), both of which are not exhaustive but give details of bus, train, ferry and flight times. KTDC publishes an excellent walking tour map and guide to Fort Cochin (free; available from all KTDC tourist offices) which describes the fascinating histories of many of the buildings you will see in the fort area.

Accommodation

The romantic atmosphere of **Fort Cochin** is being rashly exploited, with a growing number of budget guesthouses and upmarket hotels, which are drastically altering the face of this lovely town. Property developers with no family connections in the town are coming to build here with little interest in restoration and conservation, creating eyesores such as the *Park Avenue* hotel. The biggest crisis however, is the **clean water shortage** problem that has hit the locals very hard, especially in the high season; if you must stay in Fort Cochin, keep your daily water consumption to a minimum. To help preserve the fort area, you could opt to stay in **Ernakulam**, which lacks the old-world ambience, but is far more convenient for travel connections. The eighteenth-century Dutch palace on the tip of **Bolghatty Island** is a congenial three-star complex, although, after years of endless renovation it now possesses little of its once very grand charm.

Ernakulam

Ernakulam has plenty of accommodation, although its guesthouses and hotels tend to fill up by late afternoon, so **book** in advance.

Abad Plaza, MG Road ☎0484/381122. Comfortable and pleasant business-style high-rise in the centre of Ernakulam, with restaurant and bar, swimming pool and health club. ❽
Aiswarya, Jos Junction ☎0484/364454. Caters to most mid-range budgets, where the cheaper

non-a/c rooms are excellent value; the a/c rooms on the top floors come with balconies. There is a good restaurant downstairs serving "meals" and fish *molee* (fish in coconut sauce). ❺–❻
Avenue Regent, MG Road ☎0484/372662, ℻370129. Very comfortable, centrally a/c four-

star, close to the railway station and main shopping area, with a restaurant, 24hr coffee shop and bar. Expect only the highest standards, as this place doubles as a well-respected hotel-management training college. ⑥

Basoto Lodge, Press Club Road ⓣ0484/352140. Dependable backpackers' lodge with twelve basic non-a/c rooms and no restaurant. Two rooms have small balconies. ②

Bharat, Gandhi Square, Durbar Hall Road ⓣ0484/353501, ⓕ370502. Large, modern hotel heavily endowed with the ethnic tribal look. Comfortable rooms, 24hr coffee shop and three restaurants. The non-a/c rooms are not as expensive as you would imagine. ⑥–⑦

Biju's Tourist Home, corner of Canon Shed and Market roads ⓣ0484/381881. Pick of the budget bunch, with thirty clean and spacious rooms, some with a/c, close to the main boat jetty. TVs may be rented, and they have an inexpensive same-day laundry service. Friendly, very popular and recommended. ④–⑤

Cochin Tourist Home, opposite railway station ⓣ0484/364577. Cleanest of the cheap hotels lined up outside Ernakulam Junction, but often full of noisy family and pilgrim groups. There's a resident astro-palmist. ③–⑤

Deepak Lodge, Market Road ⓣ0484/353882. One of a handful of well-maintained and inexpensive lodges along this road with big, very basic rooms and communal bathrooms; an extra Rs20 gets you a huge attached bathroom. ②

Excellency, Nettipadam Road, Jos Junction ⓣ0484/374001, ⓕ374009. Just a 5min walk from Ernakulam Junction railway station. Smart, modern mid-range place, which has mostly a/c rooms and a 24hr coffee shop. ⑤–⑥

Grand, MG Road ⓣ0484/382061. A slightly kitsch place with a 1950s feel to it – lots of lino and varnished wood; despite this, all the rooms are well appointed and have a/c and cable TV. There is a multicuisine restaurant and bar. ⑦–⑧

Hakoba, Shanmugham Road ⓣ0484/369839. Conveniently midway between Main and High Court Jetties. Dowdy, but all rooms have cable TV, and both the a/c and non-a/c front rooms overlooking the street and harbour are excellent value. There's a good "meals" joint on the ground floor. ③–⑤

Maple Guest House, XL/271 Canon Shed Road ⓣ0484/355156. After *Biju's*, this is the best deal in the district. The rooms are spartan but clean, cheap and central and there are some with a/c. Don't be pushed into paying the extra Rs100 for a deluxe room, all you get is a rather unnecessary carpet. ③

Metropolitan, near Ernakulam Junction railway

station ⓣ0484/369931. Smart business hotel good for late night arrivals or early morning trains, but a bit too far from all the tourist attractions and any decent views. There is a multicuisine restaurant, 24hr coffee shop and bar. ⑦

Modern Guest House, XL/6067, Market Road ⓣ0484/352130. Popular place above a (noisy) Keralan veg restaurant, with simple non-a/c rooms with attached bathrooms. If full try their annexe, the *Modern Rest House* (ⓣ0484/361407), which has sixteen plain but pleasant rooms that are slightly more expensive. ②

Paulson Park, Carrier Station Road ⓣ0484/382179. Close to Ernakulam Junction. Good value, with large, well-appointed rooms, some with a/c, and a ground-floor restaurant featuring a surreal fake rock garden. ⑤–⑥

Sangeetha, 36/1675 Chittoor Rd, near stations ⓣ0484/368736. Comfortable rooms, if small for the price; the non-a/c ones can be stuffy. Complimentary bed tea and breakfast is included in the tariff. Very convenient for the 24hr bus station next door, and they operate a left-luggage store and foreign exchange. ⑤

Sealord, Shanmugham Road ⓣ0484/382472, ⓕ370135. High-rise and centrally a/c hotel near High Court jetty. Standard rooms are excellent value; the best are on the top floor. Rooftop restaurant, bar and foreign exchange. ⑦

Taj Residency, Marine Drive ⓣ0484/371471, ⓕ371481. Ernakulam's top business hotel, with central a/c, luxury rooms and a pleasant open-air restaurant, enjoys a prime location overlooking the harbour. If you want a pool and more leisure space, however, head over to the *Taj Malabar* on Willingdon Island. ⑨

Woodlands, Woodlands Junction, MG Road ⓣ0484/382051. A central, stylish place primarily aimed at Indian tourists, with cosy a/c and non-a/c rooms and spotless marble bathrooms. Next door there's a new, more upmarket sister outfit with central a/c and lots of glitz. Beware of the 8am checkout. ⑥

Fort Cochin

Adams Old Inn, Burgher Street ⓣ0484/217595. Great family-run guesthouse in a well-restored period building; the rooms are modern and just one has a/c. There is a decent rooftop dorm (Rs100). ③

Brunton Boatyard, next to Fort Cochin Jetty ⓣ0484/215461. A new Casino group hotel, built on the site of an eighteenth-century British boatyard; the look is Keralan carved wood and whitewash, with beautifully designed breezy rooms with a/c and balconies overlooking bay. Three speciality

The tradition of kalam ezhuttu (pronounced "kalam-erroo-too") – detailed and beautiful ritual drawings in coloured powder, of deities and geometric patterns (mandalas) – is very much alive all over Kerala. The designs usually cover an area of around thirty square metres, often outdoors and under a *pandal*, a temporary shelter made from bamboo and palm fronds. Each powder, made from rice flour, turmeric, ground leaves and burnt paddy husk, is painstakingly applied using the thumb and forefinger as a funnel. Three communities produce *kalams*; two come from the temple servant (*amblavasi*) castes, whose rituals are associated with the god Ayappa (see p.373) or the goddess Bhagavati; the third, the *pullavans*, specialize in serpent worship. Iconographic designs emerge gradually from the initial grid lines and turn into startling figures, many of terrible aspect, with wide eyes and fangs. Noses and breasts are raised, giving the whole a three-dimensional effect. As part of the ritual, the significant moment when the powder is added for the iris or pupil, "opening" the eyes, may well be marked by the accompaniment of *chenda* drums and *elatalam* hand-cymbals.

Witnessing the often day-long ritual of drawing is an unforgettable experience. The effort expended by the artist is made all the more remarkable by the inevitable destruction of the picture shortly after its completion; this truly ephemeral art cannot be divorced from its ritual context. In some cases, the image is destroyed by a fierce-looking vellichapad ("light-bringer"). He is a village oracle who can be recognized by shoulder-length hair, red *dhoti*, heavy brass anklets and the hooked sword he brandishes either while jumping up and down on the spot (a common sight), or marching purposefully about to control the spectators. At the end of the ritual, the powder, invested with divine power, is thrown over the onlookers. *Kalam ezhuttu* rituals are not widely advertised, but check at tourist offices.

restaurants and a pool edging onto the lake. ⑨
Chiramel Residency, 1 Lilly St ☎0484/217310.
A great seventeenth-century heritage guesthouse, with five carefully restored rooms around a congenial communal sitting room; the lofty non-a/c rooms all have big wooden beds, teak floors, some with a balcony, and modern bathrooms. The welcoming and warm family live downstairs. ⑤
Delight, opposite the Parade Ground
☎0484/217658. Beautiful home with distinctive blue latticework overlooking the ground. Six spacious, comfortable and airy rooms around a leafy courtyard, run by a friendly and very helpful family, whose conservation and restoration efforts are admirable. Breakfast available. Book ahead. ③–⑤
Elite, Princess Street ☎0484/215733. Several floors of basic but clean and cheap non-a/c rooms with attached bathrooms, in a friendly guesthouse above a popular restaurant. ②–③
Fort Avenue, Tower Road (☎0484/221219). A family house in a quiet but convenient location, with small but pleasant non-a/c rooms upstairs. ③
Fort Heritage, 1/283 Napier St ☎0484/225333. A seventeenth-century restored Dutch mansion, with comfortable airy a/c rooms, a restaurant and loads of character. However, the walls are hung with

tacky imitations of Rubens, the management is a little surly and it's pricey at $65 a night, breakfast included. ⑨
Fort House, 2/6A Calvathy Rd ☎0484/226103.
Pleasant a/c rooms and cheaper bamboo huts ranged around an interesting if eccentric compound, littered with pots and statues with a good café that serves delicious seafood, and a brilliant jetty. None of the rooms look onto the water however. ⑥
Malabar House Residency, 1/268 Parade Rd
☎0484/217099. Beautiful, historic mansion renovated with a highly successful mix of old-world charm and bright and brash European designer chic. The Keralan temple-style pool in the minimalist courtyard is stunning. Tariff includes breakfast. Recommended. ⑨
The Old Courtyard, Princess Street
☎0484/216302. Owned by the Casino family group, this is the latest heritage hotel to hit the scene. The rooms have been expertly restored and decorated with antique Dutch furniture, solid teak floorboards and beams, and modern bathrooms; all look onto a courtyard with a pleasant restaurant under a mango tree. ⑥–⑧
Seagull, Calvathy Road ☎0484/228128. Assorted rooms with attached bathrooms, a couple with a/c,

KERALA | Kochi and Ernakulam and around

but none makes the most of the location next to the water's edge (stand on a chair to see out of the window). It also suffers from lethargic staff and noise from its own popular bar and restaurant. ❸–❺

Spencer Tourist Home, 1/298 Parade Rd ⊕0484/225049. A place with loads of character set in an old, rambling Portuguese house. It has five large spotless non-a/c rooms to offer and a beautiful little garden to relax in, but no food is available and it's not as well maintained as the *Delight* close by. ❷–❸

Sree Venkateswara, 1/653B Peter Celli St (no phone). Clean, non-a/c doubles and attached bathrooms in a small, central guesthouse. ❷

Tharavadu Tourist Home, Quinose Street (the road behind the post office), Fort Cochin ⊕0484/216897. Eight simple, clean rooms (2 without bathrooms) in a quaint old Dutch house; breakfast and cool drinks are available and there's a cheap laundry service. They don't always honour advance bookings. ❷–❹

Willingdon and Bolghatty islands

Casino, Willingdon Island, 2km from airport, close to Cochin Harbour Terminus railway station ⊕0484/668221, ⊕668001. Deluxe and efficient place, but utterly characterless and shut in by the grey docks. Small pool, travel agent, foreign exchange and a choice of excellent restaurants. Very popular with tour groups, so book ahead. ❾

KTDC Bolghatty Palace, Bolghatty Island ⊕0484/ 525862, ⊕354879. Extensively renovated palace in beautiful location, a short hop from High Court Jetty. The main building, built by the Dutch in 1744 and later home of the British Resident, is now a three-star hotel with deluxe rooms; "honeymoon" cottages stand on stilts right on the water's edge. Reserve through any KTDC tourist office, and come armed with mosquito repellent. At weekends, the adjacent KTDC canteen and bar is noisy with day-trippers. ❽

Taj Malabar, Willingdon Island, by Tourist Office Jetty ⊕0484/666811, ⊕668297. Pinky-orange tower block in a superb location on the tip of the island with sweeping views of the bay; the old "heritage" wing, waterfront gardens and pool have recently been extensively refurbished, and the whole placed oozes *Taj* style and quality. ❾

Trident, Bristow Road, Willingdon Island ⊕0484/669595, ⊕669393. Despite the grey dockyard environs, this new hotel is the most intimate and congenial of the five stars on the island, with interesting displays of Keralan tribal and household artefacts, a pool in a tropical oasis, two restaurants, a bar and a range of luxurious rooms. Recommended. ❾

Mattancherry

With high-rise development restricted to Ernakulam, across the water, the old-fashioned character of **Mattancherry** and **Fort Cochin** remains intact. Within an area small enough to cover on foot, bicycle or auto-rickshaw, glimpses of Kochi's past greet you at virtually every turn. As you approach by ferry (get off at Mattancherry Jetty), the shoreline is crowded with tiled buildings painted in pastel colours – a view that can't have changed for centuries.

Despite the large number of tourists visiting daily, trade is still the most important activity here. Many of the streets are busy with barrows, loaded with sacks of produce, trundling between *godowns* (warehouses), and there are little shops everywhere with dealers doing business in tea, jute, rubber, chillies, turmeric, cashew, ginger, cardamom and pepper.

Jew Town

The road heading left from Mattancherry Jetty leads into the district known as **Jew Town**, where NX Jacob's tailor shop and the offices of J.E. Cohen, advocate and tax consultant, serve as reminders of a once-thriving Jewish community. Nowadays, the ever-entrepreneurial Kashmiris have moved in and the shops all sell expensive antiques, Hindu and Christian wood-carvings, oil lamps, wooden spice boxes and other bric-a-brac.

Turning right at the India Pepper & Spice Trade Building, usually resounding with the racket of dealers shouting the latest spice prices, and then right again, brings you into Synagogue Lane. The **Pardesi (White Jew)**

Synagogue (daily except Sat 10am–noon & 3–5pm) was founded in 1568, and rebuilt in 1664. Its interior is an attractive, if incongruous, hotchpotch; note the floor, paved with hand-painted eighteenth-century blue-and- white tiles from Canton, each unique, depicting a love affair between a mandarin's daughter and a commoner. The nineteenth-century glass oil-burning chandeliers suspended from the ceiling were imported from Belgium. Above the entrance, a gallery supported by slender gilt columns was reserved for female members of the congregation. Opposite the entrance, an elaborately carved Ark houses four scrolls of the *Torah* (the first five books of the Old Testament), encased in silver and gold, on which are placed gold crowns presented by the maharajas of Travancore and Cochin, testifying to good relations with the Jewish community. The synagogue's oldest artefact is a fourth-century copperplate inscription from the Raja of Cochin.

An attendant is usually available to show visitors around and answer questions, and his introductory talk features as part of the KTDC guided tour (see p.384). Outside, in a small square, several antique shops are well worth a browse but don't expect a bargain.

Draavidia, on Jew Street, is a small but active art **gallery**, which has an emphasis on contemporary art. Draavidia also puts on daily live Indian **classical music**; the programme is called Sadhana (6–7pm), and admission is on a membership basis of Rs100.

The Jews of Kochi

According to tradition, the Myuchasim Jews ("Black") were the first group of Jews to arrive on the Malabar coast, having fled the occupation of Jerusalem by Nebuchadnezzar, in 587 BC. Another legend, however, claims that the Jews initially came in the eleventh century BC, as part of a trade fleet that belonged to King Solomon. Whatever, the truth, the Jews settled in Cranganore, just north of Cochin, to trade in spices. They remained respected members of Keralan society and even had their own ruler, until the Portuguese embarked upon a characteristic "Christian" policy of persecution of non-believers early in the sixteenth century.

At that time, when Jews were being burned at the stake in Goa and forced to leave their settlements elsewhere on the coast, the Raja of Cochin gave them a parcel of land adjoining the royal palace in Mattancherry. A new Jewish community was created in the area now known as Jew Town, and a synagogue was built. The Jews were in demand as they spoke Malayalam, and trading was in their blood; the community thrived during the great trading period under the more liberal and supportive Dutch and later British rule.

There were three distinct groups of Jews in Kerala. The Black Jews were employed as labourers in the spice business, and their community of some thousands resulted from the earliest Jewish settlers marrying and converting Indians; the Brown Jews are thought to have been slave converts. The White (Pardesi) Jews considered both groups inferior to themselves; they were orthodox and married only among their number. However, by the early 1950s, most of Kochi's Jews disappeared, when they were given free passage to Israel, where they could more easily uphold their customs and rules. The remaining White Jews are on the verge of extinction as they are determined to stay racially pure. At the time of writing only seven families survive, a total of 22 people with just enough males over the age of 13 to perform the rituals in the synagogue – and no rabbi.

Mattancherry Palace (daily except Fri 10am–5pm; free, but donations welcome), stands on the left side of the road a short walk from the Mattancherry Jetty in the opposite direction to Jew Town. The gateway on the road is, in fact, its back entrance; although the most sensible side to approach from the ferry, it inexplicably remains locked with a loose chain. Visitors slim enough can, and do, enter through the gap, saving the walk around the block. In the walled grounds stands a circular tiled Krishna temple (closed to non-Hindus).

Although known locally as the **Dutch Palace**, the two-storey palace was built by the Portuguese as a gift to the Cochin Raja, Vira Keralavarma (1537–61), and the Dutch were responsible for subsequent additions. While its appearance is not particularly striking – squat with whitewashed walls and tiled roof – the interior is captivating.

The **murals** that adorn some of its rooms are among the finest examples of Kerala's much underrated school of painting (see Contexts, p.681): friezes illustrating stories from the *Ramayana*, on the first floor, date from the sixteenth century. Packed with detail and gloriously rich colour, the style is never strictly naturalistic; the treatment of facial features is pared down to the simplest of lines for the mouth, and characteristically aquiline noses. Downstairs, the women's bedchamber holds several less complex paintings, possibly dating from the 1700s. One shows Shiva dallying with Vishnu in his female form, the enchantress Mohini; a second portrays Krishna holding aloft Mount Govardhana; another features a reclining Krishna surrounded by *gopis*, or cowgirls. His languid pose belies the activity of his six hands and two feet, intimately caressing adoring admirers.

Keralan murals

The quality and unique style of the murals at Mattancherry Palace in old Kochi (see above), along with those in as many as sixty other locations in Kerala, are probably the best kept secrets in Indian art. Most are on the walls of functioning temples; they are not marketable, transportable, or indeed even *seen* by many non-Hindus. Few date from before the sixteenth century, depriving them of the aura of extreme antiquity; their origins may go back to the seventh century, probably influenced by the Pallava style of Tamil Nadu, but only traces in one tenth-century cave temple survive from the earliest period. Castaneda, a traveller who accompanied Vasco da Gama on the first Portuguese landing in India, described how he strayed into a temple, supposing it to be a church, and saw "monstrous looking images with two inch fangs" painted on the walls, causing one of the party to fall to his knees exclaiming, "if this be the devil, I worship God".

Technically classified as Fresco-Secco, Kerala murals employ vegetable and mineral colours, predominantly ochre reds and yellows, white and blue-green, and are coated with a protective sheen of pine resin and oil. Their ingenious design, strongly influenced by the canonical text, *Shilparatna*, incorporates intense detail with clarity and dynamism in the portrayal of human (and celestial) figures; subtle facial expressions are captured with the simplest of lines, while narrative elements are always bold and arresting. In common with all great Indian art, they share a complex iconography and symbolism.

Non-Hindus can see fine examples in Kochi, Padmanabhapuram (see p.346), Ettumanur (see p.369) and Kayamkulam (see p.357). Visitors interested in how they are made should head for the Mural Painting Institute at Guruvayur. A paperback book, *Murals of Kerala*, by M.G. Shashi Bhooshan (Kerala Govt Dept of Public Relations) serves as an excellent introduction to the field.

While the paintings are undoubtedly the highlight of the palace, the collection also includes interesting Dutch maps of old Cochin, coronation robes belonging to past maharajas, royal palanquins, weapons and furniture. Without official permission from the Archaeological Survey of India, photography is strictly prohibited.

Fort Cochin

Moving northwest from Mattancherry Palace along Bazaar Road, you pass wholesale emporia where owners, sitting behind scales surrounded by sacks of spices, may well be prepared to talk about their wares. Keep walking in a northerly direction, over the canal and then westwards into the area known as **Fort Cochin**. The architecture of the quiet streets in this enclave is very definitely European, with fine houses built by wealthy British traders and Dutch cottages with split farmhouse doors. If you have been travelling around India for a while, the sedate and sleepy streets, the look of the houses and village atmosphere is enough to induce a potent sense of culture shock; most Westerners wander around amazed at the familiarity of it all.

Just north of the Chinese fishing nets is the bus stand and Government Jetty, and behind them are several food and drinks stalls in Vasco da Gama Square. This area and nearby Princess Street (which has a few budget and mid-range

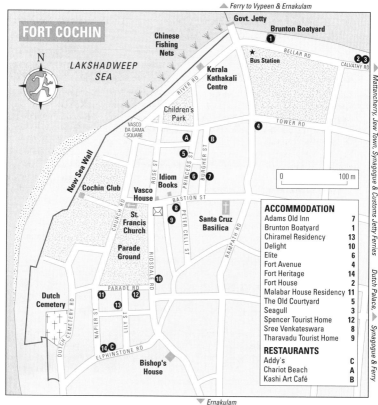

hotels) attracts backpackers and the consequent local hustlers. To fully appreci-ate the idiosyncratic nature of Fort Cochin, try the excellent **Fort Cochin: Walking Tour Map and Guide**, produced by Kerala Tourism, and available for free at the KTDC tourist office (see p.386). The tour takes you around some of the more important houses, the Dutch Cemetery, the Bishop's House and other strategic landmarks that make up the Fort area's unique and colour-ful past.

Today, Fort Cochin is home to a unique community of Eurasians, common-ly known as **Anglo-Indians**, who have developed a distinct and lively culture. With the development of tourism and the arrival of guesthouses, the changes to Fort Cochin are threatening the fragile infrastructure of this community and altering the unparalleled face of the area. The saving grace is that Fort Cochin is being preserved as a **Heritage Zone** now, with specific regulations on building renovation and tourist developments.

The *Kashi Art Café* on Burgher Street is an interesting and lively contempo-rary **art gallery** and restaurant, as well as a centre for imaginative eco-projects to protect the environment and community of Fort Cochin. The Kerala Kathakali Centre at the Cochin Aquatic Club organizes performances of **Kathakali** everyday (see box on p.395).

Chinese fishing nets

The huge, elegant **Chinese fishing nets** that line the northern shore of Fort Cochin – adding grace to an already characterful waterside view and probably the single most familiar photographic image of Kerala – are said to have been introduced to the region by traders from the court of Kublai Khan. Known in Malayalam as *cheena vala*, they can also be seen throughout the backwaters fur-ther south. The nets, which are suspended from arced poles and operated by levers and weights, require at least four men to control them. You can buy fresh fish from the tiny market here and have it grilled on the spot with sea salt, gar-lic and lemon at one of the ramshackle stalls nearby.

St Francis Church

Walking on from the Chinese fishing nets brings you to a typically English village green, especially when the local boys play cricket on a warm and sunny evening. In one corner stands the church of **St Francis**, the first European church to be built in India. Originally built in wood and named Santo Antonio, it was probably associated with Franciscan friars from Portugal. Exactly when it was founded is not known, but the stone struc-ture is likely to date from the early sixteenth century. The facade, with multi-curved sides, became the model for most Christian churches in India. Vasco da Gama was buried here in 1524, but his body was later removed to Portugal.

Under the Dutch, the church was renovated and became Protestant in 1663, then Anglican with the advent of the British in 1795 and since 1949 has been attached to the Church of South India. Inside, various tombstone inscriptions have been placed in the walls, the earliest of which is from 1562. One hang-over from British days is the continued use of *punkahs*, large swinging cloth fans on frames suspended above the congregation; these are still operated by people sitting outside pulling on cords.

The interior of the late twentieth-century **Santa Cruz Cathedral**, south of St Francis church, will delight fans of the colourful (verging on the downright gaudy) Indo-Romano-Rococo school of decoration.

- END -

Ernakulam

ERNAKULAM presents the modern face of Kerala, with more of a city feel than Thiruvananthapuram, but small enough not to be too daunting. Other than the fairly dull **Parishath Thamburan Museum** (Tues–Sun 9.30am–noon & 3–5.30pm; free) in Durbar Hall Road, there's little in the way of sights. Along the busy, long, straight **Mahatma Gandhi (MG) Road**, which more or less divides Ernakulam in half, the main activities are shopping, eating and movie-going. Here you can email and phone to your heart's content, and choose from an assortment of great places to eat Keralan food. This area is particularly good for cloth, with an infinite selection of colours; if there's a jazzy style in *lunghis* this year, you'll get it on MG Road.

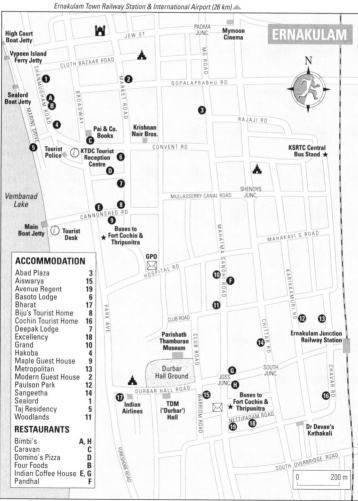

Ernakulam Town Railway Station & International Airport (26 km) ▲

ERNAKULAM

High Court Boat Jetty

Vypeen Island Ferry Jetty

Sealord Boat Jetty

Tourist Police

KTDC Tourist Reception Centre

Pai & Co. Books

Krishnan Nair Bros.

Vembanad Lake

Main Boat Jetty

Tourist Desk

Buses to Fort Cochin & Thripunitra

JEW ST

PADMA JUNC.

Mymoon Cinema

MG ROAD

CLOTH BAZAAR ROAD

MARKET ROAD

BROADWAY

SHANMUGHAM ROAD

MARINE DRIVE

GOPALAPRABHU RD

RAJAJI RD

CONVENT RD

KSRTC Central Bus Stand ★

SHENOYS JUNC.

MULLASSERRY CANAL ROAD

CANNONSHED RD

MAHAKAVI G ROAD

MAHATMA GANDHI ROAD

KARIKKAMURI RD

CHITTARD RD

GPO

HOSPITAL RD

PARK AVE

CLUB ROAD

Parishath Thamburan Museum

Durbar Hall Ground

JOSS JUNC.

SOUTH JUNC.

Ernakulam Junction Railway Station

DURBAR HALL ROAD

Indian Airlines

TDM ('Durbar') Hall

WARRIOM ROAD

Buses to Fort Cochin & Thripunitra

NETTIPADAM ROAD

Dr Devan's Kathakali

FORESHORE ROAD

SOUTH OVERBRIDGE ROAD

CHAVAR RD

0   200 m

ACCOMMODATION

Abad Plaza	3
Aiswarya	15
Avenue Regent	19
Basoto Lodge	6
Bharat	17
Biju's Tourist Home	8
Cochin Tourist Home	16
Deepak Lodge	7
Excellency	18
Grand	10
Hakoba	4
Maple Guest House	9
Metropolitan	13
Modern Guest House	2
Paulson Park	12
Sangeetha	14
Sealord	1
Taj Residency	5
Woodlands	11

RESTAURANTS

Bimbi's	A, H
Caravan	C
Domino's Pizza	D
Four Foods	B
Indian Coffee House	E, G
Pandhal	F

Cochin Cultural Centre, Fort Cochin & Willingdon Island ▼

Kathakali in Kochi

Kochi is the only city in the state where you are guaranteed the chance to see live Kathakali, the uniquely Keralan form of ritualized theatre (see p.706). Whether in its authentic setting, in temple festivals held during the winter or at the shorter tourist-orientated shows that take place year round, these mesmerizing dance dramas are an unmissable feature of Kochi's cultural life.

Four venues in the city hold daily recitals. Beginning at 6.30pm, the hour-long shows are preceded by an introductory talk. You can also watch the dancers being made up if you arrive an hour or so early, and keen photographers should arrive well before the start to ensure a front-row seat. Tickets cost Rs100 and can be bought on the door. Most visitors only attend one show, but you'll gain a much better sense of what Kathakali is all about if you take in at least a couple. This should be followed, ideally, with an all-night recital at a temple festival, or at least one of the recitals given by the Ernakulam Kathakali Club. For further details contact the tourist desk at the Main Boat Jetty, Ernakulam. The four principal venues are listed below:

Cochin Cultural Centre, Souhardham, Manikath Road ⓣ0484/367866. The least commendable option: the dancing at this a/c theatre ("sound-proof, insect-proof, and dust-proof") is accomplished, but performances are short, with only two characters, and you can't see the musicians. Worst of all, large tour groups monopolize the front seats, and the PA speakers at the back are excruciatingly loud.

Kerala Kathakali Centre, Cochin Aquatic Club, River Road (near the bus stand), Fort Cochin waterfront. Performed by a company of young graduates of the renowned Kalamandalam Academy (see p.412), and hugely enjoyable. What the actors may lack in expertise, they make up for with enthusiasm, and the small, dilapidated performance space, whose doors open on to the water, adds to the atmosphere. You also get to see three characters, and the music is particularly good. Come early to see them getting into their costumes and to grab a front-row seat.

Dr Devan's Kathakali, See India Foundation, Kalathiparambil Lane, near Ernakulam train station ⓣ0484/369471 or 371759. The oldest-established tourist show in the city, introduced by the inimitable Dr Devan, who steals the stage with his lengthy discourse on Indian philosophy and mythology. An entertaining performance, but maybe too much chat and not enough Kathakali.

Art Kerala, Kannanthodathu Lane, Valanjambalam ⓣ0484/366231. Next door to the See India Foundation, Art Kerala also puts on Kathakali performances that have proved popular with large tour groups; so expect a crowd.

At Netoor, 10km to the southeast of the centre, the ENS Kalari school of **Kalarippayat** (ⓣ0484/700810, ⓦwww.richsoft.com/enskalari, ⓔenskalari@eth.net) is one of the leading centres of the peculiarly Keralan martial art form (see box on p.333). The well-organized centre, established in 1954, is unusual in that it blends both the northern and the southern systems of Kalarippayat. Twice-daily training sessions start early at 4am; visitors are welcome to attend demonstrations (6–7pm), and there's an open session on Sundays (3–7pm). Alternatively, you can enrol on one of their Kalarippayat certificate courses, which run from one week to one year and are tailored to the needs of the student. The centre also offers lessons in the unique **Uzhichil massage** – a treatment derived from Ayurvedic medicine, designed as a cure to Kalari-related injuries – which concentrates on the lymph glands to improve tone and circulation. To get to the school take a bus from the KSRTC or the Kaloor bus stands to the Netoor INTUC bus stand, and walk down the road for half a kilometre; the school is opposite the Mahadevar Temple.

An eight-day annual **festival** at the Shiva temple in Ernakulam (Jan/Feb) features elephant processions and *panchavadyam* (drum and trumpet groups) out in the street. As part of the festival, there are usually night-time performances of Kathakali, and the temple is decorated with an amazing array of electric lights: banks of coloured tubes and sequenced bulbs imitating shooting stars.

Eating

Unusually for Keralan cities, Kochi offers a wide choice for **eating out**, from the delicious fresh-cooked fish by the Chinese fishing nets at Fort Cochin to the sophistication of the *Brunton Boatyard*. Between the two extremes, various popular modest places in Ernakulam include authentic Keralan dishes on their menus. The ferries run all evening, so it's possible to enjoy an evening meal on one of the more atmospheric islands before heading back to Ernakulam at about 9pm.

Ernakulam

Bimbi's, Shanmughan Road and Jos Junction. Brisk new Indian-style fast food joints. Hugely popular for inexpensive Udupi, North Indian and Chinese snacks and meals, and the tangiest *wadasambars* in town. They also do a great selection of shakes and ice creams.

The Brasserie, *Taj Residency*, Marine Drive. Luxury coffee shop serving pricey snacks and a particularly good range of Western cakes (Dundee, plum, palmettes and fudge).

Caravan, Broadway, near the KTDC tourist office. A/c ice-cream parlour that's a good place to chill out over a banana split or milkshake. Open until midnight so you can nip in for a late dessert.

Domino's, Esplanade Complex, Canal Road (free delivery ☎ 1600-111-123). Sometimes dhal-rice just cannot do justice to that pizza craving, although pizzas here all come with extra chilli and the topping options reflect Keralan cuisine. They will deliver to your hotel. *Baskin Robbins* ice-cream parlour is in the same complex if you want to go the whole hog.

Four Foods, Shanmugham Road. Busy, clean and popular roadside restaurant serving veg and non-veg meals, including blow-out thalis and good-value "dish of the day". For dessert, try their Mumbai-style *faloodas*, vermicelli steeped in syrup with dry fruits and ice cream.

Fry's Village Restaurant, adjacent to Mymoor Cinema, Chittoor Road. Moderately priced, ultra-spicy Keralan and "ethnic" specialities you rarely find served in such style, including the Calicut Muslim delicacy *patthri*, wafer-thin rice pancakes, *idliappam* dumplings, and *puthoo* (steamed rice cakes).

Indian Coffee House, on the corner of Cannonshed Road and Park Avenue, and another branch on Durbar Hall Road. The usual excellent coffee (ask for "pot coffee" if you don't want it with sugar), veg and non-veg lunch-time "meals", and simple snacks such as *dosa* and scrambled egg and omelettes.

Lotus Cascades, *Woodlands Hotel*, Woodlands Junction, MG Road. Classy veg Indian food, with plenty of tandoori options, at bargain prices. Great service too. Recommended.

Pandhal, MG Road. Very smart upmarket restaurant owned and managed by the Casino Group of hotels. Excellent Keralan fish dishes, as well as good North Indian cuisine and a sprinkling of continental food.

Sealord, in *Sealord* hotel, Shanmugham Road. Pricey rooftop restaurant serving good Chinese, Indian and sizzlers – but the portions are a bit mean, and the view of the harbour is not what it was since the shopping centre opposite was built. Great for a chilled beer, though.

Utsav, *Taj Residency*, Marine Drive. Expensive a la carte Indian restaurant. The Rs200 lunch-time buffets are better value and you get a matchless view over the harbour and bay at noon. At night, the twinkling lights make this the place for a very romantic dinner *à deux*.

Fort Cochin and Mattancherry

Addy's, Elphinstone Road. Open 8am until midnight, in a lovely, rambling seventeenth-century house, with lanterns, gingham cloths and loads of family atmosphere. The place gets enthusiastic reviews, with a high entertainment rating and praise for the meat dishes in particular, although Keralan dishes and fresh fish are also on the menu.

Brunton Boatyard, next to Fort Cochin Jetty. The expensive menu is a wonderful collection of dishes designed to reflect all the cultural influences that have played a part in the history of Cochin: Lebanese, Portuguese, British Raj, Dutch, Jewish and, of course, Keralan. Unfortunately, it is *à la carte* and you end up just wanting to try everything.

Chariot Beach, Princess Street. Dishes up a huge variety of seafood and Chinese dishes at reasonable prices, and you can eat alfresco on their small terrace.

Sadya, which means "feast" in Malayalam, is an unforgettable gastronomic affair that is an essential part of the Kerala experience. Whether you enjoy it on a longboat on the backwaters, in a family home or at a festival, you will never forget sitting down to a vast array of colourful food displayed on a lush green banana leaf. True to the all-India fashion of eating the main meal at noon, a *sadya* is invariably a lunch-time meal. There are strict guidelines regarding the placing of food, and the ingredients, the two main ones being tamarind (*muli*), used to give the dish a slightly sour and tangy taste, and coconut, which adds a rich and creamy flavour and takes the edge off the chillies. It is not uncommon for fourteen or so different preparations to be included in a *sadya*, each with a distinctive taste, depending on the combination of freshly ground spices. Most importantly, however, the meal should follow the principles of Ayurveda (see p.338) – there should be a perfect balance between hot, cold, sweet, sour and savoury to enhance digestion and bodily harmony.

A plantain (banana) leaf is always used as a plate, and is thrown away at the end of the meal; the tapering end should point to your left. You eat with your right hand and must try not to get any food or gravy on your palm – this is considered inauspicious. To eat with you hands enhances the whole sensory experience of the meal: it is considered just as important to feel the food as it is to taste and smell it. As a guest of honour, your plate must never be empty, and no matter how full you may be, your host will consider it his or her duty to keep giving you more, to avoid appearing stingy or poor. The best way to let the host know that you are full is to stop eating and leave a little food untouched on the plate.

The meal begins with a small cup of parippu, a soup made of gram (lentils) and coconut. Then comes the main course. In Kerala, a Hindu will tend to give you vegetarian dishes, whereas a Muslim or a Christian household will include Kozhi curry (chicken), biriyani and fish and shellfish dishes. First steamed rice is put on the lower half of the leaf. Spoonfuls of condiments such as sweet ginger chutney, coconut chutney and mango and lime pickles, as well as the savoury dishes, are placed in a semicircle on the upper half of the leaf. The essential dish in a *sadya* is sambar, a spicy vegetable and lentil stew that you eat with the steamed rice and savouries. The *sambar* is used to combine more dry preparations with rice, so you get a mush that is easy to eat with your hand. There will also be *upperi* – deep fried plantain (banana) chips that are very yellow in colour and have a distinctive taste as they are fried in local coconut oil, and a *pappadam* (poppodom), crumbled into the rice mixture. The other vegetarian dishes may include: *pazham* (steamed yellow plantains), *kitchadi* (curd with cucumber or okra, curry leaves and coconut), *mizhukki puratti* (fried green beans and plantains), *thoran* (green vegetables simmered in fresh coconut, red chillies and tumeric), *pulisseri* (yoghurt-based curry), *aviyal* (mixed vegetables, coconut and green chillies), *koottu curry* (potatoes, red and green chillies and coconut) and *olan* (pumpkin with red chickpeas or black eyed beans in coconut milk).

The third course is the dessert, taken on the same banana leaf. You will be served a sweet pancake known as *boli*, or *payasam*, which is a delicious hot and very sweet combination of brown molasses, coconut milk, spices, cashew nuts and raisins. There are several varieties of *payasam*, including *lentil payasam, jackfruit payasam,* and the rich *apapradhaman payasam* which comes with rice wafers. *Palppayasam* is made with milk and *ghee*, which makes it sacred and pure.

Then, just as you are fit to burst, you are given yet more steamed rice and hot, tangy rasam, a watery concoction that is poured on the rice. Mulligatawney soup, the broth so loved by the colonial Brits, is an adaptation of *rasam*.

Elite, Princess Street. Popular and lively haunt for both travellers and locals as it's so cheap and the menu is extensive.

Kashi Art Café, Burgher Street. Great café and exhibition space in a restored old building with a cosmopolitan yet zen-like atmosphere. A good place to check the notice boards, learn about local campaigns and festivals, and just find some tranquil space. Healthy light meals, cakes, an excellent breakfast and wonderful coffees are served all day.

Rahmathula Hotel (aka Kaika's), New Road, near Mattancherry Palace. Kaika, the chef, is renowned for his inexpensive mutton and chicken biryanis cooked in traditional Keralan style and served at breakfast and lunch; you'll need to ask directions as it is tucked away and difficult to find.

Seagull, Calvetty Road. Average restaurant in good location overlooking the water. Their seafood in Chinese sauce is particularly tasty, but be prepared for a long wait. Serves chilled beer and spirits.

Willingdon Island

Fort Cochin, Casino Hotel, Willingdon Island (☎0484/668 8421). This seafood restaurant is considered to create some of the best fish dishes in India. You select from the display of the catch of the day, and then choose the style of preparation, which is all done in front of you. Absolutely delicious maybe, but its very expensive and the decor is dull.

Taj Malabar, Willingdon Island (☎0484/666811). Two restaurants: the Jade Pavilion for Chinese, and Rice Boats serving Western, North Indian and Keralan dishes in a beautiful waterside location. The food is excellent and prices reflect this; the Rs200 lunch-time buffet includes veg and non-veg dishes and is good value.

Listings

Airlines, domestic: Indian Airlines, Durbar Hall Road (daily 9.45am–1pm & 1.45–4.45pm; ☎0484/370242 & 141); Jet Airways, Bab Chambers, Atlantis, MG Road ☎0484/369423; and Alliance NEPC in the Chandrika Building, also on MG Road ☎0484/367720.

Airlines, international: Air India, 35/1301 MG Rd, Ravipuram ☎0484/351295; British Airways, c/o Nijhwan Travels, MG Road ☎0484/364867; Air France, Alard Building, Wariam Road ☎0484/361702; Egypt Air, c/o ABC International, Old Thevara Road ☎0484/353457; Gulf Air, Bab Chambers, Atlantice Junction, MG Road ☎0484/369142; Kuwait Airways, c/o National Travels, Pulinat Building, MG Road ☎0484/360123; PIA, c/o ABC International, Old Thevara Road ☎0484/353457; Saudi Arabian Airlines, c/o Arafat Travels, MG Road ☎0484/352689; Singapore Airlines & Swissair, Aviation Travels, 35/2433 MG Rd, Ravipuram ☎0484/367911. Spencer & Co, Arya Vaidya Sala Buildings, 35/718 MG Rd ☎0484/362064, are the local agents for Air Maldives, Cathay Pacific, KLM and Northwest Airlines.

Ayurvedic treatment Although widely advertised, the following two come highly recommended – Kerala Ayurveda Pharmacy, Warriom Road, off MG Road (☎0484/361202; Rs350–400 for 1hr 30min), and PNVM Shanthigiri, Thrikkakara (☎0484/558879; Rs250 per session), on the northern outskirts.

Banks along MG Road in Ernakulam include: ANZ Grindlays, the State Bank of India, which also has a branch opposite the KTDC Tourist Reception Centre and the efficient Andhra Bank, which advances money on Visa cards. The State Bank of Travancore is virtually the only place in the state where you can trade in torn bank notes; it also has an evening counter (4–6pm). To exchange travellers' cheques, however, the best place is Thomas Cook (Mon–Sat 9.30am–6pm; ☎0484/373829), near the Air India Building at Palal Towers, MG Road; or try Surana Financial Corporation (☎0484/353724), next door. There's a new 24hr ATM (Visa and Mastercard) in the HDFC building on the junction of MG Road and Ravipuram Road, just south of Thomas Cook.

Bookstores Bhavi Books, Convent Road (☎0484/354003); Higginbothams, TD Road (☎0484/368834); and Pai & Co, MG Road (☎0484/355835), Broadway (☎0484/361020), New Road (☎0484/225607). Idiom Bookstore, opposite the Synagogue, Jew Town, Mattancherry and on Bastion Street near Princess Street, Fort Cochin (☎0484/220432; this branch also deals in secondhand books) is a wonderful place to browse for books on travel, Indian and Keralan culture, flora and fauna, religion and art and there's an excellent range of non-fiction.

Cinemas Sridhar Theatre, Shanmughan Road, near the Hotel Sealord, screens English-language movies daily; check the listings pages of the Indian Express or Hindu (Kerala edition) to find out what's on. For the latest Malayalam and Hindi releases, head for the comfortable a/c Mymoon Cinema at the north end of Chitoor Road, or the Saritha Savitha Sangeetha, at the top of Market Road.

Handicrafts CI Company, Broadway
(☎0484/352405), Kairali (☎0484/354507), Khadi
Bhavan (☎0484/355279), Khataisons Curio Palace
(☎0484/369414), Surabhi Kerala State
Handicrafts (☎0484/382278). Coir carpets can be
found at the Coirboard Showroom. All these shops
are on MG Road. For good quality Keralan,
Portuguese and Dutch antiques, head over to Jew
Street, although you'll have to bargain extremely
hard.

Hospitals General, Hospital Road
(☎0484/360002); City, MG Road
(☎0484/368970); Government, Fort Cochin
(☎0484/224444).

Internet access is available on almost every
street in the city, including Fort Cochin (all charge
Rs60/hr), where it is available in travel agencies
and hotel receptions around Princess Street – just
look out for the sign ouside. In Ernakulam, the
most efficient and speedy internet point (Rs30/hr)
is on the third floor, Pepta Menaka Complex,
Shanmugham Road.

Music stores Sargam, XL/6816 GSS Complex,
Convent Road, opposite the Public Library
(☎0484/374216), stocks the best range of music
tapes in the state, mostly Indian (Hindi films and
lots of Keralan devotional music), with a couple of
shelves of Western rock and pop. Music world,
MKV Building, MG Road (☎0484/355632) is
Cochin's answer to a music superstore with
Western pop, classical, compilations, world music
and Indian *filmi* music. Sound of Melody, DH Road,
near the Ernakulam Junction station, also has a
good selection of traditional South Indian and contemporary Western music. Sea Breeze, 248, GCDA
Complex, Marine Drive (☎0484/362561), is a
smart upmarket shop with a strong emphasis on
Western music.

Musical instruments Manual Industries, Bannerji
Road, Kacheripady Junction (☎0484/352513), is
the best for Indian classical instruments. For traditional Keralan drums, ask at Thripunitra bazaar
(see below).

Photography City Camera, Lovedale Building,
Padma Junction, MG Road (☎0484/380109),
repair cameras and come recommended; Krishnan
Nair Bros, Convent Road (☎0484/352098), stocks
the best range of camera film, including black and
white, Kodachrome and Fujichrome and professional colour transparency; Royal Studio,
Shanmugham Road (☎0484/351614), is also
worth a try. Several others are located along MG
and Shanmugham roads.

Police The city's tourist police have a counter at
the railway station and are on hand to answer
queries and assist if you get into difficulties.

Post office The head post office is on Hospital
Road, not far from the Main Jetty (Mon–Fri
8.30am–8pm, Sat 9.30am–2.30pm & 4–8pm, Sun
10am–4pm); the city's poste restante is at the
GPO, behind St Francis Church in Fort Cochin.

Tour and travel agents Clipper Holidays,
40/6531 Convent Rd (☎0484/364443), are experienced agents good for wildlife and adventure
tours in Kerala and Karnataka. Trio Travels,
XL/180 Hospital Rd (☎0484/369571), is a friendly tour operator which organizes local sightseeing
and backwater tours as well as trips into the
interior. Other all-round travel agents specializing
in tours and air-ticketing include Travel
Corporation of India, MG Road (☎0484/351646),
Princy World Travels, Marine Drive
(☎0484/352751), Trade Wings, MG Road
(☎0484/367938), and Pioneer Travels, Bristow
Road (☎0484/666148).

Around Kochi and Ernakulam

Within easy distance of Kochi and Ernakulam are the small suburban town of
Thripunitra, a former royal seat, and the three-kilometre stretch of sand called
Cherai Beach, which offers a taste of both beach- and backwater-life. Visitors
to Kochi and Ernakulam who really want to get away from it all, however, and
have time and a lot of money to spare, could do no better than to head from
here for Lakshadweep (see p.422), the "one hundred thousand islands", which
lie between 200km and 400km offshore, in the deep blue of the Arabian Sea.

Thripunitra

THRIPUNITRA, 12km southeast of Ernakulam, is worth a visit for its
colonial-style **Hill Palace** (Tues–Sun 9am–12.30pm & 2–4.30pm), now an
eclectic museum a short auto-rickshaw ride from the busy bus stand. The royal
family of Cochin at one time maintained around forty palaces; this one was
confiscated by the state government after Independence, and has slipped into
dusty decline over the past decade.

For an overview of travel services to and from Kochi/Ernakulam, see Travel Details on p.424.

By air

The new international airport (℡484/610050, 610115, or 610116) at Nedumbassery, near Alwaye (aka Alua) 26km to the north of Ernakulam has been designed to attract international flights, especially from the Gulf. Jet Airways has three flights a day to Mumbai, and Indian Airlines operates daily flights to Mumbai, Bangalore, Delhi and Thiruvananthapuram. Jet Airways flies daily and Indian Airlines flies six days a week to Chennai; Indian Airlines flies twice a week to Goa, Coimbatore, Hyderabad and Calicut. If you want to fly to the Lakshadweep Islands contact *Casino Hotel*, Willingdon Island (℡0484/666821; see p.389). Indian Airlines flies twice each week to Doha, Sharjah, Kuwait and Muscat. For details of airlines and travel agents, see Listings on p.398.

The Indian Airlines "red eye" flight to Mumbai every Tuesday at 2.30am gets you there in time for the 7.10am Air India flight direct to New York or London.

By bus

Buses leave Ernakulam's KSRTC Central bus stand for virtually every town in Kerala, and some beyond; most, but not all, are bookable in advance at the bus station, reservation enquiries (℡0484/372033). Travelling south, dozens of buses each day run to Thiruvananthapuram; most go via Alappuzha and Kollam, but a few go via Kottayam. It is also possible to travel all the way to Kanniyakumari (9hr). However, for destinations further afield in Karnataka and Tamil Nadu, you're much better off on the train, although KSRTC's "super express" and private "luxury" buses travel to these destinations. If travelling to Mysore, go early to book a seat on the 8pm bus (10hr). One of several private luxury bus companies travelling daily between Kochi/Ernakulam and Mangalore, as well as to Bangalore, is Sharma Travels, based at the Grand Hotel near Jos Junction, MG Road (℡0484/350712) and Indira Travels, Jos Junction (℡0484/360693). NTC Travels at Jos Junction (℡0484/370046) runs daily luxury buses to Madurai; and SMP Travels, Jos Junction (℡0484/353080) travels daily to Chennai.

By train

Kochi lies on Kerala's main broad-gauge line, and sees frequent trains down the coast to Thiruvananthapuram, via Kottayam, Kollam and Varkala. Heading north, there are plenty of services to Thrissur, and thence northeast across Tamil Nadu to

---

One of the museum's finest exhibits is an early seventeenth-century wooden *mandapa* (pavillion) removed from a temple in Pathanamthitta, featuring fine carvings of the coronation of the monkey king Sugriva and other themes from the *Ramayana*. Of interest too are the silver filigree jewel boxes, gold and silver ornaments, and ritual objects associated with grand ceremonies. The **epigraphy** gallery contains an eighth-century Jewish *Torah*, and Keralan stone and copper-plate inscriptions. Sculpture, ornaments and weapons in the **bronze** gallery include a *kingini katti* knife, whose decorative bells belie the fact that it was used for beheading, and a body-shaped cage in which condemned prisoners would be hanged for birds to peck them to death. Providing the place isn't over-run with noisy school groups, you could check out the nearby **deer park**, and the **garden** behind the palace is a peaceful spot to picnic beneath the cashew trees.

Performances of theatre, classical music and dance, including consecutive all-night Kathakali performances, are held over a period of several days during the

Chennai, but only a couple run north to Mangalore, where a poorly served branch line veers inland to Hassan and Mysore in Karnataka.

Although most long-distance express and mail trains depart from Ernakulam Junction, a short way southeast of the city centre, a couple of key services leave from Ernakulam Town, 2km north. To confuse matters further, some also start at Cochin Harbour station, on Willingdon Island, so be sure to check the departure point when you book your ticket. The main reservation office, good for trains leaving all three stations, is at Ernakulam Junction (⊕0484/390920; (131 for general enquiries).

The trains listed below are recommended as the fastest and/or most convenient services from Kochi. If you're heading to Alappuzha for the backwater trip to Kollam, take the bus, as the only train that can get you there in time invariably arrives late. With the opening of the Konkan Railway, a number of superfast trains travel along the coast to Goa and beyond.

Recommended trains from Kochi/Ernakulam

Destination	Name	Number	Station	Frequency	Departs	Total time
Bangalore	Kanniyakumari–Bangalore Express	#6525	ET	daily	4.40pm	14hr
Mumbai	Kanniyakumari Express	#1081	EJ	daily	12.35pm	40hr
Chennai	Trivandrum–Chennai Mail	#6320	ET	daily	7.05pm	13hr
Delhi	Rajdhani Express*	#2431	EJ	Fri & Sat	11.40pm	40hr 30min
	Kerala Express	#2625	EJ	daily	3.50pm	48hr 45min
Goa	Rajdhani Express*	#2431	EJ	Tues & Thurs	11.40pm	12hr 35min
	Mangala–Lakshadweep Express	#2617	EJ	daily	12.15pm	16hr 18min
Mangalore	Malabar Express	#6329	ET	daily	10.53pm	10hr 30min
	Parasuram Express	#6349	ET	daily	10.50am	10hr
Thiruvanantha-puram	Parasuram Express	#6350	EJ	daily	1.55pm	4hr 55min
Varkala	Parasuram Express	#6350	EJ	daily	1.55pm	3hr 43min

EJ = Ernakulam Junction
ET = Ernakulam Town
* = a/c only, meals included.

annual **festival** (Oct/Nov) at the **Shri Purnatrayisa** temple, on the way to the palace. Inside the temple compound, both in the morning and at night, massed drum orchestras perform *chenda melam* in procession with fifteen caparisoned elephants (decked out in golden regalia). At night, the outside walls of the sanctuary are covered with thousands of tiny oil lamps. Although the temple is normally closed to non-Hindus, admittance to appropriately dressed visitors (women should wear a sari; men must wear a *lungi* and remove their shirt) is usually allowed at this time.

Cherai Beach

The closest decent beach to Kochi is **Cherai Beach**, 35km to the north. The beach shelters a backwater and supports an active fishing community, some of whom use Chinese fishing nets (see p.393). The **Sri Goureeswara Temple**, closed to non-Hindus, is dedicated to the deity Sri Subramanya Swami and holds its annual nine-day festival (*utsavam*) between January and February each year. The *utsavam* is a great time to see traditional dance, including Kathakali performances, but the highlight of the festival is on the seventh day, when eighteen caparisoned elephants take to the streets in a spectacular procession. Ask at a tourist office in Kochi for details on dates.

To get to Cherai Beach, take a ferry to Vypeen Island and then a bus for 18km to the Devaswamnada Junction near Cherai, from where an auto-rickshaw will cost around Rs20 for the three-kilometre journey to the beach. You can stay at the north end of the beach, at *Sea Men's Cottage* (☎0484/489795; ❸), a quiet place offering a couple of double rooms and a café, which serves up seafood on demand. Trio Travels in Ernakulam (☎0484/353234) organizes trips to the area including boat trips on the backwaters.

Thrissur

The pleasant town of **THRISSUR** (Trichur), roughly midway between Kochi, 74km south, and Palakaad, 79km northeast, is an obvious base for exploring the cultural riches of central Kerala. Due to its convenient location near the Palghat (Palakaad) Gap – an opening between Kerala and Tamil Nadu in the natural border made by the Southern Ghat mountain range – it presided over the main trade route into the region from Tamil Nadu and Karnataka. For years Thrissur was the capital of Cochin State, controlled at various times by both the *zamorin* of Kozhikode and Tipu Sultan of Mysore.

Modern Thrissur dates from the eighteenth century, when Raja Rama Varma (aka the Maharajah Sakthan Thampuran), renowned as the "architect of Thrissur", developed the city, laying out roads and establishing markets with which Christian merchants were invited to trade. Although a Hindu himself, the Raja helped further ensure the welfare of the Christian communities by establishing Christian enclaves to the east and south of the city centre. The majority of the Christians living here today are Catholic, but there is also a small and unique pocket of Nestorians (see p.370).

Today, Thrissur prides itself as the cultural capital of Kerala and is home to several influential art institutions. The town centres on Kerala's largest temple complex, **Vaddukanatha**, surrounded by a *maidan* (green) that sees all kinds of public gatherings, not least Kerala's most extravagant, noisy and sumptuous festival, **Puram**.

Arrival and information

The principal point of **orientation** in Thrissur is the **Round**, a huge and busy roundabout subdivided into North, South, East and West, which encircles the Vaddukanatha temple and *maidan* at the centre. Once you've established which side of the Round you're on, you can save yourself long walks along the busy pavement by striking out across the green in the middle.

Thrissur's **railway station**, 1km southwest of Round South, is on the mainline to Chennai and other points in Tamil Nadu, and also has good connections to Kochi and Thiruvananthapuram. There are three main bus stands in Thrissur: the **KSRTC long-distance bus stand**, near the railway station; **Priya Darshini** (also known as "North", "Shoranur" and "Wadakkancheri") bus stand, close to Round North, which serves Palakaad and Shoranur; and the **Shakthan Thampuran** stand, on TB Road, 1km from Round South, which serves local destinations south of Thrissur such as Irinjalakuda, Kodungallur and Guruvayur.

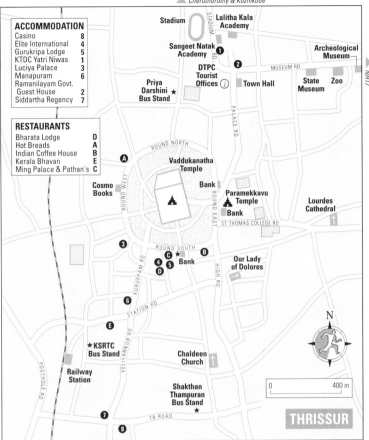

ACCOMMODATION

Casino	8
Elite International	4
Gurukripa Lodge	5
KTDC Yatri Niwas	1
Luciya Palace	3
Manapuram	6
Ramanilayam Govt. Guest House	2
Siddartha Regency	7

RESTAURANTS

Bharata Lodge	D
Hot Breads	A
Indian Coffee House	B
Kerala Bhavan	E
Ming Palace & Pathan's	C

Stadium

Lalitha Kala Academy

Sangeet Natak Academy

Archeological Museum

DTPC Tourist Offices (i)

Town Hall

State Museum

Zoo

Priya Darshini Bus Stand

MUSEUM RD

PALACE RD

STADIUM RD

NH17

ROUND NORTH

Vaddukanatha Temple

Cosmo Books

Bank

Paramekkavu Temple

Bank

Lourdes Cathedral

ROUND WEST

ROUND EAST

ST THOMAS COLLEGE RD

ROUND SOUTH

Bank

Our Lady of Dolores

KURUPPAM RD

HIGH RD

STATION RD

★ KSRTC Bus Stand

Chaldeen Church

VELIYANNUR RD

Railway Station

POOTHOLE RD

Shakthan Thampuran Bus Stand

N

0   400 m

THRISSUR

4

KERALA | Thrissur

The DTPC **tourist office** on Palace Road, opposite the Town Hall (Mon–Sat 10am–5pm), is where you can pick up maps of Thrissur, but little else. It's run on a voluntary basis and its primary purpose is to promote the elephant festival. KTDC have a small information counter at their hotel *Yatri Niwas*, Stadium Road (Mon–Sat 10am–5pm; ☎0487/332333). If you need to **change money**, the main branch of the State Bank of Travancore, next to the Paramekkavu temple (Mon–Fri 10am–2pm, Sat 10am–noon), accepts American Express travellers' cheques, but not Thomas Cook, currency or credit cards. Opposite the same temple near the Sapna Theatre, the State Bank of India (same hours) changes dollars, sterling and travellers' cheques, as does the Canara Bank (same hours) on Round South. The **GPO** lies on the southern edge of town, near the *Casino Hotel* off TB Road. **Internet** access is available at the excellent Internet Thissur.com on the second floor of City Centre Shopping Complex, Round West (daily 9am–10pm; Rs45/hr), while Space Net at the United Shopping Complex, Shankar Agar Road, Poothole charges Rs50/hr.

Accommodation

Thrissur has a fair number of mid-price **hotels**, but only a couple of decent budget places. The best bargain in this bracket is the palatial *Ramanilayam Government Rest House*, which offers star-hotel comfort at economy lodge rates but the constant stream of government officials gets priority. Almost all of Thrissur's hotels follow a 24hr checkout policy.

Casino, TB Road, near the railway station ℡0487/424699, ℻442037. Once Thrissur's poshest hotel but it has seen better days; the rooms are decent (non-a/c and a/c) and there's a multi-cuisine restaurant, bar and foreign exchange (residents only). ❺–❼

Elite International, Chembottil Lane, off Round South ℡0487/421033. Pronounced *Ee-light*. A big tower block of standard rooms, with friendly staff, a good restaurant and some balconied rooms overlooking the green (booked months ahead for Puram, when they cost ten times more than normal). ❹–❼

Gurukripa Lodge, Chembottil Lane, off Round South ℡0487/421895. Lots of rooms (including several great-value singles) in a large compound, all painted in blue; the non-a/c rooms are all large and simple with cool tiled floors and attached bathrooms. Recommended. ❷

KTDC Yatri Niwas, off Museum Road ℡0487/332333. Friendly motel-type place with spotless rooms (some a/c and with cable TV), a beer parlour and restaurant. ❷–❹

Luciya Palace, Marar Road ℡0487/424731, ℻427290. Recently revamped Neoclassical/tradi-

tional Keralan fantasy; a good mid-range choice. Some a/c rooms, but the standard non-a/c rooms, with coir mats and cane furniture, are the best deals. Single occupancy rates available. ❺–❼

Manapuram, Kuruppam Road ℡0487/440933. Modern and efficient two-star business hotel in the heart of a lively market area. A good range of rooms with cable TV, some a/c, and a few singles. Boasts two restaurants; credit cards are accepted. ❺–❼

Ramanilayam Government Rest House, Palace Road ℡0487/332016. Very good-value, huge, clean, comfortable suites with balconies; non-a/c rooms are a mere Rs45 while a/c doubles cost Rs275. It's officially for VIPs, and they're not obliged to give you a room, but smart clothes will help. It's hugely popular, and often full; the rate doubles after five nights. Breakfast is served; other meals by advance order only. ❶–❸

Siddartha Regency, Veliyannur Road, Kokkalai ℡0487/424773. Centrally a/c and comfortable Indian tourist-orientated hotel in the southwestern corner of town, near the railway, KSRTC and Shakthan Thampuran bus stations. Restaurant, a bar and gardens. ❻–❼

The Town

The focus of Thrissur is the **Vaddukanatha temple** (closed to non-Hindus) a walled complex of fifteen shrines, dating from the twelfth century and earlier, the principal of which is dedicated to Shiva. Inside the walls, the grassy compound is surprisingly quiet and spacious, with a striking apsidal shrine dedicated to Ayappa (see box on p.373). Sadly, many of the temple's treasures, such as the wood-carvings and murals, are not as well maintained as they might be. Once an essential ingredient of the temple's cultural life, but now underused and neglected, the long, sloping-roofed **Kuttambalam theatre** (closed to non-Hindus), with carved panels and lathe-turned wooden pillars, is the venue for the ancient Sanskrit performance forms of Chakyar Kuttu and Kutiyattam.

The **State Museum** and **Zoo** (both Tues–Sun 10am–5pm; Rs2) stand together on Museum Road, ten minutes' walk from the temple. Although small, the museum has excellent local bronzes, jewellery, fine wood-carvings of fanged temple guardians and a profusion of bell-metal oil lamps. The zoo, however, houses a miserable collection of tenants and, although it can be grimly fascinating to observe the variety of snakes that slither locally (king cobra, krait, viper), you may also be expected to watch an attendant prod cobras with a stick so they spit at the glass that separates you from them. Next door to the *Yatri Niwas*, the **Kerala Sangeet Natak Academy** (℡0487/332548) has a large auditorium where occasional music and dance concerts are held, as well as Keralan theatre, which has an enthusiastic following and tends to be heavily political. Around the corner is the **Kerala Lalitha Kala Academy** (daily 10am–6pm; free) whose gallery often holds exhibitions of contemporary Indian art.

One of the most important churches for Thrissur's large Christian population is the Syrian Catholic **Lourdes Cathedral**, along St Thomas College Road. Three daily masses serve a regular congregation of nine hundred. Like many of Kerala's Indo-Gothic churches, the exterior of dome and spires is more impressive than the interior, with its unadorned metal rafters and corrugated iron ceiling. Steps lead down from the altar to the crypt, a rather dilapidated copy of the grotto in Lourdes. The **Church of Our Lady of Dolores**, a short way to the south of the Round, is another important Catholic church and boasts Neo-Gothic spires and the largest interior of any church in South India. Slightly further south, the **Chaldean Church** (services Mon–Sat 7am–9am & Sun 7.30am–9.30am), dedicated to Mary, is the most ancient of all Keralan Christian centres; it is the focal point of the unique Nestorian Syrian community, which also runs a school here. Not much of the original structure remains, as the church was extensively renovated in the nineteenth century. Owing to this renovation the gabled facade is the most remarkable part of what remains of the original structure. The friendly and welcoming office by the entrance to the church will open the door to the church for you. Inside, the plain chamber is hung with chandeliers and the extraordinary pulpit is ornately carved in teak.

Shopping

Thrissur is a great place to pick up distinctive Keralan **crafts**. The main shopping area is on the Round; on Round West, the Kerala State Handicraft Emporium specializes in wood, while a few doors along a small branch of Khadi Gramodyog sells a limited range of handloom cloth. A far better selection of handloom can be found in Co-optex at the top of Palace Road. At Chemmanur's, Round South, near the *Elite International Hotel*, you'll find the usual carved-wooden-elephant-type souvenirs, and, on the ground floor, a kitsch Aladdin's Cave of nodding dogs, Jesus clocks, Mecca table ornaments and parabolic nail-and-string art. Sportsland, further west on Round South, aside from sports equipment, also sells crudely painted wooden toys, such as buses and cars. Alter Media at Utility Building, Nehru Bazaar, Nayarangadi, is a small but interesting bookshop, devoted to women's studies. **Cosmos Books**, on Round West, is a treasure-trove of romantic novels, die-hard academic criticism and books on art, drama and culture; you can even buy the latest edition of *Vogue* – at a price.

Kuruppam Road, which leads south towards the train station from the western end of Round South, is one of the best places in Kerala to buy **bell-metal** products, particularly oil lamps made in the village of Nadavaramba, near Irinjalakuda (see box on p.410). Nadavaramba Krishna & Sons and Bell-metal Craft both specialize in brass, bronze and bell-metal. Lamps cost Rs80–25,000, and "superfine" bell-metal is sold by weight, at over Rs250 per kilo. Continuing south on Kuruppam Road to the next junction with Railway Station Road, you'll find a number of small shops selling cheap Christian, Muslim and Hindu pictures etched on metal, and places that supply festival accessories, including umbrellas similar to those used for Puram (see p.406).

Thrissur is best known to outsiders as the venue for Kerala's biggest annual festival, Puram, which takes place on one day in April/May (ask at a tourist office for the exact date). Introduced by the Kochi (Cochin) Raja, Shaktan Tampuran (1789–1803), Puram is today the most extreme example of the kind of celebration seen on a smaller scale all over Kerala, whose main ingredients invariably include caparisoned elephants, drum music and fireworks.

On this day, at the hottest time of year, the centre of Thrissur fills to capacity as a sea of people gravitate towards Round South, where a long wide path leads to the southern entrance of the Vaddukanatha temple complex. Two majestic processions, representing the Tiruvambadi and Paramekkavu temples in Thrissur, compete to create the more impressive sights and sounds. They eventually meet, like armies on a battlefield, facing each other at either end of the path. Both sides present fifteen tuskers sumptuously decorated with gold ornaments, each ridden by three brahmins clutching objects symbolizing royalty: silver-handled whisks of yak hair, circular peacock feather fans and orange, green, red, purple, turquoise, black, gold or patterned silk umbrellas fringed with silver pendants. At the centre of each group, the principal elephant carries an image of the temple's deity. Swaying gently, the elephants stand still much of the time, ears flapping, seemingly oblivious to the mayhem engendered by the crowds, bomb-like firework bangs and the huge orchestra that plays in front of them.

Known as chenda melam, this quintessentially Keralan music, featuring as many as a hundred loud, hard-skinned, cylindrical *chenda* drums, crashing cymbals and wind instruments, mesmerizes the crowd while its structure marks the progress of the procession. Each kind of *chenda melam* is named after the rhythmic cycle (*tala* or, in Malayalam, *talam*) in which it is set. Drummers stand in ranks, the most numerous at the back often playing single beats. At the front, a line of master drummers, the stars of Keralan music, try to outdo each other with their speed, stamina, improvizational skills and showmanship. Facing the drummers, musicians play long double-reed, oboe-like *kuzhals* (similar to the North Indian *shehnai*) and C-shaped *kompu* bell-metal trumpets. The fundamental structure is provided by the *elatalam* – medium-sized, heavy, brass band cymbals that resolutely and precisely keep the

Eating and drinking

Thrissur's big **hotels** offer Indian, Western and Chinese food, and Keralan lunches, while several quality, inexpensive "meals" places are clustered near the **Round**. Late at night, on the corner of Round South and Round East, opposite the Medical College Hospital, you'll find a string of chai and omelette stalls, frequented by auto-rickshaw-wallahs, hospital visitors, itinerant mendicants, Ayappa devotees and student revellers.

Bharata Lodge, Chembottil Lane, next door to *Elite Hotel*. Excellent South Indian breakfasts, evening snacks and unlimited Keralan "meals" at lunch time. Inexpensive.

Bimbi's, *Hotel Manapuram*. A branch of the popular Kochi South Indian fast-food joint; dependably fresh, hot meals, snacks, ice creams, sweets and a good sociable atmosphere.

Hot Breads, ground floor, City Centre Shopping Complex, Round West. A pukka branch of the excellent South Indian bakery chain with a chic café area, selling delicious stuffed savoury

croissants, fresh breads, cream cakes and biscuits, and veg or non-veg doughy pizzas.

Indian Coffee House, Round South. The better of two in town; it's very busy and serves snacks, meals and excellent filter coffee. The branch on Station Road is very run-down.

Kerala Bhavan, Railway Station Road. Recommended for breakfast and cheap Keralan "meals". A 10min walk south of Round South (most rickshaw-wallahs know where it is).

Luciya Palace, Marar Road ☏ 0487/424731. Indian and Chinese dishes. The main appeal is that

tempo, essential to the cumulative effect of the music. Over an extended period, the *melam* passes through four phases of tempo, each a double of the last, from a grand and graceful dead slow through to a frenetic pace.

The arrival of the fastest tempo is borne on a wave of aural and visual stimulation. Those astride the elephants stand at this point, to manipulate their feather fans and hair whisks in coordinated sequence, while behind, unfurled umbrellas are twirled in flashes of dazzling colour and glinting silver in the sun. Meanwhile, the cymbals crash furiously, often raised above the head, requiring extraordinary stamina (and causing nasty weals on the hands). The master drummers play their loudest and fastest, frequently intensified by surges of energy emanating from single players, one after another. A chorus of trumpets, in ragged unison, accompanies the cacophony, creating a sound that has altered little since the origins of this jubilant festival.

All this is greeted by tremendous firework explosions and roars from the crowd; many people punch the air, while others are clearly *talam branthans*, rhythm "madmen", who follow every nuance of the structure. When the fastest speed is played out, the slowest tempo returns and the procession edges forward, the *mahouts* leading the elephants by the tusk. Stopping again, the whole cycle is repeated. At night, the Vaddukanatha temple entrances are a blaze of coloured lights and a spectacular firework display takes place in the early hours of the morning.

If you venture to Thrissur for Puram, be prepared for packed buses and trains. Needless to say, hotel accommodation should be booked well in advance and be aware that room rates sky-rocket for the few days around the festival; if you are on a budget it is better to just visit on the day itself. An umbrella or hat and a good supply of water is highly recommended. Female visitors are advised to dress conservatively and to either watch the festivities in the morning, go with a group, or stand with the Keralan women, who maintain a safe distance.

Similar but much smaller events take place, generally from September onwards, with most during the summer (April & May). Enquire at a tourist office or your hotel, or ask someone to check a local edition of the newspaper, *Mathrabhumi*, for local performances of *chenda melam* and other drum orchestras such as *panchavadyam* and *tyambaka*.

they serve dinner in the evening in a pleasant garden illuminated by fairy lights.

Ming Palace, Pathan Building, Round South. Inexpensive "Chindian", serving chop suey, noodles and lots of chicken and veg dishes; dim lighting and cheesy muzak.

Pathan's, Round South. Deservedly popular veg restaurant, with a cosy a/c family (female) annexe and a large canteen-like dining hall. Generous portions and plenty of choice, including *koftas*, kormas and lots of tandoori options, as well as Keralan thalis and wonderful Kashmiri naan.

Around Thrissur

The chief appeal of exploring the area around Thrissur is for the chances it provides to get to grips with Kerala's cultural heritage. Countless festivals, at their peak before the monsoon hits in May, enable visitors to catch some of the best drummers in the world, **Kathakali** dance drama (see p.706) and **Kutiyattam**, the world's oldest surviving theatre form (see p.708).

Irinjalakuda

The village of **IRINJALAKUDA**, 20km south of Thrissur, has a unique temple five minutes' walk west from the bus stand, dedicated to **Bharata**, the brother of Rama. Visitors are usually permitted to see inside (men must wear a *dhoti*) but, as elsewhere, the inner parts of the temple are closed to non-Hindus. It boasts a superbly elegant tiled *kuttambalam* **theatre** within its outer courtyard, built to afford an unimpeded view for the maximum number of spectators (drawn from the highest castes only), and known for excellent acoustics. A profusion of painted wood-carvings of mythological animals and stories from the epics decorates the interior. On the low stage, which is enclosed by painted wooden columns and friezes of female dancers, stand two large copper *mizhavu* drums, for use in the Sanskrit drama *Kutiyattam* (see p.708), permanently installed in wooden frames into which a drummer climbs to play. Traditionally, *mizhavus* were considered sacred objects; Nandikeshvara, Shiva's rhythm expert and accompanist, was said to reside in them. The drama for which they provided music was a holy ritual, and in the old days the instrument was never allowed to leave the temple and only played by members of a special caste, the Nambyars. Since then, outsiders have learned the art of *mizhavu* playing; some are based near the temple, but the orthodox authorities do not allow them to play inside.

Natana Kairali is an important cultural centre dedicated to the performance, protection and documentation of Kerala's lesser known but fascinating and vibrant theatre arts, including Kutiyattam, Nangiar Koothu (female monoacting) and shadow and puppet theatres. Left of the Bharata temple as you leave, it is based in the home of one of Kerala's most illustrious acting families, Ammanur Chakyar Madhom; cite that name when you ask for directions. Natana Kairali's director, Shri G. Venu (℡0488/825559), is a mine of information about Keralan arts, and can advise on forthcoming performances.

Irinjalakuda is best reached by **bus** from the Shakthan Thampuran stand at Thrissur rather than by train, as the train station is an inconvenient 8km east of town.

Kodungallur

Virtually an island, surrounded by backwaters and the sea, the small country town of **KODUNGALLUR** (Cranganore), 35km south of Thrissur, is rich in Keralan history. The dearth of information regarding the modern town contrasts with tales of its illustrious past. Kodungallur has been identified as the site of the ancient cities of **Vanji**, one-time capital of the Chera kingdom, and **Muziris**, described in the first century AD by the Roman traveller, Pliny, as *primum emporium Indiae*, the most important port in India. Other accounts describe the harbour as crowded with great ships, warehouses, palaces, temples and *Yavanas* (a generic term for foreigners) who brought gold and left with spices, sandalwood, teak, gems and silks. The Romans are said to have built a temple in Kodungallur; nothing remains, but their presence has been shown through finds of coins, the majority of which date from the reigns of Augustus to Nero (27 BC–68 AD). Its life as a great port was curtailed in 1341 by floods that silted up the harbour, leading to the development of Kochi (Cochin). Today, travellers will find that Kodungallur's "sights", with one exception, require some imagination. The town is best visited in a day-trip by **bus** from Thrissur's Shakthan Thampuran stand (1hr 30min), or en route between Thrissur and Kochi.

Standing on a large piece of open ground at the centre of Kodungallur, the ancient and typically Keralan **Kurumba Bhagavati temple** is the site of an extraordinary annual event that some residents would prefer didn't happen at all. The **Bharani** festival, held during the Malayalam month of Meenom

(March/April), attracts droves of devotees, both male and female, mainly from "low caste" communities previously excluded from the temple. Their devotions consist in part of drinking copious amounts of alcohol and taking to the streets to sing Bharani *pattu*, sexually explicit songs about, and addressed to, the goddess Bhagavati, which are considered obscene and highly offensive by many other Keralans. On Kavuthindal, the first day, the pilgrims run en masse around the perimeters of the temple three times at breakneck speed, beating its walls with sticks. Until the mid-1950s, chickens were sacrificed in front of the temple; today, a simple red cloth symbolizes the bloody ritual. An important section of the devotees are the crimson-clad village oracles, wielding scythe-like swords with which they sometimes beat themselves on the head in ecstatic fervour, often drawing blood. Despite widespread disapproval, the festival draws plenty of spectators.

Cheraman Juma Masjid, 1.5km south of Kodungallur centre on NH-17, is thought to be the earliest mosque in India, founded in the seventh century by **Cheraman Perumal**, the legendary Keralan king who converted to Islam, abdicated and emigrated to Mecca. The supposed site of his palace, Cheraman Parambu, is today nothing more than a few broken columns on open ground. The present building, which dates from the sixteenth century, was until recently predominantly made of wood, of a style usually associated with Keralan Hindu temples. Unfortunately, due to weather damage, it has recently had to be partly rebuilt, and the facade, at least, is now rather mundane, with concrete minarets. The wooden interior remains intact, however, with a large Keralan oil lamp in the centre. Introduced five centuries ago for group study of the Koran, the lamp has taken on great significance to other communities, and Muslims, Christians and Hindus alike bring oil for the lamp on the auspicious occasion of major family events. In an anteroom, a small mausoleum is said to be the burial place of Habib Bin Malik, an envoy sent from Mecca by the convert king Cheraman Perumal. Women are not allowed into the mosque at any time ("they pray at home"), but interested male visitors should contact the assistant *mukhari* (*imam*, or priest), K.M. Saidumohamed, who lives directly opposite and will show you around.

Less than 500m south from the Cheraman Juma Masjid, past a bend in the main highway (NH-17), a wide avenue leads past tall lamps to the **Mahadeva Temple**, dedicated to the god Shiva at Thirvanchikulam. A fine example of Keralan temple architecture, the temple allows access to the outer courtyard via a majestic gateway with a sloping roof and carvings of elephants, protective deities, gods and goddesses. Inside the enclosure, past a large multitiered metal lamp, a porch adorned with carvings dedicated to the heroes of the great Hindu epic, the *Ramayana*, marks the furthest non-Hindus are allowed. Within the restricted enclosure, an impressive columned hall shelters Shiva's ever faithful bull Nandi, and the inner sanctum houses a plain stone *lingam*. Despite the restriction, low retaining walls allow a good view of the extensive complex, which is well worth the short detour. Be careful of the heavy traffic, however, when walking along the narrow highway between the mosque and the temple.

The **Mar Thoma Pontifical Shrine**, fronted by a crescent of Neoclassical colonnades at Azhikode (pronounced "Arikode") Jetty (6km), marks the place where the Apostle Thomas is said to have arrived in India in 52AD, soon after the death of Christ. Despite the ugly waterside promenade and the tacky visitor centre it is a moving spot, on the edge of backwaters, but not worth a detour unless you're desperate to see the shard of the saint's wrist bone enshrined within the church.

Keralan nights are made more enchanting by the use of oil lamps. The most common type, seen all over the state, is a slim free-standing metal column surmounted by a spike that rises from a circular receptacle for coconut oil, using cloth or banana plant fibre wicks. Every classical theatre performance keeps a large lamp burning centre-stage all night. The special atmosphere of temples is also enhanced by innumerable lamps, some hanging from chains; others, *deepa stambham*, are multitiered and stand metres high.

The village of Nadavaramba, near Irinjalakuda, is an important centre for the manufacture of oil lamps and large cooking vessels, known as *uruli* and *varppu*. Alloys made from brass, copper and tin are frequently used, but the best are made from bell-metal, said to be eighty percent copper, which give a sonorous chime when struck. Shops in Thrissur that specialize in Nadavaramba ware will arrange visits to see the craftsmen at work.

If you want **to stay** at Kodungallur, the *Hotel Indraprastham* close to the town centre (℡0488/602678; ❷–❹) has standard non-a/c and a/c rooms as well as a cheap "meals" restaurant and an a/c "family" restaurant and they also have a bar.

Guruvayur

Kerala's most important Krishna shrine, the high-walled temple of **GURU-VAYUR** (3am–1pm & 4–10pm; closed to non-Hindus), 29km northwest of Thrissur, attracts a constant flow of pilgrims, second only in volume to Ayappa's at Sabarimala (see box on p.373). Its deity, **Guruvayurappan**, has inspired numerous paeans from Keralan poets, most notably Narayana Bhattatiri, who wrote the *Narayaniyam* in the sixteenth century, when the temple, whose origins are legendary, seems to have first risen to prominence.

One of the richest temples in Kerala, Guruvayur is from very early morning to late at night awash with **pilgrims** in their best white clothes, often trimmed with gold. The market outside is a particularly intense combination of commercial activity, noise and stalls full of glitter and trinkets such as two-rupee plastic Guruvayurappan signet rings, and there is a palpable air of excitement, particularly when events inside spill out into the streets. A temple committee stall outside the main gates auctions off the gifts, including bell-metal lamps, received at the shrine but, according to superstition, if you buy any of these items they must be returned to the temple as gifts.

Of the temple's 24 annual festivals, the most important are Ekadashi and Ulsavam. During the eighteen days of Ekadashi, in the month of Vrischikam (Nov/Dec), marked by processions of caparisoned elephants outside the temple, the exterior of the building may be decorated with the tiny flames of innumerable oil lamps. On certain days (check dates with a KTDC office) programmes staged in front of the temple attract the cream of South Indian classical music artists.

During *Ulsavam*, in the month of Kumbham (Feb/March), tantric rituals are conducted inside, an **elephant race** is run outside on the first day, and elephant processions take place during the ensuing six days. On the ninth day, the Palivetta, or "hunt" occurs; the deity, mounted on an elephant, circumambulates the temple accompanied by men dressed as animals, who represent human weaknesses such as greed and anger, and are vanquished by the god. The next night sees the image of the god taken out for ritual immersion in the temple

The founding of the Guruvayur temple is associated with the end of Krishna's life. After witnessing the massacre of family and compatriots, Krishna returned to his capital, Dvarka, in Gujarat, to end his earthly existence. However, knowing that Dvarka would disappear into the sea on his death, he was concerned that the form of Vishnu there, which he himself worshipped, should be spared its fate.

Krishna invited Brihaspati, also known as Guru, the preceptor of the gods, and a pupil, Vayu, the god of wind, to help him select a new home for Vishnu. By the time they arrived at Dvarka, the sea (Varuna) had already claimed the city, but the wind managed to rescue Vishnu. Krishna, Guru and Vayu travelled south, where they met Parasurama, who had just created Kerala by throwing his axe into the sea. On reaching a beautiful lake of lotuses, Rudratirtha, they were greeted by Shiva and Parvati who consecrated the image of Vishnu; Guru and Vayu then installed it, the temple was named after them, and so the deity received the title Guruvayurappan ("Lord of Guruvayur").

tank; devotees greet the procession with oil lamps and throw rice. It is considered highly auspicious to bathe in the tank at the same time as the god.

The Punnathur Kotta Elephant Sanctuary

When they are not involved in races and other arcane temple rituals, Guruvayur's tuskers hang out at the **Punnathur Kotta Elephant Sanctuary** (daily 9am–6pm; Rs5, Rs25 extra for camera), 4km north of town. Forty elephants, aged from 6 to 93, live here, munching for most of the day on specially imported piles of fodder. Each tusker is faithfully cared for by three personal *mahouts*, who wash and scrub them several times a week in the sanctuary pond – a great photo opportunity. Definitely avoid the bulls on heat – the *mahouts* will warn you which ones they are – as they become aggressive and unpredictable; only approach an elephant if a *mahout* allows you.

All the animals are the personal possession of Lord Guruvayur, given to the temple by wealthy patrons from as far afield as Bihar and Assam. All the elephants – apart from the most elderly who are allowed an honourable retirement – are gainfully employed in local temples, especially at the Guruvayur temple itself. All temples demand pretty elephants for their elaborate festivals, and the competition to rent a particularly favoured pachyderm can become a bitter auction between villages; the standard daily charge of Rs3500 per elephant once reached a record Rs75,000.

Practicalities

Buses from Thrissur (40min) arrive at the main **bus stand** at the top end of E Nada Street, five minutes east of the temple. **Accommodation** is concentrated along this street; it's often packed with pilgrims, but the two KTDC hotels are usually good bets. The pilgrim-oriented KTDC *Anjanam,* near the entrance of the Krishna temple (℗0487/552408; ❷) has basic double non-a/c rooms and a devotional atmosphere. The one-star deluxe, KTDC *Nandanam,* near the railway station (℗0487/556266; ❸–❺), offers clean a/c and non-a/c doubles with a few more creature comforts. The town is crammed with pure veg "meals" **restaurants**, and there is an *Indian Coffee House* on the southern side of E Nada Street that serves South Indian snacks, filter coffee and yet more "meals".

Cheruthuruthy

The village of **CHERUTHURUTHY** is an easy day-trip 32km north of Thrissur through gently undulating green country. It consists of a few lanes and one main street, which runs in a southwards direction from the bank of Kerala's longest river, the **Bharatapuzha** (pronounced *Bharatapura*). Considered holy by Hindus, the great river has receded in recent years, leaving a vast expanse of sand. Although of little consolation to locals, who have to deal with the problems of a depleted water supply, it has produced a landscape of incomparable beauty.

Cheruthuruthy is famous as the home of **Kerala Kalamandalam**, the state's flagship training school for Kathakali and other indigenous Keralan performing arts, which was founded in 1927 by the revered Keralan poet Vallathol (1878–1957). At first patronized by the Raja of Cochin, the school has been funded by both state and national governments and has been instrumental in the large-scale revival of interest in Kathakali, and other unique Keralan art forms. Despite conservative opposition, it followed an open-door recruitment policy, based on artistic merit, which produced "scheduled caste" Muslim and Christian graduates along with the usual Hindu castes, something that was previously unimaginable. During the 1960s, Kalamandalam's dynamic leadership forged international links with cultural organizations. Foreign students were accepted and every attempt was made to modernize, extending into the way in which the traditional arts were presented. Kalamandalam artists perform in the great theatres of the world, many sharing their extraordinary skills with outsiders; luminaries of modern theatre, such as Grotowski and Peter Brook, are indebted to them. Nonetheless, many of these trained artists are still excluded from entering, let alone performing in, temples, a popular venue for Hindu art forms, especially music.

Non-Hindus can see Kathakali, Kutiyattam and Mohiniattam performed in the school's superb theatre, which replicates the wooden, sloping-roofed traditional theatres, known as *kuttambalams*, found in Keralan temples. If you are interested in seeing how this extraordinary technique is taught, don't miss the chance to sit in on the rigorous training sessions, which have to be seen to be believed (Mon–Fri 4.30am–5pm; closed on public holidays). A handful of foreigners each year also come to the Kalamandalam academy to attend full-time **courses** in Kathakali and other traditional dance and theatre forms. Those interested should first apply in writing. Short courses last for a minimum of one month, or there are condensed courses of between three and six months. Full courses usually last between four and six years; foreign students with the necessary student visas are allowed to attend for a maximum of four years. Applications may be made from abroad (write to the Secretary, Kerala Kalamandalam, Vallathol Nagar, Cheruthuruthy, Thrissur Dist, Kerala 679 531), but it's a good idea to visit before committing yourself. The students' lot here is not an easy one – to say the least. For information contact the school office (☎0488/462418, ☏462019).

A good time to visit is during their week-long festival starting on Christmas Day. Held at the *kuttambalam* and at their original riverside campus amongst the trees, the festival presents all the art forms of Kerala and is free, although the dearth of accommodation in the area can be a problem. A short walk past the old campus leads to a small but exquisite **Shiva temple** in classic Keralan style, where the early evening worship, when the exterior is lit with candles, is particularly rewarding.

Practicalities

Cheruthuruthy's **accommodation** is limited, with some students staying as guests in private accommodation or at the new on-site, self-catering

International Hostel (●). The village has a couple of simple guesthouses and the atmospheric *Government Rest House* (℡0488/462760; ●), a short distance along the Shoranur road from Kalamandalam, has eight vast and very basic rooms, some with Western-style toilets, and all sharing a veranda. For a touch of luxury, try the *River Retreat*, on Palace Road (℡0488/462922; ●) with deluxe a/c rooms and a smart a/c multicuisine restaurant in a grand old heritage palace on the banks of the river. Other than the *River Retreat*, the only places to **eat** here are in the simple "meals" shops in the centre of village; of these, the *Mahatma*, serving vegetarian food, is by far the best.

Buses heading to Shoranur from Thrissur's Wadakkancheri stand stop outside Kalamandalam, just before Cheruthuruthy. The nearest **railway** station is Shoranur Junction, 3km to the south. It's on the main line and served by express trains to and from Mangalore, Chennai and all major stations south of here on the coastal route through Kerala.

Palakkad

PALAKKAD (Palghat), surrounded by paddy fields, lies on NH-47 between Thrissur (79km) and Coimbatore, Tamil Nadu (54km), and on the railway line from Karnataka and Tamil Nadu. Historically, thanks to the natural twenty-kilometre-wide Palakkad Gap in the Western Ghats, this area has been one of the chief entry points into Kerala. The environs are beautiful, but the town itself doesn't warrant a stop, other than to break a journey. Arriving from Tamil Nadu, Palakkad, with its dry, Deccan-like landscape, unlike most of the state, gives a misleading first impression of Kerala.

The well-preserved **fort**, built in 1766 by Haider Ali of Mysore, is the nearest thing to a "sight"; it gets plenty of visitors at weekends, despite having little to offer. However, many travellers in search of **Kathakali** and **teyyattam** performances find themselves directed here. Particularly during April and May, hundreds of one-off events take place in the area. The local Government Carnatic Music College has an excellent reputation, and a small open-air amphitheatre next to the fort often hosts first-class music and dance performances. Ask at the tourist office (see below) for details. The landscaped gardens and amusement park at **Malampuzha** (10km north; Rs80, includes all rides), watered by the large adjacent dam, is a great attraction during the weekends when crowds come to ride the cable car (known as the "ropeway"). In the same grounds, the fantasy rock garden created by the artist Nek Chand of Chandigarh fame is illuminated on Saturday and Sunday nights (open until 9pm).

Practicalities

Palakkad is well connected to the rest of Kerala and most of the main express trains travelling through to Chennai, Bangalore and points further north stop at Palakkad's **railway station**, 6km to the northeast. The KSRTC **bus stand** is slap in the centre of town; most **accommodation**, in budget lodges, is nearby. The *Ammbadi*, on TB Road, opposite the town bus stand and 500m from the KSRTC bus stand (℡0491/531244; ●–●) has comfortable rooms (some a/c) and the restaurant serves Indian and Chinese food. Far more upmarket, the modern *Hotel Indraprastha*, English Church Road (℡0491/534641; ℱ539531; ●–●), boasts large rooms (some with a/c), a gloomy but blissfully cool a/c restaurant serving a mixed menu of Indian, Western and Chinese cuisine, a bar and a pleasant lawn. *Fort Palace*, W Fort Road (℡0491/534621; ●–●), is also reasonable, with some a/c rooms, a bar and a restaurant serving good North and South Indian food. Another option is to head out to KTDC's *Garden House* at Malampuzha (℡0491/815217; ➌–➎), which has a range that includes large, ordinary non-a/c doubles as well as some comfortable a/c rooms.

Around the corner from the *Indraprastha*, the DTPC's **tourist office** is at Fort Maidan (Mon–Sat 10am–5.30pm; ℡0491/538996). They offer colourful leaflets but not much else, though you can coax them for travel information. Both the *Indraprastha* and the *Fort Palace* **change money** for residents and, in theory, so can the State Bank of India, next door to the *Indraprastha*.

➍ Kozhikode (Calicut)

The busy coastal city of **KOZHIKODE** (Calicut), 225km north of Kochi, occupies an extremely important place in Keralan legend and history. It is also significant in the story of European interference in the subcontinent, as Vasco da Gama first set in India at Kozhikode in 1498. However, as a tourist destination, it's a dud, with precious few remnants of its historic past. The few foreigners who pause here invariably do so only to break the long journey between Mysore and Kochi.

Kozhikode's roots are shrouded in myth. According to Keralan tradition, the powerful king Cheraman Perumal is said to have converted from Hinduism to Islam and left for Mecca "to save his soul", never to return. Before he set sail he divided Kerala between his relatives, all of whom had to submit to his nephew, who was given the kingdom of Kozhikode and the title *zamorin*, equivalent to emperor. The city prospered and, perhaps because of the story of the convert king, became the preferred port of Muslim traders from the Middle East in search of spices, particularly pepper. During the Raj, it was an important centre for the export of printed Indian cotton, hence the term "calico", an English corruption of the name Calicut – itself an anglicized version of the city's original Malayalam name, now reinstated. Today, due to strong ties

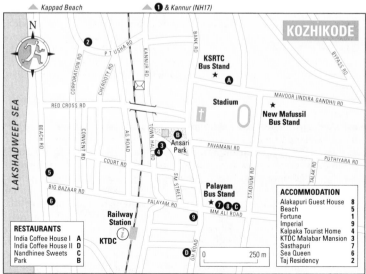

with the Gulf, where numerous sons, uncles and brothers of the city work, Kozhikode is flourishing with the injection of new wealth.

Arrival and information

The **railway station** (℡0495/701234), close to the centre of town, is served by coastal expresses and slower passenger trains; superfast express trains from Delhi, Mumbai, Kochi and Thiruvananthapuram stop here. There are three **bus stands**. All buses from destinations as far afield as Bangalore, Mysore, Ooty, Madurai, Coimbatore and Mangalore pull in at the **KSRTC stand**, on Mavoor Road (aka Indira Gandhi Road). Local buses and services from northern Kerala stop at the **New Mafussil private stand**, 500m away, on the other side of Mavoor Road. The **Palayam stand** serves city buses, infrequent long-haul buses and those from destinations further south, such as Palakaad, Thrissur and Guruvayur. Private deluxe buses from Thiruvananthapuram or Kochi stop in front of the KSRTC bus stand.

Kozhikode's **airport** is at Karippur, 23km south of the city. A taxi into the city costs Rs300 or take an **auto–rickshaw** to the Kozhikode–Palakkad highway, from where you can catch a bus. Indian Airlines **fly** here twice a day from **Mumbai**, daily from **Delhi** and **Coimbatore**, and four times a week from **Chennai**; Jet Airways also fly twice a week from Mumbai. Indian Airlines have two departures per week (Thurs & Sun) from **Goa** and **Kuwait**, and daily from **Sharjah** and **Bahrain** in the **Gulf**.

The friendly **KTDC tourist information** booth (Mon–Sat 10am–5pm; (℡0495/700097) at the railway station can tell you about travel connections and sites around Kozhikode. The KTDC tourist office (℡0495/722391) in the *Malabar Mansion Hotel* at the corner of SM Street can supply only limited information about the town and area. There is a **24hr left luggage** facility at the railway station but, as is always the case, they only accept locked luggage. With so much Gulf money floating around, you shouldn't have any difficulty **changing money** in Kozhikode. A good place to change any currency or travellers' cheque is at PL Worldways, 3rd Floor, Semma Towers, Mavoor Road (℡0495/722564). Banks that change money include the Standard Chartered Bank on Town Hall Road and the State Bank of India at Manachira Park. **Internet** facilities are available on the first floor of the block to the right of *Nandhiniee Sweets*, MM Ali Road (daily 10am–10pm; Rs30/hr).

If you want to fly out of Kozhikode, you can purchase **airline tickets** at Century Travels, Bank Road (℡0495/766522); directly at Indian Airlines, Eroth Centre, 5/2521 Bank Rd (℡0495/753966); or Jet Airways, 29 Mavoor Rd (℡0495/356518). Air India is also at Eroth Centre (℡0495/673001).

For **backwater cruises** in the Kozhikode region try the small, friendly and efficient Malabar House Boats at either of their three city offices including 1/335 Purakkatri, Thalakalthur (℡0495/452045, ℻765066). Their *kettu vallam* cruises start at Purakkatri, 12km north of the city, but they will arrange transport to the boat with prior notice. A 24hr cruise costs Rs6250 for two people, including meals; a day cruise will set you back Rs3000 for up to 6 people.

Accommodation and eating

Kozhikode's reasonably priced city-centre **hotels**, most of which operate a 24hr check-out, can fill up by late afternoon, especially during conventions; the beach area is a quiet alternative. Your best bet for a proper **meal** is to eat at your hotel, though you can get South Indian snacks and great omelette and coffee breakfasts at the dependable *Indian Coffee Houses* on Kallai Road and GH Road. Open-air *Park Restaurant*, by Mananchira tank, makes an appealing central oasis in the evenings and dishes up excellent local Malabari cuisine – try the fish. *Nandhiniee Sweets*, on MM Ali Road, is an ultra-hygienic sweets, nuts and savoury snacks pit-stop, where you can also get great fresh fruit cocktails, *badam* milk and *falooda* shakes.

Alakapuri Guest House, MM Ali Road, near the railway station, 1km from KSRTC bus stand ☎0495/723451. Built around a courtyard, the a/c rooms have huge bathtubs, polished wood and easy chairs; the cheaper, non-a/c options are rather spartan. The first-floor café serves great South Indian food all day; in the evening go down to the restaurant out in the courtyard garden. Single rates available. ❸–❻

Beach Hotel, Beach Road ☎0495/365363. Built in 1890 as the Malabar English Club, this well-conserved and atmospheric building has been a hotel since the 1940s. Comfortable rooms overlooking the beach have teak floors and large verandas; cheaper non-a/c rooms surround a garden at the back. A restaurant serves Malabari and seafood dishes. ❺–❼

Fortune, Kannur Road, 3km north of the centre ☎0495/768888, ☎768111. New Welcomgroup hotel for business travellers with plush rooms and central a/c. There's also a rooftop swimming pool, fitness suite and sauna, foreign exchange, bar, 24hr coffeeshop and Indian restaurant. The tariff includes buffet breakfast. ❼–❽

Imperial, Kallai Road ☎0495/753966. Large hotel around a courtyard with basic, very cheap rooms and a very good veg restaurant; not recommended for single women. ❶

Kalpaka Tourist Home, Corner of SM Road and Town Hall Road ☎0495/720222. Five storeys

ranged around a weirdly shaped courtyard-cum-sari store. The rooms are plain and functional (some a/c), and those on the eastern side have the best views. 24hr check-out. ❸–❻

KTDC Malabar Mansion, SM Street ☎0495/722391. Modern high-rise hotel, near the railway station. Huge a/c suites with cable TV, reasonable non-a/c rooms, beer parlour and a good South Indian restaurant. Good value. ❸–❻

Sasthapuri, MM Ali Road ☎0495/723281. Small budget place with well-maintained non-a/c and a/c rooms and a decent roof garden restaurant and a bar. It's tucked away down a side street to the right of Palayam bus station. ❷–❺

Sea Queen, Beach Road ☎0495/366604. Quiet, comfortable but ageing middle-class hotel close to the beach. The a/c and non-a/c rooms are comfortable but dark and stuffed with furniture; there's a popular South Indian restaurant and bar on the ground floor. Watch out for the rather disorientating and eye-boggling tile work on the stairs. ❺–❻

Taj Residency, PT Usha Road ☎0495/765354, ☎7664480. The grandest hotel in town but it lacks the ubiquitous *Taj* style; nonetheless, the centrally a/c rooms are very comfortable and there is a pool, coffee shop, multicuisine restaurant, and health and Ayurvedic centre. Breakfast is included in the tariff. ❾

The City

Few traces remain of the model city laid out in the fourteenth century, which followed a Hindu grid formula based on a sacred diagram containing the image of the cosmic man, Purusha. The axis and energy centre of the diagram was dictated by the position of the ancient **Tali Shiva temple** (closed to non-Hindus), which survives to this day. Everything, and everybody, had a place. The district around the port in the northwest was reserved for foreigners. Here a Chinese community lived in and around Chinese Street (now Silk Street) and later the Portuguese, Dutch and British occupied the area. Keralan Muslims (Mappilas) lived in the southwest. The northeast of the city was a commercial quarter, and in the southeast stood the Tali temple. Here too was a palace and fort; all the military *kalaris* (martial art gymnasia) that stood around the perimeter have now gone.

Considering its history, there is very little to see in Kozhikode, though it is good for shopping. Around SM Street, many good fabric and ready-made clothes shops sell the locally produced cotton cloth, particularly as stylish *lungis*. You cannot fail to be dazzled by the sheer number of gold jewellery shops, full of ladies spending lavish amounts of the money faithfully sent by relatives in the Gulf. This district is also a good place to try the local *halva* sweets, especially popular with the large Mappila community. Some shops specialize in piping-hot banana chips, straight from the frying pan.

Locals enjoy a promenade on or near the **beach** (3km from the centre) in the late afternoon and early evening. Although not suitable for swimming, it's a restful place, where you can munch on roasted peanuts sold in the many stalls while scanning the seas for jumping dolphins. After dark it's difficult to find an auto-rickshaw to take you back into town, but on the land side of the road regular buses run into the centre. You will have to travel to find better beaches such as the historic beach of **Kappad**, 16km to the north, where Vasco da Gama is said to have landed in 1498 with 170 sailors; a small memorial marks the spot. A gentle and partly rocky beach with cottage accommodation at nearby *Kappad Beach Resort* (℡0496/683760; ❼–❺), Kappad lies 4km from Thiruvangoor on the Kozhikode–Badagara route serviced by numerous buses.

The **Pazhassirajah and Krishnamenon Museums and Art Gallery** (Mon, Tues & Thurs–Sun 10am–12.30pm & 2.30–5pm, Wed 2.30–5pm; free) stand together 5km from the centre on East Hill. The Pazhassirajah collection includes copies of murals, coins, bronzes and models of the umbrella-shaped, stone megalithic remains peculiar to Kerala, while the museum houses a collection of memorabilia associated with the left-wing Keralan politician V.K. Krishnamenon, and a gallery of works by Indian artists.

The experimental handloom centre, the **Tasara Creative Weaving Centre**, is hidden in a tropical compound in Beypore North, 7km south of Kozikode, just off the Kozikode–Beypore Road. Rugs, bedspreads and wall hangings are produced here as works or art, not simply household furnishings. The designs range from a minimalist block pattern to the intricate and unique, where an artist has painted a picture onto the loom, and then woven the picture. Visitors are welcome to visit the weaving centre and art gallery (daily 9am–6pm; free) and to buy: prices range from $15 to $1000. You can also stay here and take a course on the art of the handloom under the tutelage of Mr Vasudevan Balakrishanan (℡0495/414832, ⓦwww.tarasindia.com), with the aim of taking home a wall-hanging of your own design and making.

Wayanad

One of the most beautiful regions of Kerala is the hill district of **WAYANAD**, situated 70km east of Kozhikode, with tracts of forest covering the western flanks of the Nilgiris. Due to the relative isolation and the lack of major roads, the various tribal groups that populate the area around Wayanad have so far managed to preserve their traditional identities, despite the gradual intrusion of modernization. The scenery is rich and varied, ranging from plantations of tea, spice, coffee and cocoa to the dry scruffy jungles of the **Muthanga Wildlife Sanctuary**. For those with time on their hands, Wayanad makes an alternative and rewarding route between coastal Kerala and Mysore in neighbouring Karnataka, or Ooty in Tamil Nadu.

Travelling from Kozhikode, a beautiful but tortuous road climbs a series of hairpin bends up the Southern Ghats through unspoiled forests, where macaques forage along the roadside, impervious to the groaning, diesel-belching trucks and buses going past. As the road arrives at the lip of the great plateau there are sweeping views back towards the coast of lush, green cover, and you can glimpse the sea in the hazy distance. On the highway to Mysore and Ooty, **Kalpetta**, the district capital, makes a good base from which to discover most of Wayanad, but **Mananthavady**, 35km from Kalpetta, is more convenient for exploring the northern jungles.

Kalpetta and around

Surrounded by plantations and rolling hills, **KALPETTA**, 72km east of Kozhikode, is a quiet market town with little to commend it except its pleasant location on the edge of the Muthanga Wildlife Sanctuary. Along with the settlement of **Vythiri**, 5km to the west, Kalpetta provides ample amenities and excellent walking country, including the ranges around the spectacular **Chembra Peak** (2100m), the highest mountain in Wayanad.

Although not as evocative as Periyar, the **Muthanga Wildlife Sanctuary**, 40km southeast of Kalpetta, forms part of the **Nilgiri Biosphere Reserve** along with national parks such as Bandipur and Nagarhole in Karnataka, and Madumalai across the border in Tamil Nadu. Like neighbouring Bandipur National Park, Muthanga, with its dry deciduous forests, is noted for elephants and also shelters deer, wild boar, bear and tiger. The highway from Kalpetta to Mysore and Ooty via the scruffy town of **Sultan's Battery** passes through part of the sanctuary, and provides an opportunity, if you're lucky, to see wild elephants crossing the road on ancient migratory trails.

Accessible from Meppady and 12km south of Kalpetta, **Chembra Peak** (2100m) has soaring ridges and expansive meadows on one side, thick forests on the other. It makes a good stiff climb, but take plenty of water. The peak towers over Vythiri, dominating the countryside, and provides stunning views over Wayanad and out to sea. To get to Meppady, turn off the main Kozhikode highway at Chundale and follow the Ooty road for a further 8km; you can take a bus from Kalpetta.

Practicalities

The state **bus** stand in the centre of town of Kalpetta has connections to Kozhikode (72km; 2hr), Ooty (115km; 3hr), Mysore (42km; 4hr) and Mananthavady (35km; 1hr). **Auto-rickshaws** and **Jeeps** are available for local transport.

The DTPC **tourist office** (Mon–Sat 10am–5pm; ☏0493/602134) is in Kalpetta North, 1km from the bus stand; although they are not accustomed to foreign visitors, with a little encouragement they will supply information on buses and the area in general. They also organize **guided tours** by minibus whenever there is enough demand. Their day tour (Rs100) takes in the **Edakkal caves**, 12km south of Sultan's Battery, with prehistoric carvings dating back to around 1000BC, and some nearby waterfalls, but doesn't spend nearly enough time at Muthanga Sanctuary. They also organize longer two-day tours that include Muthanga and Mananthavady wildlife sanctuaries, which are a little less frenetic and offer more time at the sanctuaries. The tourist office is able to assist with hiring a **forest guide** at Rs250 a day, and negotiating a Jeep with driver (Rs8/km and Rs100 vehicle entrance fee) for those going independently to the wildlife sanctuaries. To enter Muthanga sanctuary you need to buy a **permit**, for which you have to locate the elusive permit-giving authority in one of four warden's offices over a fifty-kilometre area. For up-to-date information on permits, enquire at the DFO on Garage Road, Sultan's Battery (no phone).

Accommodation and eating

Kalpetta has ample **accommodation**, most within easy striking distance of the bus stand, including the *Arun Tourist Home* on Main Road

(℡0493/602039; ❷), which has cheap basic rooms. For a bit more comfort, try the large, rambling modern *Harita Giri*, close by on Emily Road (℡0493/602673; ❷–❺). Although the hotel has seen better days it offers a wide range of rooms from budget (including singles) to deluxe a/c suites; there is a garden, bar and a restaurant and they arrange tours on demand. By far the best hotel in town, however, is *Green Gates* above the tourist office, TB Road, Kalpetta North (℡0493/602001; ❼), offering well-appointed standard and a/c rooms and a pleasant restaurant. For inexpensive **food**, the ever-dependable *India Coffee House*, opposite the tourist office, serves good South Indian snacks, lunch-time "meals" and filter coffee.

For a bit of luxury, head out to **Vythiri** where, tucked away on tea, coffee and spice plantations, lie two excellent **resorts**. The first and most accessible is the *Vythiri Resort* (book through Prime Holdings ℡&℻0493/655366; ❾); to reach it, turn off the main road which runs south to Kozhikode, by the spice shop, onto an estate road and continue for 3km. Jeeps from Kalpetta out to the resort charge Rs100. Set in a beautiful seven-acre plot with three boulder-strewn mountain streams flowing through it, *Vythiri* boasts tasteful "cottages" and serves exquisite Keralan cuisine in its restaurant. The resort will arrange forest and sightseeing tours, including a visit to the Harrison Malayalam Tea Factory. The nature resort *Green Magic* (book accommodation and transport through Tourindia, Thiruvananthapuram (℡0471/330437, ℻331407; ❾, full board), a further 4km up the same track and only accessible by four-wheel drive with the final 1.5km on foot, is even more exotic. It consists of luxurious treehouses nestled under a canopy of lush rain forest, each accessed by a unique pulley system made with cane that relies on a counterweight of water to lift you over 20m off the ground. Energy sources include solar power and *gobar* (cow-dung) gas, and meals are prepared from organically grown vegetables and served, according to Keralan tradition, on banana leaves. Several forest trails lead out from the resort offering plenty of opportunities for guided walks; tours of the sanctuaries can also be arranged.

Thirunelli

One of Wayanad's most celebrated temples, **Thirunelli**, lies in a remote part of the district 32km north of Kalpetta, off the Kodagu road. The temple is dedicated to the god Vishnu and is often referred to as the "Kashi of the South", which equates it in veneration with the holy city of Varanasi. An unusual mix of Keralan tiled roofs and northern North Indian-style pillared halls, Thirunelli is, like Kashi, considered to be a *tirtha*, or crossing, between the mundane world and the divine. Following tradition, devout pilgrims bathe in the nearby **Papanasini River**, which is said to absolve them of their worldly sins. More interesting still – especially during the annual festival (14–28 March), when it comes alive with tribal colour, is the **Valliyurkavu Bhagavathi temple**, 8km to the east. It's an unassuming Keralan-style temple in a pastoral setting, dedicated to the goddess Durga. For the last hundred years, however, the temple has played host to a tribal labour mart and, although bonded labour is now extinct, the festival continues as a celebration and attracts tribal people from all over Wayanad.

Practicalities

Buses from Kalpetta, Kozhikode and Kannur pull into the **bus stand** in the centre of **Mananthavady**, the nearest town to the temples. From here the easiest mode of travel is by Jeep, available for rent in the bazaar or through *Haksons*

There are sixteen tribes in Wayanad, which make up over seventeen percent of the region's population. Surrounded by a sea of change, many have found their traditional way of life under threat; some tribes are adapting to modern life and others are resisting change.

One of the largest of the Wayanad tribes is the Paniya who, until early this century, were sold as bonded labour to plantation owners. Traditional Paniya women are distinctive, as they wear large round earrings made of palmyra leaves studded with bright red *kunnikkuru* seeds. Like the Paniyas, the Adiyas were another tribe who worked as bonded labour. "Adiyar" literally means "slave" and some of their songs celebrate their serfdom. However, Adiya legends also trace their roots back to the legend of the hero Maveli, who lived at a time when there was no caste or divisions of tribes. The legend relates the coming of outsiders in the form of three celestial beings who, with the help of the ferocious mother goddess Mali, helped subjugate the people and create the tribes of Wayanad.

The Kattunaykan live in the forests of Wayanad and adjacent districts, and are more shy and primitive. Resisting change, the Kattunaykan continue to live, by and large, as hunter-gatherers and honey-collectors. In contrast, the Mullukurman were once hunter-gatherers but now thrive as subsistence farmers and live in small hamlets, called *kudis*, consisting of ten to twelve houses. The Mullukurman practice a form of ritualistic religion centred on the *daivapura*, a sacred meeting place found in every *kudi*. Some Mullukurman have abandoned their roots and now work in modern-day India, in areas such as local and state government. Although a small section of Kurichiyans has followed a similar direction, for the most part they continue to live within matrilineal joint families and to work the land. The Kurichiyans have baffled modern medicine with their longevity, as many live to be 100, a fact which has been put down to healthy living, hard work and the pleasant climate of Wayanad.

Hotel. Local buses do go to Thirunelli, but be careful you don't miss the last bus back as there is no accommodation at the temple. Buses leave here for Kodagu and Mysore, among other destinations in Karnataka and Tamil Nadu, but there are no express services. Mananthavady is also the only place to find decent **accommodation**; *Haksons* at KT Junction (T0493/540118; ②–③) a short distance down the Kozhikode road, has a good **restaurant** and is excellent value with clean doubles and deluxe rooms.

The far north

The beautiful coast of Kerala **north of Kozhikode** is a seemingly endless stretch of coconut palms, wooded hills and virtually deserted beaches. The towns hold little of interest for visitors, most of whom bypass the area completely. The main reason to stop here today is to look for **teyyattam**, the extraordinary masked trance dances and oracle readings that take place villages throughout the region between November and May every year.

Kannur (Cannanore)

KANNUR (Cannanore), 92km north of Kozhikode, was for many centuries the capital of the Kolathiri rajas, who prospered from the thriving maritime spice trade through its port. In the early 1500s, after Vasco da Gama passed through, the Portuguese took it and erected an imposing bastion, **St Angelo's fort**, overlooking the harbour, but today this is occupied by the Indian army and closed to visitors. In Kannur itself, the popular town beach can get quite crowded; for a bit more quiet head down to the small **Baby Beach** (4km) in the army's cantonment area (daily access 9am–5pm).

Most visitors use Kannur as a base while they search out **teyyattam**, spectacular spirit-possession rituals that are an important feature of town and village life in the area (see p.709). There are over 400 different varieties of *teyyattam*, so you could spend days and nights enthralled in it, and never see the same ritual twice. Locating these events is exciting and an essential part of the whole experience – you can often hear the loud and frenetic drumming miles away, but the actual temple where the *teyyam* is performing may be hidden deep within the forest or coconut groves. The best way to start looking for *teyyattam* is to ask at the local tourist office or at *Costa Malabari* (see below) and they will point you in the right direction. If you are short of time, head out to the daily ritual at **Parassinikadavu** (see p.422).

Practicalities

Straddling the main coastal transport artery between Mangalore and Kochi/Thiruvananthapuram, Kannur is well connected by **bus** and **train** to most major towns and cities in Kerala. In addition, buses travel to Mysore turning inland at Thalassery (aka Tellycherry) and climb the beautiful wooded Ghats to Virajpet in Kodagu. The State Bank of India (Mon–Fri 10am–2pm, Sat 10am–noon) on Fort Road will **change money**, travellers' cheques and advance cash on Visa and Mastercard. **Internet** access is widely available; try Internet, Wheat House Building, opposite the Civil Station, which charges Rs30/hr.

Decent budget **accommodation** is available at *Plaza Tourist Home* (℡0497/360031; ②), close to the railway station gates on Fort Road, which has reasonable rooms and an *Indian Coffee House* **restaurant** downstairs. *Madan,* a few metres up the road (℡0497/768204; ②), is a sunny yellow, friendly budget lodge set in a courtyard with simple rooms. *Swadeshi Woodlands Lodge* a few minutes away on Aarat Road (℡0497/701434; ②), is a quiet old hotel with character in a large yard with basic rooms and a reasonable South Indian restaurant. More upscale is the plush, centrally a/c, business-oriented *Kamala International* (℡0497/766910; ③), in the town centre on SM Road; it has a rooftop garden restaurant. The excellent value *Government Guest House* in the cantonment area (℡0497/706426; ②), stands on the crest of a cliff overlooking the sea, and boasts huge, simple non-a/c rooms that catch the breezes; it's primarily for visiting VIPs but there are usually a few spare rooms. The brilliantly located *Mascot Beach Resort* (℡0497/708445; ④–⑤), 300m before Baby beach, perches on a rocky shoreline with large well-appointed a/c rooms with views across the cove to the lighthouse. They change money and serve great food in their restaurant, but there is no bar.

However, for a total escape, head 10km south to the very warm and welcoming *Costa Malabari* in **Tottada** village; book through the Tourist Desk at Ernakulam (℡0484/371761; ④–⑥). Hidden deep in the cashew and coconut groves, the informal house has four airy and comfortable non-a/c rooms, and you are served outstanding home-cooked Malabari cuisine, seafood and tropical fruits from the garden. Five minutes' walk away through toddy and cashew plantations are two very private golden beaches, where you can swim out to the mussel fishermen and dolphins. This is an ideal base if you want to learn more about *teyyattam* and catch the local temple rituals. You can be collected from the station by prior arrangement (Rs120).

The only place you can be absolutely guaranteed a glimpse of *teyyattam* is the village of **PARASSINIKADAVU**, 20km north of Kannur beside the Valapatanam River, where the head priest, or *madayan*, of the **Parassini Madammpura** temple performs every day during winter before assembled devotees. Elaborately dressed and accompanied by a traditional drum group, he becomes possessed by the temple's presiding deity – Lord Muthappan, Shiva in the form of a *kiratha*, or hunter – and enacts a series of complex offerings. The two-hour ceremony culminates when the priest/deity dances forward to bless individual members of the congregation. Even by Keralan standards, this is an extraordinary spectacle, and well worth taking time out of a journey along the coast for.

Regular local buses leave Kannur **for Parassinikadavu** from around 7am, dropping passengers at the top of the village, ten minutes on foot from the temple. However, if you want to get there in time for the dawn **teyyattam**, you'll have to splash out on one of the Ambassador taxis that line up outside Kannur bus stand. The cabbies sleep in their cars, so you can arrange the trip on the spot by waking one up; you can also arrange a taxi through one of the

Lakshadweep

Visitors in search of an exclusive tropical paradise may well find it in LAKSHAD-WEEP, the "one hundred thousand islands" which lie between 200km and 400km offshore, in the deep blue of the Arabian Sea. The smallest Union Territory in India, it consists of clear blue lagoons, reefs, white sand banks and 27 tiny coconut-palm-covered coral islands. Only ten are inhabited, with a total population of just over 50,000 people, the majority of whom are Malayalam-speaking Sunni Muslims, said to be descended from seventh-century Keralan Hindus who converted to Islam.

The main sources of income are fishing, coconuts and related products. Fruit, vegetables and pulses are cultivated in small quantities but staples such as rice and many other commodities have always had to be imported. The Portuguese, who discovered the value of coir rope, spun from coconut husk, controlled Lakshadweep during the sixteenth century; when they imposed an import tax on rice, locals retaliated by poisoning some of the forty-strong Portuguese garrison – and terrible reprisals followed. As Muslims, the islanders enjoyed friendly relations with Tipu Sultan of Mysore, which naturally aroused the ire of the British, who moved in at the end of the eighteenth century and remained until Independence, when Lakshadweep became a Union Territory.

At present, accommodation is available for non-residents of India on only two of the islands – Bangaram and Kadmat. Beautiful Kadmat is primarily being developed as a popular destination for well-heeled Indian tourists, who are also allowed to visit the neighbouring islands of Kavarattu and Minicoy (both closed to foreigners). This option may also appeal to foreign visitors who wish to visit the islands but are travelling on a more limited budget; you can only visit the island if you book through the Society for Promotion of Recreational Tourism and Sports (SPORTS) on IG Road, Willingdon Island (☎0484/668387, ℗668155). SPORTS offers a six–day package cruise to Lakshadweep on one of two ships, the *Tipu Sultan* or the *Bharat Seema*. You spend two days at sea and four days lying on the beach. SPORTS will arrange all permits and the package is for full board ($450 for non-a/c, $500 for a/c).

Bangaram

The teardrop-shaped uninhabited 128-acre islet of Bangaram welcomes a limited number of foreign tourists at any one time, and expects them to pay handsomely for

more upmarket hotels but you'll have leave around 4.30am. Alternatively, head out to Parassinikadavu for the early afternoon ritual, which starts around 2pm, allowing you plenty of time to get there and back by bus, with half an hour or so to browse the temple bazaar (whose stalls do a great line in kitsch Lord Muthappan souvenirs). Note that the second performance of the day does not always take place, so it's a good idea to phone to check in advance (☏ 0497/780722).

Kasargode and Bekal

The old-fashioned little town of **KASARGODE**, 153km north of Kozhikode near the Karnataka border, has a predominantly Muslim population and is principally a fishing community – though some say smuggling is not unknown. It currently gets few foreign visitors, but the number is increasing, as it is the nearest town of any size to the beaches and fort at **BEKAL** (16km south). At present, this is as unexploited an area as you could hope to find, with hardly a beachside shack café, let alone a five-star hotel. The local fishermen are completely unused to the sight of semi-naked Westerners, while some stretches of sand serve as communal toilets. The undertow can be dangerously strong in some places.

the privilege. Bangaram is an archetypal tropical hideaway, edged with pristine white sands and surrounded by a calm lagoon where average water temperature stays around 26°C all year. Beyond the lagoon lies the coral reef, home to sea turtles, dolphins, eagle rays, lionfish, parrotfish, octopus and predators like barracudas and sharks. Islanders come to Bangaram and its uninhabited neighbours, which are all devoid of animal and bird life, to fish and to harvest coconuts.

Theoretically, it's possible to visit Bangaram all year round; the hottest time is April and May, when the temperature can reach 33°C; the monsoon (May–Sept) attracts approximately half the total rainfall seen in Kerala, in the form of passing showers rather than a deluge, although seas are rough. The island remains incredibly peaceful, and there are concerted attempts to minimize the ecological impact of tourism. The *Bangaram Island Resort* (☉) accommodates up to thirty couples in simple thatched cottage rooms, each with a veranda. Cane tables and chairs sit outside the restaurant on the beach, and a few hammocks are strung up between the palms. There's no air-conditioning, TV, radio, telephone, newspapers or shops, let alone discos. The tariff, if expensive for India, compares favourably with other exotic holiday destinations; during peak season (Dec 21 to Jan 20) it rises to $350 full board for a double room; in low season (April–Sept except Aug) it may be as much as 25 percent less. Facilities include scuba diving (from $45 per dive; lessons with qualified instructor); glass-bottomed boat trips to neighbouring uninhabited islands; and deep-sea fishing (Oct to mid-May; $50–75). Kayaks, catamarans and a sailing boat are available free, and it's possible to take a day-trip to Kadmat.

At present, the only way for foreigners to reach Bangaram is on the staggeringly expensive flights on small aircraft run by Indian Airlines out of Kochi (one daily, except Sun) and Goa (Mon, Wed & Fri) and bookable through the *Casino Hotel* on Willingdon Island (see p.389). Foreigners pay $300 for the round trip, which takes an hour and a half. Flights arrive in Lakshadeep at the island of Agatti, 8km southwest from where the connecting boat journey to Bangaram takes two hours, picking its way through the shallows to avoid the corals. During the monsoon (May 16–Sept 15), helicopters are used so as to protect the fragile coral reefs that lie just under the surface. All arrangements, including flights, accommodation and the necessary entry permit, are handled by the *Casino Hotel*, Willingdon Island, Kochi (☏ 0484/668221, ☏ 668001). Some foreign tour operators, however, offer all-in packages combining Lakshadweep with another destination, usually Goa.

A popular weekend day-trip destination, Bekal's **fort** (daily 9am–5.30pm; Rs2, Fri free) stands on a promontory between two long, classically beautiful palm-fringed **beaches**. Although this is one of the largest forts in Kerala and has been under the control of various powers including Vijayanagar, Tipu Sultan and the British, it's nothing to get excited about. The bastion's commanding position, with views across the bays to north and south, is impressive enough, but only four watchtowers and the outer walls survive. An adjacent Hindu temple, next to the gates, with garish stucco images of the gods, draws a steady stream of visitors, while others clamber along the battlements or climb down to the beach through hidden passages. A short walk south of the main gates leads to Bekal Resort's visitor centre where the café and shops only open at the weekends.

Practicalities

The nearest major town to Kasargode is Mangalore, 50km north in Karnataka. Long-distance **buses** usually call at both its bus stands: a new private one on the main highway (NH-17) on the outskirts and the KSRTC city bus stand at the centre of town. Among regular buses along the smaller coastal road, those south to Kanhangad, also on NH-17, stop at Bekal. Kasargode **railway station** is 3km from town. Bekal Resorts (℡0499/736937), a government-funded project to promote the area with careful consideration of environmental and social issues, runs a **tourist information office** at their visitor centre next to Bekal Fort, which is only staffed sporadically and at weekends. When open, they are happy to give you advice about the area and information on transport and accommodation.

Near the bus stand in **Kasargode**, the *Enjay Tourist Home* (℡0499/421164; ❷) has some a/c rooms, a South Indian restaurant and car rental, while *Aliya Lodge* (℡0499/430744; ❷), near the town centre on MG Road, has very cheap non-a/c doubles, which get booked early, and a restaurant. At the top (east) end of MG Road, near the new bus stand, the easily recognizable monolith of the *City Tower* (℡0499/430400; ❷–❸) is Kasargode's fanciest hotel with reasonably priced doubles, some a/c rooms and a travel desk, but their "meals" restaurant is disappointingly dull.

The most atmospheric place to stay at **Bekal** is the *Travellers Bungalow* (❶) which has two basic rooms in a superb location at the furthest point of the promontory inside the fort. It's a great place to spend a night, except at weekends, when bus loads of ghetto-blaster-toting day-trippers hang out on the veranda. If you want to stay here, you have to book through the Kasargode District Collector, Civil Station, Kasargode, ℡0499/430400. *Eeyam Lodge* at Palakannu, 2km from the fort in the direction of Kasargode (℡0499/736343; ❷–❹), is friendly and not too far from the sea at Kappil Beach, with very reasonable rooms including some with a/c, a restaurant and **money–changing** facilities.

Travel details

For details of ferry services on the backwaters – primarily between Alappuzha and Kollam – see p.362.

Trains

Thiruvananthapuram (9–11 daily; 4hr 20min–5hr); Thrissur (12–14 daily; 1hr 30min–2hr).

Kozhikode to: Kannur (9–11daily; 1hr 55min–2hr 30min); Kochi (6–7 daily; 4hr 30min–5hr 10min); Mangalore (3–4 daily; 5hr 40min–6hr); Mumbai (2–3 daily; 16hr 20min–23hr); Thirvananthapuram (4–6 daily; 8hr 35min–13hr 20min); Thrissur (6–7daily; 2hr 25min–3hr 25min).

Thiruvananthapuram to: Alappuzha (2 daily; 3hr); Bangalore (1–2 daily; 18hr 40min–19hr 20min); Calcutta (3 weekly; 49hr); Chennai (1–3 daily; 18–19hr); Delhi (1–2 daily; 52hr 35min–56hr 30min); Kanniyakumari (1–2 daily; 2hr 15min); Kochi (8 daily; 3hr 30min–5hr); Kollam (hourly; 1hr 30min–1hr 50min); Kozhikode (3 daily; 8hr–11hr 30min); Madgaon (for Goa; 4 weekly; 16hr 25min–20hr 30min); Mumbai (1–2 daily; 24hr 20min–46hr 40min); Thrissur (5–6 daily; 6–7hr); Varkala (6 daily; 38–55min).

Thrissur to: Chennai (3–4 daily; 12hr 5min–12hr 30min); Kochi (10–12 daily; 1hr 30min–2hr 10min); Thiruvananthapuram (9–10 daily; 5hr 15min–7hr 20min).

Buses

Kochi/Ernakulam to: Alappuzha (every 30min; 1hr 30min); Kanniyakumari (6 daily; 9hr); Kollam (every 30min; 3hr); Kottayam (every 30min; 1hr 30min–2hr); Kozhikode (hourly; 5hr); Periyar (10 daily; 6–7hr); Thiruvananthapuram (every 30min; 4–6hr); Thrissur (every 30min; 2hr).

Kozhikode to: Kalpetta (6 daily; 3hr); Kannur (every 30mins; 2–3hr); Kochi (hourly; 6hr); Mananthavady (4 daily; 4hr); Mysore (2 daily; 10hr); Ooty (4 daily; 6hr); Sultan's Battery (10 daily; 3hr); Thiruvananthapuram (12–15 daily; 11–12hr); Thrissur (10 daily; 3hr 30min–4hr).

Munnar to: Kochi (5 daily; 4hr 30min); Kottayam (5 daily; 5hr); Kumily (4 daily; 4hr 30min); Madurai (6 daily; 5hr); Thiruvananthapuram (5 daily; 7–8hr).

Periyar to: Kochi (8 daily; 6–7hr); Kottayam (every 30min; 3–4hr); Kozhikode (hourly; 8hr); Madurai (10 daily; 5hr 30min); Munnar (4 daily; 4hr 30min); Thiruvananthapuram (10–12 daily; 8–9hr).

Thiruvananthapuram to: Alappuzha (every 30min; 3hr 15min); Chennai (8 daily; 17hr); Kanniyakumari (12 daily; 2hr); Kochi (every 30min; 4–6hr); Kollam (every 30min; 1hr 30min); Kottayam (every 30min; 4hr); Madurai (10 daily; 7hr); Periyar (5 daily; 8hr); Ponmudi (4 daily; 2hr 30min); Varkala (hourly; 1hr 30min).

Thrissur to: Chennai (1 daily; 14hr); Guruvayur (10 daily; 40min); Kochi (every 30min; 2hr); Mysore (2 daily; 10hr); Palakkad (6 daily; 2hr); Thiruvananthapuram (15 daily; 6–7hr).

Flights

Kochi/Ernakulam to: Bangalore (1 daily; 55min); Chennai (1–2 daily; 1hr–2hr 15min); Coimbatore (2 weekly; 30min); Delhi (1 daily; 4hr 10min); Goa (2 weekly; 55min); Hyderabad (2 weekly; 1hr 40min); Lakshadweep (1 daily, except Sun; 1hr 30min); Mumbai (1–2 daily; 1hr 45min–3hr 5min); Thiruvananthapuram (3 weekly; 40min).

Kozhikode to: Chennai (4 weekly; 1hr–2hr 15min); Coimbatore (1 daily; 30min); Delhi (1 daily; 5hr 40min); Goa (2 weekly; 1hr 5min); Kochi (2 weekly; 30min); Mumbai (2 daily; 1hr 40min–3hr).

Thiruvananthapuram to: Bangalore (1 daily; 2hr 5min); Chennai (1 daily; 1hr 10min); Colombo (Sri Lanka) (2 weekly; 1hr 25min); Delhi (2 daily; 4hr 35min–5hr 20min); Malé (Maldives) (5 weekly; 40min); Mumbai (1 daily; 1hr 55min).

Chennai

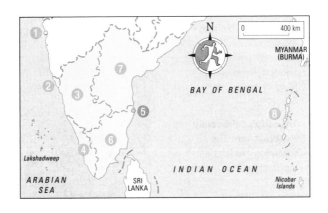

CHAPTER 5   # Highlights

* **Fort St George** The eighteenth-century fort was the centre of the Madras Presidency during the Raj, and today houses an excellent museum documenting the British occupation. See p.441

* **Government Museum** Home to the best collection of Chola bronzes in the world, beautiful stone temple carvings and fine Rajput and Moghul miniatures. See p.442

* **Theosophical Society Headquarters** The sprawling gardens and fascinating library where Krishnamurti sought to understand divine truth, and preached harmony to all humanity under a spreading banyan tree. See p.446

Chennai

Tucked into the northeastern corner of Tamil Nadu, on the Bay of Bengal, **CHENNAI** (still often referred to by its former British name, **Madras**) is India's fourth largest city, boasting a population of about six million. A hot, frenetic and congested metropolis, it is the major transportation hub of the far south and the eastern coastline, with excellent road, rail and flight connections to the rest of the subcontinent. The major international airport here makes a marginally less stressful entry point to the subcontinent than Mumbai or Delhi – but most travellers stay just long enough to book a ticket for somewhere else. The attractions of the city itself are sparse, though it does boast some fine specimens of Raj architecture, Christian pilgrimage sites connected with the apostle "Doubting Thomas", superb Chola bronzes at its Government museum and plentiful music and dance performances.

The state capital of Tamil Nadu, Chennai is, like Mumbai and Calcutta, a comparatively modern creation. It was founded by the **British East India Company** in 1639, on a narrow five-kilometre strip of land between the Cooum and Adyar rivers, a few kilometres north of the ancient Tamil port of **Mylapore** and the Portuguese settlement of San Thome, which was established in 1522. The site had no natural harbour; it was selected by Francis Day, the East India Company agent, in part because he enjoyed good relations with the local Nayak governor Dharmala Ayyappa, who could intercede with the Vijayanagar Raja of Chandragiri, to whom the territory belonged. In addition, the land was protected by water on the east, south and west; cotton could be bought here twenty percent cheaper than elsewhere; and, apparently, Day had acquired a mistress in San Thome. A fortified trading post, completed on St George's Day (April 23) 1640, was named, rather aptly, **Fort St George**. By 1700, the British had acquired neighbouring territory including Triplicane and Egmore, while over the course of the next century, as capital of the **Madras Presidency**, which covered most of South India, the city mushroomed to

▲ Enfield Factory

▼ Vellore & Kanchipuram

BAY

OF

George Town

Directorate of Shipping

Chennai Beach

GPO

RAJAJI SALAI (NORTH BEACH RD)

Parry's Corner

High Court

Fort St George

PRAKASAM RD

NSC BOSE RD

(POPHAM'S BROADWAY)

Express Bus Stand ★

Fort Museum

St Mary's Church

Anna Park

MGR Samadhi

Broadway Bus Stand ★

Fort

KAMARAJAR SALAI

Senate House

(SOUTH BEACH RD)

GEORGE TOWN

FLAG STAFF RD

HIGH RD

The Island

V.O.C. RD

WALL TAX RD

PALLAVAN SALAI BODY GUARD RD

ANNA SALAI

Cooum River

WALLAJAH RD

TYPCROFTS RD

BESANT RD

QUAID-E-MILLETH

TRIPLICANE

Chennai Central

U Rent

TRIPLICANE HIGH RD

TDC

St Andrew's Kirk

PERIYAR EVR

ARUNACHALA NAICKEN ST

Head Post Office

BHARATHI SALAI

BESANT RD

VEPERY

Egmore

See Egmore, Anna Salai and Triplicane map for detail

Government of India Tourist Office (GIRTO)

WOODS RD

WHITES RD

WESTCOTT RD

PETERS RD

ROYAPETTAH

ELEPHANT GATE BRIDGE

BUCKINGHAM CANAL

HUNTERS RD

RITHERDON RD

PANTHEON RD

POONAMALLEE HIGH RD

Government Museum

GREAMS RD

PERAMBUR BARRACKS RD

STRAHAMS RD

PURASAWALKAM HIGH RD

PURASAWALKAM

UK High Commission

COLLEGE RD

Foreigners' Registration Office

MAHATMA GANDHI RD

EGMORE

DR GURUSWAMY MCNICHOLS RD BRIDGE

STERLING RD

VILLAGE RD

M G R SALAI

KONNUR HIGH RD

KILPAUK GARDEN RD

NEW AVADI RD

CHETPUT

NUNGAMBAKKAM HIGH RD

Cooum River

Valluvar Kottam

PURIYA EVR HIGH RD

NELSON MANICKA MUSTALLAR RD

NUNGAMBAKKAM

N.S.K. RD (ARCOT RD)

2ND AVE

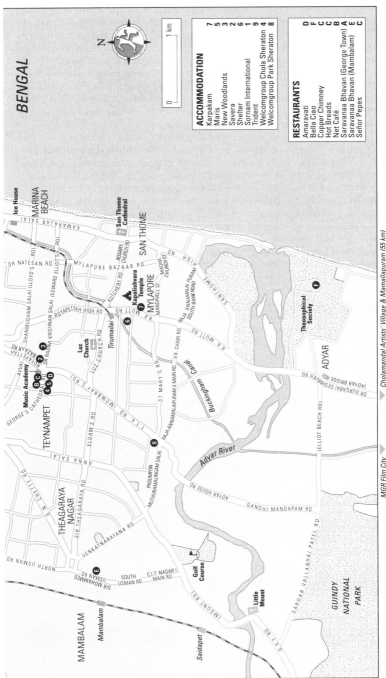

BAY OF BENGAL

5
CHENNAI

ACCOMMODATION

Karpakam	7
Maris	5
New Woodlands	3
Savera	2
Shelter	6
Sornam International	1
Trident	9
Welcomgroup Chola Sheraton	4
Welcomgroup Park Sheraton	8

RESTAURANTS

Amaravati	D
Bella Ciao	F
Copper Chimney	C
Hot Breads	B
Net Café	A
Saravanaa Bhavan (George Town)	A
Saravanaa Bhavan (Mambalam)	E
Señor Pepes	C

N

0   1 km

Cholamandal Artists' Village & Mamallapuram (55 km)

MGR Film City

St Thomas's Mount, Airport (16km) & Trisulam Railway Station

St Thomas's Mount & Airport

include many surrounding villages. The French, who had settled a little way down the coastline in Pondicherry, repeatedly challenged the British, and in 1746, they finally managed to destroy much of the city and bring it under their control. **Robert Clive** ("Clive of India"), then a clerk, was taken prisoner, an experience said to have inspired him to become a military campaigner. Clive was among the first to re-enter Madras when it was retaken by the British three years later, and continued to use it as his base. Following this, fortifications were strengthened and the British survived a year-long French siege in 1759, completing the work in 1783. By this time, however, Calcutta was in the ascendancy and Madras lost its national importance.

The city's renaissance began after Independence, when it became the centre of the Tamil **movie industry**, and a hotbed of **Dravidian nationalism**. The rise of the DMK – which ousted Nehru's Congress government in 1967 and has shared power with its rival pro-Dravidian party, the AIADMK, ever since – owed a lot to the DMK's control of the major film studios in Chennai. Later, **MGR**, Tamil Nadu's godlike film-star chief minister, exploited the same propaganda potential throughout his eleven-year rule. These days, cutouts of smiling politicians and strings of pennants in party colours are still ubiquitous, but industry and commerce have taken over as the city's prime obsessions. Renamed Chennai in 1997 (to assert its pre-colonial identity; the fishing village upon which the city was built was named Chennaipatnam), the metropolis has boomed as a result of the Indian economy opening up to foreign investment under Prime Ministers Rajiv Gandhi and Narasima Rao in the early 1990s. The flip side of this rapid economic growth is that the city's infrastructure has been stretched to breaking point; overwhelming poverty, oppressive heat and pollution are more likely to be your lasting impressions of Chennai, rather than the conspicuous affluence of its modern marble shopping malls.

Arrival and information

Chennai's main bus and railway stations are central, but its airport lies a long slog south of the city, around an hour from the hotel districts. If you are on a budget, finding an inexpensive place to stay can be difficult late at night, so hunt around for a vacancy by phone before arriving.

By air

Chennai airport at Trisulam, 16km southwest of the city centre on NH45, is comprehensively served by international and domestic flights, and the two terminals are a minute's walk from each other. Out in the main concourse, you'll find a 24-hour post office, Thomas Cook and State Bank of India foreign exchange counters, several STD telephones and a couple of snack bars. It's by no means certain that anyone will be staffing the 24hr **TTDC Tourist Information Centre** booth at the arrivals exit, but if you're lucky you may be able to fix up accommodation from here, or at the "Free Fone" desk nearby.

Also worth knowing about if you plan to leave Chennai by train is the Southern Railways' handy computerized **ticket reservation** counter (daily 10am–5pm), immediately outside the domestic terminal exit.

To **get away from the airport**, there are pre-paid minibus and taxi counters at the international arrivals exit. **Taxis** cost around Rs220–250 for the

It's just as well Chennai boasts some of India's most sophisticated medical facilities, because it is officially one of the unhealthiest places in the world. Exponential, unplanned economic growth, coupled with inadequate investment in the municipal infrastructure, has resulted in chronic pollution problems.

Exhaust emissions are the prime cause of poor air quality. Over the last decade the number of vehicles clogging Chennai's roads has more than quadrupled, and 75 percent of them are dirty, two-stroke two-wheelers. As a result, carbon monoxide levels are double the permitted maximum, while the amount of "suspended particulate matter" in the air is more than seven times the World Health Organization's prescribed limits. So, if you suffer from asthma or any other respiratory disorders, don't aim to spend long here.

Water quality is equally bad: in a recent survey, only two out of twenty groundwater samples collected from around the city were drinkable due to leakages of untreated sewage from the main waterways into reservoirs. As a result there is a disturbing rise in the incidence of mosquito-borne diseases. Chennai alone accounts for around half of the total number of reported malaria cases in Tamil Nadu, with an increase over the past three years of sixty percent in the number of patients developing the deadly falciparum strain (which can develop into cerebral malaria). There has also been an upsurge in less common diseases such as dengue fever and Japanese encephalitis. So take extra malaria precautions while you're in Chennai – always sleep under a net and cover yourself with repellent – especially during, and immediately after, the monsoons, and take extra care over what you eat and drink.

thirty-five-minute ride to the main hotels or railway stations; rickshaws charge around Rs150–175, but you'll have to lug your gear out to the main road as they're not allowed to park inside the airport forecourt. A taxi to **Mamallapuram** will cost in the in the region of Rs450; auto-rickshaws charge about Rs500. Shuttle **buses** (Rs50) run to Egmore and Central railway stations and the Thiruvalluvar (Express) bus stand, but they call at several of the large hotels en route, and are certainly not "Express". The cheapest way to get downtown is to walk to the main road and take any bus marked "Broadway" from the near side. Ask to be let off at the central LIC (Life Insurance Company) stop on Anna Salai, Chennai's main thoroughfare in the downtown area, close to hotels, restaurants and tourist information.

Trains run every 15 or 20 minutes (4.30am–11pm) from **Trisulam** station, 500m from the airport on the far (east) side of the road, to Park, Egmore and North Beach stations, taking roughly 45 minutes.

By train

Arriving in Chennai by train, you come in at one of two **long-distance railway stations**, 1.5km apart on Periyar EVR High Road, towards the north of the city. **Egmore station**, in the heart of the busy commercial Egmore district, is the arrival point for most trains from Tamil Nadu and Kerala. On the whole, all other trains pull in at **Central station**, further east, on the edge of George Town, which has a 24-hour left-luggage office (Rs7 per item/24hr; all luggage must be securely locked) and STD phone booths outside the exit. Both stations have poorly staffed and badly equipped Tourist Information kiosks, but there are always plenty of taxis and auto-rickshaws to be had; Central has a pre-paid auto-rickshaw booth in the forecourt.

By bus

Buses from elsewhere in Tamil Nadu arrive at two bus stands, **Express** and **Broadway**, opposite each other in George Town, near the High Court complex off NSC Bose Road. Both stands are unbearably crowded and confusing but Broadway, which also sees services from Karnataka, Kerala and Andhra Pradesh, is the worst: little more than a dirty, chaotic, pot-holed yard, and a nightmare to negotiate with luggage. If you need to pick up a rickshaw, walk out of the southern exits of either station, and you will find plenty parked around the petrol station on the main road. For details of buses to **Mamallapuram** from Broadway, see p.454.

Information

At the highly efficient and very helpful **Government of India Regional Tourist Office** (GOIRTO) at 154 Anna Salai (Mon–Fri 9.15am–5.45pm, Sat 9am–1pm; Ⓣ044/846 0285 or 846 1459, Ⓔgoirto@vsnl.com, Ⓦwww.tourismindia.com), you can pick up maps and leaflets, and arrange accommodation. They also supply the names of reliable tour agents for car rental, and keep a list of approved **guides** who can arrange a private tour of the city, either for a full day (Rs350–750), or half-day (Rs250–500).

A ten-minute walk across town, the **Tamil Nadu Tourism Development Corporation** (TTDC), 4 EVR Periyar Road (Mon–Fri 10am–5pm; Ⓣ044/536294, Ⓔttdo@md3.vsnl.net.in, Ⓦwww.tamilnadutourism.com) can only book accommodation in their hotels across the state. At the **ITDC** office at 29 Victor Crescent, C-in-C Road (Mon–Sat 6am–8pm, Sun 6am–2pm; Ⓣ044/827 8884, Ⓔitdc.ros@gems.vsnl.net.in), advance bookings for ITDC hotels across the whole country can be made, and tours of the city, state and country are arranged. Tourist offices for other states, including Himachal Pradesh, Kerala, Rajasthan and Uttar Pradesh, are at 28 C-in-C Road. *Hallo! Chennai* (see below) has full details of these and other state offices, as does the GOIRTO on Anna Salai.

The long-established **Hallo! Chennai** (monthly; Rs10) is an accurate directory to all the city's services, with full moon dates (useful for estimating temple festivals), exhaustive flight and train details, and an outline of Chennai bus

Name changes

The city's former name, "Madras", is not the only one to have been weeded out over the last few years by pro-Dravidian politicians. Several major roads in the city have also been renamed as part of an ongoing attempt to "Dravidify" the Tamil capital and, rather unsurprisingly, most of the new names immortalize former nationalist politicians. However, far from all of Chennai's inhabitants are in favour of the recent changes, while some (notably a large contingent of auto-rickshaw *wallahs*) seem completely oblivious to them. The confusing result of this is that both old and new names remain in use. We have used the new ones throughout the chapter. Thus Mount Road, the main shopping road through the centre of town, is now called Anna Salai. To the east, Triplicane High Road, near *Broadlands Hotel*, has become Quaide Milleth Salai. Poonamallee High Road, which runs east–west across the north of the city is now Periyar EVR High Road. North Beach Road, along the eastern edge of George Town is now known as Rajaji Salai, and South Beach Road, the southern stretch of the coastal road, is Kamaraj Salai. Running west, Edward Elliot's Road has been renamed as Dr Radha Krishnan Salai, and Mowbray's Road is called TTK Road. Nungambakkam High Road is now Uttamar Gandhi Salai.

timetables. Alternatively, there is a new, even more comprehensive bimonthly directory called **Madura Welcome, Chennai** (Rs30), that lists every bus service and route in Chennai, and from Chennai to other towns in the state. Both are available at all book and stationery shops. Unfortunately, neither have a "What's On" section: for forthcoming music and dance performances, consult the events column on page three of *The Hindu*, or ask at a tourist office. Alternatively, try and get hold of a copy of **Chennai: This Fortnight**, available for free from all moderate to expensive hotels (just walk into a hotel and ask for one).

City transport

The offices, sights, railway stations and bus stands of Chennai are spread over such a wide area that it's impossible to get around without using some form of **public transport**. Most visitors jump into auto-rickshaws, but outside rush hours you can travel around comfortably by **bus** or suburban **train**.

Incidentally, the city's drastic dry-season water shortage explains the **water carriers** trundling along its congested streets. Watch out for unofficial ones as you cross the road; tractors pull tankers so heavy that they either topple over or fail to stop when brakes are applied, causing fatal accidents.

Buses

To ride the bus in most Indian cities you need to be incredibly resilient and a master of the art of hanging onto open doorways with two fingers. Buses in Chennai, on the other hand, are regular, reliable, inexpensive, well labelled and only cramped during rush hours. On Anna Salai, they have special stops; on smaller streets, flag them down, or wait with the obvious crowd. Buses in Egmore gather opposite the railway station. The numbers of services to specific places of interest in the city are listed in the relevant account, or for a full directory of bus routes, buy a copy of *Madura Welcome, Chennai* (see above).

Trains

If you want to travel south from central Chennai to Guindy (Deer Park), St Thomas Mount or the airport, the easiest way to go is by **train**. Services run every 15 minutes (on average) between 4.30am and 11pm, prices are minimal, and you can guarantee a seat at any time except rush hour (9am & 5pm). First-class carriages substitute padded seats for wooden slatted benches and are a little cleaner, and there's always a carriage reserved for ladies which is usually clearly signed. Buy a ticket before boarding.

City trains follow the route: Chennai Beach (opposite the general post office), Fort, Park (for Central), Egmore, Nungambakkam, Kodambakkam, Mambalam (for T Nagar and silk shops), Saidapet (for Little Mount Church), Guindy, St Thomas Mount and Trisulam (for the airports).

Taxis and rickshaws

Chennai's yellow-top Ambassador **taxis** gather outside Egmore and Central railway stations, and at the airport. All have meters, but they often prefer to set a fixed price before leaving, and invariably charge a return fare, whatever the destination. At around Rs150 for Central to Triplicane, they're practically pricing themselves out of business.

Flocks of auto- and cycle-rickshaws wait patiently outside tourist hotels, and not so patiently outside railway stations. **Auto-rickshaw** drivers in Chennai are notorious for their demand for high fares from locals and tourists alike. A rickshaw from Triplicane to either of the bus stations, Egmore and Central railway stations should cost no more than Rs30–40. All rickshaws have meters; a few drivers use them if asked, but in many cases you'll save a lot of frustrating bargaining by offering a small sub above the meter reading (a driver may offer you a rate of "meter plus 5", meaning Rs5 above the final reading). If you need to get to the airport or station early in the morning, book a rickshaw, and negotiate the price (Rs150–200) the night before; the driver may well sleep in his vehicle outside your hotel.

Only take **cycle-rickshaws** on the smaller roads; riding amid Chennai traffic on a fragile tricycle seat can be extremely hair-raising.

Car, motorbike and bicycle rental

Car rental, with driver, is available at many of the upmarket hotels, or the Government of India Tourist Office (see p.434) can supply you with a list of approved, safe drivers. It's a great, relatively stress-free way to get about if you can afford it. Ambassadors cost Rs600–700 per day (or Rs1100–1200 for a/c).

Anyone brave enough to rent a **moped** or **motorcycle** for short rides around the city, or tours of Tamil Nadu, should head for U-Rent Services, at 36, 2nd Main Road, Poonamallee High Road (Mon–Sat, ☏044/441 1985). You'll need an international driving licence. Prices range from Rs150 to Rs350 per day, and you have to pay a flat Rs250 annual membership fee regardless of how long you rent a bike for.

Bicycles may be rented by the hour from dozens of stalls around the city, but you'll have to keep your wits about you riding through the centre, especially on Anna Salai.

Bus tours

One good way to get around the sights of Chennai is on a TTDC **bus tour**; bookings are taken in the relevant offices. Albeit rushed, they're good value, and the guides can be very helpful.

The **TTDC half-day tour** (daily 8am–1pm or 1.30pm–6.30pm; Rs105 non-a/c, or Rs150 a/c) starts at their office on EVR Periyar Salai. It takes in Fort St George, the Government Museum, the Snake Park, Kapalishvara Temple, Elliot's Beach and Marina Beach (on Friday, the Government Museum is closed, so the tour goes to the Birla Planetarium instead).

Among longer TTDC tours are good-value **day-trips** incorporating visits to Mamallapuram, Kanchipuram, and Pondicherry; meals are included in the tariff.

Accommodation

Finding a **place to stay** in Chennai can be a problem, as hotels are often full. Demand has pushed prices up, so only a couple of places offer anything for less than Rs200. Standards in the less expensive places are not high; in contrast Chennai's starred hotels offer luxury and quality.

The main concentration of mid-range and inexpensive hotels is in **Egmore**, around the railway station. Head for the ones listed below first; if they're full, a bit of hunting around should turn up a reasonable fallback. Other popular areas include **Anna Salai**, which tends to be more expensive, and **Triplicane**, an atmospheric Muslim area boasting some of the city's best budget guesthouses (among them *Broadlands*). The bulk of the top hotels are in the south of the city, along Nungambakkam, Dr Radha Krishnan Salai and Cathedral roads; several offer courtesy buses to and from the airport. Note that if you're arriving late at night, it pays to book a room well in advance (most of the places listed below accept telephone reservations). Finding a room, particularly one in a reasonably priced mid-range place, in the small hours of the morning after a long flight or train ride can be an ordeal.

Due to frequent shortages, visitors should use **water** as sparingly as possible.

Egmore

The accommodation listed is marked on the Egmore, Anna Salai and Triplicane **map** below.

Chandra Towers, 9 Gandhi Irwin Rd ⏀ 044/823 3344, ⏀ 825 1703. The station district's plushest hotel has all the comforts you'd expect, including

central a/c, foreign exchange, 24hr coffee shop, bar and rooftop restaurant. ❼–❽

Dayal De Lodge, 486 Pantheon Rd ⏀ 044/822

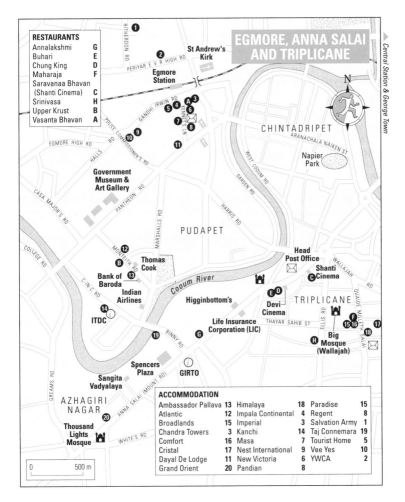

RESTAURANTS

Annalakshmi	G
Buhari	E
Chung King	D
Maharaja	F
Saravanaa Bhavan (Shanti Cinema)	C
Srinivasa	H
Upper Krust	B
Vasanta Bhavan	A

EGMORE, ANNA SALAI AND TRIPLICANE

Central Station & George Town

ACCOMMODATION

Ambassador Pallava	13	Himalaya	18	Paradise	15
Atlantic	12	Impala Continental	4	Regent	8
Broadlands	15	Imperial	3	Salvation Army	1
Chandra Towers	3	Kanchi	14	Taj Connemara	19
Comfort	16	Masa	7	Tourist Home	5
Cristal	17	Nest International	9	Vee Yes	10
Dayal De Lodge	11	New Victoria	6	YWCA	2
Grand Orient	20	Pandian	8		

0   500 m

27328, ☎8251159. Popular with backpackers, this is an old-fashioned town house set back from the main road. No frills, but welcoming, clean, and quiet except during the daily 12pm siren blasts from the rifle range opposite. It's a 10min walk from the station, so jump in an auto if you're weighed down. ③

Impala Continental, 12 Gandhi Irwin Rd ☎044/825 0484. Run-of-the-mill lodge with impersonal but clean non-a/c and a/c en-suite rooms. Good value, so often full. ③–⑤

Imperial, 6 Gandhi Irwin Rd ☎044/825 0376. Large, convenient hotel set in its own enclosed courtyard opposite the station, but sorely in need of a facelift and totally overshadowed by a glitzy new place being built behind it. Range of rooms include a/c suites. Restaurant, bar and travel services. ⑤–⑥

Masa, 15/1 Kennet's Lane ☎044/825 2966. Variously priced non-a/c and a/c en-suite rooms in a very clean, modern building, close to the station. Polite staff, and good value. *Hotel Regal* (☎044/823 1766; ④–⑤) next door is identical, except the exact dimensions have been thoughtfully provided outside each light and airy room. ②–④

Nest International, 31 Gandhi Irwin Rd ☎044/828 0113, ☎824 0599. Smart, business-oriented place surrounded by trees and overpriced. The a/c rooms are small and stuffy with ethnic cotton-print decor, and the bathrooms are tiny. Restaurant, bar and room service available. ⑦–⑧

New Victoria, 3 Kennet's Lane ☎044/825 3638. Friendly, upscale hotel; all rooms a/c with hot showers and some with balconies. Non-residents can use the bar (11am–11pm) and internet centre (Rs40/hr) while waiting for a train. Rate includes breakfast; works out as good value if you pay in dollars. ⑦–⑧

Pandian, 9 Kennet's Lane ☎044/825 2901, ☎825 8459. Pleasant, clean and modern mid-scale place

within walking distance of the railway station. Ask for a room on the Church Park side of the building for green views. Some rooms are a/c. ⑥–⑦

Regent, 8 Kennet's Lane ☎044/825 3347. Quiet, respectable lodge with non-a/c and a/c rooms, all a bit shabby for the price, but spotless bathrooms. Fine for a night. ④–⑤

Salvation Army Red Shield Guest House, 15 Ritherdon Rd ☎044/532 1821. Tucked away in a leafy suburban backstreet behind the station, this old-established Sally Army place has six- to eleven-bed dorms (Rs70; not advised for single women), doubles with attached baths (non-a/c and a/c), and a four-bedded non-a/c room (Rs350). The management is very helpful and friendly. A very dependable budget option. ③–⑧

Southern Railway Retiring Rooms, 1st floor (turn right out of the main exit). Dorm beds for Rs50, and spacious, if run-down, doubles presided over by stern matron in a regulation blue sari. The latter are excellent value, so they tend to fill up quickly. ①–④

Tourist Home, 21 Gandhi Irwin Rd ☎044/825 0079. Popular hotel directly opposite the railway station: fresher and better ventilated than many, but it suffers badly from early morning noise. Spotless rooms (some a/c) have showers, telephones, clean sheets and towels; there are also three- and six-bedded rooms. Good value. ④–⑥

Vee Yes, 35 Gandhi Irwin Rd ☎044/825 7801. Average city hotel, a 5min walk from the station; badly ventilated corridors but clean enough rooms (some a/c) with carpets and hot showers. ④–⑤

YWCA International Guest House, 1086 Periyar EVR High Rd ☎044/532 4234, ☎532 4263. Attractive hotel in quiet gardens behind Egmore station. Spotless, spacious rooms with attached bathrooms, safe deposit and a good restaurant. One of the best-value places in the city, so book ahead. The rates include an excellent buffet breakfast. ⑤–⑥

Anna Salai and Triplicane

The accommodation listed below is marked on the Egmore, Anna Salai and Triplicane **map** on p.437.

Ambassador Pallava, 30 Montieth Rd ☎044/855 4476, ☎855 4492. Colossal four-star, close to Anna Salai, with great views from its upper storeys. Amid all the cool, white marble and old-plated mirrors there is a pool, night club and health club. Rooms start at $90. ⑨

Atlantic, 2 Montieth Rd ☎044/855 3914, ☎855 3239. Huge block hotel and restaurant complex near the government museum. It's a favourite with Tamil movie directors (who often use the "deluxe"

rooms as sets). The regular a/c rooms are on the dowdy side, but large, with balconies and views, but the "deluxe" annexe is more upmarket. ⑥

Broadlands, 16 Vallabha Agraham St, Triplicane ☎044/854 5573. A whitewashed old house, with crumbling stucco and stained glass, ranged around a leafy courtyard; the kind of budget travellers' enclave you either love or loathe. It has a large roof terrace and clean, non-a/c rooms, a few with attached shower, private balcony and views of the mosque. Inexpensive left-luggage facility is available, but a reprehensible "No Indians" policy is very strictly enforced. ③ –④

Comfort, 22 Vallabha Agraham St, Triplicane ☎ 044/858 7661. A chaotic place with yards of dimly lit corridors. If you can hack this, the rooms (some a/c) are clean but on the small side, all with attached bathrooms. ④ –⑤

Cristal, 34 CNK Rd, Triplicane ☎ 044/858 5605. A very safe and friendly place run by a team of brothers; it is busy with locals sipping coffee in reception all day. The non-a/c rooms are tiled and clean, all with attached showers in a modern building just off Quaide Milleth Salai. There is no restaurant. ②

Grand Orient, 693 Anna Salai ☎ 044/852 4111, ⑤ 852 3412. Very swish, recently refurbished place on the main drag, with modern decor, central a/c and a multicuisine restaurant. ⑧

Himalaya, 54 Quaide Milleth Salai ☎ 044/854 7522. Clean, spacious rooms and efficient service. Cable TV, hot showers and a balcony in all rooms; some a/c. There is a good restaurant and 24hr

internet access (open to non-residents). ⑥ –⑧

Kanchi, 28 C-in-C Rd ☎ 044/827 1100, ⑤ 827 9000. A soulless skyscraper hotel with indifferent staff, it is redeemed by the superb views from its spacious rooms (some a/c), two excellent restaurants (one rooftop) and bar. ⑥ –⑦

Paradise, 17/1 Vallabha Agraham St, Triplicane ☎ 044/854 1542. Next door to *Broadlands*, and a dependable choice if you're after an inexpensive non-a/c room with an attached shower-toilet. There are chairs up on a large roof terrace, and food can be ordered in for you. ③ –④

Taj Connemara, Binny Road ☎ 044/852 0123, ⑤ 852 3361. Dating from the British era, this whitewashed Art Deco five-star hotel is a Chennai institution situated near Anna Salai. The best rooms are the big, characterful heritage suites, each with a dressing room and verandah overlooking the pool. The "standard" rooms are, by contrast, very overpriced and disappointing; they catch the unpleasant smells from the polluted river nearby. There is a pool, several good restaurants and a bar. Rooms start at $155. ⑨

Outside the centre

The accommodation listed below is marked on the Chennai **map** on p.431.

Karpakam, 41 South Mada St, Mylapore ☎ 044/494 2987. Very ordinary, slightly dingy place with clean but shabby rooms (some a/c), but its location overlooking the Kapalishvara Temple is unrivalled and it's also on the right side of the city for the airport, 12km away. ⑤ –⑥

Maris, 9 Cathedral Rd ☎ 044/827 0541, ⑤ 825 4847. Spruce, efficient 1970s concrete block hotel right next to the *Sheraton*, but a fraction of the price. Their spotless a/c rooms are a particularly good deal for the area. You can book TTDC city tours here. ⑥ –⑦

New Woodlands Hotel, 72–75 Dr Radha Krishnan Salai Rd ☎ 044/827 3111. Popular with honeymooners, this complex has deluxe a/c rooms, restaurants, a billiards room, gardens and pool. The single rooms are great value at only Rs300. ⑥

Ranjith, 9 Nungambakkam High Rd ☎ 044/827 0521. Comfortable non-a/c and a/c en-suite rooms with cable TV. Veg and non-veg restaurants, bar and travel agent. ⑥ –⑦

Savera, 69 Dr Radha Krishnan Salai Rd ☎ 044/827 4700, ⑤ 827 3475. Slightly older than the competition, but boasting all mod cons, including a pool, good pastry shop, bar, excellent South Indian speciality restaurant, and rooftop restaurant with great views. ⑧ –⑨

Shelter, 19–21 Venkatesa Agraharam St, Mylapore ☎ 044/495 1919, ⑤ 493 5646. Sparklingly clean

and modern luxury hotel with central a/c. It's just a stone's throw from the Kapalishvara Temple, and better value than most upscale places at this price. ⑧ –⑨

Sornam International, 11 Stringer St ☎ 044/535 3060. The best of a generally ropey budget bunch around the Central station. Clean and respectable enough, but really only worth considering if you can't face an auto-rickshaw ride across town, or have an early train to catch. There is a veg restaurant. ③

Trident, 1/24 GST Rd ☎ 044/234 4747, ⑤ 234 6699. Comfortable five-star hotel in lovely gardens with swimming pool. Conveniently near the airport (3km), but long (albeit complimentary) drive into town. Good restaurants, one of which serves great Thai cuisine. ⑨

Welcomgroup Chola Sheraton, Cathedral Road ☎ 044/811 0101, ⑤ 811 0202. Palatial five-star in the city centre, with all the trimmings, including a pool. The hefty US$160 per night room tariff includes a buffet breakfast and a very welcome "cocktail hour". ⑨

Welcomgroup Park Sheraton, 132 TTK Rd ☎ 044/499 4101, ⑤ 499 7101. Last word in American-style executive luxury, with bow-tied valets and in-room fax machines, yet somehow not too ostentatious. Three excellent restaurants, 24hr coffee shop, health suite and pool. ⑨

The City

Chennai divides into three main areas: north, central and south. The northern district, separated from the rest by the Cooum River, is the site of the first

The Chennai Festival and the sabhas

The sabhas of Chennai – the city's arts societies and venues, of which the most illustrious is the Chennai Music Academy – stage regular public performances of Carnatic classical music and Bharatanatyam dance. Here, ambitious artists have to undergo the scrutiny of an often fanatical audience and a less-than-generous bevy of newspaper critics, whose reviews can make or break a career.

Musicians are expected to interpret correctly the subtleties of any given composition, *raga* or *tala*. The sets of notes that make up a *raga* occupy a place midway between melody and scale; they must be played imaginatively in improvisation, but in strict sequences and with correct emphasis. The worst crime, the sign of an amateur, is to slip accidentally into a different *raga* that might share the same scale. *Tala*, the rhythmic cycle and bedrock of the music, will often be demonstrated by someone on stage, and consists of a series of claps and waves; unlike in North India, this element is overt in the South and the audience delights in clapping along to keep the often-complex time signatures. The pleasure is heightened during percussion improvisations on the barrel-shaped *mridangam* drum or *ghatam* clay pot that accompany many performances.

The Chennai Festival is an annual event held from December 15th until January 1st, during which up to five hundred events are staged, primarily at the Music Academy (Ⓣ044/811 2231) on T.T.K. Road. It is a real orgy of classical music and dance recitals, in which many of India's greatest artistes, from all over the country, can be seen at work.

Female vocalists to look out for include Mani Krishnaswamy, Charumathi Ramachandran, Sudha Raghunathan and Bombay Jayashree; duos such as the Bombay and Hyderabad Sisters are also popular. Top-ranking male singers, K.V. Narayanaswamy, B. Rajam Iyer and younger artists like Thrissur Ramachandran and T.N. Seshagopalan should not be missed. Among the best of the instrumentalists are E. Gayatri and Rama Varma on the gentle melodic *vina*, a stringed instrument unique to the South; Ramani on flute; violinists such as T.N. Krishnan, D. Ananda Raman; and N. Ravikiran on *gottuvadyam*, a rare member of the *vina* family, laid flat on the floor and played much like a slide guitar. Carnatic music's answer to John Coltrane is Kadri Gopalnath, whose soaring saxophone and flamboyant dress have made him one of the most distinctive figures on the circuit. Former child prodigy, U. Sriniwas, is a maestro on the electric mandolin. Cassettes and CDs of all the above artistes are available at *Music World* in Spencer Plaza. For addresses of good musical instrument shops in the city, see Listings, p.452.

The predominant dance style is Bharatanatyam, as performed by stars such as Alarmail Valli, and the Dhananjayans. Dance dramas are also staged by the *Kalakshetra Academy*, a school of dance and music set in a beautiful hundred-acre compound near the sea in Tiruvanmiyur, on the southern outskirts of the city.

Outside the festival period, to find out about performances of music and dance, ask at the government tourist office on Anna Salai, consult the listings pages of local papers such as *The Hindu*, or have a look in *Chennai: This Fortnight* (see p.435). You may also like to pay a visit to the Sangita Vadyalaya, behind the HDF Bank on Anna Salai (Mon–Fri 9.15am–5.45pm), which displays an impressive array of Indian musical instruments. The centre, recently shifted to this new ground-floor building in the centre of town, was set up to preserve and restore antique pieces, but resident artisans also revive rare instruments which are no longer commonly played. You can try your hand at a few of them yourself, and experiment with an amazing horde of old percussion pieces.

British outpost in India, **Fort St George**, and the commercial centre, **George Town**, which grew up during British occupation. At the southern end of Rajaji Salai, is **Parry's Corner**, George Town's principal landmark – look for the tall grey building labelled "Parry's". It's a major stop for city buses.

Central Chennai, sandwiched between the Cooum river and Dr Radna Krishnan Salai, and crossed diagonally by the city's main thoroughfare, **Anna Salai**, is the modern, commercial heart of the metropolis. To the east, this gives way to the atmospheric old Muslim quarters of **Triplicane** and a long straight **Marina** where fishermen mend nets and set small boats out to sea, and hoards of Indian tourists hitch up saris and trousers for a quick paddle.

The southern district, near the coast, **Mylapore**, inhabited in the 1500s by the Portuguese, boasts **Kapalishvara Temple** and **San Thome Cathedral**, both tourist attractions and places of pilgrimage. Further out, south of the Adyar river, is the Portuguese church on **St Thomas Mount**.

Fort St George

Quite unlike any other fort in India, **Fort St George** stands amid state offices facing the sea in the east of the city, just south of George Town on Kamaraj Salai. It looks more like a complex of well-maintained colonial mansions than a fort; indeed many of its buildings are used today as offices, a hive of activity during the week as politicians and peons rush between the Secretariat and the State Legislature.

The fort was the first structure of Madras town, and the first territorial possession of the British in India. Construction began in 1640, but most of the original buildings were replaced later that century, after being damaged during French sieges. The most imposing structure is the eighteenth-century colonnaded **Fort House**, coated in deep-slate-grey and white paint. Next door, in the more modestly proportioned **Exchange Building** – site of Madras's first bank – is the excellent fort **museum** (daily except Fri 10am–5pm; $5, or the rupee equivalent). The collection within faithfully records the central events of the British occupation of Madras with portraits, regimental flags, weapons, coins minted by the East India Company, medals, stamps and thick woollen uniforms that make you wonder how the Raj survived as long as it did. Some of the most evocative mementos are letters written by figures such as Robert Clive, reporting on life in the colony. The squat cast-iron cage on the ground floor was brought to Madras from China, where for more than a year in the nineteenth century it was used as a particularly sadistic form of imprisonment for a British captain. The upper floor, once the public exchange hall where merchants met to gossip and trade, is now an **art gallery**, where portraits of prim officials and their wives sit side by side with fine sketches of the British embarking at Madras in aristocratic finery, attended by Indians in loin cloths. Also on display are etchings by the famous artist **Thomas Daniells**, whose work largely defined British perceptions of India at the end of the eighteenth century.

South of the museum, past the State Legislature, stands the oldest surviving Anglican church in Asia, **St Mary's Church** (daily 9am–5pm), built in 1678, and partly renovated after a battle with the French in 1759. The church, built with thick walls and a strong vaulted roof to withstand the city's many sieges, served as a store and shelter in times of war. It's distinctly English in style, crammed with plaques and statues in memory of British soldiers, politicians and their wives. The grandest plaque, made of pure silver, was presented by Elihu Yale, former Governor of Fort St George (1687–96) and founder of Yale

University in the USA. A collection of photographs of visiting dignitaries, including Queen Elizabeth II, is on display in the entrance porch. Nearby, **Robert Clive's house** is in a rather sorry state, and is currently used by the Archaeological Survey of India as offices.

George Town

North of Fort St George, the former British trading centre of **George Town** (bus #18 from Anna Salai) remains a focus for banks, offices and shipping companies. This confusing – if well-ordered – grid of streets harbours a fascinating medley of architecture: eighteenth- and nineteenth-century churches, Hindu and Jain temples and a scattering of mosques, interspersed with grand mansions. However, despite its potential charm, this is Chennai's most chaotic and crowded area, a dirty and uninviting warren clogged by particularly persistent hawkers and thick traffic. Probably the best way to appreciate the area is from its edges. In the east, on Rajaji Salai, the **General Post Office** (daily 8am–8pm) occupies a robust earth-red Indo-Saracenic building, constructed in 1884. George Town's southern extent is marked by the bulbous white domes and sandstone towers of the **High Court** and the even more opulent towers of the **Law College**, both showing strong Islamic influence.

It can be fun to take a quick rummage around George Town's **bazaars**, lines of rickety stalls selling clothes, bags, umbrellas, watches, shoes and perfume, concentrated along Rajaji Salai and NSC Bose Road.

Government Museum

It's well worth setting aside at least half a day to explore the Chennai **Government Museum** (daily except Fri; 9.30am–5pm; Rs3; camera Rs20), hop on bus #11H from Anna Salai for Pantheon Road, south of Egmore railway station. It houses remarkable archeological finds from South India and the Deccan, stone sculptures from major temples and an unsurpassed collection of Chola bronzes.

A deep red circular structure, fronted by Italian-style pillars and built in 1851, the **main building** stands opposite the entrance and ticket office. The first gallery is devoted to archeology and geology, with tools, pots, jewellery and weapons from the Stone and Iron Ages, and maps of principal excavations. Later exhibits include a substantial assortment of dismantled panels, railings and statues from the second century AD stupa complex at **Amaravati**, Andhra Pradesh (see p.594). Depicting episodes from the Buddha's life and scenes from the *Jataka* stories from ancient Hinayana Buddhist texts, these sensuously carved marble reliefs are widely regarded as the finest achievements of early Indian art, outshining even the Sanchi *toranas*. Sadly, they are poorly lit and inadequately labelled; some have even been defaced with graffiti, while others are blackened and worn from constant rubbing. To the left of the Amaravati gallery, high, arcaded halls full of stuffed animals and the like lead to the **ethnology gallery**, where models, clothes and weapons, along with photographs of expressionless faces in orderly lines, illustrate local tribal societies, some long since wiped out. A fascinating display of wind and string instruments, drums and percussion includes the large predecessor of today's *sitar* and several very old *tabla*. Nearby, a group of wooden doors and window frames from Chettinad, a region near Madurai, are exquisitely carved with floral and geometric designs much like those found in Gujarati *havelis*. This section is currently under major renovation, and at the time of writing was temporarily closed to the public.

The museum's real treasure, however, is the modern, well-lit gallery, left of the main building, which contains the world's most complete and impressive selection of **Chola bronzes** (see p.680). Large statues of Shiva, Vishnu and Parvati stand in the centre, flanked by glass cases containing smaller figurines, including several sculptures of Shiva as **Nataraja**, the Lord of the Dance, encircled by a ring of fire and standing with his arms and legs poised and head provocatively cocked. One of the finest models is **Ardhanarishvara**, the androgynous form of Shiva (united with Shakti in transcendence of duality), the left side of the body is female and the right male, and the intimacy of detail is astounding. A rounded breast, a delicate hand and tender bejewelled foot are counterpoints to the harsher sinewy limbs and torso, and the male side of the head is crowned with a mass of matted hair and serpents.

A **children's museum** demonstrates the principles of electricity and irrigation with marginally diverting, semi-functional models, while the magnificent Indo-Saracenic **art gallery** houses old British portraits of figures such as Clive and Hastings, Rajput and Moghul miniatures and a small display of ivory carvings.

St Andrew's Kirk

Just northeast of Egmore station, off Periyar EVR High Road, **St Andrew's Kirk**, consecrated in 1821, is a fine example of Georgian architecture. Modelled on London's St Martin-in-the-Fields, it is one of just three churches in India which has a circular seating plan, laid out beneath a huge dome painted blue with gold stars and supported by a sweep of Corinthian columns. Marble plaques around the church give a fascinating insight into the kind of people who left Britain to work for the imperial and Christian cause. A staircase leads onto the flat roof, surrounding the dome, from where you can climb further up into the steeple past the massive bell to a tiny balcony affording excellent views of the city.

Valluvar Kottam

In the south of the Nungambakkam district, just off Village Road, the **Valluvar Kottam** is an intriguing construction, built in classical style in 1976 as a memorial to the first-century Tamil poet Thiruvalluvar. Most impressive is the 34-metre-high stone chariot, carved from just three blocks of granite, into a likeness of the great temple car of Thiruvarur. Adjoining this veritable juggernaut is a vast public auditorium, one of the largest in Asia, with a capacity of four thousand. A stroll along the auditorium roof past shallow rectangular ponds brings you to a large statue of the poet saint, within a shrine carved into the upper reaches of the chariot. Among the many reliefs around the monument, look out for the cat in human pose, reminiscent of the figure at Arjuna's Penance in Mamallapuram.

Marina Beach

One of the longest city beaches in the world, the **Marina** (Kamarajar Salai) stretches 5km from the harbour at the southeastern corner of George Town, to San Thome Cathedral. The impulse to transform Chennai's "rather dismal beach" into a Marina, styled "from old Sicilian recollections" to function as a "lung" for the city, was conceived by Mountstuart Elphinstone Grant-Duff (Governor 1881–86) who had otherwise won himself the reputation for being "feeble, sickly" and a "failure". Over the years, numerous buildings, some of which undoubtedly would not have figured in memories of Sicily, have sprung up, among them surreal modern memorials to Tamil Nadu's chief political heroes and freedom fighters.

The **beach** itself is a sociable stretch, peopled by idle paddlers, picnickers and pony-riders; every afternoon crowds gather around the beach market. However, it suffers miserably from being just a little downstream from the port, which belches out waste and smelly fumes, as well as being the local toilet around the areas where the fishermen hang out. This does not appear to deter the crowds of tourists, but for those used to clean beaches with fresh breezes, where you can walk barefoot, this is a sore disappointment. Unsurprisingly, swimming and sunbathing are neither recommended nor approved. Nor is it advisable to take your shoes off on the beach, as the sand is full of bits of broken glass and rusty bottle tops.

There's also a rather neglected aquarium, and two parks at the northern end, the **Anna Park** and **MGR Samadhi**, where Tamil tourists flock in droves to pay their respects at the shrine of the state's most illustrious movie actor and chief minister, **M.G. Ramachandran** (see box on p.449). At the northern end, one of the oldest of the city's university buildings is the **Senate House** (1879), an uncharacteristically Byzantine-influenced design by Robert Fellowes Chisholm (1840–1915). He was one of the British leaders in developing the Indo-Saracenic hybrid style, incorporating Hindu, Jain and Muslim elements along with solid Victorian, British brickwork.

Continuing south, past the Indo-Saracenic **Presidency College** (1865–71), a number of stolid Victorian university buildings include the **Lady Willingdon Teacher Training College**. Next door, the college's hostel, a huge lump of a building with a semicircular frontage painted white and yellow, was the Madras depot of the Tudor Ice Company (see box opposite) during the nineteenth century.

Mylapore

Long before Madras came into existence, **Mylapore**, south of the Marina (buses #4, 5 or 21 from the LIC building on Anna Salai), was a major settlement; the Greek geographer Ptolemy mentioned it in the second century AD as a thriving port. During the Pallava period (fifth to ninth centuries) it was second only to Mamallapuram (see p.464), a little way down the coastline.

A significant stop – with Little Mount and St Thomas Mount – on the St Thomas pilgrimage trail, the **San Thome Cathedral** (daily 6am–8pm) marks the eastern boundary of Mylapore, lying close to the sea at the southern end of the Marina. St Thomas is credited as being the first to bring Christianity to the subcontinent in the first century AD (see p.446). Although the present Neo-Gothic structure dates from 1896, San Thome stands on the site of two earlier churches (the first possibly erected by Nestorian Christians from Persia during the tenth century) built over the tomb of St Thomas; his relics are kept inside.

Behind the church, a small **museum** houses stones inscribed in Tamil, Sanskrit (twelfth-century Chola) and early Portuguese, and also a map of India dated 1519.

The **Kapalishvara**, less than 1km west of the San Thome Cathedral, is the most famous temple in Chennai, the principal shrine being dedicated to Shiva. Seventh-century Tamil poet-saints sang its praises, but the present structure probably dates from the sixteenth century. Until then, the temple is thought to have occupied a site on the shore; sea erosion or demolition at the hands of the Portuguese led it to be rebuilt inland. The huge (40m) *gopura* towering above

Over the years, Chennai has seen its fair share of world-shaping moments, but few can have been met with the wonder and unanimous approval that greeted the arrival of an American clipper in the early 1830s. Its cargo, rolled in pine sawdust and steered through the surf in small *masula* boats, had never been seen in peninsular India before, and one can only imagine the amazement of the local coolies when they first felt the weight and burning cold of melting ice on their shoulders.

In a little over four months, the ship, the *Tuscany*, had sailed halfway around the world with its precious load, harvested from frozen ponds around Boston. Little technology was required to gather the ice: grappling hooks, lengths of blocks and tackle, a few horse-drawn sleds and one hundred Irish labourers. The real breakthrough that made the trade possible was the discovery, by one Frederic Nathaniel Jarvis, that fresh pine sawdust would insulate ice, even from high tropical temperatures. A few years earlier, his friend, Frederick Tudor Boston, had tried to transport $10,000 dollars worth of New English ice to Martinique in the Caribbean, only to watch the entire cargo melt en route. However, Jarvis's bright idea enabled Boston's Tudor Ice Company to export 180 tons of ice to Calcutta in 1833. From that initial shipment enough profit was generated to build warehouses in Bombay and Madras, and thereafter the trade continued to boom for nearly forty years, until the invention of steam-powered ice-making machines, which put the company out of business.

Overlooking Chennai's sun-scorched Marina Beach, the building erected by the Tudor Ice Company in the 1840s to store their stock, still stands as an evocative reminder of this brief, but extraordinary, episode in the city's mercantile history. It was sold to a rich lawyer when the bottom fell out of the trade, and it was with him that the famous Indian philosopher, Vivekananda stayed after his return from the States in 1897, when crowds would gather on the steps outside to hear the sage speak. In memory of this event – and in spite of the fact it now serves as a hostel for the adjacent Lady Willingdaon Teacher Training College – the local municipality have rechristened the building "Vivekananda House", but to everyone else in Chennai, the stalwart old pile, with its peeling yellow-painted walls and distinctive twin circular tiered facade, is still known simply as "The Ice House".

the main east entrance, plastered in stucco figures, is a comparatively recent addition (1906). Surrounding an assortment of busy shrines, where priests offer blessings for devotees and non-Hindus alike, the courtyard features an old tree where a small shrine to Shiva's consort, Parvati, shows her in the form of a peahen (*mayil*) worshipping a *lingam*. This commemorates the legend that she was momentarily distracted from concentrating on her lord by the enchanting dance of a peacock. Shiva, miffed at this dereliction of wifely duty, cursed her, whereupon she turned into a peahen. To expiate the sin, Parvati took off to a place called Kapalinagar, and embarked upon rigorous austerities. To commemorate her success, the town was named Mayilapore or **Mylapore**. The oldest artefacts in the Kapalishvara temple are the movable bronze images of deities and the 63 Shaivite Nayanmar poet-saints, two of whom came from Mylapore. Unusually, the main shrine faces west, towards a space dominated by an eighteenth-century water-lily tank, that appears vast in this cramped suburban district.

Important **festivals** held at Kapalishvara include *Thaipusam* (February; see p.543), when the bronze images of Shiva and Parvati are pulled around the temple tank in a decorated boat to the accompaniment of music. *Brahmotsava* (March/April) celebrates the marriage of Shiva and Parvati; in the afternoon of the eighth day, all 63 bronze images of the Nayanmar saints are clothed, garlanded and taken out in palanquins along the streets to meet the bejewelled images of Shiva and Parvati. Vasantha (May/June), the summer festival, is marked by concerts.

In the busy **market streets** that surround the temple, amid stalls selling pots and pans, flowers, religious paraphernalia and vegetables, glittering shops spill over with gold wedding-jewellery. Exquisite saris are unfolded for scrutiny in silk emporia; the finest quality comes from Kanchi and is delicately embroidered with gold and silver thread. Saris of this distinction can add as much as Rs30,000 to the cost of a wedding.

A little further west, before you come to TTK Road, the **Luz Church**, on Luz Church Road, is thought to be the earliest Christian building in Chennai, built by the Portuguese in the sixteenth century. Its founding is associated with a miracle: Portuguese sailors in difficulties at sea were once guided to land and safety by a light which, when they tried to find its source, disappeared. The church, dedicated to Our Lady of Light, was erected where the light left them.

Little Mount

St Thomas is said to have sought refuge from persecution in a group of caves on the **Little Mount**, 8km south of the city centre (bus #18 from Anna Salai), now 200m off the road between the Maraimalai Adigal Bridge and the Residence of the Governor of Tamil Nadu. Entrance to the caves is beside steps leading to a statue of Our Lady of Good Health. Inside, next to a small natural window in the rock, are impressions of what are believed to be St Thomas's handprints, made when he made his escape through this tiny opening.

Behind the new circular church of Our Lady of Good Health, together with brightly painted replicas of the Pietà and Holy Sepulchre, is a natural **spring**. Tradition has it that this was created when Thomas struck the rock, so the crowds that came to hear him preach could quench their thirst; samples of its holy water are on sale.

St Thomas Mount

Tradition has it that St Thomas was speared to death (or struck by a hunter's stray arrow), while praying before a stone cross on **St Thomas Mount**, 11km south of the city centre, close to the airport (take a suburban train to Guindy railway station, and walk from there). **Our Lady of Expectation Church** (1523) is reached by 134 granite steps marked at intervals with the fourteen stations of the Cross. At the top of the steps, a huge old banyan tree provides shade for devotees who come to fast, pray and sing. Inside the church, St Thomas's cross is said to have bled in 1558; above the altar which marks the spot of the apostle's death, a painting of the Madonna and Child is credited to St Luke. A memento stall stands nearby and cold drinks are available in the adjacent Holy Apostle's Convent.

The Theosophical Society Headquarters

The **Theosophical Society** (buses #23C or #5 from George Town/Anna Salai) was established in New York in 1875 by American Civil War veteran Colonel Henry S. Olcott, a failed farmer and journalist, and the eccentric Russian aristocrat Madame Helena Petrovna Blavatsk. Blavatsk claimed occult powers and telepathic links with "Mahatmas" in Tibet. Based on a fundamental belief in the equality and truth of all religions, the society in fact propagated a modern form of Hinduism, praising all things Indian and shunning

For a spiritual organization based on principles of inclusiveness and harmony, the Theosophical Society has suffered some acrimonious schisms over the years, particularly after the deaths of its founders Olcott and Blavatsky, when its most prominent personalities clashed in an unseemly power struggle. The most infamous rift of all, though, was one between the Society's mandarins and the young man they identified in 1905 as the "Buddha to Be", Jiddu Krishnamurti, a Telegu-speaking *brahmin* boy brought to Adyar by his father after his mother died. He was first "discovered" by Charles Webster Leadbeater, a leading light in the Theosophical Society who claimed clairvoyant powers. Among the central tenets of the movement was a belief that Lord Krishna and Christ were about to be reborn as a "World Teacher", and from the moment Leadbeater saw the ten-year-old Krishnamurti playing football on the beach at Adyar he knew he'd found the "Enlightened One". Jiddu, however, did not initially look the part. Wild, malnourished and sickly, with "crooked teeth . . . and a vacant, almost moronic expression", he seemed more like a street kid than a messiah in the making.

Informed that the "Vehicle" had been identified, Annie Besant – the then President of the Theosophical Society – was quick to take the boy under her wing. Over the coming years, Krishnamurti, with the support of the TS and its benefactors, was to receive the best education that money could buy, with places at famous colleges in England and California. Spiritual instruction, meanwhile, came from Leadbeater's own guru, a mystical Buddhist lama who lived in a remote Tibetan ravine and delivered his teachings on the "astral plane".

Not surprisingly, Krishnamurti's father resented Besant's adoption of his son and initiated custody proceedings to prevent the TS from taking him abroad. The High Court of Madras found in Krishnamurti senior's favour, but its decision was overturned after Besant took the case to London (in spite of allegations of "unnatural practices" levelled against Leadbeater). By the time the legal battle had run its course, however, Krishnamurti was legally an adult and already teaching. He'd also matured into an exceedingly handsome, suave young man, with a trademark sweep of jet black hair and a taste for fashionable clothes.

While his teachings were being received with growing enthusiasm, both within India and the US, the fledgling guru was showing definite signs of resenting the role thrust upon him by the Theosophists. Soon, this found expression in criticism of the ritual, mysticism and self-aggrandizing "wise-men" that had become features of the Society's new leadership, some of whom then began to turn against their charismatic detractor, claiming he had been "possessed by black forces". The conflict came to a head when Krishnamurti, addressing a Theosophy camp in the US, formally renounced his position as head for the OSE (Order of the Star in the East), originally formed to promote his teachings. He resigned from the TS soon afterwards, with the famous pronouncement that "Truth is a pathless land . . . you cannot approach it by any path whatsoever, by any religion, by any sect."

For the rest of his life, Krishnamurti – or "K" as he preferred to be known – wandered the world as a individual, lecturing, writing and setting up educational institutions where young people could, as he said, "flower as human beings, without fear, without confusion, with great integrity". When he died in 1986, aged 91, he was one of the most famous philosophers of his generation, but always resisted the label of guru; "mediators . . .", he said, "must inevitably step down the Truth, and hence betray it."

Christian missionaries – so its two founders were greeted enthusiastically when they transferred their operations to Madras in 1882, establishing their headquarters near Elliot's Beach in Adyar. Even after Madame Blavatsky's psychic powers were proved to be bogus, the society continued to attract Hindus and

Western visitors, and its buildings still stand today, sheltering several shrines and an excellent **library** of books on religion and philosophy (Mon–Sat 8.30–10am & 2–4pm). The collection, begun by Olcott in 1886, comprises 165,000 volumes and nearly 200,000 palm-leaf manuscripts, from all over the world, a selection of which is housed in an exhibition room on the ground floor. This includes eight hundred-year-old scroll pictures of the Buddha, a seventeenth-century treatise on embalming bodies from London, rare Tibetan xylographs written on bark paper, exquisite illuminated Korans, a giant copy of Martin Luther's *Biblia* printed in Nuremberg in the 1600s and a Bible in seven languages that's the size of a thumb nail.

The 270 acres of woodland and gardens surrounding the Society's headquarters are a serene place to sit and restore spirits, away from the noise and heat of the city streets. In the middle of the grounds, a vast four-hundred-year-old **banyan tree**, said to be the second largest in the world, provides shade for up to three thousand people at a time. J. Krishnamurthi and Maria Montessori have both given talks under its tangle of pillar-like root stems, whose growth Theosophists see as symbolizing the spread of the Society itself.

The Enfield factory

India's most stylish home-made motorcycle, the **Enfield Bullet**, is manufactured at a plant on the outskirts of Chennai, 18km north of Anna Salai (bus #1 from LIC Building or Parry's Corner). With its elegant tear-drop tank and thumping 350cc single-cylinder engine, the Bullet has become a contemporary classic – in spite of its propensity to leak oil and break down. Bike enthusiasts should definitely brave the long haul across town to see the **factory**, which is as much a period piece as the machines it turns out. Guided tours (Mon–Fri 9.30am–5.30pm; ☏044/543 3000), which last around one and a half hours and are free, have to be arranged in advance by telephoning the Enfield's Marketing General Manager, Mr K. Muralidharan. You can do this yourself, or through the Government of India Tourist Office on Anna Salai.

MGR Film City

The only one of Chennai's movie studios that actively encourages visitors is **MGR Film City** (daily 8am–8pm; Rs25, plus Rs50 for still camera permits), on the southern outskirts near Guindy National Park. You can travel to and from Film City by **bus** (#1 from the LIC Building on Anna Salai, #5C from Parry's Corner, or #23C from Egmore Station), and plenty of auto-rickshaws hang around outside the main gates. A sprawling campus of decaying film sets, it offers little of interest for foreign visitors unless there happens to be an outdoor shoot in progress. At other times, action is confined to a small amusement park, and a group of disused sets dominated by a giant concrete shark's mouth, where bus parties of posing local tourists take advantage of the site's best photo opportunity. Inexpensive meals and cold drinks are available at the busy crew canteen, next to the crossroads in the middle of the campus.

Eating

Chennai runs on indigenous fast-food restaurants and "meals" (thalis) joints, in particular the legendary *Saravanaa* chain, which serves superb South Indian food for a fraction of the cost of a coffee at one of the five-stars. That said, a

Bollywood may be better known, but the film studios of Chennai churn out more movies than any other city in the world – on average, around 900 each year. The movies feature the usual Indian masala mix of fast action, wide-eyed melodrama, romance (with just the hint of a kiss), punch-ups, shoot-outs and, of course, hip-grinding song and dance sequences with as many costume changes as camera angles. They cater for the largely illiterate rural population of Tamil Nadu, although the biggest blockbusters also get dubbed into Hindi and exported north.

One notable difference between the Chennai movie industry and its counterpart in Mumbai (see p.132) is the influence of politics on Tamil films – an overlap that dates from the earliest days of regional cinema, when stories, stock themes and characters were derived from traditional folk ballads about low-caste heroes vanquishing high-caste villains. Already familiar to millions, such Robin Hood-style stereotypes were perfect propaganda vehicles for the nascent Tamil nationalist movement, the Dravida Munnetra Kazhagam, or DMK. It is no coincidence that the party's founding father, C.N. Annadurai, was a top screenplay and script writer. Like prominent Tamil Congress leaders and movie-makers of the 1930s and 1940s, he and his colleagues used both popular film genres of the time – "mythologicals" (movie versions of the Hindu epics) and "socials" (dramas set around caste conflicts) – to convey their political ideas to the masses. Audiences were actively encouraged by party workers to boo the villains and cheer each time the proletarian hero, or DMK icons and colours (red and black), appeared on the screen. From this tradition were born the fan clubs, or *rasigar manrams*, that played such a key role in mobilizing support for the nationalist parties in elections.

The most influential fan club of all time was the one set up to support the superstar actor Marudur Gopalamenon Ramachandran, known to millions simply as "MGR". By carefully cultivating a political image which mirrored the folk-hero roles he played in films, the maverick matinee idol generated fanatical grass-roots support in the state, especially among women, and rose to become chief minister in 1977. His eleven-year rule is still regarded by liberals as a dark age in the state's history, as chronic corruption, police brutality, political purges and rising organized crime were all rife during the period. Even the fact that his bungled economic policies penalized precisely the rural poor who voted for him never dented MGR's mass appeal. When he suffered a paralytic stroke in October 1984, 22 people cut off limbs, toes and fingers as offerings to pray for his recovery, while more than a hundred followers attempted to burn themselves to death. For the next three years he was barely able to speak let alone govern effectively, yet the party faithful and fan club members still did not lose faith in his leadership. When he died in 1988, two million people attended his funeral, and 31 grief-stricken devotees committed ritual suicide Even today, MGR's statue, sporting trademark sunglasses and lamb's-wool hat, is revered at tens of thousands of wayside shrines across Tamil Nadu.

MGR's political protege, and eventual successor, was a teenage screen starlet called Jayalalitha, a convent-educated brahmin's daughter whom he spotted at a school dance and, despite an age difference of more than thirty years, recruited to be both his leading lady and mistress. The couple would star opposite each other in 25 hit films, and when MGR eventually moved into politics, Jayalalitha followed him, becoming leader of the AIADMK (the party MGR set up after being expelled from the DMK in 1972) after a much publicized power struggle with his widow. Larger-than-life in voluminous silver ponchos and heavy gold jewellery, the now portly Puratchi Thalavi ("Revolutionary Leader") has taken her personality cult to extremes brazen even by Indian standards. On her forty-sixth birthday in 1994, Rs50,000 of public money was spent on giant cardboard cut-outs depicting her in academic and religious robes, while 46 of her more

449

continued overleaf

continued from previous page

fervent admirers rolled bare-chested along the length of Anna Salai. Jayalalitha's spell as Chief Minister, however, was brought to an ignominious end at the 1996 elections, after allegations of fraud and corruption on an appropriately monumental scale. Despite being found guilty by the High Court, she still managed to bring down the national government and force a general election in 1999 (by withdrawing AIADMK support from Prime Minister Vajpayee's shaky, BJP-led coalition) and later ousted her arch rival, **M. Karunanidhi**, leader of the DMK, to regain her old job as Chief Minister of Tamil Nadu. One of her first acts was to exact revenge on Karunanidhi, throwing him and one thousand of his supporters into prison on corruption charges.

Working as an extra

If your interest in the Chennai movie industry is more fervent you can rub shoulders with today's Tamil movie stars by appearing as an extra in a film at MGR or one of the other major studios on the outskirts of Chennai. Scouts regularly trawl the tourist spots downtown (notably the *Maharaja Restaurant* around the corner from *Broadlands Hotel* in Triplicane; see opposite) for foreigners to spice up crowd and party scenes. People with long blond hair stand a better chance of getting picked, but being in the right place at the right time is more important. If you're really keen, though, do the rounds of the studios yourself (details available from the Government of India Tourist Office). If someone does approach you with an offer of work as a movie extra, be sure to check their credentials (scouts always carry laminated cards from the studio with their photos on; you can also ask to see their business card), and the conditions of the job (approximately Rs300 per day, plus meals and transport to and from your hotel are standard). For obvious reasons, it's also advisable to refuse any work offered to one person only, especially if you're female.

---

minor splurge at *Annalakshmi* on Anna Salai or the *Park Sheraton* on TTK Road is well worth considering,

The restaurants listed below are marked on either the Egmore, Anna Salai and Triplicane **map** on p.437 or the Chennai **map** on p.431.

Amaravati, corner of Cathedral/TKK Road. One of four good regional speciality restaurants, in a garden complex just south of Anna Salai. This one does excellent Andhran food, including particularly tasty biriyanis (Rs40–70).

Annalakshmi, 804 Anna Salai ☎ 044/855 0296. The very best in Indian vegetarian cuisine, served in appropriately sumptuous, a/c surroundings on Chennai's main drag. Profits go to charitable organisations sponsored by the Rishikesh-based guru Shivanjali; it is run by his devotees, whose mothers do the cooking. Extremely popular with the city's affluent set, so book ahead. Most main dishes around Rs200, with a Rs100 per person cover charge.

Bella Ciao, 32 2nd Ave, Besant Nagar, near the Theosophical Headquarters ☎044/491 9171. The genuine article – a tiny Italian restaurant under Italian ownership, serving the only "real" pizza in town, fresh gnocchi with blue cheese and mushrooms, lamb in red wine and even pork chops, 18

different organic salads, and then maybe a little tiramisu and Pavarotti to complete the evening. About Rs200 per head (officially no alcohol, although beer can be "arranged"). Book in advance.

Buhari, 83 Anna Salai. Idiosyncratic 1950s-style dining hall overlooking the main street. For some reason, Russian chicken dishes are the house speciality ("à la Moscow, Kiev or Leningrad"), but they also offer a full tandoori menu, cold beers and freshly baked cakes.

Chung King, Anna Salai, down an alley next to Buhari. Genuine Chinese cuisine prepared by pukka Chinese chef. Moderately priced.

Copper Chimney, 74 Cathedral Rd ☎ 044/827 5770. Franchise of the famous Mumbai restaurant. Quality tandoori cuisine, opulent decor and a/c comfort. The meat-eater's equivalent of *Annalakshmi*. Count on Rs200–250 per head.

Geetham, *Kanchi Hotel*, 28 C-in-C Rd. Circular, glass-sided restaurant on rooftop of nine-storey tower block. The multicuisine menu is surprisingly inexpensive, and the views superb. Open 11am–noon & 7–10pm only.

Hot Breads, opposite *Hotel Maris*, Cathedral Road. Wholewheat breads, baguettes, fresh quiches and an impressive range of cakes, biscuits and pastries. Decent espresso coffee, too. Eat in or take away.

Maharajah, 307 Quaide Milleth Salai. Simple vegetarian restaurant, popular with budget travellers staying in the area. Their veg dishes are wonderful – innovative *cashew masala*, and a rich *chana masala*, laden with red onion and coriander. There is a range of Rs30 set meals and a good range of cheap and filling snacks (try their great *uttapams* or huge paper *dosas*); also ice creams, lassis and good coffee. Open till midnight.

Saravanaa Bhavan, Thanigai Murugan Rathinavel Hall, 77 Usman Rd, T Nagar. This famous South Indian fast-food chain is an institution among the Chennai middle class, with branches opposite the bus stand in George Town, and in the forecourt of the Shanti cinema (at the top of Anna Salai). Try their delicious *rawa idlys*, rounded off with a couple of their delicious *ladoo* or *barfi* milk sweets from the counter outside.

Señor (Don) Pepés, First Floor, above *Hot Breads*, Cathedral Road. Swish new a/c Tex-Mex joint, serving a predictable menu of fajitas, enchiladas, tortillas, burritos and so-so pasta dishes (dubbed "Euro-Mex"). Main courses Rs120; open only in the evening.

Srinivasa, Ellis Road, Triplicane. Excellent South Indian breakfasts – try their *kitchadi* and *vada pongal* – for next to nothing, and the coffee is genuine Coorg. Open the rest of the day for very cheap meals and snacks. There is a separate area for women and families.

Upper Krust, Alsa Mall, Montieth Road. If you are longing for that nostalgic smell of baking bread, head here. Ceiling high rows of fresh pizza slices, stuffed or plain croissants, sweet pastries, home made biscuits and soft white bread. Unfortunately there is nowhere to sit and have a coffee with your cake. Open 9.30am–8.30pm.

Vasanta Bhavan, 20 Gandhi Irwin Rd. Easily the best "meals" joint among many around Egmore station, with ranks of attentive waiters and delicious pure veg food – just Rs24 for an unlimited thali. It's busy, spotlessly clean, and their coffee and sweets are delicious.

Verandah, *Taj Connemara*, Binny's Road ☎044/852 0123. The ideal venue for a posh Sunday morning breakfast buffet (Rs236): crisp newspapers and fresh coffee served in silver pots. The blow-out lunch-time buffets (Rs413) are also recommended, and they serve à la carte Italian food in the evening (around Rs350 per head). *The Rain Tree* is the second Taj eatery, with great Chettinad (South Indian) specialities included in the weekend dinner buffets (about Rs400 per head). Reserve in advance.

Welcomgroup Chola Sheraton, 10 Cathedral Rd ☎044/828 0101. Upmarket hotel with two good restaurants; the *Peshawari* serves lavish (and expensive) northwestern frontier food, while the excellent rooftop *Sagari* specializes in Chinese dishes.

Welcomgroup Park Sheraton, 132 TTK Rd ☎044/499 4101, ☏499 7101. More – extremely good – upmarket hotel restaurants. The *Residency* serves Indian, Western and Chinese, the *Khyber* is a meaty poolside barbecue, but best of all is the *Dakshin*, one of the country's top South Indian restaurants. It offers an excellent choice of unusual dishes from the four southern states, including seafood in marinated spices, Karnataka mutton biriyani and piping-hot *idlyappam* and *appam* made on the spot. There is live Carnatic music and costs around Rs600 per head, with beer.

Listings

Airlines Air India, 19 Marshalls Rd ☎044/855 4477, airport ☎044/234 7400; Air France, Thaper House, 43–44 Monteith Rd ☎044/855 4899; Air Lanka, Nagabrahma Towers, 76 Cathedral Rd ☎044/826 1535; British Airways, Khaleeli Centre, Monteith Road ☎044/855 4680; Gulf Air, 52 Montieth Rd ☎044/855 3091; Indian Airlines, 19 Marshalls Rd ☎044/855 3039, ☏855 5208 (open round the clock, but for bookings daily 8am–5pm); Jet Airways, Thaper House, 43–44 Monteith Rd ☎044/855 5353; Lufthansa, 167 Anna Salai ☎044/852 5095; KLM, *Hotel Taj Connemara*, Binny Road ☎044/852 0123;

Malaysia Airlines, Karumuttu Centre, 498 Anna Salai ☎044/434 9632; Qantas, Eldorado Building, 112 Nungambakkam High Rd ☎044/827 8680; Sahara, Lokesh Towers, 18 Kodambakkam High Rd ☎044/828 3180; Singapore Airlines, 108 Dr Radhakrishnan Salai ☎044/852 2871; Swissair, 191 Anna Salai ☎044/852 2541; Thai International, GSA, Malavikas Centre, 144 Kodambakkam High Rd, Nungambakkam ☎044/822 6149; for American, Air Canada, Biman, Philippine, Royal Jordanian and TWA, contact Jetair, Apex Plaza, 3 MG Rd ☎044/826 2409.

Banks and exchange Tourists have few difficulties changing money in Chennai: there are plenty of banks, and the upmarket hotels offer exchange facilities to residents. A conveniently central option is American Express, G-17, Spencer Plaza, 769 Anna Salai (daily 9.30am–5.30pm, Sat 9.30am–2.30pm). Thomas Cook (Mon–Sat 9am–6pm) has offices at: the Ceebros Centre, 45 Monteith Road, Egmore; at the G-4 Eldorado Building, 112 Nungambakkam High Road; and also at the airport (open to meet flights). For encashments on Visa cards, go to Bobcards, next door to the Bank of Baroda on Monteith Road, near the *Ambassador Pallava Hotel.* You can use Visa and Mastercard at the 24hr ATM at Citibank, 766 Anna Salai.

Bookstores Higginbothams on Anna Salai is Chennai's oldest bookshop, with a vast assortment of titles at rupee rates. Its main competitor, Bookpoint, at 160 Anna Salai, has a more up-to-date selection of fiction, and handy free publicity newsletters with reviews of the latest Indian releases. Serious bookworms should, however, head for the hole-in-the-wall Giggles, in the *Taj Connemara Hotel,* where, stacked in precariously high piles, you'll find a matchless stock of novels, academic tomes on the region and coffee-table books. Unlike other bookstores in the city, this one will take credit cards and post purchases abroad for you at nominal charges. Giggles & Scribbles, Wellingdon Estate, 24 C-in-C Rd (Mon–Sat 9.30am–7.30pm), is a larger branch, set back 50m from the road, selling rare reprints of historical books on India and Indian music cassettes, and with an efficient mail-order system. Karnatic Music Book Centre, 14 Sripuram First St, Royapettah, is an excellent bookshop for Carnatic classical music and Indian dance fanatics, with mail-order service. Finally, the Theosophical Society's bookshop (Mon–Fri 8–11am & 2–5pm, Sat 8–11am & 2–4pm), at the entrance to the campus in Adyar, is the best place in Chennai to pick up literature on yoga, meditation and religion.

Cinemas such as the Abhirami and Lakshmi along Anna Salai show English-language films, but for the full-on Tamil film experience, take in a show at the Shanti, off the top of Anna Salai, which boasts the city's biggest screen and a digital stereo sound system. Nearby, the equally massive Devi hosts the latest Bollywood blockbusters.

Consulates Canada, 3rd Floor Dhun Bldg, 827 Anna Salai ☎ 044/852 9828; France, Kothari Bldg, 114 Nungambakkam High Rd ☎ 044/472131; Germany, 22 C-in-C Rd ☎ 044/827 1747; Indonesia, 5 North Leith Castle Rd, San Thome ☎ 044/245 1095; Netherlands, 738 Anna Salai ☎ 044/811566; Norway, Royal Parry House, 43

Moore St ☎ 044/517950; 10am–5pm; Sri Lanka, 9-D Nawab Habibullah Rd ☎ 044/827 0831; Sweden, 6 Cathedral Rd ☎ 044/827 5792; UK, 24 Anderson Rd, Nungambakkam ☎ 044/827 3136; USA, 220 Anna Salai ☎ 044/827 3040.

Cultural institutions Alliance Française, 3/4-A College Rd, Music Academy, 306 TTK Rd ☎ 044/811 2231, Nungambakkam ☎ 044/827 2650; British Council, 737 Anna Salai ☎ 044/826 9402; Max Mueller Bhavan, 13 Khadar Nawaz Khan Rd ☎ 044/826 1314.

Galleries The Vinyasa Art Gallery is in an annexe to the right of the Music Academy, 306 TTK Nagar (☎ 044/811 5073; daily 11am–7pm). The Gallery is dedicated to showcasing contemporary Indian artists, exhibiting works from all over India. For information about current exhibitions, check the daily newspapers.

Hospitals The best-equipped private hospital in Chennai is the Apollo, 21–22 Greams Rd (☎ 044/829 4870). For an ambulance, try ☎ 102, but it's usually quicker to jump in a taxi.

Internet access Chennai has no shortage of places offering internet access, albeit at wildly varying rates; almost every main road now offers at least one cyber point. The snazziest option is Net Café, at 101/1 Kanakasri Nagar, down an alleyway off Cathedral Road (daily 7am–midnight) – look for the neon @ sign, but rates are high and they're reluctant to let you compose off-line. SRIS Netsurfing Café on the first floor of Spencer Plaza is a cheaper, though smaller, alternative, and if you're staying at *Broadlands* or one of the other hotels in Triplicane, Gee Gee Net, is next door to *Hotel Comfort* and is open 24hrs. It's a tiny place, but extremely helpful and you never have to wait long; the biggest appeal, however, is the cost – only Rs15 per hour between 11pm and 1pm, or Rs25 between 1pm and 11pm. Otherwise, head for *Hotel Himalaya* on Quaide Milleth Salai, which is also open 24hrs and only Rs25 per hour.

Left luggage Counters at Egmore and Central railway stations store bags for Rs7 per 24hr; they demand that your luggage is securely locked and need to see proof that you are making an onward journey. The airport and some hotels (such as *Broadlands*) also guard luggage at a daily rate.

Music stores Musee Musical, 67 Anna Salai (☎ 044/849380), stocks sitars, percussion, flutes and the usual shoddy selection of Hoffner/Gibson-copy guitars. For the best range of concert quality Indian instruments, including *vinas*, check out Saptaswara Music Store, on Raipetha Road, Mylapore (☎ 044/499 3274). Music World, on the first floor of Spencer Plaza, has the best selection of audio cassettes and CDs in the city.

Opticians Eye tests, glasses and contact lenses are available at Lawrence and Mayo, 68 Anna Salai.
Pharmacy Lalitha's Medical and General Store, 11 Gandhi Irwin Rd; Spencer & Co, Spencer Plaza, Anna Salai (Mon–Sat 8am–7pm; ℡ 044/826 3611).
Photographic equipment Dozens of stores around town offer film and developing services on modern machines, but the only Kodak-approved Q-Lab in the city (recommended for transparency processing) is Image Park, GEE Plaza, 1 Craft Rd, Nungambakkam (℡ 044/827 6383). Reliance Opticals, at 136 Anna Salai stocks Fuji Provia and Sensia II. For camera repair, your best bet is Camera Crafts, 325/8A Quaide Milleth High Rd, Triplicane, near the Broadlands Hotel. Delhi Photo Stores, in an arcade directly behind the big Konica shop on Wallajah Road, is crammed with spare parts and other useful Indian-made bits and bobs.
Post and telephone Chennai's Head Post Office is on Anna Salai (daily 8am–8pm). If you're using it for poste restante, make sure your correspondents mark the envelope "Head Post Office, Anna Salai", or your letters could well end up across town at the General Post Office, north of Parry's Corner on Rajaji Salai (same hours). The post office on Quaide Milleth Salai, in Triplicane (Mon–Sat 7am–3pm) is convenient if you're staying at Broadlands or the Comfort Hotel. The easiest way

to make a local or international phone call is at one of the thousands of orange-yellow booths across the city offering PCO/STD/ISD, all whom charge as per a set government rate. Most of these places offer fax and photocopy services also, or can point you to one that can. If you need to send a telegram, the Head Post Office offers the most efficient service.
Tax clearance To get a tax clearance certificate (see Basics, p.20) take exchange documents and passport to 121 Uttamar Gandhi Rd, and allow for 3–4hr of tedious form-filling.
Travel agents Reliable travel agents include American Express, G-17 Spencer Plaza, 768–769 Anna Salai ℡ 044/852 3592; Diana World Travels, 45 Monteith Rd ℡ 044/826 1716; PL Worldways, G-11 Ground Floor, Spencer Plaza ℡ 044/852 1192; Surya Travels, F-14 First Floor, Spencer Plaza ℡ 044/855 0285; Thomas Cook, Chebroos Centre, Monteith Road, Egmore (℡ 044/827 3092).
Yoga Chennai may seem like an insalubrious place to study yoga, but some of South India's most renowned schools are based here. The following offer short courses: Adyar Yoga Research Institute, 15 III Main Rd, Kasturba Nagar, Adyar, near the Theosophical Society Headquarters; Bharatiya Vidya Bhavan, East Mada Street, Mylapore; Prof T. Krishnamacharya's Yoga Mandiram, 103 St Mary's Rd (℡ 044/499 7602).

Moving on from Chennai

If you're short of time, you might consider employing one of the **travel agents** listed above to book your plane, train or bus ticket for you. This doesn't apply to boat tickets for the Andaman Islands, which have to be booked in person.

By plane

Chennai's domestic airport stands adjacent to the international terminal, 16km southwest of the centre at **Meenambakkam**. The easiest way to get there is by taxi or auto-rickshaw, but if you're not too weighed down with luggage you can save money by jumping on a suburban train to **Trisulam station**, 500m from the airport.

Indian Airlines flies from Meenambakkam to 21 destinations around the country. In addition, Jet Airways operates services to Bangalore, Coimbatore, Delhi, Hyderabad, Mumbai, Pune Port Blair and Thiruvananthapuram; Sahara flies daily to Delhi and Air India has domestic departures for Mumbai and Delhi. A full summary of flights appears on p.456.

By boat

Boats leave Chennai every week to ten days for **Port Blair**, capital of the **Andaman Islands**. However, getting a ticket and the relevant permit can be a complete rigmarole, compounded by the absence of a regular schedule. The first thing you'll need to do is head up to the Chennai Port Trust, next to the Directorate of Shipping on Rajaji (North Beach) Road, George Town, where a small hut houses the Andaman Administration Office. A chalkboard on the wall advertises details of the next sailing, and you buy a ticket from the hatch around the corner, at the front of the main building. There are no ticket sales on the day of sailing.

The authorities may demand that you register at the Foreigners' Registration Office (Mon–Fri 9.30am–5pm), a twenty-minute auto-rickshaw ride south-west across town on Haddow's Road (between the UK High Commission and French Consulate). You also are required to buy a permit, which can be obtained from the Foreigner's Registration Office (FRO) in Chennai, Delhi, Mumbai, Calcutta, or now you can even get it on arrival in Port Blair. Bear in mind, however, that the permit is only valid for one month, from the date of purchase. To get the permit, you have to go to the FRO and fill in a form and supply three passport photos; hand it in before lunch and you should be able to pick up the permit later that same day.

The three- to four-day crossing gets mixed reviews. Conditions, especially in the rock-bottom bunk-class at Rs1150, can be hot and squalid, so go for the most expensive ticket you can afford. Cabin fares (per bed) are Rs2700 for B-Class (six-berth, common bathroom) and Rs3420 for a 1st Class 4-berth cabin (attached bath). Rs4140 gets you a deluxe two-berth cabin with a private bathroom. Meals of dal, rice and vegetables are served for around Rs100 per day, but vary little, so take some snacks, lots of water and fruit.

By bus

Most long-distance **buses** leave from the **Express Bus Stand**, on Esplanade Road, near Parry's Corner, George Town, which has a computerized **reservations** hall on the first floor (7am–9pm; ☎044/534 1835–6, but don't bet on anyone speaking English). Here you can make advance bookings for all State Express Transport Corporation (SETC) services, as well as reserve a seat on interstate buses to neighbouring Andhra, Kerala and Karnataka. A full run-down of these, giving frequency and journey times, appears in Travel Details opposite.

The chaotic **Broadway Bus Stand** is on the opposite side of Prakasam Road. All buses to Mamallapuram, Pondicherry and Chidambaram depart from here. The fastest services to **Mamallapuram** are #188, #188A and anything marked "East Coast Express" (every 30min; less than 2hr); #19A, #19C, #119 and #119A takes an hour longer.

Whether you like it or not, local slum kids will ask you which service you want and then proceed to take you to the right bus for a couple of rupees. They are, in fact, a very useful service as there are dozens of buses, and there's not a single sign in English.

By train

Trains to Tiruchirapalli (Trichy), Thanjavur, Pudukottai, Rameshwaram, Kodaikanal Road, Madurai, and most other destinations in south Tamil Nadu leave from **Egmore Station**. All other trains leave from **Central**. Left of the main building, on the first floor of the Moore Market Complex, the efficient **tourist reservation counter** (Mon–Sat 8am–8pm, Sun 8am–2pm) sells "tourist quota" tickets for trains from either station, which you can pay for in dollars, sterling, traveller's cheques or rupees (providing you have a recent encashment certificate). The booking office at Egmore, up the stairs left of the main entrance (same hours), also handles bookings for both stations, but has no tourist counter. If you're arriving in Chennai by plane, note that Southern Railways also has a reservation counter (daily 10am–5pm) outside the domestic terminal at the airport.

Destination	Name	Number	From	Departs	Total time
Bangalore	Shatabdi Exp*	#2007	Central	6am**	4hr 45min
	Bangalore Mail	#6007	Central	10.10pm	7hr 15min
Bhubaneswar	Coromandel Exp	#2843	Central	9.05am	20hr 10min
	Howrah Mail	#6004	Central	10.30pm	23hr 45min
Calcutta	Coromandel Exp	#2842	Central	9.05am	28hr 15min
	Howrah Mail	#6004	Central	10.30pm	32hr 25min
Coimbatore	Shatabdi Exp*	#2023	Central	3.10pm	6hr 50min
	Kovai Exp	#2675	Central	6.15am	7hr 35min
Delhi	Tamil Nadu Exp	#2621	Central	10pm	33hr
	Grand Trunk Exp	#2615	Central	11pm	36hr 45min
Hyderabad	Charminar Exp	#2759	Central	6.10pm	14hr 15min
Kanyakumari	Kanyakumari Exp	#6721	Central	1pm	17hr 15min
Kochi/Ernakulam	Alleppey Exp	#6041	Central	7.35pm	13hr
	Trivandrum Mail	#6319	Central	6.55pm	12hr
	Kodaikanal				
	Pandyan Exp	#6717	Egmore	7.30pm	10hr
Madurai	Madurai Exp	#6717	Egmore	7.30pm	11hr 20min
Mettuppalayam (for **Ooty**)	Nilgiri Exp	#6605	Central	8.15pm	12hr 15min
Mumbai	Mumbai Exp	#6012	Central	11.45am	27hr 20min
	Chennai Exp	#1064	Central	6.40am	24hr 15min
Mysore	Shatabdi Exp*	#2007	Central	6am**	4hr 45min
	Mysore Exp	#6222	Central	10.30pm	11hr 20min
Rameshwaram	Sethu Exp	#6701	Egmore	8.25pm	18hr 10min
Thanjavur	Cholan Exp	#6153	Egmore	8am	9hr 15min
	Sethu Exp	#6701	Egmore	8.25pm	9hr 30min
Tirupathi	Saptagiri Exp	#6057	Central	6.25am	3hr
Thiruvananthapuram	Trivandrum Mail	#6319	Egmore	6.55pm	17hr
Varanasi	Ganga Kaveri Exp**	#6039	Central	5.30pm	38hr 30min

*a/c only
**Mon & Sat only

Travel details

Trains

Chennai to: Bangalore (7 daily; 4hr 45min–8hr 10min); Bhubaneswar (7 daily; 20hr 10min–24hr); Calcutta (2–3 daily; 28hr 15min–32hr 50min); Chengalpattu (5 daily*; 1hr); Coimbatore (2 daily; 6hr 50min–8hr 55min); Delhi (3 daily; 29hr–43hr); Dindigul (5 daily*; 5hr 45min–9hr); Hyderabad (2 daily; 14–15hr); Kanniyakumari (1–2 daily; 15hr 45min–17hr 15min); Kochi (5 weekly; 10–13hr); Kodaikanal Road (4 daily*; 9hr); Kumbakonam (3 daily*; 7hr 20min); Madurai (5–6 daily*; 8hr–11hr 20min); Mumbai (3 daily; 24hr 15min–31hr 30min); Mysore (2 daily; 4hr 45min–11hr 20min); Pune (3 daily; 20–25hr 30min); Rameshwaram (2–3 daily*; 14hr 30min–24hr); Salem (10 daily; 4–6hr); Thanjavur (3 daily*; 8–9hr 30min); Thiruvananthapuram (1–2 daily; 16hr 45min–20hr); Tiruchirapalli (7–8 daily*; 5hr 20min–7hr); Tirupati (3 daily; 3hr); Vijayawada (12 daily; 7–8hr).
* Trains from Egmore; all others from Central.

Buses

Chennai to: Bangalore (29 daily; 8–11hr); Chengalpattu (60 daily; 1hr 30min–2hr); Chidambaram (20 daily; 5–7hr); Coimbatore (9 daily; 11–13hr); Dindigul (10 daily; 9–10hr); Hyderabad (1 daily; 18–20hr); Kanchipuram (every 20min; 1hr 30min–2hr); Kanniyakumari (9 daily; 16–18hr); Kodaikanal Road (10 daily; 14–15hr); Kumbakonam (17 daily; 7–8hr); Madurai (37 daily; 10hr); Mamallapuram (every 10min; 2–3hr); Pondicherry (every 10min; 4–5hr); Rameshwaram (5 daily; 14hr); Salem (20 daily; 5–7hr); Thanjavur (18 daily; 8hr 30min); Thiruvananthapuram (9 daily; 20hr); Tindivanam (every 20min; 3–4hr); Tiruchirapalli (every 30min; 8–9hr); Tirupati (every 20 min; 4–5hr); Tiruvannamalai (every 20min; 4–6hr); Udhagamandalam (Ooty) (3 daily; 15hr); Vedanthangal (3 daily; 2–3hr); Vellore (every 30min; 2–4hr); Vijayawada (1 daily; 13–16hr).

Flights

Chennai to: Bangalore (2–4 daily; 45min); Bhubaneswar (4 weekly; 2hr 30min); Calcutta (2 daily; 2hr 5min); Coimbatore (2–3 daily; 55min–1hr 55min); Delhi (3–4 daily; 2hr 30min); Hyderabad (2–3 daily; 1hr); Kochi (1–2 daily; 1hr–2hr 15min); Madurai (1 daily; 55min); Mumbai (3–4 daily; 1hr 45min); Port Blair (1 daily; 2hr 5min); Thiruvananthapuram (1–2 daily; 1hr 10min); Tiruchirapalli (5 weekly; 50min); Tirupati (2 weekly; 25min).

Tamil Nadu

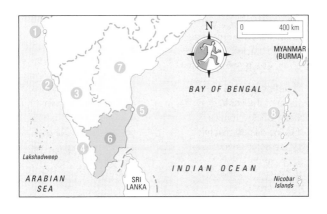

CHAPTER 6 # Highlights

✳ **Mamallapuram** Stone-carvers' workshops, a long sandy beach and a bumper hoard of Pallava monuments have made this the state's principal tourist attraction.
See p.464

✳ **Pondicherry** Former French colony that has retained the ambience of a Gallic seaside town: croissants, a promenade and gendarmes wearing *képis*. See p.486

✳ **Thanjavur** Home to some of the world's finest Chola bronzes, this town is dominated by the colossal shrine tower of the Brihadishwara Temple.
See p.505

✳ **Madurai** This major temple, the love-nest of Shiva and his consort Meenakshi, hosts a constant round of festivals.
See p.521

✳ **Kanniyakumari** Sacred meeting point of the Bay of Bengal, Indian Ocean and Arabian Sea, at the tip of the subcontinent.
See p.544

✳ **The Ghats** The spine of southern India, where you can trek through forested mountains and tea plantations from the refreshingly cool hill stations of Ooty, Conoor and Kodaikanal.
See p.547

Tamil Nadu

When Indians refer to "the South", it's usually **TAMIL NADU** they're talking about. While Karnataka and Andhra Pradesh are essentially cultural transition zones buffering the Hindi-speaking north, and Kerala and Goa maintain their own distinctively idiosyncratic identities, the peninsula's Tamil-speaking state is India's Dravidian Hindu heartland. Traditionally protected by distance and the military might of the southern Deccan kingdoms, the region has, over the centuries, been less exposed to northern influences than its neighbours. As a result, the three powerful dynasties dominating the South – the Cholas, the Pallavas and the Pandyans – were able, over a period of more than a thousand years, to develop their own unique religious and political institutions, largely unmolested by marauding Muslims. The most visible legacy of this protracted cultural flowering is a crop of astounding temples, whose gigantic gateway towers, or *gopuras*, still soar above just about every town large enough to merit a train station. It is the image of these colossal wedge-shaped pyramids, presiding over canopies of dense palm forest, or against patchworks of vibrant green paddy fields, which Edward Lear described as "stupendous and beyond belief", and which linger longest in the memory of most modern travellers.

The great Tamil temples are merely the largest landmarks in a vast network of **sacred sites** – shrines, bathing places, holy trees, rocks and rivers – interconnected by a web of ancient pilgrims' routes. Tamil Nadu harbours 274 of India's holiest Shiva temples, and 108 others which are dedicated to Vishnu; in addition, five shrines devoted to the five Vedic elements (earth, wind, fire, water and ether) are to be found here, and eight to the planets, as well as other places revered by Christians and Muslims. Scattered from the pale orange crags and forests of the Western Ghats, across the fertile deltas of the **Vagai** and **Kaveri** rivers to the Coromandel Coast on the Bay of Bengal, these sites were celebrated in the hymns of the Tamil saints, between one and two thousand years ago. It is an extraordinary fact that the same songs are still widely sung and understood today in the region, little changed since they were first composed.

The Tamils' living connection with their ancient Dravidian past has given rise to a strong **nationalist movement**. With a few fleeting lapses, one or other of the pro-Dravidian parties has been in power here since the 1950s, spreading their anti-brahmin, anti-Hindi proletarian message to the masses principally through the medium of movies. Indeed, since Independence, the majority of Tamil Nadu's political leaders have been drawn from the state's prolific **cinema** industry. Indians from elsewhere in the country love to caricature their southern cousins as "reactionary rice growers" led by "fanatical film stars". While such stereotypes should be taken with a pinch of salt, it is undeniable

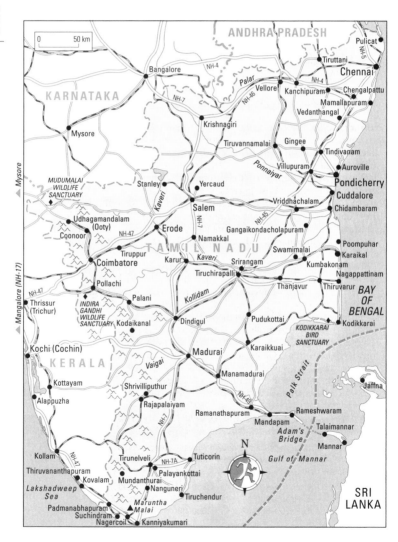

that the Tamil way of life, which has evolved along an unbroken path since pre-historic times, sets it apart from the rest of the subcontinent. This remains, after all, one of the last, if not the only, places in the world where a Classical culture has survived into the present – "India's Holy Land", described by Marco Polo as "the most splendid province in the world".

Visiting Tamil Nadu

Despite its seafront fort, grand mansions and excellence as a centre for the performing arts, the state capital **Chennai** – large enough to warrant a separate chapter in this guide – is probably its least appealing destination: a scruffy, dusty, noisy city with faint echoes of the Raj. Much the best place to start a **temple tour** is nearby **Mamallapuram** (also known as **Mahabalipuram**), a seaside village that, quite apart from some exquisite Pallava rock-cut architecture (fifth–ninth centuries) boasts a long stretch of white beach. Inland, the pilgrimage town of **Kanchipuram** is filled with reminders of an illustrious past under successive dynastic rulers, while further down the coast is one of India's rare French colonial possessions, **Pondicherry**, where Auroville has found a new role as a "New Age" focal point. The road south from Pondicherry puts you back on the temple trail, leading to the tenth-century **Chola kingdom** and the extraordinary architecture of **Chidambaram**, **Gangaikondacholapuram**, **Kumbakonam** and **Darasuram**. For the best Chola bronzes, however, and a glimpse of the magnificent paintings that flourished under Maratha rajas in the eighteenth century, travellers should head for **Thanjavur**. Chola capital for four centuries, the city boasts almost a hundred temples and was the birthplace of **Bharatanatyam** dance, famous throughout India.

In the very centre of Tamil Nadu, **Tiruchirapalli**, a commercial town just northwest of Thanjavur, held some interest for the Cholas but reached its heyday under later dynasties, when the temple complex in neighbouring **Srirangam** became one of South India's largest. Among its patrons were the Nayaks of **Madurai**, whose erstwhile capital further south, bustling with pilgrims, priests, peddlers, tailors and tourists, is an unforgettable destination.

Rameshwaram, on the long spit of land reaching towards Sri Lanka, and **Kanniyakumari**, at India's southern tip (the auspicious meeting point of the Bay of Bengal, the Indian Ocean and the Arabian Sea) are both important pilgrimage centres, with the added attraction of welcome cool breezes and vistas over the sea.

While Tamil Nadu's temples are undeniably its major attraction, it would take months to see them all, and there are plenty of other distractions for even the most ardent architecture buff. In the west of the state, where the hill stations of **Kodaikanal** and **Ootacamund (Ooty)** are the premier attractions, verdant hills offer mountain views, and a network of trails winds through forests and tea and coffee plantations. **Mudumalai Wildlife Sanctuary**, a vast spread of deciduous forest dominated by teak, offers a relaxing stopover on the route to or from Mysore. Sadly, its protected forest area, like that of Tamil Nadu's other major national park, the Anamalai sanctuary, closer to Kodaikanal in the Palani hills, has been closed to visitors for a couple of years due to local terrorist activities. To get close to any real wildlife, you'll have to head for the coast, where areas of wetland provide perfect resting places for migratory birds, whose numbers soar during the winter monsoon at **Vedanthangal**, near Chennai, and **Point Calimere**.

Temperatures in Tamil Nadu, which usually hover around 30°C, peak in May and June when they often soar above 40°, and the overpowering heat makes all but sitting in a shaded café exhausting. The state is barely affected by the southwest monsoon that pounds much of India from June to September: it receives most of its **rain** between October and January. Cooler, rainy days bring their own problems; widescale flooding can disrupt road and rail links and imbue everything with an all-pervasive dampness.

Accommodation prospects are good; all but the smallest towns and villages have something for every budget. Most hotels have their own dining halls which, together with local restaurants, sometimes serve sumptuous thalis, tinged with tamarind and presented on banana leaves. **Indigenous dishes** are almost exclusively vegetarian; for North Indian or Western alternatives, head for the larger hotels or more upmarket city restaurants.

Some history

Since the fourth millennium BC, Tamil Nadu has been shaped by its majority **Dravidian** population, of uncertain origins and physically quite different from North Indians. Their language developed separately, as did their social organization; the difference between high-caste brahmins and low-caste workers has always been more pronounced here than in the north – divisions that continue to dominate the state's political life. The influence of the powerful *janapadas*, established in the north by the fourth and third centuries BC, extended as far south as the Deccan, but they made few incursions into **Dravidadesa** (Tamil country). Incorporating what are now Kerala and Tamil Nadu, it was ruled by three dynasties: the **Cheras**, who held sway over much of the Malabar coast (Kerala), the **Pandyas** in the far south, and the **Cholas**, whose realm stretched along the Coromandel Coast in the east. Indo-Roman trade in spices, precious stones and metals flourished at the start of the Christian era, when **St Thomas** arrived in the South, but dwindled when trade links began with Southeast Asia.

The prosperity of the early kingdoms having faded by the fourth century AD, the way was clear for the Pallavas, who emerged in the sixth century as leaders of a kingdom centred around **Kanchipuram**. By the seventh century, the successors of the first Pallava king, Simhavishnu, were engaged in battles with the southern Pandyas and the forces of the Chalukyas, based further west in Karnataka. However, the centuries of Pallava dominion were not marked simply by battles and territorial expansion; this was also an era of social development. **Brahmins** became the dominant community, responsible for lands and riches donated to temples. The emergence of *bhakti*, devotional worship, placed temples firmly at the centre of religious life, and the inspirational *sangam* literature of saint-poets fostered a tradition of dance and music that has become Tamil Nadu's cultural hallmark.

In the tenth and eleventh centuries, the Cholas experienced a period of profound expansion and revival; they soon held sway over much of Tamil Nadu, Andhra Pradesh, and even made inroads into Karnataka and Orissa. In the spirit of such glorious victories and power, the Cholas ploughed their new wealth into the construction of splendid and imposing **temples**, such as those at Gangaikondacholapuram, Kumbakonam and Thanjavur.

The Vijayanagars, who gained a firm footing in Hampi (Karnataka) in the fourteenth century, resisted Muslim incursions from the north and spread out to cover most of South India by the sixteenth century. This prompted a new phase of architectural development in the building of new temples, the expansion of older ones and the introduction of colossal *gopuras*. In Madurai, the Vijayanagar governors, Nayaks, set up an independent kingdom whose impact spread as far as Tiruchirapalli.

Much more significant was the arrival of **Europeans**. First came the Portuguese, who landed in Kerala and monopolized Indian trade for about a century before they were joined by parties of British, Dutch and French traders. Though mostly on cordial terms with the Indians, the Western powers soon found themselves engaged in territorial disputes. The most marked were between the French, based in **Pondicherry**, and the British, whose stronghold since 1640 had been Fort St George in **Madras**. After battles at sea and on land, the French were confined to Pondicherry, while British ambitions reached their apex in the eighteenth century, when the East India Company occupied Bengal (1757) and consolidated its bases in Bombay and Madras.

As well as rebellions against colonial rule, Tamil Nadu also saw anti-brahmin protests, in particular those led by the Justice Party in the 1920s and 1930s. Independence in 1947 signalled the need to reorganize state boundaries, and by 1956 areas had been demarcated on a linguistic basis. Andhra Pradesh and Kerala were formed, along with Mysore state (later Karnataka) and **Madras Presidency**, a slightly smaller area than that governed from Madras by the British, where Tamil was the predominant language. In 1965 Madras Presidency became Tamil Nadu, the latter part of its name coming from the Chola agrarian administrative units known as *nadus*.

Since Independence, Tamil Nadu's industrial sector has mushroomed. Initially the state was led by the Congress Party, but in 1967 the **DMK** (Dravida Munnetra Kazhagam), championing the lower castes and reasserting Tamil identity, won a landslide victory. Anti-Hindi and anti-central government rule, the DMK flourished until the film star "**MGR" (M.G. Ramachandran)** broke away to form the All India Anna Dravida Munnetra Kazhagam (**AIADMK**) and won an easy victory in the 1977 elections. Virtually deified by his fans-turned-supporters, MGR remained successful until his death in 1987, when the Tamil government fell back into the hands of the DMK. Soon after, the AIADMK were reinstated, led by **Sri Jayalalitha Jayaram**, an ex-film star and dancer once on close terms with MGR (see p.449). The AIDMK is now back in power and the DMK is skulking in the background while former Chief Minister M. Karunanidhi fights his ground over corruption charges.

The northeast

Fazed by the fierce heat and air pollution of the capital, Chennai, most visitors escape as fast as they can, heading down the Coromandel Coast to India's stone-carving capital, **Mamallapuram** (also known as **Mahabalipuram**), whose ancient monuments include the famous Shore temple and a batch of extraordinary rock sculpture. En route, it's well worth jumping off the bus at the artists' village of **Cholamandal**, just beyond the city limits, and at **Dakshina Chitra**, a superb folk museum 30km south of Chennai, where traditional buildings from across South India have been beautifully reconstructed and restored. Further inland, **Kanchipuram** is an important pilgrimage and silk-sari-weaving town. From Kanchipuram you can loop west towards the Andhran border, taking in the fourteenth-century fort at **Vellore** on the way to **Tiruvannamalai**, a wonderfully atmospheric temple town clustered at the base of the sacred mountain, Arunachala. The sprawling ruins of **Gingee** fort stand midway between here and the coast, where you can breakfast on croissants and espresso in the former French colony of **Pondicherry**. A short way north, **Auroville**, the utopian settlement founded by followers of the Shri Aurobindo Ghose's spiritual successor, "The Mother", provides a New Age foil to the hedonism of the modern world.

Both Mamallapuram and Pondicherry are well connected to Chennai by nail-bitingly fast bus services, running along a smooth new coastal highway; if you can, stick to state buses as the private ones have a dangerous disregard for safety as they race to pick up as many passengers as possible. You can also get to Pondy by train, but this involves a change at the junction town of **Villupuram**, from where services are slow and relatively infrequent.

Mamallapuram (Mahabalipuram)

Scattered around the base of a colossal mound of boulders on the Bay of Bengal, **MAMALLAPURAM** (aka Mahabalipuram), 58km south of Chennai, is dominated less by the sea, as you might expect, than by the smooth volcanic rocks surrounding it. From dawn till dusk, the rhythms of chisels chipping granite resound through its sandy lanes – evidence of a stone-carving tradition that has endured since this was a major port of the Pallava dynasty, between the fifth and ninth centuries. Little is known about life in the ancient city, and it is only possible to speculate about the purpose of much of the boulder sculpture, which includes one of India's most photographed monuments, the **Shore Temple**. It does appear, however, that the well preserved friezes and shrines were not made for worship at all, but rather as a permanent showcase for the talents of local artists. Due in no small part to the maritime activities of the Pallavas, their style of art and architecture had wide-ranging influence, spreading from South India as far north as Ellora, as well as to Southeast Asia. This international cultural importance was recognized in 1995 when Mamallapuram was granted World Heritage Site status by UNESCO.

Given the coexistence of so many stunning archeological remains with a long white-sand **beach**, it was inevitable this would become a major hangout for Western travellers. Over the past two decades, Mamallapuram has orientated its economy to the needs of tourists, with persistent Kashmiri trinket sellers, bus loads of city dwellers at the weekends, hawkers on the beach and lots of backpacker-style budget hotels and little restaurants. Alas, the Shore Temple, now protected from the corrosive effects of the salt spray by a wall of fir trees and stone blocks, is a shadow of the exotic spectacle it used to be when the waves lapped its base. However, the atmosphere generated by the busy fishermen on the beach, the steady hammering of the stone carvers and the mesmerizing ancient rock-art backdrop is unique in India. This village is worth at least a couple of days if you're heading to or from Chennai; many people actually prefer to stay here and travel into the city for the day to book tickets or pick up mail.

Arrival, information and transport

Numerous daily **buses** ply to and from Chennai, Thiruvannmalai, Kanchipuram and Pondicherry. The bus stand is in the centre of the village. The nearest **railway station**, at Chengalpattu (Chingleput), 29km northeast on the

bus route to Kanchipuram, is on the main north–south line, but not really a convenient access point. A **taxi** or an **auto rickshaw** from Chennai costs around Rs500 (or Rs450 from the airport, Rs500 by night); book through the tourist office, or the pre-paid taxi both at Chennai airport. If you're travelling to Mamallapuram by night in a taxi or a rickshaw, make sure the price is clearly agreed before setting off. There have been recent reports of the driver stopping short of the village and demanding more money, or claiming that the fare was Rs500 per person, not per vehicle as it should be.

The **Government of Tamil Nadu Tourist Office** (Mon–Sat 9.45am–5.45pm; ☎04114/42232) is one of the first buildings you see in the village; on your left as you arrive from Chennai. It is a good place to find out about local festivals, and keeps a comprehensive list of bus times posted.

Unless you're staying at one of the upscale hotels, there are only two official places to **change money** in the village: the Indian Overseas Bank, on TK

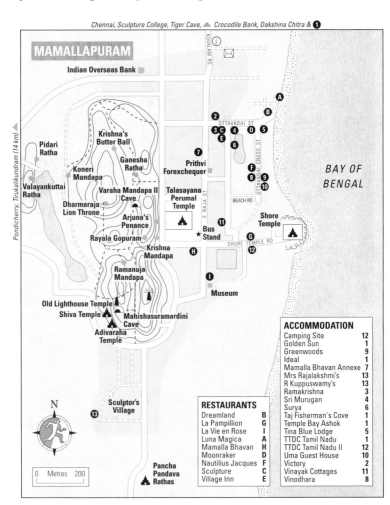

MAMALLAPURAM

Chennai, Sculpture College, Tiger Cave, ▲ Crocodile Bank, Dakshina Chitra & ●

Indian Overseas Bank

Pondicherry, Tirukalikundram (14 km) ▲

Pidari Ratha
Krishna's Butter Ball
Koneri Mandapa
Ganesha Ratha
Valayankuttai Ratha
Varaha Mandapa II Cave
Dharmaraja Lion Throne
Arjuna's Penance
Rayala Gopuram
Krishna Mandapa
Ramanuja Mandapa
Old Lighthouse Temple
Shiva Temple
Mahishasuramardini Cave
Adivaraha Temple

KOVALAM RD

OTTAVADAI ST
OTTAVADAI CROSS ST

Prithvi Forexchequer
Talasayana Perumal Temple
BEACH RD
Bus Stand
Shore Temple
SHORE TEMPLE RD

E RAJA ST

Museum

BAY OF BENGAL

N

Sculptor's Village

Pancha Pandava Rathas

0 Metres 200

RESTAURANTS
Dreamland	B
La Pampillion	G
La Vie en Rose	I
Luna Magica	A
Mamalla Bhavan	H
Moonraker	D
Nautilius Jacques	F
Sculpture	C
Village Inn	E

ACCOMMODATION
Camping Site	12
Golden Sun	1
Greenwoods	9
Ideal	1
Mamalla Bhavan Annexe	7
Mrs Rajalakshmi's	13
R Kuppuswamy's	13
Ramakrishna	3
Sri Murugan	4
Surya	6
Taj Fisherman's Cove	1
Temple Bay Ashok	1
Tina Blue Lodge	5
TTDC Tamil Nadu	1
TTDC Tamil Nadu II	12
Uma Guest House	10
Victory	2
Vinayak Cottages	11
Vinodhara	8

Kunda Road, or the more efficient Prithvi Forexchequer, 55 East Raja St, opposite *Mamalla Bhavan Annexe*. The most reputable **travel agent** in the village is JRS Travels on East Raja Street (look for the aeroplane and train painted on the outside window); otherwise head into Chennai to make your travel arrangements.

You will notice that almost every hotel advertises an "in-house" **masseur**. A number of women have, however, reported that the massage experience was not relaxing in the least. If you want to avoid any potentially problematic situations, the Ayurvedic massage hut at the *Sri Murugan Guest House* on Ottavadi Road is reputable. Mr M. Kumar and his wife at 7/A Thirukula St (℡04114/42112) are also highly recommended; they are both fully qualified in Ayurveda and a range of massage techniques, and there is the option of a steam bath at the end of the session. Book both places in advance.

Mamallapuram village itself is little more than a few sandy roads, and the sights are all an easy stroll away. By far the best way to get to the attractions outside the centre is by **bicycle**, which you can rent from shops on E Raja Street (Kovalam Road), opposite the entrance to the *Temple Bay Ashok Beach Resort*, or MK Cycle Centre, 28 Ottavadai St, for around Rs20 per day. **Scooters** and Enfield **motorcycles** are also available for Rs150–300 a day, from Poornima Travels, next to *Moonraker* restaurant.

Accommodation

With more than twenty years' experience of tourism, Mamallapuram is not short of **accommodation**. The bulk of cheap and mid-range lodges are within the village, some distance from the beach, which is the preserve of the more expensive places. Along a six-kilometre stretch of coast north of the village are a few large resort hotels with swimming pools; they tend to be booked out by tour groups, so reserve a room well in advance. It's easy enough to take a rickshaw out to these hotels from the village, but not in the other direction. However, the walk back into Mamallapuram along the beach is pleasant.

Long-term lodgings can be arranged in the sculptors' village behind the workshops on the way to the Pancha Pandava *rathas*. The two oldest established guesthouses are *R. Kuppuswamy's* and *Mrs Rajalakshmi's*, next door, but there are plenty of other places who don't use commission touts. They're all pretty basic, with thatched roofs and common shower-toilets in the yard, but have serviceable fans and are clean and homely. At around Rs350 per week, they're also just about the cheapest places to stay in the area.

Golden Sun, 3km from town, 59 Kovalam Rd ℡04114/498 5246, ℻498 2669. Not as smart as the *Ideal Beach Resort* but the large garden compound is attractive and the rooms are comfortable; the sea-facing ones are the best value. Health club, swimming pool and restaurant. ❻–❽

Greenwoods, Ottavadi Cross Street ℡04114/43318. A very friendly family-run place, set in a lush garden lovingly tended by the numerous ladies of the house. Simple a/c and non a/c rooms just a stone's throw from the beach, each with a little thatched balcony. There is a good internet café here (Rs60/hr). ❸–❹

Ideal Beach Resort, 4km from town, Kovalam Road ℡04114/42240, ℻42243. Very appealing cottages in a landscaped compound a little way

before the Tiger Cave, plus a large swimming pool and a pleasant al fresco restaurant. Popular with tour groups, so reserve well ahead. ❽–❾

Mamalla Bhavan Annexe, E Raja Street ℡04114/42260, ℻42160. Efficient and modern hotel on the main drag through the village, with spotless (mostly a/c) rooms overlooking a courtyard. Non-a/c rooms have mosquito nets. Unfortunately it's away from the beach, but there's a very good a/c restaurant to compensate. ❹–❻

Rama Krishna Lodge, 8 Ottavadai St ℡04114/42331. Clean rooms in the heart of the tourist enclave, all with bathrooms but no a/c, set round a courtyard filled with pot plants. The newest ones are on the top storey, and have sea views. There's a backup generator, and it tends to have vacancies when everywhere else is full, because of its size. ❶–❷

Sea Shore, 30A, Fisherman's Colony (☎ 04114/42074). Slap on the beach, at the end of Ottavadi Street. Above the beach restaurant there are the standard clean, tiled rooms, but they are overshadowed by a huge wood-panelled "honeymoon" room bang in front. This room has no balcony but a window in front of the bed looks straight out to sea. ❹–❺.

Sri Murugan Guest House, Ottavadai Street ☎ 04114/42552. Good-value place next door to the *Rama Krishna*. Small and peaceful, with courteous service: one of the nicest options in the area. ❸–❹

Surya, Thirukula Street ☎ 04114/42292. Lakeside hotel set in a leafy compound, dotted with rather broken sculpture. Run by a retired archeologist, the hotel seems rather peripheral to his sculpture school and gallery, which share the same space (open to the public). There's a range of rooms, some with a/c and balconies; mosquito nets are available and, considering the proximity of the lake, essential. There is a new pool (residents only), but bathtub is probably a more appropriate term to use. ❷–❻

Taj Fisherman's Cove, Covelong Beach, 30min drive north from Mamallapuram ☎ 04114/04128. Four-star hotel with a pool, bar and restaurants. The centrally a/c and comfortable rooms in the main building overlook a tropical beachside garden, while the more romantic a/c circular cottages stand at the ocean's edge. ❾

Temple Bay Ashok (ITDC) Beach Resort ☎ 04114/42251, ☏ 42257. A great location – on the beach near the village, with views of the Shore Temple. Thatched, basic a/c cottages on the beach all have sea-facing balconies, and there are huge a/c rooms in the main building, plus a swimming pool and restaurant. ❾

Tina Blue Lodge, Ottavadi Street ☎ 04114/42319. A well established family business with pleasant, simple turquoise and whitewashed rooms with mosquito nets and attached bathrooms. The blue roof terrace is fantastic, with a great sound system, a decent restaurant and a karam board. ❷–❸

TTDC Hotel Tamil Nadu Beach Resort, Kovalam Road ☎ 04114/42235, ☏ 42268. A predictably overpriced, shabby state-run place made up of huge split-level cottages (some non-a/c) with sea-facing "sitouts", a very large pool, bar and multicuisine restaurant. Also has a campsite. ❺–❼

TTDC Hotel Tamil Nadu Unit II & Camping Site, Shore Temple Road ☎ 04114/42287. Just behind the beach, adjacent to the village tank. The site is slightly rundown, but has a cheap dorm (Rs50 per bed), as well as new a/c rooms, and shabbier standard non-a/c. ❺–❼

Uma Guest House, 11 Ottavadi Cross St ☎ 04114/ 42697. An extremely new quiet hotel run by a man called Lion. Mostly spotless and tiled non-a/c rooms; if your budget can stretch to it, it's worth paying that bit more for one of the two a/c rooms, just behind the beach (no view) with breezy, private balconies. ❸–❻

Victory, 5 Ottavadai St ☎ 04114/42179. A small, European-run guesthouse with comfortable non-a/c rooms and its own garden restaurant. ❸

Vinayak Cottages, 68 E Raja St ☎ 04114/42445. Four spacious thatched cottages set in a leafy garden a stone's throw from the bus stand. Offers Western toilets, and tables outside. Good value but it's a bit removed from the beach scene. ❸–❹

Vinodhara, 4 Ottavadi Cross St ☎ 04114/42694. A large place opposite *Lakshmi Lodge*. Immaculately tiled, all non-a/c but the rooms catch cooling sea breezes, and you can see the Shore Temple from the top floor. Great value for the price. ❷–❸

The Monuments

Mamallapuram's monuments divide into four categories: open-air **bas–reliefs**, structured **temples**, man-made **caves** and **rathas** ("chariots", carved in situ from single boulders, to resemble temples or the chariots used in temple processions). The famous bas-reliefs, **Arjuna's Penance** and the **Krishna Mandapa**, adorn massive rocks near the centre of the village, while the beautiful **Shore temple** presides over the beachfront. Sixteen man-made caves in different stages of completion, are scattered through the area, but the most complete of the nine *rathas* are in a group, named after the five Pandava brothers of the *Mahabharata*.

The **entrance fee** for the Shore Temple and the Panch Rathas is now $10 [Rs10], available from the ticket booth outside the Shore Temple. The ticket is valid for one day only (6.30am–5.30pm), and will give you access to all the sights in Mamallapuram. Alternatively, you can peek through the wiremesh fence at all the restricted access sights, and the bas-reliefs are free.

The Krishna Mandapa and Arjuna's Penance

A little to the west of the village centre, the enormous bas-relief known as the **Krishna Mandapa** shows Krishna raising Mount Govardhana aloft in one hand. The sculptor's original intention must have been for the rock above Krishna to represent the mountain, but the seventeenth-century Vijayanagar addition of a columned *mandapa* (or entrance hall), prevents a clear view of the carving. Krishna is also depicted seated milking a cow and standing playing the flute. Other figures are *gopas* and *gopis*, the cowboys and girls of his pastoral youth. Lions sit to the left, one with a human face, and above them a bull.

Another bas-relief, **Arjuna's Penance** – also referred to as the "Descent of the Ganges" – is a few metres north, opposite the modern Talasayana Perumal temple. The surface of this rock erupts with detailed carving, most notably the endearing and naturalistic renditions of animals. A family of elephants dominates the right side, with tiny offspring asleep beneath a great tusker. Further still to the right, separate from the great rock, is a free-standing sculpture of an adult monkey grooming its young.

On the left-hand side, Arjuna, one of the Pandava brothers and a consummate archer, is shown standing on one leg. He is looking at the midday sun through a prism formed by his hands, meditating on Shiva, who is nearby represented by a statue, fashioned by Arjuna himself. The *Shiva Purana* tells that Arjuna made the journey to a forest on the banks of the Ganges to do penance, in the hope that Shiva would part with his favourite weapon, the *pashupatashastra*, a magic staff or arrow. Shiva eventually materialized in the guise of Kirata, a wild forest-dweller, and picked a fight with Arjuna over a boar they both claimed to have shot. Arjuna only realized he was dealing with the deity after his attempts to drub the wild man proved futile; narrowly escaping death at the playful hand of Shiva, he was finally rewarded with the weapon. Not far away, mimicking Arjuna's devout pose, an emaciated (presumably ascetic) cat stands on its hind legs, surrounded by mice.

To the right of Arjuna, a natural cleft represents the **Ganges** river, complete with *nagas* – water spirits in the form of cobras. Near the bottom, a fault in the rock that broke a *naga* received a quick-fix of cement in the 1920s. Evidence of a cistern and channels remain at the top, which at one time must have carried water to flow down the cleft, simulating the great river. It's not known if there was some ritual purpose to all this, or whether it was simply an elaborate spectacle to impress visitors. You may see sudden movements among the carved animals: lazing goats often join the permanent features.

A little way north of Arjuna's Penance, precipitously balanced on the top of a ridge, is a massive, natural, almost spherical boulder called **Krishna's Butter Ball**. Picnickers and goats often rest in its perilous-looking shade.

Ganesha Ratha and Varaha cave

Just north of Arjuna's Penance a path leads west to a single monolith, the **Ganesha Ratha**. Its image of Ganesh dates from this century; some say it was installed at the instigation of England's King George V. An interesting sculpture at one end, of a protecting demon with a tricorn headdress, is reminiscent of the Indus Valley civilization's 4000-year-old horned figure known as the "proto-Shiva".

Behind Arjuna's Penance, southwest of the Ganesha Ratha, is the **Varaha Mandapa II cave**, whose entrance hall has two pillars with horned lion bases and a cell flanked by two *dvarpalas* (guardians). One of four **panels** shows the boar incarnation of Vishnu, who stands with one foot resting on the *naga* snake-king as he lifts a diminutive Prithvi – the earth – from the primordial ocean. Another is of Gajalakshmi, the goddess Lakshmi seated on a lotus being bathed by a pair of elephants. Trivikrama, the dwarf brahmin who becomes huge and bestrides the world in three steps to defeat the demon king Bali, is shown in another panel, and finally a four-armed Durga is depicted in another.

For more background on the temples of Tamil Nadu, see Contexts, p.675.

The Shore temple

East of the village, a distinctive silhouette above the crashing ocean, Mamallapuram's **Shore temple** (see p.468 for entrance details) dates from the early eighth century and is considered to be the earliest stone-built temple in South India. The design of its two finely carved towers was profoundly influential as it was exported across South India and eventually to Southeast Asia; today, due to the combined forces of wind, salt and sand, much of the detailed carving has eroded, giving the whole a soft, rounded appearance.

The taller of the towers is raised above a cell that faces out to sea – don't be surprised to see mischievous monkeys crouching inside. Approached from the west through two low-walled enclosures lined with small Nandi (bull) figures, the temple comprises two *lingam* shrines (one facing east, the other west), and a third shrine between them housing an image of the reclining Vishnu. Recent excavations, revealing a tank containing a structured stone column thought to have been a lantern, and a large Varaha (boar incarnation of Vishnu) aligned with the Vishnu shrine, suggest that the area was sacred long before the Pallavas chose it as a temple site.

The Lighthouses and the Mahishasuramardini cave

At the highest point in an area of steep paths, unfinished temples, ruins, scampering monkeys and massive rocks, south of Arjuna's Penance, the **New Lighthouse** affords fine views east to the Shore Temple, and west across paddy fields and flat lands littered with rocks. Next to it, the **Olakanesvara** ("flame-eyed" Shiva), or **Old Lighthouse temple**, used as a lighthouse until the beginning of the twentieth century, dates from the Rajasimha period (674–800 AD) and contains no image.

Nestling between the two lighthouses is the **Mahishasuramardini cave**, whose central image portrays Shiva and Parvati with the child Murugan seated on Parvati's lap. Shiva's right foot rests on the back of the bull Nandi, and Parvati sits casually, leaning on her left hand. On the left wall, beyond an empty cell, a panel depicts Vishnu reclining on the serpent, his attitude of repose contrasted with the weapon-brandishing demons, Madhu and Kaithaba. Other figures seek Vishnu's permission to chase them.

Opposite, in one of the most celebrated sculptures in Indian art, a carved panel shows the eight-armed goddess **Durga** as Mahishasuramardini, the "crusher" of the buffalo demon **Mahishasura**. The story goes that Mahishasura became so powerful that he took possession of heaven, causing great misery to its inhabitants. To deal with such a dangerous foe, Vishnu and Shiva hit upon the idea of combining all the gods' powers into a single entity. This done, fiery jets appeared, from which emerged the terrifying "mother of the universe", Durga. In the ensuing battle, Durga caught Mahishasura with a noose, and he changed into a lion; she beheaded the lion, and he transformed into a human wielding a sword. Then she fired off a flight of arrows, only to see him turn into a huge trumpeting elephant; she cut off his trunk, whereupon the buffalo returned. Now furious, Durga partook of her favourite beverage – blood, "the supreme wine". Climbing on top of the buffalo, she kicked him about the neck and stabbed him with her trident. The impact of her foot forced him halfway out of his own mouth, only to be beheaded by his own sword, at which point he fell. The panel shows Durga riding a lion, in the midst of the struggle. Accompanied by dwarf *ganas*, she wields a bow and other weapons; Mahishasura equipped with a club, can be seen to the right, in flight with fellow demons.

The tiny **Archaeological Survey of India Museum** (daily 9am–1pm & 2–5pm; Rs2, Rs10 extra for camera) on W Raja Street, near the lighthouse, has a rather motley collection of unlabelled Pallava sculpture found in and around Mamallapuram.

Pancha Pandava Rathas

In a sandy compound 1.5km south of the village centre stands the stunning group of monoliths known – for no historical reason – as the **Pancha Pandava Rathas** (see above for entrance details), the five chariots of the Pandavas. Dating from the period of Narasimhavarman I (c.630–70 AD), and consisting of five separate free standing sculptures that imitate structured temples plus some beautifully carved life-size animals; they were carved either from a single gigantic sloping boulder or from as many as three distinct rocks.

The "architecture" of the *rathas* reflects the variety of styles employed in temple building of the time, and stands almost as a model for much subsequent development in the **Dravida**, or southern, style. The Arjuna, Bhima and Dharmaraja *rathas* show strong affinities with the Dravidian temples at Pattadakal in Karnataka. Carving was always executed from top to bottom, enabling the artists to work on the upper parts with no fear of damaging anything below. Any unfinished elements there may be are always in the lower areas.

Intriguingly, it is thought that the *rathas* were never used for worship. A Hindu temple is only complete when the essential pot-shaped finial, the *kalasha*, is put in place – which would have presented a physical impossibility for the artisans, as the *kalasha* would have had to have been sculpted first. *Kalashas* can be seen next to two of the *rathas* (Dharmaraja and Arjuna), but as part of the base, as if they were perhaps to be put in place at a later date.

The southernmost and tallest of the *rathas*, named after the eldest of the Pandavas, is the pyramidal **Dharmaraja**. Set on a square base, the upper part comprises a series of diminishing storeys, each with a row of pavilions. Four corner blocks, each with two panels and standing figures, are broken up by two pillars and pilasters supported by squatting lions. Figures on the panels include Ardhanarishvara (Shiva and female consort in one figure), Brahma, the king Narasimhavarman I and Harihara (Shiva and Vishnu combined). The central tier includes sculptures of Shiva Gangadhara, holding a rosary with the adoring river goddess Ganga by his side and one of the earliest representations in Tamil Nadu of the dancing Shiva, Nataraja, who became all-important in the region. Alongside, the **Bhima** *ratha*, the largest of the group, is the least complete, with tooling marks all over its surface. Devoid of carved figures, the upper storeys, as in the Dharmaraja, feature false windows and repeated pavilion-shaped ornamentation. Its oblong base is very rare for a shrine.

The Arjuna and Draupadi *rathas* share a base. Behind the **Arjuna**, the most complete of the entire group and very similar to the Dharmaraja, stands a superb unfinished sculpture of Shiva's bull Nandi. **Draupadi** is unique in terms of rock-cut architecture, with a roof that appears to be based on a straw thatched hut (a design later copied at Chidambaram; see p.495). There's an image of Durga inside, but the figure of her lion vehicle outside is aligned side-on and not facing the image, a convincing reason to suppose this was not a real temple. To the west, close to a life-size carving of an elephant, the *ratha* named after the twin brothers **Nakula** and **Sahadeva** is, unusually, apsidal-ended. The elephant may be a visual pun on this, as the Sanskrit technical name for a curved ended building is *gajaprstika*, "elephant's backside".

The road out to the *rathas* resounds with incessant hammering and chiselling from sculptors' workshops. Much of their work is excellent, and well worth a browse – the sculptors produce statues for temples all over the world and are used to shipping large-scale pieces. Some of the artists are horrifyingly young; children often do the hard donkey work on large pieces, which are then completed by master craftsmen.

Eating

Mamallapuram is crammed with small restaurants, most of which specialize in **seafood** – tiger prawns, pomfret, tuna, shark and lobster – all of which can be mouth-wateringly succulent and relatively inexpensive. Prices are higher at the **beach hotels**, but the atmosphere and often the food are usually worth it. Wherever you eat, avoid a nasty shock at the end of your meal by establishing exactly how much your fish is going to cost in advance, as the price quoted is often just the cost per kilo.

Beer is available in most restaurants for about Rs7, but most restaurants don't have a liquor licence, so you have to ask for a beer rather surreptitiously, and the restaurant will go out and buy it for you.

Dreamland, Ottavadi Street. Run by Swarmy and Ganesh, a delightful team that makes this place the most welcoming and relaxed place to sit and chill all day. Both the filter coffee and the lassis are superb and comes in a huge glass, and the house speciality is "pasta dreamland", a yummy seafood concoction. They also run a café opposite, serving coffees, cakes, home-made bread and hummus sandwiches

Golden Palette, *Mamalla Bhavan Annexe*, E Raja Street. Blissfully cool café with a/c and tinted windows, serving pukka veg dishes (Rs50 thalis at lunch time, North Indian tandoori in the evenings), and wonderful ice-cream sundaes. Worth popping in just for a coffee to beat the heat.

La Palais Croisette, *Ramakrishna Hotel*, Ottavadi Street. A new German Bakery place with smashing croissants, several different set breakfasts, and lots of innovative dishes alongside the usual lasagne, pasta, pizza, mousaka theme.

La Pampillion, Shore Temple Road, opposite *Hotel Tamil Nadu*. A tiny thatched hut with a cosy, romantic atmosphere. The emphasis is on traditional home-style cooking, and the speciality is tiger prawns in a lemon, garlic and tomato sauce. Their unusual lime lassi (Rs9) is very refreshing.

La Vie En Rose, next to the sculpture museum at the south end of the village. The usual Westerner-orientated menu, plus salads, pasta dishes (their spaghetti's great) and chicken specialities. Get a balcony seat overlooking the stone carvers' workshops and lighthouse.

Luna Magica, beyond Ottavadai Street. Slap on the beach, this is the place to splash out on top-notch seafood, particularly tiger prawns and lobster, which are kept alive in a tank. The big specimens cost a hefty Rs600–800, but are as tasty as you'll find anywhere, served in a rich tomato, butter and garlic sauce. They also do passable sangria, made with sweet Chennai red wine, and cold beer, with plenty of less expensive dishes for budget travellers – including a new line in veg and non-veg sizzlers.

Mamalla Bhavan, opposite the bus stand, Shore Temple Road. The best no-frills pure-veg "leaf meals" joint for miles, and invariably packed. Equally good for *iddli-wada* breakfasts, and evening dosas and other snacks. Thalis cost Rs20.

Moonraker, Ottavadai Street. Cool jazz and blues sounds, chess sets and slick service, ensure this place is filled year-round with foreign tourists. The food is good: sharkfish and fresh calamari are a speciality, but their curd-fruit-and-muesli breakfasts are delicious too.

Nautilus Jacques, Ottavadi Cross Street. New place opened by an affable Frenchman who was a former partner in *La Vie en Rose* restaurant, and dishes up delicious salads and seafood. The service is slow, but everything is made fresh, and there's nowhere to hurry to anyway.

Sculpture, Ottavadai Street. A new place owned by a master sculptor who will try and sell you his works of art as you eat. Luckily, the food is well worth staying around for – a feast of succulent coconut fish in a heavenly marinade, chapatis,

rice, vegetables and salad will cost about Rs100.

Tina Blue Lodge, Ottavadi Street. Think deep-blue and sea-green, cane furniture, eclectic music, karam boards, good beach views and beer. This is what draws people all day, as well as their excellent honey-banana pancakes. Evenings of music and dance are soon to start in the little garden.

Village Inn, Thirukula Street. Now in a new location, this little thatched eatery is still popular, and serves up seafood grilled on a charcoal fire, as well as an established favourite – their superb butter-fried chicken in a tomato-garlic sauce (Rs55).

Around Mamallapuram

The sandy hinterland and flat estuarine paddy fields around Mamallapuram harbour a handful of sights well worth making forays from the coast to see. A short way north along the main highway, the **Government College of Sculpture** and elaborately carved **Tiger Cave** can easily be reached by bicycle, but to get to the **Crocodile Bank**, where rare reptiles from across South Asia are bred for release into the wild, or **Dakshina Chitra**, a museum devoted to South Indian architecture and crafts, you'll need to jump on and off buses or rent a moped for the day. Further north still, the **Cholamandal Artists' Village** is a showcase for less traditional arts that's best visited en route to or from Chennai. Finally, a good target for a day-trip inland is the hilltop temple at **Tirukalikundram**, west of Mamallapuram across a swathe of unspoilt farmland.

Government College of Sculpture

A visit to the **Government College of Sculpture**, 2km north of Mamallapuram on the Kovalam (Covelong) Road (☎04114/42261) gives a fascinating insight into the processes of sculpture training. You can watch anything from preliminary drawing, with its strict rules regarding proportion and iconography, through to the execution of sculpture, both in wood and stone, in the classical Hindu tradition. Contact the college office to make an appointment.

Tiger Cave

Set amid groves close to the sea, 5km north from Mamallapuram on the Kovalam (Covelong) Road, the extraordinary **Tiger Cave** contains a shrine to Durga, approached by a flight of steps that passes two subsidiary cells. Following the line of an irregularly shaped rock, the cave is remarkable for the elaborate exterior, which features multiple lion heads surrounding the entrance to the main cell.

Crocodile Bank

The **Crocodile Bank** (Tues–Sun 8am–5.30pm; Rs15, Rs10 extra for camera) at Vadanemmeli, 14km north of town on the road to Chennai, was set up in 1976 by the American zoologist Romulus Whittaker, to protect and breed indigenous crocodiles. The bank has been so successful (fifteen crocs to five thousand in the first fifteen years) that its remit now extends to saving endangered species, such as turtles and lizards, from around the world.

Low-walled enclosures in its garden compound house hundreds of inscrutable crocodiles, soaking in ponds or sunning themselves on the banks. Breeds include the fish-eating, knobbly-nosed gharial and the world's largest species, the saltwater *crocodylus porosus*, which can grow to 8m in length. You can watch feeding time at about 4.30pm each Wednesday. The temptation to take photos is tempered by the sight of those hungry saurians clambering over each other to chomp the chopped flesh, within inches of the top of the wall.

Another important field of work is conducted with the collaboration of local Irula people, whose traditional expertise is with snakes. Cobras are brought to the bank for **venom collection**, to be used in the treatment of snakebites. Elsewhere, snakes are repeatedly "milked" until they die, but here at the bank only a limited amount is taken from each snake, enabling them to return to the wild. Coastal-route buses #117 and #118 stop at the entrance.

Dakshina Chitra

Occupying a patch of sun-baked sand dunes midway between Chennai and Mamallapuram, **Dakshina Chitra** (daily except Tues 10am–6pm; Rs50), literally "Vision of the South", is one of India's best-conceived folk museums, devoted to the rich architectural and artistic heritage of Kerala, Karnataka, Andhra Pradesh and Tamil Nadu. The museum was set up by the Chennai Craft Foundation with support from local government and American sponsors. Apart from giving you the chance to look around some immaculately restored old buildings, a permanent display exposes visitors to many disappearing traditions of the region which you might otherwise not be aware of, from tribal fertility cults and *Ayyannar* field deities to pottery and leather shadow puppets.

The visit kicks off with a short introductory video, followed by a guided tour of the campus, where a selection of traditional buildings from across peninsular India have been painstakingly reconstructed using authentic materials. Highlights include an airy Tamil brahmins' dwelling, a Chettinad merchant's mansion filled with Burmese furniture and Chinese laquerware, a Syrian Christian home from the backwaters of Kerala, with a fragrant jackwood interior, and a north Keralan house that has separate rooms for the women – a unique feature reflecting the area's strongly matrilineal society. Exhibitions attached to the various structures convey the environmental and cultural diversity of the south, most graphically expressed in a wonderful textile collection featuring antique silk and cotton saris from various castes and regions. There is also a pottery demonstration, where you can try your hand at throwing clay on a Tamil wheel, and a memorable slapstick shadow puppet (*tolu bommalaatam*) display.

Cholamandal Artists' Village

Tucked away on the scruffy southern edge of Chennai, the **Cholamandal Artists' Village** (daily 10am–7pm; free) was established in the mid-1960s to encourage contemporary Indian art. In a country where visual culture is so comprehensively dominated by convention, fostering innovation and artistic experimentation proved no easy feat. Despite an initially hostile response from the Madrasi establishment (who allegedly regarded the tropical storm that destroyed the artists' first settlement as an act of nemesis), the village has prospered. Today, Cholamandal's thirty-strong community has several studios and a large gallery filled with paintings, sketches, sculpture and metalwork, and a shop selling work produced here. For those with more than a passing interest in the village, there's also a small **guesthouse** (☏044/492 6092; ❷).

Tirukalikundram

The village of **TIRUKALIKUNDRAM**, 16km west on the road to Kanchipuram, is famous locally for its hilltop Shiva temple. A pair of white Egyptian vultures (*Neophron percnopterus*), believed to be reincarnated saints on their way between Varanasi and Rameshwaram, used to swoop down at noon to be fed by the temple priests. No one knew how long these visits had been going on, nor why the vultures suddenly stopped coming in 1994. Their absence, however, was taken as a bad omen and, sure enough, that year massive cyclones ravaged the Tamil Nadu coast.

Four hundred hot stone steps need to be scaled to reach the top, but don't let that – or the various individuals, including the priests, who give you the impression that you require their multifarious services and paid company – deter you. Once on the hilltop, the views are sublime, especially at sunset. Visits to Tirukalikundram are made more worthwhile if you take the time to explore the vast **Vijayanagar temple** at its heart, which harbours a collection of conches said to manifest themselves each year in the large tank on the edge of town.

Regular **buses** run to Tirukalikundram from Mamallapuram, en route to Kanchipuram, but it's more fun to rent a moped or motorcycle for the trip (see p.467). You could conceivably peddle out here, too (the route is flat all the way), but start out early in the day to avoid the worst of the heat.

Kanchipuram

Ask any Tamil what **KANCHIPURAM** (aka Kanchi) is famous for, and they'll probably say silk saris, shrines and saints – in that order. A dynastic capital throughout the medieval era, it remains one of the seven holiest cities in the subcontinent, sacred to both Shaivites and Vaishnavites, and among the few surviving centres of goddess worship in the South. Year round, pilgrims pour through for a quick puja stop on the Tirupati tour circuit and, if they can afford it, a spot of shopping in the sari emporia. For non-Hindu visitors, however, Kanchipuram holds less appeal. Although the temples are undeniably impressive, the town itself is unremittingly hot and dusty, with few decent options on the accommodation and restaurant front. You'll enjoy its attractions a whole lot more if you come here on a **day-trip** from Chennai or Mamallapuram, a two-hour bus ride east.

The Town and temples

Established by the **Pallava** kings in the fourth century AD, Kanchipuram served as their capital for five hundred years, and continued to flourish throughout the Chola, Pandya and Vijayanagar eras. Under the Pallavas, it was an important scholastic forum, and a meeting point for Jain, Buddhist and Hindu cultures. Its **temples** dramatically reflect this enduring political prominence, spanning the years from the peak of Pallava construction to the seventeenth century, when the ornamentation of the *gopuras* and pillared halls was at its most elaborate (for more on Tamil Nadu's temples, see Contexts, p.675). All can be easily reached by foot, bike or rickshaw, and are closed daily between noon and 4pm. You'll be offered a panoply of services – from sanctuary priests, shoe bearers, guides, women giving out food for fish in the temple tanks, and well-trained temple elephants that bless you with their trunks – so go prepared with a pocketful of change. Always animated, the temples really come alive during major festivals such as the **Car Festival** (May) and **Navaratri** (Oct/Nov).

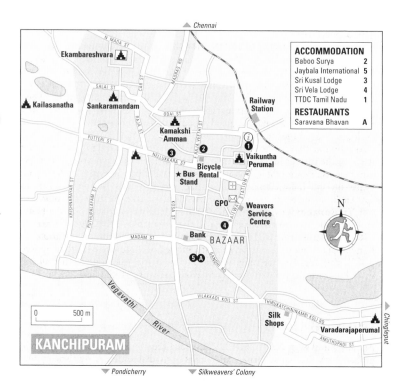

ACCOMMODATION
Baboo Surya   2
Jaybala International   5
Sri Kusal Lodge   3
Sri Vela Lodge   4
TTDC Tamil Nadu   1
RESTAURANTS
Saravana Bhavan   A

Ekambareshvara

Kailasanatha   Sankaramandam

Railway Station

Kamakshi Amman

Vaikuntha Perumal

Bicycle Rental
Bus Stand

GPO   Weavers Service Centre

Bank   BAZAAR

N

KANCHIPURAM

Silk Shops
Varadarajaperumal

Chingleput

Pondicherry   Silkweavers' Colony

Ekambareshvara temple

Kanchipuram's largest temple and most important Shiva shrine, the
Ekambareshvara temple – also known as Ekambaranatha – is easily identified by its colossal whitewashed *gopuras*, which rise to almost 60m, on the north
side of town. The main temple contains some Pallava work, but was mostly
constructed between the sixteenth and seventeenth centuries, and stands within a vast walled enclosure beside some smaller shrines and a large fish-filled
water tank.

The entrance, through a high-arched passageway beneath an elaborate *gopura* in the south wall, leads to an open courtyard and a majestic "thousand-
pillared hall" (*kalyan mandapa*), whose slightly decaying grey stone columns are
modelled as nubile maidens, animals and deities. This hall faces the tank in the
north and the sanctuary in the west that protects the emblem of Shiva (here in
his form as **Kameshvara**, Lord of Desire), an "earth" *lingam* that is one of five
lingam in Tamil Nadu representing the elements. Legend connects it with the
goddess **Kamakshi** (Shiva's consort, "Wanton-Eyed"), who angered Shiva by
playfully covering his eyes and plunging the world into darkness. Shiva repri-
manded her by sending her to fashion a *lingam* from the earth in his honour;
once it was completed, Kamakshi found she could not move it. Local myths
tell of a great flood that swept over Kanchipuram and destroyed the temples,
but did not move the *lingam*, to which Kamakshi clung so fiercely that marks
of her breasts and bangles were imprinted upon it.

Behind the sanctum, accessible from the covered hallway around it, an eerie
bare hall lies beneath a profusely carved *gopura*, and in the courtyard a venerable

mango tree represents the tree under which Shiva and Kamakshi were married. This union is celebrated during a festival each April, when many couples are married in the *kalyan mandapa*. Believed to symbolize the four Vedas, the four branches of the tree are supposed to yield different-tasting fruit, collected by the temple priests and given to women who come here to petition for fertility. For Rs50 you can perform a special problem-solving puja: walk three times around the tree to sort out financial difficulties or to find a husband for your daughter. Finally, don't miss the temple's other "thousand-pillared *mandapa*", beneath the *gopura* on the west wall, which houses the extraordinary **Pictorial Depication of Historical Episodes in Sound and Light by Electronic Meriods** (sic), a collection of bizarre gizmos elucidating the basic tenets of Hinduism. One involves thrusting your head into a contraption to hear electronically triggered excerpts from the *Vedas*.

The somewhat neglected twelfth-century **Jvaraheshvari temple**, in leafy gardens to the south, is the only Chola (tenth–twelfth centuries) structure in Kanchipuram not to have been modified and overshadowed by later buildings. Unlike the Pallava constructions, it is built of hard grey stone and its sculpted pyramidal roof is an early form of the *gopuras* used extensively by the Pandyas.

Sankaramandam

Kanchipuram is the seat of a line of holy men bearing the title **Acharya**, whose line dates back to 1300–482 BC, to the saint Adi Sankaracharya. The 68th Acharya, the highly revered Shri Chandrasekharendra Sarasvati Swami, died in January 1994 at the age of 101. Buried in the sitting position, as is the custom for great Hindu sages, his mortal remains are enshrined in a *samadhi* at the **Sankaramandam**, a *math* down the road from the Ekambareshvara temple. The present incumbent, the 69th Acharya, has his quarters on the opposite side of a marble meditation hall to the shrine, and gives *darshan* to the public during the morning and early evening, when the *math*'s two huge elephants are given offerings. Lined with old photographs from the life of the former swami, young brahmin students chanting Sanskrit verses in the background, it's a typically Tamil blend of simple sanctity and garish modern glitz.

Kailasanatha temple

The **Kailasanatha temple**, the oldest structure in Kanchipuram and the finest example of Pallava architecture in South India, is situated among several low-roofed houses just over 1km west of the town centre. Built by the Pallava king Rajasimha early in the eighth century, its intimate size and simple carving distinguish it from the town's later temples. Usually quieter than its neighbours, the shrine becomes the focus of vigorous celebrations during the Mahashivratri festival each March. Like the contemporaneous Shore temple at Mamallapuram, it is built of soft sandstone, but its relatively sheltered position inland has spared it from wind and sand erosion and it remains remarkably intact, despite some rather clumsy recent renovation work.

Topped with a modest pyramidal spire, the small temple stands within a rectangular courtyard, enclosed by a wall inlaid with tiny meditation chambers and sculpted with images of Shiva, Parvati and their sons, as well as rearing mythical lions (*yalis*). On the south side of the spire Shiva is depicted as a begging ascetic (Bhikshatana); on the north he's in the pose of the dance of destruction (Samhara-Tandava). Walls in the dim interior bear traces of frescoes, and the ceilings are etched with religious verses written in Pali. The sanctum, inaccessible to non-Hindus, shelters a sturdy sixteen-sided black *lingam*, guarded by elephant-headed Ganesh and Shiva's other son, Skanda, the god of war, with whom the king Rajasimha was closely associated. Double walls were built round the sanctuary to support the weighty tower above; the passage between them is used as a circumambulatory path as part of the ritual worship of Shiva.

Kamakshi Amman temple

Built during Pallava supremacy and modified in the fourteenth and seventeenth centuries, the **Kamakshi Amman Temple**, northwest of the bus stand, combines several styles, with an ancient central shrine, gates from the Vijayanagar period, and high, heavily sculpted creamy *gopuras* set above the gateways in a later period.

To the right of the central shrine, inaccessible to non-Hindus, a raised *mandapa* is now an art gallery, housing many pictures of the recent **Acharyas** (see account on Sankaramandam temple). This is one of India's three holiest shrines to Shakti, Shiva's cosmic energy depicted in female form, usually as his consort. The goddess Kamakshi, a local form of Parvati, shown with a sugar-cane bow and arrows of flowers, is honoured as having lured Shiva to Kanchipuram, where they were married, and thus having forged the connection between the local community and the god. In February or March, deities are wheeled to the temple in huge wooden "cars", decked with robed statues and swaying plantain leaves. During the rest of the year, the intricately carved "cars" are kept behind bars on Gandhi Road.

Vaikuntha Perumal temple

Built shortly after the Kailasanatha temple at the end of the eighth century, the smaller **Vaikuntha Perumal temple**, a few hundred metres south of the train station, is dedicated to Vishnu. Its lofty carved *vimana* (towered sanctuary) crowns three shrines containing images of Vishnu, stacked one on top of the other. Unusual scenes carved in the walls enclosing the temple yard depict events central to Pallava history, among them coronations, court gatherings and battles with the Chalukyas who ruled the regions to the northwest. The temple's pillared entrance hall was added by Vijayanagar rulers five centuries later, and is very different in style, with far more ornate sculpting.

Varadarajaperumal temple

The Vaishnavite **Varadarajaperumal temple** stands within a huge walled complex in the far southeast of town, guarded by high gates topped with *gopuras*. The inner sanctuary boasts superb carving and well preserved paintings, but non-Hindus only have access to the outer courtyards and the elaborate sixteenth-century pillared hall close to the Western entrance gate. The outer columns of this *mandapa* are sculpted as lions and warriors on rearing horses, to celebrate the military vigour of the Vijayanagars, who believed their prowess was inspired by the power of Shakti.

Practicalities

Flanked on the south by the Vegavathi River, Kanchipuram lies 70km southwest of Chennai, and about the same distance from the coast. **Buses** from Chennai (1hr 30min–2hr), Mamallapuram (2hr–2hr 30min), and Chengalpattu (1hr) arrive at the potholed and chaotic stand in the centre on Raja Street. The sleepy **train station** in the northeast sees only five daily passenger services from Chengalpattu (one of them, the #161, starts in Chennai) and two from Anakkonam.

As most of the main roads are wide and traffic rarely unmanageable, the best way **get around** Kanchi is by **bicycle** – available for minimal rates (Rs1.50/hr) at stalls west and northeast of the bus stand. The town's vegetable markets, hotels, restaurants and bazaars are concentrated in the centre of town, near the bus stand.

Note that unless you have used dollars and are happy to chance the black market, there is nowhere in the town to **change money**; the nearest official foreign exchange places are in Chennai and Mamallapuram.

Accommodation and eating

There's not a great choice of **accommodation** in Kanchipuram, but the hotels are sufficient for an overnight stay. The less expensive lodges offer minimal comfort, while the pricier places, if not exactly elaborate, are clean and comfortable and generally serve good South Indian dishes in their own **restaurants**. However, the most highly rated place to eat in town is **Saravana Bhavan** on Gandhi Road, an offshoot of the famous Chennai chain of pure veg restaurants. They offer superb Rs30 "meals" at lunch time, and a long list of delicious South Indian snacks and good coorg coffee the rest of the day; they open at 6am for breakfast, and there's a cool a/c annexe inside. It's also marginally less like bedlam than the other "meals" joints in the centre, which tend to get swamped by shaven-headed pilgrims from Tirupati.

Baboo Surya, 85 E Raja Veethi St ⊤ 04112/22555. Kanchee's top hotel: large and modern with immaculate a/c and non-a/c rooms, glass elevator and a good veg/tandoori restaurant. Ask for a room with a "temple view". ❺–❻

Jaybala International, 504 Gandhi Rd ⊤ 04112/24348. Slightly more old-fashioned than the *Baboo Surya*, but with huge clean rooms (some a/c) and lower tariffs. They also offer excellent-value single occupancy rates, and *Saravana Bhavan* (see above) is on the doorstep. ❹–❺

Sri Kusal Lodge, 68C Nellukkara St ⊤ 04112/22356. Very friendly, marble-lined lodge – the best of the budget bunch. The basic rooms are all non-a/c and have attached bathrooms but they open onto a rather dismal corridor. Good English is spoken here. ❷

Sri Rama Lodge, 21 Nellukkara St ⊤ 04112/22435. Good, fairly clean budget lodge with attached bathrooms and some a/c rooms. Best bet if *Sri Kusal* is booked. ❷–❸

Sri Vela Lodge, Railway Station Road ⊤ 04112/21504. Another run-of-the-mill lodge, a 10min walk across town from the bus stand. Larger than average rooms, with attached shower-toilets and fans, but still airless. Busy "meals" restaurant downstairs. ❷

TTDC Tamil Nadu, Railway Station Road ⊤ 04112/22553. A friendly and dependable place, although rather overpriced; the rooms are large and clean enough, but are on the shabby side. The restaurant has a snazzy new menu card, but it is still undeniably dingy and best avoided. ❺–❼

Vellore

Unless you are a connoisseur of military architecture, or have succumbed to a tropical disease, you're unlikely to find much inspiration in **VELLORE**, 150km west of Chennai. The limited charms of its vast sixteenth-century Hindu fort, whose blue-grey granite ramparts form an incongruous backdrop to the fast-moving traffic dominating the centre, are less memorable than the mayhem of its main streets. The streets of Vellore are more jammed than average because of the presence in the middle of town of the **CMC Hospital**, one of South India's foremost medical centres. Patients and their relatives travel here for treatment from all over India, giving Vellore a more upbeat feel than you'd expect for a city of its size, but the only foreign visitors that spend a night here tend to be those breaking the long haul between Bangalore and Chennai.

The approach to the **fort** (daily 7am–8pm; free) is from the east, over a modern bridge that straddles a wide moat, once filled with crocodiles. Locals assert that the giant four-sided structure, with its impressive crenellated walls, was built in the late sixteenth century by Chinna Bomma Reddi, viceroy of the Aravidu kings of Chandragiri. Over time, his reign gave way to the Vijayanagar dynasty, but the fort held off attacks until it fell to the Muslim Adi Shahis of Bijapur in the seventeenth century. Later the Marathas ousted their Muslim enemies, only to be overthrown in turn by Daud Khan of Delhi in the early 1700s. British officers took control in 1768, and remained overlords until Independence.

Close to the northern wall, the magnificent *kalyan mandapa* (thousand-pillared hall) in the outer courtyard of the **Jalakanteshvara temple** boasts a vitality and richness of carving matched only at Srirangam (see p.518). The outer pillars depict rearing steeds, mythical dragons and warriors, while the central columns support sculptures of *yalis*, mythical lions prominent in much earlier Pallava temples. The temple shrine is dedicated to Shiva, represented by a *lingam*. Although it was never pillaged, the presence of Muslim and European troops during successive occupations was considered a desecration, and worship was suspended until 1981 when a new Nataraja bronze was installed.

A **cemetery** to the right of the fort entrance holds the graves of the British soldiers who died during a swiftly defeated mutiny in 1806, when *sepoys* rose in protest against demands for them to shave their beards and adopt a common dress code. Nearby, a small **archeological museum** (daily except Fri 10am–1pm & 2–4.30pm; free) houses fragments of sculpture, hero stones and inscriptions found on the site. The only other building of interest, Tipu Sultan's palace, lie within the confines of the Police Cadet College and are off-limits to casual visitors.

Practicalities

Regular **buses**, from the two adjacent bus stands just east of the fort's entrance, connect Vellore with Chennai (every 5–10min; 3–4hr), Kanchipuram (every 5–10min; 2hr 30min) and Bangalore (10 daily; 5–6hr). Buses to and from Tiruvannamalai (every 5–10min; 2hr), however, leave from a smaller stand at the southeast corner of the fort, ten minutes' walk down Town Hall Road. The nearest main-line **railway station** lies 3km north of the city at **Katpadi Junction**, where you can pick up direct services to and from Chennai (2hr–2hr 30min), Bangalore (4hr 15min) and beyond. Trains on the metregauge line between Vellore and Tirupathi, Tiruvannamalai and Pondicherry pull in to the **Cantonment Station**, 2km south of the bus stand.

Finding **accommodation** in Vellore can be a problem, as most rooms tend to be booked out by people visiting relatives in the hospital. In the narrow road opposite the CMC Hospital, dozens of modest lodges offer the best deal in the way of budget options. These include the very friendly *VDM Lodge*, at 13/1 Beri Bakkali St (⌂0416/24008; ❷–❸), whose cosy "deluxe" rooms on the fifth floor have great views of the city and air coolers, or the large and well run *Gayathri*, on 22 Babu Rao St (⌂0416/27714; ❷). The *Solai*, a couple of doors down the same street (⌂0416/222876; ❷–❹), has a few decent a/c rooms. As a last resort, *Mayura*, 85 Babu Rao St (⌂0416/225788; ❷), has small rooms in need of a lick of paint, but it is clean, cheap and within walking distance of the bus stand. The top hotel in the town centre is *Prince Manor*, on Katpadi Road next to the hospital (⌂0416/227106; ❻); it's a comfortable three-star with a choice of spacious a/c and non-a/c rooms, and two restaurants. Offering similar standards, but 1.5km north of town on New Katpadi Road, is the more modern, business-orientated *River View* (⊤0416/25568; ❻–❼), which is nowhere near the river, but perfectly pleasant, cool and quiet, with a choice of quality in-house restaurants.

For **eating** options in the town centre, you've the usual string of simple veg "meals" joints along Ida Scudder Street, opposite the hospital, of which the *Anand* is about the brightest. Further down the street, past the hospital and on the first floor of the *Susil Hotel* (look for the giant neon hoarding), is an excellent little Chinese restaurant, *Chinatown*, which serves tasty mild chicken and vegetable dishes in a dark, blissfully cool a/c dining room. Their chicken in lemon sauce is delicious, and they have plenty of vegetarian and North Indian options on the menu, priced at around Rs40-70, as well as piping hot naans and *parathas* from the tandoor. A greater choice of North Indian dishes, most of them chicken-based, is offered at the *Prince Manor*'s fourth-floor a/c restaurant, where you can stretch your legs on a roof terrace between courses. Downstairs, on the ground floor, is Vellore's only "deluxe" South Indian vegetarian; it's your usual marble-lined *udipi* canteen, but has a/c and a colour TV blaring Tamil movies, and is not as chaotic at lunch time as the competition on Ida Scudder Street.

Vedanthangal

One of India's most spectacular bird sanctuaries lies roughly 1km east of the village of **VEDANTHANGAL**, a cluster of squat, brown houses set in a patchwork of paddy fields 30km from the east coast and 86km southwest of Chennai. It's a tiny, relaxed place, bisected by one road and with just two chai stalls.

The **sanctuary** (daily dawn–dusk) a low-lying area less than half a kilometre square, is at its fullest between December and February, when it is totally flooded. The rains of the northeast monsoon, sweeping through in October or November, bring indigenous water birds ready to nest and settle until the dry season (usually April), when they leave for wetter areas. Abundant trees on mounds above water level provide perfect nesting spots, alive by January with fledglings. Visitors can watch the avian action from a path at the water's edge, or from a watchtower (fitted out with strong binoculars). Try to come at sunset, when the birds return from feeding. Common Indian species to look out for are openbill storks, spoonbills, pelicans, black cormorants and **herons** of several types. You may also see ibises, grey pelicans, migrant cuckoos, sandpipers, egrets, which paddle in the rice fields, and tiny, darting bee-eaters. Some migrant birds pass through and rest on their way between more permanent sites; swallows, terns and redshanks are common, while peregrine falcons, pigeons and doves are less regularly spotted.

Practicalities

Getting to Vedanthangal can present a few problems. The nearest town is Maduranthakam, 8km east, on NH-45 between Chengalpattu and Tindivanam. Head here to wait for the hourly buses to the sanctuary, or catch one of the four daily services from Chengalpattu. Taxis make the journey from Maduranthakam for Rs200–250, but cannot be booked from Vedanthangal.

Vedanthangal's only accommodation is the two-roomed **forest lodge** (❶) near the bus stand, school and chai stall. Rooms, spacious and comfortable with attached bath, have to be booked through the Wildlife Warden, 50, 4th Main

Gandhi Nagar, Adyar, Chennai (☏044/413947); if you turn up on spec, it may well be full, especially in December and January. They'll prepare food if given enough notice.

Tiruvannamalai

Synonymous with the fifth Hindu element of fire, **TIRUVANNAMALAI**, 100km south of Kanchipuram, ranks, along with Madurai, Kanchi, Chidambaram and Trichy, as one of the five holiest towns in Tamil Nadu. Its name, meaning "Red Mountain", derives from the spectacular extinct volcano, **Arunachala**, which rises behind it, and which glows an unearthly crimson colour at dawn. This awesome natural backdrop, combined with the presence in the centre of town of the colossal Arunchaleshvara temple, make Tiruvannamalai one of the region's most memorable destinations. Far removed from the tourist trail, it is a perfect place to get to grips with life in small-town Tamil Nadu. For those searching for the spiritual south, the countless shrines, sacred tanks, *ashrams* and paved pilgrim paths scattered around the sacred mountain (not to mention the legions of dreadlocked *babas* who line up for alms outside the main sites) will keep anyone interested in Hinduism absorbed for days.

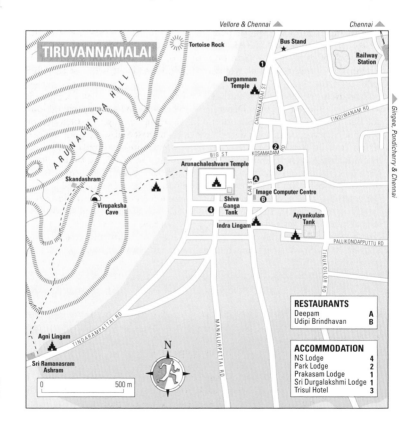

Mythology identifies Arunachala as the place where Shiva asserted his power over Brahma and Vishnu by manifesting himself as a *lingam* of fire, or **agnilingam**. The two lesser gods had been disputing their respective strengths when Shiva pulled this primordial pyro-stunt, challenging his adversaries to locate the top and bottom of his blazing column. They couldn't (although Vishnu is said to have faked finding the head) and collapsed on their knees in a gesture of supreme submission. The event is commemorated each year at the rising of the full moon in November/December, when the **Deepam ceremony**, bringing to an end the ten-day **Karttigai festival**, culminates with the illumination of gallons of camphor in the temple courtyard. This acts as a signal for brahmins stationed on the summit of Arunachala to light a vast vat of ghee and paraffin, which blazes for days and can be seen from a radius of more than 20km. It represents the fulfilment of Shiva's promise to reappear each year to vanquish the forces of darkness and ignorance with firelight. The massive *agnilingam* attracts tens of thousands of pilgrims, who rush from the temple below to the summit in time to fuel the inferno with their own offerings. The whole event, best enjoyed from the relative safety of a rooftop in town, is one of the great spectacles of sacred India. The latest incarnation of a prehistoric fire-worshipping cult, it has probably been performed here in some form or another, without interruption, for four thousand years.

The alleged regenerative and healing powers of the sacred Red Mountain also explain why the famous twentieth-century saint **Shri Ramana Maharishi** chose this as the site for his 23-year meditation retreat, in a cave on the side of the hill. Shri Ramana's subsequent teachings formed the basis of a worldwide movement, and his former ashram on the edge of Tiruvannamalai attracts a stream of Western devotees. A crop of other smaller ashrams have mushroomed alongside it, some of them more authentic than others, and the ranks of white-cotton-clad foreigners floating between them have become a defining feature of the area south of town over the past five or six years.

Arunchaleshvara temple

Known to Hindus as the "Temple of the Eternal Sunrise", the enormous **Arunchaleshvara temple**, built over a period of almost a thousand years and incorporating several distinct styles, consists of three concentric courtyards whose gateways are topped by tapering *gopuras*, the largest of which cover the east and north gates. The best spot from which to view the precinct, a breathtaking spectacle against the sprawling plains and lumpy, granite Shevaroy Hills, is the path up to Shri Ramana Maharishi's meditation cave, Virupaksha (see below), on the lower slopes of Arunachala. To enter it, however, head for the huge eastern gateway, which leads through the thick outer wall carved with images of deities, local saints and teachers, to a paved inner courtyard. The large stepped Shivaganga tank to the left originally lay outside the temple precincts; on the right stands a vast "thousand-pillared" *mandapa*, where the temple elephant lives when not taking part in rituals. In the basement of a raised hall to the right before entering the next courtyard is the Parthala *lingam*, where Shri Ramana Maharishi is said to have sat in a state of Supreme Awareness while ants devoured his flesh.

The second enclosure, built a couple of centuries earlier, in the 1200s, is much smaller, with a large Nandi bull facing the sanctuary and a shrine to the goddess (Shiva's consort) on its northern edge. In the temple kitchens in its southeastern corner, food is prepared for the gods. A nineteenth-century roof shelters the central courtyard, surveyed by numerous deities etched into its

During the annual Karttigai festival, Hindu pilgrims are supposed to perform an auspicious circumambulation of Arunachala, known as the Pradakshana (*pra* signifies the removal of all sins, *da* the fulfilment of desires, *kshi* freedom from the cycle of rebirth and *na* spiritual liberation). Along the way, offerings are made at a string of shrines, tanks, temples, *lingams*, pillared meditation halls, sacred rocks, springs, trees and caves related to the Tiruvannamalai legends. Although hectic during the festival, the paved path linking them all together is quiet for most of the year and makes a wonderful day hike, affording fine views of the town and its environs.

An even more inspiring prospect is the ascent of Arunachala itself, which can be completed in two to three hours if you're fit and can cope with the heat (if you can't, don't attempt this hike). The path is less easy to follow than the Pradakshana, and you may feel like employing one of the guides who offer their services at the trailhead, just above the Shri Ramanasram ashram. At the summit, where you can see remnants of the annual Deepam blaze, sits Swami Narayana, a renunciate who has been performing an austerity of silence here for more than fourteen years.

outer walls, among them Shiva, Parvati, Venugopala (Krishna), Lakshmi, Ganesh and Subrahmanya. In the dim interior, arcaded cloisters supported by magnificently carved columns lead to the main shrine dedicated to Shiva and accessible to non-Hindus: a *lingam* raised on a platform bearing tenth-century inscriptions. This is the location of six daily puja, or acts of worship, when the *lingam* is bathed, clothed and strewn with flower garlands amid the heady smell of incense and camphor and the sound of bells and steady chanting.

In one of the outer courtyards on the north side, drenched devotees – mostly women – circumambulate an ancient hybrid *neem* and *bodhi* tree, draping it with offerings for the health of offspring and the success of married life.

Virupaksha and Skandashram caves

Opposite the western entrance of the temple complex, a path leads up a holy hill (15min) to the **Virupaksha cave**, where Shri Ramana Maharishi stayed between 1899 and 1916. He personally built the bench outside and the hill-shaped *lingam* and platform inside, where all are welcome to meditate in peace. When this cave became too small, constantly crowded with relatives and devotees, Shri Ramana shifted to another, hidden away in a clump of trees a few minutes further up the hill. He named this one, and the small house built onto it, **Skandashram**, and lived there from 1916 to 1922. The inner cave here is also set aside for meditation, and the front patio affords splendid views across the temple, town and surrounding plains.

Shri Ramanasram ashram

The caves can also be reached via a pilgrims' path winding uphill from the **Shri Ramanasram ashram**, 2km south of the temple along the main road. This simple complex is where the sage lived after returning from his retreat on Arunachala, and where his body is today enshrined (Hindus customarily bury saints in the sitting position rather than cremate their bodies). The *samadhi* has become a popular place for Shri Ramana's devotees on pilgrimage, but interested visitors are welcome to stay in the dorms here. There's also an excellent bookshop stocking a huge range of titles on the life and teachings of the guru, as well as quality postcards, calendars and religious images.

Tiruvannamalai is served by regular buses from Vellore (every 5-10min; 2hr), and by less frequent services from Pondicherry (11 daily; 2hr). Coming from the coast, it's easiest to make your way from Tindivanam, picking up one of the numerous buses to Tiruvannamalai from there. The town bus stand is north of the temple; 500m east of there, the **railway station** is on the line between Tirupati and Madurai, with a daily service in each direction.

Amazingly, you can access the internet from Tiruvannamalai, at the Image Computer Centre, 52 Car Street (daily 10am–10pm; Rs60/hr).

Accommodation and eating

For such an important pilgrimage place, Tiruvannamalai has surprisingly few decent **hotels**. If your budget can stretch to it, stay at the two-star *Trisul*, a couple of minutes' walk from the main temple entrance at 6 Kanakaraya Mudali St (☎04175/22219; ❺–❻), which has huge, immaculately clean rooms (some with a/c), courteous staff and a good restaurant. Its only drawback is that it gets booked for long periods by Westerners studying at one or other of the ashrams. The next best option, and excellent value for money, is *NS Lodge*, facing the Arunachaleshvara Temple's south entrance at 47 Thiruvoodal St (☎04175/25388; ❷–❹). Its rooms are neat and clean, some have a/c and all have cable TV and attached shower-toilets; there's also a great view of the temple towers from the roof. Moving down the scale, pick of the budget lodges is the *Sri Durgalakshmi*, just west of the bus stand at 73 Chinnakadai St (☎04174/26041; ❷). If it's full, try the shabbier *Prakasam* next door (☎04175/26041; ❶–❷), owned by the same family. Otherwise, a reliable option is further into town towards the temple: the *Park* (☎04175/22471; ❷–❺), 26 Kosmadam St, just northeast of the main temple entrance. It has a range of rooms, from basic but clean to a/c and comfortable and there's a busy vegetarian canteen on the ground floor.

For **food**, you've a choice of a dozen or so typical South Indian "meals" joints, of which the *Udipi Brindhavan Hotel*, just off the bottom of Car Street, is the most traditional (though not the most hygienic). Delicious hot ghee chapatis are served here all afternoon, as well as all the usual rice specialities. The other commendable *udipi* restaurant in town is the *Deepam*, also on Car Street opposite the temples' east entrance, which boasts a cooler a/c "deluxe" wing next door (same name), where you can order ice creams and milk shakes; both branches serve excellent *parottas* for under Rs10. If you feel like a change from South Indian, head for the *Trisul*, whose posh ground-floor restaurant serves a North Indian buffet for around Rs100, as well as a full tandoori menu.

Gingee

An epic landscape of huge boulder hills, interspersed by lush splashes of rice paddy and banana plantations, stretches east of Tiruvannamalai towards the coast. The scenery peaks at **GINGEE** (pronounced "*Shinjee*"), 37km east of the Red Mountain along the Pondicherry highway, where the ruins of Tamil Nadu's most spectacular **fort** (whole complex, including palace: daily sunrise–sunset; $10 [Rs10]) sprawl over a vast swathe of sun-scorched granite. If this were anywhere except India, you wouldn't be able to move for interpretative panels and Walkman posts, but here the miles of crumbling ramparts and temple masonry have been left to the mercy of the weeds and tropical weather. Only on weekends, when bus parties pour around the most accessible monuments, does the site receive more than a trickle of visitors. Come here in the week, and you may well have the place to yourself, save for the odd troupe of monkeys and inquisitive tree squirrels.

Dissected by the main Tiruvannamalai–Pondicherry road, Gingee fort comprises three separate citadels, crowning the summits of three dramatic hills: Krishnagiri to the north, Rajagiri to the west and Chandrayandurg to the southeast. Connecting them to form an enormous triangle, 1.5km from north to south, are twenty-metre-thick walls, punctuated by bastions and gateways giving access to the protected zones at the heart of the complex. It's hard to imagine such defences ever being overrun, but they were, on numerous occasions following the fort's foundations by the Vijayanagars in the fifteenth century. The Muslim Adil Shahis from Bijapur, Shivaji's Maharatas and the Moghuls all conquered Gingee, using it to consolidate the vulnerable southern reaches of their respective empires. The French also took it in 1750, but were ousted by the British after a bloody five-week siege eleven years later.

A network of raised, paved paths links the site's principal landmarks. From the road, head south to the main **east gate**, where a snaking passage emerges after no fewer than four changes of direction, inside the **palace** enclave. Of the many structures unearthed by archeologists here, the most distinctive is the square seven-storey **Kalyana Mahal tower**, focal point of the former governor's residence; featuring an ingenious hydraulic system that carried water to the uppermost levels, it is crowned by a tapering pyramidal tower. Continue west through a gateway, and you'll pick up the path to **Rajagiri**, Gingee's loftiest citadel; at 165m above the surrounding plain it's a very stiff climb in the heat, but the views are well worth the effort.

The other ruins worth exploring lie a short way beyond the east gate. Typifiying Gingee's position at the interface between the warring powers of north and South India is the **mosque of Sadat Ullah Khan I**, built in the early years of the eighteenth century. It stands a stone's throw from the sixteenth-century **Venkatarama temple**, dedicated to an aspect of Vishnu known as "Lord of the Venkata Hills". A dilapidated seven-storey *gopura* caps the east entrance, its passageway carved with scenes from the *Ramayana*.

Practicalities

Gingee is easily accessible by frequent **buses** from Tiruvannamalai 37km west and Pondicherry 68km southeast. You can either alight at the site itself, 2km west of **Gingee** town, or, if you intend to spend the night there, dump your bags at the hotel and continue to the ruins by auto-rickshaw. The only **accommodation** to speak of (and the only dependable place to leave luggage while you visit the fort), is the *Shivasand Hotel*, on MG Road, opposite the main bus stand (☎04145/22218; ③–⑤), whose *Vasantham* South Indian restaurant is Gingee's classiest place to eat. Auto-rickshaws charge Rs80–90 for the return trip from the town centre to the fort; you'll have to settle an additional fee for waiting time. Note that there are no refreshments, not even drinking water, available at the site, so take your own, or wander 500m back down the road towards town to the small roadside chai stall in the village.

Pondicherry and around

First impressions of **PONDICHERRY**, the former capital of French India, can be unpromising. Instead of the leafy boulevards and *pétanque* pitches you might expect, its messy outer suburbs and bus stand are as cluttered and chaotic as any other typically Tamil town. Closer to the seafront, however, the atmosphere grows tangibly more Gallic as the bazaars give way to rows of houses whose shuttered windows and colour-washed facades wouldn't look out of place in Montpellier. For anyone familiar with the British colonial imprint, it can induce culture shock to see richly ornamented Catholic churches, French

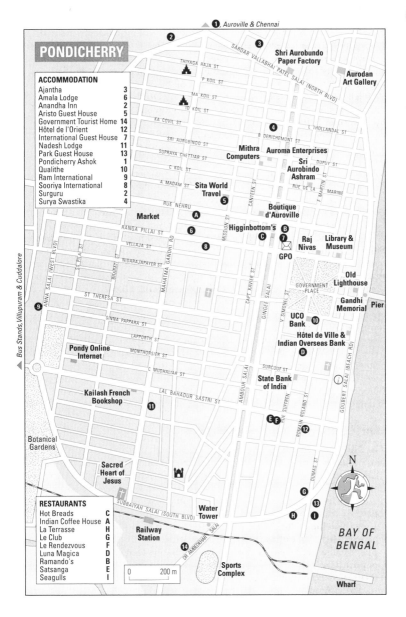

PONDICHERRY

ACCOMMODATION

Ajantha	3
Amala Lodge	6
Anandha Inn	2
Aristo Guest House	5
Government Tourist Home	14
Hôtel de l'Orient	12
International Guest House	7
Nadesh Lodge	11
Park Guest House	13
Pondicherry Ashok	1
Qualithe	10
Ram International	9
Sooriya International	8
Surguru	2
Surya Swastika	4

RESTAURANTS

Hot Breads	C
Indian Coffee House	A
La Terrasse	H
Le Club	G
Le Rendezvous	F
Luna Magica	D
Ramando's	B
Satsanga	E
Seagulls	I

Auroville & Chennai

Shri Aurobundo
Paper Factory

Aurodan
Art Gallery

Mithra
Computers

Auroma Enterprises

Sri
Aurobindo
Ashram

Sita World
Travel

Boutique
d'Auroville

Market

Higginbottom's

Raj
Nivas

Library &
Museum

GPO

Old
Lighthouse

GOVERNMENT
PLACE

Gandhi
Memorial

Pier

UCO
Bank

Hôtel de Ville &
Indian Overseas Bank

Pondy Online
Internet

State Bank
of India

Kailash French
Bookshop

Botanical
Gardens

Sacred
Heart of
Jesus

Water
Tower

Railway
Station

Sports
Complex

BAY OF
BENGAL

N

Bus Stands, Villupuram & Cuddalore

0   200 m

Wharf

road names and policemen in de Gaulle-style kepis. Even today, it is common to hear French spoken in the street and to see elderly men playing a late afternoon game of *boules* in the dusty squares around Ambour Salai and Gingee Salai.

Known to Greek and Roman geographers as "Poduke", Pondicherry was an important staging post on the second-century maritime trade route between Rome and the Far East (a Roman amphitheatre has been unearthed at nearby Arikamedu). When the Roman empire declined, the local Pallava and Chola kings took control, followed by a succession of colonial powers, from the Portuguese in the sixteenth century to the French, Danes and British. The enclave was exchanged several times between them during the various battles and treaties of the Carnatic Wars in the early eighteenth century, finally leaving the small territory in peace, in the hands of the French. Finally left in peace, Pondicherry's heyday dates from the arrival of **Dupleix**, who accepted the governorship in 1742 and immediately set about rebuilding a town decimated by its former British occupants. It was he who instituted the street plan of a central grid encircled by a broad oblong boulevard, bisected north to south by a canal dividing the "Ville Blanche", to the east, from the "Ville Noire", to the west.

Although relinquished by the French in 1954 – when the town became the headquarters of the **Union Territory of Pondicherry**, administering the three other former colonial enclaves scattered across South India – Pondicherry's split personality still prevails. West of the canal stretches a bustling South Indian market town, while to the east, towards the sea, the streets are emptier, cleaner and decidedly European. The seaside promenade, **Goubert Salai** (formerly Beach Road), has the forlorn look of an out-of-season French resort, complete with its own white Hôtel de Ville. Tanned sun-worshippers share space with grave Europeans drifting about in white robes, busy about their spiritual quest. It was here that **Shri Aurobindo Ghose** (1872–1950), a leading figure in the freedom struggle in Bengal, was given shelter after it became unwise to live close to the British in Calcutta. His **ashram** attracts thousands of devotees from all around the world, but particularly from Bengal.

Ten kilometres north, the utopian experiment-in-living **Auroville** was inspired by Aurobindo's disciple, the charismatic Mirra Alfassa, a Parisian painter, musician and mystic better known as "The Mother". Today this slightly surreal place is populated by numbers of expats and visited by long-stay Europeans eager to find inner peace. Nearby are two beaches – Auroville and Serenity – that are suitable for sunbathing and swimming.

Arrival and information

The **New Bus Stand** on the western edge of town, is the arrival point for most long-distance services from Chennai, Madurai and Bangalore, and Mamallapuram via the new "ECR" (East Coast Road); for a summary of routes, see "Travel Details" on p.570. Pondicherry's **railway station** is south of the centre, five minutes' walk from the sea; on a branch line, it's connected by four daily trains to the main line at Villupuram (departures 5.10am, 7.50am, 4.15pm & 7.45pm; 2hr). The first of these services, train #46, continues on to Chennai. There is a **computerized reservation centre** here.

The friendly and helpful staff at the **Pondicherry Tourism Development Corporation** office on Goubert Salai (daily 8.45am–1pm & 2–5.30pm; ☎0413/339497) can give you their leaflet and city map, and provide information about Auroville. You can also book a seat on the PTDC **city tour**

(2–5.30pm; Rs52.50) and arrange **car rental** (Rs1300 per day, including fuel). Recommended places to **change money** include: the Indian Overseas Bank in the Hôtel de Ville; Sita World Travels, 124 Mission St; the State Bank of India on Surcouf Street; and UCO Bank, rue Mahe de Labourdonnais. The **GPO** is on Ranga Pillai Street (Mon–Sat 10am–7.30pm).

The cheapest **internet access** is available at Mithra Computers, at 55 Canteen St, one block east of Mission Street in the northeast of town (daily 7am–9.30pm; Rs40). A slightly more expensive but more comfortable option is the a/c Pondy On Line Internet centre, 125 Candappa St (Mon–Sat 9.30am–12.30pm & 4–9pm). Otherwise, there are several decent internet centres along Rue Nehru that charge about Rs40 per hour.

Pondicherry is well served with both **auto–** and **cycle-rickshaws** which make sense if you are travelling from and to the New Bus Stand, but most tourists **rent a bicycle** from one of the many stalls dotted around town (Rs20 per day, plus Rs200 refundable deposit). If you're staying at the *Park Guest House*, hire one of theirs (they're all immaculately maintained). The tourist office (see above) also rent out good bikes from their *Lake Café*, on the seafront promenade, but at the rather expensive rate of Rs5 per hour. For trips further afield (to Auroville, for example), you may want to rent a moped or scooter. Of the rental firms operating in town, Auroma Enterprises, 9 Sri Aurobindo St (℡0413/36179) is the cheapest and has the best reputation, with new Honda Kinetics for Rs100/day. You'll have to pay a Rs500 deposit and leave your passport as security.

Accommodation

Pondicherry's **basic lodges** are concentrated around the main market area, Ranga Pillai Street and rue Nehru. Throughout Pondicherry, guesthouses belonging to the **Sri Aurobindo Ashram** offer fantastic value for money, but come with a lot of baggage apart from your own (regulations, curfews and overpowering "philosophy of life" notices). Although supposedly open to all, they are not keen on advertising, or on attracting misguided individuals indulging in "spiritual tourism".

Ajantha, 3, Zamindar Garden, SV Patel Salai ℡0413/334756. A newly refurbished hotel which is nothing fancy, but the rooms (some a/c) are clean with attached bathrooms, and the management very friendly and helpful. ❸–❻

Amala Lodge, 92 Ranga Pillai St ℡0413/338910. A leafy little budget place off MG Road, hemmed in by "Job Typing" offices. The non-a/c rooms are simple but acceptably clean, some with attached bath, otherwise there are communal facilities. A good fall-back, but you can get better value elsewhere for the same price and with less early morning noise. ❷

Anandha Inn, Sardar Vallabhai Patel Road ℡0413/330711, ℻331241. Seventy luxurious rooms, two restaurants and a pastry shop, in a gleaming white marble environment. Good value but popular with tour groups so book in advance. ❼

Aristo Guest House, 124 Mission St ℡ 0413/336728, ℻330057. Hard to find (look for the blue-and-white "Sita World Travels" sign). Budget rooms (some a/c) ranged around a raised courtyard; it's a bit dingy and not advised for single women, but fine for a short stay. ❷–❻

Government Tourist Home, Dr Ambedkhar Salai, Uppalam ℡0413/36376. Charmless, neon-lit concrete block, at the bottom end of town and within earshot of the railway line, but an unbelievable bargain (doubles only Rs30). All rooms with attached shower-toilets and there are two ultra-cheap a/c rooms. ❶

Hotel de l'Orient, 17, Rue Romain Rolland ℡0413/343067, ℻227829, ✉orient1804@satyam.net.in. Pondy's newest and grandest address. A large, beautiful French house with ten cool rooms, individually decorated with French antiques, overlooking a tiled leafy courtyard. A very romantic place, but the restaurant isn't great. ❽–❾

International Guest House, Gingee Salai, near the GPO ℡0413/336699. The largest Aurobindo establishment, with dozens of very large and spot-less rooms, some a/c and all with attached bath-rooms. Recommended as a budget option, and safe for single women. Daily tours of Auroville can be reserved and depart from here. ② –④

Nadesh Lodge, 539 Mahatma Gandhi Rd, near Small Market Clock Tower ☎ 0413/339221. A wel-coming and popular backpackers' lodge, in a bustling neighbourhood bazaar. Twenty non-a/c simple rooms face onto an elongated courtyard filled with pot plants. There is an in-house camera repair-wallah and a small library. ②

Park Guest House, at the south end of Goubert Salai ☎ 0413/334412. A Sri Aurobino Society pad, with very comfortable, spotless rooms slap on the seafront, with new mozzie nets and "sitouts" over-looking a well watered garden. Cycle rental, laun-dry and cafeteria. Great value. ④

Pondicherry Ashok, Chinnakalapet, 12km from Pondicherry on the old coastal road to Mamallapuram, near Auroville ☎ 0413/655160, ℗ 655140. Twenty comfortable a/c rooms in a quiet, breezy location on the seashore, with a chil-dren's playground, restaurant, barbecue and bar. Generous discounts for stays of three days or more. ⑧

Qualithe, 3 Rue Mahe de Labourdonnais ☎ 0413/334325. Despite the row of wine shops and the dingy bar downstairs, this is Pondy's most characterful budget lodge. Upstairs, large, simple rooms lead off a pleasant balcony with wicker chairs and great views over Government Place. You may have to share a room, as each one has four big beds. ④

Ram International, 398 Anna Salai ☎ 0413/337230, ℗ 337238. Very good-value, effi-cient, modern place on the western edge of town. Advance booking recommended. ⑤ –⑥

Sooriya International, 55 Ranga Pillai St ☎ 0413/338910. Large, immaculate a/c rooms in a slightly ageing central hotel. An ostentatious exte-rior, but the tariffs are reasonable. ⑥

Surguru, 104 Sardar Vallabhai Patel Salai (North Blvd) ☎ 339022, ℗ 334377. Best value among Pondy's mid-price hotels. Spruce, spacious rooms, brisk service and most mod cons, including an excellent veg restaurant (see Eating, below). ⑤ –⑥

Surya Swastika, 11 ID Koil St ☎ 0413/343092. Traditional Tamil guesthouse in a quiet corner of town, with nine basic rooms around a central courtyard that doubles as a pilgrims' canteen at lunch time. Incredibly cheap and cleaner than most of the bazaar lodges, and it provides an interesting insight into the lives of modern Hindu pilgrims. ①

The Town

Pondicherry's beachside promenade, **Goubert Salai**, is a favourite place for a stroll, with cafés and bars to idle in and cooling breezes blowing in off the sea. There's little to do, other than watch the world go by, but the Hôtel de Ville, today housing the municipal offices, is still an impressive spectacle, and a four-metre-high Gandhi memorial, surrounded by ancient columns, dominates the northern end. Nearby, inland facing, a French memorial commemorates French Indians who lost their lives in World War I.

Just north of the Hôtel de Ville, a couple of streets back from the promenade, is the leafy old French-provincial-style square now named **Government Place**. A fountain stands at the centre, and among its paths and lawns are a number of sculptures carved in nearby Gingee. On its northern side, guarded by policemen in red képis, the impressive, gleaming white **Raj Nivas**, official home to the present lieutenant governor of Pondicherry Territory, was built late in the eighteenth century for Joseph Francis Dupleix, who became gover-nor of French India. Unfortunately, the home of Ananda Ranga Pillai (1709–61), *dubash*, or close adviser of Dupleix – once one of the highlights of a visit to Pondicherry – is now closed to the public.

The **Pondicherry Museum** (Tues–Sun 10am–5pm), on Ranga Pillai Street, opposite Government Place, has an archeological collection comprising Neolithic and 2000-year-old remains from Arikamedu, a few Pallava (sixth–eighth centuries) and Buddhist (tenth-century) stone sculptures, bronzes, weapons and paintings. Alongside these are displayed a bizarre assem-bly of French salon furniture and bric-a-brac from local houses, including a velvet S-shaped "conversation seat".

The **Sri Aurobindo Ashram** on rue de la Marine (daily 8am–noon & 2–6pm; no children under 3; photography with permission) is one of the best known and wealthiest ashrams in India, founded in 1926 by the Bengali philosopher-guru Aurobindo Ghose and his chief disciple, personal manager and mouthpiece, "The Mother". It now serves as the headquarters of the Sri Aurobindo Society (or SAS) which today owns most of the valuable property and real estate in Pondicherry, and wields what many consider to be a disproportionate influence over the town. A beautifully maintained small rockery, cactus and flower garden greets you as you enter the compound. The **samadhi**, or mausoleum, of Sri Aurobindo and "The Mother" is covered daily with flowers and usually surrounded by supplicating devotees with their hands and heads placed on the tomb. Inside the main building, an incongruous and very bourgeois-looking Western-style room, complete with three-piece suite, is where "The Mother" and Sri Aurobindo chilled out. Make sure not to tread on the Persian carpet on the floor, as devotees prostrate here also. A bookshop in the next room sells tracts, and frequent cultural programmes are presented in the building opposite (ask at the bookshop for information).

In the southwest of town, near the train station, you can hardly miss the huge cream and brown **Sacred Heart of Jesus**, one of Pondicherry's finest Catholic churches, built by French missionaries in the 1700s. Nearby, the shady **Botanical Gardens** established in 1826, offer many quiet paths to wander (daily 8.45am–5.45pm; free). The French planted nine hundred species of imported trees, shrubs and flowers here, experimenting to see how they would do in Indian conditions; one, the *khaya senegalensis*, has grown to a height of 25m. You can also see an extraordinary fossilized tree, found 25km away in Tiravakarai.

The **Aurodhan Art Gallery**, at 11 Thillai Nattar St, just off SV Patel Salai (Mon–Sat 9am–1pm, 3–6pm; free) is a peaceful sanctuary dedicated to contemporary Indian art. The permanent exhibition showcases the talent of local artists, who have produced a prodigious amount – pictures and sculptures line the rooms and corridors over several floors. Many of the exhibits reflect the influence of Sri Aurobino or the environment of Auroville, and there are some excellent portraits. Five minutes' walk away is the **Sri Aurobindo Paper Factory**, on SV Patel Salai (Mon–Sat 8.30am–5pm), where you can watch the fascinating and laborious process of making the handmade paper that is sold in tourist spots all over India.

Eating

If you've been on the road for a while and are hankering for healthy salads, fresh coffee, crusty bread, cakes and real pastry, you'll be spoilt for choice in Pondicherry. Unlike the traveller-orientated German-bakery-style places elsewhere in the country, the Western **restaurants** here cater for a predominantly expatriate clientele, with discerning palettes and fat French-franc pay cheques. Pick of the bunch has to be the sophisticated *Le Club*, but you can eat well for a lot less at the more atmospheric *Satsanga*. **Beer** is available just about everywhere except the SAS-owned establishments.

Café Luna, Rue Suffren, near State Bank of India. A little hole in the wall where old men gather to drink coffee and pass the time of day. The coffee is prepared with great pomp and style, and the lunch-time plate of lemon rice and *vada* (Rs5) is absolutely superb.

Hot Breads, 42 Ambour Salai. Crusty croissants, fresh baguettes and delicious savoury pastry snacks, served in a squeaky clean French boulangerie-café: the espresso's a dream.

Indian Coffee House, rue Nehru. Not their cleanest branch, but the coorg filter coffee and *ottapams* are good, and the waiters as picturesque in their ice-cream-wafer hats.

La Terrasse, 5, Subbiah Salai (closed Wed). The most popular French restaurant for the European backpacker crew to hang out at, opening at 8.30am for croissants and coffee al fresco in the garden. Excellent prawn dishes start at Rs55, and there are crepes, pizzas and a variety of salads on offer all day, to sustain the postcard-writing clientele.

Le Club, 33 Dumas St (closed Mon). Beyond the pocket of most travellers, not to mention locals, but far and away the town's top restaurant complex. The predominantly French menu features their famous coq au vin, steak au poivre, plenty of seafood options and a full wine list, rounded off with cognac at Rs200 a shot. Count on Rs300 per head (if you forsake the shorts). Now there is also a cheaper bistro that is great for Sunday brunch, a *tapas* and cocktail bar, and a Vietnamese and Southeast Asian restaurant (open daily).

Le Rendezvous, 30 rue Suffren. Filling seafood sizzlers, a range of delicious pizzas and tandoori brochettes are specialities of this popular expat-orientated restaurant. They also serve fresh croissants and espresso for breakfast, either indoors or up on the more romantic thatched rooftop, with jazz sounds and chilled beer in discreet ceramic jugs. Most main dishes Rs80–130.

Ramanas, corner of rue Nehru and Gingee Salai. Filled with a hard-core *iddli*-eating office crowd; service is fast, and the South Indian food is cheap and good. Opens at 7am for breakfast.

Satsanga, Lal Bahadur Sastri Street. If you only eat once in Pondy, it should be here. Served on the colonnaded veranda of an old colonial mansion, the menu (devised by the French patron) is carefully prepared and exactly the kind of thing you dream about elsewhere in India: organic salads with fresh herbs, tsatsiki and garlic bread, sauté potatoes, tagliatelle à la carbonara, and mouthwatering pizzas washed down with chilled Kingfisher beer. Check their *plat du jour* for fresh fish dishes. Around Rs250 per head for three courses with drinks.

Seagulls Restaurant and Bar, 19 Dumas St. Reasonably priced, open-air rooftop restaurant in a breezy spot right next to the sea, new pier and cargo harbour. Huge menu, with veg dishes, meat, seafood, Indian, Chinese and even some Italian dishes (pizza, risotto, spaghetti). Inexpensive.

Auroville

AUROVILLE, the planned "City of Dawn" and New Age capital of India, is 10km north of Pondicherry, just outside the Union Territory in Tamil Nadu. Founded in 1968, Auroville was inspired by "The Mother", the spiritual successor of Sri Aurobindo. Around 1350 people live in communes (two-thirds of them are non-Indians), with such names as Fertile, Certitude, Sincerity, Revelation and Transformation, in what it is hoped will eventually be an ideal city for a population of 50,000. Architecturally experimental buildings, combining modern Western and traditional Indian elements, are set in a rural landscape of narrow lanes, deep red earth and lush greenery. Income is derived from ecofriendly agriculture, handicrafts and home-made foodstuffs, alternative technology, educational and development projects and Aurolec, an alternative computer software company. The entire complex is run on natural energy generated by solar panels and windmills, and water is drawn using wind turbines.

The avowed aim of the commune is harmony, leading a life made meaningful through hard physical work backed up by a spiritual discipline of inner consciousness, rather than dogma, rule or ritual behaviour. Nonetheless, the place has had its ups and downs, not least of which have been the **disputes** between the community and the Sri Aurobindo Society (SAS) over ownership since the death of "The Mother" in 1973. Rejecting the Aurovillians' calls for self-determination, the SAS cut off funds to the community, forcing its members to become financially self-sufficient. The power struggle intensified in the mid-1970s, erupting into full-blown violence on a couple of occasions before the police were called in. At one stage, the war of attrition got so tough that some Western countries had to provide aid to the Aurovillians. Eventually, however, the High Court ruled in their favour, and in 1988, the Auroville Foundations

Act was passed, placing responsibility for the administration of the settlement in the hands of a seven-member council, with representatives from the state government, the SAS and Auroville itself.

One of the accusations levelled at the settlers around this time was that, although Auroville was supposedly an egalitarian community, most of the Indians involved were being relegated to the status of labourers. Aurovillians countered these attacks by pointing to the numerous ways they had worked to improve the lives of low-caste Tamils in the surrounding villages, many of whom had been given full-time jobs manufacturing textiles, software and non-polluting unbaked bricks. The site also has a school for local Tamil children, started by a retired policeman from Essex in England.

Considering how little there is to see here, Auroville attracts a disproportionately large number of day-trippers – much to the chagrin of its inhabitants, who rightly point out that you can only get a sense of what the settlement is all about if you stay a while. Interested visitors are welcomed as paying guests in most of the communes, where you can work alongside permanent residents (see "Practicalities" below).

The Matri Mandir

The various conflicts of the past two decades have inevitably spawned divisions among the Aurovillians themselves. While some still treat the teachings of "The Mother" with the same uncritical devotion as the Pondicherry ashramites, others have strayed from the orthodoxy. One thing, however, unites the whole community: the **Matri Mandir**, or "dwelling place of The Mother", is a gigantic hi-tech meditation centre at the heart of the site, 36m in diameter. An information booth is open daily 8.30am to 5.15pm (☎0413/622373).

Begun in 1970, the space-age structure was conceived as "a symbol of the Divine's answer to man's inspiration for perfection". Soil from 126 countries and 23 Indian states was symbolically placed in an urn, now kept in a concrete cone from which a speaker can address an audience of 3000 without amplification. In accordance with the instructions of "The Mother", this is open to all (daily 4–4.45pm; arrive at least one hour in advance; the Mandir is closed if there is rain), although the Aurovillians' reluctance to admit outsiders is palpable. After a long wait for tickets to be issued, accompanied by strict instructions on how to behave while inside, visitors are ushered in silence to the Matri Mandir's ramped entrance. You are allowed a fleeting glimpse of the seventy-centimetre crystal ball that forms its focal point, made by the Swiss optical company, Karl Zeiss, and believed to be the largest of its kind in the world. Contrary to the intentions of the architects, the whole experience can leave a bad taste in your mouth; the Aurovillians clearly hate having to herd day-trippers through what most of them regard as the soul of their community. However, you'll get a different response if you express more than a passing interest; your original entry ticket allows you to return later for an hour of silent meditation. If you are keen to come back again after this, you may be granted permission for a visit out of normal hours (apply at the information booth between 3.30pm & 4.30pm). Only then, Aurovillians claim, will you appreciate the real significance of the place.

Practicalities

Auroville lies 10km north of Pondicherry on the main Chennai road; you can also get there via the new coastal **highway**, turning off at the village of Chinna Mudaliarchavadi. **Bus** services are frequent along both routes but – as Auroville is so spread out, covering some fifty or so square kilometres – it's best to come with your own transport, at the very least a bike. Most people rent a scooter or **motorcycle** from Pondicherry and ride up. Alternatively, book onto Pondicherry Tourism's daily **tour** from Pondicherry (depart 2pm, return 5.30pm; Rs52.50).

For a pre-visit primer, call in at the **visitor centre** (daily 9.30am–5.30pm), bang in the middle of the site near the Bharat Niwas, which holds a permanent exhibition on the history and philosophies of the settlement. You can also pick up some inexpensive literature on Auroville in the adjacent bookshop and check out a notice board for details of **activities** in which visitors may participate (these typically include yoga, reiki and Vipassana meditation, costing around Rs50 per session). In addition, there's a handicrafts shop and several pleasant vegetarian cafés serving snacks, wholesome meals and cold drinks.

The information desk at the visitor centre is also the place to enquire about **paying guest accommodation** in Auroville's thirty or so communes. Officially there's no lower limit on the time you have to stay, but visitors are encouraged to stick around for at least a week, helping out on communal projects; tariffs are in the range of Rs100–500 per day, depending on levels of comfort. Alternatively, you can arrange to stay in one of four **guesthouses**, offering simple non-a/c rooms from US$5–15 (payable in rupees). Beds in these, and in the communes, are always in short supply, especially during the two peak periods of December to March and July to August. It is advisable to book well in advance by telephone (c/o Auroville Guest Programmes, Auroville 605 101, Tamil Nadu ☎0413/622704), ✉avguests@auroville.org.in). Otherwise, the only rooms in the area are just outside Auroville. In the village of Chinna Mudaliarchavadi, the *Palm Beach Cottage Centre* (❶) is nothing of the kind (the sea is fifteen minutes' walk away), but has passably clean rooms with communal bathrooms and a small garden, where meals are served. Nearby, the *Cottage Guesthouse* (❷) offers a little more comfort in thatched huts or a recently built block boasting en-suite rooms. For **food**, you won't do better than the simple, filling veg meals served in Auroville itself.

Central Tamil Nadu: The Chola heartland

To be on the banks of the Cauvery listening to the strains of Carnatic music is to have a taste of eternal bliss.

Tamil proverb

Continuing south from Pondicherry along the Coromandel Coast, you enter the flat landscape of the **Kaveri** (aka Cauvery) **Delta**, an intensely green world of paddy fields cut by thirty major rivers, canals, dams, dykes and rivulets that has been intensively farmed since ancient times. Only a hundred miles in diameter, it forms the rice-bowl core of Tamil Nadu. The **Kaveri** is the largest river, known in Tamil as Ponni, "The Lady of Gold" (a form of the Mother

Goddess), and is revered as a conduit of liquid *shakti*, the primordial female energy that nurtures the millions of farmers who live on her banks and tributaries. Three bumper crops each year are coaxed from the giant patchwork of paddy, which Colonel Fullarton in his *View of English Interests in India* (1785) described as " …teeming with an industrious race expert in agriculture". Amid the stifling heat of mid-July, on the eighteenth day of the solar month Adi, villagers have for hundreds, possibly thousands, of years gathered in vast numbers to mark the rising of the river. During the festival, money, cloth, jewellery, food, tools and household utensils are thrown into the river as offerings, so that the goddess will have all she needs for the coming year. From October until December, the delta is washed with the powerful second annual monsoon, bringing a rich harvest of rainwater for the paddy. This is one of the most beautiful periods of the year, as diagonal swathes of rain sweep across the endless green fields between bursts of dazzling sunshine, and the sunrise is pure and clear after stormy nights.

This mighty delta formed the very heartland of the **Chola** empire, which reached its apogee between the ninth and thirteenth centuries, an era often compared to classical Greece and Renaissance Italy, both for its cultural richness and the sheer scale and profusion of its architectural creations. Much as the Cholas originally intended, every visitor immediately stands in awe of their huge temples, not only in cities such as **Chidambaram**, **Kumbakonam** and **Thanjavur**, but also out in the countryside at places like **Gangaikondacholapuram**, where the temple is all that remains of a once-great city.

Exploring the area for a few days will bring you into contact with the more delicate side of Cholan artistic expression, such as the magnificent **bronzes** of Thanjavur, and the incantatory **saints' hymns** of the *Sangam* and *Tevaram* – bodies of oral poetry that emerged in the delta more than a thousand years ago. Its composers were wandering poets who travelled the length and breadth of the south, singing, dancing and spreading a new devotional brand of Hinduism known as **bhakti**. Phrased in classical Tamil and with a richness rarely equalled since, their verses praise the beauty of the delta's natural landscape and recall the significance of the countless shrines and sacred sites (more than half of the 274 holy Shaivite places in Tamil Nadu are found here). Considering many were not set down in Sanskrit until centuries after they were composed, it is a miracle that the hymns have survived at all. But today, they form the basis of a thriving oral tradition, sung in temples, *maths* (religious institutions), pilgrims' buses and homes wherever Tamil is the lingua franca. The poems have also provided the raw material for many a hit mythological movie, and you'll hear modern versions of the better-known ones, jazzed up with electric guitars and synthesizers, blaring out of audio-cassette stores.

Nowhere else in the world has a classical civilization survived till the twenty-first century, and the knowledge that the ancient culture of the Cholas endures here alongside their awesome monuments lends a unique resonance to any journey across the Kaveri Delta.

Chidambaram

CHIDAMBARAM, 58km south of Pondicherry, is so steeped in myth that its history is hard to unravel. As the site of the *tandava*, the cosmic dance of Shiva as **Nataraja**, King of the Dance, it is one of the holiest Hindu sites in South

India. A visit to the **Sabhanayaka Nataraja temple** affords a fascinating glimpse into ancient Tamil religious practice and belief. The legendary king **Hiranyavarman** is said to have made a pilgrimage here from Kashmir, seeking to rid himself of leprosy by bathing in the temple's Shivaganga tank. In thanks for a successful cure, he enlarged the temple. He also brought 3000 brahmins, of the Dikshitar caste, whose descendants are to this day the ritual specialists of the temple, distinguishable by topknots of hair at the front of their heads.

Few of the fifty *maths*, or monasteries, that once stood here remain, but the temple itself is still a hive of activity and hosts numerous **festivals**. The two most important are ten-day affairs, building up to spectacular finales: on the ninth day of each, temple chariots process through the four Car streets in the **Car festival**, while on the tenth day, **abhishekham**, the principal deities in the *raja sabha* (thousand-pillared hall) are anointed. For exact dates (one is in May/June, the other in Dec/Jan), contact any TTDC tourist office and plan well ahead, as they are very popular. Other local festivals include fire-walking and *kavadi* folk dance (dancing with decorated wooden frames on the head) at the Thillaiamman Kali (April/May) and Keelatheru Mariamman (July/Aug) temples.

The town also has a hectic market, and a large student population, which is based at Annamalai University, a centre of Tamil studies, to the east. Among the simple thatched huts in the flat, sparsely populated countryside, which becomes very dry and dusty in summer, the only solid-looking structures are small road-side temples. Many local people honour Aiyannar, the village deity who protects borders, and whose shrines are flanked with *kudirais*, brightly painted terracotta or wooden figures of horses.

Arrival and information

The town revolves around the Sabhanayaka Nataraja temple and the busy market area that surrounds it, along North, East, South and West Car streets. Though little more than a country halt, the **railway station**, 2km southeast of the centre, has good connections both north and south, plus retiring rooms and a **post office** on platform 1 (Mon–Sat 9am–1pm & 1.30–5pm). Buses from Chennai, Thanjavur, Mamallapuram, and Madurai pull in at the **bus stand**, also in the southeast, but nearer the centre, about 1km from the temple.

The TTDC **tourist office**, next to the *TTDC Tamil Nadu Hotel* on Railway Feeder Road, has helpful staff but they only have a small pamphlet to give to visitors. None of the **banks** in Chidambaram changes money.

Accommodation and eating

To cope with the influx of devotees, Chidambaram abounds in pilgrim **accommodation**, but there are few upper-bracket options beyond the *Saradharam* hotel, near the bus stand. Ask at the Station Master's Office, platform 1 for the **railway retiring rooms** (Rs100) which provide the best deal in town – huge, clean non-a/c rooms, though the bathrooms are a little dilapidated. Plenty of basic, wholesome "meals" places can be found on and around the Car streets: *Shri Ganesa Bhavan*, on West Car Street, gets the locals' vote, but for quality, inexpensive South Indian food you can't beat *Pallavi* at the *Saradharam* hotel, which is packed at lunch times for its good-value thalis. The *Annu Pallai* behind it is an equally commendable, though somewhat dingy, non-veg alternative. The small *Indian Coffee House*, on Venugopal Pillai Street, is a dependable and pleasant place to read the morning papers over filter coffee and omelette.

Akshaya, 17–18 East Car St ☎04144/20192. Pleasant mid-range hotel, backing onto the temple wall, with thirty rooms (three a/c; non-a/c is better value) and helpful staff. ②–⑤

Mansoor Lodge, 91 East Car St ☎04144/21072. Walls are on the grubby side, but otherwise a good, friendly cheapie with spotless, tiled floors and clean bathrooms. ②

Raja Rajan, 162 West Car St ☎04144/22690. Neat and clean rooms close to the temple, with tiled bathrooms and low tariffs; the a/c ones are good value. ②–④

Sabanayagam, 22 East Sannathi, off East Car Street ☎04144/20896. Despite a flashy exterior, this is a run-of-the-mill budget place. Ask for a room with a window, preferably on the second floor overlooking the temple entrance. There's a good veg restaurant downstairs. Some a/c. ②–⑤

Saradharam, 19 Venugopal Pillai St, opposite the bus stand ☎04144/21336, ℻22656. Chidambaram's poshest hotel. Large, clean and well kept rooms (some a/c) in modern buildings, with internet, two decent restaurants as well as a pizza place, small garden, bar, laundry and foreign exchange. ④–⑦

TTDC Hotel Tamil Nadu, Railway Feeder Road, located between the train station and bus stand ☎04144/38056. Friendly, but some rooms are woefully neglected: check the bedding is clean, and if the a/c works. Also dorm beds (Rs50), an Indian-Chinese restaurant, bar, and *iddli* restaurant. ⑤–⑥

Sabhanayaka Nataraja temple

For South India's Shaivites, the **Sabhanayaka Nataraja temple** (daily 4am–noon & 4pm–10pm), where Shiva is enthroned as Lord of the Cosmic Dance, Nataraja, is the holiest of holies. Its huge *gopuras*, whose lights are used as landmarks by sailors far out to sea in the Bay of Bengal, soar above a 55-acre complex, divided by four concentric walls. The oldest parts now standing were built under the Cholas, who adopted Nataraja as their chosen deity and crowned several kings here. The rectangular outermost wall, of little interest in itself, affords entry on all four sides, so if you have the time the best way to tackle the complex is to work slowly inwards from the third enclosure in clockwise circles. **Guides** are readily available but tend to shepherd visitors towards the central shrine too quickly. Frequent devotional (puja) ceremonies take place at the innermost sanctum, the most popular being at noon and 6pm, when a fire is lit in the inner sanctum, great gongs are struck and devotees rush forward to catch a last glimpse of the *lingam* before the doors are shut. On Friday nights before the temple closes, during a particularly elaborate puja, Nataraja is carried on a palanquin accompanied by music and attendants carrying flaming torches and tridents. At other times, you'll hear ancient devotional hymns from the *Tevaram*.

The third enclosure

Four gigantic *gopura* towers rise out of the irregular third wall, each with a granite base and a brick-built superstructure of diminishing storeys covered in a profusion of carved figures. The western *gopura* is the most popular entrance, as well as being the most elaborately carved and probably the earliest (c.1150 AD). Turning north (left) from here, you come to the colonnaded **Shivaganga tank**, the site of seven natural springs. From the broken pillar at the tank's edge, all four *gopuras* are visible.

Facing the tank, on the left side, is the **Shivakamasundari temple**, devoted to Parvati, consort of Shiva. Step inside to see the Nayak (sixteenth-century) ceiling paintings arranged in cartoon-like frames in muted reds and yellows. On the right as you enter, the story of the leper king Hiranyavarman is illustrated, and at the back, frames form a map of the temple complex. Next door, in the northwest corner, a shrine to Subrahmanya, the son of Shiva, is adorned with paintings illustrating stories from the *Skanda Purana*. Beyond this, in front of the northern *gopura*, stands a small shrine to the Navagraha (nine planets).

In the northeast corner, the largest building in the complex, the **Raja Sabha** (fourteenth–fifteenth century) is also known as "the thousand-pillared hall", although tradition holds that there are only nine hundred and ninety-nine actual pillars, the thousandth being Shiva's leg. During festivals the deities Nataraja and Shivakamasundari are brought here and mounted on a dais for the anointing ceremony, *abhishekha*.

The importance of **dance** at Chidambaram is underlined by the reliefs of dancing figures inside the east *gopura* demonstrating 108 *karanas* (a similar set is to be found in the west *gopura*). A *karana* (or *adavu*, in Tamil) is a specific point in a phase of movement prescribed by the extraordinarily comprehensive Sanskrit treatise on the performing arts, the *Natya Shastra* (c.200 BC–200 AD) – the basis of all forms of classical dance, music and theatre in India. A caption from the *Natya Shastra* surmounts each *karana* niche. Four other niches are filled with images of patrons and *stahapatis* – the sculptors and designers responsible for the iconography and positioning of deities.

A pavilion at the south *gopura* houses an image of Nandi, Shiva's bull. Although not accessible from here, the central Nataraja shrine faces south; as with all Shiva temples, Nandi sits opposite the god. In the southwest corner, a shrine contains one of the largest images in India of the elephant-headed son of Shiva, Ganapati (Ganesh). If you stand inside the entrance (*mandapa*), with your back to Ganapati, you'll see at the base of the two pillars nearest the shrine, carvings of the two important devotees of Nataraja at Chidambaram (see box opposite). To the right is the sage Patanjali, with a snake's body, and on the left Vyaghrapada, with a human body and tiger's feet.

The second enclosure

To get into the square second enclosure, head for its **western entrance** (just north of the west *gopura* in the third wall) which leads into a circumambulatory passageway. Once beyond this second wall it's easy to become disorientated, as the roofed inner enclosures see little light and are supported by a maze of colonnades. The atmosphere is immediately more charged, reaching its peak at the very centre.

On the north side, the **Mulasthana** houses the *svayambhulingam* worshipped by Patanjali and Vyaghrapada. The **Deva Sabha**, or "hall of the gods", on the east, shelters as many as a hundred bronze images used in processions and is a meeting place for members of the three hundred Dikshitar brahmin families who own and maintain the temple. Beyond it lies the other, eastern entrance to the second enclosure.

The **Nritta Sabha**, or "dance hall", stands on the site where Shiva outdanced Kali (see box opposite), now the southwest corner of the second enclosure. Probably the oldest surviving structure of the two inner areas, its raised platform was fashioned in stone to resemble a wooden temple chariot, or *ratha*. Before they were inexplicably concreted over in the mid-1950s, the east and west sides of the base were each adorned with a wheel and a horse; all that can be seen now are fragments.

The innermost enclosure

Passing through the southern entrance (marked by a gold flagstaff) to the **innermost enclosure** brings you immediately into a hallway, which leads west to the nearby **Govindaraja shrine**, dedicated to Vishnu – a surprise in this most Shaivite of environments. Govindaraja is attended by non-Dikshitar brahmins who, it is said, don't always get along with the Dikshitars. From outside the shrine, non-Hindus can see through to the most sacred part of the

The thousand-headed cosmic serpent, Adisesha, upon whose coiled body Vishnu reclines in the primordial ocean, once expressed a wish to see Shiva's famed dance. Having arranged time off from his normal duties with Vishnu, Adisesha prayed to Shiva, who was so impressed by the serpent's entreaties that he promised to dance in the forest of Tillai (the site of Chidambaram). Adisesha was reborn as the human sage Patanjali (represented as half-man, half-snake) and made straight for Tillai. There he met another sage who shared his wish to see Shiva dance, Vyaghrapada – "Tiger Feet", who had been granted the claws of a tiger to help him climb trees and pluck the best flowers to offer Shiva. Together, they worshipped a *svayamb-hulingam*, a *shivalingam* that had "self-manifested" in the forest, now housed in the Mulasthana shrine of Sabhanayaka temple. However, the guardian of the forest, who turned out to be the goddess Kali, refused to allow Shiva to dance when he arrived. In response, he challenged her to a dance competition for possession of the forest. Kali agreed but, perhaps due to modesty she could not match a pose of Shiva's – it involved raising the right foot above the head. Defeated, Kali was forced to move off a little way north, where a temple now stands in her honour.

temple, the **Kanaka Sabha** and the **Chit Sabha**, adjoining raised structures, roofed with copper and gold plate and linked by a hallway. Two huge bells and extremely loud *nagaswarams* (double-reed wind instruments), *tavils* (drums) and *nattuvangams* (cymbals) call worshippers for ceremonies. The only entrance – closed to non-Hindus – is up five silver-plated steps into the Chit Sabha, guarded by the devotees Vyaghrapada and Patanjali and lit by an arc of flickering oil lamps.

The Chit Sabha houses bronze images of Nataraja and his consort Shivakamasundari. Behind and to the left of Nataraja, a curtain, sacred to Shiva and strung with rows of leaves from the bilva tree, demarcates the most potent area of all. Within it lies the **Akashalingam**, known as the Rahasya, or "secret", of Chidambaram: made of the most subtle of the elements, Ether (*akasha*) – from which air, fire, water and earth are born – the *lingam* is invisible. This is said to signify that God is nowhere, only in the human heart.

A crystal *lingam*, said to have emanated from the light of the crescent moon on Shiva's brow, and a small ruby Nataraja are worshipped in the Kanaka Sabha. They are ritually bathed in the flames of the priests' camphor fire or oil lamps six times a day. This inner area is where you're most likely to hear **oduvars**, hereditary singers from the middle, non-brahmin castes, intoning verses of ancient Tamil poetry. The songs with which they regale the deities at puja time, drawn from compilations such the *Tevaram* or earlier *Sangam*, are more than a thousand years old

Gangaikondacholapuram

Devised as the centrepiece of a city built by the Chola king Rajendra I (1014–42 AD) to celebrate his conquests, the magnificent **Brihadishwara temple** stands in the tiny village of **GANGAIKONDACHOLAPURAM**, in Trichy District, 35km north of Kumbakonam. The tongue-twisting name means "the town of the Chola who took the Ganges". Under Rajendra I, the Chola empire did indeed stretch as far as the great river of the north, an unprecedented achievement for a southern dynasty. Aside from the temple and the rubble remains of Rajendra's palace, 2km east at Tamalikaimedu, nothing of the city remains. Nonetheless, this is among the most extraordinary archeological sites of South India, outshone only by Thanjavur, and devoid of visitors most of the time, which gives it a memorably forlorn feel.

Buses run here from Kumbakonam every five minutes (and pass through on the way to Kumabakonam every 10min), and it is also served by some between Trichy and Chidambaram Be sure not to get stuck here between noon and 4pm when the temple is closed. Parts of the interior are extremely dark, and a torch is useful. Facilities in the surrounding village are minimal; there's little more than a couple of chai shops.

Brihadishwara temple

The **Brihadishwara temple** (daily 6am–noon & 4–8pm; free) is enclosed by a rectangular wall; visitors enter through a gateway to the north, separated from the main road by a car park. You must remove your shoes and leave them at the hut in the corner of the car park, to the right of the main gateway entrance. From the gateway, you arrive at a well maintained, grassy courtyard, flanked by a closed hallway (*mandapa*). Over the sanctuary, to the right, a massive pyramidal tower (*vimana*) rises 55m in nine diminishing storeys. Though smaller than the one at Thanjavur, the tower's graceful curve gives it an impressive refinement. At the entrance you're likely to meet an ASI caretaker, who can act as a guide to all the deities sculpted on the temple; you will also be shown the lovingly tended gardens.

Turning left (east) inside the courtyard you pass a small shrine to the goddess **Durga**, containing an image of Mahishasuramardini (see p.470). Just beyond, steps climb from a large seated lion, known as Simha-kinaru and made from plastered brickwork, to a well. King Rajendra is said to have had Ganges water placed in it to be used for the ritual anointing of the *lingam* in the main temple. The lion, representing Chola kingly power, bows to the huge Nandi respectfully seated before the eastern entrance of the temple, in line with the Shiva *lingam* contained within the temple sanctum.

Set into the east wall, the remains of a *gopura* entranceway lead directly to a large water tank. Directly in front, before the eastern entrance to the temple, stands a small altar for offerings and the huge Nandi bull. Two flights of steps on the north and south ascend to a porch, the *mukhamandapa*, where a large pair of guardian deities flank the entrance to the long pillared *mahamandapa* hallway.

If you'd like to climb up onto the roof for views of the vicinity and of the tower, ask the guide. Access to the tower is from within the temple, up steep steps. Immediately inside, on either side of the doorway, sculptures of Shiva in his various benevolent (*anugraha*) manifestations include him blessing Vishnu, Devi, Ravana and the saint Chandesha (see p.504). In the northeast corner an unusual square, stone block features carvings of the nine planets (*navagraha*). A number of **Chola bronzes** (see p.680) stand on the platform; the figure of Karttikeya, the war god, carrying a club and a shield, is thought to have had particular significance.

The base of the main temple sanctuary is decorated with lions and scrollwork. Above this decoration, running from the southern to the northern entrance of the *ardhamandapa*, a series of sculpted figures in plastered niches portray different images of Shiva. The most famous is at the northern entrance, showing Shiva and Parvati garlanding the saint Chandesha, who here is sometimes identified as Rajendra I. For more on the temples of Tamil Nadu, see Contexts, p.676.

Two minutes' walk east along the main road (turn right from the car park), the tiny **Archeological Museum** (daily except Fri 10am–1pm & 2–5.45pm) contains Chola odds and ends, discovered locally. The finds include terracotta lamps, coins, weapons, tiles, bronze, bangle pieces, palm-leaf manuscripts and an old Chinese pot.

Kumbakonam and around

Sandwiched between the Kaveri (Cauvery) and Arasalar Rivers, is the busy town of **KUMBAKONAM**, 74km southwest of Chidambaram and 38km northeast of Thanjavur. Kumbakonam is believed by Hindus to be the place where the water pot (*kumba*) of *amrita*, the ambrosial beverage of immortality, was washed up by a great deluge from atop sacred Mount Meru in the Himalayas. Shiva, who just happened to be passing the pot in the guise of a wild forest-dwelling hunter; for some reason fired an arrow at the pot, causing it to break. From the shards, he made the *lingam* that is now enshrined in the **Kumbareshwara temple**, whose *gopuras* tower over the town, along with those of some seventeen other major shrines. A former capital of the Cholas, who are said to have kept a high-security treasury here, Kumbakonam is today the chief commercial centre for the Thanjavur region. The main bazaar, **Big Street**, is especially renowned for its quality costume jewellery.

The main reason to stop in Kumbakonam is to admire the exquisite sculpture of the **Nageshwara Swami Shiva temple**, which contains the most refined Chola stone carving still in situ. The town also lies within easy reach of the magnificent Darasuram and Gangaikondacholapuram temples, both spectacular ancient monuments that see very few visitors. In addition, the village of

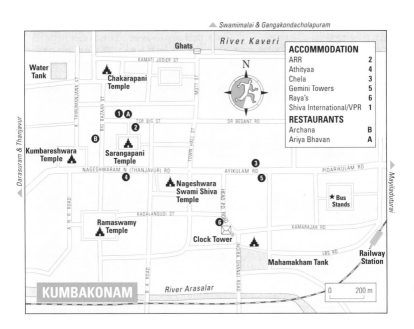

ACCOMMODATION	
ARR	2
Athityaa	4
Chela	3
Gemini Towers	5
Raya's	6
Shiva International/VPR	1

RESTAURANTS	
Archana	B
Ariya Bhavan	A

KUMBAKONAM

0   200 m

Swamimalai, only a bike ride away, is the state's principal centre for traditional **bronze–casting**.

Arrival and information

Kumbakonam's small **railway station**, in the southeast, 2km from the main bazaar, is well served by trains both north and south, and has a left-luggage office (24hr) and decent **retiring rooms** [Rs100]. The hectic **Moffussil** (local) and **Aringannar** (long-distance) bus stands are opposite each other in the southeast of town, between the train station and the Mahamakham tank. All the timetables are in Tamil, but there's a 24hr enquiry office. Buses leave for Gangaikondacholapuram, Pondicherry and Thanjavur every few minutes, many via Darasuram. Frequent services run to Chennai, Trichy, and several daily to Bangalore.

Accommodation

Kumbakonam is not a major tourist location, and has limited **accommodation**, with only one upper-range hotel, the *Sterling Swamimalai*, 10km southeast of town on the outskirts of Swamimalai village (see p.505). The good news for budget travellers is that most of the inexpensive places are clean and well maintained.

ARR, 21 TSR Big St ☎0435/421234. Fifty large, clean rooms (some a/c) over five floors; bland, but comfortable enough and the top-floor rooms have temple views. There is an a/c restaurant, with a bar to while away a quiet evening in and you can hire a TV for a bit extra. ④ – ⑥
Athityaa, Nageshwaram N (Thanjavur) Road ☎0435/421794, ☎430194. This place was once smart but is now is rather worn and grubby, especially for the price, although the a/c and non-a/c rooms are spacious – ask for one on the west side, facing the temple. ④ – ⑥
Chela, 9 Ayikulam Rd ☎0435/430336, ☎431592. Another large mid-range place, between the bus stand and centre, distinguished by its horrendous mock-Classical facade. Soap, fresh towels and TVs are offered as standard. They also have a bar and backup generator. ④ – ⑥
Gemini Towers, 18 Ayikulam Rd ☎0435/423559.

Opposite the *Chela*, with a grand name for a welcoming but very run-of-the-mill budget lodge. All the rooms are non-a/c, tidy and good value. ②
Raya's, 28–29 Head Post Office Rd ☎0435/432170, ☎422479. A central, well maintained hotel whose rooms are a little small for the price, but clean, comfortable, and near the sights. The saucy "Royal Suite" has mirrors on all four walls and ceiling. ④ – ⑥
Shiva International/VPR Lodge, 101/3 TSR Big St ☎0435/424013. After the temple *gopuras*, these huge co-owned, adjacent lodges are the largest buildings in town. *VPR* offers cheap rates for cleanish rooms and a prison-block atmosphere; *Shiva* is altogether more pleasant, with very spacious, airy doubles. Their standard non-a/c is a bargain (ask for #301, which has great views on two sides and a choice of toilets). ② – ④

The Town

Surmounted by a multicoloured *gopura*, the eastern entrance of Kumbakonam's seventeenth-century **Kumbareshwara temple**, home of the famous *lingam* from where the town derived its name, is approached via a covered market selling a huge assortment of cooking pots, a local speciality, as well as the usual glass bangles and trinkets. As you enter, you pass the temple elephant, Manganal, with painted forehead and necklace of bells. Beyond the flagstaff, a *mandapa* houses a fine collection of silver *vahanas* (vehicles of the deities, used in festivals), and *pancha loham* (compound of silver, gold, brass, iron and tin) figures of the 63 Nayanmar poet-saints (see p.639).

The principal and largest of the Vishnu temples in Kumbakonam is the thirteenth-century **Sarangapani temple**, entered through a ten-storey pyramidal *gopura* gate, more than 45m high. The **central shrine** dates from the late Chola period with many later accretions. Its entrance, within the innermost court, is guarded by huge *dvarpalas*, identical to Vishnu whom they protect. Between them are carved stone *jali* screens, each different, and in front of them stands the sacred, square *homam* fireplace. During the day, pinpoints of light from ceiling windows penetrate the darkness around the sanctum, designed to resemble a chariot with reliefs of horses, elephants and wheels. A painted cupboard contains a mirror for Vishnu to see himself when he leaves the inner sanctum.

The small **Nageshwara Swami Shiva temple**, in the centre of town, is Kumbakonam's oldest temple, founded in 886 AD and completed a few years into the reign of Parantaka I (907–c.940 AD). First impressions are unpromising, as much of the original building has been hemmed in by later, Disney-coloured accretions, but beyond the main courtyard, occupied by a large columned *mandapa*, a small *gopura*-topped gateway leads to an inner enclosure where the earliest Chola shrine stands. Framed in the main niches around its sanctum wall are a series of exquisite stone figures, regarded as the finest surviving pieces of **ancient sculpture** in South India. With their languid stance and mesmeric, half-smiling facial expressions, these modest-sized masterpieces far outshine the more monumental art of Thanjavur and Gangaikondacholapuram. The figures show Dakshinamurti (Shiva as a teacher, on the south wall), Durga and a three-headed Brahma (north wall) and Ardanari, half-man, half-woman (west wall). Joining them are near-life-size voluptuous maidens believed to be queens or princesses of King Aditya's court.

The most famous and revered of many sacred **water tanks** in Kumbakonam, the **Mahamakham tank** in the southeast of town, is said to have filled with ambrosia (*amrit*) collected from the pot broken by Shiva. Every twelve years, when Jupiter passes the constellation of Leo, it is believed that water from the Ganges and eight other holy rivers flows into the tank, thus according it the status of *tirtha*, or sacred river crossing. At this auspicious time, as many as four million pilgrims come here for an absolving bathe. On the last occasion, on February 18, 1992, the former chief minister of Tamil Nadu, Jayalalitha Jayaraman (see box on p.449), numbered among them. Her visit, billed by the spin-doctors as coinciding with her birthday, had been advertised throughout the state by giant roadside hoardings and headlines imploring Hindus to "Come, have a holy dip on the auspicious day." However, the publicity stunt backfired tragically. As Jayalalitha was being showered with sacred water in a specially reserved corner of the tank, the crowds pressed forward to get a closer look, provoking a *lathi* charge from her police bodyguard. In the ensuing stampede, 48 pilgrims were crushed to death. Newspaper reports over the following weeks ascribed the accident to "collapsing walls" and "general mayhem".

Eating

There's nothing very exciting about **eating out** in Kumbakonam, and most visitors stick to their hotel restaurant. For a change of scene, though, a few places stand out.

Archana, Big Bazaar Street. Right in the thick of the market. Popular among shoppers for its good-value banana leaf "meals", and South Indian snacks, although it can get hot and stuffy inside.

Ariya Bavan, TSR Big Street. Convenient if you're staying in *VPR/Shiva* two doors down, and a dependable all-rounder, serving the usual South Indian menu, with tasty biriyani and piping hot chapatis.

Arogya, ground floor of the *Athityaa*, Nageshwaram N (Thanjavur) Road. By general consent, the best veg restaurant in town. No surprises on the menu, but their lunch-time "unlimited meals" (Rs30) are excellent, and they serve North Indian tandoor in the evenings. No alcohol.

The delta lands **around Kumbakonam** are scattered with evocative vestiges of the Cholas' golden age, but the most spectacular has to be the crumbling Airavateshwara temple at **Darasuram**, 6km southwest. Across the fields to the north, the bronze-casters of **Swamimalai** constitute a direct, living link with the culture that raised this extraordinary edifice, using traditional "lost wax" techniques, unchanged since the time when Darasuram was a thriving medieval town, to create graceful Hindu deities.

You can combine the two sights in an easy half-day trip from Kumbakonam. The route is flat enough to cycle, although you should keep your wits about you when pedalling the main Thanjavur highway, which sees heavy traffic. To reach Swamimalai from Darasuram, return to the main road from the temple and ask for directions in the bazaar. Swamimalai is only 3km north, but travelling between the two involves several turnings, so expect to have to ask a local to wave you in the right direction at regular intervals. From Kumbakonam, the route is more straightforward; cross the Kaveri at the top of Town Hall Road (north of the centre), turn left and follow the main road west through a ribbon of villages.

Darasuram

The **Airavateshwara temple**, built by King Rajaraja II (c.1146–73 AD), stands in the village of **DARASURAM**, 6km southwest of Kumbakonam. This superb if little-visited Chola monument ranks alongside those at Thanjavur and Gangaikondacholapuram but while they are grandiose, emphasizing heroism and conquest, it is far smaller, exquisite in proportion and detail and said to have been decorated with *nitya-vinoda*, "perpetual entertainment", in mind. Shiva is here known as Airavateshwara, because he was worshipped at this temple by Airavata, the white elephant of the king of the gods, Indra.

The entrance is through a large *gopura* gateway, a metre below ground level, in the main wall, which is topped with small reclining bull figures. Inside, the main building is set in a spacious courtyard. Next to the inner sanctuary, fronted by an open porch, the steps of the closed *mandapa* feature elegant, curled balustrades decorated with elephants and *makaras* (mythical crocodiles with floriate tails). At the corners, rearing horses and wheels make the whole into a chariot. Elsewhere, clever sculptural puns include the head of an elephant merging with that of a bull.

Fine Chola black basalt images in wall-niches in the *mandapa* and the inner shrine include Nagaraja, the snake-king, with a hood of cobras, and Dakshinamurti, the "south-facing" Shiva as teacher, expounding under a banyan tree. One rare image shows Shiva as Sharabha, part man, beast and bird, destroying the man-lion incarnation of Vishnu, Narasimha – indicative of the animosity between the Shaivite and Vaishnavite cults.

Outside, a unique series of somewhat gruesome panels, hard to see without climbing onto the base, form a band along the top of the basement of the closed *mandapa* and the sanctum sanctorum. They illustrate scenes from Sekkilar's *Periya Purana*, one of the great works of Tamil literature. The poem tells the stories of the Tamil Shaivite saints, the Nayanmars, and was commissioned by King Kulottunga II, after the poet criticized him for a preoccupation with erotic, albeit religious, literature. Sekkilar is said to have composed it in the Raja Sabha at Chidambaram; when it was completed the king sat every day for a year to hear him recite it.

Each panel illustrates the lengths to which the saints were prepared to go to demonstrate devotion to Shiva. The boy Chandesha, for example, whose job it was to tend the village cows, discovered one day that they were involuntarily producing milk. He decided to bathe a *lingam* with the milk as part of his daily worship. Appalled by this apparent waste, the villagers complained to his father, who went to the field, cursed the boy, and kicked the *lingam* over. At this affront to Shiva, Chandesha cut off his father's leg with an axe; he is shown at the feet of Shiva and Parvati, who have garlanded him. Another panel shows a man who frequently gave food to Shiva devotees. When his wife was reluctant to welcome and wash the feet of a mendicant who had previously been their servant, he cut off her hands. Elsewhere, a Pallava queen has her nose cut off for inadvertently smelling a flower, rendering it useless as an offering to Shiva. The last panel shows the saint **Sundara** who sang a hymn to Shiva, and for doing so, Shiva rescued a child who had been swallowed by a crocodile.

Swamimalai

SWAMIMALAI, 8km west of Kumbakonam, is revered as one of the six sacred abodes of Lord Murugan, Shiva's son, whom Hindu mythology records became his father's religious teacher (*swami*) on a hill (*malai*) here. The site of this epic role reversal now hosts one of the Tamils' holiest shrines, the **Swaminatha temple**, crowning the hilltop of the centre of the village. Of more interest to non-Hindus, however, are the hereditary **bronze–casters'** workshops dotted around the bazaar and the outlying hamlets.

Known as **sthapathis**, Swamimalai's casters still employ the "lost wax" process (*madhuchchishtavidhana* in Sanskrit) perfected by the Cholas to make the most sought-after temple idols in South India. Their finished products are displayed in numerous showrooms along the main street, from where they are exported worldwide, but it can be more memorable to watch the *sthapathis* in action, fashioning the original figures from beeswax and breaking open the moulds to expose the mystical finished metalwork inside. One of most welcoming workshops lies 2km south of the village, sheltered under a coconut coppice along the main road to Darasuram (look out for it on the right if you're coming from this direction). At any one time, you can see most stages of the manufacturing process, and they keep a modest selection of souvenir pieces for sale. For more on Tamil bronze-casting, see p.680.

The nearby hamlet of **Thimmakkudy**, 2km back towards Kumbakonam, is the site of the area's grandest **hotel**, the *Sterling Swamimalai*, (⊤0435/420044, Ⓕ421705; ⓪), a beautifully restored nineteenth-century brahmins' mansion kitted out with mod cons, such as fans and fridges. They also have an in-house yoga teacher and Ayurvedic massage room, and in the evenings there is a cultural performance in front of a vast stone sculpture of the face of Shiva.

Thanjavur

One of busiest commercial towns of the Kaveri delta, **THANJAVUR** (aka Tanjore), 55km east of Tiruchirapalli and 35km southwest of Kumbakonam, is often overlooked by travellers. However, its history and treasures – among them the breathtaking **Brihadishwara temple**, Tamil Nadu's most awesome Chola monument – give it a crucial significance to South Indian culture. The home of the world's finest Chola bronze collections, the town holds enough of interest to keep any visitors who stay here enthralled for at least a couple of days, and is the most obvious base for trips to nearby Gangaikondcholapuram, Kumbakonam, Darasuram and Swamimalai.

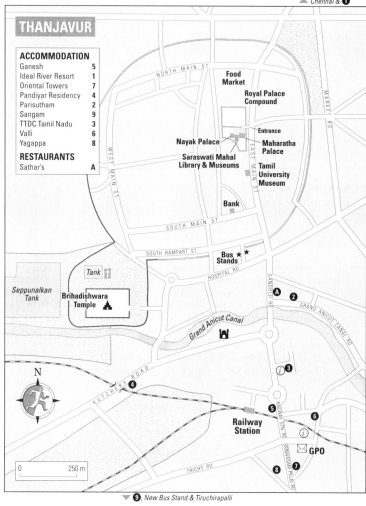

THANJAVUR

ACCOMMODATION
Ganesh	5
Ideal River Resort	1
Oriental Towers	7
Pandiyar Residency	4
Parisutham	2
Sangam	9
TTDC Tamil Nadu	3
Valli	6
Yagappa	8

RESTAURANTS
Sathar's	A

NORTH MAIN ST

Food Market

Royal Palace Compound

Entrance

Nayak Palace

Maharatha Palace

Saraswati Mahal Library & Museums

Tamil University Museum

Bank

SOUTH MAIN ST

SOUTH RAMPART ST

Bus Stands ★ ★

HOSPITAL RD

Tank

Seppunalkan Tank

Brihadishwara Temple ▲

Grand Anicut Canal

GANDHIJI RD

GRAND ANICUT CANAL RD

A 2

i 3

4

5

6

i

GPO

Railway Station

RAILWAY STN RD

SRINIVASAN PILLAI RD

N

WEST MAIN ST

EAST MAIN ST

MARKET RD

KUTCHERY ROAD

0   250 m

TRICHY RD

8

7

Thanjavur is roughly split in two by the east–west **Grand Anicut Canal**. The **old town**, north of the canal and once entirely enclosed by a fortified wall, was between the ninth and the end of the thirteenth centuries chosen as the capital of their extensive empire by all the Chola kings save one. None of their secular buildings survives, but you can still see as many as ninety temples, of which the Brihadishwara most eloquently epitomizes the power and patronage of Rajaraja I (985–1014), whose military campaigns spread Hinduism to the Maldives, Sri Lanka and Java. Under the Chola kings, as well as the later Nayaks and Marathas, literature, painting, sculpture, Carnatic classical music and Bharatanatyam dance all thrived here. Quite apart from its own intrinsic interest, the Nayak **Royal Palace compound** houses an important library and museums including the aforesaid collection of bronzes.

TAMIL NADU | Thanjavur

6

Of major local **festivals**, the most lavish celebrations at the Brihadishwara temple are associated with the birthday of King Rajaraja, in October. An eight-day celebration of **Carnatic classical music** is also held each January at the Panchanateshwara temple at **Thiruvaiyaru**, 13km away, to honour the great Carnatic composer-saint, Thyagaraja.

Arrival and information

Buses from Chennai, Pondicherry, Madurai and Tiruchirapalli pull in at the long-distance State Bus Stand, opposite the City Bus Stand, in the south of the old town. Other services from Tiruchirapalli, and those to and from local destinations such as Kumbakonam, stop at the New Bus Stand, inconveniently located 4km southwest of the centre, in the middle of nowhere. Rickshaws into town from here cost Rs40–50, or you can jump on one of efficient "city buses" (about Rs2) that shuttle to and from the city centre every few minutes.

Daily express **trains** from Chennai, Tiruchirapalli and Rameshwaram pull in at the station, just south of the centre. There are also several fast passenger services daily from Thiruvarur, Nagappattinam and Nagore. The station has a new **computerized reservation system** (Mon–Sat 8am–2pm & 3–5pm, Sun 8am–2pm). The red and cream station itself has an antiquated air, with its decorated columns in the main hall and sculptures of dancers and musicians. Luggage can be left in the parcel office for a small baksheesh.

The **GPO** and most of the hotels and restaurants lie on or around **Gandhiji Road** (aka Railway Station Road), which crosses the canal and leads to the railway station in the south. The **TTDC Tourist Office**, opposite the post office (Mon–Fri 10am–5.45pm; ☎04362/30984), is a good source of local information; there's a smaller, less efficient branch in the compound of the *TTDC Tamil Nadu* hotel on Gandhiji Road (daily 8am–4pm).

You can **change money** at Canara Bank on South Main Street and, with a bit of gentle persuasion, at the *Parishutham Hotel* – useful out of banking hours, although the rates are not always favourable. The Government **hospital** is on Hospital Road, and there are plenty of pharmacies on Gandhiji Road.

For **internet access**, head for Gemini Soft on the first floor of the *Oriental Towers* hotel, Srinivasam Palai Road (☎04362/34459); as you pass through the main gate, take the white external staircase on your left.

Accommodation

Most of Thanjavur's **hotels** are concentrated in the area between the railway station and bus stands and as a rule charge higher rates than you'd pay elsewhere in the state. A flurry of building activity in the run-up to the 1995 World Tamil Conference led to a proliferation of upper-range options, many of them south of the centre, but there's very little choice at the bottom of the market. If you're travelling on a tight budget, this may be somewhere to consider treating yourself to an upgrade. For the **railway retiring rooms**, contact the matron on the first floor of the train station; the rooms comprise six big, clean double rooms opening out onto a large communal veranda, overlooking station approach. Offering great value, as ever, they're invariably full by noon.

Ganesh, 314 Srinivasam Pillai Rd, Railady ☎04362/31113. It's self-proclaimed selling point is that is "very, very near the railway station", but it is also on a very, very noisy, busy road. The rooms are not overly large, but they're clean, and there's a good veg restaurant downstairs. Some rooms are a/c. ②–⑤

Ideal River Resort, Vennar Bank, Palli Agrharam ☎04362/34533, ☎34933. Luxurious chalet-rooms in a self-contained campus slap on the riverside, 12km towards Kumbakonam. A very pleasant location, but too far from the city without your own transport. Popular with tour groups so book in advance. ⑥–⑦

Oriental Towers, 2889 Srinivasam Pillai Rd ℡04362/31467, ℻ 30770. Huge, all mod cons hotel-cum-shopping complex, with small swimming pool on the fourth floor and very comfortable a/c rooms. Good value at this price, but it lacks the quality of the *Sangam*. ⑦–⑧

Pandiyar Residency, 14 Kutchery Rd ℡04362/39875. A newish hotel across the canal from the Brihadishwara Temple, next to a busy flyover; it's gone rapidly downhill, and the rooms are small for the price, but the a/c deluxe options have good temple views. ④–⑤

Parishutham, 55 Grand Anicut Canal Rd ℡04362/31801, ℻ 30318. A deluxe hotel boasting spacious, centrally a/c rooms overlooking a large, palm-fringed pool (residents only), a swish multi-cuisine restaurant, craft shop, foreign exchange, travel agent, and attentive service. Popular with tour groups, so book ahead. ⑨

Sangam, Trichy Road ℡04362/34151 or 34026, ℻ 36695. Thanjavur's newest luxury hotel is 2km southwest of the centre. International four-star standards, with an excellent restaurant, new pool and beautiful Tanjore paintings (the one in the lobby is worth a trip here in itself). Great value and recommended. ⑦–⑧

TTDC Tamil Nadu, Gandhiji Road, 10min from the bus and railway stands ℡04362/31421. Once the raja's guesthouse, now a typically shabby state-run hotel, with more character than modern alternatives. Large, comfortable carpeted rooms (some with a/c), set around a leafy enclosed garden. ④–⑤

Valli, 2948 MKM Rd ℡04362/31584. A real find – an exceptionally friendly place with super-clean rooms opening onto bright green corridors; the rooms range around a leafy courtyard, and there's a popular busy canteen downstairs. Some rooms are a/c. The best budget option in town. ②–⑤

Yagappa, Trichy Road ℡04362/30421 or 33548. Offering spacious, well appointed rooms with "sitouts", large, tiled bathrooms and friendly staff; there's also a bar and restaurant. Reception features intriguing furniture made from coffee roots. The twenty-percent discount for all foreigners makes this place particularly good value. ③–⑥

Brihadishwara temple

Thanjavur's skyline is dominated by the huge tower of the **Brihadishwara temple**, although for all its size it lacks the grandiose excesses of later periods. The site has no great significance; the temple was constructed as much to reflect the power of its patron, King Rajaraja I, as to facilitate the worship of Shiva. Profuse **inscriptions** on the base of the main shrine provide incredibly detailed information about the organization of the temple. They show it to have been rich, both in financial terms and in ritual activity. Among recorded **gifts** from Rajaraja, taken from booty acquired in conquest, are the equivalent of 1320kg of silver, 1100kg of gold and 550kg of assorted jewels, plus income from agricultural land throughout the Chola empire. No fewer than four hundred female dancers, **devadasis** (literally "slaves to the gods", married off to the deity) were employed, and each provided with a house. Other staff – another two hundred people – included dance teachers, musicians, tailors, potters, laundrymen, goldsmiths, carpenters, astrologers, accountants and the attendants who were required at all manner of rituals and processions.

The entrance to the complex is on the east, through two **gopura** gateways some way apart. Although the outer one is the larger, both are of the same pattern: massive rectangular bases topped by pyramidal towers with carved figures and vaulted roofs. At the core of each is a monolithic sandstone lintel, said to have been brought from Tiruchirapalli, over 50km away. The outer facade of the inner *gopura* features mighty fanged *dvarpala* door guardians, mirror images of each other, and thought to be the largest monolithic sculptures in any Indian temple. Panels illustrating scenes from the *Skanda Purana* decorate the base, including the marriage of Shiva and Parvati.

Once inside, the gigantic **courtyard** gives plenty of space to appreciate the temple buildings. A sixteenth-century pavilion, fronted by a tall lamp column and facing the main temple, holds the third largest Nandi (Shiva's bull-vehicle) in India.

The **main temple**, constructed of granite, consists of a long pillared *mandapa* hallway, followed by the *ardhamandapa*, or "half-hall", which in turn leads to the inner sanctum, the *garbha griha*. The plinth of the central shrine measures 46 square metres; above it, the pyramidal *vimana* tower (at just under 61m high, the largest and tallest in India when it was built in 1010) rises in thirteen diminishing storeys, the apex being exactly one-third of the size of the base. Such a design is quite different from later temples, where the *vimanas* become smaller as the *gopura* entranceways increasingly dominate – a desire to protect the sanctum sanctorum from the polluting gaze of outsiders.

The long pillared *mandapa* from the Vijayanagar period (sixteenth century) has been roughly adjoined to the *ardhamandapa*; you can see the mouldings do not match. Inside, the walls are decorated with eighteenth-century Maratha portraits. The *vimana* is an example of a "structured monolith", a stage removed from the earlier rock-cut architecture of the Pallavas, whereby blocks of stone are assembled and then carved. The profusion of carvings, aside from the inscriptions, include the *dvarpala* door guardians, Shiva, Vishnu, Durga, Ganapati (Ganesh), Bhu-devi (the female goddess Earth) and Lakshmi, arranged on three sides in two rows.

As the stone that surmounts the *vimana* is said to weigh eighty tons, there is considerable speculation as to how it got up there; the most popular theory is that it was hauled up a six-and-a-half-kilometre-long ramp. Others have suggested the use of a method comparable to the Sumer ziggurat style of building, whereby logs were placed in gaps in the masonry and the stone raised by leverage. The simplest answer, of course, is that perhaps it's not a single stone at all.

The black *shivalingam,* over 3.5m high, in the **inner sanctum** is called Adavallan, "the one who can dance well" – a reference to Shiva as Nataraja, the King of the Dance, who resides at Chidambaram and was the *ishtadevata*, chosen deity, of the king. The *lingam* is not always on view, but during puja ceremonies (8 & 11am, noon & 7.30pm), to the accompaniment of clanging bells, a curtain is pulled revealing the god to the devotees.

Surrounding the *garbha griha*, an **ambulatory passage** contains some of South India's greatest art treasures, including a frieze of beautiful **frescoes** dating from the reign of Rajaraja I. Unfortunately, the passage was recently closed to the public to protect the paintings. They were only recovered in the 1930s, having remained hidden for nearly one thousand years behind layers of inferior murals from the seventeenth century. Featuring uncannily lifelike portraits of the royals, deities, celestials and dancing girls – naked save for their jewellery and ornate hairstyles – the frieze is a swirl of rich pigments made from lapis lazuli, yellow and red ochre, lime, and lamp soot. In the upper ambulatory, also kept under lock and key, a sculpted series of reliefs showing the 108 classical dance poses predates the famous sets at Chidambaram (see p.498).

Outside, the walls of the courtyard are lined with **colonnaded passageways** – the one along the northern wall is said to be the longest in India. The one on the west, behind the temple, contains 108 *linga* from Varanasi and (heavily graffitied) panels from the Maratha period. At the centre stands a small shrine to Varuna (the Vedic god, associated with water and the sea), next to an image of the goddess Durga, usually kept clothed.

Other **shrines** in the enclosure include one behind the main temple to a devotee-saint, Karuvurar, supposedly able to cure barrenness. To the northwest, a seventeenth-century temple to Subrahmanya (a son of Shiva) has a base finely decorated with sculptures of dancers and musicians. Close to the figure of Nandi is a thirteenth-century Devi shrine; in the northeast corner, a *mandapa*

In an old house in the suburb of Karanthattangudi, ten minutes by auto-rickshaw from the centre of Thanjavur, V.R. Govindarajan's shop at 31 Kuthirakkatti St (℡04362/30282) contains an amazing array of antiques, including brass pots, betel nut boxes, oil lamps, coins and Tanjore paintings. Small, modern and simple examples of Tanjore paintings cost around Rs500, while large, recently made pictures with twenty-four-carat gold decoration may cost as much as Rs20,000, and for a fine hundred-year-old painting you can expect to part with Rs80,000 or more. Upstairs, seven artists work amid a chaotic collection of clocks and bric-a-brac, and you can watch the various stages in the process of Tanjore painting.

The owner of the small craft shop in the *Parishutham* hotel is very knowledgeable about local craftsmen who produce Tanjore paintings, copper "art plates" and musical instruments like the classical *vina*. A branch of the government chain, Poompuhar Handicrafts, on Gandhiji Road (next to the *TTDC Tamil Nadu Hotel*), stocks copper Thanjavur "art plates", brass oil lamps and sandalwood carvings, and there's also a cooperative handicrafts shop above the Sangeeta Mahal concert hall in the Royal Palace compound.

For more background on Tanjore paintings, see Contexts, p.682.

houses images of Nataraja, his consort and a devotee, and is also used for decorating icons prior to processions. A **path** leads from between the two *gopuras* the length of the main wall where, behind the temple, the manicured lawn lined with benches is a haven of quiet. The temple water tank lies just beyond, next to the northwest corner.

In the southwest corner of the courtyard, the small **Archeological Museum** (daily 9am–1pm & 4–8pm; free) houses an interesting collection of sculpture, including an extremely tubby, damaged Ganesh, before-and-after photos detailing restoration work to the temple in the 1940s and displays about the Cholas. You can also buy the excellent ASI booklet *Chola Temples*, which gives detailed accounts of Brihadishwara and the temples at Gangaikondacholapuram and Darasuram. For more on Tamil Nadu's temples, see Contexts, p.676.

The Royal Palace Compound

The **Royal Palace Compound**, where members of the erstwhile royal family still reside, is on E Main Street (a continuation of Gandhiji Road), 2km northeast of Brihadishwara Temple. Dotted around the compound are several reminders of Thanjavur's past under the Nayaks and the Marathas, including an exhibition of oriental manuscripts and a superlative museum of **Chola bronzes**. The dusty and run-down **Tamil University Museum** contains coins and musical instruments, while near the entrance to the complex, the rambling **Royal Museum** (daily 9am–6pm; Rs1, Rs20 extra for camera) houses a modest collection of costumes, portraits, musical instruments, weapons, manuscripts and courtly accessories.

Just after the ticket office for the Royal Museum is a new collection – the **H.H. Raja Serfoji II Memorial Hall and Museum** (daily 9am–6pm; Rs1, Rs20 extra for camera). In the eighteenth century, the youthful Serfoji II was a victim of a violent family feud between two regional ruling families, the Pandayas and Haysalas, and ended up in a pitch-black prison cell for years. Despite several attempts to kill him by burning red chillies in his cell to suffocate him, Serfoji survived and was eventually rescued by a Danish missionary

TAMIL NADU | Thanjavur

in 1789. Serfoji II then accepted his rightful position as Maharajah of Thanjavur, and never forgot his debt to the missionary, who remained a close adviser and taught the ruler about Christianity, a religion he grew to hold in great respect. The collection is the outcome of a lifetime investigation into the turbulent life and reign of Serfoji II by his grandson; sadly, however, the museum doesn't do much to illuminate his life. The permanent exhibition comprises a clutter of ivory desk sets and silver ware, newspaper cut-outs, immature royal portraits and decaying royal finery, all in a damp upper room of the palace.

The palace buildings have been in a sorry state for years; hopes were raised for their preservation when the responsibility for maintenance passed in 1993 to the Indian National Trust for Cultural Heritage (INTACH), but almost immediately some suffered extensive damage in storms. The Sarja Madi, "seven-storey" bell tower, built by Serfoji II in 1800, is closed to the public due to its unsafe condition.

Work on the palace began in the mid-sixteenth century under Sevappa Nayak, the founder of the Nayak kingdom of Thanjavur; additions were made by the Marathas from the end of the seventeenth century onwards. Remodelled by Shaji II in 1684, the **Durbar Hall**, or hall of audience, houses a throne canopy decorated with the mirrored glass distinctive to Thanjavur. Although damaged, the ceiling and walls are elaborately painted. Five domes are striped in primary red, green and yellow, and on the walls, European influence is evident in the friezes of leaf and pineapple designs, and trumpeting angels in a night sky.

Niches in the walls hold sculptures of deities, including the figure of Shiva devotee Patanjali (see box on p.499), with a snake winding around his leg, and an Englishman said to be in the unlikely position of learning classical dance from a young woman, to whom he is presenting a gift. Visible on the left wall, as you face the throne, are traces of a Nayak mural of deer in a forest. Next to this, two holes in the floor, once entrances to a secret passageway, are allegedly home to cobras and not recommended for exploration. Some of the later paintings portray the entertainers who as recently as the 1960s revelled in the now overgrown square outside: fighters, circus performers and wrestlers.

The **courtyard** outside the Durbar Hall was the setting for one of the more poignant moments in Thanjavur's turbulent history when, in 1683, the last of the Nayak kings gave himself up to the king of Madurai, whose forces were swarming through the city after a long siege. Legend has it that the attackers gained the upper hand after the Raja of Madurai's chief guru-magician filled the Kaveri with rotten pumpkins, casting a spell to ensure that whoever drunk its water would defect to their side. Finding himself deserted by his troops, the Nayak king is said to have donned his ceremonial gem-studded robes, pinned his bushy eyebrows back with gold wires and marched to his death intoning Vishnavite verses. As he did so, a massive explosion behind him signalled the destruction of the palace harem, along with all its inhabitants, whose honourable deaths the king had ensured by packing the ground floor with gunpowder.

Saraswati Mahal Library and Museum

The **Saraswati Mahal Library**, one of the most important Oriental manuscript collections in India, is closed to the public, but used by scholars from all over the world. Over eighty percent of its 44,000 manuscripts are in Sanskrit, many on palm-leafs, and some very rare or even unique. The Tamil works include treatises on medicine and commentaries on works from the Sangam period, the earliest literature of the South.

A small **museum** (daily except Wed 10am–1pm & 2pm–5pm; free) displays a bizarre array of books and pictures from the collection. Among the palm-leaf manuscripts is a calligrapher's tour-de-force in the form of a visual mantra, where each letter in the inscription "Shiva" comprises the god's name repeated in microscopically small handwriting. Most of the Maratha manuscripts, produced from the end of the seventeenth century, are on paper; they include a superbly illustrated edition of the *Mahabharata*. Sadists will be delighted to see that the library managed to hang onto its copy of the explicitly illustrated **Punishments in China**, published in 1804. Next to it, full rein is given to the imagination of French artist, **Charles Le Brun** (1619–90), in a series of pictures on the subject of physiognomy. Animals such as the horse, bullock, wolf, bear, rabbit and camel are drawn with painstaking care above a series of human faces which bear an uncanny, if unlikely, resemblance to them. You can buy postcards of this scientific study and exhibits from the other palace museums in the **shop** next door.

Nayak Durbar Hall Art Museum and Rajaraja Cholan Museum

A magnificent collection of **Chola bronzes** – the finest of them from the Tiruvengadu hoard unearthed in the 1950s – fills the **Nayak Durbar Hall Art Museum** (daily 9am–1pm & 2pm-5pm; Rs1), a high-ceilinged audience hall with massive pillars, dating from 1600. The elegance of the figures and delicacy of detail are unsurpassed. A tenth-century statue of Kannappa Nayannar (#174), a hunter-devotee, shows minutiae right down to his embroidered clothing, fingernails and the fine lines on his fingers. The oldest bronze, four cases left of the main doorway (#58) shows Vinadhra Dakshinamurti ("south-facing Shiva") who, with a deer on one left hand, would have originally been playing the *vina* – the musical instrument has long since gone. However, the undisputed masterpiece of the collection shows Shiva as Lord of the Animals (#86), sensuously depicted in a skimpy loin cloth, with a turban made of snakes. Next to him stands an equally stunning Parvati, his consort (# 87), but the cream of the female figures, a seated, half-reclining Parvati (#97), is displayed on the opposite side of the hall.

The **Rajaraja Cholan Museum** (same hours) houses Chola stone sculpture and small objects excavated at Gangaikondacholapuram (see p.499) such as tiny marbles, games boards, bangles and terracotta pieces. Two illuminated maps show the remarkable extent of the Chola empire under the great kings Rajaraja I and his son, Rajendra I. Towering over these buildings is the Nayak-period **arsenal**, cunningly designed to resemble a temple *gopura*, with fine views of Thanjavur from the top.

To find out more about Chola bronzes, see p.680 of Contexts.

Eating and drinking

For **food**, there's the usual crop of busy and cheap "meals" canteens dotted around town, the best of which are *Annantha Bhavan* and the *Sri Venkantan*, both on Gandhiji Road near the textile stores. The *Sangam* hotel's swish *Thillana* restaurant is a lot pricier, but worth it for the live Carnatic music. Of Thanjavur's dingy bars, *King's* in the *Yagappa* hotel, is the best choice for a quiet beer.

Annam, *Pandiyar Residency*, 14 Kutchery Rd (☎04362/30574). Small, inexpensive and impeccably clean veg restaurant that's recommended for its cut-above-the-competition unlimited lunch-time thalis (Rs25), and evening South Indian snacks (especially the delicious cashew *uttapams*).

King's, *Yagappa*, Trichy Road. Seven kinds of beer are served in the usual dimly lit room, or on the "lawn" – read: "sandy back yard" – where decor includes a stuffed lizard and plastic flowers in fish tanks. They also serve tasty chicken and pakora plate snacks.

Sathar's, Gandhiji Road. This is the town's most popular non-veg restaurant, and a pretty safe place to eat chicken (because of the constant turnover); seating is downstairs or on a covered terrace. Dishes are around Rs60–80. There's a mostly male clientele.

Thillana, *Sangam*, Trichy Road. Swish multi-cuisine restaurant that's renowned for its superb lunch-time South Indian thalis (11am–3pm; Rs75). Evenings feature an extensive à la carte menu (their *chettinad* specialities are superb). Worth a splurge just for the live Carnatic music (*veena*, flute and vocals on alternate days). Count on Rs250–300 per head.

Moving on from Thanjavur

Travelling to Trichy, it's best to catch a bus (from the less crowded new bus stand, 4km southwest of the centre), rather than the train, as most services from Thanjavur junction are slower passenger ones that frequently run late. The same applies to buses for Kumbakonam. For most other destinations, you're better off going by train. The best services for Chennai are the *Cholan Express* (#6154; departs 9.15am; 9hr 45min), which goes via Chidambaram (2hr 50min), and the overnight *Sethu Express* (#6702; departs 10.45pm; 10hr 30min). In the opposite direction, the latter train (as #6701) runs as far as Rameshwaram (departs 5.50am; 8hr 30min). For Madurai, you have to travel to Trichy and pick up a train from there.

Thiruvarur

Often bypassed by visitors travelling between Thanjavur and the coast, **THIRUVARUR**, 55km east of Thanjavur, is famed as the birthplace of the musical saint Thyagaraja, to whom the town's huge temple is dedicated. According to Hindu myth, the first temple was built on this spot after Shiva and Parvati, at rest in a garden at the foot of Mount Kailash, were disturbed by a handful of bilva leaves scattered over them by a playful monkey. Shiva, delighted, blessed the beast, who was reincarnated as the kindly King Muchukunda of the Manu dynasty. The king built many temples but later got involved in a fight with the demon Vala, who was finally killed by the god Indra. Muchukunda was offering puja in thanks for his salvation when Shiva appeared and instructed him to build a temple at Thiruvarur. Today, the **Thyagarajaswamy temple**, on the north side of town, dating mainly from the fourteenth and fifteenth centuries, measures nearly three hundred metres by more than two hundred metres. Its three successive enclosed courtyards contain a number of shrines, including one to Thyagaraja with an unusual line of the nine *navagralias* (planet deities) peering in at the saint's image. The inner sanctum houses a bronze *lingam* crowned with a seven-headed cobra, its outer walls and ceilings brightly painted with vivid images of Shiva and accompanying deities.

In March the town hosts the **Arulmigu Thyagarajaswamy car festival**, when for ten days animated crowds pull, push and wish the great temple car (the largest in Tamil Nadu) and its smaller companions well on their laborious path around the surrounding streets – worth stopping for.

6

Frequent **buses** and **trains** arrive in Thiruvarur from Thanjavur and Nagappattinam; there are also a few train services from Mayiladuturai in the north. The train station and bus stand are five minutes' walk apart in the south of town. To reach the temple, cross the bridge just north of the bus stand, and carry straight on for ten minutes or so. It's not difficult to find **accommodation**, even during the car festival. Several adequate lodges (all ❶) are situated close to the bus stand on Thanjavur Road: try the *President* (☎04366/22748) or *Sekar* (☎04366/22525), which is next to the post office. If you're not on a rock-bottom budget, the best option by far, though, is the *Royal Park Hotel*, just over 1km out of the centre on Bye-Pass Road (☎04366/21020, ℉21024; ❸–❺). It has a choice of a/c and non-a/c rooms, and two decent **restaurants** serving South and North Indian cuisine.

Kodikkarai (Point Calimere)

On a small knob of land jutting out into the sea, 65km south of Nagappattinam and 80km southeast of Thanjavur, **KODIKKARAI BIRD SANCTUARY** plays host to around 250 species in an area of swampland, known as "the great swamp", and dry evergreen forest. On the way to the sanctuary, you pass through fifty thousand acres of salt marshes around **Vedaranyam**, the nearest town, 11km north. Vast salt fields, traditionally the mainstay of the local economy, line the road, the salt drying in thatched mounds. During the struggle for Independence this was an important site for demonstrations in sympathy with Gandhi's famous salt protest. Over the last few years, however, salt has been pushed into second place by prawn cultivation, which brings a good income, but has necessitated widespread forest clearance and has reduced the numbers of birds visiting Kodikkarai.

The **best time** to visit the sanctuary is between November and February, when migratory birds come, mostly from Iran, Russia and Poland, to spend the winter. The rarest species include black bittern, barheaded goose, ruddy shelduck, Indian black-crested baza and eastern steppe eagle. During December and January the swamps host spotted billed pelicans and around ten thousand flamingos, who live on tiny shrimps (the source of the lurid pink colouring of their plumage); their numbers have dropped from the 30,000 that wintered here in the days before prawn production took off. The deep forest is also the home of one of the most colourful birds in the world, the Indian pitta (*pitta brachyura*).

Prodigiously well informed local **guides**, equipped with powerful binoculars, can take you to key wildlife haunts. The Forest Department works with the Mumbai Natural History Society to ring birds and trace their migrating patterns, and occasionally the MNHS organizes **field trips** around the area.

From the jetty, you might be lucky enough to spot a school of dolphins. To do so, however, you need to seek permission from the Navy Command – Kodikkarai is only 40km across the Palk Strait from Jaffna, and from the grounds of the *Rest House* (see opposite) the navy monitors all seaborne activity between Sri Lanka and the Indian coast.

Kodikkarai can only be reached (by regular bus) via Vedaranyam, connected by **bus** to Nagappattinam, Thanjavur, Trichy, Chennai and Ramanathapuram (for Rameshwaram). Chennai buses can be booked in advance in a house next door to Shitharthan Medical Stores on Vedaranyam's E Main Street (over the road from the bus stand). The nearest **railway station** is 30km away at Tiruthuraipondi.

The only **accommodation** in the area, the Forest Department's exceptionally cheap *Poonarai Rest House* (reserve through DFO, 281/1846 W Main St, Thanjavur, 613 009, or the wildlife warden in Nagapattinam; ⊕), has ten plain, spacious rooms, each with chairs, desk, fan, bedding, bath and balcony. Apart from in January, when the rest house is invariably full, it's usually possible to turn up without a reservation. **Food** is limited to a couple of chai shops outside the gate, although staff will bring it in if asked. If you need to eat in **Vedaranyam** turn left out of the bus stand, and again at a T-junction, into the main bazaar, Melai Street. The best place is the simple *Karaivani*, on the left-hand side, which serves veg "leaf" meals.

Tiruchirapalli and around

TIRUCHIRAPALLI – more commonly referred to as **Trichy** – stands in the plains between the Shevaroy and Palani hills, just under 100km north of Madurai. Dominated by the dramatic Rock Fort, it's a sprawling commercial centre with a modern feel; the town itself holds little attraction, but pilgrims flock through en route to the spectacular **Ranganathaswamy temple** in **Srirangam**, 6km north.

The precise date of Trichy's foundation is uncertain, but though little early architecture remains, it is clear that between 200 and 1000 AD control of the city passed between the Pallavas and Pandyas. The Chola kings who gained supremacy in the eleventh century embarked upon ambitious building projects, reaching a zenith with the Ranganathaswamy temple. In the twelfth century, the Cholas were ousted by the Vijayanagar kings of Hampi, who stood proudly against invading Muslims until 1565, when they were eventually overthrown by the sultans of the Deccan. Less than fifty years later the Nayaks of Madurai came to power, constructing the fort and firmly establishing Trichy as a trading city. After almost a century of struggle against the French and British, who both sought lands in southeast Tamil Nadu, the town came under British control until it was declared part of Tamil Nadu state in 1947.

Arrival and information

Trichy's **airport**, 8km south of the centre, has flights from Chennai (daily except Thurs & Sun; 50min), Cochin (3 weekly; 40min) and Kozikode (Wed & Sun only; 45min). The journey into town, by taxi (Rs100) or bus (#7, #28, #59, #63, #122 or #K1) takes less than half an hour; for enquiries and bookings go to Indian Airlines, at 4A Dindigul Rd (⊕0431/480233). There are also flights (4 weekly) from **Colombo** on Air Lanka (based in the *Femina* hotel; ⊕0431/460844).

Trichy's main train station, **Trichy Junction** – which has given its name to the southern district of town – provides frequent rail links with Chennai, Madurai and the eastern coastline. From here you're within easy reach of most hotels, restaurants and banks, as well as the **bus stands**. There are two stands – **Central** and **State Express** – opposite each other, but no fixed rules about where a particular bus will depart from: you just have to keep asking. State Express buses run frequently to major towns such as Madurai (#137), Kodaikanal, and Pondicherry, right around the clock. Private buses (if you really want to risk their manic and dangerous driving) line up along Rockins Road and the conductors hussle people aboard. The efficient local city service (#1) that leaves from the long platform on Rockins Road, opposite the *Shree Krishna* restaurant, is the most convenient way of getting to the Rock Fort (Rs1.50), the temples (Rs2) and Srirangam (Rs2). **Auto-rickshaws** are also widely available.

The **tourist office** (Mon–Fri 10am–5.45pm; ☎0431/460136), which proffers travel information but no maps, is opposite the State bus stand, just outside the *Tamil Nadu* hotel. **Banks** for foreign exchange include the State Bank of India on Dindigul Road, but they will only change travellers' cheques that are American Express (dollars only), or Thomas Cook (sterling only). Far more efficient is the forex dealer (Mon–Sat 10am–6pm) in the Jenney Plaza Building, a mall just beyond the *Jenney's Residency* hotel. Here you can change any travellers' cheques or currency, but you can't get a cash advance on a credit card.

Internet access is available at the Grace Soft Netcafé, on the ground floor of Jenney's Plaza, for Rs35 per hour (Mon–Sat 9.15am–11pm, Sun 5–10pm).

Accommodation

Trichy has no shortage of **hotels** to accommodate the thousands of pilgrims that visit the town. Most offer good value for money, keeping tariffs just below the Rs200 mark to avoid incurring luxury taxes. Dozens of characterless lodges, as well as some more comfortable upmarket hotels, cluster around the bus stand. Traffic noise can be a real problem in this area, so ask for a room on the rear side of any hotel you check into.

Ajanta, Rockins Road ☎0431/415504. A huge, 86-room complex centred on its own Vijayanagar shrine, and with an opulent Tirupati deity in reception. Plain, clean rooms, some with a/c and TVs; the singles are particularly good value. Popular with middle-class pilgrim tour groups, so book ahead. ②–④

Aristo, 2 Dindigul Rd ☎0431/415858. A jaded offbeat 1960s hotel, set back from the road in its own quiet compound. The bargain standard rooms have a fair amount of superficial grime, but are huge for the price, and open onto a deep common veranda. Cosier "cottages" are the honeymooners' alternative: pebble-strewn verandas, whacky colour schemes and mouldy bathrooms. ③–⑤

Ashby, 17A Junction Rd ☎0431/460652. This atmospheric old-fashioned Raj-era place is most foreign tourists' first choice. The rooms are large and impeccably clean, with fresh towels, soap, cable TV and mozzie coils. There's a little courtyard restaurant that the staff will press you to use (but only eat here if the place is doing brisk business), and a decent bar. Some rooms suffer from the all-night din of outside traffic. Great value. ②–③

Femina, 14C Williams Rd ☎0431/414501, ℱ410615. well maintained place east of the state bus stand: a sprawling block of comfortable rooms and suites, some with balconies looking to the Rock Fort. Plush restaurants, travel services, shops, and a 24hr coffee bar. ⑤–⑦

Jenney's Residency, 3/14 McDonald's Rd ☎0431/461301, ℱ461451. A slightly jaded marble and mirrors place with comfortable a/c rooms. It features a "Wild West" bar, and two good restaurants – including an upmarket Chinese place – cocktail bar and swimming pool (open to non-residents for Rs100). ⑨

Mathura, 9C Rockins Rd ☎0431/414737. Large modern block opposite the bus stand. One of the best budget deals in the area, but noisy – ask for a back room. ②–③

Modern Hindu, 6B McDonald's Rd ☎0431/417858. Best of the rock-bottom lodges: an old-fashioned place with extremely basic rooms (those on the top floor open onto a large common veranda and shady wall of trees), some with attached bath. The rules include "no bad character women". Single occupancy rates available. ②

Sangam, Collector's Office Road ☎0431/464700. Trichy's top hotel boasts all the facilities of a four-star, including an excellent pool. ⑧

Supa, 5 Royal Rd, behind *Savera* hotel ☎0431/460055. The mansion home of a famous 1940s Tamil singer that's somehow become a dilapidated budget lodge run by elderly staff, with huge two-, three- and four-bed rooms, and rank bathroomless singles. It's grimy and cheap but atmospheric, with a certain melancholic charm. ②

TTDC Tamil Nadu, McDonald's Road ☎0431/414346. One of their better hotels, and just far enough from the bus stand to escape the din. Best value are the non-a/c doubles, though even these are dowdier than most of the competition; all rooms have cable TV. ②–⑤

517

The Town

Although Trichy conducts most of its business in **Trichy Junction**, the southern district, the main sights are at least 4km north. The **bazaars** immediately
north heave with locally made cigars, textiles and fake diamonds made into inexpensive jewellery and used for dance costumes. Thanks to the town's frequent,
cheap air connection with Sri Lanka, you'll also come across boxes of smuggled
Scotch and photographic film. Head north along Big Bazaar Road (a continuation of Dindigul Road) and you're confronted by the dramatic profile of the
Rock Fort, topped by the seventeenth-century Vinayaka (Ganesh) temple.

North of the fort, the wide Kaveri River marks the boundary between
Trichy's crowded streets and its more serene temples; the incredible
Ranganathaswamy temple is so large it holds much of the village of
Srirangam within its courtyards. Also north of the Kaveri is the elaborate **Shri
Jambukeshwara temple**, while several British **churches** in Trichy town
make for an interesting contrast. The **Shantivanam Ashram**, a bus ride away,
is open daily to interested visitors all year round (see p.520).

The Rock Fort

Trichy's **Rock Fort** (daily 6am–8pm; Rs1, Rs10 extra for camera), looming
incongruously above the bazaars in the north of town, is best reached by bus
(#1) from outside the train station, or from Dindigul Road; auto-rickshaws
will try to charge you Rs50 or more for the five-minute ride.

The massive sand-coloured rock on which the fort rests towers to a height of
more than eighty metres, its irregular sides smoothed by wind and rain. The
Pallavas were the first to cut into it, but it was the Nayaks who grasped the site's
potential as a fort, adding only a few walls and bastions as fortifications. From
the entrance, at the north end of China Bazaar, a long flight of red and white
painted steps cuts steeply uphill, past a series of Pallava and Pandya rock-cut
temples (closed to non-Hindus), to the **Ganesh temple** crowning the hilltop.
The views from its terrace are spectacular, taking in the Ranganathaswamy and
Jambukeshwara temples to the north, their *gopuras* rising up from a sea of palm
trees, and the cubic concrete sprawl of central Trichy to the south.

Shri Jambukeshwara temple

By the side of the Chennai-bound road north out of Trichy, the **Shri
Jambukeshwara temple**, dedicated to Shiva, is smaller and later than the
Ranganathaswamy temple. Much of it is closed to non-Hindus, but the sculptures that adorn the walls in its outer courts, of an extravagance typical of the
seventeenth-century Nayak architects, are worth the short detour.

Srirangam: Ranganathaswamy temple

The **Ranganathaswamy temple** at **Srirangam**, 6km north of Trichy, is
among the most revered shrines dedicated to Vishnu in South India, and also
one of the largest and liveliest, engulfing within its outer walls homes, shops and
markets. Enclosed by seven rectangular walled courtyards and covering more
than one-hundred-and-twenty acres, it stands on an island defined by a tribu-
tary of the Kaveri River. This location symbolizes the transcendence of Vishnu,
housed in the sanctuary reclining on the coils of the snake Adisesha, who in legend formed an island for the god, resting on the primordial ocean of chaos.

Frequent **buses** from Trichy pull in and leave from outside the southern gate;
bus #1 is the most regular and efficient in both directions. The temple is
approached from the south. From here, a gateway topped with an immense and

heavily carved *gopura*, plastered and painted in bright pinks, blues and yellows, and completed as recently as 1987, leads to the outermost courtyard, the latest of seven built between the fifth and seventeenth centuries. Most of the present structure dates from the late fourteenth century, when the temple was renovated and enlarged after a disastrous sacking by the Delhi armies in 1313. The outer three courtyards, or *prakaras*, form the hub of the temple community, housing ascetics, priests and musicians, and the streets are lined with food stalls and shops selling souvenirs, ritual offerings and fresh flower garlands to be presented to Vishnu in the inner sanctuary. You can people-watch for hours here as the narrow streets are filled with pilgrims and locals going about their daily business and devotional activities.

At the fourth wall, the entrance to the temple proper, visitors remove footwear before passing through a high gateway, topped by a magnificent *gopura* and lined with small shrines to teachers, hymn-singers and sages. In earlier days, this fourth *prakara* would have formed the outermost limit of the temple, and was the closest members of the lowest castes could get to the sanctuary. It contains some of the finest and oldest buildings of the complex, including a temple to the goddess **Ranganayaki** in the northwest corner where devotees worship before approaching Vishnu's shrine. On the eastern side of the *prakara*, the heavily carved "thousand pillared hall" (*kalyan mandapa*) was constructed in the late Chola period. During the month of Margali (Dec/Jan) Tamil hymns are recited from its southern steps as part of the Vaikuntha Ekadasi festival.

The pillars of the outstanding **Sheshagiriraya Mandapa**, south of the *kalyan mandapa*, are decorated with rearing steeds and hunters armed with spears. These are splendid examples of **Vijayanagar** style, which depicts chivalry defending the temple against Muslim invaders, and represents the triumph of good over evil. On the southern side of the *prakara*, the Venugopala shrine, dedicated to Krishna, probably dates from the Nayak period (late sixteenth century).

To the right of the gateway into the fourth courtyard, a small museum (daily 10am–noon & 2–5pm) contains a modest collection of stone and bronze sculptures, and some delicate ivory plaques.

Inside the gate to the third courtyard – the final section of the temple open to non-Hindus – is a pillared hall, the Garuda Mandapa, carved throughout in typical Nayak style. Maidens, courtly donors and Nayak rulers feature on the pillars that surround the central shrine to Garuda, the man-eagle vehicle of Vishnu. Other buildings in the third courtyard include the vast kitchens, which emanate delicious smells as dosas and *vadas* are prepared for the deity, while devotees ritually bathe in the tanks of the moon and the sun in the northeast and southeast corners. It is well worth looking for the booth in the wall on the left-hand side; here you pay Rs2 to climb to the roof of the third courtyard. All around the viewing point, richly painted *gopuras* soar towards the sky, dramatically increasing in size from the centre outwards. In the middle of the complex is the central tower, crowning the holy sanctuary and coated in gold and carved with images of Vishnu's incarnations, on each of its four sides.

The dimly lit fifth and innermost courtyard, the most sacred part of the temple, shelters the image of Vishnu in his aspect of Ranganatha, reclining on the serpent Adisesha. The shrine is usually entered from the south, but for one day each year, during the **Vaikuntha Ekadasi festival**, the north portal is opened; those who pass through this "doorway to heaven" can expect great merit. Most of the temple's daily festivals take place in this enclosure, beginning each morning with *vina*-playing and hymn-singing as Vishnu is awakened in the presence of a cow and an elephant, and ending just after 9pm with similar ceremonies.

For more on Ranganathaswamy and Tamil Nadu's other great temples, see Contexts, p.676.

Eating

To **eat** well in Trichy, you won't have to stray far from the bus stand, where the town's most popular "meals" joints do a day-long roaring trade. For more atmosphere, stroll further up McDonald's Road to *Vincent's*, where you can eat alfresco.

Abhirami, 10 Rockins Rd, opposite the bus stand. Trichy's most famous South Indian serves up unbeatable value lunch-time "meals" (Rs20), and the standard range of snacks the rest of the day. They also have a "fast food" counter where you can get dosas and *uttapams* at any time. It opens at 6.30am for piping hot *wada-pongal* breakfasts.

English Bakery, 4 Madurai Rd, opposite Jenney's Plaza. This new bakery-cum-snack bar is the place to buy fresh bread, cream cakes, biscuits, cinnamon rolls and filled sandwiches. You can choose from a seemingly limitless variety of ice-cream sundaes, served up by a gaggle of giggling girls.

Gajapriya, on the ground floor of the *Gajapriya* hotel, Royal Road. Non-veg North Indian and noodle dishes are specialities of this small, but bliss-

fully cool and clean a/c restaurant. A good place to chill out over coffee; there's a separate "family" room for women.

Shree Krishna, 9C Rockins Rd, opposite the bus stand. Delicious and very filling American or South Indian "set breakfasts" (Rs23), specialities from all over the South after 6.30pm, and unlimited Rs20 banana leaf thalis served between 11am and 3pm, and all served with a big smile.

Vincent's Restaurant, on the junction of Dindigul Road and Madurai Road. A bit shabby now, but it's an escape from the hectic bus stand area. An "Oriental" theme restaurant, set back from the road in its own terrace, with mock pagodas, concrete bamboo, and a multicuisine menu that includes tasty chicken tikka and other tandoori dishes. No alcohol; opens at 5pm.

Shantivanam Ashram

Situated on the banks of the Kaveri, the **Shantivanam** (Sanskrit for "Forest of Peace") **ashram** is in the small village of **THANNEEPALLI**, about forty minutes by bus on the route to Kullithalai, northwest of Trichy. The programme here is based on a fusion of Christianity and Hinduism, and is the work of the Benedictine monk, Bede Griffiths, who died in 1993 at an advanced age. In the ashram's chapel, lines from the *Bhagavad Gita* and *om* symbols share space with crosses and biblical verses. Visitors can participate in as much or as little of the programme as they wish, staying in dorms or private rooms, and sharing meals, in exchange for a donation and chores. The ashram is usually full during Christian celebrations.

The far south

The **far south** of Tamil Nadu comprises a great amphitheatre of the Vaigai plains, enfolded in the west by the bare brown Alagar Hills, arching south from the edge of the Kaveri Delta to the tip of peninsular India. Studded with massive outcrops of pink and pale brown granite, the region is rich in ancient myths, where the daredevil Shiva turned evil elephants into stone boulders and rivers were formed to quench the thirst of giant pot-bellied dwarfs. Many of these stories probably pre-date the earliest traces of human settlement, but most were set down when this was the heartland of the mighty **Pandyans**, the southernmost of South India's three great warring dynasties. Their former capital, **Madurai**, is today the state's second city and, as the site of the famous Meenakshi-Sundareshwarar temple, the region's spiritual root, often dubbed "The Varanasi of the South". Further east, **Rameshwaram**, occupying a narrow spit that fractures into dozens of islets as it nears the war-torn north coast of neighbouring Sri Lanka, is equally sacred to Hindus. It forms the eastern point of a sacred triangle whose apex, at **Kanniyakumari**, combines the heady intensity of an age-old pilgrimage place with all the gimcrackery you'd expect from India's own Land's End.

Madurai

[Madurai is] a city gay with flags, waving over homes and shops selling food and drinks; the streets are broad rivers of people, folk of every race, buying and selling in the bazaars, or singing to the music of wandering bands and musicians…[around the temple], amid the perfume of ghee and incense, [are stalls] selling sweet cakes, garlands of flowers, scented powder and betel paan…[while nearby are] men making bangles of conch shells, goldsmiths, cloth dealers, tailors making up clothes, coppersmiths, flower sellers, vendors of sandalwood, painters and weavers.

The Garland of Madurai, traditional Tamil poem, second century AD

One of the oldest cities in south Asia, **MADURAI**, on the banks of the Vaigai River, has been an important centre of worship and commerce for as long as there has been civilization in South India. Megasthenes, the Greek ambassador who came here in 302 BC, wrote of its splendour and its queen, Pandai, "a daughter of Herakles", while the Roman geographer Strabo complained how the city's silk, pearls and spices were draining the imperial coffers of Rome. It was this lucrative trade, meticulously detailed in an Alexandrian mariner's manual dating from the first century AD, *The Periplus of the Erythraean Sea*, that enabled the **Pandyan** dynasty to erect the mighty **Meenakshi–Sundareshwarar temple**. Although today surrounded by a sea of modern concrete cubes, the massive gopuras of this vast complex, writhing with multicoloured mythological figures and crowned by golden finials, remain the greatest man-made spectacle of the south. Any day of the week no fewer than 15,000 people pass through its gates, increasing to 25,000 on Friday (sacred to the goddess Meenakshi), while the temple's ritual life spills out into the streets in an almost ceaseless round of festivals and processions. The chance to experience sacred ceremonies that have persisted largely unchanged since the time of the ancient Egyptians is one that few travellers pass up.

Madurai is the subject of an extraordinary number of myths. Its origins stem from a *sthala* (a holy site where legendary events have taken place) where Indra, the king of the gods, bathed in a holy tank and worshipped Shiva. Hearing of this, the Pandyan king Kulashekhara built a temple on the site and installed a *shivalingam*, around which the city grew. The name Madurai is popularly derived from the Tamil word *madhuram*, meaning "sweetness"; according to legend, Shiva shook his matted locks over the city, coating it with a fine sprinkling of *amrita*, the nectar of immortality.

MADURAI

ACCOMMODATION
Madurai Ashok	1
Pandyan	3
Taj Garden Retreat	4
TTDC Tamil Nadu (Star) II	2

Madurai's urban and suburban sprawl creates traffic jams to rival India's very worst. Chaos on the narrow, potholed streets is exacerbated by political demonstrations and religious processions, wandering cows, demanding right of way with a peremptory nudge of the haunch, and put-upon pedestrians forced onto the road by ever-increasing numbers of street traders. Open-air kitchens extend from chai-shops, where competing paratha-wallahs literally drum up custom for their freshly fried breads with a tattoo of spoon-on-skillet signals. Given the traffic problems, it's just as well that Madurai, with its profusion of markets and intriguing corners, is an utterly absorbing city to walk around.

Some history

Although invariably interwoven with myth, the traceable history and fame of Madurai stretches back well over 2000 years. Numerous natural **caves** in local hills and boulders, often modified by the addition of simple rock-cut beds, were used both in prehistoric times and by ascetics, such as the Ajivikas and Jains, who practised withdrawal and penance.

Madurai appears to have been the capital of the Pandyan empire without interruption for at least a thousand years. It became a major commercial city, trading with Greece, Rome and China through the Pandyan seaports along the Tamil coastline. Some y*avanas* (a generic term for foreigners) were employed in Madurai as palace guards and policemen; the Tamil epics describe them walking around town with their eyes and mouths wide open with amazement, much as foreign tourists still do when they first arrive. Long a seat of Tamil culture, Madurai under the Pandyas is credited with being the site of three literary **sangams**, "literary academies", said to have lasted 10,000 years and supported some 8000 poets; despite this fanciful reckoning, the most recent of these academies does have a historical basis. The "Sangam period" is generally taken to mean the first three to four centuries of the Christian era.

The Pandyas' capital finally fell in the tenth century, when the **Chola** King Parantaka took the city; they briefly regained power in the thirteenth century. Early in the 1300s, however, the notorious **Malik Kafur**, the Delhi Sultanate's "favourite slave", made an unprovoked attack during a plunder-and-desecration tour of the south, and destroyed much of the city. Forewarned of the raid, the Pandya king, Sundara, fled with his immediate family and treasure, leaving his uncle and rival, Vikrama Pandya, to repel Kafur. Nevertheless, the latter returned to Delhi with booty said to consist of "six hundred and twelve elephants, ninety-six thousand *mans* of gold, several boxes of jewels and pearls and twenty thousand horses".

Shortly after this raid Madurai became an independent Sultanate; in 1364, it joined the Hindu **Vijayanagar** empire, ruled from Vijayanagar/Hampi (see p.289) and administered by governors, the **Nayaks**. In 1565, the Nayaks asserted their own independence. Under their supervision and patronage, Madurai enjoyed a renaissance, being rebuilt on the pattern of a lotus centring on the Meenakshi temple. Part of the palace of the most illustrious of the Nayaks, **Thirumalai** (1623–55), survives today.

The city remained under Nayak control until the mid-eighteenth century when the **British** gradually took over. A hundred years later the British de-fortified Madurai, filling its moat to create the four Veli streets that today mark the boundary of the old city.

Arrival and information

Madurai's small domestic **airport** (☎0452/671333, or 670433), 12km south of the city, is served by daily flights to and from Chennai and Mumbai. Theoretically you should be able to get information at the **Government of Tamil Nadu Tourist Information Centre** booth by the exit, but it's not always open to meet flights. Very simple snack meals ("bread-omelette") are served at the **restaurant** (daily 9am–5pm). There's also a bookshop and a branch of Indian Bank, but they can't change money. **Taxis** into the city charge a fixed rate of around Rs200. City Bus #10A leaves frequently from near the exit and will drop you at Periyar Bus Stand in town.

Arriving in Madurai by **bus**, you come in at one of five stands, all served by long-distance and city buses. In the centre, only local city buses operate from either **STC bus stand**, or **Periyar stand** next door. Both are on W Veli Street in the western side of the old city, and very close to the train station and most accommodation. **Arapalayam bus stand** (serves all state buses to and from towns in the west, including Kodaikanal and Coimbatore, and Kerala) is in the northwest, close to the south bank of the river, about 2km from the train station. The **new bus stand** lies 5km southwest of the centre, and is where all State Express buses stop, and it serves all major long-distance destinations, including Trichy, Kanniyakumari, Chennai, Kerala, Bangalore, Karnataka and Andhra Pradesh. **Anna bus stand** (points north, such as the Chola cities, and Rameshwaram) is 5km out in the northeast, north of the Vaigai. Wherever you arrive, the easiest and cheapest way in is to take one of the frequent city buses to a central bus stand, then jump in an auto-rickshaw to your hotel, although from W Veli Street stands it's feasible to reach most of the budget places on the western side of town by cycle-rickshaw or on foot.

Madurai's clean and well maintained **railway station** is just west of the centre off W Veli Street. You can leave your luggage at the cloakroom (24hr) next to the reservations office (Mon–Sat 8am–2pm, 2.15pm–8pm; Sun 8am–2pm) in the main hall, where you'll also find a very helpful TTDC Tourist Office (daily 6.30am–8.30pm). There's a good veg canteen on Platform 1 and, unusually, a pre-paid auto-rickshaw and taxi booth outside the main entrance, open to coincide with train arrivals.

Information

The main **TTDC Tourist Office** is on W Veli Street (Mon–Fri 10am–5.45pm, sometimes Sat 10am–1pm; ☏0452/734757). However, its staff are less helpful than their charming counterparts at the **railway station office** (see above), which is the best place for general information and maps for Madurai and the surrounding areas, and they provide details of **car rental**. They will also arrange, with a little notice, **city tours** (7am–noon, or 3–8pm; Rs100 per head) in a minibus with one of the government-approved **guides**, who can otherwise usually be found at the southern entrance to the temple. Find out their names first at the tourist office as they usually speak better English and are reliable. Unregistered guides may be cheaper but you may well find yourself being dragged around commission-paying shops rather than the sights. Official guided city tours, for one to four visitors, cost around Rs250 for a half-day, and Rs350 for up to eight hours. The fee for a temple tour is negotiable. If you want to rent a **taxi** to see the outlying sights, the rank at the main train station abides by government set rates (on a board outside the station entrance); a full-day city tour costs around Rs550.

Madurai's **post office** is at the corner of Scott Road and N Veli Street. For postal services, enter on the Scott Road side (Mon–Sat 8am–7.30pm, Sun & hols 9am–4.30pm; speedpost 10am–7pm). For **poste restante** (Mon–Sat 9.30am–5.30pm), go to the Philatelic Bureau on the southwest corner of the building, and remember to take along your passport.

Internet access is offered everywhere, but by far the most efficient place is Net Tower (13/8 Kaka Thoppu Street, in the side street by *Hotel International*, and at 60/42 West Tower St, just in front of *West Tower* hotel). Both have rows of private cubicles, charge an extremely reasonable Rs20 per hour, and are open 8am–midnight every day.

The best place in Madurai to **change money** is Alagendran Forex Services, 168 N Veli St, opposite the Head Post Office (Mon–Sat 9am–6.30pm), which offers more or less the same rates as the State Bank of India at 6 W Veli St. Mastercard and Visa are accepted at the Andhra Bank on W Chitrai Street, but currency or travellers' cheques are not. If you get caught out by a public holiday or need to change money in the night, head for the *Supreme* hotel, whose 24hr foreign exchange desk is open to non-residents.

Bike rental at low fixed rates is available at SV, West Tower Street, near the west entrance to the temple, or the stall on West Veli Street, opposite the *TTDC Tamil Nadu* hotel.

Accommodation

Madurai has a wide range of **accommodation**, from rock-bottom lodges to good, clean mid-range places that cater for the flocks of pilgrims and tourists. There's a cluster of hotels on West Perumal Maistry Street. Upmarket options lie a few kilometres out of the town centre, north of the Vaigai River. You'll find **railway retiring rooms**, on the first floor of the station (Rs100–150); take the stairway on platform 1 (turn right from the main entrance hall). There are huge, cleanish rooms (some a/c) and are often booked up.

Aarathy, 9 Perumalkoil, W Mada Street ☏0452/731571. In a great location, overlooking the Kudalagar Temple near the STC bus stand. All rooms have attached bathrooms and a TV, some have a/c and a balcony. There is a busy open-air restaurant that is especially popular when the temple elephant, Mahalakshmi, is led through each morning and evening. Usually full of foreigners so book ahead, but ask to see the room before checking in, as not all rooms are up to standard. ④–⑤

Duke, 6 N Veli St, close to the junction with W Veli Street ☏0452/741154. A modern hotel, with larger-than-average non-a/c rooms; ask for one on the "open side", with a window. Good value. ③

International, 46 W Perumal Maistry St (☏0452/741553). Newly renovated, this is a rather chaotic lodge with laid-back service, but the rooms are fine, some have a/c, and all have 72-channel cable TV, just in case you get a tad templed-out. ③–⑤

Madurai Ashok, Alagarkoil Road ☏0452/537531, ℻537530. Plush hotel on the northern outskirts, with 24hr room service, bar, currency exchange, craft shops and a pleasant swimming pool. ⑨

New College House, 2 Town Hall Rd ☏0452/742971. Currently undergoing a major refit, this is a huge maze with more than 200 rooms that range from the very dingy and basic to the decent a/c variety. The ground floor is home to

one of the town's best "meals" canteen (see Eating, p.533), shops and an Internet centre. Likely to have vacancies when everywhere else is full. ②–⑤

Padman, 1 Perumal Tank West St ☏0452/740702, ℻743629. The views from the front rooms of this modern hotel, overlooking the ruined Perumal tank, are worth paying extra for. Clean, comfortable and central with a rooftop restaurant. Again, another popular place with foreign visitors, so book in advance. ⑥

Pandyan, Race Course, north of the river ☏0452/537090, ℻533424. A comfortable, centrally a/c hotel with a good restaurant, bar, exchange facilities, travel agency, bookstores and several craft shops. Nice garden, too. ⑧–⑨

Prem Nivas, 102 W Perumal Maistry St ☏0452/742532, ℻743618. From the outside this place looks a lot swankier than it is, but the spacious rooms make it among the best mid-price deals in the city. ④–⑤

Sri Devi, 20 W Avani Moola St ☏0452/747431. Good-value, spotless non-a/c doubles right next to the temple, which means this place is always filled with foreigners. There have been recent complaints about indecent behaviour of staff towards women; keep your corridor-facing bathroom window tightly closed. For a romantic splurge, splash out on their "deluxe" a/c rooftop room (⑥), which has matchless views over the western *gopura*. No restaurant, but they will order in food and beer for you. ❷

Supreme, 110 W Perumal Maistry St ☎0452/743151, ☏742637. A large, swish and central hotel, with a great rooftop restaurant (see p.534) for sundowners. There is a 24-hr forex desk, internet facilities and travel counter. A "duplex" room gets you views of Yanna Malai hill range. Book in advance. ❻–❼

Taj Garden Retreat, Pasumalai hills ☎0452/601020. Madurai's most exclusive hotel: a beautifully refurbished colonial house in the hills overlooking the city and temples, albeit 6km out. There are three kinds of rooms: "Standard" ($120); "Superior", in the period block ($145); and "Deluxe" modern cottages with the best views ($160). Facilities include gourmet restaurant, pool, bar and tennis court. ❾

TM, 50 W Perumal Maistry St ☎0452/741651. Despite the rather unfriendly reception and institutional atmosphere, this is an immaculately clean

option, with spotless attached bathrooms; the top-floor rooms are the airiest. It's the one of the best among the budget places on this street. ❸–❻

TTDC Hotel Tamil Nadu I, W Veli St ☎0452/737471, ☏731945. Somewhat removed from the atmosphere of the temples and the bazaar, but with newly refurbished spacious rooms overlooking a leafy courtyard. The cheapest rooms are especially good value. ❷–❻

TTDC Tamil Nadu II (Star), Alagarkoil Road ☎0452/537461, ☏533203. Another government hotel, even further from the atmosphere of the temples, 5km north of the centre. Good-sized rooms (some a/c) and a veg restaurant, though service can be rather half-hearted. ❹–❻

West Tower, 60 W Tower St ☎0452/746908. The selling point is its proximity to the temple, and the great views from the rooftop, where there's a pleasant little thatched terrace. However, the rooms are extremely basic and very over-priced; some have a/c. ❹–❻

The City

Although considerably enlarged and extended over the years, the overall layout of Madurai's **old city**, south of the Vaigai River, has remained largely unchanged since the first centuries AD. It comprises a series of concentric squares, centred on the massive Shri Meenakshi–Sundareshwarar temple and aligned with the cardinal points. The intention of the ancient architects was clearly to follow the dimensions of an auspicious mandala, or sacred diagram, set down in canonical texts known as the *Vastu Shastras*. These provided the blueprints for the now lost cities of the Vedic age, 3000 years ago, and were believed to represent the laws governing the universe; they are also abstract depictions of the Hindu creator god, Brahma, in the form of the primeval being, Parusha. Whereas rectangular grid plans symbolize temporal or royal power, squares are used by Hindus to indicate the Absolute, which is why the streets boxed around Madurai's temple, each named after the different Tamil months, are of even lengths. The reason many of the city's mass rituals involve circuits of these streets in a strictly clockwise direction is because circumambulation of a powerful shrine, such as the Meenakshi temple, is believed to activate the sacred properties of the giant mandala.

North of the river, Madurai becomes markedly more mundane and irregular. You're only likely to cross the Vaigai to reach the city's more expensive hotels, the Gandhi Museum and the Anna bus stand.

Shri Meenakshi-Sundareshwarar temple

Enclosed by a roughly rectangular six-metre-high wall, in the manner of a fortified palace, the **Meenakshi–Sundareshwarar temple** (daily 5am–12.30pm & 4–9.30pm) is one of the largest temple complexes in India. Much of it was constructed during the Nayak period between the sixteenth and eighteenth centuries, but certain parts are very much older. The principal shrines (closed to non-Hindus) are those to Sundareshwarar (Shiva) and his consort Meenakshi (a form of Parvati); unusually, the goddess takes precedence and is always worshipped first.

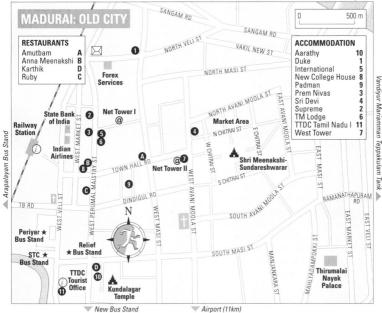

For the first-time visitor to the temple, when confronted with a confusing maze of shrines, sculptures and colonnades, and unaware of the logic employed in their arrangement, it's very easy to get disorientated. However, if you're not in a hurry, this should not deter you. Quite apart from the estimated thirty-three million sculptures to arrest your attention, the life of the temple is absolutely absorbing, and many visitors find themselves drawn back at several different times of the day. Be it the endless round of puja ceremonies, loud *nagaswaram* and *tavil* music, weddings, brahmin boys under religious instruction in the *Vedas*, the prostrations of countless devotees, the busy glittering market stalls inside the east entrance or, best of all, a festival procession, something is always going on to make this quite simply one of the most riveting places in Tamil Nadu.

Approximately fifty priests work in the temple, and live in houses close to the north entrance. They are easily identified – each wears a white *dhoti* (*veshti* in Tamil) tied between the legs; on top of this, around the waist, is a second, coloured cloth, usually of silk. Folded into the cloth, a small bag contains holy white ash. The bare-chested priests invariably carry a small towel over the shoulder. Most wear earrings and necklaces including *rudraksha* beads, sacred to Shiva. As Shaivite priests, they place three horizontal stripes of white ash on the forehead, arms, shoulders and chest and a red powder dot, sacred to the goddess, above the bridge of the nose. The majority wear their long hair tied into a knot, with the forehead shaved. Inside the temple they also carry brass trays holding offerings of camphor and ash.

Madurai takes the **gopura**, so prominent in other southern temples, to its ultimate extreme. The entire complex has no fewer than twelve such towers; set into the outer walls, the four largest rise to a height of around forty-six metres, and are visible for miles outside the city. Each is covered with a lavish profusion of painted stucco gods and demons, with the occasional live monkey scampering and chattering among the divine images. After a referendum in the 1950s, the *gopuras*, which had become monochrome and dilapidated, were repainted in the vivid kingfisher greens, blues and bright reds you can see today; they have to be completely redone every ten years or so (the last repaint was in the mid-1990s). It may be possible, for a small fee, to climb the southern and tallest tower, to enjoy superb views over the town.

The most popular **entrance** is on the eastern side, where the *gopura* gateway has reopened after a period of closure following the inauspicious suicide of a temple employee who leapt from the top. You can also enter nearby through a towerless gate that is directly in line with the Meenakshi shrine deep inside. In the **Ashta Shakti Mandapa** ("Eight Goddesses Hallway"), a sparkling market sells puja offerings and souvenirs, from fat garlands of flowers to rough-hewn sky-blue plaster deities. Sculpted pillars illustrate different aspects of the goddess Shakti, and Shiva's 64 miracles at Madurai. Behind this hall, to the south, are stables for the temple elephants and camels.

If you continue straight on from here, cross East Ati Street, and go through the seven-storey **Chitrai gopura**, you enter a passageway leading to the eastern end of the **Pottamarai Kulam** (Tank of Golden Lotuses), where Indra bathed before worshipping the *shivalingam*. From the eastern side of the tank you can see the glistening gold of the Meenakshi and Sundareshwarar *vimana* towers. Steps lead down to the water from the surrounding colonnades, and in the centre stands a brass lamp column. People take a ritually cleansing bath here, prior to entering the inner shrines, or just sit, gossip and rest on the steps.

The ceiling paintings in the open corridors are modern, but Nayak murals around the tank illustrate scenes from the *Gurur Vilayadal Puranam,* which describe Shiva's Madurai miracles. Of the two figures located halfway towards the Meenakshi shrine on the north side, one is the eighth-century king Kulashekhara Pandyan, said to have founded the temple; opposite him is a wealthy merchant patron.

On the western side of the tank is the entrance to the **Meenakshi shrine** (closed to non-Hindus), popularly known as **Amman Koyil**, literally the "mother temple". The immovable green stone image of the goddess is contained within two further enclosures that form two ambulatories. Facing Meenakshi, just past the first entrance and in front of the sanctum sanctorum, stands Shiva's bull-vehicle, Nandi. At around 9pm, the movable images of the god and goddess are carried to the **bedchamber**. Here the final puja ceremony of the day, the **lalipuja**, is performed, when for thirty minutes or so the priests sing lullabies (*lali*), before closing the temple for the night.

The corridor outside Meenakshi's shrine is known as the **Kilikkutu Mandapa** or Parrot Cage Hallway. Parrots used to be kept just south of the shrine as offerings to Meenakshi; a practice discontinued in the mid-1980s, as the birds suffered due to "lack of maintenance". Sundareshwarar and Meenakshi are brought every Friday (6–7pm) to the sixteenth-century **Oonjal Mandapa** further along, where they are placed on a swing (*oonjal*) and serenaded by members of a special caste, the Oduvars. The black and gold, almost fairground-like decoration of the *mandapa* dates from 1985.

Across the corridor, the small **Rani Mangammal Mandapa**, next to the tank, has a detailed eighteenth-century ceiling painting of the marriage of Meenakshi and Sundareshwarar, surrounded by lions and elephants against a blue background. Sculptures in the hallway portray characters such as the warring monkey kings from the *Ramayana*, the brothers Sugriva (Sukreeva) and

Bali (Vahli), and the indomitable Pandava prince, Bhima, from the *Mahabharata*, who was so strong that he uprooted a tree to use as a club.

Walking back north, past the Meenakshi shrine, through a towered entrance, leads you to the area of the Sundareshwarar shrine. Just inside, is the huge monolithic figure of Ganesh, **Mukkuruni Vinayaka**, said to have been found during the excavation of the Mariamman Teppakulam tank (see below). Chubby Ganesh is well known for his love of sweets, and during his annual **Vinayaka Chathurti festival** (Sept), a special *prasad* (gift offering of food) is concocted for him from ingredients that include 300 kilos of rice, 10 kilos of sugar and 110 coconuts.

Around a corner, a small image of the monkey god **Hanuman**, covered with *ghee* and red powder, stands on a pillar. Devotees take a little with their finger for a *tillak*, to mark the forehead. A figure of Nandi and two gold-plated copper flagstaffs face the entrance to the **Sundareshwarar shrine** (closed to non-Hindus). From here, outsiders can just about see the *shivalingam* beyond the blue and red neon Tamil *om* sign.

Causing a certain amount of fun, north of the flagstaffs are figures of Shiva and Kali in the throes of their dance competition (see box on p.499). A stall nearby sells tiny **butter balls** from a bowl of water, which visitors throw at the god and goddess "to cool them down". If you leave through the gateway here, on the east, you'll find in the northeast corner the fifteenth-century **Ayirakkal Mandapa** (thousand-pillared hall), now transformed into the temple's **Art**

Meenakshi, the fish-eyed goddess

The goddess Meenakshi of Madurai emerged from the flames of a sacrificial fire as a three-year-old child, in answer to the Pandyan king Malayadvaja's prayer for a son. The king, not only surprised to see a female, was also horrified that she had three breasts. In every other respect, she was beautiful, as her name, Meenakshi ("fish-eyed"), suggests – fish-shaped eyes are classic images of desirability in Indian love poetry. Dispelling his concern, a mysterious voice told the king that Meenakshi would lose the third breast on meeting her future husband.

In the absence of a son, the adult Meenakshi succeeded her father as Pandyan monarch. With the aim of world domination, she then embarked on a series of successful battles, culminating in the defeat of Shiva's armies at the god's Himalayan abode, Mount Kailasah. Shiva then appeared at the battlefield; on seeing him, Meenakshi immediately lost her third breast. Fulfilling the prophecy, Shiva and Meenakshi travelled to Madurai, where they were married. The two then assumed a dual role, firstly as king and queen of the Pandya kingdom, with Shiva assuming the title Sundara Pandya ("King Shiva"), and secondly as the presiding deities of the Madurai temple, into which they subsequently disappeared.

Their shrines in Madurai are today the focal point of a hugely popular fertility cult, centred on the gods' coupling; the temple priests maintain that this ensures the preservation and regeneration of the Universe. Each night, the pair are placed together in Sundareshwarar's bedchamber, but not before Meenakshi's nose ring has been carefully removed so that it won't cut her husband in the heat of passion. Their celestial lovemaking is consistently earth-moving enough to ensure that Sundareshwarar remains completely faithful to his consort (exceptional for the notoriously promiscuous Shiva). Nevertheless, this fidelity is never taken for granted, and has to be ritually tested each year when the beautiful goddess Cellattamman is brought to Sundareshwarar "to have her powers renewed". After she is spurned, she flies into a fury that can only be placated with the sacrifice of a buffalo – one among the dozens of arcane ceremonies that make up Madurai's round of temple rituals.

Museum (daily 10am–5.30pm; Rs1). In some ways it is a great shame, as screens have been erected and dusty educational displays replace a clear view of this gigantic hall full of dramatically sculpted columns. It is said that each column emits a different musical note when tapped. However, there's a fine, if rather dishevelled, collection of wood, copper, bronze and stone sculpture, an old nine-metre-high teak temple door and general miscellanea.

For more on the temples of Tamil Nadu, see Contexts, p.676.

Vandiyur Mariamman Teppakulam tank and the floating festival

At one time, the huge **Vandiyur Mariamman Teppakulam** tank in the southeast of town (bus #4 or #4A; 15min) was full with a constant supply of water, flowing via underground channels from the Vaigai. Nowadays, thanks to a number of accidents, it is only filled during the spectacular **Teppa floating festival** (Jan/Feb), when pilgrims take boats out to the goddess shrine in the centre. Before their marriage ceremony, Shiva and Meenakshi are brought in procession to the tank, where they are floated on a raft decorated with lights, which devotees pull by ropes three times, encircling the shrine. The boat trip is believed to be the overture to a seduction that reaches its passionate conclusion later that night in the temple. This traditionally makes the period during the Teppa festival the most auspicious time of year to get married.

During the rest of the year the tank and the central shrine remain empty. Accessible by steps, the tank is most often used as an impromptu cricket green, and the shade of the nearby trees makes a popular gathering place. Tradition states that the huge image of Ganesh, Mukkuruni Vinayaka, in the Meenakshi temple, was uncovered here when the area was originally excavated to provide bricks for the Thirumalai Nayak palace.

Thirumalai Nayak palace

Of the seventeenth-century **Thirumalai Nayak palace** (daily 9am–1pm & 2–5pm; free), 1.5km southeast of the Meenakshi temple, only around a quarter survives. Much of it was dismantled by Thirumalai's grandson, Chockkanatha Nayak, and used for a new palace at Tiruchirapalli. What stands here today is a result of the restoration and renovation in 1858 by the Governor of Chennai, Lord Napier, and again in 1971 for the Tamil World Conference. The palace originally consisted of two residential sections, plus a theatre, private temple, harem, royal bandstand, armoury and gardens.

The remaining building, the **Swargavilasa** ("Heavenly Pavilion") is a rectangular courtyard, flanked by eighteen-metre-tall colonnades. As well as occasional live performances of music and dance, the Tourism Department arranges a nightly **Sound and Light Show** (in English 6.45–7.30pm; Rs5), which relates the story of the Tamil epic, *Shilipaddikaram*, and the history of the Nayaks. Some find this spectacle edifying, and others soporific – especially when the quality of the tape is poor. In an adjoining hall, the palace **museum** (same hours as the palace; free) includes Pandyan, Jain and Buddhist sculpture, terracottas and an eighteenth-century print showing the palace in a dilapidated state; sadly, there is no information and no exhibit is labelled.

All that remains of the **Rangavilasa** – the palace where Thirumalai's brother Muthialu once lived – are ten pillars, wedged in a tiny back street. Take Old Kudiralayam Street, right of the palace as you face it, pass the Archaeological Department Office and turn right into Mahal Vadam Pokki Street. The third turning on the left (opposite the New India Textile Shop) is the unmarked Ten Pillars South Lane. One pillar contains a **shivalingam**, worshipped by passers-by.

Date	Name	No. of days
Jan/Feb	Teppa	12
Feb/March	Machi Mantala	10
March/April	Kotaivasanta	9
April/May	Chittirai	12
May/June	Vasanta	10
June/July	Unchal	10
July/Aug	Ati Mulaikkottu	10
Aug/Sept	Avani Mula	12
Sept/Oct	Navaratri	9
Oct/Nov	Kolatta	6
Nov/Dec	Tirukkarttikai	10
Dec/Jan	Ennai Kappu	9

TAMIL NADU | Madurai

The date of each of the Madurai temple's annual festivals varies each year; check with a tourist office when you plan your visit. The principal and most exciting component of most of them is the procession (*purappatu*, or "setting forth"), held on the morning and evening of every day. Each procession is accompanied by officiating brahmins, temple employees bearing royal insignia, umbrellas, silver staffs and, at night, flaming torches. The entourage is invariably preceded by the penetrating orchestra of *tavil* (barrel drum), hand cymbals and the distinctive *nagaswaram* (double-reed oboe-like wind instrument), for which the Madurai area is particularly famous.

Processions circumambulate clockwise inside the temple, and many leave its precincts, starting from the east entrance, passing along the Chitrai, Avani Moola or Masi streets and, on special occasions such as the floating festival (days 10 and 11 of the Teppa ceremonies), leave the centre of the city altogether. Locals and visiting pilgrims crowd the streets for *darshan*, a view of the deities. The evening processions, weaving through the starlit night, are undoubtedly the most atmospheric.

Icons from the temple, special movable images, are taken out, lavishly clothed in silk and ornaments of rubies, sapphires, pearls, silver and gold. When the festival celebrates both Meenakshi and Sundareshwarar, the contingent is usually led by Vinayaka (Ganesh, son of Shiva), as the "remover of obstacles", followed in succession by Subrahmanya (another son of Shiva), Sundareshwarar (a multiple image of the marriage of Shiva), Meenakshi and Chandeshwarar (another form of Shiva). On some occasions, the deities may be enshrined on a simple canopy, but on others, they ride on silver or gold vehicles (*vahanas*) such as horses, elephants or, most auspiciously, huge silver bulls.

At the Avani Mula festival, the coronation of Shiva is celebrated and his Maduran miracles are enacted in a series of plays (*lilas*). During the greatest festival of all, Chittirai, more plays are staged, telling the story of Meenakshi. The eighth day sees the goddess crowned as queen of the Pandyas and, on the tenth, her marriage to Shiva draws as many as fifty thousand people to the temple. Out in the streets the next morning, mayhem ensues when the most elaborate transport is brought into use for procession. The god and goddess travel in fifteen-metre-high chariots, with giant wooden wheels, hauled through the streets by hundreds of devotees, all tugging on long ropes. Rising from a wooden platform, the massive pyramidal bamboo superstructures are decorated in colourful appliqué and fronted by a row of rearing wooden horses.

The god and goddess are taken to the banks of the Vaigai River, to meet Meenakshi's brother who, in southern mythology, is Lord Kallalagar (Vishnu). The icon of Vishnu is brought from the forested hilltop temple at Alagarkovil, 20km northeast of Madurai. Vishnu travelled to Madurai to give his sister away at the wedding, only to find on reaching the river that the ceremony had already occurred. Because of this, to appease the deity, the festivities always take place on the northern bank of the river.

Tamukkam palace: the Gandhi and Government museums

Across the Vaigai, 5km northeast of the centre near the Central Telegraph Office, stands **Tamukkam** (bus #2, #3, #4 or #26; 20min), the seventeenth-century multi-pillared and arched palace of Queen Rani Mangammal. Built to accommodate such regal entertainment as elephant fights, Tamukkam was taken over by the British, used as a courthouse and collector's office, and in 1955 became home to the Gandhi and Government museums.

Madurai's **Gandhi Memorial Museum** (daily 10am–1pm & 2–5.30pm; free), far better organized than most of the species, charts the history of India since the landing of the first Europeans, viewed in terms of the freedom struggle. Generally the perspective is national but, where appropriate, reference is made to the role played by Tamils. Wholeheartedly critical of the British, it states its case clearly and simply, quoting the Englishman John Sullivan: "We have denied to the people of the country all that could raise them in society, all that could elevate them as men; we have insulted their caste; we have abrogated their laws of inheritance; we have seized the possessions of their native princes and confiscated the estates of their nobles; we have unsettled the country by our exactions, and collected the revenue by means of torture." One chilling artefact, kept in a room painted black, is the bloodstained *dhoti* the Mahatma was wearing when he was assassinated. Next door to the museum, the **Gandhi Memorial Museum Library** (daily except Wed 10am–1pm & 2–5.30pm; free) houses a reference collection, open to all, of 15,000 books, periodicals, letters and microfilms of material by and about Gandhi.

Opposite, the small **Government Museum** (daily except Fri 9am–5pm; closed 2nd Sat each month; free) displays stone and bronze sculptures, musical instruments, paintings (including examples of Tanjore and Kangra styles) and folk art such as painted terracotta animals, festival costumes and hobby horses. There's also a fine collection of shadow puppets, said to have originated in the Thanjavur area and probably exported to southeast Asia during the Chola period. A small house in which **Gandhi** once lived stands in a garden within the compound. Beside it, a number of unfinished latrines may have been intended as an exhibit, or a public amenity. It's rather hard to tell.

Kochadai Aiyannar temple

The village of **Kochadai**, a northwestern suburb of Madurai, has a beautifully maintained temple dedicated to **Aiyannar**, the Tamil village deity and guardian of borders. Travelling through Tamil Nadu, you often see such shrines from the road, but it may not always be possible, or appropriate, to investigate them. Here, however, they are accustomed to visitors. Flanked by two huge garish *dvarpalas* (doorkeepers), the entrance opens directly onto two gigantic horses with riders and furious-looking armed attendants. The shrine on the left houses the god Rama and his brother Lakshmana and, facing the entrance, is the shrine to Aiyannar. To the right, the *alamaram* tree, also a shrine, apparently houses a **cobra**, fed with eggs and milk. According to the priests he only comes out during full moon. During a big **festival** in the Tamil month of Panguni (March/April), Aiyannar is taken around the village to the accompaniment of music and fireworks.

Kochadai is served by frequent buses (#68 or #54) en route to Solavandan.

Old Madurai is crowded with textile and tailors' shops, particularly in area around West Veli, Avani Moola and Chitrai streets and Town Hall Road. It's worth taking up at least one "come see my tailor shop" demand in the immediate vicinity of the temple; many of these shops will allow potential customers to climb up onto their roofs for great views over the Meenakshi complex. If you are looking to have some tailoring done, the locally produced textiles are generally good value, and tailors pride themselves on turning out faithful copies of favourite clothes in a matter of hours. South Avani Moola Street is packed with jewellery, particularly gold shops, while at 10 North Avani Moola St, you can plan for the future at the Life & Lucky Number Numerology Centre.

Madurai is also a great place to pick up South Indian crafts. Among the best outlets are All India Handicrafts Emporium, 39–41 Town Hall Rd; Co-optex, West Tower Street, and Pandiyan Co-op Supermarket, Palace Road, for hand-woven textiles; and Surabhi, West Veli Street, for Keralan handicrafts. For souvenirs such as sandalwood, temple models, carved boxes and oil lamps head for Poompuhar, 12 West Veli St (℡ 0452/25517), or Tamilnad Gandhi Smarak Nidhi Khadi Gramodyog Bhavan, West Veli Street, opposite the train station, which sells crafts, oil lamps, Meenakshi sculptures and khadi cloth and shirts.

The old purpose-built, wooden-pillared fruit and vegetable market, between North Chitrai and Avani Moola streets, provides a slice of Madurai life that can't have changed for centuries. Beyond it, on the first floor of the concrete building at the back, the flower market (24hr) is a riot of colour and fragrance. Weighing scales spill with tiny white petals, and plump pink garlands hang in rows. Varieties such as orange, yellow or white marigolds (*samandi*), pink jasmine (*arelli*), tiny purple spherical vanameli and holy tulsi plants come from hill areas such as Kodaikanal and Kumily. These are bought in bulk and distributed for use in temples, or to wear in the hair; some are made into elaborate wedding garlands (*kalyanam mala*). The very friendly traders will show you each and every flower, and if you've got a camera will more than likely expect to be recorded for posterity. It's a nice idea to offer to send them a copy of any photograph you take.

Eating

As with accommodation, the range of places to eat in Madurai is wide, and standards are generally high, whether you're eating at one of the numerous utilitarian-looking "meals" places around the temple, or in an upscale hotel. When the afternoon heat gets too much, head for one of the **juice bars** dotted around the centre, where you can order freshly squeezed pomegranate, pineapple, carrot or orange juice for around Rs20 per glass. To make the most of Madurai's exotic skyline though, you'll have to seek out a **rooftop restaurant** – another of the modern city's specialities. Rock-bottom-budget travellers should try the street-side stalls at the bottom of West Perumal Maistry Street, where old ladies dish up filling leaf plates of freshly steamed *iddli* and spicy fish masala for Rs10 per portion and delicious melt-in-the-mouth flaky *parotas*.

Aarathy, *Aarathy Hotel*, 9 Perumalkoil, W Mada Street. Tasty tiffin (dosas, *iddlis* and hot *wada sambar*), served on low tables in a hotel forecourt, where the temple elephant turns up at 6am and 6pm. For more filling, surprisingly cheap, South and North Indian meals, step into their blissfully cool a/c annexe.

Amutbam, 30 Town Hall Rd. A huge menu featuring everything from full-on chicken sizzlers to Western-style snacks, via the usual range of noodles, North Indian and veg dishes. Ask for a table in their a/c section, where you can chill out for an extra Rs2 per head.

Anna Meenakshi, opposite *TM Lodge*, W Perumal Maistry Street. An upmarket branch of *New College House*'s more traditional canteen, serving top tiffin to a discerning, strictly vegetarian clientele. This one's smaller and brighter, with shiny marble tables and an ornate bell metal lamp in the doorway. Arguably the most hygienic, best-value food in the centre. Opens 6am–9.30pm; absolutely delicious coconut or lemon "rice meals", and cheap banana leaf thalis are served from 10.30am to 4pm.

Apollo 96, *Supreme Hotel*, 110 W Perumal Maistry St. Boasting 75,000 flashing diodes and a punchy sound system, Tamil Nadu's hi-tech bar looks like the set of a low-budget 1970s sci-fi movie. Beers cost Rs75. Closes at 11pm sharp.

Karthik, W Perumal Maistry Street (around the corner from the *Aarathy Hotel*, near the relief bus stand). Run-of-the-mill from the outside, but this pure veg "meals" joint is famous for its delicious *iddli-fry*-masala – mini *iddlis* turned in a spicy chilli paste (served in late afternoon and evening only). Eat in or ask for a "parcel".

New College House, 2 Town Hall Rd. Huge meals-cum-tiffin hall in old-style hotel. Lunch time, when huge piles of pure veg food are served on banana leaves to long rows of locals, is a real deep South experience; and the coffee's pure Coorg.

Ruby, W Perumal Maistry Street. Ignore the "Alcohol Strictly Prohibited" note on the menu card: this is essentially an unlicensed bar, periodically raided by the police but a popular meeting place for foreign travellers. Cold beers (Rs60) are served in a leafy courtyard or in more claustrophobic compartments indoors, and they do hot snacks and dishes, including a fiery "Chicken 65", noodles and biriyani.

Supreme, *Supreme Hotel*, 110 W Perumal Maistry St. Arguably Madurai's best and breeziest rooftop restaurant and, with sweeping views of the city and temple, it is the ideal venue for a sundowner. Open 4pm–midnight, with an eclectic multicuisine menu.

Around Madurai

Stretching west towards the blue haze of the Alagar Hills, the Vaigai plains **around Madurai** are broken by colossal outcrops of granite, some of them weathered into weird forms like petrified monsters. Each occupies a place in the mythological landscape of the Pandyan heartland. To the northeast of the city is "Elephant Hill", said to have been created by Shiva to punish a rampaging pachyderm. The holiest rock hereabouts, however, looms over the southwest fringes of the city, where the Muslim conquerors of the early fourteenth century consolidated their fleeting colonization of the far south by founding a capital at the foot of an ancient Hindu site. Referred to by Islamic historians as "**City of Ma'bar**", the orderly grid-planned town served as the headquarters of the **Madurai Sultanate**, whose origins remain obscure. The sultanate endured for eight generations until the army of the mighty Hindu Vijayanagar empire swept south to mop up the remnants of Muslim rule left after Malik Kafir's bloody sack of 1311. The last sultan, **Sikander Shah**, allegedly died defending the town, and his tomb crowns the top of the 365-metre-monolith, known to Muslim pilgrims throughout India as **Sikandermalai**, "Hill of Sikander" (see below).

For Hindus, however, the sheer-sided rock at **TIRUPPARAKUNRAM**, 8km southwest of Madurai (buses #4A & #32 from the STC bus stand), is revered as **Sikandermalai**, one of the six abodes of Shiva's son and the Tamils' favourite god, Lord Murugan. Identified in mythology as the site of Murugan's marriage to Indra's daughter, Deivani, it is one of the most sacred shrines in Tamil Nadu. At the auspicious time of Murugan's wedding anniversary in early February, thousands of newlyweds come here to be blessed. In the summer, the god's birthday is celebrated with displays of fire-walking and body-piercing, along with other acts of ostentatious masochism, such as devotees dragging ox carts along with chains fastened to the flesh of their shoulders.

Outside festival time, however, Tirupparakunram is a peaceful spot offering a welcome respite from the frenzy of Madurai. Its **temple**, built around an eighth-century shrine cut into the rock 35m above the town's rooftops,

By air

Indian Airlines fly daily to Mumbai via Chennai; their office at 7a W Veli St, near the post office (☎ 0452/741234/6), is efficient and helpful. To get to the airport, catch a taxi for around Rs200, or take city bus #10A from Periyar bus stand.

By bus

At the last count, five different stations operated long-distance buses from Madurai (see p.524); if you are still unsure which one you need, ask at the tourist office in the railway station and ignore the unscrupulous hustlers hanging around the STC bus stand.

From the New Bus Stand, numerous government buses leave day and night to Chennai (11hr). Destinations in Karnataka include Bangalore, for which there are nineteen TTC buses (first 6am, last 10.15pm) and two KSRTC (7.45am & 10.30pm). Night services also leave for Mysore (departs 4pm; 10hr). For Kerala there are three JJTC and two PRC buses a day to Ernakulam/Kochi (10hr), via Kottayam. This stand also serves northern destinations, such as Thanjavur, Tiruchirapalli and Kumbakonam, Rameshwaram (every 30min; 4hr), Kanniyakumari (every 30min; 6hr) and Thiruvananthapuram.

There are no direct services from Madurai to Ooty, but buses to Coimbatore (6hr) leave from the Arapalayam stand, 3km west of the centre, every 30min during the day. Kodaikanal (4hr) is equally well served with departures from here every 15min or so. You can also get buses to Kumily (for Periyar Wildlife Sanctuary; every 30min), and one a day to Palakaad (9hr).

By train

Madurai is on the main broad-gauge line and well connected to most major towns and cities in South India.

For reservations (Mon–Sat 8am–2pm & 2.15pm-8pm, Sun 8am–2pm), ask for a reservation form at the enquiry counter, then join the long queues in the forecourt at the station; the best time to book trains is in the evening or early morning. For timetable details, ask the Tourism Department information centre, to the right of the ticket counters.

It's possible to reach the railhead for Kodaikanal by train, but the journey is much faster by Express bus. For Thiruvananthapuram and Alleppey, head over to Coimbatore (see table below), and then catch the super fast New Delhi–Trivandrum Express #2626 (departs daily at 5.55am). For Ooty, catch any train to Coimbatore, where you should spend the night in order to pick the early morning Nilgiri Express to Mettupalayam, departure point for the Blue Mountain Railway (see p.559).

Recommended trains from Madurai

Destination	Name	No.	Departs	Total time
Bangalore	Madurai–Bangalore Express	#6731	8pm	12hr
Chennai	Vaigai Express	#2636	5.20am	9hr 40min
	Pandyan Express	#6718	7.35pm	11hr 15min
Coimbatore (Ooty)	Madurai–Coimbatore Fast Passenger	#778	2.30pm	5hr 20min
Kanyakumari	Madurai–Kanyakumari Express	#6721	12.30am	5hr 45min
Rameshwaram	Coimbatore–Rameshwaram Express	#6115	6am	4hr 50min
Trichy	Vaigai Express	#2636	5.20am	2hr 45min

comprises a series of huge terraces and halls, interconnected by stone staircases. At ground level, the main colonnaded *mandapa*, adorned with brightly painted horses and *yalis*, served as a field hospital for British soldiers in the 1760s, when the temple was badly vandalized (one local priest allegedly burned himself to death in protest at the British vandalism). Perhaps as a consequence of this, non-Hindus are not always allowed to visit the upper levels (if you're refused entry, ask at the temple office). It is definitely worth making the climb to see the ancient rock-carvings in, around and below the walls of the central shrine, where Murugan's vehicle (*vahana*) the peacock, features prominently; these are some of the best surviving examples of Pallava rock art in the South.

Crowning the windswept summit of the hill, amid gnarled old umbrella trees that cling to the bare rock, the **Dargah of Sikander Shah** is the region's holiest Muslim shrine. The ruler whose heroic death on this spot failed to save his capital from the Viyayanagar reconquest is today revered as a saint. His tomb complex – known as Skandermalai to Muslim pilgrims – made up of a domed mosque and covered colonnade dating from the fifteenth century, attracts pilgrims from across the country. Sikander's reputation for piety, however, doesn't square with the account of the Madurai Sultanate featured in the chronicles of Shams Siraj of Delhi, in which Sikander is accused of having succumbed to the decadence of neighbouring Madurai:

He began to perform acts of indecency in public . . . when he held court in the audience hall he wore women's ornaments on his wrists and ankles, and his neck and fingers were adorned with feminine decorations. His indecent acts with pederasts were performed openly . . . (and) the people of Ma'bar were utterly and completely weary and out of patience with him and his behaviour.

Given the paucity of other historical sources relating to this brief period of Muslim supremacy in South India, it is hard to know which version of the story – Sikander as valiant sage or as sybaritic sultan – is the more apocryphal. The **views** of Madurai and the surrounding plains from the tomb are unambiguously impressive.

Rameshwaram and around

The sacred island of **RAMESHWARAM**, 163km southeast of Madurai and less than 20km from Sri Lanka across the Gulf of Mannar is, along with Madurai, South India's most important pilgrimage site. Hindus tend to be followers of either Vishnu or Shiva, but Rameshwaram brings them together, being where the god Rama, an incarnation of Vishnu, worshipped Shiva in the *Ramayana*. The **Ramalingeshwara temple** complex, with its magnificent pillared walkways, is the most famous on the island, but there are several other small temples of interest, such as the **Gandhamadana Parvatam**, sheltering Rama's footprints, and the **Nambunayagi Amman Kali temple**, frequented for its curative properties. **Dhanushkodi**, "Rama's bow", at the eastern end of the peninsula, is where Rama is said to have bathe. The boulders that pepper the sea between here and Sri Lanka, known as "Adam's Bridge", are the stepping stones used by Hanuman in his search for Rama's wife, Sita, after her abduction by Ravana, the demon king of Lanka.

Rameshwaram is always crowded with day-trippers, and ragged mendicants who camp outside the Ramalingeshwara and the **Ujainimahamariamman**, the small goddess shore temple. An important part of their pilgrimage is to

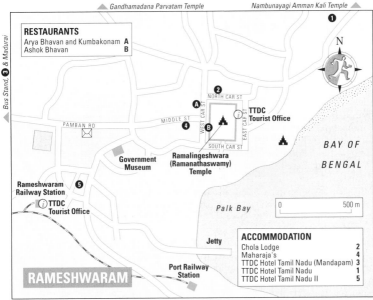

bathe in the main temple's sacred tanks and in the sea; the narrow strip of beach is shared by groups of bathers, relaxing cows and mantra-reciting *swamis* sitting next to sand *linga*. As well as fishing – prawns and lobsters for packaging and export to Japan – the coastal villages make a lot of money selling shells to pilgrims- a symbol that they have been to Rameshwaram and worshipped Vishnu (he is always portrayed as holding a conch).

The heavy military presence along the approach roads to Rameshwaram warns you of the proximity of the **war in Sri Lanka**, a short boat ride east across the Palk Strait. As the crow flies, Jaffna, the epicentre of the protracted and bloody conflict between the Tamil Tigers and the Sri Lankan army, is actually a lot closer to Rameshwaram than Madurai. The strait between India and Sri Lanka has long served as a key supply line for the separatists – a trade covertly tolerated by the state's pro-Tamil DMK government. However, after the Tigers assassinated Rajiv Gandhi in 1991 for supporting the Sri Lankan government, it looked temporarily as if the war might spread to the mainland (the coast around Rameshwaram supports a huge population of Tamil refugees), and the Indian army was drafted in to keep the peace. More recently, **caste conflicts** in the town of **Ramanathapuram** (Ramnad), opposite Rameshwaram, have claimed many lives; locals live their lives around 24hr curfews and frequent outbreaks of rioting. If you do plan to make a trip here, it is important to check the current political situation first in the newspapers; if there is a fresh outburst of fighting in Sri Lanka, avoid this area altogether. Once you've crossed the bridge over the Pamban Channel, the oppressive atmosphere of the mainland gives way to Rameshwaram's infectious devotional intensity.

Arrival and information

The NH-49, the main road from Madurai, connects Rameshwaram with Mandapam on the mainland via the impressive two-kilometre-long Indira

Gandhi bridge, originally built by the British in 1914 as a rail link, and reopened in 1988 by Rajiv Gandhi for road traffic. Armed guards at checkposts at either end keep a watchful eye on travellers. **Buses** from Madurai (via Ramnad), Trichy, Thanjavur, Kanniyakumari and Chennai pull in at the bus stand, 2km west of the centre. The **railway station**, 1km southwest of the centre, is the end of the line for trains from Chennai, Coimbatore, Thanjavur, Madurai and Ramnad, and boasts decent **retiring rooms**, a veg restaurant and a left-luggage office (5.30am–10pm). There are two daily express trains to and from Chennai, and one (the *Rameshwaram–Coimbatore Express* #6116) for Coimbatore, via Madurai. Buses run half-hourly to Madurai (4hr) and four times daily to Kunniyakumari (9–10hr). Travel agents around the temple run faster and more comfortable **minibuses** around South India.

Red-and-white city buses run every ten minutes from the bus stand to the main temple; otherwise, **local transport** consists of unmetered cycle- and auto-rickshaws that gather outside the bus stand. Jeeps are available for rent near the train station, and bicycles can be rented from shops in the four Car streets around the temple. There is no **ferry service** to and from Sri Lanka, due to the troubles there.

The tiny TTDC **tourist office**, 14 East Car St (Mon–Fri 10am–5pm; ☎ 04573/21371), gives out information about guides, accommodation and boat trips. TTDC also have a counter at the railway station (☎ 04573/21373), which opens to coincide with the arrival of trains, and a small booth at the bus stand (daily except holidays 10am–5.45pm). The **post office** is on Pamban Road.

Accommodation

Apart from the TTDC hotels, **accommodation** in Rameshwaram is restricted to basic lodges, mostly in the Car streets around the temple. The temple authorities have a range of rooms for pilgrims; ask at the Devasthanam Office, East Car Street (☎ 04573/21292). Six large double and three triple rooms comprise the **railway retiring rooms** (Rs100), which are generally cleaner (and quieter) than town lodges for the same price, plus there's a dorm (Rs40).

Chola Lodge, N Car Street ☎ 04573/21307. A basic pilgrim place in the quietest of the Car streets. ❷

Maharaja's, 7 Middle St ☎ 04573/21271. Located next to the temple's west gate. Good clean rooms with attached bathrooms, two with a/c and TV; there are temple views from balconies. There's no restaurant here, although management will bring restaurant food in. ❸–❺

TTDC Hotel Tamil Nadu, near the beach ☎ 04573/21064. The best place in Rameshwaram,

in a pleasant location and with a bar and restaurant. They offer comfortable, sea-facing rooms, some a/c, along with a cheap dorm (Rs40). However, it's often full, so book in advance from another TTDC hotel or office in the state. ❷–❺

TTDC Hotel Tamil Nadu II, near the train station on Railway Feeder Road ☎ 04573/20171. New hotel, far cheaper than the other TTDC outfit, but in a far less attractive location. The rooms are decidedly grubby and non-a/c but they all have attached bathrooms. ❷

Ramalingeshwara temple

The core of the **Ramalingeshwara** (or Ramanathaswamy) **temple** was built by the Cholas in the twelfth century to house two much venerated **shivalinga** associated with the *Ramayana*. After rescuing his wife Sita from the clutches of the demon Ravana, Rama was advised to atone for the killing of the demon king – a brahmin – by worshipping Shiva. Rama's monkey lieutenant, Hanuman, was despatched to the Himalayas to fetch a *shivalingam*, but when he failed to return by the appointed day, Sita fashioned a *lingam* from sand (the *Ramanathalingam*) so the ceremony could proceed. Hanuman eventually showed up with his *lingam* and in order to assuage the monkey's guilt Rama decreed that in future, of the two, Hanuman's should be worshipped first. Both the *linga* are now housed in the inner section of the Ramalingeshwara, which is not open to non-Hindus. Much of what can be visited by non-Hindu's dates from the 1600s, when the temple received generous endowments from the Sethupathi rajas of Ramanathapuram (see p.540).

High walls enclose the temple, forming a rectangle with huge pyramidal *gopura* entrances on each side. The gateways lead to a spacious closed ambulatory, flanked to either side by continuous platforms with massive pillars set on their edges. These **corridors** are the most famous attribute of the temple, their extreme length – 205m, with 1212 pillars on the north and south sides – giving a remarkable impression of receding perspective. Delicate scrollwork and brackets of pendant lotuses supported by *yalis*, mythical lion-like beasts, adorn the pillars.

Before entering the inner sections, pilgrims are expected take a ritual bathe in water from each of the 22 **tirthas** (tanks) in the temple. The groups of dripping-wet pilgrims, most of them fully clothed, make their way from one tank to the next to be doused in a bucket of water by a temple attendant. Each tank is said to have special benefits: the Rama Vimosana Tirtha provides relief from debt, the Sukreeva Tirtha gives "complete wisdom" and the attainment of *Surya Loka*, the realm of the Sun, and the Draupadi Tirtha ensures long life for women and "the love of their spouses".

Monday is Rama's auspicious day, when the Padilingam puja takes place. **Festivals** of particular importance at the temple include **Mahashivaratri** (10 days during Feb/March), **Brahmotsavam** (10 days during March/April) and **Thirukalyanam** (July/Aug), celebrating the marriage of Shiva to Parvati.

Minor temples

The **Gandhamadana Parvatam** (daily 6–11am & 3.30–6.30pm), on a hill 2km north of Rameshwaram town centre, is a venerable shrine housing Rama's footprints. On some days, ceremonies are conducted here after the 5.30am puja at the Ramalingeshwara temple, encouraging pilgrims to climb the hill to continue their devotions. From the roof, fine views extend over the surrounding country and on clear nights you can see the lights of Jaffna.

Three kilometres east of town towards the old fishing village of Dhanushkodi, the small **Nambunayagi Amman Kali temple**, set in a quiet sandy grove 200m off the main road, attracts people in search of cures for illnesses. Inside a banyan tree next to it is a shrine dedicated to the spirit Retatalai, "the two-headed". A pair of wooden sandals with spikes, said to belong to the spirit, is left in the shrine and locals say they can hear them clip-clopping at night when Retatalai chooses to wander. Pieces of cloth are tied to the branches of the tree to mark thanks for such boons as pregnancy after barrenness and the healing of family feuds. The bus terminates at Dhanushkodi, from where you can walk along the ever-narrowing spit of sand until the sea finally closes in and the island peters out, tantalizingly short of Sri Lanka.

Eating

Eating in Rameshwaram is more about survival than delighting the taste buds; most places serve up fairly unexciting "meals". *Arya Bhavan* and Kumbakonam on W Car Street are both run by the same family and dish up standard veg "meals", while *Ashok Bhavan*, also on W Car Street, offers regional varieties of thalis and South Indian "meals". Near the beach, *TTDC Hotel Tamil Nadu* is a gigantic, noisy, high-ceiling glasshouse near the sea, serving good South Indian snacks and "meals"; many items on the menu turn out to be unavailable, however.

Around Rameshwaram

RAMANATHAPURAM (aka Ramnad) offers a possible break on the bus or train between Madurai (120km northwest) and Rameshwaram (36km east). It's worth stopping here to see the neglected but atmospheric **Ramalinga Vilas**, palace of the Sethupati rajas, who by tradition were guardians of the mythical Sethu bridge built by Rama to cross to Lanka. **Caste conflicts** in the winter of 1998, however, during which riots resulted in the deaths of more than a dozen people and closed the bazaar for weeks amid extended curfews, meant this town was off-limits to tourists; check in the newspapers or ask at a tourist office beforehand to ensure it's not in the midst of another flare-up.

The entrance to the **palace** (daily except Fri 9am–1pm & 2–5pm; Rs2), 2km from the bus stand, takes you into the big and dusty **Durbar Hall**, whose central aisle is hung with oil portraits of the rajas of the last few hundred years. Ceilings and walls throughout the building are decorated with early eighteenth-century murals depicting subjects such as business meetings with the English and battles with the Maratha king Sarabhoji, as well as scenes from the epics. One battle scene shows soldiers fighting with boomerangs, and there's a real Indian boomerang on display. Also on show are palm-leaf manuscripts, a Ravi Varma painting (see p.333) with appliquéd brocade and sculptures of Vishnu from the eighth and thirteenth centuries. From the **throne room**, a secret passageway once gave an escape route to a local temple. The raja's throne, supported on carved elephant legs, is decorated with a coat of arms, given by the British, featuring a lion and unicorn. As further proof of the royal family's compliance with the foreign power, the raja, at the end of the eighteenth century, allowed them to use the bedchambers upstairs – decorated with erotic murals – as a meeting hall. This cosy relationship did not find unanimous approval among his subjects. Influential local landowners showed their contempt for the British by responding to tax demands with bags of stones and, in 1798 and 1801, rebellions took place, sometimes dubbed the "South Indian War of Independence". In 1803, at the request of the British, the Ramnad raja was obliged to accept the lesser rank of *zamindar* (feudatory chieftain).

On the roof is a stone bed on which the raja would lounge in the evenings to enjoy panoramic views of the town and surrounding country. The buildings immediately below were royal guesthouses, in one of which a descendant of the rajas now resides.

Tirunelveli and around

Separated by the only perennial river in the far south, the Tambraparni, **TIRUNELVELI** and its modern counterpart, **PALAYANKOTTAI**, together form the largest conurbation in the densely populated red-soil region south of Madurai. Aside from the huge **Nellaiyappa temple**, built by the Pandyas in the thirteenth century with a towering pyramidal *gopura*, situated 2km west of the river, neither holds much of specific interest. However, you may want to use Tirunelveli as a base for day-trips to nearby **Thiruppudaimarudur**, 25km west, whose old riverside temple is famed for its wood-carvings, or further west to **Kuttalam**, in the foothills of the Ghats, where a series of dramatic waterfalls attract streams of day-trippers. An hour or so east on the Coromandel

Coast, the traditional Tamil pilgrimage town of **Tiruchendur** has the region's most spectacular shore temple, dominating an appropriately impressive sweep of surf-lashed beach. The sea between the Coromandel and Sri Lanka is rich enough to support a string of fishing settlements, but the most lucrative harvest yielded by the Gulf of Mannar are the pearls gathered by divers from the port of **Tuticorin**, an hour north of Tiruchendur. The Portuguese founded one of their first colonies in India here.

Tirunelveli's **bus stand**, in the town centre just across the river from Palayankottai, has services to and from Madurai (3hr), Nagercoil (1hr 30min), Tuticorin (1hr), Tiruchendur (1hr) and Kollam (5hr). For Kuttalam, you have to head to Tenkasi (1hr) and change onto a local bus. **Trains** from Chennai, Madurai, Nagercoil and Kollam pull in at the main-line station, five minutes' walk west on the opposite side of Madurai Road.

Most of the **accommodation** in town is lined up outside the bus stand, on Madurai Road. Pick of the bunch is the *Sri Jankiran* (℡0462/331941; ❺), which has some a/c rooms, a cosy **restaurant** and roof terrace. Next door, the *Barani* (℡0462/333234; ❸–❹) is marginally cheaper, but dependably clean, as is the *Aryaas* (℡0462/339001; ❸), a short walk further down the road.

Thiruppudaimarudur

THIRUPPUDAIMARUDUR, a small riverside village 25km west of Tirunelveli, is the site of a temple renowned throughout the region for its splendid medieval wood-carvings and murals. The best preserved of these murals line the interior of the temple's east tower, which you can scale via flights of precariously steep wooden steps. Pillars and brackets propping up a succession of ceilings have been sumptuously decorated, while the walls (which you'll need a flashlight to see clearly) are covered with vibrant paintings, depicting scenes from the *Ramayana*, Vishnu's various incarnations and mythical battles.

Buses to Thiruppudaimarudur leave more or less hourly from Tirunelveli, and take fifty minutes. The village doesn't have any hotels or guesthouses.

Kuttalam (Courtalam)

An image familiar to collectors of exotic prints and engravings in Victorian Britain was that of the great waterfalls at **KUTTALAM** (**Courtalam**), 136km northwest of Kanniyakumari, where the Chittar River plunges down a sheer cliff on the very edge of the Western Ghats. A couple of centuries ago, when the famous Raj-era artist, Thomas Daniells, came to sketch the falls, this was still a remote spot, overgrown with vegetation and frequented only by wandering *sadhus* and the odd party of sickly Brits. A hydro project upstream has somewhat diminished the falls' splendour, and the barrage of film music and hoardings in the modern concrete village that has sprung up at their feet does little to enhance the overall atmosphere, but it is still worth coming here for an invigorating bathe. Bussing in from all over the state, thousands of Tamils do just that each day, especially at weekends and between July and late September, when water levels are at their highest. From late January until May, the falls can dry up completely.

In all, nine major cascades are dotted around Kuttalam, but only one, known for obvious reasons as **Main Falls**, is located in the village proper. This is where the largest crowds congregate – the "ladies" to the left, fully dressed in soaking saris; old folk and kids to the right; and men, in regulation voluminous underpants, taking the full force of the central flow. It's worth pointing out that few foreigners come to Kuttalam, so expect to create a bit of a stir if you strip off; for a little more privacy, try jumping onto one of the minibuses that run throughout the day to smaller waterfalls around Kuttalam.

To reach Kuttalam by bus, you first have to head for **Tenkasi**, which is well connected to Tirunelveli (2hr) and Madurai (3hr), from where local buses run the final twenty minutes to the falls. The only **accommodation** and **restaurant** to speak of when you get here is *TTDC Hotel Tamil Nadu I,* opposite Parasakthi Women's college (℡04633/22423; ●), with overpriced and uniformly shabby double rooms, some with a/c. *TTDC Hotel Tamil Nadu II,* is next door (℡04633/22663; ●), and has the same range of rather dilapidated a/c and non-a/c rooms but at a slightly cheaper rate. Both offer good off-season discounts.

Tuticorin

TUTICORIN, 51km east of Tirunelveli on the NH-7 or 130km northeast of Kanniyakumari, developed as a flourishing Portuguese colony in the sixteenth century and later expanded under the Dutch and British. Eclipsed by Madras in the late 1700s, it is nowadays the state's second port and would be an entirely forgettable, gritty Tamil town were it not for the prodigious quantities of **pearl**-bearing saltwater molluscs, *Pinctada martensi,* that grow in the shark-infested shallows offshore. These are harvested for one month each year (normally in March–April) by divers equipped with little more than antiquated face masks. The pearls they collect are said to rank among the finest in the world, on a par with those found in the Persian Gulf, which is presumably why you won't easily find any for sale in the bazaar; all but a tiny proportion are exported.

Tuticorin is largely industrial and not a particularly appealing place to stay, but if you find yourself in need of a hotel, head for VE Road, a short rickshaw ride from the centre of town. The business traveller-orientated *Jony International* (℡0461/328350; ●) has decent rooms with a/c and cable TV; nearby, the *Sugam* (℡0461/328172; ●) is a clean and dependable budget option.

Tiruchendur

TIRUCHENDUR means "beautiful holy town" in Tamil, and for once the epithet fits, thanks to the awesome presence on its shoreline of the mighty **Subramanya temple**. The shrine – one of the six sacred abodes of the Tamils' favourite god, **Lord Murugan** (Shiva's son, Subramanya), here in the form of the Ascetic ("renouncer of the transitory and illusory") – presides over a spectacular sandy beach, with breakers crashing in off the Gulf of Mannar. Corrosive salt winds have taken their toll on the original building erected by the Pallavas in the ninth century, and large sections of what you see today are modern, dating from 1941. However, references to the deity inside occur in some of the Tamils' oldest scriptures, while archeological digs conducted in the 1890s on the banks of the Tambraparni River nearby yielded evidence of a three-thousand-year-old religious cult focused on a spear-wielding deity very similar to Murugan. More extraordinary still were the prehistoric mouth locks that came to light at the same time, identical to those worn by more fervent devotees at Murugan festivals in Tamil Nadu today.

The Subramanya temple is approached via a long colonnaded walkway, running 700m through a packed sacred precinct lined with shops selling puja paraphernalia and pilgrims' souvenirs. Non-Hindus are permitted to enter the central shrine on payment of a small donation. The deity inside is among the

During the month of *Thai* (February) in the Tamil calendar, the usual intensity of the devotional activities among the thousands of Shaivite pilgrims trailing around Tamil Nadu, reaches a fanatical peak on the occasion of Thaipusam. Thaipusam is the full moon festival in honour of Lord Murugan (aka Lord Subramaniam), son of Shiva and Parvati, who represents the triumph of good over evil. Thaipusam recalls the day that Parvati gave Murugan the *vel*, a magical weapon that destroys all wickedness, sins and banishes negativity from the soul.

The archaic rituals seen today are rooted in myth and legend. The most popular version is that there was a devotee, Idumban, who, on the night of the full moon in the month of *Thai*, was instructed in a dream to go to Shivagiri hill to worship Lord Murugan. Idumbam dutifully set off, taking with him two pots of milk as an offering, and along the way he sang devotional hymns.

Today, the practice continues as Shaivite pilgrims from all over India congregate to venerate Lord Murugan; there are temples dedicated to Murugan throughout Tamil Nadu, and a few in Kerala. Each pilgrim has to take an offering, called a kavadi, meaning "sacrifice at each step", to remind them of their previous sin and their personal vow to Lord Murugan. In accordance with the tradition set by Idumbam, most devotees carry a milk *kavadi* (a pot filled with milk), which is covered in fruit and flowers and carried on the head in a long and winding procession. The pilgrims sing hymns as they wander from temple to temple to do puja to Murugan.

A *kavadi*, however, can also be a huge metal or wooden structure. These *kavadis* are strung with razor-sharp hooks and lavishly decorated with flowers, bells and peacock feathers. In an extreme act of personal penance and homage to Murugan, a devotee may volunteer to be hooked up to one of these frames. Before they can be pierced, the volunteer has to undergo a whole month of inner cleansing, with a strict vegetarian diet, celibacy and spiritual nourishment to give them strength. On the day of *Thaipusam*, with the help of the frantic drumming and the chanting by the crowds, the devotee enters a deep trance to make the pain disappear, then spears and hooks are pushed through the flesh. Alternatively, a devotee may pull a wagon or chariot by a set of hooks pierced in the skin of their back.

The tradition of bringing milk *kavadis* remains very popular in Tamil Nadu – it is not uncommon for up to 20,000 people to gather at a shrine to offer their *kavadi* on Thaipusam. The most famous Mururgan temples are at Palani (see p.553) and Tiruchendur (see opposite); ask at a TTDC tourist office to find out exact places and dates (which change each year). The act of piercing, however, is now officially prohibited in India, although the practice may still be witnessed on extremely rare occasions in the very rural areas. Piercing continues unabated in those countries, such as Thailand, Singapore and Malaysia, where there are significant populations of Tamil Hindus.

---

most revered in South India, attracting crowds of more than a million during the temple's annual festival, just before the monsoon, when 108 different herbs and auspicious preparations are offered to the god, symbolizing the renewal of the earth. The ritual is accompanied by the chanting of some of the oldest Sanskrit verses surviving in India. In his 1995 travelogue *The Smile of Murugan*, the British historian Michael Wood speculates that these may even predate human speech; scholars have shown their nearest analogue is birdsong, lending credence to the theory that ritual came before verbal language in human evolution.

Tiruchendur is well connected by bus to Tirunelveli (1hr), Madurai's Palankanathan bus stand (4hr), Tuticorin (40min) and Nagercoil (2hr), and there are four daily trains to and from Tirunelveli. Aside from a handful of spartan pilgrims' hostels in the sacred precinct, the only **accommodation** in the town is the *TTDC Hotel Tamil Nadu* (⊤04638/44268; ❸–❺), a typically lacklustre and shabby government-run place with a/c and non-a/c options. The inexpensive **restaurant** here serves veg and non-veg food.

Kanniyakumari and around

KANNIYAKUMARI, at the southernmost extremity of India, is almost as compelling for Hindus as Rameshwaram. It is significant not only for its association with a virgin goddess, Kanya Devi, but also as the meeting point of the Bay of Bengal, Indian Ocean and Arabian Sea. Watching the sun rising and setting is the big attraction, especially on full moon day in April, when it's possible to see both the setting sun and rising moon on the same horizon. Although Kanniyakumari is in the state of Tamil Nadu, most foreign visitors arrive on daytrips from Thiruvananthapuram (Trivandrum), the capital of Kerala, 86km northwest. While the place is of enduring appeal to pilgrims, other visitors may find it bereft of atmosphere, with nature's power to engender wonder in the human spirit obliterated by ugly buildings and hawkers selling shells and trinkets.

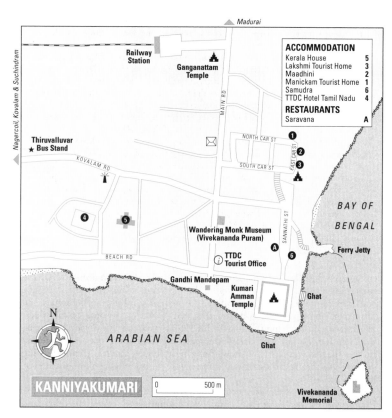

Arrival and local transport

Trains from Thiruvananthapuram, Mumbai, Bangalore – and even Jammu, at 86hr the longest rail journey in India – stop at the **railway station** in the north of town, 2km from the seafront. **From Madurai**, the best train service is the #6721 *Tuticorin Express*, which leaves Madurai Junction at 12.30am, and arrives at 6.15am the following morning, just in time for sunrise. You can leave **luggage** in the generator room behind the ticket office for Rs7 each item/24hr.

The new and well organized **Express bus stand** in the west of town is served by regular buses from Thiruvananthapuram (hourly; 2hr), Kovalam (12 daily; 1hr 30min–2hr), Madurai (13 daily; 6hr), Rameshwaram (4 daily; 9–10hr; change at Madurai during the rainy season in Nov & Dec) and Chennai (11 daily; 14–16hr). Auto-rickshaws and taxis provide **local transport**.

Accommodation

As Kanniyakumari is a "must see" for Indian tourists and pilgrims, **hotels** tend to fill up by noon. However, recent hotel developments have raised standards, and relieved the pressure on space.

Kerala House, seafront ☎04652/71257. A large colonial-era building, converted to a rest house for Keralan civil servants, whose cavernous doubles (two of them are a/c) have dressing cases and bathrooms; some rooms have sea views. Book in advance through the Political Department of the State Secretariat in Thiruvananthapuram. ❸–❹

Lakshmi Tourist Home, E Car Street ☎04652/71333. All rooms are clean and smart, some with a/c and views out to sea. There's an excellent non-veg restaurant. ❹–❺

Maadhini, E Car Street ☎04652/71787, ✆716570. Large, newly built hotel right on the seafront above the fishing village. It has fine sea views, comfortably furnished rooms and one of the best restaurants in town. ❸–❺

Manickam Tourist Home, N Car Street ☎04652/71387. Spacious and modern rooms, some with a/c and sea views. Faces the sunrise and the Vivekananda rock. Good value. ❸–❺

Samudra, Sannathi Street ☎04652/71162. Smart new hotel near the temple entrance, with well furnished deluxe rooms facing the sunrise. Facilities include satellite TV and a veg restaurant. ❹–❺

TTDC Hotel Tamil Nadu, seafront ☎04652/46257. Cottages (some are a/c) and clean rooms (a/c on the first floor), most with a sea view. There are cheaper and very basic "mini" doubles at the back and a youth hostel dorm (Rs50). Good square meals are served in functional surroundings. ❷–❼

The Town

The seashore **Kumari Amman temple** (daily 4.30–11.30am & 5.30–8.30pm) is dedicated to the virgin goddess **Kanya Devi**, who may originally have been the local guardian deity of the shoreline, but was later absorbed into the figure of Devi, or Parvati, consort of Shiva. One version of Kanya Devi's story relates how she did penance to win the hand of Shiva. The god was all in favour and set out from Suchindram for the wedding, due to take place at midnight. The celestial *devas*, however, wanted Kanya Devi to remain a virgin, so that she could retain her full quota of *shakti*, or divine power, and hatched a plot. Narada the sage assumed the form of a cock and crowed; on hearing this, Shiva, thinking that it was dawn and that he had missed the auspicious time for the ceremony, went home. The image of Kanya Devi inside the temple wears a diamond nose stud of such brilliance that it's said to be visible from the sea. Male visitors must be shirtless and wear a *dhoti* before entering the temple; non-Hindus are not allowed in the inner sanctum. It is especially auspicious for pilgrims to wash at the bathing *ghat* here.

Resembling a prewar British cinema, the **Gandhi Mandapam** (daily 6.30am–12.30pm & 3–7.30pm), 300m northwest of the Kumari Amman temple, was actually conceived as a modern imitation of an Orissan temple. It was designed so that the sun strikes the auspicious spot where the ashes of

545

Mahatma Gandhi were laid (prior to their immersion in the sea) at noon on his birthday, October 2.

Possibly the original sacred focus of Kanniyakumari are two rocks, about 60m apart, half-submerged in the sea 500m off the coast, which came to be known as the Pitru and Matru *tirthas*. In 1892 they attracted the attention of the Hindu reformer Vivekananda (1862–1902) and he swam out to the rocks to meditate on the syncretistic teachings of his recently dead guru, Ramakrishna Paramahamsa. Incorporating elements of architecture from around the country, the 1970 **Vivekananda Memorial** (daily except Tues 7–11am & 2–5pm), reached by the Poompuhar ferry service from the jetty on the east side of town (every 30min; same hours), houses a statue of the saint. The footprints of Kanya Devi can also be seen here, at the spot where she performed her penance.

For more on the life and teachings of Vivekananda, visit the **Wandering Monk museum (Vivekananda Puram)**, just north of the tourist office at the bottom of town (daily 8am–noon & 4–8pm; free). A sequence of 41 panels (in English, Tamil and Hindi) recounts the *swami's* odyssey around the subcontinent at the end of the nineteenth century. Born in Calcutta, Vivekananda received a Western education, which he subsequently rejected – largely as a result of a "defiling encounter" with the West during a visit to the Parliament of Religions in Chicago. Based on the Vedic scriptures (in spite of the fact Vivekananda never mastered Sanskrit), he countered the traditional Hindu dogma that the universe is a delusion beyond the sole reality of Brahma. He suggested a proactive ethos based on social work and reform – a kind of early Indian *engagement* without Jean-Paul Sartre's baggy suits and strong coffee.

Eating

Aside from the usual "meals" places and hotel dining rooms, there are a few popular veg and non-veg **restaurants** in the centre of town, most attached to one or other of the hotels. *Archana* in the *Maadhini Hotel* on E Car Street has an extensive veg and non-veg multicuisine menu, served inside a well ventilated dining hall, or alfresco on a sea-facing terrace (evenings only). They also serve the town's best selection of ice cream. On Sannathi Street, *Saravana* is arguably Kanniyakumari's best "meals" restaurant, dishing up all the usual snacks, cold drinks and huge Tamil thalis at lunch time to hoards of hungry pilgrims. Their coffee is good too.

Around Kanniyakumari

Construction of the **Stanunathaswami temple** at **SUCHINDRAM**, 12km northwest of Kanniyakumari, extended over a period of at least six hundred years. Parts date back as far as the ninth or tenth century, others are from the fifteenth, and a huge seven-storey pyramidal *gopura* was erected during the sixteenth. Its oldest and most remarkable feature, however, is a series of beautifully preserved **epigraphs** carved on a huge boulder in the main *mandapa*. Some are in the ancient Pali language, dating from the third century BC when this was the most southerly outpost of the Mauryan empire. Later inscriptions in classical Tamil are the first known references to the three traditional dynasties of the South, the Cholas, the Pandyas and the Pallavas. Although its main sanctuary houses a *shivalingam*, the temple is jointly dedicated to Brahma, Vishnu and Shiva. Its proudest boasts, aside from the epigraphs and some remarkably extravagant stone sculpture, are **musical pillars**, which emit a chime when struck, and an extraordinary three-metre-high figure of Hanuman. A special puja takes place at sunset (around 6pm) every Friday, with music and a procession. The temple is open to non-Hindus and all castes, although male visitors must remove their shirts before entering.

As you head along the NH-47 towards Kerala, the spectacular crags of the Travancore Hills encroach upon the flats of iridescent rice paddy lining the coastal strip, completely dominating the landscape to Thiruvananthapuram. The most prominent peak in the area is the pyramidal **Maruntha Malai** (aka "Maruval Malai"), 13km from Kanniyakumari, renowned among Tamils as "Medicine Mountain". During the monsoon, its steep green slopes sprout a profusion of medicinal herbs. Local healers must have been aware of this fact for thousands of years because the hill crops up time and again in Hindu mythology, most famously in the *Ramayana*. According to the epic, Hanuman had been dispatched to Mount Kailash in the Himalayas to look for herbs for Rama, who had been wounded by a poisoned arrow during the battle with the evil demon Ravana's army in Lanka. Instead of picking the plants, however, Hanuman had ripped up the whole mountain to keep them fresh. On his way back to Rama, Hanuman dropped a piece of Mount Kailash at this spot on his way. Today, the Maruntha Malai remains an important source of curative herbs, used in the preparation of Ayurvedic medicines. It's also home to a scattering of *sadhus* who, when they aren't away wandering, live in a string of caves that dot the pilgrim path to the *shivalingam* crowning the summit. Taking around six hours, the **hike** to it is especially popular with pilgrims who have walked to Kanniyakumari in fulfilment of a vow. It should not be attempted without a guide as the route is hard to follow; the best place to find a guide is in the village of **Pothayadi**, near the trailhead.

The Southern Ghats

Sixty or more million years ago, what we know today as peninsular India was a separate land mass drifting northeast across the ocean towards central Asia. Current geological thinking has it that this mass must originally have broken off the African continent along a fault line that is today discernible as a north–south ridge of volcanic mountains, stretching 1400km down the west coast of India, known as the **Southern Ghats**. The range rises to a height of around 2500m, making it India's second highest mountain chain after the Himalayas.

Forming a natural barrier between the Tamil plains and coastal Kerala and Karnataka, the Ghats (literally "steps") soak up the bulk of the southwest monsoon, which drains east to the Bay of Bengal via the mighty Kaveri and Krishna river systems. The massive amount of rain that falls here between June and October (around 2.5m) allows for an incredible **biodiversity**. Nearly one third of all India's flowering plants can be found in the dense evergreen and mixed deciduous forests cloaking the Ghats. The woodland undergrowth supports the subcontinent's richest array of wildlife, from jungle civets, muntjac and the rare tahr antelope, to gaur (Indian bison), herds of wild Asian elephant and tigers.

It was this abundance of game, and the cooler temperatures of the range's high valleys and grasslands, that first attracted the sun-sick British, who were quick to see the economic potential of the temperate climate, fecund soil and plentiful rainfall. As the forests were felled to make way for tea plantations, and the region's many tribal groups – among them the Todas – were forced deeper into the mountains, permanent **hill stations** were established. Today, as in the days of the Raj, these continue to provide welcome escapes from the fierce summer heat for the fortunate middle-class Tamils, and foreign tourists, who can afford the break.

Much the best known of the hill resorts – in fact better known, and more visited, than it deserves – is **Udhagamandalam** (formerly Ootacamund, still often "Ooty"), in the **Nilgiris** (from *nila-giri*, "blue mountains"– named after the profusion of blue gum trees). The ride up to Ooty, on the **miniature railway** via Coonoor, is fun, and the views breathtaking but, in general, unless you have the means to stay in the best hotels here, the grey and concrete centre of the town itself comes as a rude shock. The other main hill station, founded by American missionaries, is leafy and quiet **Kodaikanal**, further south near Madurai.

Accessed via the hill stations, the forest areas lining the state border harbour Tamil Nadu's principal wildlife sanctuaries, **Annamalai** and **Mudumalai**, which, along with Wayanad in Kerala, and Nagarhole and Bandipur in Karnataka, form the vast **Nilgiri Biosphere Reserve**, the country's most extensive tract of protected forest. Road building, illegal felling, hydroelectric projects and overgrazing have gradually whittled away at this huge wilderness area over the past two decades. In recent years a more pressing threat has arisen in the form of the infamous sandalwood smuggler, **Veerapan** (see p.570), whose kidnappings of a Tamil film star, forest wardens and government officials have led to the parks being indefinitely closed to the public. However, as the main route between Mysore and the cities of the Tamil plains wriggles through the Nilgiris, you may well find yourself pausing for a night or two along the way, if only to enjoy the cold air and serene landscape of the tea terraces. Whichever direction you're travelling in, a brief stopover at the dull and congested textile-producing city of **Coimbatore** is hard to avoid.

The **best time to visit** the Ghats is between late November and early March. At other times, either the weather is too cloudy and wet, or the hill stations are swarming with hoards of summer tourists. Winter is also the optimum period for **trekking** in the Nilgiris, which allows you to visit some of the region's most unspoilt forest areas, the traditional homeland of the Todas.

Kodaikanal

Perched on top of the Palani range, around 120km northwest of Madurai, **KODAIKANAL**, also known as **Kodai**, owes its perennial popularity to the hilltop position of the town, which, at an altitude of over 2000m, affords breathtaking views over the blue-green reaches of the Vagai plain. Raj-era houses and flower-filled gardens add atmosphere, while short walks out of the centre lead to rocky outcrops, waterfalls and dense *shola* forest. With the wildlife sanctuaries and forest areas of the Ghats now officially closed to visitors, Kodai's outstandingly scenic hinterland also offers South India's best **trekking** terrain. Even if you're not tempted by the prospect of the open trail and cool air, the jaw-dropping **bus ride** up here from the plains makes the detour into this easternnmost spur of the Ghats an essential one.

Kodaikanal's history, with an absence of wars, battles for leadership and princely dominion, is uneventful, and the only monuments to its past are the neat British bungalows that overlook the lake and Law's Ghat Road on the eastern edge of town. The British first moved here in 1845, to be joined later by members of the American Mission who set up schools for European children. One remains as Kodai International School; despite the name, it has an almost exclusively Indian student population. The school lays a strong emphasis on music, particularly guitar playing, and occasionally holds workshops, as well as concerts on the green just east of the lake.

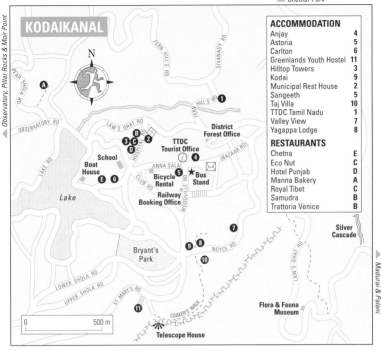

KODAIKANAL

N

◄ Observatory, Pillar Rocks & Moir Point

FERN HILL'S RD

SIVANADY RD

BEAR SHOLA RD

OBSERVATORY RD

LAKE RD

LAW'S GHAT RD

HOSPITAL RD

FERN HILL'S RD

District
Forest Office

TTDC
Tourist Office

School
Boat
House

ANNA SALAI

(BAZAAR RD)

CLUB RD

Bicycle
Rental

Bus
Stand

Railway
Booking Office

WOODVILLE RD

Lake

Bryant's
Park

NOYCE RD

LOWER SHOLA RD

UPPER SHOLA RD

ST MARY'S RD

COAKER'S WALK

Telescope House

Silver
Cascade

LAW'S GHAT RD

Flora & Fauna
Museum

▶ Madurai & Palani

0   500 m

ACCOMMODATION	
Anjay	4
Astoria	5
Carlton	6
Greenlands Youth Hostel	11
Hilltop Towers	3
Kodai	9
Municipal Rest House	2
Sangeeth	5
Taj Villa	10
TTDC Tamil Nadu	1
Valley View	7
Yagappa Lodge	8

RESTAURANTS	
Chetna	E
Eco Nut	C
Hotel Punjab	D
Manna Bakery	A
Royal Tibet	C
Samudra	B
Trattoria Venice	B

6

TAMIL NADU | The Southern Ghats

After a while in the plains of South India, a retreat to Kodai's cool heights is more than welcome. However, in the height of summer (June–Aug), when temperatures compete with those in the lowlands, it's not worth the trip – nor is it a good idea to come during the monsoon (Oct–Dec), when the town is shrouded in mists and drenched by heavy downpours. In late February and early March the nights are chilly; the busiest tourist season therefore, is from April to June, when prices soar.

Arrival, information and getting around

The **buses** from Madurai and Dindigul that climb the spectacular road up the steep hillside to Kodai from the plains below pull in at the stand in the centre of town. Unless you're coming from as far as Chennai or Tiruchirapalli, buses are much more convenient than trains: the nearest **railhead**, Kodaikanal Road – also connected to Dindigul (30min) and Madurai (50min) – is three hours away by bus. Note, too, that **the road from Palani** is by far the most spectacular approach, although the least travelled (except during the monsoons when the other is invariably blocked). If you plan to spend a few days in Kodai, it's worth visiting Palani, an atmospheric destination in itself (see p.553), as a day-trip and just to travel this route.

Tickets for onward rail journeys from Kodaikanal Road can be booked at an office above the *Hilltop Inn* restaurant next to the *Hilltop Towers* hotel on Club Road (Mon–Sat 9am–1pm & 1.30–5pm, Sun 1.30–5pm). King Tours and Travels on Woodville Road can reserve trains, buses and planes for travel within South India. The **tourist office** (daily 10am–5.30pm), on the main road,

Anna Salai (Bazaar Road), offers little information except unclear sketch maps of the area. For **internet access**, *Alpha Net* (daily 9am–9pm; Rs60 per hour) is next to Royal Tibet restaurant, on P.T. Road.

Taxis line Anna Salai in the centre of town, offering sightseeing at high but fixed rates. Most tourists, however, prefer to amble around the area at their own pace. Compact and hilly as it is, Kodaikanal is best explored on foot, or by **bicycle**, which you can rent from a stall on Anna Salai for Rs10 per day (those on offer at the lakeside are much more expensive); it may be fun to freewheel downhill, but most journeys will involve a hefty uphill push too.

If you need to **change money**, head for the State Bank of India on Anna Salai.

Accommodation

Kodaikanal's inexpensive **lodges** are grouped at the lower end of Anna Salai. Many are dim and poky, however, so hunt around. Always ask whether blankets and hot water are provided (this should be free in the moderate to expensive places, but you may be charged in budget hotels). **Mid–range hotels** are usually good value, especially if you get a room with a view, but they hike their prices drastically during high season (April–June). For its stunning location alone, *Greenland's Youth Hostel* offers unbeatable value for money at the bottom of the range.

Anjay, Anna Salai, near the bus stand ⊤04542/41089. A simple budget lodge slap in the centre, which has smarter rooms than you'd expect from the outside, but does suffer from traffic noise. If they're full, check out the equally good value *Jaya* behind. ❷–❸

Astoria, Anna Salai ⊤04542/40524. Well kept hotel opposite the bus stand, with homely rooms and a good, mid-priced restaurant. No views, but comfortable enough. ❻

Carlton, off Lake Road ⊤04542/40071. The most luxurious hotel in Kodaikanal, in a spacious, tastefully renovated and well maintained colonial house overlooking the lake, with a restaurant, bar and comfortable lounge. Cottages within the grounds are available at higher prices; all rates include meals. ❾

Greenland's Youth Hostel, St Mary's Road ⊤04542/41099. Attractive old stone house offering unrivalled views and sunsets from its deep verandas. The rooms are pleasant and simple with huge wooden beds, blankets, open and working fireplaces and attached bathrooms, and there is a cheap bunk-bed dorm (Rs50). Unfortunately, the staff here are surly and constantly demand baksheesh. Trekking information and guides are available. Book ahead. ❶–❸

Hilltop Towers, Club Road ⊤04542/40413, ⑫40415. Modern, comfortable rooms and good service. Very near the lake and school, with two South Indian restaurants. ❻–❼

Kodai, Noyce Road ⊤04542/41301, ⑫42108. Large campus of fifty incongruous but very pleasant chalets situated at the top of the hill, with good views of the town, and a quality restaurant. ❺–❻

Municipal Rest House, Hospital Road ⊤04542/41253. A very welcoming and friendly budget place with basic but spacious rooms with coir carpets and attached shower-toilets (bucket hot water is extra). The new "deluxe" annexe offers slightly more comfortable beds, extra blankets and hot water. Great value. ❶–❷

Sangeeth, Anna Salai ⊤04542/40456. Reasonably sized, warm and comfortable rooms with bath. Centrally located and convenient for the bus stand, but with no views over the plains. ❸–❹

Taj Villa, Coaker's Walk, off Club Road ⊤04542/40940. Comfortable old stone house, with more character than most, in lovely gardens with superb views. All rooms have attached bathrooms, but you'll have to get hot water by the bucket. A touch overpriced, but the sunset is fabulous. Internet access is available here. ❺–❻

TTDC Tamil Nadu, Fern Hill's Road ⊤04542/41336. Large, government-run hotel block northwest of town, primarily aimed at Indian family groups. Standard rooms with TVs, family cottages and a cheap dorm (Rs75). Good off-season discounts. ❺–❼

Valley View, Post Office Road ⊤04542/40181, ⑫40189. Swish modern place on the eastern side of town, popular with honeymooners. All the rooms are warm, comfortable and have satellite TV; rooms #308 and #309 have good views over the valley below. There is a good Gujarati restaurant here. ❼.

Yagappa Lodge, Noyce Road, off Club Road ⊤04542/41235 or 42116. Small, clean lodge in old buildings ranged around a dusty courtyard with good views; the best budget deal after *Greenland's*

The Town

Kodai's focal point is its **lake**, sprawling like a giant amoeba over a full 24 hectares just west of the town centre. This is a popular place for strolls, or bike rides along the five-kilometre path that fringes the water's edge, and pedal- or rowboats can be rented on the eastern shore (Rs40/30min, plus Rs10 if you require an oarsman). Horse-riding is also an option down by the lake, but it's pricey (Rs80) and rather tame to be led along the lakeside. Shops, restaurants and hotels are concentrated in a congested area of brick, wood and corrugated iron buildings east and downhill from the lake. To the south is **Byrant's Park**, with tiered flowerbeds against a backdrop of pine, eucalyptus, rhododendron and wattle, which stretches southwards to Shola Road, less than 1km from the point where the hill drops abruptly to the plains. A recently restored path, known as **Coaker's Walk**, skirts the hill, winding from the *Taj Villa* to *Greenland's Youth Hostel* (10min), and offering remarkable views that on a clear day stretch as far as Madurai, and fantastic sunsets.

If it's raining or you are at a loose end in the evening, head over to the **skating rink** on Post Office Road, just behind the bus stand. Open daily 9am–9pm (Rs35/hr, including skate hire), the rink has a wonderfully uneven wooden floor where local teenage boys gracefully show their skating skills; everyone else stumbles gamely around the edge.

One of Kodai's most popular natural attractions is **Pillar Rocks**, 7km south of town, a series of granite cliffs rising more than 100m above the hillside. To get there, follow the westbound Observatory Road from the northernmost point of the lake (a steep climb) until you come to a crossroads. The southbound road passes gentle **Fairy Falls** on the way to Pillar Rocks. Observatory Road continues west to the **Astrophysical Observatory**, perched at Kodai's highest point (2347m). Visitors can't go in, but a small **museum** (daily 10am–noon & 2–5pm; closed Fri July–March) displays assorted instruments. Closer to the north shore of the lake, **Bear Shola Falls** are at their strongest early in the year, just after the second annual monsoon.

East of the town centre, about 3km south down Law's Ghat Road (towards the plains), the **Flora and Fauna Museum** (Mon–Sat 10am–noon & 3–5pm; Rs1) has a far from inviting collection of stuffed animals. However, the orchid house is spectacular, and well worth a look on the way to **Silver Cascade** waterfalls a further 2km along.

Chettiar Park, on the very northwest edge of town, around 3km from the lake at the end of a winding uphill road, flourishes with trees and flowers all year round, and every twelve years is flushed with a haze of pale-blue **Kurinji blossoms** (the next flowering will be in 2006). These unusual flowers are associated with the god Murugan, the Tamil form of Karttikeya (Shiva's second son), and god of Kurinji, one of five ancient divisions of the Tamil country. A temple in his honour stands just outside the park.

Eating

If you choose not to eat in any of the **hotel restaurants**, head for the food stalls along **PT Road** just west of the bus stand. Menus include Indian, Chinese, Western and Tibetan dishes, and some cater specifically for vegetarians. Look out, too, for the **bakeries**, with their wonderful, fresh, warm bread and cakes each morning.

Kodai has become something of a low-key trekking centre in recent years. As you wander around town, guides continually approach offering their services on day hikes to local view points and beauty spots, or for longer trips involving night halts in villages. Scrutinize their recommendation books for comments by other tourists, and before you employ anyone, go for a coffee to discuss the possible routes, costs and nature of the walks they're offering. While most are relatively straightforward, some tackle unstable paths and steep climbs for which you'll need sturdy footwear. You should also clarify accommodation and food arrangements, transport costs and also their fees, in advance.

Generally, simple meals and tiffin are available at villages along the routes of longer hikes, so you don't need to carry much more than a sleeping bag, water, emergency food supplies and warm clothes for the evening. Maps of the area tend to be hopelessly inaccurate, but the one featured in the booklet *Beauty in Wilderness* (Rs10), available from the DFO (District Forest Office) near the *Hotel Tamil Nadu*, gives you a rough idea of distances, if not the lie of the land. While at the DFO, get permission to stay in the Forest Rest Houses, which provide rudimentary accommodation for around Rs25–50 per night; most have fireplaces, but bear in mind that any wood you might burn contributes to the overall deforestation of the Palanis. Local environmental groups are concerned about the potential long-term impact of trekking on the economy and ecology of the range, and as a result encourage walkers to carry all rubbish, bury their faeces where toilets are not available and use purification tablets rather than bottled water.

If you'd prefer to hike without a guide, the following route is worth considering; most of it follows forest roads, and there are settlements at regular intervals, many of them connected to Kodai by daily bus services. You don't get to explore the wild tops of the range, but the views and countryside throughout are beautiful, with patches of indigenous *shola* forest accessible at various points.

First head out of town on the Pillar Rocks road towards Berijam; if you can hitch a ride, you'll avoid the horn beeping that otherwise accompanies your progress as far as the end of the road at Moir Point. Berijam (23km), a picturesque lake surrounded by dense pine and acacia forest, is little more than an outpost for forest wardens. From here, however, you can follow quiet back-country roads, taking local herders' and wood gatherers' paths that cut between the bends, to Kavunji, which is served by six daily buses to Kodai – handy if you're short of time. This sleepy Palani village is the home of a small NGO that promotes children's health projects, run by S.A. Iruthyaraj (look for the house with a white chicken painted on the wall), who is highly knowledgeable about local *shola* forests and off-track routes in the area. Further along the trail at Polur (8km) are some spectacular waterfalls. The locals say it is impossible to get close to them, but you can, by scrambling down the hillside via a muddy overgrown cattle path – and it's well worth it for the refreshing shower.

For more information on environmentally friendly trekking in the Kodai area, contact the Palani Hills Conservation Council (PHCC), Amarville House, Lower Shola Road, Kodaikanal 62410 (☏04542/40711). This excellent environmental organization also welcomes foreign volunteer workers to help with their various campaigns and grass-roots projects in the Palanis.

Carlton, *Carlton Hotel*, off Lake Road. Splash out on a buffet spread at Kodai's top hotel (Rs300), rounded off with a *chhota* peg of IMFL scotch in the bar.

Chetna, next to the *Charlton* hotel, by the lake. A minuscule place with a sweet pink attic and flower-filled balcony. Run by an enthusiastic and health-conscious couple from Rajasthan, you can get simple thalis (Rs25), coffee, Indian sweets and snacks here.

Eco Nut, J's Heritage Complex, PT Road. One of South India's few bona fide Western-style wholefood shops and a great place to stock up on trekking supplies: muesli, home-made jams, breads, pickles and muffins, high-calorie "nutri-balls" and delicious cheeses from Auroville.

Hotel Punjab, PT Road. Top North Indian cuisine and reasonably priced tandoori specialities; try their great butter chicken and hot naan.

Manna Bakery, Bear Shola Road. The fried breakfasts, pizzas and home-baked brown bread and cakes served in this eccentric, self-consciously ecofriendly café-restaurant are great, but some might find the bare concrete dining hall dingy.

Royal Tibet, PT Road. The better of the town's two Tibetan joints, with dishes ranging from thick home-made bread to particularly tasty *momos* and noodles, and some Indian and Chinese options.

Samudra, PT Road. Moderately priced seafood specialities, trucked in weekly by freezer lorry from Kochi and served in an attractive raffia- and fishing-net-filled dining room. Try their tandoori pomfret or filling "fish fry" budget option; the tiger prawns are good for a splurge, but they do plenty of chicken dishes too, steeped in tasty Chinese sauces.

Trattoria Venice, PT Road. Warming minestrone, fresh home-made pastas and pizzas and delicious tiramisu, all finished up with a cappuccino made with home-grown coffee beans. If this isn't enough, come for an endlessly amusing performance by the eccentric manager-entertainer-chef-waiter, Ganesh.

Palani

Few sacred sites in South India enjoy as dramatic a location as **PALANI**, just over 100km northwest of Madurai. Crowning a smooth-sided, perfectly dome-shaped outcrop of granite, the town's principal shrine overlooks a vast lake, **Vyapuri**, enfolded by the pale yellow crags of the Palani Hills, rising sheer to the south. During the monsoons, the torturous road that scales the mountains from here provides the only dependable access to Kodaikanal. At other times, relatively few travellers are aware of its existence, but the views outstrip those from the busier southern approach to the hill station, while Palani itself, a busy little Tamil pilgrimage town, warrants at least a day-trip or stopover between Kodai and Ooty.

Praised for over two thousand years in the songs of the wandering Tamil saints, Palani's red and white striped **Malaikovil temple** attracts thousands of Hindu pilgrims each day. Each visitor is expected to perform two important rituals. The first involves an auspicious circuit of the base of the hill, via a two-kilometre-long sandy path known as the **Giri–Veedhi**, which is punctuated with shrines and stone-carved peacocks (Murugan's *vahana*, or vehicle). The second is an ascent of the sacred walkway via its 659 steps, illuminated from dusk onwards with tiny camphor lamps left by the devotees (and interrupted by more prosaic billboards advertising the names of the temple's corporate sponsors), to the hilltop shrine itself. During Palani's main festival in April/May, thousands of devotees – mostly male and clad in black *dhotis* – pour up the winding flight to worship the image, said to be formed from an aggregate of poisonous minerals, that, if mixed with coconut milk, fruits and flowers, produces medicinal herbs. Some carry pails of milk on yokes as offerings for Lord Murugan, while the more fervent among them perform austerities (cheek-piercing with metal leaf-shaped skewers is a favourite). Those unable to climb the steps can ascend in a carriage pulled slowly up the steep incline by electric winch (Rs1) but it can take a lot of queuing to get on. From the summit, the **views** across the Vyapuri lake and Vaigai plain, with the Ghats looming behind, are unforgettable.

Apart from the numerous simple *choultries* – pilgrims' hostels owned by various caste associations from all over South India – Palani has two proper **hotels**. A small new unit of *TTDC Tamil Nadu*, West Giri Street, opposite the Winch Station (⊕04545/41156; ③–⑤) has decent a/c and non-a/c doubles with attached bathrooms and hot water, as does the smart new *Subam Hotel*, 7 North

Giri St near the main temple entrance (☎04545/42672; ③–⑤). **Buses to Palani** from Kodaikanal (every 1hr 30min; 3hr) are often full, so it's wise to reserve a seat a day in advance. The town is also well connected by train and bus to Coimbatore, via Pollachi (for the Indira Gandhi wildlife sanctuary), and Madurai, and a private "deluxe" service passes through each morning en route to Ooty.

Indira Gandhi (Anamalai) Wildlife Sanctuary

Anamalai Wildlife Sanctuary, officially renamed the **Indira Gandhi Wildlife Sanctuary**, is a 958-square-kilometre tract of forest on the southern reaches of the Cardamom Hills, southwest of the busy junction town of **Pollachi**. Vegetation ranges from dry deciduous to tropical evergreen, and the sanctuary is home to lion-tailed **macaques** (black-maned monkeys), wild elephants, crocodiles, *sambar*, spotted- and barking deer, as well as fifteen **tigers** at the last count.

The Indira Gandhi Wildlife Sanctuary has been at the centre of several water and land rights disputes over the past few years, mostly between local tribal people and the government, which have been developing major hydroelectric and irrigation projects in the area. Access to visitors was always strictly limited, but in 1998, the park was closed altogether, ostensibly for the same reasons the Forest Department have shut the other wildlife sanctuaries in Tamil Nadu. Until the "Veerapan problem" (see box on p.570) is resolved, the Indira Gandhi Wildlife Sanctuary will remain out of bounds, which can, in the long run, only benefit its fragile population of predators.

Coimbatore

Visitors tend only to use the busy industrial city of **COIMBATORE** as a stopover on the way to Ooty, 90km northwest. Once you've climbed up to your hotel rooftop to admire the blue, cloud-capped haze of the Nilgiris in the west, there's little to do here other than kill time wandering through the nuts-and-bolts bazaars, lined with lookalike textile showrooms, "General Traders" and shops selling motor parts.

Coimbatore earned its reputation as the "Manchester of South India" in the 1930s, when the nearby **Pykara Falls** hydroelectric project was built to provide cheap power for its huge textile mills and spin-off industries. Since then, the city has never looked back. If you arrive here from more traditional corners of Karnataka or the deep south you'll find it distinctly prosperous, modern and orderly: new office buildings and business hotels dominate the skyline, while in the street, trousers far outnumber *lunghis* and virtually every man sports a pen in his shirt pocket.

Practicalities

Coimbatore's two main **bus stands**, Central and Thiruvalluvar, are close together towards the north of the city centre; the busy town bus stand is sandwiched in between. From Central bus stand on Dr Nanjappa Road, buses leave for Ooty every fifteen minutes. Buses to Bangalore and Mysore can be booked in advance at the **reservation office** (9am–noon & 1–8pm). There are also frequent services to and from Madurai, Chennai and Tiruchirapalli (Trichy). A third stand, Ukkadam bus stand, serves local towns and destinations in northern Kerala, such as Pollachi, Palghat, Munnar, Trissur and Kannur; it's 4km from the others, in the southwest of the city next to the lake.

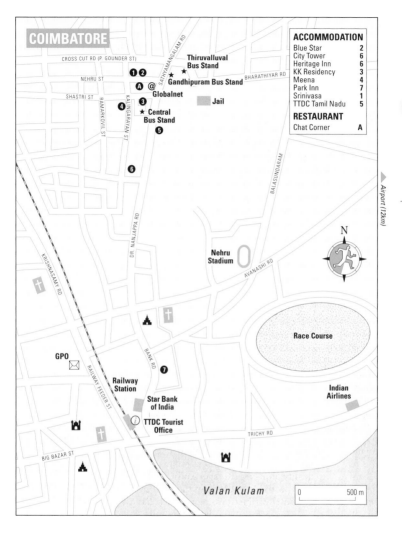

CROSS CUT RD (P. GOUNDER ST)

NEHRU ST

SHASTRI ST

SATHYAMANGALAM RD

Thiruvalluval
Bus Stand

Gandhipuram Bus Stand

BHARATHIYAR RD

Globalnet

Jail

Central
Bus Stand

RAMAKOVIL ST

KALINGARAYAN ST

DR. NANJAPPA RD

BALASUNDARAM

Airport (12km)

KRISNASAMY RD

Nehru
Stadium

AVANASHI RD

N

Race Course

GPO

RAILWAY FEEDER ST

BANK RD

Railway
Station

Star Bank
of India

TTDC Tourist
Office

Indian
Airlines

TRICHY RD

BIG BAZAR ST

Valan Kulam

0   500 m

ACCOMMODATION

Blue Star	2
City Tower	6
Heritage Inn	6
KK Residency	3
Meena	4
Park Inn	7
Srinivasa	1
TTDC Tamil Nadu	5

RESTAURANT

| Chat Corner | A |

TAMIL NADU | The Southern Ghats

The **railway station**, 2km south of two central bus stands, is well connected to major southern destinations. To catch the Nilgiri Blue Mountain Railway
to **Ooty** (see p.559), join the #6005 Nilgiri Express **from Chennai**, which
leaves Coimbatore at 5.30am (1hr), and change onto the narrow-gauge steam
railway at **Mettupalayam**, from where a train departs at 7.30am. The other
connection leaves Coimbatore at 10.50am, to meet up with the 1.15pm from
Mettupalayam. If you're catching the early service, try to stay near the train station, or arrange transport the night before, as auto-rickshaws are few and far
between at this early hour of the morning. Alternatively, jump on a bus to
Mettupalayam from the Central bus stand before 6am, which will get you to
the head of the narrow gauge line in time for the 7.30am departure.

Coming **from Ooty**, you'll get into Mettupalayam at either 12.45pm or 6.30pm, leaving you plenty of time to grab something to eat and catch onward overnight trains from Coimbatore to Chennai and Madurai (if you intend to do this, reserve tickets in advance at Ooty). Of the overnight services to **Chennai**, the Cheran Express #2674 (daily 11.05pm; 9hr) is marginally quicker than the Nilgiri Express #6606 (daily 8.40pm; 9hr 35min), but nowhere near as smart and fast as the swish #2024 Shatabdi Express, (daily 7.25am; 6hr 35min). The daily #6115 Rameshwaram Express leaves at 11.25pm for **Rameshwaram** via **Madurai** (arrive 6am). For Cochin, catch the daily #6865 Tiruchi Express (daily depart 12.45am; 5hr 30min). The best train for **Mangalore** is the #6627 West Coast Express (daily depart 7.55pm; 9hr).

Coimbatore **airport** lies 12km northeast of town and is served by buses to and from the town bus stand (taxis charge around Rs175). Indian Airlines and Jet Airways fly daily to and from Mumbai, Chennai, Delhi, Kozhikode and Bangalore, and twice a week to Cochin. Indian Airlines' office is 2km northeast of the railway station on Trichy Road (☎0422/399833 or 399821); Jet Airways can be found 4km along the same road (☎0422/212036).

You can **change money** at the State Bank of India and Bank of Baroda, near the railway station or, more quickly and efficiently, at TT Travels, #102 A-Block Raheja Centre, Avanashi Road (☎0422/212854), a five-minute rickshaw ride northeast of the train station. The latter is the only bank open on Sundays (daily 9.30am–5.30pm). **Internet** booths are springing up all over Coimbatore, most places charging a reasonable Rs30/hr. Two of the most convenient places are: Globalnet, on the first floor of the *Krishna Towers*, on the corner of Nehru Street and Dr Nanjappa Road, just north of the bus stands; and the STD place directly opposite the *Blue Star* hotel.

Accommodation and eating

Most of Coimbatore's **accommodation** is concentrated around the bus stands. The cheapest places line Nehru Street and Shastri Street but, whatever you do, avoid the rock-bottom places facing the bus stand itself, which are plagued with traffic noise from around 4am onwards.

As for **eating**, your best bets are the bigger hotels such as the *City Tower*, whose excellent rooftop restaurant, *Cloud 9*, serves a topnotch multicuisine menu to a predominantly business clientele. The *Malabar*, on the first floor of the *KK Residency*, is a less pricey option, popular with visitors from across the Ghats for its quality non-veg Keralan cuisine. For vegetarian South Indian food, however, you won't do better than the ultra-modern *Chat Corner*, opposite the *Blue Star* hotel on Nehru Street, which has a squeaky clean "meals" restaurant, open-air terrace and excellent little juice bar.

Blue Star, 369 Nehru St ☎ 0422/230635. Impeccably clean rooms, all with balconies, quiet fans and bathrooms, in a modern multistorey building five minutes' walk from the bus stands. The best moderately priced place in this area. ❸–❹

City Tower, Sivaswamy Road, just off Dr Nanjappa Road, a two-minute-walk south of the Central bus stand ☎ 0422/230681, ℗ 230103. A smart upscale hotel situated in the city centre with modern interiors (heavy on leatherette and vinyl); the "Executive" rooms are more spacious. Some rooms are a/c. ❻–❼

Heritage Inn, 38 Sivaswamy Rd ☎ 0422/231451, ℗ 233223. Coimbatore's top hotel, featuring more than sixty centrally a/c rooms, a couple of quality restaurants and foreign exchange. Credit cards accepted. ❼–❽

KK Residency, 7 Shastri St ☎ 0422/232433. Large tower-block hotel around the corner from the main bus stands; very clean rooms and a couple of decent restaurants. ❹–❺

Meena, 109 Kalingarayan St ☎ 0422/235420. Tucked away off the main drag, but handy for the bus stand. The rooms are clean, with attached shower-toilets and small balconies. A good choice for budget travellers. ❷

ⓕ 301291. Business-orientated hotel that's the smartest option around the railway station. Immaculate, quiet and good value; room rates include breakfast. ❺–❼.
Srinivasa, 365 Nehru St, next door to *Blue Star* ☎ 0422/230116. Near the bus stands and the cleanest of the cheap lodges in this area, which isn't saying much. ❷
TTDC Tamil Nadu, Dr Nanjappa Road ☎ 0422/236311. Opposite Central bus stand; convenient, clean and reliable. Better than most in the chain with a/c and non a/c rooms. It is often fully booked, so phone ahead. ❹–❻

Coonoor and Kotagiri

COONOOR, a scruffy bazaar and tea planters' town on the Nilgiri Blue Mountain Railway (see box on p.559), lies at the head of the Hulikal ravine, 27km north of Mettupalayam and 19km south of Ooty, at an altitude of 1858m, on the southeastern side of the Dodabetta mountains. Often considered second best to its more famous neighbour, Coonoor has luckily avoided Ooty's over-commercialization, and can make a pleasant place for a short stop. In addition to an atmospheric little hill market specializing in leaf tea and fragrant essential oils, it is rejuvenating to take a stroll or two in the outlying hills and valleys. Accommodation in the town is in short supply, limited to a couple of flea-infested lodges in the bazaar; it's a better idea to stay somewhere else and travel here for the day.

Coonoor loosely divides into two sections, with the bus stand (regular services to Mettupalayam, Coimbatore and elsewhere in the Nilgiris), railway station and market huddled together in **Lower Coonoor**. In **Upper Coonoor**, **Sim's Park** is a fine botanical garden on the slopes of a ravine, with hundreds of rose varieties (daily 8am–6.30pm; Rs5).

Visible from miles away as tiny orange or red dots amid the green vegetation, **tea-pickers** work the slopes around Coonoor, carrying wicker baskets of fresh leaves and bamboo rods that they use like rulers to ensure that each plant is evenly plucked. Once the leaves reach the factory, they're processed within a day, producing seven grades of tea. **Orange Pekoe** is the best and most expensive; the seventh and lowest grade, a dry dust of stalks and leaf swept up at the end of the process will be sold on to make instant tea. To visit a tea or coffee plantation, contact UPASI (United Planters' Association of Southern India), "Glenview", Coonoor.

Around the town, rolling hills and valleys, carpeted with spongy green tea bushes and stands of eucalyptus and silver oak, offer some of the most beautiful scenery in the Nilgiris, immortalised in many a Hindi movie dance sequence. Cinema fans from across the south flock here to visit key locations from their favourite blockbusters, among them **Lamb's Rock** (5km) and **Dolphin's Nose** (9km), former British picnicking spots with paved pathways and dramatic views of the Mettupalayam plains. Buses run out here from Coonoor every two hours. It's a good idea to catch the first one at 7am, which gets you to Dolphin's Nose before the mist starts to build up, and walk the 9km back into town via Lamb's Rock – an enjoyable amble that takes you through tea estates and dense forest.

The only other major settlement hereabouts, **KOTAGIRI**, lies a winding one-hour bus ride from Coonoor, at an altitude of just under 2000m. High on the cloudy hilltops, it's even more given over to tea planting than Coonoor, and as a result has little to recommend it as a tourist destination. The one reason you might want to venture up here is to shop at the **Women's Cooperative** off Ramchand Square, which stocks the region's best selection of locally made handicrafts, including traditional red-and-black **Toda embroidery** (see

You can maximize the beneficial effects of Coonor's mountain air with a short *yoga course* at the *YWCA*. Yoga therapist Dr A.R. ("Raj") Hirudhayaraj, co-warden of the hostel, offers introductory tuition in the basic *asanas* (postures), *pranayama* (breathing exercises), dietary prescriptions and meditation techniques of Hatha Yoga. He's also a qualified herbalist and a mine of information on Tamil culture in general. Lessons cost Rs150 per hour, or Rs2100 for a seven-day course, comprising two hours of teaching each day. Bookings can be made in advance by telephone (☎0423/233426), or on spec at the *YWCA*.

box on p.564). Hand-woven woollen shawls are the most expensive items on offer, but they also keep smaller souvenir items such as spectacle cases and wallets, all at very fair fixed prices. Income from the shop is used to fund women's development projects in the area, principally among the Todas; they've an interesting frieze of photos on the wall showing where the money goes.

Kotagiri is connected to Coonor (every 15min; 1hr) and Mettupalayam (every 30min; 2hr) by regular and reliable **bus** services. You can also get here from Ooty, 28km west (hourly; 2hr), via one of the highest motorable roads in the Nilgiris.

Practicalities

When it comes to finding somewhere to **stay** or **eat**, there's not a lot of choice in Coonor, and it's not a good idea to leave looking for a room till too late in the day. By and large the hotels are dotted around Upper Coonor, within 3km of the station; you'll need an auto-rickshaw to find most of them. As ever, ignore any rickshaw-wallahs who tell you the hotel you want to go to is "full" or "closed". The correct fare from the bus stand to Bedford Circle/*YWCA* is Rs20–25.

If you're staying at the *YWCA*, or one of the upmarket hotels, your best bet is to eat there. In the bazaar, the only commendable **restaurants** are *Hotel Tamizhamgam* (pronounced "Tamirangum"), on Mount Road near the bus stand, which is Coonor's most popular vegetarian meals-cum-tiffin joint. For good-value non-veg North Indian tandoori and Chinese food, try the *Greenland* hotel, up the road.

The Travancore Bank, on Church Road in Upper Ooty, near Bedford Circle, **changes currency**, but not always travellers' cheques. Otherwise, the nearest place is the State Bank of India in Ooty (see p.562).

Accommodation

The tariffs included here are for the low season, as high season tariffs may increase from anywhere between twenty and a hundred percent, depending on the tourist influx.

Blue Hills, Mount Road, 1km up from the bus stand ☎ 0423/230103. This place offers clean doubles, complete with Formica furnishing. The concrete building is an eyesore and its popularity among all-male holiday groups means its not recommended for female travellers, but it's cheap and the non-veg restaurant is good. ③–⑤

La Barrier Inn, Coonoor Club Road ☎ 0423/232561. Located way up above the bazaar, with great views of surrounding hills (and cricket nets). The rooms are spotless and very large, opening onto flower-filled balconies. A recommended and comfortable mid-range option. ⑤

Riga, Appleby Road ☎ 0423/234405. A tower block 2km out of the centre in Wellington. Plush rooms and a restaurant with great views, but there's little atmosphere or history to this place. ⑦

Taj Garden Retreat, Hampton Manor

⊤ 0423/230021, ⊕ 232775. Old colonial-era hotel with cottage accommodation, tea-garden lawns and spectacular views, and a good range of sports and activities on offer – including freshwater fishing. Luxurious, but way overpriced, especially for foreigners, who pay thirty percent more. The restaurant serves spectacular lunch-time buffets. ➒

Venlan (Ritz), Ritz Road, Bedford ⊤ 0423/230632, ⊕ 230600. Recently refurbished, this luxury hotel is in a great location on the outskirts. Very spacious with carpeted rooms, deep balconies and fine views. Much better value than the *Taj Garden Retreat* but it lacks any *fin-de-siecle* charm. ➐–➑

Vivek, Figure of Eight Road, nr Bedford Circle

⊤ 0423/230658. Catch a town bus to Bedford Circle and walk from there. Managed by a very amiable lady, offering clean rooms (some with tiny balconies overlooking the tea terraces) and a great value dorm (Rs40). Just beware of the "monkey menace". ➋–➌

YWCA Guest House, Wyoming, near the hospital ⊤ 0423/234426. A characterful Victorian-era house on a bluff overlooking town, with flower garden, tea terraces and fine views from relaxing verandas. There are five spotless double rooms and two singles; yoga lessons are on offer (see above) and superb home-cooked meals are available at very reasonable rates (Rs70 non-veg; Rs40 veg). This is among the most congenial budget hotels in South India. No alcohol. ➍

The Nilgiri Blue Mountain Railway

The famous narrow-gauge Nilgiri Blue Mountain Railway climbs up from Mettupalayam on the plains, via Hillgrove (17km) and Coonoor (27km) to Udhagamandalam, a journey of 46km passing through sixteen tunnels, eleven stations and nineteen bridges. It's a slow haul of four and a half hours or more – sometimes the train moves little faster than walking pace, and always takes much longer than the bus – but the views are absolutely magnificent, especially along the steepest sections in the Hulikal ravine.

The line was built between 1890 and 1908, paid for by the tea planters and other British inhabitants of the Nilgiris. It differs from India's two comparable narrow-gauge lines, to Darjeeling and Shimla, for its use of the so-called Swiss rack system, by means of which the tiny locomotives are able to climb gradients of up to 1 in 12.5. Special bars were set between the track rails to form a ladder, which cogs of teeth, connected to the train's driving wheels, engage like a zipper mechanism. Because of this novel design, only the original locomotives can still run the steepest stretches of line, which is why the section between Mettupalayam and Coonoor has remained one of South Asia's last functioning steam routes. The chuffing and whistle-screeches of the tiny train, echoing across the valleys as it pushes its blue and cream carriages up to Coonoor (where a diesel locomotive takes over) rank among the most romantic sounds of South India. It conjures up the determined gentility of the Raj era even more strongly than Ooty's faded colonial monuments. Even if you don't count yourself as a train spotter, a boneshaking ride on the Nilgiri Blue Mountain Railway should be a priority when crossing the Nilgiris between southern Karnataka and the Tamil plains.

Timetable details for the line appear in the account of Coimbatore (see p.554), and in the Moving On from Ooty box on p.568.

Udhagamandalam (Ootacamund) and around

Mr John Sullivan, a British *burra-sahib*, is credited with "discovering" **UDHAGAMANDALAM** – still more commonly referred to by its anglicized name, **Ootacamund**. When he first clambered into this corner of the Nilgiris through the Hulikal ravine in the early nineteenth century, the territory was the traditional homeland of the pastoralist **Toda** hill-tribe, who lived in almost

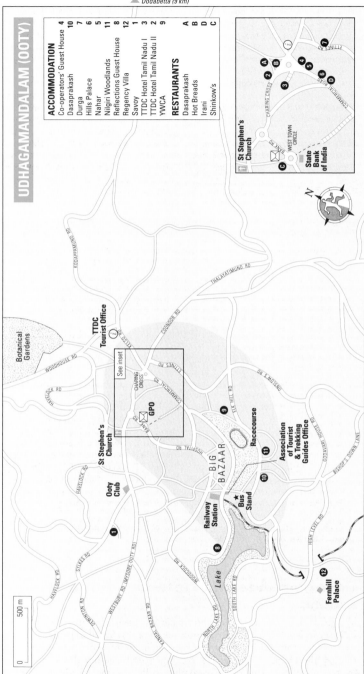

▲ *Dodabetta (9 km)*

UDHAGAMANDALAM (OOTY)

ACCOMMODATION

Co-operators' Guest House	4
Dasaprakash	10
Durga	7
Hills Palace	6
Nahar	5
Nilgiri Woodlands	11
Reflections Guest House	8
Regency Villa	12
Savoy	1
TTDC Hotel Tamil Nadu I	3
TTDC Hotel Tamil Nadu II	2
YWCA	9

RESTAURANTS

Dasaprakash	A
Hot Breads	B
Irani	D
Shinkow's	C

St Stephen's Church

State Bank of India

West Town Circle

Charing Cross

Botanical Gardens

TTDC Tourist Office

St Stephen's Church

Ooty Club

GPO

See inset

Racecourse

BIG BAZAAR

Association of Tourist & Trekking Guides Office

Railway Station

★ Bus Stand

Lake

Fernhill Palace

▼ *Coonoor & Coimbatore*

◀ Mysore ▼

500 m

total isolation from the cities of the surrounding plains and Deccan plateau lands. Realizing the agricultural potential of the area, Sullivan acquired tracts of land for Rs1 per acre from the Todas, and set about planting flax, barley and hemp, as well as potatoes, soft fruit and, most significantly, **tea**, which all flourished in the mild climate. Within twenty years, the former East India Company clerk had made himself a fortune and drawn the attention of the British residents sweating it out on the southern plains. Sullivan and his business cronies planned and founded Ootacamund, a town complete with artificial lake, churches and stone houses that wouldn't have looked out of place in Surrey or the Scottish Highlands. Ootacamund quickly become the most popular hill retreat in peninsular India, known fondly by the *burra-* and *memsahibs* of the south as "**Ooty**", the "Queen of Hill Stations".

Of the Todas, little further note was made beyond a couple of anthropological monographs, references to their *munds*, or settlements, in the *Madras Gazette*, and the financial transactions that deprived them of the traditional lands. Christianized by missionaries and uprooted by tea planters and forest clearance, they retreated with their buffalo into the surrounding hills and wooded valleys where, in spite of hugely diminished numbers, they continued to preserve a more or less traditional way of life (see box on p.564).

By a stroke of delicious irony, the Todas outlived the colonists whose cash crops originally displaced them – but only just. Until the mid-1970s "Snooty Ooty" (as the notoriously snobby town became known) was home to some of the subcontinent's last British inhabitants who chose to "stay on", living out their final days on tiny pensions that only here would allow them to keep a lifestyle to which they had become accustomed. Over the past two decades, travellers have continued to be attracted by Ooty's cool climate and peaceful green hills, forest and grassland. However, if you come in the hope of finding quaint vestiges of the Raj, you're likely to be disappointed; what with indiscriminate development and a deluge of holiday-makers, they're few and far between.

The **best time to come** is between January and March, avoiding the high-season crowds (April–June & Sept–Oct). In May, the summer festival brings huge numbers of people and a barrage of amplified noise – worlds away from the peaceful retreat envisaged by the *sahibs*. From June to September, and during November, it'll be raining and misty, which appeals to some. The skies are clear between October or November until February, when it can get really cold at night but it's pleasantly warm in the midday sunshine.

Arrival, information and local transport

Most visitors arrive in Ooty either by bus from Mysore in Karnataka (the more scenic, if steeper, route goes via Masinagudi), or on the **miniature mountain railway** from Coonoor and Mettupalayam. The bus and train stations are fairly close together, at the western end of the big bazaar and racecourse. **Local transport** consists of auto-rickshaws and taxis, which meet incoming trains and gather outside the bus stand and also on Commercial Road around Charing Cross. You can **rent bikes** (no gears) but the steep hills make cycling very hard work.

The **TTDC tourist office** (Mon–Sat 10am–5.45pm; ☎0423/43977) is on Kelso Road, just northeast of Charing Cross, and they are eager to help, but the information is not always reliable. You can book **day tours** here, among them the Ooty, Pykara and Mudumalai tour (daily 9am–7.30pm; Rs150), which calls at Pykara dam, falls and boathouse and Mudumalai Wildlife Sanctuary, making for a very long day. The Ooty and Coonoor tour (daily

9am–6pm; Rs80) goes to Sim's Park, the botanical gardens, the lake, Dodabetta Peak, Lamb's Rock and Dolphin's Nose. If you get caught out by arriving on a Sunday, there is a **private tourist office** (daily 8am–8.30pm) in Charing Cross that can give out leaflets and advise on hotels, sightseeing and restaurants.

Ooty's **post office**, northwest of Charing Cross at West Town Circle, off Spencers Road and near St Stephen's Church, has a poste restante counter (enquiries and stamps Mon–Fri 9am–5pm; parcels Mon–Fri 9am–3pm & Sat 9am–2pm). For **internet access**, there are now numerous outlets across town, especially around Charing Cross, all charging about Rs50–60 per hour, for a frustratingly slow and unreliable service.

The only **bank** in Ooty that changes travellers' cheques and currency is the very pukka State Bank of India, on West Town Circle. While you're waiting for your cash, check out the photos in the hallway connecting the old and new blocks, dating from the era when this was the "Imperial Bank of India": stalwart, stiff-backed *burra-sahibs* pose with pipes, wives and mandatory Scottish terriers in front of the old bank building.

Accommodation

Ooty is a lot more expensive than many places in India; during April and May prices mentioned below can double. It also gets very crowded, so you may have to hunt around to find what you want. The best by far are the grand old Raj-era places; otherwise, the choice is largely down to average hotels at above-average prices. In winter (Nov–Feb), when it can get pretty cold, most hotels provide heating at extra cost.

Co-operators Guest House, Charing Cross ☏0423/444046. Slightly back from the main road so its relatively quiet. A Raj-era building with clean rooms and turquoise balconies looking down to a courtyard. Unfortunately the place has become somewhat cramped by a huge new concrete block next door. Cheap and central. ❷

Dasaprakash, south of the racecourse ☏0423/442434. This is a solid, old-style Indian hotel, clean and reasonably quiet, overlooking the racecourse. Their cheapest ("deluxe") rooms are a bit gloomy, but the "first class" doubles are fine. There is an excellent and inexpensive South Indian veg restaurant and a travel agent. ❹–❺

Durga, Ettines Road ☏0423/443837. The best deal among the many mid-range places around Charing Cross. It's clean, comfortable and central, but the buses which constantly stop outside create a lot of unwelcome noise and dust. ❹–❺

Hills Palace, Commercial Road ☏0423/442239, ℻443430. Spanking new place that's just below the main bazaar, but secluded, quiet and spotlessly clean inside. Great value in the low season. ❹

Nahar, Commercial Road, Charing Cross ☏0423/442173, ℻445173. One of Ooty's smartest hotels, offering spacious, well furnished rooms in the centre (the best rooms are in the modern building at the back) and two veg restaurants. A favourite with large Indian family holiday parties, so book ahead. ❼

Nilgiri Woodlands, Racecourse Road, 1km from bus stand and train station ☏0423/442451, ℻442530. A grand Raj-era building, with a wood-panelled lobby, hunting trophies and bare, clean rooms that are particularly good value in winter. The little cottages around the garden are worth the extra. Friendly, helpful staff and a good restaurant. ❹–❼

Reflections Guest House, North Lake Road ☏0423/443834. Homely, relaxing guesthouse by the lake, five minutes' walk from the train station, with rooms opening on to a small terrace. Easily the best budget option in Ooty, but its small and fills up quickly so book in advance. ❷

Regency Villa, Fernhill ☏0423/443097. The maharaja of Mysore's former guesthouse, now a rather run-down, atmospheric old hotel. If you're here for faded traces of the Raj, this is the place. The palatial suites in the main block are locked in a time warp, with frayed nineteenth-century furniture, original bathtubs, and old sepia photos of the Ooty hunt. By contrast, the second- and third-rate rooms, in separate blocks, are cheerless and not at all good value. Even if you can't afford to stay here, come out for a nose around and coffee on the lawn. ❺–❼

Savoy, 77 Sylkes Rd ☏0423/444142. Long-established pukka hotel, now run by the *Taj* group. It has manicured lawns, immaculate and chintzy old-world cottages with working fireplaces, wood and brass fittings. Pricey for foreigners, who pay an inflated dollar rate of $75 a night. ⑨

Unit I is in the northwest corner above Charing Cross, reached by a flight of stairs, and Unit II is in the northeast corner of Charing Cross. ☎0423/444371, ⑨ 444369. Two identical large, characterless complexes in the centre, but with good-value restaurants, a bar and billiards rooms. ②–⑥

Elk Hill Road ☎0423/442218. Charming 1920s building, set amid spacious grounds near the racecourse. Seven varieties of rooms and chalets, all immaculate, with bucket hot water and bathrooms. There is a sunny dining room and you can while away the evening in the cosy "English parlour", or by the piano. Excellent value, and very safe. An inexpensive laundry facility is available. Book ahead. ②–④

The Town

Ooty sprawls over a large area of winding roads and steep climbs. The obvious focal point is **Charing Cross**, a busy junction on dusty **Commercial Road**, the main, relatively flat, shopping street that runs south to the big bazaar and municipal vegetable market. Goods on sale range from fat plastic bags of cardamom and Orange Pekoe tea to presentation packs of essential oils (among them citronella, which is a highly effective natural mosquito repellent). A little way northeast of Charing Cross, the **Botanical Gardens** (daily 8am–6.30pm; Rs5, camera Rs5, video Rs25), laid out in 1847 by gardeners from London's Kew Gardens, consist of forty acres of immaculate lawns, lily ponds and beds, with more than a thousand varieties of shrubs, flowers and trees. There's a refreshment stand; stalls around the entrance gate sell candyfloss, peanuts and snacks.

Northwest of Charing Cross, the small Gothic-style **St Stephen's Church** was one of Ooty's first colonial structures, built in the 1820s on the site of a toda temple; timber for its bowed teak roof was taken from Tipu Sultan's palace at Srirangapatnam and hauled up here by elephant. The area around the church gives you some idea of what the hill station must have looked like in the days of the Raj. To the right of the church is the rambling and rather dilapidated Spencer's store, which opened in 1909 and sold everything a British home in the colonies could ever need; it's now it is a computer college. Nearby, in the same compound as the post office, gowned lawyers buzz around the red-brick **Civil Court**, a quasi-Gothic structure with leaded diamond-shaped windows, corrugated-iron roofs and a clock tower capped with a weather vane. Over the next hill (west), the snootiest of Ooty's institutions, the **Club**, dates from 1830. Originally the house of Sir William Rumbold, it became a club in 1843 and expanded thereafter. Its one claim to fame is that the rules for snooker were first set down here (although the members of Jabalpur Club in Madhya Pradesh are supposed to have originated the game in the first place). Entry is strictly restricted to members and their guests or members of affiliated clubs. Further along Mysore Road, the modest **Government Museum** (daily except Fri & second Sat of month 9am–1pm & 2–5pm) houses a few paltry tribal objects, sculptures and crafts.

West of the railway station and racecourse (races mid-April to mid-June), the **Lake**, constructed in the early 1800s, is one of Ooty's main tourist attractions, despite being heavily polluted (most of the town's raw sewage gets dumped here – worth bearing in mind if you're tempted to venture out on it). Honeymoon couples in particular go boating (8am–6pm; rowing, paddle and motor Rs3–120) and horse-riding (short rides Rs30–75, or Rs100 per hour).

Fernhill Palace, not far from the southeast end of the lake and once the summer residence of the Maharaja of Mysore, is now a hotel (see p.562). It's an extraordinary pile, built in the fullest expression of Ooty's characteristic

Until the arrival of the British, the Todas of the Nilgiri Hills maintained their own language and customs in villages (*munds*) of wagon-shaped huts of bamboo, thatch and reeds. Today the Toda tribal community still exists, albeit in depleted numbers. Some wear traditional costume: plain white waist-cloths under thick white woven shawls (*puthikuzhi*) striped with red and black. Once, all adult women had their upper body tattooed and their hair oiled and curled into long ringlets at the front; feminine beauty is judged by the narrowness of the feet and facial hair is admired. Men keep their hair and beards long.

Toda culture centres around the buffalo, which is held sacred; the only product they use is its milk, consuming it in vast quantities. Toda temples are dairies, off-limits to everyone save the officiating priests. The community is divided into fourteen patriarchal clans, though its polyandrous social system is fast breaking down. "Marriages" were arranged at birth with partners from another clan; at the age of 15 the female moved in with the husband's family and automatically became the wife of his younger brothers too. She could also seek further partners from other families, with the permission of her principal partner, who would generally assume the paternal role for any resultant offspring.

Traditionally, the Todas lived in interdependence with four other tribal groups, based on a barter system under which their main responsibility was to supply the others with dairy products. Of these, the Irulus, Vishnu-worshipping tool-makers and ritual specialists who are regarded by the Todas as caste inferiors, are today the most numerous, with a population of around seven thousand. Fears of caste pollution also determine relations between the Todas and the Kotas, ironsmiths and potters who provide music for rituals. The jungle-dwelling Kurumbas, known for their aptitude in magic, gathered honey and wood, while the Badagas, who arrived in the fourteenth century after being displaced by the Muslim invasions, kept the others supplied with grain and beans.

At present there are about seventeen hundred Todas, of whom a quarter are Christian. Due to high infant mortality and the introduction of life-threatening diseases by the British, their population had dwindled to little more than six hundred by the 1940s. This alarming situation was dramatically reversed though, largely through the efforts of an exceptional Toda woman, Evam Piljain-Wiedemann, who trained as a nurse in England, and succeeded in winning the confidence of other Todas to take advantage of a mobile medical clinic. She continues to work to secure rights for the Todas, and to protect the natural environment.

Blame for the threat to the survival of the Nilgiris cannot simply be laid at the door of colonial exploitation, though the story does begin with the arrival of the

---

Swiss-chalet style, with carved wooden bargeboards and ornamental cast-iron balustrades. Among the compound of firs, cedars and monkey-puzzle trees, a bizarre church-like building was erected as an indoor badminton court. Just down the road from Fernhill, a lane with a mouldering, indecipherable sign board leads to the former **Palace Hotel**, the Nizam of Hyderabad's old hill mansion. The Andhran millionaire sold it a few years back, but one of his wives (a former Miss Turkey) sued him, claiming it was hers. As the case limps slowly through the Indian courts, the building lapses into what looks like terminal dereliction, inhabited by monkeys and squatters.

Eating

Many of the **mid-range hotels**, such as *Dasaprakash,* serve up good South Indian food, but Ooty has yet to offer a gourmet **restaurant**. The *Regency Villa*, however, is well worth checking out for its colonial ambience. For an

British in 1821. Despite the British penchant for hunting (panther, tiger and deer) and fishing, they were aware, within the vision of the time, of protecting the natural landscape. The most destructive period came after Independence. From 1952, a series of "five-year plans" towards "development" were implemented. Widespread planting of exotic trees, principally eucalyptus, wattle and pine, provided a generous income for the government, but has had far-reaching effects on local ecology. A new synthetic fibre industry, established in the foothills, requires huge amounts of pulp to make fibre. Despite local fears and protests, including a *satyagraha*-style public fast, more and more acreage is cleared in order to feed factories.

Traditional *shola* forest, once destroyed, takes thousands of years to replace, and newly planted eucalyptus draws water from miles around. For the first time in its history, this once swampy region suffers from water shortages. The Todas can no longer get enough thatching grass to build houses and temples, and their traditional homes are being replaced by concrete. Nothing grows under eucalyptus and pine, and the sacred buffalo have nowhere to graze. Many Todas have been forced to sell their stock, and barely enough are left to perform the ceremonies at the heart of Toda life.

Visiting the Todas

In recent years, the Todas have become something of a tourist curiosity, particularly among the groups of well heeled foreigners passing through the Nilgiris, and numerous trekking agencies and guides offering day-trips, or longer treks, to their settlements from Ooty. Although nothing on the scale of Thailand's Hill Tribe tourist circuit, the experience has to be a hollow one, consisting of a brief visit, and possibly a meal, followed up with the inevitable photo session. That said, the Todas in the more commonly visited villages do little to discourage foreigners from coming; on the contrary, they seem only too happy to pose in traditional costume for the pre-arranged fee handed over to them by the tour leaders.

A recommended guide for trips to Toda settlements around Ooty is R. Seniappan (aka "Sinni"), contactable through the official guides' office on the corner between the bus stand and railway station. He has been running tours into the area for years, is highly knowledgeable about local customs and etiquette and enjoys cordial relations with Toda people in the villages visited. Count on around Rs250 per day for his fee, and additional costs for meals and transport. You'll probably learn just as much, however, if not more, about the Todas' way of life by reading Anthony Walker's definitive anthropological study, *The Todas of South India: A New Approach*, researched in the 1970s.

---

inexpensive *udipi* breakfast, just head for one of the "meals" restaurants around Charing Cross serving *iddli*-dosa and filter coffee.

Chandan, *Nahar Hotel*, Commercial Road, Charing Cross ☎ 0423/442173. Carefully prepared North Indian specialities (their *paneer kofta* is particularly good), and a small selection of tandoori vegetarian dishes, served inside a smart restaurant or on a lawnside terrace. They also do a full range of lassis and milkshakes.

Dashprakash, *Hotel Dashprakash*, south of the racecourse ☎ 0423/442434. Congenial and inexpensive *tiffin* café, serving unlimited, tasty South Indian thalis (Rs45; lunch and dinner) dosas, and excellent *uttapams* (the coconut chutney is sublime). There is

a sister outlet in Charing Cross with a more varied menu, including North Indian dishes and thalis.

Hot Breads, Charing Cross. French-established franchise selling the usual range of quality pastries, cheesy and plain breads and savouries from a bakery outlet downstairs, as well as pizzas and other tasty snacks in a wood-lined first-floor café.

Irani, Commercial Road. A gloomy old-style Persian joint run by Bahais. Uncompromisingly non-veg (the menu's heavy on mutton and liver), but an atmospheric coffee stop, and a popular hangout for both men and women.

The best way to appreciate the Nilgiri Hills is to get well away from the towns by trekking, which gains you access to the most unspoilt and dramatic parts of the range, where settlements, let alone visitors, are few and far between. Unfortunately, the activities of the renowned bandit and sandalwood smuggler, Veerapan (see box on p.570), at large in the thick forests along the Tamil border, recently forced the Forest Department to ban trekking in the less accessible areas. In fact, at the time of writing no permits had been issued since March 1998. The stand-off between Veerapan and the authorities cannot last forever, but pending the bandit's long-promised surrender, the following guidelines currently apply only to a handful of shorter routes around Ooty, for which permits are still issued.

The landscape of the upper Nilgiris is astonishingly diverse. Treks in the west of the region (best Dec–May) take you across former Toda territory: largely uninhabit-ed grassland and natural *shola* forest where wild flowers include rhododendron and orchids. Other areas comprise man-made forest of eucalyptus, wattle and pine – reminiscent of Australia (from where much of the vegetation was originally intro-duced). On the far western edge of the escarpment, forming the western border of Mukurti Sanctuary, thousand-metre drops plummet to the heavy evergreen rainfor-est of Kerala.

The lower areas in the north and east are completely different: a dry, rough, rocky terrain with patches of dense thorny scrub, populated by diverse wildlife, including *sambar*, sloth bear and some gaur (Indian bison). Trekking in this area is possible all year round, but the intense heat between March and May is not conducive to long walks.

Animals indigenous to the Nilgiris include the rare Nilgiri tahr (see p.691) and sambar (deer), wild dog, elephant, and even panther and tiger. The bird population is small: grey jungle fowl, hawks and harriers. At higher altitudes, bright daytime sunshine with temperatures of around 20°C is followed by a dramatic cooling to freezing point at night, and warm clothing is essential.

Trekking practicalities

Unlike most areas of the Indian Himalayas, trekking in the environmentally sensitive (and Veerapan-plagued) Nilgiris can involve lots of forward planning and, above all, bureaucracy. Permits have to be obtained from the Forest Department at least a week to ten days in advance for just about any itinerary that wanders off-road. However, it can be difficult to establish which office you need to apply to for which route, and even harder to gain the requisite forms, never mind the signatures and stamps. As a rule of thumb, the Deputy Forest Officer (North Division), at Udhagamandalam Forest Department, behind the police station (Mon–Fri 10am–5.30pm; ☎0423/443968), issues permits for the northern and eastern Nilgiris. Therefore, the DFO (South Division), in the same building (same hours; ☎0423/444083), is the man to see if you want to head south beyond Avalanchi and Parson's Valley (18km west). Just to confuse matters, there's also the Wildlife Warden's Office, five minutes' down Coonoor Road from Charing Cross, on the first floor of the Mahalingam Petrol Company (look for the green building behind the petrol pump on the right as you head out of town), who deals with the Upper Bhavani area and Mudumalai.

As stated above, the Forest Department officially ceased issuing trekking passes when the "Veerapan problem" forced the closure of the nearby national parks. However, you may be able to obtain permission for some routes if you employ a guide to help you through the paperwork; without one, you'll also find it hard to arrange accommodation and food along your chosen route. Most trekking groups stay in Forest Department and Electricity Rest Houses or bungalows, with the odd night in local village temple *choultries*, homes or schools – all of which a Tamil-speaking guide will be able to sort out a lot more easily than you. In addition, cooking equipment and provisions have to be bought or ordered along the way, and then, of course, there's the route to follow (no simple matter given the total absence of marked paths and reliable topographical maps).

Official guides, distinguished by their blue shirts, can be contacted in Ooty through their office opposite the bus stand. One of the most knowledgeable and dependable is R. Seniappan (aka "Sinni"); if he's not around, ask for "Sherif" or "Carlton". All three charge fixed rates of Rs200–250 per day depending on the length and nature of the trek. Before you leave, be sure to check the cost of accommodation and meals, and whether you'll be expected to pay for transport by jeep to the trailhead. Note, too, that it's standard practice for punters to feed their guides and porters while trekking, and to tip at the end of the route if things have gone well. Finally, remember to allow plenty of time for the processing of passes.

If you'd rather, you can book an all-in package – saving you the hassle of arranging your own permits – with guides, food, accommodation and transport covered in a single price. Contact one of the following agencies, who are all reliable and experienced (although not necessarily the cheapest) operators in the Nilgiri area:

Clipper Holidays, Suite 406, Regency Enclave, 4 Margath Rd, off Brigade Road, Bangalore ☏ 080/221 0454, ☏ 559 9833, ✉ cliphol@clipper.wiprobt.ems.vsnl.net.in. A highly professional and admirably eco-conscious outfit run by conservationist Ranjan Abraham.

Jungle Tours & Travel, Masinagudi, near the entrance to Madumalai Wildlife Sanctuary ☏ 0423/56336. Check out this place if you're staying in Madumalai – its packages are slightly cheaper than those offered in the resort hotels.

Nilgiri Trekking Association (NTA), Kavitha Nilayam, 31-D Bank Rd, Udhagamandalam ☏ 0423/441887, ☏ 442883. A relatively inexpensive option, and good source of general information on the area, although their Nilgiri treks are infrequent these days.

Ozone, 55th Main, 12th Block, Kumara Park West, Bangalore ☏&☏ 080/331 0441, ✉ nomads@giasbga.vsnl.net.in. Typically dynamic Bangalorean agent, offering a range of outdoor activities in the Nilgiri area.

Routes

When this book went to press, trekking routes in the Nilgiris were severely limited by the permit restrictions, but you can be pretty confident of obtaining a pass to hike in the Mukurthi area, on the fringes of the Mukurthi National Park, around 32km west of Ooty via Pykhara village. Although access to the core area of the reserve is not allowed, you can still cross the rolling high pastureland along the Kerala border, roamed by herds of elephant and Nilgiri tahr, and take in sweeping views of conical Mukurthi Peak (2467m), an extinct volcano known to the Todas as "Gateway to the World of the Dead". When the current access restrictions are eased, it should also be possible to explore the virgin tropical forest lining Silent Valley, for which you'll need at least three days.

The other most popular trekking area currently open to tourists is around Avalanchi, a high region of windswept grassland southwest of Ooty. The resthouse in the village serves as an ideal base for circular day-hikes to reservoirs and mountains in the area, or (if permits are issued) you can head northwest, skirting the Keralan border towards Mukurthi peak.

Also open at present is a network of trails starting at Parson's Valley, another area of open grassland, 18km west, from where you can hike to the Portmund Dam via Mukurthi Peak (one day). A paved road runs to the valley from Ooty (17km), for which you don't need a permit; alternatively, catch a bus (four daily). In the other direction, a rewarding route from Dodabetta (see p.568), the region's second high-

continued overleaf

continued from previous page

est peak, takes you northwards via Ebanad village to the edge of the Mudumalai wildlife sanctuary – a four-day round trip from Ooty. This is probably the most adventurous option currently open to tourists, passing through a string of Toda villages and some truly isolated country, but don't attempt it without a guide.

Trekking tips

To minimize your impact on this ecologically vulnerable area while trekking, try to observe the following "golden green rules" (you may need to impress some of them upon your porters or guides): pack out all rubbish; never burn plastics; purify your own water rather than use bottled water; never use toothpaste or any kind of detergent (even biodegradable ones) in streams, rivers or lakes (wash up with metal scourers); cook with kerosene or multi-fuel stoves, not on wood fires; and where you are unable to use a toilet, bury your faeces and carefully burn the paper after you (better still use water).

Nilgiri Woodlands, Racecourse Road, 1km from bus stand and railway station ☎0423/42551, ☎42530. There is an à la carte menu, but the inexpensive lunch-time and evening thalis (Rs45) are good too. Checked tablecloths and cane chairs give it the look of a village hall. No alcohol.

Shinkow, 42 Commissioners Rd ☎0423/442811. Good-value, authentic Chinese restaurants serving up good-sized portions on the spicy and pricey side – a main course will set you back about Rs130.

Around Ooty

Regular local bus services to outlying villages and plantations allow you to reach the less developed regions **around Ooty**. The most popular destination for a day-trip is the Nilgiris' second highest mountain, **Dodabetta** (2638m), 10km east along the Kotagiri road. Sheltering Coonoor from the southwest monsoon (and, conversely, Ooty from the reach of the northwest monsoon of October and November), the peak is the region's most prominent landmark. It's also easily accessible by road: buses run every couple of hours from Ooty (10am–3.30pm) to the summit, where a viewing platform and telescope make

Moving on from Ooty

Ooty railway station has a reservation counter (10am–noon & 3.30–4.30pm) and a booking office (6.30am–7pm), where you can buy tickets for the Nilgiri Blue Mountain Railway, as well as onwards services to most other destinations in the South. From Ooty, four trains run along the narrow-gauge line to Coonoor each day, with two (9.15am & 2.30pm) continuing down the Mettapalayam, on the main broad-gauge network. If you are heading to Chennai, take the second service, which meets up in Mettupayalam with the fast #6606 *Nilgiri Express* (departs 7.25pm; 10hr 30min).

You can also book buses in advance, at the reservation offices for both state buses (daily 9am–12.30pm & 1.30–5.30pm) and the local company, Cheran Transport (daily 9am–1pm & 1.30–5.30pm), at the bus stand. Towns served include Bangalore and Mysore (half-hourly buses to both pass through Mudumalai), Kodaikanal, Thanjavur, Thiruvananthapuram and Kanniyakumari, as well as Kotagiri, Coonoor and Coimbatore nearer to hand. Private buses to Mysore, Bangalore and Kodaikanal can be booked at hotels, or agents in Charing Cross; be aware though that even when advertised as "super-deluxe", many turn out to be cramped minibuses.

the most of a stunning panorama. To enjoy it, however, you'll have to get here before the daily deluge of bus parties.

For details of other possible day-trips from Ooty, notably to **Avalanchi** and **Mukuthi**, see box Trekking in the Nilgiris on p.566.

Mudumalai Wildlife Sanctuary

Set 1140m up in the Nilgiri Hills, the **MUDUMALAI WILDLIFE SANC-TUARY** is one of the most accessible in the South, covering 322 square kilometres of deciduous forest, split by the main road from Ooty (64km to the southeast) to Mysore (97km to the northwest). Unfortunately, the park has been **closed** to visitors for the past few years, amid fears that the sandalwood smuggler, **Veerapan** may abduct tourists or Forest Department wardens (see box on p.570). You can, however, still stop here en route to or from Mysore to sample the peace and fresh air of the Nilgiri forest after the bus parties of day-trippers from Ooty have all gone home.

At **Theppakkadu**, the main access point to the sanctuary, the big event of the day – now that the van tours of the park have been suspended – is an **Elephant Camp show** (daily 6pm; Rs20): the put-upon pachyderms perform puja or play soccer to a Boney M accompaniment.

Coming from Ooty, the approach to Mudumalai is spectacular, twisting and turning down 36 hairpin bends, through wooded hills and past waterfalls (in season). Monkeys dart and play in the trees, and you may glimpse a tethered elephant from the camp at **Kargudi**, where wild elephants are tamed for work in the timber industry. Mudumalai has one of the largest populations of elephants in India, along with wild dogs, gaur (Indian bison), common and Nilgiri langur and bonnet macaques (monkeys), jackal, hyena and sloth bear, and even a few tigers and panthers.

Practicalities

Until the Forest Department relaxes restrictions on trekking in the remote woodland areas around the Mudumalai, you can only reach the park by road. The fastest and most spectacular route, via Sighur Ghat, is not negotiable by large vehicles, but private minibuses and a regular Cheran Transport bus service run to Masinagudi (1hr) from Ooty. Travelling on the longer, less steep route via Gudalur, standard buses to Mysore and Bangalore from Ooty take 2hr 30min to reach **Theppakkadu**, which is connected to Masinagudi, 8km away, by bus and jeep. You can also walk this route, but should beware of animals, especially wild elephant.

Accommodation

Standards in Mudumalai are generally high, with most of the hotels in gorgeous, peaceful settings. The best of them are up to 5km off the main road from Masinagudi in **Bokkapuram**, although two budget options overlook the main road. Book in advance, and arrange for your hosts to pick you up from the bus stop – taxis or jeeps are rare in the village. Most places expect guests for full board, as Masinagudi only has a few simple restaurants.

Bamboo Banks Guest House, 2km from the main road, Masinagudi ☏0423/56222. Two comfortable rooms, and four cottages in a beautiful environment. Delicious meals are served alfresco in the garden. ⑥–⑦

Chitral Walk (Jungle Trails), near Valaitotam

village, 7km southeast of Masinagudi ☏0423/56256. The most remote and atmospheric option; it's well off the beaten track with comfortable rooms and a good cook. By far the best place in this price category. ⑥

Dreamland, next to the Masinagudi crossroads

The delicate scent of sandalwood – *chandan* in Hindi – is one of the quintessential fragrances of South India, particularly around Mysore in Karnataka, where specialist craftsmen carve combs, beads, elephants and gods and use its oil to make incense and soap. Mashed into a paste, the valuable heartwood of the tree is regarded as a powerful antiseptic capable of curing migraine and skin ailments. Vaishnavites (devotees of the god Vishnu) also smear their foreheads with sandalwood powder before performing puja, a practice recorded in the two-thousand-year old epic, the *Ramayana*, as well as the poetry of the sage Kalidasa, dating from the third century BC.

Sandalwood may be an essential element in traditional Indian culture, but it is fast becoming a rare commodity due to demand from foreign markets, which has forced the price skywards in recent years (a kilo of sandalwood oil will now fetch around US\$14,000). The largest importer is the US perfume industry, which uses vast quantities of the oil as a base and fixative, followed by the Gulf states, where sandalwood (along with myrrh, jasmine and amber) ranks among the few fragrances permitted by Islamic law.

The vast bulk of India's sandalwood comes from mixed, dry deciduous forests of the southern Deccan Plateau, around Bangalore, where trees – if allowed to grow for at least thirty years – reach an average height of 20m. Extraction and oil-pressing are strictly controlled by the Indian government, in accordance with a law passed by the Sultan of Mysore in 1792, who declared that no individual other than himself could own a sandalwood tree, even if it grew on private land. This law is still enforced, although these days foresters receive seventy percent of the sale value if they can prove they have grown and protected the wood.

In spite of having the law on their side, the Indian government has been failing miserably in its attempts to control sandalwood stocks and trade over the past decade or so. This is due largely to the activities of the notorious smuggler Veerapan, whose cartel handles an estimated seventy percent of Karnataka's total export, amounting to billions of rupees of lost revenue each year. South India's most infamous brigand began his career at the age of 14, when he poached his first elephant. Two thousand pachyderm carcasses later, he jacked in ivory smuggling for the sandalwood racket and, apart from a brief period of imprisonment in 1986 (when he managed to escape), has been on the run ever since.

⌖0423/56127. The cheapest place within reach of the park; it lacks atmosphere but it's clean and safe. ❸

Jungle Hut, 5km from the road, Bokkapuram, Masinagudi ⌖ & ⌖0423/56240. The park's most expensive option: twelve very comfortable cottages, restaurant and a swimming pool. ❼

TTDC Hotel Tamil Nadu, Theppakkadu

⌖0423/56249. Functional hotel, with clean four-bedded rooms and a very cheap dorm (Rs50 weekdays, Rs75 at weekends). Meals are by arrangement and there's a seven-night maximum stay. Officially, you should book at the TTDC office in Ooty, but you may be lucky on spec if they're not full. ❶–❻

Travel details

Trains

Chidambaram to: Chengalpattu (4 daily; 5hr 40min–8hr); Kumbakonam (3 daily; 2hr); Rameshwaram (2 daily; 12hr); Thanjavur (4 daily; 3hr); Tiruchirapalli (4 daily; 4–5hr); Tirupati (1 daily; 11hr 15min); Tiruvannamalai (1 daily; 4hr

40min).

Coimbatore to: Bangalore (2 daily; 7hr); Calcutta (4 weekly; 38hr–39hr 30min); Chennai (5–6 daily; 7hr 15min–9hr 10min); Delhi (1–2 daily; 35–43hr); Hyderabad (1 daily; 20hr 50min); Kanniyakumari (3 daily; 12hr–13hr 30min); Kochi (7 daily; 5hr–6hr

Moving continually between sixty camps in the dense jungle lining the Karnataka–Tamil Nadu border, Veerapan and his men, with their regulation green army fatigues and swaggering moustaches, keep one step ahead of the crack army forces out to arrest them, to manage their lucrative operation over a massive area. Because of the sums his smuggling generates, the bandit can afford to pay local villagers Rs30 per day to cut and transport wood – more than double what the Forest Service pays for the same work. This, combined with rumours of extravagant gifts to poor people and temples, have earned him a near mythical Robin Hood status across a 6000 square kilometre swathe of forest, despite the policy of systematic and violent intimidation which he employs to discourage informers and punish those who cross him.

Veerapan's treatment of Forest Service and government officials who fall into his clutches has been brutal over the years, with regular murders, kidnappings and incidents of torture to enhance his already fearsome reputation. The worst atrocity to date, however, was in April 1993, when 21 policemen were lured into an ambush and killed by landmines. The Indian government responded swiftly by launching the largest manhunt in history; six hundred border security troops were flown in for the operation, but somehow Veerapan still managed to slip through the net. In 2000, Veerapan again made the headlines when he kidnapped and held hostage an ageing but still popular Tami film actor, Rajkumar. As the weeks went by, the public began to ask questions when mediators and journalists demonstrated that they were able to meet with Veerapan, yet a crack squad of National Security Force officers failed and failed again to corner the brigand and save Rajkumar. The eventual release of Rajkumar after 107 days is shrouded in speculation, but was conducted by the mysterious Dr Banu, a female doctor who appeared from nowhere and is suspected of having connections with the local and illegal quarrying business; the shadowy Veerapan was allowed to retreat back into the jungle undergrowth. Today he continues to elude the massive army presence in the forests, and operates his shady business with an impressively large "dead-or-alive" bounty on his head.

Veerapan and his band are the reason why the government has closed huge tracts of protected forest in the Western Ghats to tourists, among them all the region's major wildlife reserves. The only hope for resolution is that the arch smuggler, following the example of equally notorious Indian bandits such as Phoolan Devi (India's "Bandit Queen") and Malkhan Singh from the Chambal Valley in Uttar Pradesh, will surrender.

30min); Madurai (2 daily; 5–6hr); Mumbai (1 daily; 35hr); Ooty (2 daily; 5hr); Rameshwaram (1 daily; 14hr 20min); Salem (13–14 daily; 2hr 15min–3hr); Thiruvananthapuram (3 daily; 9hr 50min–11hr); Tiruchirapalli (2 daily; 5hr 30min–8hr 50min). Kanniyakumari to: Chennai (1–2 daily; 15hr 45min–17hr 15min); Coimbatore (2 daily; 13hr 25min–16hr 45min); Delhi (Fri only; 58hr); Kochi (2–3 daily; 7hr 30min–9hr); Madurai (1–2 daily; 4hr 45min–5hr 15min); Mumbai (1 daily; 48hr); Salem (1 daily; 15hr); Thiruvananthapuram (2–3 daily; 2hr–2hr 30min); Tiruchirapalli (1–2 daily; 8hr 25min–9hr 30min). Madurai to: Bangalore (1 daily; 12hr); Chengalpattu (4–5 daily; 9hr); Chennai (5–6 daily; 7hr 45min–11hr 15min); Coimbatore (2 daily; 5hr 20min–7hr); Kanniyakumari (1–2 daily; 5hr 45min–6hr 10min); Kodaikanal Road (4–5 daily;

23min–51min); Rameshwaram (2 daily; 4hr 50min–7hr); Tiruchirapalli (5–6 daily; 2hr 20min–4hr); Tirupati (2 weekly; 11hr 20min). Tiruchirapalli to: Bangalore (1 daily; 9hr 30min); Chengalpattu (5–6 daily; 5hr 50min); Chennai (7–8 daily; 5–7hr); Cochin (1 daily; 10hr 50min); Coimbatore (2 daily; 5hr 30min–6hr); Kanniyakumari (1–2 daily; 10hr); Kodaikanal Road (5 daily; 2hr 40min); Madurai (5–6 daily; 3hr 10min–4hr 40min); Thanjavur (4 daily; 1hr 40min); Villupuram (1 daily; 6hr 55min).

Buses

Chidambaram to: Chengalpattu (20 daily; 4hr 30min–5hr); Chennai (10 daily; 5–6hr); Coimbatore (5 daily; 7hr); Kanchipuram (8–10 daily; 7–8hr); Kanniyakumari (3 daily; 10hr); Kumbakonam (every 10min; 2hr 30min); Madurai (8 daily; 8hr);

571

Pondicherry (every 20 min; 2hr); Thanjavur (every 20 min; 4hr); Tiruchirapalli (every 30min; 5hr); Tiruvannamalai (15 daily; 3hr 30min); Vellore (5 daily; 4hr 30min).

Coimbatore to: Bangalore (10 daily; 8–9hr); Chennai (15 daily; 10–12hr); Kanchipuram (3 daily; 9–10hr); Kanniyakumari (3 daily; 14hr); Kodaikanal Road (10 daily; 6hr); Madurai (25 daily; 5–7hr); Pondicherry (6 daily; 7hr); Rameshwaram (2 daily; 14hr); Salem (40 daily; 3–4hr); Thiruvananthapuram (10–15 daily; 12hr); Tiruchirapalli (every 30min; 4–6hr).

Kanchipuram to: Chennai (every 10 min; 1hr 30min–2hr); Coimbatore (4 daily; 9–10hr); Madurai (4 daily; 10–12hr); Pondicherry (12–15 daily; 7hr); Tiruchirapalli (6 daily; 7–8hr); Tiruvannamalai (15–20 daily; 3hr); Vellore (every 10min; 2hr 30min).

Kanniyakumari to: Chennai (11 daily; 14–16hr); Kovalam (10 daily; 2hr); Madurai (every 30min; 6hr); Pondicherry (10–12 daily; 12–13hr); Rameshwaram (4 daily; 9–10hr); Thiruvananthapuram (20 daily; 2hr 45min–3hr 30min); Tiruchirapalli (every 30min; 10hr).

Madurai to: Bangalore (21 daily; 8–9hr); Chengalpattu (37 daily; 9hr); Chennai (hourly; 11hr); Chidambaram (5 daily; 7–8hr); Coimbatore (every 30 min; 6–10hr); Kanchipuram (6–7 daily; 10–12hr); Kanniyakumari (hourly; 6hr); Kochi (8

daily; 10hr); Kodaikanal Road (11 daily; 4hr); Mysore (5 daily; 10hr); Pondicherry (14 daily; 11–13hr); Rameshwaram (26 daily; 4hr); Thanjavur (every 30 min; 4–5hr); Thiruvananthapuram (18 daily; 7hr); Tiruchendur (15 daily; 4hr); Tiruchirapalli (every 30 min; 4–6hr); Tirunelveli (20 daily; 3hr); Tirupati (6 daily; 15hr).

Pondicherry to: Bangalore (4 daily; 10–12hr); Chennai (every 30min; 2hr 30min–3hr); Chidambaram (every 20min; 2hr); Coimbatore (10 daily; 10hr); Kanchipuram (8 daily; 3–4hr); Kanniyakumari (15–20 daily; 12–13hr); Madurai (hourly; 11–13hr); Mamallapuram (every 20min; 3hr); Thanjavur (20 daily; 5hr); Tiruchirapalli (every 30min; 5–6hr); Tiruvannamalai (every 20min; 2hr).

Tiruchirapalli to: Chengalpattu (every 20min; 7–8hr); Chennai (hourly; 5–6hr); Coimbatore (every 30min; 4–6hr); Kanchipuram (2 daily; 6–7hr); Kanniyakumari (15–20 daily; 10–12hr); Kodaikanal Road (8–12 daily; 5hr); Madurai (every 30 min; 4–6hr); Pondicherry (20 daily; 5–6hr); Thanjavur (every 10 min; 1hr–1hr 30min); Tiruvannamalai (5 daily; 6hr).

Flights

Coimbatore to: Bangalore (1 daily; 40min); Chennai (1–2 daily; 1hr 5min–1hr 55min); Kochi (2 weekly; 30min); Mumbai (1 daily; 1hr 50min).

Andhra Pradesh

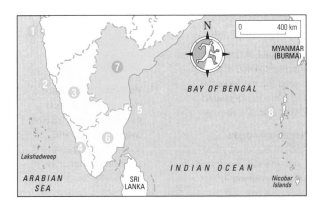

CHAPTER 7

Highlights

* **Hyderabad** This predominately Islamic city offers a compelling combination of monuments, museums and lively bazaars. See p.577

* **Golconda Fort** Set in a lush landscape just west of Hyderabad, the capital of the Qutb Shahi dynasty boasts a dramatic fort. See p.586

* **Warangal** Features two important Hindu monuments: the medieval fort and a thousand-pillared Shiva temple. See p.590

* **Nagarjunakonda** Ancient Buddhist sculptures and stupas, dotted around an island in Nagarjuna Sagar lake. See p.591

* **Amaravati** At this village on the banks of the Krishna, fine carvings surround the remains of a great stupa. See p.594

* **Tirumala Hill, Tirupati** The most visited pilgrimage centre in the world, Tirumala Hill is crowned by the Venkateshwara Vishnu temple. See p.598

* **Puttaparthy** Sai Baba's main ashram attracts modern pilgrims from all over the world, and forms the centrepiece of a thriving community. See p.599

Andhra Pradesh

A lthough **ANDHRA PRADESH** is the largest state in South India and occupies a great swathe of land, stretching for over 1200km along the coast from Orissa to Tamil Nadu and reaching far inland from the fertile deltas of the Godavari and Krishna rivers to the semi-arid Deccan Plateau, it's not a place that receives many tourists. Most foreign travellers pass through en route to its more attractive neighbours, which is understandable as places of interest are few and far between. However, the sights that Andhra

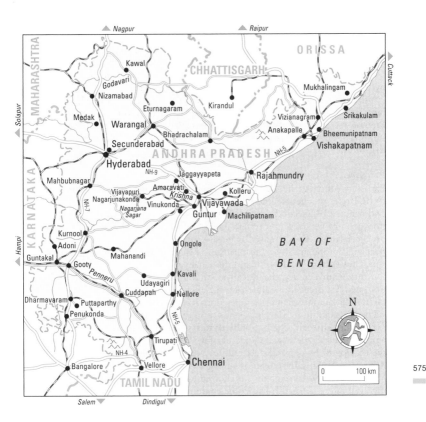

All accommodation prices in this book have been categorized using the price codes below. Prices given are for a double room, and all taxes are included. For more details, see p.46.

① up to Rs100	④ Rs300–400	⑦ Rs900–1500
② Rs100–200	⑤ Rs400–600	⑧ Rs1500–2500
③ Rs200–300	⑥ Rs600–900	⑨ Rs2500 and upwards

Pradesh does have to offer are absorbing and well enough connected to warrant at least a few stops on a longer tour of South India.

The state capital, **Hyderabad**, is a run-down but undoubtedly atmospheric city dating from the late sixteenth century. Its endless bazaars, eclectic Salar Jung museum and the mighty **Golconda Fort** nearby make it an enticing place to spend a day or two. Outlying areas are home to the spanking new towers of hi-tech companies. By contrast, its modern twin, commercial **Secunderabad**, excels only in characterlessness. **Warangal**, 150km northeast of Hyderabad, has both Muslim and Hindu remains from the twelfth and thirteenth centuries, while the region's Buddhist legacy – particularly its superb sculpture – is preserved in museums at sites such as **Nagarjunakonda** (south of Hyderabad) and **Amaravati**, the ancient Satavahana capital. In the east, the big cities of **Vishakapatnam** and **Vijayawada** have little to recommend them, though the latter makes a convenient access point for Amaravati. The temple town of **Tirupati** in the far southeast – best reached from Chennai in Tamil Nadu – is one of India's great Hindu phenomena, a fascinating and impossibly crowded pilgrimage site. In the southwest of the state, the small town of **Puttaparthy** attracts a more international pilgrim crowd, drawn here by the prospect of *darshan* from spiritual leader Sai Baba.

Although modern industries have grown up around the capital, and shipbuilding, iron and steel are important on the coast, most people in Andhra Pradesh remain poor. Away from the Godavari and Krishna deltas, where the soil is rich enough to grow rice and sugar cane, the land is virtually impossible to cultivate.

Some history

Earliest accounts of the region, dating back to the time of **Ashoka** (third century BC), refer to a people known as the Andhras. The **Satavahana dynasty** (second century BC–second century AD), also known as the Andras, came to control much of central and southern India from their second capital at Amaravati on the Krishna. They enjoyed extensive international trade with both eastern Asia and Europe, and were great patrons of Buddhism. Subsequently, the Pallavas and Cholas from Tamil Nadu and the Chalukyas from Karnataka held sway. By the thirteenth century, the Kakatiyas of Warangal were under constant threat from Muslim incursions, while later on, after the fall of their city at Hampi, the Hindu Vijayanagars transferred operations to Chandragiri near Tirupati.

The next significant development was in the mid-sixteenth century, with the rise of the **Muslim Qutb Shahi dynasty**. In 1687, the son of the Moghul emperor Aurangzeb seized Golconda. Five years after Aurangzeb died in 1707, the Viceroy of Hyderabad declared independence and established the Asaf Jahi dynasty of Nizams. In return for allying with the British against Tipu Sultan of Mysore, the **Nizam** dynasty was allowed to retain a certain degree of autonomy even after the British had come to dominate all India.

During the struggle for Independence, harmony between Hindus and Muslims in Andhra Pradesh disintegrated, and **Partition** brought matters to a bloody climax (see box, p.579). Andhra Pradesh state was created in 1956 from Telegu-speaking regions (although Urdu is widely spoken in Hyderabad) that had previously formed part of the Madras Presidency on the east coast and the princely state of Hyderabad to the west. Today almost ninety percent of the population is Hindu, with Muslims largely concentrated in the capital.

Hyderabad/Secunderabad

A melting-pot of Muslim and Hindu cultures, the capital of Andhra Pradesh comprises the twin cities of **HYDERABAD** and **SECUNDERABAD**, with a combined population of around six million. Secunderabad, of little interest to

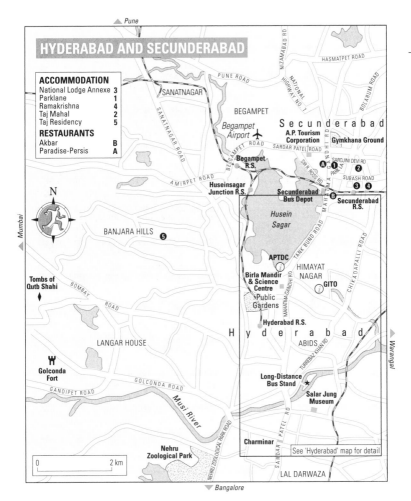

visitors, is the modern administrative city founded by the British, whereas Hyderabad, the old city, with its seething bazaars, Muslim monuments and Salar Jung Museum has heaps of charm. Despite this, Hyderabad went into decline after Independence with tensions often close to the surface due to lack of funding – the old city only received 25 percent of the budget despite having 45 percent of the population. In recent years, however, the area has received a new lease of life from the computer industry, and Hyderabad is now at the forefront of software training, rivalling Bangalore as the south's hi-tech capital. This upturn has increased the optimism of Hyderabadis, whether they are reaping direct benefits or not, who now gleefully refer to their city as "Cyberabad".

The last Nizam

Picking your way through the sprawl of modern Hyderabad, it's hard to imagine that a little over fifty years ago this was the capital of a vast and powerful state, whose sumptuous palaces, mosques and ornamental gardens made it among the most splendid cities ever seen in south Asia. That the last outpost of living Moghul grandeur in the subcontinent could be so quickly and so thoroughly reduced hints at the terrible events surrounding the demise of the state's last ruler. Direct descendents of the prophet Mohammed on one side, and the prophet's right-hand man, the Khalifa, on the other, the Asaf Shah dynasty of Hyderabad – known since the seventeenth century by its honorific Moghul title, **Nizam** – rose to pre-eminence in the twilight of Muslim rule in India. Feuds of succession nearly consumed the family, but it survived the colonial incursions of the French, East India Company and Marathas, and by the twentieth century presided over the premier princely state in British India, home to a population of between fifteen and twenty thousand.

Marooned amid the vast ocean of Hindu India, the state capital, Hyderabad, emerged from the collapse of the Moghul empire and Deccan Sultanates as a lone outpost of courtly Muslim culture in India. Its nobles, merchants, craftsmen and artists, drawn from as far afield as Turkey, Persia and Central Asia, as well as the fading Indo-Islamic capitals of the north, lived in a splendid isolation epitomized by the extravagant lifestyles of the Nizams. Behind the high walls of the King Kothi palace, some 10,000 people – ranging from the Arab mercenaries and Abyssinian amazons who guarded the harem, to the legions of wives, courtesans and servants who attended on the ruler – lived an increasingly anachronistic, introverted life, regulated by complex medieval etiquette and old-world courtly manners.

When he ascended to the throne in 1911, the tenth and last Nizam, **Mir Osman Ali**, was reputedly the richest man in the world. Memoirs of former British diplomats and local aristocrats describe his collection of 300 vintage Daimlers and Rolls Royce cars; of the famously huge, 185-carat "Jacobi" diamond, thought to be the largest ever found, which the Nizam used as a paperweight; and of trucks stacked with pearls, precious stones and gold ingots – a portable fortune that could be spirited away in the event of revolution or attack.

Taciturn, paranoid and addicted to opium, the last Nizam grew progressively more eccentric as British rule waned. The city was as rife with rumours of his extreme stinginess as of his unsurpassed wealth. Visitors, it was said, were limited to one biscuit when they called for tea, while the Nizam wore the same threadbare clothes for thirty or more years. One British resident mistook him for "a snuffly old clerk too old to be sacked". He even reputedly knitted his own socks, and ate all his meals off a tin plate on his bedroom floor, surrounded by the contents of overspilling wastepaper baskets. Perhaps the most surprising facet of the last Nizam's eccentricity, however, was his prodigious sexual appetite; he is said to have fathered

Hyderabad was founded in 1591 by **Muhammad Quli Shah** (1562–1612), beside the Musi River, 8km east of Golconda, the fortress capital of the Golconda empire which by now was suffering from overcrowding and a serious lack of water. Unusually, this new city was laid out on a grid system, with huge arches and stone buildings that included Hyderabad's most famous monument, **Charminar**. At first it was a city without walls; these were only added in 1740, as defence against the Marathas. Legend has it that a secret tunnel linked the spectacular **Golconda Fort** with the city, dotted with dome-shaped structures at suitable intervals to provide the unfortunate messengers who had to use it with the opportunity to come up for fresh air.

more than 100 illegitimate children. Hidden cameras installed inside the guest quarters of his palaces also enabled him to compile what is thought to be India's largest collection of pornographic photographs.

When the end of the Raj finally came in 1947, Mir Osman Ali was given one year in which to decide whether to throw his lot in with India or faraway Pakistan. In the event, much to the amazement of Prime Minister Nehru and Home Affairs minister Patel, he chose instead to tough it out alone, declaring himself ruler of a fully autonomous **Hyderabad State**. The decision, symptomatic of the Nizam's introversion and bull-headed cupidity, was an act of hubris that would cost the lives of hundreds of thousands of this former subjects.

Often glossed over by historians as a bloodless formality, the ensuing assault on Hyderabad ordered by Nehru in 1948 – in which a fully mechanized Indian army attacked a feudal force armed with little more than 300 rifles – turned into one of the ugliest episodes in the history of Independent India. After being held at bay for four days, Nehru's troops rampaged through Hyderabad state, looting and leaving a trail of destruction in their wake. Taking advantage of the mayhem, gangs of Hindu *goondas* also ran amuck, slaughtering their Muslim neighbours and systematically raping the women. Although outwardly unruffled, Nehru was privately outraged by reports of the atrocities committed by the Indian army in "**Operation Polo**", and commissioned an official enquiry once the dust had settled. The report, entitled *Hyderabad: After the Fall*, concluded that as many as 200,000 Muslims were massacred in the wake of the army action.

While tens of thousands of his former supporters, staff and nobles fled to escape execution and imprisonment, Nizam Mir Osman Ali was accorded the usual princely rights, along with privy purse amounting to Rs5 million per year. He was also allowed to retain income derived from his estates and keep his treasure. Nevertheless, he died in 1967 complaining that the annexation of Hyderabad had reduced him to poverty.

Among the Nizam's surviving assets being squabbled over by his heirs is a mysterious million, deposited in a London bank account shortly before the 1948 debacle. Following Partition, both the Indian and Pakistani governments laid claim to the sum, along with a several of the Nizam's descendents and an Indian Princess called Tahera, who told the High Court of Andhra Pradesh that a stake of the money was owed to her as a *mehr*, the dowry given by a Muslim woman's family upon marriage which is traditionally returned in the event of divorce. So far the only beneficiary of the unending legal wrangle over the lost million has been the UK's Natwest bank. Since it was deposited in 1947, the £1,007,940 and nine shillings are estimated to have grown to between £25 and 80 million. The bank insists it cannot relinquish the money until all the parties involved in the dispute are in agreement – an unlikely prospect indeed, given the perennially turbulent state of Indo-Pak relations, and the refusal of the various protagonists involved to recognize each others' claims.

For the 300 years of Muslim reign, there was harmony between the predominantly Hindu population and the minority Muslims. Hyderabad was the most important focus of Muslim power in South India at this time; the princes' fabulous wealth derived primarily from the fine gems mined in the Kistna Valley at Golconda, which, in the 1600s, was the diamond centre of the world. The famous **Koh-i-Noor** diamond was found here, and the only time it was ever captured was by Moghul emperor Aurangzeb, when his son seized the Golconda Fort in 1687. It ended up, cut, in a British royal crown.

Arrival and information

The old city of **Hyderabad** straddles the Musi River. Most places of interest lie south of the river, while much of the accommodation is to the north. Further north, separated from Hyderabad by the Husain Sagar Lake, is the modern twin city of **Secunderabad**, where some long-distance trains terminate, and where all through trains deposit passengers. If you do have to get off at Secunderabad, your ticket is valid for any connecting train to Hyderabad; and if none is imminent, many buses including #5, #8 and #20 ply between both stations. Hyderabad **airport**, 8km north of the city at Begampet, is served by auto-rickshaws, taxis and buses #9m or #10 via Nampally station, and a number of routes including #10, #45, #47 and #49 from Secunderabad. Hyderabad **railway station** (also known as Nampally) is close to all amenities and offers a fairly comprehensive service to major destinations. The well-organized **long-distance bus stand** occupies an island in the middle of the Musi River, 3km southeast of the railway station.

The main **tourist office** in Hyderabad is the **APTDC office** (daily 7am–7pm; ☎040/345 3036, ☏345 3086, ✉ *apttdc@satyam.net.in*) on Secretariat Road just before it becomes Tank Bund, opposite a large public building known as the BRK; the other APTDC office, at Yatri Nivas, Sardar Patel Road, Secunderabad (daily 7am–7pm; ☎040/781 6375), is of little use unless you want to book one of their tours. The **Government of India tourist office**, Sandozi Buildings, Himayatnagar Road, Hyderabad, offers a few brochures (Mon–Fri 9am–5pm; ☎040/7630037). However, the best source of tourist information is the monthly listings **magazine**, *Channel 6*, widely available from bookstalls for Rs12.

Guided tours

APTDC operates a number of guided tours. All times quoted below are when the tours set off from the Secunderabad office; pick-up time in Hyderabad is 45min later. The better of the two city tours (daily 8am–5.15pm; Rs130) includes Husain Sagar, the Birla temple and planetarium, Qutb Shahi tombs (not Fri), Salar Jung Museum (not Fri), Charminar and Golconda. There are also shorter morning and afternoon city tours and one to Golconda Fort's sound and light show (daily 4.15pm–9.15pm; Rs100 including entrance fee), which also drives past Hi-Tech City. Ramoji Film City, 35km south, also has its own tour (daily 7.45am–6pm; Rs350 including entry). The Nagarjuna Sagar tour (daily 6.30am–9.30pm; Rs225) covers 360km in total, and is rather rushed, but is a convenient way to get to this fascinating area (see p.591). The longer tours to Tirupati/Tirumala, more conveniently reached from Chennai, and further afield in South India are not worth considering.

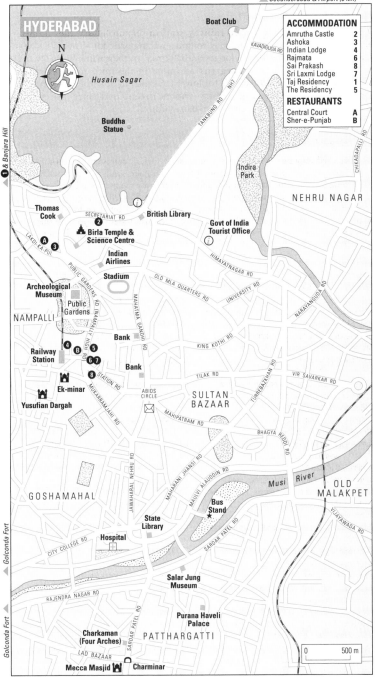

HYDERABAD

N

Secunderabad & Airport (8 km)

Boat Club

Husain Sagar

Buddha
Statue

KAVADIGUDA RD

TANKBUND RD

NH7

CHIKADAPALLI RD

ACCOMMODATION
Amrutha Castle	2
Ashoka	3
Indian Lodge	4
Rajmata	6
Sai Prakash	8
Sri Laxmi Lodge	7
Taj Residency	1
The Residency	5

RESTAURANTS
Central Court	A
Sher-e-Punjab	B

Indira
Park

NEHRU NAGAR

1 & Banjara Hill

Thomas
Cook

SECRETARIAT RD

British Library

Govt of India
Tourist Office

Birla Temple &
Science Centre

HIMAYATNAGAR RD

LAKDI-KA-PUL

Indian
Airlines

Stadium

OLD MLA QUARTERS RD

UNIVERSITY RD

NARAYANGUDA RD

PUBLIC GARDENS RD

NAMPALLY HIGH RD

Archeological
Museum

Public
Gardens

NAMPALLI

Bank

MAHATMA GANDHI RD

KING KOTHI RD

Railway
Station

STATION RD

Bank

TILAK RD

VIR SAVARKAR RD

Ek-minar

ABIDS
CIRCLE

SULTAN
BAZAAR

TURREBAZKHAN RD

Yusufian Dargah

MUKARRAMJAHI RD

MAHIPATRAM RD

BHAGYA REDDY RD

GOSHAMAHAL

JAWAHARLAL NEHRU RD

MAHARANI JHANSI RD

MAULVI ALAUDDIN RD

Musi River

OLD
MALAKPET

Golconda Fort

State
Library

Bus
Stand

SARDAR PATEL RD

VIJAYAWADA RD

Hospital

CITY COLLEGE RD

Golconda Fort

Salar Jung
Museum

RAJENDRA NAGAR RD

SARDAR PATEL RD

Purana Haveli
Palace

PATTHARGATTI

Charkaman
(Four Arches)

LAD BAZAAR

Mecca Masjid

Charminar

0   500 m

Accommodation

The area in front of Hyderabad **railway station** (Nampally) has the cheapest accommodation, but you're unlikely to find anything basic for less than Rs200. The grim little enclave of five lodges with "Royal" in their name is usually full and best avoided. The real **bargains** are more in the mid- to upper-range hotels, which offer better facilities for lower rates than in other big cities. About 2km north of Secunderabad railway station, decent mid-range places line **Sarojini Devi Road**, near the Gymkhana Ground.

Hyderabad addresses

Hyderabadis appear to have a deep mistrust of logical, consistent road-naming, mapping and addresses. One road merges into another, some addresses refer to nothing more specific than a locality, and others identify themselves as being opposite buildings that no longer exist. Just as confusing are those that have very specific addresses consisting of a string of hyphenated numbers referring to house and plot numbers, incomprehensible to anybody other than town surveyors. All this is somewhat ironic in a city that is home to one of the major sections of the Survey of India.

Hyderabad

Amrutha Castle, Secretariat Road, Saifabad ℡040/329 9899, ℻324 1850, ℮amruthacastle @pol.net.in. Affiliated to *Best Western*, this extraordinary hotel, designed like a fairy castle with round turret rooms, offers full international facilities at fair prices. With its rooftop swimming pool, it's a good place to splash out. ⑧–⑨

Ashoka, 6–1–70 Lakdi-ka-Pul ℡040/323 0105, ℻323 3739. Standard mid-range hotel with a variety of clean attached rooms, including cable TV and some a/c. ⑤–⑥

Indian lodge, Nampally Station ℡040/657 3840. The best of the basic lodges in the station area. All rooms attached with TV. ③.

Rajmata, Nampally High Road, opposite railway station ℡040/320 1000. Set back from the road in the same compound as the various *Royal* lodges. Large, clean non-a/c deluxe rooms. Their adjacent *Lakshmi* restaurant offers good South Indian veg. ⑤

The Residency, Nampally High Road ℡040/320 4060, ℻320 4040, ℮reservations @theresidency-hyd.com. Swish, modern hotel belonging to the *Quality Inn* group; the most upmarket option near the station. The restaurant serves good veg food, beautifully presented in plush surroundings. ⑦–⑨

Sai Prakash, Station Road ℡040/461 1726, ℻461 3355. Less than 5mins walk from the station. Modern hotel, complete with capsule lift. Comfortable, carpeted rooms (all with cable TV) set around atrium. High standards (non-a/c in particular), and very popular. Good restaurants and bar. ⑥–⑦

Sri Laxmi Lodge, Gadwal Compound, Station Road ℡040/320 1551. Quiet place with clean attached rooms down a lane opposite the *Sai Prakash*. Very good value. ②.

Taj Residency, Road No. 1, Banjara Hills ℡040/339 3939, ℻339 2218, ℮trhres.hyd@tajhotels.com. One of three Taj Group hotels in the vicinity with the usual top-notch facilities, overlooking a lake, 4km from the centre of Hyderabad. Cheapest room around $100. Good restaurant and coffee shop. ⑨

Secunderabad

National Lodge annexe, opposite Secunderabad Railway station ℡040/770 5572. No-frills lodge; but the best of the bunch if you need to catch an awkwardly timed train. To the left of the older *National* as you come out from the station. ②

Parklane, 115 Park Lane ℡040/784 0466, ℻784 0599. Large rooms (ordinary and deluxe), with views onto other buildings, very clean bathrooms, Star TV, restaurant and friendly staff. ⑤–⑥

Ramakrishna, St. John's Road ℡040/783 4567, ℻782 0933. Comfy mid-range option in a large concrete block opposite the railway reservation complex. Some a/c rooms. Smartest place in the station area. ⑤–⑥

Taj Mahal, 88 Sarojini Devi Rd ℡040/812105. Clean and efficient but old-fashioned hotel with character, built in 1949, but bearing no detectable relation to the Taj Mahal. Rooms are clean, comfortable and spacious, although a bit dark. Veg restaurant with snacks and spicy Andhra meals. No bar. ④–⑥

The City

Hyderabad is divided into three: **Hyderabad**, the old city; **Secunderabad**, the new city (originally called Husain Shah Pura); and **Golconda**, the old fort. The two cities are basically one big sprawl, separated by a lake, **Husain Sagar**, which was created in the 1500s and named after the noble Husain Shah Wali, who had helped Ibrahim Quli Qutb Shah recover from a serious illness. A huge stone Buddha stands in the centre of the lake.

The most interesting area, south of the River Musi, holds the **bazaars**, **Charminar** and the **Salar Jung Museum**. It must be a long time since the Musi amounted to very much. Even after the rains the river is about a tenth the width of the bridge; most of the area under the bridge is grassed over, some planted with palms and paddy. North of the river, the main shopping areas are centred around Abids Circle and the Sultan Bazaar (ready-made clothes, fruit, veg and silk), ten minutes' walk east of the railway station. Abids Circle is connected to MG Road, which runs north to join Tankbund Road at Husain Sagar and on to Secunderabad, while to the south it metamorphoses into Nehru Road.

Salar Jung Museum

The unmissable **Salar Jung Museum** (daily except Fri 10.30am–5pm; Rs150), on the south bank of the Musi, houses part of the huge collection of Salar Jung, one of the Nizam's prime ministers, and his ancestors. A well travelled man of wealth, with an eye for objets d'art, he bought whatever took his fancy from both the east and west, from the sublime to, in some cases, the ridiculous. His extraordinary hoard includes Indian jade, miniatures, furniture, lacquer work, Moghul opaque glassware, fabrics, bronzes, Buddhist and Hindu sculpture, manuscripts and weapons. There are also good examples of *bidri*, decorated metalwork cast from an alloy of zinc, copper and tin, that originated in Bidar in northern Karnataka. Avoid weekends, though, when the museum gets very crowded.

Charminar, Lad Bazaar and the Mecca Masjid

A maze of bazaars teeming with people, the old city has at its heart the **Charminar**, or "Four Towers", a triumphal arch built at the centre of Muhammad Quli Shah's city in 1591 to commemorate an epidemic. As its name suggests, it features four graceful minarets, each 56m high, housing spiral staircases to the upper storeys. Although a secular building, it has a mosque (now closed) on the roof; the oldest in Hyderabad, it is said to have been built to teach the royal children the Koran. The yellowish colour of the whole building is thanks to a special stucco made of marble powder, *gram* (a local pulse), and egg yolk.

Charminar marks the start of the fascinating **Lad Bazaar**, which leads to Mahboob Chowk, a market square featuring a mosque and Victorian clock tower. Lad Bazaar specializes in everything you could possibly need for a Hyderabadi marriage; it's full of old stores where you can buy jewellery, rosewater, herbs and spices, exotic materials and more mundane *lunghis*. You'll also find silver filigree jewellery, antiques and *bidri* ware, as well as boxes, plates, *hookah*-paraphernalia and the like, delicately inlaid with silver and brass. Hyderabad is the centre of the trade in **pearls** – so beloved of the Nizams (see p.578) that they not only wore them but apparently liked nothing more than having them ground into powder to eat. Pearls can be bought, for good prices, in the markets near the Charminar. Southeast of Lad Bazaar, the complex of

Royal Palaces includes Chaumahalla, four palaces set around a central courtyard.

Southwest, behind the Charminar, is **Mecca Masjid**, the sixth largest mosque in India, constructed in 1598 by the sixth king, Abdullah Qutb Shah, from locally hewn blocks of black granite and small red bricks from Mecca, which are slotted over the central arch. The mosque itself can hold 3000

The fish miracle

In a land of a thousand-and-one holy healers, miracle cures and all round weird phenomena, one stands out as the fishiest. Each year from the 6th to the 8th of June, on "mrigasira karti", the traditional arrival of the monsoon in Andhra, more than half a million asthmatics wheeze their way across India to Hyderabad on a quest to solve their breathing problems. With the summer heat at its fiercest and most humid, they stand for hours in the sun clutching little plastic bags containing live merrel fish. Once the patient is at the head of the mile-long queue, the fish, together with a nut-sized pellet of marzipan-coloured paste, are rammed wriggling down their throat.

The secret recipe for the wonder seafood cure is jealously guarded by the three brothers of a family of Hyderabadi toddy tappers, the Bathini Gouds. It was revealed in 1845 to one of their ancestors, Veerana Goud, by a *rishi* (saint) returning after a pilgrimage to the Himalayas, to thank the Gouds for their hospitality and kindness. The holy man, however, insisted the fish cure would only be efficacious if administered once each year, free of charge and using the exact ingredients prescribed by him, among them "holy water" from the so-called "Milk-well" (*Doodhbaowli*) in the toddy tappers' back yard.

Over the century and a half or so since the first fish cure, the treatment's fame has grown to such an extent that the Gouds are now unable to host the annual dispensary at their home, in the cramped confines of Gandhinagar bazaar, around 1km from the Charminar. Instead, the local municipality has set aside the city's vast Exhibition Ground to accommodate the hundreds of thousands of asthmatics and their families who pour in. Indian Railways also lay on several special trains from Delhi, Guwahati and Thiruvananthapuram, and extra divisions of police are drafted in to cope with the crowds, who numbered around 600,000 in 2000.

To keep up with the ever increasing demand, the Gouds employ a team of dozens to prepare the paste in the months leading up to the break of the monsoon. But none of the old *rishi*'s provisos are ignored. The expense of making and administering the cure – roughly Rs20,000 annually – is still met entirely by the three brothers, although patients are these days required to bring their own fish (unless they're vegetarian, in which case bananas may be used).

If you're tempted to take the treatment, it's a good idea to contact the Goud family in advance by post (128, State Bank of India Colony, Gandhinagar, Kavadiguda, Hyderabad 500 038). Get to Hyderabad a couple of days in advance, and they will issue you with a pass that will save you having to queue for hours in the heat. Bear in mind too, that to benefit fully from the fish cure you should have the treatment three times on successive years, and stick to a special Ayurvedic diet for 45 days after each one.

Finally, watch out for the crop of soundalike Goud impostors trying to cash in on the fish cure, who prey on unsuspecting new arrivals at the railway station. Not only do these fly-by-nights charge for the treatment, but none are likely to have mastered the deft finger-down-the-throat stab required to speedily shove the merrel on its wiggly way.

For a vivid account of what the fish cure actually feels like, hunt out a copy of Tahir Singh's *The Sorcerer's Apprentice* (see Books, p.713).

worshippers with up to 10,000 in the courtyard; on the left of the courtyard are the tombs of the Nizams. Outside the mosque is a stall where they will change your torn, cut rupee bills at good rates.

The **Charkaman**, or "Four Arches", north of Charminar, were built in 1594 and once led to the parade ground of royal palaces to the south (now long gone). The surrounding narrow streets spill over with interesting small shops; through **Doulat-Khan-e-Ali** – the western arch, which originally led to the palace – stores sell lustrous brocade and antique saris. The arch itself is said to have been once hung with rich gold tapestries.

North of the river

The **Yusufian Dargah**, with a striking bulbous yellow dome, is set in a leafy courtyard not far south of the railway station (follow the road that runs down from the Ek-minar mosque and look for an alley on the right). It's the shrine of a seventeenth century Sufi saint of the venerable Chisti order and you can enter (with covered head) and perambulate the flower-decked tomb. About a kilometre north of the station, set in Hyderabad's tranquil public gardens, the **A.P. state museum** (daily except Fri 10.30am–5pm; Rs2) displays a modest but well-labelled collection of bronzes, prehistoric tools, copper inscription plates, weapons, household utensils and even an Egyptian mummy. There's a gallery of modern art in the new extension, too. The nearby **health museum** (Mon–Sat 10.30am–1.30pm & 2–5pm; free) is dowdy and uninspiring.

The **Birla Venkateshwara temple** (daily 7am–noon & 3–9pm), on Kalabahad ("black mountain") Hill, north of the Public Gardens, is open to all. Constructed in Rajasthani white marble in 1976 by the Birla Trust, it was set up by the wealthy industrialist Birla family. Although the temple itself is not of great interest, it affords fine views. Nearby, and built by the same organization, is the **planetarium** (shows are in English: Mon–Sat 11.30am, 4pm & 6pm; Sun & hols 11.30am, 3.45pm & 6pm; Rs10) and a brand new **science centre** (daily 10.30am–8.30pm; Rs10) with lots of satellite hardware and photos, machines demonstrating sensory perceptions and a small dinosaur display.

Husain Sagar

Husain Sagar, the large expanse of water separating Hyderabad from Secunderabad, lends a welcome air of tranquillity to the busy conurbation. People come here to stroll along Tank Bund, the road that runs around the eastern side of the lake, and to relax in the small parks dotted along the water's edge. The parks contain numerous statues of prominent local figures over the last several centuries, and come alive with ice-cream and snack stalls, particular as sunset approaches and people gather to witness its natural splendour across the lake.

In the centre of the lake, stands an enormous, modern stone statue of the Buddha Purnima or "Full Moon Buddha", which was eventually erected onto its plinth by a salvage company in 1992, after spending a couple of years underwater. It had sunk at the first disastrous attempt to transport it there by barge in 1990, a tragedy that caused the deaths of eight people in an inauspicious effort to place the huge figure, which had taken five years to build, measuring 55ft high and weighing 350 tons. Boats regularly chug out to the statue from Lumbini Park, just off Secretariat Road, every hour from 9am to 6pm, the half-hour round trip costing Rs10.

Golconda Fort and the tombs of the Qutb Shahi Kings

Golconda Fort 122m above the plain of Hyderabad and 11km west of old Hyderabad, was the capital of the seven Qutb Shahi kings from 1518 until the end of the sixteenth century, when the court moved to Hyderabad. Well preserved and set in lush green scrubland, it is one of the most impressive forts in India. Large portions of its battlements are draped in grasses, lending it a soft, natural air. Its outer wall reached 18m, and the citadel boasted 87 semicircular bastions and eight mighty gates, four of which are still in use, complete with gruesome elephant-proof spikes.

To get **to the fort**, bus #119 runs from Nampally, and both the #66G direct bus from Charminar and #80D from the railway station in Secunderabad stop outside the main entrance. **For the tombs**, take #123 and #142S from Charminar. From Secunderabad the #5, #5S, #5R all go to Mehdipattanam, where you should hop onto #123. Or, take an auto-rickshaw and agree a waiting fee in advance. Set aside a day to explore the fort, which covers an area of around four square kilometres; it's well worth hiring one of the many guides who gather at the entrance, or at least buying one of the handy little pamphlets, including map, sold by vendors.

Entering the **fort** (daily 9am–5pm; $5 [Rs5]) by the Balahisar gate, you come into the grand portico, where guards clap their hands to show off the fort's acoustics; the claps can be clearly heard as far as the Durbar hall. To the right is the **mortuary bath**, where the bodies of deceased nobles were ritually bathed prior to burial. If you follow the arrowed anti-clockwise route, you pass

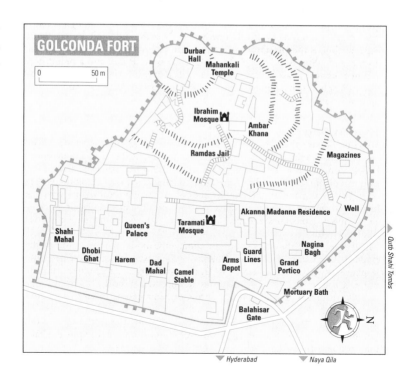

GOLCONDA FORT

0   50 m

Durbar Hall
Mahankali Temple
Ibrahim Mosque
Ambar Khana
Ramdas Jail
Magazines
Akanna Madanna Residence
Well
Shahi Mahal
Queen's Palace
Taramati Mosque
Dhobi Ghat
Harem
Dad Mahal
Camel Stable
Arms Depot
Guard Lines
Nagina Bagh
Grand Portico
Mortuary Bath
Balahisar Gate

N

▼ *Hyderabad*   ▼ *Naya Qila*

▶ *Qutb Shahi Tombs*

Quli, destined to become the first king of the Qutb Shahi dynasty, came from Persia with his uncle to sell horses to the Bahmani kingdom at Gulbarga and Bijapur. After a spell as a popular governor, he was titled Quli Qutb Shah by the Bahmani ruler Mamu Shbahmani who had appointed him. By 1518 the power of the Bahmanis was waning and Quli Qutb Shah raised an army and established independence for his state, ruling for twenty-five years and making Golconda his dynastic capital. When he was in his nineties, his eldest son Jamshed – who had briefly succeeded to the throne – conspired to have his father beheaded while praying in the mosque and his brothers exiled. However, an outraged people prevented Jamshed's coup by forcibly deposing him. Quli Qutb Shah preferred, thereafter, one of his younger sons, Ibrahim, to inherit his throne.

Ibrahim Quli Qutb Shah returned from exile to take over the kingdom at the age of eighteen. He was a learned man who wrote poetry in both Urdu and Telugu and he oversaw the construction of many of Golconda's most important buildings, including the stone fort. His reign saw the dynasty reach the height of its power, despite occasional conflicts with the neighbouring states of Bijapur and Ahmadnagar. These three kingdoms later formed an alliance to defeat the powerful Vijayanagars in 1565.

The reigns of Ibrahim's only son, Muhammad Quli Qutb Shah (1580–1612), and grandson, Muhammad Qutb Shah (1612–26), both cultured men, saw the expansion of Golconda and foundation of Hyderabad after a bridge had been built over the Musi River in 1578. Despite the growing threat from the Moghuls to the north, these were peaceful times and prosperous trade was established with the European merchants on the coast, including diamonds. Rumour has it that a mine still exists in the fort, its exact location known only to the government.

Increasing pressure came from the Moghuls during the long reign of Abdullah Qutb Shah (1626–72), and the dynasty finally ended with the surrender of his son, Abdul Hasan Qutb Shah in 1687 to the forces of Aurangzeb. This followed an eight-month battle, which, as the story goes, only ended when Aurangzeb bribed a doorman to allow his troops in to secure victory.

along a straight, walled path before coming to the two-storey residence of ministers Akkana and Madanna, and start the proper ascent to the Durbar hall. Halfway along the steps, which pass assorted water channels and wells that supplied the fort's water system, you come to a small, dark cell named after the court cashier **Ramdas**, who during his incarceration here, produced the clumsy carvings and paintings that litter the gloomy room. Nearing the top, you come across the small, pretty mosque of Ibrahim Qutb Shah; beyond this, set beneath two huge granite stones, is an even smaller temple dedicated to Durga in her manifestation as Mahakali.

The steps are crowned by the three-storey **Durbar Hall** of the Qutb Shahs. The lower level of the hall has vaulted bays and the rooftop pavilion gave the monarchs uninterrupted views over their domain. Their accompaniment was the lilting strains of court musicians, as opposed to the cacophony of incessant clapping heard today from far below.

The ruins of the **Queen's Palace**, in the southern end of the fort, stand in a courtyard centred on an original copper fountain that used to be filled with rosewater. The Queen's palace was once elaborately decorated with multiple domes. Traces of the "necklace" design on one of the arches can still be seen at the top of which a lotus bud sits below an opening flower with a cavity at its centre that once contained a diamond. Petals and creeper leaves are dotted with tiny holes that formerly gleamed with rubies and diamonds; parrots, long gone, had rubies for their eyes. Today visitors can only speculate how splendid it must all have looked, especially at night, when flaming torches illuminated the glittering decorations. At the entrance to the palace itself, four chambers provided protection from intruders. Passing through two rooms, the second of which is overgrown, you come to the **Shahi Mahal**, the royal bedroom. Originally, it had a domed roof and niches on the walls that once sheltered candles or oil lamps, and it is said that the servants used silver ladders to get up there to light them. Golconda Fort's **sound and light** show (spoken in English; March–Oct Wed, Sat & Sun 7pm; Nov–Feb 6.30pm; Rs25) is suitably theatrical and you do not have to pay the extra foreigner entry fee.

There are 82 **Qutb Shahi tombs** (daily except Fri 9am–4.30pm; Rs2) about 1km north of the outer wall. Set in peaceful gardens, they commemorate commanders, relatives of the kings, dancers, singers and royal doctors, as well as all but two of the Qutb Shahi kings. Faded today, they were once brightly coloured in turquoise and green; they all have an onion dome on a block, with a decorative arcade. You can reach them by road or, more pleasantly, by picking your way across the quiet grassy verges and fields below the fort's battlements.

Eating

In addition to the hotel restaurants, plenty of "meals" places around town specialize in **Hyderabadi cuisine**, such as authentic biriyanis, or the famously chilli-hot Andhra cuisine. Hyderabadi cooking forms a unique blend of Moghul court cuisine, featuring sumptious meat dishes with northern ingredients such as cinnamon, cardamon, cloves and garlic, and traditional southern vegetarian dishes with an array of flavourings like cassia buds, peanuts, coconut, tamarind leaves, mustard seeds and red chillies.

Akbar, 1-7-190 MG Rd, Secunderabad. Hyderabadi cuisine at moderate prices.

Amrutha Castle, Secretariat Road, Saifabad. Dine at the ground floor *Hare and Hound*, presided over by suits of armour. Great value evening buffet with a delicious range of soups, meat, fish, veg and sweets for around Rs200.

Ashoka, 6-1-70 Lakdi-ka-Pul. Hotel with a/c *Saptagiri* cafeteria serving good-value south Indian snacks and some north Indian dishes.

Central Court, Lakdi-ka-Pul. The hotel's *Touch of Class* restaurant offers good Hyderabadi non-veg plus some veg options and barbecue kebabs on a small patio; also Mughlai, Western and Chinese food. Good value lunch buffet at Rs55–75, evenings pricier buffet and à la carte.

Paradise-Persis, MG Road, Secunderabad. Very popular multi-restaurant complex bashing out fine Hyderabadi cuisine at moderate prices.

Sai Prakash, Station Road. The *Woodlands* serves good-value veg South Indian snacks and North Indian dishes. *Rich'n'Famous* is much posher and pricier, with comfy chairs and imaginative daily specials including crab, prawns and specialities from both Hyderabad and further afield.

Sher-e-Punjab, corner of Nampally High Road and station entrance. Basic basement restaurant with good tasty North Indian food at cheap rates.

Taj Residency, Road No. 1, Banjara Hills. The *Dakhni* restaurant inside the hotel serves excellent, pricey, authentic south Indian cuisine, and Hyderabadi specialities.

Listings

Airlines Air France, Gupta Estate 1st floor, Basheerbagh ☎ 040/323 0947; Air India, 5-9-193 HACA BHAVAN, opposite Public Garden Saifabad ☎ 040/323 2747; British Airways, Nijhawan Travel Services, 5–9–88/4 Ainulaman Fateh Maidan Rd

☎ 040/324 1661; Delta/Sabena/Swissair/Singapore Airlines, GSA: Aviation Travels, Navbharat Chambers, 6–3–1109/1 Raj Bhavan Rd ☎ 040/331 2380; Gulf Air/TWA/Bangladesh Biman/Air Canada/Royal

Jordanian, Jet Air, Flat 202, 5–9–58 Gupta Estate, Basheerbagh ℡040/324 0870; Indian Airlines, opposite Assembly Saifabad: office ℡040/329 9333; general flight information ℡140; pre-recorded flight info ℡142; Jet Airways, 6-3-1109/1 GF Nav Bharat Chambers, Raj Bhavan Rd ℡040/330 1222; Lufthansa, 3–5–823 Shop#B1–B3, Hyderaguda ℡040/323 5537; Qantas, Transworld Travels, 3A 1st floor, 5–9–93 Chapel Rd ℡040/329 8495.

Banks and exchange Oddly for a state capital, most banks still don't do foreign exchange, two exceptions being the State Bank of Hyderabad, MG Road and Federal Bank, 1st floor, Orient Estate, MG Road. Both are open Mon–Fri 10.30am–2.30pm, the latter also Sat 10.30am–12.30pm It's better to head for an agency such as Thomas Cook (℡040/329 6521) at Nasir Arcade, Secretariat Road; or L.K.P. Forex (℡040/321 0094) on Public Gardens Road, only ten minutes' walk north of Nampally station. Both are open Mon–Sat 9.30am–5.30pm. In Secunderabad try the Allahabad bank, next to Park Lane hotel.

Bookstores Higginbothams, 1 Lal Bahadur Stadium, Hyderabad; Gangarams, 62 DSD Rd, near *Garden Restaurant* in Secunderabad; and Kalaujal, Hill Fort Road, opposite the Public Gardens, which specializes in art books. Both shops offer a wide selection of literature, non-fiction titles and reference books.

Car rental Air Travels in Banjara Hills (℡040/335 3099, ℡335 5088) and Classic Travels in Secunderabad (℡040/775 5645) both provide a 24-hour service, with or without driver.

Crafts Leepakshi, the A.P. state government emporium at Gunfoundry on MG Road, has a wide range of handicrafts, including *Bidri* metalwork, jewellery and silks. Utkalika (Government of Orissa handicrafts), House no. 60-1-67, between the Ravindra Bharati building and *Hotel Ashoka*, has a modest selection of silver filigree jewellery, hand-loom cloth, *ikhat* tie-dye, Jagannath papier-mâché figures and buffalo bone carvings. Cheneta Bhavan is a modern shopping complex a little south of the railway station, stuffed with handloom cloth shops from various states, including Tamil Nadu, Uttar Pradesh, Rajasthan, Madhya Pradesh and Andhra Pradesh. For silks and saris, try Meena Bazaar, Pochampally Silks and Sarees, and Pooja Sarees, all on Tilak Road.

Cycles Bicycles can be rented for Rs20 per 24hrs at a friendly stall on the right as you approach Hyderabad station from Nampally High Road.

Hospitals The government-run Gandhi Hospital is in Secunderabad ℡040/770 2222. The private CDR Hospital is in Himayataagar ℡040/322 1221. There's a Tropical Diseases Hospital in Nallakunta ℡040/766 7843.

Internet access The most convenient internet access is available from Satyam Online at Modern Xerox (daily 9am–10pm; ℡040/460 3894), near the Ek-minar mosque, behind Nampally station, for Rs35 per hour. Other outlets are to be found in the Abids area.

Library The British Library, Secretariat Road (Tues–Sat 11am–7pm; ℡040/323 0774) has a wide selection of books and recent British newspapers. Officially you must be a member or a British citizen to get in but if you look western you're unlikely to be asked to prove it.

Pharmacies Apollo Pharmacy (℡040/323 1380) and Health Pharmacy (℡040/331 0618) are both open 24hr.

Police ℡040/323 0191.

Travel agents General agents for airline and private-bus tickets include: Travel Club Forex (℡040/323 4180), Nasir Arcade, Saifabad, close to Thomas Cook, and Kamat Travels, in the *Hotel Sai Prakash* complex (℡040/461 2096). There is a host of private bus agents on Nampally High Road outside Hyderabad railway station.

Around Hyderabad

Heading north from Hyderabad towards the borders of Maharashtra and Madhya Pradesh, the landscape becomes greener and more hilly, sporadically punctuated by attractive black granite formations. There is little to detain visitors here except the small town of **Warangal**, conveniently situated on the main railway line as it loops across to the east, which warrants a stop to visit the nearby medieval fort and Shiva temple. Heading south from the capital, flat farmland stretches for miles into the centre of the state, where the Nagarjuna Sagar dam has created a major lake, with the important Buddhist site of **Nagarjunakonda**, now an island, in its midst.

Daily train services from Hyderabad railway station (Nampally) include: the Charminar Express #2760 to Chennai (7pm; 14hr); the Hyderabad–Cochin Express #7030 (12 noon; 27hr); the Andhra Pradesh Express #2723 to Delhi (6.40am; 26hr); the Hyderabad–Mumbai Express #7032 (8.40pm; 17hr); the East Coast Express #7046 to Calcutta (7am; 33hr 15min) via Vijayawada, Vishakapatnam and Bhubaneshnar; and the Rayasaleema Express #7429 to Tirupati (5.30pm; 15hr 30min). All northeast-bound services call at Warangal and most at Vijayawada. From Secunderabad, there are some originating services and many through trains in all directions. Useful services include the Konark Express #1020 to Mumbai (10.50am; 17hr 30min) Secunderabad–Bangalore Express #7085 (5.40pm: 13hr 35min), the Kacheguda–Mandad Express #7664 to Aurangabad (6pm; 14hr 20min) and the Secunderabad–Varanasi Express #7091 (Mon & Wed 10.30pm; 30hr 15min).

The railways reservations office at Hyderabad (Mon–Sat 8am–2pm & 2.30–8pm, Sun 8am–2pm) is to the left as you enter the station. Counter #211 (next to enquiry counter) is supposedly for tourist reservations, but it's also used for group bookings and lost tickets. Foreign visitors can make bookings at the Chief Reservation Inspector's Office on platform 1 (daily 9am–5pm). The Secunderabad reservation complex is by the major junction with St John's Road over 400m to the right as you exit the station. Counter 134 is for foreigners.

From the Central bus stand, regular bus services run to Amaravati, Bangalore, Bidar, Chennai, Mumbai, Nagarjuna Sagar, Tirupati, Vijayawada and Warangal. Also various deluxe and video buses depart for Bangalore, Chennai, Mumbai and other major destinations, from outside Nampally station, where you will find a cluster of private agencies.

Between them, Indian Airlines and Jet Airways offer three daily flights to Bangalore, at least seven to Mumbai, three to Delhi, three or four to Chennai, two to Vishakapatnam, at least one to Tirupati and one or two to Calcutta, via Bhubaneshwar on three of those days. There are also flights to Ahmedabad and Cochin on some days. Indian Airlines runs at least one flight daily to one or other of the Gulf states. Air India also has flights to Mumbai, and a new service twice weekly direct to Singapore (2hr 30min).

Warangal

WARANGAL – "one stone" – 150km northeast of Hyderabad, was the Hindu capital of the Kakatiyan empire in the twelfth and thirteenth centuries. Like other Deccan cities, it changed hands many times between the Hindus and the Muslims – something that is reflected in its architecture and the remains you see today.

Warangal's **fort**, 4km south, is famous for its two circles of fortifications: the outer made of earth with a moat, and the inner of stone. Four roads into the centre meet at the ruined temple of **Svayambhu**, built in 1162 and dedicated to Shiva. At its southern, free-standing gateway, another Shiva temple, from the fourteenth century, is in much better shape; inside, the remains of an enormous *lingam* came originally from the Svayambhu shrine. Also inside the citadel is the **Shirab Khan**, or audience hall, an early eleventh-century building.

The largely basalt Chalukyan-style "thousand-pillared" **Shiva temple** (daily 10am–6pm; $5 [Rs5]), just off the main road, beside the slopes of Hanamkonda Hill (6km north), was constructed by King Rudra Deva in 1163. A low-roofed building, on several stepped stages, it features superb carvings and three shrines to Vishnu, Shiva and Surya. They lead off the *mandapa* whose numerous finely carved columns give the temple its name. In front, a polished Nandi bull was carved out of a single stone. A Bhadrakali temple stands at the top of the hill.

Practicalities

If you make an early start, it's just about possible to visit Warangal in a day-trip from Hyderabad. Frequent buses and trains run to the site (roughly 3hr). Warangal's bus stand and railway station are opposite each other, served by local buses and auto-rickshaws. The easiest way to cover the site is to rent a bicycle from one of the stalls on Station Road (Rs2 per hr). As you follow Station Road from the station, if you are heading for the fort turn left just beyond the post office, under the railway bridge and left again at the next main road. For Hanamkonda turn right onto JPN Road at the next main junction after the post office, left at the next major crossroads onto MG Road, and right at the end on to the Hanamkonda main road. The temple and hill are on the left.

Accommodation is limited; the *Hotel Ashok* (℡08712/85491; ❹–❺) on Main Road, Hanamkonda, 6km from the railway and bus stand, which has a/c rooms, a restaurant and bar, is rather more upmarket than *Hotel Ratna* (℡08712/60645, ℻60096; ❸–❹), 2km from the station on MG Road. Basic lodges nearer the station include the *Vijaya* (℡08712/25851; ❷–❸) on Station Road, which is the closest and best value, and the *Urvasi* (℡08712/61760; ❷–❹) at the junction of Station and JPN Roads, which has some a/c rooms. There are several decent **places to eat** along Station Road – the upstairs *Titanic*, halfway along on the right, serves good *tandoori* and other non-veg items. **Internet** facilities are available at Grace@Net on JPN Road for Rs30 per hour.

Nagarjunakonda

NAGARJUNAKONDA, or "Nagarjuna's Hill", 166km south of Hyderabad and 175km west of Vijayawada, is all that now remains of the vast area, rich in archeological sites, submerged when the huge Nagarjuna Sagar Dam was built across the Krishna River in 1960. Ancient settlements in the valley were first discovered in 1926; extensive excavations carried out between 1954 and 1960 uncovered more than one hundred sites dating from the early Stone Age to late medieval times. Nagarjunakonda was once the summit of a hill, where a fort towered 200m above the valley floor; now it's just a small oblong island near the middle of Nagarjuna Sagar Lake, accessible by boat from the mainland. Several Buddhist monuments have been reconstructed, in an operation reminiscent of that at Abu Simbel in Egypt, and a **museum** exhibits the more remarkable ruins of the valley. **VIJAYAPURI**, the village on the shore of the lake, overlooks the colossal dam itself, which stretches for almost 2km. Torrents of water flushed through its 26 flood-gates produce electricity for the whole region, and irrigate an area of almost 800 square kilometres. Many villages had to be relocated to higher ground when the valley was flooded.

The island and the museum

Boats arrive on the northeastern edge of Nagarjunakonda island, unloading passengers at what remains of one of the gates of the fort, built in the fourteenth century and considerably renovated by the Vijayanagar kings in the mid-sixteenth century. Low, damaged stone walls skirting the island mark the edge of the fort, and you can see ground-level remains of the Hindu temples that served its inhabitants.

Well-kept gardens lie between the jetty and the museum, beyond which nine Buddhist monuments from various sites in the valley have been rebuilt. West of the jetty, there's a reconstructed bathing *ghat*, built entirely of limestone during the reigns of the Ikshvaku kings (third century AD). A series of levels and steps leads to the water's edge; boards etched into some of its slabs were probably used for dice games.

The **maha–chaitya**, or *stupa*, constructed at the command of King Chamtula's sister in the third century AD, is the earliest Buddhist structure in the area. It was raised over relics of the Buddha – said to include a tooth – and has been reassembled in the southwest of the island. Nearby, a towering **statue** of the Buddha stands draped in robes beside a ground plan of a monastery that enshrines a smaller **stupa.** Other *stupas* stand nearby; the brick walls of the *svastika chaitya* have been arranged in the shape of swastikas, common emblems in early Buddhist iconography.

In the **museum** (daily except Fri 9am–5pm; free), **Buddhist sculptures** include large stone friezes decorated with scenes from the Buddha's life: his birth; his mother's vision of an elephant and a lotus blossom; his renunciation; and his subversion of evil as he meditated and realized enlightenment under the *bodhi* tree. Twelve statues of standing Buddhas – one of which reaches 3m – show the Buddha in various postures of teaching or meditation. Many pillars are undamaged, profusely carved with Buddha images, bowing devotees, elephants and lotus medallions.

Earlier artefacts include stone tools and pots from the Neolithic age (third millennium BC), and metal axe heads and knives (first millennium BC). Among later finds are several inscribed pillars from Ikshvaku times, recording in Prakrit or Sanskrit the installation of Buddhist monasteries and statues. The final phase of art at Nagarjunakonda is represented by sculptures: a thirteenth-century *tirthankara* (Jain saint), a seventeenth-century Ganesh and Nandi, and a set of eighteenth-century statues of Shiva and Shakti, his female consort. Also on display is a model showing the excavated sites in the valley.

Practicalities

Organized **APTDC tours** from Hyderabad to Nagarjunakonda (see box on p.580), taking in the sites and museum, the nearby Ethiopothala waterfalls and an engraved third-century Buddhist monolith known as the Pylon, can be a bit rushed: if you want to spend more time in the area you can take a bus from the Central bus stand in Hyderabad (4hr; all the regular Macherla services stop at Vijayapuri) or Vijayawada (6hr; a direct service runs daily at 11am and frequent services leave from Guntur). It can be quicker to change at Macherla.

Accommodation at Vijayapuri is limited, and you need to decide in advance where you are going to stay to know where to get off the bus, as there are two distinct settlements 6km apart on either side of the dam. For easy access to the sites it is better to stay near the jetty on the right bank of the dam. Ask the bus to leave you at the launch station. The drab-looking concrete *Nagarjuna Motel Complex* (☏08642/78188; ❷) has adequate rooms and some a/c. Five hundred metres away in the village, the *Golden Lodge* (☏08642/78148; ❶) is much more basic. Both APTDC places are on the other side of the dam approaching the lake from the direction of Hyderabad. The APTDC *Vijay Vihar Complex* (☏08680/76633; ❺), which has spacious rooms with balconies and a good restaurant, is 2km further up the hill from the APTDC project house (☏08680/76540; ❸–❺) in the left bank village. However, if you want to stay in these more comfortable surroundings, there is a frequent shuttle bus to the right bank and it's a pleasant walk to the dam and lake shore.

Tickets for **boats** to the island (daily 9am & 1.30pm; 45min; Rs25) are on sale 25 minutes before departure. Each boat leaves the island ninety minutes after it arrives, which allows reasonable time to see the museum and walk briskly round the monuments, but if you want to take your time and soak up the pleasant atmosphere without the crowds from the boat, take the morning boat and return in the afternoon. A cafeteria on the island serves drinks and occasionally biscuits, but only opens when the boat is in, so take provisions.

Eastern Andhra Pradesh

Perhaps India's least visited area, eastern Andhra Pradesh is sandwiched between the Bay of Bengal in the east and the red soil and high peaks of the Eastern Ghats in the north. Its one architectural attraction is the ancient Buddhist site of **Amaravati**, near the city of **Vijayawada**, whose sprinkling of historic temples is far overshadowed by impersonal, modern buildings. Some 350km north, the major port of **Vishakapatnam** is not as grim as it first seems, but it's not a place to linger. For anyone with a strong desire to explore, however, pockets of natural beauty along the coast and in the hills of eastern Andhra Pradesh can offer rich reward. In this sleepy landscape, little affected by modernization, bullocks amble between swaying palms and the rice fields are viridescent against rusty sands. However, unless you have the patience to endure the excruciatingly slow public transport system, your own vehicle is essential.

Vijayawada

Almost 450km north of Chennai, a third of the way to Calcutta, **VIJAYAWADA** is a bustling commercial centre on the banks of the Krishna delta, hemmed in by bare granite outcrops 90km from the coast. This mundane city, alleviated by the mountain backdrop and some urban greenery, is seldom visited by tourists, but it does, however, make the obvious stop-off point for visits to the third-century Buddhist site at **Amaravati**, 60km west.

A handful of temples in Vijayawada merit a quick look. The most important, raised on the low Indrakila Hill in the east, is dedicated to the city's patron goddess **Kanaka Durga** (also known as Vijaya), goddess of riches, power and benevolence. Though it is believed to be thousands of years old, what you see today, with the exception of a few pillared halls and intricate carvings, is largely renovated (and freshly whitewashed). Across the river, roughly 3km out of town, there's an ancient, unmodified cave temple at **Undavalli**, a tiny rural village set off the main road, easily reached on any Guntur-bound bus, or the local #13 service. The temple is cut out of the granite hillside in typical Pallava style: simple, solid and bold. Each of its five levels contains a deep low-roofed hall, with small rock-cut shrines to Vishnu, Shiva and Parvati, and pillared verandahs guarded by sturdy grey statues of gods, saints and lions. Views from the porches take in a sublime patchwork of rivulets, paddy fields and banana plantations.

Practicalities

Vijayawada's **railway station**, on the main Chennai–Calcutta line, is in the centre of town. Buses arriving from Vishakapatnam, Guntur, Amaravati and as far afield as Hyderabad and Chennai pull into the **bus stand** further west. Specific ticket offices cater for each service, and a **tourist office**

(☎0866/523966) has details on local hotels and sights. APTDC also has an office in the centre of town at Hotel Ilapuram Complex, Gandhi Nagar (☎0866/570255). You can **change money** at Zen Global Finance, 40-6-27 Krishna Nagar in Labbipet. Between the bus stand and railway station, Ryes Canal flows through the heart of town.

Vijayawada is a major business centre, with a good selection of mid-range **hotels**, all less than 2km from the railway station and bus stand. Most have reasonably priced restaurants serving Andhra thalis and à la carte items. Budget options include *Monika Lodge* (☎0866/571334; ❷–❸), just off Elluru Road about 500m from the bus stand: very simple, and slightly grubby. Two better-value places, both on Atchutaramaiah Street, which links the railway station to Elluru Road, are the *Hotel Narayana Swamy* (☎0866/571221; ❸), and the *Sri Ram* (☎0866/579377; ❹–❺) with spotless rooms, some a/c and all with cable TV. A posher option is the modern *Hotel Swarna Palace* on Elluru Road at the junction with Atchutaramaiah Street (☎0866/577222, ⓕ574602; ❻–❼). The rooms are comfortably furnished, with cable TV. The fourth-floor restaurant provides large portions of Indian, Chinese and continental food with city views and something of a disco appearance without the music. The *Raj Towers* (☎0866/571311, ⓕ571317; ❹–❼), also on Elluru Road, is a tall modern block with good mid-range rooms.

Guntur

Another sprawling and bustling commercial city 30km southwest of Vijayawada, **GUNTUR** has no merits of its own but makes an even more convenient jumping-off point for Amaravati than Vijayawada, especially if coming from the area of Nagarjuna Sagar. There are buses every ten to fifteen minutes to Vijayawada (45min–1hr), and every half-hour to Amaravati from the old bus stand (adjacent to the main bus stand). If you decide to spend the night here, there are some perfectly adequate lodges right opposite the bus stands. *Annapurna Lodge* (☎0863/356493; ❷–❹) has decent-sized clean rooms and some a/c; *Padmasri Lodge* (☎0863/223813; ❷–❹) also has a/c and cheaper singles.

Amaravati

AMARAVATI, a small village on the banks of the Krishna River 30km west of Vijayawada, is the site of a Buddhist settlement, formerly known as Chintapalli, where a *stupa* larger than those at Sanchi was erected over relics of the Buddha in the third century BC, during the reign of Ashoka. The *stupa* no longer stands, but its great size is evident from the large mound that formed its base. It was originally surrounded by grey stone railings with a gateway at each of the cardinal points, one of which has been reconstructed in an open courtyard. Its decoration, meticulously carved and perfectly preserved, shows the themes represented on all such Buddhist monuments: the Buddha's birth, renunciation and life as an emaciated ascetic, enlightenment under the *bodhi* tree, his first sermon in the Deer Park, and *parinirvana*, or death. Several foundation stones of monastic quarters remain on the site.

Exhibits at the small but fascinating **museum** (daily except Fri 10am–5pm; $5 [Rs5] inc site) range in date from the third century BC to the twelfth century AD. They include statues of the Buddha, with lotus symbols on his feet, a head of tightly curled hair, and long ear lobes, all traditional indications of an enlightened teacher. Earlier stone carvings represent the Buddha through such symbols as the *chakra* (wheel of *dharma*), a throne, a *stupa*, a flaming pillar or a *bodhi* tree – all being worshipped. The lotus motif, a central symbol in early Buddhism, is connected with a dream the Buddha's mother had shortly after conception, and has always been a Buddhist symbol of essential purity: it appears repeatedly on railings and pillars. Later sculptures include limestone statues of the goddess Tara and *bodhisattva* Padmapani, both installed at the site in medieval times when the community had adopted Mahayana teachings in place of the earlier Hinayana doctrines. What you see here are some of the finer pieces excavated from the site – other remains have been taken to the Madras Government Museum and the British Museum in London.

Practicalities

Theoretically buses run hourly from Vijaywada to Amaravati but the service seems to be unreliable, so it's best to take a bus to Guntur (every 15min; 45min–1hr), where you can pick up a connection to Amaravati (1hr–1hr 30min). Buses return to Guntur every half-hour, and during the monsoon boats gather at the jetty in Amaravati and follow the Krishna River all the way to Vijayawada. Organized tours run from the APTDC *Krishnaveni Motel*, next to the main bridge, on the south bank of the Krishna in Vijiyawada, to Amaravati and back for Rs50 when the river is high enough, not often in recent years. The excavated site and museum are roughly 1km from the bus stand. Tri-shaws – miniature carts attached to tricycles and brightly painted with chubby film stars – take tourists to the site and the river bank, where there are several drink stalls. APTDC has two small guest houses on the banks of the Krishna beside the attractive Sri Amareshwara Swamy temple at the far end of the main street,; the *Dharani* (☏08645/55332; ❷), which also has cheap dorm beds for Rs50, and the slightly more comfortable *Poonami* (☏08645/65332; ❸). Their canteen provides basic meals and snacks.

Vishakapatnam and around

One of India's most rapidly growing industrial cities, and its fourth largest port, **VISHAKAPATNAM** (aka Vizag), 350km north of Vijayawada, is a big unpleasant city choked with the smells and dirt of a busy shipbuilding industry, an oil plant and a steel factory. Such is its sprawl that it has overtaken and polluted much of the neighbouring town of Waltair, once a health resort. Although there's little to warrant a stop at Vishakapatnam, the district of Waltair with its uncrowded treelined roads and attractive seafront makes for a pleasant stroll. If you head that way, you can visit the modest collection of art and sculpture at the Visakha museum, (Tues–Sun 4–8pm; Rs1.50) on Beach Road near the *Hotel Park*. The beach around here is far enough from the port for the sea to be reasonably clean, though the best beach for swimming is at Kalshagiri further north, reached by regular buses from the RTC complex.

   Various traces of older civilizations lie within a day's journey of the city. At **Bheemunipatnam**, 30km north, you can see the remains of a Dutch fort and a peculiar cemetery where slate-grey pyramidal tombs are abandoned to nature. **Borra**, 70km inland on a minor road that winds through the Eastern Ghats and the Araku forests, boasts a set of eerie limestone caves whose darkness is pierced with age-old stalactites and stalagmites (daily 10am–12.30pm & 2–5pm; Rs12). You'll need a car to get to **Mukhalingam**, 100km north of Bheemunipatnam, where three Shaivite temples, built between the sixth and twelfth centuries, rest in low hills. Their elaborate carvings and well-preserved towering *shikharas* display slight local variations to the otherwise standard Orissan style. There's nowhere to stay in Mukhalingam.

Vishakapatnam's **railway station**, on the Chennai–Calcutta coastal route, is in the old town, towards the port. The ride to Delhi takes a tedious two days. The **bus stand**, known as RTC Complex, is in a newer area, 3km from the coast. There's an **airport**, 12km west of town, with daily connections to Hyderabad and Mumbai, and several weekly to Calcutta and Bhubaneshwar. Bus #38 runs from the airport to the centre. Irregular **ships** make the three-day crossing from here to Port Blair on the Andaman Islands.

The **tourist office** (Mon–Sat 10.30am–5pm; ☏0891/546446) at the Vuda complex, Siripuram, is difficult to find and only of use if you want to book a tour: city tour (daily 8.30am–6pm; Rs90) or Borra caves (daily 7am–9pm; Rs250 including lunch); this can be done more easily in any case at the APTDC booth in the RTC complex. The Andhra Bank near the RTC complex will **change money**.

If you arrive late by bus, head for the well-maintained **retiring rooms** (❶) in the bus stand. Otherwise, most **hotels** are in the old town, near the railway station: turn right out of the station and walk for a few minutes. The best is *Hotel Karanths*, 33-1-55 Patel Marg (☏0891/502048; ❸–❺), whose spotless rooms have balconies, pressed sheets, colour TV and attached bathrooms. The downstairs restaurant serves unbeatable thalis and tiffin at low prices. Next door, *Dakshayani* (☏0891/561798; ❷) offers simple grotty rooms, some with private bathrooms. Round the corner in Bowdara Road, the *Sri Ganesh Hotel* (☏0891/563274; ❷) is a better budget option with simple clean rooms. Vishakapatnam's nicest upmarket hotel, the *Park* on Beach Road (☏0891/554488; ❻), has luxurious rooms, a swimming pool, a bar, restaurant, and access to the beach. Adjacent to the *Park* is the smart *Palm Beach* (☏0891/554026; ❻), which also offers full amenities.

Southern Andhra Pradesh

The further south you travel from the fertile lands watered by the great Krishna and Godavari rivers, the less hospitable the terrain becomes, especially in the rocky southwest of the state. For Hindus, the main attraction in southern Andhra Pradesh is the tenth-century **Shri Venkateshvara temple**, outside **Tirupati**, the most popular Vishnu shrine in India, where millions of pilgrims come each year to receive *darshan*. **Puttaparthy**, the home town of the spiritual leader Sai Baba, is the only other place in the region to attract significant numbers of visitors, mostly devotees of the guru from many parts of India and the world. Both Tirupati and Puttaparthy are closer to Bangalore and Chennai than to other points in Andhra Pradesh, and for many tourists, constitute their only foray into the state.

Tirupati

Set in a stunning position, surrounded by wooded hills capped by a ring of vertical red rocks, the **Shri Venkateshvara temple** at Tirumala, an enervating drive 700m up in the Venkata hills, 11km from **TIRUPATI** and 170km northwest of Chennai, is said to be the richest and most popular place of pilgrimage in the world, drawing more devotees than either Rome or Mecca. Apart from the main temple, other shrines like the **Ganesh temple** at the foot of the hill and the **Tiruchanur Padmavati temple** are also firmly on the pilgrim trail and so the whole area around Tirumala Hill provides a fascinating insight into contemporary Hinduism practised on a large scale. If you are not particularly keen on waiting in line for hours at a time, choose the day of your visit with care; avoid weekends, public and school holidays, and particularly special festivals, at which times you are likely to meet at least 10,000 other visitors.

Arrival and information

The best way of getting to Tirupati is by train from Chennai; the trip can be done in a day if you get the earliest of the three daily services (3hr 30min). From Hyderabad it takes sixteen hours. An APTDC counter at the railway station (daily 7.30am–7pm; ☏08574/56877) is accessible from the entrance hall and platform 1, where there's a 24-hour left-luggage office and a self-service veg refreshment room. Stands sell English copies of TKT Viraraghava Charya's *History of Tirupati*, and there's a Vivekananda religious bookshop next door. Tirupati's APSRTC Central bus station – also with 24-hour left luggage – is about 1km east of the railway station. Frequent express services run from Chennai (4hr), but the train is far more comfortable. However, if you're travelling south and want to avoid Chennai, there are hourly buses to Kanchipuram (5hr), three of which continue to Mahabalipuram (7hr). There is also a useful daily train that stops at the Tamil Nadu temple towns of Tiruvannamalai, Chidambaram, Thanjavur and Trichy. Local transport is provided by beautifully decorated cycle-rickshaws, with silver backs, colourfully painted, and some covered by appliquéd cloth, as well as auto-rickshaws.

A special section at the back of the bus stand has services every few minutes **to Tirumala** and the Venkateshvara temple. You shouldn't have to queue too long unless it's a weekend or festival. An easier option is to take a **taxi**, best organized through the APTDC **tourist counter** at the railway station; avoid the unlicensed taxis outside the station as they could be stopped by the Tirumala police. The tourist office also runs a tour (10am–5.30pm; Rs125 not including entrance tickets) which takes in Chandragiri **Fort** (except Fri) and a number of temples, but does not include the Venkateshvara temple owing to the long queues.

Accommodation and eating

Unless you're a pilgrim seeking accommodation in the *dharamshalas* near the temple, all the decent places to stay are in Tirupati, near the railway and bus stand. The *Bhima* chain are probably the best-maintained hotels in town. **Eating** is recommended in the bigger hotels, although there are, of course, cheap "meals" places in town and near the temple.

Bhimas Deluxe, 34–38 G Car St, near railway station ☏08574/25521, ☏25471, ☏bhimas-deluxe@bhimas.com. Decent, comfortable rooms (all have optional a/c). The *Maya* veg restaurant serves South Indian snacks in the morning, and North Indian plus some Chinese dishes in the evenings. ⑤–⑥

Bhimas Paradise, Renigunta Road ☏08574/25747, ☏25568. This and the sister *Bhimas Residency* next door offer clean functional rooms, some a/c, with tiny balconies. Star TV, pool, garden and 24hr coffee shop, but an ugly location on the main road. The restaurant, *Bharani*, is clean and dark, serving veg South Indian snacks, thalis and North Indian dishes. ⑥–⑦

Indira Rest House, Tiruchanur Road ☏08574/23125. Basic, no-nonsense lodge, a few minutes' walk behind the railway lines from the bus stand. Some new a/c rooms ②–⑤

Maurya, 149 TP Area ☏08574/24894, ☏53859. Well-maintained hotel east of temple tank with some a/c rooms, and cable TV. Good value. ③–⑤

Mini Bhimas, 191 Railway Station Rd ☏08574/25930. Very basic but cleanish en-suite rooms. ②

Raghunadha, 191 Railway Station Rd ☏08574/23130. Good, simple, clean lodge; one of the better cheap places. Cable TV in all rooms and some a/c. ②–⑤

Sindhuri Park, beside bathing tank

ment *Vrinda* restaurant serves quality veg food, including a range of thalis. ❻–❼

Govindarajaswamy temple

Just a five-minute walk from the railway station, the one temple in Tirupati itself definitely worth a visit is Govindarajaswamy, whose modern grey *gopura* is clearly visible from many points in town. Begun by the Nayaks in the sixteenth century, it's an interesting complex with large open courtyards decorated with lion sculptures and some ornately carved wooden roofing. The temple's **inner sanctum** is open to non-Hindus and contains a splendid large black reclining Vishnu, coated in bronze armour and bedecked in flowers. The *sanadarsanan* (daily 9.30am–12.30pm; Rs5) will let you in to glimpse the deity, and participate in fire blessings at the main and subsidiary shrines.

Tucked away at the back of the complex, just inside the south *gopura*, there is also the Venkateshvara Museum of Temple Arts. Set in a colonnaded compound, the single hall displays photographs, models and diagrams of buildings and various ritual objects. The temple's impressive bathing tank lies 200m to the east.

Tiruchanur Padmavati temple

Between Tirupati and Tirumala Hill, the **Tiruchanur Padmavati temple** is another popular pilgrimage halt. A gold *vimana* tower with lions at each corner surmounts the sanctuary, which contains a black stone image of goddess Lakshmi with one silver eye. At the front step, water sprays wash the feet of the devotees. A Rs5 ticket allows you to jump the line to enter the sanctuary. If you'd like to donate a sari to the goddess, you may do so, on payment of Rs1200. Cameras are prohibited.

Tirumala Hill, the Venkateshvara temple and Kapilateertham

There's good reason for the small shrine to Ganesh at the foot of **Tirumala Hill**. The journey up is hair-raising and it's worth saying a quick prayer when embarking on it, but at least separate routes up and down preclude head-on crashes. Overtaking is strictly forbidden, but drivers do anyway; virtually every bend is labelled "blind" and every instruction to drive slowly is blithely ignored. The fearless sit on the left for the best views; the most devout, of course, climb the hill by foot. When you get to the top, you will see barbers busying themselves giving pilgrims tonsures as part of their devotions. Temple funds support a university, hospital, orphanages and schools at Tirupati as well as providing cheap, and in some cases free, accommodation for pilgrims.

The **Venkateshvara temple**, dedicated to **Vishnu** and started in the tenth century, has been recently renovated to provide facilities for the thousands of pilgrims who visit daily; a rabbit warren of passages and waiting rooms wind their way around the complex in which pilgrims interminably shuffle towards the inner sanctum. Non-Hindus are permitted to enter the inner sanctum, but for everyone, *darshan*, a view of the god, is the briefest of brief experiences. Unless your visit is intended to be particularly rigorous, on reaching the temple you should follow the signs for the special *darshan* that costs Rs50 (daily 6–10am ex Fri and noon–9pm). This will reduce the time it takes to get inside by hours, if not days. You have to sign a declaration of faith in Lord Venkateshvara and give your passport number. There is a seated waiting area.

Once inside, you'll see the somewhat incongruous sight of *brahmins* sitting at video monitors, observing the goings-on in the inner sanctum; the constant to-ing and fro-ing includes temple attendants bringing in supplies, truckloads of oil and other comestibles, and huge cooking pots being carried across the courtyard. You may also catch deities being hauled past on palanquins to the accompaniment of *nagesvaram* (a South Indian oboe-like double-reed wind instrument) and *tavil* drum, complete with an armed guard. At the entrance is a colonnade, lined with life-sized statues of royal patrons, in copper or stone. The *gopura* gateway leading to the inner courtyard is decorated with sheets of embossed silver; a gold *stambha* (flagstaff) stands outside the inner shrine next to a gold upturned lotus on a plinth. Outside, opposite the temple, is a small museum, the **Hall of Antiquities** (daily 8am–8pm). Your special *darshan* ticket entitles you to enter the museum via a shorter queue opposite the exit and to pick up two free *laddu* sweets. **Kapilateertham**, a temple at the bottom of the hill, has a gaily painted little Hindu pleasure garden at the entrance; after the rains, a powerful waterfall crashes into a large tank surrounded by colonnades, and everyone piles in for a bath, with typically good-natured pilgrim bedlam ensuing.

Chandragiri Fort
In the sixteenth century, Chandragiri, 11km southwest of Tirupati, became the third capital of the Vijayanagars, whose power had declined following the fall of the city of Vijayanagar (Hampi) in Karnataka. It was here that the British negotiated the acquisition of the land to establish Fort St George, the earliest settlement at what is now Chennai. The original fort, thought to date from c.1000 AD, was taken over by Haider Ali in 1782, followed by the British in 1792. A small museum of sculpture, weapons and memorabilia (daily except Fri 10am–5pm; $5 [Rs5]) is housed in the main building, the Indo-Saracenic Raja Mahal. Another building, the Rani Mahal, stands close by, while behind that is a hill with two free-standing boulders that was used as a place of public execution during Vijayanagar times. A small temple from the Krishna Deva Raya period and a freshwater tank stand at the top of the hill behind the Raja Mahal. In the evening there is a 45min sound and light show (English version Nov–Feb 7.30pm, Mar–Oct 8pm; Rs20), which is a good way of glimpsing the fort without having to pay big bucks.

Puttaparthy
Deep in the southwest of the state, amid the arid rocky hills bordering Karnataka, a thriving community has grown up around the once insignificant village of **PUTTAPARTHY**, birthplace of spiritual leader Sai Baba, whose followers believe him to be the new incarnation of God. Indeed, you will not be in the town long before being greeted by the oft-heard salutation of "Sai Ram". Centring on **Prasanthi Nilayam**, the ashram where Sai Baba resides from July to March, the town has schools, a university, a hospital and sports centre which offer up-to-date, free services to all. There's even a small airport. The **ashram** itself is a huge complex with room for thousands, canteens, shops, a museum and library, and a vast assembly hall where Sai Baba gives *darshan* twice daily (6.40am & 3pm). Queues start more than an hour before the appointed time, and a lottery decides who gets to sit near the front.

The **museum** (daily 10am–noon), situated up a small hill to the left after entering the main gates, is undoubtedly the most interesting place for the casual visitor. The ground floor contains a detailed, fascinating display on the **major faiths** with illustrations and quotations from their sacred texts, punctuated by Sai Baba's comments. These are invariably intended to point out the underlying unity of the different belief systems. The first floor has more colourful exhibits, focusing on various places of worship and one dedicated to Sai Baba's predecessor, the Shirdi Sai Baba (see box below). Finally, the third floor displays bring the animistic tribal religions of Africa into the universal fold, as well as the beliefs and philosophy of the ancient Greeks. It is noteworthy that the divinity of Socrates is accorded special emphasis.

Practicalities

Puttaparthy is most accessible from Bangalore in Karnataka (see p.232), from where seven daily **buses** (4hr) run to the stand outside the ashram entrance. The town is also connected to Hyderabad (3 daily; 10hr) and Chennai (1 nightly; 11hr). Regular buses make the 42-kilometre run to **Dharmavaram**, the nearest **railhead**, which has good services north and south. There are also two **flights** a week from Mumbai.

Most visitors **stay** at the ashram in large bare sheds or smaller rooms if available. Except in the case of families, accommodation is strictly segregated by sex, as are meals and *darshan*. Overt socializing is discouraged and there is a strict policy of lights-out at 9pm. Costs are minimal, and though you can't book in advance, you can enquire about availability at the secretary's office (☏08555/87583). Space is only usually a problem around the time of Sai Baba's birthday in late November. If you do want to stay, you have to register by filling out forms and surrendering your passport at the office before being allocated a bed by the Public Relations Officer. Your passport is returned after attending the first orientation session. Outside the ashram, many of the basic

Shri Satya Sai Baba

Born Satyanarayana Raju on November 23, 1926 in Puttaparthy, then an obscure village in the Madras Presidency, Satya is reported to have shown prodigious talents and unusual purity and compassion from an early age. His apparently supernatural abilities initially caused some concern to his family, who took him to Vedic doctors and eventually to be exorcised. Having been pronounced to be possessed by the divine rather than the diabolical, at the age of fourteen, he calmly announced that he was the new incarnation of Sai Baba, a saint from Shirdi in Maharashtra who died eight years before Satya was born.

Gradually his fame spread, and a large following grew. In 1950 the ashram was inaugurated and a decade later Sai Baba was attracting international attention; today he has millions of devotees worldwide, a considerable number of whom turn out for his birthday celebrations in Puttaparthy, when he delivers a message to his devotees. His smiling, diminutive, saffron-clad figure is seen on posters, framed photos and murals all over South India. Though his miraculous powers reportedly include the ability to materialize *vibhuti* – sacred ash – with curative properties, Sai Baba claims this to be an unimportant activity, aimed at those firmly entrenched in materialism, and emphasizes instead his message of universal love. Indeed, he prefers the ash to be seen as a representation of the final condition of worldly things and the desire to give them up in search of the divine.

In recent years a number of ex-followers, some of whom had obtained high positions, have made serious allegations of coercion and even sexual abuse on the part of the guru himself, which have been vehemently denied. Whatever your feelings about the divinity of Sai Baba, the atmosphere around the ashram is undeniably peaceful, and the growth of such a vibrant community in this once-forgotten backwater is no small miracle in itself.

lodges are rather overpriced. However, the *Sai Ganesh Guest House* near the police station (☏08555/87079; **②**) is friendly and a good cheap option. The new, great-value *Sri Sai Sadam* is at the far end of the main street (☏08555/87507; **③–④**); all rooms have fridge, TV and balcony with views of the countryside or the ashram, and there's a meditation room and rooftop restaurant. At the top end, the all a/c *Sai Towers*, near the ashram entrance (☏0855/87270; **⑦**) charges a lot for its smallish rooms, but has a good restaurant downstairs. Even non-residents can **eat** in the ashram canteen, and there are simple snack stalls along the main street.

Travel details

Trains

Hyderabad/Secunderabad to: Aurangabad (1 daily; 12hr 22min); Bangalore (3–4 daily; 11hr 45min–15hr 50min); Bhubaneshwar (3 daily; 19hr 50min–22hr 55min); Calcutta (2 daily; 27hr 40min–33hr 15min); Chennai (2 daily; 14hr 5min–14hr 15min); Delhi (2–3 daily; 22hr 10min–32hr 50min); Mumbai (3 daily; 15hr 35min–17hr 40min); Tirupati (3–4 daily; 14hr–15hr 30min); Varanasi (2 weekly; 30hr 15min); Vijayawada (12–13 daily; 5hr 10min–7hr 45min); Vishakapatnam (5–6 daily; 11hr 30min–19hr 10min); Warangal (9–10 daily; 2hr 8min–3hr 18min).

Tirupati to: Chennai (3 daily; 3hr 15min); Hyderabad/Secunderabad (3–4 daily; 13hr 20min–17hr 10min); Tiruchirapalli (1 daily; 14hr 15min); Varanasi (1 daily; 36hr); Vijayawada (3–6 daily; 6hr 25min–8hr 45min); Vishakapatnam (2–3 daily; 13hr 25min–19hr 5min).

Vijayawada to: Calcutta (5–7 daily; 21hr 55min–33hr 20min); Chennai (7–12 daily; 5hr 45min–8hr 50min); Delhi (4–6 daily; 23hr 10min–32hr 50min); Hyderabad/Secunderabad (12–13 daily; 5hr 15min–8hr 10min); Tirupati (3–6 daily; 6hr 25min–8hr 15min); Vishakapatnam (12–16 daily; 6hr 5min–12hr 30min).

Vishakapatnam to: Bhubaneshwar (5–7 daily; 6hr 45min–9hr 50min); Calcutta (5–7 daily; 15hr 15min–23hr); Chennai (2–4 daily; 12hr 45min–15hr 55min); Delhi (1–2 daily; 34hr 40min–39hr 45min); Hyderabad/Secunderabad (5–6 daily; 11hr 50min–15hr 40min); Tirupati (2–3 daily; 14hr 30min–16hr 50min); Vijayawada (12–16 daily; 5hr 55min–11hr 10min).

Buses

Hyderabad to: Amaravati (2 daily; 7hr); Bangalore (hourly; 13hr); Bidar (19 daily; 4hr); Chennai (1 daily; 16hr); Mumbai (8 daily; 17hr); Puttaparthy (3 daily; 10hr); Tirupati (7 daily; 12hr); Vijayapuri (10 daily; 4hr); Vijayawada (every 15min; 6hr); Warangal (every 15–30min; 3hr).

Tirupati to: Chennai (every 30min; 3hr 30min–4hr); Hyderabad (7 daily; 12hr); Kanchipuram (hourly; 3hr 30min); Mahabalipuram (3 daily; 5hr 30min); Puttaparthy (1 daily; 10hr).

Vijayawada to: Amaravati (hourly; 2hr); Guntur (every 15min; 1hr–1hr 30min); Hyderabad (every 15min; 6hr).

Flights

Hyderabad to: Ahmedabad (4 weekly; 1hr 40min); Bangalore (2–3 daily; 1hr); Calcutta (1–2 daily; 2–3hr); Chennai (3–4 daily; 1hr–1hr 45min); Cochin (2 weekly; 2hr 40min); Delhi (3 daily; 2hr–2hr 10min); Mumbai (6–7 daily; 1hr 15min–3hr); Tirupati (1–2 daily; 55min–1hr 20min); Vishakapatnam (2 daily; 1hr–1hr 30min).

Puttaparthy to: Mumbai (2 weekly; 1hr 20min).

Vishakapatnam to: Bhubaneshwar (4 weekly; 55min); Calcutta (4 weekly; 2hr 20min); Chennai (4 weekly; 1hr 5min); Delhi (4 weekly; 3hr 35min); Hyderabad (2 daily; 1hr–1hr 30min); Mumbai (1 daily; 2hr 45min).

The Andaman Islands

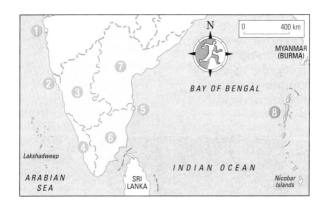

CHAPTER 8

Highlights

※ **Scuba-diving** Beautiful coral reefs teem with vivid underwater life. See p.610

※ **Port Blair** The Cellular Jail stands as a reminder of the hilly Andaman capital's bleak colonial past. See p.615

※ **Wandoor** The white sandy beach and islets of the Mahatma Gandhi National Marine Park are the archipelago's most popular day-trip destination, and a good appetizer for more remote parts. See p.620

※ **Havelock Island** Cruise by boat to the Andamans' most popular holiday hang-out, very laid-back, friendly and great for diving. See p.622

※ **North Andaman** The long haul on the road from Port Blair is worthwhile for the backdrop of thick rainforest and the dazzling tropical beaches when you get there. See p.625

The Andaman Islands

The **ANDAMAN ISLANDS** – India's most remote state – are situated 1000km off the east coast in the middle of the Bay of Bengal, connected to the mainland by flights and ferries from Calcutta, Chennai and Vishakapatnam. Thickly covered by deep green tropical forest, the archipelago supports a profusion of wildlife, including some extremely rare species of bird, but the principal attraction for tourists lies offshore, around the pristine reefs ringing most of the islands. Filled with colourful fish and kaleidoscopic corals, the crystal-clear waters of the Andaman Sea feature some of the world's richest and least spoilt marine reserves – perfect for **snorkelling** and **scuba diving**. Potential visitors may, however, consider that the expense or effort required to get there, the lack of infrastructure and certain increased health risks, as well as ethical concerns about ecological and tribal issues, rather outweigh the benefits of a trip.

For administrative purposes, the Andamans are grouped with the **Nicobar Islands**, 200km further south but, as yet, strictly off-limits to foreigners. Approximately two hundred islands make up the Andaman group and nineteen the Nicobar. They are islands of varying size, the summits of a submarine mountain range stretching 755km from the Arakan Yoma chain in Burma to the fringes of Sumatra in the south. All but the most remote of these are populated in parts by **indigenous tribes** whose numbers have been slashed dramatically as a result of nineteenth-century European settlement and, more recently, rampant **deforestation**. Today felling is supposed to be restricted, and 86 percent of the islands' forests are officially "protected". Nevertheless, *padauk* and teak are still extensively used for building materials, furniture and tourist knick-knacks, and those areas of woodland still open to the lumberjacks are being stripped of valuable foreign-currency-earning timber ahead of the all-out ban on extraction expected in the next few years.

Foreign tourists are only permitted to visit certain parts of the Andaman group, separated by the deep Ten Degree Channel from the Nicobar Islands.

Accommodation price codes

All accommodation prices in this book have been categorized using the price codes below. Prices given are for a double room, and all taxes are included. For more details, see p.46.

① up to Rs100	④ Rs300–400	⑦ Rs900–1500
② Rs100–200	⑤ Rs400–600	⑧ Rs1500–2500
③ Rs200–300	⑥ Rs600–900	⑨ Rs2500 and upwards

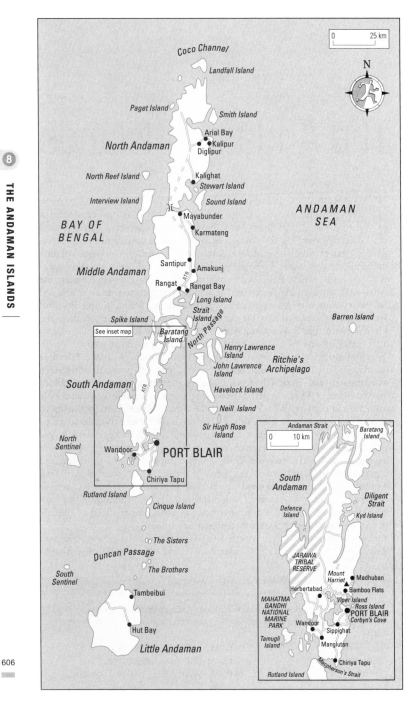

The point of arrival for boats and planes is **South Andaman**, where the predominantly Tamil and Bengali community in the small but busy capital, **Port Blair**, accounts for almost half the total population. **Permits** obtainable on the mainland or on arrival by air are granted for a stay of one month. The most beautiful beaches and coral reefs are found on outlying islands. A healthy get-up-and-go spirit is essential if you plan to explore these, as connections and transport can be erratic, frequently uncomfortable and severely limited, especially on the smaller islands. Once away from the settlements, you enter a Coca-Cola-free zone where you'll need your own camping supplies and equipment. It's also worth pointing out that a surprising number of travellers fall sick in the Andamans. The dense tree cover, marshy swamps and high rainfall combine to provide the perfect breeding ground for mosquitoes, and **malaria** is endemic in even the most remote settlements. Sandflies are also ferocious in certain places and **tropical ulcer** infections from scratching the bites is a frequent hazard.

The climate remains tropical throughout the year, with temperatures ranging from 24° to 35°C and humidity never below seventy percent. By far the best time to visit is between January and May. From mid-May to October, heavy rains flush the islands, often bringing violent cyclones that leave west-coast beaches strewn with fallen trees, while in November and December less severe rains arrive with the northeast monsoon. Despite being so far east, the islands run on Indian time, so the sun rises as early as 4.30am in summer and darkness falls soon after 5pm.

Some history

The earliest mention of the Andaman and Nicobar Islands is found in Ptolemy's geographical treatises of the second century AD. Other records from the Chinese Buddhist monk I'Tsing some five hundred years later and Arabian travellers who passed by in the ninth century depict the inhabitants as fierce and cannibalistic. Marco Polo arrived in the thirteenth century and could offer no more favourable description of the natives: "The people are without a king and are idolaters no better than wild beasts. All the men of the island of Angamanian have heads like dogs…they are a most cruel generation, and eat everybody they catch…" It is unlikely, however, that the Andamanese were cannibals, as the most vivid reports of their ferocity were propagated by Malay pirates who held sway over the surrounding seas, and needed to keep looters well away from trade ships that passed between India, China and the Far East.

During the eighteenth and nineteenth centuries European missionaries and trading companies turned their attention to the islands with a view to colonization. A string of unsuccessful attempts to convert the Nicobaris to Christianity was made by the French, Dutch and Danish, all of whom were forced to abandon their plans in the face of hideous diseases and a severe lack of food and water. Though the missionaries themselves seldom met with any hostility, several fleets of trading ships that tried to dock on the islands were captured, and their crews murdered, by Nicobari people.

In 1777 the British Lieutenant Blair chose the South Andaman harbour now known as Port Blair as the site for a penal colony, based on the deportation of criminals that had proved successful in Sumatra, Singapore and Penang. Both this scheme, and an attempt to settle the Nicobar Islands in 1867, were thwarted by adverse conditions. However, this latest attempt at colonization was more successful, and in 1858 Port Blair finally did become a penal settlement, where political activists who had fuelled the Mutiny in 1857 were made to clear land and build their own prison. Out of 773 prisoners, 292 died, escaped or were

Quite where the indigenous population of the Andaman and Nicobar Islands originally came from is a puzzle that has preoccupied anthropologists since Radcliffe-Brown, the English social anthropologist, conducted his famous field work among the Andamanese at the beginning of the twentieth century. Asian-looking groups such as the Shompen (see below) may have migrated here from the east and north when the islands were connected to Burma, or the sea was sufficiently shallow to allow transport by canoe, but this doesn't explain the origins of the black populations, whose appearance suggests African roots. Wherever they came from, the survival of the islands' first inhabitants has been threatened by traders and colonizers, who introduced disease and destroyed their territories by widespread felling. Thousands also died from addiction to alcohol and opium, which the Chinese, Japanese and British exchanged for valuable shells. Of perhaps 5000 aborigines in 1858, from six of the twelve native tribal groups, only five percent remain.

On the Nicobar Islands, the distinctly Southeast-Asian Nicobaris, who claim descent from a Burmese prince and were identified as *lojenke* (naked people) by I'Tsing, have integrated to some extent with recent settlers, following widespread conversion by Christian missionaries. While they continue to live in small communities of huts raised on stilts, most have adopted modern agricultural methods, raising pigs and cultivating fruit and vegetables gardens rather than hunting. One of the largest communities of Nicobaris is at John Richardson Bay, near the town of Hut Bay on Little Andaman. The Shompen of Great Nicobar, on the other hand, have not assimilated, and fewer than two hundred survive, living predominantly on the coast, where they barter in honey, cane and nuts with the Nicobaris.

The indigenous inhabitants of the Andamans, divided into *eramtaga* (those living in the jungle), and *ar-yuato* (those living on the coast), traditionally subsisted on fish, turtles, turtle eggs, pigs, fruits, honey and roots. Although they comprised the largest group when the islands were first colonized, less than thirty Great Andamanese remain, forcibly settled on Strait Island, north of South Andaman as a "breeding centre" and reliant on the Indian authorities for food and shelter. In the 1860s, the Rev H. Corbyn set up a "home" for them to learn English on Ross Island, insisting that they wear clothes and attend reading and writing classes. Five children and three adults from Corbyn's school were taken as curiosities to Calcutta in 1864, where they were shown around the sights. The whole experience, however, proved more fascinating for the crowds who'd come to ogle the "monkey men" than for the Andamanese themselves, who, one of the organizers of the trip ruefully remarked, ". . . never evinced astonishment or admiration at anything which they beheld, however wonderful in its novelty we might suppose it would appear to them". From the foreign settlers the Andamanese tragically contracted diseases such as syphilis, measles, mumps and influenza, and fell prey to opium addiction. Within three years almost the entire population had died.

The Jarawas, who shifted from their original homes when land was cleared to build Port Blair, now live on the remote western coasts of Middle and South

hanged in the first two months. Many also lost their lives in attacks by Andamanese tribes who objected to forest clearance, but the settlement continued to fill with people from mainland India, and by 1864 the number of convicts had grown to 3000. In 1896 work began on the jail made up of hundreds of tiny solitary cells, which still stands today and is one of Port Blair's few "tourist attractions".

In 1919 the British government in India decided to close down the penal settlement, but it was subsequently used to incarcerate a new generation of

Andaman, hemmed in by the Andaman Trunk Road which since the 1970s has cut them off from hunting grounds and fresh water supplies. Over the past two decades, encroachments on their land by loggers, road builders and Bengali settlers have met with fierce resistance. Dozens, possibly hundreds, of people have died in skirmishes. In one incident a party of Burmese was caught poaching on Jarawa land; of the eleven men involved, six limped out with horrific injuries, two were found dead, and the other three were never seen again. Most of the incidents have occurred on or near the Andaman Trunk Road, which is why armed escorts board the buses at several points during the journey north from Port Blair to Mayabunder. Some contact with the Indian government used to be made through gift-exchanges at each full moon, when consignments of coconuts, bananas and red cloth were taken to a friendly band of Jarawas on a boat, but the initiative was later cancelled. The damage may well have been done though, for some Jarawas have become curious about what "civilisation" has to offer and since 1997 have taken to holding their hands out for goodies to passing vehicles and even visiting Indian settlements near their territory. When the initially generous reception waned, their visits evolved into surreptitious raids and there was an attack on a police outpost in March 1998. So tensions remain high and government plans in the pipeline for the permanent settlement and "development" of the Jarawas does not bode well for the independent survival of some of the planet's last hunter-gatherers.

Aside from a couple of violent encounters with nineteenth-century seamen (seventy were massacred on first contact in 1867), relations with the Onge, who call themselves the Gaubolambe, have been relatively peaceful. Distinguished by their white-clay and ochre body paint, they continue to live in communal shelters (*bera*) and construct temporary thatched huts (*korale*) on Little Andaman. The remaining population of around one hundred retain their traditional way of life on two small reserves. The Indian government has erected wood and tin huts in both, dispatched a teacher to instruct them in Hindi, and encouraged coconut cultivation, but to little avail. Contact with outsiders is limited to an occasional trip into town to purchase liquor, and visits from rare parties of anthropologists. The reserves are strictly off-limits to foreigners, but you can learn about the Onges' traditional hunting practices, beliefs and rituals in Vishvajit Pandya's wonderful ethnography study, *Above the Forest*.

The most elusive tribe of all, the Sentinelese, live on North Sentinel Island west of South Andaman. Some contact was made with them in 1990, after a team put together by the local administration had left gifts on the beaches every month for two years, but subsequent visits have invariably ended in a hail of arrows. Since the early 1990s, the AAJVS, the government department charged with tribal welfare, has effectively given up trying to contact the Sentinelese, who are estimated to number around eighty. Flying in or out of Port Blair, you pass above their island, ringed by a spectacular coral reef, and it's reassuring to think that the people sitting at the bottom of the plumes of smoke drifting from the forest canopy have for so long resisted contact with the outside world.

freedom fighters from India, Malabar and Burma. During World War II the islands were occupied by the Japanese, who tortured and murdered hundreds of indigenous islanders suspected of collaborating with the British, and bombed the homes of the Jarawa tribes. British forces moved back in 1945, and at last abolished the penal settlement.

After Partition, refugees, mostly low-caste Hindus from Bangladesh and Bengal, were given land in Port Blair and North Andaman, where the forest was clear-felled to make room for rice paddy, cocoa plantations and new industries. Since

1951 the population has increased by more than ten times, further swollen by repatriated Tamils from Sri Lanka, thousands of Bihari labourers, ex-servicemen given land grants, economic migrants from poorer Indian states and the legions of government employees packed off here on two-year "punishment postings". This replanted population greatly outnumbers the Andamans' indigenous people, who currently comprise around half of one percent of the total. Contact between the two societies is limited, and is not always friendly. In addition, there exists within Port Blair a clear divide between the relatively recent incomers and the so-called "pre-42s" – descendants of the released convicts and freedom fighters whose families settled here before the major influx from the mainland. This small but influential minority, based at the exclusive Browning Club in the capital, has been calling for curbs on immigration and new property rules to slow down the rate of settlement. While doubtless motivated by self-interest, their demands nevertheless reflect growing concern for the future of the Andamans, where rapid and largely unplanned development has wrought havoc on the natural environment, not to mention on the indigenous population.

With the days of the timber-extraction cash cow now numbered, the hope is that **tourism** will replace tree felling as the main source of revenue. However, the extra numbers envisaged are certain to overtax an already inadequate infrastructure, aggravating seasonal water shortages and sewage disposal problems. Given India's track record with tourism development, it's hard to be optimistic. Perhaps the greatest threat looming on the horizon is the plan to extend the airport runway in 2002, which will allow long-haul flights from Southeast Asia to land here. In the meantime smaller **charter planes** from Bangkok and Singapore may have started arriving by the end of 2001. If only a trickle of the tourist traffic flooding between Thailand and India is diverted through the Andamans, the impact on this culturally and ecologically fragile region could be catastrophic.

Getting to the Andaman Islands

Port Blair, on South Andaman, is served by Indian Airlines **flights** from Calcutta (daily except Wed & Fri) and Chennai (Mon, Wed, Fri & Sun); Jet Airways now runs a daily flight from Chennai, which means that availability is a lot easier than it used to be on that sector. Tickets for the two hour flights remain expensive though, at around $200 one way, unless you qualify for a discount.

It's also possible to get to Port Blair by **ship**. Services to and from Chennai have stabilised and can now be reasonably relied upon to leave in each direction every Friday. Those from Calcutta every two weeks and Vishakapatnam once every month are still somewhat erratic. Although far cheaper than flying, the crossings are long (3–4 days; from $25), uncomfortable and often delayed by bad conditions and bureaucracy.

Tourists arriving by plane can pick up the **permit** necessary to visit the islands on arrival at Port Blair airport; passengers travelling on a ship should obtain one at a foreigners' registration office before leaving mainland India. Refer to the relevant chapters for full details on obtaining permits from Chennai (see p.453) and Vishakapatnam (see p.595); permits are also available in Calcutta. Permits are usually extendible for fifteen days beyond the original thirty but the authorities sometimes only allow you to stay in Port Blair for that period, not an appealing prospect.

Scuba diving in the Andaman Islands

The seas around the Andaman and Nicobar Islands are some of the world's most unspoiled. Marine life is abundant, with an estimated 750 species of fish existing on one reef alone. Parrot, trigger and angel fish live alongside manta rays, reef sharks and loggerhead turtles. Many species of fish and coral are unique to the area and fascinating life-systems exist in ash beds and cooled lava based around the volcanic Barren Island (see p.629).

For a quick taste of marine life, you could start by **snorkelling**; most hotels can supply masks and snorkels, though some equipment is in dire need of replacement. The only way to get really close, however, and venture out into deeper waters, is to **scuba dive** (see below). The experience of weaving in and out of coral beds, coming eye to eye with fish or swimming with dolphins and barracudas is unforgettable.

At present, the islands only have three proper **dive centres**. Two are based in the Port Blair area, reputable and PADI registered, but far from cheap; **Samudra** (℡01392/33159, ℻31824), occupies a former Japanese bunker at the *Sinclairs Bay View Hotel* (see p.615), while the Swiss-run **Andaman Divers** (℡01392/33461 or 6–9pm 35771, ℻33463) has an office in the *Peerless Resort* at Corbyn's Cove. Both charge qualified divers around Rs2500 for two local dives and Rs3200 for trips to Wandoor and beyond. Beginners can do introductory dives with basic training at Rs1800/2800 for a half/full day. For a hefty Rs15,000, you can also do a three- or four-day PADI open-water course. When booking dives with either, check which sites they use: Cinque Island offers arguably the best diving in the area, and is worth shelling out a little extra to visit as it's otherwise difficult to reach. It is best to avoid the occasional fly-by-night unregistered operations that pop up offering cut-price diving trips, as neither their equipment nor expertise can be counted on.

The most congenial and cheapest of the bona fide centres is the **Andaman Scuba Club** (✉info@AndamanScubaClub.com) on Havelock Island (see p.622). Run by a friendly Swiss duo and their Indian partner, all PADI-certified instructors, they offer dives at prime sites in the area to those qualified at Rs1000 each plus Rs500 daily for equipment rental, open-water courses at Rs12,900 and advanced courses at Rs10,000. "Discover Scuba" theory, training and intro dives cost Rs2500 and they allow unlimited free snorkelling trips to anyone who has dived with them. They are completely reliable, safe and fun to dive with. They also accept foreign currency or travellers cheques as payment.

Underwater in the Andamans, it is not uncommon to come across schools of reef sharks, which rarely turn hostile, but one thing to watch out for and avoid is the **black-and-white sea snake**. Though the snakes seldom attack – and, since their fangs are at the back of their mouths, would find it difficult to get a grip on any human – their bite is twenty times more deadly than that of the cobra.

Green Coral Code

Increased tourism inevitably puts pressure on the delicate marine ecosystem, and poorly funded wildlife organizations can do little to prevent damage from insensitive visitors. You can ensure your presence in the sea around the reefs does not harm the coral by observing the following **Green Coral Code** while diving or snorkelling:

❐ Never touch, or walk on, living coral as it will die.

❐ Try to keep your feet away from reefs while wearing fins; the sudden sweep of water caused by a flipper kick can be enough to destroy coral.

❐ Always control the speed of your descent while diving; enormous dam age can be caused by divers' landing hard on a coral bed.

❐ Never break off pieces of coral from a reef, and remember that it is ille gal to export dead coral from the islands, even fragments you may have found on a beach.

South Andaman

South Andaman is today the most heavily populated of the Andaman Islands – particularly around the capital, **Port Blair** – thanks in part to the drastic thinning of tree cover to make way for settlement. Foreign tourists can only visit its southern and east central reaches – including the beaches at **Corbyn's Cove** and **Chiriya Tapu**, the fine reefs on the western shores at **Wandoor**, 35km southwest of Port Blair and the environs of **Madhuban** and **Mount Harriet** on the east coast across the bay from the capital.

With your own transport it's easy to find your way along the narrow bumpy roads that connect small villages, weaving through forests and coconut fields, and skirting the swamps and rocky outcrops that form the coastline.

Port Blair

PORT BLAIR, a characterless cluster of tin-roofed buildings tumbling towards the sea in the north, east and west and petering into fields and forests in the south, merits only a short stay. There's little to see here – just the **Cellular Jail** and a few small **museums** – but as the point of arrival for the islands, and the only place with a bank, tourist offices and hotels, it can't be avoided. If you plan to head off to more remote islands, this is also the best place to stock up on supplies and buy necessary equipment.

Arrival and information

Port Blair has two jetties: **boats** from the mainland moor at **Haddo Jetty**, nearly 2km northwest of **Phoenix Jetty**, arrival point for inter-island ferries. The Director of Shipping Services at Phoenix Jetty has the latest information on boats and ferries, but you can also check the shipping news column of the local newspaper, the *Daily Telegrams*, for details of forthcoming departures. Advice on booking ferry tickets appears in the box on p.618.

The smart new **airport** terminal is 4km south of town at Lamba Line. Entry **permits** are issued to foreigners from the immigration counters as you enter the arrivals hall. **Taxis** are on hand for short trip into town (Rs40–50), but if you have booked a room in any of the middle or upper range hotels or do so at the counter in the airport, you should find a shuttle bus waiting outside.

The counter at the airport (☎03192/32414) hands out a useful brochure, but the main **A&N tourist office** (Mon–Sat 10am–5pm; ☎03192/32694) is situated in a modern building, diagonally opposite Indian Airlines on the southern edges of the town. Unless you want to book accommodation in an ANIIDCO hotel or a seat on one of their tours (such as to Wandoor), it's hard to think of a reason to go there; they don't keep transport timetables or any useful information about the rest of the archipelago. North of the centre on Junglighat Main Road, the **Government of India Tourist Office** (Mon–Fri 8.30am–5pm; ☎03192/33006) is little better.

Road names are not used much in Port Blair, with most establishments addressing themselves simply by their local area. The name of the busiest

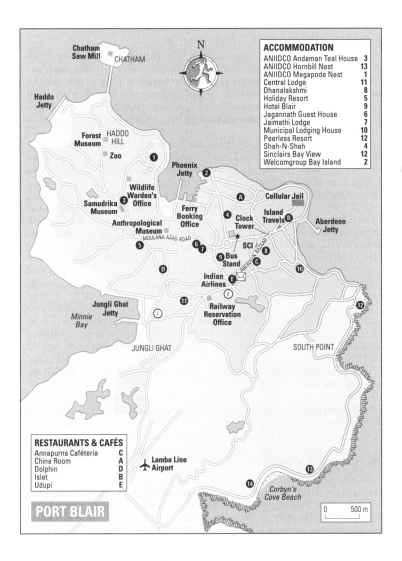

ACCOMMODATION

ANIIDCO Andaman Teal House	3
ANIIDCO Hornbill Nest	13
ANIIDCO Megapode Nest	1
Central Lodge	11
Dhanalakshmi	8
Holiday Resort	5
Hotel Blair	9
Jagannath Guest House	6
Jaimathi Lodge	7
Municipal Lodging House	10
Peerless Resort	12
Shah-N-Shah	4
Sinclairs Bay View	12
Welcomgroup Bay Island	2

RESTAURANTS & CAFÉS

Annapurna Caféteria	C
China Room	A
Dolphin	D
Islet	B
Udupi	E

PORT BLAIR

and most central area is **Aberdeen Bazaar**, where you'll find the superintendent of police (for permit extensions), the SCI office for onward bookings by sea (☏03192/33590), and the State Bank of India (Mon–Fri 9am–1pm, Sat 9–11am). Some hotels will change travellers' cheques, but you'll get faster service and better rates at Island Travels (☏03192/33034; Mon–Sat 2–5pm), which has a licence to change money, and is just up the road from the clocktower in Aberdeen Bazaar. You can email or use the internet for Rs60 per hour at Kembu's NetJoint (☏03192/34949) on Moulana Azad Road near *Jagannath Guest House*. There is also a net café in the *Hotel Blair* complex.

Local transport and tours

Walking is tiring and time-consuming in hilly Port Blair – even taking into account the minimal amount of sightseeing the place offers – making transport essential. Yellow-top **taxis** gather opposite the bus stand. They all have meters, but negotiating the price before leaving is usual practice. Expect to pay Rs50 for a trip from the centre of town to Corbyn's Cove. In 1999 the islands received the first fleet of **auto-rickshaws** but they tend to charge almost as much as taxis.

Local **buses** run infrequently from the bus stand in central Port Blair to Wandoor and Chiriya Tapu, and can be used for day-trips, though it's best to rely on your own transport to get around South Andaman. **Bicycles** can be rented from Aberdeen Bazaar, at Rs5 per hour, but the roads to the coasts are most easily covered on a **Vespa** or **motorcycle**, both available for rent at TSG Travels (Mon–Sat 8.30am–7pm; ℡03192/32894) on Moulana Azad Road behind Phoenix Bay. They require a licence and Rs500 deposit. Singh Travels at the Singh cloth store near the Aberdeen Bazaar clocktower have a few old scooters with gears. They are less fussed about showing a licence but ask for a Rs1000 deposit. Rental rates at both places are Rs120 per day. The petrol pump is on the crossroads west of the bus stand, and there's another on the road towards the airport. Fill up before you leave town, as petrol is hard to come by elsewhere.

Cramming the island's few interesting sights together with a string of dull destinations, most of the ANIIDCO **tours** are a complete waste of time; you're better off renting a scooter or taxi and taking in the jail and museums at your own pace. However, more worthwhile are their **harbour cruises** (daily 3–5pm; Rs20) that depart from Phoenix Jetty for fleeting visits to the floating docks and **Viper Island** (see p.617), and the day-trips to **Wandoor** and the **Mahatma Gandhi marine park** (see p.620). The bus tour to Wandoor (8am; Rs75) connects with the 10am boat to the islands of Red Skin (Rs90) and Jolly Buoy (Rs125). You can also spend an evening cruising the harbour with a buffet dinner and entertainment on the Atlantis, ANIIDCO's floating restaurant (daily 7pm; Rs225) but it's primarily aimed at wealthy Indian visitors.

Accommodation

Port Blair boasts a fair selection of places to stay. Concentrated mainly in the centre of town, the bottom-range **accommodation** can be as dour as any port town on the mainland; assume if a lodge isn't listed below, it's not worth looking at, let alone sleeping in. More comfortable hotels occupy correspondingly more salubrious locations on the outskirts. Wherever you intend to stay, it's definitely worth booking ahead during peak season.

ANIIDCO Andaman Teal House, Delanipur ℡03192/34060. High on the hill above Haddo port this place offers great views, spacious and pleasant rooms, and is very good value, although can be inconvenient without your own transport. ❸–❹

ANIIDCO Hornbill Nest, 1km from Corbyn's Cove ℡03192/34305. Clean, roomy cottages on a hillside by the coast. Great location, catching the sea breezes, but transport to and from town is a problem unless you rent a scooter. ❸

ANIIDCO Megapode Nest, Haddo Hill ℡03192/33659, ℻32702. A&N Tourism's upscale option has 25 comfortable rooms, and pricier self-contained "cottages", ranged around a central lawn, with good views, and a quality restaurant. ❼

Central Lodge, Middle Point ℡03192/33632. Ramshackle wooden building situated in a secluded top corner of town. A rock-bottom option, offering basic rooms or garden space for hammocks. ❶

Dhanalakshmi, Aberdeen Bazaar ℡03192/33952. Friendly, clean and very central but not particularly good value. The rooms are all en suite and tiled, but can get stuffy (you have to keep the front windows closed because of traffic noise, and the back ones shut to keep out the mosquitoes). ⑤–⑦

Holiday Resort, Premnagar, a fifteen-minute walk from the centre ☎03192/30516. This is the best mid-price deal in the town centre; it's clean and spacious, with some a/c, a bar and a TV lounge. ⑤–⑥

Hotel Blair, HSKP Complex, five minutes from the bus stand ☎03192/38109, ℱ34062. Reasonable value modern hotel with large clean rooms in a fairly quiet location. Airy rooftop restaurant serving standard fare. ⑤–⑦

Jagannath Guest House, Moulana Azad Road ☎03192/32148. One of the better value basic lodges: clean, central and convenient for the jetty. The front-side rooms are the nicest, though marginally more expensive. No telephone bookings taken. ③

Jaimathi Lodge, Moulana Azad Road ☎03192/33457. Popular place with Westerners and Indians alike. Large, fairly clean rooms with communal balconies. Slightly cheaper than the *Jagannath* next door and more likely to have rooms free. ②–③

Municipal Lodging House, opposite Municipal Swimming Pool ☎03192/34919. Port Blair's best budget deal: clean rooms with good beds, fans,

bathrooms, balconies and sea views, but it's often booked up with Bengali tourists and inter-island travellers. ②

Peerless Resort, Corbyn's Cove ☎03192/33461, ℱ33463. Perfect setting amid gardens of palms, jasmine and bougainvillea, opposite a white sandy beach. Balconied a/c rooms, cottages, bar, and a mid-priced restaurant where the evening buffet doesn't always match up to what is served in simpler places elsewhere. Ideal for families. ⑨

Shah-N-Shah, Mohanpura, near the bus stand ☎03192/33696. Set between the bus stand and the boat jetty, this is basic but comfortable, with en-suite rooms and a sociable terrace. ③–④

Sinclairs Bay View, on the coast road to Corbyn's Cove ☎03192/33159, ℱ31824, ℮sinclairs@vsnl.com. Clifftop hotel offering spotless carpeted rooms, balconies, en-suite bathrooms, dramatic views, bar and restaurant, in-house diving school and airport shuttle bus. ⑧

Welcomgroup Bay Island, Marine Hill, Port Blair ☎03192/20881. Port Blair's swishest hotel; elegant, airy and finished with polished teak wood. All rooms have carpets and balconies overlooking Phoenix Jetty (the less expensive ones are a little cramped); quality restaurant, gardens and open-air sea-water swimming pool, though tariffs are decidedly steep at over $100 per double. ⑨

The Town

Port Blair's only firm reminder of its gloomy past, the sturdy brick **Cellular Jail** (Mon–Sat 9am–noon & 2–7pm), overlooks the sea from a small rise in the northeast of town. Built between 1896 and 1905, its tiny solitary cells were quite different and far worse than the dormitories in other prison blocks erected earlier. Only three of the seven wings that originally radiated from the central tower now remain. Visitors can peer into the cells (3 x 3.5m), and imagine the grim conditions under which the prisoners existed. Cells were dirty and ill ventilated, drinking water was limited to two glasses per day, and the convicts were expected to wash in the rain as they worked clearing forests and building prison quarters. Food, brought from the mainland, was stored in vats where the rice and pulses became infested with worms; more than half the prison population died long before their twenty years' detention was up. Protests against conditions led to hunger strikes in 1932, 1933 and 1937, resulting in yet more deaths, and frequent executions took place at the gallows that still stand in squat wooden shelters in the courtyards, in full view of the cells. The **sound and light show** (daily in English 7.15pm; in Hindi 6pm; not during the rainy season of May–Sept & Nov; Rs10) outlines the history of the prison, and a small **museum** by the entrance gate (same hours as the jail) exhibits lists of convicts, photographs and grim torture devices.

South of the jail near the surprisingly well-equipped Water Sports Complex, you can see tanks full of fish and coral from the islands' reefs at the **Aquarium** (daily 9am–1.30pm & 2–5.30pm; free). In the Haddo area in the west side of town, exhibits in the **Anthropological Museum** (Mon–Sat 9am–noon & 1–4pm; free), devoted to the Andaman and Nicobar tribes, include weapons, tools and also rare photographs of the region's indigenous people taken in the 1960s. Among the most striking of these is a sequence featuring the Sentinelese, taken on April 26, 1967, when a party of Indian officials made the first contact with the tribe. After scaring the aborigines, the visitors marched into one of their hunting camps and made off with the bows, arrows and other artefacts now displayed in the museum. The anthropologist charged with documenting the expedition noted afterwards that "the whole atmosphere was that of conquering hordes over-running conquered territory."

Further northwest in Delanipur opposite T&N Tourism's *Teal House* hotel, the **Samudrika Naval Maritime Museum** (Tues–Sun 9am–noon & 2–5.30pm; Rs10) is an excellent primer if you're heading off to more remote islands, with a superlative shell collection and informative displays on various aspects of local marine biology. One exhibit features a cross-section of the different corals you can expect to see on the Andamans' reefs, followed up with a run-down of the various threats these fragile animals face, from mangrove depletion and parasitic starfish to clumsy snorkellers.

Wildlife lovers are advised to steer clear of the grim little zoo (Tues–Sun 8am–5pm; Rs1), further down towards Haddo, whose only redeeming feature is that it has successfully bred rare crocodiles and monkeys for release into the wild. The adjoining **Forest Museum** (Mon–Sat 8am–noon & 2–5pm; free) is an equally dismal spectacle, feebly attempting to justify the Indian Forest Service's wholesale destruction of the Andamans' forests with a series of lacklustre photographs of extraction methods. However, if you really want to confront the grim reality of the local timber industry, press on north to **Chatham Sawmill** (daily 7am–2.30pm), at the end of the peninsula marking the northernmost edge of Port Blair. One of the oldest and largest wood-processing plants in Asia, it seasons and mills rare hardwoods taken from various islands – a sad testimony to the continued abuse of international guidelines on tropical timber production; photography is prohibited.

Eating

Between them, Port Blair's restaurants offer dishes from North and South India, Burmese specialities and a wide variety of seafood. For rock-bottom budget travellers, there are roadside stalls selling plates of grilled fish at Rs10, in addition to the usual crop of cheap but run-of-the-mill "meals" cafés in the main bazaar: of these, the *Majestic*, *Gagan* and *Milan* on AB Road are the best, but you should steer clear of the *Dhanalakshmi*'s notoriously dreadful canteen.

In Port Blair, as throughout the Andamans, attitudes to **alcohol** lag somewhat behind the mainland, and you'll be lucky to find a cold beer outside the upscale hotels, though there is one cheap and cheerful bar underneath the *Jaimathi*. For the usual range of IMFLs, you'll have to join the drunken scrum at the seedy state liquor shop, tucked away down the alley running alongside the *Shah-N-Shah* hotel.

Annapurna Cafeteria, Aberdeen Bazaar, towards the post office. Far and away Port Blair's best South Indian joint, serving the usual range of huge crispy *dosas*, North Indian and Chinese plate meals, delicious coffee, and wonderful *pongal* at breakfast. The lunch-time thalis are also great.
China Room, on the hill above the Phoenix Jetty ☏03192/30759. The most tourist-oriented restaurant in town, run by a Burmese-Punjabi couple whose roots are vividly reflected in the chilli-and-

ginger-rich cuisine. Particularly recommended for seafood, which comes in a range of tasty sauces. Roomy courtyard but reserve a table inside if it's raining.
Dolphin, Marthoma Church Complex, Golghar. Pleasantly decorated new restaurant serving carefully prepared dishes. Mostly Indian and Chinese but some continental and a few house specialities involving chicken and seafood.
Islet, below the Cellular Jail. A safe option for non-

veg north Indian tandoori, especially chicken, although they offer a good selection of vegetarian dishes, too. Snappy service and good views of the bay from the window seats or balcony.

New India Cafe, Moulana Azad Road. In the basement of *Jaimathi Lodge*, this cheap restaurant is popular with westerners and Indians alike. Wide menu of veg and meat dishes but expect to wait if you order anything that's not already prepared.

Udupi, near Post Office. North and South Indian standards served on a pleasant covered terrace. Good cheap thalis, including some with fish.

Waves, *Peerless Resort*, Corbyn's Cove. Pricey, but very congenial alfresco hotel restaurant under a shady palm grove, and one of the few places in town you can order a beer with your meal. Most dishes around Rs100.

Around Port Blair

At some point, you're almost certain to find yourself killing time in Port Blair, waiting for boats to show up or tickets to go on sale. Rather than wasting days in town, it's worth exploring the **coast** of South Andaman which, although far more densely populated than other islands in the archipelago, holds a handful of easily accessible beauty spots and historic sites. Among the latter, the ruined colonial monuments on **Viper** and **Ross** islands can be reached on daily harbour cruises or regular ferries from the capital. For **beaches**, head southeast to **Corbyn's Cove**, or cross South Andaman to reach more secluded **Chiriya Tapu**, both accessible in easy day-trips if you rent a moped or taxi. By far the most rewarding way to spend a day out of town, however, is to catch the tourist boat from **Wandoor** to **Jolly Buoy** or **Red Skin** islands in the **Mahatma Gandhi Marine Reserve**, which boasts some of the Andamans' best snorkelling. The other area worth visiting is **Mount Harriet** and **Madhuban** on the central part of South Andaman, north across the bay from Port Blair.

Viper and Ross islands

First stop on the harbour cruise from Port Blair (daily 3–5pm; Rs20) is generally **Viper Island**, named not after the many snakes that doubtless inhabit its tangled tropical undergrowth, but a nineteenth-century merchant vessel that ran aground on it during the early years of the colony. Lying a short way off Haddo Wharf, it served as an isolation zone for the main prison, where escapees and convicts (including hunger strikers) were sent to be punished. Whipping posts and crumbling walls, reached from the jetty via a winding brick path, remain as relics of a torture area, while occupying the site's most prominent position are the original gallows.

No less eerie are the decaying colonial remains on **Ross Island**, at the entrance to Port Blair harbour, where the British sited their first penal settlement in the Andamans. Originally cleared by convicts wearing iron fetters (most of them sent here in the wake of the 1857 Mutiny, or First War of Independence), Ross witnessed some of the most brutal excesses of British colonial history, and was the source of the prison's infamy as **Kalapani**, or Black Water. Of the many convicts transported here, distinguished by their branded foreheads, the majority perished from disease or torture before the clearance of the island was completed in 1860. Thereafter, it served briefly as the site of Revd Henry Corbyn's "**Andaman Home**" – a prison camp created with the intention of "civilizing" the local tribespeople – before becoming the headquarters of the revamped penal colony, complete with theatre hall, tennis courts, swimming pool, hospitals and grand residential bungalows. Rather ambitiously dubbed "the Paris of the East", the settlement typified the stiff-upper-lipped spirit of the Raj at its most cruel: while the *burra-* and

Port Blair is the departure point for all flights and ferry crossings to the Indian mainland; it is also the hub of the Andamans' inter-island bus and ferry network. Unfortunately, booking tickets (especially back to Chennai, Calcutta or Vishakapatnam) can be time-consuming, and many travellers are obliged to come back here well before their permit expires to make reservations, before heading off to more pleasant parts to spend their remaining days.

To the mainland

If you've travelled to the Andamans by ship, you'll know what a rough ride the sixty-hour crossing can be in bunk class, and how difficult tickets are to come by (see p.453). It's also a good idea to talk to fellow travellers about current conditions, which vary from year to year and vessel to vessel. The one factor you can be sure about is that the ship offers the cheapest route back. The downside is that schedules can be erratic, and accurate information about them difficult to obtain – annoying when you only have a one-month permit. For Chennai, whose weekly service on Fridays run by the DSS is the most reliable, you'll have to head down to the ticket office at Phoenix Jetty. Basically, the only sure way of finding out when the next ship is leaving and securing a ticket to Calcutta and Vishakapatnam is to join the "queue" outside the SCI office (℡03192/33590), opposite the *Dhanalakshmi* hotel in Aberdeen Bazaar. In theory, tickets are supposed to go on sale a week in advance of departure, but don't bank on it. Bear in mind, too, if you're reading this a couple of days' journey away from the capital, and with only a week or less left on your permit, that the local police can get heavy with foreigners who outstay their allotted time.

Returning to the mainland by plane in just two hours instead of sixty can save lots of time and hassle, but at $200 one-way, air tickets to Chennai and Calcutta are far from cheap. With the introduction of Jet Airways' daily service on top of Indian Airlines four flights a week, tickets to Chennai are usually easy to obtain at short notice apart from peak times like Diwali or Christmas. Booking on one of the five weekly IA flights to Calcutta needs more advance planning but if you're in a hurry polite persistence at their office can work wonders as they often don't know exactly how many seats are available till the last minute because of strict payload limits. The IA office (℡03192/34744) is diagonally opposite the ANIIDCO office, while Jet Airways (℡03192/36911) is on the first floor at 189 Main Road, Junglighat, next to the GITO office.

memsahibs dressed for dinner and sang hymns in church, convicts languished in the most appalling conditions less than a mile away. In the end, the entry of the Japanese into World War II, hot on the heels of a massive earthquake in 1941, forced the British to evacuate, and in the coming years most of the buildings were dismantled by the new overlords, who themselves founded a POW camp here.

Little more than the hilltop Anglican church, with its weed-infested graveyard, has survived the onslaught of tropical creepers and vines, and the island makes a peaceful break from Port Blair. To get here, jump on one of the regular launches from Phoenix Jetty (daily except Wed; departing 8.30am, 10.30am & 12.30pm and returning 8.45am, 10.45am, 12.40pm; Rs15).

Corbyn's Cove and Chiriya Tapu

The best beach within easy reach of the capital lies 10km southeast at **Corbyn's Cove**, a small arc of smooth white sand backed by a swaying curtain of palms. There's a large hotel here (*Sinclairs Bay View*, see p.615), but the

On the day of your flight, be sure to check in at least ninety minutes before the scheduled departure time (security formalities can be protracted), and expect to have to "click" your camera to prove it is just that. Note, too, that Indian law strictly forbids the removal of coral from the Andamans. Get caught with any in your luggage and you'll lose your flight, and probably have to pay a hefty bribe to the police.

Travellers intending to catch onward trains from their port of arrival on the mainland should note that Port Blair has an efficient computerized Southern Railways reservation office near the Secretariat (Mon–Sat 8.30am–1pm & 2–4pm).

Inter-island services

Buses connect Port Blair with most major settlements on South and Middle Andaman, mainly via the Andaman Trunk Road. From the crowded, disorganized bus stand at the bottom of town, one daily government service at 5am runs via Rangat (6hr) as far as Mayabunder (9hr), from where you have to catch a boat across the straits to Kalighat on North Andaman in order to press on north to Diglipur and Arial Bay. There is another daily service to Rangat at 6am. Several private companies including Geetanjali Travels (tickets at Tillai tea shop by the bus stand) and the cheaper Ananda (☎03192/33252) run deluxe or video coach (ear plugs essential) services, which leave from the road outside the bus stand also at 5am

Most of the islands open to foreign tourists, including Neill, Havelock, Middle and North Andaman, are also accessible by boat from Phoenix Jetty. Details of forthcoming departures are posted in the shipping news columns of the local newspapers, but the most reliable source of information is the office on the first floor of the Harbour Authority building, Phoenix Jetty, where you can also book tickets in advance. Schedules change frequently but you can expect a boat most days to Havelock, roughly four weekly to Neill and Rangat and twice weekly to Diglipur. If possible try to travel on a newer vessel like the *Ramanujam*. The journeys on older boats can be a lot longer and more uncomfortable than you might expect. From 9am onwards, the heat on board is intense, with only corrugated plastic sheets for shade, while the benches are highly uncomfortable and the toilets generally dismal. You should take adequate supplies of food and water with you; only biscuits and simple snacks are sold on the boats. More details of boat services to destinations outside the capital appear in the relevant accounts.

water isn't particularly clear, and bear in mind that lying around scantily clothed will bring you considerable attention from crowds of local workers.

For more isolation, rent a moped or take a taxi 30km south to **Chiriya Tapu** ("Bird Island"), at the tip of South Andaman. The motorable track running beyond this small fishing village leads through thick jungle overhung with twisting creepers to a large bay, where swamps give way to shell-strewn beaches. Other than at lunch time, when it often receives a deluge of bus parties, the beach offers plenty of peace and quiet, forest walks on the woodcutters' trails winding inland from it and easy access to an inshore reef. However, the water here is nowhere near as clear as at some spots in the archipelago, and serious snorkellers and divers may be tempted to try for a boat out to volcanic Cinque Island (see p.629), a couple of hours further south. Groups from the big hotels in Port Blair use inflatables with outboard motors to reach Cinque, but it is also possible to charter your own fishing boat here; ask around the bar in the village, and expect to pay around Rs3000 per boat for the return trip.

Wandoor and the Mahatma Gandhi National Marine Park

Much the most popular excursion from Port Blair is the boat ride from **Wandoor**, 30km southwest, to one or other of the fifteen islets comprising the **Mahatma Gandhi National Marine Park**. Although set up purely for tourists, the trip is worth doing, gaining you access to one of the richest coral reefs in the region. Boats depart from Wandoor at 10am (daily except Mon; Rs90–125, plus Rs10 entry permit to the park); you can get there on A&N Tourism's **tour** (Rs75) or by local bus, but it is more fun to rent a moped and ride down to meet the boat yourself.

The long white beach at **Wandoor** is littered with the dry, twisted trunks of trees torn up and flung down by annual cyclones, and fringed not with palms, but by dense forest teeming with birdlife. You should only snorkel here at high tide. From the jetty, the boats chug through broad creeks lined with dense mangrove swamps and pristine forest to either **Red Skin Island** or, more commonly, **Jolly Buoy**. The latter, an idyllic deserted island, boasts an immaculate shell-sand beach, ringed by a bank of superb coral. The catch is that the boat only stops for around an hour, which isn't nearly enough time to explore the shore and reef. While snorkelling off the edges of the reef, however, beware of strong currents.

Mount Harriet and Madhuban

The richly forested slopes of **Mount Harriet** make for decent exercise and can easily be done as a day-trip from Port Blair. You can take one of the hourly passenger ferries from Chatham to **Bamboo Flats** or, if you want to have your own transport on the other side, there are five daily vehicle ferries from Phoenix Bay. From Bamboo Flats it's a pleasant seven-kilometre stroll east along the coast and north up a path through trees hung with thick vines and creepers to the 365-metre summit, which affords fine views back across the bay. An intermittent bus service connects Bamboo Flats and Hope Town, where the path starts, that can save you 3km. Alternatively, jeeps and taxis are available to take you all the way to the top, but they charge at least Rs200. There is a Rs10 charge to enter Mount Harriet National Park but the checkpost is on the road so you probably won't be asked if you take the path. If you have your own wheels or strong legs you can reach **Madhuban** on the coast 5km northeast of the mountain. There's a decent beach, and the area is still used for training logging **elephants** so you stand a good chance of seeing them learning their trade.

Islands north of Port Blair

Printed on the permit card you receive on arrival in the Andamans is a list of all the other islands you're allowed to visit in the archipelago; the majority of them are north of Port Blair. Given the great distances involved, not to mention the often erratic connections between them (and the time limit imposed by the one-month permit), it definitely pays to know where to head for as soon as you arrive rather than drift off on the first promising ferry out of Phoenix Jetty. The best way of doing this is to talk to fellow travellers arriving back in the capital. The following accounts will give you a good idea of what to expect upcountry, but new islands are opened up to tourists each year and these may well offer the kind of wilderness experience you're here for.

Having travelled all the way to the Andamans, it is surprising how many visitors make a beeline for the two only developed islands in the group, **Neill** and **Havelock**, both within easy reach of Port Blair. To get further north, where tourism of any kind has thus far had very little impact, you can take a ferry from Havelock to ramshackle **Rangat**, at the south end of **Middle Andaman**, or bypass the whole east coast by catching a bus from Port Blair direct to **Mayabunder**, the main market town for the central and north Andamans. Either way, you'll be lucky not to be marooned from time to time in some truly grim little settlements, interspersed with a few long hard slogs up the infamous **Andaman Trunk Road** (or "ATR").

On Middle and North Andaman, and their satellite islands, **accommodation** is scarce, to say the least. Aside from a handful of new ANIIDCO hotels (bookable in advance in Port Blair), the only places to stay are APWD rest houses set aside for government officials and engineers, where you may (or may not) be granted a room if one is free. Settlements such as Rangat, Mayabunder and Diglipur, in the far north, also have very rudimentary lodges. To escape the settled areas you have to be **prepared to rough it**, travelling on inshore fishing dugouts, sleeping on beaches and cooking your own food. The rewards, however, are great. Backed by dense forest filled with colourful birds and insects, the beaches, bays and reefs of the outer Andamans teem with wildlife, from gargantuan crabs, pythons and turtles, to dolphins, sharks, giant rays and the occasional primeval-looking dugong.

Essential **kit** for off-track wanderings includes a sturdy mosquito net, mats to sleep on (or a hammock), a large plastic container for water, some strong antiseptic for cuts and bites (sand flies are a real problem on many of the beaches) and, most important of all, **water purification** tablets or a water purifier since bottled water is virtually non-existent. Wherever you end up, preserve the goodwill of local people by packing your rubbish out – carrying it in your backpack – or burning it, and being sensitive to scruples about dress and nudity, especially in areas settled by conservative Bengali or Tamil Hindus.

Neill

Tiny, triangular-shaped **Neill** is the most southerly inhabited island of **Ritchie's Archipelago**, three hours' ferry ride northeast of Port Blair. The source of much of the capital's fresh fruit and vegetables, its fertile centre, ringed by a curtain of stately tropical trees, comprises vivid patches of green paddy dotted with small farmsteads and banana plantations. The beaches are mediocre by the Andamans' standards, but worth a day or two en route to or from Havelock. **Boats** leave Port Blair four or five times each week for Neill, continuing on to Havelock and Rangat.

Neill boasts three **beaches**, all of them within easy cycling distance of the small bazaar just up the lane from the hotel (you can rent **cycles** from one or other of the stall holders from Rs20–30 per day). The best place to swim is **Neill Kendra**, a gently curving bay of white sand, which straddles the jetty and is scattered with picturesque wooden fishing boats. A more secluded option, **Lakshmangar,** lies a little over 3km north: head right at the ANIID-CO hotel (see below) and follow the road for around twenty minutes until it dwindles into a surfaced track, then turn right. Wrapped around the headland, the beach is a broad spur of white shell sand with shallow water offering good snorkelling. Exposed to the open sea and thus prone to higher tides, **Sitapur** beach, 6km south at the tip of the island, is less appealing, but the ride across Neill's central paddy land is pleasant.

The island now has three **places to stay**. From the jetty, a two-minute walk brings you to the ANIIDCO *Hawabill Nest;* ⊤03192/82630; ➍–➏), a dozen or so clean, carpeted rooms with sit-outs, ranged around a central courtyard and restaurant, best booked in advance from Port Blair. The two private options are both at Lakshmangar; the *Pearl Park Hotel* (⊤03192/82510; ➋–➐) has some small huts and posher a/c bungalows, while the *Tango* (no phone; ➊–➋) offers much more basic bamboo huts. Apart from the **restaurants** at these three establishments and a few stalls around the jetty, the only other place to eat is the highly recommended *Gyan,* halfway along the road to Lakshmangar.

Havelock

Havelock is the largest island in Ritchie's Archipelago, and the most intensively cultivated, settled like many in the region by Bengali refugees after Partition. Thanks to its regular ferry connection with the capital, it is also visited in greater numbers than anywhere else in the Andamans. In peak season, as many as three hundred tourists may be holed up here, and at such times Havelock's much photographed Radhnagar beach, often touted as the most beautiful in India, can feel overwhelmed. Party-lovers from Goa have also turned up over the past few winters, complete with rave gear and full-on sound systems, so the writing may well be on the wall for Havelock. On the plus side, the boat journey here from Neill, skirting a string of uninhabited islets with shadowy views of South Andaman to the west, is wonderful, and wildlife – both on land and in the sea – remains abundant despite intensive settlement and deforestation.

Havelock's main **jetty** is on the north side of the island, at the village known as **Havelock #1.** There are three small **lodges** as you turn right from the jetty, on the mangrove-lined outskirts of the village. Best of these is the friendly *Maya Sea View* (⊤03192/82367; ➊–➌), which has attached and non-attached rooms as well as a couple of open bamboo shacks. Further along is the similar seafront *M.S. Guest House* (⊤03192/82439; ➊–➋) and there is the *U.S. Lodge* (no phone; ➊–➋) as a fallback. There are basic **restaurants** at the lodges and snacks to be had at stalls in the village. Otherwise, rent a **moped** (Rs150 per day) or **cycle** (Rs50 per day) for a few days and head straight inland to the bazaar, two kilometres south. Further accommodation listed below is available at beaches #2 to #5, really one long unbroken strand, which you get to by turning left at the main junction, or at Radhnagar (aka #7 beach), 12km southwest, reached by turning right. An intermittent bus service also covers these routes, but you could find yourself waiting all day for it and missing out on a room.

The first place to stay on the **east coast** is *Eco Villa* (no phone; ➌) at beach #2, whose ten huts are not the best value but the cook is famous for concocting rare culinary delights. At beach #3 is the base of the excellent

Andaman Scuba Club (see p.611 for details). Next up is the *Sunrise* (℡03192/82387; ❷) with more huts set in a picturesque palm grove, followed by the rather overpriced cottages of ANIIDCO's *Dolphin Yatri Niwas* (℡03192/82411, ℻82444; ❸–❼) at beach #5. This is also the only place on the island to **change money** in an emergency but the rates are dire. The last and best of the places along this stretch is the *Coconut Grove* (℡03192/82427; ❷), which has sturdy huts of varying sizes and the most sociable restaurant.

Heading past a string of thatched villages hemmed in by banana groves and paddy fields, the road towards **Radhnagar** drops through some spectacular woodland to a kilometre-long arch of perfect white sand, backed by stands of giant *mowhar* trees. The water is a sublime turquoise colour, and although the coral is sparse, marine life here is diverse and plentiful, especially among the rocks around the corner from the main beach (to get there on foot, backtrack along the road and follow the path through the woods and over the bluff). Radhnagar has two **places to stay**: ANIIDCO's *Tent Camp* (no phone; ❷–❺), rows of canvas tents of varying size and comfort and a toilet block, and the upmarket *Jungle Resort* (℡03192/37656, ℻37657; ❸–❼), run by a Swiss-Andaman family, who offer luxurious wood-and-thatch cottages and a few more basic huts in a clearing behind the beach. They also have a good restaurant and there is a string of basic food shacks lining the road down to the beach, of which *Travellers* is justifiably the most popular. As the nesting site for a colony of Olive Ridley **turtles**, Radhnagar is strictly protected by the Forest Department, whose wardens ensure tourists do not light fires or sleep on the beach.

Long Island

Just off the southeast coast of Middle Andaman, **Long Island** is dominated by an unsightly plywood mill, but don't let this put you off. Served by only two boats per week from the capital (usually Wed & Sat), and two daily lumber launches from Rangat, it sees far fewer visitors than either Neill or Havelock, but boasts a couple of excellent beaches, at **Marg Bay** and **Lalaji Bay**, both most easily reached by chartering a fisherman's dingy from the jetty. The latter beach is earmarked as the site of a new private tented accommodation enterprise. Otherwise, you could try your luck at the APWD *Rest House* (❷), or camp. This is a good island to head for if you want to sidestep the hordes at Havelock, but don't have time to tackle the long trip north.

Middle Andaman

For most travellers, **Middle Andaman** is a charmless rite of passage to be endured en route to or from the north. The sinuous Andaman Trunk Road, hemmed in by walls of towering forest, winds through miles of jungle, crossing the strait that separates the island from its neighbour, Baratang Island, by means of rusting flat-bottomed ferry. The island's frontier feeling is heightened by the presence on the buses of armed guards, and the knowledge that the impenetrable forests west of the ATR are the **Jarawa Tribal Reserve** (see p.608). Of its two main settlements, the more northerly **Mayabunder** is slightly more appealing than characterless inland **Rangat** because of its pleasant setting by the sea, but neither town gives any reason to dally for long.

Rangat and around

At the southeast corner of Middle Andaman, **RANGAT** consists of little more than two rows of unsanitary *chai* shops and general stores divided by the ATR, which in the monsoon degenerates into a fly-infested mud slick, churned at regular intervals by over-laden buses. However, as a major staging post on the journey north, it's impossible to avoid; just don't get stranded here if you can help it.

Ferries to and from Port Blair (9hr) dock at **Rangat Bay** (aka **Nimbutala**), 8km east; some stop at Havelock Island (4 weekly) and Long Island (2 weekly), and there are also two daily lumber boats to Long Island. In addition, the village is served by two daily government **buses** to Port Blair (7–8hr) as well as some private services, which pass through in the morning en route from Mayabunder. The APWD *Rest House* (☎03192/74237; ❷), pleasantly situated up a winding hill from the bazaar with views across the valley, is the best **place to stay** and eat, providing good filling fish thalis. Otherwise, the most bearable lodge is the *Avis* (☎03192/27554; ❷) on Church Road. The town's best **restaurant**, is the *Hotel Vijay*, whose amiable proprietor serves up copious thalis and, if the boat is in, crab curry, along with the usual range of soft drinks and mineral water.

If you do get stuck here, rather than staying put in Rangat jump on a bus heading north, or find a jeep to take you to **Amakunj beach** aka Cuthbert Bay, 9km along the road from Nimbutala to Mayabunder. On the right of the road just beyond the helipad, a Forest Department signboard saying "Sand Collection Point" marks the start of a track running the remaining 500m to the sea. The beach has little shade to speak of, but the snorkelling is good and, best of all, there's the very comfortable ANIIDCO *Hawksbill Nest* (☎03192/79022; ❸–❹) **hotel** on the main road, which is invariably empty.

Mayabunder

About two hours further north by road, perched on a long promontory right at the top of the island and surrounded by mangrove swamps, is **MAYABUNDER**, springboard for the remote northern Andaman Islands. The village, which is home to a large minority of former Burmese **Karen** tribal people who were originally brought here as cheap logging labour by the British, is more spread out and more appealing than Rangat, but again there is little to hold your interest for long. At the brow of the hill before it descends to the jetty a small hexagonal wooden structure houses the Forest Museum cum Interpretation Centre (Mon–Sat 8am–noon & 1–4pm; free), which holds a motley collection of turtle shells, snakes in formaldehyde, dead coral, a crocodile skull and precious little information. Next door the APWD *Rest House* (☎03192/73211; ❶–❷) is large and very comfortable, with a pleasant garden and gazebo overlooking the sea, and a dining room serving good set meals. The only other reasonable **accommodation** nearby is back in the centre of the bazaar at the *S&S Lodge* (☎03192/73449; ❶), which has clean but unattached rooms, while the dilapidated and cockroach-infested *Lakshminarayan Lodge* should be avoided at all costs. Further afield at **Karmateng beach**, 14km southeast, there is another ANIIDCO hotel, the *Swiftlet Nest* (☎03192/73495; ❸–❹) but nothing else. Two buses are supposed to go there daily, failing which there are taxis or auto-rickshaws.

Interview Island

Mayabunder is the jumping-off place for **Interview Island**, a windswept nature sanctuary off the remote northwest coast of Middle Andaman. Only

Until the last stretch of the Andaman Trunk Road and a bridge across the narrow strait to North Andaman Island just west of Mayabunder are completed in 2002, the shortest crossing is the ferry ride to Kalighat (2 daily; 3hr). The first departure of the day leaves at 9.30am, on a boat that's hopelessly small and cramped, so come prepared for hours of relentless sun (or torrential rain in the monsoons). That said, the journey is very memorable, especially towards its latter stages when the mangrove-lined sides of the creek close in as you approach Kalighat. The other boat leaves at 3pm when the early morning buses from Port Blair have arrived, making it possible to get all the way from the capital to North Andaman in a day, though it is a back-breaking journey to attempt in one go.

Heading in the opposite direction, buses to Port Blair are regular but it is advisable to book ahead, with tickets for the daily government departure (at 6am) going on sale from 3pm the previous day at the bus stand, 2km from the jetty near the bazaar. Of the private services, the fastest and most comfortable is the one operated by Geetanjali Travels, which links up with the arrival of the first ferry from Kalighat, leaving the jetty at 7.30am (you can buy tickets on the bus). The trip takes 9 to 10 hours, depending on how long you have to wait at the two ferry crossings along the way. There are also four or five additional services to Rangat, the first at 8.30am from the bus stand.

opened to tourists in 1997, it's large and mainly flat, and completely uninhabited save for a handful of unfortunate forest wardens, coast guards and policemen, posted here to ward off poachers. As foreigners aren't permitted to spend the night on the island, few tourists ever make it to Interview, but those that do are rarely disappointed. If you've come to the Andamans to watch **wildlife**, this should be top of your list.

The only way to reach Interview is to charter a private fishing dingy from Mayabunder jetty. Arrange one the day before and leave at first light. Approaching the island, you'll be struck by its wild appearance, particularly noticeable on the northwest where the monsoon storms have wrecked the shoreline forest. If you can, however, get your boatman to pull up on to the **beach** at the southern tip of the island, which has a perennial freshwater pool inside a low cave; legend has it that the well, a nesting site for white-bellied **swifts**, has no bottom. At the forest post, where you have to sign an entry ledger, ask the wardens about the movements of Interview's feral **elephants**, descendants of trained elephants deserted here by a Calcutta-based logging company after its timber operation failed in the 1950s. When food (or potential mates) are scarce, the elephants take to the sea and swim to other islands (sometimes, it is said, all the way to Mayabunder).

North Andaman

Shrouded in dense jungle, **North Andaman** is the least populated of the region's large islands, crossed by a single road linking its scattered Bengali settlements. Timber extraction is proceeding apace here, despite the decision by the Island Development Authority to phase out logging by the year 2000, but the total absence of motorable roads into northern and western areas has ensured blanket protection for a vast stretch of convoluted coastline, running from Austin Strait in the southeast to the northern tip, Cape Price. Even if it were physically possible to reach this region, you wouldn't be allowed to, but it's reassuring to know at least one extensive wilderness survives in the Andamans. That said, the imminent completion of the ATR's final section, which will connect the far north to Mayabunder, may herald the start of a new settlement influx, with the same disastrous consequences for the environment seen elsewhere.

There is no reason to spend more time in **Kalighat**, where the boat arrives from Mayabunder, than it takes to get a bus out, nor longer in North Andaman's ugly main town of **Diglipur** than it takes to get a connection down to **Arial Bay** for **Smith Island** or on to the attractive coastal area round **Kalipur**.

Kalighat

Until the new road is finished, **KALIGHAT**, where the river becomes unnavigable and the ferryboat from Mayabunder turns around, serves as the main entry point to North Andaman. A cluttered little bazaar unfolds from the top of the slipway, hemmed in by dense mangrove swamps, and when you arrive you should hope a bus is standing here to take you to Diglipur. If there isn't, head for one of the village's dismal little chai stalls and dig in for a wait, or turn right to see if there's a room in the three-roomed **Government Rest House** (no phone; ❷) on the hill overlooking the end of the street. The *chowkidar* in this quaint wooden house is friendly, but refuses to cook for tourists so you'll have to chance the chai stalls for a meal.

The one worthwhile place to visit in this area is **Radhnagar**, 10km out of town and served by hourly buses, where there's a beautiful sandy beach backed by unspoilt forest where camping is feasible. Try to rent a **cycle** from one of the stalls in Kalighat though, as the beach is 2km outside Radhnagar bazaar, providing the nearest source of fresh water.

In principle, four **buses** per day run north from Kalighat to **Diglipur** (at 12.30pm, 1pm, 3pm & 5.30pm); they're crammed full, but the trip takes only 45 minutes. Look out for logging elephants beside the road shortly after leaving Kalighat. Heading south, the **boat** leaves at 5am and 12.30pm for Mayabunder. If you're continuing on to **Port Blair** (only possible if you take the early crossing), buy a through bus ticket for Geetanjali Travels' express video coach (Rs100) at P.V.L. Sharma's grocery store, in the bazaar; this service is timed to leave from Mayabunder just after the boat arrives from Kalighat.

Diglipur and Arial Bay

Known in the British era as Port Cornwallis, **DIGLIPUR**, North Andaman's largest settlement, is another disappointing market where you're only likely to pause long enough to pick up a local bus further north to the coast. On the hill above the bus stand, the APWD *Rest House* (☎03192/72203; ❶) offers the

village's only **accommodation**, but the *chowkidar* is less than welcoming and you're better off pressing on 9km to **ARIAL BAY**, where a smaller but much more congenial APWD *Rest House* (no phone; ❶) stands on a hillock overlooking the settlement's small bazaar. Better still, continue another 9km to **Kalipur**, served by several daily buses, where ANIIDCO recently opened and must rank among the region's biggest white elephant. Occupying a perfect spot on a hilltop, with superb views inland and to sea, the *Turtle Resort* (☎03192/72553; ❸–❹), an unfeasibly large concrete hotel for such a remote location, has spacious, clean rooms with fans and a restaurant (residents only). Only five minutes' walk from the hotel down the path by the sharp bend in the road there is an excellent deserted beach, backed by lush forest and covered in photogenic driftwood. Swimming is best at high tide because the water recedes across rocky mudpools.

The staff at the hotel claim it's possible to walk from here to **Saddle Peak**, at 737m the highest mountain in the Andamans, which rises dramatically to the south, swathed in lush jungle. Permission to make the three- to four-hour climb must be obtained from the Range Officer at Arial Bay, but don't attempt the hike without a guide and plenty of drinking water. The majority of tourists who find their way up here, however, do so in order to explore the various **islands** dotted around the gulf north of Arial Bay, particularly **Smith** (see below).

The best **place to eat** in this area is the *Mohan Restaurant*, at the far end of the bazaar in Arial Bay, which serves cold drinks and huge portions of fresh local seafood to a surreal backdrop of lurid cherubs and a poster of the racehorse Red Rum. From Arial Bay the **boat** that has made its way up from the capital returns direct (Wed & Sat 4pm; 13–14hr) to Port Blair overnight.

Smith Island

Over recent years **Smith** has become one the most popular escapes for travellers wishing to live out their Robinson Crusoe fantasies. Although it has not yet been included on the list printed on foreign tourist permits, it has achieved semi-official status and Rs10 permits are issued at the Port authority in Arial Bay because of its proximity to the protected wildlife reserve at **Ross Island** (not to be confused with the one near Port Blair). The typically densely forested island has a small settlement at the ferry jetty, about half an hour's journey from Arial bay. There are no roads but a walking trail (2hr) leads across to the main beach, where up to thirty Westerners may be camping at any one time. There's a fresh-water spring behind the beach but no food and only basic rice, vegetables and fruit are available at the village so all camping gear and other provisions must be taken along from the mainland. It is likely, however, that permanent rentable tents and even huts may appear soon. Fishing boats will ferry people direct to the beach for around Rs50 per head, as long as they've got a few takers. At low tide Smith is connected to Ross by a sandbar which people walk across though they are not strictly allowed onto the protected island.

Other islands

The remaining islands open to foreign tourists in the Andaman group are all hard to get to and, with the exception of **Little Andaman** – where a vestigial population of Onge tribespeople has survived a massive influx of Indian Tamils and native Nicobars – uninhabited. Two hours' boat ride south of Chiriya Tapu on South Andaman, **Cinque Island** offers superlative diving, outshone only by distant **Barren Island**, whose volcanic sand beds teem with marine life.

Cinque Island

Cinque Island actually comprises two islets, joined by a spectacular sand isthmus, with shallow water either side that covers it completely at high tide. The main incentive to come here is the superlative diving and snorkelling around the reefs. However, heaps of dead coral on the beach attest to damage recently wrought by the Indian navy during the construction of the swish air-conditioned "cottages" overlooking the beach. Rumour has it that these were built for the visit of a Thai VIP in 1996, but local government officials now use them as bolt holes from Port Blair.

Although there are no **ferries** to Cinque, it is possible to arrange dinghies from Chiriya Tapu village on South Andaman (see p.619). The two dive centres in Port Blair also regularly come here with clients. Currently, your permit only allows you to spend the day on the island; overnights stays are prohibited.

Barren Island

The most intriguing island open to tourists in the Andaman group has to be **Barren Island**, twenty hours' sea voyage east of Port Blair. India's only active **volcano**, the arid brown mountain blew its top in May 1991 after lying dormant for 188 years, and has done so on two occasions since between 1994 and 1995. The only living creatures on Cinque are a herd of **goats**, released in 1891 by the British to provide sustenance for any shipwrecked sailors. There are no ferries to the island, but diving expeditions regularly make the trip as the seas around Barren are the richest in the region.

Little Andaman

Little Andaman is the furthest point south in the archipelago you can travel to on a standard one-month tourist permit. Located ten hours by sea from Port Blair, most of the island has been set aside as a tribal reserve for the **Onge** (see p.609) and is thus off-limits. The only areas you're allowed to visit lie on either side of the main settlement, Hut Bay, which sits halfway down the east coast. The northern part of this stretch has been mercilessly clear-felled, leaving a stark wasteland flanking the main road to the largest beach at **Butler Bay**,

16km from Hut Bay, while the coast to the south boasts few beaches to compare with those further north in the Andamans. Given the discomfort involved in getting here (the boat journey can be a hideous experience), it's not hard to see why so few travellers bother.

Those that do rarely venture far out of **Hut Bay**, a scruffy agglomeration of chai shacks, hardware and provision stores ranged along Little Andaman's single surfaced road. The only remarkable features of this insalubrious, unwelcoming place is an extraordinarily high incidence of cerebral **malaria** and the most ferocious **sandflies** in all the islands – more reasons not to come here. Unfortunately, the late afternoon arrival time of the ferry means that unless you're kitted out to camp and have enough provisions, you'll have to spend at least a night in town (see below). As soon as you can, though, head north to Butler Bay or south down the coast, beyond the Christian Nicobari settlements around **John Richardson Bay** (3km), to the island's only other accessible **beaches**; be prepared for sandflies and long walks to water sources, and try not to wander into the Onges' reserve, which begins at the lighthouse.

Practicalities

Boats leave Port Blair for Little Andaman around twice a week; the service to aim for is the one that continues south to Car Nicobar, capital of the Nicobar Islands, as the ferry is larger and marginally more comfortable. Both arrive at the main jetty (specially enlarged for the full-on logging operation still underway here), a 3km plod from the bazaar, where you'll find the island's only established **accommodation**. Before leaving Port Blair, it's worth making a reservation at head office for the APWD *Rest House* (no phone; ❷), 1km north of the shops behind the **hospital**, which has clean and spacious en-suite rooms. Otherwise your only option is the bleak *GM Lodge* (no phone; ❶) in the bazaar, whose rooms wouldn't look out of place in Port Blair's Cellular Jail. If you find yourself having to sleep here, take your mattress and mosquito net onto the roof as constant power cuts render the fans useless. At the time of writing, basic huts were being knocked up at Butler Bay.

Travel details

Flights

Port Blair to: Calcutta (5 weekly; 2hr); Chennai (1–2 daily; 2hr).

Boats

Arial Bay to: Port Blair (2 weekly; 12–14hr); Smith Island (1–2 daily; 30min).
Havelock to: Long Island (2 weekly; 2–3hr); Neill Island (4 weekly; 1hr–1hr 30min); Port Blair (6 weekly; 4–6hr); Rangat Bay (4 weekly; 4–5hr).
Mayabunder to: Kalighat (2 daily; 2hr 30min–3hr).
Port Blair to: Arial Bay (2 weekly; 12–14hr); Calcutta (1 every 2 weeks; 60hr); Chennai (1 weekly; 60hr); Havelock Island (6 weekly; 4–6hr); Little Andaman (2 weekly; 9–10hr); Long Island (2 weekly; 7hr 30min–9hr); Neill Island (4 weekly; 3–4hr); Rangat Bay (4 weekly; 8–10hr); Vishakapatnam (1 monthly; 56hr).

Rangat Bay to: Havelock Island (4 weekly; 4–5hr); Long Island (1–2 daily; 1hr 30min–2hr); Neill Island (2 weekly; 5–6hr); Port Blair (4 weekly; 8–10hr).

Buses

Diglipur to: Arial Bay (every 1–2hr; 20min); Kalighat (4 daily; 45min); Kalipur (5 daily; 40min).
Mayabunder to: Karmateng beach (2 daily; 30min); Port Blair (3–5 daily; 9–10hr); Rangat (5 daily; 2hr–2hr 30min).
Port Blair to: Chiriya Tapu (3 daily; 1hr 15min); Mayabunder (3–5 daily; 9hr–10hr); Rangat (5 daily; 7–8hr); Wandoor (4 daily; 1hr 15min).
Rangat to: Mayabunder (5 daily 2hr–2hr 30min); Port Blair (5 daily; 7–8hr).

contexts

contexts

History

South India – the vast triangular-shaped peninsula beyond the Narmada River – is separated from the North by the Vindhya Range, a barren band of sheer-sided table mountains. For many centuries, this geographical obstacle discouraged the movement of peoples between the two regions. The South thus remained largely isolated from the changes imported by successive waves of invaders who swept across the Gangetic plains from the northwest. Tracing the progress of these newcomers, written histories of the subcontinent have tended to focus on the impact of North upon South. Influences did traverse the Vindhyas and Deccan Plateau, but they invariably did so slowly, by a process of gradual assimilation rather than conquest, enabling the societies of the peninsula to develop in their own way. Moreover, some of India's most defining cultural traits and traditions originated in the deep Dravidian south, from where they spread northwards.

Prehistory

By comparison with the extraordinary wealth of archeological finds in north-western India, evidence of **prehistoric settlement** in the South is scant. Yet one of the oldest human artefacts ever unearthed in Asia was discovered at Pallavaram, near Chennai (Madras). In 1863, British archeologist Bruce Foote found an oval-shaped hand-axe, flaked on both faces to produce a clean cutting edge, that he surmised must have originated in the Lower Paleolithic era. Since this initial discovery, similar tools have come to light as far south as the Kaveri River delta, indicating that the region was inhabited by **nomadic hunter-gatherers** at the same time as similar groups emerged in the distant north, between 400,000 and 10,000 years ago.

The first archeologist to establish a sequence for the various stone implements discovered in the South was **Mortimer Wheeler**, whose work on the Coromandel Coast near Pondicherry in 1945 showed that metal was introduced comparatively late to the region. Fixing the date-spans of upper strata with the Roman coins he found in them, Wheeler showed how copper made its first appearance midway through the second millennium BC, by which time rudimentary **agriculture** and the **domestication of animals** were widespread along open coastal areas and river deltas.

It has never been proven, but new technologies, including metal, were probably imported into South India from the northwest, where sophisticated urban civilizations of the Indus Valley – the region straddling the present-day India–Pakistan border – were already well established by 3000 BC. Recent paleobotanical studies have shown that a sharp rise in rainfall occurred around this time, which probably explains why agriculture was able to flourish and cities emerge. The inhabitants of **Harappa** and **Mohenjo Daro**, large urban centres that reached their peaks between 2300 and 1800 BC, were certainly expert water managers. Amid the ruins of their well organized cities, remnants of elaborate sewerage and irrigation systems have been found, along with scales and weights, metal jewellery, weapons, precious stones, seals and delicate pottery. Huge communal granaries stored the surplus grain that underpinned a flourishing foreign trade, and the existence of palaces and spacious houses show that this was a highly stratified society, with its own script and formalized religion.

After the sensational rediscovery of the Harappan ruins in the 1920s, it was long assumed that invasions from the northwest brought about the eventual demise of the Indus Valley civilizations, but it now seems more likely that prolonged drought caused the decline. The same climatic changes may also explain how **metal** technology and knowledge of **rice cultivation** first found their way south: as rainfall decreased, the corresponding drop in agricultural output impoverished the once-thriving cities of the Indus Valley, forcing its inhabitants to flee south in search of more fertile land.

The Dravidians

Some historians have advanced this migration theory to account for the origins of the so-called **Dravidians**, who are believed to have colonized the South around the same time as the Indus Valley civilization went into decline in the second millennium BC. However, the most compelling evidence that the Dravidians originated in the northwest is linguistic. Kanad, Telegu, Malayalam and Tamil – the principal modern languages of South India – have a completely different root from the main languages of the North, which derive from the so-called Indo-Aryan group, and are based principally on Sanskrit. Over the years, some wild comparisons have been made between Dravidian and other Asian tongues (most notably Japanese), but the only surviving Asian language with definite Dravidian antecedents is Brahui, spoken by the transhumant people of the Baluchistan uplands on the Iran–Pakistan border. This fact suggests that the Dravidians almost certainly came from the Baluchi grasslands in the fourth or third millennium BC, via the Indus Valley, where they would have acquired the metalwork and farming techniques that subsequently allowed them to establish permanent settlements in the far south.

Although far less technologically advanced than the Indus Valley civilizations, the Dravidian tribes, based around fertile riverine lands that were separated by densely wooded hills and mountain ranges, forged a strong agrarian base and gradually evolved into distinct chiefdoms. Like the Harappans, their essentially agricultural economies were supplemented by trade in luxury goods such as shells, precious stones and pearls (the Old Testament records that King Solomon sent ships every three years to South India to buy silver, gold, ivory, monkeys and peacocks). This maritime trade expanded steadily over the centuries, enabling the region's chiefs to extend their rule inland and create larger settlements away from the coast.

The Aryans

For most of the twentieth century, archeologists believed the dramatic demise of the Indus Valley cities, between 1800 and 1700 BC, was precipitated by the arrival of invaders from the northwest. Recent carbon-dating techniques, however, have shown that the decline occurred between two and three centuries before the first appearance on the northern plains of a fairer-skinned nomadic people, who called themselves the *Aryas*, or **Aryans**.

The precise route of this migration remains a moot point among historians. Some argue that the newcomers travelled southeast through Persia, while others claim they came via Afghanistan. There is, however, a general consensus that they originated in a region around the Caucasus Mountains, and were part of an ancient diaspora that spread as far as western Europe (their language, an antiquated form of Sanskrit, has astonishingly close affinities with Latin, Greek and Celtic).

The main historical source for this era is the **Rig Veda**, a vast body of 1028 hymns, epic chants, spells, songs and instructions for religious rituals equal in length to the *Iliad* and *Odyssey* combined. Phrased in 10,600 elaborate metered verses, this laboriously sophisticated work includes sections composed between 1400 and 1500 BC, transmitted orally and only set down in writing in the modern era. The Aryans' sacred scriptures contain a wealth of detail about their daily life, philosophical ideas and religious practices. Frequent references to Agni, the "God of Fire", and Indra, the "Fort Breaker", are indicative of violent encounters with the dark-skinned indigenous inhabitants of northern Indian, known as *Dasa* or *Dasyas*, whom the warrior bands swept aside in their slow expansion eastwards over the middle of the second millennium BC. These conquests were facilitated by the Aryans' use of horse-drawn, spoke-wheeled **chariots**, an incomparably fast and effective way of crossing the dry plains.

By the dawn of the **Iron Age** early in the first millennium BC, the dominion of the Aryans, by now a loose confederacy of tribes who fought each other as much as their indigenous enemies, stretched south as far as the Vindhya Range and the rich soils of the Deccan Plateau. Beyond lay the wild unexplored territory of **Dakshinapatha**, "the Way South", blocked by dense forests and ravine-scarred hills.

Sanskritization of the South

The *Rig Veda* records the reluctance of the Ayrans to press south along this route, but it is clear some of their priests (brahmins) and wandering ascetics (*rishis*) did, probably in search of patronage. Along with their sacred verses, Vedic philosophies and knowledge of iron, they took with them concepts of racial discrimination derived from centuries of war with the Dyasas, who by this time seem to have become a sub-class below the three existing grades in Aryan society: priests (brahmins), warriors (*kshatriyas*) and artisans (*vaishyas*). A product of the transition from nomadic to settled society, the **caste** system – based on notions of **varna**, or colour, and ritual pollution – seemed to have found favour among the tribal chiefs of southern India, who deployed the new ideas and scriptures of the brahmins to legitimize their rule.

The transmission of cultural influences from north to south was slow, but pervasive. By the sixth century BC, brahmanical philosophies formed the religious bedrock of the many petty chiefdoms and larger principalities that had proliferated in the South, where village culture had by now firmly taken root under the tutelage of the brahmins – a way of life that would remain largely intact in the region for another two thousand years.

The Mauryan era

In the Gangetic basin, meanwhile, small tribal kingdoms (*janapadas*) were beginning to merge with others to form larger confederacies (*mahajanapadas*) governed by single rulers from fortified capitals. Two new reforming religious movements were also gaining ground in the North. The first, **Buddhism** (see p.670), arose from the teachings of a young prince from the Nepalese foothills, Siddharta, or **Gautama Buddha** (563–483 BC). In addition, **Jainism**, founded by the prophet **Mahavira** (599–527 BC) around the same time, began to attract followers, most notably among the ruling elite of a dynasty that was destined to become the most powerful in the subcontinent.

Stepping into the vacuum left by the departure of **Alexander the Great** from the northwest, the **Mauryans**, who ruled the region southeast of the Ganges, usurped the throne of their arch-adversaries, the Nandas, in 320 BC to make their king, **Chandragupta Maurya**, the first *de facto* emperor of India, with an empire that stretched from the Punjab to Karnataka. A strict Jain, he eventually renounced his throne and starved himself to death on a hilltop at

Sravanabelgola (still an important South Indian pilgrimage centre), thereby achieving the status of a saint.

From their capital at Pataliputra (in Bihar, near present-day Patna), the Mauryans ruled over a vast swathe of the subcontinent, greatly enlarged during the reign of Chandragupta's grandson, **Ashoka**, who defeated the mighty Kalingas on the east coast (modern Orissa). It was the bloody aftermath of that battle, in which 100,000 people were killed and 150,000 abducted, that the emperor embraced Buddhism and the path of non-violence. Edicts proclaiming the tenets of the new imperial faith were erected throughout the empire, and missionaries and ambassadors dispatched to spread the message of "right conduct", or *dhamma*, abroad. No such edicts, however, have so far come to light further south than the goldfields around Mysore, and it seems likely that most of the Deccan and peninsular India, including all of modern Andhra Pradesh, Kerala and Tamil Nadu, remained outside Mauryan influence.

The Mauryans may never have conquered the far south, but their way of life and system of government strongly influenced developments in the region. Through trade and interaction with Jain and Buddhist monk-missionaries, concepts of statehood gradually filtered south, encouraging the dominant powers in the peninsula to expand their realms.

Dravidadesa: the Early Kingdoms

Inscribed on the eight rock-cut edicts that Ashoka raised on the frontiers of his empire in the third century BC are verses expressing goodwill towards his "undefeated neighbours" (*avijita*). The list includes the earliest known references to the three ancient ruling clans who dominated the far south in the final centuries of the first millennium BC: the **Cholas** of the Coromandel region and Kaveri basin; the **Pandyas**, whose capital was at Madurai; and the **Cheras**, from southwest Kerala. Collectively, the kingdoms of these three dynasties comprised a domain known to northerners as **Dravidadesa**, "Land of the Tamils".

A wealth of historical detail relating to the early kingdoms of the South has survived, most of it in a remarkable body of classical Tamil poetry known as the **Sangam**, composed between the first and third centuries AD in the literary academies (*sangam*) of Madurai. The texts, which were only rediscovered in the nineteenth century, refer to an era when the indigenous Dravidian culture of the deep south was being transformed by Sanskritic influences from the North. Nevertheless, they vividly demonstrate that some of the most distinctive characteristics of Indian civilization – including yoga, *tantra*, the cult of the god Murugan and goddess worship – were almost certainly indigenous to the South, and widespread well before the Aryans came to dominate the region completely.

The Sangam also records the stormy political relations between the three dynasties, who were frequently at war with each other, or with the rulers of neighbouring Sri Lanka. Ultimately, however, all three seem to have succumbed to an enigmatic fourth dynasty, the **Kalabhras**, about whom the Sangam poems say very little other than that they were "bad kings" (*kaliarasar*). Buddhist texts from a later period suggest the Kalabhras were originally hill tribes who swept down from the Deccan to harass the inhabitants of the river valleys and coastal areas, and later took up Jainism and Buddhism, deposing the Dravidian kings and persecuting the brahmins.

The expansion of trade

The cultural flowering of the Sangam era in the South, during the first two centuries AD, was stimulated by a rapid growth in **maritime trade** throughout the region. As well as Arab merchants, the ports of the Malabar and Coromandel coasts now began to welcome **Roman** ships. After a century of relentless civil war, peace had returned to Rome, bringing with it renewed demand in the imperial capital for luxury goods such as pearls, spices, perfumes, precious stones and silk. When Augustus conquered Egypt to open up the Red Sea, and Hippalus discovered that the monsoon winds would blow a ship from there across the Arabian Sea in around a fortnight, the means to supply this appetite for exotic oriental merchandise was within the Romans' grasp.

A vivid picture of the boom that ensued has survived in an extraordinary mariners' manual entitled the *Periplus of the Erythraean Sea,* written by an anonymous Alexandrian merchant-adventurer. Featuring meticulous descriptions of the trade, ports and capital cities of the far south, it reveals that the region was an entrepôt for valuable foreign goods – notably Chinese silk and oil from the Gangetic basin – and that the Coromandel was gradually eclipsing the Malabar as peninsular India's principal trade platform.

This fact has been borne out by Mortimer Wheeler's discovery of the Romans' main trading post at **Arikamedu**, just south of modern Pondicherry in Tamil Nadu, where large brick buildings, water reservoirs, baths and a huge number of artefacts – including shards of pre-Christian ceramics from Arezzo and hoards of coins – suggest it was largely the lust for Roman gold that fuelled the ancient trade in the South. Indeed, the Roman chronicler, Strabo, famously complained that the Indian merchants were threatening to completely empty the treasuries of Rome of gold coins. Prodigious quantities of these have been unearthed in recent times, especially in the area around the ancient port of **Muziris**, near present-day Kannur in northern Kerala.

The Satavahanas

Coupled with the advances in knowledge of state administration made by the Mauryans, the vast trade wealth pouring into South India around the turn of the millennium enabled the region's rulers to create larger and more organized kingdoms, backed by well equipped armies. Conditions were ripe for the rise of a major power, and this came in the first century BC with the advent of the **Satavahanas**, an obscure tribal dynasty from the Deccan who, in the space of a hundred years, assumed the imperial mantle of the Mauryans. By the time Ptolemy was writing his *Geography*, midway through the second century AD, the empire, based in **Pratisthana** (near modern Paithan in Maharashtra), comprised thirty fortified cities and stretched from coast to coast. Administered by a network of noblemen, it was upheld by semi-autonomous military garrisons, with an army said by the Roman chronicler Pliny to consist of 30,000 cavalry and 9000 war elephants.

Thanks to their control of the region's lucrative foreign trade, the Satavahanas (or Andhras as they are referred to in some ancient texts) were also prolific patrons of the arts, responsible for the greatest monuments in India at that time, notably the famous ornamental gateways (*toranas*) of the Buddhist stupa at **Sanchi** (in Madhya Pradesh), and many of the most accomplished rock-cut caves of the northwest Deccan. However, the crowning glory of Andhran art was to be the Great Stupa complex at **Amaravati**, in Andhra Pradesh (see p.594), whose exquisite bas-reliefs (now housed in the Government Museum, Chennai; see p.442) are considered by many scholars to be the finest ancient Indian sculpture.

The Early Middle Ages: 600–1200 AD

The history of the early middle ages in South India, from the time of the Satavahanas' demise to the arrival of the Muslims, hinges on the rise and fall of a mosaic of **regional dynasties**. These invariably fought each other to gain supremacy for short periods, and then found their rule usurped by one or other of their adversarial neighbours. Not until the sword of Islam descended on the Deccan in the thirteenth century did the peninsula succumb to a single overlord.

Various theories have been advanced to explain this, but the most convincing is that the warring kingdoms were generally too small to exert control over large territories for long. Bringing rebellious chiefdoms to heel meant costly military expeditions, which would inevitably render the ruler's own region vulnerable to attack.

Despite this, the ongoing power balance mitigated against the rise of an empire and the long-term political stability it afforded allowed for the development of distinct regional cultures. The wealth of historic monuments scattered across South India today graphically exemplifies the differences between these cultures, and the way in which they interacted over the centuries.

Chalukyas, Pallavas and Cholas

Foremost among the states of the southern Deccan were the **Chalukyas**, who had been underlings of the Kadamabas (Hindu rulers of the region that later became Goa) until **Pulakeshin I** broke away and founded a capital at Vatapi (**Badami**; see p.299). Here, atop a rocky escarpment overlooking a lake, the king and his descendants erected a series of magnificent stone temples. From simple rock-cut excavations, these evolved into more sophisticated free-standing structures, embellished with elaborate iconographic sculpture, that were among the first buildings in the region to fuse indigenous architectural styles with those of northern India.

The Chalukyas' conspicuous wealth inevitably attracted the attentions of their neighbours. After fending off two invasions, they eventually succumbed in 753 AD to the **Rashtrakutas**, whose domain extended most of the way across the Deccan.

The Chalukyas' southern enemies, the **Pallavas**, emerged after defeating the Kalabhras, the "bad kings" who originally routed the region's three early dynasties. Originally Buddhists, they converted to brahmanism sometime in the fifth century and thereafter carved out a kingdom that would spread from the mouth of the Krishna River to the edge of the Kaveri basin in the South. From the outset, the Pallavas seem to have been keen seafarers, trading with Greeks, Satavahanas and Romans, whose coins have all been found amid the ruins of ancient **Mamallapuram** (see p.464), just south of Chennai. The extraordinary crop of stone temples, open-air bas-reliefs and finely carved caves dotted around this fishing and stone-carving village recall the era when it ranked among the busiest ports in Asia.

The majority of Mamallapuram's monuments were begun in the mid-seventh century, during the reign of Narasimha Varman I (aka *Mamalla*, "the Great Wrestler"), and completed over the following two generations. Of them all, the best known is the **Shore temple**, overlooking the beach and thought to be the first shrine built of loose stone blocks in the subcontinent. Surmounted by a steep pyramidal tower (*vimana*), it closely resembles the better preserved Kailasanatha temple in the Pallavas' former capital, **Kanchipuram**, where, in the mid-seventh century, the Chinese pilgrim, Hsiuen-tsang, reported seeing one hundred Buddhist monasteries as well as eighty major Hindu temples.

The Shore temple at Mamallapuram provided the main architectural inspiration for the **Cholas**, an offshoot of the ancient dynasty of the same name who asserted their independence from the Pallavas in 897 AD, when the latter had their hands full fighting off the Rastrakutas. During their two-hundred-and-fifty-year rule, the Cholas expanded out of their royal capital, **Thanjavur**, in the Kaveri basin, defeating both the Pandyas and Cheras, and later conquering Sri Lanka, the Maldives and the Andamans, in addition to enclaves in Java and Sumatra, which they captured in order to control trade with Southeast Asia.

Combined with the huge sums in plunder yielded by their military campaigns, the Cholas' trade monopoly financed an awesome building spree. The dynasty's most visionary ruler was **Rajaraja I** (985–1014), who erected the colossal Brihadishwara temple, in its day the largest in India. Decorating the walls of the shrine, beneath its soaring tower, exquisite frescoes recall the opulence and sophistication of the Chola court, where keen patronage of the arts – most famously bronze-casting, but also Karnatic music, sculpture, dance and literature – produced works that have never been surpassed since.

Bhakti and the Tamil poets

From the eighth century onwards, the devotional form of Hinduism known as **bhakti**, which first blossomed in Tamil Nadu, spread north into the rest of India to become, as it still is, the dominant strain of Hinduism throughout the country. This was essentially a popular movement, whose emphasis that each individual devotee could form a personalized, emotionally charged relationship with a chosen god (*ishtadevata*) revolutionized Hindu practice by offering a religious path and goal open to all castes.

The great champions of *bhakti* were the **poet–saints** of Tamil Nadu, often said to have "sung" the religions of Jainism and Buddhism out of South India. Although in practice a variety of deities was worshipped, the movement had two strands: the **Nayanmars**, devoted to Shiva, and the **Alvars**, centred on Vishnu. Collections of their poetry, the greatest literary legacy of South India, remain popular today, and the poets themselves are almost deified, featuring in carvings in many temples.

The four most prominent of the 63 Nayanmar poet-saints were **Campantar**, who converted the king of Madurai from Jainism and had a great cult centre at Chidambaram; **Cuntarar**, a brahmin who had two low-caste wives; **Appar**, himself a convert from Jainism; and **Manikkavachakar**, whose mystical poems are still sung in homes and temples throughout Tamil Nadu. The Vaishnavite movement centred on Srirangam (near Trichy), its poets including men and women of all social classes. The most celebrated Alvar was **Nammalvar**, a *shudra* who spent his life in fasting and meditation. **Antal**, the most popular female Alvar, is said to have married Vishnu's statue at Srirangam, and was thereafter regarded as an incarnation of Vishnu's consort, Shri.

All the poems tell of the ecstatic response to intense experiences of divine favour, an emotion frequently described in terms of conjugal love, and expressed in verses of great tenderness and beauty. They stress selfless love between man and god, claiming that such love alone can lead to everlasting union with the divine. Devotees travelled the South, singing, dancing and challenging opponents to public debates.

Among the most significant consequences of the *bhakti* revolution in Hinduism was the emergence of **temple cities**. By stressing the importance of the individual's devotion to a particular god or goddess, *bhakti* inspired a massive upsurge in popular worship and, inevitably, a proliferation of shrines to accommodate worshippers. This process went hand in hand with the assimilation of important regional deities into the Hindu pantheon. Thus, trees, rocks, caves or bodies of water held sacred in a given place began to be "legitimized" through identification with Shiva or Vishnu. Notable examples include the deities of Chidambaram and Madurai, two of South India's most important religious centres, whose importance was firmly established well before the Sanskritization that associated them with Shiva in the sixth century.

In time, the same happened to lesser local gods and village deities, until innumerable cult centres across the South became bound in a complex web of interconnections. The institution of **pilgrimage**, linking local and distant deities, emerged for the first time as an essential element of Hinduism during the era of the Tamil saints, and has remained an important unifying force in India ever since. It is no coincidence that some of the most defining texts of the *bhakti* movement are the *Mahatmyas*, oral chants intoned by brahmins that elucidate the significance of individual temples and their relationship to other shrines.

Muslim incursions

At the start of the eleventh century, a new player appeared on the political map of northern India. **Mahmud**, a Turkish chieftain who had established a powerful kingdom at Ghazni, near Kabul in Afghanistan, made seventeen plundering raids into the plains of India between 1000 and 1027 AD. His was the first of many Muslim incursions from the northwest that would, after two hundred years of constant infighting and wars with local rulers, lead to the creation of an Islamic empire based in Delhi.

Founded in 1206 AD, the **Delhi Sultanate** made little impact on the South during its formative years. In 1309, however, the redoubtable Sultan **Allauddin Khilji**, set his sights southwards. Having heard rumours of the treasures stored in the great Tamil temples (Rajaraja had not long before donated 880kg of gold to the Brihadishwara temple), he took advantage of the Cholas' decline to mount a raid. It is recorded that his general, the ruthless military genius and former Hindu slave, **Malik Kafur**, returned with a thousand camels bearing booty, including the famous Kohinoor diamond.

This, however, was merely a prelude to the Sultanate's second expedition of 1310–1311, in the course of which Allauddin's army pressed into the deep south itself. Raiding towns and desecrating the splendid Chola temples of the Kaveri Delta, it reached Madurai on April 10, 1311 and mercilessly sacked the Pandyas' capital, massacring the few of its inhabitants who had not fled. Forewarned of Kafur's approach, many temples had hidden or buried their treasures. Some, like the eighty priceless Chola bronzes that came to light in Chidambaram in the 1960s, were rediscovered; others remain lost.

Aside from the wholesale destruction of art treasures, the main legacy of Allauddin's plunder was the creation of a short-lived **Muslim Sultanate** at Tirupparakunram (see p.534), near Madurai. Overlooking the town from the top of a huge sandstone outcrop, the tomb of its eighth and last Sultan, **Sikander Shah**, remains one of the far south's few bona fide Muslim shrines.

The Deccan Sultanates

The Delhi Sultanates possessed sufficient military strength to subdue most of India, but time and again showed themselves incapable of consolidating their territorial gains with strong administrations. In the end, the despot **Muhamed Tuqluq**'s incessant wars, together with his crackpot plan to relocate the capital from Delhi to Daulatabad, 1000km south on the Deccan, saw the Sultanates' reign degenerate into one of terror and profligacy. Forced by drought, famine and the threat of Moghul invasion to abandon Daulatabad and return to Delhi, Tuqluq struggled until his death to hold onto power. By the mid-fourteenth century, his successor, **Feroz Shah**, had completely lost control of the Deccan.

In the wake of the Daulatabad debacle, one of Tuqluq's former generals, **Zafar Shah**, aka **Bahman Shah**, saw his chance to found his own dynasty, which he located at a safe distance south of the old capital, at **Gulbarga** (in present-day northern Karnataka). The **Bahmanis'** rule lasted around two hundred years, and was as bloody as the old Delhi Sultanate's; Zafar Shah's son, Mohammed Shah (1358–73) is said to slaughtered half a million people in his wars with neighbouring states, which included the Vijayanagars, who founded their empire at around the same time (see below).

In the fifteenth century AD, the Bahmanis shifted their capital further northeast to **Bidar**, constructing a massive fortress that still survives. Under the careful stewardship of **Mahmud Gawan**, a talented prime minister who served several successive sultans, the dynasty flourished, but went into a dramatic decline after his death. The ensuing power struggle saw the governors of the four largest districts in the kingdom – Bijapur, Ahmadnagar, Bidar and Golconda – declare independence, with Bijapur eventually emerging as the major power by the sixteenth century. Their rule, however, was bedevilled by conflict with both Vijayanagar and the Portuguese; they lost the port of Goa to the latter in 1510.

The power balance between the Deccan kingdoms was decisively turned in the Muslims' favour after 1565 when, following years of fighting each other, the sultanates formed a pact to wage war on their common Hindu enemies, the Vijayanagars. At the battle of Talikota that year, the alliance crushed the Hindu army and set about the most destructive sack of a city the subcontinent had ever seen. Within twenty-one years, however, the Deccan sultanates had succumbed completely to the might of the Moghuls.

Vijayanagar: 1346–1565

To the south of the Bahmanis' territory, the Krishna River formed the border with the mighty Hindu kingdom of **Vijayanagar**, which emerged in response to the threat of Muslim invasions. Its founders were two brothers from Andhra Pradesh, **Harihara** and **Bukka**, who were allegedly captured by Tuqluq during his sack of Kampili in 1327 AD and taken as prisoners to Delhi, where they converted to Islam before being dispatched as governors to their native town to restore order after an uprising. Legend has it that the sage Vidyaranya then reconverted the brothers to Hinduism and encouraged them to defect (although some Indian historians have disputed this, claiming Harihara and Bukka were actually offshoots of the Hoysalas).

Whatever its roots, the dynasty the brothers founded on the banks of the Tungabadhra River (at modern-day Hampi; see p.289) quickly flourished. Following a series of short wars with the Hoysalas, Madurai and the Gajapatis of eastern Indian, the rulers of the southern kingdoms pragmatically threw in their lot with the ambitious newcomers, realizing their best chance of protection from marauding Muslims lay in a strong Hindu front to the north. This proved to be the case. At a time when the influence of Turkish, Persian and Afghan culture on northern India was most marked, the South, insulated by

On May 18, 1498, three Portuguese *caravelas* dropped anchor off the coast of northern Kerala at a beach called Kappad, having sailed from Lisbon via the Cape of Good Hope in a little over ten months. Five hundred years later, to the day, groups of angry protesters gathered on the same beach to burn effigies of the explorer who stepped ashore, Vasco da Gama. By rounding the tip of Africa and opening up a maritime route to the spice markets of western India, da Gama would change the pattern of world history, for which he has been feted as a national hero ever since by the Portuguese public. Among the educated classes of India, however, he is reviled as a pirate and looter, who committed acts of appalling barbarism out of greed for "black gold" – the pepper of the Malabar Coast.

While the ramifications of da Gama's voyages remain a subject of heated debate, the essential facts of his three expeditions to India have survived, thanks to the diaries of Alvaro Velho, one of da Gama's soldiers. These describe in detail how the small fleet of five ships set sail from Lisbon in July 1497, with an aura of messianic resolve as the sacred symbol of Christ billowed in their sails. Their route took them around the islands of Cabo Verde (Cape Verde) and four thousand miles southeast to round the Cape of Good Hope at the beginning of November.

At Malindi, da Gama was granted the services of an expert navigator, an Arab sea captain called Ibn' Masjid, who piloted the three remaining *caravelas* across the Indian Ocean to Calicut. However, news of atrocities committed by the Portuguese en route had preceded their arrival, and the local *zamorin*, Mana Vikrama, briefly imprisoned da Gama before he was allowed to fill his holds with pepper and leave – an insult the proud Portuguese admiral would never forget.

Four years later he returned to Calicut, this time bent on revenge. In addition to what he perceived as his own "contumely treatment" at the hands of the Hindu ruler, he intended to avenge the murder of 53 Portuguese killed during a previous expedition in 1500. As a prelude to the onslaught, da Gama waylaid a Muslim ship en route from Mecca and burned alive all 700 of its passengers and crew. Then he set about bombarding the city. While the cannonade decimated Calicut's temples and houses, da Gama ordered the crews of a dozen or so trade ships anchored in

Vijayanagar, remained outside the sway of Islam – a fact that accounts perhaps better than anything else for the striking cultural differences that still exist between the north and the south of the subcontinent.

Vijayanagar's golden period was during the reign of **Krishna Deva Raya** (1509–29), before its monopoly over the trade in spices and Arabian horses had been undermined by the Portuguese and other European powers. While the Bijapuris were a constant and costly source of irritation, the king's well organized administration, together with his control of some thirty or so rich ports, ensured a steady flow of wealth.

The dynastic capital, Vijayanagar ("City of Victory") became, for an all too brief period, among the most splendid in the world. Travellers such as Domingo Paes, who stayed there between 1522 and 1524, marvelled at the opulence of its royal court, the richness of its bazaars and the sumptuousness of its festivals. Krishna Deva Raya's rule was also the period when the South acquired some of its most impressive **temple towers** (*gopuras*), erected by the king to foster loyalty among brahmins and inhabitants of distant regions over which Vijayanagar's hold was precarious.

After Krishna Deva Raya's death in 1529, internal struggles and conflicts with the Portuguese weakened the empire. However, it was the Vijayanagars' old foe, the Bijapuris, who eventually brought their glorious rule to an abrupt and bloody end. Having benefited from the Deccan Sultanates' constant feuding for

the harbour to be rounded up. Before killing them, he had the prisoners' hands, ears and noses hacked off and the pieces sent ashore piled in a small boat.

This horrific act set the precedent, and genocide became a hallmark of early Portuguese colonialism in Asia, as the Europeans extended their trade links up the South Indian coast to Goa. And so it was with some astonishment that, five centuries later, Goan nationalist politicians and journalists greeted Portugal's invitation to participate in the festivities marking the quincentennial of Vasco da Gama's voyage. Quite apart from those original atrocities, Goan freedom fighters, who had struggled to oust the Portuguese, found it particularly absurd that they should now be expected to celebrate the start of their rule. An organization called Deshpremi Samiti was duly formed to campaign against the celebrations, stirring up acrimonious debate in the Goan press. While some maintained the quincentennial glorified colonial oppression, pro-Portuguese Goans advocated a "forgive-and-forget" approach (epitomized by comments in the *Navhind Times* by former MP Erasmo Sequeira, who wrote that "… whatever [Vasco da Gama] was, he was. It is historians who must involve themselves in critical appreciation. The rest of us can just enjoy the celebrations."

The controversy eventually came to a head with the Kerala Tourism Development Corporation's announcement that they were intending to stage a full-blown re-enactment of da Gama's landing, complete with wooden replicas of the three caravels and tourists acting the parts of Portuguese mariners. The plans provoked large protest marches in Goa, and the Delhi government was forced to issue a statement saying India would not under any circumstances participate in the so-called "celebrations" of 1498.

In the event, the anniversary passed off peacefully, though clearly the raking over of da Gama's unsavoury conduct did little to enhance relations between India and its first colonizer. Significantly however, the controversy did serve to fix in Indian minds a parallel between the exploitation of colonial times and the activities of today's multinationals, who use current trade agreements to open up emerging markets in India. It is no coincidence that alongside the effigies of Vasco da Gama being burned on Kappad beach were others of Coca-Cola and Pepsi bottles.

more than a century, the Vijayanagars made a fatal mistake when they desecrated mosques during campaigns in the 1550s. This finally galvanized the sultans to set aside their differences and march on Vijayanagar. The armies met at Talikota in 1565. At first, the battle seemed to be going the Hindus' way, but suddenly turned against them when two of their Muslim generals defected. The Vijayanagar regent, Rama Raya, was captured and beheaded, while his brother, Tirumala, fled with what was left of the army, leaving the capital defenceless.

The ensuing sack lasted six months and reduced Asia's most illustrious city to rubble. Predictably, the Deccan sultans squabbled over the spoils and spent the next century fighting each other, leaving the region vulnerable to invasion by the Moghuls.

The Portuguese

Around the same time as Vijayanagar was enjoying its period of greatest prosperity, the harbinger of a new regional power appeared on the horizon of the Arabian Sea. Driven by the lust for "Christians and Spices", Vasco da Gama's arrival on the Malabar Coast in 1498 (see box on p.642) blazed a trail that would, after only fifteen years, result in the creation of Europe's first bona fide colony in the East.

Formerly a Vijayanagar port, **Goa** had been taken by the Bahmanis, whom the Portuguese, under **Admiral Alfonso Albuquerque**, expelled in 1510. Thereafter, despite repeated attempts by the Muslims to regain their possession, the colony expanded at a breathless pace. At the height of its power, the city was the linchpin of a trade network extending from the Philippines to the north Atlantic, with cathedrals to rival Rome's and a population that at one time was greater even than Lisbon's.

Yet, despite enjoying an early monopoly on maritime trade in Asia, ruthlessly enforced by their insurmountable naval supremacy, the Portuguese were unable to sustain an early lead over their European rivals. Repeated outbreaks of disease depleted the population of Goa, while the defeat in 1565 of Vijayanagar, which by that time accounted for a significant portion of the city's trade, had a disastrous effect on the whole Portuguese economy. Unable to maintain control of the sea lanes, Portugal gradually saw its trade empire whittled away, first by the Dutch, and later by the French and British. Goa actually survived as a Portuguese colony until 1961, but was effectively a spent force by the end of the seventeenth century.

The Moghul Empire

Descendants of Timur and Genghis Khan's Mongols from Samarkhand in Central Asia, the **Moghuls** staked their claim to North India with Babur's defeat of the Delhi Sultan, Ibrahim Lodi, in 1526. Through the revolutionary deployment of small arms and mobile artillery, the invaders routed an army ten times their size. The victory inaugurated an empire that would, by the time of its demise two hundred years later, become the largest and most powerful since Ashoka's, eighteen centuries earlier. Keen patrons of the arts as well as fearsome military strategists, successive emperors blended Persian and Indian culture to create some of the subcontinent's greatest treasures, including the Red Fort in Delhi and the Taj Mahal in Agra.

Aurangzeb and the Marathas

The Moghuls' influence, however, had little impact on the South until the reign of **Shah Jehan** (1627–58), when the northernmost of the Deccan Sultanates, Ahmadnagar, was annexed. A hundred years after their sack of Vijayanagar, Bijapur and Golconda also succumbed, this time to the last of the Great Moghuls, **Aurangzeb** (1658–1707).

The most expansionist ruler of the dynasty, Aurangzeb was also a devout Sunni, notorious for his rough treatment of Hindus, and for reinstating the much-hated *jizya* tax on non-Muslims that his great-grandfather, Akbar, had repealed. Aurangzeb's arch-adversaries in the Deccan region were a confederacy of low-caste Hindu warriors called the **Marathas**. Unlike the Moghuls, they attacked not with large, formal armies, but by mounting guerrilla-style raids, retreating to the safety of impregnable fortresses perched on the top of table mountains.

Under their most audacious and gifted leader, **Shivaji**, whom Aurangzeb named "The Mountain Rat", the Marathas managed on numerous occasions to outwit the Moghul's superior forces, and over time came to dominate a large chunk of western India. The year of Shivaji's death in 1680, Aurangzeb's son, Akbar, slipped south from Delhi to form an alliance with his opposite number, with whose help he hoped to overthrow his father. But the plot ended in a heavy defeat for the usurper and his Hindu allies. Soon afterwards, Aurangzeb moved his court from Delhi to Aurangabad in order personally to supervise the subjugation of the Marathas. It was from there, too, that he mounted the victorious campaigns against Bijapur and Golconda which would extend Moghul rule to its eventual highwater mark.

Aurangzeb may have pushed the empire's boundaries further south than any of his predecessors, but his policies ultimately brought about the dynasty's downfall. To win over the nobles of his new acquisitions in the Deccan, the emperor demanded lower taxes from them, which left an administrative shortfall that he subsequently made up for by over-taxing his farmers. This duly provoked **peasant uprisings**, made more deadly by the proliferation of small arms at that time, which Aurangzeb's cumbersome, elephant-based army was ill suited to quell. In addition, the burden on the shattered Deccan states of reprovisioning an army whose annual losses were calculated at 100,000 men and around 300,000 animals was enormous. In 1702–3, famine and pestilence wiped out an estimated two million people in the region.

After the last Great Moghul's death in 1707, half a century of gradual decay was presided over by a succession of eight incompetent emperors. The final blow to the Moghul dynasty came in 1779, when the Persian Nadir Shah raided Delhi and made off with a vast loot that included the Peacock Throne itself. "The streets", wrote one eyewitness, "were strewn with corpses like a garden with weeds. The city was reduced to ashes and looked like a burnt plain."

Dutch, British and French

The Portuguese domination of the Indian Ocean was complete by the time Babur descended on Delhi, and neither he nor his Moghul successors felt in the least threatened by the presence of foreign powers on their coastal borders. In fact, they welcomed the traders as providers of silver and gold which they could use to mint money. In the course of the seventeenth and eighteenth centuries, however, the European powers would become a force to be reckoned with, eventually replacing the Moghuls as India's rulers.

The first challengers of the Portuguese trade supremacy were the **Dutch**, whose cheaper and more manoeuvrable *fluyt* ships easily outsailed the more old-fashioned, ungainly *caravelas* from Lisbon. Determined not to allow Asia to be carved up by the proselytizing Roman Catholics, the Protestant Dutch East India Company – founded in 1602, only a couple of decades after Holland's victorious war of independence over Spain – systematically took control of the international spice trade, relieving the Portuguese of the strategically essential Mollaccas in 1641, Ceylon in 1663 and their chief ports on the Malabar Coast soon after.

Although established two years before its Dutch counterpart, the **English** East India Company lagged behind initially, operating on a more modest scale with a fleet of smaller, privately run ships. Following the example of the Dutch, they set up a string of trading posts, or **factories**, around the coast, where goods – mostly **textiles** – could be stored awaiting annual shipment. Its first headquarters (from 1612), in Surat, Gujarat, was relocated to Bombay (Mumbai) in 1674 – the company had acquired the headquarters for a pittance from Charles II after he gained possession of it as a dowry gift on his marriage to the Portuguese Infanta, Catherine of Braganza. By the mid-seventeenth century, the British possessed 27 such outposts, the largest being **Fort St George** on the Coromandel Coast – the forerunner of Madras (modern Chennai). Over time, as the nature of the textile trade in India changed, the factories evolved from mere warehouses into large financial centres whose influence spread far inland. Gradually, communities of weavers settled around them, while growing numbers of recruits arrived to staff ever-expanding administrations and the military apparatus required to protect them.

The greatest threat to Britain's early Indian colonies was not local rulers, but rival Europeans. In the case of Fort St George, the **French** – whose own East India Company, started in 1664, was based further south on the Coromandel Coast at **Pondicherry** – were to prove the most troublesome. Initially, agreements between the two rival companies forestalled any armed encounters. But with the outbreak of the War of the Austrian Succession in 1740, Britain and France found themselves members of opposing coalitions in a conflict which, although rooted in central Europe, proved a turning point in the history of South Asia.

The first clash between France and Britain came in 1746 when the French governor of Pondicherry the wily diplomat **Joseph François Dupleix**, captured Fort St George with the help of a French fleet commanded by **Admiral La Bourdonnais**. Among those imprisoned during the short French occupation (the fort was handed back two years later) was a young East India Company clerk whose humiliation at the hands of the French is often used to explain his sudden career change from pen-pushing to soldiering. Considered one of the founders of the British Raj, **Robert Clive** cut his military teeth in the politically unstable Carnatic region around Madras.

Dupleix had long since learned that the best way to extend French influence, and trade, was to forge alliances with whichever local ruler looked likely to emerge victorious from the furious in-fighting that wracked the South during the break-up of the Moghul empire. In this way, the British and the French were drawn into the conflicts of regional rulers, often facing each other from opposite ends of a battlefield.

In one such encounter, where the European powers pitched in to support rival sons of the Nawab of **Arcot** in 1751, Clive, then only 26 years old, distinguished himself by holding a breached and sprawling fortress for fifty days with only two hundred men against a vastly superior force of 15,000 French and their Indian allies. The first great triumph of British arms in the history of India, this feat made Clive a hero, a reputation he consolidated soon afterwards by marching through the monsoons to intervene decisively at the siege of **Trichinopoly**. The French lost half their army in this second battle, and saw their protégé, Chandra Sahib, captured and killed. Dupleix's reputation never recovered; he was recalled two years later and died destitute.

The British went on to defeat the French again at Wandiwash in 1760, and finally took Pondicherry after an eight-month siege, effectively bringing to an end the French bid for power in India. For Robert Clive, the Carnatic war was but a local skirmish compared to the significance of his later achievements in Bengal, where his victory at **Plassey** in 1757 laid the foundations of a British rule that would last for two hundred years. It did, however, teach him and his compatriots lessons that would serve them well in the future: not least of all, how effective a relatively small number of highly disciplined troops could be against a far larger undisciplined army.

Haider Ali and Tipu Sultan of Mysore

After the heavy defeats in the Carnatic, the French were certainly down, but they were not yet quite out, thanks to the one remaining thorn in the side of British territorial ambitions: **Haider Ali**. A former general of the Maharaja of Mysore, Haider Ali had usurped his master's throne in 1761 and within a short time ruled over virtually the entire South. The secret of his dramatic success lay in his readiness to learn from the Europeans, in particular the French, whose military tactics he emulated, and who provided him with officers to train his infantry. Between 1767 and 1769, he fought a series of battles with the British, whom he had always, unlike other Indian rulers, regarded as a threat to India as a whole, and whom he eventually coerced into a highly favourable treaty after threatening to attack Madras.

Held back by corrupt officials in both Madras and Calcutta, the British failed to provide a robust response, but rallied during the governorship of **Warren Hastings**. In 1778, they were once again at war with the French, and fending off Marathas in the west, which Haider Ali took as his cue to launch a major offensive. Assisted by the French, who landed troops by sea to join the battle, Haider again forced the British to sue for peace.

This was far from the most honourable period in the imperial history of France and Britain. During their various marches and skirmishes across the Carnatic, temples were regularly desecrated and massacres were commonplace; in all, a million Tamils were killed. On one occasion, four hundred wounded Hindu women were raped by rioting British soldiers, while in the Kaveri region, the French general, Lally, fired brahmin priests from his cannons for refusing to tell him where their temple treasure was hidden.

After Haider's death in 1782, his son, **Tipu Sultan**, aka "the Tiger of Mysore" carried on his father's campaigns, but did so with diminished support from the French, who had by this time begun to wind down their Indian operations. In the end, Tipu Sultan was let down badly by his father's former allies. In 1799, they failed to dispatch troops to reinforce him when an army, led by Lord Wellesley and his brother Arthur (later the Duke of Wellington, of Waterloo fame) marched on **Srirangapatnam**. Tipu Sultan died defending a breach in his capital's walls (a story that later inspired Wilkie Collins's novel, *The Moonstone*), and Mysore was returned to the old Hindu dynasty Haider Ali had deposed. After more than a century of continual conflict between the European powers and their various allies, the struggle for control of India was finally won by the British.

British rule in the South

Following their victory at Srirangapatnam, the British, under Hastings' successor, **Lord Cornwallis**, annexed the coastal areas and interior plains that had been under Tipu Sultan's sway, settling down to a period of relatively trouble-free rule. Stretching from the Telegu-speaking region of present-day Andhra Pradesh to the Malabar Coast, the **Madras Presidency** was a notoriously "hands-off" regime, with vast administrative districts on which colonial officers could make very little impact. Life basically continued as it had before the advent of the British Raj. Unlike in the North, where the economic changes brought about by the Industrial Revolution in England had a huge impact, the South's output was geared towards domestic consumption; when the Lancashire mills forced the bottom out of the cotton industry in Bengal, the weavers of Madras were largely unaffected.

Nevertheless, resentment at British rule was not confined to the northern plains, where the so-called **Indian Mutiny** (redubbed "the First War of Independence" by nationalist politicians) broke out in Lucknow in 1857. **Uprisings** also occurred in forest regions of Andhra Pradesh, and the Mopilah Muslims of the Malabar mounted small insurrections. Generally, however, opposition to the British came not from low-caste or tribal populations, but ironically from members of the English-speaking, university-educated elite in Madras, where the nineteenth century saw the emergence of a nascent **nationalist movement**. Based at the Theosophical Society's headquarters in Adyar, Annie Besant's Home Rule League openly objected to the colonial regime, while publications such as *The Hindu* spread the nationalist message among the literate classes.

The South since Independence

Independence passed off relatively peacefully in South India in 1947, as the North succumbed to the horrors of Partition. With the exception of the Nizam of Hyderabad, who tried to retain his dominions and had to be ousted by the new Indian army (see box on p.578), the Princely States – namely Cochin, Travancore and Mysore – acceded gracefully to the Indian Union. Although deprived of their privy purses and most of their land, many of the former rulers used their privileged backgrounds to secure powerful roles in their new states, becoming members of parliament or industrialists.

The dissolution of British rule also generated an upsurge in regional sentiments. In the South, calls to restructure state boundaries along linguistic lines gained pace, culminating in the 1956 **State Reorganization Act**, when the region was divided into four main states: the Kanada-speaking area became Mysore (later changed to Karnataka); the Telegu zone made up Andhra Pradesh; the former Tamil region of the Madras Presidency became Madras (subsequently renamed Tamil Nadu); and Kerala was created from the Malayalam-speaking Malabar coastal zone. Goa, meanwhile, remained under Portuguese control until 1961, when India's first Prime Minister, **Jawaharlal Nehru**, lost his patience with the Portuguese dictator Salazar and sent in the troops.

From the start, Nehru vociferously opposed the creation of language-based states, predicting such a move would lead to fragmentation, schisms and regionalism. The political upheavals of the past fifty years have proved him right. With the rise in popularity of the pro-Dravidian **DMK** in Tamil Nadu and the **Telegu Desam** in Andhra Pradesh, the South's political scene has been completely dominated by **regional parties** in one guise or another, reflecting widespread mistrust of central government rule from Delhi. This has been most vehemently expressed in resistance to the imposition of Hindi – the most widely spoken language in northern India – as the medium of education and law. As these parties gained larger shares of the vote, state-specific issues and calls for greater regional autonomy have increasingly dominated the political agendas of all four states.

Caste and communal conflict

The period since Independence has also seen a marked rise in **caste conflict**. Caste (see p.660) has always been more firmly rooted in South Indian society than the more Muslim-influenced north, but political legislation passed over the previous two decades to encourage greater participation in government and education of low, tribal and "Other Backward Castes" (OBCs) has somewhat deepened these age-old social divisions. Adopted in 1950, the Constitution of India paved the way for laws to combat caste discrimination, with clauses obliging the states to implement policies of "positive discrimination". "Untouchables" and OBCs were given **quotas** in educational institutions, parliament, regional assemblies and state sector jobs.

The Mandal Commission, set up in 1979 to look at the impact of quotas, came out strongly in favour of positive discrimination, and in August 1990 Prime Minister **V.P. Singh** announced that his party would implement its recommendations. Cynics accused him of trying to poach the Muslim and low-caste vote blocks from the opposition Congress Party, but the ensuing backlash was a strong contributory factor in the downfall of V.P. Singh's Janata Dal coalition in the elections of 1991.

The issue of quotas remains a contentious one in the South. "Affirmative action" policies, as quotas have been euphemistically dubbed, have certainly increased the level of scheduled caste participation in government, but they have had some negative effects too. Inevitably, sought-after university places and public sector jobs are often granted to unqualified people instead of better qualified members of higher castes, creating sectarian resentment that has increasingly spilled into violence. Several times in the past decade, violent clashes between brahmins and low-caste farmers have led to whole districts of Tamil Nadu being placed under martial law.

The other harmful repercussion of positive discrimination has been the **politicization** of caste. In order to be elected or to form power-wielding coalitions, Indian politicians these days have to galvanize **vote banks** – blocks of support from specific caste or ethnic groups. In return, these vote banks look to their leaders to advance their agendas in government, a process that all too often results in national or state interests being subordinated to the demands of minority groups.

With the expansion of the quota system under Prime Minister **Narasimha Rao** in 1994 to include disadvantaged Muslims and other "ethnic" minorities, state and national politics have become increasingly dominated not only by caste, but by communal issues – precisely the kind of sectarianism that the Mandal report and India's resolutely secular Constitution sought to eradicate.

The South has traditionally been spared the kind of **communal conflict** that has so often plagued the North. Over the past five years, however, the steady rise of communal parties, such as the far right pro-Hindu BJP, has been accompanied by violent confrontations between Hindus and Muslims, particularly in Tamil Nadu. The spiralling violence came to a head on February 14, 1998, when fifteen bombs exploded in crowded districts of Coimbatore, killing sixty people. The Home Affairs Minister and BJP leader at that time, L.K. Advani, was due to address a rally in the city, which the Islamic extremist organization **Al-Umma** decided to use as a pretext to settle communal scores for earlier attacks on Muslims in the region.

Tamil nationalism and the war in Sri Lanka

The highest profile victim of communal violence in India since the assassination of Mahatma Gandhi by Hindu extremists in 1948 was the former prime minister **Rajiv Gandhi** (son of Indira), who was killed while electioneering in Tamil Nadu on May 21, 1991. The murder was a reprisal for Rajiv's intervention in the war of neighbouring Sri Lanka – a conflict that has dominated foreign policy in the South over the past fifteen years and made a lasting impression on the coastal regions of Tamil Nadu.

The ongoing **ethnic conflict** between the majority (Buddhist) Sinhala and minority Tamil populations of Sri Lanka escalated into full-scale war in 1987. With the help of various foreign powers, the Sinhala president, Jayawardene, mounted an invasion of the Tamil guerrillas' stronghold on the Jaffna peninsula, in the north of the island. Jayawardene was furious when it transpired that Rajiv's Indian government had air-dropped supplies for the beleaguered Tamil freedom fighters. The two countries signed a peace accord in July 1987, part of which permitted the Indian army to intervene and disarm the Tamils. But in the event, India became bogged down in a messy war with high casualties on both sides. Tamil refugees, meanwhile, poured in their millions across the Palk Straits to settle in camps around Rameshwaram, Tamil Nadu, where they

Among the major changes to rural life in South India since Independence have been those brought about by the so-called Green Revolution. From the 1960s, encouraged by Western governments and aid donors, India introduced modern farming techniques to intensify wheat and rice production. Based on the use of new high-yield varieties of seed, together with chemical fertilizers, the new methods led to a dramatic increase in agricultural output (India survived a severe drought in 1988 and even managed to contribute grain to famine-stricken farmers in the African Sahel at around the same time). Their longer-term impact, however, remains under scrutiny.

One of the major drawbacks of the Green Revolution has been a growing disparity between the wealthy land-owning farmers and their landless share-cropping tenants. Unable to afford the expensive seeds and accompanying chemicals, poor farmers and their families have been forced, by mounting debts, to leave the countryside in search of waged employment. The majority end up living on the streets, or in the vast slum encampments that have sprung up on the edges of all South Indian cities over the past two decades.

Recent global economic trends have also been felt in the South Indian countryside. The General Agreement on Tariffs and Trade, or GATT, is potentially the most significant of these. Signed in 1994, the treaty aims to promote free trade by defending foreign investors from economic protectionism. While popular with the business community, however, GATT and other policies like it have proved controversial in a country as sensitive to its colonial history as India (particularly one brought up on the Gandhian ideals of *svadeshi*, or small-scale, non-polluting self-reliance).

A component of the treaty that has come in for particular criticism in India is its promotion of genetic patenting. This enables the large multinationals who manufacture seed used by South Indians to patent their products, making it illegal for farmers to replant them. No matter that the seeds may have originated in developing countries such as India, where generations of peasant farmers have painstakingly experimented to create pest- and drought-resistant strains. If a company can prove that it has modified the seed in any way, it is entitled by GATT to patent it.

The issue prompted indignation in India, but little more than that until it transpired the expensive seeds didn't even produce the promised increased yields – their one redeeming feature in the eyes of small farmers. In 1993, on the anniversary of Gandhi's birthday, half a million farmers issued "Quit India" notices to the US company Cargill, whose genetically modified sunflower seeds had been used by many farmers in northern Karnataka. Angry protesters succeeded in dismantling the company's plant in Bangalore within half an hour. The police, most of whom had family in the countryside, did not offer any significant resistance.

The Seed Satyagraha, as this grassroots farmers' movement became known, makes explicit the connection with the anticolonial struggle by using the name

remain, awaiting the end of a war that looks set to rumble on for some years to come.

India was only able to extricate itself after the defeat of Rajiv Gandhi in the 1989 elections, after which, in March 1990, the new government withdrew all troops from the island. It was during the campaign for the following elections, in May 1991, that Rajiv and sixteen others were **assassinated** by a female suicide bomber. Seven years later, an Indian court convicted 26 people for the killing; they were all Sri Lankan militants or Indian allies of the Liberation Tigers of Tamil Eelam (LTTE) conspirators. The assassination had been a

chosen by Gandhi for his campaign of non-violent civil disobedience, or *satyagraha*. Replacing the spinning wheel with a seed as the movement's symbol, it has been seen by many as a second freedom struggle and its ideas have spread from Karnataka through Andhra Pradesh, Tamil Nadu and Kerala in recent years.

Government support for the seed satyagraha, however, did not materialize until the late 1990s, following rumours that the giant corporation Monsanto planned to unleash the new so-called "Terminator Gene" on the region. Designed to protect the company's patents, the new genetically modified gene produces plants that yield sterile seeds (ie ones that cannot be re-sown, and thus oblige farmers to purchase new ones – and the accompanying fertilizers – each season). Moreover, it is widely feared that cross-pollination would render other crops sterile, resulting in complete dependence on foreign companies. To draw attention to this risk, a coalition of ten million Karnatakan farmers, the KRSS, mounted "Operation Cremate Monsanto", pulling up cotton crops at test sites and organizing mass rallies against the WTO. Its leader, the maverick Professor Najundasmamy, also staged much publicized laugh-in, when 6000 farmers laughed all day outside the town hall in Bangalore at their elected representatives, for "subverting democracy". To diffuse the crisis, and the prospect of a full-scale rural uprising, the Indian government banned the technology and required all exporting countries to guarantee that seeds entering India are "terminator free".

Another change that has had serious implications for millions of Indian farmers over the past decade or so has been the government's relationship with the International Monetary Fund (IMF) and its sister organization, the World Bank. In order to qualify for a £90 billion loan in the late 1980s, India was obliged to end its programme of subsidies to farmers, who for years had been entitled to free or cheap electricity, diesel, fertilizers and pesticides. According to the World Trade Organization, such state aid constituted "interference with the free market" and was illegal.

Farmers were instead encouraged by a raft of incentives and publicity drives to grow cash crops such as cotton, which offered the additional benefit of generating foreign currency (needed to repay the IMF loans). Using specially developed high-yield seeds and chemicals, improved harvests and profits were assured, and within a couple of years, huge chunks of the country (as much as sixty percent of farm land in Andhra Pradesh) had been given over to the "White Gold".

The advertising campaigns mounted by the multinational agri-manufacturers, however, failed to warn that cotton prices might suddenly drop; that pests might develop immunities to the chemicals; that the new hybrid seeds didn't always grow; or that much greater quantities of water would be needed to cultivate them. When all these disasters struck at once, as they did in 1999–2000, millions of farmers in South India were ruined. Their only option was to borrow money from the *aarthis*, or "money lenders" who had sold them the seeds and chemicals in the first place. In Andhra Pradesh alone, around 500 farmers committed suicide by drinking the useless insecticide, lying down to die amid their failed crops.

revenge attack for Rajiv's enforcement of the 1987 peace accord, which resulted in Indian troops being sent to fight Tamil separatist guerrillas.

Ripples from the war in Sri Lanka have also had a marked influence on political life in the Tamil Nadu, home to an estimated 60 million Tamil speakers. Following its resounding defeat in the wake of Rajiv's assassination, when it was accused of harbouring and training **separatist guerrillas** to fight the war, the **DMK**, the then dominant (Tamil nationalist) party has had to distance itself from the LTTE. Its increasingly high profile within central government also required it to adhere to New Delhi's "hands off" line. In the background, however, DMK ministers and parliament representatives in the capital have been able to exert influence over foreign policy, keeping Indian troops out of the war and banning pro-Tiger demonstrations. Tamil Nadu's previous Chief Minister, M. Karunanidhi, had an additional reason to downplay his party's connections with the LTTE. Through the late 1990s, he made several speeches insisting that the Tigers should not be seen as the only legitimate representatives of the Tamil people, hinting that he saw himself as a potential pan-Tamil leader if and when the north of Sri Lanka ever gained Independence. At the same time, Tamil nationalist leaders such as Karunanidhi cannot afford to overtly oppose the LTTE, who command huge popular support in Tamil Nadu, and thus considerable influence at election time. The current ruling party, the **AIADMK**, led by the maverick ex-film starlet **Jayalalitha** (see p.449), have consistently exploited this fact to kindle support, forming coalitions with more openly pro-Tiger nationalist parties and leaders.

The elections of 1998–99

With the demise of the Congress Party (and corresponding rise of the pro-Hindu, nationalist BJP) throughout the 1990s, politics at national level became increasingly fragmented. No longer dominated by a single party, the succession of short-lived governments in New Delhi tended to be formed by shaky coalitions, brought together by political expediency more than any common agenda. Thus regionalist parties such as the pro-Tamil DMK and AIADMK, who had for decades enjoyed massive support in their home state but wielded disproportionately little influence at national level, emerged as a potent new force.

The strength of this new political element was dramatically demonstrated in the wake of the 1998 national elections, won by a BJP-led coalition. To bring it down, Congress – now led by Sonia Gandhi, the Italian-born widow of the former prime minister Rajiv Gandhi – collaborated with Jayalalitha, leader of the AIADMK. When she pulled out of the BJP-led coalition, Prime Minister Vajpayee lost a vote of no confidence and was forced to call yet another general election in April 1999 – the third in three years.

At the start of the campaign, Congress hopes were high that with a Gandhi once again as party leader, it could revive the popular support lost after years of in-fighting and corruption scandals. Moreover, to compound the BJP's problems, Vajpayee's caretaker government was saddled with a worsening financial deficit and a welter of domestic difficulties. Events took an unexpected turn following a sudden and dramatic flare up in the long-standing border war between India and Pakistan in Kashmir. The conflict was contained, but Pakistan took a bloody nose from the encounter before Pak Premier, Nawaz Sharif, bowed to international pressure and withdrew his forces.

The wave of patriotism that swept India after the victory was a godsend for Vajpayee (cynics argued it may well have been the hidden policy behind the army's uncompromising response to the crisis). Riding high on the feel-good factor, his party inflicted the biggest defeat Congress had sustained since it first came to power in 1947. Vajpayee's majority was far from as large as he might have hoped, and the BJP-led National Democratic Alliance (NDA) coalition was fractured and tenuous, but Sonia's second election defeat seemed to herald, at last, the end of dynastic politics in India (in spite of the entrance on to the political stage of her charismatic 26-year-old daughter, Priyanka).

Having betrayed the former BJP government, Jayalalitha was capitulated into something of a political wilderness, with her party soundly beaten by BJP-led coalition that included the DMK, led by her arch rival, the then Chief Minister of Tamil Nadu, **M. Karunanidhi**. No longer a minister, she lacked protection against the raft of **corruption** charges dating from the period when she was the state's chief minister (1991–96). Finally, in October 2000, the High Court in Chennai (Madras) found her guilty of accepting bribes from businessmen to permit illegal construction projects, and issued a three-year suspended prison sentence. In the riots that followed 5000 demonstrators were arrested, as Jayalalitha's supporters set fire to a bus full of students, killing three innocent women – an incident filmed and broadcast by Star TV news.

The new millennium

To rub salt in Jayalalitha's wounds, her appeal against the conviction was quashed by the High Court of Chennai in April 2001, casting doubts on whether she would be able to run in the state assembly **elections** the following month (Indian electoral law debars candidates who've been sentenced to a prison term of more than two years). However, the ruling only seems to have intensified her desire to get even with her arch adversary, Karunanidhi. Despite having her nomination papers rejected by the election officials, "Jaya", as the redoubtable ex-starlet is known to her fans, announced she would run anyway, expecting that the corruption charges could be overturned at a later date. In the run up to the election, her AIADMK-led coalition comprised the Tamil Maanila Congress, the (overtly pro-Tamil Tiger) Pattali Makkal Katchi (or PMK), two communist parties and two Muslim parties.

From the outset, the thrust of Jayalalitha's campaign was to personally target Karunanidhi, now heading a sixteen-party coalition dominated by the DMK and BJP. Speeches appealing to the memory of her former lover, matinee idol and charismatic chief minister, the late M.G. Ramchandran (aka "MGR"; see p.449), depicted her as a lone woman persecuted by a regime hell-bent on keeping out of public life. On several occasions she even vowed that if she were re-elected she would incarcerate Karunanidhi in the same cell she'd been locked up in, and make him eat off the same tin plate. Jayalalitha's **vendetta** seemed to capture the imagination of Tamil voters, who returned her coalition with a landslide majority. The new chief minister wasted no time in settling scores with her opponents, ordering Karunanidhi's arrest on corruption charges, along with that of around one thousand of his supporters. Television audiences across the country were shocked by film footage of the 78-year-old former CM being roughly pulled down the stairs of his house by police and bundled into a van by police. The indignity of the arrest, followed by that of two federal cabinet ministers who tried to intervene, caused a political storm in Delhi. The governor of the state, who had been criticized for allowing Jayalalitha to run despite her criminal record, was sacked and pressure applied to secure Karunanidhi's release.

This came a few days later (having been allegedly granted "on humanitarian grounds"), but the ageing former premier will almost certainly have to face the charges that he accepted bribes from road constructors in Chennai while in power. As this book went to print, India was bracing itself for violent repercussions in the South. One Tamil farmer had already burned himself to death in protest at Karunanidhi's arrest, and pundits were predicting a 1975 Emergency-style purge of Jayalalitha's political opponents. A high-ranking BJP government official, despatched by prime minister Vajpayee from New Delhi to investigate the situation, reported that "no law of the land prevails in Tamil Nadu".

Recent political life in the South may been dominated by the power struggle in Tamil Nadu, but for millions of villagers, the start of the third millennium will forever be associated with the catastrophic **tropical storms** that ripped across the region during the monsoons. In 2000, record rainfalls wrought havoc in the southern state of Andhra Pradesh. An estimated 12 million were left marooned or homeless as river levels rose by as much as 4m in places. With transport and communications at a standstill for weeks, food distribution and rescue efforts all but ground to a halt. Riots broke out in camps set up by the army for **flood** victims, as supplies of food and plastic sheets ran out.

Ironically, only the previous year the chief ministers of Tamil Nadu and Karnataka had been locked in a bitter dispute about **water shortages**. Karnataka had repeatedly withheld supplies of water on the Cavery River, guaranteed by the terms of an accord forged by Prime Minister Vajpayee (a treaty which his party waved as a vote winner in the 1999 elections, and whose failure was a huge source of embarrassment for the BJP generally and the prime minister in particular).

Many commentators at the time regarded the fallout from the "**River Dispute**", as the Kaveri controversy became known, as symptomatic of the **regionalism** that has been on the rise in the South over the past few years. The inexorable growth of parties such as the DMK, AIADMK and Telegu Desam has been accompanied by a marked weakening of New Delhi's grip. Incapable of raising adequate tax revenue, and rotten to its core with corruption, the centre no longer commands the power it used to. Chronic political instability has also taken its toll. The absence of consistent policies has meant that big business and the affluent classes have increasingly had to look after themselves, and provided a spur for more radical nationalist political parties, particularly in the countryside, where few of the improvements in life vaunted by state governments have made much impact.

As it struggles to balance the ambitions of its privileged elite with the basic needs of its poor, Indian society at the start of the twenty-first century is rife with ironies. The country recently chosen by Bill Gates as the site of Microsoft's new Hi-Tech City in Hyderabad, capable of launching satellites and nuclear rockets, is unable to provide clean drinking water, adequate nutrition and basic education for millions of its inhabitants. Its capacity to close this yawning gap will depend on the extent to which the India's politicians are, over the coming years, able to deliver stable government, and curb the corruption and self-interest that have come to dominate public life, particularly in the South.

Religions

This great and ancient nation was once the fountain of human light, the apex of human civilization, the exemplar of courage and humanity, the perfection of good government and settled society, the mother of all religions, the teacher of all wisdom and philosophy.

Shri Aurobindo (1907)

Long regarded as the bastion of Hindu values, South India boasts many of the finest, oldest and most extravagant temples in the country. The devotion displayed by the millions of pilgrims is just the most obvious aspect of the fact that Hinduism permeates every element of life here, from social structures to education and politics. The vast pantheon of Hindu deities is manifest everywhere, from soaring temple gateways to *bidi* packets and the little mobile shrines erected in houses, buses, cars and shops.

The South is also home to a substantial Muslim community; since the twelfth century, Muslims have settled in the South as traders and rulers, constructing pearl-domed mosques throughout the region. Today, Muslims are largely concentrated in the major cities and Kerala. Christians, believed to have been living in South India since the first century AD, have developed distinct denominations, and worship in buildings that range from simple thatched huts to the grand basilicas and churches erected by the Portuguese, French and British. Although Jains and Buddhists are now a minute fraction of the southern population, several magnificent temples stand testament to an impressive presence in the past. The once influential Keralan Jews are now a pitifully small group, originally attracted here from both the Arab world and Europe by the rich pickings of the Malabar Coast and its spice belts, but their influence can still be strongly felt in Fort Cochin (Kochi). Mumbai features a rapidly dwindling society of Zoroastrian Parsis (see p.672); both groups continue to intermarry to preserve their unique heritage and identity.

Hinduism

Contemporary **Hindu society** – which represents over 85 percent of South Indians – is the product of several thousand years of evolution and assimilation. The South has played a vital role in the development if Hinduism in the subcontinent, producing reformers like **Shankara**, who travelled throughout India in the ninth century, bringing about sweeping reforms by utilizing Buddhist models to establish a revitalized Hindu monastic order that is still in use today. Later, in the thirteenth century, in the face of a Muslim onslaught on Hindu institutions, South Indian **Vaishnavas** (worshippers of Vishnu and his incarnations) were pivotal in the development of Krishna worship, establishing centres in Krishna's mythological homeland of Braj, to the south of Delhi. Ever since, Vaishnavism has been at the heart of South Indian Hindu life.

The Hindu religion boasts no founder or prophet, no single creed and no single prescribed practice or doctrine; it takes in hundreds of gods, goddesses, beliefs and practices, and widely variant cults and philosophies. Some Hindu deities are recognized by only two or three villages; others, such as Vishnu and Shiva, are popular right across the subcontinent, with devotion tending to

Vishnu

The chief function of Vishnu, "pervader", is to keep the world in order, preserving, restoring and protecting. With four arms holding a conch, discus, lotus and mace, Vishnu is blue-skinned, and often shaded by a serpent, or resting on its coils, afloat on an ocean. He is usually seen alongside his half-man-half-eagle vehicle, Garuda.

Vaishnavites, often distinguishable by two vertical lines on their foreheads, recognize Vishnu as supreme lord, and hold that he has manifested himself on earth nine times. These incarnations, or *avatars*, have been as fish (Matsya), tortoise (Kurma), boar (Varaha), man-lion (Narsingh), dwarf (Vamana), axe-wielding brahmin (Parasuram), Rama, Krishna and Balaram (though some say that the Buddha is the ninth *avatar*). Vishnu's future descent to earth as Kalki, the saviour who will come to restore purity and destroy the wicked, is eagerly awaited.

The most important *avatars* are Krishna and Rama, star of the epic *Ramayana* (see p.721). Krishna is the hero of the *Bhagavad Gita*, in which he proposes three routes to salvation (*moksha*): selfless action (*karmayoga*), knowledge (*jnana*) and devotion to god (*bhakti*), and explains that *moksha* is attainable in this life, even without asceticism and renunciation. This appealed to all castes, as it denied the necessity of ritual and officiating brahmin priests, and evolved into the popular *bhakti* cult that legitimized love of God as a means to *moksha*, and also found expression in emotional songs of the quest for union with God. Through *bhakti*, Krishna's role was extended, and he assumed different faces: most popularly he is the playful cowherd who seduces and dances with cowgirls (*gopis*), giving each the illusion that she is his only lover. He is also pictured as a small, chubby, mischievous baby, known for his butter-stealing exploits, who inspires tender motherly love in women. Like Vishnu, Krishna is blue, and is often shown dancing and playing the flute.

Vishnu is worshipped especially in the form of Lord Venkateshvara at Tirumala in Andhra Pradesh and the huge popularity of this pilgrimage centre is largely due to his role as the granter of wishes, leading many thousands to his shrine daily to pray for favours.

Shiva

Shaivism, the cult of Shiva, was also inspired by *bhakti*, requiring selfless love from devotees in a quest for divine communion, but Shiva has never been incarnate on earth. He is presented in many different aspects, such as Nataraja, Lord of the Dance, Mahadev, Great God, and Maheshvar, Divine Lord, source of all knowledge. Though he does have several terrible forms, his role extends beyond that of destroyer, and he is revered as the source of the whole universe.

Shiva is often depicted with four or five faces, holding a trident, draped with serpents, and bearing a third eye in his forehead. In temples, he is identified with the *lingam*, or phallic symbol, resting in the *yoni*, a representation of female sexuality. Whether as statue or *lingam*, Shiva is guarded by his bull-vehicle, Nandi, and often accompanied by a consort, who also assumes various forms and is looked upon as the vital energy, *shakti*, that empowers him. Their erotic exploits were a favourite sculptural subject between the ninth and twelfth centuries.

Shiva is the object of popular veneration all over India; devotees are identifiable by the horizontal lines (between one and three) painted on their foreheads. In particular, Shaivite ascetics worship Shiva in the aspect of the terrible Bhairav. The ascetics renounce family and caste ties and perform extreme meditative and yogic practices. Many, though not all, smoke *ganja*, Shiva's favourite herb; all see renunciation and realization of God as the key to *moksha*. Some ascetic practices enter the realm of tantrism, in which confrontation with all that's impure, such as alcohol, death and sex, is used to merge the sacred and the profane, and bring about the profound realization that Shiva is omnipresent.

Ganesh

Tubby and smiling, elephant-headed Ganesh, the first son of Shiva and Parvati, is invoked before every undertaking (except funerals). Seated on a throne or lotus, his image is often placed above temple gateways, in shops and in houses. In his four arms he holds a conch, discus, bowl of sweets (or club) and a water lily, and he's always attended by his vehicle, a rat. Credited with writing the *Mahabharata* as it was dictated by the sage Vyasa, Ganesh is regarded by many as the god of learning, the lord of success, prosperity and peace. In the South he is often known as Vinayaka and as such there is a huge festival, *Vinayakapuja*, in his honour in late monsoon, where he is thrown into the sea; the celebration in Mumbai is the most ostentatious and famous.

Other gods and goddesses

Pictured as a triumphant youth, bedecked with flowers, images of Murugan, son of Shiva and his consort Pavarti, are particularly common in Tamil Nadu and rural Kerala (see box on p.543). He provides protection from evil and negative actions, which makes him a popular family deity. It is possible that he derives from a pre-Aryan fertility god.

Another son of Shiva, this time from a peculiar mythological union with Vishnu (see box on p.656), Ayappa is also associated with the role of protection, and his shrine in northern Kerala is a huge magnet to pilgrims, making the black-clad, mostly male, devotees a familiar sight. The common depiction of Ayappa riding a tiger with an entourage of leopards denotes his victory over evil.

Durga, the fiercest of the female deities, is an aspect of Shiva's consort, Parvati (also known as Uma), who is remarkable only for her beauty and fidelity. In whatever form, Shiva's consort is *shakti*, the fundamental energy that spurs him into action. Among Durga's many aspects, each a terrifying goddess eager to slay demons, are Chamunda, Kali and Muktakeshi, but in all her forms she is Mahadevi (Great Goddess). Statues show her with ten arms, holding the head of a demon, a spear, and other weapons; she tramples demons underfoot, or dances upon Shiva's body. A garland of skulls drapes her neck, and her tongue hangs from her mouth, dripping with blood – a particularly gruesome sight on pictures of Kali. In all her temples, animal sacrifices are a crucial element of worship, to satisfy her thirst for blood and deter her ruthless anger.

The comely goddess Lakshmi, usually shown sitting or standing on a lotus flower, and sometimes called Padma (lotus), is the embodiment of loveliness, grace and charm, and the goddess of prosperity and wealth. Vishnu's consort, she appears in different aspects alongside each of his *avatars*; the most important are Sita, wife of Rama, and Radha, Krishna's favourite *gopi*. In many temples she is shown as one with Vishnu, in the form of Lakshmi Narayan.

Though some legends claim that his mother was Ganga, or even Agni, Karttikeya is popularly believed to be the second son of Shiva and Parvati. Primarily a god of war, he was popular among the northern Guptas, who worshipped him as Skanda, and the southern Chalukyas, for whom he was Subrahmanya. Usually shown with six faces, and standing upright with bow and arrow, Karttikeya is commonly petitioned by those wishing for male offspring.

India's great monkey god Hanuman features in the *Ramayana* as Rama's chief aide in the fight against the demon king of Lanka. Depicted as a giant monkey clasping a mace, Hanuman is the deity of acrobats and wrestlers, but is also seen as Rama and Sita's greatest devotee, and an author of Sanskrit grammar. As his representatives, monkeys find sanctuary in temples across southern India.

The most beautiful Hindu goddess, Saraswati, the wife of Brahma – with her flawless milk-white complexion – sits or stands on a water lily or peacock, playing a lute, *sitar* or *vina*. Associated with the Saraswati River, mentioned in the *Rig Veda*,

CONTEXTS | Religions

continues over

she is seen as a goddess of purification and fertility, but is also revered as the inventor of writing, the queen of eloquence and goddess of music.

Closely linked with the planet Saturn, Sani is feared for his destructive powers. His image, a black statue with protruding blood-red tongue, is often found on street corners; strings of green chillies and lemon are hung in shops and houses each Saturday (*Saniwar*) to ward off his evil influences.

Mention must also be made here of the sacred cow, Khamdenu, who receives devotion through the respect shown to all cows, left to amble through streets and temples all over southern India. The origin of the cow's sanctity is uncertain; some myths record that Brahma created cows at the same time as brahmins, to provide *ghee* (clarified butter) for use in priestly ceremonies. To this day cow dung and urine are used to purify houses (in fact the urine keeps insects at bay), and the killing or harming of cows by any Hindu is a grave offence. The cow is often referred to as mother of the gods, and each part of its body is significant: its horns symbolize the gods, its face the sun and moon, its shoulders Agni (god of fire) and its legs the Himalayas. Hindus touch the hip of a cow to give them fertility and prosperity.

border on fanaticism in the South. Hindus (from the Persian word for Indians) call their beliefs and practices **dharma**, which embraces natural and moral law to define a way of living in harmony with a natural order, while achieving personal goals and meeting the requirements of society.

Early developments

In the second millennium BC, the foundations of Hinduism as a religion and way of life were laid down by the Aryans, semi-nomads who had wandered into the Indus valley in the North. They brought a belief in gods associated with the elements, including **Agni**, the god of fire and sacrifice, **Surya**, the sun god, and **Indra**, the chief god. Most of these deities faded in later times, but Indra is still regarded as the father of the gods, and Surya was widely worshipped until the medieval period.

Aryan beliefs were set out in the **Vedic** scriptures as they had been "heard" (*shruti*) by "seers" (*rishis*). Transmitted orally for centuries, they were finally written, in Sanskrit, between 1000 BC and 500 AD. The earliest were the *Samhitas*, or hymns; the *Brahmanas*, sacrificial texts, and *Aranyakas*, or "forest treatises" came later.

The earliest and most important *Samhita*, the **Rig Veda**, contains hymns to deities and *devas* (divine powers), and is supplemented by other books detailing rituals and prayers for ceremonial use. The **Brahmanas** stress correct ritual performance, drawing heavily on concepts of **purity and pollution** that persist today and concentrating on sacrificial rites. Pedantic attention to ritual soon supplanted the importance of the *devas*, and they were further undermined by a search for a single cosmic power thought to be their source, eventually conceived of as **Brahma**, the absolute creator, personified from earlier mentions of Brahman, an impersonal principle of cosmic unity.

The **Aranyakas** focused on this all-powerful godhead, and reached their final stage in the **Upanishads**, which describe in beautiful and emotive verse the mystic experience of unity of the soul (*atman*) with Brahma, ideally attained through asceticism, renunciation of worldly values and meditation. In the *Upanishads* the concepts of **samsara**, a cyclic round of death and rebirth characterized by suffering and perpetuated by desire, and **moksha**, liberation from *samsara*, became firmly rooted. Fundamental aspects of the Hindu world view, both are accepted by all but a handful of Hindus today, along with the belief in **karma**, the belief that one's present position in society is determined by the effect of one's previous actions in this and past lives.

Philosophical trends

The complications presented by Hinduism's view of deities, *samsara*, *atman* (the human soul) and *moksha* naturally encouraged philosophical debate, and led eventually to the formation of six schools of thought, known as the **Darshanas**. Each presented a different exposition of the true nature of *moksha* and how to attain it.

Foremost among these was the **Advaita Vedanta** school of **Shankara** (c.788–850 AD), who interpreted Hinduism as pure monotheism verging on monism (the belief that all is one: in this case, one with God). Drawing on Upanishadic writings, he claimed that they identified the essence of the human soul with that of God (*tat tvam asi*, "that thou art"), and that all else – the phenomenal world and all *devas* – is an illusion (*maya*) created by God. Shankara is revered as saint-philosopher at the twelve **jyotirlinga**, the sacred Shaivite sites associated with the unbounded *lingam* of light, which as a manifestation of Shiva once persuaded both Brahma and Vishnu to acknowledge Shiva's supremacy.

Another important *Darshana* centred around the age-old practice of **yoga** (literally "the action of yoking [to] another"), elucidated by **Patanjali** (second century BC) in his *Yoga Sutras*. Interpreting yoga as the yoking of mind and body, or the yoking of the mind with God, Patanjali detailed various practices, which used in combination may lead to an understanding of the fundamental **unity** of all things. The most common form of yoga known in the West is *hatha-yoga*, whereby the body and its vital energies is brought under control through physical positions and breathing methods, with results said to range from attaining a calm mind to being able to fly through the air, enter other bodies or become invisible. Other practices include *mantra-yoga*, the recitation of formulas and meditation on mystical diagrams (mandalas), *bhakti-yoga* (devotion), *jnana-yoga* (knowledge) and *raja-yoga* (royal) – the highest form of yoga when the mind is absorbed in God.

Popular deities

Alongside the *Dharma Shashtras* and *Dharma Shutras*, the most important works of the *smriti* tradition, thought to have been completed by the fourth century AD at the latest, were the **Puranas**, long mythological stories focused on the Vedic gods and their heroic actions, and Hinduism's two great epics, the **Mahabharata** and the **Ramayana** (see box p.721). Through these texts, the main gods and goddesses became firmly embedded in the religion. Alongside **Brahma**, the creator, **Vishnu** was acknowledged as the preserver, and **Shiva** ("auspicious, benign"), referred to in the *Rig Veda* as Rudra, was recognized for his destructive powers. The three are often depicted in a trinity, *tri-murti*, but in time Brahma's importance declined, and Shiva and Vishnu became the most popular deities. Nearly all Hindus belong to sects that actively worship Shiva or Vishnu in one form or another (see box on p.656).

Other gods and goddesses who came alive in the mythology of the *Puranas* – each depicted in human or semi-human form and accompanied by an animal "**vehicle**" – are still venerated across South India. River goddesses, ancestors, guardians of particular places and protectors against disease and natural disaster are as central to village life as the major deities.

Caste and social structure

The stratification of Hindu society is rooted in the **Dharma Shashtras** and **Dharma Shutras**, scriptures written from "memory" (*smriti*) at the same time as the *Vedas*. These defined four hierarchical classes, or **varnas**, each assigned specific religious and social duties known as **varnashradharma**, and established Aryans as the highest social class. The **Aryans** already had a class system in place before reaching the subcontinent; their nobility was known as the *kshatra* and the ordinary tribesman as the *vish*. However, their contact with darker-skinned people known as the **Dasas** caused them concern about racial purity, resulting in a division of society based on **varna** – literally "colour" – a unique institution of **racism** that has lasted over three thousand years. In descending order the *varnas* are: **brahmins** (priests and teachers), **kshatryas** (rulers and warriors), **vaishyas** (merchants and cultivators) and **shudras** (menials). The first three classes, known as "twice-born"– initially to distinguish those born in their native place and then born again during their induction as an Aryan – are distinguished by a sacred thread worn from the ceremony of initiation, and are granted full access to religious texts and rituals. Below all four categories, groups whose jobs involve contact with dirt or death (such as undertakers, leather workers and cleaners) were classified as **Untouchables**. Though discrimination against Untouchables is now a criminal offence, in part thanks to the campaigns of Gandhi – he renamed Untouchables *Harijans*, "Children of God" – the lowest stratum of society has by no means disappeared. Today, the word "**dalit**" is the politically correct term to use when talking about this class. Children, widows and ascetics remained outside the *varna* system.

When at the end of the Vedic age new ideas threatened the absolute power of the priesthood, and religions such as Buddhism and Jainism preached equality, the priesthood responded with the manuscript **Manu-smriti** (the words of Manu, the original man, remembered). Composed by a succession of brahmin authors some time around the third century BC, *Manu-smriti* laid out the *varna* system in detail and defined the role and tasks of each *varna*, as well as the strict interaction between each group. The moral grounds laid out for the system of division was that one should perform every task well and with pride rather than to try and take on someone else's tasks. This argument, combined with **karma** (the result of one's deeds), and the concept of rebirth which developed from the late Vedic period onwards, proposes that you are what you are born. Through good deeds you may have the fortune of being reborn at a higher level in the next life.

These ethics are also carried through to the **Bhagavad Gita**, where Aryan beliefs are protected against reformers and non-believers by singing the virtues of each of the four divisions – wisdom for the brahmin, valour for the *kshatriya*, industry for the *vaishya* and service for the *shudra*. Interaction between the divisions had become clearly defined. *Manu-smriti*, which continues to act as the foundation of **Hindu law**, lays down the rules of purity – for example, a *shudra*'s shadow may never cross a brahmin and if it does the brahmin will have to perform a ritual to purify himself.

Within the four *varnas*, social status is further defined by **caste**, which refers to numerous social groupings within Hindu society. When the Portuguese first came to India in the sixteenth century, they came across these divisions and referred to them as "*castas*" (tribes, clans or families), a term which led to the word "*caste*". Caste lays restrictions on all aspects of life from food consumption, religious obligations and contact with other castes, to the choice of marriage partners. Those that belong to other faiths have been given a caste status to clarify their position in the general social hierarchy; Christians in Kerala have actually adopted this system of classification and developed a caste system of their own.

Within the broader caste identity, there are sub-groups known as **jati**, which classify individuals by family and precise occupation (for example, a *vaishya* may be a jewellery-seller, cloth merchant, cowherd or farmer). There are almost three thousand *jatis*; the divisions and restrictions they have enforced have become, time and time again, the substance of reform movements and the target of critics. Whereas *varna* and caste is fixed from birth to death, there is a degree of flexibility to a *jati* identity, and some have a tendency to be upwardly mobile, in which case the members try and assume that ethics, manners and ways of the *jati* group they would like to be. Their tenure at this new rung in the hierarchy depends solely on whether the other *jatis* are willing to accept their new position. Despite this, Hindus still tend to marry members of the same caste and *jati* – marrying someone of a different caste often results in ostracism from both family and caste, leaving the couple stranded in a society where caste affiliation takes primacy over all other aspects of individual identity.

Castes have distinctive patterns of intra-caste relationships within themselves while at the same time interacting with other castes along strict rules of behaviour. Although castes maintain their structural place in society through both interaction and segregation, there is an element of fraternity, especially with castes close to each other in the hierarchy. Horizontal caste relations are limited by the diversity of India's geography and culture; while *varna* has its roots in theology, caste and *jati* is able to adapt itself to its local environment. Each region has such strong ritual and linguistic traits that would mean that a brahmin in Goa is unable to directly relate to a brahmin in Tamil Nadu.

The left hand versus the right

Literature suggests that caste came late to Tamil country, in about the ninth century. As Tamil society was fundamentally agrarian, there were few families who could claim to be *kshatriyas* (warriors) and so most of the population was divided between brahmins, *shudras* and untouchables. The largest group among the Tamils, the *shudras*, divided itself into a further two groups, the left-handed and the right-handed castes – the Idangai and the Valangai. The left and right hands allude to which hand was considered pure by either group (in most of Hindu India, the right hand is the pure hand while the left is menial). These two seemingly innocuous divisions have been at odds with each other ever since their inception, leading to bitter conflict and rivalry. The left-hand group includes craftsmen, weavers, some cultivators, cowherds and leather workers; the right-hand one includes traders, most cultivators, some weavers, musicians, barbers, washermen, potters and labourers.

Practice

A Hindu has three aims in life: **dharma**, fulfilling one's duty to family and caste and acquiring religious merit (*punya*) through right living; **artha**, the lawful making of wealth; and **karma**, desire and satisfaction. The primary concern of most Hindus is to reduce bad *karma* and acquire merit (*punya*), by honest and charitable living within the restrictions imposed by caste and worship, in the hope of attaining a higher status in rebirth.

These goals are linked with the four traditional stages in life. The first is as a child and student, devoted to learning from parents and a guru. Next comes the stage of householder, expected to provide for a family and raise sons. That accomplished, he or she may then take up a life of celibacy and retreat into the forest to meditate alone, and finally renounce all possessions to become a homeless ascetic, hoping to achieve the ultimate goal of *moksha*. According to ancient custom, the life of a high-class Hindu man progressed through four distinct phases – *brahmachari* (celibate) following his initiation or "thread ceremony", *grhastha* (householder), *vanaprashta* (forest dweller) following middle age and after his children have grown up, and finally, *sannyasin* (a renunciate). However, in practice, few follow this course in life and the *vanaprashta* is no more; in general, life is meant to progress along ordered lines from initiation (for high caste Hindus) through education, career and marriage. A small number of Hindus who follow this ideal life, including some women, assume the final stage as **sannyasis**, saffron-clad **sadhus** who wander throughout India, begging for food and retreating to isolated caves, forests and hills to meditate. They're a common feature in most Indian towns, and many stay for long periods in particular temples. Not all have raised families: some assume the life of a *sadhu* at an early age as a *chella* (pupil or disciple) to an older *sadhu*.

However, strict rules still address the dharmic principles of **purity** and **pollution**, the most obvious of them requiring high-caste Hindus to limit their contact with potentially polluting lower castes. All bodily excretions are polluting (hence the strange looks Westerners receive when they blow their noses and return the handkerchief to their pocket or request toilet paper). Above all else, **water** is the agent of purification, used in ablutions before prayer, and revered in all rivers, especially Ganga (the Ganges).

In most Hindu homes and businesses, a small shrine is set up with pictures of chosen deities, and scriptures are read. Outside the home, worship takes place in temples, and consists of **puja**, or devotion to God. This may be a simple act of prayer, but more commonly it is a complex process when the god's image is circumambulated, offered flowers, rice, sugar and incense, and anointed with water, milk or sandalwood paste (which is usually done on behalf of the devotee by the temple priest, the *pujari*). The aim in puja is to take **darshan** – glimpse the god – and thus receive his or her blessing. Whether devotees simply worship the deity in prayer, or make requests – for a healthy crop, a son, good results in exams, a vigorous monsoon or a cure for illness – they always leave the temple with *prasad*, an offering of food or flowers from the holy sanctuary, given to them by the *pujaris*.

Communal worship and get-togethers en route to pilgrimage sites are celebrated with *kirtan* or *bhajan*, singing of hymns, perhaps verses in praise of Krishna taken from the *Bhagavad Purana*, or repetitive cries of "Jay Shankar!" (Praise to Shiva). Temple ceremonies are conducted in Sanskrit by *pujaris* who tend the image in daily rituals that symbolically wake, bathe, feed and dress the god, and finish each day by preparing the god for sleep. The most elaborate is the evening ritual, **arthi**, when lamps are lit, blessed in the sanctuary, and passed around devotees amid the clanging of drums, gongs and cymbals. In many villages, shrines to *devatas*, village deities who function as protectors and may bring disaster if neglected, are more important than temples.

Each of the great stages in life – birth, **initiation** (when boys of the three twice-born castes are invested with a sacred thread, and a mantra is whispered into their ear by their guru), marriage, death and cremation – are marked by fervent prayer, energetic celebration and feasting. The most significant event in a Hindu's life is **marriage**, which symbolizes ritual purity, and for women is so important that it takes the place of initiation. Feasting, dancing and singing among the bride and groom's families, usually lasting for a week or more before and after the marriage, are the order of the day all over India. The actual marriage is consecrated when the couple walks seven times round a sacred fire, accompanied by sacred verses read by an officiating brahmin. Relatives pour in from all over the country and abroad to witness not just the union of man and wife, but also to reaffirm the group's social standing. Traditionally, Hindu marriage customs bind caste groups together, sometimes through inter-caste marriage, where one caste marries another. Today, most Hindu marriages traditionally involve the parents, who negotiate or even insist on the match; love marriages are increasingly common, especially in urban areas, but still tend to depend on parental consent and collusion.

The age-old Indian tradition of giving **dowry**, a gift of money, jewellery and goods from the bride's family to the groom's, is now officially illegal but still widely demanded and invariably given, for fear that a daughter's welfare will be in jeopardy if it is withheld. Dowry is prevalent in both Hindu and Christian communities, and is as much practised by the upper and middle class-es as it is by the poor, but for the latter it can represent an endless cycle of sav-ing and debt with each new generation. Among more wealthy and cosmopol-itan families, scooters, TVs and holidays are now the essential elements of a modern dowry. As it is a "gift", dowry is undeclared income, and the groom's family can place relentless pressure on the bride's family to continue providing "gifts" long after the wedding. The abuse, torture and burning of wives whose family provides a dowry that is below expectations is still all too common, especially in rural areas where there is little female literacy and the new brides are not aware of their rights under the constitution. Despite active opposition by progressive women's groups, dowry is a practice that is too deeply ingrained in Indian culture to easily eradicate, and the government seems unable to put a stop to it.

As a rule, Hindu society frowns upon **divorce**, but with increasing modern-ization, especially among the middle classes, it has become more common. Hindu law does not recognize divorce, and the legal procedure is relatively complicated.

For Hindus, **death** is an essential process in an endless cycle of rebirth in the grand illusion (*maya*) until the individual attains enlightenment and freedom (*moksha*) from *samskara* (transmigration). Hindus cremate their dead except for young children, whom they bury or cast into a river. The eldest son is entrust-ed to light the funeral pyre and the ashes are scattered, usually on a sacred river, such as the Ganges in northern India. Rites after death can be lengthy and complicated according to each Hindu community, and the role of the *purohit* (priest) is indispensable. **Widows** traditionally wear white and, according to ancient Hindu belief, are considered to be outside society.

Pilgrimage

The Hindu calendar is jam-packed with **festivals** devoted to deities, re-enacting mythological stories and commemorating holy sites. The grandest festivals are held at places made holy by association with gods, goddesses, miracles and great teachers, or at sacred rivers and mountains; throughout the year these are all important **pilgrimage** sites, visited by devotees eager to receive *darshan*, glimpse the world of the gods, and attain merit. The journey, or *yatra*, to a pilgrimage site is every bit as significant as reaching the sacred location, and bands of Hindus (particularly *sadhus*) often walk from site to site. Modern transport, however, has made things easier, and every state lays on pilgrimage tours, when buses and Jeeps full of chanting families roar from one temple to another, filling up with religious souvenirs as they go.

South India has many important sites. The Venkateshvara temple atop Tirumala Hill in Andhra Pradesh claims to draw more pilgrims than any other holy place in the world. Every year, another two million or so devotees head up to the Ayappa Forest Temple at Sabarimala in Kerala. At Kanniyakumari, the southern tip of India, the waters of the Indian Ocean, the Bay of Bengal and the Arabian Sea are thought to merge at an auspicious point. Pilgrimages here are often combined with visits to the great temples of Tamil Nadu, where Shaivite and Vaishnavite saints established cults and India's largest temples were constructed. Madurai, Thanjavur, Chidambaram and Srirangam are major pilgrimage centres, representing the pinnacle of the architectural development that began at Mamallapuram. Their festivals often involve the tugging of deities on vast wooden chariots through the streets, lively and noisy affairs that make for an unforgettable experience. As well as specific temples sacred to particular gods, historical sites, such as the former Vijayanagar capital at Hampi, remain magnets for pilgrims. More than a common ideology, it is this map of sacred geography, entwined with popular mythology, that unites hundreds of millions of Hindus, who have also been brought together in nationalistic struggles, particularly in response to Christian missionaries and Muslim and British domination.

Islam

Across South India, **Muslims** – some ten percent of the total population – form a significant presence in almost every town, city and village. In most of the southern states, the percentage is slightly lower, the exception being Kerala, where nearly a quarter of the populace are Muslims, and are concentrated in fishing and trading communities right along the Malabar coast. The only major southern city with a distinctly Islamic flavour is Hyderabad in Andhra Pradesh, although Mumbai and Chennai also boast well established Muslim quarters.

The belief in only one god, **Allah**, the condemnation of idol worship and the observance of strict dietary laws and specific festivals sets Muslims apart from their Hindu neighbours, with whom they have coexisted for centuries, although not always peaceably. Such differences have helped fuel communal tensions, most notably during Partition in 1947, and more recently in the violent wake of the destruction of the Babri Masjid in Ayodhya in Uttar Pradesh in 1992. Although most of southern India managed to avoid the worst excesses of the early 1990s, Mumbai became a violent bloodbath, an experience documented in the magnificent film, *Bombay*, directed by M. Ratnam.

The origin and development of Islam

Islam, "submission to God", was founded by **Mohammed** (570–632 AD), who was regarded as the last in a succession of prophets, and who transmitted God's final and perfected revelation to mankind through the writings of the divinely revealed "recitation", the **Koran** (Qur'an). The Koran is the authoritative scripture of Islam that sets down the basics of Islamic belief: that there is one god, Allah (though he is also attributed with 99 beautiful names), and his prophet is Mohammed. The true beginning of Islam is dated at 622 AD, when Mohammed and his followers, exiled from Mecca, made the **hijra**, or migration, north to Yathrib, later known as Medina, "City of the Prophet". The *hijra* marks the start of the Islamic lunar calendar; the Gregorian year 1995 is for Muslims 1416 AH (*Anno Hijra*).

From Medina, Mohammed ordered raids on caravans heading for Mecca, and led his community in battles against the Meccans, inspired by *jihad*, or "striving" on behalf of God and Islam. This concept of holy war was the driving force behind the incredible expansion of Islam – by 713 Muslims had settled as far west as Spain, and on the banks of the Indus in the east. When **Mecca** was peacefully surrendered to Mohammed in 630, he cleared the sacred shrine, the Ka'ba, of idols, and proclaimed it the pilgrimage centre of Islam.

Mohammed was succeeded as leader of the *umma*, the Islamic community, by Abu Bakr, the prophet's representative, or Caliph, the first in a line of Caliphs who led the orthodox community until the eleventh century AD. However, a schism soon emerged when the third Caliph, Uthman, was assassinated by followers of Ali, Mohammed's son-in-law, in 656 AD. This new sect, calling themselves **Shi'as**, "partisans" of Ali, looked to Ali and his successors, infallible *Imams*, as leaders of the *umma* until 878 AD, and thereafter replaced their religious authority with a body of scholars, the *ulema*.

By the second century after the *hijra* (ninth century AD), orthodox, or **Sunni**, Islam had assumed the form in which it endures today. A collection of traditions about the prophet, **Hadith**, became the source for ascertaining the **Sunna**, customs, of Mohammed. From the Koran and the Sunna, seven major **articles of belief** were laid down: belief in one God, in angels as his messengers, in prophets (including Jesus and Moses), in the Koran, in the doctrine of predestination by God, in the Day of Judgement, and in the bodily resurrection of all people on this day. Religious practice was also standardized under the Muslim law, **Sharia**, in the **Five Pillars of Islam**. The first "pillar" is the confession of faith, *shahada*, that "There is no god but God, and Mohammed is his messenger." The other four are: prayer (*salat*) five times daily, almsgiving (*zakat*), fasting (*saum*), especially during the month of Ramadan and, if possible, pilgrimage (*hajj*) to Mecca, the ultimate goal of every practising Muslim.

Islam in South India

The first Muslims to settle in India were traders who arrived on the south coast in the seventh century, probably in search of timber for shipbuilding. Later, in 711, Muslims entered Sind, in the northwest, to take action against Hindu pirates, and dislodged the Hindu government. Their presence, however, was short-lived. Much more significant was the invasion of North India, first under **Mahmud of Ghazni**, who in the spirit of *jihad*, engaged in a war against infidels and idolaters, then under the Turkish **sultanates** from the twelfth century on. It was the powerful **Moghuls** (see p.644) who succeeded them and pushed Islam deep into central and northern India, although the South remained largely unconquered.

The Muslims of the Malabar Coast and especially Kerala owe their roots not to migration from central Asia, but to the long history of trade and interaction with the Arab world. These Muslims of the **Moplah** community have nurtured a unique heritage alongside their Hindu and Christian neighbours. More recently, returning expatriate workers from the Gulf have helped to inject new wealth into the Moplah community and provide a facelift to towns like Kozhikode.

Many of the Muslims who settled in South India intermarried with Hindus, Buddhists and Jains, and the community spread. A further factor in its growth was the arrival of the **Sufis**, whose proselitizing missions in what is now northern Karnataka intensified with the rise of the Deccani Sulltans in the fourteenth century. Their teachings emphasized abstinence and self-denial in service to God, and stressed the attainment of inner knowledge of God through meditation and mystical experience. The Sufi teachings particularly appealed to Shaivites and Vaishnavites, who shared their passion for personal closeness to God. This similarity meant that Sufis were more easily able to adapt to the cultural landscape of medieval India – although not all groups of Sufis were benign; some took to the task of spreading the word with zeal and with the occasional use of force.

For sufis, music (particularly *qawwali* singing) and dance is a significant medium of expression, and for this reason they have always been shunned by orthodox Muslims. However, this devotional music appealed to Hindus, for whom *kirtan* (singing) has played an important role in religious practice. One *qawwali*, relating the life of the Sufi saint Waris Ali Shah, draws parallels between his early life and the childhood of Krishna – an outrage for hardline Muslims, but attractive to Hindus. Sufi shrines, or *dargahs*, all over India bridge the gap between Islam and Hinduism. The most important in the region are Hazrat Gesu Daraz in Gulbarga, Northern Karnataka, the hilltop shrine of Sikaner Shah, near Madurai and Golgumbaz in Bijapur.

Practice

Muslims are enjoined to pray five times daily, following a routine of utterances and positions. They may do this at home or in a **mosque**; the latter are always full at noon on Friday, for communal prayer. (Only the Druze, an esoteric sect based in Mumbai, hold communal prayers on Thursdays.) All mosques are distinguishable by the bulbous white domes and high minarets, from which a *muezzin* calls the faithful to prayer. Mosques all over India display a bold linear grandeur quite different to the delicacy of Hindu temples; in South India this is most evident in Hyderabad. By contrast, in rural areas of Karnataka for example, the landscape is scattered with mosques that are no more than a simple wall supported by two token minarets, standing in a field outside the village. Nonetheless, all mosques feature a *mihrab*, or niche indicating the direction of prayer (to Mecca), and some may also include a *mimbar* or pulpit, from which the Friday sermon is read, a source of water for ablutions, and a separate balcony for women.

The position of **women** in Islam is a subject of great debate. It is customary for women to be veiled, and in strictly orthodox communities most wear a *burqa*, usually black, that covers them from head to toe. In larger cities, however, many women do not cover their head. Like other Indian women, Muslim women take second place to men in public, but in the home, where they are often shielded from men's eyes in an inner courtyard, they wield great influence. In theory, **education** is equally available to boys and girls, but girls tend to forgo learning soon after sixteen, encouraged instead to assume the traditional role of wife and mother.

On **marriage**, a woman *receive*s a **dowry** from her husband as financial security and a sign of respect. Contrary to popular belief, polygamy is not widespread; while it does occur, and Mohammed himself had several wives, many Muslims prefer monogamy, and several sects actually stress it as the duty of Muslims.

In Islam, **divorce** may occur through the Indian court, or according to Muslim law, but a woman can only divorce her husband if there is mutual consent.

Christianity

Around fifteen million out of India's twenty-two million **Christians** live in the South, practising in one or another of the largely indigenized versions of established Church denominations. There is also a spread of alternative experiments, such as the ashrams that practise a synthesis of Hindu and Christian elements, a concept of retreat and meditation not so different from the traditional role of monasteries in the West.

Christianity in South India

The Christian presence in South India goes back a long way – the **Apostle Thomas** ("Doubting Thomas") is said to have arrived in Kerala, in 54 AD, to convert itinerant Jewish traders living in the flourishing port of Muziris. There are many tales of the miracles performed by **Mar Thoma**, as St Thomas is known in Malayalam. One legend tells of how he approached a group of Hindu brahmins of Palur (now Malabar) who were trying to appease the gods by throwing water into the air; if the gods accepted the offerings, the droplets would hang above them. St Thomas also threw water in the air, which miraculously remained suspended, leading the brahmins to convert to Christianity there and then. It is customarily believed in the South that St Thomas was martyred and buried on December 21, 72 AD, at Mylapore in Chennai, whose former name, Madras, comes from the Syriac, "*madrasa*" meaning "monastery". His tomb has since been a major place of pilgrimage and, in recognition of this, in the late nineteenth century the Portuguese built the San Thome Cathedral on the site. By oral tradition, this is the **oldest Christian denomination** in the world, but actual documentary evidence of Christian activity in the subcontinent can only be traced to the sixth century, when immigrant Syrian communities were granted settlement rights along the Malabar coastline by royal charter. Ever since, Christianity has flourished in Kerala, aided by magnanimous Hindu rulers.

Christianity then spread across the South by attracting indigenous congregations; the concept of a Godhead and soul, simplicity and prayer, was not dissimilar to traditional Indian mysticism and spirituality. In the pre-colonial era, the manner in which Christianity developed was largely affected by the local cultural environment and retained Indian customs, with congregations bringing their social beliefs and habits to church. The Syrian Christians, especially, developed a social hierarchy that had overtones of the Hindu caste system.

The history of **foreign domination** from the sixteenth century in India is closely affiliated to the spread of Christianity across the whole subcontinent. **St Francis Xavier** arrived in the Portuguese trading colony of Goa in 1552 to convert and establish missions to reach out to the Hindu "untouchables"; his tomb and alleged relics are retained in the Basilica of Bom Jesus in Old Goa. In 1559, the bloody and brutal Inquisition in Goa by Portuguese Jesuit missionaries, at the behest of their king, marked the height of a campaign to "cleanse" the small colony of Hindu and Muslim religious practice, although it was actually set up primarily to purge the colony of Jews.

The **British** initially took the attitude that the subcontinent was a heathen and polytheistic civilization waiting to be proselytized. By the nineteenth century, conversion to Christianity was particularly appealing to those of the lower and sub-castes, and in the South mass conversions took place in Andhra Pradesh. Later, the British realized that conversion did not necessarily incur a change in moral and educational standards; they gradually became less zealous in their missionary efforts and content to provide social welfare among the more established Christian communities and to build very English-looking churches in their cantonments.

Christian society

Today, Christians in Goa and Kerala number nearly a third and a fifth of the population respectively. While most in Goa follow the **Catholicism** of their former Portuguese rulers, Kerala is home to an array of denominations, ranging from Catholic through Syrian and Malankara **Orthodox** to the Church of South India, modelled on **Anglicanism**; see p.370 for more on this.

As Christianity, based on the equality and brotherhood expounded by its founder Jesus Christ, is intended to be free of caste stigmas, it is attractive to those seeking social advancement and consequently there have always been conversions among disaffected tribal peoples and untouchables. Although, the generic nature of Christianity in southern India has mean that it has largely avoided the situation in some of the northern states, where there has recently been a rise in tension between Christian communities and Hindu extremists.

Practice

The strong sense of international history and culture has distinctly influenced the presence of Christianity in southern India. The Mar Thoma Christians congregate in small white churches, decorated with colourful pictures and statues of figures from the New Testament. These are visibly different from the great twin-steepled basilicas of Goa, Pondicherry and Chennai, with their heavy gold interiors and candlelit shrines to the Virgin Mary. In the fishing villages such as Mamallapuram, the fishermen's "church" is a tiny thatched hut with wattle walls, distinguishable only by a tiny cross and the sound of singing on a Sunday morning.

In Tamil Nadu, Christian **festivals** are highly structured along "caste" ranks and, like their Hindu brethren, Tamil Christians never eat beef or pork as it is considered polluting. By contrast, in Goa Christians eat beef and pork as a feature of their Portuguese heritage. In many churches across the South, you will often see devotees offering the Hindu *arati*-plate of coconut, sweets and rice, and the women will wear a tilak dot on their forehead.

Christians carry plates of food to the graves of their ancestors to honour their dead, on the anniversary of their death, in much the same manner that a Hindu family will share a feast on such a day. At **Christmas** time you cannot fail to notice the brightly coloured paper stars and small nativity scenes glowing and flashing outside schools, houses, shops and churches throughout South India.

In the same way that Hindus and Muslims consider the **pilgrimage** to be an integral part of life's journey, Indian Christians tend to visit churches where there is a relic, such as a shard of finger bone alleged to have belonged to St Thomas. Most churches in Kerala and Goa make claim to at least one part of the saint's body, especially his fingers and toes. These relics are brought out on special feast days, and huge crowds will jostle to catch a rare sight of the tiny bit of yellowing bone lying in a casket.

Christians in India have never adopted the practice of giving or receiving **dowry** on the occasion of marriage, although in an arrangement similar to Hindu practice, a Christian **marriage** tends to take place between a man and woman who are members of the same denomination or sect. In most cases, the parents of the couple play a central role in the selection process, paying particular attention to the social status and education of the prospective bride or groom. If a woman becomes a **widow**, she is not socially ostracized as a Hindu woman would be, but instead she is encouraged to remarry.

Buddhism

For several centuries, **Buddhism** dominated India, with adherents in almost every part of the subcontinent. However, having reached its height in the fifth century, it was all but eclipsed by the time of the Muslim conquest. Today, Buddhists are a minute fraction of the population in South India, but a collection of superb monuments are firm reminders of the prior importance of the faith, and essential elements in southern India's cultural legacy.

Origins and development

The founder of Buddhism, **Siddhartha Gautama**, known as the **Buddha**, "the awakened one", was born into a wealthy *kshatrya* family in Lumbini, north of the Gangetic plain in present-day Nepal, around 566 BC. Brought up in luxury as a prince and a Hindu, he married at an early age, and renounced family life when he was thirty. Unsatisfied with the explanations of worldly suffering proposed by Hindu gurus, and convinced that asceticism did not lead to spiritual realization, Siddhartha spent years in meditation, wandering through the ancient kingdom, or *janapada*, of Magadha. His enlightenment (*bodhi*) is said to have taken place under a *bodhi* tree in **Bodhgaya** (Bihar), after a night of contemplation during which he resisted the worldly temptations set before him by the demon, Mara. Soon afterwards he gave his first sermon in **Sarnath**, now a major pilgrimage centre. For the rest of his life he taught, expounding **Dharma**, the true nature of the world, human life and spiritual attainment. Before his death (*c*.486 BC) in Kushinagara (Uttar Pradesh, North India), he had established the **sangha**, a community of monks and nuns, who continued his teachings.

The Buddha's view of life incorporated the Hindu concepts of *samsara* and karma, but remodelled the ultimate goal of religion, calling it **nirvana**, "no wind". Indefinable in worldly terms, since it is by nature free from conditioning, *nirvana* is represented by clarity of mind, pure understanding and unimaginable bliss. Its attainment signals an end to rebirth, but no communion of a "soul" with God; neither has independent existence. The most important concept outlined by the Buddha was that all things, subject to change and dependence, are characterized by **impermanence**, and there is **no self**, no permanent ego, so **attachment** to anything (possessions, emotions, spiritual attainment and *devas*) must be renounced before impermanence can be grasped, and *nirvana* realized.

Disregarding caste and priestly dominance in ritual, the Buddha formulated a teaching open to all. His followers took refuge in the three jewels: *Buddha*, *Dharma*, and *Sangha*. The teachings became known as **Theravada**, or "Doctrine of the Elders". By the first century BC the **Tripitaka**, or "Three Baskets" (a Pali canon in three sections), had set out the basis for early Buddhist practice. *Dana* (selfless giving) and *sila* (precepts which aim at avoiding harm to oneself and others), were presented as the most important guidelines for all Buddhists, and the essential code of practice for the lay community.

Carried out with good intentions, *dana* and *sila* maximize the acquisition of good karma, and minimize material attachment, thus making the individual open to the more religiously oriented teachings, the **Four Noble Truths**. The first of these states that all is suffering (*dukkha*), not because every action is necessarily unpleasurable, but because nothing in the phenomenal world is permanent or reliable. The second truth states that *dukkha* arises through attachment, the third refers to *nirvana*, the cessation of suffering, and the fourth details the path to *nirvana*. Known as the **Eightfold Path** – right understanding, thought, speech, action, livelihood, effort, mindfulness and concentration – it aims at reducing attachment and ego and increasing awareness, until all four truths are thoroughly comprehended, and *nirvana* is achieved. Even this should not be clung to – those who experience it are advised by the Buddha to use their understanding to help others to achieve realization.

The Sanskrit word **bhavana**, referred to in the West as **meditation**, translates literally as "bringing into being". Traditionally meditation is divided into two categories: **Samatha**, or calm, which stills and controls the mind, and **Vipassana**, or insight, during which thought processes and the noble truths are investigated, leading ultimately to a knowledge of reality. Today, both methods are taught.

At first, Buddhist iconography represented the Buddha by symbols such as a footprint, *bodhi* tree, parasol or vase. These can be seen on stupas (domed monuments containing relics of the Buddha) built throughout India from the time of the Buddhist emperor Ashoka (see p.636), and in ancient Buddhist caves, which served as meditation retreats and *viharas* (monasteries). Though the finest examples are to be found in the North, there are interesting sites in the South, such as the stupas at Amaravati and Nagarjunakonda in Andhra Pradesh and caves at Aihole and Badami in Karnataka.

This artistic development coincided with an increase in the devotional side of Buddhism, and the recognition of **bodhisattvas** – those bound for enlightenment who delayed their self-absorption in *nirvana* to become teachers, spurred by selfless compassion and altruism.

The importance of the *bodhisattva* ideal grew as a new school, the **Mahayana**, or "Great Vehicle", emerged. By the twelfth century it had become fully established and, somewhat disparagingly, renamed the old school **Hinayana**, or "Lesser Vehicle". Mahayanists proposed emptiness (*sunyata*) as the fundamental nature of all things, taking to extremes the belief that nothing has independent existence. The **wisdom** necessary to understand *sunyata*, and the **skilful means** required to put wisdom into action in daily life and teaching, and interpret emptiness in a positive sense, became the most important qualities of Mahayana Buddhism. Before long *bodhisattvas* were joined in both scripture and art by female consorts who embodied wisdom.

Hinayana Buddhism survives today in Sri Lanka, Burma, Thailand, Laos and Cambodia. Mahayana Buddhism spread from India to China, Japan, Korea and Vietnam, where it incorporated local gods and spirits into a family of *bodhisattvas*. In many places further evolution saw the adoption of magical methods, esoteric teachings and the full use of sense experience to bring about spiritual transformation, resulting in a separate school known as **Mantrayana** or **Vajrayana** based on texts called *tantras*. Mantrayana encouraged meditation on *mandalas* (symbolic diagrams representing the cosmos and internal spiritual attainment), sexual imagery and sometimes sexual practice, in which the female principle of wisdom could be united with skilful means.

Practice

For Buddhist monks and nuns, and some members of the lay community, meditation is an integral part of religious life. Most lay Buddhists concentrate on *dana* and *sila*, and on auspicious days, such as *Vesak* (marking the Buddha's birth, enlightenment and death), make **pilgrimages** to Bodhgaya, Sarnath, Lumbini and Kushinagar (all are in northern India). After laying offerings before Buddha statues, devotees gather in silent meditation, or join in chants taken from early Buddhist texts.

Uposathas, full moon days, are marked by continual **chanting** through the night. Temples are lit by glimmering butter lamps, often set afloat on lotus ponds, among the flowers that represent the essential beauty and purity to be found in each person in the thick of the confusing "mud" of daily life.

Jainism

The **Jain** population in South India today is tiny, with most families involved in commerce and trade. This dwindling community represents a tradition that has been tremendously influential for at least 2500 years. Similarities to Hindu worship, and a shared respect for nature and non-violence, have contributed to the decline of the Jain society through conversion to Hinduism, but there is no antagonism between the two faiths.

Origins and development

The Jain doctrine is based upon the teachings of **Mahavira**, or "Great Hero", the last in a succession of 24 **tirthankaras** ("crossing-makers") said to appear on earth every 300 million years. Mahavira (*c*.599–527 BC) was born as Vardhamana Jnatrputra into a *kshatrya* family near modern Patna, in northeast India. Like the Buddha, Mahavira rejected family life at the age of thirty, and spent years wandering as an ascetic, renouncing all possessions in an attempt to conquer attachment to worldly values. Firmly opposed to sacrificial rites and caste distinctions, after gaining complete understanding and detachment, he began teaching others, not about Vedic gods and divine heroes, but about the true nature of the world, and the means required for release, *moksha*, from an endless cycle of rebirth.

His teachings were written down in the first millennium BC, and Jainism prospered throughout India, under the patronage of kings such as Chandragupta Maurya (third century BC). Not long after, there was a schism, in part based on linguistic and geographical divisions, but mostly due to differences in monastic practice. On the one hand the **Digambaras** ("sky-clad") believed that nudity was an essential part of world renunciation, and that women are incapable of achieving liberation from worldly existence. The ("white-clad") **Svetambaras**, however, disregarded the extremes of nudity, incorporated nuns into monastic communities and even acknowledged a female *tirthankara*.

In an incredibly complicated process of philosophical analysis known as **Anekanatavada** (many-sidedness), Jainism approaches all questions of existence, permanence and change from seven different viewpoints, maintaining that things can be looked at in an infinite number of valid ways. Thus it claims to remove the intellectual basis for violence, avoiding the potentially damaging result of holding a one-sided view. In this respect Jainism accepts other religious philosophies, and it has adopted, with a little reinterpretation, several Hindu festivals and practices.

Focusing on the practice of **ahimsa** (non-violence), Jains follow a rigorous discipline to avoid harm to all **jivas**, or "souls", which exist in animals and humans, and in plants, water, fire, earth and air. They assert that every *jiva* is pure, omniscient and capable of achieving liberation, or *moksha*, from existence in this universe. However, *jivas* are obscured by **karma**, a form of subtle matter that clings to the soul, is born of action, and binds the *jiva* to physical existence. For the most orthodox Jain, the only way to dissociate karma from the *jiva*, and thereby escape the wheel of death and rebirth, is to follow the path of asceticism and meditation, rejecting passion, wrong view, attachment, carelessness and impure action.

Practice

Today the two sects worship at different temples, but the number of naked Digambaras is minimal. Many Svetambara monks and nuns wear white masks to avoid breathing in insects, and carry a "fly-whisk", sometimes used to brush their path; none will use public transport, and they often spend days or weeks walking barefoot to a pilgrimage site. Practising Jain householders vow to avoid injury, falsehood, theft (extended to fair trade), infidelity and worldly attachment.

Jain **temples** are wonderfully ornate, with pillars, brackets and spires carved by *silavats* into voluptuous maidens, musicians, saints and even Hindu deities; the swastika symbol commonly set into the marble floors is central to Jainism, representing the four states of rebirth as gods, humans, "hell beings" or animals and plants. Worship in temples consists of prayer and puja before images of the *tirthankaras*; the devotee circumambulates the image, chants sacred verses and makes offerings of flowers, sandalwood paste, rice, sweets and incense. It's common to fast four times a month on *parvan* (holy) days, the eighth and fourteenth days of the moon's waxing and waning periods. While reducing attachment to the body, this emulates the fast to death (while in meditation), or *sallekhana*, accepted by Jain mendicants as a final rejection of attachment, and a relatively harmless way to end worldly life.

To enter a monastic community, lay Jains must pass through eleven *pratimas*, starting with right views, the profession of vows, fasting and continence, and culminating in renunciation of family life. Once a monk or nun, a Jain aims to clarify understanding through meditation, hoping to extinguish passions and sever the ties of karma and attachment, entering fourteen spiritual stages, *gunasthanas*, to emerge as a fully enlightened, omniscient being. Whether pursuing a monastic or lay lifestyle, however, Jains recognize the rarity of enlightenment, and religious practice is, for the most part, aimed at achieving a state of rebirth more conducive to spiritual attainment.

Pilgrimage sites are known as **tirthas**, but this does not refer to the literal meaning of "river crossing", sacred to Hindus because of the purificatory nature of water. One of the foremost Svetambara *tirthas*, Shatrunjaya, where over nine hundred temples crown a single hill, is in Gujarat in northern India. There is also an important Digambara *tirtha* at **Sravanabelagola** in Karnataka, where an eighteen-metre-high image of Bahubali (recognized as the first human to attain liberation), at the summit of a hill, is anointed in the huge *abhisheka* festival every twelve years.

Zoroastrianism

Of all South India's religious communities, Western visitors are least likely to come across – or recognize – **Zoroastrians**, who have no distinctive dress and few houses of worship. Most live in Mumbai, where they are known as **Parsis** (Persians) and are active in business, education, and politics. Today, the most famous Parsis are the Tata family – leading industrialists who have long held an unprecedented monopoly over a vast range of commercial interests that range from trucks, cars and scooters to several major steel and chemical factories, tea plantations and even lipsticks. Nonetheless, economic successes aside, Zoroastrian numbers (roughly 90,000) are rapidly dwindling, mainly due to the strict rule of intermarriage and a sharp decline in the birth rate; Parsis are increasingly forced to marry into the wider community and their distinct identity is slowly becoming diluted.

Origin and development

The religion's founder, **Zarathustra** (Zoroaster), who lived in Iran in 6000 BC (according to Zoroastrians), or between 1700 and 1400 BC, was the first religious prophet to expound a dualistic philosophy, based on the opposing powers of good and evil. For him, the absolute, wholly good and wise god, **Ahura Mazda**, together with his holy spirit and six emanations present in earth, water, the sky, animals, plants and fire, is constantly at odds with an evil power, **Angra Mainyu**, who is aided by **daevas**, or evil spirits.

Mankind, whose task on earth is to further good, faces judgement after death, and depending on the proportion of good and bad words, thoughts and actions, will find a place in heaven or suffer the torments of hell. Zarathustra looked forward to a day of judgement, when a saviour, **Saoshyant**, miraculously born of a seed of the prophet and a virgin maiden, will appear on earth, restoring Ahura Mazda's perfect realm and expelling all impure souls and spirits to hell.

The first Zoroastrians to enter India arrived on the Gujarati coast in the tenth century, soon after the Arabian conquest of Iran, and by the seventeenth century most had settled in Mumbai.

Practice

Zoroastrian practice is based on the responsibility of every man and woman to choose between good and evil and to respect God's creations. Five daily prayers, usually hymns (*gathas*), uttered by Zarathustra and standardized in the main Zoroastrian text, the **Avesta**, are said in the home or in a temple, before a fire, which symbolizes the realm of truth, righteousness and order. For this reason, Zoroastrians are often, incorrectly, called "fire-worshippers".

No Ruz, or "New Day", which celebrates the creation of fire and the ultimate triumph of good over evil, is the most popular Zoroastrian festival.

Members of other faiths may not enter Zoroastrian temples, but one custom that is evident to outsiders is the method of disposing of the dead. A body is laid on a high open rooftop (or isolated hill) known as *dakhma* (often referred to as a "tower of silence" see p.118), for the flesh to be eaten by vultures, and the bones cleansed by the sun and wind. Recently, some Zoroastrians, by necessity, have adopted more common methods of cremation or burial; in order not to bring impurity to fire or earth, they only use electric crematoria, and shroud coffins in concrete before laying them in the ground.

Sacred art
and architecture

It is often said that South India is the most religious place on earth, and if the region's vast storehouse of sacred art and architecture is anything to go by, this is probably true. For thousands of years, successive chieftains, emperors, nawabs and *nizams* – whether Hindu, Buddhist, Jain or Muslim – have assigned huge sums of money and human resources towards raising religious structures, as much to symbolize the power of their earthly rule as the superhuman power of the gods and natural forces. Some, like the towering temple *gopuras* of Tamil Nadu or the gigantic Golgumbaz tomb at Bijapur, were conceived on an awesome scale; others, such as the rock-cut shrines of the Pallava period in Mamallapuram or the meticulously crafted architecture of the Hoysalas in Karnataka, were more intimate. Yet the South's religious monuments have one thing in common: nearly all of them testify to the Indians' enduring love of elaboration. Even the most austere Muslim Sultans of the Deccan couldn't resist decorating their tombs and mosques with exquisite geometric shapes, while the attention to fine detail demonstrated by the sculptors of the Cholas is astonishing juxtaposed with the sheer size of the buildings.

Another common feature of South Indian religious art and architecture is the extent to which the various mediums have, over the centuries, been governed by **convention**. In the same way as ritual follows precise rules passed through generations, buildings and their decor conform to the most exacting specifications, set down in ancient canonical texts. This is particularly true of **iconography** – the complex language of symbols used to represent gods, goddesses and saints, in their many and diverse forms. Even nowadays, the stone-carvers of Mamallapuram spend years learning how to render the exact size and lines of their subjects. Without such exactitude, an icon or religious building is deemed to be devoid of its essential power. If the proportions are incorrect, the all-important sequence of auspicious numbers through which the magical power of the gods become manifest is disrupted, and the essential order of the universe compromised.

Such rigorous adherence to tradition would seem to leave little scope for innovation, but somehow South Indian artists have devised an amazing variety of **regional styles**. One of the most absorbing aspects of travelling around the peninsula is comparing these. After a while, you'll begin to be able to differentiate between them and, in the process, gain a more vivid sense of the people and period that created them. The following notes are intended as a primer; for more in-depth explorations, hunt out some of the titles listed under "The Arts and Architecture" in Books on p.717.

Stupas

Among the very earliest sacred structures built in India were hemispherical mounds known as **stupas**, which have been central to Buddhist worship since the sixth century BC, when the Buddha himself modelled the first prototype.

Asked by one of his disciples for a symbol to help disseminate his teachings after his death, the Master took his begging bowl, teaching staff and a length of cloth – his only worldly possessions – and arranged them into the form of a stupa, using the cloth as a base, the upturned bowl as the dome and the stick as the projecting finial, or spire.

Originally, stupas were simple burial mounds of compacted earth and stone containing relics of the Buddha and his followers. As the religion spread, however, the basic components multiplied and became imbued with **symbolic significance**. The main dome, or *anda* – representing the sacred mountain, or "diving axis" linking heaven and earth – grew larger, while the wooden railings, or *vedikas*, surrounding it were replaced by massive stone ones. A raised ambulatory terrace, or *medhi*, was added to the vertical sides of the drum, along with two flights of stairs and four ceremonial entrances, carefully aligned with the cardinal points. Finally, crowing the tip of the stupa, the single spike evolved into a three-tiered umbrella, or *chhattra*, representing the Three Jewels of Buddhism: the Buddha, the Law and the community of monks, or *Sangham*.

The *chhattra*, usually enclosed within a low square stone railing, or *harmika* (a throwback to the days when sacred *bodhi* trees were surrounded by fences) formed the topmost point of the axis, directly above the reliquary in the heart of the stupa. Ranging from bits of bone wrapped in cloth, to fine caskets of precious metals, crystal and carved stone, the reliquaries were the "seeds" and their protective mounds the "egg". Excavations on the estimated eighty-four thousand stupas scattered around the subcontinent have shown that the solid interiors were also sometimes built as elaborate **mandalas** – symbolic patterns that exerted a beneficial influence over the stupa and those who walked around it. The ritual of **circumambulation**, or *pradakshina*, which enabled the worshipper to tap into a magical force-field and be transported from the mundane to the divine realms, was always carried out in a clockwise direction from the east, in imitation of the sun's passage across the heavens.

In South India, the **Satavahana** (or Andhra) dynasty, who ruled a vast tract of the country towards the end of the first millennium (see History, p.637), erected stupas across the region, among them the Great Stupa at **Amaravati** in Andhra Pradesh (see p.594). Little of this once-impressive monument remains in situ, but you can admire some of the outstanding sculpture that decorated its ornamental gateways (*toranas*) in the Government Museum in Chennai (see p.442). To see a stupa in action, however, you have to follow in the footsteps of the emperor Ashoka's missionaries southwards to Sri Lanka, where, as dagobas, stupas are still revered as repositories of sacred energy.

Temples

To make sense of Hindu **temples**, you need to be able to identify their common features. Many of these conventions are recorded in the **Shilpa Shastras** – Sanskrit manuals that set out, in meticulous detail, ancient building specifications and their symbolic significance.

Unlike Christian churches or Muslim mosques, temples are not simply places of worship, but are objects of worship in themselves – recreations of the "Divine-Cosmic-Creator-Being" or the particular deity enshrined within them. For a Hindu, to move through a temple is akin to entering the very body of the God and to be glimpsed in the shrine-room during the moment of darshan, or ritual viewing of the deity, is the culmination of an act of worship. In South India, this concept also finds expression in the technical terms used in the Shastras to designate different parts of the structure: the foot, shin, torso, neck, head and so forth.

The temples of Tamil Nadu

No Indian state is more dominated by its **temples** than Tamil Nadu, whose huge temple towers dominate most towns and villages. The majority were built in honour of Shiva, Vishnu and their consorts; all are characterized not only by their design and sculptures, but by constant activity – devotion, dancing, singing, pujas, festivals and feasts. Each is tended by brahmin priests, recognizable by their *dhotis* (loincloths), a sacred thread draped over the right shoulder and marks on the forehead. One to three horizontal (usually white) lines distinguish Shaivites; vertical lines (yellow or red), often converging into a near-V shape, are common among Vaishnavites.

Dravida, the temple architecture of Tamil Nadu, first took form in the **Pallava** port of **Mamallapuram**. A step up from the cave retreats of Hindu and Jain ascetics, the earliest Pallava monuments were **mandapas**, shrines cut into rock-faces and fronted by columns. The magnificent **bas-relief** at Mamallapuram, **Arjuna's Penance**, shows the fluid carving of the Pallavas at its most exquisite. This sculptural skill was transferred to free-standing temples, **rathas**, carved out of single rocks and incorporating the essential elements of Hindu temples: the dim inner sanctuary, the *garbhagriha*, capped with a modest tapering spire featuring repetitive architectural motifs. In turn, the Shore temple was built with three shrines, topped by a *vimana* similar to the towering roofs of the *rathas*; statues of Nandi, Shiva's bull, later to receive pride of place, surmount its low walls. In the finest structural Pallava temple, the Kailasanatha temple at **Kanchipuram**, the sanctuary, again crowned with a pyramidal *vimana*, stands within a courtyard enclosed by high walls. The projecting and recessing bays of the walls, carved with images of Shiva, his consort and ghoulish mythical lions, *yalis*, were the prototype for later styles.

Pallava themes were developed in Karnataka by the Chalukyas and Rashtrakutas, but it was the Shaivite **Cholas** who spearheaded Tamil Nadu's next architectural phase, in the tenth century. In **Thanjavur**, Rajaraja I created the Brihadeshwara temple principally as a status symbol. Its proportions far exceed any attempted by the Pallavas. Set within a vast walled courtyard, the sanctuary, fronted by a small pillared hall (*mandapa*), stands beneath a sculpted *vimana* that soars over sixty metres high. Most sculptures once again feature Shiva, but the *gopuras*, or towers, each side of the eastern gateway to the courtyard, were a new innovation, as were the lions carved into the base of the sanctuary walls, and the pavilion erected over Nandi in front of the sanctuary. The second great Chola temple was built in **Gangaikondacholapuram** by Rajendra I. Instead of a mighty *vimana*, he introduced new elements, adding subsidiary shrines and placing an extended *mandapa* in front of the central sanctuary, its pillars writhing with dancers and deities.

By the time of the thirteenth-century **Vijayanagar** kings, the temple was central to city life, the focus for civic meetings, education, dance and theatre. The Vijayanagars extended earlier structures, adding enclosing walls around a series of *prakaras*, or courtyards, and erecting free-standing *mandapas* for use as meeting halls, elephant stables, stages for music and dance, and ceremonial marriage halls. Raised on superbly decorated columns, these *mandapas* became known as **thousand-pillared halls** (*kalyan mandapas*). **Tanks** were added, doubling as water stores and washing areas, and used for festivals when deities were set afloat in boats surrounded by glimmering oil lamps.

Under the Vijayanagars, the gopuras were enlarged and set at the cardinal points over the high gateways to each prakara, to become the dominant feature. Rectangular in plan, and embellished with images of animals and local saints or rulers as well as deities, gopuras are periodically repainted in pinks, blues, whites and yellows, a sharp and joyous contrast with the earthy browns and greys of halls and sanctuaries below. **Madurai** is the place to check out Vijayanagar architecture, and experience the timeless temple rituals. Dimly lit halls and sun-drenched courtyards hum with murmured prayers, and regularly come alive for festivals in which Shiva and his "fish-eyed" consort (see p.529) are hauled through town on mighty wooden chariots tugged by hordes of devotees. Outside Tiruchirapalli, the temple at **Srirangam** was extended by the Vijayanagar Nayaks to become South India's largest. Unlike that in Madurai, it incorporates earlier Chola foundations. The ornamentation, with pillars formed into rearing horses, is superb.

Hoysala temples

The Hoysala dynasty ruled southwestern Karnataka between the eleventh and thirteenth centuries. From the twelfth century, after the accession of King Vishnu Vardhana, they built a series of distinctive temples centred primarily at three sites: **Belur** (see p.253) and **Halebid** (see p.251) close to modern Hassan, and **Somnathpur** (see p.245), near Mysore.

At first sight, and from a distance, Hoysala temples appear to be modest structures, compact and even squat. On closer inspection, however, their profusion of fabulously detailed and sensuous sculpture, covering every inch of the exterior, is astonishing. Detractors are prone to class Hoysala art as decadent and overly fussy, but anyone with an eye for craftsmanship is likely to marvel at these jewels of Karnatakan art.

The intricacy of the carvings was made possible by the material used in construction: a soft **steatite soapstone** that on oxidization hardens to a glassy, highly polished surface. The level of detail, similar to that seen in sandalwood and ivory work, became increasingly freer and fluid as the style developed, and reached its highest point at Somnathpur. Beautiful bracket figures, often delicate portrayals of voluptuous female subjects, were placed under the eaves, fixed by pegs top and bottom. A later addition (except possibly in the Somnathpur temple), these serve no structural function.

Another technique more usually associated with wood is the unusual treatment of the massive stone pillars: lathe-turned, they resemble those of the wooden temples of Kerala. They were probably turned on a horizontal plane, pinned at each end, and rotated with the use of a rope. It may be no coincidence that, to this day, wood-turning is still a local speciality. Only the central shaft of each pillar seems to have been turned; in the base and capitals, a less precise, presumably handworked imitation of turning is evident.

The architectural style of the Hoysala temples is commonly referred to as vesara, or "hybrid" (literally "mule"), rather than belonging to either the northern, nagari, or southern, Dravidian styles. However, they show great affinity with nagari temples of western India, and represent another fruit of contact, like music, painting and literature, facilitated by the trade routes between the North and the South. All Hoysala temples share a star-shaped plan, built on high plinths (jagati) that follow the shape of the sanctuaries and mandapas to provide a raised surrounding platform. Such northern features may have been introduced by the designer and artists of the earliest temple at Belur, who were imported by Vishnu Vardhana from further north in Andhra Pradesh. Also characteristic of the Hoysala style is the use of ashlar masonry, without mortar. Some pieces of stones are joined by pegs of iron or bronze, or mortice and tenon joints. Ceilings inside the mandapas are made up of corbelled domes, looking similar to those of the Jain temples of Rajasthan and Gujarat; in the Hoysala style they are only visible from inside.

Keralan temples

As you'd expect from one of India's most culturally distinct regions, Kerala's temples are quite unlike those elsewhere in the South. Their most striking features – to accommodate the torrential downpours – are the sloping tiled roofs that crown the sanctuaries, colonnades and gateways. In addition, the innermost shrines are invariably circular, or apsidal ended – perhaps in imitation of earlier indigenous styles.

In the corner of the spacious temple courtyards (which are often very broad to make room for the annual elephant processions) stands a covered hall with beautiful lathe-turned pillars and wooden panels, where performances of Kathakali and other forms of ritualized theatre are held (see p.706). In some older temples, **murals** also adorn the inner faces of the high enclosing walls (see p.681).

Keralan temples are generally closed to non-Hindus, but many make exceptions during festivals, when drum bands, tuskers and ritual dances comprise some of the most compelling spectacles in all of South India (see "Thrissur Puram", p.406).

Goan temples

Stick to the former Portuguese heartland of Goa, and you'd be forgiven for thinking the state was exclusively Christian. It isn't, of course, as the innumerable brightly painted Hindu temples hidden amid the lush woodland and areca groves of the more outlying areas confirm. The oldest-established and best known lie well away from the coastal resorts, but are worth hunting out if you've an eye for quirky religious buildings.

Goa's first stone temples date from the rule of the Kadamba dynasty, between the fifth and fifteenth century AD. From the few fragments of sculpture and masonry unearthed at the ruins of their old capital, it is clear that these were as skilfully constructed as the famous monuments of the neighbouring Deccan region. However, only one, the richly carved Mahadeva temple at **Tamdi Surla** in east Goa, has survived. The rest were systematically destroyed, first by Muslim invaders, and later by the Portuguese.

Goan temples incorporate the main elements of Hindu architecture, but boast some unusual features of their own – some necessitated by the local climate, or the availability of building materials, others the result of outside influences. The impact of European–Portuguese styles (inevitable given the fact that the majority of Goan temples were built during the colonial era, but ironic considering the Portuguese destroyed the originals) is most evident on the exterior of the buildings. Unlike conventional Hindu temple towers, which are curvilinear, Goan *shikharas*, taking their cue from St Cajetan's church in Old Goa (see p.160), consist of octagonal drums crowned by tapering copper domes. Hidden inside the top of these is generally a pot of holy water called a **poornakalash**, drawn from a sacred Hindu river or spring. The sloping roofs of the *mandapas*, with their projecting eves and terracotta tiles are also distinctively Latin, while the glazed ceramic Chinese dragons often perched above them, originally imported from Macau, add to the colonial feel. Embellished with Baroque-style balustrades and pilasters, Islamic arches and the occasional bulbous Moghul dome, the sides of larger temples also epitomize Goan architecture's flair for fusion.

Always worth looking out for inside the main assembly halls are **woodcarvings** and panels of **sculpture** depicting mythological narratives, and the opulently embossed solid silver **doorways** around the entrance to the shrines, flanked by a pair of guardians, or **dvarpalas**. The most distinctively Goan feature of all, however, has to be the **lamp tower**, or *deepmal*, an addition introduced by the Marathas, who ruled much of Goa during the seventeenth and eighteenth centuries. Also known as *deep stambhas*, literally "pillars of light", these five- to seven-storey whitewashed pagodas generally stand opposite the main entrance. Their many ledges and windows hold tiny oil lamps that are illuminated during the *devta*'s weekly promenade, when the temple priests carry the god or goddess around the courtyard on their shoulders in a silver sedan chair known as a **palkhi**.

Near the deepmal you'll often come across a ornamental plant pot called a **tulsi vrindavan**. The straggly sacred shrub growing inside it, tulsi, represents a former mistress of Vishnu whom his jealous consort Lakshmi turned into a plant after a fit of jealous pique.

Hindu sculpture

Hindu sculpture has traditionally been an integral part of temple architecture. Masons and stone-carvers often laboured for decades, even a whole lifetime, on the same site, settled in camps with their families, in much the same style as modern construction workers live around what they are building in India today. Each grade of artisan – from the men who cut the stone blocks or etched bands of decorative friezes, to the master-artists who fashioned the main idols – was a member of a **guild** that functioned along the same lines as caste, determining marriages and social relations. Guilds also controlled the handing down of tools, specialist knowledge and techniques to successive generations, through years of rigorous apprenticeship.

Another role of the guilds was to apply the rules of iconography set in the *Shilpa Shastras*, still followed today. Measurement always begins with the proportions of the artist's own hand and the image's resultant face-length as the basic unit. Then follows a scheme which is allied to the equally scientific rules applied to classical music, and specifically *tala* or rhythm. Human figures total eight face-lengths, eight being the most basic of rhythmic measures. Figures of deities are *nava-tala*, nine face-lengths.

Like their counterparts in medieval Europe, South Indian sculptors remained largely anonymous. Even though the most talented artists may have been known to their peers – in some rare cases earning renown in kingdoms at opposite ends of the subcontinent – their names have become lost over time. An explanation often advanced for this is the *Shastras*' insistence that the personality of an individual artist must be suppressed in order for divine inspiration to flow freely. For this reason, only a tiny number of stone sculptures in India bear inscriptions that preserve the identity of their creators.

With the entry of Indian religious sculpture into the international art market, the old conventions of anonymity are beginning to break down. A handful of sculptors at South India's stone-carving capital, **Mamallapuram** in Tamil Nadu (see p.464), have become well known, as the demand for pieces to adorn temples and shrines in the homes of expatriate Indians has increased.

However, age-old guidelines governing iconographic sculpture are still applied here as rigorously as they have been for more than a thousand years, which makes it somewhat difficult to differentiate between the work of masters and less experienced apprentices.

You can watch sculptors in action, and buy their work, at innumerable workshops around Mamallapuram, while the Government Sculpture College nearby welcomes visitors, offering you the chance to see how students learn to measure out the proportions of the sculpture with their hands, and memorize the extraordinary body of iconographic lore that must be fully internalized before they graduate.

Chola bronzes

Originally sacred temple objects, **Chola bronzes** are another art form from Tamil Nadu that has become highly collectable (even if their price tags are considerably higher than stone sculptures). The most memorable bronze icons are the **Natarajas**, or dancing Shivas. The image of Shiva, standing on one leg encircled by flames, with wild locks caught in mid-motion, has become almost as recognizably Indian as the Taj Mahal, and few Indian millionaires would feel their sitting rooms were complete without one.

The principal icons of a temple are usually stationary and made of stone. Frequently, however, ceremonies require an image of the god to be led in procession outside the inner sanctum, and even through the streets. According to the canonical texts known as *Agamas*, these moving images should be made of metal. Indian bronzes are made by the **cire perdu** ("lost-wax") process, known as *madhuchchistavidhana* in Sanskrit. Three layers of clay mixed with burned grain husks, salt and ground cotton are applied to a figure crafted in bees' wax, with a stem left protruding at each end. When that is heated, the wax melts and flows out, creating a hollow mould into which molten metal – a rich five-metal alloy (*panchaloha*) of copper, silver, gold, brass and lead – can be poured through the stems. After the metal has cooled, the clay shell is destroyed, and the stems filed off, leaving a unique completed figure, which the caster-artist, or *sthapathi*, remodels to remove blemishes and add delicate detail.

Knowledge of bronze-casting in India goes back at least as far as the Indus Valley civilization (2500–1500 BC), and the famous **"Dancing Girl"** from Mohenjo Daro. The earliest produced in the South were made by the Andhras, whose techniques were continued by the Pallavas, the immediate antecedents of the Cholas. The few surviving **Pallava** bronzes show a sophisticated handling of the form; figures are characterized by broad shoulders, thick-set features and an overall simplicity that suggests all the detail was completed at the wax stage. The finest bronzes of all, however, are from the **Chola** period, from the late ninth to early eleventh centuries. As the Cholas were predominantly Shaivite, Nataraja, Shiva and his consort Parvati (frequently in a family group with son Skanda) and the sixty-three Nayanmar poet-saints are the most popular subjects. Chola bronzes display more detail than their predecessors. Human figures are invariably slim-waisted and elegant, with the male form robust and muscular and the female graceful and delicate.

As with stone sculpture, the design, iconography and proportions of each figure are governed by the strict rules laid down in the *Shilpa Shastras*, which draw no real distinction between art, science and religion.

Those bronzes produced by the few artists practising today invariably follow the Chola model; the chief centre is now **Swamimalai**, 8km west of Kumbakonam (see p.505). Original Chola bronzes are kept in many Tamil temples, but as temple interiors are often dark it's not always possible to see them properly. Important **public collections** include the Nayak Durbar Hall Art Museum at Thanjavur, the Government State Museum at Chennai and the National Museum, New Delhi.

Murals

Fragments of paint indicate that murals adorned the walls and ceilings of India's oldest rock-cut prayer halls, dating from the third century BC. Only a couple of hundred years later, the art form reached its peak in the sumptuous Satavahana paintings at Ajanta, in the northwest Deccan, where the walls of huge caves were covered in the most exquisite images, rendered in muted reds, greens and blues. For the most part, these show religious scenes – episodes from the life of the Buddha (*jatakas*) – but they also incorporate pictures of courtly life, battles and a host of secular detail. However, remnants of ancient murals in the far south are scant, limited to a few patches at **Badami** in Karnataka (see p.299), and the Kailasanatha temple at **Kanchipuram** (see p.475).

Not until the resurgence of the Tamil Cholas in the ninth and tenth centuries did mural painting flourish again in the region. The finest examples – showing in the most sensuous detail vignettes from life at the royal court of Rajaraja I – are those decorating the interior of the main sanctum of the Brihadishwara temple at **Thanjavur** (see p.508). Sadly, these are closed to the public, but you can still enjoy the wonderful ceiling paintings of the Nayak rulers at the Shivakamasundari temple in **Chidambaram** (see p.497), which illustrate Shaivite myths and legends.

Keralan murals

One of the best-kept secrets of South Indian art has to be the quality and unique style of the murals at Mattancherry Palace in old Kochi (see below), along with those in as many as sixty other locations in Kerala. Most are on the walls of functioning temples, not marketable, transportable or indeed even seen by many non-Hindus. Few date from before the sixteenth century, depriving them of the aura of extreme antiquity. Their origins may go back to the seventh century, however, and are probably influenced by the Pallava style of Tamil Nadu; unfortunately only traces in one tenth-century cave temple survive from the earliest period. The traveller Castaneda, who accompanied Vasco da Gama on the first Portuguese landing in India, described how he strayed into a temple, supposing it to be a church, and saw "monstrous looking images with two inch fangs" painted on the walls, causing one of the party to fall to his knees exclaiming, "if this be the devil, I worship God."

Technically classified as fresco-secco, Keralan murals employ vegetable and mineral colours, predominantly ochre reds and yellows, white and blue-green, and are coated with a protective sheen of pine resin and oil. Their ingenious design, strongly influenced by the canonical text, Shilparatna, incorporates intense detail with clarity and dynamism in the portrayal of human (and celestial) figures; subtle facial expressions are captured with the simplest of lines, while narrative elements are always bold and arresting. In common with all great Indian art, they share a complex iconography and symbolism. Non-Hindus can see fine examples in **Kochi**, **Padmanabhapuram** (see p.345), **Ettumanur** (see p.369) and **Kayamkulam** (see p.357). Visitors interested in how they are made should head for the Mural Painting Institute at **Guruvayur** (see p.410). A paperback book, Murals of Kerala, by M.G. Shashi Bhooshan

(Kerala Government Department of Public Relations) serves as an excellent introduction to the field.

Tanjore (Thanjavur) painting

The name **Tanjore painting** is given to a distinctive form of southern picture-making that came to prominence in the eighteenth century, encouraged by the Maratha Raja of Thanjavur, Serfoji. The term "painting", however, is misleading, and inadequate to describe work of the Tanjore school. It is distinctive because – aside from a painted image – details such as clothing, ornaments, and any (typically Baroque) architectural elements are raised in low plaster relief from the surface, which is then decorated by the sumptuous addition of glass pieces, pearls, semiprecious or precious stones and elaborate gold leaf work. Other variations include pictures on mica, ivory and glass.

Figures are delineated with simple outlines; unmixed primary colours are used in a strict symbolic code, similar to that found in the make-up used in the classical dramas of Kerala, where each colour indicates qualities of character. Other schools of painting normally show Krishna with blue-black skin; in the Tanjore style, he is white.

Traditionally, most depicted Vaishnavite deities, with the most popular single image probably being that of **Balakrishna**, the chubby baby Krishna. In the tenth-century Sanskrit *Bhagavata Purana*, Balakrishna was portrayed as a rascal who delighted in stealing and consuming milk, butter balls and curd. Despite his naughtiness, all women who came into contact with him were seized with an overflowing of maternal affection, to the extent that their breasts spontaneously oozed milk. Thanks to such stories, Krishna as a child became the chosen deity par excellence of mothers and grandmothers. Tanjore paintings typically show him eating, accompanied by adoring women.

Although Tanjore painting went into decline after the nineteenth century, in recent years there has been new demand for domestic, rather than temple, shrines. High-quality work is produced in Thanjavur (see p.508), Kumbakonam (see p.501) and Tiruchirapalli (see p.515).

Kalam ezhuttu

The tradition of **kalam ezhuttu** (pronounced "kalam-erroo-too") – detailed and beautiful ritual drawings in coloured powder, of deities and geometric patterns (*mandalas*) – is very much alive all over **Kerala**, although few visitors to the region even know of its existence. The designs usually cover an area of around thirty square metres, often outdoors and under a *pandal* – a temporary shelter made from bamboo and palm fronds. Each colour, made from rice flour, turmeric, ground leaves and burnt paddy husk, is painstakingly applied using the thumb and forefinger as a funnel. Three communities produce *kalams*; two come from the temple servant (*amblavasi*) castes, whose rituals are associated with the god Ayappa (see pp.373 and 378) or the goddess Bhagavati; the third, the *pullavans*, specialize in serpent worship. Iconographic designs emerge gradually from the initial grid lines and turn into startling figures, many of terrible aspect, with wide eyes and fangs. Noses and breasts are raised, giving the whole a three-dimensional effect. As part of the ritual, the significant moment when the powder is added for the iris or pupil, "opening" the eyes, may well be marked by the accompaniment of *chenda* drums and *elatalam* hand-cymbals.

Witnessing the often day-long ritual is an unforgettable experience. The effort expended by the artist is made all the more remarkable by the inevitable destruction of the picture shortly after its completion; this truly ephemeral art cannot be divorced from its ritual context. In some cases, the image is destroyed by a fierce-looking vellichapad ("light-bringer"), a village oracle who can be recognized by shoulder-length hair, red dhoti, heavy brass anklets and the hooked sword he brandishes either while jumping up and down on the spot (a common sight), or marching purposefully about to control the spectators. At the end of the ritual, the powder, invested with divine power, is thrown over the onlookers. Kalam ezhuttu rituals are not widely advertised, but check at tourist offices.

The architecture of Islam

South India may be best known for its Hindu monuments, but the southern **Deccan** region, encompassed by the modern states of Karnataka and western Andhra Pradesh, is littered with wonderful Muslim **mosques** and **tombs**, dating from an era when this was the buffer zone between the ancient Indian cultures of the Dravidian south and the dynasties who succeeded the Delhi Sultans (see "History" p.640).

The buildings that survive from this era illustrate the extraordinary cross-fertilization that took place between indigenous art forms and Islamic styles from distant Central Asia. Thus, some of the oldest Muslim constructions at **Bidar** (see p.313) and **Gulbarga** (see p.311), look Afghan, whereas the later masterpieces of the Bahmani dynasty, such as the Ibrahim Rauza at **Bijapur** (see p.305), incorporate motifs that wouldn't have looked out of place on a temple. This fusion occurred both because of a certain stylistic tolerance on the part of later Muslim rulers in southern India, and because the craftsmen they employed were often Hindus to whom lotus flowers and fancy floral scrollwork came more easily to hand than Persian geometric patterns.

The most famous Muslim monument in the South is the **Golgumbaz** at **Bijapur** (see p.308) – India's largest domed structure – but enough superb buildings stand in the same town, and in the other old capitals of the former Deccan Sultans, dotted along the northern border of Karnataka between Bijapur and Hyderabad, to keep enthusiasts of Islamic architecture occupied for weeks.

Wildlife

A fast-growing population and the rapid spread of industries have inflicted pressures on the rural landscape of South India, but the region still supports a wealth of distinct flora and fauna. Although many species have been hunted out over the past fifty years, enough survive to make a trip into the countryside well worthwhile. Walking on less frequented beaches or through the rice fields of the coastal plain, you'll encounter dozens of exotic birds, while the hill country of the interior supports an amazing variety of plants and trees. The majority of the peninsula's larger mammals keep to the dense woodland of the Western Ghat mountains, where a string of contiguous reserves affords them some protection from the hunters and loggers that have wrought such havoc in India's fragile forest regions over the past few decades.

Flora

Something like 3500 species of flowering plants have been identified in South India, as well as countless lower orders of grasses, ferns and brackens. The greatest floristic diversity occurs in the Western Ghats, where it is not uncommon to find one hundred or more different types of trees in an area of one hectare. Many were introduced by the Portuguese from Europe, South America, Southeast Asia and Australia, but there are also a vast number of indigenous varieties which thrive in the moist climate.

Along the coast, the rice **paddy** and **coconut** plantations predominate, forming a near-continuous band of lush foliage. Spiky **spinifex** also helps bind the shifting sand dunes behind the miles of sandy beaches lining both the Malabar and Coromandel coasts, while **causerina** bushes form striking splashes of pink and crimson during the winter months.

In towns and villages, you'll encounter dozens of beautiful **flowering trees** that are common in tropical parts of India but unfamiliar to most Europeans and North Americans. The Indian **labernum**, or cassia, throws out masses of yellow flowers and long seed pods in late February before the monsoons. This is also the period when mango and Indian **coral trees** are in full bloom; both produce bundles of stunning red flowers.

Among the most distinctive trees that grow in both coastal and hill areas is the stately **banyan**, which propagates by sending out shoots from its lower branches. The largest specimens grow over an area of two hundred metres. The banyan is also revered by Hindus, and you'll often find small shrines at the foot of mature trees. The same is true of the *peepal*, which has distinctive spatula-shaped leaves. Temple courtyards often enclose large *peepals*, usually with strips of auspicious red cloth hanging from their lower branches.

Tree lovers and botanists should not miss an opportunity to visit the Western Ghats, which harbour a bewildering wealth of flora, from flowering trees and plants, to ferns and fungi. **Shola** forests, lush patches of moist evergreen woodland that carpet the deeper mountain valleys, exhibit some of the greatest biodiversity. Sheltered by a leafy canopy, which may rise to a height of twenty metres or more, buttressed roots and giant trunks tower above a luxuriant undergrowth of brambles, creepers, and bracken, interspersed by brakes of bamboo. Common tree species include the **kadam, sisso** or **martel, kharanj** and **teak**, while rarer **sandalwood** thrives on the higher, drier plateaulands south of Mysore – homeland of the infamous smuggler and bandit, Veerapan (see box on p.570). There are dozens of representatives of the Ficus, or fig, family too, as well as innumerable (and ecologically destructive) eucalyptus and rubber trees, planted as cash crops by the Forest Department.

Mammals

During a field expedition to Goa in the 1970s, the eminent Indian naturalist, Salim Ali, complained the only animal he spotted was a lone leopard cat dead at the roadside. For although peninsula India boasts more than fifty species of wild mammals, visitors who stick to populated coastal areas are unlikely to spot anything more inspiring than a monkey or tree squirrel. Most of the larger animals have been hunted to the point of extinction; the few that remain roam the dense woodland lining the Western Ghats, in the sparsely populated forest zones of the **Nilgiri Biosphere Reserve**.

The largest Indian land mammal is, of course, the Asian **elephant**, stockier and with much smaller ears than its African cousin, though no less venerable. Travelling around Kerala and Tamil Nadu, you'll regularly see elephants in temples and festivals, but for a glimpse of one in the wild you'll have to venture into the mountains where, in spite of the huge reduction of their natural habitat, around six and a half thousand still survive. Among the best places for sightings are Periyar in Kerala (see p.371) and Nagarhole in Karnataka (see p.278). In the era when it was a maharaja's hunting reserve, the latter became infamous as the place where the British hunter, G.P. Sanderson, devised the brutal *khedda* system for trapping elephants: herds were driven into lethal stockades and captured, or killed. Between 1890 and 1971, 1536 were allegedly caught in this way, while 225 of them died – a figure that probably only represents the tip of the iceberg. Today, wild elephants, which are included under the Endangered Species Protection Act, are under increasing pressure from villagers: each adult animal eats roughly two hundred kilos of vegetation and drinks one hundred litres of water a day, and their search for sustenance inevitably brings them into conflict with neighbouring rural communities.

Across India, local villagers displaced by wildlife reserves have often been responsible for the poaching that has reduced **tiger** populations to such fragile levels. These days in South India sightings are very rare indeed; however, several kinds of big cat survive. Among the most adaptive and beautiful is the leopard or **panther** (*Panthera panthus*). Prowling the thick forests of the Ghats, these elusive cats prey on monkeys and deer, and occasionally take domestic cattle and dogs from the fringes of villages. Their distinctive black spots make them notoriously difficult to see amongst the tropical foliage, although their mating call (reminiscent of a saw on wood) regularly pierces the night air in remote areas. The **leopard cat** (*Felis bengalensis*) is a miniature version of its namesake, and more common. Sporting a bushy tail and round spots on soft buff or grey fur, it is about the same size as a domestic cat and lives around villages, picking off chickens, birds and small mammals. Another cat with a penchant for poultry, and one which villagers occasionally keep as a pet if they can capture one, is the docile Indian civet (*Viverricual indica*), recognizable by its lithe body, striped tail, short legs and long pointed muzzle.

Wild cats share their territory with a range of other mammals unique to the subcontinent. One you've a reasonable chance of seeing is the **gaur**, or Indian bison (*Bos gaurus*). These primeval-looking beasts, with their distinctive sleek black skin and knee-length white "socks", forage around bamboo thickets and shady woods. The bulls are particularly impressive, growing to an awesome height of two metres, with heavy curved horns and prominent humps.

Feared, adored, immortalized in myth and used to endorse everything from breakfast cereals to petrochemicals, few animals command such universal fascination as the tiger. Only in India, however, can this rare and enigmatic big cat still be glimpsed in the wild, stalking through the teak forests and terai grass to which it is uniquely adapted. A solitary predator at the apex of the food chain, it has no natural enemies save one.

As recently as the turn of the century, up to 100,000 tigers still roamed the subcontinent, even though shikar (tiger hunting) had long been the "sport of kings". An ancient dictum held it auspicious for a ruler to notch up a tally of 109 dead tigers, and nawabs, maharajas and Moghul emperors all indulged their prerogative to devastating effect. But it was the trigger-happy British who brought tiger hunting to its most gratuitous excesses. Photographs of pith-helmeted, bare-kneed burrasahibs posing behind mountains of striped carcasses became a hackneyed image of the Raj. Even Prince Philip (now president of the Worldwide Fund for Nature) couldn't resist bagging one during a royal visit.

In the years following Independence, demographic pressures nudged the Indian tiger perilously close to extinction. As the human population increased in rural districts, more and more forest was cleared for farming – thereby depriving large carnivores of their main source of game and of the cover they needed to hunt. Forced to turn on farm cattle as an alternative, tigers were drawn into direct conflict with humans; some animals, out of sheer desperation, even turned man-eater and attacked human settlements.

Poaching has taken an even greater toll. The black market has always paid high prices for live animals – a whole tiger can fetch up to $100,000 – and for the various body parts believed to hold magical or medicinal properties. The meat is used to ward off snakes, the brain to cure acne, the nose to promote the birth of a son and the fat of the kidney – applied liberally to the afflicted organ – as an antidote to male impotence.

By the time an all-India moratorium on tiger shooting was declared in the 1972 Wildlife Protection Act, numbers had plummeted to below 2000. A dramatic

With its long fur and white V-shaped bib, the scruffy **sloth bear** (*Melursus ursinus*) – whose Tamil name (*bhalu*) inspired that of Rudyard Kipling's character in *The Jungle Book* – ranks among the weirder-looking inhabitants of the region's forests. Sadly, it's also very rare, thanks to its predilection for raiding sugar-cane plantations, which has brought it, like the elephant, into direct conflict with man. Sloth bears can occasionally be seen shuffling along woodland trails, but you're more likely to come across evidence of their foraging activities: trashed termite mounds and chewed-up ants' nests. The same is true of both the portly Indian **porcupine** (*Hystrix indica*), or *sal*, which you see a lot less often than the mounds of earth it digs up to get at insects and cashew or teak seedlings, and the **pangolin** (*Manis crassicaudata*), or *tiryo*: a kind of armour-plated anteater whose hard grey overlapping scales protect it from predators.

Full-moon nights and the twilight hours of dusk and dawn are the times to look out for nocturnal animals such as the **slender loris** (*Loris tardigradus*). This shy creature – a distant cousin of the lemur, with bulging round eyes, furry body and pencil-thin limbs – grows to around twenty centimetres in length. It moves as if in slow motion, except when an insect flits to within striking distance, and is a favourite pet of forest people. The **mongoose** (*Herpestes edwardsi*) is another animal sometimes kept as a pet. Rudyard Kipling's "Rikitikitavi" keeps dwellings free of scorpions, mice, rats and other vermin. It will also readily take

response geared to fire public imagination came the following year, with the inauguration of **Project Tiger**. At the personal behest of Indira Gandhi, nine areas of pristine forest were set aside for the last remaining tigers. Displaced farming communities were resettled and compensated, and armed rangers employed to discourage poachers. Demand for tiger parts did not end with Project Tiger, however, and the poachers remained in business, aided by organized smuggling rings. In August 1993, undercover investigators recovered a 400-kilo haul of tiger bones, together with forty fresh carcasses, from a team of Tibetan smugglers in Delhi which had promised to supply 1000kg more on demand. Unfortunately, such exposure is rare and perpetrators are most likely to get off with bail, free to return to their trade. The maximum punishment for tiger poaching is a $125 fine, or one year in prison. Well organized guerrilla groups thus operate with virtual impunity out of remote national parks, including Corbett, Dudhwa and Kanha, where inadequate numbers of poorly armed and poorly paid wardens offer little more than token resistance, particularly as increased use of poison is making it more and more difficult to track poachers. Project Tiger officials are understandably reluctant to jeopardize lucrative tourist traffic by admitting that sightings are getting rarer, but the prognosis looks very gloomy indeed.

Today, even though there are 23 Project Tiger sites, numbers continue to fall. Official figures optimistically claim a **population** of up to 3000–3500, but independent evidence is more pessimistic, putting the figure at under 2000. The population rise indicated by counts based on pug marks – thought to be like human finger prints, unique to each individual – that gave such encouragement in the early 1990s has been declared inaccurate. Poorly equipped park wardens are still fighting a losing battle against the failure of bureaucratic and legal systems to face the seriousness of the situation. It was estimated in 1996 that one tiger was being poached every eighteen hours and the situation is believed to be still as depressing today. The most pessimistic experts even claim that at the present rate of destruction, India's most exotic animal could face extinction early in the new millennium.

on snakes, which is why you often see it writhing in a cloud of dust with king cobras during performances by snake charmers.

Late evening is also the best time for spotting **bats**. South India boasts four species, including the fulvous fruit bat (*Rousettus leshenaulti*), or *vagul* – so-called because it gives off a scent resembling fermenting fruit juice – Dormer's bat (*Pipistrellus dormeri*), the very rare rufous horseshoe bat and the Malay fox vampire (*Magaderma spasma*), which feeds off the blood of live cattle. **Flying foxes** (*Pteropus gigantus*), the largest of India's bats, are also present in healthy numbers. With a wingspan of more than one metre, they fly in cacophonous groups to feed in fruit orchards, sometimes falling foul of electricity cables on the way: frazzled flying foxes dangling from live cables are a common sight in the interior.

Other species to look out for in forest areas are the Indian **giant squirrel** (*Ratufa indica*), or *shenkaro*, which has a coat of black fur and red–orange lower parts. Two and a half times larger than its European cousins, it lives in the canopy, leaping up to twenty metres between branches. The much smaller three-striped squirrel (*Funambulus palmarum*), or *khadi khar*, recognizable by the three black markings down its back, is also found in woodland. However, the five-striped palm squirrel (*Funambulus pennanti*) is a common sight all over the state, especially in municipal parks and villages.

Forest clearings and areas of open grassland are grazed by four species of deer. Widely regarded as the most beautiful is the **cheetal** (*Axis axis*), or spotted axis deer, which congregates in large groups around water holes and salt licks, occasionally wandering into villages to seek shelter from its predators. The plainer buff-coloured **sambar** (*Cervus unicolor*) is also well represented, despite succumbing to diseases spread by domestic cattle during the 1970s and 1980s. Two types of deer you're less likely to come across, but which also inhabit the border forests, are the **barking deer** (*Muntiacus muntjak*), whose call closely resembles that of a domestic dog, and the timid **mouse deer** (*Tragulus meminna*), a speckled-grey member of the *Tragulidae* family that is India's smallest deer, growing to a mere thirty centimetres in height. Both of these are highly secretive and nocturnal; they are also the preferred snack of Goa's smaller predators: the **striped hyena** (*Hyaena hyaena*), **jackal** (*Canis aureus*), or *colo*, and **wild dog** (*Cuon alpinus*), which hunt in packs.

Long-beaked **dolphins** are regular visitors to the shallow waters of South India's more secluded bays and beaches. They are traditionally regarded as a pest by local villagers, who believe they eat scarce stocks of fish. However, this long-standing antipathy is gradually eroding as local people realize the tourist-pulling potential of the dolphins: Palolem beach, in Goa (see p.205), is a dependable dolphin-spotting location.

Finally, no rundown of South Indian mammals would be complete without some mention of **monkeys**. The most ubiquitous species is the mangy pink-bottomed **macaque** (Macaca mulatta), or makad, which hangs out anywhere scraps may be scavenged or snatched from unwary humans: temples and picnic spots are good places to watch them in action. The black-faced Hanuman **langur**, by contrast, is less audacious, retreating to the trees if threatened. It is much larger than the macaque, with pale grey fur and long limbs and tail. In forest areas, the langur's distinctive call is an effective early-warning system against big cats and other predators, which is why you often come across herds of cheetal grazing under trees inhabited by large colonies of them.

Reptiles

Reptiles are well represented in the region, with more than forty species of snakes, lizards, turtles and crocodiles recorded. The best places to spot them are not the interior forests, where dense foliage makes observation difficult, but open cultivated areas: paddy fields and village ponds provide abundant fresh water, nesting sites and prey (frogs, insects and small birds) to feed on.

Your house or hotel room, however, is where you are most likely to come across tropical India's most common reptile, the **gecko** (*Hemidactylus*), which clings to walls and ceilings with its widely splayed toes. Deceptively static most of the time, these small yellow-brown lizards will dash at lightning speed for cracks and holes if you try to catch one, or if an unwary mosquito, fly or cockroach scuttles within striking distance. The much rarer chameleon is even more elusive, mainly because its constantly changing camouflage makes it virtually impossible to spot. They'll have no problem seeing you, though: independently moving eyes allow them to pinpoint approaching predators, while prey is slurped up with their fast-moving forty-centimetre-long tongues. The other main lizard to look out for is the **Bengal monitor**. This giant brown speckled reptile looks like a refugee from *Jurassic Park*, growing to well over a metre in length. It used to be a common sight in coastal areas, where they basked on roads and rocks. However, monitors are often killed and eaten by villagers, and have become increasingly rare. Among the few places you can be sure of sighting one is South Andaman, in the Andaman archipelago.

The monsoon period is when you're most likely to encounter **turtles**. Two varieties paddle around village ponds and wells while water is plentiful: the flap-shell (*Lissemys punctata*) and black-pond (*Melanochelys trijuga*) turtles, neither of which are endangered. Numbers of marine turtles (*Lepidochelys olivacea*), by contrast, have plummeted over the past few decades because villagers raid their nests when they crawl onto the beach to lay their eggs. This amazing natural spectacle occurs each year at a number of beaches in the region, notably Morgim in north Goa and Havelock Island in the Andamans (see p.622). Local coastguards and scientists from the Institute of Oceanography in Goa monitor the migration, patrolling the beaches to deter poachers, but the annual egg binge remains a highlight of the local gastronomic calendar, eagerly awaited by fisher families, who sell the illegal harvest in local markets. Only in Orissa, in eastern India, where a special wildlife sanctuary has been set up to protect them, have the sea turtles (also known as Olive Ridleys) survived the seasonal slaughter to reproduce in healthy numbers.

An equally rare sight nowadays is the **crocodile**. Populations have dropped almost to the point of extinction, although the Cambarjua Canal near Old Goa, and more remote stretches of the Mandovi and Zuari estuaries, support vestigial colonies of saltwater crocs, which bask on mud flats and river rocks. Dubbed "salties", they occasionally take calves and goats, and will snap at the odd human if given half a chance. The more ominously named mugger crocodile, however, is harmless, inhabiting unfrequented freshwater streams and riversides. You can see all of India's indigenous crocodiles at the wonderful Crocodile Bank near Mamallapuram (see p.473).

Snakes

Twenty-three species of snake are found in South India, ranging from the gigantic **Indian python** (*Python molurus*, or *har* in Konkani) – a forest-dwelling constrictor that grows up to four metres in length – to the innocuous worm snake (*Typhlops braminus*), or *sulva*, which is tiny, completely blind and often mistaken for an earthworm.

The eight poisonous snakes present in the region include India's four most deadly species: the cobra, the krait, the Russel's viper and saw-scaled viper. Though these are relatively common in coastal and cultivated areas, even the most aggressive snake will slither off at the first sign of an approaching human. Nevertheless, ten thousand Indians die from snake bites each year, and if you regularly cut across paddy fields or plan to do any hiking, it makes sense to familiarize yourself with the following four or five species just in case; their bites nearly always prove fatal if not treated immediately with anti-venom serum – available at most clinics and hospitals.

Present in most parts of the state and an important character in Hindu mythology, the Indian **cobra** (*naja naja*), or *naga*, is the most common of the venomous species. Wheat-brown or grey in colour, it is famed for the "hood" it unfurls when confronted and whose rear side usually bears the snake's characteristic spectacle markings. Its big brother, the king cobra *(Naja hannah)*, or *Raj naga*, is much less often encountered. Inhabiting the remote forest regions along the Karnatakan border, this beautiful brown, yellow and black snake, which grows to a length of four metres or more, is very rare, although the itinerant snake charmers that perform in markets occasionally keep one. Defanged, they rear up and "dance" when provoked by the handler, or are set against mongooses in ferocious (and often fatal) fights. The king cobra is also the only snake in the world known to make its own nest.

Distinguished by their steel-blue colour and faint white cross markings, **kraits** (*Bungarus coerulus*) are twice as deadly as the Indian cobra: even the bite of a newly hatched youngster is lethal. **Russel's viper** (*Viperi russeli*), is another one to watch out for. Distinguished by the three bands of elliptical markings that extend down its brown body, the Russel hisses at its victims before darting at them and burying its centimetre-long fangs into their flesh. The other common poisonous snake in South India is the **saw–scaled viper** (*Echis carinatus*). Grey with an arrow-shaped mark on its triangular head, it hangs around in the cracks between stone walls, feeding on scorpions, lizards, frogs, rodents and smaller snakes. They also hiss when threatened, producing the sound by rubbing together serrated scales located on the side of their head. Finally, **sea snakes** (*Enhdrina schistosa*), are common in coastal areas and potentially lethal (with a bite said to be twenty times more venomous than a cobra's), although rarely encountered by swimmers as they lurk only in deep water off the shore.

Harmless snakes are far more numerous than their killer cousins and frequently more attractive. The beautiful **golden tree snake** (Chrysopelea ornata) for example, sports an exquisitely intricate geometric pattern of red, yellow and black markings, while the **green whip snake** (Dryhopis nasutus), or sarpatol, is stunning parakeet green with a whip-like tail extending more than a metre behind it. The ubiquitous **Indian rat snake**, often mistaken for a cobra, also has beautiful markings, although it leaves behind it a foul stench of decomposing flesh. Other common non-poisonous snakes include the wolf snake (Lycodon aulicus), or kaidya, the Russel sand boa (Eryx conicus), or malun, the kukri snake (Oligodon taeniolatus), or pasko, the cat snake (Boiga trigonata), or manjra, and the keelbacks (Natrix).

Birds

You don't have to be an aficionado to enjoy South India's abundant birdlife. Travelling around the region, you can see breathtaking birds regularly flash between the branches of trees or appear on overhead wires at the roadside.

Thanks to the internationally popular brand of Goan beer, the **kingfisher** has become that state's unofficial mascot: it's not hard to see why the brewers chose it as their logo. Three common species of kingfisher frequently crop up amid the paddy fields and wetlands of the coastal plains, where they feed on small fish and tadpoles. With its enormous bill and pale green-blue wing feathers, the stork-billed kingfisher (*Perargopis capensis*) is the largest and most distinctive member of the family, although the white-breasted kingfisher (*Halcyon smyrnensis*) – which has iridescent turquoise plumage and a coral-red bill – and the common, or small blue, kingfisher (*Alcedo althis*) are more alluring.

Other common and brightly coloured species include the grass-green, blue and yellow **bee-eaters** (*Merops*), the stunning **golden oriole** (*Oriolus oriolus*), and the **Indian roller** (*Coracias bengalensis*), famous for its brilliant blue, flight feathers and exuberant aerobatic mating displays. **Hoopoes** (*Upupa epops*), recognizable by their elegant black-and-white tipped crests, fawn plumage and distinctive "hoo…po…po" call, also flit around fields and villages, as do **purple sunbirds** (*Nectarina asiatica*) and several kinds of **bulbuls**, **babblers** and **drongos** (*Dicrurus*), including the fork-tailed black drongo (*Dicrurus adsimilis*) – a winter visitor that can often be seen perched on telegraph wires. If you're lucky, you may also catch a glimpse of the **paradise flycatcher** (*Tersiphone paradisi*), which is widespread and among the region's most exquisite birds, with a thick black crest and long silver, tail streamers.

The South Indian states covered in this book harbour a total of 96 separate wildlife sanctuaries and national parks – if you include the various protected islets of the Andaman and Nicobar Islands, and the many minor reserves dotted around the region. What follows is a selection (listed in alphabetical order) of those we found most rewarding, both in terms of their wildlife and the natural environment. Bear in mind that, at the time this book went to press, those in the Western Ghats were closed pending the surrender or capture of the sandalwood smuggler Veerapan (see box on p.570). Before heading into the countryside, therefore, check with the local tourist office to ensure the park you hope to visit is currently accessible.

Cotigao Wildlife Sanctuary (Goa). Tucked away in the extreme south of Goa, near Palolem beach, its extensive mixed deciduous forest and hilly backdrop make up for a relative paucity of wildlife. Best time: November to March. See p.212.

Eravikulam National Park (Kerala). Located 17km northeast of Munnar in the lap of the Western Ghats. Famous for its thriving population of Nilgiri tahr, a rare antelope that lives only here, on the high rolling grasslands. See them on the hard hike up Anamudi, South India's biggest mountain. Best time: January to April. See p.381.

Indira Gandhi (Anamalai) Wildlife Sanctuary (Tamil Nadu). On the southernmost reaches of the Cardamom Hills, this park is more remote than Mudumalai, and consequently less visited, but encompasses some beautiful mountain scenery as well as abundant fauna. Best time: January to March. See p.554.

Kodikkarai (Point Calimere) (Tamil Nadu). On a promontory jutting into Palk Bay, some 250 species of birds, mostly migrants, descend on a swathe of mixed swampland and dry deciduous forest in the wake of the monsoon. Best time: November to February. See p.514.

Mahatma Gandhi National Marine Park (Andaman Islands). The islets in this reserve, encircled by vivid coral reefs, rise out of crystal-clear water that teems with tropical fish, turtles and other marine life. Can be reached by daily excursion boats, via bus links, from the capital Port Blair. Best time: January to March. See p.620.

Mudumalai Wildlife Sanctuary (Tamil Nadu). Set 1140m up in the Nilgiri Hills, Mudumalai is one of the most easily reached reserves in the South. It offers a full range of accommodation and trails and gives access to huge areas of protected forest. Best time: January to March. See p.569.

Periyar Wildlife Sanctuary (Kerala). A former Maharaja's hunting reserve, centred on an artificial lake high in the Cardamom Hills. Occasional tiger sightings, but you're much more likely to spot an elephant. Well placed for trips into the mountains and tea plantations, with good accommodation, including remote observation tower which you have to trek to. Best time: October to March. See p.371.

Vadanemmeli Crocodile Bank (Tamil Nadu). Endangered species of indigenous crocodiles, lizards and turtles are bred here, 15km north of Mamallapuram, for release into the wild. Local Irula tribes people collect venom from poisonous snakes to make serum. Open year round. See p.473.

Vedanthaangal Bird Sanctuary (Tamil Nadu). A wonderful mixed heronry, 86km southwest of Chennai, where you can sight 250 species of migrant wetland birds, blown in by the northwest monsoon. Best time: December and February. See p.481.

Paddy fields, ponds and saline mudflats are teeming with water birds. The most ubiquitous of these is the snowy white **cattle egret** (*Bubulcus ibis*), which can usually be seen wherever there are cows and buffalo, feeding off the grubs, insects and other parasites that live on them. The large egret (*Ardea alba*) is also pure white, although lankier and with a long yellow bill, while the third member of this family, the little egret (*Egretta garzetta),* sports a short black bill and, during the mating season, two long tail feathers. Look out too for the mud-brown **paddy bird**, India's most common heron. Distinguished by its pale green legs, speckled breast and hunched posture, it stands motionless for hours in water waiting for fish or frogs to feed on.

The hunting technique of the beautiful **white-bellied fish eagle** (*Haliaetus leucogaster*), by contrast, is truly spectacular. Cruising twenty to thirty metres above the surface of the water, this black and white osprey stoops at high speed to snatch its prey – usually sea snakes and mackerel – from the waves with its fierce yellow talons. More common birds of prey such as the **brahminy kite** (*Haliastur indus*) – recognizable by its white breast and chestnut head markings – and the **pariah kite** (*Milvus migrans govinda*) – a dark-brown buzzard with a fork tail – are widespread around towns and fishing villages, where they vie with raucous gangs of house **crows** (*Corvus splendens*) and **white-eyed jackdaws** (*Corvus monedula*) for scraps. Gigantic pink-headed **king vultures** (*Sarcogyps clavus*) and the **white-backed vulture** (*Gyps bengalensis*), which has a white ruff around its bare neck and head, also show up whenever there are carcasses to pick clean.

Other birds of prey to keep an eye open for, especially around open farm-land, are the **white-eyed buzzard** (Butastur teesa), the **honey buzzard** (Pernis ptilorhyncus), the **black-winged kite** (Elanus caeruleus) – famous for its blood-red eyes – and **shikra** (Accipiter badius), which closely resembles the European sparrowhawk.

Forest birds

The region's forests may have lost many of their larger animals, but they still offer exciting possibilities for bird-watchers. One species every enthusiast hopes to glimpse while in the woods is the magnificent **hornbill**, of which three species have been spotted: the grey hornbill (*Tockus birostris*), with its blue-brown plumage and long curved beak, is the most common, although the Indian pied hornbill (*Anthracoceros malabaricus*), distinguished by its white wing and tail tips and the pale patch on its face, often flies into villages in search of fruit and lizards. The magnificent great pied hornbill (*Buceros bicornis*), however, is more elusive, limited to the densest forest areas where it may occasionally be spotted flitting through the canopy. Growing to 130 centimetres in length, it has a black-and-white striped body and wings, and a huge yellow beak with a long curved casque on top.

Several species of **woodpecker** also inhabit the interior forests, among them two types of goldenback woodpecker: the lesser goldenback (*Dinopium bengalensis*), is the more colourful of the pair, with a crimson crown and bright splashes of yellow across its back. The Cotigao sanctuary in south Goa (see p.212) is one of the last remaining strongholds of the Indian great black wood-pecker, which has completely disappeared from the more heavily deforested hill areas further north. In spite of its bright red head and white rump, this shy bird is more often heard than seen, making loud drumming noises on tree trunks between December and March.

A bird whose call is a regular feature of the Western Ghat forests, particu-larly in teak areas, is the wild ancestor of the domestic chicken – the **jungle fowl**. The more common variety is the secretive but vibrantly coloured, red junglefowl (*Gallus gallus*), which sports golden neck feathers and a metallic black tail. Its larger cousin, the grey or sommerat's jungle fowl (*Galolus sommeratii*), has darker plumage scattered with yellow spots and streaks. Both inhabit clearings, and are most often seen scavenging for food on the verges of forest roads.

Wildlife viewing

Although you can expect to come across many of the species listed above on the edge of towns and villages, a spell in one or other of South India's nature reserves offers the best chance of **viewing wild animals**. Administered by poorly funded government bodies, they're a far cry indeed from the well organized and well maintained national parks you may be used to at home. Information can be frustratingly hard to come by and the staff running them can be less than helpful.

That said, at the larger, more easily accessible wildlife reserves – such as Periyar and Mudumalai – a reasonable infrastructure exists to transport visitors around, whether by jeep, minibus, coach or, in the case of the former, boat. Don't, however, expect to see much if you stick to these standard excursion vehicles laid on by the park authorities. Most of the rarer animals wisely keep well away from noisy groups of trippers. Wherever possible, try to organize **walking safaris** with a reliable, approved guide in the forest, while bearing in mind that not all guides may be as knowledgable and experienced as they claim, and that an untrained, unconfident guide may actually lead you into life-endangering situations; before parting with any money, ask to see recommendation books.

Accommodation is generally available at all but the most remote sanctuaries and reserves, although it may not always be very comfortable. Larger parks tend to have a batch of luxurious, Western-style resort campuses for tour groups. In all cases, you'll find reviews of the accommodation on offer in the descriptions of individual parks featured in the Guide section of this book, along with full details of how to travel to, from and around the site. Our accounts will also advise you on the best times of year to visit in each case, and indicate the kind of wildlife present.

Finally, it's worth stating the bad news that for the past few years, some of the main parks in the Nilgiri Biosphere region – notably Mudumalai, Anamalai, Bandipur and Nagarhole – have been **closed** because of the threat of abduction or violence from the sandalwood smuggler **Veerapan** (see box on p.570). This is particularly annoying for travellers making their way between Mysore in Karnataka and Ooty in Tamil Nadu. If you intend to stop off at any of the parks in this area, check before you set off that they're open.

Websites

Ⓦ www.indev.nic.in/wwf
Home page of the World Wildlife Fund, India, dedicated to conservation and environmental protection in the subcontinent. Useful primarily as a source for volunteer work and news.

Ⓦ www.5tigers.org
Everything you ever wanted to know about tigers, and more besides.

Ⓦ http://environment:123india.com
Features, safaris reviews and the latest wildlife news from across the country.

Ⓦ www.camacdonald.com/birding/asiaindia.htm
Exhaustive reviews of India's bird-watching hotspots, online resources and printed material, with dozens of pretty pics and reports from recent field trips by bona fide enthusiasts.

Ⓦ www.nbs.it/tiger
Background on India's disappearing big cat, including detailed poaching statistics – depressing reading indeed.

Music

One who is an expert in playing the veena, well versed in shruti and other forms of musical sound, and has a deep understanding of thaalam, will attain enlightenment with ease.

Tyagaraja (1767–1847)

Hindustani music from North India may be better known internationally, but the classical music of the South – called Karnatic – is by far the more ancient. Its tenets, once passed on only orally, were codified in Vedic literature between 4000 and 1000 BC, long before Western classical music was even in its infancy. Visiting the region, you'll have ample opportunity to attend Karnatic recitals, a key feature of cultural life in major cities such as Chennai, while religious rituals in South Indian temples invariably feature some kind of musical accompaniment. Styles of music – whether secular or religious – vary greatly from state to state, but among the most singular South Indian idioms are Keralan percussion, and the heavily Portuguese-accented music of Goa, both of which convey the cultural distinctiveness of these two regions more vividly than anything else.

Karnatic instrumental music

The Karnatic music of South India might be labelled "classical", but it's nothing like classical music anywhere else in the world. Rather than being the province of an urbane elite, it's an explosion of colour, sound and Hindu worship. While Hindustani music developed close associations with court and palace, Karnatic music remained part of the warp and weft of the South Indian culture, both religious and secular. The other major difference is that Karnatic music, lacking written notation, is taught by demonstration and learned by ear or, in the case of its highly sophisticated rhythmic system, taught by a marvellous, mathematical structure of "finger computing" which enables a percussionist to break down a complex *thaalam* (rhythmic cycle) into manageable units. Indian percussion maestros readily admit the supremacy of Karnatic concepts of rhythm, and increasing numbers of Hindustani percussionists have studied in the South.

The music and the faith which inspired Karnatic music have remained inseparable. Visitors to the vast temples of South India are much more likely to encounter music than in the North. It's usually the piercing sound of the *nagaswaram* (shawm) and the *tavil* (barrel drum). More than likely it accompanies flaming torches and a ceremonial procession of the temple deity.

While devotional and religious in origin, Karnatic music is as much a vehicle for education and entertainment as for spiritual elevation. **Kritis**, a genre of Hindu hymn, are hummed and sung as people go about their daily business. In their tunefulness and recognizability, they hold a similar position in popular culture to the Christian hymn in Western societies.

The association of music and **dance** with Hindu thought has a long heritage, beginning with Shiva Himself as Nataraja, the Cosmic Dancer, whose potent image is ever present in Hindu iconography. His temple at Chidambaram, for example, is rich with sculptures of *natya* dance poses, music-making and musical instruments, and the *devadasis*, the servants of God, were traditionally temple dancers.

BANSURI Transverse bamboo flute (venu in Sanskrit), typically shorter than its Hindustani counterpart of the same name.

BHARATA NATYAM Literally "Dance of India", the classical dance of South India formerly known as *dasi attam* or the dance of the *devadasis*.

CLARIONET An alternative local name for the Western clarinet; its introduction into chenda melam (see box on p.702) is attributed to the nineteenth-century musician Madadeva Nathamuni.

DEVADASI Female temple- or courtesan-dancers, trained in music and dance.

GHATAM Tuned clay pot played with the hands or, for effect, by bouncing off the belly.

JALATARANGAM A half-ring of water-filled china bowls tuned so the biggest vessel produces the deepest note. Musicians such as M.S. Chandrasekharian (also a renowned vina player), Krishnarajapuram Dhanam, the instrument's first female player, and Seeta Doraiswamy (featured on *An Anthology of South Indian Classical Music*) are amongst its exponents.

JAVALI Type of composition, often playfully erotic in content.

KANJIRA Tambourine-like hand drum, lacking the Western tambourine's side jingles.

MORSING Jew's harp.

MRIDANGAM Double-headed barrel drum, termed the "king of percussion and the queen of melody".

MUKHAVINA Soft-toned, double-reeded woodwind instrument.

TANPURA Four- or sometimes five-stringed drone instrument; some "modernists" substitute an electronic version called a shruti box.

TAVIL Double-headed barrel drum, closely associated with nagaswaram ensembles and the Pillai caste.

TILLANA Type of composition, associated with the Bharata Natyam style of classical dance.

VINA or **VEENA** Fretted seven-string instrument, three of the strings being for rhythmic purposes.

VIOLIN The European violin, tuned to meet the Indian ear.

Karnatic composers, too, are looked upon with some reverence. Indeed, the music's three great composers – **Tyagaraja** (1767–1847), **Muttuswamy Dikshitar** (1776–1835) and **Syama Sastri** (1762–1827) – are known as the *Trimurti* or "Holy Trinity" and are regarded as saint-composers. Between them, the trinity were responsible for hundreds of compositions: Tyagaraja alone is credited with some six hundred kritis.

Indians compare the music of the Trimurti to the grape, the coconut and the banana. Tyagaraja can be consumed and enjoyed immediately; appreciating Muttuswamy Dikshitar is like cracking open a shell to get to the contents; and with Syama Sastri you have to remove the soft outer layer to get to the fruit. Their era has become known as the **Golden Period**, and their music is revered and celebrated year in, year out, at various music conferences (festivals) and on a never-ending stream of recordings.

In performance

In concert, Karnatic music often seems to lack Hindustani music's showmanship and flamboyance. But neither does it require the same sustained level of concentration. A Karnatic **ragam** (raga) might be said to resemble a miniature beside a large-scale Hindustani canvas.

Karnatic musicians will distil the essence of a ragam into six to eight minutes. In part this is because a *kriti*, the base of many performances, is a fixed composition without improvisation. Karnatic musicians' creativity lies in their ability to interpret that piece faithfully while shading and colouring the composition appropriately. The words of a *kriti* affect even non-vocal compositions: instrumentalists will colour their interpretations as if a vocalist were singing along; the unvoiced lyric determines where they place an accent, a pause or melodic splash.

Improvization has its place too, most noticeably in a sequence known as **ragam-thanam-pallavi**. This is a full-scale flowering of a Karnatic ragam and is every bit the equal of a Hindustani performance, although it is employed more sparingly, tending to be the centrepiece or climax of a Karnatic concert.

Whereas Karnatic music tends to break down into three strands: temple music, temple dance-accompaniment, and music for personal and private devotional observance, **sabha** or paying concert performances have somewhat blurred these distinctions. During the 1890s, the sabha associations in **Madras** (now Chennai) took an innovative path, moving from music performances into dance recitals. Chennai remains a centre of excellence and its music conferences, especially around December and January, attract devout audiences each year.

Concert-giving led to other changes: **microphones** came into use during the 1930s. They lent soft-voiced instruments such as members of the *vina* family (see below a new lease of life, and replaced full-tilt vocal power with greater subtlety. Nowadays, concerts will typically feature a named principal soloist (either vocal or instrumental) with melodic and rhythmic accompaniment and a *tanpura* or drone player. Percussionists of standing are often included in concert announcements and advertising as they are attractions in their own right. Female musicians involved in a principal role tend to be vocalists, *vina* players or violinists. Male musicians have access to a wider range of musical possibilities as well as outnumbering female principal soloists or accompanists by roughly three to one.

Traditional Karnatic instruments

The **vina** (or *veena*) is the foremost Karnatic **stringed instrument**, the southern equivalent (and ancestor) of the sitar. A hollow wooden fingerboard with 24 frets is supported by two resonating gourds at each end. The *vina* has seven strings, four used for the melody and the other three for rhythm and drone. Current leading players include V. Doreswamy Iyengar, Chitti Babu, S. Balachandar and Sivasakti Sivanesan. The **chitra vina** (or *gotuvadyam*) is an unfretted 21-string instrument with sets for rhythm and drone as well as sympathetic strings. It has a characteristic soft voice which, before amplification, meant it was best suited to intimate surroundings. The best-known player is the young N. Ravikiran, who has switched to a hollow cylinder of teflon for his slide.

As in the North, the transverse bamboo flute goes under the name of **bansuri** or **venu**, although it is typically shorter and higher in pitch than the

Hindustani instrument. Watch out for recordings by N. Ramani and the younger S. Shashank. The **nagaswaram** (or *nadaswaram*) is a piercing double-reed shawm-like instrument. It's longer and more deep-toned than the Hindustani *shehnai* and is associated with weddings, processions and temple ceremonies. It's often paired with a drone nagaswaram or *ottu*. Besides its ceremonial functions – and it is perhaps best heard in the open air – it is sometimes employed in formal classical concert settings. Leading players include Sheik Chinnamoulana and the brothers M.P.N. Sethuraman and M.P.N. Ponnuswamy.

The Karnatic counterpart to the tabla is the **mridangam**, a double-headed, barrel-shaped drum made from a single block of jackwood. Both heads are made from layers of hide and can be tuned according to the ragam being performed. Vellore Ramabhadran and Mysore Rajappa Sainatha are two of the top players. Other percussion instruments include the **tavil**, a folk-style barrel drum commonly found in ceremonial nagaswaram ensembles and the **ghatam**, a clay pot tuned by firing. The latter is frequently found in South Indian ensembles, and unlikely as it may seem, in the hands of a top player like T.H. "Vikku" Vinayakram it can contribute some spectacular solos. The **morsing** (or morching) is a Jew's harp, often part of the accompanying ensemble, but frequently dropped when groups tour to save on the air fare. The **jalatarangam** (or jalatarang) is something of a curiosity, a melodic percussion instrument comprising a semicircle of water-filled porcelain bowls. It can create a sound of extraordinary beauty as the lead melody instrument in a typical Karnatic ensemble with violin, mridangam and ghatam. Players include Mysore M.S. Chandrasekharian and the brothers Anayampatti S. Dhandapani and Anayampatti S. Ganesan.

New instruments

Both of the subcontinent's two classical systems give pride of place to the voice while melodic instruments, to some degree, are played to mimic it. Nevertheless, Karnatic music makes use of a fascinating array of stringed, wind and percussion instruments, many unique to the subcontinent.

From the nineteenth century, Karnatic music began to appropriate **Western instruments**, notably the violin and clarinet. More recent additions include the mandolin and saxophone. In the South – where the northern *sarangi* is a stranger – the violin's fluidity, grace, speed and penetrative volume guaranteed it a complement of converts during the nineteenth century, most notably **Tanjore Vadivelu** of the Tanjore Quartette.

Nowadays Karnatic music without the **violin** is inconceivable. Credit for introducing it and adapting its Western tuning is given to **Balaswamy Dikshitar** (1786–1859), younger brother of the saintly composer – though some traditionalist scholars claim it as really a descendant of the earlier *dhanur vina*. Maestros such as Lalgudi G. Jayaraman, V.V. Subrahmanyam and L. Subramaniam are major artists, while A. Kanyakumari typifies the female violinists who are coming to the fore. In South India, the violin is played sitting on the floor with the body of the violin against the upper chest and the scroll wedged against the ankle leaving the left hand free to slide more freely up and down the strings. **Shankar**, brother of L. Subramaniam, has devised his own electric double violin with an extended bottom range and dark tone.

The introduction of the **clarinet**, or to give it its local name *clarionet*, is credited to Mahadeva Nattuvanar, in around 1860. Until around 1920, the clarinet

Compilations

An Anthology of South Indian Classical Music (Ocora, France).
A substantial work compiled by the eminent violinist Dr L. Subramaniam. This four-CD primer gathers many of Karnatic music's vocal and instrumental giants with detailed descriptions of the music they make and the instruments they play. M.S. Subbulakshmi (vocals), T.R. Mahalingam (flute), A.K.C. Natarajan (clarinet), Raajeshwari Padmanabhan (*vina*), N. Ravikiran (*chitra vina*), Subashchandran (morsing), V.V. Subrahmanyam (violin) and T.H. Vinayakram (*ghatam*) are among the concentration of virtuosi.

Vocal music

M. Balamuralkrishna
Born in 1930 into a musical family, Balamuralikrishna was a child prodigy. He is also credited as a composer of new ragam formulations and some four hundred classical compositions.

Vocal (Moment, US).
A kriti in Lathangi lasting nearly an hour, followed by a spectacular *tillana* performance using four different ragams in succession to create a *tillana ragamalika* (garland of ragams). Zakir Hussain (tabla) and T.H. Vinayakram (ghatam) provide rhythmic support.

Sudha Ragunathan
On very rare occasions along comes a new musician whose presence and musicality simply transport the listener. Since her debut, Sudha Ragunathan (b.1958) has proved herself to be one of the most illuminating female singers in Karnatic music. Although she has recorded for labels such as EMI India and Inreco, her prime work is to be found on Winston Panchacharam's New York-based Amutham label.

Kaleeya Krishna (Amutham, US).
Released in 1994, this album of devotional music finds Ragunathan in the company of a full Indian orchestra conducted by Vazhuvoor R. Manikkavinayakam. The record celebrates the work of the composer Ventatasubbaiyar (1700–65), whose muse was Krishna. An uplifting performance, even for non-Hindus. The more intimate, violin, mridangam and ghatam instrumentation on *San Marga* (Amutham, US) is similarly recommended.

M.S. Subbulakshmi
M.S. Subbulakshmi (b. 1916) is a cultural ambassador for Indian arts on a par with Ravi Shankar. In the 1960s she enjoyed a great deal of attention by virtue of her albums also being available on the World Pacific label. But unlike Ravi Shankar she did not support her recording career with constant touring although she appeared at the Edinburgh Festival (1963) and at Carnegie Hall (1977). She has been heaped with honours, and is considered a national treasure.

M.S. Subbulakshmi at Carnegie Hall (Gramophone Company of India, India).
This double CD captures Subbulakshmi in New York in October 1977 with her daughter Radha Viswanathan, the violinist Kandadevi Alagiriswami and the percussionist Guruvayur Dorai.

Instrumental artists

S. Balachander
The *vina* maestro S. Balachander (1927–90) was one of the best known Karnatic instrumentalists, having been one of the influential World Pacific label's major artists

with groundbreaking issues such as *Sounds of the Veena* featuring the flute of Ramani and *The Magic Music of India*. Unlike most Karnatic performers, his recorded work is peppered with interpretations of ragams that are longer than normal.

The Virtuoso of Veena (Denon, Japan).
Ragam Chakravaakam is at the centre of this disc. Track one comprises alapana and thanam while track two explores Tyagaraja's devotional employment of the same ragam. Taeko Kusano's touching notes marvellously capture the spirit of this maverick musician.

Kadri Gopalnath
Gopalnath's father started on his father's instrument, the *nagaswaram*, but got turned on to the saxophone after hearing the palace band at Mysore. He studied initially under N. Gopalkrishna Iyer of Mangalore and the vocalist and mridangam player T.V. Gopalkrishnan and pioneered saxophone in a Karnatic classical setting. He typifies the duality of Karnatic music in playing a modern instrument in a tradition that goes back centuries.

Gem Tones: Saxophone Supreme, South Indian Style (Globestyle, UK).
A fervent and thrilling collection with accompaniment by A. Kanyakumari on her low-tuned violin, sounding for all the world like a tenor sax, plus *mridangam* (M. R. Sainatha) and *morsing* (B. Rajasekhar).

Lalgudi Jayaraman
Violin may only be a relatively recent South Indian import – merely a few centuries old – but it is difficult to imagine Karnatic music without it and Jayaraman is one of the finest contemporary violinists.

Violin (Moment, US).
An interesting North–South excursion with a *kriti*, a *bhajan* (a Hindu devotional song form) and a *tillana* (a light dance-derived form using drum syllables as well as lyrics proper). Percussion accompaniment is from Vellore Ramabhadran (*mridangam*) and Moment's founder Zakir Hussain (tabla).

The Karnataka College of Percussion
The Karnataka College have worked with German fusionists Dissidenten on their Germanistan and Jungle Book albums, and have made a number of records in their own right. Despite the ensemble's percussive-sounding identity, KCP also features the voice of Ramamani and melody instruments such as *vina* (played by leader Raghavendra), violin (M.S. Govindaswamy) and flute (V.K. Raman).

River Yamuna (Music of the World, US).
This 1997 album is an edited, reworked and reordered version of *Shiva Ganga*, the 1995 album produced by Dissidenten's Marlon Klein. An accessible introduction for beginners testing the heat of Karnatic water.

N. Ramani
The flautist Dr N. Ramani (b. 1934), like Balachander and M.S. Subbulakshmi, came to attention through Richard Bock's World Pacific label. Born in Tiruvarur in Tamil Nadu, the birthplace of Tyagaraja, by the age of 12 he was accomplished enough to be appearing on All India Radio. The *venu*, as the Indian flute is known, is Lord Krishna's instrument and therefore holds a special place in Indian music.

Classical Karnatic Flute (Nimbus, UK).
A recording with a great deal of presence dating from 1990. Ramani is accompanied by violin from T.S. Veeraraghavan, *mridangam* from Srimushnam Rajarao and *ghatam* from E.M. Subramaniam in pieces by Tyagaraja and Ramani himself.

continues over

N. Ravikiran

The magisterial Ravikiran (b. 1967), who gave his first vocal recital at the age of five, is the foremost exponent of the *chitra vina*. In his hands, it is a joy, capable of arcane and ethereal sounds that in the West are associated with electronic instruments such as the *theremin*, but are typically Indian melodic properties. Ravikiran is also the author of the first-rate introductory guide, *Appreciating Carnatic Music* (Ganesh & Co., Madras, 1997). Log on to ⌨ www.ravikiranmusic.com for more information.

Young Star of Gottuvadyam (Chhanda Dhara, Germany).
Accompanied on mridangam by Trichur R. Mohan and on ghatam by T.H. Subashchandran, Ravikiran's repertoire and performances here are mesmerizing. The nearly nineteen-minute long performance of Shankara Bharanam is especially good and after the kriti the piece goes into a percussion duet. A northern *bhajan* in Sindhu Bhairavi closes.

Shankar

L. Shankar (b. 1953) played in a violin trio with his brothers L. Vaidyanathan and L. Subramaniam, and accompanied Karnatic vocalists, before embarking on a solo career, and founding the Indo-Jazz fusion group Shakti with guitarist John McLaughlin. He is renowned for creating his own ten-string double violin with its startling extended range.

Raga Aberi (Music of the World, US).
A spectacular ragam-thanam-pallavi performance growing out the growling low notes of Shankar's extraordinary violin. The performance also features spectacular vocal percussion and solos from Zakir Hussain (tabla) and Vikku Vinayakram (ghatam).

U. Srinivas

Mandolin-player U. Srinivas (b. 1969) uses a five-string, solid body instrument, akin to a cut-down electric guitar, rather than the eight-string Western mandolin, which he claims is ideally suited to the ragas of South Indian music. Like many Karnatic musicians he was a child prodigy and has excited listeners the world over, notably in the West with a successful fusion album, *Dream* (1995 – see below), with Michael Brook. He sometimes performs mandolin duets with his brother U. Rajesh.

Rama Sreerama (RealWorld, UK).
A well recorded and inspiring introduction to Srinivas's music, including pieces by Srinivas himself and Tyagaraja. Strongly devotional in character, with violin, *mridangam* and *ghatam* accompaniment.

L. Subramaniam

L. Subramaniam (b. 1947) is from a dynasty of violinists (his brothers are L. Vaidyanathan and Shakti-founder L. Shankar). He is one of the most recorded

---

was mostly used as an ensemble instrument in *cinna melam*, a dance accompaniment form. Thereafter, it was gradually established as a soloist's instrument. Balaraman of the Nadamuni Band was one of the twentieth century's first clarionet maestros and his work has been continued by musicians like A.K.C. Natarajan.

The **mandolin** has gained acceptance thanks to another of South India's child prodigies, **U. Srinivas**, often known as Mandolin Srinivas. He started playing the instrument aged six and has since toured worldwide and proved that the mandolin (albeit heavily modified) is highly effective at spinning gossamer webs of Tyagaraja improvisations. He is a very devout musician and his performances usually have a devotional ingredient.

The **saxophone** is another recent import and its champion, Kadri Gopalnath,

Karnatic artists in the West and has regularly played in non-Karnatic contexts – with Hindustani musicians, jazz-fusion groups, Western orchestras and in films (including Mira Nair's Salaam Bombay and Mississippi Masala).

Electric Modes (Water Lily Acoustics, US).
A two-CD set, one volume of which consists of original compositions, the second of which focuses on traditional ragams. The album's title recalls Muddy Waters' album *Electric Mud*. "From the mud of the past emerges a brave new world of music", wrote Kavichandran Alexander, alluding to both the Buddhist image of the lotus or water lily and his label's name.

Fusion
Michael Brook
Toronto-born composer and producer Michael Brook has had an eclectic career, with early stints in rock bands (Martha and the Muffins) leading to ambient/minimalist-influenced soundtrack work. But he is perhaps best known as a producer, working on albums for Peter Gabriel's Realworld label with U. Srinavas and Nusrat Fateh Ali Khan amongst others.

Dream (Realworld, UK)
An album that began with the idea of Brook producing Srinavas and turned into a full-blown East–West collaboration, including contributions from Canadian singer Jane Siberry.

John McLaughlin/Shakti
Guitarist John McLaughlin has been a linchpin of East–West fusion since introducing Miles Davis to India music back in the 1960s, moving through solo work, the jazz-rock Mahavishnu Orchestra and, most impressively, the all-acoustic group Shakti, formed in 1974 with tabla player Zakir Hussain. With L. Shankar (violin) and T.H. Vinayakram (ghatam), Shakti toured and recorded to great acclaim through until 1977 when Columbia, used to massive-selling albums from McLaughlin, withdrew support. The group has since continued to perform in various permutations, including the Remember Shakti revival in 1997 with musicians such as Selvaganesh (percussion), Debashish Bhattacharya (guitar) and U. Srinavas (mandolin) in place of L. Shankar.

Remember Shaki *The Believer* (Verve, UK)
In this wonderful live recording, made during a tour in 2000, McLaughlin teams up with mandolin maestro U. Srinavas and percussion virtuosos Zakir Hussain and V. Selvaganesh, to rework the successful Shakti formula. The result is some of the most inspired improvization ever captured on disc.

is one of South India's most popular musicians, with dozens of recordings to his credit. Gopalnath demonstrates Karnatic music's particular ability to be ancient and modern at the same time. When he plays the Karnatic ragams the powerful sound of the saxophone echoes the ancient *nagaswaram*, but its tone and attitude are also distinctively contemporary.

Ken Hunt

Goan music

With reggae and techno blaring out of so many beach bars, you'd be forgiven for thinking **Goa's music and dance scene** started with the invention of the synthesizer. However, the state boasts a vibrant musical tradition of its own: a

The noisiest, rowdiest and most intense phase of any Keralan temple festival is the one presided over by the local drum orchestra, or chenda melam, whose ear-shattering performances accompany the procession of the deity around the sacred precinct and into the shrine. As impressive for their mental arithmetic as percussion technique and sheer bodily stamina in the intense heat, the musicians play an assortment of upright barrel drums (chenda) supported over the shoulder, bronze cymbals and wind instruments – the oboe-like kuzhal and the spectacular C-shaped brass trumpets (kombu) which emphasise and prolong the drum beating.

Performances invariably begin with an impressive "ghrr" and "dhim" produced on the drums. This is said to symbolize a lion's roar and was probably once performed in support of a lion hunt. After this mighty introduction, the drums drop the tempo and the music builds up like a pyramid. It starts slowly with long-lasting musical cycles and works up to a short, fast, powerful climax. During the performance, the elephant, musicians and crowd process round the temple precinct, and after more than two hours, the excited crowd and sweating musicians celebrate the conclusion and follow the elephant and deity into the inner temple.

The first stage broadly symbolizes the ordinary life of men, while the peak of the last stage shows the ideal human or divine aspect of reality. The music must please the god on top of the elephant and, of course, the assembled temple crowd. While the main beats are provided by beating the underside of the chenda, the skilled solo chenda players create intricate patterns over the top. Different players may gather for each event, but they are capable of playing together perfectly with no rehearsal. The concept is more like a big jazz band than a European classical orchestra.

A typical setup for a medium-sized temple festival kicks off with a turn from the panchavadyam orchestra, comprising three types of drums, cymbals and the kombu trumpets. A conch is blown three times, symbolizing the holy syllable "Om", and the performance begins its first stage with a slow, 1792-beat rhythmic cycle. The next cycle has 896 beats, half that number, then 448, half again, then 224 and so on. The speed increases until fast 56-beat cycles round it off. Fireworks, a large crowd and elephants trumpeting support the ecstatic climax.

For the evening, performances of tayambaka, keli and kuzhal pattu are announced. Each is a solo performing style, with players from the chenda melam and panchavadyam orchestras. Tayambaka is the main attraction, an improvised chenda solo played with a small ensemble of accompanying treble and bass chenda and cymbals. The other solo styles, keli (with a soloist on the *maddalam*, horizontally slung barrel drum) and kuzhal pattu (oboe), precede the midnight performance of the last chenda melam.

Rolf Killius

typically syncretic blend of east and west that is as spicy and distinctive as the region's cuisine. You won't hear the calypso-like rhythms of Konkani pop or haunting Kunbi folk songs at the full-moon parties, though. Rooted in village and religious life, Goan music is primarily for domestic consumption, played at temple festivals, harvest celebrations, as an accompaniment to popular theatre and, most noticeably, on the crackly cassette machines of local buses.

Wander into almost any Hindu village on the eve of an important puja, particularly around harvest time after the monsoons, and you'll experience Goan roots music and dance at its most authentic. The torchbearers of the region's thriving **folk tradition** are the Kunbi class of landless labourers, most often seen bent double in rice paddy, the women with garish coloured cotton saris tied *dhoti*-style around their legs. Agricultural work – planting, threshing and grinding grain, raking salt pans, and fixing fishing nets – provide the essential rhythms for Konkani songs, known as **Kunbi geet**.

More rehearsed performances take place during the Hindu month of Paush (late Feb), when groups of women gather in the village square-cum-dance ground (*mannd*) to sing *dhalos* and *fugdis*. The singing may run over seven or more nights, culminating with outbreaks of spirit possession and trances.

The most famous Goan folk song and dance form, though, has to be the **mando**. Originally, this slow and expressive dance (whose name derives from the Sanskrit mandala, meaning circular pattern) was traditionally performed in circles, but these days tends to be danced by men and women standing opposite each other in parallel lines, waving fans and coloured handkerchiefs. *Mandos* gather pace as they progress and are usually followed by a series of **dulpods**, quick-time tunes whose lyrics are traditionally satirical, exposing village gossip about errant housewives, lapsed priests and so on. *Dulpods*, in turn, merge into the even jauntier rhythms of **deknis**, bringing the set dances to a tumultuous conclusion.

The basic rhythmic cycles, or *ovis*, of Goan folk songs were exploited by early Christian missionaries in their work. Overlaid with lyrics inspired by Bible stories, many were eventually assimilated into the local Catholic tradition: today, the mando, for example, is usually danced by Christians on church *festas* and wedding days. It also became the favourite dance of the Goan gentry, who, dressed in ball gowns and dinner suits with fans and flamboyant handkerchiefs, used to perform it during the glittering functions held in the reception rooms of the territory's top houses.

Fados

The most European-influenced of all the Goan folk idioms is the **fado**. Rendered in a turgid mock operatic style, these melancholic songs epitomize the colonial predilection for nostalgia or longing for the home country, known in Portuguese as *saudades*. Ironically, though, few *fadistas* actually laid eyes on the fabled lights of Lisbon or Coimbra they eulogized in their lyrics, and today the fado is a dying art form. However, a couple of renowned folk singers, notably the band leader **Oslando** and singer-guitarist **Lucio Miranda**, invariably include a couple of old fado numbers on their albums. Lucio, the greatest living exponent of the form, also gives the odd performance in the five-star hotels around Panjim.

Konkani pop

Rave music aside, most of the sounds you hear around Goa these days are either *filmi* hits from the latest blockbuster Hindi movies, or a mishmash of folk tunes and calypso rhythms known as **Konkani pop**. Backed by groups of women singers and fanfaring mariachi-style brass sections, Konkani lead vocalists croon away with the reverb cranked up against a cacophony of electric guitar and keyboard accompaniment.

Konkani pop is best experienced live (the costumes tend to be as lurid as the music), but if you don't manage to get to a gig, every kerbside cassette-wallah stocks a range of popular tapes. No particular artist is worth singling out – nor are many likely to find fans among Western visitors. However, world-music aficionados should definitely check out a couple of cassettes to sample the sometimes surreal blend of musical influences. Underpinning the Portuguese-style melodies are conga-driven African and Caribbean rhythms, Brazilian syncopations, and almost Polynesian-sounding harmonies. The only part of the world Konkani pop sounds like it doesn't come from is India.

Dance

Among the most magical experiences a visitor to South India can have is to see one of the dances that play such an important part in the cultural life of the region. India's most prevalent classical dance style, Bharatanatyam, originated in the South and still fills concert halls in Tamil towns, while other types of ritualized theatre, such as Kathakali, Kuttiyattam and Teyyam, remain integral to temple worship in Kerala. If you're lucky enough to catch an authentic performance in situ, you'll never forget it: the stamina of the performers and the spectacle of an audience sitting up all night to see the finale of a dance drama at dawn is utterly remarkable.

The Natya Shastra

All forms of Indian dance share certain broad characteristics and can be traced back to principles enshrined in the **Natya Shastra**, a Sanskrit treatise on dramaturgy dating from the first century BC. The text covers every aspect of the origin and function of **Natya**, the art of dance-drama, which combines music, stylized speech, dance and spectacle, and characterizes theatre throughout South Asia.

The spread of this art form occurred during the centuries of cultural expansion from the second BC to the eighth AD, when South Indian kings sent trade missions, court dancers, priests and conquering armies all over the region. Even in countries that later embraced Buddhism or Islam, dances continue to show evidence of Indian forms, and Hindu gods and goddesses still feature, mixed with indigenous heroes and deities.

Indian dance is divided into two temperaments: **tanava**, which represents the fearful male energy of Shiva, and **lasya**, representing the grace of his wife Parvati. Dances can fall into one or other category (Kathakali is *tanava* and Bharatanatyam, *lasya*), or combine the two elements. Equally, they include in differing degrees the three main components of classical dance: **nritta**, pure dance in which the music is reflected by decorative movements of the body; **natya**, which is the dramatic element of the dance and includes the portrayal of character; and **nritya**, the interpretive element, in which mood is portrayed through hand and facial gestures and the position of the feet and legs.

The term **abinaya** describes the resources at the disposal of a performer in communicating the meaning of a dance; they include costume and make-up, speech and intonation, psychological understanding and, perhaps the most distinctive and complex element, the language of gestures. Stylized gestures are prescribed for every part of the body – there are seven movements for the eyebrows, six for the nose and six for the cheeks, for example – and they can take a performer years of intensive training to perfect.

Once complete control of the body has been mastered, a performer will have a repertoire of several thousand meanings. In combination with other movements a single hand gesture, with the fingers extended and the thumb bent for example, can be used to express heat, rain, a crowd of men, the night, a forest, a flight of birds or a house. Similarly, up to three characters can be played by a single performer by alternating facial expressions.

Despite frequent feats of technical brilliance, performers are rarely judged by their skill in executing a particular dance, but by their success in communicating certain specific emotions, or **bhava**, to the audience. This can only be measured by the quality of **rasa**, a mood or sentiment, one for each of the nine bhava, which the audience experiences during a performance.

Bharatanatyam

The best-known Indian classical dance style, **Bharatanatyam**, is a graceful, gestural form performed by women. A popular subject for temple sculptures throughout South India (especially Tamil Nadu), it originated in the dances of the **devadasis**, temple dancing girls who originally performed as part of their devotional duties in the great Tamil shrines. Usually "donated" to a temple by their parents, the young girls were formally "wedded" to the deity and spent the rest of their lives dancing or singing as part of their devotional duties. Later, however, the *devadasis* system became debased, and the dancers, who formerly enjoyed high status in Hindu society, became prostitutes controlled by the brahmins, whom male visitors to the temple would pay for sexual services.

In the latter half of the nineteenth century, four brothers set themselves the task of saving the dance from extinction and pieced together a reconstruction of the form through study of the *Natya Shastra*, the images on temple friezes and through information gleaned from former *devadasis*. Although the dance today is largely based on their findings, this was only the first step in its revival, as Bharatanatyam continued to be confined to the temples and was danced almost exclusively by men – the only way, as the brothers saw it, of preventing its moral decline. Not until the 1930s, when **Rukmini Devi**, a member of the Theosophical Society, introduced the form to a wider middle-class audience, did Bharatanatyam begin to achieve popularity as a secular art form.

As ward of the nineteenth-century British rebel **Annie Besant**, Devi had greater exposure to foreign arts than many women of her generation. She developed an interest in Western dance while accompanying her husband, George Arundale, former principal of the Theosophical Society's school in Adyar, Chennai, on lecture tours and had studied under Pavlova, among others. In 1929, however, after witnessing a performance of the dance she later named "Bharatanatyan", she dedicated her life to its revival. The dance school she founded at Adyar is now known as Kalakshetra and continues to develop some of the world's most accomplished exponents.

In her determination to make the art form socially respectable, Devi eliminated all erotic elements and was known to be rigid and authoritarian in her views about how Bharatanatyam should be danced. Many ex-pupils have gone on to develop their own interpretations of the style, but the form continues to be seen as an essentially spiritual art. Its theme is invariably romantic love, with the dancer seen as a devotee separated from the object of her devotion. In this way, she dramatizes the idea of **sringara bhakti**, or worship through love.

As with other classical dance forms, training is rigorous. Performers are encouraged to dissolve their identity in the dance and become instruments for the expression of divine presence. The order in which the phases of the dance are performed and practised is considered to be the one best suited to this goal. A recital usually lasts about two hours and consists of the following phases: *alarippu, jatiswaram, sabdam, varnam, padams javalis, tillana* and *mangalam*.

All performances are preceded by a namaskaram, a salutation to the gods, offered by the stage, musicians and audience; a floral offering is made to a statue of the presiding deity, which stands at the right of the stage. The pivotal part of the performance is **varnam**, which the preceding three phases build up to through *nritta* (pure dance based on rhythm), adding melody and then lyrics. In *varnam*, every aspect of the dancer's art is exercised through two sections, the first slow, alternating *abinhaya* with rhythmic syllables, and the second twice the pace of the first, alternating *abinhaya* with melodic syllables. In the following two phases the emphasis is on the expression of mood through mime, and in the penultimate phase, the *tillana*, the dancer reverts again to the pure rhythm which began the dance. A *mangalam*, or short prayer, marks the end of a performance.

Kathakali

Here is the tradition of the trance dancers, here is the absolute demand of the subjugation of body to spirit, here is the realization of the cosmic transformation of human into divine.

Mrinalini Sarabhai, classical dancer

The image of a Kathakali actor in a magnificent costume with extraordinary make-up and a huge gold crown has become Kerala's trademark, seen on anything from matchboxes to TV adverts for detergents. Traditional performances, of which there are still many, usually take place on open ground outside a temple, beginning at 10pm and lasting until dawn, illuminated solely by the flickers of a large brass oil lamp centre stage. Virtually nothing about Kathakali is naturalistic, because it depicts the world of gods and demons. Both male and female roles are played by men.

Standing at the back of the stage, two musicians play driving rhythms, one on a bronze gong, the other on heavy bell-metal cymbals; they also sing the dialogue. Actors appear and disappear from behind a handheld curtain and never utter a sound, save the odd strange cry. Learning the elaborate hand gestures, facial expressions and choreographed movements, as articulate and precise as any sign language, requires rigorous training that can begin at the age of eight and last ten years. At least two more drummers stand left of the stage; one plays the upright **chenda** with slender curved sticks, the other plays the **maddalam**, a horizontal barrel-shaped hand drum. When a female character is "speaking", the chenda is replaced by the hourglass-shaped *ettaka*, a "talking drum" on which melodies can be played. The drummers keep their eyes on the actors, whose every gesture is reinforced by their sound, from the gentlest embrace to the gory disembowelling of an enemy.

Although it bears the unmistakable influences of Kutiyattam and indigenous folk rituals, Kathakali, literally "story-play", is thought to have crystallized into a distinct theatre form during the seventeenth century. The plays are based on three major sources: the *Mahabharata*, *Ramayana* and the *Bhagavata Purana*. While the stories are ostensibly of god-heroes such as Rama and Krishna, the most popular characters are those that give the most scope to the actors – the villainous, fanged, red-and-black-faced *katti* ("knife") anti-heroes. These types, such as the kings Ravana and Duryodhana, are dominated by lust, greed, envy and violence. David Bolland's handy paperback *Guide to Kathakali*, widely available in Kerala, gives invaluable scene-by-scene summaries of the most popular plays and explains in simple language a lot more besides.

When attending a performance, arrive early to get your bearings before it gets dark, even though the first play will not begin much before 10pm. Members of the audience are welcome to visit the dressing room before and during the performance, to watch the **masks** and **make-up** being applied. The colour and design of these, which specialist artists take several hours to apply, signify the personality of each character. The principal characters fall into the seven following types.

- **Pacca** ("green" and "pure") characters, painted bright green, are the noble heroes, including gods such as Rama and Krishna.
- **Katti** ("knife") are evil and clever characters such as Ravana. Often the most popular with the audience, they have green faces to signify their noble birth, with upturned moustaches and white mushroom knobs on the tips of their noses.
- **Chokannatadi** ("red beard") characters are power-drunk and vicious, and have black faces from the nostrils upwards, with blood-red beards.
- **Veluppadi** ("white beard") represents Hanuman, monkey son of the wind god and personal servant of Rama. He always wears a grey beard and furry coat, and has a black and red face and green nose.
- **Karuppadi** ("black beard") is a hunter or forest-dweller and carries a sword, bow and quiver. He has a coal-black face with a white flower on his nose.
- **Kari** ("black") characters, the ogresses and witches of the drama, have black faces, marked with white patterns, and huge breasts.
- **Minnukku** ("softly shaded") characters are women, brahmins and sages. The women have pale yellow faces sprinkled with mica and the men wear orange *dhotis*.

Once the make-up is finished, the performers are helped into their costumes – elaborate wide skirts tied to the waist, towering head-dresses and long silver talons fitted to the left hand. Women, brahmins and sages are the only characters with a different style of dress: men wear orange, and the women wear saris and cover their heads. The transformation is completed with a final prayer before the performance begins.

Visitors new to Kathakali will undoubtedly get bored during such long programmes, parts of which are very slow indeed. If you're at a village performance, you may not always find accommodation, so you can't leave during the night. Be prepared to sit on the ground for hours, and bring some warm clothes. Half the fun is staying up all night to witness, just as the dawn light appears, the gruesome disembowelling of a villain or a demon asura.

Kuchipudi

Kuchipudi, which originated in Andhra Pradesh, was only accorded the status of Classical Dance Form by the Sangeet Natak Academi in New Delhi in 1958. Before this – although considered to follow the **Natya Shastra** more closely than any other form – it was seen essentially as a folk idiom, a means of presenting scenes from mythology and the Hindu epics to relatively unsophisticated audiences.

Similar in form to Bharatanatyam, it also shares a history of decline and regeneration. Its present form is thought to date back to the seventeenth century when a local man capsized his boat while on the way to his wedding and prayed that his life might be saved. On finding his prayers answered, he wrote, in his new incarnation as **Siddhappa Yogi**, a dance drama in praise of Krishna and gathered a troupe of brahmin men to perform it. When presented at court in 1675, it so impressed the resident *nawab* that he granted the village of Kuchipudi to the artists so that they might pass on their art to future generations. Taking its name from the village, the dance has been practised by the same fifteen brahmin families ever since.

Traditionally performed only by groups of men, Kuchipudi requires seven years of rigorous training, with parallel education in music, Sanskrit, the ancient scriptures and mythology. Since the turn of the century, however, there has been an increase in the numbers of women dancing, as well as solo performances.

Like Bharatanatyam, Kuchipudi follows a fixed sequence of phases and uses similar techniques and costume, but it is distinguished by the importance of dialogue and song, and differs from other forms in that the dancers sing for themselves, usually in Telugu. Humour and spectacle are other important elements that distinguish it from the more restrained mood of Bharatanatyam: the highlight of most performances is a scene in which one dancer carries a pot of water on her head while balancing on the edge of a brass plate.

Mohiniyattam

A semiclassical form from Kerala, **Mohiniyattam** has its origins, like Bharatanatyam, in the temple dances of the *devadasis*. It, too, was revived through the efforts of enthusiastic individuals, first in the nineteenth century by Swati Thirunal, the king of Travancore, and again in the 1930s, after a period of disrepute, by the poet Vallathol.

Mohiniyattam ("the dance of the enchantress") takes its name from the mythological maiden **Mohini**, who evoked desire and had the ability to steal the heart of the onlooker. Usually a solo dance performed by women, it is dominated by the mood of **lasya**, with graceful movements distinguished by a rhythmic swaying of the body from side to side. The central theme is one of love and devotion to god, with Vishnu or Krishna appearing most frequently as the heroes. The mark of a successful performance is if the dancer successfully communicates her dreams and ambitions to the audience.

Dancers of Mohiniyattam wear realistic make-up and the white, gold-bordered Kasavu sari of Kerala. The music which accompanies the dancer is classical Carnatic with lyrics in Malayalam.

Kutiyattam

Three families of the Chakyar caste and a few outsiders perform the Sanskrit drama **Kutiyattam**, the oldest continually performed theatre form in the world. Until recently it was only performed inside temples and then only in front of the uppermost castes. Visually it is very similar to its offspring, Kathakali, but its atmosphere is infinitely more archaic. The actors, eloquent in sign language and symbolic movement, speak in the bizarre, compelling intonation of the local brahmins' Vedic chant, unchanged since 1500 BC.

A single act of a Kutiyattam play can require ten full nights; the entire play forty. A great actor, in full command of the subtleties of gestural expression, can take half an hour to do such a simple thing as murder a demon, berate the audience or simply describe a leaf falling to the ground. Unlike Kathakali, Kutiyattam includes comic characters and plays. The ubiquitous Vidushaka, narrator and clown, is something of a court jester, and traditionally has held the right to criticize openly the highest in the land without fear of retribution.

Teyyattam

In northern Kerala, a wide range of ritual "performances", loosely known as *teyyattam*, are extremely localized, even to particular families. They might include *bhuta* (spirit or hero worship), trance dances, the enactment of legendary events and oracular pronouncements. Performers are usually from low castes, but during the ritual, a brahmin will honour the deities they represent, so the status of each individual is reversed.

Although teyyattam can nowadays be seen in government-organized cultural festivals, the powerful effect is best experienced in the courtyard of a house or temple, in a village setting. Some figures, with painted faces and bodies, are genuinely terrifying; costumes include headgear metres high, sometimes doubling as a mask, and clothes of leaves and bark.

The only place you can be sure of seeing teyyattam is at **Parassinikadavu**, a small village 20km north of Kunnur, in the far north of Kerala, where the head priest of the local temple dances each day. This is an extraordinary spectacle that shouldn't be missed if you're in the area. For more typical village teyyattam, you have to be in the right place at the right time. First, head for Kannur and ask the local tourist officer to point you in the right direction; after a few days' of waiting around, someone will hear you're looking for teyyattam and take you back to their village if a performance is planned – an experience anyone with more than a passing interest in ritual theatre and costume should definitely not miss.

Vicki Maggs

Books

Appropriately for a part of the world with a written history dating back nearly two and a half thousand years, South India has spawned an extraordinary wealth of books. What follows is merely a selection of those that have proved most useful or enjoyable during the preparation of this guide. Most are available in the UK and US, and frequently in India too, where they tend to be much cheaper. Where separate editions exist in the UK and USA, publishers are detailed below in the form "UK publisher/US publisher", unless the publisher is the same in both countries. Where books are published in India only, this follows the publisher's name. O/p signifies an out-of-print recommended book (try finding these through ⓦ www.amazon.com/ⓦ www.amazon.co.uk).

History

Jad Adams and Phillip Whitehead *The Dynasty: the Nehru-Gandhi Story* (Penguin). A brilliant and intriguing account of India's most famous – or infamous – family and the way its various personalities have shaped post-Independence India, although Sonia Gandhi's recent prominence rather begs an update.

A.L. Basham *The Wonder that was India* (South Asia Books, India). Scholarly survey of Indian history, society, music, art and literature from 400 BC to the coming of the Muslims. Volume II, by S.A. Rizvi, brings it up to the arrival of the British. An undergraduate set text on Indian history courses the world over.

Larry Collins and Dominique Lapierre *Freedom at Midnight* (HarperCollins). Readable, if shallow, account of Independence, highly sympathetic to the British and, particularly, to Mountbatten, who was the authors' main source of information.

Charles Dellon, *L'Inquisition de Goa* (Editions Chandeigne, Paris). The only surviving first-hand account of the Goan Inquisition, by a French traveller who survived it in the seventeenth century. Dellon's chilling narrative, in this French edition illustrated with the original engravings, was the *Papillon* of its day, and remains a shocking indictment of the genocide perpetrated by the colonial clergy – at least, if you can read French (its English translation is out of print and extremely rare).

☆ **Patrick French** *Liberty or Death* (HarperCollins). The definitive account of the last years of the British Raj. Material from hitherto unreleased intelligence files shows how Churchill's "florid incompetence" and Atlee's "feeble incomprehension" contributed to the debacle that was Partition, which French concludes was doomed through "confusion, human frailty and neglect". All in all, a damning indictment of Britain's role, that debunks many myths; it also shows up *Freedom at Midnight* as fundamentally flawed.

Richard Hall *Empires of the Monsoon* (HarperCollins). An impeccably researched account of early colonial expansion into the Arabian Sea and Indian Ocean, which traces the web of trade connections binding Europe, Africa and the subcontinent. It features a particularly vivid account of Vasco da Gama's expeditions, in all its brutality, and the subsequent conquest of Goa.

Lawrence James *Raj: the Making and Unmaking of British India* (Abacus, UK). A door-stopping 700-page history of British rule in India, drawing on recently released official papers and private memoirs. The most up-to-date, erudite survey of its kind, and unlikely to be bettered as a general introduction.

Gordon Johnson *Cultural Atlas of India* (Andromeda). A lavishly illustrated general introduction to the religions, societies, arts and sciences of the subcontinent, written by top scholars and presented in accessible coffee-table format. Colour maps and boxes bring a particularly strong history section to life.

 John Keay *India: a History* (HarperCollins). In this, the most recent of his five consistently excellent books on India, John Keay manages to coax clear, impartial and highly readable narrative from 5000 years of fragmented events. Arguably the best single-volume history currently in print.

 Bhermann Kulke & Dietmar Rothermund *A History of India* (Routledge). Among the few complete histories of India to give adequate coverage to the South (one of the authors' specialist subjects), from the Mesolithic era (100,000 BC) to the war in Sri Lanka.

Amaurg de Riencourt *The Soul of India* (Honeyglen). A wide-ranging exploration of India's past, from the Indus Valley civilization to Indira's death. The focus is squarely philosophical, which makes it hard going in places, but this is one of the most erudite reference books in print.

Robert Sewell, *A Forgotten Empire* (reprinted in facsimile by Asian Educational Services, New Delhi). The definitive history of the Vijayanagars, supplemented with the translated chronicles of Domingo Paes and Fernao Nuniz, two Portuguese travellers who visited in the royal city at the height of its splendour. Essential reading if you want to get to grips with the history behind Hampi's ruins.

Percival Spear's *History of India* Volume II covers the period from the Moghul era to the death of Gandhi. Among the most readable offerings of its kind, and the most easily available.

Romila Thapar *History of India* Volume I (Penguin/Viking). Concise paperback account of early Indian history, ending with the Delhi Sultanate.

Gillian Tindall *City of Gold* (Penguin, India). Definitive, if rather dry biography of Mumbai, from colonial trading post to modern metropolis.

Society

 Pramila Jayapal *Pilgrimage* (Penguin India). Sensitive account of diverse social situations, problems and experiences in far-flung parts of India (including Kerala, Karnataka and Tamil Nadu) by Jayapal, an academic and development expert. Also provides insight into the experience of a Westernized Indian returning after most of her life abroad.

Gita Mehta *Karma Cola: Marketing the Mystic East* (Minerva/Fawcett Books). Satirical look at the psychedelic 1970s freak scene in India, with some hilarious anecdotes, and many a wry observation on the whackier excesses of spiritual tourism. Her latest book, *Snakes and Ladders* (Vintage/Fawcett Books), is a brilliant overview of contemporary urban India in the form of a pot-pourri of essays, travelogues and interviews. It covers issues from Bollywood and the sex industry, to caste, gender, ecology and the contradiction between Indian poverty and the country's multi-million-dollar arms and business sector.

 V.S. Naipaul *India: a Wounded Civilisation* (Penguin). This bleak political travelogue, researched and written during and shortly after the Emergency, gained Naipaul, an Indian Trinidadian, a reputation as one of India's harshest critics. Two decades later, he returned to see what had happened to the country his parents left. The result, *A Million Mutinies Now*, is an altogether more sympathetic and rounded portrait – a superbly crafted mosaic of individual lives from around the subcontinent, including a memorable portrait of a staunchly traditional Tamil brahmin. One of the best books on India ever written.

Ramesh Thakur *The Government and Politics of India* (Macmillan). For the most part, this critical overview of contemporary Indian government and politics is as dry as its title suggests, but there are no more succinct, comprehensive treatments of the subject in print. Includes strong essays on caste and the quota controversy, the police force, regionalism and why religion has dominated politics over the past two decades.

 Mark Tully *No Full Stops in India* (Penguin/Viking). Crystallizing a lifetime's experience as the BBC's man in India, Tully's thesis – that Indians should seek inspiration for their future in their own great traditions rather than those of the West – provoked widespread scorn from the country's Westernized elite. Yet this remains among the best-informed critiques on India of its generation. Most of the ten essays in it refer to the North, but the issues tackled are equally relevant to the South.

Various *India* (Granta). To commemorate the fiftieth anniversary of Indian Independence, Granta published this mixed bag of new fiction, comment, poetry, reportage and memoirs from an impressive cast of Indian and foreign contributors. Among its many highlights are notes from the diary of V.S. Naipaul and Sebastião Salgado's photographic essay on Mumbai.

Travel

 William Dalrymple *The Age of Kali* (HarperCollins). Though not quite in the same league as *City of Djinns*, Dalrymple's latest offering – a collection of stylish essays from ten years of journalistic assignments – is rich with insights drawn from encounters and interviews with a vast range of personalities. Madurai's Meenakshi temple and the extraordinary history of the Nizam of Hyderabad comprise the South India content. Published in India as *In the Court of the Fish-Eyed Goddess*.

Alexander Frater *Chasing the Monsoon* (Penguin). Frater's wet-season jaunt down the west coast and across the Ganges plains took him through an India of muddy puddles and grey skies: an evocative account of the country as few visitors see it, and now something of a classic of the genre.

Geoffrey Moorhouse *Om* (Sceptre). Not Moorhouse's best, but nevertheless an absorbing account of his 1992 journey to South India's key spiritual centres, following the death of his daughter, with typically well informed asides on history, politics, contemporary culture and religion.

Dervla Murphy *On a Shoestring to Coorg* (Flamingo/Overlook Press). Murphy stays with her young daughter in the little-visited tropical mountains of Coorg, Karnataka. Arguably the most famous modern Indian travelogue, and a manifesto for single-parent budget travel.

François Pryard *Voyage to the East Indies, the Maldives, the Moluccas and Brazil* (Hakluyt Society, India). Albert Gray's translation of the famous French chronicler's travelogue includes a vivid first-hand description of the Portuguese colony during its decadent heyday. Goa was Pryard's first port of call after being shipwrecked in the Maldives in 1608.

Jeremy Seal *The Snake Bite Survivor's Club* (Picador). Includes three chapters on snake-obsessed corners of India by someone whose fascination only just outweighs his phobia. The best of them describes a visit to a snake-venom extraction centre near Chennai.

Tahir Shah *Sorcerer's Apprentice* (Weidenfeld & Nicolson). A journey through the weird underworld of occult India. Travelling as apprentice to a master conjurer and illusionist, Shah encounters hangmen, baby renters, skeleton dealers, sadhus and charlatans. If it were set anywhere else in the world, this would be an unbelievable story.

David Tomory, *Hello Goodnight* (Lonely Planet). An upbeat account of Goa through the ages, enlivened with a seamless bricolage of anecdote, experiences and encounters distilled from over thirty years' of visiting and reading about the region. Its all in here: from Albuquerque to Wendell Rodricks and Jungle Barry to the Nine Bar, crammed into 23 chapters of poppy prose that faithfully capture Goa's essential quirkiness. Some will find it short on analysis, but the book's depiction of contemporary tourist culture, in particular, is spot on.

Michael Wood *The Smile of Murugan* (Viking). A supremely well crafted and affectionate portrait of Tamil Nadu and its people in the mid-1990s, centred on a video-bus pilgrimage tour of the state's key sacred sites. Indispensable if you plan to explore the deep southeast.

Fiction

Anita Desai *Feasting and Fasting* (Vintage). The most recent novel by one of India's leading female authors eloquently portrays the frustration of a sensitive young woman stuck in the stifling atmosphere of home while her spoilt brother is packed off to study in America.

Clive James *The Silver Castle* (Picador/Random House). A delightful story of a street urchin's rise from the roadside slums of outer Mumbai to the bright lights of Bollywood. James succeeds in balancing his witty celebration of the Hindi film world with an earnest attempt to dissect the ironies of the Maharashtran capital.

Rohinton Mistry *A Fine Balance* (Faber/Vintage). Two friends seek promotion from their low-caste rural lives to the glitz of the big smoke. A compelling and savage triumph-of-the-human-spirit novel exposing the evils of the caste system and of Indira Gandhi's brutal policies during the Emergency Years. Mistry's *Such a Long Journey* (Faber/Vintage) is a highly acclaimed account of a Mumbai Parsi's struggle to maintain personal integrity in the face of betrayals and disappointment.

R.K. Narayan *Gods, Demons and Others* (Minerva/University of Chicago Press). Many of Narayan's beautifully crafted books, full of subtly drawn characters and good-natured humour, are set in the fictional South Indian territory of Malgudi. This one tells classic Indian folktales and popular myths through the voice of a village storyteller.

★ **Arundhati Roy** *The God of Small Things* (Flamingo/HarperCollins). Haunting Booker Prize-winning novel about a well-to-do South Indian family caught between the snobberies of high-caste tradition, a colonial past and the diverse personal histories of its members. Seen through the eyes of two children, the assortment of scenes from Keralan life are as memorable as the characters themselves, while the comical and finally tragic turn of events says as much about Indian history as the refrain that became the novel's catchphrase: "things can change in a day."

★ **Salman Rushdie** *The Moor's Last Sigh* (Jonathan Cape/Pantheon). Set in Kerala and Mumbai, Rushdie's follow-up to *The Satanic Verses*, a characteristically lurid and spleen-ridden evocation of the Maharashtran capital's paradoxes, caused a stir in India, and was the subject of a defamation case brought by Shiv Sena leader Bal Thackeray.

Manohar Shetty (ed) *Ferry Crossing: Short Stories From Around Goa* (Penguin, India). This long-awaited anthology of Goan fiction, compiled by a local poet, comprises broadly themed short stories woven around the local landscape and people. Translated from Konkani, Marathi, and Portuguese, none are what you might call world-class, but they offer fresh perspectives on Goan life, particularly the impact of modernization on villages.

William Sutcliffe *Are You Experienced?* (Penguin). Hilarious easy read sending up a "typical" backpacker trip around India.

Biography and autobiography

Charles Allen *Plain Tales from the Raj* (Abacus). First-hand accounts from erstwhile *sahibs* and *memsahibs* of British India, organized thematically ("The Club", "The Barracks", "The Hot Weather" and so on).

James Cameron *An Indian Summer* (Penguin). Affectionate and humorous description of the veteran British journalist's visit to India in 1972, and his marriage to an Indian woman. An enduring classic.

M.K. Gandhi *Experiments with Truth* (Penguin/Dover). Gandhi's fascinating records of his life, including the spiritual and moral quests, changing relationship with the British Government in India, and gradual emergence into the fore of politics.

 Robert Harvey **Clive**: *The Life and Death of a British Emperor* (Sceptre). The most recent biography of the man often dubbed the "founding father" of the British empire. Although more famous for his role in the battle of Plassey, he pulled off some extraordinary military feats during a formative early spell in the Carnatic, based in Madras, which are recounted here in engaging style.

Women

Chantal Boulanger *Saris: an Illustrated Guide to the Indian Art of Draping* (Shakti Press International). The fruit of six years' fieldwork by a French anthropologist, this astonishingly comprehensive book catalogues the numerous styles of sari tying, and their sociocultural significance (check out their site @ www.devi.net).

 Elizabeth Bumiller *May You Be the Mother of a Hundred Sons* (Fawcett Books/Penguin India). Lucid exploration of the Indian woman's lot, drawn from dozens of first-hand encounters, by an American journalist. Subjects tackled include dowries, arranged marriages, *sati*, magazines, and film stars.

Sashi Deshpande *The Binding Vine* (Virago). Disturbing story of one woman's struggle for independence, and her eventual acceptance of the position of servitude traditionally assumed by an Indian wife.

Anees Jung *The Night of the New Moon* (Penguin UK/India). Revealing and poetic stories woven around interviews with Muslim women from all sectors of Indian society. Jung's *Unveiling India* is a compelling account of the life of a Muslim woman who has chosen to break free from orthodoxy.

Vrinda Nabar *Caste as Woman* (Penguin India). Conceived as an Indian counterpart to Greer's *The Female Eunuch*, this is a wry study of the pressures brought to bear during the various stages of womanhood. Drawing on scripture and popular culture, Nabar looks at issues of identity and cultural conditioning.

Viramma, Josiane Racine & Jean-Luc Racine *Viramma: Life of an Untouchable* (Verso). Unique autobiography of an untouchable woman told in her own words (transcribed by French anthropologists), over a fifteen-year period, offering frank, often humorous insights into life in rural Tamil Nadu, the universe and everything.

Development and the environment

Julia Cleves Mosse *India: Paths to Development* (Oxfam). Concise analysis of the economic, environmental and political changes affecting India, focusing on the lives of ordinary poor people and the exemplary ways some have succeeded in shaping their own future. The best country brief on the market; only available through Oxfam.

 Jeremy Seabrook *Notes from Another India* (Pluto Press). Life histories and interviews – compiled over a year's travelling and

skilfully contextualized. They reveal the everyday problems faced by Indians from a variety of backgrounds, and how grassroots groups have tried combat them. One of the soundest, and most engaging, overviews of Indian development issues ever written.

Paul Sinath *Everybody Loves a Good Drought* (Review). A classic report on India's poorest districts, telling the stories of individual villages that are usually lost in a maze of development statistics.

Wildlife

Salim Ali, Dillon and Ripley *The Handbook of the Birds of India and Pakistan* (OUP, UK). Covers all of South Asia's birds in a single volume, with plates and maps: the definitive work, although hard to come by.

Claude Alvares (ed.) *Fish Curry and Rice: a Citizens' Report on the Goan Environment* (Ecoforum, India). A comprehensive overview of Goan green issues, giving a region-by-region rundown of the state's natural habitats, followed by articles outlining the principal threats to the environment from tourism, transport policy, changes in local farming practices and a host of other eco-evils.

P.V. Bole and Yogini Vaghini *Field Guide to the Common Trees of India* (OUP, UK/US). A handy-sized, indispensable tome for tree-spotters.

 Bikram Grewal *Birds of India, Bangladesh, Nepal, Pakistan and Sri Lanka* (Odyssey). Five hundred species are detailed in this glossy and practical field guide – most with excellent colour photographs. Based on Salim Ali & Co's authoritative work, and the best of

the bunch available in UK and US high-street bookshops.

Insight Guides *Indian Wildlife* (APA Publications, UK). An excellent all-round introduction to India's wildlife, with scores of superb colour photographs, features on different animals and habitats and a thorough bibliography. Recommended.

S. Prater *The Book of Indian Animals* (OUP/Bombay Natural History Society, India). The most comprehensive single-volume reference book on the subject, although only available in India.

Romulus Whitaker *Common Indian Snakes* (Macmillan, UK). A detailed illustrated guide to the subcontinent's snakes, with all the main species included.

Martin Woodcock *Handguide to the Birds of the Indian Subcontinent* (Collins, UK). For years the market leader, although now superseded by Grewal's guide. Available in light-weight, pocket-sized paperback form, and very user-friendly, with nearly every species illustrated (some in black and white).

The arts and architecture

Roy Craven *Indian Art* (Thames & Hudson). Concise general introduction to Indian art, from Harappan seals to Moghul miniatures, with lots of illustrations.

Mohan Khokar *Traditions of Indian Classical Dance* (Clarion Books, India). Detailing the religious and social roots of Indian dance, this lavishly illustrated book, with sections on regional traditions, is an excellent introduction to the subject.

George Michell *The Hindu Temple* (University of Chicago Press). The definitive primer, introducing Hindu temples, their significance, and architectural development.

Bonnie C. Wade *Music in India: the Classical Traditions* (Manmohar, India). A scrupulous catalogue of Indian music, outlining the most commonly used instruments, with illustrations and musical scores.

Religion

 Wendy O'Flaherty (transl) *Hindu Myths* (Penguin). Translations of key myths from the original Sanskrit texts, providing an insight into the foundations of Hinduism.

Dorf Hartsuiker *Sadhus: Holy Men of India* (Inner Traditions International). The weird world of India's itinerant ascetics exposed in glossy colour photographs and erudite but accessible text.

J.R. Hinnelle (ed) *A Handbook of Living Religions* (Penguin). The beliefs, practices, iconography and historical roots of all India's major faiths explained in accessible language, with full bibliographies to back up each chapter. Deservedly the most popular book of its kind in print, and an ideal introduction.

 Roger Hudson *Travels through Sacred India* (o/p). Knowledgeable and accessible introduction to religious India, with a gazetteer of holy places, listings of ashrams and lively essays on temples, *sadhus*, gurus and sacred sites. Hudson derives much of his material from personal encounters, which brings the subjects to life. Includes sections on all India's main faiths, and an excellent bibliography.

Language

No fewer than seventeen major languages, officially recognized by the constitution, numerous minor ones and over a thousand dialects are spoken across
India. When Independent India was organized, the present-day states were
largely created along linguistic lines, which helps the traveller at least make
some sense of the complex situation. Considering the continuing prevalence
of English, there is rarely any necessity to speak a local language but some
theoretical knowledge of the background and having at least a few words of
one or two can only enhance your visit.

While the main languages of northern India are all Indo-Aryan, in South
India the picture changes completely. The four most widely spoken languages,
Tamil (Tamil Nadu), Telugu (Andhra Pradesh), Kannada (Karnataka) and
Malayalam (Kerala), all belong to the **Dravidian** family, the world's fourth
largest group. These and related minor languages grew up quite separately
among the non-Aryan peoples of southern India over thousands of years. The
exact origins of the Dravidian group have not been established but it is possible that proto-Dravidian was spoken further north in prehistoric times before
the people were driven south by the Aryan invaders.

The earliest written records of **Tamil**, the most dominant and oldest language of the family, date back to the second century AD, while **Malayalam** is
the most closely related to Tamil but also the newest, dating from the tenth
century. In between those two in age, **Telugu** (seventh century) has the

Indian English

Over the period of the British Raj, Indian English developed its own
characteristics, which have survived to the present day. The lilting stress and
intonation patterns are owing to crossover from the Indian languages, as is the
sometimes bewildering pace of delivery. Likewise, certain vowel sounds, for
example the lack of distinction between the pronunciation of "cot" and "caught",
and the utterance of some consonants, such as the common retroflex nature of
"d", "t" and "r" with the tongue touching the soft palate, are also due to strong local
linguistic features.

Indian languages have contributed a good deal of vocabulary to everyday
English as well, including words like veranda, bungalow, sandal, pyjamas, shampoo,
jungle, turban, caste, chariot, chilli, cardamom and yoga. The traveller to India soon
becomes familiar with other terms in common usage that have not spread so widely
outside the subcontinent: *dacoit, dhoti, bandh, panchayat, lakh* and *crore* are but a few
(see Glossary p.728 for definitions).

Perhaps the most endearing aspect of Indian English is the way it has preserved
forms now regarded as highly old-fashioned in Britain. Addresses such as "Good
sir" and questions like "May I know your good name?" are commonplace, as are
terms like "tiffin", "cantonment" or "top-hole". This type of usage reaches its
apogee in the more flowery expressions of the media which regularly feature in the
vast array of daily newspapers published in English. Thus headlines often appear
such as "37 perish in mishap", referring to a train crash, or passages like this splendid
report of a bank robbery: "The miscreants absconded with the loot in great haste.
They repaired immediately to their hideaway, whereupon they divided the
iniquitous spoils before vanishing into thin air."

second most speakers and **Kannada** (fourth century) follows closely on the heels of Tamil in terms of both antiquity and literary tradition. The beautiful flowing **scripts**, especially the exquisite curls of Kannada, add a constant aesthetic quality to any tour of the South. They developed that way thanks to the palmyra and talipot palm leaves prevalent in the South, which were turned under a firmly held hard stylus – a technique also adopted in Southeast Asian scripts like Burmese, Thai and Khmer.

Of the non-Dravidian languages, two have a substantial number of speakers: **Konkani**, only recognized as the official language of Goa in 1992, is Indo-Aryan and closely related to Marathi; while **Dakhani**, an old form of Urdu, dates back to the fourteenth century and remains the first language in the Muslim communities of Karnataka and Andhra Pradesh, especially noticeable in Hyderabad. Of course, the trained ear may catch numerous **minor languages** or dialects while travelling in South India – indigenous peoples, such as the tribes of the Andaman Islands, all have their own languages, some of very uncertain linguistic origins.

Literary traditions

The rich will make temples for Shiva,
What shall I, a poor man, do?
My legs are pillars, the body the shrine,
The head a cupola of gold.
Listen, O lord of the meeting rivers,
Things standing shall fall, but the moving shall stay forever

Basavanna (Kannada poet, tenth century AD)

Of South India's main languages, **Tamil** boasts a literary tradition that goes back to pre-Pallava times. According to popular belief, three literary academies or **Sangam** met at Madurai, the earliest of which was attended by the gods and is no longer in existence. The Second Sangam is supposed to have been responsible for the **Tolkappiyam** – a treatise on Tamil grammar – but on close examination this would seem to have appeared later than the **Ettutogai**, the "Eight Anthologies" ascribed to the Third Sangam. Although in archaic Tamil, and barely readable by ordinary Tamils today, the Eight Anthologies, consisting of over 2000 poems composed by around two hundred authors, and the **Pattuppattu**, or "Ten Songs", represent the greatest works of ancient Tamil literature. Even from this early stage, literature was subject to the Tamil love of classification, and the poems were divided into two main categories: *agam* (internal), dealing with love, and *puram* (external), laudatory poems in praise of the kings.

Although the Aryan influence on Tamil culture was already evident in Sangam literature, the influence of northern civilization grew and, in the sixth century, Hindu, Buddhist and Jain practices were widespread in the far south. Sanskrit left an indelible impression on Tamil literature, and the epic style of Sanskrit was emulated by long narrative poems such as **Shilappadigaram** (*The Jewelled Anklet*). Unlike the Sanskrit epics, however, Tamil poems such as the *Shilappadigaram* deal with the lives of ordinary people – in this case the hapless couple, Kovalan and Kannagi – and provide an invaluable insight into everyday life of the time. Shortly after the *Shilappadigaram* was written, Sattan, a poet from Madurai, composed the **Manimegalai**, a sort of anthology to the *Shilappadigaram*, but with a philosophical bent and a Buddhist message. The **Shivaga Shidamani**, another great early Tamil epic, was written by the Jain

Eight times as long as the *Iliad* and *Odyssey* combined, the Mahabharata is the most popular of all Hindu texts. Written around 400 AD, it tells of a feuding *kshatrya* family in upper India (Bharata) during the fourth millennium BC. Like all good epics, the *Mahabharata* recounts a gripping tale, using its characters to illustrate moral values. In essence it attempts to elucidate the position of the warrior castes, the *kshatryas*, and demonstrate that religious fulfilment is as accessible for them as it is for *brahmins*.

The chief character is Arjuna, a superb archer, who with his four brothers – Yudhishtra, Bhima, Nakula and Sahadeva – represents the Pandava clan, upholders of righteousness and supreme fighters. Arjuna won his wife Draupadi in an archery contest, but wishing to avoid jealousy she agreed to be the shared wife of all five brothers. The Pandava clan is resented by their cousins, the evil Kauravas, led by Duryodhana, the eldest son of Dhrtarashtra, ruler of the Kuru kingdom.

When Dhrtarashtra handed his kingdom over to the Pandavas, the Kauravas were far from happy. Duryodhana challenged Yudhishtra (known for his brawn but not his brain) to a gambling contest. The dice game was rigged; Yudhishtra gambled away not only his possessions, but also his kingdom and his shared wife. The Kauravas offered to return the kingdom to the Pandavas if they could spend thirteen years in exile, together with their wife, without being recognized. Despite much scheming, the Pandavas succeeded, but on return found that the Kauravas would not fulfil their side of the bargain.

Thus ensued the great battle of the *Mahabharata*, told in the sixth book, the Bhagavad Gita – immensely popular as an independent story. Vishnu descends to earth as Krishna, and steps into battle as Arjuna's charioteer. The *Bhagavad Gita* details the fantastic struggle of the fighting cousins, using magical weapons and brute force. Arjuna is in a dilemma, unable to justify the killing of his own kin in pursuit of a rightful kingdom for himself and his brothers. Krishna consoles him, reminding him that his principal duty, his *varnashradharma*, is as a warrior. What is more, Krishna points out, each man's soul, or *atman*, is eternal, and transmigrates from body to body, so Arjuna need not grieve the death of his cousins. Krishna convinces Arjuna that by fulfilling his *dharma* he not only upholds law and order by saving the kingdom from the grasp of unrighteous rulers, he also serves God in the spirit of devotion (*bhakti*), and thus guarantees himself eternal union with the divine in the blissful state of *moksha*.

The Pandavas finally win the battle, and Yudhishtra is crowned king. Eventually Arjuna's grandson, Pariksit, inherits the throne, and the Pandavas trek to Mount Meru, the mythical centre of the universe and the abode of the gods, where Arjuna finds Krishna's promised *moksha*.

author Tiruttakkadevar and emulates Sanskrit court poetry, but concerns itself with the fantastic heroics of Shivaga (aka Jivaka) who eventually embraces the faith and becomes a monk.

Perhaps the greatest of all Tamil epics is Kamban's **Ramayanam**, composed in the ninth century – not just a translation from the Sanskrit *Ramayana* (see p.721) but a reinterpretation, with additional story lines, and, on occasion, markedly different interpretations of the main characters. Rama is not always shown as heroic, while Ravana, the demon king, occasionally is. During this period, inspired by the *Bhagavad Purana*, Vaishnavism became a predominant force in Tamil literature, promoting the new-found hero and man-god, Krishna.

In terms of antiquity, **Kannada**, the language of Karnataka, comes second only to Tamil amongst the Dravidian languages, with its earliest literature dating back to the ninth century AD and evidence from inscriptions that traces the language back to the fourth century. The golden age of Kannada literature was between

Rama is the seventh of Vishnu's ten incarnations and the story of his life unfolds in the epic Ramayana. Although possibly based on a historic figure, Rama is seen rather more as a representation of the qualities of Vishnu. Rama was the oldest of four sons born to Dasaratha, King of Ayodhya, by his three wives and was heir to the throne. At the time of the coronation one of the king's wives, Kaikeya, seized the moment to ask for the two favours he had previously promised her in a moment of rash appreciation. Her first request was that her oldest son Bharata be anointed king instead of the rightful Rama. Her second request was that Rama be banished to the forest for fourteen years.

Rama in an exemplary show of filial piety accepted his father's unfortunate request and left the city together with his wife Sita and brother Laksmana. From their place of exile they continued their long battle against the demon forces led by Ravana, the evil king of Lanka. One day Ravana's sister Suparnakhi spotted Rama in the woods and immediately fell in love with him. Being a faithful and ideal husband Rama rebuffed her advances; Suparnakhi as a result tried to kill Sita, seeing her as the obstacle to Rama's heart. Laksmana intervened and cut off her nose and ears in retaliation. Suparnakhi fled to her brother, who mobilized fourteen giants to dispose of Rama. Rama destroyed them single-handedly and then similarly killed 14,000 warriors. Ravana was furious but heeded his advisers who suggested they should no more fight Rama but just kidnap his beloved, hinting that he would then quickly die of a broken heart. Sita was thus captured and flown by chariot to one of Ravana's palaces on the island of Lanka.

Determined to find Sita, a distraught Rama enlisted the help of Hanuman, lord of the monkeys. Rama and Laksmana then start their search for Sita, which leads to the discovery that she is being held on the island of Lanka. Hanuman leaps across the strait and makes his way surreptitiously into Ravana's palace where he hears the evil king trying to persuade Sita to marry him instead of the squeaky clean Rama – offering her the choice of consummation or consumption – become my bride or "My cooks shall mince thy limbs with steel and serve thee for my morning meal." Hanuman reports back to Rama who gathers an army and prepares to attack. This time the monkeys form a bridge across the straits allowing the army to cross and after much fighting Sita is rescued and reunited with the victorious Rama.

During the long journey back to Ayodhya Sita's honour was brought into question. To verify her innocence she asks Laksmana to build a funeral pyre. She prays to Agni before stepping into the flames and asks for protection before walking through them. Agni walks her through the fire to a delighted Rama. They march into Ayodhya guided by a trail of lights put there by the local people and this enlightened homecoming has long since been celebrated as Divali – the festival of lights. Soon after, Rama is finally crowned as rightful king, his younger brother gladly stepping down.

the tenth and the twelfth centuries, when the poet-saints of the **Virashaiva** sect composed their **Vacanas** or "sayings". Also known as the **Lingayatas**, or "those who wear the *linga*", the Virashaiva poets dedicated their lives to the god Shiva. Although the sect, distinguished by the *lingam* encased in a small stone casket and worn around the neck, is still in existence, and *vacanas* are still composed, the four greatest poet-saints – **Basvanna**, **Dasimayya**, **Allama** and **Mahadeviyakka** – all flourished in the early medieval period. Basvanna, the most illustrious of all, epitomized the spirit of Virashaiva, with an uncompromising view of life and society and a single-minded devotion to the pursuit of truth through homage to Shiva. Basvanna and the Virashaivas rejected caste and believed the true path was open to all; they believed in the equality of women and the right of widows to remarry. They also rejected the highly structured poetic devices of classical Sanskrit poetry and composed simple free verse with

Tamil

Basic words

Yes	Aamaam
No	Illai
Goodbye (will return again)	Varavaanga
Please	Koncham dhayavuseydhu
Thanks	Nauri
Thank you very much	Romba nanringa
Excuse me	Enga
Pardon	Mannikkavum
This	Idhu
That	Adhu
What is this/that?	Idhu/adhu ennaanga
Very good	Romba nallayirukkudhu
Not bad	Paravaayillai
Come (inviting someone in)	Vaanaga
Stop	Neruthu
These	Evaikal
Big	Pareya
Small	Sarreya
Much	Athekam
Little	Kuvrairu

Time

Today	Enrru
Tomorrow	Naalai
Yesterday	Neerru
Day	Pakal/kezhamai
Night	Eravu
Early morning	Athekaalai
Morning	Kaalai
Afternoon	Matiyam
Evening	Maalai
Monday	Thengal
Tuesday	Chavvaay
Wednesday	Buthan
Thursday	Veyaacha
Friday	Valle
Saturday	Chane
Sunday	Gnaayetrru/ Kezhama

Communicating

I don't understand	Enakku puriya-villaiye
I understand	Enakku puriyudhu
I don't know Tamil	Enakku thamizh theriyaathunga
Do you know someone who knows English?	Inge aangilam therinchavanga yaaraavadhu irukkiraangalaa?
Could you speak slowly?	Koncham methuvaa pesuveengalaa
Could you speak loudly	Koncham balamaa pesunga
What does he say?	Avar enna sollugiraar

Food and shopping

I am hungry	Enakku pasikkudhul
I am thirsty	Enakku dhaga maayirukkudhu
How much is it?	Athanudaiya vilai enna?
I want only coffee	Enakku kapi maththi-ram than vendum
Please show me	Koncham kan-pikkireengalaa
Coffee	Kapi
Tea	Teyneer
Milk	Paal
Sugar	Sakkaray
Water	Neer
Rice	Arese
Cooked Rice	Satham
Vegetables	Kaaykarikal
Cooked vegetables	Kane
Curd/yoghurt	Thayer
Coconut	Thaenkaay

Directions

Far	Turam
Near	Arukkil
Where is… ?	Enge iruk-kuthunga…?
From here is it near?	Athu ingeyirundhu pakkam thaane?
How far is it from here?	Athu ingeyirundhu evvalavu dhoora-mayirukkunga?

Where can I get an auto?	*Enga auto enga kidaikunga?*
What is the charge to get there?	*Empaa, anga povad hukku evvalavu?*
Where is the bank?	*Vangi enge irukkuthunga?*
Where is the bus stand?	*Bas staandu enge irukki radhu?*
Where is the train station?	*Tireyn staashan enge iruk-kuthunga?*
Where is the restroom?	*Kakkoos enge irukkudhu*
Where is the enquiries (information) office?	*Visaranai enge irukki radhu?*
Where is... road?	*... theru enge irukkiradhu?*
Post office	*Anja lagam*
Temple	*Kohvil*

Numbers

1	*onru*
2	*eranndu*
3	*mundru*
4	*naangu*
5	*iyendhu*
6	*aaru*
7	*aezshu*
8	*ayttu*
9	*nbathu*
10	*patthu*
11	*pathenonrru*
12	*panereynndu*
13	*pathemoonrru*
14	*pathenaangu*
15	*pathenainthu*
16	*pathenaaru*
17	*pathnaezshu*
18	*pathenayttu*
19	*pathenthonbathu*
20	*erapathu*
30	*muppathu*
40	*naarpathu*
50	*iymbathu*
60	*arupathu*
70	*azhupathu*
80	*aennapathu*
90	*thonnoorru*
100	*noorru*
1000	*aayeram*
100,000	*latcham*

Malayalam

Basic words

Yes	*Aanaate*
No	*Alla*
Hello	*Namaste*
Please	*Dayavuchetu*
Thank you	*Nanni*
Excuse me	*Ksamikkuu*
How much is it?	*Etra?*
I don't understand	*Enikka arriyilla*
Do you speak English?	*Ninal englisha samsaarik-kumo?*
My name is...	*Ente pero...*
Where is... ?	*Eviteyaannaa...?*
How much is it?	*Etra?*
Coffee	*Kaappi*
Tea	*Chaaya*
Milk	*Paalu*
Sugar	*Panchasara*
Medicine	*Marunnu*
Water	*Vellam*
Vegetables	*Pachakkari*
Fish	*Meen*
Curd	*Tairu*
Rice	*Ari*
Banana	*Eyttappalam*
Coconut	*Teynna*

Numbers

1	*onnu*
2	*randu*
3	*muunu*
4	*naalu*
5	*anchu*
6	*aaru*
7	*eylu*
8	*ettu*
9	*ombatu*
10	*pattu*
11	*pationnu*
12	*pantrantu*
13	*pati-muunu*
14–18	*pati-...*
19	*pattonpattu*
20	*irupatu*
21	*irupattonnu*
22	*irupatti-randu*
30	*muppatu*
31	*muppati-yonnu*
40	*nalpatu*
50	*anpatu*
60	*arupatu*
70	*elapatu*
80	*enpatu*

90	*tonnuru*
100	*nuura*
1000	*aayiram*
100,000	*laksham*

Telugu

Kannada

11	hannondu
12	hanneradu
13	hadi- mooru
14–18	hadi-...
19	hattombhattu
20	ippattu
21	ippattondu
30	muvattu
31	muvattondu
40	naalvattu
50	aivattu
60	aravattu
70	eppattu
80	embattu
90	tombattu
99	tombattombattu
100	nooru
1000	ondu saavira
100,000	laksha

Konkani

Basic words

Yes	Hoee
No	Na
Hello	Paypadta
Goodbye	Miochay
Please	Upkar kor
Thank you	Dio borem korunc
Excuse me	Upkar korkhi
How much?	Kitlay?
How much does it cost?	Kitlay poisha lakthele?
I don't want it	Mhaka naka tem
I don't understand	Mhaka kay samzona na
Where is... ?	Khoy aasa... ?
Beach	Prayia
Road	Rosto
Coffee	Kaafi
Tea	Chai
Milk	Dudh
Sugar	Shakhar
No sugar	Shakhar naka
Rice	Tandul
Water	Oodak
Coconut	Nal
Tender coconut	Adzar

Numbers

1	ek
2	dohn
3	teen
4	char
5	paanch

6	soh
7	saht
8	ahrt
9	nou
10	dha
20	vees
30	tees
40	cha-ees
50	po-nas
100	chem-bor
1000	ek-azaar
100,000	laakh

Hindi/Urdu

(Not spoken in Tamil Nadu, Kerala, Karnataka [except in the northeast] or much of Andhra Pradesh)

Basic words and phrases

Greetings	Namaste (said with palms together at chest height as in prayer – not used for Muslims)
Greetings (to a Muslim)	Aslaam alequm
In reply	U ale qum aslaam
We will meet again (goodbye)	Phir milenge
Goodbye (to a Muslim)	Khudaa Haafiz (may god bless you)
How are you? (formal)	Aap kaise hain
How are you? (familiar)	Kya hal hai
Brother (a common address to a stranger)	Bhaaii/bhaayaa
Sister	Didi
Sir (Sahib)	Saaheb
Yes	Haan
OK/good	Achhaa
No	Nahiin
How much?	Kitna?
Bad	Kharaab
My name is...	Mera nam... hai
What is your name? (formal)	Aapka naam kya hai?
What is your name? (familiar)	Yumhara naam kya hai?

			Numbers	
I don't understand	*Samaj nahin aayaa*		1	*ek*
It is OK	*Thiik hai*		2	*do*
How much?	*Kitna?*		3	*tin*
Where is the... ?	*... Kahaan hai?*		4	*char*
How far?	*Kitnaa duur?*		5	*paanch*
Stop	*Ruko*		6	*chey*
Wait	*Thero*		7	*saat*
Medicine	*Dawaaii*		8	*aatth*
Pain	*Dard*		9	*now*
Stomach	*Pet*		10	*das*
Eye	*Aankh*		100	*saw*
Nose	*Naakh*		1000	*hazaar*
Ear	*Kaan*		100,000	*laakh*
Back	*Piit*			
Foot	*Paao*			

a direct and universal philosophical wisdom which has caused some to refer to their work as the **Kannada Upanishads**.

The Lingayatas also composed their *vacanas* in **Telugu**, the language of Andhra Pradesh and parts of northern Tamil Nadu and southeast Karnataka. Telugu literature did not really develop until the twelfth century, and not as strongly as those of Tamil and Kannada until the sixteenth century, when it was adopted at the court of the Vijayanagar empire at Hampi (see p.289). Telugu-speaking brahmins – most dedicated Vaishnavas (devotees of the god Vishnu and his incarnations) – were attracted to the court of King Krishna Deva Raya, who was also an accomplished composer of Sanskrit and Telugu verse. After the fall of Vijayanagar, the cultural centre shifted to the court of Tanjore where, despite its location in the heart of Tamil country, Telugu continued to enjoy its privileged status, partly due to the high calibre of religious poets who travelled to Tanjore and the surrounding country. In its heyday Tanjore was home to the merging of devotional literature with theatre, music and dance – nowhere better seen than in the work of the saint, poet and songwriter Tyagaraja (1767–1847), another Telugu-speaking brahmin, who was to leave an indelible impression on Karnatic music (see p.694).

Post Independence issues

With **Independence** it was decided by the government in Delhi that Hindi should become the **official language** of the newly created country. Interestingly, the idea of using Hindustani, a more recent colloquial hybrid of Hindi and Urdu, popular with Gandhi and others in an effort to encourage communal unity during the fight for freedom, was never pursued; this was due to a mixture of political reasons following Partition and the fact that the language lacked the necessary refinement. A drive to teach Hindi in all schools followed and over half the country's population are now reckoned to have a decent working knowledge of the language. However, the **Tamil-led** Dravidian south has always been at the forefront of a strong **resistance** to the imposition of Hindi, which has even led to riots over the issue on occasions. The practical outcome of this southern distaste for Hindi is that vast majority of people living below the Deccan plateau have little or no knowledge of it.

This is where English, the language of the ex-colonists, becomes an important means of communications. Not surprisingly, given India's rich linguistic diversity, **English** remains a **lingua franca** for many people (see box on p.718). It is still the preferred language of law, higher education, much of commerce and the media, and to some degree political dialogue. For many educated Indians, not just those living abroad, it is actually their first language. All this explains why the Anglophone visitor can often soon feel surprisingly at home despite the huge cultural differences. It is not unusual to overhear everyday contact between Indians from different parts of the country being conducted in English, and surprisingly stimulating conversations can often be had, not only with students or businesspeople, but also with chai-wallahs or shoeshine boys.

Glossary

See p.695 for a glossary of musical terms.

acharya religious teacher

adivasi official term for tribal person

agarbati incense

ahimsa non-violence

amrita nectar of immortality

anda literally "egg": the spherical part of a stupa

anicut irrigation dam

ankusha elephant goad

anna coin, no longer minted (16 annas to one rupee)

apsara heavenly nymph

arak liquor distilled from rice or coconut

arata evening temple puja of lights

asana yogic seating posture; small mat used in prayer and meditation

ashram centre for spiritual learning and religious practice

asura demon

atman soul

avatar reincarnation of Vishnu on earth, in human or animal form

ayurveda ancient system of medicine employing herbs, minerals and massage

baba respectful term for a *sadhu*

bagh garden, park

baksheesh tip, donation, alms, occasionally meaning a corrupt backhander

bandh general strike

bandhani tie-and-dye

baniya another term for a *vaishya*; a money lender

banyan vast fig tree, used traditionally as a meeting place, or shade for teaching and meditating; also, in South India, a cotton vest

bastee slum area

basti Jain temple

bazaar commercial centre of town; market

begum Muslim princess; Muslim women of high status

betel leaf chewed in *paan*, with the nut of the areca tree: loosely applies to the nut

bhajan song

bhakti religious devotion expressed in a personalized or emotional relationship with the deity

bhang pounded marijuana, often mixed in lassis

bhawan (also *bhavan*) palace or residence

bhumi earth, or earth goddess

bhumika storey

bidi tobacco rolled in a leaf; the "poor man's puff"

bidri inlaid metalwork as produced in Bidar

bindu seed, or the red dot (also *bindi*) worn by women on their foreheads as decoration

biradiri summer house, pavilion

bodhi enlightenment

bodhi tree/bo tree *peepal* tree, associated with the Buddha's enlightenment (*Ficus religiosa*)

bodhisattva Buddhist saint

brahmin a member of the highest caste group; priest

bundh (also *bandh*) general strike

burkha body-covering shawl worn by orthodox Muslim women

burra-sahib colonial official, boss or a man of great importance

cantonment area of town occupied by military quarters

caste social status acquired at birth

cella chamber in temple, often housing the image of a deity

cenotaph ornate tomb

chaat snack

chaddar large head-cover or shawl

chaitya Buddhist temple

chakra discus; focus of power; energy point in the body; wheel, often representing the cycle of death and rebirth

chandan sandalwood paste

chandra moon

chappal sandals or flip-flops (thongs)

charas hashish

charbagh garden divided into quadrants (Moghul style)

charpoi string bed with wooden frame

chaumukh image of four faces placed back to back

chauri fly whisk, regal symbol

chela pupil

cheruvu lake

chhatri tomb; domed temple pavilion

chillum cylindrical clay or wood pipe for smoking *charas* or *ganja*

chital spotted deer

choli short, tight-fitting blouse worn with a sari

chor robber

choultry quarters for pilgrims adjoining South Indian temples

chowgan green in the centre of a town or village

chowk crossroads or courtyard

chowkidar watchman, caretaker

coolie porter, labourer

crore ten million

cupola small delicate dome

dacoit bandit

dalit "oppressed", "out-caste"; the term, introduced by Dr Ambedkar, is preferred by so-called "untouchables" as a description of their social position

danda staff or stick

dargah sufi shrine

darshan vision of a deity or saint; receiving religious teachings

darwaza gateway, door

dawan servant

deg cauldron for food offerings, often found in *dargahs*

deva god

devadasi temple dancer

devi goddess

dhaba food hall selling local dishes

dham important religious site, or a theological college

dharamshala rest house for pilgrims

dharma sense of religious and social duty (Hindu); the law of nature, teachings, truth (Buddhist)

dhobi laundry

dholak double-ended drum

dholi sedan chair carried by bearers to hilltop temples

dhoop thick pliable block of strong incense

dhoti white ankle-length cloth worn by males, tied around the waist, and sometimes hitched up through the legs

dhurrie woollen rug

digambara literally "sky-clad": a Jain sect, known for the habit of nudity among monks, though this is no longer commonplace

dikpalas guardians of the four directions

diwan (*dewan*) chief minister

diwan-i-am public audience hall

diwan-i-khas hall of private audience

dowry payment or gift offered in marriage

dravidian of the southern culture

dukka tank and fountain in courtyard of mosque

dupatta veil worn by Muslim women with *salwar kamise*

durbar court building; government meeting

dvarpala guardian image placed at sanctuary door

eve-teasing sexual harassment of women, either physical or verbal

fakir ascetic Muslim mendicant

feni Goan spirit, distilled from coconut or cashew fruits

finial capping motif on temple pinnacle

gada mace (the weapon)

gadi throne

gandharvas Indra's heavenly musicians

ganj market

ganja marijuana buds

garbha griha temple sanctuary, literally "womb-chamber"

garh fort

gari vehicle, or car

gaur Indian bison

ghat mountain, landing platform, or steps leading to water

ghazal melancholy Urdu songs

ghee clarified butter

giri hill

godown warehouse

gompa Tibetan, or Ladakhi, Buddhist monastery

goonda ruffian

gopi young cattle-tending maidens who feature as Krishna's playmates and lovers in popular mythology

gopura towered temple gateway, common in South India

gumbad dome on mosque or tomb

guru teacher of religion, music, dance, astrology etc

gurudwara Sikh place of worship

haj Muslim pilgrimage to Mecca

hajji Muslim engaged upon, or who has performed, the *haj*

hammam sunken hot bath, Persian-style

harijan title – "Children of God" – given to "untouchables" by Gandhi

hartal one-day strike

haveli elaborately decorated (normally wooden) mansion

hijra eunuch or transvestite

hinayana literally "lesser vehicle": the name given to the original school of Buddhism by later sects

hookah water pipe for smoking strong tobacco or marijuana

howdah bulky elephant saddle, sometimes made of pure silver, and often shaded by a canopy

idgah area laid aside in the west of town for prayers during the Muslim festival Id-ul-Zuhara

imam Muslim leader or teacher

imambara tomb of a Shi'ite saint

imfl Indian-made foreign liquor

inam *baksheesh* in Tamil

indo-saracenic overblown Raj-era architecture that combines Muslim, Hindu, Jain and Western elements

ishwara God; Shiva

iwan the main (often central) arch in a mosque

jaghidar landowner

jali lattice work in stone, or a pierced screen

jangha the body of a temple

jatakas popular tales about the Buddha's life and teachings

jati sub-caste, determined by family and occupation

jawan soldier

jhuta soiled by lips: food or drink polluted by touch

-ji suffix added to names as a term of respect

jihad striving by Muslims, through battle, to spread their faith

jina another term for the Jain *tirthankara*

johar old practice of self-immolation by women in times of war

jyotirlinga twelve sites sacred by association with Shiva's unbounded *lingam* of light

kabutar khana pigeon coop

kailasa or **kailash** Shiva's mountain abode

kalam school of painting

kalasha pot-like capping stone characteristic of South Indian temples

kama satisfaction

kamise women's knee-length shirt, worn with *salwar* trousers

karan *wallah* in Tamil

karma weight of good and bad actions that determine status of rebirth

katcha the opposite of pukka, unacceptable

kathakali traditional Keralan dance-drama

kavad small decorated box that unfolds to serve as a travelling temple

khadi home-spun cotton; Gandhi's symbol of Indian self-sufficiency

khan honorific Muslim title

khol black eyeliner, also known as *surma*

khud valley side

kirtan hymn-singing

kot fort

kothi residence

kotla citadel

kovil term for a Tamil Nadu temple

kshatrya the warrior and ruling caste

kumkum red mark on a Hindu woman's forehead (widows are not supposed to wear it)

kund tank, lake, reservoir

kurta men's long shirt worn over baggy pyjamas

lakh one hundred thousand

lama Tibetan Buddhist monk and teacher

lathi heavy stick used by police

lingam phallic symbol in places of worship representing the god Shiva

liwan cloisters in a mosque

loka realm or world, eg *devaloka*, world of the gods

lunghi male garment; long wrap-around cloth, like a *dhoti*, but usually coloured

madrasa Islamic school

maha- common prefix meaning great or large

mahadeva literally "Great God", a common epithet for Shiva

mahal palace; mansion

maharaja (*Maharana, Maharao*) king

maharani queen

mahatma great soul

mahayana literally "great vehicle": a Buddhist school that has spread throughout Southeast Asia

mahout elephant driver or keeper

maidan large open space or field

makara crocodile-like animal featuring on temple doorways, and symbolizing the River Ganges; also the vehicle of Varuna, the Vedic god of the sea

mala necklace, garland or rosary

mandala religious diagram

mandapa hall, often with many pillars, used for various purposes, eg *kalyan(a) mandapa* for wedding ceremonies and *nata mandapa* for dance performances

mandi market

mandir temple

mantra sacred verse or word

maqbara Muslim tomb

marg road

masjid mosque

mataji female *sadhu*

math Hindu or Jain monastery

maund old unit of weight (roughly 20kg)

mayur peacock

medhi terrace

mela festival

memsahib respectful address to European woman

mihrab niche in the wall of a mosque indicating the direction of prayer (to Mecca); in India the *mihrab* is in the west wall

mimbar pulpit in a mosque from which the Friday sermon is read

minaret high slender tower, characteristic of mosques

mithuna sexual union, or amorous couples in Hindu and Buddhist figurative art

moksha blissful state of freedom from rebirth aspired to by Hindus and Jains

mor peacock

mudra hand gesture used in Vedic rituals, featuring in Hindu, Buddhist and Jain art and dance, and symbolizing teachings and life stages of the Buddha

muezzin man behind the voice calling Muslims to prayer from a mosque

mullah Muslim teacher and scholar

mund village

munda male garment like *lunghi*

mutt Hindu or Jain monastery

nadi river

naga mythical serpent

nala stream gorge in the mountains

natak dance

natya drama

nautch performance by dancing girls

nawab Muslim landowner or prince

nilgai blue bull

nirvana Buddhist equivalent of *moksha*

niwas building or house

nizam title of Hyderabad rulers

nullah stream gorge in the mountains

om (aka *AUM*) symbol denoting the origin of all things, and ultimate divine essence, used in meditation by Hindus and Buddhists

paan betel nut, lime, calcium and aniseed wrapped in a leaf and chewed as a digestive Mildly addictive

pada foot, or base, also a poetic metre

padma lotus; another name for the goddess Lakshmi

pagoda multistoreyed Buddhist monument

paise small unit of currency (100 paisa = 1 rupee)

palanquin enclosed sedan chair, shouldered by four men

pali original language of early Buddhist texts

palli old mosque or church in Kerala

panchayat village council

panda pilgrims' priest

parikrama ritual circumambulation around a temple, shrine or mountain

parsi Zoroastrian

pir Muslim holy man

pole fortified gate

pradakshina patha processional path circling a monument or sanctuary

prakara enclosure or courtyard in a South Indian temple

pranayama breath control, used in meditation

prasad food blessed in temple sanctuaries and shared among devotees

prayag auspicious confluence of two or more rivers

puja worship

pujari priest

pukka correct and acceptable, in the very English sense of "proper"

punya religious merit

purdah seclusion of Muslim women inside the home, and the general term for wearing a veil

purnima full moon

purohit priest

qabr Muslim grave

qawwali devotional singing popular among sufis

qila fort

raga or **raag** series of notes forming the basis of a melody

raj rule; monarchy; in particular the period of British imperial rule 1857–1947

raja king

rakshasa demon (demoness: *rakshasi*)

rangoli geometrical pattern of rice powder laid before houses and temples

rath processional temple chariot of South India

rawal chief priest (Hindu)

rishi "seer"; philosophical sage or poet

rudraksha beads used to make Shiva rosaries

sadhu Hindu holy man with no caste or family ties

sagar lake

sahib respectful title for gentlemen; general term of address for European men

salabhanjika wood nymph

salwar kamise long shirt and baggy ankle-hugging trousers worn by Muslim women

samadhi final enlightenment; a site of death or burial of a saint.

samsara cyclic process of death and rebirth

sangam sacred confluence of two or more rivers, or an academy

sangeet music

sannyasin homeless, possessionless ascetic (Hindu)

sarai resting place for caravans and travellers who once followed the trade routes through Asia

sari usual dress for Indian women: a length of cloth wound around the waist and draped over one shoulder

sarovar pond or lake

sati one who sacrifices her life on her husband's funeral pyre in emulation of Shiva's wife; no longer a common practice, and officially illegal

satsang teaching given by a religious figurehead

satyagraha literally "grasping truth": Gandhi's campaign of non-violent protest

scheduled castes official name for "untouchables"

sepoy an Indian soldier in European service

seth merchant or businessman

seva voluntary service in a temple or community

shaivite Hindu recognizing Shiva as the supreme god

shankha conch, symbol of Vishnu

shastra treatise

shikar hunting

shikhara temple tower or spire

shishya pupil

shloka verse from a Sanskrit text

shri respectful prefix; another name for Lakshmi

shudra the lowest of the four castes or *varnas;* servant

singha lion

soma medicinal herb with hallucinogenic properties used in early Vedic and Zoroastrian rituals

stambha pillar, or flagstaff

sthala site sacred for its association with legendary events

stupa large hemispherical mound, representing the Buddha's presence, and often protecting relics of the Buddha or a Buddhist saint

surma black eyeliner, also known as *kohl*

surya the sun, or sun god

sutra (*sutta*) literally "thread": verse in Sanskrit and Pali texts

svetambara "white-clad" sect of Jainism, that accepts nuns and shuns nudity

swami title for a holy man

swaraj "self-rule"; synonym for independence, coined by Gandhi tala rhythmic cycle in classical music; in sculpture a *tala* signifies one face-length; in architecture a storey

taluka district

tandava vigorous, male form of dance; the dance of Shiva Nataraja

tandoor clay oven

tapas literally "heat": physical and mental austerities

tempo three-wheeled taxi

thali combination of vegetarian dishes, chutneys, pickles, rice and bread served, especially in South India, as a single meal; the metal plate on which a meal is served

theravada "Doctrine of the Elders": the original name for early Buddhism, which persists today in Sri Lanka and Thailand

tiffin light meal

tiffin carrier stainless steel set of tins used for carrying meals

tika devotional powder-mark Hindus wear on forehead, usually after puja

tilak red dot smeared on the forehead during worship, and often used cosmetically

tirtha river crossing considered sacred by Hindus, or the transition from the mundane world to heaven; a place of pilgrimage for Jains

tirthankara "ford-maker" or "crossing-maker": an enlightened Jain teacher who is deified – 24 appear every 300 million years

tola the weight of a silver rupee: 180 grains, or approximately 116g

tonga two-wheeled horse-drawn cart

topi cap

torana arch, or free-standing gateway of two pillars linked by an elaborate arch

trimurti the Hindu trinity

trishula Shiva's trident

tuk fortified enclosure of Jain shrines or temples

tulku reincarnated teacher of Tibetan Buddhism

untouchables members of the lowest strata of society, considered polluting to all higher castes

urs Muslim saint's day festival

vahana the "vehicle" of a deity; the bull Nandi is Shiva's *vahana*

vaishya member of the merchant and trading caste group

varna literally "colour": one of four hierarchical social categories – brahmins, *kshatryas*, *vaishyas* and *shudras*

vedas sacred texts of early Hinduism

vedika railing around a stupa

vihara Buddhist or Jain monastery

vilasa hall or palace

vimana tower over temple sanctuary

wada mansion or palace

wallah suffix implying occupation, eg dhobi-wallah, rickshaw-wallah

wazir chief minister to the king

yagna Vedic sacrificial ritual

yaksha pre-Vedic folklore figure connected with fertility and incorporated into later Hindu iconography

yakshi female *yaksha*

yali mythical lion

yantra cosmological pictogram, or model used in an observatory

yatra pilgrimage

yatri pilgrim

yogi *sadhu* or priestly figure possessing occult powers gained through the practice of yoga (female: *yogini*)

yoni symbol of the female sexual organ, set around the base of the *lingam* in temple shrines

yuga aeon: the present age is the last in a cycle of four *yugas*, kali-yuga, a "black age" of degeneration and spiritual decline

zamindar landowner

zenana women's quarters; segregated area for women in a mosque

index

and small print

Index

Maps are listed in coloured text.

INDEX

INDEX

INDEX

INDEX

Rough Guide credits

Text editors : Helena Smith and Clifton
Wilkinson
Series editor : Mark Ellingham
Editorial : Martin Dunford, Jonathan Buckley,
Jo Mead, Kate Berens, Ann-Marie Shaw,
Paul Gray, Judith Bamber, Orla Duane, Olivia
Eccleshall, Ruth Blackmore, Geoff Howard,
Claire Saunders, Gavin Thomas, Alexander
Mark Rogers, Polly Thomas, Joe Staines,
Richard Lim, Duncan Clark, Peter Buckley,
Lucy Ratcliffe, Alison Murchie, Matthew
Teller, Karoline Densley (UK); Andrew
Rosenberg, Stephen Timblin, Yuki Takagaki,
Richard Koss (US)
Production : Susanne Hillen, Andy Hilliard,
Link Hall, Helen Prior, Julia Bovis, Michelle
Draycott, Katie Pringle, Mike Hancock, Zoë

Nobes, Rachel Holmes, Andy Turner
Cartography : Melissa Baker, Maxine Repath,
Ed Wright, Katie Lloyd-Jones
Picture research : Louise Boulton, Sharon
Martins
Online : Kelly Cross, Anja Mutic-Blessing,
Jennifer Gold, Audra Epstein, Suzanne
Welles (US)
Finance : John Fisher, Gary Singh, Edward
Downey, Mark Hall, Tim Bill
Marketing & Publicity : Richard Trillo, Niki
Smith, David Wearn, Chloë Roberts, Demelza
Dallow, Claire Southern (UK); Simon Carloss,
David Wechsler, Kathleen Rushforth (US)
Administration : Tania Hummel, Julie
Sanderson

Publishing information

This second edition published November
2001 by Rough Guides Ltd ,
62–70 Shorts Gardens, London WC2H 9AH
Penguin Putnam, Inc. 375 Hudson Street,
NY 10014, USA
Distributed by the Penguin Group
Penguin Books Ltd,
80 Strand, London WC2R ORL
Penguin Putnam, Inc.
375 Hudson Street, NY 10014, USA
Penguin Books Australia Ltd,
487 Maroondah Highway, PO Box 257,
Ringwood, Victoria 3134, Australia
Penguin Books Canada Ltd,
10 Alcorn Avenue, Toronto, Ontario,
Canada M4V 1E4
Penguin Books (NZ) Ltd,
182–190 Wairau Road, Auckland 10,
New Zealand
Typeset in Bembo and Helvetica to an
original design by Henry Iles.

Printed in Italy by LegoPrint S.p.A.

© David Abram, Devdan Sen, Nick Edwards,
Mike Ford and Beth Wooldridge 2001

No part of this book may be reproduced in
any form without permission from the
publisher except for the quotation of brief
passages in reviews.

752pp includes index
A catalogue record for this book is available
from the British Library.

ISBN 1-85828-745-6

The publishers and authors have done their
best to ensure the accuracy and currency of
all the information in The Rough Guide to
South India , however, they can accept no
responsibility for any loss, injury, or
inconvenience sustained by any traveller as a
result of information or advice contained in
the guide.

Help us update

We've gone to a lot of effort to ensure that
the third edition of The Rough Guide to
South India is accurate and up-to-date.
However, things change – places get
"discovered", opening hours are notoriously
fickle, restaurants and rooms raise prices or
lower standards. If you feel we've got it
wrong or left something out, we'd like to
know, and if you can remember the address,
the price, the time, the phone number, so
much the better.

We'll credit all contributions, and send a
copy of the next edition (or any other Rough
Guide if you prefer) for the best letters.
Everyone who writes to us and isn't already a
subscriber will receive a copy of our full-
colour twice-yearly newsletter. Please mark
letters: "Rough Guide South India Update"
and send to: Rough Guides, 62–70 Shorts
Gardens, London WC2H 9AH, or Rough
Guides, 4th Floor, 345 Hudson St, New York,
NY 10014. Or send an email to:
mail@roughguides.co.uk

Acknowledgements

The authors would like to thank Helena Smith for the equanimity and unfailing good humour with which she faced the task of editing two fully redesigned Indias back-to-back. If the whacky race of producing them to such tight deadlines earned medals, many indeed would have been won along the way. Thanks (and more imaginary medals), too, to Clifton Wilkinson, whose speedy work eased the burden. We also greatly appreciate the help of Jo Mead, for pushing ahead with the redesign and generally managing the various Indias and their respective crews so deftly. Thanks also to everyone in production who helped with this title, especially Katie Pringle for dedicated typesetting and picture layout and Susannah Wight for proofreading.

David: Thanks to friends old and new for their support: Ajit and Lily Sukhija and family (Panjim), Shelly and Teresa and family (Candolim), Sarah and Francis and family (Morjim), Axel and Lucie (Arambol), Nicola and Hayley and staff at IAR, and Frederick Noronha.

Nick: Many thanks to the following for assistance: Mr Gupta, Mr Kotrappa and Mr Ratnakar of KSTDC, Bangalore; Sharad Kanp, APTDC, Hyderabad; and Jijo Thomas, ANIIDCO, Port Blair. Danke for great diving and general merriment to Ule, Marcus and Ajay of Andaman Scuba Club, Havelock Island. Among fellow travellers thanks for vital info to Vicky and Brett (UK) re Little Andaman, Rob and Chloe (UK) re Neill Island and Shira (Israel) and Ola (Poland) re Smith (but not for stranding me at Radhnagar beach!). Bravo to Michael Eleftheriou for the mugshot. Finally, cheers to my oldest mate and best man, Graham, for high times on the Karnatic Coast and hugs of thanks to lovely Maria for not grumbling too much on those bone-shaking buses and letting me share the wonder of South India with her.

Beth: Above all, my sincere thanks go to Dr A. Jayathilak IAS, of Kerala Tourism and Mr P.J. Vargheese of the tourist desk in Kochi, who together made Kerala such a joy to explore. For help and insight, I thank the GOITRO in Chennai, the TTDC in Madurai, KTDC in Thiruvananthapuram, Pondy Tourism and the ADTC in Alappuzha. For pure enthusiasm, two great drivers, Shashi and Gopal, both tried so hard to teach me Malayalam and took me way off the beaten track; Kireon of Costa Malabari treated me to the very finest Keralan dishes and an absolutely unforgettable all-night teyyattam fire ritual. For friendship and hospitality, I thank Swarmi, Paul and Ganesh in Mamallapuram, Ananda, Shernez Varma in Pondicherry, St Stephen's church in Ooty, and Sajheeta in Patnem. Finally, a massive hug to Mum and Dad, and to Nick for extricating me from a sticky situation between two buses in Chennai.

SMALL PRINT

Photo credits

Colour powder shop, Mysore – Dinodia
Picture Agency

Mamallapuram – Andrew Morris

Tea plantation at Munnar – Dinodia Picture
Agency

Film poster – Jerry Dennis

Thanjavur – David Abram

Teyyattam dancer – Dinodia Picture Agency

Stuffing peppers – Paul Harris

Beach and fishing boats at dawn, Kerala –
Carolyn Bates

Meenakshi Temple, Madurai – Hutchison

Kodaikanal – Reuben Knutson

Worshipper at Sravanabelgola – Jeroen
Snijders

View from Palani Temple – Reuben Knutson

Film and political hoardings – David Abram

Kovalam Beach – Andrew Morris

Tail end of cyclone, Tiruvannamalai –
F. Good/TRIP

Allepey boat, Kottayam – Reuben Knutson

Srirangam's Ranganathaswamy shrine –
Colin Pantall

Dussehra – Rajesh H. Sharma/Dinodia
Picture Agency

Reef – Louise Murray/Robert Harding

Temple chariot festival, Thiruvarur, Tamil
Nadu – M. Amirtham/Dinodia Picture
Agency

Ayurvedic massage, Kovalam – Dinodia
Picture Agency

Jog Falls, Karnataka – Shama M. Ketkar/
Dinodia Picture Agency

Achyutaraya Temple, Hampi – Andrew Morris

Garuda, Chidambaram – Colin Pantall

Toddy tapper, Goa – Andrew Morris

Goats relaxing at Arjuna's Penance,
Mamallapuram – David Abram

Thelavadi, Kerala – Paul Harris

Keralan ritual theatre – Paul Harris

Flower market – Paul Harris

Gokarn, Karnataka – Dinodia Picture Agency

Cricket match on the Oval Maidan, Mumbai
– Nick Whitney/Images of India

Ashram sign – F. Good/TRIP

Cantilevered fishing nets, Kochi – Andrew
Morris

Curved horns of a panchavadyam orchestra,
Shiva Temple, Ernakulam – Steve
Davey/La Belle Aurore

Madurai – David Abram

Sravanabelgola – Devdan Sen

Periyar Wildlife Sanctuary – Paul Harris

Vizhinjam – Andrew Morris

Chola bronze – Dinodia Picture Agency

Nilgiri Blue Mountain Railway – H.K. Poladia/
Dinodia Picture Agency

Elephanta Caves – Dinodia Picture Agency

Basilica of Bom Jesus, Old Goa – Steve
Jones/AXIOM

Varkala – Dinodia Picture Agency

St Sebastian Church, Kochi – Alain
Evrard/Robert Harding

Golgumbaz, Bijapur – Devdan Sen

Store keeper – Orde Eliason/Link Picture
Library

Ganesh Festival – Dinodia Picture Agency

Arambol Beach, early morning – Mike Jones

Fishing boat on Palolem beach – Greg Evans

Jog Falls – M. Amirtham/Dinodia Picture
Agency

Thrissur Puram – Vinay Parelkar/ Dinodia
Picture Agency

Boating on the backwaters – Paul Harris

Krishna's Butter Ball, Mamallapuram – David
Abram

Parathasarathy Temple, Chennai – Steve
Davey/La Belle Aurore

Tirupati – Dinodia Picture Agency

Cellular jail, Port Blair – R.A. Acharya/
Dinodia Picture Agency

Kalipur beach – Nick Edwards

SMALL PRINT

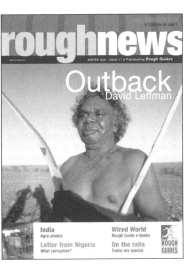

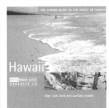

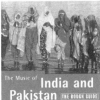

Will you have enough stories to tell your grandchildren?
©2000 Yahoo! Inc.
Do You Yahoo!?
Yahoo! Travel

The ideas expressed in this code were developed by and for independent travellers.

Learn About The Country You're Visiting

Start enjoying your travels before you leave by tapping into as many sources of information as you can.

The Cost Of Your Holiday

Think about where your money goes - be fair and realistic about how cheaply you travel. Try and put money into local peoples' hands; drink local beer or fruit juice rather than imported brands and stay in locally owned accommodation. Haggle with humour and not aggressively. Pay what something is worth to you and remember how wealthy you are compared to local people.

Embrace The Local Culture

Open your mind to new cultures and traditions - it will transform your experience. Think carefully about what's appropriate in terms of your clothes and the way you behave. You'll earn respect and be more readily welcomed by local people. Respect local laws and attitudes towards drugs and alcohol that vary in different countries and communities. Think about the impact you could have on them.

Exploring The World – The Travellers' Code

Being sensitive to these ideas means getting more out of your travels - and giving more back to the people you meet and the places you visit.

Minimise Your Environmental Impact

Think about what happens to your rubbish - take biodegradable products and a water filter bottle. Be sensitive to limited resources like water, fuel and electricity. Help preserve local wildlife and habitats by respecting local rules and regulations, such as sticking to footpaths and not standing on coral.

Don't Rely On Guidebooks

Use your guidebook as a starting point, not the only source of information. Talk to local people, then discover your own adventure!

Be Discreet With Photography

Don't treat people as part of the landscape, they may not want their picture taken. Ask first and respect their wishes.

We work with people the world over to promote tourism that benefits their communities, but we can only carry on our work with the support of people like you. For membership details or to find out how to make your travels work for local people and the environment, visit our website.

www.tourismconcern.org.uk

Tourism Concern
Campaigning for Ethical and Fairly Traded Tourism